Élisabeth Vigée Le Brun,
Portrait of Countess Golovina, ca. 1797–1800

This portrait by the French painter Élisabeth Vigée Le Brun (1755–1842) shows Countess Varvara Golovina, a Russian noblewoman and writer, in an informal pose holding her shawl and looking frankly at the viewer. The immensely talented Vigée Le Brun painted over six hundred portraits in her long life, receiving commissions from aristocrats, statesmen, and others across Europe. She was granted membership in ten academies of fine arts, highly unusual for a female artist. Her patrons included Queen Marie Antoinette, of whom she painted thirty portraits. Vigée Le Brun fled France during the French Revolution and ended up in Moscow, where she painted this and numerous other works. The portrait suggests a sympathetic connection between the artist and Countess Golovina, who had traveled to Paris, composed music, and later wrote a memoir of her time as a court lady for Catherine the Great.

Elisabeth Vigée Le Brun (1755–1842), *Portrait of Countess Nathalie Golovine* (Varvara Nikolaevna Golovina) (1724–1767). Oil on canvas. Photo © Photo Josse/Bridgeman Images

A History of Western Society

FOURTEENTH EDITION

Merry E. Wiesner-Hanks
University of Wisconsin–Milwaukee

Clare Haru Crowston
University of Illinois at Urbana-Champaign

Joe Perry
Georgia State University

John P. McKay
University of Illinois at Urbana-Champaign

bedford/st.martin's
Macmillan Learning
Boston | New York

Vice President: Leasa Burton
Senior Program Director: Erika Gutierrez
Senior Executive Program Manager: William J. Lombardo
Director of Content Development: Jane Knetzger
Development Manager: Caroline Thompson
Development Editor: Will Stonefield
Editorial Assistant: Kalinda Collins
Director of Media Editorial: Adam Whitehurst
Media Editor: Cara Kaufman
Senior Marketing Manager: Melissa Rodriguez
Senior Director, Content Management Enhancement:
   Tracey Kuehn
Senior Managing Editor: Michael Granger
Executive Content Project Manager: Christina M. Horn
Assistant Content Project Manager: Esther Saks
Lead Digital Asset Archivist and Workflow Project Manager:
   Jennifer Wetzel

Production Supervisor: Brianna Lester
Director of Design, Content Management:
   Diana Blume
Interior Design: Boynton Hue Studio
Cover Design: William Boardman
Cartographer: Mapping Specialists, Ltd.
Text Permissions Editor: Michael McCarty
Text Permissions Researcher: Elaine Kosta,
   Lumina Datamatics, Inc.
Executive Permissions Editor: Robin Fadool
Photo Researcher: Cheryl Du Bois, Lumina Datamatics, Inc.
Director of Digital Production: Keri deManigold
Assistant Director of Digital Production: Michelle Camisa
Copyeditor: Susan Zorn
Indexer: Rebecca McCorkle
Composition: Lumina Datamatics, Inc.
Printing and Binding: Lakeside Book Company

Library of Congress Control Number: 2022938788

ISBN 978-1-319-32988-4 (Combined Edition)
ISBN 978-1-319-34370-5 (Volume 1)
ISBN 978-1-319-34371-2 (Volume 2)
ISBN 978-1-319-48047-9 (Since 1300)

Printed in the United States of America.

1 2 3 4 5 6   27 26 25 24 23 22

For information, write: Bedford/St. Martin's, 75 Arlington Street, Boston, MA 02116

ACKNOWLEDGMENTS

Text acknowledgments and copyrights appear at the back of the book on pages 975–976, which constitute an extension of the copyright page. Art acknowledgments and copyrights appear on the same page as the art selections they cover.

A History of Western Society grew out of the initial three authors' desire to infuse new life into the study of Western civilization. The three current authors, Merry E. Wiesner-Hanks, Clare Haru Crowston, and Joe Perry, who first used the book as students or teachers and took over full responsibilities with the eleventh edition, continue to incorporate the latest and best scholarship in the field and to give special attention to the history of daily life, which has long been a popular distinction of this text. All three of us bring insights into the text from the classroom, as well as from new secondary works and our own research in archives and libraries.

In this new fourteenth edition we continue to add tools to help students think historically and master the material. Because our colleagues and current adopters say they like to teach with primary sources in a variety of ways, features throughout the book foreground primary sources. Every chapter now includes the popular feature **Thinking Like a Historian** (one per chapter), which groups at least five sources around a central question; **Evaluating Visual Evidence** (one per chapter) and **Evaluating Written Evidence** (one per chapter), each of which features an individual primary source; and **Viewpoints**, which pairs two written or visual primary sources on the same issue. We have also focused on ways to help students think about the big picture as they read. To help students look for and understand the most important points conveyed in each chapter, **section heading questions drive the narrative**. To help students see how developments are related to each other, **visual timelines** at the start of each chapter provide an appealing and engaging way to foster the development of chronological reasoning skills.

For the first time, *A History of Western Society* is available with **Achieve**—a fully mobile, accessible, and flexible learning platform. Achieve offers powerful assessment tools and content to support students at all levels of preparation in an intuitive and user-friendly system. These tools easily integrate with your school's LMS for a seamless experience. For more information, see "Achieve with *A History of Western Society*" on page ix.

The Story of *A History of Western Society*: Bringing the Past to Life for Students

When *A History of Western Society* was first conceptualized, social history was dramatically changing the ways we understood the past, and the original authors decided to create a book that would re-create the lives of ordinary people in appealing human terms, while also giving major economic, political, cultural, and intellectual developments the attention they unquestionably deserve. The current authors remain committed to advancing this vision for today's classroom, with a broader definition of social history that brings the original vision into the twenty-first century.

History as a discipline never stands still, and over the last several decades cultural history has joined social history as a source of dynamism. Because of its emphasis on the ways people made sense of their lives, *A History of Western Society* has always included a large amount of cultural history, ranging from foundational works of philosophy and literature to popular songs and stories. We have enhanced this focus on cultural history in recent editions in a way that highlights the interplay between people's lived experiences and the ways they reflect on these experiences to create meaning. The joint social and cultural perspective requires—fortunately, in our opinion—the inclusion of objects as well as texts as important sources for studying history, which has allowed us to incorporate the growing emphasis on material culture in the work of many historians. We know that engaging students' interest in the past is often a challenge, but we also know that the text's hallmark approach—the emphasis on daily life and individual experience in its social and cultural dimensions—connects with students and makes the past vivid and accessible.

Chapters and Features That Humanize the Past

Because students often have trouble engaging with the past, we seek to make it more approachable in human terms. One way we do this is by discussing social and cultural history, particularly in the acclaimed **"Life" chapters**, which emphasize daily life in a particular time period. The five chapters are Chapter 4: *Life* in the Hellenistic World, 338–30 B.C.E.; Chapter 10: *Life* in Villages and Cities of the High Middle Ages, 1000–1300; Chapter 18: *Life* in the Era of Expansion, 1650–1800; Chapter 22: *Life* in the Emerging Urban Society, 1840–1914; and Chapter 30: *Life* in an Age of Globalization, 1990 to the present.

To make the past even more discernible and memorable, we give students a chance to see it through individual people's lives in the popular **Individuals in Society biographical essays**. Appearing in each chapter, these essays offer brief studies of individuals and the societies in which they lived. We have found that students empathize with these human beings as they seek to define their own identities. The spotlighting of individuals, from the master artist Leonardo da Vinci to the former enslaved woman and Moravian missionary Rebecca Protten to Russian dissident leader Alexei Navalny, perpetuates the book's continued attention to cultural and intellectual developments and highlights human agency. The fourteenth edition includes new "Individuals in Society" features on Epicurus (Chapter 4), Macrina the Younger (Chapter 7), Cecilia Panifader (Chapter 10), and Vincent Ogé (Chapter 19).

Primary Sources and Historical Thinking

Because understanding the past requires that students engage directly with sources on their own, this edition features an expansive primary source program within its covers. These primary source assignments help students master a number of key learning outcomes, among them **critical thinking**, **historical thinking**, **analytical thinking**, and **argumentation**. Foremost among these assignments is **Thinking Like a Historian** (one in each chapter), which groups three to six sources around a central question, with additional questions to guide students' analysis of the evidence and suggestions for essays that will allow them to put these sources together with what they have learned in class. Topics include "Land Ownership and Social Conflict in the Late Republic" (Chapter 5); "Humanist Learning" (Chapter 12); "The Rights of Which Men?" (Chapter 19); "The Republican Spirit in 1848" (Chapter 21); "Normalizing Eugenics and 'Racial Hygiene' in Nazi Germany" (Chapter 27); and "The Conservative Reaction to Immigration and Islamist Terrorism" (Chapter 30).

To encourage comparative analysis, our **Viewpoints** feature pairs two written or visual sources that show contrasting or complementary perspectives on a particular issue. We hope that teachers will use these passages to get students thinking about diversity within and across societies, as well as across cultures. The thirty "Viewpoints" assignments—one in each chapter—introduce students to working with sources, encourage critical analysis, and extend the narrative while giving voice to the people of the past. Each includes a brief introduction and questions for analysis. Carefully chosen for accessibility, each pair of documents presents views on a diverse range of topics, such as "Greek Playwrights on Families, Fate, and Choice" (Chapter 3); "Roman and Byzantine Views of Barbarians" (Chapter 7); "Italian and English Views of the Plague" (Chapter 11); "Rousseau and Wollstonecraft Debate Women's Equality" (Chapter 16); "Contrasting Visions of the Sans-Culottes" (Chapter 19); "White Man's Burden or Capitalist Exploitation?" (Chapter 24); and "Cold War Propaganda" (Chapter 28).

The final types of original source features, **Evaluating Visual Evidence** (one per chapter) and **Evaluating Written Evidence** (one per chapter), supply an individual visual or written source, which are often more substantial in length than in other features, with headnotes and questions that help students understand the source and connect it to the information in the rest of the chapter. Selected for their interest and carefully integrated into their historical context, these sources provide students with firsthand encounters with people of the past and should, we believe, help students "hear" and "see" the past. With twenty-four written

and visual sources new to this edition, students can evaluate evidence such as "Thucydides on the Great Plague at Athens" (Chapter 3); "Charlemagne and His Second Wife, Hildegard" (Chapter 8); "Apprenticeship Contract for a Money-Changer" (Chapter 10); "Lucas de Heere, *Allegory of the Tudor Succession*, 1572" (Chapter 13); "Portrait of Don Francisco de Arobe and His Sons, 1599" (Chapter 14); "Gonzales Coques, *The Young Scholar and His Wife*, 1640" (Chapter 15); "New Ideas About Race and Identity" (Chapter 17); "Hogarth's Satirical View of the Church" (Chapter 18); "Wartime Propaganda Posters" (Chapter 25); "De-Stalinization and Khrushchev's 'Secret Speech'" (Chapter 28); "The Supermarket Revolution" (Chapter 29); and more.

To give students abundant opportunities to hone their textual and visual analysis skills, as well as a sense of the variety of sources on which historians rely, the primary source program includes a mix of canonical and lesser-known sources; a diversity of perspectives representing ordinary and prominent individuals alike; and a wide variety of source types, from tomb inscriptions, diaries, sermons, letters, and poetry, to artifacts, paintings, architecture, and propaganda posters. In addition, we have quoted extensively from a wide range of primary sources in the narrative, demonstrating that such quotations are the "stuff" of history. We believe that our extensive use of primary source extracts as an integral part of the narrative as well as in extended form in the primary source boxes will give students ample practice in thinking critically and historically.

New Coverage and Updates to the Narrative

This edition is enhanced by the incorporation of a wealth of new scholarship and subject areas that immerse students in the dynamic and ongoing work of history. Revisions to the fourteenth edition include expanded coverage of the medieval Muslim world in Chapters 8 and 16, including more analysis and attention to the role of Muslim women as well as to economic, cultural, and intellectual exchange between Muslims, Jews, and Christians. Meanwhile, Chapters 12, 14, and 16 all spotlight changing ideas about race and identity among Europeans during the Renaissance and Enlightenment periods, and collectively these chapters aim to explain how these ideas influenced Europeans' actions and attitudes toward the peoples they colonized. Chapter 14 additionally spotlights the roles of Indigenous and European women in the Americas during the early colonial period. New coverage in Chapter 24 further explores the interactions of race and gender during European colonization of Africa.

Chapter 15 features a new section about the Polish-Lithuanian Commonwealth, an early example of a constitutional monarchy characterized by remarkable religious and ethnic diversity. Several chapters present new scholarship about the environment and its role in history: for example, Chapter 11 foregrounds the Little Ice Age and its impacts on medieval Europe; and Chapter 20 has a new section emphasizing environmental effects of the Industrial Revolution.

In Chapter 27, a new section about the Spanish Civil War explains this conflict in context as a prelude to World War II. Chapter 27 also features expanded coverage of the eastern European front and of living conditions for ordinary people in the Soviet Union. Lastly, Chapter 30 has been extensively revised to cover recent events in historical context, including Russia's 2022 invasion of Ukraine; the COVID-19 pandemic's economic, social, and political effects; the rise of China as a global superpower; and the success of right-wing populist movements across the Western world.

Helping Students Understand and Engage with the Narrative

We know firsthand and take seriously the challenges students face in understanding, retaining, and mastering so much material that is often unfamiliar. The pedagogy and tools throughout *A History of Western Society* are designed to prompt active reading and comprehension of the continuities and changes that are the driving forces of historical development. Our book has a wealth of pedagogical aids that help students understand where they are going in their reading and where they have been. To focus students' reading, questions drive the narrative. Not only does each chapter open with **a chapter preview that poses questions**, but **each major heading is now one of these questions**. These questions are repeated again in the **Review & Explore section** at the end of each chapter.

We also provide tools that anchor the narrative in the big picture. Today's students are visually oriented, and our **visual timelines** assist them in developing chronological reasoning skills and making connections among events. To help students understand the bigger picture, each chapter includes **Looking Back, Looking Ahead conclusions** that provide an insightful synthesis of the chapter's main developments, while connecting to events that students will encounter in the chapters to come. In this way students are introduced to history as an ongoing process of interrelated events. These conclusions are followed by **Make Connections questions** that prompt students to assess larger developments across chapters, thus allowing them to develop skills in evaluating change and continuity, making comparisons, and analyzing context and causation.

To help students prepare for exams, in addition to repeating the major section heading questions in **Review the Main Ideas**, each Review & Explore section includes an **Identify Key Terms** prompt. For students who wish to know more, this section concludes with a **Suggested Resources** listing that supplies up-to-date readings on the vast amount of new work being done in many fields, as well as recommended documentaries, feature films, television programs, and websites.

To promote clarity and comprehension, boldface **key terms** in the text are defined in the margins and listed in the chapter review. **Phonetic spellings** are located directly after terms that readers are likely to find hard to pronounce. The topic-specific **thematic chronologies** that appear in many chapters provide a more focused timeline of certain developments. Once again, we also provide a **unified timeline** at the end of the text. Comprehensive and easy to locate, this timeline allows students to compare developments over the centuries. We are also proud of the text's high-quality art and map program, which has been thoroughly revised and features hundreds of **contemporaneous illustrations** (20 percent new). To make the past tangible, and as an extension of our attention to cultural history, we include images of numerous **artifacts** — from swords and fans to playing cards and record players. As in earlier editions, all illustrations have been carefully selected to complement the text, and all include captions that inform students while encouraging them to read the text more deeply. High-quality **full-size maps** contextualize major developments in the narrative, and helpful spot maps are embedded in the narrative to locate areas under discussion. We recognize students' difficulties with geography, and the new edition includes the popular **Mapping the Past map activities**. Included in each chapter, these activities give students valuable skills in reading and interpreting maps by asking them to analyze the maps and make connections to the larger processes discussed in the narrative.

Acknowledgments

It is a pleasure to thank the instructors who read and critiqued the book and Achieve in preparation for its revision:

Lara Apps, *Athabasca University*
Elizabeth Collins, *Triton College*
Celeste Cunningham, *Massachusetts Bay Community College*
Robert C. Feinberg, *Community College of Rhode Island*
Jennifer Foray, *Purdue University*
Peter Frizsche, *University of Illinois at Urbana-Champaign*
Chad Fulwider, *Centenary College of Louisiana*
Hal Goldman, *Carleton University*
Erika Huckestein, *Widener University*
Peter Manos, *Cleveland State University*
Bruce Nye, *Front Range Community College*
Nathan Orgill, *Georgia Gwinnett College*
Rebecca Reeves, *Wallace State Community College*
James Reibman, *Northampton County Area Community College*
Claire Sanders, *Texas Christian University*
Matthew West, *Lawson State Community College*
Matthew Zembo, *Hudson Valley Community College*

It is also a pleasure to thank the many editors who have assisted us over the years, first at Houghton Mifflin and now at Bedford/St. Martin's (Macmillan Learning). At Bedford/St. Martin's these include development editor Will Stonefield, executive content project manager Christina Horn, media editor Cara Kaufman, associate editor Stephanie Sosa, editorial assistant Kalinda Collins, senior executive program manager William J. Lombardo, and senior program director Erika Gutierrez. Other key contributors are director of rights and permissions Hilary Newman, executive permissions editor Robin Fadool, digital production assistant director Michelle Camisa, copyeditor Susan Zorn, and cover designer William Boardman.

Many of our colleagues at the University of Illinois, the University of Wisconsin–Milwaukee, and Georgia State University continue to provide information and stimulation, often without even knowing it. We thank them for it. We also thank the many students over the years with whom we have used earlier editions of this book. Their reactions and opinions helped shape the revisions to this edition, and we hope it remains worthy of the ultimate praise that they bestowed on it: that it's "not boring like most textbooks." We thank the Foundation for Civic Space and Public Policy (Warsaw) and all who participated in its seventeenth annual conference, "Recovering Forgotten History: The Image of East-Central Europe in English-Language Academic and Text Books," in 2019. Their insight and critical yet supportive commentary helped shape our revisions to Chapters 14 through 30.

Merry Wiesner-Hanks would, as always, also like to thank her husband, Neil, without whom work on this project would not be possible. Clare Haru Crowston thanks her husband, Ali, and her children, Lili, Reza, and Kian, who are a joyous reminder of the vitality of life that we try to showcase in this book. Joe Perry thanks his colleagues and students at Georgia State for their intellectual stimulation and is grateful to Joyce de Vries for her unstinting support and encouragement.

Each of us has benefited from the criticism of our coauthors, although each of us assumes responsibility for what he or she has written and revised. Merry Wiesner-Hanks takes responsibility for Chapters 1–13; Clare Crowston takes responsibility for Chapters 14–20; and Joe Perry takes responsibility for Chapters 21–30.

We'd especially like to thank the founding authors, John P. McKay, Bennett D. Hill, and John Buckler, for their enduring contributions and for their faith in each of us to carry on their legacy.

MERRY E. WIESNER-HANKS
CLARE HARU CROWSTON
JOE PERRY

Achieve sets a new standard for driving student learning in your history course by way of powerful learning content, engaging activities, and actionable student insights and analytics. Achieve brings together all of the features that instructors and students loved about our previous platform, LaunchPad—interactive e-textbook, LearningCurve adaptive quizzing and other assessments, interactive learning activities, and extensive instructor resources—all within a new, enhanced technology platform.

Proven Student Success

Macmillan Learning's Learning Science & Insights team has conducted extensive research to inform the development of Achieve. Their research has shown that students who completed more of the assigned material and who had higher grades on those assignments in Achieve had higher exam scores.* In addition:

- 88% of students said Achieve was easy to use.
- 82% of students agreed that Achieve helped them develop, practice, and apply skills associated with their course.
- 80% of instructors agreed that Achieve helped students improve their knowledge of the course material.

Benefits

Powerful Learning Content.

- *E-textbook.* Macmillan Learning's e-textbook is an interactive version of the textbook that offers highlighting, bookmarking, and note-taking. Students can download the e-textbook to read offline, or to have it read aloud to them. Achieve allows instructors to assign chapter sections as homework.

- *Adaptive Quizzing.* LearningCurve Adaptive Quizzing provides personalized question sets and clear feedback based on each student's correct and incorrect answers, offering an easy way for students to prepare for class by reviewing the e-textbook and then assessing their understanding of the key concepts.

| ← Back to Study Plan | Score: 15/750 | | Question Value: 15 points |

How did King Charles I react in 1629 to his ongoing tension with the House of Commons?

- ○ He began a civil war, splitting the people between the houses of York and Lancaster.
- ○ He turned to the courts to support his rule.
- ○ He dismissed the archbishop of Canterbury, William Laud.
- ○ He refused to summon Parliament for the next eleven years.

Need help on this question?

| Read the ebook page on this topic (no penalty) | Get a hint (fewer points) | Show answer (no points) |

*Based on a survey of Achieve users in Fall of 2021 with over 200 instructor responses and over 3,000 student responses.

- *Integrated Reader.* The integrated companion reader, *Sources for Western Society,* contains at least five additional primary source readings for each chapter. Comprehension quizzes then test students' understanding of each primary source.

▼ *Bedford Tutorials for Western Civilization.* Twelve guided tutorials with assessment help students build essential skills for the course, such as avoiding plagiarism, working with primary sources, and learning to think and read like a historian.

Working with Primary Sources

As a student in a history course, you probably have some preconceived ideas about what you will be studying and how you will study it. But your college-level history may surprise you. You may have thought that the study of history is about "facts," when the study of history has as much to do with working with and evaluating sources and as evidence as it does with learning dates, names, events, and places from the past. In this tutorial, you will learning the following:

- What exactly are historical sources
- The difference between primary and secondary sources
- How to read and analyze a written source
- How to read and analyze a visual source

What Are Historical Sources?

The stories historians tell in books, articles, and lectures are pieced together from hundreds, often thousands, of documents, objects, and artifacts. The challenge is to turn all of those individual pieces of evidence into a convincing, compelling version of the past. That's no easy task. Most historical evidence was produced by people with no direct interest in telling the story of their times. While historians do have access to the occasional

---

Working with Primary Sources

Please read the Bedford Tutorial, "Working with Primary Sources." Then, answer these questions to demonstrate your understanding of working with primary sources.

A primary source is

○ an interpretation or analysis of the past.

○ a textbook or scholarly journal article.

● a document, object, or image created during the time period under study.

○ always a text document.

Engaging Activities.

▼ *New Video Activities.* The ten Video Activities in Achieve invite students to draw connections in history. Each video tells an engaging story related to an important theme or topic in the chapter. Assessment that follows each video helps students understand and reflect on the big themes that have shaped Western society.

To complete this activity, watch the video and answer the questions.

▶ 0:00 | 3:39   🔊   CC   AD   ▤   1x   ⛶

Which of the following crops was first introduced to Europe as a result of the Columbian exchange?

○ wheat

○ peaches

○ maize

○ cucumbers

In this activity, you will view a historical image and then answer a series of questions. You will need to scroll down in order to access the questions and complete the activity.

This painting depicts a fifty-six-year-old man, Don Francisco de Arobe (center), and two young men, Don Pedro and Don Domingo, believed to be his sons. De Arobe was the leader of a settlement in the province of Esmeraldas on the north coast of modern-day Ecuador. In this tropical, coastal region, Africans who escaped from slavery in the 1550s joined, intermarried with, and eventually became the majority in some Indigenous communities suffering population loss due to Spanish-spread disease. The men in this painting are probably of African and Indigenous descent. Their fine clothing displays a mixture of European and Indigenous styles: they wear imported Spanish silk cloaks and lace collars and cuffs, combined with gold nose- and earplugs that had been worn by Indigenous people since before contact with the Spanish. A Spanish official commissioned the painting in 1599 for the king of Spain to commemorate de Arobe's conversion to Christianity and his

▲ *New Evaluating Visual Evidence Activities.* Extending the Evaluating Visual Evidence feature in the book, each chapter in Achieve has an interactive activity that presents an image related to a major chapter topic, and assessment then guides students in understanding the image's significance in the broader context of the chapter.

• *Instructor Activity Guides.* The ten Instructor Activity Guides provide instructors with a structured plan for using Achieve's active learning opportunities in both face-to-face and remote learning courses. Each guide offers step-by-step instructions—from pre-class reflection to in-class engagement to post-class follow-up. The guides include suggestions for discussion questions and group work, with estimated class time, implementation effort, and Bloom's taxonomy level for each activity.

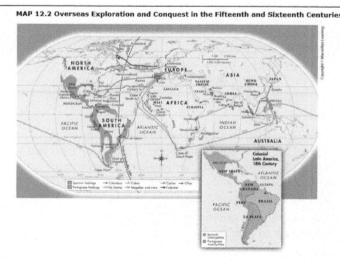

MAP 12.2 Overseas Exploration and Conquest in the Fifteenth and Sixteenth Centuries

The Spanish and Portuguese were the two most prominent European countries to settle the Americas. Which other European states, according to this map, sent out exploring expeditions by the end of the seventeenth century?
A. Switzerland and Denmark
B. Italy and Greece
C. France and England
D. Finland and Russia

▶ *iClicker Classroom Response System.* Achieve seamlessly integrates iClicker, Macmillan Learning's highly acclaimed classroom response system. iClicker can help make any classroom—in person or virtual—more lively, engaging, and productive.

- *Instructor Resources.* Achieve provides a full suite of instructor resources to foster active learning, all in one place. These include the Instructor's Resource Manual, Lecture Slides, iClicker Slides, and more.

Actionable Data and Insights.

- *Summative Assessment.* Chapter quizzes and test bank questions provided in Achieve allow students to demonstrate what they've learned. Exam/Quiz results report to a Gradebook that lets instructors monitor student progress individually and classwide. The test bank contains hundreds of questions meticulously checked against the updated content of the text. Instructors can assign out-of-the-box exams or create their own by:
  - Choosing from thousands of questions in our database.
  - Filtering questions by type, topic, difficulty, and Bloom's level.
  - Customizing multiple-choice questions.
  - Integrating their own questions into the exam.

▼ *Learning Objectives, Reports, and Insights.* Achieve's Insights and Reports provides powerful analytics, viewable in an elegant dashboard, that offer instructors a window into student progress against Learning Objectives and facilitate lessons that are specifically tailored to students' needs.

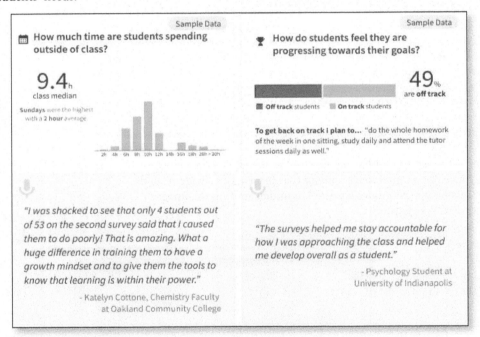

Enhanced Platform.

- *Next-Generation Technology.* Achieve provides a cleaner, more intuitive, mobile-friendly interface. Designed for the Cloud, it has better monitoring tools and allows faster response to issues, allowing us to improve on our uptime. It is generally more scalable and extensible, so it can support future products and customer needs.
- *Integration.* Achieve can all be integrated with the tools of your choice—including the iClicker Student Response system or your LMS (Blackboard, Canvas, D2L or Moodle). For more information, talk to your local sales representative.
- *Accessibility.* Macmillan Learning strives to create products that are usable by all learners and that meet universally applied accessibility standards.

For more information about print and digital versions of *A History of Western Society,* visit the online catalog page at macmillanlearning.com.

BRIEF CONTENTS

CONTENTS

1 Origins
to 1200 B.C.E.   2

photo: Art Images/Hulton Fine Art Collection/Getty Images

6   The Roman Empire

27 B.C.E.–284 C.E.   138

7   Late Antiquity

250–600   168

photo: De Agostini/A. DAGLI ORTI/Getty Images

photo: De Agostini/G. DAGLI ORTI/Getty Images

8 Europe in the Early Middle Ages
600–1000

9 State and Church in the High Middle Ages
1000–1300

photo: G. Dagli Orti/© NPL — DeA Picture Library/Bridgeman Images

photo: © Musée Condé, Chantilly, France/Bridgeman Images

photo: Photo © Mauro Ranzani/Bridgeman Images

photo: Musée des Beaux-Arts, Valenciennes, France/Bridgeman Images

photo: De Agostini/Getty Images

photo: Charles Le Brun [1619–1690], 1678/Museum of Fine Arts, Budapest, Hungary/
Erich Lessing/Art Resource, NY

photo: Fine Art Photographic/Getty Images

photo: DeAgostini/DEA/A. DAGLI ORTI/Getty Images

24 The West and the World
1815–1914   728

photo: Prisma/Universal Images Group/Getty Images

25 War and Revolution
1914–1919   762

photo: Imperial War Museum/Bridgeman Images

26 Opportunity and Crisis in the Age of Modernity
1880–1940   800

27 Dictatorships and the Second World War
1919–1945   832

photo: Photo by Staff/Mirrorpix/Getty Images

photo: De Agostini/Getty Images

30 *Life* in an Age of Globalization

1990 to the present   938

MAPS, FIGURES, AND TABLES

Maps

Figures and Tables

SPECIAL FEATURES

EVALUATING VISUAL EVIDENCE

EVALUATING WRITTEN EVIDENCE

VIEWPOINTS

THINKING LIKE A HISTORIAN

INDIVIDUALS IN SOCIETY

MAPPING THE PAST

A History of
Western Society

1

Origins

to 1200 B.C.E.

For most of their time on the earth, humans were foragers moving through the landscape, inventing ever more specialized tools. Previous generations of historians have generally tended to view that long foraging past not as "history," but as "prehistory." History only began, for them, when writing began. This leaves out most of the human story, however, and today historians no longer see writing as such a sharp dividing line. They explore all eras of the human past using many different types of sources, sometimes using technologies that were unavailable until recently, such as DNA analysis and radiocarbon dating, although they do still tend to pay more attention to written sources.

About 11,000 years ago, people in some places domesticated plants and animals and began to live in permanent villages, some of which grew into cities. They created structures of governance to control their more complex societies, and some invented writing to record taxes, inventories, and payments; later writing was put to other uses. These new technologies and systems were first introduced in the Tigris and Euphrates River Valleys of southwest Asia and the Nile Valley of northeast Africa, areas that became linked through trade connections, military conquests, and migrations. ■

CHAPTER PREVIEW

- What do we mean by "the West" and "Western civilization"?

- How did early human societies create new technologies and cultural forms?

- What kind of civilization did the Sumerians build in Mesopotamia?

- How did the Akkadian and Old Babylonian empires develop in Mesopotamia?

- How did the Egyptians establish a prosperous and long-lasting society?

Plowing in New Kingdom Egypt
In this wall painting from the tomb of an official painted between 1500 and 1300 B.C.E., a man guides a wooden ox-drawn plow through the soil, while the woman walking behind throws seed in the furrow. The painting was designed not to show real peasants working but to depict the servants who would spring to life to serve the deceased in the afterlife. Nevertheless, the gender division of labor and the plow itself are probably accurate. (Art Images/Hulton Fine Art Collection/Getty Images)

What do we mean by "the West" and "Western civilization"?

Human groups have long made distinctions between themselves and others. Some of these distinctions are between small groups such as neighboring tribes, some between countries and civilizations, and some between vast parts of the world. Among the most enduring of the latter are the ideas of "the West" and "the East."

Describing the West

Ideas about the West and the distinction between West and East derived originally from the ancient Greeks. Greek civilization grew up in the shadow of earlier civilizations, especially Egypt and Mesopotamia. The Greeks defined themselves in relation to these more advanced cultures, which they saw as "Eastern." They were also the first to use the word *Europe* for a geographic area, taking the word from the name of a minor goddess. They set Europe in opposition to "Asia" (also named for a minor goddess), by which they meant both what we now call western Asia and what we call Africa.

The Greeks passed these ideas on to the Romans, who saw themselves clearly as part of the West. To Romans, the East was more sophisticated and more advanced, but also decadent and somewhat immoral. Roman value judgments have continued to shape preconceptions, stereotypes, and views of differences between the West and the East to this day.

Greco-Roman ideas about the West were passed on to people who lived in western and northern Europe, who saw themselves as the inheritors of this classical tradition and thus as the West. When these Europeans established colonies outside Europe beginning in the late fifteenth century, they regarded what they were doing as taking Western culture with them. With colonization, *Western* came to mean those cultures that included significant numbers of people of European ancestry, no matter where on the globe they were located.

In the early twentieth century, educators and other leaders in the United States became worried that many people, especially young people, were becoming cut off from European intellectual and cultural traditions. They encouraged the establishment of college and university courses focusing on "Western civilization," the first of which was taught at Columbia University in 1919. In designing the course, the faculty included cultures that, as far back as the ancient Greeks, had been considered Eastern, such as Egypt and Mesopotamia. This conceptualization and the course spread to other colleges and universities, developing into what became known as the introductory Western civilization course, a staple of historical instruction for generations of college students.

After World War II, divisions between the West and the East changed again, with *Western* coming to imply a capitalist economy and *Eastern* the Communist Eastern bloc. Thus, Japan was considered Western, and some Greek-speaking areas of Europe became Eastern. The collapse of communism in the Soviet Union and eastern Europe in the 1980s brought yet another refiguring, with much of eastern Europe joining the European Union, originally a Western organization.

In the early twenty-first century, *Western* still suggests a capitalist economy, but it also has certain cultural connotations, such as individualism and competition. Islamist radicals often describe their aims as an end to Western cultural, economic, and political influence, though Islam itself is generally described, along with Judaism and Christianity, as a Western monotheistic religion. Thus, throughout its long history, the meaning of "the West" has shifted, but in every era it has meant more than a geographical location.

What Is Civilization?

Just as the meaning of the word *Western* is shaped by culture, so is the meaning of the word *civilization*. In the ancient world, residents of cities generally viewed themselves as more advanced and sophisticated than rural folk. They saw themselves as more "civilized," a word that comes from the Latin adjective *civilis*, which refers to a citizen, either of a town or of a larger political unit.

This depiction of people as either civilized or uncivilized was gradually extended to whole societies. Beginning in the eighteenth century, European scholars described any society in which political, economic, and social organizations operated on a large scale, not primarily through families and kin groups, as a **civilization**. Civilizations had cities; laws that governed human relationships; codes of manners and social conduct that regulated how people were to behave; and scientific, philosophical, and theological beliefs that explained the larger world. Civilizations also had some form of political organization through which one group was able to coerce resources out of others to engage in group

■ **civilization** A large-scale system of human political, economic, and social organizations; civilizations have cities, laws, states, and often writing.

■ **Paleolithic era** The period of human history up to about 9000 B.C.E., when tools were made from stone and bone and people gained their food through foraging.

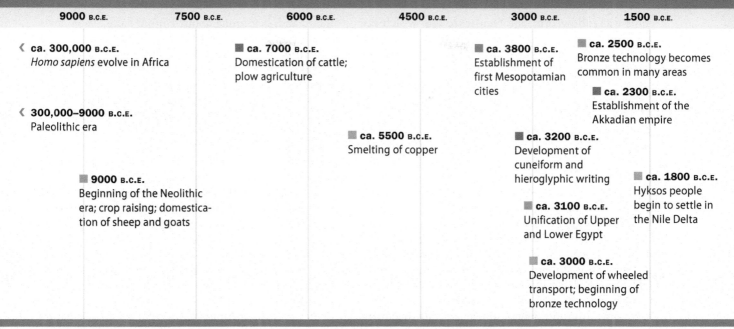

9000 B.C.E.	7500 B.C.E.	6000 B.C.E.	4500 B.C.E.	3000 B.C.E.	1500 B.C.E.

‹ ca. 300,000 B.C.E.
Homo sapiens evolve in Africa

‹ 300,000–9000 B.C.E.
Paleolithic era

■ 9000 B.C.E.
Beginning of the Neolithic era; crop raising; domestication of sheep and goats

■ ca. 7000 B.C.E.
Domestication of cattle; plow agriculture

■ ca. 5500 B.C.E.
Smelting of copper

■ ca. 3800 B.C.E.
Establishment of first Mesopotamian cities

■ ca. 3200 B.C.E.
Development of cuneiform and hieroglyphic writing

■ ca. 3100 B.C.E.
Unification of Upper and Lower Egypt

■ ca. 3000 B.C.E.
Development of wheeled transport; beginning of bronze technology

■ ca. 2500 B.C.E.
Bronze technology becomes common in many areas

■ ca. 2300 B.C.E.
Establishment of the Akkadian empire

■ ca. 1800 B.C.E.
Hyksos people begin to settle in the Nile Delta

A note on dates: This book generally uses the terms B.C.E. (Before the Common Era) and C.E. (Common Era) when giving dates, a system of chronology based on the Christian calendar and now used widely around the world.

endeavors, such as building large structures or carrying out warfare. States established armies, bureaucracies, and taxation systems. Generally only societies that used writing were judged to be civilizations.

Until the middle of the twentieth century, historians often referred to the places where writing and cities developed as "cradles of civilization," proposing a model of development for all humanity patterned on that of an individual life span. However, the idea that all human societies developed (or should develop) in a uniform process from a "cradle" to a "mature" civilization has now been largely discredited, and some historians choose not to use the term *civilization* at all because it could imply that some societies are superior to others.

Just as the notion of "civilization" has been questioned, so has the notion of "Western civilization."

Ever since the idea of "Western civilization" was first developed, people have debated what its geographical extent and core values are. Are there certain beliefs, customs, concepts, and institutions that set Western civilization apart from other civilizations, and, if so, when and how did these originate? How were these values and practices transmitted over space and time, and how did they change? No civilization stands alone, and each is influenced by its neighbors. Whatever Western civilization was — and is — it has been shaped by interactions with other societies, cultures, and civilizations. Even so, the idea that there are basic distinctions between the West and the rest of the world in terms of cultural values has been very powerful for thousands of years, and it still shapes the way many people view the world.

How did early human societies create new technologies and cultural forms?

Scientists who study the history of the earth use a variety of systems to classify and divide time. Geologists and paleontologists divide time into periods that last many millions of years and that are determined by the movements of continents and the evolution and extinction of plant and animal species. During the nineteenth century, European archaeologists coined labels for eras of the human past according to the primary material out of which

surviving tools had been made. Thus the earliest human era became the Stone Age, the next era the Bronze Age, and the next the Iron Age. They further divided the Stone Age into the Paleolithic and Neolithic eras. During the **Paleolithic era**, people used stone and other natural products to make tools and gained food largely by foraging, that is, by gathering plant products, trapping or catching small animals and birds, and hunting larger prey.

This was followed by the **Neolithic era**, which saw the beginning of agriculture and animal domestication; this change occurred at various times around the world, but the earliest was around 9000 B.C.E., so this date is often used to mark the transition between the Paleolithic and the Neolithic.

From the First Hominids to the Paleolithic Era

Using many different pieces of evidence from all over the world, archaeologists, paleontologists, and other scholars have developed a view of human evolution that has a widely shared basic outline, though there are disagreements about details. Sometime between 7 and 6 million years ago in southern and eastern Africa, groups of human ancestors (members of the biological "hominid" family) began to walk upright, which allowed them to carry things. About 3.4 million years ago, some hominids began to use naturally occurring objects as tools, and around 2.5 million years ago, one group in East Africa began to make simple tools, a feat that was accompanied by, and may have spurred, brain development. Groups migrated into much of Africa and then into Asia and Europe; by about 600,000 years ago, there were hominids throughout much of Afro-Eurasia.

About 300,000 years ago, again in East Africa, some of these early humans evolved into *Homo sapiens* ("thinking humans"), which had still larger and more complex brains that allowed for symbolic language and better social skills. *Homo sapiens* invented highly specialized tools made out of a variety of materials. They made regular use of fire for heat, light, and cooking. They also migrated, first across Africa, and by 130,000 years ago, and perhaps earlier, out of Africa into Eurasia. Eventually they traveled farther still, reaching Australia using rafts about 50,000 years ago and the Americas by about 15,000 years ago, or perhaps earlier. They moved into areas where other types of hominids lived, interacting with them and in some cases interbreeding with them. Gradually other types of hominids became extinct, leaving *Homo sapiens* as the only survivors and the ancestors of all modern humans.

In the Paleolithic period, humans throughout the world lived in ways that were similar to one another. Archaeological evidence and studies of modern foragers suggest that people generally lived in small groups of related individuals and moved throughout the landscape in search of food. They ate mostly plants, and much of the animal protein in their diet came from foods gathered or scavenged rather than hunted directly. Paleolithic peoples did, however, hunt large game, often hunting in groups. Groups working together forced animals over cliffs, threw spears to kill

them, and, beginning about 15,000 B.C.E., used bows to shoot projectiles so that they could stand farther away from their prey while hunting.

Paleolithic people were not differentiated by wealth. Most foraging societies that exist today, or did so until recently, have some type of division of labor by sex and also by age. Men are more often responsible for hunting and women for gathering plant and animal products. This may or may not have been the case in the Paleolithic era, or there may have been a diversity of patterns in different areas around the world.

Beginning in the Paleolithic era, human beings have expressed themselves through what we would now term the arts or culture: painting and decorating walls and objects, making music, telling stories, dancing alone or in groups. Paleolithic evidence of culture, particularly from after about 50,000 years ago, includes flutes, carvings, jewelry, and amazing paintings done on cave walls and rock outcroppings that depict animals, people, and symbols. Burials, paintings, and objects suggest that people may have developed ideas about supernatural forces that controlled some aspects of the natural world and the humans in it, what we now term spirituality or religion. Spiritually adept men and women communicated with that unseen world, and objects such as carvings or masks were probably thought to have special healing or protective powers.

Total human population grew very slowly during the Paleolithic. One estimate proposes that there were perhaps 500,000 humans in the world about 30,000 years ago. By about 10,000 years ago, this number had grown to 5 million — ten times as many people. This was a significant increase, but it took twenty thousand years. The low population density meant that human impact on the environment was relatively small, although still significant.

Domestication

Foraging remained the basic way of life for most of human history, and for groups living in extreme environments, such as tundras or deserts, it was the only possible way to survive. In a few especially fertile areas, however, the natural environment provided enough food that people could become more settled. About 15,000 years ago, the earth's climate entered a warming phase, and more parts of the world were able to support people who did not move very much or at all. Archaeological sites in many places begin to include storage pits and grindstones, evidence that people were intensifying their work to get more food from the surrounding area, becoming sedentary or semi-sedentary rather than nomadic. They also acquired more objects and built more permanent housing.

Cave Painting at Altamira   The Cave of Altamira in northern Spain contains spectacular polychrome paintings of animals, along with hand markings made by blowing red ochre pigment and charcoal through a tube. The oldest paintings date from about 36,000 B.C.E., and others were added over many thousands of years. Paleolithic finger and hand markings have been found all over the world. (Universal History Archive/Universal Images Group/Getty Images)

In several of these places, along with gathering wild grains, roots, and other foodstuffs, people began planting seeds in the ground and selected the seeds they planted to get crops that had favorable characteristics, such as larger edible parts. Through this human intervention, certain crops became domesticated, that is, modified by selective breeding so as to serve human needs. Scholars used to think that crop raising was the cause of sedentism, or a sedentary way of life, but they now know that in many places villages preceded intentional crop raising by thousands of years, so the primary line of causation runs the other way: people began to raise crops because they were living in permanent communities. Thus people were "domesticated," meaning settled down, before plants and animals were.

Intentional crop planting first developed around 9000 B.C.E., in the area archaeologists call the **Fertile Crescent**, which runs from present-day Lebanon, Israel, and Jordan north to Turkey and then south and east to the Iran-Iraq border. Over the next two millennia, a similar process — first sedentism, then domestication — happened elsewhere as well, in the Nile River Valley, western Africa, China, India, Papua New Guinea, and Mesoamerica.

Along with domesticating certain plants, people also domesticated animals. Dogs were the first to be domesticated, and in about 9000 B.C.E., at the same time they began to raise crops, people in the Fertile Crescent domesticated wild goats and sheep. They began to breed the goats and sheep selectively for qualities that they wanted. Sheep and goats allow themselves to be herded, and people developed a new form of living, **pastoralism**, based on herding and raising livestock. Eventually other grazing animals, including cattle, camels, horses, yak, and reindeer, also became the basis of pastoral economies in Central and West Asia, many parts of Africa, and far northern Europe.

The domestication of certain large animals had a significant impact on human ways of life. Cattle, water buffalo, donkeys, and horses can be trained to carry people or burdens on their backs and pull against loads dragged behind them. They can be used to pull plows, which began with cattle about 7000 B.C.E. The use of animals dramatically increased the power available to humans to carry out their tasks, which had both an immediate effect in the societies in which

■ **Neolithic era** The period after 9000 B.C.E., when people developed agriculture, domesticated animals, and used tools made of stone and wood.

■ **Fertile Crescent** An area of mild climate and abundant wild grain where agriculture first developed, in present-day Lebanon, Israel, Jordan, Turkey, and Iraq.

■ **pastoralism** An economic system based on herding flocks of goats, sheep, cattle, or other animals beneficial to humans.

this happened and a long-term effect when these societies later encountered other societies in which human labor remained the only source of power. Domesticated animals eventually far outnumbered their wild counterparts and were used for destruction in war as well as food production and transport.

The shift from hunting and gathering to the domestication of plants and animals grew out of a combination of demographic, social, and cultural changes. In terms of demographic factors, populations may have slowly grown beyond the readily available food supply, despite the warming climate that had boosted the supply of foraged foods and allowed sedentary villages to develop. This increase in population resulted from lower child mortality and longer life spans, and perhaps also from higher fertility rates resulting from a sedentary village lifestyle. Naturally occurring foods often included grains or other crops that could be ground and cooked into a mush soft enough for

Pillar at Göbekli Tepe　The huge limestone pillars arranged in rings at the Paleolithic site Göbekli Tepe are somewhat humanoid in shape, and the carvings are of dangerous animals, including lions, boars, foxes, snakes, vultures, and scorpions. The structure shown here required enormous skill and effort of the people who built it, and clearly had great importance to them. (uchar/E+/Getty Images)

babies to eat. This mush — for which there is widespread archaeological evidence — allowed women to decide to stop nursing their children at a younger age and instead put their energies elsewhere. In so doing, women lost the contraceptive effects of breast-feeding, and children were born at more frequent intervals. But instead of moving to a new area — the solution that foragers relied on when faced with the problem of food scarcity — people chose to stay with or near the physical and social structures of the sedentary villages they had built. So they developed a different way to increase the food supply to keep up with population growth — plant and animal domestication. Thus began cycles of expanding population and intensification of land use that have continued to today.

A very recent archaeological find at Göbekli Tepe (guh-BEK-lee TEH-peh) in present-day Turkey suggests that cultural factors may have played a role in the development of agriculture as well, interweaving with demographic and social factors. Here around 9000 B.C.E. hundreds of people came together to build rings of massive, multi-ton, elaborately carved limestone pillars, and then covered them with dirt and built more. Archaeological remains indicate that the people who created this site ate wild game and plants, not crops. Once these pillars were carved and raised in place, however, their symbolic, cultural, or perhaps religious importance may have made people decide to adopt a subsistence strategy that would allow them to stay nearby. Indeed, it is very near here that evidence of the world's oldest domesticated wheat has been discovered. So while the people who built Göbekli Tepe were foragers, their descendants who decided to stay nearby became crop raisers. Archaeologists speculate that, at least in this case, the symbolic, cultural, or perhaps religious importance of the structure can help explain why the people who built it changed from foraging to agriculture.

Implications of Agriculture

Whatever the reasons for the move from foraging to agriculture, within several centuries of initial crop planting, people in the Fertile Crescent, parts of China, and the Nile Valley were relying primarily on domesticated food products. Some historians view this change as the most important development in human history, as it made everything else possible. They term it the "Agricultural Revolution" or sometimes the "Neolithic Revolution," because according to the periodization of the human past developed in the nineteenth century, agriculture marked the transition from Paleolithic to Neolithic.

A field of planted and weeded crops yields ten to one hundred times as much food — measured in calories — as the same area of naturally occurring plants. It also requires much more labor, however, which was provided both by the greater number of people in the community and by those people working longer hours. In contrast to the twenty hours a week foragers spent on obtaining food, farming peoples were often in the fields from dawn to dusk. Some scientists, in fact, describe the development of agriculture as a process of codependent domestication: humans domesticated crops, but crops also "domesticated" humans so that they worked long hours spreading particular crops around the world, especially wheat, rice, and later corn. Early farmers were also less healthy than foragers were; their narrower range of foodstuffs made them more susceptible to disease and nutritional deficiencies. They did have the consolation of alcohol, which should perhaps be added to the list of reasons for the development and spread of crop raising, as planted crops provided a reliable supply of raw material people could transform into this high-energy substance that also became their principal painkiller. Alcohol became part of social events, and its consumption was often ritualized, with beer and wine among the offerings given to spirits and deities, or consumed by shamans, priests, and worshippers.

Sometime in the seventh millennium B.C.E., people attached wooden sticks to frames that animals dragged through the soil, thus breaking it up and allowing seeds to sprout more easily. These simple scratch plows, pulled by cattle and water buffalo, allowed Neolithic people to produce a significant amount of surplus food. Some people in the community could now spend their days performing other tasks, thus increasing the division of labor. Some people specialized in making tools, houses, and other items needed in village life, or in producing specific types of food. Families and households became increasingly interdependent, trading food for other commodities or services.

The division of labor allowed by plow agriculture contributed to the creation of social hierarchies based on wealth and power, which have been a central feature of human society since the Neolithic period. Although no written records were produced during this era, archaeological evidence provides some clues about how the hierarchies might have developed. Compared to foragers, villagers needed more complex rules about how food was to be distributed and how different types of work were to be valued. Certain individuals must have begun to specialize in the determination and enforcement of these rules, and informal structures of power gradually became more formalized. Religious specialists probably developed more elaborate rituals to celebrate life passages and to appeal to the gods for help in times of difficulty, such as illness.

Individuals who were the heads of large families or kin groups had control over the labor of others, and this power became more significant when that labor brought material goods that could be stored. Material goods — plows, sheep, cattle, sheds, pots, carts — gave one the ability to amass still more material goods, and the gap between those who had them and those who did not widened. Through violence, purchase, and other processes, some individuals came to own other people as well. Slavery predates written records, but it developed in almost all agricultural societies. Enslaved people were another source of physical power for their enslavers, allowing them to amass still more wealth and influence. In the long era before the invention of fossil fuel technology, the ability to exploit animal and human labor was the most important mark of distinction between elites and the rest of the population. Such social hierarchies were reinforced over generations as children inherited goods and status from their parents. By the time writing was invented, social distinctions between elites — the nobles, hereditary priests, and other privileged groups — and the rest of the population were already in existence.

Along with hierarchies based on wealth and power, the development of agriculture was intertwined with a hierarchy based on gender. In many places, plow agriculture came to be a male task. Men's responsibility for plowing and other agricultural tasks took them outside the household more often than women's duties did, enlarging their opportunities for leadership. As a result, they may have been favored as inheritors of family land and of the right to farm communally held land. Accordingly, over generations, women's independent access to resources decreased. The system in which men have more power and access to resources than women of the same social level, and in which some men are dominant over other men, is called **patriarchy** and is found in every society in the world with written records, although the level of inequality varies. Men's control of property was rarely absolute, because the desire to keep wealth and property within a family or kin group often resulted in women's inheriting, owning, and in some cases managing significant amounts of wealth. Hierarchies of wealth and power thus intersected with hierarchies of gender in complex ways.

Trade and Cross-Cultural Connections

By 7000 B.C.E. or so, some agricultural villages in the Fertile Crescent may have had as many as ten thousand residents. One of the best known of these, Çatal Hüyük (CHAH-tahl huh-yuk) in what is now Turkey,

■ **patriarchy** A social system in which men have more power and access to resources than women of the same social level, and in which some men are dominant over other men.

which existed from about 7500 to about 5700 B.C.E., shows evidence of trade as well as specialization of labor. Çatal Hüyük's residents lived in densely packed mud-brick houses with walls covered in white plaster that had been made with burned lime. Along with planting crops and raising sheep, Çatal Hüyük's residents made textiles, pots, figurines, baskets, carpets, copper and lead beads, and other goods, and they decorated their houses with murals showing animal and human figures. They gathered, sharpened, and polished obsidian, a volcanic rock that could be used for knives, blades, and mirrors, and then traded it with neighboring towns to obtain seashells and flint. From here the obsidian was exchanged still farther away, for Neolithic societies slowly developed local and then regional networks of exchange and communication.

Among the goods traded in some parts of the world was copper, which people hammered into shapes for jewelry and tools. Like most metals, in its natural state copper usually occurs mixed with other materials in a type of mixed rock material called ore, and by about 5500 B.C.E., people in the Balkans had learned that copper could be extracted from ore by heating it in a smelting process. Smelted copper was poured into molds and made into spear points, axes, chisels, beads, and other objects. Pure copper is soft, but through experimentation artisans learned that it would become harder if they mixed it with other metals during heating, creating an alloy called bronze.

Because it was stronger than copper, bronze had a far wider range of uses, so much so that later historians decided that its adoption marked a new period in human history: the **Bronze Age**. The Bronze Age began about 3000 B.C.E., and by about 2500 B.C.E.,

bronze technology was having an impact in many parts of the world. The end of the Bronze Age came with the adoption of iron technology, which occurred from 1200 B.C.E. to 300 B.C.E. (see Chapter 2). All metals were expensive and hard to obtain, however, so stone, wood, and bone remained important materials for tools and weapons long into the Bronze and even Iron Age. Metals were not available at all in many parts of the world, so in some places stone, wood, and bone tools never lost their importance.

Objects were not the only things traded over increasingly long distances during the Neolithic period, for people also carried ideas as they traveled. Knowledge about the seasons and the weather was vitally important for those who depended on crop raising, and agricultural peoples in many parts of the world began to calculate recurring patterns in the world around them, slowly developing calendars. Using their own observations and ideas that came from elsewhere, they built earth and stone structures to help them predict the movements of the sun and stars. These included Nabta Playa, erected about 4500 B.C.E. in the desert west of the Nile Valley in Egypt, and Stonehenge, erected about 2500 B.C.E. in southern England.

The rhythms of the agricultural cycle and patterns of exchange also shaped religious beliefs and practices. In many places multiple gods came to be associated with patterns of birth, growth, death, and regeneration in a system known as **polytheism**. Like humans, the gods came to have a division of labor and a social hierarchy. There were rain gods and sun gods, sky goddesses and moon goddesses, gods that ensured the health of cattle or the growth of corn, and goddesses of the hearth and home.

What kind of civilization did the Sumerians build in Mesopotamia?

The origins of Western civilization are generally traced to an area that is today not seen as part of the West: Mesopotamia (mehs-oh-puh-TAY-mee-uh), the Greek name for the land between the Euphrates (yoo-FRAY-teez) and Tigris (TIGH-grihs) Rivers (Map 1.1), which today is in Iraq. The earliest agricultural villages in Mesopotamia were in the northern, hilly parts of the river valleys, where there is abundant rainfall for crops. By about 5000 B.C.E., farmers had brought techniques of crop raising southward to the southern part of Mesopotamia, called Sumer. In this arid climate farmers developed irrigation on a large scale, which demanded organized group effort but allowed the population to grow. By about 3800 B.C.E., one of the agricultural villages, Uruk (OO-rook), had expanded significantly, becoming what many historians view as the world's first city, with a population

that eventually numbered more than fifty thousand. People living in Uruk built large temples to honor their chief god and goddess, and they also invented the world's first system of writing. Over the next thousand years, other cities also grew in Sumer, trading with one another and adopting writing.

Environment and Mesopotamian Development

From the outset, geography had a profound effect on Mesopotamia because here agriculture is possible only with irrigation. Consequently, the Sumerians and later civilizations built their cities along the Tigris and Euphrates Rivers and their branches. They used the rivers to carry agricultural and trade goods, and also to

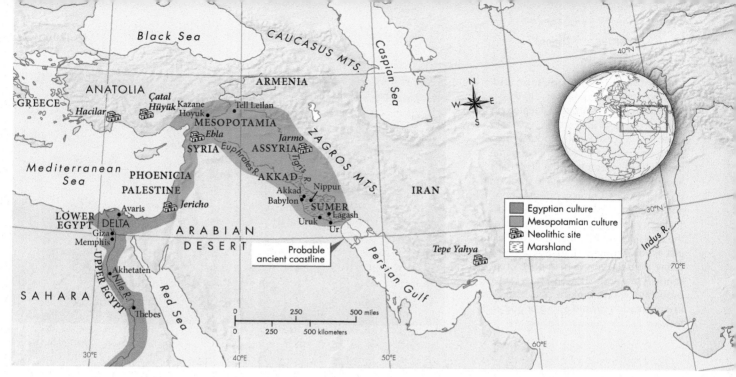

MAP 1.1 Spread of Cultures in the Ancient Near East, ca. 3000–1640 B.C.E.   This map illustrates the spread of the Mesopotamian and Egyptian cultures through the semicircular stretch of land often called the Fertile Crescent. From this area, the knowledge and use of agriculture spread throughout western Asia, North Africa, and Europe.

provide water for vast networks of irrigation channels. The Tigris and Euphrates flow quickly at certain times of the year and carry silt down from the mountains and hills, causing floods. To prevent major floods, the Sumerians created massive hydraulic projects, including reservoirs, dams, and dikes as well as canals. In stories written later, they described their chief god, Enlil, as "the raging flood which has no rival" and believed that at one point there had been a massive flood, a tradition that also gave rise to the biblical story of Noah:

> A flood will sweep over. . . . A decision that the seed of mankind is to be destroyed has been made. The verdict, the word of the divine assembly, cannot be revoked.[1]

Judging by historical records, however, actual destructive floods were few.

In addition to water and transport, the rivers supplied fish, a major element of the Sumerian diet, and reeds, which were used for making baskets and writing implements. The rivers also provided clay, which was hardened to create bricks, the Sumerians' primary building material in a region with little stone. Clay was fired into pots, and inventive artisans developed the potter's wheel so that they could make pots that were stronger and more uniform than those made by earlier methods of coiling ropes of clay. The potter's

wheel in turn appears to have led to the introduction of wheeled vehicles sometime in the fourth millennium B.C.E. Wheeled vehicles, pulled by domesticated donkeys, led to road building, which facilitated settlement, trade, and conquest, although travel and transport by water remained far easier.

Cities and villages in Sumer and farther up the Tigris and Euphrates traded with one another, and even before the development of writing or kings, it appears that colonists sometimes set out from one city to travel hundreds of miles to the north or west to found a new city or to set up a community in an existing center. These colonies might well have provided the Sumerian cities with goods, such as timber and metal ores, that were not available locally. The cities of the Sumerian heartland continued to grow and to develop governments, and each one came to dominate the surrounding countryside, becoming city-states independent from one another, though not very far apart.

The city-states of Sumer continued to rely on irrigation systems that required cooperation and at least some level of social and political cohesion. The authority to run this system was, it seems, initially assumed by Sumerian priests. Encouraged and directed by their religious leaders, people built temples on tall platforms in the center of their cities. Temples grew into elaborate complexes of buildings with storage

---

■ **Bronze Age** The period in which the production and use of bronze implements became basic to society.

■ **polytheism** The worship of many gods and goddesses.

Clay Letter Written in Cuneiform and Its Envelope, ca. 1850 B.C.E. In this letter from a city in Anatolia, located on the northern edge of the Fertile Crescent in what is now Turkey, a Mesopotamian merchant complains to his brother at home, hundreds of miles away, that life is hard and comments on the trade in silver, gold, tin, and textiles. Correspondents often enclosed letters in clay envelopes and sealed them by rolling a cylinder seal across the clay, leaving the impression of a scene, just as you might use a stamped wax seal today. Here the very faint impression of the sender's seal at the bottom shows a person, probably the owner of the seal, being led in a procession toward a king or god. (© The Trustees of the British Museum/Art Resource, NY)

space for grain and other products and housing for animals. (Much later, by about 2100 B.C.E., some of the major temple complexes were embellished with a huge stepped pyramid, called a ziggurat, with a shrine on the top.) The Sumerians believed that humans had been created to serve the gods, who lived in the temples. To support the needs of the gods, including the temple constructions, and to support the religious leaders, temples owned large estates, including fields and orchards. Temple officials employed individuals to work the temple's land.

By 2500 B.C.E. there were more than a dozen city-states in Sumer. Each city developed religious, political, and military institutions, and judging by the fact that people began to construct walls around the cities and other fortifications, warfare between cities was quite common. Presumably their battles were sometimes sparked by disputes over water, as irrigation in one area reduced or altered the flow of rivers in other areas.

The Invention of Writing and the First Schools

The origins of writing probably go back to the ninth millennium B.C.E., when Near Eastern peoples used clay tokens as counters for record keeping. By the fourth millennium, people had realized that impressing the tokens on clay, or drawing pictures of the tokens on clay, was simpler than making tokens. This breakthrough in turn suggested that more information could be conveyed by adding pictures of still other objects. The result was a complex system of pictographs in which each sign pictured an object. These pictographs were the forerunners of the Sumerian form of writing known as **cuneiform** (kyou-NEE-uh-form) (Figure 1.1), from the Latin term

for "wedge shaped," used to describe the indentations made by a sharpened stylus in clay; cuneiform was invented about 3200 B.C.E.

Pictographs were initially limited in that they could not represent abstract ideas, but the development of ideograms—signs that represented ideas—made writing more versatile. Thus the sign for star could also be used to indicate heaven, sky, or even god. The development of the Sumerian system of writing was piecemeal, with scribes making changes and additions as they were needed. Over time, the system became so complicated that scribal schools were established; by 2500 B.C.E., these schools flourished throughout Sumer. Students at the schools were all male, and most came from families in the middle range of urban society. Each school had a master, teachers, and monitors. Discipline was strict,

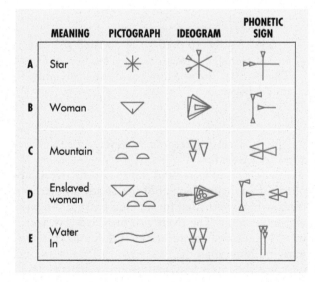

	MEANING	PICTOGRAPH	IDEOGRAM	PHONETIC SIGN
A	Star			
B	Woman			
C	Mountain			
D	Enslaved woman			
E	Water In			

FIGURE 1.1 Sumerian Writing
(Source: S. N. Kramer, *The Sumerians: Their History, Culture, and Character.* Copyright © 1963 by The University of Chicago Press.)

■ **cuneiform** Sumerian form of writing; the term describes the wedge-shaped marks made by a stylus.

and students were caned for sloppy work and misbehavior. One graduate of a scribal school had few fond memories of the joy of learning:

> My headmaster read my tablet, said:
> "There is something missing," caned me.
>
> . . .
>
> The fellow in charge of silence said:
> "Why did you talk without permission," caned me.
> The fellow in charge of the assembly said:
> "Why did you stand at ease without permission," caned me.[2]

Scribal schools were primarily intended to produce individuals who could keep records of the property of temple officials, kings, and nobles. Thus writing first developed as a way to enhance the growing power of elites, not to record speech, although it later came to be used for that purpose, and the stories of gods, kings, and heroes were also written down. Hundreds of thousands of hardened clay tablets have survived from ancient Mesopotamia, and from them historians have learned about many aspects of life, including taxes and wages. Sumerians wrote numbers as well as words on clay tablets, and some surviving tablets show multiplication and division problems.

Religion in Mesopotamia

To Sumerians, and to later peoples in Mesopotamia as well, the world was controlled by gods and goddesses, who represented cosmic forces such as the sun, moon, water, and storms. The king of the gods was Enlil, who was believed to rule over the gods just as the king of a city-state ruled his population. Almost as powerful were the gods of the sun, of storms, and of freshwater. Each city generally had a chief god or goddess, or sometimes several, with a large temple built in his or her honor. In Uruk, for example, one of the central temples was dedicated to the goddess Inanna, the goddess of love and sexuality, who was also associated with the planet Venus. In one widely told myth, Inanna descends to the underworld, setting off a long struggle among her worshippers to find a replacement. Another deity is found to take her place, but then Inanna returns, just as Venus sets and rises.

People believed that humans had been created to serve the gods and generally anticipated being well treated by the gods if they served them well. The best way to honor the gods was to make the temple as grand and impressive as possible because the temple's size demonstrated the strength of the community and the power of its chief deity. Once it was built, the temple itself was often off-limits to ordinary people, who did not worship there as a spiritual community. Instead the temple was staffed by priests and priestesses who carried out rituals to honor the god or

Sacrificial Procession Scene　　In this fragment from a wall painting from the palace of King Zimri-Lim of Mari on the middle Euphrates from about 1800 B.C.E., a giant deity in a scalloped robe strides in front of priests, one of whom is leading a bull to be sacrificed. Mari was an important city-state in Mesopotamia, and the public rooms of its palace were decorated with scenes showing the close link between kings and deities. (Musée du Louvre, Paris, France/Bridgeman Images)

goddess. Kings and other political leaders might also visit the temple and carry out religious ceremonies from time to time, particularly when they thought the assistance of the gods was especially needed.

The peoples of Mesopotamia had many myths to account for the creation of the universe. According to one told by the Babylonians, in the beginning was the primeval sea, known as the goddess Tiamat, who gave birth to the gods. When Tiamat tried to destroy the gods, Marduk, the chief god of the Babylonians, proceeded to kill her and divide her body and thus created the sky and earth. These myths are the earliest known attempts to answer the question, how did it all begin? They traveled with people when they moved and were eventually written down, but not until long after they had first been told, and they often had many variations. Written texts were not an important part of Sumerian religious life, nor were they central to the religious practices of most of the other peoples in this region.

In addition to stories about gods, the Sumerians told stories about heroes and kings, many of which were eventually reworked into the world's first epic poem, the *Epic of Gilgamesh* (GIL-guh-mesh). An epic poem is a narration of the achievements, the labors, and sometimes the failures of heroes that embodies peoples' ideas about themselves. Historians can use epic poems to learn about various aspects of a society, and to that extent epics can be used as historical sources. This epic recounts the wanderings of Gilgamesh—the semihistorical king of Uruk—and his search for eternal life, and it grapples with enduring questions about life and death, friendship, humankind and deities, and immortality.

Sumerian Politics and Society

Exactly how kings emerged in Sumerian society is not clear. Scholars have suggested that during times of emergencies, a chief priest or perhaps a military leader assumed what was supposed to be temporary authority over a city. Temporary power gradually became permanent kingship, and sometime before 2450 B.C.E. kings in some Sumerian city-states began transferring their kingship to their sons, establishing patriarchal hereditary dynasties in which power was handed down through the male line. This is the point at which written records about kingship began to appear. The symbol of royal status was the palace, which came to rival the temple in grandeur.

Kings made alliances with other powerful individuals, often through marriage. Royal family members were depended upon for many aspects of government. Kings worked closely with religious authorities and relied on ideas about the kings' connections with the gods, as well as the kings' military might, for their power. Acting together, priests, kings, and officials in Sumerian cities used force, persuasion, and taxation to maintain order, keep the irrigation systems working, and keep food and other goods flowing.

The king and his officials held extensive tracts of land, as did the temple; these lands were worked by the palace's or the temple's clients, free men and women who were dependent on the palace or the temple. They received crops and other goods in return for their labor. Some individuals and families owned land outright and paid their taxes in the form of agricultural products or items they made. At the bottom rung of society were enslaved people, some of whom were most likely prisoners of war and criminals who had lost their freedom as punishment for their crimes; others perhaps came into slavery to repay debts. Compared to many later societies, slavery was not widespread in Sumer, where most agricultural work was done by dependent clients. Enslaved people in Sumer also engaged in trade and made profits. They could borrow money, and many were able to buy their freedom.

Sumerian society made distinctions based on gender. Most elite landowners were male, but women who held positions as priestesses or as queens ran their own estates, independently of their husbands and fathers. Some women owned businesses and took care of their own accounts. They could own property and distribute it to their offspring. Sons and daughters inherited from their parents, although a daughter received her inheritance in the form of a dowry, which technically remained hers but was managed by her husband or husband's family after marriage. The Sumerians established the basic social, economic, and intellectual patterns of Mesopotamia, and they influenced their neighbors to the north and east.

Mesopotamian Harpist
This small clay tablet, carved between 2000 B.C.E. and 1500 B.C.E., shows a seated woman playing a harp. Her fashionable dress and hat suggest that she is playing for wealthy people, perhaps at the royal court. Images of musicians are common in Mesopotamian art, indicating that music was important in Mesopotamian culture and social life. (Musée du Louvre, Paris, France/Erich Lessing/ Art Resource, NY)

to 1200 B.C.E.

How did the Akkadian and Old Babylonian empires develop in Mesopotamia?

15

How did the Akkadian and Old Babylonian empires develop in Mesopotamia?

The wealth of Sumerian cities also attracted non-Sumerian conquerors from the north, beginning with the Akkadians and then the Babylonians. Both of these peoples created large states in the valley of the Tigris and Euphrates, and Hammurabi, one ruler of Babylon, proclaimed an extensive law code. Merchants traveled throughout the Fertile Crescent and beyond, carrying products and facilitating cultural exchange.

The Akkadians and the Babylonians

In 2331 B.C.E., Sargon, the king of a city to the north of Sumer, conquered a number of Sumerian cities with what was probably the world's first permanent army and created a large state. The symbol of his triumph was a new capital, the city of Akkad (AH-kahd). Sargon also expanded the Akkadian empire westward to north Syria. He encouraged trading networks that brought in goods from as far away as the Indus River and what is now Turkey. Sargon spoke a different language than did the Sumerians, one of the many languages that scholars identify as belonging to the Semitic language family, which includes modern-day Hebrew and Arabic. However, Akkadians adapted cuneiform writing to their own language, and Akkadian became the diplomatic language used over a wide area.

Sargon tore down the defensive walls of Sumerian cities and appointed his own sons as their rulers to help him cement his power. He also appointed his daughter, Enheduana (2285–2250 B.C.E.), as high priestess in the city of Ur. Here she wrote a number of hymns, especially those in praise of the goddess Inanna, becoming the world's first author to put her name to a literary composition. (See "Thinking Like a Historian: Addressing the Gods," page 16.) For hundreds of years Enheduana's works were copied on clay tablets, which have been found in several cities in the area, indicating that people may have recited or read them.

Sargon's dynasty appears to have ruled Mesopotamia for about 150 years, during which time the Tigris and Euphrates Valleys attracted immigrants from many places. Then his empire collapsed, in part because of a period of extended drought, and the various city-states became independent again. One group of immigrants into Mesopotamia were the Amorites (AM-uh-rites), who migrated from the west. The Amorites were initially nomadic pastoralists, not agriculturalists, but they began to raise crops when they settled throughout Mesopotamia. They founded several city-states after Sargon's dynasty ended, one of which was Babylon along the middle Euphrates, where that river runs close to the Tigris. Babylon became more than a city-state, growing to

Sargon of Akkad This bronze head, with elaborately worked hair and beard, might portray the great conqueror Sargon of Akkad (though his name does not appear on it). The eyes were originally inlaid with jewels, which have since been gouged out. Produced around 2300 B.C.E., this head was found in the ruins of the Assyrian capital of Nineveh, where it had been taken as loot. (INTERFOTO/Alamy)

include smaller territories whose rulers recognized the king of Babylon as their overlord.

Life Under Hammurabi

Hammurabi of Babylon (r. 1792–1750 B.C.E.) was initially a typical king of his era, but late in his reign he conquered several other kingdoms, uniting most of Mesopotamia under his rule. The era from his reign to around 1595 B.C.E. is called the Old Babylonian period. As had earlier rulers, Hammurabi linked his success with the will of the gods. He encouraged the spread of myths that explained how Marduk, the primary god of Babylon, had been elected king of the gods by the other deities in Mesopotamia. Marduk later became widely regarded as the chief god of Mesopotamia, absorbing the qualities and powers of other gods.

Hammurabi's most memorable accomplishment was the proclamation of an extensive law code, introduced about 1755 B.C.E. Like the codes of the earlier lawgivers, **Hammurabi's law code** proclaimed that he issued his laws on divine authority "to establish law and justice in the language of the land, thereby promoting the welfare

■ **Hammurabi's law code** A proclamation issued by Babylonian king Hammurabi to establish laws regulating many aspects of life.

Addressing the Gods

Hymns and incantations to the gods are among the earliest written texts in Mesopotamia and Egypt, and sculpture and paintings also often show people addressing the gods. The sources here are examples of such works. What ideas about the gods and the way humans should address them are shared in all these sources, and how do ideas in Egypt differ from those in Mesopotamia?

1 **Enheduana's "Exaltation of Inanna."** Enheduana (2285–2250 B.C.E.), the daughter of Sargon of Akkad, was appointed by her father as high priestess in the Sumerian city of Ur, where she wrote a number of literary and religious works that were frequently recopied long after her death, including this hymn to the goddess Inanna.

~ Your divinity shines in the pure heavens. . . . Your torch lights up the corners of heaven, turning darkness into light. The men and women form a row for you and each one's daily status hangs down before you. Your numerous people pass before you, as before Utu [the sun-god], for their inspection. No one can lay a hand on your precious divine powers; all your divine powers. . . . You exercise full ladyship over heaven and earth; you hold everything in your hand. Mistress, you are magnificent, no one can walk before you. You dwell with great An [the god of the heavens] in the holy resting-place. Which god is like you in gathering together . . . in heaven and earth? You are magnificent, your name is praised, you alone are magnificent!

I am En-hedu-ana, the high priestess of the moon god. . . . Mercy, compassion, care, lenience and homage are yours, and to cause flood storms, to open hard ground and to turn darkness into light. My lady, let me proclaim your magnificence in all lands, and your glory! Let me praise your ways and greatness! Who rivals you in divinity? Who can compare with your divine rites? . . . An and Enlil [the chief god of Sumer] have determined a great destiny for you throughout the entire universe. They have bestowed upon you ladyship in the assembly chamber. Being fitted for ladyship, you determine the destiny of noble ladies. Mistress, you are magnificent, you are great! Inanna, you are magnificent, you are great! My lady, your magnificence is resplendent. May your heart be restored for my sake! Your great deeds are unparalleled, your magnificence is praised! Young woman, Inanna, your praise is sweet!

(Werner Forman/Universal Images Group/Getty Images)

2 **Babylonian cylinder seal showing a man addressing the deities.** Dating from the Old Babylonian period (1800–1600 B.C.E.), this seal shows a man (left) addressing two deities, the one on the right holding the rod and ring, symbols of authority. The cuneiform inscription reads, "Ibni-Amurru, son of Ilima-ahi, servant of the god Amurru."

3 **Pyramid text of King Unas.** This incantation, designed to assist the king's ascent to the heavens after his death, was inscribed on a wall of the royal burial chambers in the pyramid of the Egyptian king Unas (r. 2375–2345) at Saqqara, a burial ground near the Nile.

~ Re-Atum [the sun-god], this Unas comes to you,
A spirit indestructible
Who lays claim to the place of the four pillars!
Your son comes to you, this Unas comes to you
May you cross the sky united in the dark,

ANALYZING THE EVIDENCE

1. In Source 1 from Mesopotamia, what powers and qualities of the goddess Inanna does Enheduana praise? In Source 2, what qualities do the deities in the cylinder seal exhibit?
2. In Sources 3–5 from Egypt, what powers and qualities does the sun-god exhibit?
3. What common features do you see across all the sources in the powers ascribed to the gods and the proper attitude of humans in addressing them?
4. Continuing to think about similarities, bear in mind that Enheduana was a member of the ruling dynasty of Akkad, and Unas and Akhenaton were kings of Egypt. How did their social position shape their relationship to the gods?
5. The pharaohs of Egypt were also regarded as gods; how does this make the relationship of Unas and Akhenaton to the sun-god distinctive?

May you rise in lightland, the place in which you
    shine!
Osiris, Isis, go proclaim to Lower Egypt's gods
And their spirits:
"This Unas comes, a spirit indestructible,
Like the morning star above Hapy [the god of the
    flooding of the Nile],
Whom the water-spirits worship;
Whom he wishes to live will live,
Whom he wishes to die will die!"

. . .

Thoth [the god of law and science], go proclaim
    to the gods of the west
And their spirits:
"This Unas comes, a spirit indestructible,
Decked above the neck as Anubis
Lord of the western height
He will count hearts, he will claim hearts,
Whom he wishes to live will live,
Whom he wishes to die will die!"

5 **Relief depicting Akhenaton,
Nefertiti, and their daughter,
Meritaton, making an
offering to Aton.** This carved
alabaster relief comes from the
royal palace at Tell el-Amarna.

(Egyptian National Museum, Cairo, Egypt/Bridgeman Images)

4 **Hymn to Aton.** When the pharaoh Akhenaton (r. 1351–1334 B.C.E.) promoted the worship of the
sun-god Aton instead of older Egyptian gods, new hymns were written for the pharaoh to sing in
honor of the god.

Thou appearest beautifully on the horizon of heaven
Thou living Aton, the beginning of life!
When thou art risen on the eastern horizon,
Thou hast filled every land with thy beauty.
Thou art gracious, great, glistening, and high over every land;
Thy rays encompass the lands to the limit of all that thou hast made

. . .

Thy rays suckle every meadow.
When thou risest, they live, they grow for thee.
Thou makest the seasons in order to rear all that thou hast made,
The winter to cool them,
And the heat that they may taste thee.
Thou hast made the distant sky in order to rise therein,
In order to see all that thou dost make.
While thou wert alone,
Rising in thy form as the living Aton,

Appearing, shining, withdrawing or approaching,
Thou madest millions of forms of thyself alone.
Cities, towns, fields, road, and river —
Every eye beholds thee over against them,
For thou art the Aton of the day over the earth . . .
Thou art in my heart,
And there is no other that knows thee
Save thy son Nefer-kheperu-Re Wa-en-Re [Akhenaton],
For thou hast made him well versed in thy plans and in thy
    strength . . .
Since thou didst found the earth
And raise them up for thy son
Who came forth from thy body:
The king of Upper and lower Egypt, . . . Akhenaton . . . and the
    Chief Wife of the King . . . Nefertiti, living and youthful forever
    and ever.

PUTTING IT ALL TOGETHER

Using the sources above, along with what you have learned in class and in this chapter, write
a short essay that compares ideas about the gods in Mesopotamia and Egypt. How do these
ideas reflect the physical environment in which these two cultures developed, and how do they
reflect their social and political structures?

Sources: (1) J. A. Black et al., *Electronic Text Corpus of Sumerian Literature* (http://etcsl.orinst.ox.ac.uk/), Oxford 1998–2006; (3) Miriam Lichtheim, *Ancient
Egyptian Literature: A Book of Readings*, vol. 1, *The Old and Middle Kingdoms* (Berkeley: University of California Press, 1973), p. 31; (4) John A. Wilson,
trans., in James B. Pritchard, ed., *Ancient Near Eastern Texts Relating to the Old Testament — Third Edition with Supplement* (Princeton, N.J.: Princeton University
Press, 1969), pp. 370–371.

of the people." Its 282 laws set a variety of punishments, primarily fines, but also physical punishment such as mutilation, whipping, and burning. It is unknown whether its provisions were always or even generally followed, but it influenced other law codes of the area, including those later written down in Hebrew Scripture.

Hammurabi's code began with legal procedure. There were no public prosecutors or district attorneys, so individuals brought their own complaints before the court. Each side had to produce witnesses to support its case. In cases of murder, the accuser had to prove the defendant guilty; any accuser who failed to do so was put to death. Another procedural regulation declared that once a judge had rendered a verdict, he could not change it. Hammurabi's code provides a wealth of information about daily life in Mesopotamia. Because of farming's fundamental importance, the code dealt extensively with agriculture. Tenants faced severe penalties for neglecting the land or not working it at all. Because irrigation was essential to grow crops, tenants had to keep the canals and ditches in good repair. Anyone whose neglect of the canals resulted in damaged crops had to bear all the expense of the lost crops. Those tenants who could not pay the costs were forced into slavery. Those who helped enslaved people escape were to be put to death.

Babylon was a society in which business was important, so many of the laws are about contracts and what happens if someone breaks them. Those who defrauded others were to pay back ten times the amount, and a merchant who tried to increase the interest rate on a loan forfeited the entire amount. Laws about business indicate that many women carried out trade on their own; provisions about wine sellers refer to them as "she," and women were specifically allowed to sell property. There was also a form of consumer protection: a boat builder who did sloppy work had to repair the boat at his own expense.

About one-third of the laws relate to marriage and the family. As elsewhere in southwest Asia, marriage had aspects of a business agreement. The groom or his father offered the prospective bride's father a gift, called a marriage settlement, and if this was acceptable, the bride's father provided his daughter with a dowry. As in Sumer, after marriage the dowry belonged to the woman and was a means of protecting her rights and status. Expectations for how husbands and wives should behave were embedded in the law code, with differential treatment of cases depending on whether the spouses had lived up to these. (See "Evaluating Written Evidence: Hammurabi's Code on Marriage and Divorce," page 19.) Reproduction was clearly important: a man was specifically allowed to bring a concubine into the household or have children with servants or enslaved women if his wife could not bear children.

The penalty for adultery, defined as sex between a married woman and a man not her husband, was death. A husband had the power to spare his wife by obtaining a pardon for her from the king. He could, however, accuse his wife of adultery even if he had not caught her in the act. In such a case she could try to clear herself, and if she was found innocent, she could take her dowry and leave her husband.

Norms about how parents and children should behave toward one another were also embedded in the code. A father could not disinherit a son without just cause, and the code ordered the courts to forgive a son for his first offense. Men could adopt children into their families and include them in their wills, which artisans sometimes did to teach them the family trade, or wealthy landowners sometimes did to pass along land to able younger men, particularly if they had no children of their own.

The Code of Hammurabi demanded that the punishment fit the crime, calling for "an eye for an eye, and a tooth for a tooth," at least among equals. However, a higher-ranking man who physically hurt a commoner or an enslaved person, perhaps by breaking his arm or putting out his eye, could pay a fine to the victim instead of having his arm broken or losing his own eye. As long as criminal and victim shared the same social status, however, the victim could demand exact vengeance.

Cultural Exchange in the Fertile Crescent

Law codes, preoccupied as they are with the problems of society, provide a bleak view of things, but other Mesopotamian documents give a happier glimpse of life. Wills and financial documents reveal couples who respected one another and women who were engaged in business. The Mesopotamians enjoyed a vibrant and creative culture that left its mark on the entire Fertile Crescent, as other groups adopted Mesopotamian practices. Mesopotamian writing, mathematics, merchandise, and other aspects of the culture spread far beyond the Tigris and Euphrates Valleys. Overland trade connected Sumer, Akkad, and Babylon with the eastern Mediterranean coast, where cities flourished under local rulers. (See "Viewpoints: Faulty Merchandise in Babylon and Egypt," page 20.) These cities were mercantile centers rich not only in manufactured goods but also in agricultural produce, textiles, and metals. People in Syria and elsewhere in the Middle East used Akkadian cuneiform to communicate in writing with their more distant neighbors.

Southern and central Anatolia (modern Turkey) presented a similar picture of extensive contact between cultures. Major Anatolian cities with large local populations were also home to colonies of traders from Mesopotamia. Thousands of cuneiform tablets testify to centuries of commercial and cultural exchanges with Mesopotamia, and eventually with Egypt, which rose to power in the Nile Valley.

Hammurabi's Code on Marriage and Divorce

Most of the provisions in Hammurabi's law code concern what we today term civil law rather than criminal law, including a great many on the family. The following are only some of many that concern marriage and the relationship between husbands and wives.

~

128. If a man take a wife and do not arrange with her the (proper) contracts, that woman is not a (legal) wife. . . .

137. If a man set his face to put away a concubine who has borne him children or a wife who has presented him with children, he shall return to that woman her dowry and shall give to her the income of field, garden and goods and she shall bring up her children; from the time that her children are grown up, from whatever is given to her children they shall give to her a portion corresponding to that of a son and the man of her choice may marry her.

138. If a man would put away his wife who has not borne him children, he shall give her money to the amount of her marriage settlement and he shall make good to her the dowry which she brought from her father's house and then he may put her away.

139. If there were no marriage settlement, he shall give to her one mana of silver for a divorce.

140. If he be a freeman [i.e., a formerly enslaved man], he shall give her one-third mana of silver.

141. If the wife of a man who is living in his house, set her face to go out and play the part of a fool, neglect her house, belittle her husband, they shall call her to account; if her husband say: "I have put her away," he shall let her go. On her departure nothing shall be given to her for her divorce. If her husband say: "I have not put her away," her husband may take another woman. The first woman shall dwell in the house of her husband as a maid servant.

142. If a woman hate her husband, and say: "Thou shalt not have me," they shall inquire into her reasons for this; and if she have been a careful mistress and be without reproach and her husband have been going about and greatly belittling her, that woman has no blame. She shall receive her dowry and shall go to her father's house.

143. If she have not been a careful mistress, have gadded about, have neglected her house and have belittled her husband, they shall throw that woman into the water.

EVALUATE THE EVIDENCE

1. According to the law code, what must a husband who wants to divorce his wife do, and what factors shape the consequences?
2. According to the law code, what must a wife who wants to divorce her husband do, and what factors shape the consequences?
3. What do these laws reveal about norms for male and female behavior in ancient Babylon, that is, what people thought made a good husband and a good wife?

Source: *The Code of Hammurabi, King of Babylon*, translated by Robert Francis Harper (Chicago: University of Chicago Press, 1904), pp. 62, 63–64.

How did the Egyptians establish a prosperous and long-lasting society?

At about the same time that Sumerian city-states expanded and fought with one another in the Tigris and Euphrates Valleys, a more cohesive state under a single ruler grew in the valley of the Nile River in North Africa. This was Egypt, which for long stretches of history was prosperous and secure behind desert areas on both sides of the Nile Valley. At various times groups migrated into Egypt seeking better lives or invaded and conquered Egypt. Often these newcomers adopted aspects of Egyptian religion, art, and politics, and the Egyptians also carried their traditions with them when they established an empire and engaged in trade.

The Nile and the God-King

No other single geographical factor had such a fundamental and profound impact on the shaping of

Goods of all sorts were bought, sold, and transported throughout the ancient world, and, as happens today, some were not of the quality those receiving them expected. The following documents discuss faulty merchandise. The first is from an inscribed clay tablet from Babylon, sent about 1750 B.C.E. by a copper merchant named Nanni to a copper smelter named Ea-nasir. Nanni complains about the copper received and the rude treatment given to his agent. It is probably the world's oldest customer-service complaint. The second is a letter written on papyrus in hieratic script, sent about 1200 B.C.E. by Khay, an official at the temple for the god Harakhti (Horus), to Montuhi, the mayor of Elephantine, a city on an island in the Nile. Khay comments about the poor-quality honey Montuhi had sent.

Nanni's Letter

Tell Ea-nasir Nanni sends the following message:

When you came, you said to me as follows: "I will give Gimil-Sin (when he comes) fine quality copper ingots." You left then but you did not do what you promised me. You put ingots which were not good before my messenger (Sit-Sin) and said: "If you want to take them, take them; if you do not want to take them, go away!"

What do you take me for, that you treat somebody like me with such contempt? I have sent as messengers gentlemen like ourselves to collect the bag with my money (deposited with you) but you have treated me with contempt by sending them back to me empty-handed several times, and that through enemy territory. Is there anyone among the merchants who trade with Telmun [a trading center on the Persian Gulf] who has treated me in this way? You alone treat my messenger with contempt! On account of that one (trifling) mina of silver which I owe (?) you, you feel free to speak in such a way, while I have given to the palace on your behalf 1,080 pounds of copper. . . . How have you treated me for that copper? You have withheld my money bag from me in enemy territory; it is now up to you to restore (my money)

to me in full. Take cognizance that (from now on) I will not accept here any copper from you that is not of fine quality. I shall (from now on) select and take the ingots individually in my own yard, and I shall exercise against you my right of rejection because you have treated me with contempt.

Khay's Letter

The [title lost] of the chapel of Harakhti, Khay, greets [the mayor] of Elephantine Montuhi [prosperity] and health and in the favor of Amon-Re, King of the Gods! . . .

I opened the jar of honey which you had procured for the god and proceeded to draw out ten *hin*-measures of honey from it for the divine offering, but I found it was all full of lumps of (congealed) ointment. So I resealed it and sent it back south to you. If it is someone else who gave it to you, let him inspect it. And you shall see whether you might locate a good (jar of honey) and send it on to me. Then shall Pre [a god] keep you healthy. But if there isn't any, you shall send the *menet*-jar of incense by the hand of the priest Netjermose until you locate some honey.

And you shall send me the timbers of seasoned sycamore wood. Then shall Amon-Re keep you healthy, and Harakhti let you achieve a long lifetime.

QUESTIONS FOR ANALYSIS

1. In Nanni's letter, along with the poor-quality copper Ea-nasir offered, why else is he upset? What does he threaten to do?
2. Nanni is a merchant, and Khay a priest. How do their occupations shape what they suggest will be the consequences for bad merchandise?
3. How does the information in these letters provide evidence for the economic and cultural developments discussed in this chapter?

Sources: Nanni's letter: A. Leo Oppenheim, ed., *Letters from Mesopotamia: Official, Business, and Private Letters on Clay Tablets from Two Millennia* (Chicago: University of Chicago Press, 1967), pp. 82–83; Khay's letter: Edward Wente, ed., *Letters from Ancient Egypt* (Athens, Ga.: Scholars Press, 1990), pp. 128–129.

Egyptian life, society, and history as the Nile River. The Nile flooded once a year for a period of several months, bringing fertile soil and moisture for farming, and agricultural villages developed along its banks by at least 6000 B.C.E. Although the Egyptians worried at times that these floods would be too high or too low, they also praised the Nile as a creative and comforting force:

> Hail to thee, O Nile, that issues from the earth
>   and comes to keep Egypt alive! . . .
> He that waters the meadows which Re [Ra] created,
> He that makes to drink the desert . . .
> He who makes barley and brings emmer [wheat]
>   into being . . .
> He who brings grass into being for the cattle . . .
> He who makes every beloved tree to grow . . .
> O Nile, verdant art thou, who makest man and
>   cattle to live.[3]

Egyptians Pulling Building Blocks   In this stylized painting on papyrus from the early Third Intermediate Period, men in a procession pull a sledge with building blocks, led by a man wearing a leopard-skin cape. Egyptians used sledges to haul massive stone blocks and construction materials for pyramids, temples, and monumental buildings, though other aspects of their construction techniques are open to debate, speculation, and attempts at reenactment. (Ancient Art and Architecture/Alamy)

The Egyptians based their calendar on the Nile, dividing the year into three four-month periods: *akhet* (flooding), *peret* (growth), and *shemu* (harvest).

Through the fertility of the Nile and their own hard work, Egyptians produced an annual agricultural surplus, which in turn sustained a growing and prosperous population. The Nile also unified Egypt. The river was the region's principal highway, promoting communication and trade throughout the valley.

Egypt was fortunate in that it was nearly self-sufficient. Besides having fertile soil, Egypt possessed enormous quantities of stone, which served as the raw material of architecture and sculpture, and abundant clay for pottery. Moreover, the raw materials that Egypt lacked were close at hand. The Egyptians could obtain copper from Sinai (SIGH-nigh) and timber from Lebanon, and they traded with peoples farther away to obtain other materials that they needed.

The political power structures that developed in Egypt came to be linked with the Nile. Somehow the idea developed that a single individual, a king, was responsible for the rise and fall of the Nile. This belief came about before the development of writing in Egypt, so, as with the growth of priestly and royal power in Sumer, the precise details of its origins have been lost. Egyptian kingship was linked with divinity, and the ruler was regarded as the living embodiment of the god Horus, the source of law and morality and the mediator between gods and humans. (See "Thinking Like a Historian: Addressing the Gods," page 16.) This divine force was found in all members of the pharaoh's family, and rulers or rulers-to-be occasionally married close relatives to increase the amount of divinity in the royal household and to imitate the behavior of the gods in Egyptian mythology. This concentrated divine blood set the pharaonic family apart from other Egyptians, who did not marry close relatives.

Political unification most likely proceeded slowly, but stories told about early kings highlighted one who had united Upper Egypt — the upstream valley in the south — and Lower Egypt — the delta area of the Nile that empties into the Mediterranean Sea — into a single kingdom around 3100 B.C.E. Historians later divided Egyptian history into dynasties, or families of kings, and modern historians divide Egyptian history into periods (see the chronology "Periods of Egyptian History"). The political unification of Egypt in the Archaic Period (3100–2660 B.C.E.) ushered in the period known as the Old Kingdom (2660–2180 B.C.E.), an era remarkable for prosperity and artistic flowering.

The focal point of religious and political life in the Old Kingdom was the king, who commanded wealth, resources, and people. The king's surroundings had to be worthy of a god, and only a magnificent palace was suitable for his home; in fact, the word **pharaoh**, which during the New Kingdom came to be used for the king, originally meant "great house." Just as the kings occupied a great house in life, so they reposed in great pyramids after death. Built during the Old Kingdom, these massive stone tombs contained all the things needed by the king in his afterlife. The pyramid also symbolized the king's power and his connection with the sun-god. After burial the entrance was blocked and concealed to ensure the king's undisturbed peace, although grave robbers later found the tombs fairly easy to plunder.

To ancient Egyptians, the king embodied the concept of **ma'at**, a cosmic harmony that embraced truth, justice, and moral integrity. Ma'at gave the king the right, authority, and duty to govern. To the people,

■ **pharaoh** The title given to the king of Egypt in the New Kingdom, from a word that meant "great house."

■ **ma'at** The Egyptian belief in a cosmic harmony that embraced truth, justice, and moral integrity; it gave the kings the right and duty to govern.

the king personified justice and order—harmony among themselves, nature, and the divine.

Kings did not always live up to this ideal, of course. The two parts of Egypt were difficult to hold together, and several times in Egypt's long history, there were periods of disunity, civil war, and chaos. During the First Intermediate Period (2180–2080 B.C.E.), rulers of various provinces asserted their independence from the king, and Upper and Lower Egypt were ruled by rival dynasties. There is evidence that the Nile's floods were unusually low during this period because of drought, which contributed to instability just as it helped bring down the Akkadian empire. Warrior-kings reunited Egypt in the Middle Kingdom (2080–1640 B.C.E.) and expanded Egyptian power southward into Nubia.

Egyptian Religion

Like the Mesopotamians, the Egyptians were polytheistic, worshipping many gods of all types, some mightier than others. They developed complex ideas of their gods that reflected the world around them, and these views changed over the many centuries of Egyptian history as gods took on new attributes and often merged with one another. During the Old Kingdom, Egyptians considered the sun-god Ra the creator of life. He commanded the sky, earth, and underworld. Ra was associated with the falcon-god Horus, the "lord of the sky," who served as the symbol of divine kingship.

Much later, during the New Kingdom (see the chronology "Periods of Egyptian History"), the pharaohs of a new dynasty favored the worship of a different sun-god, Amon, whom they described as creating the entire cosmos by his thoughts. Amon brought life to the land and its people, they wrote, and he sustained both. Because he had helped them overthrow their enemies, Egyptians came to consider Amon the champion of fairness and justice, especially for the common people. As his cult grew, Amon came to be identified with Ra, and eventually the Egyptians combined them into one sun-god, Amon-Ra.

The Egyptians likewise developed views of an afterlife that reflected the world around them

and that changed over time. During the later part of the Old Kingdom, the walls of kings' tombs were carved with religious texts that provided spells; these spells would bring the king back to life and help him ascend to Heaven, where he would join his divine father, Ra. Toward the end of the Old Kingdom, the tombs of powerful nobles also contained such inscriptions, an indication that more people expected to gain everlasting life. In the Middle Kingdom, new types of spells appeared on the coffins of even more people, a further expansion in admission to the afterlife.

During the New Kingdom, a time when Egypt came into greater contact with the cultures of the Fertile Crescent, Egyptians developed more complex ideas about the afterlife, recording these in funerary manuscripts that have come to be known as the *Book of the Dead*, written to help guide the dead through the difficulties of the underworld. These texts explained that the soul left the body to become part of the divine after death, and they told of the god Osiris (oh-SIGH-ruhs) who died each year and was then brought back to life by his wife, Isis (IGH-suhs), when the Nile flooded. Osiris eventually became king of the dead, weighing dead humans' hearts to determine whether they had lived justly enough to deserve everlasting life. (See "Thinking Like a Historian: The Moral Life," in Chapter 2 on page 40.) Egyptians also believed that proper funeral rituals, in which the physical body was mummified, were essential for life after death, so Osiris was assisted by Anubis, the jackal-headed god of mummification.

Funeral Stele of a Wealthy Woman   This painted wooden stele shows Djed-amon-iu-ankh (right), a wealthy Egyptian woman who lived in the Third Intermediate Period, in a thin gown and with a cone of ointment on her head, and the sun-god Ra (left) in the form of Horus the falcon-god. Ra-Horus is holding a scepter in one hand and the ankh, the Egyptian symbol of life, in the other. Djed-amon-iu-ankh offers food and lotus flowers to the god, and the hieroglyphs above them describe the offering. Steles were erected in Egypt for funeral purposes and depicted the person memorialized in an attitude of reverence. (The Picture Art Collection/Alamy)

New Kingdom pharaohs came to associate them-selves with both Horus and Osiris, and they were regarded as avatars of Horus in life and Osiris in death. The pharaoh's wife was associated with Isis, for both the queen and the goddess were regarded as protectors.

Egyptian Society and Work

Egyptian society reflected the pyramids that it built. At the top stood the king, who relied on a sizable circle of nobles, officials, and priests to administer his kingdom. All of them were assisted by scribes, who used a writing system perhaps adapted from Mesopotamia and perhaps developed independently. Egyptian scribes actually cre-ated two writing systems: one called hieroglyphic, which was used for important religious or political texts and inscriptions, and a much simpler system called hieratic, which allowed scribes to write more quickly. Hieratic writing was used for the documents of daily life, such as letters, contracts, and accounts, and also for medical and literary works. (See "Viewpoints: Faulty Merchan-dise in Babylon and Egypt," page 20.) Students learned hieratic first, and only those from well-off families or whose families had high aspirations took the time to learn hieroglyphics. In addition to scribes, the cities of the Nile Valley were home to artisans of all types, along with merchants and other tradespeople. A large group of farmers made up the broad base of the social pyramid.

For Egyptians, the Nile formed an essential part of daily life. During the season of its flooding, from June to October, farmers worked on the pharaoh's build-ing programs and other tasks away from their fields. When the water began to recede, they diverted some of it into ponds for future irrigation and began plant-ing wheat and barley for bread and beer, using plows pulled by oxen or people to part the soft mud. From October to February farming families planted and tended crops, and then from February until the next flood they harvested them.

As in Mesopotamia, common people paid their obligations to their superiors in products and in labor, and many faced penalties if they did not meet their quota. One scribe described the scene at harvest time:

> And now the scribe lands on the river bank and is about to register the harvest-tax. The janitors carry staves and the Nubians rods of palm, and they say, Hand over the grain, though there is none. The farmer is beaten all over, he is bound and thrown into a well, soused and dipped head downwards. His wife has been bound in his presence and his children are in fetters.[4]

Peoples' labor obligations in the Old Kingdom may have included forced work on the pyramids and canals,

PERIODS OF EGYPTIAN HISTORY

Dates	Period	Significant Events
3100–2660 B.C.E.	Archaic	Unification of Egypt
2660–2180 B.C.E.	Old Kingdom	Construction of the pyramids
2180–2080 B.C.E.	First Intermediate	Political disunity
2080–1640 B.C.E.	Middle Kingdom	Recovery and political stability
1640–1570 B.C.E.	Second Intermediate	Hyksos migrations; struggles for power
1570–1070 B.C.E.	New Kingdom	Creation of an Egyptian empire; growth in wealth
1070–712 B.C.E.	Third Intermediate	Political fragmentation and conquest by outsiders (see Chapter 2)

although recent research suggests that most people who built the pyramids were paid for their work. Some young men were drafted into the pharaoh's army, which served as both a fighting force and a labor corps.

Egyptian Family Life

The lives of all Egyptians centered around the family. Just as in Mesopotamia, first marriages were generally arranged by the couples' parents, and they seem to have taken place at a young age. Once couples were married, having children, especially sons, was a high priority, as indicated by surviving charms to promote fertility and prayers for successful childbirth. Boys continued the family line, and only they could per-form the proper burial rites for their father. (See "Eval-uating Visual Evidence: Egyptian Family Life," page 24.) Second marriages, resulting from divorce or the death of a spouse, were common and were more often determined by the spouses themselves.

Wealthy Egyptians lived in spacious homes with attractive gardens and walls for privacy. For them, life included a daily bath and clean clothes, along with perfumes as deodorants. Poorer people lived in cramped quarters, with narrow rooms for living, including two small rooms for sleeping and cooking. These small houses suggest that most Egyptians lived in small family groups, not as large extended fami-lies. The very poor lived in small buildings with their animals. Egyptians of all classes generally wore linen clothes made from fibers of the flax plant.

Egyptian Family Life

This painting from the tomb of the Egyptian official Inherkau, who lived and worked during the reign of Ramesses III (r. 1184–1153 B.C.E.), toward the end of the New Kingdom, shows the deceased and his wife Wabet (left) receiving offerings. The first man holds a statuette of the god Osiris and a box carrying ushabtis, small figurines that represented servants who would carry out tasks for the deceased in the afterlife. Inherkau and Wabet's children play around their feet with birds or bird toys. According to the conventions of tomb painting, children of the deceased were always shown very young and naked, no matter what their actual ages were at the time the painting was made. They were also depicted with what Egyptologists have called the sidelock of youth, a lock of hair on the side of their heads that showed their connections with the god Horus. Inherkau oversaw artisans and workers on the royal tombs at Thebes, as had his father and grandfather before him, whose names are also on the tomb. Most of the people who worked on the tombs at Thebes were not enslaved, but were paid for their labor. Many craftsmen and officials such as Inherkau built their own underground tombs near Thebes, with burial chambers with vaulted ceilings and wall decorations.

EVALUATE THE EVIDENCE

1. How does the artist suggest emotional connections between family members in this scene? How does the scene combine family life and religious rituals?
2. Based on this scene, how would you describe the Egyptian view of the afterlife?

(From the Tomb of Ankerkhe, Workmen's Tombs, Deir el-Medina, Thebes, Egypt/Bridgeman Images)

Marriage was a family matter, not a religious ritual, and a woman brought some of her family's property to the marriage, which continued to belong to her, though her husband had the right to manage it. Both spouses could initiate divorce, and if they divorced, the woman took her marriage portion with her and could also claim a share of the profits made during her marriage. Women could own land in their own names, operate businesses, testify in court, and bring legal action against men. Some wealthy Egyptian men had several wives or concubines, but most men had only one wife. Information from literature and art depicts a world in which ordinary husbands and wives enjoyed each other's company alone and together with family and friends. Egyptian tomb monuments often show the couple happily standing or sitting together.

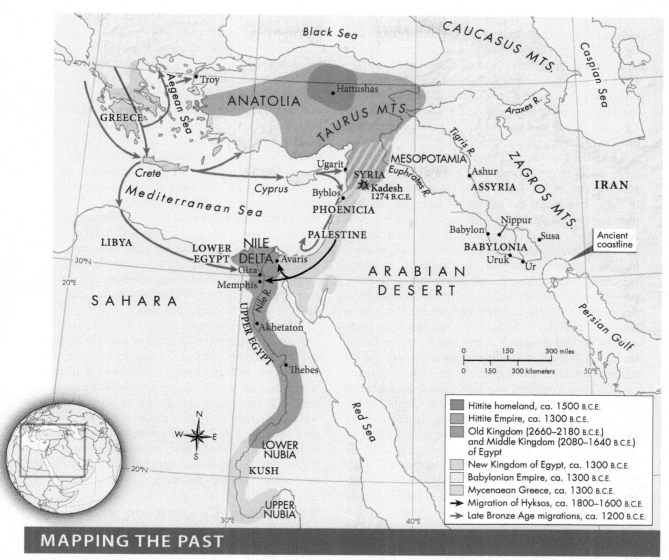

MAPPING THE PAST

MAP 1.2 Empires and Migrations in the Eastern Mediterranean

The rise and fall of empires in the eastern Mediterranean were shaped by internal developments, military conflicts, and the migration of peoples to new areas.

ANALYZING THE MAP At what point was the Egyptian empire at its largest? The Hittite Empire? What were the other major powers in the eastern Mediterranean at this point?

CONNECTIONS What were the major effects of the migrations of the Hyksos? Of the late Bronze Age migrations? What clues does the map provide about why the late Bronze Age migrations had a more powerful impact than those of the Hyksos?

The Hyksos and New Kingdom Revival

While Egyptian civilization flourished in the Nile Valley, various groups migrated throughout the Fertile Crescent and then accommodated themselves to local cultures (Map 1.2). Some settled in the Nile Delta, including a group the Egyptians called Hyksos, which means "rulers of the uplands." Although they were later portrayed as a conquering horde, the Hyksos were actually migrants looking for good land, and

their entry into the delta, which began around 1800 B.C.E., was probably gradual and generally peaceful.

The Hyksos brought with them the methods of making bronze and casting it into tools and weapons that became standard in Egypt. The Hyksos also brought inventions that revolutionized Egyptian warfare, including bronze armor and weapons as well as horse-drawn chariots and the composite bow made of laminated wood and horn, which was far more powerful than the simple wooden bow.

The migration of the Hyksos, combined with a series of famines and internal struggles for power, led Egypt to fragment politically in what later came to be known as the Second Intermediate Period (1640–1570 B.C.E.). During this time, the Egyptians adopted bronze technology and new forms of weaponry from the Hyksos, while the newcomers began to worship Egyptian deities and modeled their political structure on that of the Egyptians.

In about 1570 B.C.E., a new dynasty of pharaohs arose, pushing the Hyksos out of the delta, subduing Nubia in the south, and conquering parts of Canaan in the northeast. In this way, these Egyptian warrior-pharaohs inaugurated what scholars refer to as the New Kingdom—a period in Egyptian history characterized by not only enormous wealth and conscious imperialism but also a greater sense of insecurity because of new contacts and military engagements. By expanding Egyptian power beyond the Nile Valley, the pharaohs created the first Egyptian empire, and they celebrated their triumphs with monuments on a scale unparalleled since the pyramids of the Old Kingdom. Even today the colossal granite statues of these pharaohs and the rich tomb objects testify to the might and splendor of the New Kingdom.

The New Kingdom pharaohs include a number of remarkable figures. Among these was Hatshepsut (r. ca. 1479–ca. 1458 B.C.E.), one of the few female pharaohs in Egypt's long history, who expanded Egyptian holdings, sent trading expeditions, and promoted the arts. (See "Individuals in Society: Hatshepsut," page 27.) Amenhotep III (r. ca. 1388–ca.1350 B.C.E.) corresponded with other powerful kings in Babylonia and other kingdoms in the Fertile Crescent, sending envoys, exchanging gifts, and in some cases marrying their daughters. The kings promised friendship and active cooperation. They made alliances for offensive and defensive protection and swore to uphold one another's authority. Hence, the greatest powers of the period maintained peace, which facilitated the movement of gifts between kings and trade between ordinary people.

Amenhotep III was succeeded by his son, who took the name Akhenaton (ah-keh-NAH-tuhn) (r. 1351–1334 B.C.E.). He renamed himself as a mark of his changing religious ideas. Egyptians had long worshipped various sun-gods and aspects of the sun—Ra, Amon, Amon-Ra—but Akhenaton favored instead the worship of the god Aton (also spelled Aten), the visible disk of the sun. He was not a monotheist (someone who worships only one god), but he did order that the names of other sun-gods be erased from the walls of buildings, transferred taxes from the traditional priesthood of Amon-Ra, and built huge new temples to Aton, especially at his new capital in the area now known as Amarna. In these temples Aton was to be worshipped in bright sunlight. Akhenaton also had artists portray him in more realistic ways than they had portrayed earlier pharaohs; he is depicted interacting with his children and especially with his wife Nefertiti (nehf-uhr-TEE-tee), who supported his new religious ideas.

Akhenaton's new religion, imposed from above, failed to find a place among the people, however. After his death, traditional religious practices returned and the capital was moved back to Thebes. The priests of Amon-Ra led this restoration, but it was also supported by Akhenaton's son Tutankhamon (r. 1333–1323 B.C.E.), whose short reign was not particularly noteworthy and whose name would probably not be remembered except for the fact that his was the only tomb of an Egyptian king to be discovered nearly intact. Study of Tutankhamon's mummy also revealed that he suffered from malaria and a malformed foot, and had broken his leg shortly before he died. His high status did not make him immune to physical ailments. The wealth of "King Tut's tomb," assembled for a boy-king who died unexpectedly at nineteen, can only suggest what must have originally been in the tomb of a truly powerful pharaoh.

Tutankhamon's short reign was also marked by international problems, including warfare on several of the borders of the Egyptian empire. His grandfather and father had engaged in extensive diplomatic relations with rulers of states dependent on Egypt and with other powerful kings, but Tutankhamon was less successful at these diplomatic tasks. He also died childless. His successors were court officials, and in 1298 B.C.E. one of them established a new dynasty whose members would reassert Egypt's imperial power and respond to new challenges.

Conflict and Cooperation with the Hittites

One of the key challenges facing the pharaohs after Tutankhamon was the expansion of the kingdom of the Hittites. At about the same time that the Sumerians were establishing city-states, speakers of Indo-European languages migrated into Anatolia. Indo-European is a large family of languages that includes English, most of the languages of modern Europe, Persian, and Sanskrit. It also includes Hittite, the language of a people who seem to have migrated into this area about 2300 B.C.E.

Surviving records indicate that in the sixteenth century B.C.E. the Hittite king Hattusili I led his forces against neighboring kingdoms. Hattusili's grandson and successor, Mursili I, extended the Hittite conquests as far as Babylon. On his return home, the victorious Mursili was assassinated by members of his own family, which led to dynastic warfare. This pattern of expansion followed by internal conflict was repeated frequently, but when they were united behind a strong king, the Hittites were extremely powerful.

As the Hittites expanded southward, they came into conflict with the Egyptians, who were re-establishing their empire. The pharaoh Ramesses II engaged in

INDIVIDUALS IN SOCIETY

Hatshepsut

The familial connection between the pharaohs and the gods allowed a handful of women to rule in their own right in Egypt's long history, often during the political turmoil at a dynasty's end, forming the link to the next dynastic rule. We know the names of six female pharaohs, including Sobekneferu (r. 1806–1802 B.C.E.) at the end of the Twelfth Dynasty and Twosret (r. 1191–1189 B.C.E.) at the end of the Nineteenth Dynasty.

The longest-ruling female pharaoh was Hatshepsut (ca. 1507–1458 B.C.E.), who reigned for twenty years during the Eighteenth Dynasty. Hatshepsut expanded Egyptian holdings through military victories, sent trading expeditions, and sponsored artists and architects, ushering in a period of artistic creativity and economic prosperity. Among the magnificent monuments was one of the world's great buildings, an elaborate terraced mortuary temple at Deir el Bahri, with large statues of Hatshepsut and various gods and wall reliefs featuring scenes of royal power. Hatshepsut was born female-bodied, the daughter of the pharaoh Thutmose I and his primary wife, and married a half-brother, Thutmose II, becoming his "Great Royal Wife," or principal queen. At Thutmose II's death, Hatshepsut became the regent to Thutmose II's very young son (by a different wife), Thutmose III. Several years later, Hatshepsut assumed the position of co-pharaoh and began a complex and creative use of public gender imagery that has been a source of controversy since Hatshepsut's female-bodiedness was first discovered in the nineteenth century. (Before then, inscriptions had been read as referring to a male pharaoh.)

Hatshepsut is often depicted in ceremonial representations with the standard pharaonic regalia — a headdress topped by a cobra, a kilt, and an artificial braided metallic beard — or as the god Osiris, but in other official portraits wears the normal clothing of a wealthy Egyptian woman. The inscriptions also vary in their gender references, using both "she" and "son of Re," the Egyptian sun-god. Until recently, scholars generally referred to Hatshepsut as a woman playing a male role, but new thinking about gender has pointed out that the boundaries between gender presentation and gender identity are not always clear, and certainly difficult to discern for people who lived thousands of years ago. This ambiguity suggests that the

Granite head of Hatshepsut.

(Paul Williams/funkyfood London/Alamy)

gender-neutral "they" might be the best way to think about Hatshepsut. Just as some Egyptian deities exhibited gender duality, blending male and female attributes, so did Hatshepsut's public, royal image. After Hatshepsut's death, Thutmose III ruled as a single pharaoh and tried to destroy all evidence that Hatshepsut had ever ruled, smashing statues and scratching their name off inscriptions. Older scholarship viewed this behavior as his revenge against his "evil stepmother" or a critique of biologically female pharaohs, but newer studies suggest he may have been trying to destroy depictions of Hatshepsut as a successful ruler to lessen the power of Hatshepsut's family. In 2007, a team of archaeologists located a mummy that was likely Hatshepsut's; the mummy indicates they died from cancer, rather than from assassination, as had been one speculation.

QUESTIONS FOR ANALYSIS

1. How does Hatshepsut combine actions and imagery that are gendered female with those gendered male in Egyptian society?
2. How does the hierarchy of family and social position modify the gender hierarchy in ancient Egypt? Can you think of more recent examples?

numerous campaigns to retake Egyptian territory in Syria. He assembled a large well-equipped army with thousands of chariots and expected to defeat the Hittites easily, but he and his army were ambushed by them at the Battle of Kadesh in 1274 B.C.E. Returning to Egypt, Ramesses declared that he had won and had monuments carved commemorating his victory. In reality, neither side gained much by the battle, though both sides seem to have recognized the impossibility of defeating the other.

In 1258, Ramesses II and the Hittite king Hattusili III concluded a peace treaty, which was recorded in both Egyptian hieroglyphics and Hittite cuneiform. Returning to the language of cooperation established in earlier royal diplomacy, each side promised not to invade the other and to come to the other's aid if attacked. Each promised peace and brotherhood, and the treaty ended with a long oath to the gods, who would curse the one who broke the treaty and bless the one who kept it.

NOTES

1. J. A. Black et al., *Electronic Text Corpus of Sumerian Literature* (http://etcsl.orinst.ox.ac.uk/), Oxford 1998–2006.
2. Quoted in S. N. Kramer, *The Sumerians: Their History, Culture, and Character* (Chicago: University of Chicago Press, 1963), p. 238.
3. James B. Pritchard, ed., *Ancient Near Eastern Texts Relating to the Old Testament—Third Edition with Supplement* (Princeton, N.J.: Princeton University Press, 1969), p. 372.
4. Quoted in A. H. Gardiner, "Ramesside Texts Relating to the Taxation and Transport of Corn," *Journal of Egyptian Archaeology* 27 (1941): 19–20.

LOOKING BACK LOOKING AHEAD

The political and military story of waves of migrations, battles, and the rise and fall of empires can mask striking continuities across the Neolithic and Bronze Ages. The social patterns that were set in early agricultural societies—with most of the population farming the land and a small number of elite who lived off their labor—lasted for millennia. Disrupted peoples and newcomers shared practical concepts of agriculture and metallurgy with one another, and wheeled vehicles allowed merchants to transact business over long distances. Merchants, migrants, and conquerors carried their gods and goddesses with them, and religious beliefs and practices blended and changed. Cuneiform tablets, wall inscriptions, and paintings testify to commercial exchanges and cultural accommodation, adoption, and adaptation.

The treaty of Ramesses II and Hattusili III brought peace between the Egyptians and the Hittites for a time, which was further enhanced by Ramesses II's marriage to a Hittite princess. This stability was not to last, however. Within several decades of the treaty, new peoples were moving into the eastern Mediterranean, disrupting trade and in some cases looting and destroying cities. There is evidence of drought, and some scholars have suggested that a major volcanic explosion in Iceland cooled the climate for several years, leading to a series of poor harvests. Both the Egyptian and Hittite Empires shrank dramatically. All of these developments are part of a general "Bronze Age Collapse" that historians see as a major turning point.

Make Connections

Think about the larger developments and continuities within and across chapters.

1. What basic elements of Mesopotamian and Egyptian society can be traced back to the Neolithic period, and why do you think there were these continuities?

2. How were the societies that developed in Mesopotamia and Egypt similar to one another, and how were they different?

3. The civilizations discussed in this chapter developed in parts of the world not usually seen today as part of "the West." What customs, concepts, institutions, or other aspects of Mesopotamian and Egyptian civilization have continued in parts of the world understood today as "the West" that would explain why they are viewed as foundational?

1 REVIEW & EXPLORE

Identify Key Terms

Identify and explain the significance of each item below.

civilization (p. 4)

Paleolithic era (p. 5)

Neolithic era (p. 6)

Fertile Crescent (p. 7)

pastoralism (p. 7)

patriarchy (p. 9)

Bronze Age (p. 10)

polytheism (p. 10)

cuneiform (p. 12)

Hammurabi's law code (p. 15)

pharaoh (p. 21)

ma'at (p. 21)

Review the Main Ideas

Answer the section heading questions from the chapter.

1. What do we mean by "the West" and "Western civilization"? (p. 4)

2. How did early human societies create new technologies and cultural forms? (p. 5)

3. What kind of civilization did the Sumerians build in Mesopotamia? (p. 10)

4. How did the Akkadian and Old Babylonian empires develop in Mesopotamia? (p. 15)

5. How did the Egyptians establish a prosperous and long-lasting society? (p. 19)

Suggested Resources

BOOKS

- Fagan, Brian M., and Nadia Durrani. *People of the Earth: An Introduction to World Prehistory*, 15th ed. 2018. A thorough survey that presents up-to-date scholarship, designed for students.

- Harding, A. F. *European Societies in the Bronze Age*. 2000. A comprehensive survey of developments in Europe during the Bronze Age.

- Hawass, Zahi. *Silent Images: Women in Pharaonic Egypt*. 2000. Blends text and pictures to draw a history of ancient Egyptian women.

- Kriwaczek, Paul. *Babylon: Mesopotamia and the Birth of Civilization*. 2012. Traces Mesopotamia from the first settlements to the fall of Babylon.

- Leick, Gwendolyn. *The Babylonians*. 2002. An introduction to all aspects of Babylonian life and culture.

- McCarter, Susan Foster. *Neolithic*. 2007. An introductory survey of the development and impact of agriculture, with many illustrations.

- Podany, Amanda. *Brotherhood of Kings: How International Relations Shaped the Ancient Near East*. 2010. Examines a thousand years of diplomacy among rulers.

- Scott, James C. *Against the Grain: A Deep History of the Earliest States*. 2017. A critical view of the development of agriculture.

- Tattersall, Ian. *Masters of the Planet: The Search for Our Human Origins*. 2012. An up-to-date survey of how humans evolved, in a lively narrative written for general readers.

- Van de Mieroop, Marc. *A History of the Ancient Near East, 3000–332 B.C.E.* 3d ed., 2015. A concise history from Sumerian cities to Alexander the Great.

- Visicato, Giuseppe. *The Power and the Writing: The Early Scribes of Mesopotamia*. 2000. Studies the practical importance of early Mesopotamian scribes.

MEDIA

- *Ancient Mesopotamia and Egypt*. Two interactive websites from the British Museum with objects in the museum's fabulous collection, with maps, essays, and other resources.
  http://www.mesopotamia.co.uk/
  http://www.ancientegypt.co.uk/

- *Ancient Worlds: Come Together* (BBC, 2010). Archaeologist and historian Richard Miles explores the beginning of civilization in the cities of Mesopotamia in this documentary.

- *Cave of Forgotten Dreams* (Werner Herzog, 2010). Renowned director Werner Herzog goes inside the newly discovered Chauvet caves of southern France to film the oldest-known human artwork from around 32,000 years ago.

- *Egypt's Golden Empire* (PBS, 2002). This three-part series on the era of the New Kingdom examines the lives of pharaohs, nobles, and ordinary people in Egypt's expanding empire.

- *Eternal Egypt*. A multimedia website with over fifteen hundred examples of Egyptian art and artifacts, along with articles, maps, and animations. Run by the Egyptian Supreme Council of Antiquities, Egyptian Center for Documentation of Cultural and Natural Heritage, and IBM.
  www.eternalegypt.org/EternalEgyptWebsiteWeb/HomeServlet

- *The Kings: From Babylon to Baghdad* (History Channel, 2004). This feature-length *History Channel* special surveys the rulers of Mesopotamia from Sargon of Akkad to Saddam Hussein, with special attention to military matters.

- *Theban Mapping Project*. An interactive website run by a scholar from the American University in Cairo that highlights the excavations of palaces, tombs, and temples in the Valley of the Kings, with maps, videos, articles, and thousands of photos.
  www.thebanmappingproject.com/

2

Small Kingdoms and Mighty Empires in the Near East

1200–510 B.C.E.

The migrations, drought, and destruction of what scholars call the Bronze Age Collapse in the late thirteenth century B.C.E. ended the Hittite Empire and weakened the Egyptians. Much was lost, but the old cultures of the ancient Near East survived to nurture new societies. The technology for smelting iron, which developed in Anatolia as well as other places in the world, improved and spread, with iron weapons and tools becoming stronger and thus more important by about 1000 B.C.E. In the absence of powerful empires, the Phoenicians, Kushites, Hebrews, and many other peoples carved out small independent kingdoms until the Near East was a patchwork of states. The Hebrews created a new form of religious belief with a single god and wrote down their religious ideas and traditions in what later became the most significant written document from this period.

In the tenth century B.C.E. this jumble of small states gave way to an empire that for the first time embraced the entire Near East: the empire of the Assyrians. The Assyrians assembled a huge army that used sophisticated military technology and brutal tactics, and they also developed effective administrative techniques and stunning artistic works. The Assyrian Empire lasted for about three hundred years and then broke apart with the rise of a new empire centered in Babylon. Then, beginning in 550 B.C.E., the Persians conquered the Medes—nomadic peoples who had settled in Iran—and then the Babylonians and Assyrians, creating the largest empire yet seen, stretching from Anatolia in the west to the Indus Valley in the east. The Persians established effective methods of governing their diverse subjects and built roads for conquest, trade, and communication. ■

CHAPTER PREVIEW

■ How did iron technology shape new states after 1200 B.C.E.?

■ How did the Hebrews create an enduring religious tradition?

■ How did the Assyrians and Neo-Babylonians gain and lose power?

■ How did the Persians conquer and rule their extensive empire?

Archers in the King's Palace
In this colorful decorative frieze made of glazed brick, men wearing long Persian robes and laced ankle boots carry spears, bows, and quivers. This reconstruction in the Louvre Museum in Paris was made from bricks found in the palace of King Darius I of Persia in Susa, built about 510 B.C.E. The cultural and ethnic diversity of the Persian Empire, and its vast size, are represented in the varying skin and hair tones of the figures. (Azoor Photo/Alamy)

How did iron technology shape new states after 1200 B.C.E.?

If the Bronze Age Collapse was a time of massive political and economic disruption, it was also a period when new technologies spread, especially iron. Even though empires shrank, many small kingdoms survived that shared a common culture across a wide area while also following their own local traditions.

Iron Technology

Along with migration and drought, another significant development in the centuries around 1200 B.C.E. was the spread of iron tools and iron technology. Iron is the most common element in the earth, but most iron found on or near the earth's surface occurs in the form of ore, which must be smelted to extract the metal. This is also true of the copper and tin that are used to make bronze, but these can be smelted at much lower temperatures than iron. As artisans perfected bronze metalworking techniques, they also experimented with iron. They developed a long and difficult process for smelting iron, using charcoal and a bellows (which raised the temperature of the fire significantly) to extract the iron from the ore. This procedure was performed in an enclosed furnace, and the process was repeated a number of times as the ore was transformed into wrought iron, which could be hammered into shapes.

Iron smelting was developed independently in several different places, including western Africa in what is now Nigeria, Anatolia (modern Turkey), and most likely India. In Anatolia, the earliest smelted weapon has been dated to about 2500 B.C.E., but there may have been some smelting earlier. Most of the iron produced was too brittle to be of much use until about 1100 B.C.E., when techniques improved and iron weapons gradually became stronger and cheaper than their bronze counterparts. Thus, in the schema of dividing history into periods according to the main material out of which tools are made (see Chapter 1), the **Iron Age** began in about 1100 B.C.E. Iron weapons became important items of trade around the Mediterranean and throughout the Tigris and Euphrates Valleys, and the technology for making them traveled as well. From Anatolia, iron objects

were traded west into Greece and central Europe, and north into western Asia. By 500 B.C.E., knowledge of smelting had traveled these routes as well.

Ironworkers continued to experiment and improve their products. Near Eastern ironworkers discovered that if the relatively brittle wrought iron objects were placed on a bed of burning charcoal and then cooled quickly, the outer layer would form into a layer of much harder material, steel. Goods made of cast or wrought iron were usually traded locally, but fine sword and knife blades of steel traveled long distances, and the knowledge of how to make them followed. Because it was fairly plentiful and relatively cheap when compared with bronze, iron has been called the "democratic metal." The transition from bronze to iron happened over many centuries, but iron (and even more so, steel) would be an important factor in history from this point on.

The Decline of Egypt and the Emergence of Kush

Although the treaty between the Egyptians and Hittites in 1258 B.C.E. (see Chapter 1) seemed to indicate a future of peace and cooperation, this was not to be. Groups of seafaring peoples whom the Egyptians called Sea Peoples migrated and marauded in the eastern Mediterranean. Just who these people were and where they originated are much debated among scholars. They may have come from Greece, or islands in the Mediterranean such as Crete and Sardinia, or Anatolia, or from all of these places. Wherever they came from, their movements and their raids, combined with the expansion of the Assyrians (see "Assyria's Long Road to Power"), led to the collapse of the Hittite Empire.

Iron Monstrous Figure   This tiny figure, made mostly of iron in the second millennium B.C.E. in the Near East, combines a human face and serpentine-scaled body. Beings that combined human and animal qualities were thought to have supernatural powers in many ancient societies and were sometimes considered gods. Iron was initially used for luxury items such as jewelry and religious objects, and only later for weapons and tools. (Purchase, 2009 Benefit Fund and Friends of Inanna Gifts; Gift of Mr. and Mrs. Horiuchi, 2010/Metropolitan Museum of Art)

■ **Iron Age** Period beginning about 1100 B.C.E., when iron became the most important material for tools and weapons.

■ **Kush** Kingdom in Nubia that adopted hieroglyphics and pyramids, and later conquered Egypt.

TIMELINE

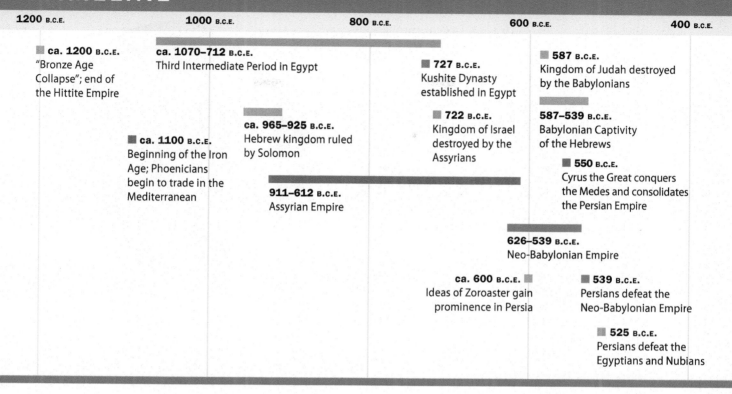

1200 B.C.E.　　　　　1000 B.C.E.　　　　　800 B.C.E.　　　　　600 B.C.E.　　　　　400 B.C.E.

ca. 1200 B.C.E.
"Bronze Age Collapse"; end of the Hittite Empire

ca. 1070–712 B.C.E.
Third Intermediate Period in Egypt

727 B.C.E.
Kushite Dynasty established in Egypt

587 B.C.E.
Kingdom of Judah destroyed by the Babylonians

ca. 1100 B.C.E.
Beginning of the Iron Age; Phoenicians begin to trade in the Mediterranean

ca. 965–925 B.C.E.
Hebrew kingdom ruled by Solomon

722 B.C.E.
Kingdom of Israel destroyed by the Assyrians

587–539 B.C.E.
Babylonian Captivity of the Hebrews

550 B.C.E.
Cyrus the Great conquers the Medes and consolidates the Persian Empire

911–612 B.C.E.
Assyrian Empire

626–539 B.C.E.
Neo-Babylonian Empire

ca. 600 B.C.E.
Ideas of Zoroaster gain prominence in Persia

539 B.C.E.
Persians defeat the Neo-Babylonian Empire

525 B.C.E.
Persians defeat the Egyptians and Nubians

In Egypt, the pharaoh Ramesses III (r. 1186–1155 B.C.E.) defeated the Sea Peoples in both a land and sea battle, but these were costly struggles, as were other military engagements. Egypt entered into a long period of political fragmentation and conquest by outsiders that scholars of Egypt refer to as the Third Intermediate Period (ca. 1070–712 B.C.E.). The long wars against invaders weakened and impoverished Egypt, causing political upheaval and economic decline. Scribes created somber portraits that no doubt exaggerated the negative, but they were effective in capturing the mood:

> The land of Egypt was abandoned and every man was a law to himself. During many years there was no leader who could speak for others. Central government lapsed, small officials and headmen took over the whole land. Any man, great or small, might kill his neighbor. In the distress and vacuum that followed . . . men banded together to plunder one another. They treated the gods no better than men, and cut off the temple revenues.[1]

The decline of Egypt allowed new powers to emerge. South of Egypt was a region called Nubia, mostly in present-day Sudan, which, as early as 2000 B.C.E., served as a conduit of trade through which ivory, gold, ebony, animal skins, and eventually iron flowed north from sub-Saharan Africa, with wine, olive oil, papyrus, and other products flowing south. Small kingdoms arose in this area. As Egypt expanded during the New Kingdom (see Chapter 1), it took over northern Nubia, incorporating it into the growing Egyptian empire. The Nubians adopted many features of Egyptian culture, many Nubians became officials in the Egyptian bureaucracy and officers in the army, and there was significant intermarriage between the two groups.

Later, with the contraction of the Egyptian empire in the Third Intermediate Period, an independent kingdom, **Kush**, rose in power in Nubia, with its capital at Napata. Kush had a rich supply of iron, which it used for weapons, tools, personal adornments, and other products. Researchers in archaeo-metallurgy (the study of ancient metals) are now using advanced technologies that detect magnetic fields and electrical resistance underground to locate and study Kushite iron production centers. The Kushites conquered southern Egypt, and in 727 B.C.E., the Kushite

The Kingdom of Kush,
1000 B.C.E.–300 C.E.

king Piye (r. ca. 747–716 B.C.E.) swept through the Nile Valley to the delta in the north. United once again, Egypt enjoyed a period of peace and prosperity. The Kushite rulers understood themselves to be a new dynasty of pharaohs and were devoted to Egyptian gods such as Amon-Ra. Piye's son Taharqa (r. 690–664 B.C.E.) launched the biggest building campaign since the New Kingdom, with temples, monuments, and pyramids throughout the Nile Valley. (See "Individuals in Society: King Taharqa of Kush and Egypt," page 35.)

Late in Taharqa's reign, invading Assyrians (see "Assyria's Long Road to Power") pushed the Kushites out of Egypt, and the Kushite rulers moved their capital slightly farther up the Nile to Meroë, which was surrounded by iron ore deposits and forests for producing the charcoal needed to smelt iron. Meroë became a center for the production of iron, which the Kushite kings may have controlled. Iron products from Meroë were the best in the world and were traded to much of Africa and across the Red Sea and the Indian Ocean to India.

The Rise of Phoenicia

While Kush expanded in the southern Nile Valley, another group rose to prominence along the Mediterranean coast of modern Lebanon, the northern part of the area called Canaan in ancient sources. These Canaanites established the prosperous commercial centers of Tyre, Sidon, and Byblos and were master shipbuilders. Between about 1100 and 700 B.C.E., the residents of these cities became the seaborne merchants of the Mediterranean. Their most valued products were purple and blue textiles that were dyed with a compound made from the secretions of murex sea snails, especially prized because the brilliant color did not fade. From this originated their Greek name, **Phoenicians** (fih-NEE-shuhnz), meaning "Purple People."

The trading success of the Phoenicians brought them prosperity. In addition to textiles and purple dye, they began to manufacture goods for export, such as tools, weapons, and cookware. They worked bronze and iron, which they shipped as processed objects or as ores, and made and traded glass products. Phoenician ships often carried hundreds of jars of wine, and the Phoenicians introduced grape growing to new regions around the Mediterranean, dramatically increasing the wine available for consumption and trade. They imported rare goods and materials, including hunting dogs, gold, and ivory, from Persia in the east and their neighbors to the south. They also

Phoenician Coin   This silver Phoenician coin shows an animal-headed ship containing soldiers with shields and helmets above the waves, and a hippocampus, a mythical beast, below. Phoenician gold and silver coins have been found throughout the Mediterranean, evidence of the Phoenicians' extensive trading network. This particular coin was most likely not used very often, as the images on it are still sharp; silver is soft, and frequent handling would have rubbed off the edges of the images. (Erich Lessing/Art Resource, NY)

expanded their trade to Egypt, where they mingled with other local traders.

Moving beyond Egypt, the Phoenicians struck out along the coast of North Africa to establish new markets in places where they encountered little competition. The Phoenicians planted trading posts and small farming communities along the coast, founding colonies in Spain, Sicily, and North Africa. Their trade routes eventually took them to the far western Mediterranean and beyond to the Atlantic coast of modern-day Portugal. The Phoenicians' voyages brought them into contact with the Greeks, to whom they introduced many aspects of the older and more urbanized cultures of Mesopotamia and Egypt.

In the ninth century B.C.E., the Phoenicians founded, in modern Tunisia, the city of Carthage, which prospered to become the leading city in the western Mediterranean; by the sixth century B.C.E., it was the center of an empire that controlled many other Phoenician colonies. Here ironsmiths began smelting and smithing wrought iron and steel on a large scale for use and export, specializing in transforming partially worked ore into finished products. They developed new technologies to improve their products; for example, they recycled the shells of murex sea snails left over from purple dye production into a flux, a chemical compound that helped rid the iron of impurities. As in Meroë, the iron industry was controlled

■ **Phoenicians**   Seafaring people from Canaan who traded and founded colonies throughout the Mediterranean and spread the phonetic alphabet.

INDIVIDUALS IN SOCIETY
King Taharqa of Kush and Egypt

Like his father Piye, who conquered and united Egypt after a long period of political disruption, Taharqa (r. 690–664 B.C.E.) was the king of Kush who was also the pharaoh of Egypt, ruling for twenty-six years after being crowned in 690 B.C.E. in the Egyptian capital of Memphis in what was termed Egypt's Twenty-Fifth Dynasty. An able military commander, he ensured peace for the first part of his reign and used the time to build and expand temples and monuments to the gods throughout the Nile Valley, especially to Amon-Ra, a powerful Egyptian god whom the Kushite kings also especially revered. These buildings were filled with statues, busts, paintings, and plaques with Taharqa's name or image, showing the black-skinned king as a sphinx or warrior, or as worshipping the gods or being protected by them. He presented himself as heir to the powerful New Kingdom pharaohs who had ruled eight centuries earlier, another period during which rulers had expanded their territories and built monuments and temples. Taharqa's construction boom included pyramids, the first built since the Middle Kingdom. Ultimately there were more pyramids in Kush (modern-day Sudan) than there were in Egypt.

During the sixth year of his rule, the Nile swelled the perfect amount from spring rains: enough to ensure excellent harvests, but not so much that any villages were flooded. Taharqa ordered this fortunate event recorded on tall columns called stelae, which noted that the floods had killed the snakes and rats, but no people, and thanked the gods for favoring Egypt and its king.

While he was a young man, Taharqa had apparently led Kushite troops against the Assyrians, who were expanding their empire in Lebanon and Judah. In 701 B.C.E. the Assyrians under King Sennacherib initially defeated the Kushites and their allies, and then turned against Jerusalem, the capital of Judah. According to biblical accounts, the Jewish king Hezekiah asked the Egyptian and Kushite troops for assistance, and there is a brief mention in the Bible (2 Kings 19:9; Isaiah 37:9) of "King Tirhakah of Kush" (older translations use "Ethiopia," a translation of the Greek word for this area) whom scholars have identified with Taharqa, setting out to fight the Assyrians. There is also a longer discussion of God sending an angel who slew thousands of Assyrians. Whatever happened to cause the death of Sennacherib's troops (and some modern scholars think this might have been a plague), he abandoned his siege and left, and the city was spared.

In 679 B.C.E., during the middle of Taharqa's reign, the Assyrians under Sennacherib's son Esarhaddon began expanding again, occupying Judah and Lebanon. When they invaded Egypt, Taharqa's forces initially defeated them, but on a second attempt the Assyrian forces captured and sacked Memphis, killing many members of the royal family or taking them away as prisoners to Assyria. Esarhaddon ordered a commemorative pillar showing Taharqa's son kneeling in front of him with a rope piercing his lips. Taharqa himself escaped south, however, and the Kushites held on to their Egyptian territories south of Memphis until he died. For several more decades Kushites, Assyrians, and others fought in the Nile Valley, and gradually a native Egyptian dynasty reasserted control. Both they and the Assyrians attempted to destroy any record of Kushite rule, erasing inscriptions and records and destroying art and artifacts. Much of what we know about Egypt's black pharaohs has only emerged in the last several decades, as statues and stelae long buried have been excavated.

Bronze life-size statue of King Taharqa.
(State Hermitage Museum, St. Petersburg, Russia/ Werner Forman Archive/ Shutterstock)

QUESTIONS FOR ANALYSIS

1. In what ways is Taharqa similar to earlier Egyptian pharaohs? In what ways is he different?
2. Why would the Egyptian dynasty that succeeded Taharqa's Kushite Dynasty be eager to destroy the record of its existence?

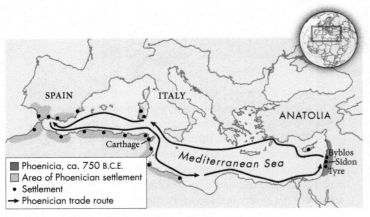

Phoenician Settlements in the Mediterranean

by the state and was a source of power that would help Carthage continue to expand its empire. In the third century B.C.E. this empire was brought into conflict with an expanding Rome (see Chapter 5).

The Phoenicians made many technological advances, and their overwhelming cultural achievement was the spread of a completely phonetic system

of writing—that is, an alphabet. Writers of both cuneiform and hieroglyphics had developed signs that were used to represent sounds, but these were always used with a much larger number of ideograms. Sometime around 1800 B.C.E., workers in the Sinai Peninsula, which was under Egyptian control, began to write only with phonetic signs, with each sign designating one sound. This system vastly simplified writing and reading, and it spread among common people as a practical way to record ideas and communicate. The Phoenicians adopted the simpler system for their own language and spread it around the Mediterranean. The Greeks modified this alphabet and then used it to write their own language, and the Romans later based their alphabet—the script we use to write English today—on Greek. Alphabets based on the Phoenician alphabet were also created in the Persian Empire and formed the basis of Hebrew, Arabic, and various alphabets of South and Central Asia. The system invented by ordinary people and spread by Phoenician merchants is the origin of most of the world's phonetic alphabets today.

How did the Hebrews create an enduring religious tradition?

The legacy of another people who took advantage of Egypt's collapse to found an independent state may have been even more far-reaching than that of the Phoenicians. For a period of several centuries, a people known as the Hebrews controlled first one and then two small states on the western end of the Fertile Crescent, Israel and Judah. Politically unimportant when compared with the Egyptians or Babylonians, the Hebrews created a new form of religious belief called **monotheism**, or worship of a single god. They called their all-powerful god **Yahweh** (YAH-way), spelled YHWH in ancient Hebrew because the written language had no vowels. (In the Middle Ages, different vowels were added by Christian scholars, first in Latin and then in other languages, which resulted in "Jehovah." Most English-language Bibles now translate YHWH as "LORD.") Beginning in the late 600s B.C.E., the Hebrews began to write down their religious ideas, traditions, laws, advice literature, prayers, hymns, history, and prophecies in a series of books. These were gathered together centuries later to form the Hebrew Bible, which Christians later adopted and termed the "Old Testament." These writings later became the core of the Hebrews' religion, *Judaism*, a word taken from the kingdom of Judah, the southern of the two Hebrew kingdoms and the one that was the

primary force in developing religious traditions. (The word *Israelite*, often used as a synonym for *Hebrew*, refers to all people in this group, and not simply the residents of the northern kingdom of Israel.) Jews today revere these texts, as do many Christians, and Muslims respect them, all of which gives them particular importance.

The Hebrew State

Most of the information about the Hebrews comes from the Bible, which, like all ancient documents, must be used with care as a historical source. Archaeological evidence has supported many of its details, and because it records a living religious tradition, extensive textual and physical research into everything it records continues, with enormous controversies among scholars about how to interpret findings. The Hebrews were nomadic pastoralists who may have migrated into the Nile Delta from the east, seeking good land for their herds of sheep and goats. According to the Hebrew Bible, they were enslaved by the Egyptians but were led out of Egypt by a charismatic leader named Moses. The biblical account is very dramatic, and the events form a pivotal episode in the history of the Hebrews and the later religious practices of Judaism. Moses conveyed God's warning to the pharaoh that a series of plagues would strike Egypt, the last of which was the threat that all firstborn sons in Egypt

■ **monotheism** Worship of a single god.

■ **Yahweh** The sole god in the Jewish religion.

would be killed. He instructed the Hebrews to prepare a hasty meal of a sacrificed lamb eaten with unleavened bread. The blood of the lamb was painted over the doors of Hebrew houses. At midnight Yahweh spread death over the land, but he passed over the Hebrew houses with the blood-painted doors. This event became known as the Passover and later became a central religious holiday in Judaism. The next day a terrified pharaoh ordered the Hebrews out of Egypt. Moses then led them in search of what they understood to be the Promised Land, an event known as the Exodus, which was followed by forty years of wandering.

According to scripture, the Hebrews settled in the area between the Mediterranean and the Jordan River known as Canaan. They were organized into tribes, each tribe consisting of numerous families who thought of themselves as all related to one another and having a common ancestor. At first, good farmland, pastureland, and freshwater sources were held in common

The Hebrew Exodus and State, ca. 1250–800 B.C.E.

→ Possible route of the Exodus, ca. 1250 B.C.E.
☐ Solomon's kingdom, ca. 950 B.C.E.
☐ Israel, ca. 800 B.C.E.
☐ Judah, ca. 800 B.C.E.

by each tribe. Common use of land was—and still is—characteristic of nomadic peoples. The Bible divides up the Hebrews at this point into twelve tribes, each named according to an ancestor.

In Canaan, the nomadic Hebrews encountered a variety of other peoples, whom they both learned from and fought. They slowly adopted agriculture and, not surprisingly, at times worshipped the agricultural gods of their neighbors, including Baal, an ancient fertility god. Like the Hyksos in Egypt, this was an example of the common historical pattern of newcomers adapting themselves to the culture of an older, well-established people.

The Bible reports that the greatest danger to the Hebrews came from a group known as the Philistines, who were most likely Greek-speaking people who had migrated to Canaan as part of the movement of the Sea Peoples and who established a kingdom along the Mediterranean coast. The Philistines' superior technology and military organization at first made them invincible, but the Hebrews found a champion and a spirited leader in Saul. In the biblical account, Saul and his men battled the Philistines for control of the land, often without success. In the meantime, Saul established a monarchy over the Hebrew tribes, becoming their king, an event conventionally dated to about 1025 B.C.E.

The Bible includes detailed discussion of the growth of the Hebrew kingdom. It relates that Saul's work was carried on by David of Bethlehem (r. ca. 1005–965 B.C.E.), who pushed back the Philistines and waged war against his other neighbors. To give his kingdom a capital, he captured the city of Jerusalem, which he enlarged, fortified, and made the religious and political center of his realm. David's military successes enlarged the kingdom and won the Hebrews

A Golden Calf According to the Hebrew Bible, Moses descended from Mount Sinai, where he had received the Ten Commandments, to find the Hebrews worshipping a golden calf, which was against Yahweh's laws. In July 1990 an American archaeological team found this model of a gilded calf inside a pot. The figurine, which dates to about 1550 B.C.E., is strong evidence for the existence in Canaan of religious traditions that involved animals as divine symbols. (www.BibleLandPictures.com/Alamy)

unprecedented security, and his forty-year reign was a period of vitality and political consolidation.

David's son Solomon (r. ca. 965–925 B.C.E.) launched a building program that the biblical narrative describes as including cities, palaces, fortresses, and roads. The most symbolic of these projects was the Temple of Jerusalem, which became the home of the Ark of the Covenant, the chest that contained the holiest of Hebrew religious articles. The temple in Jerusalem was intended to be the religious heart of the kingdom, a symbol of Hebrew unity and Yahweh's approval of the kingdom built by Saul, David, and Solomon.

Evidence of this united kingdom may have come to light in August 1993 when an Israeli archaeologist found an inscribed stone slab in northern Israel probably dating from the second half of the ninth century B.C.E. that refers to a "king of Israel" and also to the "House of David." This discovery has been regarded by most scholars as the first mention of King David's dynasty outside of the Bible. The nature and extent of this kingdom continue to be disputed among archaeologists, who offer divergent datings and interpretations for the finds that are continuously brought to light.

Along with discussing expansion and success, the Bible also notes problems. Solomon's efforts were hampered by strife. The financial demands of his building program drained the resources of his people, and his use of forced labor for building projects also fanned popular resentment.

A united Hebrew kingdom did not last long. At Solomon's death, his kingdom broke into political halves. The northern part became Israel, with its capital at Samaria, and the southern half became Judah, with Jerusalem remaining its center. War soon broke out between them, as recorded in the Bible, which weakened both kingdoms. The Assyrians wiped out the northern kingdom of Israel in 722 B.C.E. Judah survived numerous calamities until the Babylonians crushed it in 587 B.C.E. The survivors were forcibly relocated to Babylonia, a period commonly known as the Babylonian Captivity. In 539 B.C.E., the Persian king Cyrus the Great (see "Consolidation of the Persian Empire") conquered the Babylonians and permitted some forty thousand exiles to return to Jerusalem. They rebuilt the temple, although politically the area was simply part of the Persian Empire.

■ **Torah** The first five books of the Hebrew Bible, containing the most important legal and ethical Hebrew texts; later became part of the Christian Old Testament.

■ **Covenant** An agreement that the Hebrews believed to exist between themselves and Yahweh, in which he would consider them his chosen people if they worshipped him as their only god.

The Jewish Religion

During and especially after the Babylonian Captivity, the most important legal and ethical Hebrew texts were edited and brought together in the **Torah**, the first five books of the Hebrew Bible. Here the exiles redefined their beliefs and practices, thereby establishing what they believed was the law of Yahweh. Fundamental to an understanding of the Jewish religion is the concept of the **Covenant**, an agreement that people believed to exist between themselves and Yahweh. According to the Bible, Yahweh appeared to the tribal leader Abraham, promising him that he would be blessed, as would his descendants, if they followed Yahweh. (Because Judaism, Christianity, and Islam all regard this event as foundational, they are referred to as the "Abrahamic religions.") Yahweh next appeared to Moses during the time he was leading the Hebrews out of Egypt, and Yahweh made a Covenant with the Hebrews: if they worshipped Yahweh as their only god, he would consider them his chosen people and protect them from their enemies. The Covenant was understood to be made with the whole people, not simply a king or an elite, and was renewed again several times in the accounts of the Hebrew people in the Bible. Individuals such as Abraham and Moses who acted as intermediaries between Yahweh and the Hebrew people were known as prophets; much of the Hebrew Bible consists of writings in their voices, understood as messages from Yahweh to which the Hebrews were to listen.

Worship was embodied in a series of rules of behavior, the Ten Commandments, which Yahweh gave to Moses. (See "Thinking Like a Historian: The Moral Life," page 40.) These required certain kinds of religious observances and forbade the Hebrews to steal, kill, lie, or commit adultery, thus creating a system of ethical absolutes. From the Ten Commandments a complex system of rules of conduct was created and later written down as Hebrew law, most likely influenced by Hammurabi's code (see Chapter 1). This code often called for harsh punishments, but later tradition, largely the work of the prophets who lived from the eighth to the fifth centuries B.C.E., put more emphasis on righteousness than on retribution.

Like the followers of other religions in the ancient Near East, Jews engaged in rituals through which they showed their devotion. They were also expected to please Yahweh by living up to high moral standards and by worshipping him above all other gods. The first of the Ten Commandments expresses this obligation: "I am the Lord your God . . . you shall have no other gods besides me" (Exodus 20:23). Increasingly this was understood to be a commandment to worship Yahweh alone. The later prophets such as Isaiah created a system of ethical monotheism, in which goodness was understood to come from a single transcendent god, and in which religious obligations included fair and just behavior toward other people as well as rituals. They saw Yahweh as intervening directly in history and also working through individuals—both Hebrews and non-Hebrews—that he had chosen to carry out his aims. (See "Viewpoints: Rulers and Divine Favor: Views of Cyrus the Great," page 42.) Judging by the many prophets (and a few prophetesses) in the Bible exhorting the Hebrews to listen to Yahweh, honor the Covenant, stop worshipping other gods, and behave properly, adherence to this system was a difficult challenge.

Like Mesopotamian deities, Yahweh punished people, but the Hebrews also believed he was a loving and forgiving god who would protect and reward all those who obeyed his commandments. A hymn recorded in the book of Psalms captures this idea:

> Blessed is every one who fears the Lord, who
>   walks in his ways!
> You shall eat the fruit of the labor of your hands;
> you shall be happy, and it shall be well with you.
> Your wife will be like a fruitful vine within your
>   house;
> your children will be like olive shoots around your
>   table.
> Lo, thus shall the man be blessed who fears the
>   Lord. (Psalms 128:1–4)

The religion of the Hebrews was thus addressed to not only an elite but also the individual. Because kings or other political leaders were not essential to its practice, the rise or fall of a kingdom was not crucial to the religion's continued existence. Religious leaders were important in Judaism, but personally following the instructions of Yahweh was the central task for observant Jews in the ancient world.

Hebrew Family and Society

The Hebrews were originally nomadic, but they adopted settled agriculture in Canaan, and some lived in cities. The shift away from pastoralism affected more than just how people fed themselves. Communal use of land gave way to family or private ownership, and devotion to the traditions of Judaism came to replace tribal identity.

Family relationships reflected evolving circumstances. Marriage and the family were fundamentally important in Jewish life; celibacy was frowned upon, and almost all major Jewish thinkers and priests were married. Polygamy

was allowed, but the typical marriage was probably monogamous. In the codes of conduct written down in the Hebrew Bible, sex between a married woman and a man not her husband was an "abomination," as were incest and sex between men. Men were free to have sexual relations with concubines, servants, and enslaved women, however.

As in Mesopotamia and Egypt, marriage was a family matter, too important to be left to the whims of young people. Although specific rituals may have been expected to ensure ritual purity in sexual relations, sex itself was understood as part of Yahweh's creation, and the bearing of children was seen in some ways as a religious function. Sons were especially desired because they maintained the family bloodline, while keeping ancestral property in the family. As in Mesopotamia, land was handed down within families, generally from father to son. A firstborn son became the head of the household at his father's death. Mothers oversaw the early education of the children, but as boys grew older, their fathers gave them more of their education. Both men and women were expected to know religious traditions so that they could teach their children and prepare for religious rituals and ceremonies. Women worked in the fields alongside their husbands in rural areas, and in shops in the cities. According to biblical codes, menstruation and childbirth made women ritually impure, but the implications of this belief in ancient times are contested by scholars.

Children, according to the book of Psalms, "are a heritage of the lord, and the fruit of the womb is his reward" (Psalms 128:3), and newly married couples were expected to begin a family at once. The desire for children to perpetuate the family was so strong that if a man died before he could sire a son, his brother was legally obliged to marry the widow. The son born of the brother was thereafter considered the offspring of the dead man. If the brother refused, the widow had her revenge by denouncing him to the elders and publicly spitting in his face.

Jewish Blessing on Silver Scroll   This tiny silver scroll, dating from about 600 B.C.E. and found in rock-hewn burial chambers near Jerusalem, contains the oldest known citation of texts also found in the Hebrew Bible: "May Yahweh bless you and keep you, and make [his face] shine upon you." It was worn as an amulet to provide protection against evil. (The Israel Museum, Jerusalem/Bridgeman Images)

The Moral Life

Ancient peoples developed various codes of behavior and morality, which included how they were to treat other humans and often also how they were to act toward the gods. What similarities and differences do you see in the ideas of a moral life for New Kingdom Egyptians, Hebrews, and Zoroastrian Persians?

1 **The Egyptian** *Book of the Dead.* During the New Kingdom and afterward, well-to-do Egyptians were buried with papyrus scrolls on which were written magical and religious texts, now known as the *Book of the Dead*, designed to help the deceased make the crossing to the afterlife. These included a standardized list of things the deceased had not done during life, what modern scholars have called a "negative confession."

To be said on reaching the Hall of the Two Truths so as to purge N [here the name of the deceased was written] of any sins committed and to see the face of every god:

Hail to you, great God, Lord of the Two Truths!
I have come to you, my Lord,
I was brought to see your beauty. . . .

I have not done crimes against people,
I have not mistreated cattle,
I have not sinned in the Place of Truth.
I have not known what should not be known,
I have not done any harm.
I did not begin a day by exacting more than my due,
My name did not reach the bark of the mighty
    ruler.
I have not blasphemed a god,
I have not robbed the poor.
I have not done what the god abhors,
I have not maligned a servant to his master.
I have not caused pain,
I have not caused tears.
I have not killed,

I have not ordered to kill,
I have not made anyone suffer.
I have not damaged the offerings in the temples,
I have not depleted the loaves of the gods,
I have not stolen the cakes of the dead [food left
    for the deceased].
I have not copulated nor defiled myself.
I have not increased nor reduced the measure,
I have not diminished the arura [arable land],
I have not cheated in the fields.
I have not added to the weight of the balance,
I have not falsified the plummet of the scales.
I have not taken milk from the mouth of
    children,
I have not deprived cattle of their pasture.
I have not snared birds in the reeds of the gods,
I have not caught fish in their ponds.
I have not held back water in its season,
I have not dammed a flowing stream,
I have not quenched a needed fire.
I have not neglected the days of meat offerings,
I have not detained cattle belonging to the god,
I have not stopped a god in his procession.
I am pure, I am pure, I am pure, I am pure!

2 **The Ten Commandments.** According to Hebrew Scripture, where they appear twice, the Ten Commandments were given by Yahweh to Moses. HaShem (which means "the Name") is one of the names of God in Judaism, used as a sign of reverence and respect, as is writing "G-d."

Exodus 20
1: And G-d spoke all these words, saying:
2: I am HaShem thy G-d, who brought thee out of the land of Egypt, out of the house of bondage.
3: Thou shalt have no other gods before Me.
4: Thou shalt not make unto thee a graven image, nor any manner of likeness, of any thing that is in heaven above, or that is in the earth beneath, or that is in the water under the earth;
5: thou shalt not bow down unto them, nor serve them; for I HaShem thy G-d am a jealous G-d, visiting the iniquity of the fathers upon the children unto the third and fourth generation of them that hate Me;

ANALYZING THE EVIDENCE

1. In Source 1, what religious duties and personal actions does the negative confession suggest were important to Egyptians?
2. In Source 2, the Ten Commandments, what actions were required of or forbidden to Hebrews?
3. What does Zoroaster call on believers to do in Source 3?
4. In these moral codes, what will be the rewards of those who do what they are supposed to do? What will be the fate of those who do not?
5. What seems to be the most important moral duty in each of these codes?

6: and showing mercy unto the thousandth generation of them that love Me and keep My commandments.

7: Thou shalt not take the name of HaShem thy G-d in vain; for HaShem will not hold him guiltless that taketh His name in vain.

8: Remember the sabbath day, to keep it holy.

9: Six days shalt thou labour, and do all thy work;

10: but the seventh day is a sabbath unto HaShem thy G-d, in it thou shalt not do any manner of work, thou, nor thy son, nor thy daughter, nor thy man-servant, nor thy maid-servant, nor thy cattle, nor thy stranger that is within thy gates;

11: in six days HaShem made heaven and earth, the sea, and all that in them is, and rested on the seventh day; wherefore HaShem blessed the sabbath day, and hallowed it.

12: Honour thy father and thy mother, that thy days may be long upon the land which HaShem thy G-d giveth thee.

13: Thou shalt not murder; Thou shalt not commit adultery; Thou shalt not steal; Thou shalt not bear false witness against thy neighbour.

14: Thou shalt not covet thy neighbour's house; thou shalt not covet thy neighbour's wife, nor his man-servant, nor his maid-servant, nor his ox, nor his ass, nor any thing that is thy neighbour's.

3 **Zoroaster's teachings in the Avesta.** The sacred texts of the Zoroastrians, collected in the Avesta, include some written by Zoroaster himself as liturgical poems that priests were to recite during divine services. This one tells believers about aspects of Ahuramazda they should understand, such as Right and Good Thought, as they decide what to do in their lives.

Now I will speak, O proselytes, of what ye may bring to the attention even of one who knows,

praises for the Lord [Ahuramazda] and Good Thought's acts of worship

well considered, and for Right; the gladness beheld by the daylight.

Hear with your ears the best message, behold with lucid mind

the two choices in the decision each man makes for his own person

before the great Supplication, as ye look ahead to the declaration to Him.

They are the two Wills, the twins who in the beginning made themselves heard through dreaming,

those two kinds of thought, of speech, of deed, the better and the evil;

and between them well-doers discriminate rightly, but ill-doers do not.

Once those two Wills join battle, a man adopts

life or non-life, the way of existence that will be his at the last:

that of the wrongful the worst kind, but for the righteous one, best thought.

Of these two Wills, the Wrongful one chooses to do the worst things,

but the most Bounteous Will (chooses) Right, he who clothes himself in adamant;

as do those also who committedly please the Lord with genuine actions, the Mindful One.

Between those two the very Daevas [the traditional gods of Iran] fail to discriminate rightly, because delusion

comes over them as they deliberate, when they choose worst thought;

they scurry together to the violence with which mortals blight the world.

But suppose one comes with dominion for Him, with good thought and right,

then vitality informs the body, piety the soul:

their ringleader Thou wilt have as if in irons:

and when the requital comes for their misdeeds,

for Thee, Mindful One [Ahuramazda], together with Good Thought, will be found dominion

to proclaim to those, Lord, who deliver Wrong into the hands of Right.

May we be the ones who will make this world splendid,

Mindful One and Ye Lords, bringers of change, and Right,

as our minds come together where insight is fluctuating.

For then destruction will come down upon Wrong's prosperity,

and the swiftest (steeds) will be yoked from the fair dwelling of Good Thought,

of the Mindful One, and of Right, and they will be the winners in good repute.

When ye grasp those rules that the Mindful One lays down, O mortals,

through success and failure, and the lasting harm that is for the wrongful

as furtherance is for the righteous, then thereafter desire will be fulfilled.

PUTTING IT ALL TOGETHER

Using the sources above, along with what you have learned in class and in Chapters 1 and 2, write a short essay that discusses similarities and differences in ideas about the moral life for New Kingdom Egyptians, Hebrews, and Zoroastrian Persians. What is the basis of morality for these three groups, and how does this shape how people are supposed to act?

Sources: (1) Miriam Lichtheim, *Ancient Egyptian Literature: Volume II: The New Kingdom*, pp. 124–26. © 2006 by the Regents of the University of California. Published by the University of California Press. Reprinted by permission;; (2) *The Tanakh*, JPS Electronic Edition, based on the 1917 JPS translation, https://www.jewishvirtuallibrary.org/jsource/Bible/Exodus20.html; (3) M. L. West, *The Hymns of Zoroaster: A New Translation of the Most Ancient Sacred Texts of Iran* (London: I. B. Tauris, 2010), pp. 51, 53, 55.

VIEWPOINTS

Rulers and Divine Favor: Views of Cyrus the Great

In Mesopotamia — and elsewhere in the ancient world — individuals who established large empires through conquest often later proclaimed that their triumph was the result of divine favor, and they honored the gods of the regions they conquered. King Cyrus the Great of Persia appears to have followed this tradition. A text written in cuneiform on a sixth-century B.C.E. Babylonian clay cylinder presents Cyrus describing the way in which the main Babylonian god Marduk selected him to conquer Babylon and restore proper government and worship. Cyrus is also portrayed as divinely chosen in the book of Isaiah in Hebrew Scripture, which was probably written sometime in the late sixth century B.C.E. after Cyrus allowed the Jews to return to Jerusalem. Because Cyrus was not a follower of the Jewish God, however, the issue of divine favor was more complicated for Jews than it was for Babylonians.

The Cyrus Cylinder

I am Cyrus, king of the universe, the great king, the powerful king, king of Babylon, king of Sumer and Akkad, king of the four quarters of the world. . . .

When I went as harbinger of peace i[nt]o Babylon I founded my sovereign residence within the palace amid celebration and rejoicing. Marduk, the great lord, bestowed on me as my destiny the great magnanimity of one who loves Babylon, and I every day sought him out in awe. My vast troops marched peaceably in Babylon, and the whole of [Sumer] and Akkad had nothing to fear. I sought the welfare of the city of Babylon and all its sanctuaries. As for the population of Babylon, . . . [w]ho as if without div[ine intention] had endured a yoke not decreed for them, I soothed their weariness, I freed them from their bond. . . . Marduk, the great lord, rejoiced at [my good] deeds, and he pronounced a sweet blessing over me, Cyrus, the king who fears him, and over Cambyses, the son [my] issue, [and over] all my troops, that we might proceed further at his exalted command.

The Book of Isaiah, Chapter 45

Thus said the Lord to Cyrus, His anointed one — whose right hand He has grasped, Treading down nations before him, Ungirding the loins of kings, Opening doors before him, and letting no gate stay shut: I will march before you, and level the hills that loom up; I will shatter doors of bronze and cut down iron bars. I will give you treasures concealed in the dark and secret hoards — So that you may know that it is I the LORD, the God of Israel, who call you by name. For the sake of My servant Jacob, Israel My chosen one, I call you by name, I hail you by title, though you have not known Me. I am the LORD, and there is none else; beside Me, there is no God. I engird you, though you have not known Me. . . .

It was I who roused him [that is, Cyrus] for victory, and who level all roads for him. He shall rebuild My city, and let My exiled people go, without price and without payment — said the LORD of hosts.

QUESTIONS FOR ANALYSIS

1. How would you compare the portrayal of Cyrus in the two texts?
2. The Babylonians worshipped many gods, and the Hebrews were monotheistic. How does this difference shape the way divine actions and favor are portrayed in the texts?
3. Both of these texts have been very influential in establishing the largely positive historical view of Cyrus. What limitations might there be in using these as historical sources?

Sources: Cylinder inscription translation by Irving Finkel, curator of Cuneiform Collections at the British Museum, www.britishmuseum.org; "The Book of Isaiah" in *Tanakh: A New Translation of The Holy Scriptures According to the Traditional Hebrew Text* (Philadelphia: Jewish Publication Society, 1985).

The development of urban life among the Jews created new economic opportunities, especially in crafts and trades. People specialized in certain occupations, and, as in most ancient societies, these crafts were family trades. Sons worked with their father, daughters with their mother. If the business prospered, the family might be assisted by a few paid or enslaved workers. (See "Evaluating Written Evidence: Manumission of an Enslaved Woman and Her Daughter," page 43.) The practitioners of a craft usually lived in a particular section of town. Commerce and trade developed later than crafts. Trade with neighboring countries was handled by foreigners, usually Phoenicians. Jews dealt mainly in local trade, and in most instances craftsmen and farmers sold directly to their customers.

The Torah set out rules about many aspects of life. Among these was the set of dietary laws known as *kashrut* (from which we derive the English word *kosher*), setting out what plants and animals Jews were forbidden to eat and how foods were to be prepared properly. Later commentators sought to explain these laws as originating in concerns about health or hygiene, but the biblical text simply gives them as rules coming from Yahweh, sometimes expressed in terms

Manumission of an Enslaved Woman and Her Daughter

During the time of Persian rule in Egypt, Jewish soldiers were stationed in Elephantine, a military post on the Nile. Historians have since recovered papyrus documents from that location, known as the Elephantine papyri, that provide information on all sorts of everyday social and economic matters, including marriage, divorce, property, slavery, and the borrowing of money. The text below is a document releasing a woman and her daughter from slavery. It was written in Aramaic, the language of business in the Persian Empire.

~

On the 20th of Siwan, that is the 7th day of Phamenoth, the year 38 of King Artaxerxes*—at the time, Meshullam son of Zakkur, a Jew of the fortress Elephantine, of the detachment of Arpakhu, said to the woman Tapmut (as she is called) his slave, who has on her right hand the marking "Of Meshullam," as follows: I have taken kindly thought of you in my lifetime. I hereby declare you released at my death and likewise declare released the daughter Yehoyishma' (as she is called) whom you have borne to me. No son or daughter, close or distant relative, kinsman, or clansmen of mine has any right to you or to the daughter Yehoyishma' whom you have borne to me. None has any right to mark you or to deliver you as payment of money. Whoever attempts such action against you or the daughter Yehoyishma' whom you have borne to me must pay you a fine of 50 karsh of silver by the king's weights. You are released, with your daughter Yehoyishma', from the shade of the sun, and no other man is master of you or your daughter Yehoyishma'. You are released for God.

And Tapmut and her daughter Yehoyishma' declared: We shall serve you [a]s a son or daughter supports his or her father as long as you live; and when you die, we shall support your son Zakkur like a son who supports his father, just as we have been doing for you when you were alive. . . . If we ever say, "We will not support you as a son supports his father, and your son Zakkur after your death," we shall be liable to you and your son Zakkur for a fine in the amount of 50 karsh of refined silver by the king's weights without suit or process.

Written by Haggai the scribe, at Elephantine, at the dictation of Meshullam son of Zakkar.

EVALUATE THE EVIDENCE

1. What does Meshullam do in this document? Why does he say he is doing this?
2. To whom else do Meshullam's promises extend?
3. What do Tapmut and her daughter Yehoyishma' promise to do in this document?
4. What does their declaration imply about the legal status of enslaved people in ancient Egypt? How does this status compare with the legal status of enslaved people in the pre–Civil War United States?

*This is the date of the document. Siwan was a month in the Hebrew calendar, Phamenoth a seasonal period in the Egyptian calendar. Artaxerxes is most likely Artaxerxes I, king of Persia from 465 to 424 B.C.E., which means that the year this agreement was drafted was 427 B.C.E.

Source: James B. Pritchard, ed., *Ancient Near Eastern Texts Relating to the Old Testament — Third Edition with Supplement* (Princeton, N.J.: Princeton University Press, 1969), p. 548.

---

of ritual purity or cleanliness. It is not clear how these rules were followed during the biblical period, because detailed interpretations were written down only much later, during the time of the Roman Empire. As with any law code, from Hammurabi's to contemporary ones, it is much easier to learn about what people were supposed to do according to the laws of the Torah than what they actually did.

Beliefs and practices that made Jews distinctive endured, but the Hebrew states did not. Small states like those of the Phoenicians and the Hebrews could exist only in the absence of a major power, and the beginning of the ninth century B.C.E. saw the rise of such a power: the Assyrians of northern Mesopotamia. They conquered the kingdom of Israel, the Phoenician cities, and eventually many other states as well.

How did the Assyrians and Neo-Babylonians gain and lose power?

The **Assyrian Empire** originated in northern Mesopotamia, from where it expanded to encompass much of the Near East in the tenth through the seventh centuries B.C.E. After building up their military, the Assyrians conquered many of their neighbors, including Babylonia, and took over much of Syria all the way to the Mediterranean. They then moved into Anatolia, where the pressure they put on the Hittite Empire was one factor in its collapse. Assyria's success allowed it to become the leading power in the Near East, with an army that at times numbered many tens of thousands. Internal strife and civil war led to its decline, allowing the Neo-Babylonians to build a somewhat smaller empire.

Assyria's Long Road to Power

The Assyrians had inhabited northern Mesopotamia since the third millennium B.C.E., forming a kingdom that grew and shrank in size and power over the centuries. During the time of Sargon of Akkad (r. ca. 2334–2279 B.C.E.), they were part of the Akkadian empire, then independent, then part of the Babylonian empire under Hammurabi, then independent again (see Chapter 1). Warfare with the Babylonians and other Near Eastern states continued off and on, and in the thirteenth century B.C.E., the Assyrians slowly began to create a larger state.

The eleventh century B.C.E. — the time of the Bronze Age Collapse — was a period of instability and retrenchment in southwest Asia. The Assyrians did not engage in any new wars of conquest but remained fairly secure within their borders. At the end of the tenth century, however, under the leadership of King Adad-nirari II (r. 911–892 B.C.E.), Assyria began a campaign of expansion and domination. The next several turbulent centuries were marked by Assyrian military campaigns, constant efforts by smaller states to maintain or recover their independence, and eventual further Assyrian conquest.

Assyrian history is often told as a story of one powerful king after another, but among the successful Assyrian rulers there was one queen, Shammuramat, whose name in Greek became Semiramis. She ruled with her husband and then as regent for her young son in 810–806 B.C.E. Although not much can be known for certain about the historical Queen Semiramis, many legends grew up about her. Some emphasized her wisdom, beauty, and patronage of the arts, while others portrayed her as a sex-crazed sorceress. These stories cannot be used as evidence for the lives of women in the Assyrian Empire, but like the stories of Queen Cleopatra of Egypt (see Chapter 5), they can be used as evidence for the continuing fascination with the few women who held political power in the ancient world.

Eighth-century kings continued the expansion of Assyria, and the capital was established at Nineveh (NIHN-uh-vuh) on the Tigris River. In 717 B.C.E.

Sargon II (r. 721–705 B.C.E.) led his army in a sweeping attack along the coast of the eastern Mediterranean south of Phoenicia, where he defeated the armies of the Egyptian pharaoh. His successor, Sennacherib (r. 705–681 B.C.E.), besieged many cities in Judah, which was under the leadership of King Hezekiah (r. ca. 715–686 B.C.E.). Sennacherib's account of his siege of Jerusalem in 701 B.C.E. provides a vivid portrait of the Assyrian war machine:

> As to Hezekiah, the Jew, he did not submit to my yoke, I laid siege to 46 of his strong cities, walled forts and to the countless small villages in their vicinity, and conquered them by means of well-stamped earth-ramps, and battering rams brought thus near to the walls combined with the attack by foot soldiers, using mines, breaches as well as sapper work. . . . Himself I made prisoner in Jerusalem, his royal residence, like a bird in a cage. I surrounded him with earthwork in order to molest those who were leaving his city's gate.[2]

What he does not mention is that the siege of Jerusalem was not successful, a fact he also left out of the carvings and artwork that he ordered for his palace. (See "Evaluating Visual Evidence: Assyrians Besiege a City," page 45.) Although they had conquered many cities in Judah, the Assyrian armies gave up their attempts to conquer the entire kingdom and went home.

Sennacherib's campaign is also recorded several times in the Hebrew Bible. The biblical accounts attribute Judah's ability to withstand the Assyrian siege to an angel sent by Yahweh, but they also describe Hezekiah as taking practical measures to counter the Assyrian invasion, including making weapons and ordering the building of a tunnel that would divert water from the springs outside the walls of Jerusalem into the city, thus both limiting the water available for Assyrian troops and assuring the city of a steady supply. The tunnel was completed and worked as planned and is now a major tourist attraction, with water still flowing in it at certain times of the year. In addition to weapons, water, and possible divine favor, there appear to have been other reasons as well for the Assyrian withdrawal. The biblical texts also mention attacks on the Assyrians by Kushite and Egyptian troops (see "Individuals in Society: King Taharqa of Kush and Egypt," page 35), and modern scholars also suggest that there may have been a plague among the Assyrian troops.

Despite this one loss, in general by means of almost constant warfare, the Assyrians created an empire that stretched from east and north of the Tigris River to

■ **Assyrian Empire** An empire that originated in northern Mesopotamia and expanded to encompass much of the Near East in the tenth through the seventh centuries B.C.E.

Assyrians Besiege a City

In this Assyrian carving made about 700 B.C.E., from the palace of King Sennacherib at Nineveh, troops attack the Jewish fortified town of Lachish using a variety of siege machinery. On the right, defending soldiers crowd a tower, while men and women carry sacks away from the city. This attack was part of Sennacherib's campaign to conquer Judah, which he described in written accounts as well as carvings ordered for his palace. Lachish was one of the cities that Sennacherib was able to overpower and subjugate.

EVALUATE THE EVIDENCE

1. What means of attack do the Assyrians use against the besieged city in the carving?
2. How does the artist convey the idea that Assyrian military might was overwhelming?
3. Why might Sennacherib have chosen to have the siege of Lachish rather than that of the more important city of Jerusalem portrayed in his palace? What does that suggest about the purpose of art such as this?

(DEA/G. NIMATALLAH/De Agostini/Getty Images)

central Egypt (Map 2.1). Revolt against the Assyrians inevitably promised the rebels bloody battles and cruel sieges followed by surrender, accompanied by systematic torture and slaughter, or by deportations. Like many conquerors, the Assyrians recognized that relocated peoples were less likely to rebel because they were forced to create new lives for themselves far from their original homelands and that simply relocating leaders might be enough to destroy opposition.

Assyrian methods were certainly harsh, but in practical terms Assyria's success was actually due primarily to the size of its army and the army's sophisticated and effective military organization. By Sargon II's time, the Assyrians had invented the mightiest military machine the ancient Near East had ever seen, with perhaps seventy thousand men in the field, armed with iron spears and swords, in an era that typically saw armies of under ten thousand.

Assyrian military genius was remarkable for the development of a wide variety of siege machinery and techniques, including excavation to undermine city walls and battering rams to knock down walls and gates. Never before in the Near East had anyone applied such technical knowledge to warfare. The Assyrians even invented the concept of a corps of engineers, who bridged rivers with pontoons or provided soldiers with inflatable skins for swimming. And the Assyrians knew how to coordinate their efforts, both in open battle and in siege warfare.

Assyrian Rule and Culture

The Assyrians won most of their battles, and they also knew how to use their victories to consolidate their power. The key to success in all empires is to get cooperation from some people in the regions you

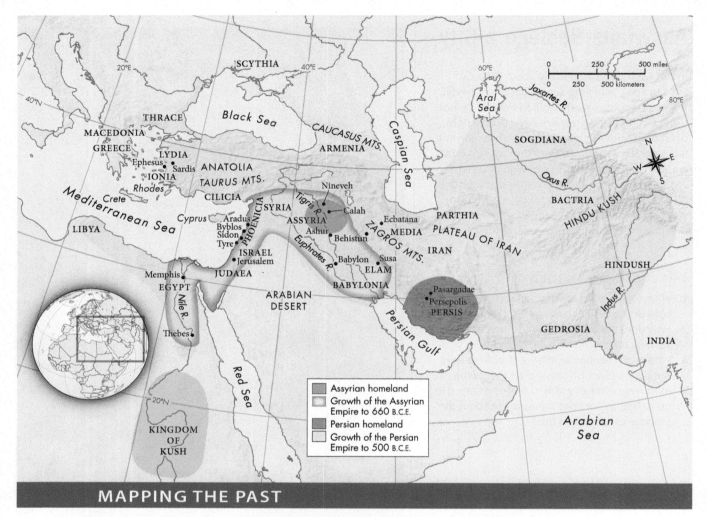

MAP 2.1 The Assyrian and Persian Empires, ca. 1000–500 B.C.E.

At its height around 650 B.C.E., the Assyrian Empire included almost all of the old centers of power in the ancient Near East. By 513 B.C.E., however, the Persian Empire was far larger.

ANALYZING THE MAP How does the Persian Empire compare in size to the Assyrian Empire? What other differences can you identify between the two?

CONNECTIONS Compare this map to Map 1.2. What changes and continuities do you see in the centers of power in the ancient Near East?

wish to dominate, and the Assyrians did this well. Although the lands closest to Assyria became provinces governed by Assyrian officials, kingdoms that were farther away were not annexed but became dependent states that followed Assyria's lead and also paid Assyria a hefty tribute. The Assyrian king chose these states' rulers either by regulating the succession of native kings or by supporting native kings who appealed to him.

In the seventh century B.C.E., Assyrian power seemed firmly established, yet the downfall of Assyria came swiftly and completely. Conflicts among various claimants to the throne, generals, and governors led to civil war, which weakened Assyria's ability to withstand opponents. Babylon won its independence from Assyria in 626 B.C.E. and joined forces with the Medes, an Indo-European-speaking people from Persia (modern Iran). Together the Babylonians and the

Medes destroyed the Assyrian Empire in 612 B.C.E., paving the way for the rise of the Neo-Babylonian and then the Persian Empire. The Hebrew prophet Nahum (NAY-uhm) spoke for many when he asked, "Nineveh is laid waste: who will bemoan her?" (Nahum 3:7). Their cities destroyed and their power shattered, the Assyrians disappeared from history, remembered only as a cruel people of the Old Testament who oppressed the Hebrews. Two hundred years later, when the Greek adventurer and historian Xenophon (ZEH-nuh-fuhn) passed by the ruins of Nineveh, he marveled at the extent of the former city but knew nothing of the Assyrians. The glory of their empire was forgotten.

Modern archaeology has brought the Assyrians out of obscurity. In 1839, the English archaeologist and traveler A. H. Layard began excavations at Nineveh. His findings electrified the world. Layard's workers unearthed masterpieces, including monumental sculpted figures—huge winged bulls, human-headed lions, and sphinxes—as well as brilliantly sculpted friezes. Among the most renowned of Layard's finds were the Assyrian palace reliefs, whose number was increased by the discoveries of twentieth-century archaeologists. For the kings' palaces, Assyrian artists carved reliefs that showed scenes of war as a series of episodes that progressed from the time the army marched out until the enemy was conquered. In doing so, they created a visual narrative of events, a form still favored by comic-book artists and the authors of graphic novels.

Equally valuable were the numerous Assyrian cuneiform documents, which ranged from royal accounts of mighty military campaigns to simple letters by common people. The biggest find was the library of King Ashurbanipal (r. 668–627 B.C.E.), the last major Assyrian king, in the city of Nineveh. Like many Assyrian kings, Ashurbanipal was described as extremely cruel, but he was also well educated and deeply interested in literary and religious texts, especially those from what was already to him the ancient Mesopotamian past. Included in the tens of thousands of texts in his library were creation accounts from ancient Babylon (some most likely simply confiscated from the city of Babylon, which was part of the Assyrian Empire), the *Epic of Gilgamesh*, and many other mythological and religious texts, as well as word lists, chronicles, and royal documents. Some texts relate to medicine and astronomy, and others to foretelling the future or practicing magic. The clay tablets on which these were written are harder than normal, which many scholars think may have happened as a result of a fire that destroyed the

Assyrian Winged Human-Headed Bull　This giant alabaster human-headed bull, from the palace of King Ashurnasirpal II (r. 888–859 B.C.E.) in Nimrud (now in Iraq), represents an Assyrian protective deity called a lamassu. Assyrians often placed pairs of lamassu at the entrance to palaces, where they stood as sentinels. This one was destroyed by the Islamic State in Iraq and the Levant (ISIL) in 2015, when they bulldozed and blew up the palace because they judged the artifacts idolatrous. (Nimrud, Iraq/Bridgeman Images)

city of Nineveh shortly after the end of Ashurbanipal's reign.

The Neo-Babylonian Empire

The decline of Assyria allowed a new dynasty of kings to create a somewhat smaller empire centered at Babylon, which historians call the Neo- (or new) Babylonian empire to distinguish it from the earlier Babylonian empire of Hammurabi. With the help of the Medes, who had established themselves in modern western Iran, people living in southern Mesopotamia overthrew Assyrian rule in 626 B.C.E. The Neo-Babylonian empire they created was marked by an attempt to restore past Babylonian greatness. Their most famous king, Nebuchadnezzar II (neh-buh-kuhd-NEH-zuhr) (r. 604–562 B.C.E.), thrust Babylonian power into Syria and Judah, destroying Jerusalem and forcibly deporting the residents to Babylonia.

The Neo-Babylonian rulers focused on solidifying their power and legitimizing their authority. Kings and priests consciously looked back to the great days of Hammurabi and other earlier kings. They instituted a religious revival that included restoring old temples and sanctuaries, as well as creating new ones in the same tradition. Part of their aim was commercial: they sought to resurrect the image of Babylonian greatness in order to revive the economy and attract new people to the area. In their hands, the city of Babylon grew and gained a reputation for magnificence and luxury. The city, it was said by later Greek and Roman writers, even housed hanging gardens, one of the "wonders of the ancient world." No contemporary written or archaeological sources confirm the existence of the hanging gardens, but they do confirm that Babylon was a bustling, thriving city.

Neo-Babylonian Figurine   This terracotta figurine, made in Babylon about 700 B.C.E., shows a female figure with an inclined head and clasped hands, a common posture indicating religious devotion. Throughout the ancient Mediterranean and Near East, people placed religious statuettes in household shrines and gravesites or carried them around, viewing them as offering protection and blessing. (Pictures From History/Newscom)

The Neo-Babylonian empire preserved many basic aspects of older Babylonian law, literature, and government, yet it failed to bring peace and prosperity to Mesopotamia. Loss of important trade routes to the north and northeast reduced income, and additional misfortune came in the form of famine and plague. The Neo-Babylonian empire was weakened and ultimately conquered in 539 B.C.E. by their former allies, the Medes, who had themselves found new allies, the Persians.

How did the Persians conquer and rule their extensive empire?

The Assyrians rose to power from a base in the Tigris and Euphrates River Valleys of Mesopotamia, which had seen many earlier empires. They were defeated by a coalition that included a Mesopotamian power—Babylon—but also a people with a base of power in a part of the world that had not been the site of earlier urbanized states: Persia (modern-day Iran), a stark land of towering mountains and flaming deserts, with a broad central plateau in the heart of the country (see Map 2.1). Beginning in the sixth century B.C.E., the Persians created an even larger empire than the Assyrians did, and one that stretched far to the east. Though as conquerors they willingly used force to accomplish their ends, they also used diplomacy to consolidate their power and generally allowed the peoples that they conquered to practice their existing customs and religions. Thus the **Persian Empire** was one of political unity and cultural diversity.

Consolidation of the Persian Empire

Iran's geographical position and topography explain its traditional role as the highway between western and eastern Asia. Nomadic peoples migrating south

from the broad steppes of Russia and Central Asia have streamed into Iran throughout much of history. Confronting the uncrossable salt deserts, most have turned either westward or eastward, moving on until they reached the advanced and wealthy urban centers of Mesopotamia and India. Cities did emerge along these routes, however, and Iran became the area where nomads met urban dwellers.

Among the nomadic groups were Indo-European-speaking peoples who migrated into this area about 1000 B.C.E. with their flocks and herds. They were also horse breeders, and the horse gave them a decisive military advantage over those who already lived in the area. One of the Indo-European groups was the Medes, who settled in a part of northern Iran later called Media. The Medes united under one king and joined the Babylonians in overthrowing the Assyrian Empire. With the rise of the Medes, the balance of power in western Asia shifted for the first time to the area east of Mesopotamia.

In 550 B.C.E., Cyrus the Great (r. 559–530 B.C.E.), king of the Persians and one of the most remarkable statesmen of antiquity, conquered the Medes. Cyrus's conquest of the Medes resulted not in slavery and slaughter but in the union of the two peoples. Having united Persia and Media, Cyrus set out to achieve two goals. First, he wanted to win control of the shore of the Mediterranean and thus of the terminal ports of

■ **Persian Empire** A large empire centered in today's Iran that used force and diplomacy to consolidate its power and that allowed cultural diversity.

Chariot with Medean Soldiers   Two men dressed in clothing of the Medes, one of the groups conquered by the Persians, drive a four-horse chariot in this small model made entirely of gold. In the nineteenth century a huge collection of silver and gold objects from the fifth and fourth centuries B.C.E. was found on the banks of the Oxus River in what is now Tajikistan. Most likely, the spot had been a ferry crossing and the objects had been buried long ago. (De Agostini/DEA PICTURE LIBRARY/Getty Images)

the great trade routes that crossed Iran and Anatolia. Second, he strove to secure eastern Iran from the pressure of nomadic invaders.

In a series of major campaigns, Cyrus achieved his goals. He conquered various kingdoms of the Tigris and Euphrates Valleys and then swept into western Anatolia. Here his forces met those of the young kingdom of Lydia, a small state where gold may have first been minted into coins. Croesus (KREE-suhs) (r. 560?–546?), the Lydian king at the time, was reputed to have been fabulously wealthy, giving rise to the phrase "richer than Croesus" for someone with enormous wealth. Croesus considered Cyrus an immediate threat and planned to attack his territory. Greek legends later related that Croesus consulted the oracle at Delphi, that is, the priestess of the temple to the god Apollo at Delphi, who was understood to convey the words of the god when she spoke. Speaking through the priestess, Apollo said of the invasion, "If you make war on the Persians, you will destroy a mighty empire" (Herodotus 1.53.3). Thinking that the oracle meant the Persian Empire, Croesus went

ahead and was defeated; the oracle meant that he would destroy his own kingdom.

Cyrus's generals subdued the Greek cities along the coast of Anatolia, thus gaining him important ports on the Mediterranean. From there, Cyrus marched to the far eastern corners of Iran and conquered the regions of Parthia and Bactria in Central Asia, though he ultimately died on the battlefield there.

After his victories, Cyrus made sure that the Persians were portrayed as liberators, and in some cases he was more benevolent than most conquerors were. According to his own account, he freed all of the captive peoples who were living in forced exile in Babylonia, including the Hebrews. He returned their sacred objects to them and allowed those who wanted to return to Jerusalem to do so, and he paid for the rebuilding of their temple. (See "Viewpoints: Rulers and Divine Favor: Views of Cyrus the Great," page 42.)

Cyrus's successors continued Persian conquests, creating the largest empire the world had yet seen. In 525 B.C.E. Cyrus's son Cambyses (r. 530–522 B.C.E.) subdued the Egyptians and the Nubians. At Cambyses's death (the circumstances of which are disputed), Darius I (r. 521–486 B.C.E.) took over the throne and conquered Scythia in Central Asia, along with much of Thrace and Macedonia, areas north of the Aegean Sea. By 510, the Persians also ruled the western coast of Anatolia and many of the islands of the Aegean. Thus, within forty years, the Persians had transformed themselves from a subject people to the rulers of a vast empire that included all of the oldest kingdoms and peoples of the region, as well as many outlying areas (see Map 2.1). Unsurprisingly, Darius began to call himself "King of Kings." Invasions of Greece by Darius and his son Xerxes were unsuccessful, but the Persian Empire lasted another two hundred years, until it became part of the empire of Alexander the Great (see Chapter 4).

The Persians also knew how to preserve the empire they had won on the battlefield. Learning from the Assyrians, they created an efficient administrative system to govern the empire based in their newly built capital city of Persepolis near modern Shiraz, Iran. Under Darius, they divided the empire into districts and appointed either Persian or local nobles as administrators called **satraps** to head each one. The satrap controlled local government, collected taxes, heard legal cases, and maintained order. He was assisted by a council, and also by officials and army leaders sent from Persepolis who made sure that the satrap knew the will of the king and that the king knew what was going on in the provinces. This system lessened opposition to Persian rule by making local elites part of the system of government, although sometimes satraps used their authority to build up independent power.

Communication and trade were eased by a sophisticated system of roads linking the empire from the coast of Asia Minor to the valley of the Indus River. On the roads were way stations where royal messengers could get food and horses, a system that allowed messages to be communicated quickly, much like the famed Pony Express in the American West. These roads meant that the king was usually in close touch with officials and subjects. The roads also simplified the defense of the empire by making it easier to move Persian armies. In addition, the system allowed the easy flow of trade, which Persian rulers further encouraged by building canals, including one that linked the Red Sea and the Nile.

Persian Religion

Iranian religion was originally tied to nature, with many gods. Ahuramazda (ah-HOOR-uh-MAZ-duh), the chief god, was the creator of all living creatures. Mithra, the sun-god whose cult would later spread throughout the Roman Empire, saw to justice and redemption. Fire was a particularly important god, and fire was often part of religious rituals. A priestly class, the Magi, developed among the Medes to officiate at sacrifices, chant prayers to the gods, and tend the sacred flame.

Around 600 B.C.E., the ideas of Zoroaster, a thinker and preacher whose dates are uncertain, began to gain prominence. Zoroaster is regarded as the author of key religious texts, later gathered together in a collection of sacred texts called the Avesta. (See "Thinking Like a Historian: The Moral Life," page 40.) He introduced new spiritual concepts to the Iranian people, stressing devotion to Ahuramazda alone instead of many gods and emphasizing the individual's responsibility to choose between the forces of creation, truth, and order and those of nothingness, chaos, falsehood, and disorder. Zoroaster taught that people possessed the free will to decide between these and that they must rely on their own conscience to guide them through an active life in which they focused on "good thoughts, good words, and good deeds." Their decisions were crucial, he warned, for there would come a time of reckoning. At the end of time, the forces of order would win, and the victorious Ahuramazda, like the Egyptian god Osiris (see "Egyptian Religion" in Chapter 1), would preside over a last judgment to determine each person's eternal fate. Those who had lived according to good and truth would enter a divine kingdom. Liars and the wicked, denied this blessed immortality, would be condemned to eternal pain, darkness, and punishment. Thus Zoroaster preached a last judgment that led to a heaven or a hell.

Scholars — and contemporary Zoroastrians — debate whether Zoroaster saw the forces of disorder as a malevolent deity named Angra Mainyu who was co-eternal with and independent from Ahuramazda, or whether he was simply using this term to mean "evil thoughts" or "a destructive spirit." Later forms of **Zoroastrianism** followed each of these lines of understanding. Most Zoroastrians believed that the good Ahuramazda and the evil Angra Mainyu were locked together in a cosmic battle for the human race, a religious conceptualization that scholars call dualism, which was rejected in Judaism and Christianity. Some had a more monotheistic interpretation, however, and saw Ahuramazda as the only uncreated god.

Whenever he actually lived, Zoroaster's writings were spread by teachers, and King Darius began to use Zoroastrian language and images. Under the protection of the Persian kings, Zoroastrian ideas spread throughout Iran and the rest of the Persian Empire, and then beyond this into central China. Zoroastrianism became the official religion of the later Persian Empire ruled by the Sassanid dynasty, and much later Zoroastrians migrated to western India, where they became known as Parsis and still live today. Zoroastrianism survived the fall of the Persian Empire to influence Christianity,

■ **satraps** Administrators in the Persian Empire who controlled local government, collected taxes, heard legal cases, and maintained order.

■ **Zoroastrianism** Religion based on the ideas of Zoroaster that stressed devotion to the god Ahuramazda alone and that emphasized the individual's responsibility to choose between good and evil.

King Darius Defeats His Enemies   King Darius of Persia proclaimed victory over his enemies with a written inscription and sculpture high on a cliff near Mount Behistun so all could see. He attributed his victory to Ahuramazda, the god of Zoroastrianism, whose symbol is carved above the chained prisoners. The proclamation itself was inscribed in three different cuneiform script languages, and it has been a vital tool for scholars as they have deciphered these ancient languages. (BIBLE LAND PICTURES/Bridgeman Images)

Islam, and Buddhism, largely because of its belief in a just life on earth and a happy afterlife. Good behavior in the world, even though unrecognized at the time, would receive ample reward in the hereafter. Evil, no matter how powerful in life, would be punished after death. In some form or another, Zoroastrian concepts still pervade many modern religions, and Zoroastrianism still exists as a religion.

Persian Art and Culture

The Persians made significant contributions to art and culture. They produced amazing works in gold and silver, often with inlaid jewels and semiprecious stones. They transformed the Assyrian tradition of realistic monumental sculpture from one that celebrated gory details of slaughter to one that showed both the Persians and their subjects as dignified. They noted and carved the physical features of their subjects: their hair, their clothing, their tools and weapons. Because they depicted both themselves and non-Persians realistically, Persian art serves as an excellent source for learning about the weapons, tools, clothing, and even hairstyles of many peoples of the area.

These carvings adorned temples and other large buildings in cities throughout the empire, and the Persians also built new cities from the ground up. The most spectacular of these was Persepolis, designed as a residence for the kings and an administrative and cultural center. The architecture of Persepolis combined elements found in many parts of the empire. Underneath the city was a system of closed water pipes, drainage canals, and conduits that allowed water from nearby mountains to flow into the city without flooding it, provided water for households and plantings inside the city, and carried away sewage and waste from the city's many residents. The Persians thus further improved the technology for handling water, which had been essential in this area since the time of the Sumerians.

The Persians allowed the peoples they conquered to maintain their own customs and beliefs, as long as they paid the proper amount of taxes and did not rebel. Persian rule resulted in an empire that brought people together in a new political system, with a culture that blended older and newer religious traditions and ways of seeing the world. Even the Persians' opponents, including the Greeks who would eventually conquer the Persian Empire, admired their art and institutions.

NOTES

1. James H. Breasted, *Ancient Records of Egypt*, vol. 4 (Chicago: University of Chicago Press, 1907), para. 398.

2. James B. Pritchard, ed., *Ancient Near Eastern Texts Relating to the Old Testament—Third Edition with Supplement* (Princeton, N.J.: Princeton University Press, 1969), p. 288.

LOOKING BACK LOOKING AHEAD

During the centuries following the Bronze Age Collapse, natives and newcomers brought order to life across the ancient Near East. As Egypt fell, small kingdoms, including those of the Nubians, Phoenicians, and Hebrews, grew and prospered. Regular trade and communication continued, and new products and ideas were transported by sea and land. Beginning about 900 B.C.E., the Assyrians created a large state through military conquest that was often brutal, though they also developed effective structures of rule through which taxes flowed to their leaders. The Persians, an Iranian people whose center of power was east of Mesopotamia, then established an even larger empire, governing through local officials and building beautiful cities.

The lands on the northern shore of the Mediterranean were beyond the borders of the urbanized cultures and centralized empires of the ancient Near East but maintained contact with them through trade and migration. As the Persian Empire continued to expand, it looked further westward toward these lands, including Greece, as possible further conquests. Greek-speaking people living in Anatolia and traveling more widely throughout the area had also absorbed numerous aspects of Persian and other more urbanized cultures they had encountered. They learned of Near Eastern religions and myths, and of the sagas of heroic wars. They also acquired many of the advanced technologies developed by their eastern neighbors, including the use of bronze and later iron, the phonetic alphabet, wine making, and shipbuilding. The Greeks combined these borrowings with their own traditions, ideas, and talents to create a distinct civilization, one that fundamentally shaped the subsequent development of Western society.

Make Connections

Think about the larger developments and continuities within and across chapters.

1. How were the Assyrian and Persian Empires similar to earlier river valley civilizations? How were they different? What might explain the pattern of similarities and differences?

2. The Persians and Assyrians became significant in history through military conquest and the establishment of empires, and the Phoenicians and Hebrews through cultural creations. Which of these were longer-lasting, and why?

3. What lessons and insights might the Persian Empire have to offer future diverse states and empires, including those of the modern world?

2 REVIEW & EXPLORE

Identify Key Terms

Identify and explain the significance of each item below.

Iron Age (p. 32)

Kush (p. 33)

Phoenicians (p. 34)

monotheism (p. 36)

Yahweh (p. 36)

Torah (p. 38)

Covenant (p. 38)

Assyrian Empire (p. 43)

Persian Empire (p. 48)

satraps (p. 50)

Zoroastrianism (p. 50)

Review the Main Ideas

Answer the section heading questions from the chapter.

1. How did iron technology shape new states after 1200 B.C.E.? (p. 32)

2. How did the Hebrews create an enduring religious tradition? (p. 36)

3. How did the Assyrians and Neo-Babylonians gain and lose power? (p. 43)

4. How did the Persians conquer and rule their extensive empire? (p. 48)

Suggested Resources

BOOKS

+ Briant, Pierre. *From Cyrus to Alexander*. 2002. A superb treatment of the entire Persian Empire.

+ Clark, Peter. *Zoroastrianism: An Introduction to an Ancient Faith*. 1998. The best introduction to the essence of Zoroastrianism.

+ Edwards, David N. *The Nubian Past*. 2004. Studies the history of Nubia and the Sudan, incorporating archaeological evidence to supplement historical sources.

+ Foster, Benjamin R. *Civilizations of Ancient Iraq*. 2009. Discusses the development of cities and the empires of Babylonia and Assyria.

+ Gates, Charles. *Ancient Cities: The Archaeology of Urban Life in the Ancient Near East and Egypt, Greece, and Rome*. 2003. Provides a survey of ancient life primarily from an archaeological point of view, but also includes cultural and social information.

+ Goldenberg, Robert. *The Origins of Judaism: From Canaan to the Rise of Islam*. 2007. Examines the development of Jewish ideas and traditions.

+ Kriwaczek, Paul. *In Search of Zarathustra: Across Iran and Central Asia to Find the World's First Prophet*.

2002. An award-winning BBC journalist follows the legacy of Zoroaster back through time.

+ Kugel, James. *The God of Old: Inside the Lost World of the Bible*. 2004. A noted biblical scholar surveys the way the ancient Israelites understood God.

+ Markoe, Glenn E. *The Phoenicians*. 2000. A fresh investigation of the Phoenicians at home and abroad in the western Mediterranean over their long history, with many illustrations.

+ Meyers, Carol. *Rediscovering Eve: Ancient Israelite Women in Context*. 2012. A brief study designed for general readers that draws on archaeology and ethnography along with biblical texts.

+ Morkot, Robert G. *The Black Pharaohs: Egypt's Nubian Rulers*. 2000. Examines the growth of the Kushite kingdom and its rule over pharaonic Egypt in the eighth century B.C.E.

+ Provan, Iain, V. Philips Long, and Tremper Longman III. *A Biblical History of Israel*. 2003. A history of ancient Israel that relies primarily on the biblical text.

MEDIA

+ *The Bible's Buried Secrets* (*Nova*, 2008). In this two-hour documentary, *Nova* examines the ancient Israelites through biblical and other ancient texts and archaeological artifacts.

+ *Engineering an Empire: The Persians* (History Channel, 2006). This hour-long documentary focuses on the engineering of the Persian Empire, especially its canals and roads.

+ *Israel Antiquities Authority*. Official website of the Israel Antiquities Authority, with a huge collection of artifacts from many periods in the "National Treasures" section. **www.antiquities.org.il /home_eng.asp**

+ *Nubia: The Forgotten Kingdom* (Discovery Channel, 2003). Archaeologists excavate temples and markets of the ancient city of Dangeil and examine Nubia's links with Egypt.

+ *Phoenicia: The Phoenician Ship Expedition*. Traces the building and voyage of a reconstruction of a Phoenician trading vessel that in 2008–2010 retraced the Phoenicians' route around Africa and in 2012 sailed to London for the Olympics. **phoenicia.org.uk/**

+ *Quest for the Phoenicians* (National Geographic, 2004). Scientists use DNA analysis and other modern technologies to examine the migrations and the sailing routes of the ancient Phoenicians.

3

The Development of Greek Society and Culture

ca. 3000–338 B.C.E.

The people of ancient Greece built on the traditions and ideas of earlier societies to develop a culture that fundamentally shaped the intellectual and cultural traditions of Western civilization. Humans came into Greece over many thousands of years, in waves of migrants whose place of origin and cultural characteristics have been the source of much scholarly debate. The first to arrive were foragers, but techniques of agriculture and animal domestication had spread into Greece from Turkey by about 6500 B.C.E., after which small farming communities worked much of the land. Early settlers to Greece brought skills in making bronze weapons and tools, which became more common around 3000 B.C.E.

Drawing on their day-to-day experiences as well as human reason, the Greeks developed ways of questioning, understanding, and explaining the world around them and the place of humans in it, ideas that later grew into modern philosophy and science. They also created new political forms such as the polis and new types of literature and art. The history of the Greeks is divided into three broad periods, two of which are covered in this chapter: the Helladic period of the Bronze Age, roughly 3000 B.C.E. to 1100 B.C.E.; and the Hellenic period, from 1100 B.C.E. to 338 B.C.E., when Greece was conquered by Macedonia. The later Hellenistic period is covered in Chapter 4. ■

CHAPTER PREVIEW

■ How did the geography of Greece shape its earliest kingdoms?

■ What was the role of the polis in Greek society?

■ How did the wars of the classical period shape Greek history?

■ What ancient Greek ideas and ideals have had a lasting influence?

Warriors and Heroes in Ancient Greece
This painting on the side of a large jar, made in the sixth century B.C.E. and used for mixing wine and water, shows warriors in the Trojan War fighting over the body of Patroclus, a Greek warrior beloved by Achilles, after he was killed by the Trojan prince Hector. Scenes from myths and epics surrounded the ancient Greeks in their homes and public spaces, communicating cultural values.
(De Agostini/G. DAGLI ORTI/Getty Images)

How did the geography of Greece shape its earliest kingdoms?

During the Bronze Age, which for Greek history is called the Helladic period, early settlers in Greece began establishing small communities contoured by the mountains and small plains that shaped the land. These communities sometimes joined together to form kingdoms, most prominently the Minoan kingdom on the island of Crete and the Mycenaean kingdom on the mainland. The Minoan and Mycenaean societies flourished for centuries until the Bronze Age Collapse, when Greece entered a period of decline known as the Dark Age (ca. 1100–800 B.C.E.). Epic poems composed by Homer and Hesiod after the Dark Age provide the poets' versions of what life may have been like in these early Greek kingdoms.

Geography and Settlement

Hellas, as the Greeks still call their land, encompassed the Greek peninsula, the islands of the Aegean (ah-GEE-uhn) Sea, and the lands bordering the Aegean, an area known as the Aegean basin (Map 3.1). Geography acts as an enormously divisive force in Greek life; mountains divide the land, and although there are good harbors on the sea, there are no navigable rivers. Much of the land is rocky and not very fertile, which meant that food availability was a constant concern.

The major regions of Greece were Thessaly and Macedonia in the north, and Boeotia (bee-OH-shuh) and the large island of Euboea (YOU-boh-ee-ah) in the center, lands marked by fertile plains that helped to sustain a strong population capable of serving as

MAP 3.1 Classical Greece, 500–338 B.C.E.   In antiquity, the home of the Greeks included the islands of the Aegean and the western shore of Turkey as well as the Greek peninsula itself. Crete, the home of Minoan civilization, is the large island at the bottom of the map.

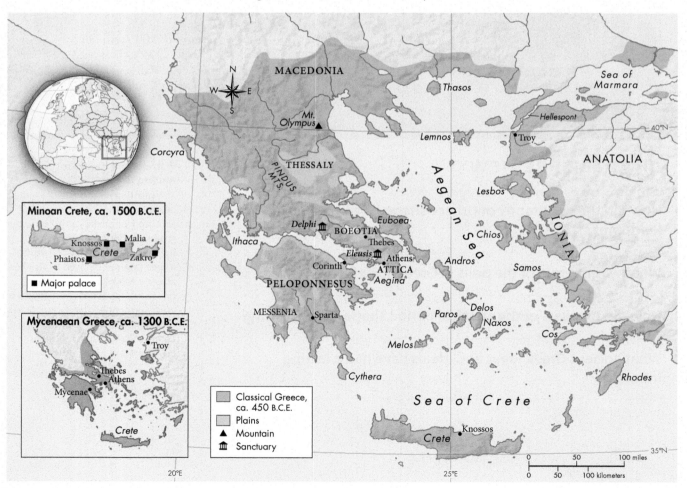

TIMELINE

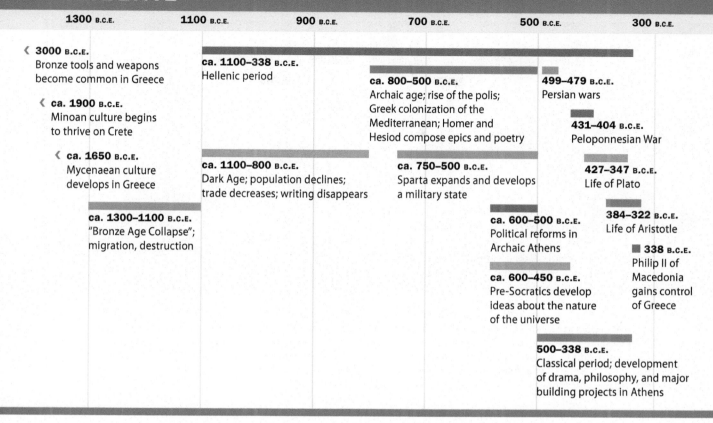

1300 B.C.E.	**1100** B.C.E.	**900** B.C.E.	**700** B.C.E.	**500** B.C.E.	**300** B.C.E.

‹ 3000 B.C.E.
Bronze tools and weapons become common in Greece

ca. 1100–338 B.C.E.
Hellenic period

ca. 800–500 B.C.E.
Archaic age; rise of the polis; Greek colonization of the Mediterranean; Homer and Hesiod compose epics and poetry

499–479 B.C.E.
Persian wars

‹ ca. 1900 B.C.E.
Minoan culture begins to thrive on Crete

431–404 B.C.E.
Peloponnesian War

‹ ca. 1650 B.C.E.
Mycenaean culture develops in Greece

ca. 1100–800 B.C.E.
Dark Age; population declines; trade decreases; writing disappears

ca. 750–500 B.C.E.
Sparta expands and develops a military state

427–347 B.C.E.
Life of Plato

ca. 1300–1100 B.C.E.
"Bronze Age Collapse"; migration, destruction

ca. 600–500 B.C.E.
Political reforms in Archaic Athens

384–322 B.C.E.
Life of Aristotle

338 B.C.E.
Philip II of Macedonia gains control of Greece

ca. 600–450 B.C.E.
Pre-Socratics develop ideas about the nature of the universe

500–338 B.C.E.
Classical period; development of drama, philosophy, and major building projects in Athens

---

formidable cavalry and infantry. Immediately to the south of Boeotia was Attica, with plains for wheat and hillier areas where olives and wine grapes flourished. Attica's harbors looked to the Aegean, which invited its inhabitants, the Athenians, to concentrate on maritime commerce. Still farther south, the Peloponnesus (peh-luh-puh-NEE-suhs), a large peninsula connected to the rest of mainland Greece by a very narrow isthmus at Corinth, was a patchwork of high mountains and small plains that divided the area into several regions. Beyond the coast, the islands of the Aegean served as stepping-stones to Anatolia, present-day Turkey.

The geographical fragmentation of Greece encouraged political fragmentation. Communications were poor, with rocky tracks far more common than roads. Early in Greek history, several kingdoms did emerge, but the rugged terrain prohibited the growth of a great empire like those of Mesopotamia or Egypt. Instead tiny states became the most common form of government.

The Minoans

On the large island of Crete, Bronze Age farmers and fishermen began to trade their surpluses with their neighbors, and cities grew, housing artisans and merchants. Beginning about 2000 B.C.E., Cretan traders voyaged throughout the eastern Mediterranean and the Aegean. Social hierarchies developed, and in many cities certain individuals came to hold power. The

Cretans began to use writing about 1900 B.C.E., in a form later scholars called Linear A. This has not been deciphered, but scholars know that the language of Crete was not related to Greek, so they do not consider the Cretans "Greek."

What we can know about the culture of Crete depends on archaeological and artistic evidence, and of this there is a great deal. At about the same time that writing began, rulers in several cities of Crete began to build large structures with hundreds of interconnected rooms. The largest of these, at Knossos (NOH-suhs), has over a thousand rooms, with pipes for bringing in drinking water and sewers to get rid of waste. The archaeologists who discovered these huge structures called them "palaces," and they named the flourishing and vibrant culture of this era **Minoan**, after a mythical king of Crete, Minos.

Few specifics are known about Minoan political life except that a king and a group of nobles stood at its head. Minoan life was long thought to have been relatively peaceful, but new excavations are revealing more and more walls around cities, which has called the peaceful nature of Minoan society into question. In terms of their religious life, Minoans appear to have worshipped goddesses far more than gods. Whether this translated into more egalitarian gender roles for real people is unclear, but surviving Minoan art shows women as well as men

---

■ Minoan A wealthy and vibrant culture on Crete from around 1900 B.C.E. to 1450 B.C.E., ruled by a king with a large palace at Knossos.

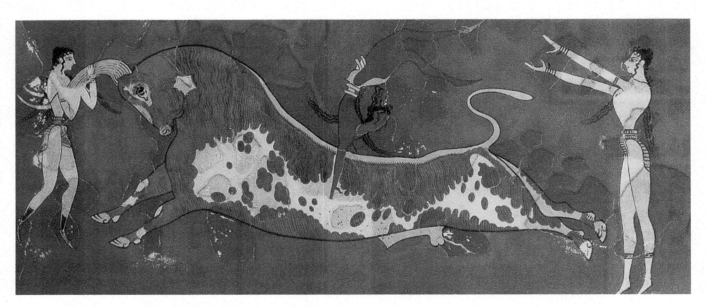

Minoan Bull-Leaping   A colorful fresco dating from around 1600 B.C.E. found at the palace of Knossos on Crete shows three people in a scene of bull-leaping. The outside figures are women, who are generally portrayed with light skin to represent women's association with the household, and the figure leaping over the bull is a man, whose reddish skin associates him with the outdoors. Bulls were venerated in Minoan culture, and this may be a scene of an actual ritual sport done at the palace, a spectacle celebrating human athletic prowess and mastery of nature. (Werner Forman/Universal Images Group/Getty Images)

leading religious activities, watching entertainment, and engaging in athletic competitions.

Beginning about 1700 B.C.E. Minoan society was disrupted by a series of earthquakes and volcanic eruptions on nearby islands, some of which resulted in large tsunamis. The largest of these was a huge volcanic eruption that devastated the island of Thera to the north of Crete, burying the Minoan town there in lava and causing it to collapse into the sea. This eruption, one of the largest in recorded history, may have been the origin of the story of the mythical kingdom of Atlantis, a wealthy kingdom with beautiful buildings that had sunk under the ocean. The eruption on Thera was long seen as the most important cause of the collapse of Minoan civilization, but scholars using radiocarbon and other types of scientific dating have called this theory into question, as the eruption seems to have occurred somewhat earlier than 1600 B.C.E., and Minoan society did not collapse until more than two centuries later. In fact, new settlements and palaces were often built on Crete following the earthquakes and the eruption of Thera.

The Mycenaeans

As Minoan culture was flourishing on Crete, a different type of society developed on the mainland. This society was founded by groups who had migrated there

after 2000 B.C.E. By about 1650 B.C.E., one group of these immigrants had raised palaces and established cities at Thebes, Athens, Mycenae (migh-SEE-nee), and elsewhere. These palace-centers ruled by local kings formed a loose alliance under the authority of the king of Mycenae, and the archaeologists who first discovered traces of this culture called it **Mycenaean** (migh-see-NEE-an).

As in Crete, the political unit in Mycenaean Greece was the kingdom, and the king and his warrior aristocracy stood at the top of society. The seat and symbol of the king's power was his palace, which was also the economic center of the kingdom. Within the palace's walls, royal artisans fashioned gold jewelry and rich ornaments, made pottery, forged bronze weapons, prepared hides and wool for clothing, and manufactured the other goods needed by the king and his supporters. The Mycenaean economy was marked by an extensive division of labor, and at the bottom of the social scale were enslaved men and women.

Palace scribes kept records with a script known as Linear B, which scholars realized was an early form of Greek and have learned to read. Thus, they consider the Mycenaeans the first truly "Greek" culture to emerge in this area. Information on Mycenaean culture comes through inscriptions and other forms of written records as well as buildings and other objects. All of these point to a society in which war was common. Mycenaean cities were all fortified by thick

■ **Mycenaean**   A Bronze Age culture that flourished in Greece from about 1650 B.C.E. to 1100 B.C.E., building fortified palaces and cities.

Mycenaean Armor and Helmet   This cuirass, a piece of armor that protects both front and back, was made in about 1500 B.C.E. from long strips of flattened bronze. The oldest armor ever found in Europe, it was unearthed at the Mycenaean cemetery at Dendra, along with this helmet made of boar's teeth. Both are in very good condition, which suggests they were ceremonial, or at least only rarely used. (GEOFF GARVEY/Archaeological Museum of Nauplion, Greece/Bridgeman Images)

stone walls, and graves contain bronze spears, javelins, swords, helmets, and the first examples of metal armor known in the world. Mycenaean kingdoms appear to have fought regularly with one another.

Contacts between the Minoans and Mycenaeans were originally peaceful, and Minoan culture and trade goods flooded the Greek mainland. But most scholars think that around 1450 B.C.E., possibly in the wake of another earthquake that left Crete vulnerable, the Mycenaeans attacked Crete, destroying many towns and occupying Knossos. For about the next fifty years, the Mycenaeans ruled much of the island. The palaces at Knossos and other cities of the Aegean became grander as wealth gained through

trade and tribute flowed into the treasuries of various Mycenaean kings. Linear B replaced Linear A as a writing system, a further sign of Mycenaean domination.

Prosperity did not bring peace, however; between 1300 and 1100 B.C.E., various kingdoms in and beyond Greece ravaged one another in a savage series of wars that destroyed both the Minoan and Mycenaean civilizations. Among these wars was perhaps one that later became known as the Trojan War, fought by Greeks in Ionia, the coastal area of Anatolia.

The fall of the Minoans and Mycenaeans was part of what scholars see as a general collapse of Bronze Age civilizations in the eastern Mediterranean (see Chapters 1 and 2). This collapse appears to have had a number of causes: internal economic and social problems; invasions and migrations by outsiders, who destroyed cities and disrupted trade and production; changes in warfare and weaponry, particularly the adoption of iron weapons, which made foot soldiers the most important factor in battles and reduced the power of kings and wealthy nobles fighting from chariots; and natural disasters, which reduced the amount of food and contributed to famines.

These factors worked together to usher in a period of poverty and disruption that historians of Greece have traditionally called the Dark Age (ca. 1100–800 B.C.E.). Cities were destroyed, population declined, villages were abandoned, and trade decreased. Pottery became simpler, and jewelry and other grave goods became less ornate. Even writing, which had not been widespread previously, was a casualty of the chaos, and Linear A and B inscriptions were no longer produced.

The Bronze Age Collapse led to the widespread and prolonged movement of Greek peoples, both within Greece itself and beyond. They dispersed beyond mainland Greece farther south to the islands of the Aegean and in greater strength across the Aegean to the shores of Anatolia, arriving at a time when traditional states and empires had collapsed. By the conclusion of the Dark Age, the Greeks had spread their culture throughout the Aegean basin and, like many other cultures around the Mediterranean and the Near East, they had adopted iron.

Homer, Hesiod, and the Epic

Archaeological sources from the Dark Age are less rich than those from the periods that came after, and so they are often used in conjunction with literary sources written in later centuries to give us a more complete picture of the era. Unlike the Hebrews, the Greeks had no sacred book that chronicled their past. Instead they had epics, poetic tales of legendary heroes and of the times when people believed the gods still walked the earth. Of these, the *Iliad* and the *Odyssey* are the most important. Most scholars think they were composed in the eighth or seventh century B.C.E. By the fifth century B.C.E. they were attributed to a poet named Homer, though whether Homer was an actual historical individual is debated. What is not debated is their long-lasting impact, both on later Greek culture and on the Western world.

The *Iliad* recounts the tale of the Trojan War of the late Bronze Age. As Homer tells it, the Achaeans (uh-KEE-uhnz), the name he gives to the Mycenaeans, sent an expedition to besiege the city of Troy and to retrieve Helen, the wife of one of the Mycenaean kings, who was abducted by Paris, the Trojan king's son. The epic is full of bloody battles, duels between individual warriors, surprise attacks, revenge killings, desperate grief, noble speeches, and interventions by the gods, who also fight among themselves. At its heart is the quarrel between the Mycenaean king, Agamemnon, and the stormy hero of the poem, Achilles (uh-KIHL-eez), whose uncontrolled anger brings suffering to all. Ancient Greeks and Romans believed that the Trojan War was a real event embellished by poetic retelling, but by the modern era most people regarded it as a myth until the ruins of Troy were discovered in the late nineteenth century. Today most scholars think that the core of the story was a composite of many conflicts, although the characters are not historical.

Homer's *Odyssey* recounts the adventures of Odysseus (oh-DIH-see-uhs), a wise and fearless hero of the war at Troy, during his ten-year voyage home. He encounters many dangers, storms, and adventures, but he finally reaches his home and unites again with Penelope, the ideal wife, dedicated to her husband and family.

Both of Homer's epics portray engaging but flawed characters who are larger than life yet human. The men and women at the center of the stories display the quality known as *arête* (ah-reh-TAY), that is, having excellence and living up to one's fullest potential. Homer also portrays the gods and goddesses as Greeks understood them, not perfect beings but instead much like humans, with emotions, needs, and desires. They generally sit on Mount Olympus in the north of Greece and watch the fighting at Troy, although they sometimes participate in the action.

Greeks also learned about the gods and goddesses of their polytheistic system from another poet, Hesiod (HEH-see-uhd), who most scholars think lived sometime between 750 and 650 B.C.E. In his poem the *Theogony*, Hesiod combined Mesopotamian myths with a variety of Greek oral traditions to forge a coherent story of the origin of the gods. In another of his poems, *Works and Days*, the gods watch over the earth, looking for justice and injustice, while leaving the great mass of men and women to live lives of hard work and endless toil.

What was the role of the polis in Greek society?

Homer and Hesiod both lived in the era after the Dark Age, which later historians have termed the Archaic age (800–500 B.C.E.). The most important political change in this period was the development of the **polis** (PAH-luhs; plural *poleis*), a word generally translated as "city-state." With the polis, the Greeks established a new type of political structure. During the Archaic period, poleis established colonies throughout much of the Mediterranean, spreading Greek culture. Two particular poleis, each with a distinctive system of government, rose to prominence on the Greek mainland: Sparta and Athens.

Organization of the Polis

The Greek polis was not the first form of city-state to emerge. The earliest states in Sumer were also city-states, as were many of the small Mycenaean kingdoms. What differentiated the new Greek model from older city-states is the fact that the polis was more than a political institution; it was a community of citizens with their own customs and laws. With one exception,

the poleis that emerged after 800 did not have kings but instead were self-governing. The physical, religious, and political forms of the polis varied from place to place, but everywhere the polis was relatively small, reflecting the fragmented geography of Greece. The smallness of the polis enabled Greeks to see how they fit individually into the overall system — and how the individual parts made up the social whole. This notion of community was fundamental to the polis and was the very badge of Greekness.

Poleis developed from Dark Age towns. When fully developed, each polis normally shared a surprisingly large number of features with other poleis. Physically a polis was a society of people who lived in a city (*asty*) and cultivated the surrounding countryside (*chora*). The countryside was essential to the economy of the polis and provided food to sustain the entire population. By the fifth century B.C.E., the city was generally surrounded by a wall. The city contained a point, usually elevated, called the acropolis, and a public square or marketplace called the agora (ah-guh-RAH). On the acropolis, people built temples, altars, public monuments, and various dedications to the gods of the polis. The agora was the political center of the polis. In the agora were shops, public buildings, and courts.

All poleis, with one exception, did not have standing armies. Instead they largely relied on their citizens for protection. Wealthy aristocrats often served as cavalry. The backbone of the army, however, was the heavily armed infantry, or **hoplites**, middle-class and upper-middle-class propertied citizens who could afford leather and bronze armor and helmets, shields, and iron-tipped weapons, which they purchased themselves. They marched and fought in a close rectangular formation known as a *phalanx*, holding their shields together to form a solid wall, with the spears of the front row sticking out over the tops of the shields. As long as the phalanx stayed in formation, the hoplites presented an enemy with an impenetrable wall. This meant that commanders preferred to fight battles on open plains, where the hoplites could more easily maintain the phalanx, rather than in the narrow mountain passes that were common throughout much of Greece.

For naval battles, cities also relied on citizens as rowers for their warships, though these citizens were usually paid. An experienced rower was valuable because he had learned how to row in rhythm with many other men, and some rowers became professionals who hired themselves out to any military leader. In times of intense warfare, cities also used enslaved men as rowers because there were not enough free men available.

Governing Structures

Each Greek polis had one of several different types of government. Monarchy, rule by a king, had been prevalent during the Mycenaean period but declined thereafter. Sporadic periods of violent political and social upheaval often led to the seizure of power by one man, a type of government the Greeks called **tyranny**. Tyrants generally came to power by using their wealth or by negotiating to win a political following that toppled the existing legal government. In contrast to its contemporary meaning, however, tyranny in ancient Greece did not necessarily mean oppressive rule. Some tyrants used their power to benefit average citizens by helping to limit the power of the landowning aristocracy, which made them popular.

Other types of government in the Archaic age were democracy and oligarchy. **Democracy** translates as "the power of the people" but was actually rule by citizens, not the people as a whole. Almost all Greek cities defined a citizen as an adult man with at least one or, at some times and places, two citizen parents. Women were citizens for religious and reproductive purposes, but their citizenship did not give them the right to participate in government. Free men who were not children of a citizen, resident foreigners, and enslaved men were not citizens and had no political voice. Thus ancient Greek democracy did not reflect the modern concept that all people are created equal, but it did permit male citizens to share equally in determining the diplomatic and military policies of the polis, without respect to wealth. This comparatively broad basis of participation made Greek democracy an appealing model to some political thinkers across the ages, although others feared direct democracy and viewed it as "mob rule."

Oligarchy, which literally means "the rule of the few," was government by citizens who met a minimum property requirement. Many Greeks preferred oligarchy because it provided more political stability than democracy did. (Many of the Founding Fathers of the United States agreed, and they established a system in which the most important elections were indirect and only property owners had the right to vote.) Although oligarchy was the government of the prosperous, it left the door open to political and social advancement. If members of the polis obtained enough wealth to meet property or money qualifications, they could enter the governing circle.

Overseas Expansion

The development of the polis coincided with the growth of the Greek world in both wealth and numbers, which brought new problems. The increase in population created more demand for food than the land could supply. The resulting social and political tensions drove many people to seek new homes outside Greece. In some cases the losers in a conflict within a polis were forced to leave.

Greeks from the mainland and Ionia traveled throughout the Mediterranean, sailing in great numbers to Sicily and southern Italy (Map 3.2). Here they conquered local peoples, though also later intermarried with them, and established prosperous cities. Some adventurous Greeks sailed farther

---

■ **polis** Generally translated as "city-state," it was the basic political and institutional unit of Greece in the Hellenic period.

■ **hoplites** Heavily armed citizens who served as infantry troops and fought to defend the polis.

■ **tyranny** Rule by one man who took over an existing government, generally by using his wealth to gain a political following.

■ **democracy** A type of Greek government in which all citizens administered the workings of government.

■ **oligarchy** A type of Greek government in which citizens who owned a certain amount of property ruled.

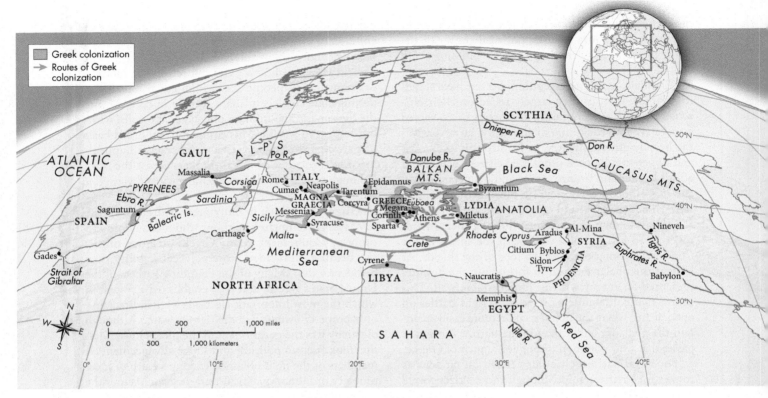

MAP 3.2 Greek Colonization, ca. 750–550 B.C.E. The Greeks established colonies along the shores of the Mediterranean and the Black Sea, spreading Greek culture and creating a large trading network.

Golden Comb This golden comb, produced about 400 B.C.E. in Scythia (see Map 3.2), shows a battle between three warriors, perhaps the three brothers who are the legendary founders of Scythia. Their dress shows a combination of Greek and Eastern details; the mounted horseman is clothed with largely Greek armor, while the warriors on foot are wearing Eastern dress. The comb may have been made by a Greek craftsman who had migrated to the Black Sea area, as the Greeks had established colonies there, but it was buried in a Scythian burial mound. (Fine Art Images/Heritage Images/Getty Images)

west to Sardinia, France, Spain, and perhaps even the Canary Islands. In Sardinia they first established trading stations and then permanent towns. From these new outposts Greek influence extended to southern France.

Colonization changed the entire Greek world, both at home and abroad. In economic terms the expansion of the Greeks created a much larger market for agricultural and manufactured goods. From the east, especially from the northern coast of the Black Sea, came wheat. In return flowed Greek wine and olive oil, which could not be produced in the harsher climate of the north. Greek-manufactured goods, notably rich jewelry and fine pottery, circulated from southern Russia to Spain. During the same period the Greeks adopted the custom of minting coins from metal, a skill first developed in the kingdom of Lydia in Anatolia. Coins provided many advantages over barter: they allowed merchants to set the value of goods in a determined system, they could be stored easily, and they allowed for more complex exchanges than did direct barter.

New colonies were planned and initially supplied by the *metropolis*, or "mother city." Once founded, however, they were independent of the metropolis, a pattern that was quite different from most later systems of colonization. Colonization spread the polis and its values far beyond the shores of Greece.

The Growth of Sparta

Many different poleis developed during the Archaic period, but Sparta became the leading military power in Greece. To expand their polis, the Spartans did not establish colonies but set out in about 750 B.C.E. to conquer Messenia (muh-SEE-nee-uh), a rich, fertile region in the southwestern Peloponnesus. This conflict, called the First Messenian War by later Greek historians, lasted for twenty years and ended in a Spartan triumph. The Spartans appropriated Messenian land and turned the Messenians into **helots** (HEH-luhts), unfree residents who lived in their own families and communities but were forced to work state lands.

In about 650 B.C.E., Spartan exploitation and oppression of the Messenian helots, along with Sparta's defeat at the hands of a rival polis, led to a massive helot revolt that became known as the Second Messenian War. The Spartan poet Tyrtaeus, a contemporary of these events, vividly portrays the violence of the war:

> For it is a shameful thing indeed
> When with the foremost fighters
> An elder falling in front of the young men
> Lies outstretched,
> Having white hair and grey beard,
> Breathing forth his stout soul in the dust,
> Holding in his hands his genitals
> Stained with blood.[1]

Finally after some thirty years of fighting, the Spartans put down the revolt. Nevertheless, the political and social strain it caused led to a transformation of the Spartan polis. After the war, non-nobles who had shared in the fighting as hoplites appear to have demanded rights equal to those of the nobility and a voice in the government. (In more recent history, similar demands in the United States during the Vietnam War led to a lowering of the voting age to eighteen, to match the age at which soldiers were drafted.) Under intense pressure, the aristocrats agreed to remodel the state into a new system.

The plan for the new system in Sparta was attributed to the lawgiver Lycurgus, who may or may not have been an actual person. According to later Greek sources, political distinctions among Spartan men were eliminated, and all citizens became legally equal. Governance of the polis was in the hands of two hereditary kings who were primarily military leaders. The kings were also part of the *Gerousia* (jeh-roo-SEE-ah), a council of men who had reached the age of sixty and thus retired from the Spartan army. The Gerousia deliberated on foreign and domestic matters and prepared legislation for the assembly, which consisted of all Spartan citizens. The real executive power of the polis was in the hands

of five ephors (EH-fuhrs), or overseers, elected from and by all the citizens.

To provide for their economic needs, the Spartans divided the land of Messenia among all citizens. Helots worked the land, raised the crops, provided the Spartans with a certain percentage of their harvest, and occasionally served in the army. The Spartans kept the helots in line by means of systematic brutality and oppression, essential because the helots vastly outnumbered citizens.

In the system attributed to Lycurgus, every citizen owed primary allegiance to Sparta. Suppression of the individual together with emphasis on military prowess led to a barracks state. Family life itself was sacrificed to the polis. Once Spartan boys reached the age of seven, they were enrolled in separate companies with other boys their age. They were required to live in the barracks and eat together in a common mess hall until age thirty. They slept outside on reed mats and underwent rugged physical and military training until they were ready to become frontline soldiers. For the rest of their lives, Spartan men kept themselves prepared for combat. In battle Spartans were supposed to stand and die rather than retreat. Because men often did not see their wives or other women for long periods, not only in times of war but also in peace, their most meaningful relations were same-sex ones. The Spartan military leaders may have viewed such relationships as militarily advantageous because they believed that men would fight even more fiercely for lovers and comrades.

Spartans expected women in citizen families to be good wives and strict mothers of future soldiers. They were prohibited from wearing jewelry or ornate clothes. They, too, were supposed to exercise strenuously in the belief that hard physical training promoted the birth of healthy children. Xenophon (ca. 430–354 B.C.E.), a later Athenian admirer of the Spartans, commented:

> [Lycurgus had] insisted on the training of the body as incumbent no less on the female than the male; and in pursuit of the same idea instituted rival contests in running and feats of strength for women as for men. His belief was that where both parents were strong their progeny would be found to be more vigorous.[2]

Spartan Expansion, ca. 750–500 B.C.E.

- Spartan homeland
- Annexed lands
- Spartan allies

Euboea · ACHAEA · ELIS · ARCADIA · PELOPONNESUS · MESSENIA · LACONIA · Sparta · Megara · ATTICA · Athens · Corinth · Argos · Cythera

■ **helots** Unfree residents of Sparta forced to work state lands.

An anecdote frequently repeated about one Spartan mother sums up Spartan military values. As her son was setting off to battle, the mother handed him his shield and advised him to come back either victorious, carrying the shield, or dead, being carried on it. Yet Spartan women were freer than many other Greek women. With men in military service much of their lives, women in citizen families owned land and ran the estates and were not physically restricted or secluded.

Along with the emphasis on military values for both sexes, the Spartan system served to instill in society the civic virtues of dedication to the state and a code of moral conduct. These aspects of Spartan society, along with Spartan military successes, were generally admired throughout the Greek world.

The Evolution of Athens

Like Sparta, Athens faced pressing social, economic, and political problems during the Archaic period, but the Athenian response was far different from that of the Spartans. Instead of creating a state devoted to the military, the Athenians created a state that became a democracy.

Statuette of a Spartan Female Athlete   This small bronze statuette from Archaic period Sparta shows a smiling female athlete with well-muscled legs holding up the edge of her short tunic. Young women were praised for their swiftness in Sparta, including in choral songs sung by girls' choirs. (CM Dixon/Print Collector/Hulton Archive/Getty Images)

For Athens, the late seventh century B.C.E. was a time of turmoil, the causes of which are unclear. In 621 B.C.E., Draco (DRAY-koh), an Athenian aristocrat, under pressure from small landholders and with the consent of the nobles, published the first law code of the Athenian polis. His code was harsh—and for this reason his name is the origin of the word *draconian*—but it embodied the ideal that the law belonged to all citizens. The aristocracy still governed Athens oppressively, however, and the social and economic situation remained dire. Despite Draco's code, noble landholders continued to force small farmers and artisans into economic dependence. Many families were sold into slavery because of debt; others were exiled, and their land was mortgaged to the rich.

One person who recognized these problems clearly was Solon (SOH-luhn), an aristocrat and poet. Reciting his poems in the Athenian agora, where anyone could hear his call for justice and fairness, Solon condemned his fellow aristocrats for their greed and dishonesty. According to later sources, Solon's sincerity and good sense convinced other aristocrats that he was no crazed revolutionary. He also gained the trust of the common people, whose problems provoked them to demand access to political life, much as commoners in Sparta had. Around 594 B.C.E., the nobles elected Solon chief *archon* (AHR-kahn), or magistrate of the Athenian polis, with authority over legal, civic, and military issues.

Solon immediately freed all people enslaved for debt, recalled all exiles, canceled all debts on land, and made enslavement for debt illegal. He allowed non-nobles into the old aristocratic assembly, where they could take part in the election of magistrates, including the annual election of the city's nine archons.

Although Solon's reforms solved some immediate problems, they did not satisfy either the aristocrats or the common people completely, and they did not bring peace to Athens. During the sixth century B.C.E., however, the successful general Pisistratus (pih-SIHS-trah-tuhs) declared himself tyrant. Under his rule, Athens prospered, and his building program began to transform the city into one of the splendors of Greece. He raised the civic consciousness and prestige of the polis by instituting new cultural festivals that brought people together. Although he had taken over control of the city by force, his reign as tyrant weakened the power of aristocratic families and aroused rudimentary feelings of equality in many Athenian men.

Athens became more democratic under the leadership of Cleisthenes (KLISE-thuh-neez), a wealthy and prominent aristocrat who had won the support of lower-status men and became the leader of Athens in

508 B.C.E. Cleisthenes created the *deme* (deem), a unit of land that kept the roll of citizens, or *demos*, within its jurisdiction. Men enrolled as citizens through their deme instead of through their family group, which brought people of different families together and promoted community and democracy. The demes were grouped into ten tribes, which thus formed the link between the demes and the central government. Each tribe elected a military leader, or *strategos* (plural *strategoi*).

The democracy functioned on the idea that all full citizens were sovereign. In 487 B.C.E., the election of the city's nine archons was replaced by reappointment by lot, which meant that any citizen with a certain amount of property had a chance of becoming an archon. This system gave citizens prestige, although the power of the archons gradually dwindled as the strategoi became the real military leaders of the city. Legislation was in the hands of two bodies, the *boule* (boo-LAY), or council, composed of five hundred members, and the *ecclesia* (ek-lay-SEE-yah), the assembly of all citizens. By supervising the various committees of government and proposing bills to the ecclesia, the boule guided Athenian political life. Nonetheless, the ecclesia had the final word. Open to all male citizens over eighteen years of age, it met at a specific place to vote on matters presented to it.

How did the wars of the classical period shape Greek history?

From the time of the Mycenaeans, violent conflict was common in Greek society, and this did not change in the fifth century B.C.E., the beginning of what scholars later called the classical period of Greek history, which they date from about 500 B.C.E. to the conquest of Greece by Philip of Macedon in 338 B.C.E. First, the Greeks beat back the armies of the Persian Empire. Then, turning their spears against one another, they destroyed their own political system in a century of warfare culminating in the Peloponnesian War. There was no enforceable international law and very little diplomacy, and each polis maintained a substantial military force and a culture of militarism. Constant armed conflicts allowed the rise of a dominant new power: the kingdom of Macedonia.

The Persian Wars

In 499 B.C.E., the Greeks who lived in Ionia rebelled unsuccessfully against the Persian Empire, which had ruled the area for fifty years (see Chapter 2). The Athenians had provided halfhearted help to the Ionians in this failed rebellion, and in 490 B.C.E., the Persians retaliated against Athens, only to be surprisingly defeated by the Athenian hoplites at the Battle of Marathon. (According to legend, a Greek runner carried the victory message to Athens. When the modern Olympic games were founded in 1896, they included a long-distance running race between Marathon and Athens, a distance of about twenty-five miles, designed to honor the ancient Greeks. The marathon was set at its current distance of 26.2 miles for the London Olympics of 1908, so that the finish would be in front of the royal box in the stadium.)

In 480 B.C.E., the Persian king Xerxes I (r. 485–465 B.C.E.) personally led a massive invasion of Greece.

Under the leadership of Sparta, many, though not all, Greek poleis joined together to fight the Persians. The first confrontations between the Persians and the Greeks occurred at the pass of Thermopylae (thuhr-MAWP-uh-lee), where an outnumbered Greek army, including three hundred top Spartan warriors, held off a much larger Persian force for several days. The Greeks at Thermopylae fought heroically, but the Persians won the battle and subsequently occupied and sacked Athens.

At the same time as the land battle of Thermopylae, Greeks and Persians fought one another in a naval battle at Artemisium off Boeotia. The Athenians, led by the general Themistocles, provided the heart of the naval forces with their fleet of triremes, large oar-propelled warships that could carry nearly two hundred rowers, along with soldiers for battles. Storms had wrecked many Persian ships, and neither side won a decisive victory. Only a month or so later, the Greek fleet met the Persian armada at Salamis, an island across from Athens. Though outnumbered, the Greek navy won an overwhelming victory by outmaneuvering the Persians. The remnants of the Persian fleet retired, and in 479 B.C.E., the Greeks overwhelmed the Persian army at Plataea. By defeating the Persians, the Greeks ensured that they would not be ruled by a foreign power.

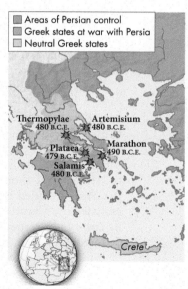

The Persian Wars, 499–479 B.C.E.

Growth of the Athenian Empire

The defeat of the Persians created a power vacuum in the Aegean, and the Athenians took advantage of the situation. Led by Themistocles, the Athenians and their allies formed the **Delian League**, a military alliance aimed at protecting the Aegean Islands, liberating Ionia from Persian rule, and keeping the Persians out of Greece. The Delian (DEE-lee-uhn) League was intended to be a free alliance under the leadership of Athens, but as the Athenians drove the Persians out of the Aegean, they also became increasingly imperialistic. Instead of treating its allies as equals, Athens treated them like subjects, collecting tribute by force and attempting to control the economic resources of the entire Delian League. Major allies revolted, and they were put down brutally. Athenian ideas of freedom and democracy did not extend to the citizens of other cities.

The Delian League, ca. 478–431 B.C.E.

Legend:
- Delian League
- Allied with Delian League, 446 B.C.E.
- Athenian military settlement

The aggressiveness of Athenian rule also alarmed Sparta and its allies. Relations between Athens and Sparta grew more hostile, particularly when Pericles (PEHR-uh-kleez) (ca. 494–429 B.C.E.), an ambitious aristocrat, became the leading statesman in Athens by gaining support among ordinary citizens through measures that broadened democracy. Like the democracy he led, Pericles was aggressive and imperialistic. In 459 B.C.E., Sparta and Athens went to war over conflicts between Athens and some of Sparta's allies. The war ended in 445 B.C.E with a treaty promising thirty years of peace, and no serious damage to either side. The treaty divided the Greek world between the two great powers, with each agreeing to respect the other and its allies.

Peace lasted about thirteen years instead of thirty. Athens continued its severe policies toward its subject allies and came into conflict with Corinth, one of Sparta's leading supporters. In this climate of anger and escalation, Pericles decided to punish the city of Megara, which had switched allegiance from Sparta to Athens and then back again. In 433/2 B.C.E., Pericles persuaded the Athenians to pass a law that excluded the Megarians from trading with Athens and its empire. In response the Spartans and their allies declared war.

Terracotta Vase with a Warrior and His Wife The painting on this lekythos, a vessel used for storing oil used for funerary rites, shows a warrior, plumed helmet and shield in hand, leaving his seated wife. Painted about 450 B.C.E. by the painter art historians have labeled the Achilles Painter — from whom more than two hundred vases have been identified — it shows a scene that was very common in militaristic classical Greece. (AGENZIA FOTOGRAFICA LUISA RICCIARINI/National Archaeological Museum, Athens, Greece/Bridgeman Images)

The Peloponnesian War

The Peloponnesian War lasted a generation and brought in its wake disease, famine, civil wars, widespread destruction, and huge loss of life (Map 3.3). During the first Spartan invasion of Attica, which began in 431 B.C.E., cramped conditions within the walls of Athens nurtured a dreadful plague that killed huge numbers, eventually claiming Pericles himself. (See "Evaluating Written Evidence: Thucydides on the Great Plague at Athens, 430 B.C.E.," page 68.) The charismatic and eloquent Cleon became the leader of Athens and urged a more aggressive war strategy, doubling the tribute of Athens's allies to pay for it. Both Cleon and the leading Spartan general were killed in battle. Recognizing that ten years of war had resulted only in death, destruction, and stalemate, Sparta and Athens concluded the Peace of Nicias (NIH-shee-uhs) in 421 B.C.E.

The Peace of Nicias resulted in a cold war, in which hostility and threats continued but there was no open warfare between Sparta and Athens. But even cold war can bring horror and misery, especially to those caught in the middle. Such was the case when, in 416 B.C.E., the Athenians sent a fleet to the largely neutral island of Melos with an ultimatum: the Melians could surrender or perish. The Melians resisted. The Athenians conquered them, killed the men of military age, and sold the women and children into slavery.

The cold war grew hotter, thanks to the ambitions of Alcibiades (al-suh-BIE-uh-dees) (ca. 450–404 B.C.E.), an aristocrat and a kinsman of Pericles. A shameless opportunist, Alcibiades widened the war to further his own career and increase the power of Athens. He convinced the Athenians to attack Syracuse, the leading polis in Sicily. Conquering Syracuse would bring Athens an immense amount of resources and would also

■ **Delian League** A military alliance led by Athens whose aims were to protect the Aegean Islands, liberate Ionia from Persian rule, and keep the Persians out of Greece.

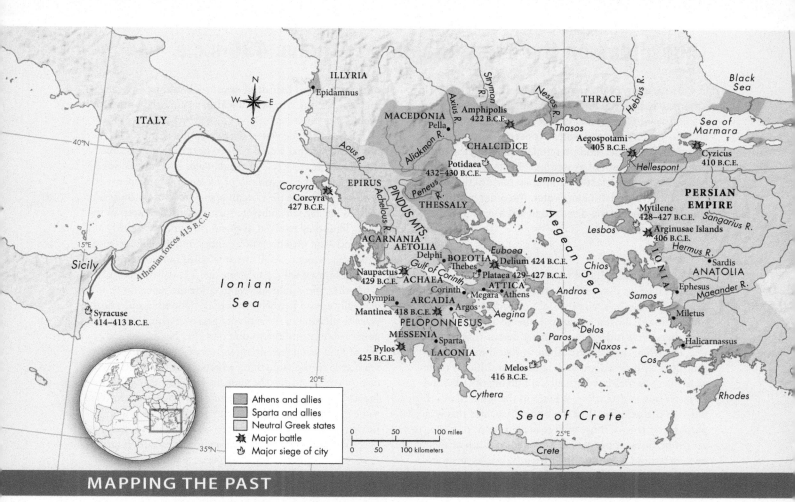

MAPPING THE PAST

MAP 3.3 The Peloponnesian War, 431–404 B.C.E.

This map shows the alignment of states during the Peloponnesian War.

ANALYZING THE MAP How would you compare the area controlled by Sparta and its allies to that of Athens and its allies? How would you expect these similarities and/or differences to affect the way that each side chose to conduct its military campaigns?

CONNECTIONS What does the location of the major battles and sieges suggest about the impact of the war throughout Greece?

cut off the grain supply from Sicily to Sparta and its allies, allowing Athens to end the war and become the greatest power in Greece. The undertaking was vast, requiring an enormous fleet and thousands of sailors and soldiers, and it ended in disaster in 413 B.C.E., with nearly the entire fleet captured or destroyed by Syracusan forces. The Athenian historian Thucydides (thoo-SIHD-ih-dees) (ca. 460–ca. 399 B.C.E.), who saw action in the war himself and later tried to understand its causes, wrote the epitaph for the Athenians: "Infantry, fleet, and everything else were utterly destroyed, and out of many few returned home."[3]

The disaster in Sicily ushered in the final phase of the war. Sparta immediately declared war on Athens, and many of Athens's allies broke their ties with

Athens. The Persians threw their support behind Sparta and built a fleet of ships for them; in exchange they expected Ionia to be returned to them once the Spartans were successful. In Athens, a coup in 411 B.C.E. led by wealthy men angry at the handling of the war overthrew the democratic government, briefly replacing it with an oligarchic one.

Now equipped with a fleet, the Spartans challenged the Athenians in the Aegean, and a long series of inconclusive naval battles followed. In 405 B.C.E., Spartan forces destroyed the last Athenian fleet at the Battle of Aegospotami, after which the Spartans blockaded Athens until it was starved into submission. In 404 B.C.E., after twenty-seven years of fighting, the Peloponnesian War was over.

Thucydides on the Great Plague at Athens, 430 B.C.E.

In 430 B.C.E. many of the people of Attica sought refuge in Athens to escape the Spartan invasion that had begun the previous year. Overcrowding, lack of proper sanitation, and the scarcity of clean water exposed the population to a virulent plague. Modern scholars studying the tooth pulp inside the teeth of its victims think that it was typhoid fever, a disease that is still common in parts of the world with contaminated drinking water. The great historian Thucydides contracted the disease and left a vivid description of its effects.

The most terrible thing of all was the despair into which people fell when they realized that they had caught the plague. Terrible, too, was the sight of people dying like sheep through having caught the disease as a result of nursing others. This indeed caused more deaths than anything else. For when people were afraid to visit the sick, then they died with no one to look after them. Indeed, there were many houses in which all the inhabitants perished through lack of attention. When, on the other hand, they did visit the sick, they lost their own lives, and this was particularly true of those who made it a point of honor to act properly. Such people felt ashamed to think of their own safety and went into their friends' houses at times when even the members of the household were so overwhelmed by the weight of their calamities that they had actually given up the usual practice of making laments for the dead. Yet still the ones who felt most pity for the sick and the dying were those who had had the plague themselves and had recovered from it. They knew what it was like and at the same time felt themselves to be safe, for no one caught the disease twice, or, if he did, the second attack was never fatal. . . .

A factor that made matters much worse than they were already was the removal of people from the country into the city, and this particularly affected the newcomers. There were no houses for them, and, living as they did during the hot season in badly ventilated huts, they died like flies. The bodies of the dying were heaped one on top of the other, and half-dead creatures could be seen staggering about in the streets or flocking around the fountains in their desire for water.

The catastrophe was so overwhelming that people, not knowing what would happen next to them, became indifferent to every rule of religion and law. Athens owed to the plague the beginnings of a state of unprecedented lawlessness. People now began openly to venture on acts of self-indulgence which before then they used to keep in the dark. Thus they resolved to spend their money quickly and to spend it on pleasure, since money and life alike seemed equally ephemeral. As for what is called honor, no one showed himself willing to abide by its laws, so doubtful was it whether one would survive to enjoy the name for it. It was generally agreed that what was both honorable and valuable was the pleasure of the moment and everything that might conceivably contribute to that pleasure. No fear of god or law of man had a restraining influence. As for the gods, it seemed to be the same thing whether one worshiped them or not, when one saw the good and the bad dying indiscriminately. As for offenses against human law, no one expected to be punished. Instead, everyone felt that already a far heavier sentence had been passed on him and was hanging over him, and that before the time for its execution arrived, it was only natural to get some pleasure out of life.

This, then, was the calamity that fell upon Athens, and the times were hard indeed, with people dying inside the city and the land outside being laid waste.

EVALUATE THE EVIDENCE

1. How does Thucydides describe the effects of the disease on individuals and Athenian society?
2. Why, in Thucydides's view, was Athens especially susceptible to a plague at this time?
3. How would you compare the actions and experience of Athenians during the plague with those of people in more recent pandemics?

Source: Rex Warner, trans., *Thucydides, History of the Peloponnesian War* (London: Penguin Classics, 1954), pp. 153, 156.

The Struggle for Dominance

The decades after the end of the Peloponnesian War were turbulent ones, with warfare continuing. Democracy was restored in Athens, but it and its chief rivals Sparta and Thebes each continued to try to create a political system in which it would dominate. When Athens surrendered to Sparta in 404 B.C.E., the Spartans used their victory to build an empire. Their decision brought them into conflict with Persia, which demanded the return of Ionia to its control. From 400 to 386 B.C.E., the Spartans fought the Persians for Ionia, a conflict that eventually engulfed Greece itself. After years of stalemate the Spartans made peace with Persia and their own Greek enemies. The result was a treaty, the King's Peace of 386 B.C.E., in which the Greeks and Persians pledged themselves to live in harmony. This agreement cost Sparta its empire but not its position of dominance in Greece.

The Spartans were not long content with this situation, however, and decided to punish cities that had opposed Sparta during the war. In 378 B.C.E., the Spartans launched an unprovoked attack on Athens. Together the Thebans and the Athenians created what was called the Second Athenian Confederacy, a federation of states to guarantee the terms of the peace treaty. The two fought Sparta until 371 B.C.E., when, due to growing fear of Theban might, Athens made a separate peace with Sparta. Left alone, Thebes defended itself until later that year, when the Thebans routed the Spartan army on the small plain of Leuctra and, in a series of invasions, eliminated Sparta as a major power.

Philip II and Macedonian Supremacy

While the Greek states exhausted themselves in endless conflicts, the new power of Macedonia arose in the north. The land, extensive and generally fertile, nurtured a large population. Macedonia had strong ties to the Greek poleis, but the government there developed as a kingdom, not a democracy or oligarchy.

The kings of Macedonia slowly built up their power over rival states, and in 359 B.C.E., the brilliant and cultured Philip II ascended to the throne. With decades of effort he secured the borders of Macedonia against invaders from the north, and he then launched a series of military operations in the northwestern Aegean. By clever use of his wealth and superb army, he gained control of the area, and in 338 B.C.E., he won a decisive victory over Thebes and Athens that gave him command of Greece. Because the Greeks could not put aside their quarrels, they fell to an invader, and 338 B.C.E. is often seen as marking the end of the classical period.

After his victory, Philip led a combined army of soldiers from Macedonia and from many Greek states in an attempt to liberate the Ionian Greeks from Persian rule. Before he could launch this campaign, however, Philip fell to an assassin's dagger in 336 B.C.E. His young son Alexander vowed to carry on Philip's mission. He would succeed beyond all expectations.

What ancient Greek ideas and ideals have had a lasting influence?

Despite the violence that dominated Greece for nearly two centuries beginning in 500 B.C.E., or to some degree because of it, playwrights and thinkers pondered the meaning of the universe and the role of humans in it, and artists and architects created new styles to celebrate Greek achievements. Although warfare was one of the hallmarks of the classical period, intellectual and artistic accomplishments were as well.

Athenian Arts in the Age of Pericles

In the midst of the warfare of the fifth century B.C.E., Pericles turned Athens into the showplace of Greece. He appropriated Delian League funds to pay for a huge building program. Workers erected temples and other buildings as patriotic memorials housing statues and carvings, often painted in bright colors, showing the gods in human form and celebrating the Greek victory over the Persians. (The paint later washed away, leaving the generally white sculpture that we think of as "classical.") Many of the temples were built on the high, rocky Acropolis that stood in the center of the city, on top of the remains of temples that had been burned by the Persians, and sometimes incorporating these into their walls.

The Athenians normally hiked up the long approach to the Acropolis only for religious festivals, of which the most important and joyous was the Great Panathenaea, held every four years to honor the

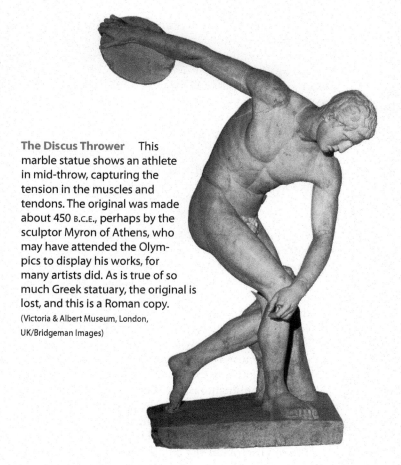

The Discus Thrower This marble statue shows an athlete in mid-throw, capturing the tension in the muscles and tendons. The original was made about 450 B.C.E., perhaps by the sculptor Myron of Athens, who may have attended the Olympics to display his works, for many artists did. As is true of so much Greek statuary, the original is lost, and this is a Roman copy. (Victoria & Albert Museum, London, UK/Bridgeman Images)

The Acropolis of Athens

The natural rock formation of the Acropolis probably had a palace on top as early as the Mycenaean period, when the palace was also surrounded by a defensive wall. Temples were constructed beginning in the sixth century B.C.E., and after the Persian wars Pericles ordered the reconstruction and expansion of many of these, as well as the building of new and more magnificent temples and an extension of the defensive walls. The largest building is the Parthenon, a temple dedicated to the goddess Athena, which originally housed a 40-foot-tall statue of Athena made of ivory and gold sheets attached to a wooden frame. Much of the Parthenon was damaged when it was shelled during a war between Venice and the Ottoman Empire in the seventeenth century C.E., and air pollution continues to eat away at the marble.

(Klaas Lingbeek- van Kranen/Getty Images)

EVALUATE THE EVIDENCE

1. Imagine yourself as an Athenian walking up the hill toward the Parthenon. What impression would the setting and the building itself convey?
2. What were the various functions of the Acropolis?

virgin goddess Athena and perhaps offer sacrifices to older deities as well. (See "Evaluating Visual Evidence: The Acropolis of Athens.") For this festival, Athenian citizens and legal noncitizen residents formed a huge procession to bring the statue of Athena in the Parthenon an exquisite robe, richly embroidered by the citizen women of Athens with mythological scenes. The marchers first saw the Propylaea, the ceremonial gateway whose columns appeared to uphold the sky. On the right was the small temple of Athena Nike, built to commemorate the victory over the Persians. As visitors walked on, they obtained a full view of the Parthenon, the chief temple dedicated to Athena at the center of the Acropolis, with a huge painted ivory and gold statue of the goddess inside. After the religious ceremonies, all the people joined in a feast.

The development of drama was tied to the religious festivals of the city, especially those celebrating the god of wine, Dionysus (see "Public and Personal Religion"). Drama was as rooted in the life of the polis as were the architecture and sculpture of the Acropolis. The polis sponsored the production of plays and required wealthy citizens to pay the expenses of their production. At the beginning of the year, dramatists submitted their plays to the chief archon of the polis. He chose those he considered best and assigned a theatrical troupe to each playwright. Many plays were highly controversial, containing overt political and social commentary, but the archons neither suppressed nor censored them.

Not surprisingly, given the incessant warfare, conflict was a constant element in Athenian drama, and playwrights used their art in attempts to portray,

VIEWPOINTS

Greek Playwrights on Families, Fate, and Choice

The plays of Aeschylus and Sophocles often involve one family member killing another, which sets off a cycle of further violence, and through these actions the playwrights address issues of fate, the will of the gods, and human moral responsibility when faced with a choice. Aeschylus's *Agamemnon*, produced in 458 B.C.E., traces the homecoming of King Agamemnon from the Trojan War, an expedition that had begun with his sacrificing his daughter Iphigenia to the goddess Artemis so the winds would shift and the Greek fleet could sail to Troy. (His wife Clytemnestra plots his murder in revenge, and she stabs him.) In Sophocles's *Antigone* (an-TIH-guh-nee), produced about 441 B.C.E., two sons of King Oedipus have killed each other in a war over who would rule. The current king Creon forbids them to be buried, but their sister Antigone disobeys him and carries out the proper funeral rituals. Creon condemns her to be walled up, so she kills herself, as does her fiancé (who is also Creon's son) and Creon's wife.

Agamemnon

Meanwhile his armed men moped along the shores,
And cursed the wind, and ate his dwindling stores . . .
Then Calchas [a soothsayer] spoke again. The wind, he said,
Was sent by Artemis; and he revealed
Her remedy—a thought to crush like lead
The hearts of Atreus' sons, who wept, as weep they must,
And speechless ground their scepters in the dust.
The elder king [Agamemnon] then spoke: "What can I say?
Disaster follows if I disobey;
Surely yet worse disaster if I yield
And slaughter my own child, my home's delight,
In her young innocence, and stain my hand
With blasphemous unnatural cruelty,
Bathed in the blood I fathered! Either way,
Ruin! Disband the fleet, sail home, and earn
The deserter's badge—abandon my command,
Betray the alliance—now? The wind must turn,
There must be sacrifice, a maid must bleed —
Their chafing rage demands it—they are right!
May good prevail, and justify my deed!"
Then he put on
The harness of Necessity.
The doubtful tempest of his soul
Veered, and his prayer was turned to blasphemy,
His offering to impiety . . .
Heedless of her tears,
Her cries of "Father!" and her maiden years,

Her judges valued more
Their glory and their war.

Antigone

Creon (to Antigone):
You—tell me not at length but in a word.
You knew the order not to do this thing?

Antigone:
I knew, of course I knew. The word was plain.

Creon:
And still you dared to overstep these laws?

Antigone:
For me it was not Zeus who made that order.
Nor did that Justice who lives with the gods below
mark out such laws to hold among mankind.
Nor did I think your orders were so strong
that you, a mortal man, could over-run
the gods' unwritten and unfailing laws.
Not now, nor yesterday's, they always live,
and no one knows their origin in time.
So not through fear of any man's proud spirit
would I be likely to neglect these laws,
draw on myself the gods' sure punishment.
I knew that I must die; how could I not?
even without your warning. If I die
before my time, I say it is a gain.
Who lives in sorrows many as are mine
how shall he not be glad to gain his death?
And so, for me to meet this fate, no grief.
But if I left that corpse, my mother's son,
dead and unburied I'd have cause to grieve
as now I grieve not.
And if you think my acts are foolishness
The foolishness may be in a fool's eye.
. . .
Look what I suffer, at whose command,
Because I respected the right.

QUESTIONS FOR ANALYSIS

1. How do Agamemnon and Antigone justify what they have done?
2. Does Aeschylus or Sophocles seem more approving of the choice made by the title character of his play?
3. Given what was going on in Athens at the time that these plays were performed, how can these plays be seen as political commentary?

Sources: Aeschylus, *Agamemnon*, trans. Philip Vellacott (1956), at: https://archive.org/details/AgamemnonAeschylustrans.Vellacott; *Sophocles I: Antigone*, trans. Elizabeth Wyckoff, in *The Complete Greek Tragedies* (Chicago: Phoenix Books, 1954), pp. 173–174, 190, 191.

understand, and resolve life's basic conflicts. The Athenian dramatists examined questions about the relationship between humans and the gods, the demands of society on the individual, and the nature of good and evil. Aeschylus (EHS-kuh-lihs) (525–456 B.C.E.), the first of the great Athenian dramatists, was also the first to express the agony of the individual caught in conflict. In his trilogy of plays, *The Oresteia* (ohr-eh-STEE-uh), Aeschylus deals with the themes of betrayal, murder, and reconciliation, urging that reason and justice be applied to reconcile fundamental conflicts. The final play concludes with a prayer that civil dissension never be allowed to destroy the city and that the life of the city be one of harmony and grace.

Sophocles (SOF-uh-klees) (496–406 B.C.E.) also dealt with matters personal and political. He wrote over one hundred plays, of which only seven survive. Among these is *Antigone* (an-TIH-guh-nee), in which the title character chooses to bury the body of her brother though the king has forbidden this because her brother had led foreign troops against the city. (See "Viewpoints: Greek Playwrights on Families, Fate, and Choice," page 71.) Sophocles later wrote *Oedipus* (EHD-uh-puhs) *the King* and its sequel, *Oedipus at Colonus*, which tell the story of Antigone's father Oedipus, doomed by the gods to kill his father and marry his mother. Try as he might to avoid his fate, his every action brings him closer to its fulfillment. When at last he realizes that he has unwittingly carried out the decree of the gods, Oedipus blinds himself and flees into exile. In *Oedipus at Colonus*, Sophocles dramatizes the last days of the broken king, whose patient suffering and uncomplaining piety win him the praise of the gods.

With Euripides (you-RIHP-uh-dees) (ca. 480–406 B.C.E.), drama entered a new and, in many ways, more personal phase. To him the gods were far less important than human beings. The essence of Euripides's tragedy is the flawed character—men and women who bring disaster on themselves and their loved ones because their passions overwhelm reason. Among these were the leaders of Athens, against whom Euripides directed his antiwar play *The Trojan Women*, produced in the spring after the slaughter and subjugation of the Melians.

Writers of comedy treated the affairs of the polis and its politicians bawdily and often coarsely. Even so, their plays were also performed at religious festivals. Best known are the comedies of Aristophanes (eh-ruh-STAH-fuh-neez) (ca. 445–386 B.C.E.), an ardent lover of his city and a merciless critic of cranks and quacks. (See "Individuals in Society: Aristophanes," page 73.) Like Aeschylus, Sophocles, and Euripides, Aristophanes used his art to dramatize his ideas on the right conduct of the citizen and the value of the polis.

Households and Work

In sharp contrast with the rich intellectual and cultural life of Periclean Athens stands the simplicity of its material life. The Athenians, like other Greeks, lived with comparatively few material possessions in houses that were rather simple. Well-to-do Athenians lived in houses consisting of a series of rooms opening onto a central courtyard. Artisans often set aside a room to use as a shop or work area. Larger houses often had a dining room at the front where the men of the family ate and entertained guests at drinking parties called *symposia*, and a **gynaeceum** (also spelled *gynaikeion*), a room or section at the back where the women of the family and enslaved women worked, ate, and slept. Other rooms included the kitchen and bathroom. By modern standards there was not much furniture.

Cooking, done over a hearth in the house, provided welcome warmth in the winter. Baking and roasting were done in ovens. Meals consisted primarily of various grains, especially wheat and barley, as well as lentils, olives, figs, grapes, fish, and a little meat, foods that are now part of the highly touted "Mediterranean diet." The Greeks used olive oil for cooking, and also as an ointment and as lamp fuel. The only Greeks who consistently ate meat were the Spartan warriors. They received a small portion of meat each day, together with the infamous Spartan black broth, a concoction of pork cooked in blood, vinegar, and salt. One Athenian, after tasting the broth, commented that he could easily understand why the Spartans were so willing to die.

In the city a man might support himself as a craftsman—a potter, bronze-smith, sailmaker, or tanner—or he could contract with the polis to work on public buildings. Certain crafts, including spinning and weaving, were generally done by women, who produced cloth for their own families and sold it. Free men and women without skills worked as paid laborers but competed with enslaved people for work.

Slavery was commonplace in Greece, as it was throughout the ancient world. Enslaved people included Greeks and non-Greeks captured in war or raids or born to enslaved mothers. Most citizen households in Athens owned at least one enslaved person. Some enslaved men were skilled workers or well-educated teachers and tutors of writing, while others were unskilled laborers in the city, agricultural workers in the countryside, or laborers in mines. Enslaved women worked in agriculture, as domestic servants and nurses for children, or as artisans. Enslaved people were often treated brutally, but they engaged in a variety of strategies to deal with the conditions of their enslavement, including running away, leveraging laws to their advantage, and purchasing their freedom. Greek thinkers such as Aristotle tried to distinguish between enslaved and free people by saying the enslaved had a "slavish nature," but in reality Greeks

■ **gynaeceum** Women's quarters at the back of an Athenian house where the free and enslaved women of the family worked, ate, and slept.

INDIVIDUALS IN SOCIETY

Aristophanes

I n 424 B.C.E., in the middle of the Peloponnesian War, citizens of Athens attending one of the city's regular dramatic festivals watched *The Knights*, in which two enslaved men complain about another enslaved man's power over the man who owned them, named Demos ("the people" in Greek), and everyone else around him. They run into a sausage seller and tell him that an oracle has predicted he will become more influential than the man they are complaining about and will eventually dominate the city, becoming what in ancient Greece was called a demagogue. The sausage seller doesn't think this possible, but the men tell him he is the perfect candidate: "Mix and knead together all the state business as you do for your sausages. To win the people, always cook them some savoury that pleases them. Besides, you possess all the attributes of a demagogue; a screeching, horrible voice, a perverse, crossgrained nature and the language of the market-place. In you all is united which is needful for governing."* This leads to a series of shouted debates between the influential enslaved man and the sausage maker, each one accusing the other of corruption and indecent behavior, and each making ever more elaborate promises to the citizens of Athens. Ultimately the sausage seller wins, and the formerly domineering enslaved man becomes a lowly sausage seller.

Although the forceful enslaved man's name is never mentioned in the play, everyone knew he represented Cleon, at that point the leader of Athens, who had risen to power through populist speeches. The real Cleon may well have been among the thousands in the audience, as front-row seats at festivals were a reward he had just been given by the citizens of Athens for a military victory. Cleon had taken legal action against the playwright two years earlier for another play, accusing him of slandering the polis, but in this case he did nothing.

That playwright was Aristophanes, the only comic playwright in classical Athens from whom whole plays survive. Not much is known about Aristophanes's life, other than a few ambiguous clues in the plays. His first play, now lost, was produced in 427 B.C.E., and his last datable play, also now lost, in 386 B.C.E. (The dates of his life are inferred from these, as there is a comment in one play suggesting he was only eighteen when his first play was produced.) He directed some of his own plays, won the theater competition several times, and had sons who were also comic playwrights. Even in his early plays,

Roman copy of a Hellenistic bust depicting what Aristophanes might have looked like. (De Agostini/DEA PICTURE LIBRARY/Getty Images)

Aristophanes seems to have opposed anything that was new in Athens: new types of leaders (like Cleon), new styles in drama (Euripides was a standard target), new kinds of educators (such as the Sophists), new philosophy (especially that of Socrates). Everything and everyone except the people of Athens themselves was open to ridicule, and the more obscene the better: poets throw turds at each other, politicians collapse drunk and vomiting in the streets, military leaders walk around with huge erections when their wives refuse to have sex with them until they call off the war. Aristophanes combined kinds of comedy that today are often separated — political satire, complicated wordplay, celebrity slamming, cross-dressing, slapstick, dirty jokes, silly props, absurdity, audience taunting — and was a master at all of these.

QUESTIONS FOR ANALYSIS

1. How might political satires such as those of Aristophanes have both critiqued and reinforced civic values in classical Athens?
2. Can you think of more recent parallels to Aristophanes's political satires? What has been the response to these?

*Aristophanes, *The Knights*, ed. Eugene O'Neill, Jr. (New York: Random House, 1938), lines 215–219. Available at Perseus Digital Library: http://www.perseus.tufts.edu/hopper/text?doc=Perseus%3Atext%3A1999.01.0034%3Acard%3D213.

relied on enslaved individuals for tasks that required literacy and numeracy, such as teaching, banking, and civic administration.

Gender and Sexuality

Citizenship was the basis of political power for men in ancient Athens and was inherited. After the middle of the fifth century B.C.E., people were considered citizens only if both parents were citizens, except for a few men given citizenship as a reward for service to the city. Adult male citizens were expected to take part in political decisions and be active in civic life, no matter what their occupation. They were also in charge of relations between the household and the wider community. Women in Athens and elsewhere in Greece, like those in Mesopotamia, brought dowries to their husbands upon marriage, which became the husband's to invest or use, though he was supposed to do this wisely.

Women did not play a public role in classical Athens. We know the names of no female poets, artists, or philosophers, and the names of very few women at all. The Athenian ideal for the behavior of a citizen's wife was a domestic one: she was to stay at home, bearing and raising children, spinning and weaving cloth, and

Young Man and Hetaera   In this scene painted on the inside of a drinking cup, a hetaera holds the head of a young man who has clearly had too much to drink. Sexual and comic scenes were common on Greek pottery, particularly on objects that would have been used at a private dinner party hosted by a citizen, known as a symposium. Wives did not attend symposia, but hetaerae and entertainers were often hired to perform for the male guests. (Photograph © 2021 Museum of Fine Arts, Boston. All rights reserved/Henry Lillie Pierce Fund/Bridgeman Images)

overseeing the household and its free and enslaved servants. (See "Thinking Like a Historian: Gender Roles in Classical Athens," page 76.) This physical seclusion kept citizen women away from men who were not family members, assuring citizen men that their children were theirs. How much this ideal was followed is debated by historians, but women in wealthier citizen families probably spent most of their time at home in the gynaeceum, leaving the house only to attend some religious and city festivals, and perhaps occasionally plays. They did visit temples to ask the gods for help in childbirth and other rituals specific to women.

Women from noncitizen families lived freer lives than citizen women, although they worked harder and had fewer material comforts. They performed manual labor in the fields or sold goods or services in the agora, going about their affairs much as men did.

Among the services that some women and men sold was sex. Women who sold sexual services ranged from poor streetwalkers known as *pornai* to middle-status hired mistresses known as *palakai*, to sophisticated courtesans known as *hetaerae*, who added intellectual accomplishments to physical beauty. Hetaerae accompanied men at dinner parties and in public settings where their wives would not have been welcome, serving men as social as well as sexual partners.

Same-sex relations were generally accepted in all of ancient Greece, not simply in Sparta. In classical Athens part of a male adolescent citizen's training might entail a hierarchical sexual and tutorial relationship with an adult man, who most likely was married and may have had female sexual partners as well. These relationships between young men and older men were often celebrated in literature and art, in part because Athenians regarded perfection as possible only in the male. Women were generally seen as inferior to men, dominated by their bodies rather than their minds. The perfect body was that of the young male, and perfect love was that between a young man and a slightly older man. The extent to which perfect love was sexual or spiritual was debated among the ancient Greeks. In one of his dialogues, the philosopher Plato (see "The Flowering of Philosophy") argues that the best kind of love is one in which contemplation of the beloved leads to contemplation of the divine, an intellectualized love that came to be known as "platonic." Plato was suspicious of the power of sexual passion because it distracted men from reason and the search for knowledge.

Along with praise of intellectualized love, Greek authors also celebrated physical sex and desire. The soldier-poet Archilochus (d. 652 B.C.E.) preferred "to light upon the flesh of a maid and ram belly to belly and thigh to thigh."[4] The lyric poet Sappho, who lived on the island of Lesbos in the northern Aegean Sea in the sixth century B.C.E., wrote often of powerful desire. One of her poems describes her reaction on seeing her beloved talking to someone else:

He appears to me, that one, equal to the gods,
the man who, facing you,
is seated and, up close, that sweet voice of yours
he listens to

And how you laugh your charming laugh. Why it
makes my heart flutter within my breast,
because the moment I look at you, right then, for me,
to make any sound at all won't work any more.

My tongue has a breakdown and a delicate
— all of a sudden — fire rushes under my skin.
With my eyes I see not a thing, and there is a roar
that my ears make.
Sweat pours down me and a trembling
seizes all of me; paler than grass
am I, and a little short of death
do I appear to me.[5]

Sappho's description of the physical reactions caused by love — and jealousy — reaches across the centuries. The Hellenic and even more the Hellenistic Greeks regarded Sappho as a great lyric poet, although because some of her poetry is directed toward women, over the last century she has become better known for her sexuality than her writing. Today the English word *lesbian* is derived from Sappho's home island of Lesbos.

Same-sex relations did not mean that people did not marry; Athenians saw the continuation of the family line as essential. Sappho, for example, appears to have been married and had a daughter. Sexual desire and procreation were both important aspects of life, but ancient Greeks did not necessarily link them.

Public and Personal Religion

Like most peoples of the ancient world, the Greeks were polytheists, worshipping a variety of gods and goddesses who were immortal but otherwise acted just like people. Migration, invasion, and colonization brought the Greeks into contact with other peoples and caused their religious beliefs to evolve. How much these contacts shaped Greek religion and other aspects of culture has been the subject of a fierce debate since the late 1980s, when in *Black Athena: The Afroasiatic Roots of Classical Civilization*, Martin Bernal proposed that the Greeks owed a great deal to the Egyptians and Phoenicians, and that scholars since the nineteenth century had purposely tried to cover this up to make the Greeks seem more European and less indebted to cultures in Africa and Asia.[6] Bernal's ideas are highly controversial, and most classicists do not accept his evidence, but they are part of a larger tendency among scholars in the last several decades — including those who vigorously oppose Bernal — to see the Greeks less in isolation from other groups and more in relation to the larger Mediterranean world.

Greek religion was primarily a matter of ritual, with rituals designed to appease the divinities believed to control the forces of the natural world. Processions, festivals, and sacrifices offered to the gods were frequently occasions for people to meet together socially, for times of cheer or even drunken excess.

By the classical era, the primary gods were understood to live metaphorically on Mount Olympus, the highest mountain in Greece. Zeus was the king of the gods and the most powerful of them, and he

Religious Procession   This painted wooden slab from about 540 B.C.E., found in a cave near Corinth, shows adults and children about to sacrifice a sheep to the deities worshipped in this area. The participants are dressed in their finest clothes and crowned with garlands. Music adds to the festivities. Rituals such as this were a common part of religious life throughout Greece. (DEA/G. DAGLI ORTI/De Agostini/Getty Images)

Gender Roles in Classical Athens

Athenian men's ideas about the proper roles for men and women, conveyed in written and visual form, became one of the foundations of Western notions of gender for millennia. How do the qualities they view as ideal and praiseworthy for men compare with those they view as ideal for women?

1 **Pericles's funeral oration, from Thucydides's *History of the Peloponnesian War*, 430 B.C.E.** In this speech given in honor of those who had died in the war, the Athenian leader Pericles glorifies the achievements of Athenian men and women.

⌐ If we look to the laws, they afford equal justice to all in their private differences; if to social standing, advancement in public life falls to reputation for capacity, class considerations not being allowed to interfere with merit; nor again does poverty bar the way; if a man is able to serve the state, he is not hindered by the obscurity of his condition. . . . Further, we provide plenty of means for the mind to refresh itself from business. We celebrate games and sacrifices all the year round, and the elegance of our private establishments forms a daily source of pleasure. . . . [I]n education, where our rivals from their very cradles by a painful discipline seek after manliness, at Athens we live exactly as we please, and yet are just as ready to encounter every legitimate danger. . . . We cultivate refinement without extravagance and knowledge without effeminacy; wealth we employ more for use than for show. . . . Again, in our enterprises we present the singular spectacle of daring and deliberation, each carried to its highest point, and both united in the same persons. . . . In short, I say that as a city we are the school of Hellas; while I doubt if the world can produce a man, who where he has only himself to depend upon, is equal to so many emergencies, and graced by so happy a versatility as the Athenian. . . .

If I must say anything on the subject of female excellence to those of you who will now be in widowhood, it will be all comprised in this brief exhortation: Great will be your glory in not falling short of your natural character; and greatest will be hers who is least talked of among the men whether for good or for bad.

2 **Xenophon, *Oeconomicus*, ca. 360 B.C.E.** In a treatise on household management, the historian, soldier, and philosopher Xenophon creates a character, Isomachus, who provides his much younger wife with advice and informs her about ideal gender roles. "God" in this selection means all of the gods, personified as male; "law" is personified as female ("law gives her consent").

⌐ ISOMACHUS: "God made provision from the first by shaping, as it seems to me, the woman's nature for indoor and the man's for outdoor occupations. Man's body and soul He furnished with a greater capacity for enduring heat and cold, wayfaring and military marches; or, to repeat, He laid upon his shoulders the outdoor works. While in creating the body of woman with less capacity for these things," I continued, "God would seem to have imposed on her the indoor works; and knowing that He had implanted in the woman and imposed upon her the nurture of new-born babies, He endowed her with a larger share of affection for the new-born child than He bestowed upon man. And since He imposed on woman the guardianship of the things imported from without, God, in His wisdom, perceiving that a fearful spirit was no detriment to guardianship, endowed the woman with a larger measure of timidity than He bestowed on man. Knowing further that he to whom the outdoor works belonged would need to defend them against malign attack, He endowed the man in turn with a larger share of courage. . . . Law, too, gives her consent—law and the usage of mankind, by sanctioning the wedlock of man and wife; and just as God ordained them to be partners in their children, so the law establishes their common ownership of house and estate. Custom, moreover, proclaims as beautiful those excellences of man and woman with which God gifted them at birth. Thus for a woman to bide tranquilly at home rather than roam abroad is no dishonour; but for a man to remain indoors, instead of devoting himself to outdoor pursuits, is a thing discreditable."

ANALYZING THE EVIDENCE

1. In Sources 1–3, what qualities do the authors see as praiseworthy in men? In women?
2. In Sources 2 and 3, what do Xenophon and Aristotle view as the underlying reasons for gender differences?
3. The two paintings in Sources 4 and 5 show scenes that were normal parts of real Athenian life, but how do they also convey ideals for men and women? What are these ideals?
4. Because no writing or art by Athenian women has survived, we have to extrapolate women's opinions from works by men. What do the body language and expression of the young woman in Source 4 suggest she thought about her situation?

4 **Vase painting showing Athenian woman at home, fifth century** B.C.E. A well-to-do young woman sits on an elegant chair inside a house, spinning and weaving. The bed piled high with coverlets on the left was a symbol of marriage.

(Musée du Louvre, Paris, France/Erich Lessing/Art Resource, NY)

3 **Aristotle, *The Politics*.** In *The Politics*, one of his most important works, Aristotle examines the development of government, which he sees as originating in the power relations in the family and household.

The city belongs among the things that exist by nature, and man is by nature a political animal. . . . The family is the association established by nature for the supply of men's everyday wants. . . .

It is clear that the rule of the soul over the body, and of the mind and the rational element over the passionate, is natural and expedient; whereas the equality of the two or the rule of the inferior is always hurtful. The same holds good of animals in relation to men; for tame animals have a better nature than wild, and all tame animals are better off when they are ruled by man; for then they are preserved. Again, the male is by nature superior, and the female inferior; and the one rules, and the other is ruled; this principle, of necessity, extends to all mankind. . . .

A similar question may be raised about women and children, whether they too have virtues: ought a woman to be temperate and brave and just, and is a child to be called temperate, and intemperate, or not? . . . Here the very constitution of the soul has shown us the way; in it one part naturally rules, and the other is subject, and the virtue of the ruler we maintain to be different from that of the subject; the one being the virtue of the rational, and the other of the irrational part. Now, it is obvious that the same principle applies generally, and therefore almost all

things rule and are ruled according to nature. . . . For the slave has no deliberative faculty at all; the woman has, but it is without authority, and the child has, but it is immature. So it must necessarily be supposed to be with the moral virtues also; all should partake of them, but only in such manner and degree as is required by each for the fulfillment of his duty. . . . Clearly, then, moral virtue belongs to all of them; but the temperance of a man and of a woman, or the courage and justice of a man and of a woman, are not, as Socrates maintained, the same; the courage of a man is shown in commanding, of a woman in obeying. . . . All classes must be deemed to have their special attributes; as the poet says of women, "Silence is a woman's glory," but this is not equally the glory of man.

5 **Lekythos (oil flask), with a wedding scene, attributed to the Amasis Painter, ca. 550** B.C.E. In this early representation of an Attic wedding procession, the bearded groom drives the cart to his home, while the bride (right) pulls her veil forward in a gesture associated with marriage in Greek art.
(Metropolitan Museum of Art, New York, NY, U.S.A./Bridgeman Images)

PUTTING IT ALL TOGETHER

Using the sources above, along with what you have learned in class and this chapter, write a short essay that compares ideals for men and women in classical Athens. How did these ideas about gender roles both reflect and shape Athenian society and political life?

Sources: (1) Thucydides, *The Peloponnesian War* (London: J. M. Dent; New York, E. P. Dutton, 1910), at Perseus Digital Library; (2) Xenophon, *The Economist*, trans. H. G. Dakyns, at http://www.gutenberg.org/files/1173/1173-h/1173-h.htm; (3) Aristotle, *Politics*, Book One, translated by Benjamin Jowett, at http://classics.mit.edu/Aristotle/politics.1.one.html.

was married to Hera, who was also his sister. Zeus and Hera had several children, including Ares, the god of war. Zeus was also the father of the god Apollo, who represented the epitome of youth, beauty, and athletic skill, and who served as the patron god of music and poetry. Apollo's half-sister Athena was a warrior-goddess who had been born from the head of Zeus.

The Greeks also honored certain heroes. A hero was born of the union of a god or goddess and a mortal, and was considered an intermediary between the divine and the human. A hero displayed his divine origins by performing deeds beyond the ability of human beings. Herakles (or Hercules, as the Romans called him), the son of Zeus and the mortal woman Alcmene, was the most popular of the Greek heroes, defeating mythical opponents and carrying out impossible (or "Herculean") tasks. Devotees to Hercules believed that he, like other heroes, protected mortals from supernatural dangers and provided an ideal of vigorous masculinity.

The polis administered cults and festivals, and everyone was expected to participate in these events, comparable to today's patriotic parades or ceremonies. Much religion was local and domestic, and individual families honored various deities privately in their homes. Many people also believed that magic rituals and spells were effective and sought the assistance of individuals reputed to have special knowledge or powers. Even highly educated Greeks sought the assistance of fortune-tellers and soothsayers, from the oracle at Delphi to local figures who examined the flights of birds or the entrails of recently slaughtered chickens for clues about the future.

Along with public and family forms of honoring the gods, some Greeks also participated in what later historians have termed **mystery religions**, in which participants underwent an initiation ritual and gained secret knowledge that they were forbidden to reveal to the uninitiated. The Eleusinian mysteries, held at Eleusis in Attica, are one of the oldest of these. They centered on Demeter, the goddess of the harvest, whose lovely daughter Persephone (per-SEH-foh-nee), as the story goes, was taken by the god Hades to the underworld. In mourning, Demeter caused drought, and ultimately Zeus allowed Persephone to return to her, though she had to spend some months of the year in Hades. There is evidence of an agrarian ritual celebrating this mythological explanation for the cycle of the seasons as early as the Bronze Age, and in the sixth century B.C.E., the rulers of nearby Athens made the ritual open to all Greeks, women and enslaved people included. Many people flocked to the annual ceremonies and learned the mysteries, which by the fourth century B.C.E. appear to have promised life after death to those initiated into them.

Another somewhat secret religion was that of Dionysus (die-uh-NIE-suhs), the god of wine and powerful emotions, who was killed and then reborn, which is why he, like Persephone, became the center of mystery religions offering rebirth. As the god of wine, he also represented freedom from the normal constraints of society, and his worshippers were reported to have danced ecstatically and even to have become a frenzied and uncontrolled mob. Whether or how often this actually happened is impossible to know, as contemporary Athenian writers who did not approve may have embellished their accounts of these wild rituals, and later scholars sometimes regarded them simply as fiction because chaotic orgies did not fit with their notions of the rational and orderly Greeks.

Greeks also shared some public Panhellenic festivals, the chief of which were sports festivals held every four years at Olympia in honor of Zeus. Their origins were attributed to the gods, though they most likely actually grew out of athletic competitions held in honor of a recently deceased person, which had been common since Mycenaean times. They included foot and chariot races, javelin throwing, wrestling, and boxing, all except chariot racing performed nude. Open to male athletes from around the Greek world, contestants won only a wreath, so they had to be fairly wealthy or find a rich patron to pay for training, transportation, and other expenses. Athletes might also receive rewards from the polis that sponsored them, as the games became a tool through which cities asserted their superiority over their rivals. The modern Olympic games, first held in 1896, have continued this pattern of mixing politics and sports.

The Flowering of Philosophy

Just as the Greeks developed rituals to honor the gods, they spun myths and epics to explain the origin of the universe. Over time, however, as Greeks encountered other peoples with different beliefs, some of them began to question their old gods and myths, and they sought rational rather than supernatural explanations for natural phenomena. These Greek thinkers, based in Ionia, are called the Pre-Socratics because their rational efforts preceded those of the Athenians. They took individual facts and wove them into general theories that led them to conclude that, despite appearances, the universe is actually simple and subject to natural laws. The Pre-Socratics began an intellectual revolution with their idea that nature was predictable, creating what we now call philosophy and science.

Drawing on their observations, the Pre-Socratics speculated about the basic building blocks of the universe. Thales (THAY-leez) (ca. 600 B.C.E.) thought the basic element of the universe was water, and Heraclitus (hehr-uh-KLIE-tuhs) (ca. 500 B.C.E.) thought it was fire. Democritus (dih-MAH-kruh-tuhs) (ca. 460 B.C.E.) broke this down further and created the atomic theory, the idea that the universe is made up of invisible, indestructible particles. The culmination of Pre-Socratic thought was the theory that four simple substances make up the universe: fire, air, earth, and water.

The stream of thought started by the Pre-Socratics branched into several directions. Hippocrates (hih-PAH-kruh-teez) (ca. 470–400 B.C.E.) became the most prominent physician and teacher of medicine of his time. Hippocrates sought natural explanations for diseases and seems to have advocated letting nature take its course and not intervening too much. Illness was caused not by evil spirits, he asserted, but by physical problems in the body, particularly by imbalances in what he saw as four basic bodily fluids: blood, phlegm, black bile, and yellow bile. In a healthy body, these fluids, called humors, were in perfect balance, and the goal of medical treatment of the ill was to help the body bring them back into balance.

The **Sophists** (SOF-ihsts), a group of thinkers in fifth-century-B.C.E. Athens, applied philosophical speculation to politics and language, questioning the beliefs and laws of the polis to understand their origin. They believed that excellence in both politics and language could be taught, and they provided lessons for the young men of Athens who wished to learn how to persuade others. Their later opponents criticized them for charging fees and also accused them of using rhetoric to deceive people instead of presenting the truth. (Today the word *sophist* is usually used in this sense, describing someone who deceives people with clever-sounding but false arguments.)

Socrates (SOK-ruh-teez) (ca. 469–399 B.C.E.), whose ideas are known only through the works of others, also applied philosophy to politics and to people. He seemed, to many Athenians, to be a Sophist because he also questioned Athenian traditions, although he never charged fees. His approach when exploring ethical issues and defining concepts was to start with a general topic or problem and to narrow the matter to its essentials. He did so by continuously questioning participants in a discussion or argument through which they developed critical-thinking skills, a process known as the **Socratic method**.

Socrates was viewed with suspicion by many because he challenged the traditional beliefs and values of Athens, including its democracy. One of his students had headed the bloody oligarchical coup in 411 B.C.E., and one of the people he insulted had been a fighting hero in the restoration of democracy after the coup. Charges were brought against Socrates for corrupting the youth of the city and for impiety, that is, for not believing in the gods honored in the city. Thus, he was essentially charged with being unpatriotic because he criticized the traditions of the city and the decisions of government leaders. He was tried and imprisoned, and though he had several opportunities to escape, in 399 B.C.E., he drank the poison ordered as his method of execution and died.

Most of what we know about Socrates, including the details of his trial and death, comes from his student Plato (427–347 B.C.E.), who wrote dialogues in which Socrates asks questions. Plato also founded the Academy, a school dedicated to philosophy. He developed the theory that there are two worlds: the impermanent, changing world that we know through our senses, and the eternal, unchanging realm of "forms" that constitute the essence of true reality. According to Plato, true knowledge and the possibility of living a virtuous life come from contemplating ideal forms — what later came to be called **Platonic ideals** — not from observing the visible world. Thus if you want to understand justice, asserted Plato, you should think about what would make perfect justice, not study the imperfect examples of justice around you. Although it is hard to separate Plato's thought from Socrates's, in his major work *The Republic*, Plato has Socrates argue that the best form of government is rule by enlightened individuals, what he called "philosopher-kings." Democracy is far too undisciplined and would lead to anarchy, so the role of the people is simply to choose a wise ruler.

Plato's student Aristotle (384–322 B.C.E.) also thought that true knowledge was possible, but he believed that such knowledge came from observation of the world, analysis of natural phenomena, and logical reasoning, not contemplation. Aristotle thought that everything had a purpose; therefore, to know something, one also had to know its function. Excellence — *arête* in Greek — meant performing one's function to the best of one's ability, whether one was a horse or a person. The range of Aristotle's thought is staggering. His interests embraced logic, ethics, natural science, physics, politics, poetry, and art. He studied the heavens as well as the earth and judged the earth to be the center of the universe, with the stars and planets revolving around it.

Plato's idealism profoundly shaped Western philosophy, but Aristotle came to have an even wider influence; for many centuries in Europe, the authority of Aristotle's ideas was second only to the Bible's. His works — which are actually a combination of his lecture notes and those of his students, copied and recopied many times — were used as the ultimate proof that something was true, even if closer observation of the phenomenon indicated that it was not. Thus, ironically, Aristotle's authority was sometimes invoked in a way that contradicted his own ideas. Despite these limitations, the broader examination of the universe and the place of humans in it that Socrates, Plato, and Aristotle engaged in is widely regarded as Greece's most important intellectual legacy.

■ **mystery religions** Belief systems that were characterized by secret doctrines, rituals of initiation, and sometimes the promise of rebirth or an afterlife.

■ **Sophists** A group of thinkers in fifth-century-B.C.E. Athens who applied philosophical speculation to politics and language and were accused of deceit.

■ **Socratic method** A method of inquiry used by Socrates based on asking questions, through which participants developed their critical-thinking skills and explored ethical issues.

■ **Platonic ideals** According to Plato, the eternal unchanging ideal forms that are the essence of true reality.

NOTES

1. J. M. Edmonds, *Greek Elegy and Iambus* (Cambridge, Mass.: Harvard University Press, 1931), I.70, frag. 10.

2. *The Works of Xenophon*, trans. Henry G. Dakyns (London: Macmillan and Co., 1892), p. 296.

3. Thucydides, *History of the Peloponnesian War,* 7.87.6. Translation by John Buckler.

4. G. Tarditi, *Archilochus Fragmenta* (Rome: Edizioni dell'Ateno, 1968), frag. 112. Translation by John Buckler.

5. Gregory Nagy, *The Ancient Greek Hero in 24 Hours* (Cambridge, Mass.: Harvard University Press, 2013), p. 119.

6. Martin Bernal, *Black Athena: The Afroasiatic Roots of Classical Civilization* (New Brunswick, N.J.: Rutgers University Press, 1991). Essays by classical scholars refuting Bernal can be found in Mary R. Lefkowitz and Guy Maclean Rogers, eds., *Black Athena Revisited* (Durham: University of North Carolina Press, 1996).

LOOKING BACK LOOKING AHEAD

The ancient Greeks built on the endeavors of earlier societies in the eastern Mediterranean, but they also added new elements, including drama, philosophy, science, and naturalistic art. They created governments that relied on the participation of citizens. These cultural and political achievements developed in societies that, for many centuries, were almost always at war with the Persians and with one another. Those conflicts led many to wonder whether democracy was really a good form of government and to speculate more widely about abstract ideals and the nature of the cosmos. The Greeks carried these ideas with them as they colonized much of the Mediterranean, in migrations that often resulted from the conflicts that were so common in Greece.

The classical Greeks had tremendous influence not only on the parts of the world in which they traveled or settled, but also on all of Western civilization from that point on. As you will see in Chapter 5, Roman art, religion, literature, and many other aspects of culture relied on Greek models. And as you will see in Chapter 12, European thinkers and writers made conscious attempts to return to classical ideals in art, literature, and philosophy during the Renaissance. In the new United States, political leaders from the Revolutionary era on decided that important government buildings should be modeled on the Parthenon or other temples, complete with marble statuary of their own heroes. In some ways, capitol buildings in the United States are perfect symbols of the legacy of Greece — gleaming ideals of harmony, freedom, democracy, and beauty that (as with all ideals) do not always correspond with realities.

Make Connections

Think about the larger developments and continuities within and across chapters.

1. How did division and conflict within and among city-states shape Greek history from the Bronze Age through the classical period?

2. How were Greek understandings of the role of the gods in public and private life similar to those of the Egyptians and Sumerians? How were they different?

3. Looking at your own town or city, what evidence do you find of the cultural legacy of ancient Greece?

3 REVIEW & EXPLORE

Identify Key Terms

Identify and explain the significance of each item below.

Minoan (p. 57)	tyranny (p. 61)	Delian League (p. 66)	Socratic method (p. 79)
Mycenaean (p. 58)	democracy (p. 61)	gynaeceum (p. 72)	Platonic ideals (p. 79)
polis (p. 60)	oligarchy (p. 61)	mystery religions (p. 78)	
hoplites (p. 61)	helots (p. 63)	Sophists (p. 79)	

Review the Main Ideas

Answer the section heading questions from the chapter.

1. How did the geography of Greece shape its earliest kingdoms? (p. 56)

2. What was the role of the polis in Greek society? (p. 60)

3. How did the wars of the classical period shape Greek history? (p. 65)

4. What ancient Greek ideas and ideals have had a lasting influence? (p. 69)

Suggested Resources

BOOKS

- Bayliss, Andrew J. *The Spartans.* 2020. A brief, readable survey that separates myth from reality.
- Beard, Mary. *The Parthenon.* 2010. A cultural history of Athens's most famous building, including the many controversies that surround it.
- Eckstein, Arthur M. 2006. *Mediterranean Anarchy, Interstate Warfare and the Rise of Rome.* Examines the long-term impact of endemic conflict in Mediterranean politics.
- Forsdyke, Sarah. *Slaves and Slavery in Ancient Greece.* 2021. Emphasizes the experiences and perspectives of enslaved men and women.
- Hansen, Mogens Herman. *Polis: An Introduction to the Ancient Greek City-State.* 2006. The authoritative study of the polis.
- Holland, Tom. *Persian Fire: The First World Empire and the Battle for the West.* 2007. Designed for general audiences, a dramatic retelling of conflict between the Greeks and the Persians.
- Kagan, Donald. *The Peloponnesian War.* 2003. A comprehensive yet accessible study that focuses on leaders and battles, but also the human costs.
- Maclachlan, Bonnie. *Women in Ancient Greece: A Sourcebook.* 2012. Source materials in translation, with texts from literary, rhetorical, philosophical, and legal sources, as well as papyri and inscriptions.
- Osborne, Robin. *Greece in the Making, 1200–479 B.C.,* 2d ed. 2009. Traces the evolution of Greek communities from villages to cities and the development of their civic institutions.
- Rhodes, P. J. *Periclean Athens.* 2018. A concise introduction, designed for students, to the major political and cultural developments of Pericles's time.
- Roochnik, David. *Retrieving the Ancients: An Introduction to Greek Philosophy.* 2004. A sophisticated and well-written narrative of ancient Greek thought designed for students.
- Worthington, Ian. *Philip II of Macedonia.* 2010. Examines Philip's life and legacy, based on literary and archaeological sources.

MEDIA

- *Ancient Apocalypse: Mystery of the Minoans* (BBC, 2008). Explores the role of the volcanic eruption on the nearby island of Thera in ending Minoan civilization; shot on location in Crete.
- *Athens: The Truth About Democracy* (BBC, 2007). Historian Bettany Hughes takes a critical look at classical Athens, with attention to slavery, imperialism, the flow of money, and restrictions on women.
- *Diotima: Materials for the Study of Women and Gender in the Ancient World.* Translated texts, images, and essays on women, gender, sexualities, race, class, enslavement, disability, and the intersections among them in the ancient Mediterranean world. **diotima-doctafemina.org**
- *The Greeks* (PBS, 2016). Three-part series made by National Geographic that explores ancient Greek history from the Bronze Age through the classical period; considers its impact on today's world.
- *The Odyssey* (Andrey Konchalovskiy, 1997). Originally made as a television miniseries, this film portrays many of Odysseus's adventures much as Homer wrote them, as they need no enhancing. Shot on location in the Mediterranean and with an international cast.
- *Perseus Digital Library.* The premier website for accessing the literature and archaeology of ancient Greek culture and now Roman as well, with hundreds of primary texts in Greek, Latin, and English translation, and thousands of images from museum collections and archaeological sites. **www.perseus.tufts.edu/hopper/**
- *The Rise and Fall of the Spartans* (History Channel, 2003). Examines the creation, maintenance, and end of Sparta's distinctive military/political system.
- *Troy* (Wolfgang Petersen, 2004). A fairly decent Hollywood film that focuses, as did Homer in his epic, on the personalities and motivations of the characters as well as on the Trojan War itself.

4

Life in the Hellenistic World

338–30 B.C.E.

When his father Philip was assassinated in 336 B.C.E., two years after he conquered Greece, twenty-year-old Alexander inherited not only his crown but also his determination to lead a united Greek force in fighting Persia. Alexander's invasion of the Persian Empire led to its downfall, but he died while planning his next campaign, only a little more than a decade after he had started. He left behind a huge empire that quickly broke into slightly smaller kingdoms, but more important, his death ushered in an era, the Hellenistic, in which Greek culture, the Greek language, and Greek thought spread as far as India, blending with local traditions. The end of the Hellenistic period is generally set at 30 B.C.E., the year of the death of Cleopatra VII—a Greek ruler—and the Roman conquest of her kingdom of Egypt. The Romans had conquered much of what had been Alexander's empire long before this, but many aspects of Hellenistic culture continued to flourish under Roman governance, adapting to Roman ways of life. Thus rather than coming to an abrupt end in one specific year, the Hellenistic world gradually evolved into the Roman.

In many ways, life in the Hellenistic world was not much different from life in Hellenic Greece or from that in any other Iron Age agricultural society: most people continued to be farmers, raising crops and animals for their own needs and for paying rents and taxes to their superiors. Those who lived in cities, however, often ate foods and drank wine that came from far away, did business with people who were quite unlike them, and adopted religious practices and ways of thinking unknown to their parents. Hellenistic cities thus offer striking parallels to those of today. ■

CHAPTER PREVIEW

- How and why did Alexander the Great create an empire, and how did it evolve?

- How did Greek ideas and traditions spread to create a Hellenized society?

- What characterized the Hellenistic economy?

- How did religion, philosophy, and the arts reflect and shape Hellenistic life?

- How did science and medicine serve the needs of Hellenistic society?

Hellenistic Married Life
This small terra-cotta figurine from Myrina in what is now Turkey, made in the second century B.C.E., shows a newly married couple sitting on a bridal bed. The groom is drawing back the bride's veil, and she is exhibiting the modesty that was a desired quality in young women. Figurines representing every stage of life became popular in the Hellenistic period and were used for religious offerings in temples and sacred places. This one was found in a tomb. (Musée du Louvre, Paris, France/Erich Lessing/Art Resource, NY)

How and why did Alexander the Great create an empire, and how did it evolve?

Fully intending to carry out Philip's designs to lead the Greeks against the Persians, Alexander (r. 336–323 B.C.E.) proclaimed to the Greek world that the invasion of Persia was to be a mighty act of revenge for Xerxes's invasion of Greece in 480 B.C.E. (see "The Persian Wars" in Chapter 3) and more recent Persian interference in Greek affairs. Although he could not foresee this, Alexander's invasion ended up being much more. His campaign swept away the Persian Empire, which had ruled the area for over two hundred years. In its place Alexander established a Macedonian monarchy, and although his rule over these vast territories was never consolidated due to his premature death, he left behind a legacy of political and cultural influence, as well as a long period of war. Macedonian kings established dynasties and Greek culture spread in this Hellenistic era.

Military Campaigns

Despite his youth, Alexander was well prepared to invade Persia. Philip had groomed his son to become king and had given him the best education possible, hiring the Athenian philosopher Aristotle to be his tutor. In 334 B.C.E. Alexander led an army of Macedonians and Greeks into Persian territory in Asia Minor. With him went a staff of philosophers to study the people of these lands, poets to write verses praising Alexander's exploits, scientists to map the area and study strange animals and plants, and a historian to write an account of the campaign. Alexander intended not only a military campaign but also an expedition of discovery.

In the next three years Alexander moved east into the Persian Empire, winning major battles at the Granicus River and Issus (Map 4.1). He moved into Syria and took most of the cities of Phoenicia and the eastern coast of the Mediterranean without a fight. His army

MAP 4.1 Alexander's Conquests, 334–324 B.C.E.   This map shows the course of Alexander's invasion of the Persian Empire. More important than the great success of his military campaigns were the founding of new cities and the expansion of existing ones by Alexander and the Hellenistic rulers who followed him.

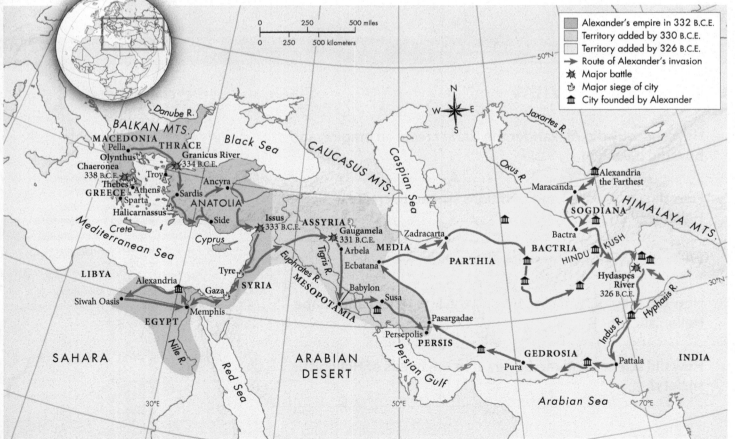

356–323 B.C.E.
Life of Alexander
the Great

323–ca. 300 B.C.E.
War of succession leads to the establishment of
Antigonid, Ptolemaic, and Seleucid dynasties

340–270 B.C.E.
Life of Epicurus, on whose
ideas Epicureanism was based

335–262 B.C.E.
Life of Zeno, on whose
ideas Stoicism was based

ca. 287–212 B.C.E.
Life of Archimedes

334–324 B.C.E.
Alexander the Great's
military campaigns

ca. 280 B.C.E.
Founding of the library of Alexandria
by the Ptolemies

ca. 330–200 B.C.E.
Establishment of new Hellenistic cities

168 B.C.E.
Roman overthrow
of the Antigonid
dynasty

166–164 B.C.E.
Revolt of the
Maccabees
in Judaea

63 B.C.E. ❯
Roman conquest
of Syria; Seleucid
dynasty ends

30 B.C.E. ❯
Roman conquest of
Egypt; Ptolemaic
dynasty ends

---

successfully besieged the cities that did oppose him, including Tyre and Gaza, executing the men of military age afterwards and enslaving the women and children. He then turned south toward Egypt, which had earlier been conquered by the Persians. The Egyptians saw Alexander as a liberator, and he seized it without a battle. After honoring the priestly class, Alexander was proclaimed pharaoh, the legitimate ruler of the country. He founded a new capital, Alexandria, on the coast of the Mediterranean, which would later grow into an enormous city. He next marched to the oasis of Siwah, west of the Nile Valley, to consult the famous oracle of Zeus-Amon, a composite god who combined qualities of the Greek Zeus and the Egyptian Amon-Ra (see "Egyptian Religion" in Chapter 1). No one will ever know what the priest told him, but henceforth Alexander called himself the son of Zeus.

Alexander left Egypt after less than a year and marched into Assyria, where at Gaugamela he defeated the Persian army, and then conquered the

Amphora with Alexander and Darius at the Battle of Issus　Alexander, riding bareback, charges King Darius III, who is standing in a chariot. This detail from a jug was made within a decade after the battle in a Greek colony in southern Italy, beyond the area of Alexander's conquests, a good indication of how quickly Alexander's fame spread. (De Agostini DEA/A. DAGLI ORTI/Getty Images)

principal Persian capital of Persepolis. There he performed a symbolic act of retribution by burning the royal buildings of King Xerxes, the invader of Greece during the Persian wars 150 years earlier. Without success Alexander pursued Persia's King Darius III (r. 336–330 B.C.E.), who appears to have been killed by Persian conspirators.

The Persian Empire had fallen and the war of revenge was over, but Alexander had no intention of stopping. Many of his troops had been supplied by Greek city-states that had allied with him; he released these troops from their obligations of military service, but then rehired them as mercenaries. Alexander then began his personal odyssey. With his Macedonian soldiers and Greek mercenaries, he set out to conquer more of Asia. He plunged deeper into the East, into lands completely unknown to the Greek world. It took his soldiers four additional years to conquer Bactria (in today's Afghanistan) and the easternmost parts of the now-defunct Persian Empire, but still Alexander was determined to continue his march.

In 326 B.C.E. Alexander crossed the Indus River and entered India (in the area that is now Pakistan). There, too, he saw hard fighting, and finally at the Hyphasis (HIH-fuh-sihs) River his troops refused to go farther. Alexander was enraged by the mutiny, for he believed he was near the end of the world. Nonetheless, the army stood firm, and Alexander relented. (See "Viewpoints: Greek Historians on Alexander the Great," page 87.) Still eager to explore the limits of the world, Alexander turned south to the Arabian Sea, and he waged a bloody and ruthless war against the people of the area. After reaching the Arabian Sea and turning west, he led his army through the grim Gedrosian Desert (now part of Pakistan and Iran). The army and those who supported the troops with supplies suffered fearfully, and many soldiers died along the way. Nonetheless, in 324 B.C.E. Alexander returned to Susa in the Greek-controlled region of Assyria, and in a mass wedding that symbolized both his conquest and his aim to unite Greek and Persian cultures, he married the daughter of Darius as well as the daughter of a previous Persian king, and at his order his high officers all married Persian wives. He gave wedding presents to Macedonian soldiers who married Persian women as well, a number reported to be 10,000. How

many of these marriages of ordinary soldiers survived is unknown, but of the high officers, only Seleucus, the founder of the vast Seleucid Empire (see "The Political Legacy"), kept his Persian wife; his son and successor in 280, Antiochus I, was thus half-Persian.

His mission was over, but Alexander never returned to his homeland of Macedonia. He died the next year in Babylon from fever, wounds, and excessive drinking. He was only thirty-two, but in just thirteen years he had created an empire that stretched from his homeland of Macedonia to India, gaining the title "the Great" along the way.

Alexander so quickly became a legend that he still seems superhuman. That alone makes a reasoned interpretation of his goals and character very difficult. His contemporaries from the Greek city-states thought he was a bloody-minded tyrant, but later Greek and Roman writers and political leaders admired him and even regarded him as a philosopher interested in the common good. That view influenced many later European and U.S. historians, but this idealistic interpretation has generally been rejected after a more thorough analysis of the sources. The most common view today is that Alexander was a brilliant leader who sought personal glory through conquest and who tolerated no opposition.

The Political Legacy

The main question at Alexander's death was whether his vast empire could be held together. Although he fathered a successor, the child was not yet born when Alexander died and was thus too young to assume the duties of kingship. (Later he and his mother, Roxana, were murdered by one of Alexander's generals, who viewed him as a threat.) This meant that Alexander's empire was a prize for the taking. Several of the chief Macedonian generals aspired to become sole ruler, which led to a civil war lasting for decades that tore Alexander's empire apart. By the end of this conflict, the most successful generals had carved out their own smaller though still vast monarchies, each in competition for power with the others, as were their successors. As in the classical period, there was no enforceable international law, and the shifting and unstable balances of power combined with the ruthlessness and ambitions of leaders led to frequent war.

Alexander's general Ptolemy (ca. 367–ca. 283 B.C.E.) claimed authority over Egypt, and after fighting off rivals, established a kingdom and dynasty there, called the Ptolemaic (TAH-luh-MAY-ihk). In 304 B.C.E. he took the title of pharaoh, and by the end of his long life he had a relatively stable realm to pass on to his son. The **Ptolemaic dynasty** would rule Egypt for nearly three hundred years, until the death of the last Ptolemaic ruler, Cleopatra VII, in 30 B.C.E. (see Chapter 5). Seleucus (ca. 358–281 B.C.E.), another of Alexander's officers, carved out a

> ■ **Ptolemaic dynasty** Dynasty of rulers established by General Ptolemy in Egypt after Alexander's conquests, which ruled until 30 B.C.E.
>
> ■ **Antigonid dynasty** Dynasty of rulers established by General Antigonus in Macedonia after Alexander's conquests, which ruled until 168 B.C.E.
>
> ■ **Seleucid Empire** Large empire established in the Near East by General Seleucus after Alexander's conquests, which remained in power until 63 B.C.E.
>
> ■ **Hellenistic** A term that literally means "like the Greek," used to describe the period after the death of Alexander the Great, when Greek culture spread.

The works of only four ancient writers about Alexander the Great survive, all from three centuries or more after Alexander's death, though they make use of now-lost much older primary sources. Diodorus was a first-century-B.C.E. Greek historian, born in Sicily, and Arrian (ca. 86–160 C.E.) was a Greek military leader and historian. Both excerpts describe Alexander's troops' refusal to go farther east in India.

Diodorus

Alexander observed that his soldiers were exhausted with their constant campaigns. They had spent almost eight years among toils and dangers, and it was necessary to raise their spirits by an effective appeal if they were to undertake an expedition against the Gandaridae [people who lived across the Hyphasis River]. There had been many losses among the soldiers, and no relief from fighting was in sight. The hooves of the horses had been worn thin by steady marching. The arms and armour were wearing out, and Greek clothing was quite gone. They had to clothe themselves in foreign materials, recutting the garments of the Indians. This was the season also, as luck would have it, of the heavy rains. They had been going on for seventy days, to the accompaniment of continuous thunder and lightning . . . he saw only one hope of gaining his wish, if he might gain the soldiers' great goodwill though gratitude. Accordingly he allowed them to ravage the enemy's country, which was full of every good thing. During these days when the army was busy foraging, he called together the wives of the soldiers and their children; to the wives he undertook to give a monthly ration, to the children he delivered a service bonus in proportion to the military records of their fathers. When the soldiers returned laden with wealth from their expedition, he brought them together for a meeting. He delivered a carefully prepared speech about the expedition against the Gandaridae but the Macedonians did not accept it, and he gave up the undertaking.

Arrian

The spirit of the Macedonians now began to flag, when they saw the king [Alexander] raising one labour after another, and incurring one danger after another. Conferences were held throughout the camp, in which those who were the most moderate bewailed their lot, while others resolutely declared that they would not follow Alexander any farther, even if he should lead the way. When he heard of this, before the disorder and pusillanimity [cowardice] of the soldiers should advance to a great degree, he called a council of the officers of the brigades and addressed them: — "Macedonians and Grecian allies, seeing that you no longer follow me into dangerous enterprises with a resolution equal to that which formerly animated you, I have collected you together into the same spot, so that I may either persuade you to march forward with me, or may be persuaded by you to return. . . . But, O Macedonians and Grecian allies, stand firm! Glorious are the deeds of those who undergo labour and run the risk of danger; and it is delightful to live a life of valour and to die leaving behind immortal glory. . . . For the land is yours, and you act as its viceroys [rulers]. The greater part also of the money now comes to you. . . ." Having said this, he retired into his tent . . . waiting to see if any change would occur in the minds of the Macedonians. . . . But on the contrary, when there was a profound silence throughout the camp, and the soldiers were evidently annoyed at his wrath, without being at all changed by it . . . he made known to the army that he had resolved to march back again.

QUESTIONS FOR ANALYSIS

1. What do the two authors say that Alexander did to try to persuade his troops to go further? What do these actions suggest about the authors' views of Alexander's character as a leader?
2. What other aspects of Alexander's campaigns do these sources reveal?

Sources: *Diodorus of Sicily*, with an English translation by C. Bradford Welles (Cambridge, Mass.: Harvard University Press, 1961), vol. 8, pp. 391–393; Arrian, *The Anabasis of Alexander*, translated by E. J. Chinook (London: Hodder and Stoughton, 1884), pp. 307–308, 314.

large state, the **Seleucid Empire** (SUH-loo-suhd), that stretched from the coast of Asia Minor to India. He was assassinated in 281 B.C.E. on the order of the ruler of the Ptolemaic kingdom, but his son succeeded him, founding a dynasty that also lasted for centuries, although the kingdom itself shrank as independent states broke off in Pergamum, Bactria, Parthia, and elsewhere. Antigonus I (382–301 B.C.E.), a third general, became king of Macedonia and established the **Antigonid** (an-TIH-guh-nuhd) **dynasty**, which lasted until it was overthrown by the Romans in 168 B.C.E. The remains of the Seleucid Empire were also conquered by the Romans, in 63 B.C.E., and the Ptolemaic kingdom ended with Roman conquest in 30 B.C.E. (see Chapters 5 and 6).

Hellenistic rulers amassed an enormous amount of wealth from their large kingdoms, and royal patronage provided money for the production of literary works and the research and development that allowed discoveries in science and engineering. To encourage

Royal Couple Cameo   This Hellenistic cameo, designed to be worn as a necklace, probably portrays King Ptolemy II and his sister Arsinoe II, rulers of the Ptolemaic kingdom of Egypt. During the Hellenistic period portraits of queens became more common because of the increased importance of hereditary monarchies. (Leemage/Universal Images Group/Newscom)

obedience and support for their militaristic ambitions, Hellenistic kings often created ruler cults that linked the king's authority with that of the gods, or they adopted ruler cults that already existed, as Alexander did in Egypt. These deified kings were not considered gods as mighty as Zeus or Apollo, and the new ruler cults probably had little religious impact on the people being ruled. The kingdoms never won the deep emotional loyalty that Greeks had once felt for the polis, but the ruler cult was an easily understandable symbol of unity within the kingdom.

Hellenistic kingship was hereditary, which gave women who were members of royal families more power than any woman had in democracies such as Athens, where citizenship was limited to men. Wives and mothers of kings had influence over their husbands and sons, and a few women ruled in their own right when there was no male heir.

Greece itself changed politically during the Hellenistic period. To enhance their joint security, many poleis organized themselves into leagues of city-states, of which the two most extensive were the Aetolian (ee-TOH-lee-uhn) League in western and central Greece and the Achaean (uh-KEE-uhn) League in southern Greece. These leagues also became involved in the frequent warfare of the Hellenistic period, contributing to the anarchy of the eastern Mediterranean.

How did Greek ideas and traditions spread to create a Hellenized society?

Alexander's most important legacy was clearly not political unity. Instead it was the spread of Greek ideas and traditions across a wide area, a process scholars later called **Hellenization**. To maintain contact with the Greek world as he moved farther eastward, Alexander founded new cities and military colonies and expanded existing cities, settling Greek and Macedonian troops and veterans in them. Besides keeping the road back to Greece open, these settlements helped secure the countryside around them. This practice continued after his death, with more than 250 new cities founded in North Africa, West and Central Asia, and southeastern Europe. These cities and colonies became powerful instruments in the spread of Hellenism and in the blending of Greek and other cultures.

Urban Life

In many respects the Hellenistic city resembled a modern city. It was a cultural center with theaters, temples, and libraries. It was a seat of learning, a

Hellenistic Statuette of an African Man   This small statue of a young African man from the third or second century B.C.E. shows him wearing a rolled cloth around his waist, a garment characteristic of artisans who worked in the heat of a foundry or forge, making iron tools and weapons. Black Africans could be found in many parts of the Hellenistic world, their presence reflected in naturalistic depictions such as this one by artists with firsthand knowledge of their subjects. (Rogers Fund, 1918/The Metropolitan Museum of Art)

■ **Hellenization** The spread of Greek ideas, culture, and traditions to non-Greek groups across a wide area.

home of poets, writers, teachers, and artists. City dwellers could find amusement through plays, musical performances, animal fights, and gambling. The Hellenistic city was also an economic center that provided a ready market for grain and produce raised in the surrounding countryside. In short, the Hellenistic city offered cultural and economic opportunities for rich and poor alike.

To the Greeks, civilized life was unthinkable outside of a city, and Hellenistic kings often gave cities all the external trappings of a polis. Each had an assembly of citizens, a council to prepare legislation, and a board of magistrates to conduct political business. Yet, however similar to the Greek polis it appeared, such a city could not engage in diplomatic dealings, make treaties, pursue its own foreign policy, or wage its own wars. The city was required to follow royal orders, and the king often placed his own officials in it to see that his decrees were followed.

A Hellenistic city differed from a Greek polis in other ways as well. The Greek polis had one body of law and one set of customs. In the Hellenistic city Greeks represented an elite class. Natives and non-Greek foreigners who lived in Hellenistic cities usually possessed lesser rights than Greeks and often had their own laws. In some instances this disparity spurred natives to assimilate Greek culture in order to rise politically and socially.

The city of Pergamum in northwestern Anatolia is a good example of an older city that underwent changes in the Hellenistic period. Previously an important strategic site, Pergamum was transformed by its new Greek rulers into a magnificent city complete with all the typical buildings of the polis, including gymnasia, baths, and one of the finest libraries in the entire Hellenistic world. The new rulers erected temples to the traditional Greek deities, but they also built imposing temples to other gods. There was a Jewish population in the city, who may have established a synagogue. Especially in the agora, the public marketplace in the center of town, Greeks and local people met to conduct business and exchange goods and ideas. Greeks felt as though they were at home, and the evolving culture mixed Greek and local elements.

The Bactrian city of Ay Khanoum on the Oxus River, on the border of modern Afghanistan, is a good example of a brand-new city where cultures met. Bactria and Parthia had been part of the Seleucid kingdom, but in the third century B.C.E. their governors overthrew the Seleucids and established independent kingdoms in today's Afghanistan and Turkmenistan (Map 4.2). Bactria became an outpost of Hellenism, from which the rulers of China and India learned of sophisticated societies other than their own. It had Greek temples and administration buildings, and on a public square was a long inscription in Greek verse

carved in stone, erected by a man who may have been a student of Aristotle and taken from a saying of the oracle at Delphi:

> In childhood, learn good manners
> In youth, control your passions
> In middle age, practice justice
> In old age, be of good counsel
> In death, have no regrets.[1]

Along with this very public display of Greek ideals, the city also had temples to local deities and artwork that blended Greek and local styles (for an example, see the metal disk in "Evaluating Visual Evidence: Bactrian Disk with Religious Figures," page 91).

Greeks in Hellenistic Cities

Like Alexander himself, the ruling dynasties of the Hellenistic world were Macedonian, and Macedonians and Greeks filled all the important political, military, and diplomatic positions. Besides building Greek cities, Hellenistic kings offered Greeks land and money as lures to further immigration.

The Hellenistic monarchy, unlike the Greek polis, did not depend solely on its citizens to fulfill its political needs, but instead relied on professionals. Talented Greek men had the opportunity to rise quickly in the government bureaucracy. Appointed by the king, these administrators did not have to stand for election each year, unlike many officials of Greek poleis. Since they held their jobs year after year, they had ample time to create new administrative techniques, and also time to develop ways to profit personally from their positions.

Greeks also found ready employment in the armies and navies of the Hellenistic monarchies. Alexander had proved the Greco-Macedonian style of warfare to be far superior to that of other peoples, and Alexander's successors, themselves experienced officers, realized the importance of trained soldiers in their campaigns for dominance. Hellenistic kings were reluctant to arm the local populations or to allow them to serve in the army, fearing military rebellions among their conquered subjects. The result was the emergence of paid professional armies and navies consisting primarily of Greeks, although drawn from many areas of Greece and Macedonia, not simply from one polis. Unlike the citizen hoplites of classical Greece, these men were full-time soldiers. Hellenistic kings paid them well, often giving them land or leasing it to them as an incentive to remain loyal.

Greeks were able to dominate other professions as well. Hellenistic kingdoms and cities recruited Greek writers and artists to create Greek literature, art, and

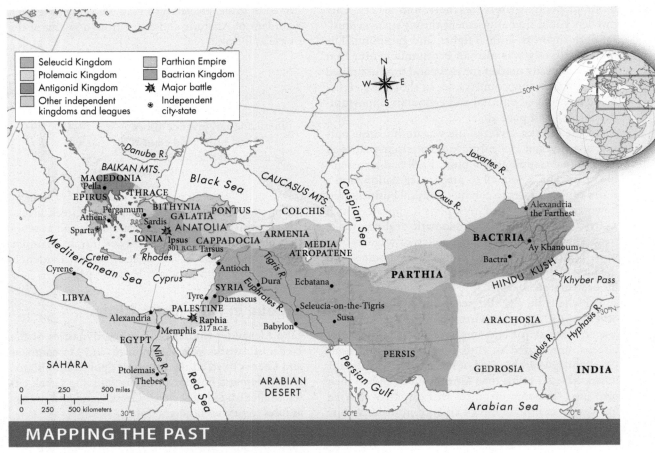

MAPPING THE PAST

MAP 4.2 The Hellenistic World, ca. 263 B.C.E.

This map depicts the Hellenistic world after Alexander's death.

ANALYZING THE MAP Compare this map to Map 4.1. After Alexander's death, were the Macedonians and Greeks able to retain control of most of the land he had conquered? What areas were lost?

CONNECTIONS What does this map suggest about the success or failure of Alexander's dreams of conquest?

culture. Greek architects, engineers, and skilled crafts-men found themselves in great demand to produce the Greek-style buildings commissioned by the Hellenistic monarchs. Architects and engineers would sometimes design and build whole cities, which they laid out in checkerboard fashion and filled with typical Greek buildings. An enormous wave of construction took place during the Hellenistic period.

Increased physical and social mobility benefited some women as well as men. More women learned to read than before, and they engaged in occupations in which literacy was beneficial, including care of the sick. During the Hellenistic period women still had to have male guardians to buy, sell, or lease land; to borrow money; and to represent them in other commercial transactions. (The requirement of a male guardian was later codified in Roman law and largely maintained in Europe into the nineteenth century.)

Yet often such a guardian was present only to fulfill the letter of the law. The woman was the real agent and handled the business being transacted.

Because of the opportunities the Hellenistic monarchies offered, many people moved frequently. These were generally individual decisions, not part of organized colonization efforts such as those that had been common earlier in Greek history (see Chapter 3). Once a Greek man had left home to take service with, for instance, the army or the bureaucracy of the Ptolemies, he had no incentive beyond his pay and the comforts of life in Egypt to keep him there. If the Seleucid king offered him more money or a promotion, he might well accept it and take his talents to Asia Minor. Thus professional Greek soldiers and administrators were very mobile and were apt to look to their own interests, not their kingdom's. Linguistic changes further facilitated the ease with which

Bactrian Disk with Religious Figures

This spectacular metal disk, about 10 inches across, was made in the Bactrian city of Ay Khanoum in the third century B.C.E. It probably depicts Cybele, a Greek earth mother goddess, and Nike, the Greek winged goddess of victory, being pulled in a chariot by lions with the sun-god Helios above. A priest holds a sun parasol — a royal symbol — above them, and a priestess is standing on a stepped altar at the right. Worship of Cybele spread into Greece from the east and was then spread by her Greek followers as they conquered, traveled, and migrated.

(Pictures From History/CPA Media Pte Ltd./Alamy)

EVALUATE THE EVIDENCE

1. Looking at the disk along with the other illustrations of divine and human figures in this chapter and Chapter 3, which elements of the imagery seem typically Greek? Which appear different, so are perhaps of Asian origin?
2. Why do you think the artist who made this might have combined Greek and non-Greek elements to create a hybrid image on this luxury item?

---

people moved. Instead of the different dialects spoken in Greece itself, a new Greek dialect called the *koine* (koy-NAY), which means "common," became the spoken language of traders, the royal court, the bureaucracy, and the army across the Hellenistic world.

As long as Greeks continued to migrate, the kingdoms remained stable and strong. In the process they drew an immense amount of talent from the Greek peninsula. However, the Hellenistic monarchies could not keep recruiting Greeks forever, in spite of their wealth and willingness to spend lavishly, as the population of Greece was not boundless. In time the huge surge of immigration slowed greatly.

Greeks and Non-Greeks

Across the Hellenistic world the prevailing institutions and laws became Greek. Everyone, Greek or non-Greek, who wanted to find an official position or compete in business had to learn Greek. Those who did gained an avenue of social mobility, and as early as the third century B.C.E. local people in some Hellenistic cities began to rise in power and prominence. They adopted a Greek name and, if they were male, went to Greek educational institutions or sent their sons there. Hoping to impress the Greek elite, priests in Babylon and Alexandria composed histories of their areas in Greek. Once a man knew Greek, he could move more

easily to another area for better opportunities, and perhaps even hide his non-Greek origins. He could also join a military unit and perhaps be deployed far from his place of origin. Thus learning Greek was an avenue of geographic mobility as well.

Cities granted citizenship to Hellenized local people and sometimes to Greek-speaking migrants, although there were fewer political benefits of citizenship than there had been in the classical period, because real power was held by monarchs, not citizens. Even a few women received honorary citizenship in Hellenistic cities because of aid they had provided in times of crisis. Being Greek became to some degree a matter of culture, not bloodlines.

Cultural influences in the other direction occurred less frequently, because they brought fewer advantages. Few Greeks learned a non-Greek language, unless they were required to because of their official position. Greeks did begin to worship local deities, but often these were somewhat Hellenized and their qualities blended with those of an existing Greek god or goddess. (See "Evaluating Visual Evidence: Bactrian Disk with Religious Figures.") Greeks living in Egypt generally cremated their dead while Egyptians continued to mummify them, although by the first century B.C.E. Greeks and Romans sometimes mummified their dead as well, attaching realistic portraits painted on wooden panels to the mummies. These portraits have served as important sources about clothing and hairstyles.

Yet the spread of Greek culture was wider than it was deep. Hellenistic kingdoms were never entirely unified in language, customs, and thought. The principal reason for this phenomenon is that Greek culture generally did not extend far beyond the reaches of the cities. Many urban residents adopted the aspects of Hellenism that they found useful, but people in the countryside generally did not embrace it, nor were they encouraged to.

Ptolemaic Egypt provides an excellent example of this situation. The Ptolemies maintained separate legal systems for Greeks and Egyptians. Indigenous Egyptians were the foundation of the kingdom: they fed it by their labor in the fields and financed its operations with their taxes. For this reason, the Ptolemies tied local people to the land more tightly than they had been before, making it nearly impossible for them to leave their villages. The bureaucracy of the Ptolemies was relatively efficient, and the Egyptian population was viciously and cruelly exploited. Even in times of hardship, the king's taxes came first, even though payment might mean starvation. The people's desperation was summed up by one Egyptian, who scrawled the warning, "We are worn out; we will run away."[2] To many Egyptians, revolt or a life of banditry was preferable to working the land under the harsh Ptolemies.

The situation was somewhat different in the booming city of Alexandria, founded by Alexander to be a new seaport, where there had been a small village earlier. Within a century of its founding, it was probably the largest city in the world, with a population numbering in the hundreds of thousands. The ruling elite was primarily Greek, and the Ptolemies tried to keep the Greek and Egyptian populations apart, but this was not always possible. Although the Ptolemies encouraged immigration from Greece, the number of immigrants was relatively low, so intermarriage increased. And the Ptolemies themselves gave privileges to local priests, building temples and sponsoring rituals honoring the local gods. Priestly families became owners of large landed estates and engaged in other sorts of business as well, becoming loyal supporters of the Ptolemaic regime. Even the processions honoring local gods still celebrated Greekness,

however, and sometimes became a flash point sparking protests by Egyptians.

In about 280 B.C.E. the Ptolemies founded a library in Alexandria that both glorified Greek culture and sponsored new scholarship. It came to contain hundreds of thousands of papyrus scrolls of Greek writings, including copies of such classic works as the poems of Homer, the histories of Herodotus and Thucydides, and the philosophical works of Plato and Aristotle, as well as newer accounts of scientific discoveries. The Ptolemies sent representatives to Greece to buy books, paid for copies made of any Greek books that were brought to Alexandria, and supported scholars who edited multiple versions of older books into a single authoritative version. The library became one of the foremost intellectual centers of the ancient world, pulling in Greek-speaking writers, scholars, scientists, and thinkers from far away and preserving Greek writings.

Greek culture spread more deeply in the Seleucid kingdom than in Egypt, although this was not because the Seleucids had an organized plan for Hellenizing the local population. The primary problem for the Seleucids was holding on to the territory they had inherited. To do this, they established cities and military colonies throughout the region to nurture a vigorous and large Greek-speaking population and to defend the kingdom from their Persian neighbors. Seleucid military colonies were generally founded near existing villages, thus exposing even rural residents to all aspects of Greek life. Many local people found Greek political and cultural forms attractive and imitated them. In Asia Minor and Syria, for instance, numerous villages and towns developed along Greek lines, and some of them grew into Hellenized cities.

The kings of Bactria and Parthia spread Greek culture even further. Some of these rulers converted to Buddhism, and the Buddhist ruler of the Mauryan Empire in northern India, Ashoka (ca. 269–233 B.C.E.), may have ordered translations of his laws into Greek for the Greek-speaking residents of Bactria and Parthia. In the second century B.C.E., after the collapse of the Mauryan Empire, Bactrian armies conquered part of northern India, establishing several small Indo-Greek states where the mixing of religious and artistic traditions was particularly pronounced.

What characterized the Hellenistic economy?

Alexander's conquest of the Persian Empire not only changed the political face of the ancient world and led to a shared urban culture, but also brought the Near East and Egypt fully into the

sphere of Greek economics. The Hellenistic period, however, did not see widespread improvements in the way most people lived and worked. The majority of people were farmers who lived in the countryside, and their lives continued to be dominated by hard work. There were relatively few advances in agricultural or production methods, and many people who lived in rural areas were actually worse off than they had been before, because of higher rents and taxes. Wealthy and middling-status people in cities flourished, but poorer people in cities who depended on wages were hurt by inflation. Alexander and his successors did link East and West in a broad commercial network, however, and the spread of Greeks throughout the Near East and Egypt created new markets and stimulated trade.

Rural Life

As in every ancient society, the vast majority of people in the Hellenistic world were subsistence farmers who lived in the countryside. For them, the most important event of the 330s B.C.E. may have been a long-lasting drought, not Alexander's conquests. Most people in this period worked on small family farms that they owned or rented, or on larger farms owned by wealthy absentee landlords. The mainstays of Hellenistic agriculture remained the triad of grain, grapevines, and olive trees, which had been the core of Mediterranean crop raising since the Bronze Age, so prominent that "grain, new wine, and olive oil" are frequently mentioned together in Hebrew Scripture.

Farmers relied on a simple plow pulled by oxen to break the ground and prepare the soil for planting. Plowing also controlled weeds and preserved soil moisture. Farmers further broke up the land with mattocks, a tool similar to a pickax. At harvest time they reaped the grain with sickles. Barley was more common than wheat because it was hardier and could grow in poorer soil; it was generally eaten as a cooked grain. Wheat, on the other hand, was the preferred grain for making bread. Lentils and beans served as food for both people and animals, and as fertilizer for the soil. Olive trees grew even in poor soil, and fruit trees added welcome sweets to the family diet. Whenever possible, farmers grew grapevines, as wine was a common drink in the Hellenistic world, where it was generally drunk mixed with water because the wine was so rough. Protein came from cheese, fish—fresh, dried, salted, and smoked—and very occasionally meat.

Men tended to do the plowing, while women and children hoed and weeded. Plowing and seeding were usually done in the autumn. Winter rains encouraged growth, and farmers harvested their crops in early summer. After the harvest, grain was spread over a circular threshing floor, where donkeys harnessed to a pole crushed the kernels. Grapes were harvested in early fall and left sitting for two weeks before being crushed into wine.

At harvest time people offered some of their crops to the gods in thanks and set aside another — no doubt larger — portion for paying their rents and taxes. Another portion was saved as seed for the next year, but the largest portion was stored to be eaten over the next months. With what was left, farmers treated themselves to a festive meal, enjoyed along with music and dancing as a short break from work. Government intervened in rural people's lives primarily in the collection of taxes, as much of the revenue for the Hellenistic kingdoms was derived from taxing land and agricultural products. Egypt had a strong tradition of central authority dating back to the pharaohs, which the Ptolemies inherited and tightened. They had the power to mobilize local labor into the digging and maintenance of canals and ditches, and they even attempted to decree what crops Egyptian farmers would plant and what animals would be raised. Such centralized planning was difficult to enforce at the local level, however, especially because the officials appointed to do so switched positions frequently and concentrated most on extracting taxes. Thus, despite some royal interest in agriculture, there is no evidence that agricultural productivity increased or that practices changed. Technology was applied to military needs, but not to those of food production.

Diodorus of Sicily, a Greek historian who apparently visited Ptolemaic Egypt around 60 B.C.E., was surprised that Egyptians could feed all their children instead of resorting to the selective exposure of infants practiced in Greece. He decided that this was because of their less formal child-rearing habits:

> They feed their children in a sort of happy-go-lucky fashion that in its inexpensiveness quite surpasses belief; for they serve them with stews made of any stuff that is ready to hand and cheap, and give them such stalks as the byblos plant [the reeds from which papyrus is made] as can be roasted in the coals and the roots and the stems of marsh plants, either raw or boiled or baked. And since most of the children are reared without shoes or clothing because of the mildness of the climate of the country, the entire expense incurred by the parents of a child until it comes to maturity is not more than twenty drachmas. These are the leading reasons why Egypt has such an extraordinarily large population.[3]

Egyptian parents would probably have given other reasons, such as rents and taxes, for why their children had simple food and no shoes.

Women Traveling on Camels   These terra-cotta statues from Alexandria in the third or second centuries B.C.E. show women on camelback carrying food items to sell, including ducks and round loaves of bread. Both camels and women selling food would have been common sights in the marketplaces of Alexandria and other Hellenistic cities, as would vendors selling inexpensive art objects such as these. (G. DAGLI ORTI/De Agostini/Getty Images)

Production of Goods

As with agriculture, although demand for goods increased during the Hellenistic period, no significant new techniques of production appear to have developed. Manual labor, not machinery, continued to turn out the raw materials and manufactured goods the Hellenistic world used.

Diodorus gives a picture of this hard labor, commenting about life in the gold mines owned by the kings:

> At the end of Egypt is a region bearing many mines and abundant gold, which is extracted with great pain and expense. . . . For kings of Egypt condemn to the mines criminals and prisoners of war, those who were falsely accused and those who were put into jail because of royal anger, not only them but sometimes also all of their relatives. Rounding them up, they assign them to the gold mines, taking revenge on those who were condemned and through their labors gaining huge revenues. The condemned—and they are very many—all of them are put in chains; and they work persistently and continually, both by day and throughout the

> night, getting no rest and carefully cut off from escape. For the guards, who are barbarian soldiers and who speak a different language, stand watch over them so that no man can either by conversation or friendly contact corrupt any of them.[4]

Apart from gold and silver, which were used primarily for coins and jewelry, bronze continued to be used for shields. Iron was utilized for weapons and tools.

Pottery remained an important commodity, and most of it was produced locally. The coarse pottery used in the kitchen for plates and cups changed little. Fancier pots and bowls, decorated with a shiny black glaze, came into use during the Hellenistic period. This ware originated in Athens, but potters in other places began to imitate its style, heavily cutting into the Athenian market. In the second century B.C.E. a red-glazed ware, often called Samian, burst on the market and soon dominated it. Pottery was often decorated with patterns and scenes from mythology, legend, and daily life. Potters often portrayed heroic episodes, such as battles from the *Iliad*, or gods, such as Dionysus at sea. Pots journeyed with Greek merchants, armies, and travelers, so these images spread knowledge of Greek religion and stories west as far as

Portugal and east as far as Southeast Asia. Pottery thus served as a means of cultural exchange—of ideas as well as goods—among people scattered across huge portions of the globe.

Commerce

Alexander's conquest of the Persian Empire had immediate effects on trade and prices. In the conquered Persian capitals Alexander had found vast sums of gold, silver, and other treasure. This wealth financed the creation of new cities, the building of roads, and the development of harbors. It also provided the thousands who participated in his expeditions with booty, with which they could purchase commodities. The release of this vast Persian horde of money into the Greek world led to inflation, however, and prices on basic commodities such as flour and olive oil doubled or more. After a high point in about 300 B.C.E., prices gradually sank, but they never returned to prices of the earlier period. Those who depended on wages for a living were badly hurt by this inflation, and they did what poor people often do as they search for a better life: migrate, which in this case meant to the new cities of the East.

Greek merchants eagerly took advantage of new opportunities for trade, which was facilitated by the coining of money. Most of the great monarchies coined their money according to a uniform system, which meant that much of the money used in Hellenistic kingdoms had the same value. Traders were less in need of money changers than in the days when each major power coined money on a different standard.

Overland trade was conducted by caravan, and the backbone of this caravan trade was the camel—a shaggy, ill-tempered, but durable animal ideally suited to the harsh climate of the caravan routes. Luxury goods that were light, rare, and expensive traveled over the caravan routes to Alexandria or to the harbors of Phoenicia and Syria, from which they were shipped to Greece, Italy, and Spain. In time these luxury items, including ivory, precious stones, and spices, became more commonplace, in part because of an increased volume of trade. Perhaps the most prominent good in terms of volume was silk, and the trade in silk later gave the major east-west route its name: the Silk Road. In return the Greeks and Macedonians sent east manufactured goods, especially metal weapons, cloth, wine, and olive oil. Although these caravan routes can trace their origins to earlier times, they became far more prominent in the Hellenistic period. Business customs and languages of trade developed and became standardized, so that merchants from different nationalities could communicate in a way understandable to all of them.

The durability and economic importance of the caravan routes are amply demonstrated by the fact that the death of Alexander, the ensuing wars of his successors, and later regional conflicts had little effect on trade. Numerous mercantile cities grew up along these routes, and commercial contacts brought people from far-flung regions together, even if sometimes indirectly. The merchants and the caravan cities were links in a chain that reached from the Mediterranean Sea to India and beyond to China, along which ideas as well as goods were passed.

More economically important than the trade in luxury goods were commercial dealings in essential commodities like raw materials and grain and such mass-produced items as pottery. The Hellenistic monarchies usually raised enough grain for their own needs as well as a surplus for export. This trade in grain was essential for the cities of Greece and the Aegean, many of which could not grow enough. Fortunately for them, abundant wheat supplies were available nearby in Egypt and in the area north of the Black Sea (see Map 4.2). Cities in Greece often paid for their grain by exporting olive oil and wine.

Most trade in bulk commodities was seaborne, and the Hellenistic merchant ship was the workhorse of the day. The merchant ship had a broad beam and relied on sails for propulsion. It was far more seaworthy than the contemporary warship, the trireme (see Chapter 3), which was long, narrow, and built for speed. A small crew of experienced sailors could handle the merchant vessel easily. Maritime trade provided opportunities for workers in other industries and trades: sailors, shipbuilders, dockworkers, accountants, teamsters, and pirates. Piracy was always a factor in the Hellenistic world, so ships' crews had to be ready to defend their cargoes as well as transport them.

Much maritime trade was shipped in large two-handled pottery jars called amphoras, which protected contents from water and rodents. They were easy and cheap to produce, were surprisingly durable, and could easily be reused. Amphoras contained all sorts of goods—wine, olive oil, spices, unguents, dried fish, olives, grapes, salt, and the pine pitch used to caulk ships so that they would not leak. Like modern containers, amphoras often had stamps, inscriptions, or other markings indicating where they were made, where they were going, and what their contents were. These markings and the remains of the amphoras' contents have provided marine archaeologists and historians with much of their information about trade in the Hellenistic world. Amphoras made specifically for wine seem to have been standardized in size and shape so that they could fit on racks in ships, making long-distance shipping of wine cheaper and easier, just as standardized steel containers have made the shipping of breakable wine bottles—and every other commodity—cheaper and easier today.

Both land and sea trade involved enslaved people as well as goods, traveling in all directions. As in classical Greece, war provided captives for slave markets, as did intentional slave raiding and piracy. Enslaved people were taken great distances and were often separated from others from their homeland, as ancient authors cautioned that having too many enslaved people from one area together might encourage them to revolt. Enslaved people were found in the cities and temples of the Hellenistic world; in the shops, fields, armies, and mines; and in the homes of wealthy people. Their price varied depending on their age, sex, health, and skill level, and also on market conditions. Large-scale warfare increased the number of people who could be enslaved, so their price went down; during periods of relative peace, fewer people were enslaved through conquest, so their price went up.

How did religion, philosophy, and the arts reflect and shape Hellenistic life?

The mixing of peoples in the Hellenistic era influenced religion, philosophy, and the arts. The Hellenistic kings built temples to the old Olympian gods and promoted rituals and ceremonies like those in earlier Greek cities, but new deities also gained prominence. More people turned to mystery religions, which blended Greek and non-Greek elements.

Others turned to practical philosophies that provided advice on how an individual should live a good life. Themes of individualism emerged in Hellenistic art and literature as well.

Religion and Magic

When Hellenistic kings founded cities, they also built temples, staffed by priests and supported by taxes, for the Olympian gods of Greece. The transplanted religions, like those in Greece itself, sponsored literary, musical, and athletic contests, which were staged in beautiful surroundings among impressive new Greek-style buildings. These festivities offered bright and lively entertainment, both intellectual and physical. They fostered Greek culture and traditional sports and were attractive to socially aspiring individuals who adopted Greek culture.

Along with the traditional Olympian gods, Greeks and non-Greeks in the Hellenistic world also honored and worshipped deities that had not been important in the Hellenic period or that were a blend of imported Greek and local gods and goddesses. Tyche (TIGH-kee), for example, the goddess and personification of luck, fate, chance, and fortune, became increasingly prominent during the chaotic years following Alexander's death. Contemporaries commented that when no other cause could be found for an event, Tyche was responsible. Temples to her were built in major cities of the eastern Mediterranean, including Antioch and Alexandria, and her image was depicted on coins and bas-reliefs.

Tyche could be blamed for bad things that happened, but Hellenistic people did not simply give in to fate. Instead they honored Tyche with public rituals and more-private ceremonies, and they also turned to professionals who offered spells for various purposes. We generally make a distinction between

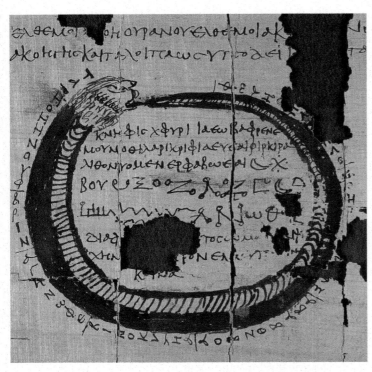

Hellenistic Magical Text   This text, written in Greek and Egyptian on papyrus, presents a magical incantation surrounded by a lion-headed snake. Both Hellenic and Hellenistic Greeks sought to know the future through various means of divination and to control the future through rituals and formulas that called on spirits and gods. (Papyrus 121 f.3r/British Library, London, UK/© British Library Board. All Rights Reserved./Bridgeman Images)

religion and magic, but for Greeks there was not a clear line. Thus they would write spells using both ordinary Greek words and special "magical" language known only to the gods, often instructing those who purchased them to carry out specific actions to accompany their words. Thousands of such spells survive, many of which are curse tables, intended to bring bad luck to a political, business, or athletic rival; or binding spells, meant to force a person to do something against his or her will. These binding spells included hundreds intended to make another person love the petitioner. They often invoke a large number of deities to assist the petitioner, reflecting the mixture of gods that was common in Hellenistic society. (See "Evaluating Written Evidence: A Hellenistic Spell of Attraction," page 98.)

Hellenistic kings generally did not suppress existing religious practices. Some kings limited the power of existing priesthoods, but they also subsidized them with public money. Priests continued to carry out the rituals that they always had, perhaps now adding the name *Zeus* to that of the local deity or composing their hymns in Greek.

Some Hellenistic kings intentionally sponsored new deities that mixed Egyptian and Greek elements. When Ptolemy I Soter established the Ptolemaic dynasty in Egypt, he thought that a new god was needed who would appeal to both Greeks and Egyptians. Working together, an Egyptian priest and a Greek priest combined elements of the Egyptian god Osiris (god of the afterlife) with aspects of the Greek gods Zeus, Hades (god of the underworld), and Asclepius (god of medicine) to create a new god, Serapis. Like Osiris, Serapis came to be regarded as the judge of souls, who rewarded virtuous and righteous people with eternal life. Like Asclepius, he was also a god of healing. Ptolemy I's successors made Serapis the protector and patron of Alexandria and built a huge temple in the god's honor in the city. His worship spread as intentional government policy, and he was eventually adopted by Romans as well, who blended him with their own chief god, Jupiter.

Many people were attracted to mystery religions, so called because at the center of each was an inexplicable event that brought union with a god and was not to be divulged to anyone not initiated into the religions. Mystery religions incorporated aspects of both Greek and non-Greek religions and provided an element of personal control in an unstable world by claiming to save their adherents from the worst that fate could do. Most taught that by the rites of initiation, in which the secrets of the religion were shared, devotees became united with a deity who had also died and risen from the dead. The sacrifice of the god and his victory over death saved the devotee from eternal death. Similarly, mystery religions demanded a period of preparation in which the converts strove to become pure and holy,

that is, to live by the religion's precepts. Once aspirants had prepared themselves, they went through the initiation, usually a ritual of great emotional intensity symbolizing the entry into a new life.

The Egyptian cult of Isis became the most widespread of the mystery religions in the Hellenistic world, and later it spread to Rome. Isis herself had not died and been reborn, but instead had brought her husband Osiris (now merged with Serapis) back to life (see "Egyptian Religion" in Chapter 1). Some of her followers believed she would provide them with a

Isis and Horus In this small statue from Egypt, the goddess Isis is shown suckling her son Horus. Worship of Isis spread throughout the Hellenistic world; her followers believed that Isis offered them life after death, just as she had brought Horus's father, Osiris, back to life. (Musée du Louvre, Paris, France/Peter Willi/Bridgeman Images)

A Hellenistic Spell of Attraction

Spells that have survived from the Hellenistic world include hundreds that are intended to make another person love the petitioner. Most of these are heterosexual, but a few involve men seeking men or women seeking women. This spell, inscribed on a lead tablet, is directed toward Anubis, the Egyptian dog-headed god of the underworld, and mentions a number of Egyptian and Greek deities associated with the underworld. Through this spell a woman named Sophia seeks to attract a woman named Gorgonia, although the spell itself is formulaic and was most likely written by a professional.

Fundament of the gloomy darkness, jagged-toothed dog, covered with coiling snakes, turning three heads, traveler in the recesses of the underworld, come, spirit-driver, with the Erinyes [or Furies, Greek goddesses of vengeance, often shown with snake hair and whips], savage with their stinging whips; holy serpents, maenads [frenzied female followers of Dionysus], frightful maidens, come to my wroth incantations. Before I persuade by force this one and you, render him immediately a fire-breathing daemon. Listen and do everything quickly, in no way opposing me in the performance of this action; for you are the governors of the earth. . . . By means of this corpse-daemon inflame the heart, the liver [which people also saw as a location of emotions], the spirit of Gorgonia, whom Nilogenia bore, with love and affection for Sophia, whom Isara bore. Constrain Gorgonia,

whom Nilogenia bore, to cast herself into the bath-house for the sake of Sophia, whom Isara bore; and you, become a bath-woman.* Burn, set on fire, inflame her soul, heart, liver, spirit with love for Sophia, whom Isara bore. Drive Gorgonia, whom Nilogenia bore, drive her, torment her body night and day, force her to rush forth from every place and every house, loving Sophia, whom Isara bore, she, surrendered like a slave, giving herself and all her possessions to her, because this is the will and command of the great god. . . . Blessed lord of the immortals, holding the scepters of Tartaros and of terrible, fearful Styx (?) and of life-robbing Lethe, the hair of Kerberos trembles in fear of you, you crack the loud whips of the Erinyes; the couch of Persephone delights you, when you go to the longed bed, whether you be the immortal Serapis, whom the universe fears, whether you be Osiris, star of the land of Egypt; your messenger is the all-wise boy; yours is Anubis, the pious herald of the dead. Come hither, fulfill my wishes, because I summon you by these secret symbols.

EVALUATE THE EVIDENCE

1. In the spell, what feelings does Sophia direct Anubis to create in Gorgonia, and what behavior is the expected result of these feelings?
2. What aspects of this spell appear distinctively Hellenistic? What aspects fit with modern understandings of sexual attraction?

*Public baths were common in Hellenistic and Roman society as places where people went for recreation and relaxation as well as cleansing, much like today's spas. Here Sophia wants Gorgonia to meet her in a public bath, and Anubis wants to change himself into a female bath attendant so he can cast his spell on her more easily.

Source: Bernadette J. Brooten, *Love Between Women: Early Christian Responses to Female Homoeroticism* (Chicago: University of Chicago Press, 1996), pp. 83–87.

better afterlife, while others worshipped Isis more for benefits she might offer in *this* life: fertility in crops and animals, protection during childbirth, safety during voyages. People saw her as embodying exotic ancient wisdom, just as some people today believe that Egyptian *ankh* symbols or pyramid shapes bring good luck or have power. Her priests asserted that she had bestowed on humanity the gift of civilization and founded law and literature. The worship of Isis was spread by merchants and others moving around the Mediterranean, with temples springing up in ports and other cities, offering her devotees a community as well as a place of worship.

Hellenism and the Jews

Jews in Hellenistic cities were generally treated the same as any other non-Greek group. At first they were seen as resident aliens. As they grew more numerous, they received permission to form a political corporation, a *politeuma* (pah-lih-TOO-mah), which gave them a great deal of autonomy. The Jewish politeuma, like the rest of the Hellenistic city, was expected to obey the king's commands, but there was virtually no royal interference with the Jewish religion. The Seleucid king Antiochus III (ca. 242–187 B.C.E.), for instance, recognized that most Jews were loyal subjects, and in his efforts to solidify his empire he endorsed their religious customs and ensured their autonomy.

Antiochus IV Epiphanes (r. 175–ca. 164 B.C.E.) broke with this pattern. He expanded the Seleucid kingdom and nearly conquered Egypt, but while he was there a revolt broke out in Judaea, led by Jews who opposed the Hellenized Jewish leader he had designated for them. Antiochus attacked Jerusalem, killing many, and restored his leader. According to Hebrew Scripture, he then banned Jewish practices and worship, ordered copies of the Torah burned, and set up altars to the Greek gods in Jewish temples. This action sparked a widespread Jewish revolt that began in 166 B.C.E., called the Revolt of the Maccabees after the name of one of its leaders. Using guerrilla tactics, the Maccabees fought Syrian troops who were fighting under Seleucid commanders, retook Jerusalem, and set up a semi-independent state in 164 B.C.E. This state lasted for about a century, until it was conquered by the Romans. (The rededication of the temple in Jerusalem after the Maccabee victory is celebrated in the Jewish holiday of Hanukkah.)

Jews living in Hellenistic cities often embraced many aspects of Hellenism. The Revolt of the Maccabees is seen by some historians, in fact, as primarily a dispute between Hellenized Jews and those who wanted to retain traditional practices. So many Jews learned Greek, especially in Alexandria, that the Hebrew Bible was translated into Greek and services in the synagogue there came to be conducted in Greek. Jews often took Greek names, participated in Greek political institutions such as citizens' assemblies, adopted Greek practice by forming their own trade associations, and put inscriptions on graves as the Greeks did. Some Jews were given the right to become full citizens of Hellenistic cities, although relatively few appear to have exercised that right. Citizenship would have allowed them to vote in the assembly and serve as magistrates, but it would also have obliged them to worship the gods of the city — a practice few Jews chose to follow.

Philosophy and the People

Philosophy during the Hellenic period was the exclusive province of the wealthy and educated, for only they had leisure enough to pursue philosophical studies (see "The Flowering of Philosophy" in Chapter 3). During the Hellenistic period, however, although philosophy was still directed toward the educated elite, it came to touch the lives of more men and women than ever before. There were several reasons for this development. First, much of Hellenistic life, especially in the new cities of the East, seemed unstable and without venerable traditions to the Greeks who migrated to these cities. Greeks were far more mobile than they had ever been before, but their very mobility left them feeling uprooted. Second, traditional religions had declined and there was a growing belief that one could do relatively little to change one's fate. One could honor Tyche, the goddess of fortune, through rituals in the hope that she would be kind, but to protect against the worst that Tyche could do, many Greeks also looked to philosophy. Philosophers themselves became much more numerous, and several new schools of philosophical thought caught the minds and hearts of many contemporary Greeks and some non-Greeks.

One of these was **Epicureanism** (eh-pih-kyou-REE-uh-nih-zuhm), a practical philosophy of serenity in an often-tumultuous world. Epicurus (eh-pih-KYOUR-uhs) (340–270 B.C.E.) used observation and logic to study the world, and also to examine the human condition (see "Individuals in Society: Epicurus," page 100). He decided that the principal goods of human life were contentment and pleasure, which he defined as the absence of pain, fear, and suffering.

Epicurus taught that individuals could most easily attain peace and serenity by ignoring politics and the rest of the outside world and looking into their personal feelings and reactions. The Epicureans were content to live under a democracy, oligarchy, monarchy, or any other form of government, and they never speculated about the ideal state.

Zeno (335–262 B.C.E.), a philosopher from Cyprus, advanced a different concept of human beings and the universe. Zeno first came to Athens to form his own school, the Stoa, named after the covered walkways where he preferred to teach, and his philosophy, **Stoicism** (STOH-uh-sih-zuhm), in turn, came to be named for his school. Zeno and his followers considered nature an expression of divine will; in their view people could be happy only when living in accordance with nature.

■ **Epicureanism** A system of philosophy based on the teachings of Epicurus, who viewed a life of contentment, free from fear and suffering, as the greatest good.

■ **Stoicism** A philosophy, based on the ideas of Zeno, that people could be happy only when living in accordance with nature and accepting whatever happened.

INDIVIDUALS IN SOCIETY

Epicurus

Epicurus was an Athenian philosopher who, like Aristotle, thought that the senses, observation, and logic provided true knowledge about the world, in contrast to Plato's notion that knowledge comes from contemplating ideal forms. Like the Pre-Socratic philosopher Democritus, Epicurus thought that the world was infinite, made up of small pieces of matter that move in space and that determine the events of the world. (For both Plato and Democritus, see "The Flowering of Philosophy" in Chapter 3.) Although he did not deny the existence of the gods, Epicurus taught that they had no effect on human life.

For Epicurus, the purpose of philosophy was to help people have a life free of pain and suffering, a tranquil, peaceful state he termed *ataraxia* that would lead to happiness, *eudaimonia* in Greek. People should behave morally, he thought, not because they feared death or punishment in the afterlife, but because acting badly would make them feel guilty and detract from happiness. By encouraging the pursuit of pleasure, he was not advocating drunken revels or sexual excess, which he thought caused pain, but moderation in food, clothing, and shelter. Epicureanism taught its followers to ignore politics and public issues, for politics led to tumult, which would disturb the desired sense of peace.

Epicurus thought that a life surrounded by friends was the best type of life, and he sought to achieve this in a school and intellectual community he established in Athens, called the Garden. In sharp contrast to Plato, Epicurus is reported to have allowed enslaved men and even women to participate in the discussions at the Garden. *Ataraxia* and *eudaimonia* were ideals to which anyone could aspire, no matter what their social standing.

The many formal writings of Epicurus survive only in fragments, but the third-century-C.E. biographer Diogenes Laertes quotes several letters in their entirety, including one written at the end of Epicurus's life, when he apparently suffered from kidney stones:

> I have written this letter to you on a happy day to me, which is also the last day of my life. For I have been attacked by a painful inability to urinate, and also dysentery, so violent that nothing can be added to the violence of my sufferings. But the cheerfulness of my mind, which

comes from the recollection of all my philosophical contemplation, counterbalances all these afflictions.... And I beg you to take care of the children of Metrodorus [another Epicurean philosopher], in a manner worthy of the devotion shown by the young man to me, and to philosophy.*

Epicureanism was popular in both Greece and Rome, though many Romans opposed it as contrary to their notions of public duty. It largely died out with the coming of Christianity, and "epicurean" came to mean someone who loves fancy food and sensual pleasures, a meaning it still has. In the seventeenth century some European philosophers became interested in the actual teachings of Epicurus again, and later U.S. thinkers did as well. Late in life, Thomas Jefferson even declared, "I too am an Epicurean. I consider the genuine (not imputed) doctrines of Epicurus as containing everything rational in moral philosophy which Greece and Rome have left us."

Today a huge trove of papyrus scrolls, carbonized and buried in the library of a luxurious villa at Herculaneum when the volcano Vesuvius exploded in 79 C.E., is known to contain major Epicurean works. Unrolling the scrolls would destroy them, so scientists are engaged in a complex process of virtual enrolling and decoding, using a sensitive imaging technique called X-ray phase-contrast tomography, to reveal letters hidden in the papyri. So far only a few individual letters have been identified from what often look like lumps of coal, but the researchers are optimistic that this virtual unwrapping will eventually work and could then be applied to other fragile texts.

QUESTIONS FOR ANALYSIS

1. How are Epicurus's ideas reflected in the quotation from the letter written while he was dying? In the community he established in the Garden?
2. In the U.S. Declaration of Independence, Thomas Jefferson wrote that unalienable rights given to all humans include "life, liberty, and the pursuit of happiness." How does this famous phrase express Epicurean ideas?

*Diogenes Laertius, *Lives of Eminent Philosophers* 10.22, trans. C. D. Yonge, at Attalus (http://www.attalus.org/old/diogenes10a.html#22).

Carbonized papyri found at Herculaneum. Many scrolls found there are thought to contain works by Epicurus.
(Antonio Masiello/Getty Images)

They stressed the unity of humans and the universe, stating that all people were obliged to help one another.

Unlike the Epicureans, the Stoics taught that people should participate in politics and worldly affairs. Yet this idea never led to the belief that individuals should try to change the order of things. The Stoics used the image of an actor in a play: the Stoic plays an assigned part but never tries to change the play. Like the Epicureans, they were indifferent to specific political forms. They believed that people should do their duty to the state in which they found themselves. To the Stoics, the important question was not whether they achieved anything, but whether they lived virtuous lives. The patient self-control and fortitude that the Stoics advocated made Stoicism a popular philosophy among the Romans later, and gave rise to the modern adjective *stoic* to convey these virtues.

The Stoics' most significant intellectual achievement was the creation of the concept of **natural law**. They concluded that because all people were kindred, partook of divine reason, and were in harmony with the universe, one law governed them all. This law was a part of the natural order of life and applicable everywhere, not something created by individual states or rulers. Natural law was thus an abstract matter of ethics for the Stoics rather than something with direct application to the violent and chaotic world of Hellenistic political life, although philosophers thousands of years later would use it to assess and even urge revolt against governments they thought were acting against it.

Art and Drama

Individualistic and individualized themes emerged in Hellenistic art and literature as well as in philosophy. Sculptors looked to the works of the classical period, such as the reliefs and statuary on the Athenian Acropolis, for their models in terms of composition, but then created works that showed powerful emotions and straining muscles. In contrast to the classical preference for the perfect human form, the artists and the people who bought their works wanted art that showed real people, including those suffering from trauma, disease, and the physical problems that came with aging. Hellenistic art was more naturalistic than Hellenic art — portraying the poor, old, and ugly as well as the young and beautiful.

As had Athens in the classical period, Hellenistic cities offered theater performances to their residents, paid for by the government. People tended to prefer revivals of the tragedies of Aeschylus,

Boxer at Rest　This magnificent life-size bronze sculpture, made most likely between the fourth and second centuries B.C.E. and discovered buried in Rome in 1885, portrays a boxer just after a bout. Naked except for his leather hand wraps, he has bruises and cuts on his face that have dripped blood (represented by inlaid copper on his thigh and arm), a broken nose and cauliflower ears from previous fights, and sunken lips, suggesting knocked-out teeth. Hellenistic art moved away from the earlier preference for idealized perfection to show more realistic human bodies and the effects of life experiences on them. (Jürgen Raible/akg-images/Newscom)

Sophocles, and Euripides (see "Athenian Arts in the Age of Pericles" in Chapter 3) over newly written tragic works, but in comedy they wanted new material. This was provided by Menander (ca. 342–291 B.C.E.), whose more than one hundred comedies poked fun at current philosophies and social trends, including love, luck, money, and marriage. Menander's comedies tended to be less political than those of Aristophanes, but they still commented on the ruler cults developed by Hellenistic kings, the dangers of the new professionalized mercenary armies to older values, and the conspicuous consumption of the newly rich.

■ **natural law**　A Stoic concept that a single law that was part of the natural order of life governed all people.

How did science and medicine serve the needs of Hellenistic society?

In the scholarly realm, Hellenistic thinkers made advances in mathematics, astronomy, and mechanical design. Physicians used observation and dissection to better understand the way the human body works and to develop treatments for disease. Many of these developments occurred in Alexandria, where the Ptolemies did much to make the city an intellectual, cultural, and scientific center.

Science

The main advances in Hellenistic science came in astronomy, geography, and mechanics. The most notable of the Hellenistic astronomers was Aristarchus (a-ruh-STAHR-kuhs) of Samos (ca. 310–230 B.C.E.). Aristarchus concluded that the sun is far larger than the earth and that the stars are enormously distant from the earth. He argued against the commonsense observation, which Aristotle had supported, that the earth was the center of the universe. Instead, Aristarchus developed the heliocentric theory — that the earth and planets revolve around the sun. His theory was discussed for several centuries, but it was later forgotten when another influential astronomer working in Alexandria, Claudius Ptolemy (ca. 90–ca. 168 C.E.) — probably no relation to the ruling Ptolemies, as the name was a common one — returned to an earth-centered universe. Aristarchus's heliocentric theory was resurrected in the sixteenth century C.E. by the brilliant Polish astronomer Nicolaus Copernicus.

In geometry Hellenistic thinkers discovered little that was new, but Euclid (YOU-kluhd) (ca. 300 B.C.E.), a mathematician who lived in Alexandria, compiled a valuable textbook of existing knowledge. His *Elements of Geometry* rapidly became the standard introduction to geometry. Generations of students from the Hellenistic period to the twentieth century learned the essentials of geometry from it.

The greatest thinker of the Hellenistic period was Archimedes (ahr-keh-MEED-eez) (ca. 287–212 B.C.E.), a native of Syracuse who was interested in nearly everything. A clever inventor, he devised a water screw to draw water from a lower to a higher level, a compound pulley to lift heavy weights, and several war machines. His chief interest, however, lay in pure mathematics. He founded the science of hydrostatics (the study of fluids at rest) and discovered the principle that the volume of a solid floating in a liquid is equal to the volume of the liquid displaced by the solid.

Archimedes was willing to share his work with others, among them Eratosthenes (ehr-uh-TAHS-thuh-neez) (285–ca. 204 B.C.E.). Like Archimedes, he was a man of almost universal interests. From his native Cyrene in North Africa, Eratosthenes traveled to Athens, where he studied philosophy and mathematics. He refused to join any of the philosophical schools, for he was interested in too many things to follow any particular dogma. Around 245 B.C.E. King Ptolemy III invited Eratosthenes to Alexandria and made him the head of the library there. Eratosthenes continued his mathematical work and by letter struck up a friendship with Archimedes.

Eratosthenes used mathematics to further the geographical studies for which he is most famous. He concluded that the earth was a spherical globe and calculated the circumference of the earth geometrically, estimating it as about 24,675 miles. He was not wrong by much: the earth is actually 24,860 miles in circumference. He drew a map of the earth and discussed the shapes and sizes of land and ocean and the irregularities of the earth's surface. His idea that the earth was divided into large landmasses influenced other geographers and later shaped ordinary people's understanding of the world as well. Using geographical information gained by Alexander the Great's scientists, Eratosthenes declared that to get to India, a ship could sail around Africa or even sail directly westward, an idea that would not be tested until the end of the fifteenth century.

Other Greek geographers also turned their attention southward to Africa. During this period the people of the Mediterranean learned of the climate and customs of Ethiopia and gleaned some information about sub-Saharan Africa from Greek sailors and merchants who had traveled there. Geographers incorporated these travelers' reports into their more theoretical works.

Hellenistic science was often used for purposes of war, as Hellenistic rulers intent on expanding their territories were willing to invest huge amounts of money to design and build offensive weapons and walls and defensive weapons to protect against invading armies. Theories of mechanics were used to build machines that revolutionized warfare. Fully realizing the practical possibilities of the first effective artillery in Western history, Philip of Macedonia had introduced the machines to the broader world in the middle of the fourth century B.C.E. The catapult became the first and most widely used artillery piece, shooting ever-larger projectiles. Generals soon realized that they could also hurl burning bundles over the walls to start fires in the city. As the Assyrians had earlier, engineers built siege towers, large wooden structures that served as artillery platforms, and put them on wheels so that soldiers could roll them up to a town's walls. Once there, archers stationed on top of the siege towers swept the enemy's ramparts with arrows, while other soldiers manning catapults added missile fire. As soon as the walls were cleared, soldiers from the siege towers swept over the enemy's ramparts and into the city. To augment the siege towers, generals added battering rams that consisted of long, stout shafts housed in reinforced shells. Inside the shell the crew pushed the ram up to the wall and then heaved the shaft against the wall. Rams proved even more effective than catapults in bringing down large portions of walls.

Diodorus provided a description of these machines in his discussion of Philip's attack on the city of Perinthos in 340 B.C.E.:

> Philip launched a siege of Perinthos, advancing engines to the city and assaulting the walls in relays day after day. He built towers 120 feet tall that rose far above the towers of Perinthos. From their superior height he kept wearing down the besieged. He mined under the wall and also rocked it with battering-rams until he threw down a large section of it. The Perinthians fought stoutly and threw up a second wall. Philip rained down great destruction through his many and various arrow-shooting catapults. . . . Philip continually battered the walls with his rams and made breaches in them. With his arrow-firing catapults clearing the ramparts of defenders, he sent his soldiers in through the breaches in tight formation. He attacked with scaling-ladders the parts of the walls that had been cleared.[5]

For the Perinthians this grim story had a happy ending when their allies arrived to lift the siege, but many cities were successfully besieged and conquered with the new machines. Over time, Hellenistic generals built larger, more complex, and more effective machines. The earliest catapults could shoot only large arrows and small stones. By the time Alexander the Great besieged Tyre in 332 B.C.E., his catapults could throw stones big enough to knock down city walls.

If these new engines made waging war more efficient, they also added to the misery of the people, as war often directly involved the populations of cities. As it had in Periclean Athens (see Chapter 3), war often contributed to the spread of disease, and battlefields gave surgeons and physicians plenty of opportunities to test their ideas about how the human body would best heal.

Medicine

Doctors as well as scientists combined observation with theory during the Hellenistic period. (See "Thinking Like a Historian: Hellenistic Medicine," page 104.) They studied the writings attributed to Hippocrates (see Chapter 3) and generally accepted his theory of the four humors, but they also approached the study of medicine in a systematic, scientific fashion. The physician Herophilus (ca. 335–280 B.C.E.), for example, who lived in Alexandria, was the first to accurately describe

the nervous system, and he differentiated between nerves and blood vessels and between motor and sensory nerves. Herophilus also closely studied the brain, which he considered the center of intelligence, and discerned the cerebrum and cerebellum. His younger contemporary Erasistratus (ca. 304–250 B.C.E.) also conducted research on the brain and nervous system and improved on Herophilus's work. To learn more about human anatomy, Herophilus and Erasistratus dissected human cadavers while their students watched. Human dissection was seen as unacceptable in most parts of the Hellenistic world, so they were probably the only scientists in antiquity to dissect human bodies, although animal dissection became very common in the Roman period. The story later spread that they had dissected living criminals provided for them by the Ptolemaic kings of Egypt, but this may have just been a legend. They wrote works on various medical and anatomical topics, but only the titles and a few fragments quoted by later authors survive.

Because Herophilus and Erasistratus followed the teachings of Hippocrates, later writers on medicine labeled them "Dogmatists" or the "Dogmatic school," from the Greek word *dogma*, or philosophical idea. Along with their hands-on study of the human body, the Dogmatists also speculated about the nature of disease and argued that there were sometimes hidden causes for illness. Opposing them was an "Empiric school" begun by a student of Herophilus; these doctors held observation and experiment to be the only way to advance medical knowledge and viewed the search for hidden causes as useless. Later Greek and Roman physicians sometimes identified themselves with one or the other of these ways of thinking, but the labels were also sometimes simply used as insults to dismiss the ideas of a rival.

Whether undertaken by Dogmatists or Empiricists, medical study did not lead to effective cures for the infectious diseases that were the leading cause of death for most people, however, and people used a variety of ways to attempt to combat illness. Medicines prescribed by physicians or prepared at home often included natural products blended with materials understood to work magically. One treatment for fever, for example, was the liver of a cat killed when the moon was waning and preserved in salt. People also invoked Asclepius, the god of medicine, in healing rituals, or focused on other deities who were understood to have power over specific illnesses. They paid specialists to devise spells that would cure them or prevent them from becoming ill in the first place (see "Evaluating Written Evidence: A Hellenistic Spell of Attraction," page 98). Women in childbirth gathered their female friends and relatives around them, and in larger cities they could also hire experienced midwives who knew how to decrease pain and assist in the birthing process if something went wrong. People in the Hellenistic world may have thought that fate determined what would happen, but they also actively sought to make their lives longer and healthier.

Hellenistic Medicine

Hellenistic medical specialists based their ideas about the body and their handling of illness on observation, and also on the writings ascribed to the Greek physician Hippocrates and his followers. These were copied, recopied, edited, and expanded over the centuries, so it is impossible to say who wrote any specific work, but they contain ideas that were widely shared. How did Hellenistic physicians view the healthy body, and what did they recommend to maintain good health and treat sickness?

1 **Hippocratic writings: *On the Nature of Man.*** This treatise discusses the structure of the human body and the causes of disease.

〜 The human body contains blood, phlegm, yellow bile and black bile. These are the things that make up its constitution and cause its pains and health. Health is primarily that state in which these constituent substances are in the correct proportion to each other, both in strength and quantity, and are well mixed. Pain occurs when one of the substances presents either a deficiency or an excess, or is separated in the body and not mixed with the others. . . .

Now the quantity of the phlegm in the body increases in winter because it is that bodily substance most in keeping with the winter, seeing that it is the coldest. . . . The following signs show that winter fills the body with phlegm: people spit and blow from their noses the most phlegmatic mucus in winter; swellings become white especially at that season and other diseases show phlegmatic signs. . . .

And just as the year is governed at one time by winter, then by spring, then by summer, and then by autumn; so at one time in the body phlegm predominates, at another time blood, at another time yellow bile and this is followed by a preponderance of black bile. In these circumstances it follows that the diseases which increase in winter should decrease in summer and vice versa. . . .

Some diseases are produced by the manner of life that is followed; others by the life-giving air that we breathe. That there are these two types must be demonstrated in the following way. When a large number of people all catch the same disease at the same time, the cause must be ascribed to something common to all and which they all use; in other words to what they all breathe. In such a disease, it is obvious that individual bodily habits cannot be responsible because the malady attacks one after another, young and old, men and women alike.

2 **Hippocratic writings: *Prognosis.*** This treatise provides guidance about how to examine a patient and determine if a disease will be fatal or not.

〜 It seems to be highly desirable that a physician pay much attention to prognosis. If he is able to tell his patients when he visits them not only about their past and present symptoms, but also to tell them what is going to happen, as well as to fill in the details they have omitted, he will increase his reputation as a medical practitioner and people will have no qualms in putting themselves in his care. . . .

The signs to watch for in acute diseases are as follows: First, study the patient's face; whether it has a healthy look and in particular whether it is exactly as it normally is. If the patient's normal appearance is preserved, this is best; just as the more abnormal it is, the worse it is. . . .

Rapid breathing indicates either distress or inflammation of the organs above the diaphragm. Deep breaths taken at long intervals are a sign of delirium. If the expired air from the mouth and nostrils is cold, death is close at hand. . . .

The most helpful kind of vomiting is that in which the matter consists of phlegm and bile, as well-mixed as possible, and is neither thick nor particularly great in quantity. If it is not well-mixed, it is less good. The vomiting of dark green, livid or dark material, no matter which of these colours, must be considered a bad sign.

In all disease of the lungs, running at the nose and sneezing is bad.

ANALYZING THE EVIDENCE

1. In Source 1, what are the basic substances in the body, and how do they create pain and illness? How is health shaped by the seasons and by people's actions? By things in the air (which we would call germs, though the Greeks thought of them as poisons)?
2. In Source 2, what does the author suggest that a physician pay attention to when diagnosing illness, and why is prognosis important? How does the technique of the physician in Source 3 fit with this advice?
3. How does the author of Source 4 suggest that infections in the pleural cavity be handled?
4. What does the author of Source 5 recommend for people who want to stay healthy, and how does this advice differ for different types of individuals?
5. Taking the sources together, what do these authors see as the most important role of physicians in preventing and treating illness? What do they see as the most important role of people themselves in maintaining their own health?

3 **Physician with young patient.** This plaster cast from ca. 350 B.C.E. shows a physician examining a child, while Asclepius, the god of healing, observes.

(Hulton Archive/Getty Images)

4 **Hippocratic writings: *Diseases*.** In this section of a long treatise, the author discusses treatment of people who have pus in the pleural cavity surrounding the lungs, which today is often linked with emphysema.

First cut the skin between the ribs with a knife with a rounded blade. Then take a sharp-pointed knife wrapped in a strip of cloth with its tip exposed a thumb-nail's length and make an incision. Next, having drained away as much pus as seems appropriate, drain the wound with a drain of raw linen, attached to a cord. Let out the pus once a day. On the tenth day, after having let out all the pus, drain the wound with a piece of fine linen. Then inject warm wine and oil through a small tube, so that the lung accustomed to being moistened by the pus might not suddenly be dried out. Let out the morning's infusion toward evening, and the evening one in the morning. When the pus becomes thick like water, sticky to the finger when touched, and scanty, insert a hollow tin drainage tube. When the [pleural] cavity is completely drained, gradually cut the drain shorter, and allow the wound to heal until you finally take out the drain.

5 **Hippocratic writings: *A Regimen for Health*.** In this treatise the author provides suggestions for preventing illness.

People with a fleshy, soft, or ruddy appearance are best kept on a dry diet for the greater part of the year as they are constitutionally moist. Those with firm and tight-drawn skins, and those with tawny and dark complexions should keep to a diet containing plenty of fluids most of the time, as such people are naturally dry. The softest and most moist diets suit young bodies best as at that age the body is dry and has set firm. Older people should take a drier diet most of the time, for at that age bodies are moist, soft, and cold. Diets then must be conditioned by age, the time of year, habit, country and constitution. They should be opposite in character to the prevailing climate, whether winter or summer. Such is the best road to health. . . .

Fat people who want to reduce should take their exercise on an empty stomach and sit down to their food out of breath. . . . [T]hey should take only one meal a day, go without baths, sleep on hard beds and walk about with as little clothing as may be. Thin people who want to get fat should do exactly the opposite. . . . A wise man ought to realize that health is his most valuable possession and learn how to treat his illnesses by his own judgment.

PUTTING IT ALL TOGETHER

Using the sources above, along with what you have learned in class and in the chapters in this book, write a short essay that analyzes ideas about health and illness in the Hellenistic world, and the treatments that resulted from these ideas. What characterized a healthy body, and how was good health to be regained in the case of illness? Many of the ideas and treatments may seem strange, given how we understand the body today, but do any sound familiar?

Sources: (1) *Hippocratic Writings*, ed. G. E. R. Lloyd, trans. J. Chadwick and W. N. Mann (Harmondsworth, U.K.: Penguin, 1983), pp. 262, 264; (2) *Hippocratic Writings*, pp. 170–171, 172, 177; (4) James Longrigg, *Greek Medicine: From the Heroic to the Hellenistic Age: A Source Book* (London: Duckworth, 1998), p. 139; (5) *Hippocratic Writings*, p. 274.

NOTES

1. Ahmad Hasan Dani et al., *History of Civilizations of Central Asia* (Paris: UNESCO, 1992), p. 107.
2. Quoted in W. W. Tarn and G. T. Griffith, *Hellenistic Civilizations*, 3d ed. (Cleveland and New York: Meridian Books, 1961), p. 199.

3. Diodorus of Sicily, *Biblioteca historica* 1.80–36, Loeb Classical Library Volume 279, with an English translation by C. H. Oldfather (Cambridge, Mass.: Harvard University Press, 1933), pp. 275, 277.
4. Diodorus of Sicily, *Biblioteca historica* 3.12.1–3.
5. Diodorus of Sicily, *Biblioteca historica* 3.12.2–3.

 LOOKING BACK LOOKING AHEAD

The conquests of Philip and Alexander broadened Greek and Macedonian horizons, but probably not in ways that they had intended. The empire that they created lasted only briefly, but the Hellenistic culture that developed afterwards took Greeks even beyond the borders of Alexander's huge empire as conquerors, merchants, artists, and sailors. Throughout the Mediterranean and western Asia, they interacted with Egyptians, Persians, Bactrians, Jews, and countless others, influencing them and being shaped in return.

The most deeply Hellenized non-Greek people were, ironically, those who conquered much of what had been Alexander's empire: the Romans. The Romans derived their alphabet from the Greek alphabet, though they changed the letters somewhat. Roman statuary was modeled on Greek statuary and was often, in fact, made by Greek sculptors, who found ready customers among wealthy Romans. Furthermore, the major Roman gods and goddesses were largely the same as the Greek ones, though they had different names. Although the Romans did not seem to have been particularly interested in the speculative philosophy of Socrates and Plato, they were drawn to the more practical philosophies of the Epicureans and Stoics. And like the Hellenistic Greeks, many Romans turned from traditional religions to mystery religions that offered secret knowledge and promised eternal life. Among these was Christianity, a new religion that grew in the Roman Empire and whose most important early advocate was Paul of Tarsus, a well-educated Hellenized Jew who wrote in Greek. Significant aspects of Greek culture thus lasted long after the Hellenistic monarchies and even the Roman Empire were gone, shaping all subsequent societies in the Mediterranean and Near East.

Make Connections

Think about the larger developments and continuities within and across chapters.

1. How was Greek society in the Hellenistic era similar to that of the earlier Hellenic era examined in Chapter 3? How was it different? What would you judge to be more significant, the continuities or the changes?

2. Cities had existed in the Tigris and Euphrates Valleys and the Near East long before Alexander's conquests. What would residents of Sumer (Chapter 1), Babylon (Chapters 1 and 2), and Pergamum find unusual about one another's cities? What would seem familiar?

3. How would you compare religion in Egypt in the Old and New Kingdoms (Chapter 1) with religion in Hellenistic Egypt? What provides the best explanation for the differences you have identified?

4 REVIEW & EXPLORE

Identify Key Terms

Identify and explain the significance of each item below.

Ptolemaic dynasty (p. 86)

Antigonid dynasty (p. 87)

Seleucid Empire (p. 87)

Hellenistic (p. 87)

Hellenization (p. 88)

Epicureanism (p. 99)

Stoicism (p. 99)

natural law (p. 101)

Review the Main Ideas

Answer the section heading questions from the chapter.

1. How and why did Alexander the Great create an empire, and how did it evolve? (p. 84)

2. How did Greek ideas and traditions spread to create a Hellenized society? (p. 88)

3. What characterized the Hellenistic economy? (p. 92)

4. How did religion, philosophy, and the arts reflect and shape Hellenistic life? (p. 96)

5. How did science and medicine serve the needs of Hellenistic society? (p. 102)

Suggested Resources

BOOKS

- Adamson, Peter. *Philosophy in the Hellenistic and Roman World.* 2015. A history of philosophy designed for nonspecialists that began life as a series of podcasts.

- Bowden, Hugh. *Mystery Cults of the Ancient World.* 2010. Examines the main mystery religions of the ancient Mediterranean, using artistic and literary evidence.

- Chaniotis, Angelos. *War in the Hellenistic World.* 2005. Covers the wars of this period, the reasons behind them, and how they were waged.

- Connelly, Joan. *Portrait of a Priestess: Women and Ritual in Ancient Greece.* 2009. A survey of the important public roles of priestesses, with many illustrations.

- Errington, R. Malcolm. *A History of the Hellenistic World, 323–30 B.C.* 2008. Easily the best coverage of the period: full, scholarly, and readable.

- Fox, Robin Lane. *The Invention of Medicine: From Homer to Hippocrates.* 2020. Explores real medical case histories to put Greek medicine into its social context.

- Freeman, Philip. *Alexander the Great.* 2010. Designed for general readers, this excellent biography portrays Alexander as both ruthless and cultured.

- Manning, J. G. *The Last Pharaohs: Egypt Under the Ptolemies, 305–30 B.C.* 2009. Examines the impact of the Ptolemies on Egyptian society and the way their state blended Greek and Egyptian elements.

- Waterfield, Robin. *Dividing the Spoils: The War for Alexander the Great's Empire.* 2011. A cultural and political narrative of this turbulent period based on up-to-date research.

MEDIA

- *Ancient Mysteries: The Lost Treasures of the Alexandria Library* (History Channel, 2004). Documentary presenting the building of the library and its collection, the research undertaken there, and the destruction of the library at the hands of a Christian mob in the fourth century C.E.

- *Brought to Life: Exploring the History of Medicine.* Interactive website from the Science Museum in London offering a thematic approach to the past three thousand years in the history of medicine that foregrounds objects and material culture. Includes many items from the ancient Mediterranean. **www.sciencemuseum.org.uk/broughttolife**

- *Infinite Secrets: The Genius of Archimedes* (*Nova*, 2004). Excellent *Nova* special that explores Archimedes's ideas, theories, and writings.

- *In the Footsteps of Alexander the Great* (BBC, 2010). Michael Wood follows Alexander's two-thousand-mile journey from Greece to India in this documentary, tracing his conquests and the meaning these have for the peoples of these areas today.

- *Pothos.* Long-standing user-generated website with articles, debates, a blog, and visual materials about Alexander the Great. **www.pothos.org/content/**

- *Travels through Greco-Roman Antiquity.* A project of the Falvey Memorial Library at Villanova University, this site centers on a map through which users can explore ancient cities and battle sites. Includes descriptions, photographs, and art. **exhibits.library.villanova.edu/ancient-greece**

5

The Rise of Rome

ca. 1000–27 B.C.E.

The Hellenistic monarchies that arose after Alexander's conquests extended eastward and southward from Greece. The Greek colonies that had been established in southern Italy were not part of these monarchies, but culturally they became part of the Hellenistic world. To the north of the Greek city-states in the Italian peninsula, other people built their own societies. Among these were the people who later became the Romans, who settled on hills along the Tiber River in central Italy. Beginning in the sixth century B.C.E., the Romans gradually took over more and more territory in Italy through conquest and annexation. At about the same time, a group of aristocrats revolted against the kings ruling Rome and established a republican government in which the main institution of power was a political assembly, the Senate. Under the direction of the Senate, the Romans continued their political and military expansion, first to all of Italy, then throughout the western Mediterranean basin, and then to areas in the east that had been part of Alexander's empire. As they did, they learned about and incorporated Greek art, literature, philosophy, and religion, but the wars of conquest also led to serious problems that the Senate proved unable to handle.

Roman history is generally divided into three periods: the monarchical period, traditionally dated from 753 B.C.E. to 509 B.C.E., in which the city of Rome was ruled by kings; the republic, traditionally dated from 509 B.C.E. to 27 B.C.E., in which it was ruled by the Senate and expanded its power first to all of Italy and then beyond; and the empire, from 27 B.C.E. to 476 C.E., in which the vast Roman territories were ruled by an emperor. This chapter covers the first two of these periods. The Roman Empire will be discussed in Chapters 6 and 7. ■

CHAPTER PREVIEW

- How did the Romans become the dominant power in Italy?

- What were the key institutions of the Roman Republic?

- How did the Romans build a Mediterranean empire?

- How did expansion affect Roman society and culture?

- What led to the fall of the Roman Republic?

Dining Under a Pergola
In this first-century-B.C.E. mosaic from an enormous temple to the goddess Fortuna at Praeneste near Rome, diners eat and drink under a pergola laden with grapes, while a man poles a small boat. The mosaic portrays an idealized view of life on the Nile River during a flood. On the highest terrace of the temple was an area where people drew lots to predict the future, small inscribed wooden tablets whose message — understood as an oracle from the goddess — was interpreted by a priest. (DEA/S. VANNINI/De Agostini/Getty Images)

How did the Romans become the dominant power in Italy?

The colonies established by Greek poleis (city-states) in the Hellenic era (see "Overseas Expansion" in Chapter 3) included a number along the coast of southern Italy and Sicily. Although Alexander the Great (see Chapter 4) created an empire that stretched from his homeland of Macedonia to India, his conquests did not reach as far as southern Italy and Sicily. Thus the Greek colonies there remained politically independent. They became part of the Hellenistic cultural world, however, and they transmitted much of that culture to people who lived farther north in the Italian peninsula. These people included the Etruscans, who built the first cities north of the Greek colonies, and then the Romans, who eventually came to dominate the peninsula.

The Geography of Italy

The Italian peninsula occupies the center of the Mediterranean basin (Map 5.1). Italian winters are rainy,

MAP 5.1 Roman Italy and the City of Rome, ca. 218 B.C.E. As Rome expanded, it built roads linking major cities and offered various degrees of citizenship to the territories it conquered or with which it made alliances. The territories outlined with a thick line that are separate from the Italian peninsula were added to Roman territory largely as a result of the Punic Wars.

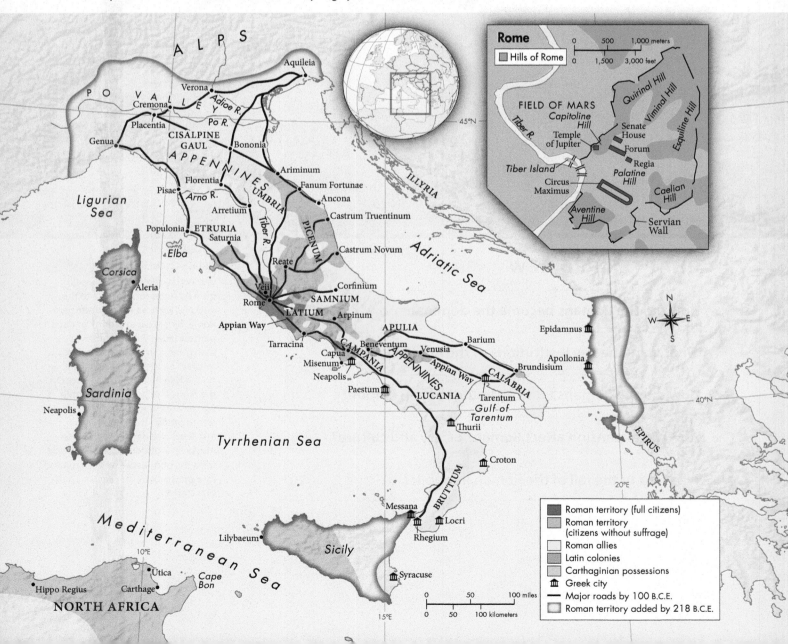

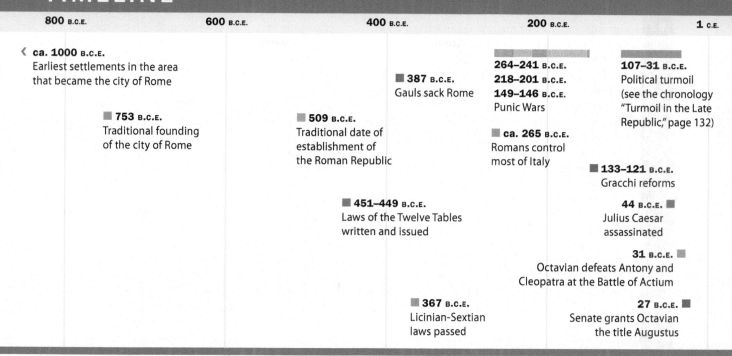

ca. 1000 B.C.E.
Earliest settlements in the area
that became the city of Rome

753 B.C.E.
Traditional founding
of the city of Rome

387 B.C.E.
Gauls sack Rome

509 B.C.E.
Traditional date of
establishment of
the Roman Republic

264–241 B.C.E.
218–201 B.C.E.
149–146 B.C.E.
Punic Wars

107–31 B.C.E.
Political turmoil
(see the chronology
"Turmoil in the Late
Republic," page 132)

ca. 265 B.C.E.
Romans control
most of Italy

451–449 B.C.E.
Laws of the Twelve Tables
written and issued

133–121 B.C.E.
Gracchi reforms

44 B.C.E.
Julius Caesar
assassinated

31 B.C.E.
Octavian defeats Antony and
Cleopatra at the Battle of Actium

367 B.C.E.
Licinian-Sextian
laws passed

27 B.C.E.
Senate grants Octavian
the title Augustus

but the summer months are dry. Because of the climate, the rivers of Italy usually carry little water during the summer. Most of Italy's rivers are unsuitable for regular, large-scale shipping and never became major thoroughfares for commerce and communications. Yet the rivers nourished a bountiful agriculture that could produce enough crops for a growing population.

Geography encouraged Italy to look to the Mediterranean. In the north, Italy is protected by the Alps, which form a natural barrier. From the north the Apennine Mountains run southward along the east coast for the entire length of the Italian boot, cutting off access to the Adriatic Sea for those to their west. This barrier induced Italy to look west to Spain and Carthage rather than east to Greece, but it did not carve up the land in a way that would prevent the development of political unity.

In their southward course, the Apennines leave two broad and fertile plains to their west: Latium and Campania. These plains attracted settlers and invaders from the time that peoples began to move into Italy. Among these peoples were those who would found Rome on the Tiber River in Latium.

This site enjoyed several advantages. The Tiber provided Rome with a constant source of water. Located at an easy crossing point on

The Etruscans, ca. 500 B.C.E.

the Tiber, Rome thus stood astride the main avenue of communications between northern and southern Italy. Positioned amid seven hills, Rome was defensible, and it was relatively close to the sea through the port of Ostia seventeen miles away. Thus Rome was in an excellent position to develop the resources of Latium and maintain contact with the rest of Italy.

The Etruscans

Before Rome rose to power, the dominant group in northern Italy was the culture that is now called Etruscan, which developed in north-central Italy about 800 B.C.E. Recent studies of DNA evidence have indicated that the Etruscans most likely originated in Turkey or elsewhere in the Near East, but they migrated to Italy by at least 3000 B.C.E. and developed their culture there. The Etruscans spoke a language that was very different from Greek and Latin, although they adopted the Greek alphabet to write it. We know they wrote letters, records, and literary works, but once the Romans conquered them, knowledge of how to read and write Etruscan died out. Also, the writings themselves largely disappeared because many were written on linen books that did not survive; what remain are inscriptions on stone or engravings in metal. Modern scholars have learned to read Etruscan to some degree, but we have little knowledge of how the Etruscans would describe themselves. Most of what we know about their civilization comes from archaeological evidence and from the writings of other peoples who lived around them at the same time; often these people were hostile because they had been conquered by the Etruscans.

The Etruscans established permanent settlements that evolved into cities and built a rich cultural life that became the foundation of civilization in much of Italy. They spread their influence over the surrounding countryside, which they farmed and mined for its abundant mineral resources. They also grew rich by trading natural products, especially iron, with their Greek neighbors to the south and east and with others throughout the Mediterranean. Once wealthy, they became militarily powerful.

Beginning about 750 B.C.E., the Etruscans expanded southward into central Italy through military actions on land and sea and through the establishment of colony cities. Written records of battles all come from the side of the Etruscans' opponents, but objects found in graves indicate that military values were important in their society, as wealthy men were buried with bronze armor and shields and iron weapons. In the process of expansion, the Etruscans

Etruscan Dancers   A fresco from an Etruscan tomb, painted about 470 B.C.E., shows dancers in an idyllic setting with olive trees, while other walls depict musicians and a banquet. The scenes are based on similar scenes on Greek pottery, evidence of the connections between the Etruscans and their Greek neighbors to the south. This tomb is one among many thousands in the Necropolis of Monterozzi in Tarquinia, just north of Rome, now a UNESCO World Heritage Site. (Pictures From History/CPA Media Pte Ltd/Alamy)

encountered a small collection of villages subsequently called Rome and for several centuries engaged in a series of wars with the Romans that also involved other groups that lived in northern and central Italy.

The Founding of Rome

Archaeological evidence indicates that the ancestors of the Romans began to settle on the hills east of the Tiber during the early Iron Age, around 1000 to 800 B.C.E. Archaeological sources provide the most important information about this earliest period of Roman history, but later Romans told a number of stories about the founding of Rome. These stories mix legend and history, as Roman historians were more concerned with telling a good story than with precision about details and dates, but mythical or not, they illustrate the traditional ethics, morals, and ideals of Rome.

The Romans' foundation myths were told in a number of different versions. In the most common of these, Romulus and Remus founded the city of Rome, an event later Roman authors dated precisely to 753 B.C.E. These twin brothers were the sons of the war-god Mars, and their mother, Rhea Silvia, was a descendant of Aeneas, a brave and pious Trojan who left Troy after it was destroyed by the Greeks in the Trojan War (see "Homer, Hesiod, and the Epic" in Chapter 3). The brothers, who were left to die by a jealous uncle, were raised by a female wolf. When they were grown, they decided to build a city in the hills that became part of Rome, but they quarreled over which hill should be the site of the city. In the end, Romulus killed Remus and named the city after himself. He also established a council of advisers later called the Senate. Romulus and his mostly male followers expanded their power over the neighboring Sabine peoples, in part by abducting and then marrying their women. The Sabine women then arranged a peace by throwing themselves between their brothers and their husbands, convincing them that killing kin would make the men cursed. The Romans, favored by the gods, continued their rise to power.

Despite its tales of murder, rape, and kidnapping, this founding myth ascribes positive traits to the Romans: they are descended from gods and heroes, can thrive in wild and tough settings, and will defend their boundaries at all costs. The story also portrays women who were ancestors of Rome as virtuous and brave, and it highlights what would become Rome's greatest achievement, marveled at by ancient Greek authors and emphasized by historians today: its ability to include conquered peoples within its fold. In contrast to Athens, where newcomers could never become citizens and were always excluded from full political participation, in most of its history Rome regularly offered citizenship to the elite members of newly conquered territories. Even enslaved men who had been freed were endowed with citizenship immediately upon receiving their freedom, something that was also never possible in Athens. Rome was thus a multiethnic society from the start, able to inspire loyalty to Rome in many different peoples.

Later Roman historians continued the story by describing a series of kings after Romulus, each elected by the Senate. According to tradition, the last three kings were Etruscan, and another tale about female virtue was told to explain why the Etruscan kings were overthrown, for ancient historians often attributed major government upheavals to the possession or loss of women. In this story, the son of King Tarquin, the Etruscan king who ruled Rome, raped Lucretia, a virtuous Roman wife, in her own home. Lucretia summoned her husband and father to the house, told them what had happened, and demanded they seek vengeance. She then died by suicide by plunging a knife into her heart.[1] Her father and husband and the other Roman nobles swore on the bloody knife to avenge Lucretia's death by throwing out the Etruscan kings, and they did. Whether any part of this story is true can never be known, but Romans generally accepted it as history and dated the expulsion of the Etruscan kings to 509 B.C.E. They saw this year as marking the end of the monarchical period and the dawn of the republic.

Most historians today view the idea that Etruscan kings ruled in the city of Rome as legendary, but fighting with groups that came from the north, such as the Etruscans, was a major early Roman experience and would shape Rome's later policies. Historians also stress the influence of the Etruscans on Rome. The Etruscans transformed Rome from a relatively large town to a real city. The Romans adopted the Etruscan alphabet, which the Etruscans themselves had adopted from the Greeks. They also adopted an Etruscan symbol, a bundle of rods tied together with an ax emerging from the center, which symbolized the Etruscan king's power. This ceremonial object was called the fasces (FAS-eez) and was carried first by Etruscan officials and then by Romans. (It was also used by later governments: in the twentieth century Mussolini would use the fasces as the symbol of his political party, the Fascists, and fasces are on the speaker's platform of the U.S. House of Representatives and form the armrests of Abraham Lincoln's chair in the Lincoln Memorial in Washington, D.C.) Even the toga, the white woolen robe worn by citizens, came from the Etruscans, as did gladiatorial combat honoring the dead. In engineering and architecture as well, the Romans adopted some design elements and the basic plan of their temples, along with paved roads, from the Etruscans.

In this early period, the city of Rome does appear to have been ruled by kings, as were most territories in the ancient world. A hereditary aristocracy also developed—again, an almost universal phenomenon; it advised the kings and may have played a role in choosing them. And sometime in the sixth century B.C.E., a group of aristocrats revolted against these kings and established a government in which the main institution of power was the **Senate**, an assembly of aristocrats, rather than a single monarch. Rome thereby became a republic. Executive power was in the hands of two members of the Senate called **consuls**, but they were elected for one-year terms only and rejoined the ranks of the Senate after their term in office.

Under kings and then the Senate, the villages along the Tiber gradually grew into a single city, whose residents enjoyed contacts with the larger Mediterranean world. Temples and public buildings began to grace Rome, and the Forum, a large plaza between two of Rome's hills, became a public meeting place similar to the Greek agora (see "Organization of the Polis" in Chapter 3). In addition, trade in metalwork became common, and wealthier Romans began to import fine Greek vases and other luxuries.

The Roman Conquest of Italy

In the period from 509 to 264 B.C.E., referred to by historians as the early republic, the Romans fought numerous wars with their neighbors on the Italian peninsula, with an army initially composed primarily of Roman citizens who volunteered or were conscripted for short terms by ballots, essentially a lottery among all male citizens ages sixteen to forty-six. Only those citizens with a certain amount of property were eligible for army service, and the units were organized by how much money a soldier could spend on arms and armor; the wealthiest citizens formed the cavalry, as only they could afford horses. Conquered territories were often turned into allies, and other territories became allies of Rome without fighting. Alliances with the towns around them in Latium gave the Romans a large population that could be tapped for military needs, though allied armies were led by Romans. Wealth gained from victories using troops from Rome's allies was split between Rome itself and all her allies, a strategy that encouraged loyalty to Rome. Rome often declared conquered territory public land, sometimes settling Roman colonists in it or selling it to private landholders, but often allowing conquered or allied people to continue to inhabit and farm it. The Romans also ensured good behavior by threatening to reassign lands if the allies rebelled.

■ **Senate** The assembly that was the main institution of power in the Roman Republic, originally composed only of aristocrats.

■ **consuls** Primary executives in the Roman Republic, elected for one-year terms in the Senate, who commanded the army in battle, administered state business, and supervised financial affairs.

These wars of the early republic later became the source of legends that continued to express Roman values. One of these involved the aristocrat Cincinnatus, who had been expelled from the Senate and forced to pay a huge fine because of the actions of his son. As the story goes, in 458 B.C.E. he was plowing the fields of his small farm when the Senate asked him to return and assume the office of dictator. This position, which had been created very early in the republic, was one in which one man would be given ultimate powers for six months in order to handle a serious crisis such as an invasion or rebellion. (Like the word *tyrant* in ancient Greece, *dictator* did not have its current negative meaning in the early Roman Republic.) At this point the armies of the Aequi, a neighboring group, had surrounded Roman forces commanded by both consuls, and Rome was in imminent danger of catastrophe. Cincinnatus, wiping his sweat, listened to the appeal of his countrymen and led the Roman infantry in victory over the Aequi. He then returned to his farm, becoming a legend among later Romans as a man of simplicity who put his civic duty to Rome before any consideration of personal interest or wealth, and who willingly gave up power for the greater good. The Roman Senate actually chose many more men

as dictator in the centuries after Cincinnatus, but no subsequent dictator achieved his legendary reputation. For George Washington and other leaders of the U.S. War of Independence, he became the symbolic model of a leader who had performed selfless service but then stepped down from power, which Washington himself did.

In 387 B.C.E., the Romans suffered a major setback when the Celts — or Gauls, as the Romans called them — invaded the Italian peninsula from the north, destroyed a Roman army, and sacked the city of Rome. (For more on the Gauls, who lived in present-day France, see Chapter 7.) More intent on loot than on conquest, the Gauls agreed to abandon Rome in return for a thousand pounds of gold. As the story was later told, when the Gauls provided their own scale and weights to measure the gold, the Romans howled in indignation, claiming these were rigged. The Gallic chieftain Brennus then threw his sword on the scale, exclaiming "*Vae victis*" (woe to the conquered), implying that those who were defeated were at the mercy of their conquerors. The Romans then had to put more gold on the scale to balance the added sword. These words, though legendary, were used by later Romans to explain why they would not surrender to other groups that sought to conquer Rome, and the city of Rome was not sacked again until 410 C.E.

The Romans rebuilt their city and continued their campaign of conquest and annexation through alliances. They brought Latium and their Latin allies fully under their control and conquered Etruria and the Etruscans (see Map 5.1). Starting in 343 B.C.E., they turned south and grappled with the Samnites in a series of bitter wars for the possession of Campania. The Samnites were a formidable enemy and inflicted serious losses on the Romans, but the Romans won in the end and continued their expansion southward.

Alarmed by Roman expansion, as were all the Greek cities in southern Italy, the city of Tarentum in southern Italy called for help from Pyrrhus (PIHR-uhs), king of Epirus in western Greece. He came to Italy with a large army, and in 280 B.C.E. he won two furious battles but suffered heavy casualties — thus the phrase "Pyrrhic victory" is still used today to describe a victory involving severe losses.

Pyrrhus then received an offer from the Greek cities in Sicily to help them drive out the Carthaginians, who were expanding their holdings throughout the Mediterranean (see "The Rise of Phoenicia" in Chapter 2 and "The Punic Wars" later in this chapter). He initially defeated Carthaginian armies and was proclaimed king of Sicily, but his demands for money and manpower to continue fighting led the Greeks in Sicily to turn against him, and he

Fresco of a Campanian Foot Soldier   This fresco from the sixth century B.C.E. shows a soldier wearing a gilded helmet with a large feather. Campania is an area in southern Italy around the present-day city of Naples, first settled by Italic people, then colonized by Greeks, and then conquered by Romans in their expansion southward. (DEA PICTURE LIBRARY/ De Agostini/Getty Images)

decided to go back to Italy, where in his absence the Romans had rebuilt their army and conquered or made alliances with almost all of the Greek cities. After an inconclusive battle, Pyrrhus and his army returned to Epirus, leaving almost all of southern Italy in Roman hands. The Romans then turned north again, and by about 265 B.C.E. they had conquered or taken into their sphere of influence most of Italy.

These campaigns meant that an army composed of wealthier citizens serving for short terms was no longer enough, and soldiers gradually served for longer and longer terms. They were organized into legions of about five thousand men, armed with iron swords and iron-tipped spears, and wearing chest plates and helmets.

Along with military conquest and diplomatic alliances, the Romans enlisted religion in their expansion. Victorious generals made sure to honor the gods of the people they had conquered and to invite those gods to settle in Rome. By doing so they transformed them into gods they could also call on for assistance in their future campaigns. In this way Greek deities and mythical heroes were absorbed into the Roman pantheon. Their names were changed to Roman names, so that Zeus (the king of the gods), for example, became Jupiter, and Herakles (the semidivine hero) became Hercules, but their personal qualities and powers were similar.

Religion for the Romans was largely a matter of honoring the state and the family, not developing a close relationship with a deity or worshipping with a congregation of fellow believers. The main goal of religion was to secure the peace of the gods, what was termed *pax deorum*, and to harness divine power for public and private enterprises. Religious rituals were an important way of expressing common values, which for Romans meant those evident in their foundation myths: bravery, morality, seriousness, family, and home. The sacred fire at the shrine of the goddess Vesta in the city of Rome, for example, was attended by the vestal virgins, young women chosen from aristocratic families. Vesta was the goddess of hearth and home, whose protection was regarded as essential to Roman well-being. The vestal virgins were important figures at major public rituals, though at several times of military loss and political crisis they were also charged with negligence of duty or unchastity, another link between female honor and the Roman state. All classes of people in Rome — including commanders before military campaigns — sought the advice of oracles, people or objects understood to communicate the will of the gods.

Along with the great gods, the Romans believed in spirits who inhabited fields, forests, crossroads, and even the home itself. These spirits were to be honored with rituals and gifts so that they would be appeased instead of becoming hostile. Family and individual religious practices varied considerably, and every household had its own guardian deities. (See "Evaluating Visual Evidence: Household Shrine to the Gods and Ancestors," page 124.)

Once they had conquered an area, the Romans built roads. These roads provided an easy route for communication between the capital and outlying areas, allowed for the quick movement of armies, and offered an efficient means of trade. Many were marvels of engineering, as were the stone bridges the Romans built over Italy's many rivers.

In politics the Romans shared full Roman citizenship with the elites of many of their oldest allies, particularly the inhabitants of the cities of Latium. In other instances they granted citizenship without the right to vote or hold Roman office. These allies were subject to Roman taxes and calls for military service but ran their own local affairs. The extension of Roman citizenship strengthened the state and increased its population and wealth, although limitations on this extension would eventually become a source of conflict (see "The Countryside and Land Reforms" later in this chapter).

The Temple of Hercules Victor This round temple, dating from the second century B.C.E., is the oldest surviving marble building in Rome, made in a Greek style of materials that were partly imported from Greece. It once contained a statue of the mythical hero Hercules, and may have been built by Mummius Achaicus, the consul and general who defeated Greek forces and destroyed the city of Corinth. In building this temple, Mummius Achaicus linked himself with Hercules and left a permanent monument to his victory. (Justin Kase z12z/Alamy)

What were the key institutions of the Roman Republic?

Along with citizenship, the republican government was another important institution of Roman political life. Roman institutions were not static; they changed over time to address problems as they emerged.

The Roman State

Most of our written sources about Roman government and history in the republican period come from upper-class authors whose families were members of the Senate, many from the late republican period (147–30 B.C.E.), so they were looking backward. They shaped their narratives to both explain and help maintain the privileges of their social, political, and economic status, and they were thus critical of change, which they generally saw as decline. They viewed the Senate favorably and emphasized its leadership in a phrase describing the Roman government: *senatus populusque Romanus*, "the Senate and the Roman people," abbreviated SPQR. That phrase shows up in legal, political, and historical writings, and its abbreviation is on coins and inscriptions, including those from the imperial period. By that point the Senate no longer had much power, and the Senate and the people (embodied in other assemblies) were often hostile to one another, so the phrase had become a traditional patriotic motto, not a description of political reality. Recent historians have used evidence left by ordinary people, along with more critical readings of the literary sources, to get a clearer picture of the development of the Roman state.

All types of sources indicate that in the early republic, social divisions determined the shape of politics. Political power was in the hands of a hereditary aristocracy — the **patricians**, whose privileged legal status was determined by their birth as members of certain families. Once a patrician, always a patrician, though belonging to a family whose members had been in the Senate did not guarantee entrance. If a patrician couldn't finance a campaign, he couldn't get elected. Aristocratic families rose and fell in power over Rome's long history, and some important leaders were what the Romans called *novi homines* (new men), the first in their families to serve in the Senate or as consul. Families that had long held power snobbishly regarded these new men with disdain or suspicion.

The common people of Rome, the **plebeians** (plih-BEE-uhns), were free citizens with a voice in politics, but initially they had few of the patricians' political and social advantages. Most plebeians were poor artisans, small farmers, and landless urban dwellers, though some increased their wealth in the course of Roman expansion and came to rival the patricians economically. Plebeians were later allowed to obtain the highest offices in Rome,

but even the most powerful among them were derided (though sometimes in whispers) as novi homines.

The Romans created several assemblies through which men elected high officials and passed legislation. The earliest was the Centuriate Assembly, in which citizens were organized into groups called centuries. Each citizen was assigned to a century depending on his status and amount of wealth, and the patricians possessed the majority of centuries. When an election was ordered, each century met separately and voted as a bloc, which meant that the patricians could easily outvote the plebeians. In 471 B.C.E., plebeian men won the right to meet in an assembly of their own, the Plebeian Assembly, and to pass ordinances.

The highest officials of the republic were the two consuls, who were elected for one-year terms by the Centuriate Assembly. The consuls commanded the army in battle, administered state business, presided over the Senate and assemblies, and supervised financial affairs. In effect, they ran the state. The consuls appointed quaestors (KWEH-stuhr) to assist them in their duties, and in 421 B.C.E. the quaestorship became an elective office open to plebeian men. In 366 B.C.E., the Romans created a new office, that of

Coin Showing a Voter   This coin from 63 B.C.E. shows a citizen wearing a toga dropping a voting tablet into a voting urn, the Roman equivalent of today's ballot box. The tablet has a *V* on it, meaning a yes vote, and the coin has an inscription giving the name of the moneyer, the official who controlled the production of coins and decided what would be shown on them. Here the moneyer, Lucius Cassius Longinus, depicted a vote held fifty years earlier regarding whether an ancestor of his should be named prosecutor in a trial charging three vestal virgins with unchastity. As was common among moneyers, Longinus chose this image as a means to advance his political career, in this case by suggesting his family's long history of public office. (Photo 12/Archives Snark/Alamy)

praetor (PREE-tuhr). When the consuls were away from Rome, the praetors could act in their place; they could also command armies, act as governors in the provinces, interpret law, and administer justice.

The most important institution was the Senate, which during the republic grew to several hundred members. Senate membership was a lifetime position, and all senators had previously been elected to one of the high positions, which automatically conferred Senate membership. Because the Senate sat year after year with the same members, it provided stability and continuity. It passed formal decrees that were technically "advice" to the magistrates, who were not bound to obey them but usually did. The Senate directed the magistrates on the conduct of war and had the power over the expenditure of public money. In times of emergency, it could name a dictator.

Within the city of Rome itself, the Senate's powers were limited by laws and traditions, but as Rome expanded, the Senate had greater authority in the outlying territories. The Romans divided the lands that they conquered into provinces, and the Senate named the governors, most of whom were former consuls or praetors, for each province. Another responsibility of the Senate was to handle relations between Rome and other powers.

A lasting achievement of the Romans was their development of civil law. Roman civil law, the *ius civile*, consisted of statutes, customs, and procedures that regulated the lives of citizens, especially in matters of concern to those who owned property, such as ownership, inheritance, and contracts. It became increasingly complex over the centuries, and later emperors would try to develop uniform codes that brought what was a bewildering group of statutes and rulings together (see Chapter 7). By contrast, Roman criminal law was brutally simple, and often harsh. As the Romans came into more frequent contact with foreigners, the consuls and praetors applied a broader *ius gentium*, the "law of the peoples," to matters such as peace treaties, the treatment of prisoners of war, and the exchange of diplomats. In the ius gentium, all sides were to be treated the same regardless of their nationality. By the late republic, Roman jurists had widened this principle still further into the concept of *ius naturale*, "natural law," based in part on Stoic beliefs (see "Philosophy and the People" in Chapter 4). Natural law, according to these thinkers, is made up of rules that govern human behavior and that come from applying reason rather than customs or traditions, and so apply to all societies. In reality, Roman officials generally interpreted the law to the advantage of Rome, of course, at least to the extent that the strength of Roman armies allowed them to enforce it. But Roman law came to be seen as one of the most important contributions Rome made to the development of Western civilization.

Social Conflict in Rome

Inequality between plebeians and patricians led to a conflict known as the **Struggle of the Orders**, which lasted for the entire early republican period. In this conflict the plebeians sought to increase their power by taking advantage of the fact that Rome's survival depended on its army, which needed plebeians to fill the ranks of the infantry. According to tradition, in 494 B.C.E. the plebeians literally walked out of Rome and refused to serve in the army. Their general strike worked, and the patricians grudgingly made important concessions. They allowed the plebeians to elect their own officials, the **tribunes**, who presided over the Plebeian Assembly, brought plebeian grievances to the Senate for resolution, could stop debate in the Senate, and could veto the decisions of the consuls if they wished. The tribunes were regarded as being legally inviolate, and if anyone harmed them, the Plebeian Assembly pledged to avenge them immediately.

The law itself was the plebeians' primary target during the Struggle of the Orders. Only the patricians knew what the law was, and only they could argue cases in court. All too often they used the law for their own benefit. According to ancient Greek and Roman historians, after much struggle, in 449 B.C.E., the patricians surrendered their legal monopoly and codified and published the Laws of the Twelve Tables, so called because they were inscribed on twelve bronze plaques. The Laws of the Twelve Tables covered many legal issues, including property ownership, guardianship, inheritance, procedure for trials, and punishments for various crimes. With legal procedures now made public, plebeians could argue cases in court. Later, in 445 B.C.E., the patricians passed a law, the *lex Canuleia*, that for the first time allowed patricians and plebeians to marry one another.

Licinius and Sextius were plebeian tribunes in the fourth century B.C.E. who mounted a sweeping assault on patrician privilege. They proposed a series of laws that the Senate passed in 367 B.C.E. Though historians continue to debate exactly what these Licinian-Sextian laws were, they apparently gave wealthy plebeians access to all the offices of Rome, including the right

---

■ **patricians** The Roman hereditary aristocracy; they held most of the political power in the republic.

■ **plebeians** The common people of Rome; they were free but had few of the patricians' advantages.

■ **Struggle of the Orders** A conflict in which the plebeians sought political representation and safeguards against patrician domination.

■ **tribunes** Plebeian-elected officials; tribunes brought plebeian grievances to the Senate for resolution and protected plebeians from the arbitrary conduct of patrician magistrates.

to hold one of the two consulships. Once plebeians could hold the consulship, they could also sit in the Senate and advise on policy. The laws also limited the amount of conquered land any single individual could hold, though this was frequently ignored. Though decisive, this victory did not end the Struggle of the Orders, which happened only in 287 B.C.E. with the passage of the *lex Hortensia*. This law gave the resolutions of the Plebeian Assembly the force of law for patricians and plebeians alike.

The long Struggle of the Orders had resulted in an expansion of power to wealthy plebeians, and by 200 B.C.E. the majority of the consuls were plebeian. This did not mean they were concerned with the problems of average people. Political power had been expanded only slightly and still resided largely in a group of wealthy families, some of whom happened to be plebeian. Access to the highest political offices was still difficult for any plebeian, who often had to get the support of patrician families if he wanted a political career.

Networks of support were actually important for all Romans involved in public life, not simply aspiring plebeians. Roman politics operated primarily through a **patron-client system** whereby free men promised their votes to a more powerful man in exchange for his help in legal or other matters. The more powerful patron looked after his clients, and his clients' support helped the patron advance his career. This system held Roman society together even as it was undergoing political upheavals.

The patron-client system even extended to foreign affairs. As Rome expanded, along with conquered territories and allies (and conquered territories turned allies), Rome also developed a number of client kingdoms along its borders, such as the Bosporan kingdom on the north shore of the Black Sea and the Votadini people in northeast England. Client kings conducted their own internal business according to their own laws and customs, but gave up their rights to independent foreign affairs. The client kingdoms enjoyed the protection of Rome while defending Rome's borders, but they were not relationships between equals: Rome always remained the senior partner. In time many of these states became provinces of the Roman Empire (see Chapters 6 and 7).

How did the Romans build a Mediterranean empire?

As the republican government was developing, Rome continued to expand its holdings beyond the Italian peninsula. Unlike Alexander the Great, the Romans did not map out grandiose strategies to conquer the world, but they became masters of the Mediterranean in a relatively short period of time, amazing their contemporaries. Historians debate the reasons they were so successful. Some view them as pathological predators among more peaceful neighbors, but the many wars in the Hellenistic period suggest that Rome's neighbors were also quite militaristic. A newer view is that Rome was one warlike state among many, successful primarily because it incorporated allies as citizens, thus maintaining a large population base despite losses in war.

The Punic Wars

As they pushed southward, incorporating the southern Italian peninsula into their growing territory, the Romans confronted another great power in the western Mediterranean, the Carthaginians. The city of Carthage had been founded by Phoenicians as a trading colony in the eighth century B.C.E. (see "The Rise of Phoenicia" in Chapter 2). By the fourth century B.C.E., the Carthaginians began to expand their holdings. They had one of the largest navies in the Mediterranean and were wealthy enough to hire mercenaries to do much of their fighting. At the end of a long string of wars, the Carthaginians had created and defended a mercantile empire that stretched from western Sicily to the western end of the Mediterranean (see Map 5.1).

Beginning in the fifth century B.C.E., the Romans and the Carthaginians made a series of treaties with one another that defined their spheres of influence, and they worked together in the 270s B.C.E. to defeat Pyrrhus. But the Greek cities that became Roman allies in southern Italy and Sicily saw Carthage as a competitor in terms of trade. This competition led to the first of the three **Punic Wars** between Rome and Carthage. The First Punic War lasted for twenty-three years (264–241 B.C.E.) and ended with the Romans in possession of Sicily, which became their first real province.

The peace treaty between Rome and Carthage brought no peace because both powers had their sights set on dominating the western half of the Mediterranean. In 238 B.C.E., the Romans took advantage of Carthaginian weakness to seize Sardinia and Corsica. The Carthaginians responded by expanding their holdings in Spain under the leadership of the commander Hamilcar Barca. With him he took his ten-year-old son, Hannibal, whom he had earlier led to an altar where he had made the boy swear to be an enemy to Rome forever. In the following years, Hamilcar and his son-in-law Hasdrubal (HAHZ-droo-buhl)

■ **patron-client system** An informal system of patronage in which free men promised their votes to a more powerful man in exchange for his help in legal or other matters.

■ **Punic Wars** A series of three wars between Rome and Carthage in which Rome emerged the victor.

subjugated much of southern Spain and in the process rebuilt Carthaginian power. Rome first made a treaty with Hasdrubal, setting the boundary between Carthaginian and Roman interests at the Ebro River, and then began to extend its own influence in Spain.

In 221 B.C.E., Hamilcar's son Hannibal became the Carthaginian commander in Spain and laid siege to Saguntum (suh-GUHN-tum), a Roman-allied city that lay within the sphere of Carthaginian interest and was making raids into Carthaginian territories. The Romans declared war, claiming that Carthage had attacked a city friendly to Rome. So began the Second Punic War. In 218 B.C.E., Hannibal marched an army of tens of thousands of troops—and, more famously, several dozen war elephants—from Spain across what is now France and over the Alps into Italy. Once there, he defeated one Roman army after another, and in 216 B.C.E. he won his greatest victory at the Battle of Cannae (KAH-nee). Hannibal also made alliances with other enemies of Rome, including King Philip V of Macedonia and the king of Syracuse. He then spread devastation throughout the Italian peninsula, and he also sowed dissension among the Roman-allied cities in central and southern Italy by exposing Rome's inequitable treatment of its allies. A number rebelled. Yet Hannibal was not able to win areas near Rome in central Italy because Roman allies there, who had been extended citizenship rights, remained loyal.

Despite Hannibal's successes, his allies did not supply him with enough food and supplies to sustain his troops. The Senate of Carthage did not reinforce Hannibal with additional troops because it wanted to use these troops to retake Sicily and Sardinia from Rome, and also because it feared that Hannibal could pose a threat to it if he were too successful.

Rome also fought back, and in 210 B.C.E. it found a counterpart to Hannibal in the young commander Scipio Africanus (SKIP-ee-oh af-rih-KAHN-us). Scipio copied Hannibal's methods of mobile warfare and guerrilla tactics and made more extensive use of cavalry than had earlier Roman commanders. He battled first in Spain, which in 207 B.C.E. he wrested from the Carthaginians. That same year, the Romans sealed Hannibal's fate at the Battle of Metaurus, where they destroyed a major Carthaginian army coming to reinforce Hannibal. Scipio then struck directly at Carthage itself, prompting the Carthaginians to recall Hannibal from Italy to defend their homeland.

In 202 B.C.E., at the town of Zama near Carthage (Map 5.2), Scipio defeated Hannibal in a decisive battle. The Carthaginians sued for peace and in 201 B.C.E. the Roman Senate agreed, on terms that were very favorable to the Romans. Hannibal himself later served as a military adviser at the Seleucid court in its battle with Rome.

The Second Punic War and the treaty that ended it contained the seeds of still other wars. Rome regarded the treaty as making Carthage permanently subordinate to Rome, unable to wage war against its neighbors without Roman approval. But Carthage did just that in 151 B.C.E., after Numidia, a kingdom in North Africa that bordered Carthage and was a client state of Rome, launched a border raid on Carthaginian territory. In response, Rome declared war on Carthage in 149 B.C.E., which became the Third Punic War. After a three-year siege, led by Scipio Aemilianus, the grandson by adoption of Scipio Africanus, the Roman army took the city in 146 B.C.E. and destroyed it. The Romans sold the remaining residents into slavery and annexed Carthage's territory, which became an important source of grain to feed the city of Rome.

During the war with Hannibal, the Romans had invaded the Iberian Peninsula, an area rich in material resources and the home of fierce warriors. They met with bloody and determined resistance. Not until 133 B.C.E., after years of brutal and ruthless warfare, did Scipio Aemilianus finally conquer Spain. Scipio's victory meant that Roman language, law, and culture would in time permeate this entire region, although it would be another century before the Iberian Peninsula was completely pacified.

The Punic Wars required huge numbers of troops, and Rome was forced to ignore its official requirement that soldiers be citizens with a certain amount of property. Although it still maintained the lottery for drafting wealthier citizens, Rome devised other ways as well to increase the number of troops. Rome's allies in the Italian peninsula were required to provide more soldiers, and poor volunteers were recruited from Rome itself with modest amounts of pay and the promise of war booty. The Roman state began providing standardized weapons and armor, as many soldiers were too poor to afford these on their own, and army service increased from six years to about twenty.

Rome Turns East

During the Second Punic War, King Philip V of Macedonia made an alliance with Hannibal against Rome. The Romans, in turn, allied themselves with the Aetolian League of city-states in central Greece. The cities of the league bore the brunt of the fighting on the Greek peninsula until after the Romans had defeated Hannibal in 202 B.C.E. Then the Roman legions were deployed against the Macedonians, who were defeated in a series of wars. Roman armies also won significant victories against the forces of the Seleucid emperors, and that empire shrank, with parts becoming Roman client kingdoms. In 148 B.C.E., Rome made Macedonia into a Roman province. Another decisive victory came in 146 B.C.E., when the Romans attacked the city of Corinth. Just as they had at Carthage earlier that year, the Romans destroyed the city, killing the

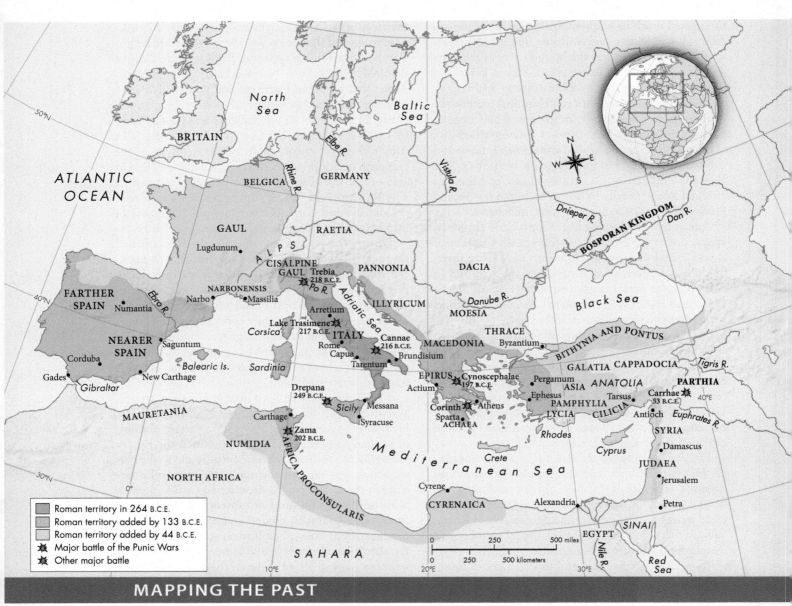

MAP 5.2 Roman Expansion During the Republic, ca. 282–44 B.C.E.

Rome expanded in all directions, first west and then east, eventually controlling every shore of the Mediterranean.

ANALYZING THE MAP Which years saw the greatest expansion of Roman power during the republic? How might the different geographic features have helped or hindered the expansion into certain areas?

CONNECTIONS What allowed the Romans to maintain their power across such a wide and diverse area?

men, sending the women and children into slavery, and looting it for treasure. Statues, paintings, and other works of art were shipped to Rome. In 133 B.C.E., the king of Pergamum bequeathed his kingdom to the Romans. The Ptolemies of Egypt retained formal control of their kingdom, but they obeyed Roman wishes in terms of trade policy.

Once the Romans had conquered the Hellenistic world, they faced the formidable challenge of governing

it, which they met by establishing the first Roman provinces in the East. Declaring the Mediterranean *mare nostrum,* "our sea," the Romans began to create political and administrative machinery to hold the Mediterranean together under a political system of provinces ruled by governors sent from Rome. Not all Romans were joyful over Rome's conquest of the Mediterranean world; some considered the victory a misfortune. The historian Sallust (86–34 B.C.E.), for example, writing from hindsight, complained that the acquisition of an empire was the beginning of Rome's troubles:

> But when through labor and justice our Republic grew powerful, great kings defeated in war, fierce nations and mighty peoples subdued by force, when Carthage the rival of the Roman people was wiped out root and branch, all the seas and lands lay open, then — fortune began to be harsh and to throw everything into confusion. The Romans had easily borne labor, danger, uncertainty, and hardship. To them leisure, riches — otherwise desirable — proved to be burdens and torments. So at first money, then desire for power grew great. These things were a sort of cause of all evils.[2]

Sallust was one of the voices creating a narrative of decline that became very powerful in the tumultuous late republic; this narrative influenced historians for long afterwards.

How did expansion affect Roman society and culture?

By the second century B.C.E., the Romans ruled much of the Mediterranean world, and tremendous wealth poured into Rome, especially from the East, though holding on to Roman provinces was also costly because of military expenditures. Roman institutions, social patterns, and ways of thinking changed to meet the new era. Some looked nostalgically back at what they fondly considered the good old days and idealized the traditional agrarian and family-centered way of life. Others embraced the new urban life and eagerly accepted Greek culture.

Roman Families

The core of traditional Roman society was the family, and the word *family* (*familia*) in ancient Rome actually meant all those under the authority of a male head of household, including nonrelated individuals who lived in the household. In poor families, this group might be very small, but among the wealthy, it could include hundreds of enslaved, freed, and free servants and household workers.

The male head of household was called the **paterfamilias**. Fathers held great power over their children, which technically lasted for their children's whole lives. Initially this seems to have included power over life and death, but by the second century B.C.E., that had been limited by law and custom. Fathers continued to have the power to decide how family resources should be spent, however, and sons did not inherit until after their fathers had died.

In the early republic, legal authority over a woman generally passed from her father to her husband on marriage, but the Laws of the Twelve Tables allowed it to remain with her father even after marriage. That was advantageous to the father, and could also be to the woman, because her father might be willing to take her side in a dispute with her husband, and she could return to her birth family if there was quarreling or abuse. By the late republic, more and more

marriages were of this type, and during the time of the empire (27 B.C.E.–476 C.E.), almost all of them were.

To marry, both spouses had to be free Roman citizens. Most citizens did marry, with women of wealthy families marrying in their mid-teens and non-elite women in their late teens. Grooms were generally somewhat older than their brides. Marital agreements, especially among the well-to-do, were stipulated with contracts between the families involved. According to Roman law, marriage required a dowry, a payment of money, property, and/or goods that went from the bride's family to the groom. People who were not citizens certainly lived together in marriage-like relationships, but these had no standing before the law and their children could not legally inherit. If allowed, enslaved people could enter a marriage-like relationship called *contubernium*, though any children produced would belong to the people who owned the parents.

Weddings were central occasions in a family's life, with spouses chosen carefully by parents, other family members, or marriage brokers. Professional fortune-tellers were frequently consulted to determine whether a match was good or what day would be especially lucky or auspicious for a couple to marry. The ceremony typically began with the bride welcoming the groom and the wedding party to her home for a feast, and then later the whole group progressed with much noise to the groom's household. It would be very unlucky if the bride tripped while going into the house, so the groom often carried her across the doorstep. The bride's entrance into the groom's house marked the point at which the two were married. As elsewhere in the ancient world, no public officials or priests were involved.

Women could inherit and own property under Roman law, though they generally received a smaller portion of any family inheritance than their brothers did. A woman's inheritance usually came as her dowry on marriage. In the earliest Roman marriage laws,

■ **paterfamilias** The oldest dominant male of the Roman family, who held great power over the lives of family members.

men could divorce their wives without any grounds, and women could not divorce their husbands. By the second century B.C.E., however, these laws had changed, and both men and women could initiate divorce. By then, women had also gained greater control over their dowries and other family property, perhaps because Rome's military conquests meant that many husbands were away for long periods of time and women needed some say over family finances.

Although marriages were arranged by families primarily for handing down property, preserving wealth, and legitimizing children, the Romans, in something of a contradiction, viewed the model marriage as one in which husbands and wives were loyal to one another and shared interests and activities. The Romans praised women who were virtuous and loyal to their husbands and devoted to their children. (See "Viewpoints: Praise of Good Women in the Eulogy for Murdia and the Turia Inscription," page 123.)

Traditionally minded Romans thought that mothers should nurse their own children and personally see to their welfare. Non-elite Roman women did nurse their own children, although wealthy women increasingly employed free or enslaved wet nurses and to help them with child rearing. Very young children were under their mother's care, and most children learned the skills they needed from their own parents. For children from wealthier urban families, opportunities for formal education increased in the late republic. Boys and girls might be educated in their homes by tutors, often enslaved Greek men, and boys also might go to a school run by a private teacher and paid for by their parents.

Most people in the expanding Roman Republic lived in the countryside. Farmers used oxen and donkeys to plow their fields, collecting the dung of the animals for fertilizer. Along with crops raised for local consumption and to pay their rents and taxes, many farmers raised crops to be sold. These included wheat, flax for making linen cloth, olives, and wine grapes.

Until the late republic most Romans, rich and poor, ate the same plain meals of bread, olives, vegetables, and a little meat or fish, with fruit for dessert. They used fingers and wooden spoons to serve themselves from simple pottery or wooden bowls and plates. They usually drank water or wine mixed with water from clay cups. Drinking unmixed wine was considered a sign of degeneracy. The Romans took three meals a day: an early breakfast, a main meal or dinner in the middle of the day, and a light supper in the evening. Dinner was also a social event, the main time for Romans to visit, chat, and exchange news. Afterward everyone who could afford the time took a long nap, especially during the hot summer months.

Most Romans worked long days, and an influx of enslaved people from Rome's wars and conquests provided additional labor for the fields, mines, and cities. To the Romans, slavery was a misfortune that befell some people and a normal outcome of imperial expansion, but it was not racialized, as captives from any ethnic group could be enslaved. Enslaved boys and girls were occasionally formally apprenticed in trades such as leatherworking, weaving, or metalworking. Enslaved well-educated men served as tutors or accountants, ran schools, and designed and made artwork and buildings. Manumission, the freeing of individuals by those who owned them, was fairly common, especially for those who worked in the household. Freedmen and women (*liberti*) then often remained part of the familia. Because they also became citizens, male liberti were part of wealthy men's networks of patronage and clientage. Despite flexibility in the Roman system of slavery, there were slave rebellions from time to time, sometimes in large-scale revolts put down by Roman armies (see "Civil War and the Rise of Julius Caesar").

Membership in a family did not end with death; the spirits of the family's ancestors were understood to remain with the family and were venerated. They and other gods regarded as protectors of the household—collectively called the *lares* and *penates*—were represented by small statues or paintings that stood in a special cupboard or a niche in the wall. (See "Evaluating Visual Evidence: Household Shrine to the Gods and Ancestors," page 124.) The statues were taken out at meals and given small bits of food, or food was thrown into the household's hearth for them. The lares and penates represented the gods at family celebrations such as weddings, and families took the statues with them when they moved. They were honored in special rituals and ceremonies, although the later Roman poet Ovid (43 B.C.E.–17 C.E.) commented that these did not have to be elaborate:

> The spirits of the dead ask for little.
> They are more grateful for piety than for an
>   expensive gift —
> Not greedy are the gods who haunt the Styx [the
>   river that bordered the underworld] below.
> A rooftile covered with a sacrificial crown,
> Scattered kernels, a few grains of salt,
> Bread dipped in wine, and loose violets —
> These are enough.[3]

New Social Customs and Greek Influence

Many aspects of life did not change greatly during the Roman expansion. Most people continued to marry and form families and to live in the countryside, with the rhythm of their days and years determined

VIEWPOINTS

Praise of Good Women in the Eulogy for Murdia and the Turia Inscription

Tombstones in Rome, like those of today, provide information about what those who erected them thought was important for later generations to know about the deceased. Those for women were often erected by their husbands or sons, including those below, both dating from the first century B.C.E. The first, a eulogy for a woman named Murdia, was erected by a son from her first marriage. The second, erected by a husband, is traditionally called the "Turia inscription," although we do not know the identity of the woman or her husband with certainty.

The Eulogy for Murdia

[O]f my mother Murdia, daughter of Lucius. . . . She made all her sons heirs in equal proportion, and gave her daughter a share as a legacy. Her maternal love was expressed by her concern for her children, and the equal shares she gave to each of them.

She left a specified sum of money to her husband so that the dowry, to which he was entitled, should be enhanced by her good opinion of him. . . . This behavior was typical of her. Her parents gave her in marriage to worthy men. Her obedience and honour preserved her marriages; as wife she endeared herself by her virtues, was beloved for her loyalty and was left the more honoured because of her judgement, and after her death to be praised in the estimation of her fellow citizens. . . .

For these reasons, praise for all good women is simple and similar, since their native goodness and the trust they have maintained do not require a diversity of words. Sufficient is the fact that they have all done the same good deeds that deserve fine reputation, and since their lives fluctuate with less diversity, by necessity we pay tribute to values they hold in common, so that nothing may be lost from fair precepts and harm what remains.

Still, my dearest mother deserved greater praise than all others, since in modesty, propriety, chastity, obedience, woolworking, industry, and loyalty she was on an equal level with other good women, nor did she take second place to any woman in virtue, work and wisdom in times of danger.

The Turia Inscription

You became an orphan suddenly before the day of our wedding, when both your parents were murdered together in the solitude of the countryside. It was mainly due to your efforts that the death of your parents was not left unavenged. . . . Then pressure was brought to bear on you and your sister to accept the view that your father's will, by which you and I were heirs, had been invalidated by his having contracted a [fictitious purchase] with his wife. . . . You defended our common cause by asserting the truth, namely, that the will had not in fact been broken. . . . They gave way before your firm resolution and did not pursue the matter any further. . . .

You provided abundantly for my needs during my flight [into political exile] and gave me the means for a dignified manner of living, when you took all the gold and jewelry from your own body and sent it to me and over and over again enriched me in my absence with servants, money and provisions, showing great ingenuity in deceiving the guards posted by our adversaries.

You begged for my life when I was abroad—it was your courage that urged you to this step—and because of your entreaties I was shielded by the clemency of those against whom you marshalled your words. But whatever you said was always said with undaunted courage.

Meanwhile when a troop of men collected by Milo, whose house I had acquired by purchase when he was in exile, tried to profit by the opportunities provided by the civil war and break into our house to plunder, you beat them back successfully and were able to defend our home.

QUESTIONS FOR ANALYSIS

1. What qualities do both men praise in their female relatives, and how might they describe the ideal Roman woman?
2. Murdia's son comments that "praise for all good women is simple and similar." Do the actions that Turia's husband highlights support this idea, or did the unrest of the late Roman Republic shape what were regarded as admirable qualities in Roman women?

Sources: Jane F. Gardner and Thomas Wiedemann, eds., *The Roman Household: A Sourcebook* (New York: Routledge, 1991), pp. 132–133; Mary R. Lefkowitz and Maureen B. Fant, eds., *Women's Life in Greece and Rome: A Source Book in Translation*, 2d ed. (Baltimore, Md.: John Hopkins University Press, 1992), pp. 135–137.

by the needs of their crops. But the conquest of the Mediterranean world and the wealth it brought gave the Romans leisure, especially in cities. The spoils of war went to build theaters, stadiums, and other places of amusement. This new urban culture reflected Hellenistic Greek influences. Some Romans, especially younger people, developed a liking for Greek literature, and it became common for an educated Roman to speak both Latin and Greek. The new Hellenism profoundly stimulated the growth and development of Roman art and literature. Roman artists copied many aspects of Greek art, but they also used art,

Household Shrine to the Gods and Ancestors

(Werner Forman/Universal Images Group/Getty Images)

In this shrine to the household gods, which the Romans called a *lararium* (pl. *lararia*), two dancing protector deities (*lares*), each holding a raised drinking horn, flank a male ancestor-spirit, or *genius*. His head is covered as a sign of reverence, and he holds a box for incense and a bowl for offerings. At the bottom a crested and bearded snake glides through plants to an altar on which there is an egg and some fruit. Snakes were common figures in lararia and were viewed as guardian spirits of the family and symbols of fertility and prosperity. This elaborate shrine was in the entryway of a large house in Pompeii, most likely owned by two wealthy brothers who were freedmen (*liberti*), as their names appear on bronze seals in the hallway and in graffiti on the exterior of the house. The house also had extensive wall frescoes of mythological scenes, all preserved when

Mount Vesuvius erupted in 79 C.E. Lararia in wealthy households could be extravagant, but even poor families had a designated space for protective lares figures.

EVALUATE THE EVIDENCE

1. Why might Romans have placed a lararium at the entranceway, where it would be the first thing visitors would see? What did it show about those who lived there?
2. This was most likely in a house owned by two freedmen. How was this altar a symbol of their prosperity and upward mobility?
3. What evidence does this altar provide for Roman adoption of Greek culture?

especially portraiture, to communicate Roman values. Portrait busts in stone were a favored art form. Those who commissioned them wanted to be portrayed as individuals, but also as representing certain admirable qualities, such as wisdom or dignity.

Greek influence was also strong in literature. Roman authors sometimes wrote histories and poetry in Greek, or translated Greek classics into Latin.

The poet Ennius (EHN-ee-uhs) (239–169 B.C.E.), the father of Latin poetry, studied Greek philosophy, wrote comedies in Latin, and adapted many of Euripides's tragedies for the Roman stage. Plautus (ca. 254–184 B.C.E.) brought a bawdy humor to his reworkings of Greek plays. The Roman dramatist Terence (ca. 195–159 B.C.E.) wrote comedies of refinement and grace that owed their essential elements to

Roman Bath　This Roman bath in Bath, England (a city to which it gave its name), was built beginning in the first century C.E. around a natural hot spring. The Romans spread the custom of bathing, which they had adopted from the Greeks, to the outer reaches of their empire. In addition to hot water, bathers used oil for massage and metal scrapers to clean and exfoliate their skin. Many Roman artifacts have been unearthed at Bath, including a number of curse tablets, small tablets made of lead calling on the gods to harm someone, which were common in the Greco-Roman world. Not surprisingly, many of the curse tablets found at Bath relate to the theft of clothing while people were bathing. (bath: Photo © Neil Holmes/Bridgeman Images; artifact: © The Trustees of the British Museum/Art Resource, NY)

Greek models. All early Roman literature was derived from that of the Greeks, but it flourished because it also spoke to Roman ways of thinking.

Many rich urban dwellers changed their eating habits by consuming elaborate meals of exotic dishes and vintage wines drawn from all over the empire. Metal spoons took the place of wooden ones, and silver and bronze platters took the place of pottery. In the early first century B.C.E. artisans in Syria developed glassblowing, a technique they took to Rome when Syria was conquered by the Romans in 64 B.C.E. Glassblowing revolutionized glass production, and glass drinking cups could soon be seen on nearly every Roman table. By the late republic and early empire, many wealthy Romans dined formally on couches around a circular table. The Romans built status recognition into their dining rooms with the order in which people were seated, how they were seated, and differences in the meals they were served.

During the second century B.C.E., the Greek custom of bathing also gained popularity in the Roman world. The Romans built more and more large public buildings containing pools and exercise rooms, and by the period of the early empire, baths had become an essential part of any Roman city. The baths were socially important places where men and women went to see and be seen. Social climbers tried to talk to the right people and wangle invitations to dinner; politicians took advantage of the occasion to discuss the affairs of the day; marriages were negotiated by wealthy fathers. Baths were also places where people could buy sex; the women and men who worked in bathhouses often made extra income through prostitution. For this reason, conservative moralists portrayed them as dens of iniquity, but they were seen by most Romans as a normal part of urban life.

Opposing Views: Cato the Elder and Scipio Aemilianus

Romans differed greatly in their opinions about the new social customs and about Greek influence. Two men, Marcus Cato (234–149 B.C.E.) and Scipio Aemilianus (185–129 B.C.E.), both of whom were military commanders and consuls, the highest office in the Roman Republic, can serve as representatives of these opposing views.

Marcus Cato was born a plebeian and owned a small rural estate, but his talent and energy caught the eye of high patrician officials and he became their client.

He fought in the Second Punic War under Scipio Africanus and then returned to Rome, where he worked his way up through various offices. In 195 B.C.E., he was elected consul. A key issue facing Cato was the heated debate over the repeal of the Oppian Law, which had been passed twenty years earlier, right after Rome's disastrous loss to Carthage at the Battle of Cannae. Rome had needed money to continue the war, and the law decreed that no woman was to own more than a small amount of gold, or wear clothing trimmed in purple, or drive a chariot in the city of Rome itself. These were all proclaimed to be luxuries that wasted money and undermined the war effort. The law was passed in part for financial reasons, but it also had gendered social implications, as there was no corresponding law limiting men's conspicuous consumption. By 195 B.C.E., the war was over and this restriction on women's spending had lost its economic rationale. Roman women publicly protested against it, and Cato led the battle to prevent its repeal, arguing that women's desire to spend money was a disease that could never be cured and that women were like wild animals and would engage in an orgy of shopping if the law were lifted. The women's political actions were more effective than Cato's speeches, however, and the law was lifted, although later in his political career Cato pushed for other laws forbidding women from wearing fancy clothing or owning property.

Women's spending was not the only thing destroying Roman society, according to Cato. He made speeches in the Senate decrying Greek influence and set himself up as the defender of what he saw as traditional Roman values: discipline, order, morality, frugality, and an agrarian way of life. He was also practical, however, and made certain his older son learned Greek as an essential tool in Roman society, though he instructed the boy not to take Greek ideas too seriously. Cato held the office of censor, and he attempted to remove from the lists of possible officeholders anyone who did not live up to his standards. He even criticized his superior Scipio Africanus for being too lenient toward his troops and spending too much money. Cato proclaimed his views through his decisions when acting as a military commander, and also in his written works, which were all in Latin.

Late in life Cato was a diplomat to Carthage, and, according to later Roman historians, after he saw that the city had recovered economically from the war with Rome, he came home declaring, "Carthage must be destroyed." Cato's words were traditionally seen as a major reason for the Third Punic War, though more recently historians have emphasized differences of opinion between Rome and Carthage about the terms of the peace treaty that had ended the Second Punic War.

The military campaign against Carthage was led by Scipio Aemilianus, in contrast to Cato an avid devotee of Hellenism. Like his grandfather, Scipio believed that broader views had to replace the old Roman narrowness. Rome was no longer a small city; it was the capital of the Mediterranean world, and Romans had to adapt themselves to that fact. Scipio became an innovator in both politics and culture. He developed a more personal style of politics that looked unflinchingly at the broader problems that the success of Rome brought to its people. He embraced Hellenism wholeheartedly and promoted its spread in Roman society. Perhaps more than anyone else of his day, Scipio represented the new Roman — imperial, cultured, and independent.

In his education and interests, too, Scipio broke with the past. As a boy he had received the traditional Roman training, learning to read and write Latin and becoming acquainted with the law. He mastered the fundamentals of rhetoric and learned how to throw the javelin, fight in armor, and ride a horse. But as a young man he formed a lasting friendship with his tutor, the Greek historian Polybius, who had been brought to Rome as a war hostage during Rome's long fight with the Antigonid dynasty in Macedonia and the leagues of city-states in Greece. Polybius actively encouraged him in his study of Greek and in his intellectual pursuits. In later life Scipio's love of Greek learning, rhetoric, and philosophy became legendary. Scipio also promoted the spread of Hellenism in Roman society, and his views became more widespread than those of Cato. In general, Rome absorbed and added what it found useful from Hellenism, just as earlier it had absorbed aspects of Etruscan culture.

What led to the fall of the Roman Republic?

The wars of conquest created serious problems for the Romans. Ever-larger armies had to be recruited to defend Rome's larger territory, with more extensive systems of administration and tax collection needed to support these armies. Roman generals, who commanded huge numbers of troops for long periods of time, acquired great power and ambition and were becoming too mighty for the Senate to control. At the

same time, ordinary citizens who fought in those armies and paid taxes to support them thought the Senate paid no attention to their concerns, and they supported alternatives to senatorial control. Another problem was that proposals to redistribute land seized from conquered people to poor citizens led those conquered people — who were often officially allies of Rome — to demand full Roman citizenship. The spoils of war seemed to many people to be unevenly distributed, with military contractors and those who collected taxes profiting greatly while average soldiers gained little. These complex and explosive problems largely account for the turmoil of the late republic (133–27 B.C.E.) and the gradual transformation of government into one in which one man held the most power.

The Countryside and Land Reforms

Following a narrative of decline that began during the late republican period itself, historians traditionally saw the long-lasting foreign wars as devastating for the Roman countryside, with the prolonged fighting drawing men away from their farms for long periods and the farms falling into wrack and ruin. There were not enough free men to keep the land under full cultivation, and women were not skilled enough to do so. Veterans and their families sold their land cheaply to wealthy landowners, who created huge estates, which the Romans called latifundia (lah-tuh-FUHN-dee-uh), worked by enslaved labor. Many veterans migrated to the cities, especially to Rome, leaving the countryside depopulated. According to this view, once they lost their land and property, men became ineligible for military service, even if they were veterans of major battles and numerous campaigns, and they were willing to support any leader who would allow them to serve again, with the pay that military service brought.

This understanding of what was going on the countryside and its causes and consequences has been challenged in the twenty-first century by historians using archaeological, demographic, genetic, and other sources rather than primarily relying on the written works of elite men. Despite the losses due to foreign wars, the countryside was not depopulated, because the birthrate went up as families adjusted to meet the needs for agricultural labor over their life cycles. Families were able to maintain small and medium-sized family farms even when several of their men were away at war, with women or other male family members running them quite successfully. There were large estates that used enslaved labor in some places, and sometimes the rich owned many small farms that became one of their sources of income, but these were not universal patterns. Thus the number of enslaved people in the countryside was much lower than previously thought. In this newer interpretation, landlessness was largely the result of overpopulation rather than simply a concentration of landholding into large estates, because when men returned from war there were too many people in the countryside. Many then did migrate to Rome, becoming urban poor who were unhappy with the way the Senate ran things. The city of Rome grew dramatically, but this did not leave the countryside empty. Thus, as with many issues in history, new evidence has made the story more complex and open to debate.

Tomb of a Roman Baker   Marcus Vergilius Eurysaces, a prosperous baker and freedman in late republican Rome, had this 30-foot-tall tomb built for himself and his wife Atistia sometime between 50 and 20 B.C.E. Over columns crammed together are odd circular openings, thought to represent basins for measuring grain or kneading dough. At the top a carved frieze shows scenes from bread production, some on a very large scale, which accounts for Eurysaces's wealth. Some of the many rural residents and formerly enslaved people who flocked to Rome became rich and celebrated their new wealth and its sources ostentatiously, upsetting the traditional elites. (Schtze/Rodemann/Bildarchiv Monheim/age footstock)

There is no debate that there were many landless poor in the city of Rome who could vote in the citizens' assemblies because they were citizens, and they tended to back anyone who offered them better prospects than the Senate did. One of these was Tiberius Gracchus (tigh-BEER-ee-uhs GRAK-uhs) (163–133 B.C.E.), an army officer in the Third Punic War who was elected tribune in 133 B.C.E. Tiberius proposed that public land in the territories of Roman allies in Italy be redistributed to the poor of the city of Rome; he also proposed that the government enforce the limit set by the Licinian-Sextian laws to the amount of land allowed to each individual. Although his reform enjoyed the support of some distinguished and popular members of the Senate, it angered those who had taken large tracts of public land for their own use, and it also upset Rome's allies, whose citizens were farming the land he proposed to give to

Land Ownership and Social Conflict in the Late Republic

Landless poor who migrated to Rome were a serious social problem and a hot-button political issue in the late republic. Landless citizens could vote in the citizens' assemblies and tended to back anyone who offered them better opportunities, especially land and the means to farm it. How did political leaders of the late republic seek to solve the problem, and why did this remain an issue?

1 Speech by Tiberius Gracchus. The general and tribune Tiberius Gracchus gave an eloquent public speech outlining the problem in 133 B.C.E., as related by the later Roman biographer Plutarch.

∼ He took his place and spoke on behalf of the poor. "The wild beasts that roam over Italy have their dens, each has a place of repose and refuge. But the men who fight and die for Italy enjoy nothing but the air and light. Without house or home they wander about with their wives and children. Their commanders lie when they exhort the soldiers in their battles to defend sepulchres and shrines from the enemy, for not one of these many Romans has either hereditary altar or ancestral tomb; they fight and die to protect the wealth and luxury of others; they are styled masters of the world, and have not a single clod of earth they can call their own." About this time King Attalus Philometor [of Pergamum] died, and Eudemus of Pergamum brought to Rome his last will, in which the Roman people were named the king's heir. Tiberius proposed a law of popular appeal providing that the king's money, when brought to Rome, should be distributed among those of the citizens receiving allotments of public land, to provide them with equipment and give them a start in farming. As for cities that were in the kingdom of King Attalus, he declared that the disposal of them was not the senate's business, but that he himself would put a resolution before the people. By this he offended the senate more than ever.

2 Reforms proposed by Tiberius Gracchus. Along with the small allotments of land for veterans paid for by King Attalus's money, Tiberius Gracchus proposed other measures, as reported by the Roman historian Appian.

∼ After speaking thus he again brought forward the existing law providing that nobody should hold more than 500 *iugera* [about 300 acres] of public domain. But he added a provision to the former law that two sons of the occupiers might each hold one half of that amount [in addition to that held by their father] and that the remainder should be divided among the poor. This was extremely disturbing to the rich because . . . they could no longer disregard the law as they had done before. . . . They collected together in groups, and made lamentation, and accused the poor of appropriating their fields of long standing, their vineyards, and their buildings. Some said they had paid the price of the land to their neighbors. Were they to lose the money with the land? . . . Others said that their wives' dowries had been expended on these estates, or that the land had been given to their own daughters as dowry. Moneylenders could show loans made on their security. All kinds of wailing and expressions of indignation were heard at once. On the other side were heard the lamentations of the poor—that they were being reduced from competence to extreme poverty, because they were unable to rear their offspring. They recounted the military services they had rendered, by which this very land had been acquired, and were angry that they should be robbed of their share of the common property. [The law was passed through procedures that many senators regarded as illegal.]

ANALYZING THE EVIDENCE

1. In Sources 1–3, what measures do Tiberius and Gaius Gracchus propose to provide land for the poor? Where would this land come from, and who might be living on it?
2. Who opposes the reforms of the Gracchi, and what do they give as their reasons?
3. In Source 4, how does the Senate seek to assure landowners they will retain their property?
4. In Source 5, what does the Flavian Bill propose, and why does the Senate oppose it? How and why is Cicero attempting to play both sides of the issue? Given what you have learned in the chapter about overpopulation in Italy, do you think there were many "deserted parts" into which people could be moved, as Cicero comments?
5. These sources stretch over more than seventy years. Why do you think this issue persisted over this long period?

Gracchus, immensely popular by reason of the law, was escorted home by the multitude as though he were the founder, not of a single city or people, but of all the nations of Italy. . . . The defeated ones remained in the city and talked the matter over, feeling aggrieved and saying that as soon as Gracchus should become a private citizen he would be sorry that he had done outrage to the sacred and inviolable office of tribune, and had sown in Italy so many seeds of future strife.

3 **The reforms of Gaius Gracchus.** Tiberius Gracchus was assassinated by a group of senators, but his brother Gaius became tribune and continued reforms, as related by Plutarch.

〜 Of the laws which he now proposed with the object of gratifying the people and destroying the power of the senate, the first concerned public lands, which were to be divided among the poor citizens; another provided that common soldiers were to be clothed at public expense without any reduction in pay, and that no one under seventeen years of age should be conscripted into military service; another concerned the allies, giving the Italians equal suffrage rights with the citizens of Rome; a fourth related to grain, lowering the market price for the poor; a fifth, dealing with the courts of justice, was the greatest blow to the power of the senators, for hitherto they alone could sit on juries, and were therefore much feared by the plebs and *equites* [wealthy commoners]. . . . He also proposed measures for sending out colonies, for constructing roads, and for building public granaries.

4 **The Agrarian Law of 111 B.C.E.** After Gaius Gracchus died by suicide in 121 B.C.E., the Senate passed several laws overturning the Gracchi reforms.

〜 With respect to the public land belonging to the Roman people within Italy . . . whatever portion of such public land or ground within Italy, or outside the city of Rome, or in a city, town, or village a land commissioner has granted or assigned and any individual shall hold or possess at the time when this measure becomes law . . . excluding such land or ground specially excepted as aforesaid, shall be private land, and for all such land, ground, or buildings there shall be the same right of purchase or sale as for other private lands, grounds, or buildings. . . . Nor shall any person take steps whereby an individual who rightfully holds or shall hold the said land, ground, or building in accordance with the law or plebiscite shall be prevented from using, enjoying, holding, or possessing the said land, ground, or building . . . nor shall any person make a proposal to that effect in the senate.

5 **Cicero discusses the Flavian Bill, 60 B.C.E.** After the law of 111 B.C.E. made almost all land in Italy private property, land for soldiers or veterans could only be found by turning to the newly conquered provinces or by using state funds to buy private land in Italy to distribute to them. In a private letter, Cicero (see "Civil War and the Rise of Julius Caesar") discusses a bill proposed by Pompey to do this.

〜 [The bill proposed] that land be purchased with the windfall which will come in from the new foreign revenues in the next five years. The senate was opposed to this whole agrarian scheme, suspecting that Pompey was aimed at getting some new powers. Pompey set his heart on carrying the law through. I, with the full approval of the applicants for land, was for confirming the holdings of all private persons—for, as you know, our strength lies in the rich landed gentry; at the same time I satisfied Pompey and the populace—which I also wanted to do—by supporting the purchase of land, thinking that if it were faithfully carried out, the dregs of the city population could be drained off and the deserted parts of Italy peopled.

PUTTING IT ALL TOGETHER

Using the sources above, along with what you have learned in class and in this chapter, write a short essay that analyzes land reform and social conflict in the later Roman Republic. How did political leaders of the late republic seek to solve the problem of increasing landlessness and a concentration of wealth, and why were their measures unsuccessful? How did this issue play into the power struggle between the Senate and charismatic military leaders during this period?

Sources: (1) Plutarch, *Life of Tiberius Gracchus,* 4.1–2, Loeb Classical Library (Cambridge, Mass.: Harvard University Press, 1921); (2) Appian, *Civil Wars,* 1.i.9–2.16, Loeb Classical Library (Cambridge, Mass.: Harvard University Press, 1913); (3) Plutarch, *Life of Gaius Gracchus,* 3–9, Loeb Classical Library (Cambridge, Mass.: Harvard University Press, 1921); (4) The Agrarian Law of 111 B.C., *Corpus Inscriptionum Latinarum,* 2d ed., vol. 1 (Berlin, 1865–), no. 585; (5) Cicero, *Letters to Atticus,* book 1, no. 29, Loeb Classical Library (Cambridge, Mass.: Harvard University Press, 1999).

Cavalry Soldier from Gaius Marius's First Legion This funeral stele shows a cavalry soldier from Gaius Marius's first legion holding a shield and lance. At the bottom right are nine *phalera*, sculpted metal disks awarded to soldiers for distinguished conduct in action, and two *armilla*, metal armbands similarly awarded as military decorations. As with military honors today, these were not worn as part of everyday wear, but on dress uniform occasions such as triumphal parades and religious ceremonies. (De Agostini/ A. DAGLI ORTI/Getty Images)

Rome's urban poor. Tiberius also acted in a way that was unprecedented, introducing his land bill in the Plebeian Assembly without officially consulting the Senate. When King Attalus III of Pergamum died and left his wealth and kingdom to the Romans in his will, Tiberius used his powers as a tribune to take the money for his reforms without asking the Senate for approval—another affront to its power, as the Senate was responsible for managing the finances of the provinces.

Many powerful Romans became suspicious of Tiberius's growing influence with the people, and Tiberius put himself forward as the champion of the

people opposed to the elites of the Senate, a populist message that many leaders since have also used to gain power. The Senate could not act against him while he was tribune; however, when he sought re-election after his term was over, riots erupted among his opponents and supporters, and a group of senators beat Tiberius to death in cold blood. The death of Tiberius was the beginning of an era of political violence.

Although Tiberius was dead, his land bill became law, and his brother Gaius (GAY-uhs) Gracchus (153–121 B.C.E.) took up the cause. The name later given to the laws championed by the brothers, the **Gracchi reforms**, reflects the fact that more than one Gracchus brother advocated them. (*Gracchi* is the Latin plural of *Gracchus*.) Gaius was also a veteran soldier with an enviable record, and when he became tribune in 123 B.C.E. he demanded even more extensive reform than had his brother. To help the urban poor, Gaius pushed legislation to provide them with cheap grain for bread, and he revived the program to send poor and propertyless people from Rome out to form colonies. To address the concerns of Rome's allies about this action, he proposed making all non-Roman Italians citizens so that they would be eligible for these benefits as well. This was not popular with many Roman citizens, rich and poor, who turned against him.

When Gaius failed in 121 B.C.E. to win the tribunate for the third time, he feared for his life. In desperation, Gaius armed his staunchest supporters, whereupon the Senate gave the consuls the license to kill him. On learning this, Gaius took his own life, and many of his supporters died in the turmoil. (See "Thinking Like a Historian: Land Ownership and Social Conflict in the Late Republic," page 128.)

Political Violence

The death of Gaius brought little peace, and trouble came from two sources: the outbreak of new wars in the Mediterranean basin and further political unrest in Rome, problems that operated together to encourage the rise of military strongmen. In 112 B.C.E., Rome declared war against the rebellious Jugurtha (joo-GUHR-thuh), king of Numidia in North Africa, one of Rome's client kingdoms whose actions had led to the Third Punic War.

The Roman legions made little headway against Jugurtha until 107 B.C.E., when Gaius Marius (MEHR-ee-uhs) (157–86 B.C.E.), a politician not from the traditional Roman aristocracy, became consul. He had no army, as the Roman troops were all fighting on Rome's northern border, and he decided to further expand the group of those eligible to be recruited to include all Roman citizens, even the poorest. He offered them armor, weapons, and most important, pay and retirement benefits in the form of land grants

■ **Gracchi reforms** Land reforms proposed by the Gracchi brothers to distribute public land to the poor of the city of Rome.

in conquered territory. Terms of service were extended to sixteen years, and training was to be all year round. Thus he completed the transformation of the Roman legions from a part-time citizens' force into a professional standing army, a process that had been going on gradually for some time. Marius also granted citizens of Rome's Italian allies full Roman citizenship if they completed a period of service in the Roman army. These Marian reforms increased the size and improved the military capabilities of the army, but they also meant that troops were loyal to the commanders who paid and rewarded them, and not the Senate.

Marius was unable to defeat Jugurtha directly, but his assistant and brother-in-law Sulla bribed Jugurtha's father-in-law to betray him, and Jugurtha was captured and executed in 104 B.C.E. in Rome. Marius later claimed this as a victory, and he was elected consul again, ultimately being elected an unprecedented seven times for the one-year term of the consul.

Fighting was also a problem on Rome's northern border, where two Germanic peoples, the Cimbri and Teutones, were moving into Gaul (present-day France) and later into northern Italy. After the Germans had defeated Roman armies sent to repel them, Marius as consul successfully led the campaign against them in 102 B.C.E., for which he was elected consul again, against the wishes of the Senate.

Rome was dividing into two political factions, both of whom wanted political power; contemporaries termed these factions the *populares* and the *optimates*. These were not political parties or consistent ideologies, but represented differences of opinion about the best way to get things done. In general the populares advocated for greater authority for the Plebeian Assembly and the tribunes and stressed the welfare of the Roman people, and the optimates upheld the leadership role of the Senate and spoke in the language of Roman traditions. Individual politicians shifted their rhetoric and tactics depending on the situation; however, both of these factions were represented in the Senate.

This division is one of many in the turmoil of the late republic, and both groups had their favored general. Marius was the general backed by the populares, who from 104 B.C.E. to 100 B.C.E. elected him consul every year, although this practice was technically illegal and put unprecedented power into a Roman military commander's hands.

The favored general of the optimates was Sulla, who was Marius's brother-in-law and had earlier been his assistant. In 91 B.C.E. many Roman allies in the Italian peninsula rose up against Rome because they were expected to pay taxes and serve in the army but had no voice in political decisions because they were not full citizens. This revolt became known as the Social War, so named from the Latin word *socius*, or "ally." Sulla's armies gained a number of victories over

the Italian allies, and Sulla gained prestige through his success in fighting them. In the end, however, the Senate agreed to give many allies Roman citizenship in order to end the fighting.

Sulla's military victories led to his election as consul in 88 B.C.E., and he was given command of the Roman army in a campaign against Mithridates, the king of a state that had gained power and territory in what is now northern Turkey and was expanding into Greece. Before he could depart, however, the populares gained the upper hand in the Plebeian Assembly, revoked his consulship, and made Marius the commander of the troops against Mithridates. Riots broke out. Sulla fled the city and returned at the head of an army, an unprecedented move by a Roman general. He quelled the riots, put down his opponents, made some political changes that reduced the power of the assembly, and left again, this time to fight Mithridates.

Sulla's forces were relatively successful against Mithridates, but meanwhile Marius led his own troops into Rome in 86 B.C.E., undid Sulla's changes, and killed many of his supporters. Although Marius died shortly after his return to power, those who supported him continued to hold Rome. Sulla returned in 83 B.C.E., and after a brief but intense civil war he entered Rome and ordered a ruthless butchery of his opponents. He then returned all power to the Senate and restored the conservative constitution as it had been before the Gracchi reforms. In 81 B.C.E., he was granted the office of dictator, a position he used to enhance his personal power. Dictators were supposed to step down after six months—many had done so in Roman history—but Sulla held this position for two years. In 79 B.C.E., Sulla abdicated his dictatorship because he was ill and believed his policies would last. Yet civil war was to be the constant lot of Rome for the next forty-eight years, and Sulla's abuse of political office became the blueprint for later leaders.

Civil War and the Rise of Julius Caesar

The history of the late republic is the story of power struggles among many famous Roman figures against a background of unrest at home and military campaigns abroad. This led to a series of bloody civil wars that raged from Spain across northern Africa to Egypt. Sulla's political heirs were Pompey, Crassus, and Julius Caesar, all of them able military leaders and brilliant politicians. Pompey (106–48 B.C.E.) began a meteoric rise to power as a successful commander of troops for Sulla against Marius in Italy, Sicily, and Africa. He then suppressed a rebellion in Spain, led naval forces against pirates in the Mediterranean, and defeated Mithridates and the forces of other rulers as well, transforming their territories into Roman provinces and providing wealth for the Roman treasury.

TURMOIL IN THE LATE REPUBLIC

104 B.C.E.	Marius and Sulla defeat Jugurtha
107, 104–100, 86 B.C.E.	Marius is elected consul
91–88 B.C.E.	Social War
88 B.C.E.	Sulla is elected consul
86 B.C.E.	Marius leads his own troops into Rome and kills Sulla's supporters
81 B.C.E.	Sulla is elected dictator
79 B.C.E.	Sulla abdicates
73–71 B.C.E.	Spartacus leads major slave revolt
70 B.C.E.	Pompey and Crassus are elected consuls
60 B.C.E.	Pompey, Crassus, and Caesar form the First Triumvirate; Caesar is elected consul
49 B.C.E.	Caesar crosses the Rubicon and takes Rome
48 B.C.E.	Caesar defeats Pompey at the Battle of Pharsalus
44 B.C.E.	Caesar is killed by a group of senators

Julius Caesar In this bust from the first century B.C.E., the sculptor portrays Caesar as a man of power and intensity. Showing individuals as representing certain virtues was common in Roman portraiture. (Art Images/Hulton Fine Art Collection/Getty Images)

Crassus (ca. 115–53 B.C.E.) also began his military career under Sulla and became the wealthiest man in Rome through buying and selling land. In 73 B.C.E., a major slave revolt broke out in Italy, led by Spartacus, a former gladiator. The slave armies defeated several Roman units sent to quash them. Finally Crassus led a large army against them and put down the revolt. Spartacus was apparently killed on the battlefield, and the rebels who were captured were crucified, with thousands of crosses lining the main road to Rome.

Pompey and Crassus then made an informal agreement with the populares in the Senate. Both were elected consuls in 70 B.C.E. and began to dismantle Sulla's constitution and initiate economic and political reforms. They and the Senate moved too slowly for some people, however, and several politicians who had been losing out in the jockeying for power, especially Catiline (108–62 B.C.E.), planned a coup, attracting people to their cause with the promise of debt relief. They planned to organize unrest in the countryside and in Rome, but the Catiline conspiracy was discovered, and Cicero (106–43 B.C.E.), who was one of the consuls in 63 B.C.E. when all this happened, denounced the conspirators on the floor of the Senate. Catiline—who was in attendance during Cicero's speech—fled Rome, and Cicero had several of the other leaders condemned to death without a trial and executed.

The man who cast the longest shadow over these troubled years was Julius Caesar (100–44 B.C.E.). Born of a noble family, he received an excellent education, which he furthered by studying in Greece with some of the most eminent teachers of the day. He had serious intellectual interests and immense literary ability. His account of his military operations in Gaul, the *Commentaries on the Gallic War*, became a classic of Western literature. (See "Evaluating Written Evidence: Julius Caesar on the Gauls," page 133.) Caesar was a superb orator, and his personality and wit made him popular. Military service was an effective stepping-stone to politics, and Caesar was a military genius who knew how to win battles and turn victories into permanent gains. He was also a shrewd politician of unbridled ambition, who knew how to use the patron-client system to his advantage. He became a protégé of Crassus, who provided cash for Caesar's needs, and at the same time helped the careers of other politicians, who in turn looked after Caesar's interests in Rome when he was away from the city. Caesar launched his military career in Spain, where his courage won the respect and affection of his troops.

■ **First Triumvirate** The name later given to an informal political alliance among Caesar, Crassus, and Pompey in which they agreed to advance one another's interests.

Julius Caesar on the Gauls

Julius Caesar described his military campaigns in Gaul from 58 to 50 B.C.E. in a firsthand account that was perhaps sent back to Rome in stages; the pieces were later put together into *Commentaries on the Gallic War*. The work is part of Caesar's campaign to win supporters, so it portrays him as decisive and brave against overwhelming odds. (See "Thinking Like a Historian: Army and Empire" in Chapter 6, page 144.) Interspersed with the accounts of battles are comments on his opponents, one of the few written sources about Gaul by someone who had actually been there. Not all are drawn from Caesar's personal experience; some are from observations by others and some from earlier writings.

Throughout Gaul there are two classes of persons of definite account and dignity. As for the common folk, they are treated almost as slaves, venturing naught of themselves, never taken into counsel. The more part of them, oppressed as they are either by debt, or by the heavy weight of tribute, or by the wrongdoing of the more powerful men, commit themselves in slavery to the nobles, who have, in fact, the same rights over them as masters over slaves. Of the two classes above mentioned one consists of Druids, the other of knights. The former are concerned with divine worship, the due performance of sacrifices, public and private, and the interpretation of ritual questions: a great number of young men gather about them for the sake of instruction and hold them in great honour. . . . In fact, it is they who decide in almost all disputes, public and private; and if any crime has been committed, or murder done, or there are any disputes about succession or boundaries, they also decide it, determining rewards and penalties: if any person or people does not abide by their decision, they ban such from sacrifice, which is their heaviest penalty. Those that are so banned are reckoned as impious and criminal; all men move out of their path and shun their approach and conversation, for fear they may get some harm from their contact, and no justice is done if they seek it, no distinction falls to their share. . . .

The Druids usually hold aloof from war, and do not pay war-taxes with the rest; they are excused from military service and exempt from all liabilities. Tempted by these great rewards, many young men assemble of their own motion to receive their training; many are sent by parents and relatives. Report says that in the schools of the Druids they learn by heart a great number of verses, and therefore some persons remain twenty years under training. And they do not think it proper to commit these utterances to writing, although in almost all other matters, and in their public and private accounts, they make use of Greek letters. I believe that they have adopted the practice for two reasons—that they do not wish the rule to become common property, nor those who learn the rule to rely on writing and so neglect the cultivation of the memory; and, in fact, it does usually happen that the assistance of writing tends to relax the diligence of the student and the action of the memory. The cardinal doctrine which they seek to teach is that souls do not die, but after death pass from one to another; and this belief, as the fear of death is thereby cast aside, they hold to be the greatest incentive to valour. . . .

The other class are the knights. These, when there is occasion, upon the incidence of a war—and before Caesar's [Caesar is here referring to himself in the third person] coming this would happen well-nigh every year, in the sense that they would either be making wanton attacks themselves or repelling such—are all engaged therein; and according to the importance of each of them in birth and resources, so is the number of liegemen and dependents that he has about him. This is the one form of influence and power known to them. . . .

Now there was a time in the past when the Gauls were superior in valour to the Germans and made aggressive war upon them. . . . At the present time, since they abide in the same condition of want, poverty, and hardship as the Germans, they adopt the same kind of food and bodily training. Upon the Gauls, however, the neighbourhood of our provinces and acquaintance with oversea commodities lavishes many articles of use or luxury; little by little they have grown accustomed to defeat, and after being conquered in many battles they do not even compare themselves in point of valour with the Germans.

EVALUATE THE EVIDENCE

1. What does Caesar view as praiseworthy qualities in Gauls? What does he say about Roman influence on them?
2. What role do Druids play in Gallic society, according to Caesar? Does he seem to approve of this role, or not?
3. How does Caesar evaluate other Gallic social groups?
4. How might Caesar's political aims have shaped how he described Gallic society to his fellow Romans?

Source: Julius Caesar, *Gallic Wars*, Loeb Classical Library (Cambridge, Mass.: Harvard University Press, 1917), vol. 72, book I, p. 3; book VI, pp. 335, 337, 339, 341, 349, 351.

In 60 B.C.E., Caesar returned to Rome from Spain, where Pompey had been sitting for three years after military victories in the East, losing some of his popularity as a conquering general as he could not convince the Senate to give his veterans land. Together with Crassus, the three concluded an informal political alliance later termed the **First Triumvirate** (trigh-UHM-veh-ruht). Crassus's money helped Caesar be elected consul, and Pompey married Caesar's daughter Julia. Crassus was appointed governor of Syria, Pompey of Hispania (present-day Spain), and Caesar of Gaul.

Cleopatra VII (69–30 B.C.E.) was a member of the Ptolemaic dynasty, the Hellenistic rulers of Egypt who had established power in the third century B.C.E. Although she was Greek, she was passionately devoted to her Egyptian subjects and was the first in her dynasty who could speak Egyptian in addition to Greek. Just as ancient pharaohs had linked themselves with the gods, she had herself portrayed as the goddess Isis and may have seen herself as a reincarnation of Isis (see "Religion and Magic" in Chapter 4).

At the time civil war was raging in the late Roman Republic, Cleopatra and her brother Ptolemy XIII were in a dispute over who would be supreme ruler in Egypt. Julius Caesar captured the Egyptian capital of Alexandria, Cleopatra arranged to meet him, and the two became lovers, although Cleopatra was much younger and Caesar was married. They apparently had a son, Caesarion, and Caesar's army defeated Ptolemy's army, ending the power struggle. In 46 B.C.E., Cleopatra arrived in Rome, where Caesar put up a statue of her as Isis in one of the city's temples.

After Caesar's assassination, Cleopatra returned to Alexandria, where she became involved in the continuing Roman civil war that now pitted Octavian, Caesar's grandnephew and heir, against Mark Antony, who commanded the Roman army in the East. Cleopatra invited Antony to come to Egypt in 41 B.C.E., and though Antony was married to the powerful Roman aristocrat Fulvia, the two became lovers and Cleopatra had twins, whom Antony acknowledged as his. When Fulvia died, Antony married Octavian's sister Octavia, an attempt to cement an alliance between the two men, but he divorced her in 32 B.C.E. and married Cleopatra. Antony's wedding present to Cleopatra was a huge grant of territory, much of it territory that officially belonged to the Roman people, which greatly increased her power and that of all her children, including Caesarion. Antony also declared Caesarion to be Julius Caesar's rightful heir.

Octavian used the wedding gift as the reason to declare Antony a traitor. He and other Roman leaders described Antony as a romantic fool captivated by the seductive Cleopatra, whom they portrayed as a decadent Eastern queen and a threat to what were considered traditional Roman values. Roman troops turned against Antony and joined with Octavian, and at the Battle of Actium in 31 B.C.E., Octavian defeated the army and navy of Antony and Cleopatra. Antony died by suicide, as did Cleopatra shortly afterward. Octavian ordered the teenage Caesarion killed, but the young children of Antony and Cleopatra were allowed to go back to Rome, where they were raised by Antony's ex-wife Octavia, as were Antony's children by Fulvia. Another consequence of Octavian's victory was that Egypt became a Roman province.

Roman sources are openly hostile to Cleopatra, and she became the model of the alluring woman whose sexual attraction led men to their doom. Stories about her beauty, sophistication, lavish spending, desire for power, and ruthlessness abounded and were retold for centuries. The most dramatic story was that she died by suicide through the bite of a poisonous snake, which may have been true and which has been the subject of countless paintings. Her tumultuous relationships with Caesar and Antony have been portrayed in plays, novels, movies, and television programs.

QUESTIONS FOR ANALYSIS

1. How did Cleopatra benefit from her relationships with Caesar and Antony? How did they benefit from their relationships with her?
2. How did ideas about gender and Roman suspicion of Greek culture combine to shape Cleopatra's fate and the way she is remembered?
3. In Chapter 1, "Individuals in Society: Hatshepsut," page 27, also focuses on a female-bodied ruler in Egypt, but one who lived more than a thousand years before Cleopatra. How would you compare the two rulers?

The only portraits of Cleopatra that date from her own lifetime are on the coins that she issued. This one, made at the mint of Alexandria, shows her as quite plain, reinforcing the point made by Cicero that her attractiveness was based more on intelligence and wit than on physical beauty. The reverse of the coin shows an eagle, a symbol of rule. (© The Trustees of the British Museum/Art Resource, NY)

Personal ambitions undermined the First Triumvirate. While Caesar was away from Rome fighting in Gaul, supporters of Caesar and Pompey formed gangs that attacked each other, and there were riots in the streets of Rome. The First Triumvirate disintegrated. Crassus died in battle while trying to conquer Parthia, and Caesar and Pompey accused each other of treachery. Fearful of Caesar's popularity and growing power, the Senate sided with Pompey and ordered Caesar to disband his army. He refused, and instead in 49 B.C.E. he crossed the Rubicon River in northern Italy—the boundary of his territorial command—with soldiers. ("Crossing the Rubicon" is still used as an expression for committing to an irreversible course of action.) Although their forces outnumbered Caesar's, Pompey and the Senate fled Rome, and Caesar entered the city and took control without a fight.

Caesar then led his army against those loyal to Pompey and the Senate in Spain and Greece. In 48 B.C.E., despite being outnumbered, he defeated Pompey and his army at the Battle of Pharsalus in central Greece. Pompey fled to Egypt, which was embroiled in a battle for control not between two generals but between a brother and a sister, Ptolemy XIII and Cleopatra VII (69–30 B.C.E.). Caesar followed Pompey to Egypt, Cleopatra allied herself with Caesar, and Caesar's army defeated Ptolemy's army, ending the power struggle. Pompey was assassinated in Egypt, Cleopatra and Caesar became lovers, and Caesar brought Cleopatra to Rome. (See "Individuals in Society: Queen Cleopatra," page 134.) Caesar put down a revolt against Roman control by the king of Pontus in northern Turkey, and then won a major victory over Pompey's army—now commanded by his sons—in Spain.

In the middle of defeating his enemies in battles all around the Mediterranean (see Map 5.2), Julius Caesar returned to Rome several times and was elected or appointed to various positions, including consul and dictator. He was acclaimed imperator, a title given to victorious military commanders and a term that later gave rise to the word *emperor*. Sometimes these elections happened when Caesar was away fighting; they were often arranged by his chief supporter and client in Rome, Mark Antony (83–30 B.C.E.), who was himself a military commander. Whatever Caesar's official position, after he crossed the Rubicon he simply made changes on his own authority, though often with the approval of the Senate, which he packed with his supporters. The Senate transformed his temporary positions as consul and dictator into ones he would hold for life.

Caesar began to make a number of legal and economic reforms. He issued laws about debt, the collection of taxes, and the distribution of grain and land. Families who had many children were to receive rewards, and Roman allies in northern Italy were to have full citizenship. He reformed the calendar, which had been based on the cycles of the moon, by replacing it with one based on the sun, adapted from the Egyptian calendar. He sponsored celebrations honoring his victories, had coins struck with his portrait, and founded new colonies, which were to be populated by veterans and the poor. He planned even more changes, including transforming elected positions such as consul, tribune, and provincial governor into ones that he appointed.

Caesar was wildly popular with most people in Rome for his generosity, and even with many senators. Other senators, led by Brutus and Cassius, favored the traditional republic and opposed Caesar's rise to what was becoming absolute power. In 44 B.C.E., they conspired to kill him and did so on March 15—the date called the "Ides of March" in the Roman calendar—stabbing him multiple times on the steps of the theater of Pompey, where the Senate was meeting that day.

The result of Caesar's assassination was yet another round of civil war. Caesar had named his eighteen-year-old grandnephew and adopted son, Octavian, as his heir. In 43 B.C.E., Octavian joined forces with two of Caesar's lieutenants, Mark Antony and Lepidus (LEH-puh-duhs), in a formal pact known later as the **Second Triumvirate**. Together they hunted down Caesar's killers and defeated the military forces loyal to Pompey's sons and to the conspirators. They agreed to divide the provinces into spheres of influence, with Octavian taking most of the west, Antony the east, and Lepidus the Iberian Peninsula and North Africa. The three came into conflict, however, and Lepidus was forced into exile by Octavian, leaving the other two to confront each other.

Both Octavian and Antony set their sights on gaining more territory. Cleopatra had returned to rule Egypt after Caesar's death, and she supported Antony. In 31 B.C.E., Octavian's forces defeated the combined forces of Antony and Cleopatra at the Battle of Actium in Greece, but the two escaped. Octavian pursued them to Egypt, and they died by suicide rather than fall into his hands. Octavian's victory at Actium put an end to an age of civil war. For his success, the Senate in 27 B.C.E. gave Octavian the name Augustus, meaning "revered one." The Senate did not mean this to be a decisive break with tradition, but because Octavian survived and began to transform the Roman government (see Chapter 6), that date is generally used to mark the end of the Roman Republic and the start of the Roman Empire.

NOTES

1. Plutarch, *Pyrrhos* 21.14. In this chapter, works in Latin with no translator noted were translated by John Buckler.
2. Sallust, *War with Catiline* 10.1–3.
3. Ovid, *Fasti* 2.535–539.

■ **Second Triumvirate** A formal agreement in 43 B.C.E. among Octavian, Mark Antony, and Lepidus to defeat Caesar's murderers.

LOOKING BACK LOOKING AHEAD

As the Greeks were creating urban culture and spreading it around the Mediterranean, other peoples, including the Etruscans and the people who later became the Romans, built their own societies on the Italian peninsula. The Romans spread their way of life throughout Italy by means of conquest and incorporation. After wars in which they defeated the wealthy city of Carthage, they expanded their political dominance throughout the western Mediterranean basin. Then they conquered in the east until they came to view the entire Mediterranean as *mare nostrum*, "our sea." As a result of these successes, Roman society and culture became Hellenized.

Yet Roman successes also brought war and civil unrest. The final days of the republic were filled with war and chaos, and the republican institutions did not survive. Rome became an empire ruled by one man. The laws and administrative practices of the republic shaped those of the empire, however, as well as those of later states in Europe and beyond. When the U.S. Constitution was drafted in 1787, its authors—well read in Roman history and law—favored a balance of powers like those they idealized in the Roman Republic, and they chose to call the smaller and more powerful deliberative assembly the Senate. They, too, were divided into those who favored rule by traditional elites and those who favored broader political power. That division is reflected in the fact that the U.S. Congress has two houses, the House of Representatives elected directly by voters, and the Senate, originally elected indirectly by state legislatures.

Make Connections

Think about the larger developments and continuities within and across chapters.

1. How would you compare ideals for male and female behavior in republican Rome with those of classical Sparta and classical Athens in Chapter 3? What are some possible reasons for the differences and similarities you have identified?

2. The Phoenicians, the Greeks, and the Romans all established colonies around the Mediterranean. How did these colonies differ, and how were they the same, in terms of their economic functions and political situations?

3. Looking over the long history of the Roman Republic, do interactions with non-Romans or conflicts among Romans themselves appear to be the most significant drivers of change, and why? How were these related to one another?

5 REVIEW & EXPLORE

Identify Key Terms

Identify and explain the significance of each item below.

Senate (p. 113)

consuls (p. 113)

patricians (p. 116)

plebeians (p. 116)

Struggle of the Orders (p. 117)

tribunes (p. 117)

patron-client system (p. 118)

Punic Wars (p. 118)

paterfamilias (p. 121)

Gracchi reforms (p. 130)

First Triumvirate (p. 133)

Second Triumvirate (p. 135)

Review the Main Ideas

Answer the section heading questions from the chapter.

1. How did the Romans become the dominant power in Italy? (p. 110)

2. What were the key institutions of the Roman Republic? (p. 116)

3. How did the Romans build a Mediterranean empire? (p. 118)

4. How did expansion affect Roman society and culture? (p. 121)

5. What led to the fall of the Roman Republic? (p. 126)

Suggested Resources

BOOKS

+ Boatwright, Mary T., et al. *The Romans: From Village to Empire*, 2d ed. 2012. An excellent survey of Roman history that emphasizes everyday life as well as political developments.

+ Canfora, Luciano. *Julius Caesar: The Life and Times of the People's Dictator.* 2007. Provides a new interpretation of Caesar that puts him fully into the context of his times.

+ Eckstein, Arthur M. *Mediterranean Anarchy, Interstate War, and the Rise of Rome.* 2006. Places the rise of the Roman Republic in the context of the wars of contemporary Hellenistic states.

+ Evans, J. K. *War, Women, and Children in Ancient Rome.* 2000. Provides a concise survey of how war affected the home front in wartime.

+ Everitt, Anthony. *The Rise of Rome: The Making of the World's Greatest Empire.* 2012. An engaging and thorough narrative written for general readers.

+ Forsythe, Gary A. *A Critical History of Early Rome from Prehistory to the First Punic War.* 2005. Uses archaeological findings as well as written sources to examine the political, social, and religious developments of early Rome.

+ Haynes, Sybille. *Etruscan Civilization: A Cultural History.* 2005. Deals with cultural history, giving special emphasis to Etruscan women.

+ Holland, Tom. *Rubicon: The Last Years of the Roman Republic.* 2005. A dramatic account of the disintegration of the republic from the Gracchi to Caesar's death.

+ Matz, David. *Daily Life of the Ancient Romans.* 2008. A brief but valuable account of the ordinary things in Roman life.

+ Miles, Richard. *Carthage Must Be Destroyed: The Rise and Fall of a Civilization.* 2011. A lively narrative of the rise and fall of Carthage, based on early sources and archaeological evidence.

+ Murell, John. *Cicero and the Roman Republic.* 2008. Looks at the late republic through Cicero's life and political career.

+ Rosenstein, Nathan. *Rome at War: Farms, Families and Death in the Middle Republic.* 2004. Detailed analysis of what was actually going on in the countryside, based on a huge range of sources.

+ Warrior, Valerie. *Roman Religion.* 2006. A relatively brief study that examines the actual practices of Roman religion in their social contexts.

MEDIA

+ *Ancient Rome: The Rise and Fall of an Empire* (BBC, 2006). A six-part docudrama; each part focuses on a turning point, with one on the Gracchi and another on Julius Caesar.

+ *Great Generals of the Ancient World: Alexander the Great, Hannibal, Julius Caesar* (History Channel, 2006). Three-part set examining the military careers, battles, and personalities of the most successful generals in the ancient world.

+ *LacusCurtius: Into the Roman World.* Website with primary and secondary resources on ancient Rome, including photographs, inscriptions, maps, and links to other Roman websites. **penelope.uchicago.edu/Thayer/E/Roman/home.htm**

+ *Mysterious Etruscans.* Informative, well-illustrated website with information on Etruscan language, art, religion, and lifestyle. **www.mysteriousetruscans.com/**

+ *Rome* (HBO and BBC, 2005, 2007). British-American historical-drama television series set in the transition from republic to empire, with real historical figures and invented characters.

+ *Spartacus* (Stanley Kubrick, 1960). Oscar-winning epic tells the story of the slave revolt led by Spartacus; starring and produced by Kirk Douglas, who considered the movie in part a response to McCarthy-era blacklisting.

6

The Roman Empire

27 B.C.E.–284 C.E.

In 27 B.C.E. the civil wars were largely over, at least for a time. With peace came prosperity, stability, and a new vision of Rome's destiny. In his epic poem the *Aeneid* celebrating the creation of the Roman people out of many different ancestors, the Roman poet Virgil expressed this vision:

> You, Roman, remember—these are your arts:
> To rule nations, and to impose the ways of peace,
> To spare the humble and to conquer the proud.[1]

This was an ideal, of course, but Augustus, now the ruler of Rome, recognized that ideals and traditions were important to Romans. Instead of creating a new form of government, he left the republic officially intact, but increasingly held more power himself. The rulers that followed him attempted to assert their power as well, though some were more successful than others and all relied on the help of the Senate and other traditional elites to run the empire. The boundaries of the Roman Empire expanded in all directions, and the army became an important means of Romanization through its forts, camps, and cities, where Roman culture mixed with local traditions. A new religion, Christianity, developed in the eastern Roman province of Judaea and spread on the roads and sea-lanes used by Roman traders and troops. By the third century C.E. civil wars had returned, however, and it seemed as if Augustus's creation would collapse. ■

CHAPTER PREVIEW

■ **How did Augustus and Roman elites create a foundation for the Roman Empire?**

■ **How did the Roman state develop after Augustus?**

■ **What was life like in the city of Rome and in the provinces?**

■ **How did Christianity grow into a major religious movement?**

■ **What political and economic problems did Rome face in the third century C.E.?**

Marketplace in Imperial Rome
In this terra-cotta relief from the third century C.E., a woman sells fruit and poultry from a shop while customers line up in front of her. Women were public merchants in imperial Rome, and some controlled their own finances, something that would have been unthinkable in ancient Athens. (De Agostini/A. DAGLI ORTI/Getty Images)

How did Augustus and Roman elites create a foundation for the Roman Empire?

After Augustus (r. 27 B.C.E.–14 C.E.) ended the civil wars that had raged off and on for decades, he faced the monumental problems of reconstruction. He first had to reconstruct a functioning government. Next he had to pay his armies for their services and care for the welfare of the provinces. Then he had to address the danger of various groups on Rome's European frontiers. Augustus was highly successful in meeting these challenges, creating a system of government in which he ruled together with the Senate and other members of the Roman elite.

Augustus and His Allies

Augustus claimed that he was restoring the republic, but he actually transformed the government into one in which he held increasing amounts of power. Historians used to see this transformation as the sole creation of Augustus and his family, but they increasingly recognize that Augustus was assisted by senators and other members of the Roman elite who wanted to play an active role in governance. Augustus and his successors turned for advice to a circle of trusted friends. Many of these were from senatorial families or those just beneath them in Rome's social hierarchy, who were called *equites*, a word meaning "horsemen" in Latin because this class had originally formed the cavalry of the Roman army.

Together the senators and equites formed a tiny elite of under ten thousand members who held almost all military, political, and economic power in Rome's expanding territory, a pattern that had started during the republican period and continued under Augustus's successors. An ambitious young man from a senatorial or equestrian family who wished to gain power and wealth generally first served as an official somewhere in the Italian peninsula. He then spent time as a high military officer, and if he was successful, he gained a post as a governor, high official, or military leader in the provinces, taking the Roman legal system and Roman culture with him. He then might try to gain a seat in the Senate, though Augustus limited these seats to around six hundred and set high minimum property requirements, so competition was fierce. Sons of sitting senators did not just inherit their fathers' seats but had to serve in the administration or high in the army first, and then run a campaign.

Although Augustus curtailed the power of the Senate, it continued to exist as the chief deliberative body of the state, and it continued to act as a court of law. Augustus and the Senate ruled together, as both needed the other to rule effectively, and the relationship between them was fluid. Augustus intentionally pursued a policy of conciliation with some of his former enemies. Toward the end of his reign, he closed the popular assemblies, so ordinary Romans could make their opinions known to him only when they saw him in person at games or during his speeches. At these times vast crowds of thousands organized themselves to clap, stomp, and shout their opinions, but these were never as important in determining policy as the opinions of Augustus's intimates.

Augustus fit his own position into the republican constitution

Augustus as Imperator   In this marble statue, found in the villa of Augustus's widow, Augustus is depicted in a military uniform and in a pose usually used to show leaders addressing their troops. This portrayal emphasizes his role as imperator, the head of the army. The figures on his breastplate show various peoples the Romans had defeated or with whom they had made treaties, along with assorted deities. Although Augustus did not declare himself a god — as later Roman emperors would — this statue shows him barefoot, just as gods and heroes were in classical Greek statuary, and accompanied by Cupid riding a dolphin, both symbols of the goddess Venus, whom he claimed as an ancestor. (Bridgeman Images)

TIMELINE

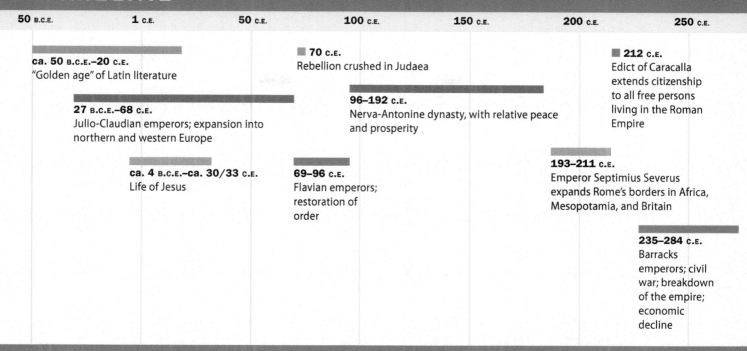

| 50 B.C.E. | 1 C.E. | 50 C.E. | 100 C.E. | 150 C.E. | 200 C.E. | 250 C.E. |

ca. 50 B.C.E.–20 C.E.
"Golden age" of Latin literature

27 B.C.E.–68 C.E.
Julio-Claudian emperors; expansion into northern and western Europe

ca. 4 B.C.E.–ca. 30/33 C.E.
Life of Jesus

70 C.E.
Rebellion crushed in Judaea

96–192 C.E.
Nerva-Antonine dynasty, with relative peace and prosperity

69–96 C.E.
Flavian emperors; restoration of order

212 C.E.
Edict of Caracalla extends citizenship to all free persons living in the Roman Empire

193–211 C.E.
Emperor Septimius Severus expands Rome's borders in Africa, Mesopotamia, and Britain

235–284 C.E.
Barracks emperors; civil war; breakdown of the empire; economic decline

---

not by creating a new office for himself but by gradually taking over many of the offices that traditionally had been held by separate people. He was elected consul, which gave him the right to call the Senate into session and present legislation to the citizens' assemblies. As a patrician, Augustus was ineligible to be a tribune, but the Senate gave him the powers of a tribune anyway, such as the right to preside over the *concilium plebis* (see Chapter 5). Recognizing the importance of religion, he had himself named *pontifex maximus*, or chief priest. An additional title that the Senate bestowed on Augustus was *princeps civitatis* (prihn-KEHPS cih-vee-TAH-tees), "first citizen of the state," and his government is called the **principate**. This title had no official powers attached to it and had been used as an honorific for centuries, so it was inoffensive to Roman ears. One of the cleverest tactics of Augustus and his allies among the Roman elite was to use noninflammatory language for the changes they were making. Only later would *princeps civitatis* become the basis of the word *prince*, meaning "sovereign ruler."

Augustus was also named **imperator**, another traditional title often given to a general by his troops after a major victory, derived from the Latin word *imperium*, which means "power to command." In the late republic more than one military commander sometimes held this title at the same time, but gradually it was restricted to the man who ruled Rome, given to him when he acceded to power, and became one of his titles. (The English word *emperor* comes from *imperator* in this more exclusive sense, and the rulers of Rome after Augustus are conventionally called emperors.) Here again Augustus and his successors used familiar language to make change seem less dramatic. They never adopted the title "king" (*rex* in Latin), as this would have been seen as too great a break with Roman traditions.

Augustus's title of imperator reflects the source of most of his power: his control and command of the army. He could declare war, he controlled deployment of the Roman army, and he paid the soldiers' wages. He granted bonuses and gave veterans retirement benefits. He could override any governor's decision about military matters in a province. Building on the earlier military reforms of Marius and Julius Caesar, Augustus further professionalized the military, making the army a recognized institution of government.

Soldiers who were Roman citizens were organized into legions, units of about five thousand men. These legionaries were generally volunteers; they received a salary and training under career officers who advanced in rank according to experience, ability, valor, and length of service. Legions were often transferred from place to place as the need arose. Soldiers served twenty-year terms, plus five in the reserves, and on retiring were to

---

principate Official title of Augustus's form of government, taken from *princeps*, meaning "first citizen."

imperator Title originally given to a Roman general after a major victory that came to mean "emperor."

be given a discharge bonus of cash or a piece of land. To pay for this bonus, Augustus ordered a tax on inheritance and on certain types of sales. The legions were backed up by auxiliaries, military forces from cities allied with Rome, which were obliged to provide a certain number of recruits each year, a situation many allies resented. Allies often had to use conscription to gain enough soldiers for what were often very long terms. Auxiliaries were paid — though at a lower rate than legionaries — and were granted Roman citizenship when they retired, which gave them legal, social, and economic privileges, but this was still not always an attractive position. Auxiliaries sometimes stayed near the area where they had been recruited, but often they served far away from home as well. They specialized in different fighting techniques than did Roman legions, and the Romans often sent the auxiliaries into the worst battles first, reserving their legions until absolutely necessary. (See "Thinking Like a Historian: Army and Empire," page 144.)

Grants of land to veterans had originally been in Italy, but by Augustus's time there was not enough land to continue this practice. Instead he gave veterans land in the frontier provinces that had been taken from the people the Romans conquered, usually near camps with active army units. Some veterans objected, and at Augustus's death they briefly revolted, but these colonies of veterans continued to play an important role in securing the Roman Empire's boundaries and controlling its newly won provinces. Augustus's veterans took abroad with them their Latin language and Roman culture, becoming important agents of Romanization and part of the cultural mixing that occurred in border areas.

Like the armies of Marius and Julius Caesar, the army that Augustus developed was loyal to him as a person, not as head of the Roman state. This form of loyalty would lead to trouble later, but the basics of the political and military system that Augustus created lasted fairly well for almost three centuries.

Roman Expansion

One of the most significant aspects of Augustus's reign was Roman expansion into central and eastern Europe and consolidation of holdings in western Europe (Map 6.1). Augustus began his work in the west by completing the conquest of Spain begun by Scipio Africanus in the third century B.C.E. In Gaul he founded twelve new towns, and the Roman road system linked new settlements with one another and with Italy. The German frontier along the Rhine River was the scene of hard fighting. In 12 B.C.E. Augustus ordered a major invasion of Germany beyond the Rhine. Roman legions advanced to the Elbe River, and the area north of the Main River and west of the Elbe was

on the point of becoming Roman. But in 9 C.E. some twenty thousand Roman troops were annihilated at the Battle of the Teutoburg Forest by an alliance of Germanic tribes led by a Germanic officer who had acquired Roman citizenship and a Roman military education. Military historians see this major defeat as an important turning point in Roman expansion, because although Roman troops penetrated the area of modern Austria, southern Bavaria, and western Hungary, the Romans never again sent a major force east of the Rhine. Hereafter the Rhine and the Danube remained the Roman frontier in central Europe, and the Romans used these rivers to supply their garrisons.

The Romans began to build walls, forts, and watchtowers to firm up their defenses, especially in the area between the two rivers, where people could more easily enter Roman territory. Romans then conquered the regions of modern Serbia, Bulgaria, and Romania in the Balkans, which gave them a land-based link between the eastern and western Mediterranean. After all the conquests under his rule, Augustus left explicit instructions in his will that Roman territory not be expanded any further, as there was plenty to do trying to subdue, Romanize, and properly govern the huge territory Rome had. Most of his successors paid no attention to his wishes.

Within the area along the empire's northern border the legionaries and auxiliaries built fortified camps. Roads linked the camps with one another, and settlements grew up around the camps. Traders began to frequent the frontier and to do business with the people who lived there. Thus Roman culture — the rough-and-ready kind found in military camps — gradually spread into the north, blending with local traditions through interactions and intermarriage. As a result, for the first time central and northern Europe came into direct and continuous contact with Mediterranean culture. Many Roman camps eventually grew into cities of several thousand people, transforming the economy of the area around them. Roman cities were the first urban developments in most parts of central and northern Europe.

As a political and religious bond between the provinces and Rome, Augustus encouraged the cult of *Roma et Augustus* (Rome and Augustus) as the guardians of the state and the source of all benefits to society. The cult spread rapidly, especially in the eastern Mediterranean, where local people already had traditions of divine kingship developed in the Hellenistic monarchies (see Chapter 4) or even earlier. Numerous temples to Rome and Augustus or just to Augustus were built throughout Roman territory. The temple at Caesarea — a new city in Judaea, built as a port and named in honor of Augustus by King Herod, ruler of the Jewish client state of Rome — was huge, as big as the Jewish

MAP 6.1 Roman Expansion Under the Empire, 44 B.C.E.–180 C.E. Following Roman expansion during the republic, Augustus added vast tracts of Europe to the Roman Empire, which the emperor Trajan later enlarged by assuming control over parts of central Europe, the Near East, and North Africa.

temple in Jerusalem. For later emperors as well, Roman officials and provincial elites who acted as patrons for their cities built celebratory arches, altars, temples, columns, and other structures to honor and show their loyalty and devotion to the ruler. (See "Evaluating Visual Evidence: Ara Pacis Augustae," page 146.)

Many of these structures were decorated with texts as well as images, chosen by those who set up the monument. For example, Augustus wrote an official account of his long career, which he included with his will, and told the Senate to set it up as a public inscription after his death. The original document, which no longer survives, was engraved on two bronze columns in front of the Mausoleum of Augustus, a large tomb erected in Rome by Augustus that is still standing. In many other places throughout the Roman Empire copies were carved into monuments on the order of provincial elites, some of which survive, and the text

became known as the *Res Gestae Divi Augusti* (The deeds of the divine Augustus).

In the late eighteenth century the English historian Edward Gibbon dubbed the stability and relative peace within the empire that Augustus created the **pax Romana**, the "Roman peace," which he saw as lasting about two hundred years, until the end of the reign of Marcus Aurelius in 180 C.E. Gibbon's term has been an influential description of this period ever since he invented it, but those the Romans conquered might not have agreed that Roman rule was so harmonious (see "Viewpoints: The Pax Romana," page 147).

Although the pax Romana was not peaceful for everyone, under Augustus and many of his successors the Romans were often able to continue doing what

■ **pax Romana** The "Roman peace," a term invented by the historian Edward Gibbon in the eighteenth century to describe the first and second centuries C.E., which he saw as a time of political stability and relative peace.

Army and Empire

Military might made it possible for the Romans to conquer and hold a huge empire. As the empire grew, it needed to recruit Romans into its legions as well as troops from allied and conquered areas into its auxiliary forces. It then needed to make these soldiers effective, loyal, and dependable. How did the Romans assemble, train, organize, and use soldiers from diverse cultures to conquer and hold their empire?

1 **Julius Caesar, *The Gallic War*, 50** B.C.E. Writing of his successful campaigns in Gaul and presenting himself as the consummate Roman military leader, Caesar (using the third person) describes his efforts to rally his wavering troops.

Such a terrible panic suddenly seized our whole army as severely affected everyone's courage and morale. Our men started asking questions, and the Gauls and traders replied by describing how tall and strong the Germans were, how unbelievably brave and skillful with weapons. . . . The panic began among the military tribunes and prefects, and the other men who, having no great military experience, had followed Caesar from Rome to court his friendship. . . . They hid themselves away in their tents and bemoaned their fate. . . . As soon as Caesar was aware of the situation he called a council, ordered centurions of all ranks to attend, and severely reprimanded them. . . . Why did they despair of their own courage, or of his anxious concern for their well-being? The danger posed by this enemy had already been experienced in the time of our fathers, when the Cimbri and Teutoni were expelled by Gaius Marius. On that occasion it was clear that the army had deserved as much credit as its commander. . . . From all this, said Caesar, they could see how crucial was firmness of purpose. . . . The Germans were the same people who had often clashed with the Helvetii—and the Helvetii had frequently beaten them, not only within their own borders but also in Germany itself—and yet the Helvetii had proved no match for our army. . . . And so, Caesar concluded, he would do at once what he had intended to put off till a later date. The very next night, during the fourth watch, they would strike camp. Then he would know as soon as possible whether their sense of shame and duty was stronger than their fear. . . . At the end of this speech the change of attitude was quite remarkable, and there arose an immense enthusiasm and eagerness to start the campaign.

2 **Augustus, *Res Gestae Divi Augusti*, ca. 14** C.E. In his account of his career, written at the end of his life, Augustus describes some of the actions he took regarding the army.

Wars, both civil and foreign, I undertook throughout the world, on sea and land, and when victorious I spared all citizens who sued for pardon. The foreign nations which could with safety be pardoned I preferred to save rather than to destroy. The number of Roman citizens who bound themselves to me by military oath was about 500,000. Of these I settled in colonies or sent back into their own towns, after their term of service, something more than 300,000, and to all I assigned lands, or gave money as a reward for military service. . . .

I settled colonies of soldiers in Africa, Sicily, Macedonia, both Spains, Achaia, Asia, Syria, Gallia Narbonensis, Pisidia. Moreover, Italy has twenty-eight colonies founded under my auspices which have grown to be famous and populous during my lifetime.

3 **Titus Flavius Josephus, *The Jewish War*, ca. 75** C.E. Josephus was a commander in the Jewish revolt against the Romans in 66 C.E. who after he was taken prisoner went over to the Roman side. Here he describes how he used the Romans as a model for the Jewish army. Like Caesar in Source 1, he writes of himself in the third person.

Josephus knew that the invincible might of Rome was chiefly due to unhesitating obedience and to practice in arms. He despaired of providing similar instruction, demanding as it did a long period of training; but he saw that the habit of obedience resulted from the number of

ANALYZING THE EVIDENCE

1. How does Julius Caesar use history and tradition in Source 1 to convince his troops to fight, and what do you think his purpose was in relating this incident as he did?
2. Why would the promise of eventual citizenship and land, as described by Augustus in Source 2 and recorded in military diplomas like the one in Source 4, have been an effective recruiting tool? How would this practice have helped maintain the empire?
3. What aspects of the Roman military does Josephus use as a model for his own forces in Source 3, and how do these compare with the qualities Vegetius identifies in Source 5 as ideal in the perfect recruit? Why would these have been important to Roman military success?
4. Julius Caesar and Augustus were military generals and rulers of Rome, Josephus was an opponent of Rome, and Vegetius was a Roman looking back at the past. How do you think their positions shaped their perspectives on the Roman army and the reasons for its success?

4 **Roman military diploma, 71 C.E.** Military diplomas were bronze sheets, wired together, that certified that a former soldier in the auxiliary forces had been honorably discharged and granted Roman citizenship by the emperor as a reward for service. They are dated, and as on this one, they often recorded the former soldier's units, tours of duty, commanders, and the names of his father, wife, and children. One copy stayed in Rome, and one was sent to the soldier himself to take to the province where he intended to live, much as members of the military today receive discharge papers.

(© Israel Museum, Jerusalem/Acquired in memory of Chaim Herzog, Sixth President of the State of Israel, by his family and Yad Chaim Herzog; the Carmen and Louis Warschaw Fund of Archaeological Acquisitions; and David and Genevieve Hendin, New York/Bridgeman Images)

5 **Vegetius, *Epitome of Military Science*, ca. 380–390 C.E.** Vegetius seems to have been a Roman imperial bureaucrat who described what he saw as ideal military recruitment and training at a point when the Roman Empire was in decline and the army faced many challenges.

In every battle it is not numbers and untaught bravery so much as skill and training that generally produce the victory. For we see no other explanation of the conquest of the world by the Roman People than their drill-at-arms, camp-discipline and military expertise. . . . But what succeeded against all [enemies] was careful selection of recruits, instruction in the rules, so to speak, of war, toughening in daily exercises, prior acquaintance in field practice with all possible eventualities in war and battle, and strict punishment of cowardice. Scientific knowledge of warfare nurtures courage in battle. No one is afraid to do what he is confident of having learned well. A small force which is highly trained in the conflicts of war is more apt to victory: a raw and untrained horde is always exposed to slaughter. . . . The rural populace is better suited for arms. They are nurtured under the open sky in a life of work, enduring the sun, careless of shade, unacquainted with bathhouses, ignorant of luxury, simple souled, content with a little, with limbs toughened to endure every kind of toil. . . . If ancient custom is to be retained, everyone knows that those entering puberty should be brought to the levy. For those things are taught not only more quickly but even more completely which are learned from boyhood. Secondly military alacrity, jumping and running should be attempted before the body stiffens with age. . . . You need not greatly regret the absence of tall stature. It is more useful that soldiers be strong than big. . . . The youth in whose hands is to be placed the defence of provinces, the fortune of battles, ought to be of outstanding breeding if numbers suffice, and morals. Decent birth makes a suitable soldier, while a sense of shame prevents flight and makes him a victor.

their officers, and he now reorganized his army on the Roman model, appointing more junior commanders than before. He divided the soldiers into different classes, and put them under decurions and centurions, those being subordinate to tribunes, and the tribunes to commanders of larger units. He taught them how to pass on signals, how to sound the advance and the retreat, how to make flank attacks and encircling movements, and how a victorious unit could relieve one in difficulties and assist any who were hard pressed. He explained all that contributed to toughness of body or fortitude of spirit. Above all he trained them for war by stressing Roman discipline at every turn: they would be facing men who by physical prowess and unshakable determination had conquered almost the entire world.

PUTTING IT ALL TOGETHER

Using the sources above, along with what you have learned in class and in Chapters 5 and 6, write a short essay that analyzes the military's role in the empire's expansion. How did the Romans assemble, train, organize, and use soldiers from diverse cultures to conquer and hold their empire? How would you assess the relative importance of various factors in this process, and why might your assessment be different from those of the authors cited here?

Sources: (1) Julius Caesar, *Seven Commentaries on the Gallic War*, trans. Carolyn Hammond (New York: Oxford University Press, 1998), pp. 24–27; (2) *Velleius Paterculus*, Loeb Classical Library, vol. 152, trans. Frederick W. Shipley (Cambridge, Mass.: Harvard University Press, 1924), pp. 347, 383; (3) Josephus, *The Jewish War*, trans. G. A. Williamson (Baltimore, Md.: Penguin Books, 1972), p. 172; (5) N. P. Milner, trans., *Vegetius: Epitome of Military Science* (Liverpool: Liverpool University Press, 1996), pp. 2–8.

Ara Pacis Augustae

In the middle years of Augustus's reign, the Roman Senate ordered a huge altar, the Ara Pacis Augustae (Altar of Augustan Peace), built to honor his return to Rome after three years in Hispania and Gaul. It was dedicated on the birthday of his wife Livia, shortly after the death of her son Drusus. The altar was decorated with life-size reliefs of Augustus and members of his family, prominent members of the Senate, and other people and deities. One side, shown here, depicts a goddess figure, most likely the goddess Peace herself, with twin babies on her lap, flanked by nymphs representing land and sea, and surrounded by plants and animals.

(DEA/G. DAGLI ORTI/De Agostini/Getty Images)

EVALUATE THE EVIDENCE

1. What do the elements depicted here most likely symbolize?
2. How did the senators who commissioned this choose to portray Augustus's reign, and why would it be in their best interests to do so?
3. The Ara Pacis Augustae and the *Res Gestae Divi Augusti* (see "Thinking Like a Historian: Army and Empire," page 144) were both works of public art designed to commemorate the deeds of Augustus. Why might the Senate and the provincial elites who set up monuments inscribed with the *Res Gestae* have commissioned such works? Can you think of contemporary parallels?

they had under the republic: create a sense of loyalty in conquered people by granting at least some of them citizenship and other privileges. Augustus also respected local customs and ordered his governors to do the same. Roman governors applied Roman law to Romans living in their territories, but they let local people retain their own laws. As long as they provided taxes, did not rebel, and supplied a steady stream of recruits for Roman armies, people could continue to run their political and social lives as they had before Roman conquest.

This policy was crucial in holding the empire together. Although the Roman army was everywhere, historians have estimated that at its height in the second century C.E. the Roman military had no more than roughly 100,000 troops. There is no way that these few men could have managed millions of rebellious subjects.

While Romans did not force their culture on local people in Roman territories, local elites with aspirations knew that the best way to rise in stature and power was to adopt aspects of Roman culture. Thus, just as

VIEWPOINTS

The Pax Romana

In 70 C.E., Roman forces under a general named Cerialis defeated groups in Gaul that had revolted against Rome and proclaimed their own kingdoms. After his victory, Cerialis apparently gave a speech to the assembled troops, proclaiming the benefits brought by Rome. The Romans continued their expansion northward into Britain, where one of their opponents was the Scottish chieftain Calgacus, who also apparently gave a speech. Both of these speeches appear in the writings of Tacitus (ca. 56–ca. 120 C.E.), a Roman official, senator, and historian.

Speech of Cerialis, from Tacitus, *History*

Cerialis then convoked an assembly of the Trevai and Lingones [two Gallic tribes] and thus addressed them: "I have never cultivated eloquence; it is by my sword that I have asserted the excellence of the Roman people. . . . Roman generals and emperors entered your territory, as they did the rest of Gaul, with no ambitious purposes, but at the solicitation of your ancestors, who were wearied to the last extremity by intestine strife, while the Germans, who they had summoned to their help, had imposed their yoke alike on friend and foe. How many battles have we fought against the Cimbri and Tuetones [two German tribes], at the cost of what hardships to our armies, and with what result have we waged our German wars, is perfectly well known. It is not to defend Italy that we occupied the borders of the Rhine, but to insure that no second Ariovistus [a Germanic leader] should seize Gaul. . . . Gaul has always had its petty kingdoms and intestine wars, till you submitted to our authority. We, though so often provoked, have used the right of conquest to burden you only with the cost of maintaining peace. For the tranquility of nations cannot be preserved without armies; armies cannot exist without pay; pay cannot be furnished without tribute; all else is common among us. . . .

Should the Romans be driven out (which God forbid) what can result but wars between all these nations? By the prosperity and order of eight hundred years has this fabric of empire been consolidated, nor can it be overthrown without destroying those who overthrow it. Yours will be the worst peril, for you have gold and wealth, and these are the chief incentives to war. Give therefore your love and respect to the cause of peace, and to that capital [i.e., Rome] in which

we, conquerors and conquered, claim an equal right. Let the lessons of fortune in both its forms teach you not to prefer rebellion and ruin to submission and safety." With words to this effect he quieted his audience, who feared harsher treatment.

Speech of Calgacus, from Tacitus, *Agricola*

Now, however, the furthest limits of Britain are thrown open . . . there are no tribes beyond us, nothing indeed but waves and rocks, and the yet more terrible Romans, from whose oppression escape is sought by obedience and submission. Robbers of the world, having by their universal plunder exhausted the land, they rifle the deep [i.e., the oceans]. If the enemy be rich, they are rapacious; if he be poor, they lust for domination; neither East nor West has been able to satisfy them. Alone among men they covet with equal eagerness the poor and the rich. To robbery, slaughter, plunder they give the lying name of empire; they create a desert and call it peace.

Nature has willed that every man's children and kindred should be his dearest objects. Yet these are torn from us by conscriptions to be slaves in foreign lands. Our wives and our sisters, even though they may escape being raped by the enemy, are seduced under the names of friendship and hospitality. Our goods and fortunes they collect for their tribute, our harvests for their granaries. Our very hands and bodies, under the lash and in the midst of insult, are worn down by the toil of clearing forests and swamps.

QUESTIONS FOR ANALYSIS

1. How do Cerialis and Calgacus differ in their opinions about Roman domination? On what aspects of Roman conquest do the two agree?
2. Tacitus was born in the provinces, and like many ancient historians, he uses speeches to make points in his narrative, even though he did not speak to eyewitnesses. How might these factors have shaped these sources and what we can learn from them?

Sources: Tacitus, *The History of Tacitus*, trans. A. J. Church and W. J. Brodribb (London: Macmillan, 1864), at: http://classics.mit.edu/Tacitus/histories.mb.txt; Tacitus, *The Agricola and Germania*, trans. A. J. Church and W. J. Brodribb (London: Macmillan, 1877), pp. 25–26.

ambitious individuals in the Hellenistic world embraced Greek culture and learned to speak Greek, those determined to get ahead now learned Latin, and sometimes Greek as well if they wished to be truly well educated.

Latin Literature

Many poets and prose writers were active in the late republic and the principate, and scholars of literature later judged their work to be of such high quality that they called the period from about 50 B.C.E. to 20 C.E. the "golden age" of Latin literature. Roman poets and prose writers celebrated the physical and emotional joys of a comfortable life in works that were polished and elegant. As had Athenian playwrights, they also responded to the political turmoil going on around them as Augustus appropriated the past, made claims about his own destiny, and promoted social change.

Rome's greatest poet was Virgil (70–19 B.C.E.), who drew on earlier traditions but gave them new twists. The *Georgics*, for example, is a poem about agriculture that used Hellenistic models to capture both the peaceful pleasures and the day-to-day harshness of rural life. Virgil's masterpiece is the *Aeneid* (uh-NEE-ihd), an epic poem that is the Latin equivalent of the Greek *Iliad* and *Odyssey*. Virgil's account of the founding of the Roman people as a hybrid created out of many different groups gave final form to the legend of Aeneas, the Trojan hero (and ancestor of Romulus and Remus) who escaped to Italy at the fall of Troy:

> I sing of warfare and a man at war,
> From the sea-coast of Troy in the early days,
> He came to Italy by destiny,
> To our Lavinian western shore,
> A fugitive, this captain, buffeted
> Cruelly on land as on the sea
> By blows from the powers of the air—behind them
> Baleful Juno [the queen of the gods] in her sleepless rage.
> And cruel losses were his lot in war,
> Till he could found a city and bring home
> His gods to Latium, land of the Latin race,
> The Alban lords, and the high walls of Rome.[2]

As Virgil told it, Aeneas became the lover of Dido, the widowed queen of Carthage, but left her because his destiny called him to found Rome. Swearing the destruction of Rome, Dido died by suicide, and according to Virgil, her enmity helped cause the Punic Wars. In leaving Dido, an "Eastern" queen, Aeneas put duty and the good of the state ahead of marriage or pleasure. The resemblances between this story and the very recent real events involving Antony and Cleopatra

were not lost on Virgil's audience. Making the public aware of these parallels, and of Virgil's description of Aeneas as an ancestor of Julius Caesar, fit well with Augustus's aims. Augustus encouraged Virgil to write the *Aeneid* and made sure it was circulated widely immediately after Virgil died. It puts sexual relations as well as war at the center of the story of Rome, just as the founding myths of the rape of the Sabine women and the suicide of Lucretia had earlier (see Chapter 5).

The poet Horace (65–8 B.C.E.) rose from humble beginnings to friendship with Augustus. His father had been enslaved, but gained his freedom and became a prosperous tax collector. He spent lavishly on Horace's education, which began in Rome and finished in Athens. Horace's most important works are a series of odes, short lyric poems often focusing on a single individual or event. One of these commemorated Augustus's victory over Antony and Cleopatra at Actium in 31 B.C.E. Horace depicted Cleopatra as a frenzied queen, drunk with desire to destroy Rome, a view that has influenced opinions about Cleopatra until today.

The historian Livy (59 B.C.E.–17 C.E.) was a friend of Augustus and a supporter of the principate. He especially approved of Augustus's efforts to restore what he saw as republican virtues. Livy's 142-volume history of Rome, titled simply *Ab Urbe Condita* (From the founding of the city), began with the legend of Aeneas and ended with the reign of Augustus. Livy used the works of earlier Greek and Roman writers, as well as his own experiences, as his source material.

Augustus actively encouraged poets and writers, but he could also turn against them. The poet Ovid (AH-vuhd) (43 B.C.E.–17 C.E.) wrote erotic poetry about absent lovers and the joys of seduction, as well as other works about religious festivals and mythology. His best-known work is *The Art of Love*, a satire of the serious instructional poetry that was common in Rome at the time. *The Art of Love* provides advice to men about how to get and keep women, and for women about how to get and keep men. (See "Evaluating Written Evidence: Ovid, *The Art of Love*," page 149.) This work was so popular, Ovid relates, that shortly after completing it he felt compelled to write *The Cure for Love*, advising people how to fall out of love and forget their former lovers. Have lots of new lovers, it advises, and don't hang around places, eat foods, or listen to songs that will make you remember your former lover. In 8 B.C.E. Augustus banished Ovid to a city on the Black Sea far from Rome. Why he did so is a mystery, and Ovid himself states only that the reason was "a poem and a mistake." Some scholars argue that Augustus banished Ovid because his poetry celebrated adultery at a time when Augustus was promoting marriage and childbearing, and others say it was because the poet knew about political conspiracies. Whatever its causes, the exile of Ovid became

Ovid, *The Art of Love*

The Art of Love is a humorous guide for lovers written by the Roman poet Ovid. Ovid addresses the first two parts to men, instructing them on how to seduce and keep women — look good, give them compliments, don't be too obvious. The third part is his corresponding advice for women, which in its main points is the same. The section below comes from the beginning of part one, advising men on where and how to meet women.

∾

Now, that you still are fancy-free, now is the time for you to choose a woman and say to her: "You are the only woman that I care for." She's not going to be wafted down to you from heaven on the wings of the wind. You must use your own eyes to discover the girl that suits you. The hunter knows where to spread his nets in order to snare the stag; he knows the valley where the wild boar has his lair. The birdcatcher knows where he should spread his lime; and the fisherman, what waters most abound in fish. And thou who seekest out the object of a lasting love, learn to know the places which the fair ones most do haunt. You won't have to put to sea in order to do that, or to undertake any distant journeys. . . .

. . . But it is especially at the theatre you should lay your snares; that is where you may hope to have your desires fulfilled. Here you will find women to your taste: one for a moment's dalliance, another to fondle and caress, another to have all for your own. . . .

Forget not the arena where mettled steeds strive for the palm of Victory. This circus, where an immense concourse of people is gathered, is very favourable to Love. . . . Sit close beside her, as close as you are able; there's nothing to prevent. The narrowness of the space compels you to press against her and, fortunately for you, compels her to acquiesce. Then, of course, you must think of some means of starting the conversation. Begin by saying the sort of thing people generally do say on such occasions. Some horses are seen entering the stadium; ask her the name of their owner; and whoever she favours, you should follow suit. And when the solemn procession of the country's gods and goddesses passes along, be sure and give a rousing cheer for Venus, your protectress. If, as not infrequently befalls, a speck of dust lights on your fair one's breast, flick it off with an airy finger; and if there's nothing there, flick it off just the same; anything is good enough to serve as a pretext for paying her attention. . . .

Dinners and banquets offer easy access to women's favour, and the pleasures of the grape are not the only entertainment you may find there; Love, with rosy cheeks, often presses in her frail hands the amphora of Bacchus [the god of wine]. As soon as his wings are drenched with wine, Cupid [the god of love] grows drowsy and stirs not from his place. But anon he'll be up and shaking the moisture from his wings, and woe betide the man or woman who receives a sprinkling of this burning dew. Wine fills the heart with thoughts of love and makes it prompt to catch on fire.

EVALUATE THE EVIDENCE

1. What metaphors and symbols does Ovid use to describe finding a lover and falling in love?
2. What does this guide indicate about leisure activities in the Rome of Ovid's day?

Source: *The Love Books of Ovid: Being the Amores, Ars Amatoria, Remedia Amoris and Medicamina Faciei Femineae of Publius Ovidius Naso*, trans. J. Lewis May (New York: Rarity Press, 1930), pp. 98, 100, 101–102, 104.

---

a symbol of misunderstood poetic genius for many later writers.

Marriage and Morality

Augustus's banishing of Ovid may have simply been an excuse to get rid of him, but concern with morality and with what were perceived as traditional Roman virtues was a matter not just for literature in Augustan Rome, but also for law. Augustus promoted marriage and childbearing through legal changes that released free women and freedwomen (women who had been enslaved, but were now free) from male guardianship if they had given birth to a certain number of children. Men and women who were unmarried or had no children were restricted in the inheritance of property. Adultery, defined as sex with a married woman or with a woman under male guardianship, was made a crime, not simply the private family matter it had been.

In imperial propaganda, Augustus had his own family depicted as a model of traditional morality, with his wife Livia at his side and dressed in conservative and somewhat old-fashioned clothing rather than the more daring Greek styles that wealthy women were actually wearing in Rome at the time. In fact, Augustus's family did not live up to this ideal. Augustus had his daughter Julia arrested and exiled for adultery and treason. Although it is impossible to tell what actually happened, she seems to have had at least one affair after her father forced her to marry a second husband — her stepbrother Tiberius.

Same-sex relationships among men were acceptable in Roman society as long as there was an age and status difference between partners and certain sexual norms were followed. Roman citizens were expected never to be sexually penetrated, for this would mean a loss of what was termed *integritas*. Thus a respectable Roman man could penetrate whomever he wished and still maintain his masculinity, but losing his *integritas* brought shame on himself and his family and could mean a loss of status. Men were expected to control their own bodily urges, however, and also control those under their power, including family, servants, inferiors, and soldiers. We do not know very much about same-sex relationships among women in Rome, though court gossip and criticism of powerful women, including the wives of Augustus's successors, sometimes included charges of such relationships, along with charges of heterosexual promiscuity and other sexual slander. Most of these were in fact personal attacks on the men who were supposed to control them, however, rather than statements about the women's actual behavior.

How did the Roman state develop after Augustus?

Augustus's success in creating solid political institutions was tested by those who ruled immediately after him, a dynasty historians later called the Julio-Claudians (27 B.C.E.–68 C.E.) after the families who comprised it. The incompetence of Nero, one of the Julio-Claudians, and his failure to deal with the army generals allowed a military commander, Vespasian (veh-SPAY-zhuhn), to claim the throne and establish a new dynasty, the Flavians (69–96 C.E.), who reasserted order. The Flavians were followed by a series of relatively successful emperors, the Nerva-Antonine dynasty (96–192 C.E.), and Rome entered a period of political stability, prosperity, and relative peace that lasted until the end of the second century C.E.

The Julio-Claudians and the Flavians

Augustus had no male children who survived, but he married his only daughter Julia to a series of male relatives and in-laws who he thought would be good heirs. Two died, but the third, Tiberius, a successful general who was the son of Augustus's wife Livia by her first marriage and thus Julia's stepbrother, survived. Adoption of an heir was a common practice among members of the elite in Rome, who used this method to pass on property to a chosen younger man—often a relative—if they had no sons. Long before Augustus's death he shared many of the powers that the Senate had given him, including the imperium over the army, with Tiberius, thus grooming him to succeed him. In his will Augustus confirmed him as heir and left him most of his vast fortune when he died in 14 C.E. The Senate confirmed Tiberius (r. 14–37 C.E.) as princeps.

For fifty years after Augustus's death the Julio-Claudians provided the rulers of Rome. They generally followed the pattern set by Augustus and adopted a nephew or great-nephew as their sons in order to promote them, though there were also often intrigues and plots surrounding the succession. Augustus's creation of an elite unit of bodyguards known as the **Praetorian** (pree-TAWR-ee-uhn) **Guard** had repercussions for his successors. In 41 C.E. the Praetorians murdered Tiberius's successor Caligula (r. 37–41 C.E.) and forced the Senate to ratify their choice of Claudius as emperor. Such events were repeated frequently. During the first three centuries of the empire, the Praetorian Guard often murdered emperors they were supposed to protect and raised to emperor men of their own choosing.

Under Claudius (r. 41–54 C.E.), Roman troops invaded Britain, and roads, canals, and aqueducts were built across the empire. Claudius was followed by his great-nephew Nero (r. 54–68 C.E), whose erratic actions and policies led to a revolt in 68 C.E. by several generals, which was supported by the Praetorian Guard and members of the Senate. He was declared an enemy of the people and died by suicide. This event opened the way to widespread disruption and civil war. In 69 C.E., the "year of the four emperors," four men claimed the position of emperor in quick succession. Roman armies in Gaul, on the Rhine, and in the east marched on Rome to make their commanders emperor. The man who emerged triumphant was Vespasian, commander of the eastern armies.

Vespasian (r. 69–79 C.E.) restored the discipline of the armies. To prevent others from claiming the throne, he designated his sons Titus (r. 79–81 C.E.) and Domitian (r. 81–96 C.E.) as his successors, thus establishing the Flavian dynasty. Although Roman policy was to rule by peaceful domination whenever possible, he used the army to suppress the rebellions that had begun erupting at the end of Nero's reign. The most famous of these was one that had burst out in Judaea in 66 C.E., sparked by long-standing popular unrest over taxes. Jewish rebels initially defeated the Roman troops stationed in Judaea, but a larger army

■ **Praetorian Guard** Imperial bodyguard created by Augustus.

THE JULIO-CLAUDIANS, THE FLAVIANS, AND THE NERVA-ANTONINES

The Julio-Claudians		The Flavians		The Nerva-Antonines	
27 B.C.E.–14 C.E.	Augustus	69 C.E.–79 C.E.	Vespasian	96 C.E.–98 C.E.	Nerva
14 C.E.–37 C.E.	Tiberius	79 C.E.–81 C.E.	Titus	98 C.E.–117 C.E.	Trajan
37 C.E.–41 C.E.	Caligula	81 C.E.–96 C.E.	Domitian	117 C.E.–138 C.E.	Hadrian
41 C.E.–54 C.E.	Claudius			138 C.E.–161 C.E.	Antoninus Pius
54 C.E.–68 C.E.	Nero			161 C.E.–180 C.E.	Marcus Aurelius
				180 C.E.–192 C.E.	Commodus

under the leadership of Vespasian and his son Titus put down the revolt. They destroyed much of the city of Jerusalem, including the Jewish temple, in 70 C.E., and took thousands of Jews as military captives, enslaving them and dispersing them throughout the empire.

The Flavians carried on Augustus's work in Italy and on the frontiers. During the brief reign of Vespasian's son Titus, Mount Vesuvius in southern Italy erupted, destroying Pompeii and other cities and killing thousands of people. (See "Individuals in Society: Pliny the Elder," page 152.) Titus gave money and sent officials to organize the relief effort. His younger brother Domitian, who followed him as emperor, won additional territory in Germany, consolidating it into two new provinces. Later in life he became more autocratic, however, and he was killed in 96 C.E. in a plot that involved his own wife, ending the Flavian dynasty.

The Nerva-Antonine Dynasty

The Flavians were succeeded by the Nerva-Antonine dynasty, which ruled from 96 C.E. to 192 C.E. In the sixteenth century the political philosopher Niccolò Machiavelli termed five of these the "five good emperors" — Nerva, Trajan, Hadrian, Antoninus Pius, and Marcus Aurelius. Machiavelli praised them because they all adopted able men as their successors during their lifetimes, thus giving Rome stability, although they may simply have been lucky, as this was a pattern set by Julius Caesar and Augustus, not something new. Eighteenth- and nineteenth-century historians generally regarded them as "good" because they were members of the Senate (thus of the class of people these historians believed should rule) and successful generals. Those people conquered by them might have had a different opinion, but they left few sources.

Dubbing emperors "good" or "bad" is not something today's historians generally do, but they view the Nerva-Antonines as able administrators and military leaders. Hadrian (r. 117–138 C.E.) is a typical example. He received a solid education in Rome and became an ardent admirer of Greek culture. He caught the attention of his elder cousin Trajan, the future emperor, who started him on a military career. At age nineteen Hadrian served on the Danube frontier, where he learned the details of how the Roman army lived and fought and saw for himself the problems of defending the frontiers. When Trajan became emperor in 98 C.E., Hadrian was given important positions in which he learned how to defend and run the empire. Although Trajan did not officially declare Hadrian his successor, at Trajan's death in 117 Hadrian assumed power.

Hadrian built or completed a number of buildings, including the circular Pantheon in Rome and new temples in Athens. He established more formal imperial administrative departments and separated civil service from military service. Men with little talent or taste for the army could instead serve the state as administrators. These innovations made for more efficient running of the empire and increased the authority of the emperor.

Under Trajan the boundaries of the Roman Empire were expanded to their farthest extent, and Hadrian worked to maintain most of these holdings, although he pulled back Roman armies from areas in the East he considered indefensible. No longer a conquering force, the army was expected to defend what had already been won. Forts and watch stations guarded the borders. Outside the forts the Romans built a system of roads that allowed the forts to be quickly supplied and reinforced in times of rebellion or unrest. Trouble for the Romans included two major revolts by Jews in the eastern part of the empire, which resulted in heavy losses on both sides and the exile of many Jews from Judaea.

Roman soldiers also built walls, of which the most famous was one across northern England built

INDIVIDUALS IN SOCIETY

Pliny the Elder

"My uncle was stationed at Misenum, in active command of the fleet. On 24 August, in the early afternoon, my mother drew his attention to a cloud of unusual size and appearance. . . . My uncle's scholarly acumen saw at once that it was important enough for a closer inspection, and he ordered a boat to be made ready." So begins a letter from the statesman and writer Pliny the Younger to the historian Tacitus, describing what happened when Mount Vesuvius erupted in 79 C.E. Pliny provided terrifying details of clouds of hot ash, raining pumice stones, and sheets of fire, and then sang the praises of his uncle, also named Pliny, whose actions, "begun in a spirit of inquiry, [were] completed as a hero." According to Pliny the Younger's account, his uncle "steer[ed] his course straight for the danger zone with the intention of bringing help to many more people. . . . He was entirely fearless, describing each new movement and phase of the portent to be noted down exactly as he observed them . . . and when his helmsman advised him to turn back he refused, telling him that Fortune stood by the courageous." The elder Pliny (23–79 C.E.) died on the beach near Pompeii, most likely from inhaling fumes that aggravated his asthma. His body was discovered several days later when the smoke and ash cleared.

The younger Pliny used this letter to portray his uncle as a model of traditional Roman virtues, but some of what he related was not an exaggeration. Like many young men of his social class — the equestrian — Pliny the Elder studied law and then joined the army as an officer. He was involved in several military campaigns in Germany and also found time to write books, including a volume on military tactics and several biographies. He left military service during Nero's reign and kept out of the limelight, writing noncontroversial books on grammar and rhetoric. After Nero died by suicide and Vespasian came to power, Pliny went back into government service, serving as the procurator (governor) of several different provinces. He again wrote biographies and histories, all of which are now lost, and the work that became his masterpiece, *Natural History*, an encyclopedia in which he sought to cover everything that was known to ancient Romans. In thirty-seven volumes, *Natural History* covers what we would now term biology, geology, astronomy, mineralogy, geography, ethnography, comparative anthropology, medicine, painting, building techniques, and many other subjects. Pliny's "spirit of inquiry" shines through this work, which he researched through the study of hundreds of sources (all carefully cited) and wrote while he was traveling around in government service. It is one of the largest works to have survived from the Roman Empire and served as a source of knowledge into the Renaissance, when it was one of the very first classical books to be published after the invention of the printing press in the fifteenth century. Pliny finished a first draft in about 77 C.E. and was working on revisions when he was appointed fleet commander in the Roman navy and sent to Misenum, near Naples. There the cloud of smoke from the erupting Vesuvius was too interesting for him to ignore, and he set off in a boat to investigate, with deadly results.

QUESTIONS FOR ANALYSIS

1. What Roman ideals does the younger Pliny portray his uncle as exemplifying through his conduct during the eruption?
2. How did army and government service in the Roman Empire provide opportunities for men of broad interests like Pliny?

Source: Quotations from Pliny the Younger, *Letters* 6.16, translated with an introduction by Betty Radice, vol. 1 (London: Penguin Classics, 1963; reprinted 1969), pp. 166, 168.

No contemporary portrait of Pliny the Elder survives, but his nephew reports that when his body was discovered, it was "still fully clothed and looking more like sleep than death." When Pompeii was excavated, archaeologists used plaster to fill the voids in layers of ash that once held human bodies, allowing us to see the exact position a person was in when he or she died. This plaster cast is not Pliny but is as close to him in death as we can come. (© SZ Photo/Manfred Storck/ Bridgeman Images)

primarily during Hadrian's reign. Hadrian's Wall, as it became known, protected Romans from attacks from the north, and it also allowed them to regulate immigration and trade through the many gates along the wall. Like all walls around cities or across territory, it served as a symbol and means of power and control as well as a defensive strategy.

As the empire expanded, the army grew larger, and more and more troops were auxiliary forces of noncitizens. Because army service could lead to citizenship, men from the provinces and even from beyond the borders of the Roman Empire sometimes joined the army willingly to gain citizenship, receive a salary, and learn a trade, though others were drafted. The army evolved into a garrison force, with troops guarding specific areas for long periods. Soldiers on active duty had originally been prohibited from marrying, but this restriction was increasingly ignored, and some troops brought their wives and families along on their assignments. At the beginning of the third century, Emperor Septimius Severus officially recognized the marriages of active duty soldiers, which allowed their families to gain citizenship and the man to legally bequeath his property to his heirs.

What was life like in the city of Rome and in the provinces?

The expansion and stabilization of the empire brought changes to life in the city of Rome and also to life in the provinces in the first two centuries C.E. The city grew to a huge size, bringing the problems that plague any crowded urban area but also opportunities for work and leisure. Roads and secure sea-lanes linked the empire in one vast web, creating a network of commerce and communication. Trade and production flourished in the provinces, and Romans came into indirect contact with China.

Life in Imperial Rome

Rome was truly an extraordinary city, and with a population of over a million it may have been the largest city in the world. Although it boasted stately palaces and beautiful residential areas, most people lived in shoddily constructed houses. They took whatever work was available, producing food, clothing, construction materials, and the many other items needed by the city's residents, or selling these products from small shops or at the city's many marketplaces.

Many residents of the city of Rome were enslaved. Enslaved people ranged from highly educated household tutors or government officials and widely sought sculptors to workers who engaged in hard physical tasks. Enslaved workers sometimes attempted to flee, but those who failed in their escape attempts were returned and often branded on their foreheads. Others had metal collars fastened around their necks. One collar discovered near Rome read: "I have run away. Capture me. If you take me back to my master Zoninus, you will receive a gold coin."[3] As in the republican period, Romans in the imperial period sometimes freed the people they owned, especially those who had long worked within their households. Manumission was limited by law, however, in part because freeing enslaved people made them citizens, allowing them to receive public grain and gifts of money, which some Romans thought debased pure Roman citizenship.

A typical day for the Roman family began with a modest breakfast, as in the days of the republic. Afterward came a trip to the outdoor market for the day's provisions. Seafood was a favorite item, as the Romans normally ate meat only at festivals. While poor people ate salt fish, the more prosperous dined on rare fish, oysters, squid, and eels. Wine was the common drink, and the rich often enjoyed rare vintages imported from abroad.

As in the republic, children began their education at home, where parents emphasized moral conduct, especially reverence for the gods and the law and respect for elders. Daughters learned how to manage the house, and sons learned the basics of their future calling from their fathers, who also taught them the use of weapons for military service. Boys boxed, swam, and learned to ride when possible, all to increase their strength, while giving them basic skills. Wealthy boys gained formal education from tutors or schools, generally favoring rhetoric and law for a political career.

Tombstones and sarcophagi (stone coffins) provide evidence about Roman attitudes toward work and family, and sometimes also insights into the deceased's personal philosophy. A simple tombstone reads: "To the spirits of the dead. T. Aelius Dionysius the freedman made this while he was alive both for Aelia Callitycena, his most blessed wife with whom he lived for thirty years with never a quarrel, an incomparable woman, and also for Amelius Perseus, his fellow freedman, and for their freedmen and those who come after them."[4] The more elaborate tombstone of a man named Marcus Antonius Encolpus left a blunt message for the living: "Do not pass by this epitaph, wayfarer, but stop, listen, hear, then go. There is no boat in Hades, no ferryman Charon. No caretaker Aecus, no Cerberus dog. All we dead below have become bones and ashes, nothing more. I have spoken the truth to you. Go now, wayfarer, lest even in death I seem garrulous to you."[5]

Approaches to Urban Problems

Fire and crime were serious problems in the city, even after Augustus created urban fire and police forces. Streets were narrow, drainage was inadequate, and sanitation was poor. Numerous inscriptions record prohibitions against dumping human refuse and even cadavers on the grounds of sanctuaries and cemeteries. Private houses generally lacked toilets, so people used chamber pots.

In the second century C.E. urban planning and new construction improved the situation. For example, engineers built an elaborate system that collected sewage from public baths, the ground floors of buildings, and public latrines. They also built hundreds of miles of **aqueducts**, sophisticated systems of canals, channels, and pipes, most of them underground, that brought freshwater into the city from the surrounding hills. The aqueducts, powered entirely by gravity, required regular maintenance, but they were a great improvement and helped make Rome a very attractive place to live. Building aqueducts required thousands and sometimes tens of thousands of workers, who were generally paid out of the imperial treasury. Aqueducts became a feature of Roman cities in many parts of the empire.

Better disposal of sewage was one way that people living in Rome tried to maintain their health, and they also used a range of treatments to stay healthy and cure illness. This included treatments based on the ideas of the Greek physician Hippocrates; folk remedies; prayers and rituals at the temple of the god of medicine, Asclepius; surgery; and combinations of all of these. The most important medical researcher and physician working in imperial Rome was Galen (ca. 129–ca. 200 C.E.), a Greek born in modern-day Turkey. Like anyone hoping to rise in stature and wealth, he came to Rome. Building on the work of Hellenistic physicians, Galen wrote a huge number of treatises on anatomy and physiology, and he became the personal physician of many prominent Romans, including several emperors. He promoted the idea that imbalances among various bodily fluids caused illness and recommended bloodletting as a cure. This would remain a standard treatment in Western medicine until the eighteenth century. His research into the nervous system and the operation of muscles—most of which he conducted on animals, because the Romans forbade dissections of human cadavers—proved to be more accurate than did his ideas about the circulation of fluids. So did his practical advice on the treatment of wounds, much of which grew out of his and others' experiences with soldiers on the battlefield.

Neither Galen nor any other Roman physician could do much for infectious diseases, and in 165 C.E. troops returning from campaigns in the East brought a new disease with them that spread quickly in the city and then beyond into other parts of the empire. Modern epidemiologists think this was most likely smallpox, but in the ancient world it became known simply as the Antonine plague, because it occurred during the reigns of emperors from the Antonine family. Whatever it was, it appears to have been extremely virulent in the city of Rome and among the Roman army for a decade or so, with total deaths estimated at about 5 million.

Along with fire and disease, food was an issue in the ever-more-crowded city. Because of the danger of starvation, the emperor, following republican practice, provided the citizen population with free grain for bread and, later, oil and wine. By feeding the citizenry, the emperor prevented bread riots caused by shortages and high prices. For those who did not enjoy the rights of citizenship, the emperor provided grain at low prices. This measure was designed to prevent speculators from forcing up grain prices in times of crisis. By maintaining the grain supply, the emperor kept the favor of the people and ensured that Rome's poor did not starve.

Popular Entertainment

In addition to supplying grain, the emperor and his family also entertained the Roman populace, often at vast expense. This combination of material support and popular entertainment to keep the masses happy is often termed "bread and circuses." The emperors gained politically from promoting public entertainment, as the arenas were places where they could be seen and honored, sitting on an elevated seat next to images of the gods.

The most popular forms of public entertainment were gladiatorial contests and chariot racing. Gladiator fights were advertised on billboards, and spectators were given a program with the names and sometimes the fighting statistics of the pairs, so that they could place bets more easily.

Men came to be gladiators through a variety of ways. Some were soldiers captured in war, and some were criminals. By the imperial period increasing numbers were volunteers, often poor immigrants who saw gladiatorial combat as a way to support themselves. All gladiators were trained in gladiatorial schools and were legally enslaved, although they could keep their winnings and

■ **aqueducts** Canals, channels, and pipes that brought freshwater into cities.

Roman Architecture These three structures demonstrate the beauty, practicality, and innovation of Roman architecture. The Pont du Gard at Nîmes in France (above) is a bridge over a river carrying an aqueduct that supplied millions of gallons of water per day to the Roman city of Nîmes in Gaul; the water flowed in a channel at the very top. Although this bridge was built largely without mortar or concrete, many Roman aqueducts and bridges relied on concrete and sometimes iron rods for their strength. The Pantheon in Rome (left), a temple dedicated to all the gods, was finished in its present form around 130 C.E., after earlier temples on this site burned down. Its dome, 140 feet in diameter, remains the largest unreinforced concrete dome in the world. Romans also used concrete for more everyday purposes. The Coliseum in Rome (below), a sports arena that could seat fifty thousand spectators built between 70 and 80 C.E., was the site of gladiatorial games, animal spectacles, and executions. For a brief time it was also used for mock naval battles, but this proved to be impractical.

(Pont du Gard: Masterfile; Pantheon: Gianni Dagli Orti/Shutterstock; Coliseum: © Gerard Degeorge/ Bridgeman Images)

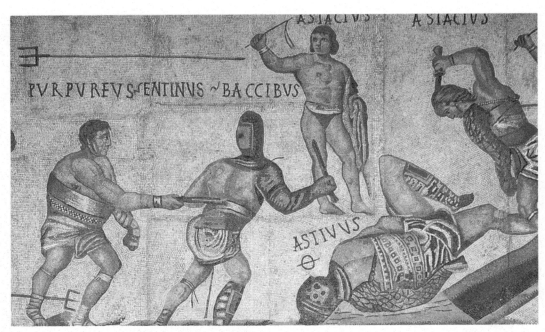

Gladiator Mosaic   Made in the first half of the fourth century, this mosaic from an estate outside Rome includes the name of each gladiator next to the figure. In the back a gladiator stands in a victory pose, while the fallen gladiator in the front is marked with the symbol Ø, indicating that he has died in combat. Many of the gladiators in this mosaic, such as those at the left, appear less fit and fearsome than the gladiators depicted in movies, more closely reflecting the reality that gladiatorial combat was a job undertaken by a variety of people. (Alinari/Bridgeman Images)

a few became quite wealthy. The Hollywood portrayal of gladiatorial combat has men fighting to their death, but this was increasingly rare, as the owners of especially skilled fighters wanted them to continue to compete. Many—perhaps most—did die at a young age from their injuries or later infections, but some fought more than a hundred battles over long careers, retiring to become trainers in gladiatorial schools. Sponsors of matches sought to offer viewers ever more unusual spectacles: left-handed gladiators fighting right-handed ones, dwarf gladiators, and for a brief period female gladiators. For a criminal condemned to die, the arena was preferable to the imperial mines, where convicts worked digging ore and died under wretched conditions. At least in the arena the gladiator might fight well enough to win freedom. Some Romans protested gladiatorial fighting, but the emperors recognized the political value of such spectacles, and most Romans enjoyed them.

The Romans were even more addicted to chariot racing than to gladiatorial shows, and they watched these in large arenas such as the Circus Maximus, which could hold 150,000 spectators. Under the empire four permanent teams competed against one another. Each had its own color—red, white, green, or blue. Two-horse and four-horse chariots ran a course of seven laps, about five miles. One charioteer, Gaius Appuleius Diocles, a Greek who had Roman citizenship, raced for twenty-four years, with over 4,000 starts and nearly 1,500 wins. His admirers honored him with an inscription that proclaimed him champion of all charioteers. Other winning charioteers were also idolized, just as sports stars are today, and the demand for races was so high that they were held on more than one hundred days a year in imperial Rome.

Prosperity in the Roman Provinces

As the empire grew and stabilized, many Roman provinces grew prosperous. Peace and security opened Britain, Gaul, and the lands of the Danube to settlers from other parts of the Roman Empire (see Map 6.2). Veterans were given small parcels of land in the provinces and became tenant farmers. The rural population throughout the empire left few records, but the inscriptions that remain point to a melding of cultures, an important reason for Rome's success. One sphere where this melding occurred was language. People used Latin for legal and state religious purposes, but gradually Latin blended with the original language of an area and with languages spoken by those who came into the area later. Slowly what would become the Romance languages of Spanish, Italian, French, Portuguese, and Romanian evolved. Religion was another site of cultural exchange and mixture. Romans moving into an area learned about and began to venerate local gods, and local people learned about Roman ones. Gradually hybrid deities and rituals developed. At first, cultural exchange occurred more in urban than in rural areas, but the importance of cities and towns to the life of the wider countryside ensured that its effects spread far afield.

The garrison towns that grew up around provincial military camps became the centers of organized political life, and some grew into major cities, including Eburacum (modern-day York), Lutetia Parisiorum (Paris), and Londinium (London). To supply these administrative centers with food, land around them was cultivated more intensively. Roman merchants became early bankers, loaning money to local people and often controlling them financially. Wealthy Roman officials also sometimes built country estates in rural areas near the city, where they did grow crops but also escaped from the stresses and unhealthy conditions of city life.

During the first and second centuries C.E., Roman Gaul became more prosperous than ever before, and its prosperity attracted Roman settlers. Roman veterans mingled with the local population and sometimes married into local families. There was not much difference in many parts of the province between the original Celtic villages and their Roman successors.

In Britain, Roman influence was strongest in the south, where more towns developed. Archaeological evidence, such as coins and amphoras that held oil or wine, indicates healthy trading connections with the north, however, as Roman merchandise moved through the gates of Hadrian's Wall in exchange for food and other local products.

Across eastern Europe, Roman influence was weaker than it was in Gaul or southern Britain, and there appears to have been less intermarriage. In Illyria (ih-LIHR-ee-uh) and Dalmatia, regions of modern Albania, Croatia, and Montenegro, the local population never widely embraced either Roman culture or urban life. To a certain extent, however, Romanization occurred simply because the peoples lived in such close proximity.

The Romans were the first to build cities in northern Europe, but in the eastern Mediterranean they ruled cities that had existed before Rome itself was even a village. Here there was much continuity in urban life from the Hellenistic period. There was also less construction than in the Roman cities of northern and western Europe because existing buildings could simply be put to new uses.

The well-preserved ruins of the ancient city of Aspendos, at the mouth of the Eurymedon (now Kopru) River on the south coast of modern Turkey

Roman Britain, ca. 130 C.E.

(see Map 6.2), give a picture of life in one of these older eastern cities. Built sometime before 500 B.C.E., the city was an important economic center in the Persian Empire and one of the earliest cities to mint coins. It was conquered by Alexander the Great and then by the Romans, but it remained prosperous. Romans and local people mixed at the city's central marketplace and in temples and public buildings. The Romans built an aqueduct to bring water into the city, although this was later destroyed in an earthquake. Over the river they also built an arched stone bridge, about thirty feet wide so that carts and chariots could easily travel on it. This may have also collapsed in an earthquake, but its foundations were so sturdy that a thousand years later the area's Turkish rulers used them to build a new bridge, which still stands. In 155 C.E. a local architect built a magnificent theater that probably held seven thousand spectators, who sat

Organist and Horn Player   Games, gladiatorial contests, and other events in the cities of the Roman Empire were often accompanied by music. In this floor mosaic from a villa in Nennig, Germany, built in the third century, a horn player plays a large curved instrument known as a *cornu*, which was also used by the military to call troops. The organist plays a water organ (*hydraulis*) in which water stored in the hexagonal podium was pumped through tubes and the force of the water pushed air through the organ pipes. (Bridgeman Images)

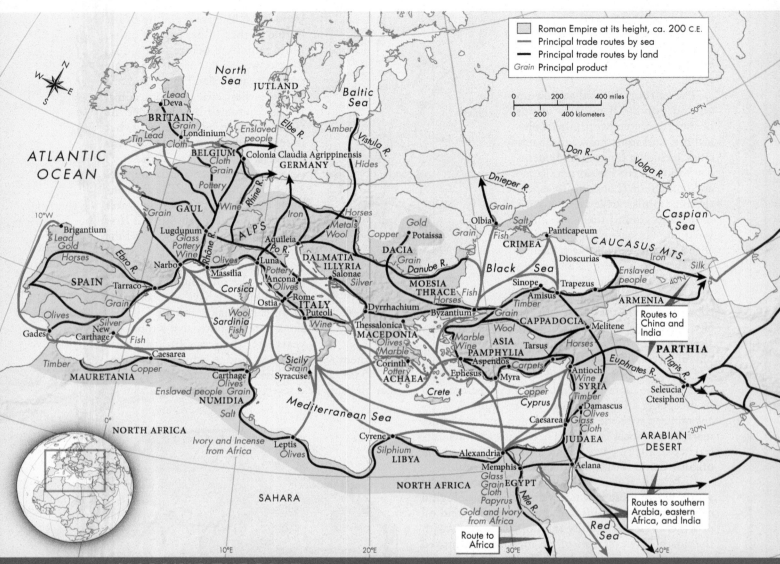

MAPPING THE PAST

MAP 6.2 Production and Trade in Imperial Rome, ca. 27 B.C.E.–180 C.E.

This map gives a good idea of the main products produced in various parts of the Roman Empire at its height and the trade routes connecting these regions. Map 10.2 on page 277 is a similar map that shows products and trade in roughly the same area nearly a millennium later. Examine both maps and answer the following questions.

ANALYZING THE MAP What similarities and differences do you see in products during these two periods?

CONNECTIONS To what extent did Roman trade routes influence later European trade routes?

---

under a retractable awning that provided shade. Here men and women enjoyed plays and gladiatorial contests, for these were popular in eastern cities, as was horse racing.

More than just places to live, cities like Aspendos were centers of intellectual and cultural life. Their residents were in touch with the ideas and events of the day, in a network that spanned the entire Mediterranean and reached as far north as Britain. As long as the empire prospered and the revenues reached the imperial coffers, life in provincial cities — at least for the wealthy — could be nearly as pleasant as that in Rome.

Trade and Commerce

The expansion of trade during the first two centuries C.E. made the Roman Empire an economic as well as a political force in the provinces (Map 6.2). Britain and Belgium became prime grain producers, with much of their harvests going to the armies of the Rhine, and Britain's wool industry probably got its start under the Romans. Italy and southern Gaul produced huge quantities of wine, which was shipped in large pottery jugs wherever merchant vessels could carry it. Roman colonists introduced the olive to southern Spain and northern Africa, which soon produced most of the oil consumed in the western part of the empire. In the East the olive oil production of Syrian farmers reached an all-time high, and Egypt produced tons of wheat that fed the Roman populace.

The growth of industry in the provinces was another striking development of this period. Cities in Gaul and Germany eclipsed the old Mediterranean manufacturing centers. Lyons in Gaul and later Cologne in Germany became the new centers of the glassmaking industry, joining older glassmaking centers in the eastern Mediterranean. Roman glass was used for perfume, wine, and other liquids, and despite its fragility it was shipped widely. The Romans also took the manufacture of pottery to an advanced stage by introducing a wider range of vessels and making

some of these on an industrial scale in kilns that were large enough to fire tens of thousands of pots at once. The most prized pottery was *terra sigillata*, reddish decorated tableware with a glossy surface. Methods for making terra sigillata spread from Italy northwards into Europe, often introduced by soldiers in the Roman army who had been trained in pottery-making in Italy. These craftsmen set up facilities to make roof tiles, amphoras, and dishes for their units, and local potters began to copy their styles and methods of manufacturing. Terra sigillata often portrayed Greco-Roman gods and heroes, so this pottery spread Mediterranean myths and stories. Local artisans added their own distinctive flourishes and sometimes stamped their names on the pots; these individual touches have allowed archaeologists to trace the pottery trade throughout the Roman Empire in great detail. Aided by all this growth in trade and industry, Europe and western Asia were linked in ways they had not been before.

As the Romans drove farther eastward, they encountered the Parthians, who had established a kingdom in what is now Afghanistan and Iran in the Hellenistic period. After the Romans tried unsuccessfully to drive out the Parthians in the second century C.E., the Parthians came to act as a link between Roman and Chinese merchants. Chinese merchants

Tomb Painting of Loading Grain　In this second- to third-century-C.E. painting from a cemetery at Ostia, the port for the landlocked city of Rome, workmen carry sacks of grain up the gangplank of a ship, identified in the painting as the *Isis Giminiana*. The cemetery was used mainly for the burial of freedmen, and the high quality of the tomb paintings shows the level of wealth they could obtain through commercial and artisanal activities. (Peter Horree/Alamy Stock Photo)

sold their wares to the Parthians, who then carried the goods overland to Mesopotamia or Egypt, from which they were shipped throughout the Roman Empire. Silk was a major commodity traded from the East to the West, along with other luxury goods. In return the Romans traded glassware, precious gems, and enslaved captives.

This was also an era of maritime trade. Roman ships sailed from Egyptian ports to the mouth of the Indus River, where they traded local merchandise and wares imported by the Parthians. In the late first century c.e. the Chinese emperor sent an ambassador, Gan

Ying, to make contact with the Roman Empire. Gan Ying made it as far as the Persian Gulf ports, where he heard about the Romans from Parthian sailors and reported back to his emperor that the Romans were wealthy, tall, and strikingly similar to the Chinese. His report became part of a group of accounts about the Romans and other "Western" peoples that circulated widely among scholars and officials in Han China. Educated Romans did not have a corresponding interest in China, however. For them, China remained more of a mythical than a real place, and they never bothered to learn more about it.

How did Christianity grow into a major religious movement?

During the reign of the emperor Tiberius in the Roman province of Judaea, which had been created out of the Jewish kingdom of Judah, a Jewish man named Jesus of Nazareth preached, attracted a following, and was executed on the order of the Roman prefect Pontius Pilate. At the time this was a minor event, but Christianity, the religion created by Jesus's followers, came to have an enormous impact first in the Roman Empire and later throughout the world.

Factors Behind the Rise of Christianity

The civil wars that destroyed the Roman Republic left their mark on Judaea, where Jewish leaders had taken sides in the conflict. The turmoil created a climate of violence throughout the area, and among the Jews movements in opposition to the Romans spread. Some of the members of these movements, such as the Zealots, encouraged armed rebellion against Roman rule, which would, indeed, break out several times in the first and second centuries c.e. Many Jews came to believe that a final struggle was near, and that it would lead to the coming of a **Messiah**, a word that means one who is anointed with holy oil, as King David was (see Chapter 2), and thus the legitimate King of the Jews. This Messiah, a descendant of King David, would destroy the Roman legions and inaugurate a period of peace, happiness, and prosperity for Jews. This apocalyptic belief was an old one among Jews, but by the first century c.e. it had become more widespread than ever, with many people prophesying the imminent coming of a Messiah and readying themselves for a cataclysmic battle.

The pagan world also played its part in the story of early Christianity. The term **pagan**, derived from a Latin word with negative connotations meaning "rural dweller" (the closest English equivalent is "redneck"),

came to refer to those who practiced religions other than Judaism or Christianity. Christianity was initially an urban religion, and those who lived in the countryside were less likely to be converts. What Christians would later term pagan practices included religions devoted to the traditional Roman gods of the hearth, home, and countryside; syncretistic religions that blended Roman and indigenous deities; the cult of the emperor spread through the erection of statues, temples, and monuments; and mystery religions that offered the promise of life after death (see Chapter 4). Many people in the Roman Empire practiced all of these, combining them in whatever way seemed most beneficial or satisfying to them, and some beliefs and practices from paganism became part of Christian worship.

The Life and Teachings of Jesus

Into this climate of Messianic hope and Roman religious blending came Jesus of Nazareth (ca. 4 B.C.E.–ca. 30/33 C.E.). According to Christian Scripture, he was born to deeply religious Jewish parents and raised in Galilee, the stronghold of the Zealots and a trading center where Greeks and Romans interacted with Jews. His ministry began when he was about thirty, and he taught by preaching and telling stories.

Like Socrates, Jesus left no writings. Accounts of his sayings and teachings first circulated orally among his followers and were later written down. The principal surviving evidence for his life and deeds is the four Gospels of the Bible (Matthew, Mark, Luke, and John), books that are part of what Christians later termed the New Testament. These Gospels — the name means "good news" — are records of Jesus's life and teachings, written to build a community of faith sometime in the late first century c.e. Many different books circulated among Jesus's followers, but the Gospels were among the most widely copied and circulated early accounts of Jesus's life. By the fourth century officials in the Christian Church decided that they, along with other types of writing such as letters and prophecies, would form Christian Scripture. The four Gospels included in the Bible are called canonical, from the Greek word that means "the rule" or "the standard," as are other writings included in scripture. Other early documents were declared noncanonical, and many were lost, though some have been rediscovered in modern times. Which books would form Christian Scripture was a source of much debate in the early church, and even today different Christian groups accept different books.

The Gospels include certain details of Jesus's life, but they were not meant to be biographies. Their authors had probably heard many different people talk about what Jesus said and did, and there are discrepancies among the four accounts. These differences indicate that early followers had a diversity of beliefs about Jesus's nature and purpose, and historians today describe this period as one of "christianities" rather than a single "Christianity."

However, almost all the early sources agree on certain aspects of Jesus's teachings: He preached of a heavenly kingdom of eternal happiness in a life after death, and of the importance of devotion to God and love of others. His teachings were based on Hebrew Scripture and reflected a conception of God and morality that came from Jewish tradition. Jesus's orthodoxy enabled him to preach in the synagogue and the temple, but he deviated from orthodoxy in insisting that he taught in his own name, not in the name of Yahweh (the Hebrew name for God). The Greek translation of the Hebrew word *Messiah* is *Christos*, the origin of the English word *Christ*. Was Jesus the Messiah, the Christ? A small band of followers thought so, and Jesus claimed that he was. Yet Jesus had his own conception of the Messiah. He would establish a spiritual kingdom, not an earthly one. As recounted in one of the Gospels, he commented:

> Do not lay up for yourselves treasures on earth, where moth and rust consume and where thieves break in and steal, but lay up for yourselves treasures in heaven, where neither moth nor rust consumes and where thieves do not break in and steal. For where your treasure is, there will your heart be also.[6]

The Roman official Pontius Pilate, who had authority over much of Judaea, knew little about Jesus's teachings. Like all Roman officials, he was concerned with maintaining peace and order, which was a difficult task in restive Judaea. According to the New Testament, crowds followed Jesus into Jerusalem at the time of Passover, a highly emotional time in the Jewish year that marked the Jewish people's departure from Egypt under the leadership of Moses (see Chapter 2). The prospect that these crowds would spark violence no doubt alarmed Pilate, as some Jews believed that Jesus was the long-awaited Messiah, while others thought him religiously dangerous. The four Gospels differ somewhat on exactly what actions Jesus took in the city and what Jesus and Pilate said to each other after Jesus was arrested. They agree that Pilate condemned Jesus to death by crucifixion because he claimed to be the legitimate king of the Jews, a claim that was reportedly stated in Latin above Jesus's head on the cross on which he was crucified. The only "king" the Jews had at this time was the Roman emperor Tiberius, so Jesus's claim was a political crime. Pilate's soldiers carried out the sentence. On the third day after Jesus's crucifixion, some of his followers claimed that he had risen from the dead. For his earliest followers and for generations to come, the resurrection of Jesus became a central element of faith.

The Spread of Christianity

The memory of Jesus and his teachings survived and flourished. Believers in his divinity met in small assemblies or congregations, often in one another's homes, to discuss the meaning of Jesus's message and to celebrate a ritual (later called the Eucharist or Lord's Supper) commemorating his last meal with his disciples before his arrest. Because they expected Jesus to return to the world very soon, they regarded earthly life and institutions as unimportant. Only later did these congregations evolve into what came to be called the religion of Christianity, with a formal organization and set of beliefs.

The catalyst in the spread of Jesus's teachings and the formation of the Christian Church was Paul of Tarsus, a well-educated Hellenized Jew who was comfortable in both the Roman and the Jewish worlds. The New Testament reports that at first he persecuted members of this new Jewish sect, but then on the road to the city of Damascus in Syria he was struck blind by a vision of light and heard Jesus's voice. Once converted, he traveled all over the Roman Empire and wrote letters of advice to many groups. These letters were copied and widely circulated, transforming Jesus's ideas into more specific moral teachings. Recognizing that Christianity would not grow if it remained within Judaism, Paul connected it with the

■ **Messiah** In Jewish belief, an anointed leader who would bring a period of peace and happiness for Jews.

■ **pagan** Originally referring to those who lived in the countryside, it came to mean those who practiced religions other than Judaism or Christianity.

Wall Painting in a Roman Catacomb This fresco from the Coemeterium Maius, a third-century set of catacombs in Rome, shows a woman praying with outstretched hands, flanked by two men. The cuts in the rock below are places where visitors could celebrate commemorative meals for the dead, a pre-Christian Roman practice that Christians continued. Christians brought food to catacombs and cemeteries to honor martyrs as well as deceased relatives, and the painting may represent the martyrs venerated here: a woman reputed to have been martyred while praying and two soldier-martyrs. (Photo 12/UIG via Getty Images)

non-Jewish world. As a result of his efforts, he became the most important figure in changing Christianity from a Jewish sect into a separate religion, and many of his letters became part of Christian Scripture.

The breadth of the Roman Empire was another factor behind the spread of Christianity. If all roads led to Rome, they also led outward to the provinces. This enabled early Christians to spread their faith easily throughout the world known to them. Though most of the earliest converts seem to have been Jews, or Greeks and Romans who were already interested in Jewish moral teachings, Paul urged that Gentiles, or non-Jews, be accepted on an equal basis. The earliest Christian converts included people from all social classes, though urban residents who were socially mobile were most likely to become Christian. Missionaries and others spread the Christian message through family contacts, friendships, and business networks.

The growing Christian communities differed about many things. Among these was the extent to which women should participate in the workings of the religion; some favored giving women a larger role in church affairs, while others were more restrictive, urging women to be silent on religious matters. Many women were active in spreading Christianity. Paul greeted male and female converts by name in his letters and noted that women often provided financial support for his activities.

People were attracted to Christian teachings for a variety of reasons. It was in many ways a mystery religion, offering its adherents special teachings that would give them immortality. But in contrast to traditional mystery religions, Christianity promised this immortality widely, not only to a select few.

Most early Christians believed that they would rise in body, not simply in spirit, after a final day of judgment, so they favored burial of the dead rather than the more common Roman practice of cremation. They began to dig tunnels in the soft rock around Rome for burials, forming huge complexes of burial passageways called catacombs. Memorial services for martyrs were sometimes held in or near catacombs, but they were not regular places of worship. Instead people worshipped in the houses of more well-to-do converts.

Along with the possibility of life after death, Christianity also offered rewards in this world to adherents. One of these was the possibility of forgiveness, for believers accepted that human nature is weak and that even the best Christians could fall into sin. But Jesus loved sinners and forgave those who repented. Christianity was also attractive to many because it gave the Roman world a cause. Instead of passivity, Christians stressed the ideal of striving for a goal. By spreading the word of Christ, Christians played their part in God's plan for the triumph of Christianity on earth. Christianity likewise gave its devotees a sense of community, which was very welcome in the often highly mobile world of the Roman Empire. To stress the spiritual kinship of this new type of community, Christians often called one another "brother" and "sister." Also, many Christians took Jesus's commandment to love one another as a guide and provided support for widows, orphans, and the poor, just as they did for family members. Such material support became increasingly attractive as Roman social welfare programs broke down in the third century.

The Growing Acceptance and Evolution of Christianity

At first most Roman officials largely ignored the followers of Jesus, viewing them simply as one of the many splinter groups within Judaism. Slowly some Roman officials and leaders came to oppose Christian practices and beliefs. They considered Christians to be subversive dissidents because they stopped practicing traditional rituals venerating the hearth and home and they objected — often publicly or in writing — to the cult of the emperor. Some Romans thought that Christianity was one of the worst of the mystery religions, with immoral and indecent rituals. For instance, they thought that the ritual of the Lord's Supper, at which Christians said that they ate and drank the body and blood of Jesus, was an act of cannibalism involving the ritual murder of Roman boys. Many in the Roman Empire also feared that the traditional gods would withdraw their favor from the Roman Empire because of the Christian insistence that these gods either did not exist or were evil spirits. The Christian refusal to worship Roman gods, in their opinion, endangered Roman lives and society. Others worried that Christians were trying to destroy the Roman family with their insistence on a new type of kinship, and they pointed to Jesus's words in the Gospels saying that salvation was far more important than family relationships. A woman who converted, thought many Romans, might use her new faith to oppose her father's choice of marital partner or even renounce marriage itself, an idea supported by the actions of a few female converts.

Governors of Roman provinces were primarily interested in maintaining order, and they hoped that Christians and non-Christians would coexist peacefully, but conflicts arose, leading governors to carry out campaigns against Christians, including torture and executions. Most persecutions were local and sporadic in nature, however, and some of the gory stories about the martyrs are later inventions, designed to strengthen believers with accounts of earlier heroes. Christians differed in their opinions about how to respond to persecution. Some sought out martyrdom, while others thought that doing so went against Christian teachings.

Responses to Christianity on the part of Roman emperors varied. Nero persecuted Christians, but Trajan forbade his governors to hunt them down. Though admitting that he considered Christianity an abomination, he decided it was better policy to leave Christians in peace. Later emperors increased persecutions again, ordering Christians to sacrifice to the emperor and the Roman gods or risk death. Executions followed their edicts, although estimates of how

Christian Oil Lamp   This terra-cotta oil lamp, showing a triumphant risen Christ flanked by angels and standing on a serpent and other animals, was made in Roman North Africa in the fourth century C.E. When Christianity spread in the Roman Empire, many believers purchased household goods with Christian symbols. (Paris Musée du Louvre/JEAN-LOUIS JOSSE/Bridgeman Images)

many people were actually martyred in any of these persecutions vary widely.

By the second century C.E. Christianity was also changing. The belief that Jesus was soon coming again gradually waned, and as the number of converts increased, permanent institutions were established instead of simple house churches. These included buildings and a hierarchy of officials often modeled on those of the Roman Empire. **Bishops**, officials with jurisdiction over a certain area, became especially important. They began to assert that they had the right to determine the correct interpretation of Christian teachings and to choose their successors. Councils of bishops determined which writings would be considered canonical, and lines were increasingly drawn between what was considered correct teaching and what was considered incorrect, or **heresy**.

■ **bishops** Christian Church officials with jurisdiction over certain areas and the power to determine the correct interpretation of Christian teachings.

■ **heresy** A religious practice or belief judged unacceptable by church officials.

Christianity also began to attract more highly educated individuals who developed complex theological interpretations of issues that were not clear in scripture. Often drawing on Greek philosophy and Roman legal traditions, they worked out understandings of such issues as how Jesus could be both divine and human, and how God could be both a father and a son (and later a spirit as well, a Christian doctrine known as the Trinity). Bishops and theologians often modified teachings that seemed upsetting to Romans, such as Jesus's harsh words about wealth and family ties. Given all these changes, Christianity became more formal in the second century, with power more centralized.

What political and economic problems did Rome face in the third century C.E.?

The prosperity and political stability of the second century gave way to a period of domestic upheaval and foreign invasion. The third century saw a long series of able but ambitious military commanders who used their legions to make themselves emperors. Many tried to establish dynasties, but most failed, and those that were established were short-lived. While they were fighting each other, the generals were not able to defend against raids across Rome's borders. The nature of the army changed, and the economy weakened because of unsound policies.

Civil Wars and Military Commanders

The reign of Marcus Aurelius (r. 161–180 C.E.) was marked by problems. The Tiber River flooded in 162, destroying crops and killing animals, which led to famine. Soldiers returning from wars in the East brought the Antonine plague back to Rome (see "Approaches to Urban Problems") and then carried it northward. Germanic-speaking groups attacked along the Rhine and Danube borders, and the emperor himself took over the campaign against them in 169. He spent most of the rest of his life in military camps along Rome's northern border, where in addition to leading troops he wrote a series of personal reflections in Greek. These *Meditations*, as they later came to be known, are advice to himself about doing one's duty and acting in accordance with nature, ideas that came from Stoic philosophy. He wrote:

The Emperor Marcus Aurelius   This larger-than-life bronze equestrian statue, sculpted either to celebrate Marcus Aurelius's military victories or shortly after his death in 180 C.E., shows the emperor holding up his hand in the conventional imperial greeting. More than twenty equestrian statues could be seen in late imperial Rome, but this is the only one to survive. In the sixteenth century Michelangelo built one of the major plazas of Rome around it, although now the original has been moved to a museum for better preservation and this is a copy that stands outdoors. (Universal Images Group/Getty Images)

> Take heed not to be transformed into a Caesar, not to be dipped in the purple dye [a color only the emperor could wear]. Keep yourself therefore simple, good, pure, grave, unaffected, the friend of justice, religious, kind, affectionate, strong for your proper work. Wrestle to continue to be the man Philosophy wished to make you. Reverence the gods, save men. . . . Do not act unwillingly nor selfishly nor without self-examination.[7]

The *Meditations* are a good key to Marcus Aurelius's character, but they appear not to have circulated very much during the centuries immediately after they were written. Certainly very few later emperors took this advice to heart.

After the death of Marcus Aurelius, misrule by his successors led to a long and intense spasm of fighting. Marcus Aurelius's son Commodus was strangled by a conspiracy that included his wife, and in 193 five men claimed the throne in quick succession, a repeat of what had happened in 69. Two of them were also assassinated, and Septimius Severus (r. 193–211 C.E.) emerged as the victor. He restored order, expanded the borders of the Roman Empire in Africa and western Asia, and invaded Scotland. He increased the size of the army significantly and paid the soldiers better. This made him popular with soldiers, though it also increased the taxes on civilians. Some of his policies regarding the army created additional problems in the long run. For example, changes in recruiting practices that emphasized local recruiting of non-Romans created a Roman army that became less acculturated to Roman values, and so was no longer the vehicle for Romanization that it had been in earlier centuries. In 212 Septimius Severus's son Caracalla (r. 198–217 C.E.) issued an edict making all free male residents of the Roman Empire citizens, which increased his standing with his supporters in the provinces. This edict made them eligible to serve in the legions — which may have been why Caracalla did this — but also made serving in the army less attractive, and so reduced the number of men willing to join.

In 235 the emperor Severus Alexander lost the respect of his troops by negotiating with Germanic chieftains raiding across Rome's northern border. They assassinated him and chose a different commander to be emperor, beginning a fifty-year period in which more than twenty different emperors seized power, which many historians refer to as the "crisis of the third century." These emperors were generally military commanders from the border provinces, and there were so many that the middle of the third century has become known as the age of the **barracks emperors**. Almost all were either assassinated or died in civil wars, and their preoccupation with overthrowing the ruling emperor left the borders unguarded. Non-Roman groups on the frontiers took full advantage of the chaos to overrun vast areas. When they reached the Rhine and the Danube, they often found gaping holes in the Roman defenses and moved deep into Roman territory.

Turmoil in Economic Life

This chaos also disrupted areas far away from the borders of the empire. Renegade soldiers and corrupt imperial officials, together with many greedy local agents, preyed on local people. In some places in the countryside, officials requisitioned villagers' livestock and compelled them to do forced labor. Farmers appealed to the government for protection so that they could cultivate the land. Although some of those in authority were unsympathetic and even violent to villagers, many others tried to maintain order. Yet even the best of them also suffered. If officials could not meet their tax quotas, which were rising to support the costs of civil war, they had to pay the deficits from their own pockets. Because the local officials were themselves so hard-pressed, they squeezed what they needed from rural families. Many farmers, unable to pay, were driven off their land, and those remaining faced ruin. As a result, agricultural productivity declined.

In response to the economic crisis, the emperors reduced the amount of silver used in coins, replacing it with less valuable metals such as copper, so that they could continue to pay their troops. This tactic, however, led to crippling inflation, which wiped out savings and sent prices soaring.

The Romans still controlled the Mediterranean, which nurtured commerce, and some parts of the empire were relatively unaffected by the uproar. The road system remained largely intact, though often roads were allowed to fall into disrepair, and unrest made it less safe for merchants to travel. Trade still flowed, but more trade became local, as did the production of food and manufactured goods.

By 284 C.E. the empire had reached a crisis that threatened its downfall. The position of emperor was gained no longer through succession ratified by the Senate but rather by victory in civil war. The government had failed at the top, and the repercussions of the disaster had dire effects throughout the empire.

NOTES

1. Virgil, *Aeneid,* trans. Theodore C. Williams (Boston: Houghton Mifflin, 1910), 6.851–853.
2. Virgil, *Aeneid,* trans. Robert Fitzgerald (New York: Vintage, 1990), 1.1–11.
3. Text in Mary Johnston, *Roman Life* (Chicago: Scott, Foresman, and Co., 1957), p. 172.
4. Elaine Fantham et al., eds., *Women in the Classical World* (New York: Oxford University Press, 1994), pp. 369–370.
5. Napthali Lewis and Meyer Reinhold, *Roman Civilization*, vol. 2 (New York: Harper Torchbooks, 1955), pp. 284–285.
6. Matthew 6:19–21.
7. Marcus Aurelius, *Meditations* 3.5, 6.30, trans. A. S. L. Farquharson (New York: Everyman's Library, 1961), pp. 5, 12.

■ **barracks emperors** The emperors of the middle of the third century, so called because they were military commanders.

LOOKING BACK LOOKING AHEAD

The first several centuries of the Roman Empire were a rich era in both economic and cultural terms. Generally working with Roman elites, rulers developed a system of government that managed vast areas of diverse people fairly effectively. The resulting stability and peace encouraged agriculture and production. Goods and people moved along roads and sea-lanes, as did ideas, including the new religion of Christianity. As they had in the republic, Romans during the empire incorporated individuals from different groups politically by granting them citizenship, and in border areas Roman and provincial culture mixed.

During a long period of internal crisis, civil war, and invasions in the third century, it seemed as if the empire would collapse, but it did not. Although emperors came and went in quick and violent succession, the basic institutions and infrastructure of the empire remained intact. Even during the worst of the ordeal, many lower-level officials and ordinary soldiers continued to do their jobs, embodying the principles of duty that Marcus Aurelius advocated. People like this would be key to passing Roman traditions on to institutions that developed later in Europe, including law courts, city governments, and nations.

Make Connections

Think about the larger developments and continuities within and across chapters.

1. What allowed large empires in the ancient world, including the Persians (Chapter 2) and the Romans, to govern vast territories and many different peoples successfully?

2. How was slavery in the Roman Empire different from that in earlier societies? How was it similar? What might account for the continuities and changes in slavery you have identified?

3. If a male resident of Athens during the time of Pericles (Chapter 3) had time-traveled to Rome during the time of Augustus, what might he have found familiar? What might have seemed strange? How might these observations have differed if the time traveler were a female resident of Athens?

6 REVIEW & EXPLORE

Identify Key Terms

Identify and explain the significance of each item below.

principate (p. 141)	Messiah (p. 160)
imperator (p. 141)	pagan (p. 160)
pax Romana (p. 143)	bishops (p. 163)
Praetorian Guard (p. 150)	heresy (p. 163)
aqueducts (p. 154)	barracks emperors (p. 165)

Review the Main Ideas

Answer the section heading questions from the chapter.

1. How did Augustus and Roman elites create a foundation for the Roman Empire? (p. 140)

2. How did the Roman state develop after Augustus? (p. 150)

3. What was life like in the city of Rome and in the provinces? (p. 153)

4. How did Christianity grow into a major religious movement? (p. 160)

5. What political and economic problems did Rome face in the third century C.E.? (p. 164)

Suggested Resources

BOOKS

- Aldrete, Gregory S. *Daily Life in the Roman City*. 2004. Reveals the significance of ordinary Roman life in the cities of Rome, its port Ostia, and Pompeii.

- Beard, Mary. *SPQR: A History of Ancient Rome*. 2016. A best-selling survey of the grand sweep of Roman history by Britain's best-known classicist.

- Campbell, Brian. *War and Society in Imperial Rome, 31 B.C.–A.D. 284*. 2002. Shows how Roman warfare and military life influenced and was influenced by Roman society.

- Clark, Gillian. *Christianity and Roman Society*. 2004. Surveys the evolution of Christian life among Christians and with their pagan neighbors.

- D'Ambra, Eve. *Roman Women*. 2006. Treats the lives of women of all social ranks.

- Everitt, Anthony. *Augustus: The Life of Rome's First Emperor*. 2007. A lively biography that traces Augustus's rise to power.

- Freeman, Charles. *A New History of Early Christianity*. 2010. A survey of the first four centuries of Christianity, written for a general audience.

- Glancy, Jennifer A. *Slavery in Early Christian Society*. 2006. Examines the impact of slavery on early Christian institutions, ideas, and practices.

- Joshel, Sandra R. *Slavery in the Roman World*. 2010. An overview of Roman slavery, including the social and family lives of enslaved people, designed for students.

- Knapp, Robert. *Invisible Romans*. 2011. A view of Roman life that focuses on ordinary men and women: soldiers, servants, laborers, housewives, gladiators, and outlaws.

- Kyle, Donald G. *Sport and Spectacle in the Ancient World*. 2007. Examines the nature and meaning of sports from Mesopotamia through Rome, including running races, fighting, and chariot racing.

- Potter, David, and David J. Mattingly. *Life, Death, and Entertainment in the Roman Empire*, 2d ed. 2010. Discusses family and gender, slavery, food, religion, and entertainment.

- Roth, Jonathan P. *Roman Warfare*. 2010. Surveys arms, tactics, strategy, and logistics from republican to imperial times.

MEDIA

- *From Jesus to Christ: The First Christians* (PBS, 1998). A four-part documentary exploring the life and death of Jesus and the transformation of Christianity from a small group to an established church. With commentary by theologians, archaeologists, and historians on many key issues.

- *Gladiator* (Ridley Scott, 2000). The Academy Award–winning historical epic about a Roman general who becomes a gladiator and avenges the murder of his family by a power-crazy emperor.

- *I, Claudius* (BBC, 1976). A highly acclaimed fictionalized version of the political intrigue in the first century, told from the viewpoint of the emperor Claudius; with Derek Jacobi and Patrick Stewart.

- *The Roman Empire in the First Century* (PBS, 2001). A four-part documentary that examines the building of the Roman Empire, highlighting ordinary people as well as emperors.

- *Rome: The Rise and Fall of an Empire* (History Channel, 2008). A thirteen-part documentary, with re-enactments — especially of battle scenes, power struggles, and lavish banquets — that trace Rome from the second century B.C.E. to the fifth century C.E.

- *Vindolanda Tablets Online*. A highly unusual find of wooden writing tablets from the second century C.E., discovered at the Roman fortress of Vindolanda behind Hadrian's Wall in Britain, that reveals many aspects of non-elite Roman society and military life. The site includes text images, transliterated texts, English translations, and historical background. **vindolanda.csad.ox.ac.uk/**

7

Late Antiquity

250–600

The Roman Empire, with its powerful — and sometimes bizarre — leaders, magnificent buildings, luxurious clothing, and bloody amusements, has long fascinated people. Politicians and historians have closely studied the reasons for its successes and have even more closely analyzed the weaknesses that led to its eventual collapse. From the third century onward, the Western Roman Empire slowly disintegrated. Scholars have long seen this era as one of the great turning points in Western history, a time when the ancient world was transformed into the very different medieval world. During the past several decades, however, focus has shifted to continuities as well as changes, and what is now usually termed "late antiquity" has been recognized as a period of creativity and adaptation, not simply of decline and fall. Historians are also now more interested in why Rome lasted so long than why it fell.

The two main agents of continuity in late antiquity were the Christian Church and the Byzantine or Eastern Roman Empire. Missionaries and church officials spread Christianity within and far beyond the borders of the Roman Empire, bringing with them the Latin language and institutions based on Roman models. The Byzantine Empire lasted until 1453, a thousand years longer than the Western Roman Empire, and preserved and transmitted much of ancient Greco-Roman law, philosophy, and institutions. The main agents of change in late antiquity were groups the Romans labeled barbarians migrating into the Roman Empire. They brought different social, political, and economic structures with them, but as they encountered Roman culture and became Christian, their own ways of doing things were also transformed. ■

CHAPTER PREVIEW

- How did Diocletian and Constantine try to reform the empire?

- How did the Christian Church become a major force in the Mediterranean and Europe?

- What were the key characteristics of barbarian society?

- How did the barbarian migrations shape Europe?

- How did the church convert barbarian peoples to Christianity?

- How did the Byzantine Empire preserve the legacy of Rome?

Battle Between Romans and Goths
Rome's wars with the Germanic-speaking groups along its northern border come to life in this relief from a Roman sarcophagus of the third century C.E., discovered in a tomb in the city of Rome. The Romans are wearing helmets, and the soldier at the right is wearing iron or bronze chain mail, a defensive technology that the Romans adapted from the Celts. This artist depicts the Romans as superior by placing them at the top, with tunics and clean-shaven faces, in contrast to the barbarous Goths, with their bare chests, long pants, and beards. (De Agostini/G. DAGLI ORTI/Getty Images)

How did Diocletian and Constantine try to reform the empire?

In the middle of the third century, the Roman Empire faced internal turmoil and external attacks. Civil wars tore the empire apart as emperors rose and fell in quick succession, and Germanic tribes and others migrated and marauded deep within the boundaries of the empire. Wars and invasions disrupted normal commerce and agriculture, the primary sources of tax revenues. The barracks emperors of the third century dealt with economic hardship by cutting the silver content of coins until money was virtually worthless. The immediate result was crippling inflation throughout the empire, made worse by the corruption of many officials. Many Romans had become Christian, but the followers of traditional Roman religion were divided in their views of what this meant for the empire. In the early fourth century the emperor Diocletian (r. 284–305), who was born of low-status parents and had risen through the ranks of the military to become emperor, restored order, and the later emperor Constantine (r. 306–337) continued his work. How Diocletian, Constantine, and their successors responded to the problems facing the empire influenced later developments.

Political Measures

Diocletian recognized that the empire had become too large for one man to handle and divided it into a western half and an eastern half (Map 7.1). Diocletian assumed direct control of the eastern part; he gave the rule of the western part to a colleague, along with the title *augustus*. Around 293 Diocletian further delegated power by appointing two men to assist the augustus and him; each of the four men was given the title *caesar*, and the system was known as the **tetrarchy** (TEH-trahr-kee), meaning "rule of four." He further divided each part of the empire into administrative units called **dioceses**, which were in turn subdivided into small provinces, all governed by an expanded bureaucracy. Although four men ruled the empire, Diocletian was clearly the senior partner and final source of authority.

Diocletian's political reforms were a momentous step. The reorganization made the empire easier to administer and placed each of the four central military commands much closer to borders or other trouble spots, so that troops could be sent more quickly when needed. Diocletian hoped that the tetrarchy would supply a clearly defined order of succession and end struggles for power over the emperorship. That did not happen, but much of Diocletian's reorganization remained.

Like Diocletian, Constantine came up through the army and took control after a series of civil wars. He eventually had authority over the entire empire, but he ruled from the East, where he established a new capital for the empire at Byzantium, an old Greek city on the Bosporus, naming it "New Rome," though it was soon called Constantinople. (Today this is Istanbul, the largest city in Turkey.) Constantine sponsored a massive building program of palaces, warehouses, public buildings, and even a hippodrome for horse racing, modeling these on Roman buildings. He built defensive works along the borders of the empire, trying hard to keep it together, and used various means to strengthen the army, as did his successors. The emperors ruling from Constantinople could not provide enough military assistance to repel invaders in the western half of the Roman Empire, however, and Roman authority there slowly disintegrated.

Economic Issues

In response to inflation and declining tax revenues, Diocletian issued an edict that fixed maximum prices and wages throughout the empire. At the same time, taxes became payable in kind, that is, in goods such

MAP 7.1 The Division of the Roman World, 293 Under Diocletian, the Roman Empire was first divided into a western and an eastern half, a development that foreshadowed the medieval division between the Latin West and the Byzantine East.

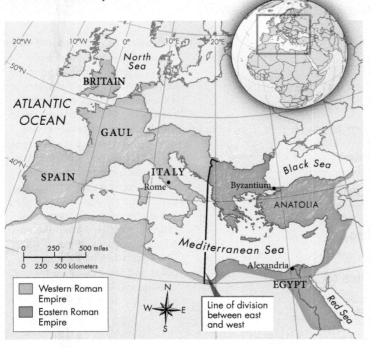

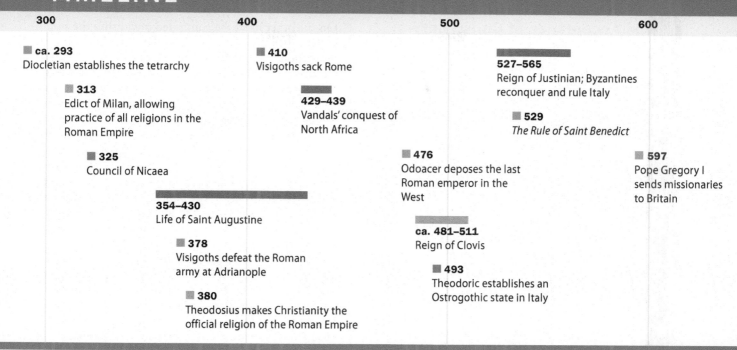

300   400   500   600

■ **ca. 293**
Diocletian establishes the tetrarchy

■ **313**
Edict of Milan, allowing practice of all religions in the Roman Empire

■ **325**
Council of Nicaea

354–430
Life of Saint Augustine

■ **378**
Visigoths defeat the Roman army at Adrianople

■ **380**
Theodosius makes Christianity the official religion of the Roman Empire

■ **410**
Visigoths sack Rome

429–439
Vandals' conquest of North Africa

■ **476**
Odoacer deposes the last Roman emperor in the West

ca. 481–511
Reign of Clovis

■ **493**
Theodoric establishes an Ostrogothic state in Italy

527–565
Reign of Justinian; Byzantines reconquer and rule Italy

■ **529**
The Rule of Saint Benedict

■ **597**
Pope Gregory I sends missionaries to Britain

as grain, sheep, or cloth instead of money, which made them difficult to transport to central authorities. Constantine continued these measures and also made occupations more rigid: all people involved in the growing, preparation, and transportation of food and other essentials were locked into their professions. In this period of severe depression, many individuals and communities could not pay their taxes. In such cases, local tax collectors, who were also bound to their occupations, had to make up the difference from their own funds. This system soon wiped out a whole class of moderately wealthy people and set the stage for the lack of social mobility that was a key characteristic of European society for many centuries to follow.

The emperors' measures did not really address Rome's central economic problems, however. Because of worsening conditions during the third and fourth centuries, many free farmers and their families were killed by invaders or renegade soldiers, or they abandoned farms ravaged in the fighting. Consequently, large tracts of land lay deserted. Landlords with ample resources began at once to reclaim as much of this land as they could, often hiring back the free farmers who had previously worked the land as paid labor or tenants. The huge villas that resulted were

Gold Coin Showing Constantine
In this gold coin, minted at Ticinum in northern Italy in 316, Constantine is shown with a halo, a symbol of his sacred character and connection to the sun-god. This iconography was later adopted in Christian art to signify divinity or sanctity. (Ashmolean Museum/Bridgeman Images)

self-sufficient and became islands of stability in an unsettled world.

Free farmers who remained on the land were exposed to raids and the tyranny of imperial officials. In return for the protection and security landlords could offer, small landholders gave over their lands and their freedom. To guarantee a supply of labor, landlords denied them freedom to move elsewhere. Henceforth they and their families worked their patrons' land, not their own. Free men and women were becoming tenant farmers bound to the land, what would later be called serfs.

■ **tetrarchy** Diocletian's four-part division of the Roman Empire.

■ **diocese** An administrative unit in the later Roman Empire; adopted by the Christian Church as the territory under the authority of a bishop.

The Acceptance of Christianity

The turmoil of the third century seemed to some emperors, including Diocletian, to be the punishment of the gods. Diocletian stepped up persecution of Christians who would not sacrifice to Rome's traditional deities, portraying them as disloyal to the empire in an attempt to wipe out the faith. These persecutions lasted only a few years, however. Increasing numbers of Romans, including members of prominent families, were converting to Christianity, and many who followed traditional Roman religions no longer saw Christianity as un-Roman. Constantine reversed Diocletian's policy and instead ordered toleration of all religions in the Edict of Milan, issued in 313.

Whether Constantine was himself a Christian by this point is hotly debated. His later biographer, the Christian bishop Eusebius, reported that he had been converted on a battlefield in 312 after seeing a vision, and other sources attribute his conversion to his Christian mother, Helena, who had become Christian earlier. Constantine sent Helena on a journey to bring sacred relics from Jerusalem to Constantinople as part of his efforts to promote Christianity in the empire.

On the other hand, he continued to worship the sun-god, and in 321 proclaimed that Sunday, "the Day of the Sun," would be the official day of rest. He was baptized only shortly before he died, although this was not uncommon for high officials. Whatever his personal beliefs at different stages of his life, there is no debate that he recognized the growing numbers of Christians in the empire and financially supported the church. He freed the clergy from imperial taxation and endowed the building of Christian churches. One of his gifts—the Lateran Palace in Rome—remained the official residence of the popes until the fourteenth century. He allowed others to make gifts to the church as well, decreeing in 321, "Every man, when dying, shall have the right to bequeath as much of his property as he desires to the holy and venerable Catholic Church. And such wills are not to be broken."[1] In return for his support, Constantine expected the assistance of church officials in maintaining order. Helped in part by its favored position in the empire, Christianity slowly became the leading religion (Map 7.2).

As they had in the first centuries of Christianity, Christians disagreed with one another about many issues,

MAP 7.2 The Spread of Christianity, to 600   Originating in Judaea, the southern part of modern Israel and Jordan, Christianity first spread throughout the Roman world and then beyond it in all directions.

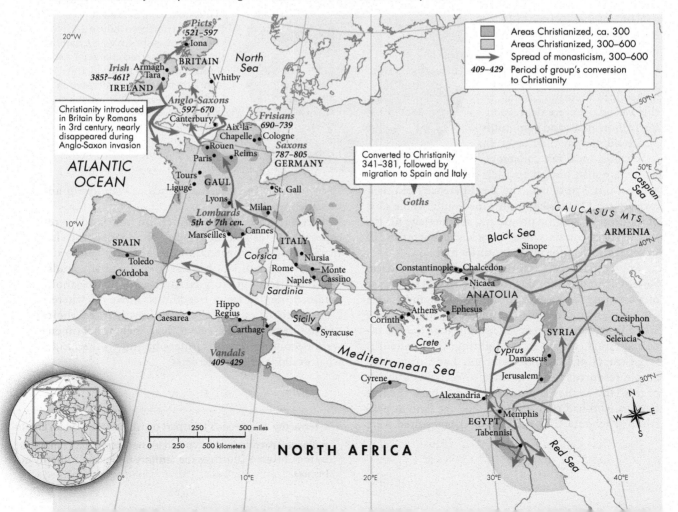

which led to schisms (SKIH-zuhms), denunciations, and sometimes violence. In the fourth and fifth centuries disputes arose over the nature of Christ. For example, **Arianism** (AI-ree-uh-nih-zuhm), developed by Arius (ca. 250–336), a priest of Alexandria, held that Jesus was created by the will of God the Father and thus was not co-eternal with him. Arian Christians reasoned that Jesus the Son must be inferior to God the Father because the Father was incapable of suffering and did not die. Arianism enjoyed such popularity and provoked such controversy that Constantine, who declared that "internal strife within the Church of God is far more evil and dangerous than any kind of war and conflict," interceded. In 325 he summoned church leaders to a council in Nicaea (nigh-SEE-uh) in Asia Minor and presided over it personally. The council produced the **Nicene Creed**, which defined the position that Christ is "eternally begotten of the Father" and of the same substance as the Father. Arius and those who refused to accept Nicene (nigh-SEEN) Christianity were banished. Their interpretation of the nature of Christ was declared a heresy, that is, a belief that contradicted the interpretation the church leaders declared was correct, which was termed orthodoxy.

These actions did not end Arianism, however. Several later emperors were Arian Christian, and Arian missionaries converted many Germanic tribes, who were attracted by the idea that Jesus was God's first-in-command, which fit well with their own warrior hierarchies and was less complicated than the idea of two persons with one substance.

The Nicene Creed says little specifically about the Holy Spirit, but in the following centuries the idea that the Father, Son, and Holy Spirit are "one substance in three persons"—the Trinity—became a central doctrine in Christianity, though again there were those who disagreed. Disputes about the nature of Christ also continued, with factions establishing themselves as separate Christian groups. The Nestorians, for example, regarded the divine and human natures in Jesus as distinct from one another, whereas the orthodox opinion was that they were united. The Nestorians split from the rest of the church in the fifth century after their position was outlawed, and settled in Persia. Nestorian Christian missionaries later founded churches in Central Asia, India, and China.

Religious and secular authorities tried in various ways to control this diversity as well as promote Christianity. In 380 the emperor Theodosius (thee-uh-DOH-shee-uhs) made Nicene Christianity the official religion of the empire. Theodosius stripped Roman pagan temples of statues, made the practice of the old Roman state religion a treasonable offense, and persecuted Christians who dissented from orthodox doctrine. Most significant, he allowed the church to establish its own courts and to use its own body of law, called canon law. The church courts, not the Roman government, had jurisdiction over the clergy

Constantine and Helena in a Nestorian Manuscript   This fifth- to sixth-century manuscript from a Nestorian Christian community in Central Asia shows Constantine with his mother Helena, holding pieces of the True Cross, one of the many relics she is traditionally credited with bringing from Jerusalem to Constantinople. Nestorian Christians had a different view of the nature of Jesus than did Constantine, but they still viewed him and his mother as important figures in their tradition. (Pictures From History/Bridgeman Images)

and ecclesiastical disputes. At the death of Theodosius, the Christian Church was considerably independent of the Roman state. The foundation for later growth in church power had been laid.

Later emperors continued the pattern of active involvement in church affairs. They appointed the highest officials of the church hierarchy; the emperors or their representatives presided at ecumenical councils; and the emperors controlled some of the material resources of the church—land, rents, and dependent peasantry.

■ **Arianism** A theological belief that originated when Arius, a priest of Alexandria, denied that Christ was co-eternal with God the Father.

■ **Nicene Creed** A statement of belief written by a group of Christian church leaders in 325 that declared God the Father and Jesus to be of the same "substance"; other interpretations were declared heresy.

How did the Christian Church become a major force in the Mediterranean and Europe?

As the emperors changed their policies about Christianity from persecution to promotion, the church grew, gradually becoming the most important institution in the Mediterranean and Europe. The able administrators and creative thinkers of the church developed permanent institutions and complex philosophical concepts that drew on the Greco-Roman tradition, which attracted learned Romans.

The Church and Its Leaders

The early Christian Church benefited from the administrative abilities of church leaders. With the empire in decay, educated people joined and worked for the church in the belief that it was the one institution able to provide some stability. Bishop Ambrose of Milan (339–397) is typical of the Roman aristocrats who held high public office, were converted to Christianity, and subsequently became bishops. Like many bishops, Ambrose had a solid education in classical law and rhetoric, which he used to become an eloquent preacher. He had a strong sense of his authority and even stood up to Emperor Theodosius, who had ordered Ambrose to hand over his major church—called a basilica—to the emperor:

> At length came the command, "Deliver up the Basilica"; I reply, "It is not lawful for us to deliver it up, nor for your Majesty to receive it. By no law can you violate the house of a private man, and do you think that the house of God may be taken away? . . . But do not burden your conscience with the thought that you have any right as Emperor over sacred things. . . . It is written, God's to God and Caesar's to Caesar. The palace is the Emperor's, the churches are the Bishop's. To you is committed jurisdiction over public, not over sacred buildings."[2]

The emperor relented. Ambrose's assertion that the church was supreme in spiritual matters and the state in secular issues was to serve as the cornerstone of the church's position on church-state relations for centuries. Ambrose came to be regarded as one of the fathers of the church, that is, early Christian thinkers whose authority was seen as second only to the Bible in later centuries.

Gradually the church adapted the organizational structure of the Roman Empire begun during the reign of Diocletian. The territory under the authority of a bishop was also called a diocese, with its center a cathedral (from the Latin *cathedra*, meaning "chair"), the church that contained the bishop's official seat of power. A bishop's jurisdiction extended throughout the diocese, and he came to control a large amount of land that was given to or purchased by the church. Bishops generally came from prominent families and had both spiritual and political power; as the Roman Empire disintegrated, they became the most important local authority on many types of issues. They claimed to trace their spiritual ancestry back to Jesus's apostles, a doctrine called **apostolic succession**. Because of the special importance of their dioceses, five bishops—those of Antioch, Alexandria, Jerusalem, Constantinople, and Rome—gained the title of *patriarch*.

After the capital and the emperor moved to Constantinople, the power of the bishop of Rome grew because he was the only patriarch in the Western Roman Empire. The bishops of Rome stressed that Rome had special significance because of its history as the capital of a worldwide empire. More significantly, they asserted, Rome had a special place in Christian history. According to tradition, Saint Peter, chief of Jesus's disciples, had lived in Rome and been its first bishop. Thus, as successors of Peter, the bishops of Rome—known as popes, from the Latin word *papa*, meaning "father"—claimed a privileged position in the church hierarchy, an idea called the **Petrine Doctrine** that built on the notion of apostolic succession. They stressed their supremacy over other Christian communities and urged other churches to appeal to Rome for the resolution of disputed doctrinal issues. Not surprisingly, the other patriarchs did not agree. They continued to exercise authority in their own regions, and local churches did as well, but the groundwork had been laid for later Roman predominance on religious matters.

Beginning in the fifth century the popes also expanded the church's secular authority, making treaties with the leaders of groups that threatened the city of Rome. One pope who did this was Gregory I (pontificate 590–604), later called "the Great," who also reorganized church lands to increase production and then distributed the additional food to the poor. He had been an official for the city of Rome before he became a church official, and his administrative and diplomatic talents helped the church expand. He sent missionaries to the British Isles and wrote letters and guides instructing bishops on practical and spiritual matters. He also promoted the ideas of Augustine, particularly those that defined church rituals as essential for salvation. The Western Christian Church headed by the pope in Rome would become the most enduring nongovernmental institution in world history.

The Development of Christian Monasticism

Christianity began and spread as a city religion. Since the first century, however, some especially pious Christians had felt that the only alternative to the decadence of urban life was complete separation from the world. This desire to withdraw from ordinary life led to the development of the monastic life. Monasticism began in third-century Egypt, where individuals like Saint Anthony (251?–356) and small groups first withdrew from cities and from organized society to seek God through prayer in desert or mountain caves and shelters, giving up all for Christ. Gradually large colonies of monks gathered in the deserts of Upper Egypt, and Christians came to believe that monks, like the early Christian martyrs executed by Roman authorities before them, could speak to God and that their prayers had special influence. These monks were called hermits, from the Greek word *eremos*, meaning "desert." Many devout women also were attracted to this eremitical (ehr-uh-MIH-tihk-uhl) type of monasticism.

In the early fourth century, the Egyptian ascetic Pachomius (puh-KOH-mee-uhs) (290–346?) drew thousands of men and women to the monastic life at Tabennisi on the Upper Nile. There were too many for them to live as hermits, so Pachomius organized communities of men and women, creating a new type of monasticism, known as cenobitic (seh-nuh-BIH-tik), that emphasized communal living. Starting in the fourth century, information about Egyptian monasticism spread throughout the Mediterranean and into Europe, and both men and women organized similar monastic communities. (See "Individuals in Society: Macrina the Younger," page 177.)

Monastery Life

In 529 Benedict of Nursia (480–543), who had experimented with both eremitical and communal forms of monastic life, wrote a brief set of regulations for the monks who had gathered around him at Monte Cassino between Rome and Naples. Benedict's guide for monastic life, known as *The Rule of Saint Benedict*, came to influence all forms of organized religious life in the Western Christian Church. Men and women in monastic houses all followed sets of rules, first those of Benedict and later those written by other individuals. For this reason, men who lived a communal monastic life came to be called **regular clergy**, from the Latin word *regulus* (rule). Priests and bishops who staffed churches in which people worshipped and who were not cut off from the world were called **secular clergy**.

The Rule of Saint Benedict outlined a monastic life of regularity, discipline, and moderation in an atmosphere of silence. Each monk had ample food and adequate sleep. The monk spent part of each day in formal prayer, which consisted of chanting psalms and other prayers from the Bible in the part of the monastery church called the choir. The rest of the day was passed in manual labor, study, and private prayer. The monastic life as conceived by Saint Benedict struck a balance between asceticism (extreme material sacrifice, including fasting and the renunciation of sex) and activity. It thus provided opportunities for men of entirely different abilities and talents—from mechanics to gardeners to literary scholars. The Benedictine form of religious life also appealed to women, because it allowed them to show their devotion and engage in study. Benedict's twin sister Scholastica (480–543) adapted the *Rule* for use by her community of nuns.

Benedictine monasticism also succeeded partly because it was so materially successful. In the seventh and eighth centuries monasteries pushed back forests and wastelands, drained swamps, and experimented with crop rotation. Benedictine houses thus made a significant contribution to the agricultural development of Europe.

Monasteries conducted schools for local young people, and monks and nuns copied manuscripts, preserving classical as well as Christian literature. Local and royal governments drew on the services of the literate men and able administrators the monasteries produced. This was not what Saint Benedict had intended, but perhaps the effectiveness of the institution he designed made it inevitable.

Christianity and Classical Culture

The growth of Christianity was not simply a matter of institutions such as the papacy and monasteries, but also a matter of ideas. The earliest Christian thinkers sometimes rejected Greco-Roman culture, but as Christianity grew from a tiny persecuted group to the official religion of the Roman Empire, its leaders and thinkers gradually came to terms with classical culture (see "The Growing Acceptance and Evolution of Christianity" in Chapter 6). They

■ **apostolic succession** The doctrine that all bishops can trace their spiritual ancestry back to Jesus's apostles.

■ **Petrine Doctrine** A doctrine stating that the popes (the bishops of Rome) were the successors of Saint Peter and therefore heirs to his highest level of authority as chief of the apostles.

■ **regular clergy** Men and women who lived in monastic houses and followed sets of rules, first those of Benedict and later those written by other individuals.

■ **secular clergy** Priests and bishops who staffed churches where people worshipped and who were not cut off from the world.

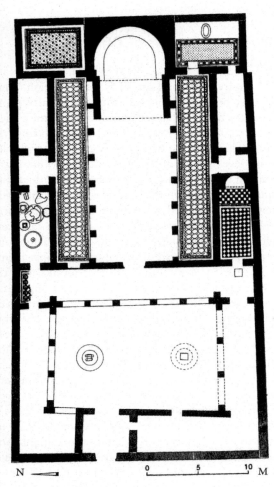

N ⟶ 0 5 10 M

Floor Plan and Foundation of Kursi Monastery Church Built on the eastern shore of the Sea of Galilee in the fifth century at a major pilgrimage site, this walled monastery had living quarters for the monks, a guesthouse, and a bath for pilgrims. It contained a church, shown here, modeled on the type of Roman public building known as a basilica, with an open courtyard with two wells (near the bottom in the pictures), mosaic floors, and a central nave separated from side aisles by rows of arched columns. In one side chapel (on the left in the pictures) was a small baptismal font, and in another a press for olive oil, a major source of income for the monastery. The skeletons of thirty monks were found in a crypt when the site was uncovered during road construction in 1970. (© Zev Radovan/Bridgeman Images)

incorporated elements of Greek and Roman philosophy and learning into Christian teachings, modifying them to fit with Christian notions.

Saint Jerome (340–419), for example, a distinguished theologian and linguist regarded as a father of the church, translated the Old and New Testaments from Hebrew and Greek into vernacular Latin. Called the Vulgate, his edition of the Bible served as the official translation until the sixteenth century, and scholars rely on it even today. Familiar with the writings of classical authors, Saint Jerome maintained that the best ancient literature should be interpreted in light of the Christian faith.

Christian Notions of Gender and Sexuality

Early Christians both adopted and adapted the then-contemporary views on women, marriage, and sexuality. In his plan of salvation, Jesus considered women the equal of men. Women were among the earliest converts to Christianity and took an active role in its spread, preaching, acting as missionaries, being martyred alongside men, and perhaps even baptizing believers. Because early Christians believed that the Second Coming of Christ was imminent, they devoted their energies to their new spiritual family of

INDIVIDUALS IN SOCIETY

Macrina the Younger

The story of early Christianity is often told as one of "church fathers"—Ambrose, Jerome, Augustine, and so on—but over the last several decades we have learned more about "church mothers," women who were important in the early development of Christianity, despite attempts by male contemporaries and later Christian authors to play down their role. One of these women was Saint Macrina the Younger (ca. 327–379), born in Caesarea, an important Byzantine trading center in the province of Cappadocia in what is now central Turkey. Her family had been Christian for several generations and eventually included a number of individuals who would later be revered as saints. According to the writings of Macrina's brother Gregory of Nyssa, her grandmother, also named Macrina (ca. 270–ca. 340), converted from paganism, fled her home during the persecutions of Diocletian, and raised her children and grandchildren in an intensely Christian atmosphere. (She became Saint Macrina the Elder, and her grandchildren included three saints: Basil of Caesarea, Gregory of Nyssa, and Macrina.)

The younger Macrina hoped to remain unmarried and devote herself to a religious life, but her father forced her to agree to a betrothal. When her fiancé died, she maintained that the betrothal had legally constituted a marriage and skillfully used the laws regarding betrothal and widowhood against the authority of her father to avoid another marriage, becoming a "virgin-widow." After her father died, she moved with her mother to a rural family estate, where they established a monastic community for women. In his biography of his sister—our main source about her life—Gregory reports that the household became a community of equals, in which all dressed alike, and Macrina performed tasks that were normally done by servants. Her household monastery became known for its intense devotional life of prayer, meditation, and asceticism, but also for its charity and hospitality toward strangers. It set the pattern for Eastern cenobitic monasticism and also influenced Western monasticism, as Saint Benedict read the works of Macrina's brothers that refer to it.

No writings from Macrina herself survive, not even letters, and historians debate how much references to her in the works of her famous brothers can be used as evidence for her own ideas. One of these, Gregory's *Dialogue on the Soul and Resurrection*, relates a long conversation he purportedly had with his sister on her deathbed, in which she argues for the immortality of the soul, using references to the natural world and classical and biblical texts. We have no idea whether this happened, but the fact that Gregory could even imagine it

An eleventh-century icon of Saint Macrina the Younger, in the Saint Sophia Cathedral in Kyiv, Ukraine. Macrina came to be widely venerated in Eastern Orthodox churches for her piety and learning. (Art Collection 3/Alamy Stock Photo)

and could portray his sister as a parallel to Socrates (who also on his deathbed argued that the soul was immortal) suggests her influence on him. Her words in this dialogue continue to provide inspiration today, particularly those about nature, which in contrast to many ascetics she saw as a reflection of the glory of God. She also felt that the soul was not separate from the mind but instead was "an intellectual essence deeply seated in our nature, acting through the operation of our bodily senses."

QUESTIONS FOR ANALYSIS

1. Why might Macrina and the other women in her community have viewed remaining unmarried as a liberating option?
2. What other examples of individuals whose ideas come down only in the writings of others have you read about?

co-believers. Women and men joyously accepted the ascetic life, renouncing marriage and procreation to use their bodies for a higher calling. Some women, either singly or in monastic communities, declared themselves "virgins in the service of Christ." All this initially made Christianity seem dangerous to many Romans, who viewed marriage as the foundation of society and the proper patriarchal order.

Not all Christian teachings about gender were radical, however. In the first century C.E. male church leaders began to place restrictions on female believers. Women were forbidden to preach and were gradually excluded from holding official positions in Christianity other than in women's monasteries. Women who chose lives of virginity in the service of God were to be praised; Saint Jerome commented that a woman "who wishes to serve Christ more than the world . . . will cease to be a woman and will be called man," the highest praise he could bestow.[3] Even such women were not to be too independent, however. Both Jewish and classical Mediterranean culture viewed women's subordination as natural and proper, so in limiting the activities of female believers the Christian Church was following well-established patterns, just as it did in modeling its official hierarchy after that of the Roman Empire.

Christian teachings about sexuality built on and challenged classical models. The rejection of sexual activity involved an affirmation of the importance of a spiritual life, but it also incorporated the hostility toward the body found in some Hellenistic philosophies and some of the other religions that had spread in the Roman Empire in this era. Christian teachings affirmed that God had created the material world and sanctioned marriage, but most Christian thinkers also taught that celibacy was the better life, and that anything that took one's attention from the spiritual world performed an evil function. For most clerical writers (who themselves were male) this temptation came from women, and in some of their writings women themselves are depicted as evil, the "devil's gateway." Thus the writings of many church fathers

contain a strong streak of misogyny (hatred of women), which was passed down to later Christian thinkers.

Saint Augustine on Human Nature, Will, and Sin

The most influential church father in the West was Saint Augustine of Hippo (354–430). Saint Augustine was born into an urban family in what is now Algeria in North Africa. His father, a minor civil servant, was a pagan; his mother, Monica, was a devout Christian. He gained an excellent classical education in philosophy and rhetoric and, as was normal for young Roman men, began relations with a concubine, who later had his son.

Augustine took teaching positions first in Rome and then in Milan, where he had frequent conversations with Bishop Ambrose. Through his discussions with Ambrose and his own reading, Augustine became a Christian. He returned to Africa and later became bishop of the seacoast city of Hippo Regius.

Augustine's autobiography, *The Confessions*, is a literary masterpiece and one of the most influential books in the history of Europe. Written in the rhetorical

Adam and Eve   This illuminated page from the book of Genesis in a ninth-century Bible tells the story of Adam and Eve; the middle part of the image links their disobedience to sexual shame, an aspect of the story often highlighted in visual depictions as well as sermons and written works. Commissioned by a nobleman who was also an abbot, this Bible was presented to Charles the Bald, king of the Franks, in 846. (DEA/G. Dagli Orti/De Agostini/Getty Images)

style and language of late Roman antiquity, it marks the synthesis of Greco-Roman forms and Christian thought. *The Confessions* describes Augustine's moral struggle, the conflict between his spiritual and intellectual aspirations and his sensual and material self. Many Greek and Roman philosophers had taught that knowledge would lead to virtue. Augustine came to reject this idea, claiming that people do not always act on the basis of rational knowledge. As he notes in *The Confessions*, even before he became a Christian he had decided that chastity was the best possible life, so he prayed to God for "chastity and continency," yet always added "but not yet." His education had not made him strong enough to avoid lust or any other evil; that would come only through God's power and grace.

Augustine's ideas on sin, grace, and redemption became the foundation of all subsequent Western Christian theology, Protestant as well as Catholic. He wrote that the basic force in any individual is the will, which he defined as "the power of the soul to hold on to or to obtain an object without constraint." The end or goal of the will determines the moral character of the individual. When Adam ate the fruit forbidden by God in the Garden of Eden (Genesis 3:6), he committed the "original sin" and corrupted the will. Adam's sin was not simply his own—it was passed on to all later humans through sexual intercourse; even infants were tainted. Original sin thus became a common social stain, in Augustine's opinion, transmitted by sexual desire. By viewing sexual desire as the result of Adam and Eve's disobedience to divine instructions, Augustine linked sexuality even more clearly with sin than had earlier church fathers. Because Adam disobeyed God and fell, all human beings have an innate tendency to sin: their will is weak. But according to Augustine, God restores the strength of the will through grace, which is transmitted in certain rituals that the church defined as **sacraments**. Grace results from God's decisions, not from any merit on the part of the individual.

When Visigothic forces captured the city of Rome in 410, horrified pagans blamed the disaster on the Christians. In response, Augustine wrote *City of God*. This original work contrasts Christianity with the secular society in which it exists. According to Augustine, history is the account of God acting in time. Human history reveals that there are two kinds of people: those who live the life of the flesh, and those who live the life of the spirit in what Augustine called the City of God. The former will endure eternal hellfire; the latter will enjoy eternal bliss. Government was a necessary evil with the power to do good by providing the peace, justice, and order that Christians need to pursue their pilgrimage to the City of God.

What were the key characteristics of barbarian society?

Augustine's *City of God* was written in response to the conquest of Rome by an army of Visigoths, one of the many peoples the Romans—and later historians—labeled "barbarians." The word *barbarian* comes from the Greek *barbaros*, meaning someone who did not speak Greek. (To the Greeks, others seemed to be speaking nonsense syllables; *barbar* is the Greek equivalent of "blah-blah" or "yada-yada.") The Romans usually used the Latin version of *barbarian* to mean the Germanic and other peoples who lived beyond the northeastern boundary of Roman territory, whom they regarded as unruly, savage, and primitive. That value judgment is generally also present when we use *barbarian* in English, but there really is no other word to describe the many different peoples who lived to the north of the Roman Empire. Thus historians of late antiquity use the word *barbarian* to designate these peoples, who spoke a variety of languages but had similarities in their basic social, economic, and political structures. (See "Viewpoints: Roman and Byzantine Views of Barbarians," page 180.) In contrast to most ancient Romans, many historians find much to admire in barbarian society.

Scholars have been hampered in investigating barbarian society because most groups did not write and thus kept no written records before Christian missionaries introduced writing. Greek and Roman authors did describe barbarian society, but they were not always objective observers, instead using barbarians to highlight what they thought was right or wrong about their own cultures. Thus written records must be combined with archaeological evidence to gain a more accurate picture. In addition, historians are increasingly deciphering and using the barbarians' own written records that do exist, especially inscriptions carved in stone, bone, and wood and written in the runic alphabet. Runic inscriptions come primarily from Scandinavia and the British Isles. Most are short and limited to names, such as inscriptions on tombstones.

Barbarians included many different ethnic groups with social and political structures, languages, laws, and beliefs that developed in central and northern

■ **sacraments** Certain rituals defined by the church in which God bestows benefits on the believer through grace.

VIEWPOINTS
Roman and Byzantine Views of Barbarians

The earliest written records about the barbarian groups that migrated, attacked, and sometimes conquered the more urbanized and densely populated areas of Europe and western Asia all come from the pens of educated Greeks, Romans, and Byzantines. They provide us with important information about barbarians, but always from the perspective of outsiders with a particular point of view. The selections below are typical of such commentary. The first is from the fourth-century Roman general and historian Ammianus Marcellinus, who fought in Roman armies against Germanic tribes, the Huns, and the Persians, and later wrote a history of the Roman Empire. The second is from the sixth-century Byzantine historian Agathias, describing recent encounters between the forces of the Byzantine emperor Justinian and various Germanic tribes.

Ammianus Marcellinus on the Huns, ca. 380

◇ The people of the Huns, but little known from ancient records, dwelling beyond the Maeotic Sea near the ice-bound ocean, exceed every degree of savagery. . . . They all have compact, strong limbs and thick necks, and are so monstrously ugly and misshapen, that one might take them for two-legged beasts or for the stumps, rough-hewn into images, that are used in putting sides to bridges. But although they have the form of men, however ugly, they are so hardy in their mode of life that they have no need of fire nor of savory food, but eat the roots of wild plants and the half-raw flesh of any kind of animal whatever, which they put between their thighs and the backs of their horses, and thus warm a little. They are never protected by any buildings, but they avoid these like tombs. . . . They are not at all adapted to battles on foot, but they are almost glued to their horses, which are hardy, it is true, but ugly. . . . They fight from a distance with missiles having sharp bone [points], instead of the usual (metal) parts, joined to the shafts with wonderful skill; then they gallop over the intervening spaces and fight hand to hand with swords, regardless of their

own lives. . . . No one in their country ever plows a field or touches a plow-handle. They are all without fixed abode, without hearth, or law, or settled mode of life, and keep roaming from place to place, like fugitives, accompanied by wagons in which they live; in wagons their wives weave for them their hideous garments, in wagons they cohabit with their husbands, bear children, and rear them to the age of puberty.

Agathias on the Franks, sixth century

◇ The Franks are not nomads, as indeed some barbarian peoples are, but their system of government, administration and laws are modelled more or less on the Roman pattern, apart from which they uphold similar standards with regard to contracts, marriage, and religious observance. They are in fact all Christians and adhere to the strictest orthodoxy. They also have magistrates in their cities and priests and celebrate the feasts in the same way we do, and, for a barbarian people, strike me as extremely well-bred and civilized and as practically the same as ourselves except for their uncouth style of dress and peculiar language. I admire them for their other attributes and especially for the spirit of justice and harmony which prevails amongst them.

QUESTIONS FOR ANALYSIS

1. What qualities of the Huns does Ammianus Marcellinus find admirable? What does he criticize?
2. What qualities of the Franks does Agathias praise? Why does he find these qualities admirable?
3. How does the fact that both Ammianus Marcellinus and Agathias come from agricultural societies with large cities shape their views of barbarians?

Sources: *Ammianus Marcellinus: Volume I*, Loeb Classical Library, vol. 300, trans. J. C. Rolfe (Cambridge, Mass.: Harvard University Press), pp. 383, 385; Agathias, *The Histories*, trans. Joseph D. Frendo (Berlin: Walter de Gruyter, 1975), p. 10.

Europe over many centuries. Among the largest groups were Celts (whom the Romans called Gauls) and Germans; Germans were further subdivided into various groups, such as Ostrogoths, Visigoths, Burgundians, and Franks. Celts, Germans, and other barbarians brought their customs and traditions with them when they moved southward, and these gradually combined with classical and Christian patterns to form new types of societies.

Village and Family Life

Barbarian groups usually resided in small villages, and climate and geography determined the basic patterns of how they lived off the land. Many groups lived in small settlements on the edges of clearings, where they raised barley, wheat, oats, peas, and beans. Men and women tilled their fields with simple wooden plows and harvested their grains with small iron sickles.

Whalebone Chest This eighth-century chest made of whalebone, depicting warriors, other human figures, and a horse, tells a story in both pictures and words. The runes along the border are one of the varieties from the British Isles. Contact with the Romans led to the increasing use of the Latin alphabet, though runes and Latin letters were used side by side in some parts of northern Europe for centuries. (Album/Newscom)

The vast majority of people's caloric intake came from grain in some form; the kernels of grain were eaten as porridge, ground up for flour, or fermented into strong, thick beer. Most people were personally free, but some had been enslaved through warfare or capture.

Ironworking represented the most advanced craft; much of northern Europe had iron deposits, and the dense forests provided wood for charcoal, which was used to provide the clean fire needed to make iron. The typical village had an oven and smiths who produced agricultural tools and instruments of war—one-edged swords, arrowheads, and shields. By the second century C.E. the swords produced by barbarian smiths were superior to the weapons of Roman troops.

In the first two centuries C.E. the quantity and quality of material goods increased dramatically. Goods were used locally and for gift giving, a major social custom. Gift giving conferred status on the giver, whose giving showed his higher (economic) status, cemented friendship, and placed the receiver in his debt. Goods were also traded, though commercial exchange was less important than in the Roman Empire.

Families and kin groups were the basic social units in barbarian society. Families were responsible for the debts and actions of their members and for keeping the peace in general. Barbarian law codes set strict rules of inheritance based on position in the family and often set aside a portion of land that could not be sold or given away by any family member so that the family always retained some land.

Barbarian society was patriarchal: within each household the father had authority over his wife, children, and other members of the household. Some wealthy and powerful men had more than

one wife, a pattern that continued even after they became Christian, but polygamy was not widespread among ordinary people. Women worked alongside men in the fields and forests, and the Roman historian Tacitus reported that at times they joined men on the battlefield, urging them to fight harder. Once women were widowed, they sometimes assumed their husbands' rights over family property and held the guardianship of their children.

Tribes and Hierarchies

The basic social and political unit among barbarian groups was the tribe or confederation, a group whose members believed that they were all descended from a common ancestor and were thus kin. Tribes were led by chieftains. The chief was the member recognized as the strongest and bravest in battle and was elected from among the male members of the most powerful family. He led the group in war, settled disputes among its members, conducted negotiations with outside powers, and offered sacrifices to the gods. The period of migrations and conquests of the Western Roman Empire witnessed the strengthening of the power of chiefs, who often adopted the title of king, though this title implies broader power than they actually had.

Closely associated with the chief in some tribes was the **comitatus**, or war band. These warriors swore loyalty to the chief, fought with him in battle, and were not supposed to leave the battlefield without him; to

■ **comitatus** A war band of young men in a barbarian tribe who were closely associated with the chief, swore loyalty to him, and fought with him in battle.

Visigothic Work and Play
This page comes from one of the very few manuscripts from late antiquity to have survived: a copy of the first five books of the Old Testament — the Pentateuch — made around 600, perhaps in Visigothic Spain or North Africa. The top shows biblical scenes, while the bottom shows people engaged in everyday activities — building a wall, drawing water from a well, and trading punches. (Bibliothèque Nationale, Paris, France/De Agostini Picture Library/Getty Images)

do so implied cowardice, disloyalty, and social disgrace. These oaths of loyalty were later more formalized in the development of feudalism (see Chapter 8).

Although initially a social egalitarianism appears to have existed among members of the comitatus because they regarded one another as kin, during the migrations and warfare of the third and fourth centuries, the war band was transformed into a system of stratified ranks. Among the Ostrogoths, for example, a warrior nobility evolved. Contact with the Romans stimulated demand for goods such as metal armbands, which the Romans produced for trade with barbarian groups. Armbands were of different widths and value, and they became a symbol of hierarchy among warriors, much as the insignia of military rank function today. During the Ostrogothic conquest of Italy, warrior-nobles also began to acquire land as both a mark of prestige and a means to power. As land and wealth came into the hands of a small elite class, social

inequalities within the group emerged and gradually grew stronger. These inequalities help explain the origins of the European noble class.

Customary and Written Law

Early barbarian tribes had no written laws. Law was custom, but certain individuals were often given special training in remembering and retelling laws from generation to generation. Beginning in the late fifth century, however, some chieftains and rulers began to collect, write, and publish lists of their customs and laws. (See "Thinking Like a Historian: Slavery in Roman and Germanic Society," page 184.)

The law code of the Salian Franks, one of the barbarian tribes, included a feature common to many barbarian codes. Any crime that involved a personal injury, such as assault, rape, and murder, was given a particular monetary value, called the **wergeld** (WUHR-gehld) (literally "man-money" or "money to buy off the spear"), that was to be paid by the

■ **wergeld** Compensatory payment for death or injury set in many barbarian law codes.

perpetrator to the victim or the family. The Salic law lists many of these:

> If any person strike another on the head so that the brain appears, and the three bones which lie above the brain shall project, he shall be sentenced to 1200 denars, which make 300 shillings. . . .
>
> If any one have killed a free woman after she has begun bearing children, he shall be sentenced to 2400 denars, which make 600 shillings.[4]

The wergeld varied according to the severity of the crime and also the social status of the victim. The fine for the murder of a woman of childbearing years was the same value as that attached to military officers of the king, to priests, and to boys preparing to become warriors, which suggests the importance of women in Frankish society, at least for their childbearing capacity.

The wergeld system aimed to prevent or reduce violence. If a person accused of a crime agreed to pay the wergeld and if the victim and his or her family accepted the payment, there was peace. If the accused refused to pay the wergeld or if the victim's family refused to accept it, a blood feud ensued.

At first, Romans had been subject to Roman law and barbarians to barbarian custom. As barbarian kings accepted Christianity and as Romans and barbarians increasingly intermarried and assimilated culturally, the distinction between the two types of law blurred and, in the course of the seventh and eighth centuries, disappeared. Instead, all who lived within an area were subject to the same law codes.

Celtic and Germanic Religion

Like Greeks and Romans, barbarians worshipped hundreds of gods and goddesses with specialized functions. They regarded certain mountains, lakes, rivers, or groves of trees as sacred because these were linked to deities. Rituals to honor the gods were held outdoors rather than in temples or churches, often at certain points in the yearly agricultural cycle. Presided over by a priest or priestess understood to have special abilities to call on the gods' powers, rituals sometimes involved animal (and perhaps human) sacrifice. Among the Celts, religious leaders called druids (DROO-ihds) had legal and educational as well as religious functions, orally passing down laws and traditions from generation to generation. Bards singing poems and ballads also passed down myths and stories of heroes and gods, which were written down much later.

The first written records of barbarian religion came from Greeks and Romans who encountered barbarians or spoke with those who had. They understood barbarian traditions through their own belief systems, often equating barbarian gods with Greco-Roman ones and adapting stories and rituals to blend the two. This assimilation appears to have gone both ways, at least judging by the names of the days of the week. In the Roman Empire the days took their names from Roman deities or astronomical bodies, and in the Germanic languages of central and northern Europe the days acquired the names of corresponding barbarian gods. Jupiter's day, for example, became Thor's day (Thursday); both of these powerful gods were associated with thunder.

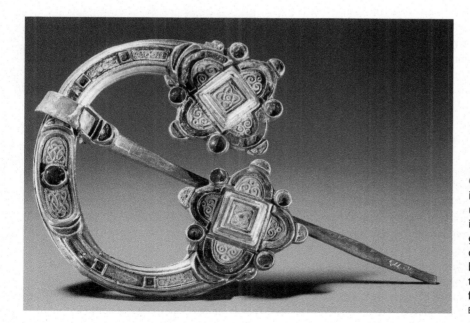

Celtic Brooch This magnificent silver and gold brooch, used to hold a heavy wool cape in place, is adorned with red garnets and complex patterns of interlace. Made in Ireland, the brooch has patterns similar to those found in Irish manuscripts from this era. (© Boltin Picture Library/ Bridgeman Images)

Slavery in Roman and Germanic Society

Slavery continued to be a common condition in the late Roman Empire and among the Germanic tribes. In both societies, it was based not on racial distinctions, but on one's personal status as free or unfree, which was increasingly regulated by law. How could a person cross the border between enslaved and free in these two societies, and what larger social values do laws regarding slavery reflect?

1 **Theodosian Code, 435–438.** Under Emperor Theodosius II (r. 408–450), imperial decrees issued since the time of Constantine that were still in effect were brought together in a single law code.

〜 If a father, forced by need, shall sell any free-born child whatsoever, the child cannot remain in perpetual slavery, but if he has made compensation by his slavery, he shall be restored to his freeborn status without the repayment of the purchase price. . . . It is established that children born from the womb of a slave woman are slaves, according to the law. . . . We have subjected the Scyrae, a barbarian nation, to Our power. Therefore We grant to all persons the opportunity to supply their own fields with men of the aforesaid race. . . . If any person should take up a boy or girl child that has been cast out of its home with the knowledge and consent of its father or owner, and if he should rear this child to strength with his own sustenance, he shall have the right to keep the said child under the same status as he wished it to have when he took charge of it, that is, as his child or as a slave, whichever he should prefer. . . . We exhort slaves, that as soon as possible they shall offer themselves for the labors of war, and if they receive their arms as men fit for military service, they shall obtain the reward of freedom. . . . [In the case of deserters] if the slave should surrender such a deserter, he shall be given his freedom.

2 **Roman tombstone.** The tombstone at right shows a man reclining on a couch, being served a drink by a small servant boy. The inscription identifies the man as a twenty-year-old soldier and freedman, and it gives his name simply as Victor, with no family name or patronymic.

3 **Justinian's Code, 529–534.** The law code of Emperor Justinian includes many provisions regarding slavery.

〜 Liberty is the natural power of doing whatever anyone wishes to do unless he is prevented in some way, by force or by law. Slavery is an institution of the Law of Nations by means of which anyone may subject one man to the control of another, contrary to nature. Slaves are so called for the reason that military commanders were accustomed to sell their captives, and in this manner to preserve them, instead of putting

(Tyne & Wear Archives & Museums/Bridgeman Images)

ANALYZING THE EVIDENCE

1. According to the Roman laws (Sources 1 and 3), how could a person become enslaved in Roman society? According to the Germanic laws (Sources 4–6), how could this happen in Germanic society? Which of these methods established more permanent conditions of servitude?
2. How could an enslaved person become free in Roman society? In Germanic?
3. Looking back at the discussions of the Roman army in Chapter 6, how did the man in the tombstone (Source 2) most likely obtain his freedom?
4. According to Justinian's Code (Source 3), is slavery natural? What types of laws establish it, and how do these laws reflect Roman notions of law?
5. In Germanic society, the kin group was responsible for the actions of its members. How do the laws in Sources 4–6 reflect this principle? From Sources 1–3 and your reading in this and earlier chapters, how did family and kin shape slavery in Roman society?

them to death. . . . Slaves are brought under our ownership either by the Civil Law or by that of Nations. This is done by the Civil Law where anyone who is over twenty years of age permits himself to be sold for the sake of sharing in his own price [that is, for debt]. Slaves become our property by the Law of Nations when they are either taken from the enemy, or are born of our female slaves. . . . Where a fugitive slave betakes himself to the arena [as a gladiator], he cannot escape the power of his master by exposing himself to this danger, which is only that of the risk of death; such a slave must, by all means, be restored to his master, either before or after the combat with wild beasts.

4 **The Burgundian Code, ca. 500.** King Gundobad (r. 474–516), who ruled the Burgundian kingdom in what is now southeastern France, drew up one of the earliest Germanic law codes for his subjects.

⚬ If anyone shall buy another's slave from the Franks [with whom the Burgundians were at war], let him prove with suitable witnesses how much and what sort of price he paid and when the witnesses have been sworn in, they shall make oath in the following manner, "We saw him pay the price in our presence, and he who purchased the slave did not do so through any fraud or connivance with the enemy." . . . If anyone wishes to manumit a slave, he may do so by giving him his liberty through a legally competent document; or if anyone wishes to give freedom to a bondservant without a written document, let the manumission thus be conferred with the witness of not less than five or seven native freemen.

5 **Lombard laws, 643–735.** The Lombards invaded Italy in 568, conquered Germanic tribes that were already there, and established a kingdom that lasted until 774. Various Lombard kings issued laws on many topics.

⚬ In the case of a natural son who is born to another man's woman slave, if the father purchases him and gives him his freedom by the formal procedure he shall remain free. But if the father does not free him, the natural son shall be a slave to him to whom the mother slave belongs. . . . He who renders false testimony against anyone else, or sets his hand knowingly to a false charter, and this fraud becomes evident, shall pay restitution, half to the king and half to him whose case it is. If the guilty party does not have enough to pay restitution, a public official ought to hand him over as a slave to him who was injured, and he [the offender] shall serve him as a slave. . . . If a man who is prodigal and ruined, or who has sold or dissipated his substance, or for other reasons does not have that with which to pay restitution, commits theft or adultery or a breach of the peace, or injures another man and the restitution for this is twenty solidi or more, then a public representative ought to hand him over as a slave to the man against whom he committed such illegal acts. . . . If a freeman has a man and woman slave, or freedman and freedwoman, who are married, and inspired by hatred of the human race, he has intercourse with that woman whose husband is the slave or with the freedwoman whose husband is the freedman, he has committed adultery and we decree that he shall lose that slave or freedman with whose wife he committed adultery and the woman as well, for it is not pleasing to God that any man should have intercourse with the wife of another.

6 **Laws of the Anglo-Saxon kings, early tenth century.** The Anglo-Saxon rulers in England issued law codes; this law is from the code of Edward the Elder (r. 899–925), king of Wessex and Mercia.

⚬ If a man, through [being found guilty of] an accusation of stealing, forfeits his freedom and gives up his person to his lord, and his kinsmen forsake him, and he knows no one who will make legal amends for him, he shall do such servile labour as may be required and his kinsmen shall have no right to his wergeld [if he is slain].

PUTTING IT ALL TOGETHER

Using the sources above, along with what you have learned in class and in Chapters 5, 6, and 7, write a short essay that analyzes ways in which the boundary between enslaved and free was established, protected, and traversed in Roman and Germanic society. How could a person cross the border between enslaved and free in these two societies, and what larger social values do laws regarding slavery reflect? How did the laws regarding slavery differ in Roman and Germanic society, and how were they similar?

Sources: (1) Clyde Pharr, ed., *The Theodosian Code* (Princeton, N.J.: Princeton University Press, 1952), 3.3.1, 5.6.3, 5.9.1, 7.13.16, 7.18.4; (3) S. P. Scott, trans., *The Civil Law* (Cincinnati: The Central Trust Company, 1932), vol. 2, p. 228; vol. 4, p. 82; (4) Katherine Fischer Drew, trans., *The Burgundian Code* (Philadelphia: University of Pennsylvania Press, 1972), Constitutiones Extravagantes 21.9; (5) Katherine Fischer Drew, trans., *The Lombard Laws* (Philadelphia: University of Pennsylvania Press, 1973), Rothair 156, Luitprand 63, Luitprand 140, Luitprand 152; (6) F. L. Attenborough, *Laws of the Earliest English Kings* (Cambridge: Cambridge University Press, 1922), Laws of Edward the Elder 6.

How did the barbarian migrations shape Europe?

Migrating groups that the Romans labeled barbarians had moved southward and eastward off and on since about 100 B.C.E. (see Chapters 5 and 6). As their movements became more organized in the third and fourth centuries C.E., Roman armies sought to defend the Rhine-Danube border of the Roman Empire, but with troop levels low because Italians were increasingly unwilling to serve in the army, generals were forced to recruit barbarians to fill the ranks. By the fourth century barbarians made up the majority of those fighting both for and against Rome, and they climbed higher and higher in the ranks of the Roman military, often intermarrying with Roman families. Toward the end of the fifth century this barbarian assumption of authority stretched all the way to the top, and the last person with the title of emperor in the Western Roman Empire was deposed by a Gothic general.

Why did the barbarians migrate? In part they were searching for more regular supplies of food, better farmland, and a warmer climate. In part they were pushed by groups living farther eastward, especially by the Huns from Central Asia in the fourth and fifth centuries. Conflicts within and among barbarian groups also led to war and disruption, which motivated groups to move (Map 7.3).

Celtic and Germanic People in Gaul and Britain

The Celts present a good example of both assimilation and conflict. Celtic peoples conquered by the Romans often assimilated Roman ways, adapting the Latin language and other aspects of Roman culture. In Roman Gaul and then in Roman Britain, towns were planned in the Roman fashion, with temples, public baths, theaters, and amphitheaters. In the countryside large manors controlled the surrounding lands. Roman merchants brought Eastern luxury goods and Eastern religions—including Christianity. The Romans suppressed the Celtic chieftains, and a military aristocracy made up of Romans—some of whom intermarried with Celtic families—governed. In the course of the second and third centuries, many Celts became Roman citizens and joined the Roman army. Celtic culture survived only in areas beyond the borders of the empire. (The modern Welsh, Bretons, Scots, and Irish are all peoples of Celtic descent.)

By the fourth century C.E. Gaul and Britain were under pressure from Germanic groups moving westward, and Rome itself was threatened (see Map 7.3). Imperial troops withdrew from Britain in order to defend Rome, and the Picts from Scotland and the Scots from Ireland (both Celtic-speaking peoples) invaded territory held by the Britons. According to the eighth-century historian Bede (beed), the Briton king Vortigern invited the Saxons from Denmark to help him against his rivals. However, Saxons and other Germanic tribes from the area of modern-day Norway, Sweden, and Denmark turned from assistance to conquest. Their goal was plunder, and at first their invasions led to no permanent settlements. As more Germanic peoples arrived, however, they took over the best lands and eventually conquered most of Britain. Historians have labeled the years 500 to 1066 (the year of the Norman Conquest) the Anglo-Saxon period of English history, after the two largest Germanic groups in England, the Angles and the Saxons.

Anglo-Saxon Helmet   This ceremonial bronze helmet from seventh-century England was found inside a ship buried at Sutton Hoo. The nearly 100-foot-long ship was dragged overland before being buried completely. It held one body and many grave goods, including swords, gold buckles, and silver bowls made in Byzantium. The unidentified person who was buried here was clearly wealthy and powerful. (British Museum, London, UK/© The Trustees of the British Museum/ Art Resource, NY)

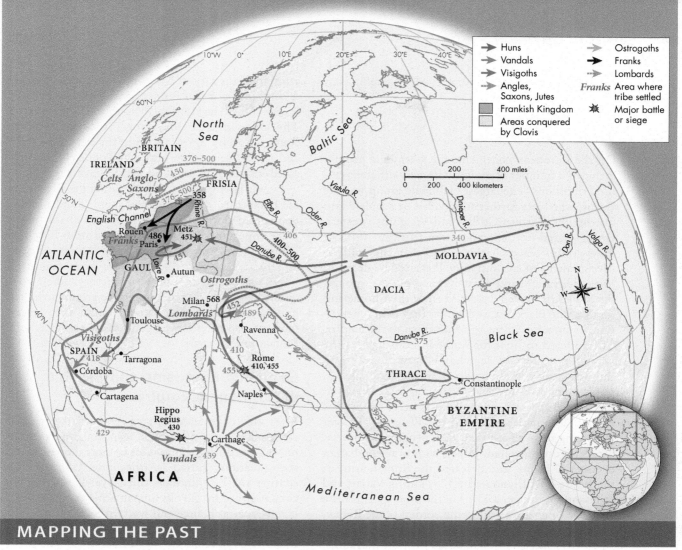

MAPPING THE PAST

MAP 7.3 The Barbarian Migrations, ca. 340–500

This map shows the migrations of various barbarian groups in late antiquity and can be used to answer the following questions.

ANALYZING THE MAP The movements of barbarian peoples used to be labeled "invasions" and are now usually described as "migrations." How do the dates on the map support the newer understanding of these movements?

CONNECTIONS Human migration is caused by a combination of push factors — circumstances that lead people to leave a place — and pull factors — things that attract people to a new location. Based on the information in this and earlier chapters, what push and pull factors might have shaped the migration patterns you see on the map?

Anglo-Saxon England was divided along ethnic and political lines. The Germanic kingdoms in the south, east, and center were opposed by the Britons in the west, who wanted to get rid of the invaders. The Anglo-Saxon kingdoms also fought among themselves, causing boundaries to shift constantly. In the ninth century, under pressure from the Viking invasions, King Alfred of Wessex (r. 871–899) created a more unified state with a reorganized army and system of fortresses for defense.

The Anglo-Saxon invasion gave rise to a rich body of Celtic mythology, particularly legends about King Arthur, who first appeared in Welsh poetry in the sixth century and later in histories, epics, and saints' lives. Most scholars see Arthur as a composite figure that evolved over the centuries in songs and stories. In their earliest form as Welsh poems, the Arthurian legends may represent Celtic hostility to Anglo-Saxon invaders, but they later came to be more important as representations of the ideal of medieval knightly chivalry and as compelling stories whose retelling has continued to the present.

Visigoths and Huns

On the European continent, the Germanic peoples included a number of groups with very different cultural traditions. The largest Germanic group was the Goths, who were further subdivided by scholars into Ostrogoths (eastern Goths) and Visigoths (western Goths) based on their migration patterns. Both of these groups played important roles in the political developments of late antiquity. Pressured by defeat in battle, starvation, and the movement of other groups, the Visigoths moved westward from their homeland north of the Black Sea, and in 376 they petitioned the Roman emperor Valens to admit them to the empire. They offered to fight for Rome in exchange for the province of Thrace in what is now Greece and Bulgaria. Seeing in the hordes of warriors the solution to his manpower problem, Valens agreed. However, the deal fell apart when crop failures led to famine and Roman authorities exploited the Visigoths' hunger by forcing them to sell their own people into slavery. The Visigoths revolted, joined with other barbarian enemies of Rome, and defeated the Roman army at the Battle of Adrianople in 378, killing Valens and thousands of Roman soldiers in the process. This left a large barbarian army within the borders of the Roman Empire, and not that far from Constantinople.

Valens's successor made peace with the Visigoths, but relations worsened as the Visigoths continued migrating westward (see Map 7.3). The Visigothic king Alaric I, who had also been a general in one of the Roman armies in the east, invaded Italy and sacked Rome in 410. The Visigoths burned and looted the city for three days. Seeking to stabilize the situation at home, the imperial government pulled its troops from the British Isles and many areas north of the Alps, leaving these northern areas vulnerable to other migrating groups. A year later Alaric died, and his successors led his people into southwestern Gaul and the Iberian Peninsula (modern Spain), where they established the Visigothic kingdom.

One significant factor in the migration of the Visigoths and other Germanic peoples was pressure from nomadic steppe peoples from Central Asia. They included the Alans, Avars, Bulgars, Khazars, and most prominently the Huns, who attacked the Black Sea area and the Byzantine Empire beginning in the fourth century.

Under the leadership of their warrior-king Attila, the Huns attacked the Byzantine Empire in 447 and then turned westward. Several Germanic groups allied with them, as did the sister of the Roman emperor, who hoped to take over power from her brother. Their troops combined with those of the Huns, and a huge army took the city of Metz, now in eastern France. A combined army of Romans and Visigoths stopped the advance of the Huns at Châlons, and they retreated. The following year they moved into the Western Roman Empire again, crossing the Alps into Italy, and a papal delegation, including Pope Leo I himself, asked Attila not to attack Rome. Though papal diplomacy was later credited with stopping the advance of the Huns, their dwindling food supplies and a plague that spread among their troops were probably much more important. The Huns retreated from Italy, and within a year Attila was dead. Later leaders were not as effective, and the Huns were never again an important factor in European history. Their conquests had pushed many Germanic groups together, however, transforming smaller bands into larger, more unified peoples who could more easily pick the Roman Empire apart.

Germanic Kingdoms and the End of the Roman Empire

After they conquered an area, barbarians generally established states ruled by kings. The kingdoms did not have definite geographical borders, however, and their locations shifted as tribes moved. In the fifth century the Burgundians ruled over lands roughly circumscribed by the old Roman army camps in what is now central France and western Switzerland. The Vandals, another Germanic tribe whose destructive ways are commemorated in the word *vandal*, swept across Spain into North Africa in 429 and took over what had been Rome's breadbasket. In 439 they established a kingdom that included Sicily and Sardinia and that lasted about a century, and in 455 they even sacked the city of Rome itself. The Visigoths pushed the Vandals out of Spain, but were themselves defeated by the Franks in 507, who took over what is now southern France. In 711 a Muslim victory ended Visigothic rule in Spain as well (see Chapter 8).

Barbarian states eventually came to include Italy itself. The Western Roman emperors were generally chosen by the more powerful successors of Constantine in the East, and they increasingly relied on barbarian commanders and their troops to maintain order. In the 470s a series of these commanders took over authority in name as well as in reality, deposing several Roman emperors. In 476 the barbarian chieftain Odoacer (OH-duh-way-suhr) deposed Romulus Augustus, the last person to have the title of Roman emperor in the West. Odoacer did not take on the title of emperor, calling himself instead the king of Italy, so this date marks the official end of the Roman Empire in the West. Emperor Zeno, the Roman emperor in the East ruling from Constantinople, worried about Odoacer's growing power and promised Theodoric (r. 471–526), the leader of the Ostrogoths who had recently settled in the Balkans, the right to rule Italy if he defeated Odoacer. Theodoric's forces were successful, and in 493 Theodoric established an Ostrogothic state in Italy, with his capital at Ravenna.

For centuries, the end of the Roman Empire in the West was seen as a major turning point in history, the fall of the sophisticated and educated classical world to uncouth and illiterate tribes. This view was further promoted by the English historian and member of Parliament Edward Gibbon, whose six-volume *The History of the Decline and Fall of the Roman Empire*, published in 1776–1788, was required reading for university students well into the twentieth century. Over the last several decades, however, many historians have put greater stress on continuities. Not only did Rome itself last for a very long time, first as a republic and then an empire, but the Ostrogoths, for example, maintained many Roman ways. Old Roman families continued to run the law courts and the city governments, and well-educated Italians continued to study the Greek classics. Theodoric's adviser Boethius (ca. 480–524) translated Aristotle's works on logic from Greek into Latin. While imprisoned after falling out of royal favor, Boethius wrote *The Consolation of Philosophy*, which argued that philosophical inquiry was valuable for understanding God. This became one of the most widely read books in the Middle Ages, though its popularity did not prevent Boethius from being executed for treason.

In other barbarian states, aspects of classical culture also continued. Barbarian kings relied on officials trained in Roman law, and Latin remained the language of scholarly communication. Greco-Roman art and architecture still adorned the land, and people continued to use Roman roads, aqueducts, and buildings. The Christian Church in barbarian states modeled its organization on that of Rome, and many bishops were from upper-class families that had governed the empire.

Very recently some historians and archaeologists have returned to an emphasis on change. They note that people may have traveled on Roman roads, but the roads were rarely maintained, and travel itself was much less secure than during the Roman Empire. Merchants no longer traded over long distances, so people's access to goods produced outside their local area plummeted. Knowledge about technological processes such as the making of glass and roof tiles declined or disappeared. There was intermarriage and cultural assimilation among Romans and barbarians, but there was also violence and great physical destruction.

The kingdom established by the Franks is a good example of this combination of peaceful assimilation and violent conflict. The Franks were a confederation of Germanic peoples who originated in the marshy lowlands north and east of the northernmost part of the Roman Empire (see Map 7.3). In the fourth and fifth centuries they settled within the empire and allied

Visigothic Church This rural church, dedicated to Saint Columba, was built in Galicia in what is now northwestern Spain during the seventh century, though the gable for bells at the top was added later. Visigothic churches, of which only several survive, were often built in the shape of a cross, with rounded arches and finely cut stone walls. According to legend, Columba was a third-century convert to Christianity from this area, saved from a forced marriage to the son of the pagan Roman emperor by a female bear, though eventually beheaded; her story was later combined with that of another virgin martyr also named Columba. (PRISMA ARCHIVO/Alamy Stock Photo)

with the Romans, some attaining high military and civil positions. The Franks believed that Merovech, a man of supernatural origins, founded their ruling dynasty, which was thus called Merovingian (mehr-uh-VIHN-jee-uhn).

The reign of Clovis (KLOH-vis) (r. ca. 481–511) marks the decisive period in the development of the Franks as a unified people. Through military campaigns, Clovis acquired the central provinces of Roman Gaul and began to conquer southern Gaul from the Burgundians and Visigoths. Clovis's conversion to Roman Christianity brought him the crucial support of the bishops of Gaul in his campaigns against tribes that were still pagan or had accepted the Arian version of Christianity. Along with brutal violence, however, the next two centuries witnessed the steady assimilation of Franks and Romans, as many

Franks adopted the Latin language and Roman ways, and Romans copied Frankish customs and Frankish personal names.

From Constantinople, Eastern Roman emperors worked to hold the empire together and to reconquer at least some of the West from barbarian tribes. The emperor Justinian (r. 527–565) waged long and hard-fought wars against the Ostrogoths and temporarily regained Italy and North Africa, but his conquests had disastrous consequences. Justinian's wars exhausted the resources of the state, destroyed Italy's economy, and killed a large part of Italy's population. The wars also paved the way for the easy conquest of Italy by another Germanic tribe, the Lombards, shortly after Justinian's death. In the late sixth century the territory of the Western Roman Empire came under barbarian sway once again.

How did the church convert barbarian peoples to Christianity?

The Mediterranean served as the highway over which Christianity spread to the cities of the Roman Empire. Christian teachings were initially carried by all types of converts, but they were often spread into the countryside and into areas beyond the borders of the empire by those who had dedicated their lives to the church, such as monks. Such missionaries were often sent by popes specifically to convert certain groups, developing new techniques to do so.

Throughout barbarian Europe, religion was not a private or individual matter; it was a social affair, and the religion of the chieftain or king determined the religion of the people. Thus missionaries concentrated their initial efforts not on ordinary people, but on kings or tribal chieftains and the members of their families, who then ordered their subjects to convert. Because they had more opportunity to spend time with missionaries, queens and other female members of the royal family were often the first converts in an area, and they influenced their husbands and brothers. Germanic kings sometimes accepted Christianity because they came to believe that the Christian God was more powerful than pagan gods and that the Christian God—in either its Arian or Roman version—would deliver victory in battle. They also appreciated that Christianity taught obedience to kingly as well as divine authority. Christian missionaries were generally literate, and they taught reading and writing to young men who became priests or officials in the royal household, a service that kings appreciated.

Missionaries' Actions

During the Roman occupation, small Christian communities were scattered throughout Gaul and Britain. The leaders of some of these, such as Bishop Martin of Tours (ca. 316–397), who founded a monastery and established a rudimentary parish system in his diocese, supported Nicene Christianity (see "The Acceptance of Christianity"). Other missionaries were Arian Christians, who also founded dioceses and converted many barbarian groups. Bishop Ulfilas (ca. 310–383), for example, an Ostrogoth himself, translated the Bible from the Greek in which it was normally written into the Gothic language, creating a new Gothic script in order to write it down. The Ostrogoths, Visigoths, Lombards, and Vandals were all originally Arian Christians, though over the sixth and seventh centuries most of them converted to Roman Christianity, sometimes peacefully and sometimes as a result of conquest.

Tradition identifies the conversion of Ireland with Saint Patrick (ca. 385–461). Born in England to a Christian family of Roman citizenship, Patrick was captured and enslaved by Irish raiders and taken to Ireland, where he worked as a herdsman for six years. He escaped and returned to England, where a vision urged him to Christianize Ireland. In preparation, Patrick studied in Gaul and was consecrated a bishop in 432. He returned to Ireland, where he converted the Irish tribe by tribe, first baptizing the chief of each tribe. By the time of Patrick's death, the majority of the Irish people had received Christian baptism.

In his missionary work, Patrick had the strong support of Bridget of Kildare (ca. 450–528), daughter of a wealthy chieftain. Bridget defied parental pressure to marry and became a nun. She and the other nuns at Kildare instructed relatives and friends in basic Christian doctrine, made religious vestments (clothing) for churches, copied books, taught children, and above all set a religious example by their lives of prayer. In this way, in Ireland and later in the European continent, women like the nuns at Kildare shared in the process of conversion.

The Christianization of the English began in earnest in 597, when Pope Gregory I sent a delegation of monks under the Roman Augustine to Britain. Augustine's approach, like Patrick's, was to concentrate on converting those who held power. When he succeeded in converting Ethelbert, king of Kent, the baptism of Ethelbert's people took place as a matter of course. Augustine established his headquarters, or *see*, at Canterbury, the capital of Kent in southern England.

In the course of the seventh century, two Christian forces competed for the conversion of the pagan Anglo-Saxons: Roman-oriented missionaries traveling north from Canterbury, and Celtic monks from Ireland and northwestern Britain. The Roman and Celtic church organizations, types of monastic life, and methods of arriving at the date of the central feast of the Christian calendar, Easter, differed completely. Through the influence of King Oswiu of Northumbria and the dynamic abbess Hilda of Whitby, the synod (ecclesiastical council) held at Hilda's convent of Whitby in 664 opted to follow the Roman practices. The conversion of the English and the close attachment of the English Church to Rome had far-reaching consequences because Britain later served as a base for the Christianization of the continent of Europe (see Map 7.2), spreading Roman Christian teachings among both pagans and Arians.

The Process of Conversion

When a ruler marched his people to the waters of baptism, the work of Christianization had only begun. Christian kings could order their subjects to be baptized, married, and buried in Christian ceremonies, and people complied increasingly across Europe.

Irish Crucifixion Plaque One of the earliest depictions of the crucifixion in Irish art, this gilt and bronze plaque from the late seventh or early eighth century shows Christ flanked by two Roman soldiers while angels hover overhead, with the figures decorated with swirls and interlace. Made by hammering a bronze sheet from behind, the plaque might have originally been on a book cover, wooden cross, or panel in a shrine. (© Boltin Picture Library/Bridgeman Images)

Churches could be built, and people could be required to attend services and belong to parishes, but the process of conversion was a gradual one.

How did missionaries and priests get masses of pagan and illiterate peoples to understand Christian ideals and teachings? They did so through preaching, assimilation, the ritual of penance, and the veneration of saints. Missionaries preached the basic teachings of Christianity in simplified Latin or translated them into the local language. In monasteries and cathedrals, men — and a few women — wrote hymns, prayers, and stories about the lives of Christ and the saints. People heard these and slowly became familiar with Christian notions.

Deeply ingrained pagan customs and practices could not be stamped out by words alone, however, or even by royal edicts. Christian missionaries often pursued a policy of assimilation, easing the conversion of pagan men and women by stressing similarities between their customs and beliefs and those of Christianity. In the same way that classically trained scholars such as Jerome and Augustine blended Greco-Roman and Christian ideas, missionaries and converts mixed pagan ideas and practices with Christian ones. Bogs and lakes sacred to Germanic gods became associated with saints, as did various aspects of ordinary life, such as traveling, planting crops, and worrying about a sick child. Aspects of existing midwinter celebrations, which often centered on the return of the sun as the days became longer, were incorporated into celebrations of

Gregory of Tours on the Veneration of Relics

Accounts of the miracles associated with the relics of saints were an important part of Christian preaching and writing, designed to win converts and strengthen their faith. Gregory of Tours (ca. 539–594), a highly educated bishop and historian from a wealthy Gallo-Roman family, described events surrounding relics in *Glory of the Martyrs*, a book of miracle stories about saints and martyrs.

∼

The cross of the Lord that was found by the empress Helena [Constantine's mother] at Jerusalem is venerated on Wednesday and Friday. Queen Radegund [a Merovingian Frankish queen], who is comparable to Helena in both merit and faith, requested relics of this cross and piously placed them in a convent at Poitiers that she founded out of her own zeal. . . .

A girl named Chrodigildis was punished by the loss of her eyesight . . . [and] she entered the rule of the aforementioned convent. With the most blessed Radegund as a guide, she bowed before the holy reliquary and there kept vigils with the other nuns. . . . In a vision it seemed to her as if someone had opened her eyes. One eye was restored to health; while she was still concerned about the other, suddenly she was awakened by the sound of a door being unlocked and regained the sight of one eye. There is no doubt that this was accomplished by the power of the cross. The possessed, the lame, and also other ill people are often cured at this place. . . .

Because he [Gregory's father] wished himself to be protected by relics of saints, he asked a cleric to grant him something from these relics, so that with their protection he might be kept safe as he set out on a long journey. He put the sacred ashes in a gold medallion and carried it with him. Although he did not even know the names of the blessed men, he was accustomed to recount that he had been rescued from many dangers. He claimed that often, because of the powers of these relics, he had avoided the violence of bandits, the dangers of floods, the threats of turbulent men, and attacks from swords.

I will not be silent about what I witnessed regarding these relics. After the death of my father my mother carried these relics with her. It was the time for harvesting the crops, and huge piles of grain had been collected on the threshing floors. . . . The threshers kindled fires for themselves from the straw. . . . Quickly, fanned by the wind, the fire spread to the piles of grain. The fire became a huge blaze and was accompanied by the shouts of men, the wails of women, and the crying of children. This happened in our field. When my mother, who was wearing these relics around her neck, learned of this, she rushed from the meal and held the sacred relics in front of the balls of flames. In a moment the entire fire so died down that no sparks were found among the piles of burned straw and the seeds. The grain the fire had touched had suffered no harm.

EVALUATE THE EVIDENCE

1. How do stories such as these about the veneration of relics link Christian beliefs with local and personal issues? Why would this have been important in the expansion of Christianity?
2. Gregory's father and mother were both from prominent upper-class families, and both received a good education. Why might Gregory have told stories such as these rather than ones about their learning as he sought to enhance people's commitment to the church?

Source: Gregory of Tours, *Glory of the Martyrs*, trans. Raymond Van Dam (Liverpool: Liverpool University, 1988), pp. 22, 107–108.

Christmas. Spring rituals involving eggs and rabbits (both symbols of fertility) were added to Easter.

The ritual of penance was also instrumental in teaching people Christian ideas. Christianity taught that certain actions and thoughts were sins, meaning that they were against God's commands. Only by confessing these sins and asking forgiveness could a sinning believer be reconciled with God. Confession was initially a public ritual, but by the fifth century individual confession to a parish priest was more common. The person knelt before the priest, who questioned him or her about sins he or she might have committed. The priest then set a penance such as fasting or saying specific prayers to allow the person to atone for the sin. The priest and penitent were guided by manuals known as penitentials (peh-nuh-TEHN-shuhlz), which included lists of sins and the appropriate penance. The seventh-century English penitential of Theodore, for example, stipulated that "if a lay Christian vomits because of drunkenness, he shall do penance for fifteen days," while drunken monks were to do penance for thirty days. Those who "commit fornication with a virgin" were to do penance for a year, as were those who perform "divinations according to the custom of the heathens."[5] Penance gave new Christians a sense of expected behavior and encouraged them to reflect on their actions, thoughts, and desires.

Most religious observances continued to be community matters, as they had been in the ancient world. People joined with family members, friends, and neighbors at their parish church to attend baptisms, weddings, and funerals presided over by a priest. The parish church often housed the **relics** of a saint, that is, bones, articles of clothing, or other objects associated with a person who had lived (or died) in a way that was spiritually heroic or noteworthy. This patron saint was understood to provide protection and assistance for those who came to worship, and the relics served as a link between the material world and the spiritual

one. (See "Evaluating Written Evidence: Gregory of Tours on the Veneration of Relics," page 192.)

Christians came to venerate the saints as powerful and holy. They prayed to saints or to the Virgin Mary to intercede with God, or they simply asked the saints to assist and bless them. The entire village participated in processions marking saints' days or points in the agricultural year, often carrying images of saints or their relics around the houses and fields. The decision to become Christian was often made first by an emperor or king, but actual conversion was a local matter, as people came to feel that the parish priest and the patron saint provided them with benefits in this world and the world to come.

How did the Byzantine Empire preserve the legacy of Rome?

Barbarian migrations and Christian conversions occurred throughout all of Europe in late antiquity, but their impact was not the same in the western and eastern halves of the Roman Empire. The Western Roman Empire gradually disintegrated, but the Roman Empire continued in the East (Map 7.4). The Byzantine or Eastern Roman Empire preserved the forms, institutions, and traditions of the old Roman Empire, and its people even called themselves Romans. Byzantine emperors traced their lines back past Constantine to Augustus, and the Senate in Constantinople carried on the traditions of the old Roman Senate. Most important, however, is how Byzantium protected the intellectual heritage of Greco-Roman civilization and then passed it on to the rest of Europe.

Sources of Byzantine Strength

While the western parts of the Roman Empire gradually succumbed to barbarian invaders, the Byzantine Empire survived attacks by Huns, Germans, Avars, Persians, and Arabs. Why didn't one or a combination of these enemies capture Constantinople as the Ostrogoths had taken Rome? The answer lies in strong military leadership and even more in the city's location and its excellent fortifications. Justinian's generals were able to reconquer much of Italy and North Africa from barbarian groups, making them part of the Eastern Roman Empire, and later generals defeated the Avars and Persians. Massive triple walls, built by the emperors Constantine and Theodosius II (r. 408–450) and kept in good repair, protected Constantinople from sea invasion. Within the walls huge cisterns provided water, and vast gardens and grazing areas supplied vegetables and meat, so the defending people could hold out far longer than the besieging

army. Attacking Constantinople by land posed greater geographical and logistical problems than a seventh- or eighth-century government could solve. The site was not absolutely impregnable, but it was almost so. For centuries the Byzantine Empire served as a bulwark for the West, protecting it against invasions from the East.

The Law Code of Justinian

One of the most splendid achievements of the Byzantine emperors was the preservation of Roman law for the medieval and modern worlds. Roman law had developed from many sources — decisions by judges, edicts of the emperors, legislation passed by the Senate, and the opinions of jurists. By the fourth century it had become a huge, bewildering mass, and its sheer bulk made it almost unusable.

Sweeping and systematic codification took place under the emperor Justinian, who appointed a committee of eminent jurists to sort through and organize the laws. The result was the *Corpus Juris Civilis* (KAWR-puhs JOOR-uhs sih-VIH-luhs) (Body of civil law), a multipart collection of laws and legal commentary issued from 529 to 534, and often called simply the **Code of Justinian**. The first part of this work, the *Codex*, brought together all the existing imperial laws into a coherent whole, eliminated outmoded laws and contradictions, and clarified the law itself. It began with laws ordering the interpretation of Christian doctrine favored by

---

■ **relics** Bones, articles of clothing, or other objects associated with the life of a saint.

■ **Code of Justinian** A collection of laws and legal commentary issued by the emperor Justinian that brought together all existing imperial laws into a coherent whole.

the emperor in opposition to groups such as the Arians and Nestorians, and affirming the power of the emperor in matters of religion, such as this decree first issued by the emperor Theodosius:

> We desire that all peoples subject to Our benign Empire shall live under the same religion that the Divine Peter, the Apostle, gave to the Romans, and which the said religion declares was introduced by himself . . . that is to say, in accordance with the rules of apostolic discipline and the evangelical doctrine, we should believe that the Father, Son, and Holy Spirit constitute a single Deity, endowed with equal majesty, and united in the Holy Trinity.
>
> We order all those who follow this law to assume the name of Catholic Christians, and consider others as demented and insane. We order that they shall bear the infamy of heresy; and when the Divine vengeance which they merit has been appeased, they shall afterwards be punished in accordance with our resentment, which we have acquired from the judgment of Heaven.[6]

The rest of the *Codex* was structured by topic and included provisions on every aspect of life, including economic issues, social concerns, and family life.

(See "Thinking Like a Historian: Slavery in Roman and Germanic Society," page 184.)

The second part of Justinian's Code, the *Digest*, is a collection of the opinions of foremost Roman jurists on complex legal problems, and the third part, the *Institutes*, is a handbook of civil law designed for students and beginning jurists. All three parts were given the force of law and formed the backbone of Byzantine jurisprudence from that point on. Like so much of classical culture, the *Corpus Juris Civilis* was lost in western Europe with the end of the Roman Empire, but it was rediscovered in the eleventh century and came to form the foundation of law for nearly every modern European nation.

Byzantine Learning and Science

The Byzantines prized education; because of them, many masterpieces of ancient Greek literature have survived to influence the intellectual life of the modern world. The literature of the Byzantine Empire was predominantly Greek, although politicians, scholars, and lawyers also spoke and used Latin. Justinian's Code was first written in Latin. More people could read in Byzantium than anywhere else in Christian Europe at the time, and history was a favorite topic.

MAP 7.4 The Byzantine Empire, ca. 600   The strategic position of Constantinople on the waterway between the Black Sea and the Mediterranean was clear to Constantine when he chose the city as the capital of the Eastern Roman Empire. Byzantine territories in Italy were acquired in Emperor Justinian's sixth-century wars and were held for several centuries.

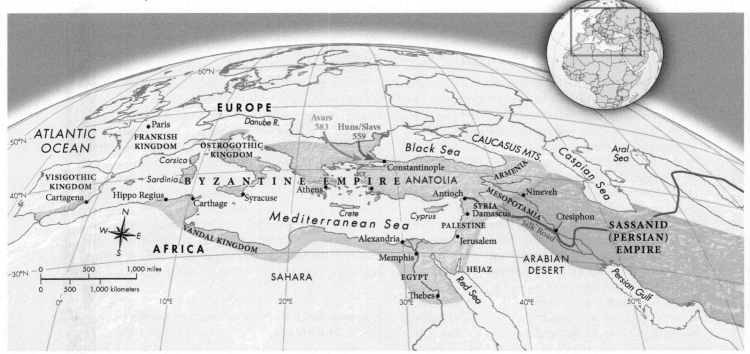

Greek Fire   In this illustration from a twelfth-century manuscript, sailors shoot Greek fire toward an attacking ship from a pressurized tube that looks strikingly similar to a modern flamethrower. The exact formula for Greek fire has been lost, but it was probably made from a petroleum product because it continued burning on water. Greek fire was particularly important in Byzantine defenses of Constantinople from Muslim forces in the late seventh century. (Bridgeman Images)

The most remarkable Byzantine historian was Procopius (ca. 500–562), who left a rousing account praising Justinian's reconquest of North Africa and Italy, but also wrote the *Secret History*, a vicious and uproarious attack on Justinian and his wife, the empress Theodora. Theodora had been a dancer and actress, dishonorable occupations in the Roman world, and many at Justinian's court were dismayed at the power she came to hold over secular and religious institutions, as Justinian consulted her about imperial policy regarding revolts, deadly epidemics, and doctrinal disputes within Christianity. (See "Evaluating Visual Evidence: Mosaic of Empress Theodora, 547" page 196.)

Although the Byzantines discovered little that was new in mathematics and geometry, they made advances in military applications. For example, they invented an explosive liquid that came to be known as "Greek fire." The liquid was heated and propelled by a pump through a bronze tube, and as the jet left the tube, it was ignited — somewhat like a modern flamethrower. Greek fire saved Constantinople from Arab assault in 678 and was used in both land and sea battles for centuries, although modern military experts still do not know the exact nature of the compound. In mechanics Byzantine scientists improved and modified artillery and siege machinery.

The Byzantines devoted a great deal of attention to medicine, and the general level of medical competence was far higher in the Byzantine Empire than in western Europe. Yet their physicians could not cope with the terrible disease, often called the Justinian plague, that swept through the Byzantine

Empire and parts of western Europe between 542 and about 560. Probably originating in northwestern India and carried to the Mediterranean region by ships, the disease was similar to what was later identified as the bubonic plague. Characterized by high fever, chills, delirium, and enlarged lymph nodes, or by inflammation of the lungs that caused hemorrhages of black blood, the Justinian plague claimed the lives of tens of thousands of people. The epidemic had profound political as well as social consequences: it weakened Justinian's military resources, thus hampering his efforts to restore unity to the Mediterranean world.

By the ninth or tenth century most major Greek cities had hospitals for the care of the sick. The hospitals might be divided into wards for different illnesses, and hospital staff included surgeons, practitioners, and aides with specialized responsibilities. The imperial Byzantine government bore the costs of these medical facilities.

The Orthodox Church

The continuity of the Roman Empire in the East meant that Christianity developed differently there than it did in the West. The emperors in Constantinople were understood to be Christ's representative on earth; their palace was considered holy and was filled with relics and religious images, called icons. Emperors convened councils, appointed church officials, and regulated the income of the church. As in Rome, there was a patriarch in Constantinople, but he did not develop the same

Mosaic of Empress Theodora, 547

(Bridgeman Images)

This intricate mosaic of the Byzantine empress Theodora from the basilica of San Vitale in Ravenna, Italy, completed the year before she died, shows her surrounded by a retinue of male and female courtiers, including the imperial princess Anicia Juliana, the wife of Justinian's general Areobindus, who is standing next to Theodora. Theodora is dressed in an imperial purple cloak, gold-embroidered gown, and pearl-encrusted crown, and she is holding a jeweled Eucharistic chalice, a symbol of her patronage of the Christian Church. Her head is surrounded by a halo, part of an artistic tradition used for members of the imperial family.

EVALUATE THE EVIDENCE

1. Theodora's background as a dancer and actress was regarded by many in the Byzantine elite as disreputable. How does the artist here suggest her power and piety to counter that negative view?
2. All of the images of members of the imperial family in this chapter show them with halos, a symbol originally connected to the sun-god adopted into Christian art for Christ, the saints, angels, and some other figures. How does this overlapping imagery help convey the idea that the Byzantine emperors had divinely given power?

powers that the pope did in the West because there was never a similar power vacuum into which he needed to step. The **Orthodox Church**, the name generally given to the Eastern Christian Church, was more subject to secular control than the Western Christian Church.

Monasticism in the Orthodox world differed in fundamental ways from the monasticism that evolved in western Europe. First, while *The Rule of Saint Benedict* gradually became the universal guide for all western European monasteries, each individual house in the Byzantine world developed its own set of rules for organization and behavior. Second, education never became a central feature of Orthodox monasteries. Monks and nuns had to be literate to perform

■ **Orthodox Church** Eastern Christian Church in the Byzantine Empire.

the appropriate rituals, but no Orthodox monastery assumed responsibility for the general training of the local young.

There were also similarities between Western and Eastern monasticism. As in the West, Eastern monasteries became wealthy property owners, with fields, pastures, livestock, and buildings. Since bishops and patriarchs of the Orthodox Church were recruited only from the monasteries, these religious leaders also exercised cultural influence.

Like their counterparts in the West, Byzantine missionaries traveled far beyond the boundaries of the empire in search of converts. In 863 the emperor Michael III sent the brothers Cyril (826–869) and Methodius (815–885) to preach Christianity in Moravia (a region in the modern Czech Republic). Cyril invented a Slavic alphabet using Greek characters, later termed the Cyrillic (suh-RIH-lihk) alphabet in his honor. In the tenth century other missionaries spread Christianity, the Cyrillic alphabet, and Byzantine art and architecture to Russia. The Byzantines were so successful that the Russians would later claim to be the successors of the Byzantine Empire. For a time Moscow was even known as the Third Rome (the second Rome being Constantinople).

NOTES

1. Maude Aline Huttman, ed. and trans., *The Establishment of Christianity and the Proscription of Paganism* (New York: AMS Press, 1967), p. 164.
2. R. C. Petry, ed., *A History of Christianity: Readings in the History of Early and Medieval Christianity* (Englewood Cliffs, N.J.: Prentice Hall, 1962), p. 70.
3. Saint Jerome, *Commentaries on the Letter to the Ephesians*, book 16, cited in Vern Bullough, *Sexual Variance in Society and History* (Chicago: University of Chicago Press, 1976), p. 365.
4. E. F. Henderson, ed., *Select Historical Documents of the Middle Ages* (London: G. Bell and Sons, 1912), pp. 176–189.
5. John McNeill and Helena M. Gamer, *Medieval Handbooks of Penance: A Translation of the Principal Libri Poenitentiales and Selections from Related Documents* (New York: Columbia University Press, 1938).
6. Justinian's Code 1.1.1, in S. P. Scott, trans., *The Civil Law*, vol. 12 (Cincinnati: The Central Trust Company, 1932), p. 9.

LOOKING BACK LOOKING AHEAD

The Christian Church and the barbarian states absorbed many aspects of Roman culture, and the Roman Empire continued to thrive in the East as the Byzantine Empire, but western Europe in 600 was very different than it had been in 250. The Western Roman Empire had slowly disintegrated under pressure from barbarian groups. Barbarian kings ruled small states from Italy to Norway, while churches and monasteries rather than emperors and wealthy individuals took on the role of constructing new buildings and providing education. The city of Rome no longer attracted a steady stream of aspiring immigrants and shrank significantly, and many other cities also shrank and were no longer centers of innovation. As the vast network of Roman urban centers dissolved, economies everywhere became more localized. Commentators such as Augustine advised people to put their faith in the eternal City of God rather than in worldly cities, because human history would always bring great change. People who lived with Augustine in Hippo would have certainly understood such counsel, for they watched the Vandals besiege their city in 430, move swiftly across North Africa, and bring an end to Roman rule there. Although Justinian's Byzantine forces reclaimed the area a little over a century later, the culture that survived was as much barbarian as Roman, with smaller cities, less trade, and fewer schools.

Two hundred years after the Vandal attack, the residents of Byzantine North Africa confronted another fast-moving army of conquest, Arabian forces carrying a new religion, Islam. This Arabic expansion dramatically shaped the development of Western civilization. Though the end of the Roman Empire in 476 has long been seen as a dramatic break in European history, the expansion of Islam two centuries later may have been even more significant. Many of the patterns set in late antiquity continued, however. Warrior values such as physical prowess, bravery in battle, and loyalty to one's lord remained central and shaped the development of the political system known as feudalism. The Frankish kingdom established by Clovis continued to expand, becoming the most important state in Europe. The economic and political power of the Christian Church expanded as well, with monasteries and convents providing education for their residents. The vast majority of people continued to live in small villages, trying to raise enough grain to feed themselves and their families, and asking the saints for help to overcome life's difficulties.

Make Connections

Think about the larger developments and continuities within and across chapters.

1. The end of the Roman Empire in the West in 476 has long been viewed as one of the most important turning points in history. Do you agree with this idea? Why or why not?

2. In what ways was the role of the family in barbarian society similar to that of the family in classical Athens (Chapter 3) and republican Rome (Chapter 5)? In what ways was it different? What might account for the similarities and differences that you identify?

3. How did the Christian Church adapt to Roman and barbarian society? How was it different in 600 from how it had been in 100?

7 REVIEW & EXPLORE

Identify Key Terms

Identify and explain the significance of each item below.

tetrarchy (p. 170)

diocese (p. 170)

Arianism (p. 173)

Nicene Creed (p. 173)

apostolic succession (p. 174)

Petrine Doctrine (p. 174)

regular clergy (p. 175)

secular clergy (p. 175)

sacraments (p. 179)

comitatus (p. 181)

wergeld (p. 182)

relics (p. 193)

Code of Justinian (p. 193)

Orthodox Church (p. 196)

Review the Main Ideas

Answer the section heading questions from the chapter.

1. How did Diocletian and Constantine try to reform the empire? (p. 170)

2. How did the Christian Church become a major force in the Mediterranean and Europe? (p. 174)

3. What were the key characteristics of barbarian society? (p. 179)

4. How did the barbarian migrations shape Europe? (p. 186)

5. How did the church convert barbarian peoples to Christianity? (p. 190)

6. How did the Byzantine Empire preserve the legacy of Rome? (p. 193)

Suggested Resources

BOOKS

+ Brown, Peter. *The Rise of Western Christendom: Triumph and Diversity, A.D. 200–1000*, 3d ed. 2013. Traces the rise of the church to a position of religious and secular power.

+ Burns, Thomas S. *Rome and the Barbarians, 100 B.C.– A.D. 400*. 2003. Argues that Germanic and Roman cultures assimilated with each other more than they conflicted.

◆ Burrus, Virginia. *Late Ancient Christianity.* 2010. A volume in the People's History of Christianity series, which focuses on the beliefs and practices of ordinary men and women.

◆ Clark, Gillian. *Late Antiquity: A Very Short Introduction.* 2011. A compact survey of the era, portraying it as a period of great transformation rather than simply decline.

◆ Clark, Gillian. *Women in Late Antiquity: Pagan and Christian Lifestyles.* 1994. Explores law, marriage, and religious life.

◆ Dunn, Marilyn. *The Emergence of Monasticism: From the Desert Fathers to the Early Middle Ages.* 2003. A thorough study of the beginnings of monasticism.

◆ Goldsworthy, Adrian. *How Rome Fell: Death of a Superpower.* 2009. A detailed narrative that emphasizes internal weaknesses caused by civil war and struggles for power.

◆ Heather, Peter. *The Fall of the Roman Empire: A New History of Rome and the Barbarians.* 2006. A masterful analysis that asserts the centrality of barbarian military actions in the end of the Roman Empire.

◆ Herrin, Judith. *Byzantium: The Surprising Life of a Medieval Empire.* 2008. Written for a general audience, this book portrays a tradition-based yet dynamic empire and discusses its significance for today.

◆ Todd, Malcolm. *The Early Germans,* 2d ed. 2004. Uses archaeological and literary sources to analyze Germanic social structure, customs, and religion and to suggest implications for an understanding of migration and ethnicity.

◆ Ward-Perkins, Bryan. *The Fall of Rome and the End of Civilization.* 2006. Uses material evidence to trace the physical destruction and economic dislocation that accompanied the barbarian migrations.

◆ Wells, Peter S. *The Barbarians Speak: How the Conquered Peoples Shaped Roman Europe.* 1999. Presents extensive evidence of Celtic and Germanic social and technical development.

MEDIA

◆ *Barbarians II* (History Channel, 2007). A four-part documentary with many battle re-enactments that views the Vandals, Saxons, Franks, and Lombards as warrior barbarian hordes with savage tactics that "drove the empire to its knees."

◆ *Christian Classics Ethereal Library.* Hosted by Calvin College, this website has hundreds of primary sources in the public domain on all aspects of the history of Christianity and is especially strong in the writings of the church fathers, including Jerome, Ambrose, Augustine, and Benedict. **www.ccel.org**

◆ *The Germanic Tribes: The Complete Four-Part Saga* (Kultur, 2003). Using computer graphics and re-enactments, this documentary examines the settlements and religion of the Germanic tribes as well as their warfare and argues that they actually preserved much of the Roman legacy.

◆ *Terry Jones' Barbarians* (BBC, 2007). A witty and lively four-part documentary by a member of the Monty Python comedy troupe that sees the barbarians as less important for Rome's fall than other factors.

8

Europe in the Early Middle Ages

600–1000

By the fifteenth century, scholars in the growing cities of northern Italy began to think that they were living in a new era, one in which the glories of ancient Greece and Rome were being reborn. What separated their time from classical antiquity, in their opinion, was a long period of darkness, to which a seventeenth-century professor gave the name *Middle Ages*. In this conceptualization, Western history was divided into three periods—ancient, medieval, and modern—an organization that is still in use today.

For a long time the end of the Roman Empire in the West was seen as the division between the ancient period and the Middle Ages, but, as we saw in the last chapter, there was continuity as well as change. The transition from ancient to medieval was also a slow process, not a single event. The agents in this process included not only Christian officials and missionaries and the barbarian migrations that broke the Roman Empire apart, but also the new religion of Islam, which deeply influenced Western civilization.

The first several centuries in this new era (ca. 600–1000), conventionally known as the "early Middle Ages," was a time of disorder and destruction, but it also marked the creation of a new type of society and a cultural revival that influenced later intellectual and literary traditions. While agrarian life continued to dominate Europe, political and economic structures that would influence later European history began to form, and Christianity continued to spread. People at the time did not know that they were living in an era that would later be labeled "middle" or sometimes even "dark," and we can wonder whether they would have shared this negative view of their own times. ■

CHAPTER PREVIEW

- What were the origins of Islam, and what impact did it have on Europe as it spread?

- How did the Franks build and govern a European empire?

- What were the significant intellectual and cultural developments in Charlemagne's era?

- How did the ninth-century invasions and migrations shape Europe?

- How and why did Europe become politically and economically decentralized in this period?

Muslim Fishermen in Spain
In this manuscript illumination from Spain, Muslim fishermen take a rich harvest from the sea. Fish were an important part of the diet of all coastal peoples in medieval Europe and were often salted and dried to preserve them for later use.
(The Granger Collection)

What were the origins of Islam, and what impact did it have on Europe as it spread?

In the seventh century C.E. two empires dominated the area today called the Middle East: the Byzantine Empire with its capital at Constantinople and the Persian Sassanid empire with its capital at Baghdad. Between the two lay the Arabian peninsula, where a merchant named Muhammad began to have religious visions around 610. By the time he died in 632, he had many followers in Arabia, and a century later his followers controlled what are now Syria, Palestine, Egypt, Iraq, Iran, northern Africa, Spain, and southern France. This expansion profoundly affected the development of Western civilization as well as the history of Africa and Asia.

The Culture of the Arabian Peninsula

In Muhammad's time Arabia was inhabited by various tribes, many of them Bedouins (BED-oo-wins). These nomadic peoples grazed goats and sheep on the sparse patches of grass that dotted the vast semi-arid peninsula. The power of the Bedouins came from their fighting skills, toughness, ability to control trade, and possession of horses and camels. Other people in the Arabian peninsula lived more settled lives in the southern valleys and coastal towns and cities along the Red Sea, such as Yemen, Mecca, and Medina, supporting themselves by agriculture and trade. Caravan routes crisscrossed Arabia and carried goods to Byzantium, Persia, and Syria, producing wealth for merchants.

For all people in the Arabian peninsula, the basic social unit was the clan—a group of blood relations connected through the male line. Clans expected loyalty from their members and in turn provided support and protection. Arabians of all types respected certain aspects of one another's customs and had some religious rules and rituals in common. For example, people throughout Arabia kept three months of the year as sacred; during that time any fighting stopped so that everyone could attend holy ceremonies in peace. The city of Mecca was the major religious and economic center of western Arabia. For centuries before the rise of Islam, many people in the Arabian peninsula prayed at the Ka'ba (KAH-buh), a temple in Mecca containing a black stone thought to be the dwelling place of a god, as well as objects connected to other gods. Economic links also connected Arabian peoples, but what eventually molded the diverse Arabian tribes into a powerful political and social unity was a new religion based on the teachings of Muhammad.

The Prophet Muhammad

Much like the earliest accounts of Jesus, the earliest account of the life of Muhammad (ca. 570–632) comes from oral traditions passed down among followers. According to these traditions, Muhammad was a merchant in the caravan trade who later married a wealthy widow, a marriage that brought him financial independence. He was extremely devout, self-disciplined, and literate, but not formally educated. He prayed regularly, and when he was about forty he began to experience religious visions, including a vision in which the angel Gabriel instructed him to preach.

Muhammad described his visions in a stylized and often rhyming prose and used this literary medium as his *Qur'an*, or "prayer recitation." The revelations were written down by his followers during his lifetime and organized into chapters, called *sura*, shortly after his death. In 651 Muhammad's third successor arranged to have an official version published, which became the **Qur'an** (kuh-RAHN), a book that is especially revered by Muslims as the direct words of God to his Prophet Muhammad. (When Muslims around the world use translations of the Qur'an, they do so alongside the original Arabic, the language of Muhammad's revelations.) At the same time, other sayings and accounts of Muhammad that gave advice on matters that went beyond the Qur'an were collected into books termed *hadith* (huh-DEETH). Muhammad's deeds and words in the Qur'an and hadith provide the normative example of Muslim traditions and practices, or *Sunna*, an Arabic word meaning "trodden path."

Muhammad's visions ordered him to preach a message of a single God and to become God's prophet, which he began to do in his hometown of Mecca. He gathered followers slowly, but he also provoked a great deal of resistance because he challenged the power of the local elite and also urged people to give up worship of the gods whose sacred objects were in the Ka'ba. In 622 Muhammad migrated with his followers to Medina, an event termed the *hijra* (HIJ-ra) that marks the beginning of the Muslim calendar. At Medina, Muhammad was much more successful, gaining converts, especially from urban areas, and working out the basic principles of the faith. That same year, through the Charter of Medina, Muhammad formed the first *umma*, a community that united his followers from different tribes and set religious ties above clan loyalty. The charter also extended rights to others living in Medina, including Jews and Christians, which set a precedent for the later treatment of Jews and Christians under Islam.

In 630 Muhammad returned to Mecca at the head of a large army, and he soon welded together most communities, settled or nomadic, in western Arabia into an even larger umma. They initially called

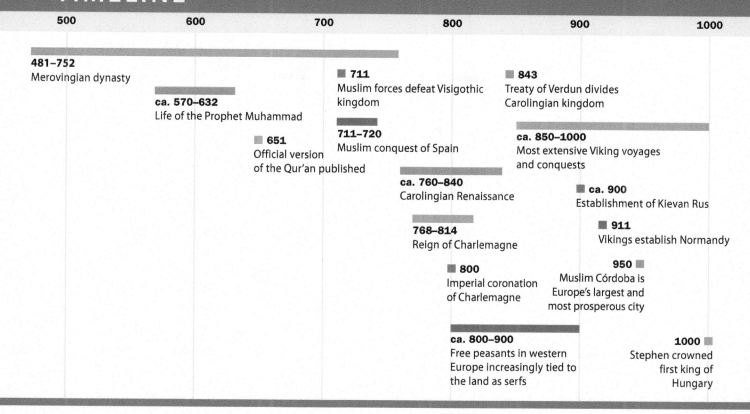

500   600   700   800   900   1000

481–752
Merovingian dynasty

ca. 570–632
Life of the Prophet Muhammad

651
Official version
of the Qur'an published

711
Muslim forces defeat Visigothic
kingdom

711–720
Muslim conquest of Spain

ca. 760–840
Carolingian Renaissance

768–814
Reign of Charlemagne

800
Imperial coronation
of Charlemagne

ca. 800–900
Free peasants in western
Europe increasingly tied to
the land as serfs

843
Treaty of Verdun divides
Carolingian kingdom

ca. 850–1000
Most extensive Viking voyages
and conquests

ca. 900
Establishment of Kievan Rus

911
Vikings establish Normandy

950
Muslim Córdoba is
Europe's largest and
most prosperous city

1000
Stephen crowned
first king of
Hungary

themselves "believers" (*mu'minun* in Arabic), but by the end of the seventh century called themselves *Muslims*, a word meaning "those who comply with God's will." The religion itself came to be called *Islam*, which means "submission to God." The Ka'ba was rededicated as a Muslim holy place, and Mecca became the most holy city in Islam.

By the time Muhammad died in 632, Muslims controlled the Arabian peninsula. During the next century one rich province of the old Roman Empire after another came under Muslim domination—first Syria, then Egypt, and then all of North Africa (Map 8.1). Long and bitter wars (572–591, 606–630) between the Byzantine and Persian Empires left both so weak and exhausted that they easily fell to Muslim attack.

The Teachings and Expansion of Islam

Muhammad's religion eventually attracted great numbers of people, partly because of the straightforward nature of its doctrines. The strictly monotheistic theology outlined in the Qur'an has only a few central tenets: Allah, the Arabic word for God, is all-powerful and all-knowing. Muhammad, Allah's prophet, preached his word and carried his message.

Muhammad described himself as the successor both of the Jewish patriarch Abraham and of Christ, and he claimed that his teachings replaced theirs. He invited and won converts from Judaism and Christianity.

Because Allah is all-powerful, believers must submit themselves to him. All Muslims have the obligation of the *jihad* (literally, "self-exertion") to strive or struggle to lead a virtuous life and to spread God's rule and law. In some cases striving is an individual struggle against sin; in others it is social and communal and could involve armed conflict, though this is not an essential part of jihad (jee-HAHD). The Islamic belief of "striving in the path of God" is closely related to the central feature of Muslim doctrine, the coming Day of Judgment. Muslims believe with conviction that the Day of Judgment will come; consequently, all of a Muslim's thoughts and actions should be oriented toward the Last Judgment and the rewards of Heaven.

To merit the rewards of Heaven, a person must follow the strict code of moral behavior that Muhammad prescribed. The Muslim must recite a profession of faith in God and in Muhammad as God's prophet: "There is no god but God and Muhammad is his prophet." The believer must pray five times a day,

■ **Qur'an** The sacred book of Islam.

fast and pray during the sacred month of Ramadan, and contribute alms to the poor and needy. If possible, the believer must make a pilgrimage to Mecca once during his or her lifetime. According to the Muslim *shari'a* (shuh-REE-uh), or sacred law, these five practices—the profession of faith, prayer, fasting, giving alms to the poor, and pilgrimage to Mecca—constitute the **Five Pillars of Islam**.

The Qur'an forbids alcoholic beverages and gambling, as well as a number of foods, such as pork, a dietary regulation adopted from the Mosaic law of the Hebrews. It condemns business usury—that is, lending money at interest rates or taking advantage of market demand for products by charging high prices for them. The hadith discourage the depiction of living beings, and Islamic art tends to favor geometric designs and calligraphy, although in some places figurative art has been created as well.

In contrast to Christianity, in which a celibate life without sex was viewed as spiritually superior, the Qur'an and hadith recommend marriage for everyone and view heterosexual sex within marriage positively. The Qur'an holds men and women to be fully equal in God's eyes; both are capable of going to Heaven and responsible for carrying out the duties of believers themselves. It does make clear distinctions between men and women, however. It allows men to have up to four wives and to divorce a wife quite easily. It orders that the Prophet's later wives be secluded, and though women played a major role in the early development of Islam, after the first generation the seclusion of women became more common. Men were expected to fulfill their religious obligations publicly, whereas women were to do so in the home, though they generally had access to a separate section of the mosque. Islamic law granted women less inheritance than their brothers, but this inheritance remained theirs and did not pass to their husbands upon marriage, as it did in most Christian societies until the mid-nineteenth century.

Sunni and Shi'a Divisions

At the same time that Islam expanded, it also split, as neither the Qur'an nor the hadith gave clear guidance about how successors to Muhammad were to be chosen. According to tradition, in 632 a group of Muhammad's closest followers chose Abu Bakr (uh-BOO BAH-kuhr), a close friend of the Prophet and a member of a clan affiliated with the Prophet's clan, as leader. He was followed by two other successors, but these provoked opposition that coalesced around Ali, Muhammad's cousin and son-in-law, who was chosen as the fourth leader in 656. Ali's supporters began to assert that the Prophet had designated

MAP 8.1 The Spread of Islam, 622–900   The rapid expansion of Islam in a relatively short span of time testifies to the Arabs' superior fighting skills, religious zeal, and economic organization as well as to their enemies' weakness.

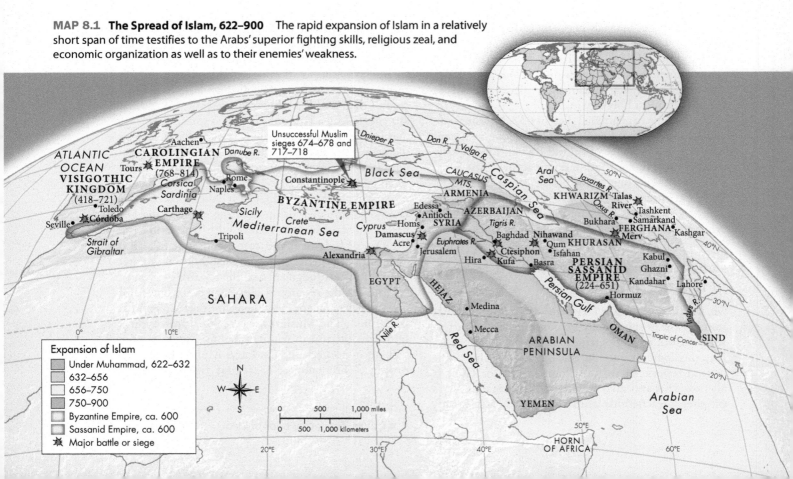

Dome of the Rock, Jerusalem   Completed in 691 and revered by Muslims as the site where Muhammad ascended to Heaven, the Dome of the Rock is the oldest surviving monument of Islamic architecture. Although influenced by Byzantine and Persian architecture, it also has distinctly Islamic features, such as Qur'anic inscriptions. (imageBROKER/Superstock)

Ali as *imam*, or leader, and that any leader who was not a descendant of Ali was a usurper. These supporters of Ali—termed Shi'ites (SHEE-ights) or Shi'a (SHEE-ah) from Arabic terms meaning "supporters" or "partisans" of Ali—saw Ali and subsequent imams as the divinely inspired leaders of the whole community. The larger body of Muslims—termed Sunnis, a word derived from *Sunna*, the practices of the community derived from Muhammad's example—accepted the original elections and saw these men as proper political leaders.

Both Sunnis and Shi'a maintain that authority within Islam lies in the Qur'an and hadith, but they disagree over who should interpret these texts. Shi'a assert that the imam does, while Sunnis hold that proper interpretation comes from the consensus of the *ulama*, the jurists, judges, and scholastics who are knowledgeable about the Qur'an and hadith. Over centuries other differences between the two groups developed, and enmity between Sunni and Shi'a Muslims sometimes erupted into violence, mixing with political and economic disputes to create conflicts that took various forms.

Conflict began with a civil war in which Ali was assassinated. The successful leaders, the Umayyad (oo-MIGH-uhd) clan, established a hereditary dynasty and moved the capital of the Islamic state to Damascus in Syria. They began to refer to themselves as "successors of the Prophet" (*khalifat rasul Allah*), from where we get the word **caliph** (KAY-luhf), which is now often used to refer to all of Muhammad's successors.

Under the Umayyad Dynasty (661–750), Islam continued to expand eastward to India and westward across North Africa. That expansion was facilitated everywhere by military strength, religious zeal, the political weakness of existing governments, and the ways Islam blended with local traditions, which made it appealing to many ethnic and social groups.

Life in Muslim Spain

In Europe, Muslim political and cultural influence was felt most strongly in the Iberian Peninsula. In 711 a Muslim force crossed the Strait of Gibraltar and easily defeated the weak Visigothic kingdom.

■ **Five Pillars of Islam** The five practices Muslims must fulfill according to the shari'a, or sacred law, including the profession of faith, prayer, fasting, giving alms to the poor, and pilgrimage to Mecca.

■ **caliph** The chief Muslim ruler, regarded as a successor to the Prophet Muhammad.

There are no contemporary descriptions from either Muslim or Christian authors of the Muslim conquest of the Iberian Peninsula that began in 711. One of the few existing documents is a treaty from 713, written in Arabic, between 'Abd al-'Aziz, the son of the conquering Muslim governor and general Musa ibn Nusair, and Tudmir, the Visigothic Christian ruler of the city of Murcia in southern Spain. Treaties such as this, and military aspects of the conquest, were also described in the earliest surviving account, an anonymous Latin chronicle written by a Christian living in Muslim Spain in 754.

Treaty of Tudmir, from 713

In the name of God, the merciful and the compassionate.

This is a document [granted] by 'Abd al-'Aziz ibn Musa ibn Nusair to Tudmir, son of Ghabdush, establishing a treaty of peace and the promise and protection of God and his Prophet (may God bless him and grant him peace). We ['Abd al-'Aziz] will not set special conditions for him or for any among his men, nor harass him, nor remove him from power. His followers will not be killed or taken prisoner, nor will they be separated from their women and children. They will not be coerced in matters of religion, their churches will not be burned, nor will sacred objects be taken from the realm, [so long as] he [Tudmir] remains sincere and fulfills the [following] conditions that we have set for him. He has reached a settlement concerning seven towns: Orihuela, Valentilla, Alicante, Mula, Bigastro, Ello, and Lorca. He will not give shelter to fugitives, nor to our enemies, nor encourage any protected person to fear us, nor conceal news of our enemies. He and [each of] his men shall [also] pay one dinar every year, together with four measures of wheat, four measures of barley, four liquid measures of concentrated fruit juice, four liquid measures of vinegar, four of honey, and four of olive oil. Slaves must each pay half of this amount.

Christian Chronicle of Events in 711, Written in 754

In Justinian's time [711], . . . Musa . . . entered the long plundered and godlessly invaded Spain to destroy it. After forcing his way to Toledo, the royal city, he imposed on the adjacent regions an evil and fraudulent peace. He decapitated on a scaffold those noble lords who had remained, arresting them in their flight from Toledo with the help of Oppa, King Egica's son [a Visigothic Christian prince]. With Oppa's support, he killed them all with the sword. Thus he devastated not only [the former Roman province of] Hispania Ulterior, but [the former Roman province of] Hispania Citerior up to and beyond the ancient and once flourishing city of Zaragoza, now, by the judgment of God, openly exposed to the sword, famine, and captivity. He ruined beautiful cities, burning them with fire; condemned lords and powerful men to the cross; and butchered youths and infants with the sword. While he terrorized everyone in this way, some of the cities that remained sued for peace under duress and, after persuading and mocking them with a certain craftiness, the Saracens [Muslims] granted their requests without delay.

QUESTIONS FOR ANALYSIS

1. What conditions and guarantees are set for Christians living under Muslim rule in the treaty between Musa and Tudmir?
2. How does the author of the chronicle view Musa and treaties such as his?
3. What evidence do these documents provide for coexistence between Christians and Muslims in Spain and for hostility between the two groups?

Source: Olivia Remie Constable, ed., *Medieval Iberia: Readings from Christian, Muslim, and Jewish Sources* (Philadelphia: University of Pennsylvania Press, 2012), pp. 30–31, 37–38.

(See "Viewpoints: The Muslim Conquest of Spain".) A few Christian princes supported by the Frankish rulers held out in northern mountain fortresses, but by 720 the Muslims controlled most of Spain. A member of the Umayyad Dynasty, Abd al-Rahman (r. 756–788), established a kingdom in Spain with its capital at Córdoba (KAWR-doh-buh).

Throughout the Islamic world, Muslims used the term **al-Andalus** to describe the part of the Iberian Peninsula under Muslim control. The name probably derives from the Arabic for "land of the Vandals," the Germanic people who swept across Spain in the fifth century. Today we often use the word *Andalusia* (an-duh-LOO-zhuh) to refer especially to southern Spain, but in the eighth century al-Andalus included the entire peninsula from Gibraltar in the south to the Cantabrian Mountains in the north (see Map 8.1). The Romans had called the Berber population of northwestern Africa *Mauri*, which became "Moor" in English and similar words in other European languages. "Moor" was also gradually used in English to describe any Muslim from North Africa or al-Andalus, whether Berber, Arab, or some other ethnicity.

The Muslim conquest of the Iberian Peninsula did not displace the existing Christian and Jewish populations. Instead Muslims, Christians, and Jews traded with and learned from one another, generally using Arabic for business transactions and much of daily life. Some scholars believe that the eighth and ninth centuries in Andalusia were an era of remarkable interfaith harmony. Jews in Muslim Spain were generally treated well, and Córdoba became a center of Jewish as well as Muslim learning. Many Christians adopted Arabic patterns of speech and dress, gave up eating pork, and developed an appreciation for Arabic music and poetry. Records describe Muslim and Christian youths joining in celebrations and merrymaking. Some Christian women of elite status chose the Muslim practice of going out in public with their faces veiled. Moorish Spain and Norman Sicily (see "Italy" in Chapter 9) were the only distinctly pluralistic societies in medieval Europe.

By 950 Córdoba had a population of about a half million, making it Europe's largest and most prosperous city. Many residents lived in large houses and easily purchased the silks and brocades made by the city's thousands of weavers. The streets were well paved and well lit — a sharp contrast to the dark and muddy streets of other cities in Europe — and there was an abundance of freshwater for drinking and bathing. The largest library contained four hundred thousand volumes, a vast collection, particularly when compared with the largest library in northern Europe at the Benedictine abbey of St. Gall in Switzerland, which had only six hundred books. Córdoba's scholars made contributions in chemistry, medicine and surgery, music, philosophy, mathematics, and geography. The Saxon nun and writer Hroswitha of Gandersheim (roz-WEETH-uh of GAHN-duhr-sheym) called the city of Córdoba "the ornament of the world."

In Spain, as elsewhere in the Arab world, Muslims had an enormous impact on agricultural development. New or more widely planted crops included rice, sugarcane, citrus fruits, dates, figs, eggplants, carrots, and, after the eleventh century, cotton. These crops, together with better methods of field irrigation and crop rotation, provided the population with food products unknown in the rest of Europe. Muslims also brought technological innovations westward, including new kinds of sails and navigational instruments, as well as paper.

Muslim-Christian Encounters

Islam built on and reformulated many teachings enshrined in Hebrew and Christian Scripture. Jesus is mentioned many times in the Qur'an, described as a

Muslim Garden in Spain   Tranquil gardens such as this one built by Muslim rulers in Granada represented paradise in Islamic culture, perhaps because of the religion's desert origins. Muslim architectural styles shaped those of Christian Spain and were later taken to the New World by Spanish conquerors. (PHAS/Universal Images Group/Getty Images)

righteous prophet chosen by God. But Muslims held that Jesus was an apostle only, not God. The Christian doctrine of the Trinity — that there is one God in three persons (Father, Son, and Holy Spirit) — posed a powerful obstacle to Muslim-Christian understanding because of Islam's emphasis on the absolute oneness of God.

Christian-Muslim relations were shaped by events as well as ideas, and they varied over time. In Spain, Muslim teachers increasingly feared that close contact with Christians would lead to

■ **al-Andalus** The part of the Iberian Peninsula under Muslim control in the eighth century, encompassing most of modern-day Spain.

Qur'an Written on Paper   This thirteenth-century Qur'an, written on paper, was produced in southern Spain, with colorful ornamental letters and gold leaf. Paper was invented in China and brought west by Muslims; by about 1100 there were paper mills in Muslim Spain, and from there papermaking spread into Christian Europe.

(Pictures From History/CPA Media Pte Ltd./Alamy Stock Photo)

Muslim contamination and become a threat to the Islamic faith, while Christian clerics worried that knowledge of Islam would lead to confusion about Christian doctrines and moral decline. Thus, beginning in the late tenth century, Muslim regulations began to officially prescribe what Christians, Jews, and Muslims could do. A Christian or Jew, however much assimilated, remained an **infidel**. An infidel was an unbeliever, and the word carried a pejorative or disparaging connotation.

In the middle of the tenth century Caliph Abd al-Rahman III (912–961) of the Umayyad Dynasty of Córdoba ruled most of the Iberian Peninsula. Christian Spain consisted of the tiny kingdoms of Castile, León, Catalonia, Aragon, Navarre, and Portugal. Civil wars among al-Rahman's descendants weakened the caliphate, and the small northern Christian kingdoms began to expand southward, sometimes working together. When Christian forces conquered Muslim territory, Christian rulers regarded their Muslim and Jewish subjects as infidels and enacted restrictive measures similar to those imposed on

Christians in Muslim lands. Interfaith contacts declined. Christians' perception of Islam as a menace would help inspire the Crusades of the eleventh through thirteenth centuries (see "Background and Motives of the Crusades" in Chapter 9).

Cross-Cultural Influences in Science and Medicine

Despite growing suspicions on both sides, the Islamic world profoundly shaped Christian European culture in Spain and elsewhere. Creative Muslim thinkers built on Greek, Persian, and Indian knowledge, translating works into and out of Arabic and writing new works. The Persian scholar al-Khwarizmi (al-KHWAHR-uhz-mee) (d. 830) wrote the important treatise *Algebra*, the first work in which the word *algebra* is used mathematically. Al-Khwarizmi adopted the Hindu system of numbers (1, 2, 3, 4), used it in his *Algebra*, and applied mathematics to problems of physics and astronomy. (Since our system of numbers is actually Indian in origin, the term *Arabic numerals*, coined about 1847, is a misnomer.) In a related field, scholars in Baghdad translated Euclid's *Elements*, the basic text for plane and solid geometry.

Muslim medical knowledge far surpassed that of the West in this era. By the ninth century Muslim physicians had translated most of the treatises of the ancient Greek physician Hippocrates and produced a number of important works of their own. The Baghdad physician al-Razi (865–925), the first physician to make a clinical distinction between measles and smallpox, produced an encyclopedic treatise on medicine that was translated into Latin and circulated widely in the West. Muslim science reached its peak in the physician, philologist, philosopher, poet, and scientist ibn-Sina of Bukhara (980–1037), known in the West as Avicenna (ah-vuh-SEH-nuh). His *Canon of Medicine* codified all Greco-Arabic medical thought, described the contagious nature of tuberculosis and the spreading of diseases, and listed 760 pharmaceutical drugs.

Muslim scholars also translated and codified the philosophical learning of Greek and Persian antiquity. In the ninth and tenth centuries that knowledge was brought to Spain, where between 1150 and 1250 it was translated into Latin, making it accessible to Europeans. The rediscovery of Aristotle (see "The Flowering of Philosophy" in Chapter 3) changed the entire direction of European philosophy and theology, as European Christian thinkers increasingly used ideas drawn from Aristotle as well as Christian texts in their writings (see "Theology and Philosophy" in Chapter 10). Thus Muslim knowledge in many fields enriched Western knowledge.

How did the Franks build and govern a European empire?

Over two centuries before the Muslim conquest of Spain, the Frankish king Clovis converted to Roman Christianity and established a large kingdom in what had been Roman Gaul (see Chapter 7). Though at that time the Frankish kingdom was simply one barbarian kingdom among many, it grew to become the most important state in Europe, expanding to become an empire. Frankish rulers after Clovis, especially Charles the Great (r. 768–814), generally known by the French version of his name, Charlemagne (SHAHR-luh-mayne), used a variety of tactics to enhance their authority and create a stable system.

The Merovingians

Clovis established the Merovingian dynasty in about 481 (see "Germanic Kingdoms and the End of the Roman Empire" in Chapter 7), and under him the Frankish kingdom included much of what is now France and a large section of southwestern Germany. Following Frankish traditions in which property was divided among male heirs, at Clovis's death the kingdom was divided among his four sons. Historians have long described Merovingian Gaul in the sixth and seventh centuries as wracked by civil wars, chronic violence, and political instability as Clovis's descendants fought among themselves. So brutal and destructive were these wars and so violent the conditions of daily life that the term *Dark Ages* was at one time used to designate the entire Merovingian period, although more recently historians have noted that the Merovingians also created new political institutions, so the era was not uniformly bleak.

Merovingian rulers also developed diverse sources of income. These included revenues from the royal estates and the "gifts" of subject peoples, such as plunder and tribute paid by peoples east of the Rhine River. New lands that might be conquered and confiscated served to replace lands donated as monastic or religious endowments. All free landowners paid a land tax, although some landowners gradually gained immunity from doing so. Fines imposed for criminal offenses and tolls and customs duties levied on roads and waterways also yielded income.

The Franks also based some aspects of their government on Roman principles. For example, the basis of the administrative system in the Frankish kingdom was the **civitas** (SIH-vih-tahs) — Latin for a city and surrounding territory — similar to the provinces of the Roman Empire. A **comites** (KOH-meh-tehs) — a senior official or royal companion, later called a

Merovingian Period Belt Buckle   This bronze belt buckle, made between 550 and 626 in Burgundy, shows the biblical story of Daniel in the lion's den, with Daniel in the middle triumphant over two fanciful lions, saved through divine intervention. Biblical stories began to appear on many types of objects in the early Middle Ages, particularly those stories that fit with barbarian values, such as boldness and valor. (JEAN-LOUIS JOSSE/Musée des Antiquités Nationales, St. Germain-en-Laye, France/Bridgeman Images)

count — presided over the civitas, as had governors in Rome. He collected royal revenue, heard lawsuits, enforced justice, and raised troops. Many comites were not conquerors from outside, but came from families that had been administrators in Roman Gaul and were usually native to the regions they administered and knew their areas well. Frankish royal administration involved another official, the *dux* (dooks) or duke. He was a military leader, commanding troops in the territory of several civitas, and thus responsible for all defensive and offensive strategies. Clovis and his descendants also issued capitularies — Roman-style administrative and legislative orders — in an attempt to maintain order in Merovingian society.

Within the royal household, Merovingian politics provided women with opportunities, and some queens not only influenced but occasionally also dominated events. Because the finances of the kingdom were merged with those of the royal family, queens often had control of the royal treasury just as more ordinary

■ **infidel** A disparaging term used for a person who does not believe in a particular religion.

■ **civitas** The city and surrounding territory that served as a basis of the administrative system in the Frankish kingdoms, based on Roman models.

■ **comites** A senior official or royal companion, later called a count, who presided over the civitas.

women controlled household expenditures. The status of a princess or queen also rested on her diplomatic importance, with her marriage sealing or her divorce breaking an alliance with a foreign kingdom or powerful noble family; on her personal relationship with her husband and her ability to give him sons and heirs; and on her role as the mother and guardian of princes who had not reached legal adulthood.

Queen Brunhilda (543?–613), for example, married first one Frankish king and at his death another. When her second husband died, Brunhilda overcame the objections of the nobles and became regent, ruling on behalf of her son until he came of age. Later she governed as regent for her grandsons and, when she was nearly seventy, for her great-grandson. Stories of her ruthlessness spread during her lifetime and were later much embellished by Frankish historians uncomfortable with such a powerful woman. The evil Brunhilda, they alleged, killed ten Frankish kings in pursuit of her political goals, and was finally executed by being torn apart by horses while cheering crowds looked on. How much of this actually happened is impossible to say, but Brunhilda's legend became a model for the wicked queen in European folklore.

Merovingian rulers and their successors traveled constantly to check up on local administrators and peoples. Merovingian kings also relied on the comites and bishops to gather and send local information to them. The court or household of Merovingian kings included scribes who kept records, legal officials who advised the king on matters of law, and treasury agents responsible for aspects of royal finance. These officials could read and write Latin. Over them all presided the mayor of the palace, the most important secular figure after the king, who governed the palace and the kingdom in the king's absence. Mayors were usually from one of the great aristocratic families, which increasingly through intermarriage blended Frankish and Roman elites. These families possessed landed wealth — villas over which they exercised lordship, dispensing local customary, not royal, law — and they often had rich and lavish lifestyles.

The Rise of the Carolingians

From this aristocracy, one family gradually emerged to replace the Merovingian dynasty. The rise of the Carolingians — whose name comes from the Latin *Carolus*, or Charles, the name of several important members of the family — rested on several factors. First, the Carolingian Pippin I (d. 640) acquired the powerful position of mayor of the palace and passed the title on to his heirs. As mayors of the palace and heads of the Frankish bureaucracy, Pippin I and his descendants were entrusted with extraordinary amounts of power and privilege by the Merovingian

kings. Although the mayor of the palace was technically employed by the ruling family, the Carolingians would use their influential position to win support for themselves and eventually subvert Merovingian authority. Second, a series of advantageous marriage alliances increased the family estates and influence in different parts of the Frankish world, and they also gave the Carolingians landed wealth and treasure with which to reward their allies and followers. Third, military victories over supporters of the Merovingians gave the Carolingians a reputation for strength and ensured their dominance. Pippin I's great-grandson, Charles Martel (r. 714–741), waged war successfully against the Saxons, Frisians, Alamanni, and Bavarians, further enhancing the family's prestige. In 732 Charles Martel defeated a Muslim force near Poitiers (pwah-tee-AY) in central France. While Muslims saw the battle as nothing more than a minor skirmish, Charles Martel and later Carolingians used it to enhance their reputation, portraying themselves as defenders of Christendom against the Muslims.

The Battle of Poitiers helped the Carolingians acquire the support of the church, perhaps their most important asset. Charles Martel and his son Pippin III (r. 751–768) further strengthened their ties to the church by supporting the work of Christian missionaries. The most important of these missionaries was the Englishman Boniface (BAH-nuh-fays) (680–754), who had close ties to the Roman pope. Boniface ordered the oak of Thor, a tree sacred to many pagans, cut down and used the wood to build a church. When the god Thor did not respond by killing him with his lightning bolts, Boniface won many converts. As missionaries preached, baptized, and established churches, they included the Christian duty to obey secular authorities as part of their message, thus extending to Frankish rulers the church's support of secular power that had begun with Constantine (see "The Acceptance of Christianity" in Chapter 7).

As mayor of the palace, Charles Martel had exercised the power of king of the Franks. His son Pippin III aspired to the title as well as the powers it entailed. Pippin's diplomats were able to convince an embattled Pope Zacharias to rule in his favor against the Merovingians in exchange for military support against the Lombards, who were threatening the papacy. Zacharias invoked his apostolic authority as pope, deposed the Merovingian ruler Chilperic in 752, and declared that Pippin should be king. An assembly of Frankish magnates elected Pippin king, and Boniface anointed him. When in 754 Lombard expansion again threatened the papacy, Pope Stephen II journeyed to the Frankish kingdom seeking help. On this occasion, he personally anointed Pippin with the sacred oils and gave him the title *Patrician of the Romans*, thus linking him symbolically with the ruling patrician class of ancient Rome. Pippin promised restitution of the papal lands and later made a gift of estates in central Italy. An important alliance had been struck between the papacy and the Frankish monarchs. When Pippin died, his son Charles, generally known as Charlemagne, succeeded him.

The Warrior-Ruler Charlemagne

Charlemagne's adviser and friend Alcuin (ca. 735–804; see "The Carolingian Renaissance") wrote that "a king should be strong against his enemies, humble to Christians, feared by pagans, loved by the poor and judicious in counsel and maintaining justice."[1] Charlemagne worked to realize that ideal in all its aspects. Through brutal military expeditions that brought wealth—lands, booty, enslaved captives, and tribute—and by peaceful travel, personal appearances, and the sheer force of his personality, Charlemagne sought to awe newly conquered peoples and rebellious domestic enemies.

If an ideal king was "strong against his enemies" and "feared by pagans," Charlemagne more than met the standard, as his reign was characterized by constant warfare. He subdued all of the north of modern France, but his greatest successes were in today's Germany, where he fought battles he justified as spreading Christianity to pagan peoples. In the course of a bloody thirty-year war against the Saxons, he added most of the northwestern German peoples to the Frankish kingdom. In his biography of the ruler, Charlemagne's royal secretary Einhard reported that Charlemagne ordered more than four thousand Saxons killed on one day and deported thousands more. Those who surrendered were forced to become Christian, often in mass baptisms. He established bishoprics in areas he had conquered, so church officials and church institutions became important means of imposing Frankish rule.

Charlemagne also achieved spectacular results in the south, incorporating Lombardy in today's northern Italy into the Frankish kingdom. He ended Bavarian independence and defeated the nomadic Avars, opening eastern Germany for later settlement by Franks. He successfully fought the Byzantine Empire for Venetia, Istria, and Dalmatia and temporarily annexed those areas to his kingdom. Charlemagne's only defeat came at the hands of the Basques of northwestern Spain. By around 805 the Frankish kingdom included all of northwestern Europe except Scandinavia and Britain (Map 8.2). Not since the Roman emperors of the third century C.E. had any ruler controlled so much of the Western world. Other than brief periods under Napoleon and Hitler, Europe would never again see as large a unified state as it had under Charlemagne. For that reason, Charlemagne is today an important symbol of European unity; the European Union

MAP 8.2 Charlemagne's Conquests, ca. 768–814 Though Charlemagne's hold on much of his territory was relatively weak, the size of his empire was not equaled again until the nineteenth-century conquests of Napoleon.

named one of its central buildings in Brussels the Charlemagne Building, and the Charlemagne Prize and Charlemagne Youth Prize are awarded for contributions to the process of European integration.

Carolingian Government and Society

Charlemagne's empire was not a state as people today understand that term; it was a collection of peoples and clans. For administrative purposes, Charlemagne divided his entire kingdom into counties based closely on the old Merovingian civitas. Each of the approximately six hundred counties was governed by a count (or in his absence by a viscount), who published royal orders, held courts and resolved legal cases, collected taxes and tolls, raised troops for the army, and supervised maintenance of roads and bridges. Counts were originally sent out from the royal court; later a person native to the region was appointed. As a link between local authorities and the central government, Charlemagne appointed officials called *missi dominici* (mih-see doh-MEH-nee-chee), "agents of the lord king," who checked up on the counts and held courts to handle judicial and financial issues.

Considering the size of Charlemagne's empire, the counts and royal agents were few and far between, and the authority of the central government was weak. Society was held together by alliances among powerful families, along with dependent relationships cemented by oaths promising faith and loyalty.

Family alliances were often cemented by sexual relations, including those of Charlemagne himself. Charlemagne had a total of four or five legal wives, most from other Frankish tribes, and at least six concubines. (See "Evaluating Visual Evidence: Charlemagne and His Second Wife, Hildegard," page 213.) Charlemagne's personal desires certainly shaped his complicated relationships—even after the age of sixty-five he continued to sire children—but the security and continuation of his dynasty and the need for diplomatic alliances were also important motives. Of his eighteen children, Charlemagne married the sons who reached adulthood to the daughters of kings and high nobles, and their descendants established most of the ruling dynasties of Europe. He prevented his daughters from marrying to avoid side branches of the family developing, though two had long-term relationships with courtiers, and their children became abbots or abbesses of major monasteries or married into noble houses. Several of Charlemagne's children born out of wedlock headed monasteries or convents as well, thus connecting his family with the church as well as the secular hierarchy. Throughout the Middle Ages, the children of kings and high nobles born out of wedlock were legally disadvantaged, but many had illustrious careers or made good marriages themselves, as there was relatively little stigma.

In terms of social changes, the Carolingian period witnessed moderate population growth. The highest aristocrats and church officials lived well, with fine clothing and at least a few rooms heated by firewood. Male nobles hunted and managed their estates, while female nobles generally oversaw the education of their children and sometimes inherited and controlled land on their own. Craftsmen and craftswomen on manorial estates manufactured textiles, weapons, glass, and pottery, primarily for local consumption. Sometimes abbeys and manors served as markets; goods were shipped away to towns and fairs for sale; and a good deal of interregional commerce existed. In the towns, artisans and merchants produced and traded luxury goods for noble and clerical patrons. When compared with earlier Roman cities or with Muslim cities of the time, such as Córdoba and Baghdad, however, Carolingian cities were small. Even in Charlemagne's main political center at Aachen, most buildings were made of wood and earth, streets were narrow and muddy, and beggars were a common sight.

The modest economic expansion benefited townspeople and nobles, but it did not significantly alter the lives of most people, who continued to live in a vast rural world dotted with isolated estates and small villages. Here life was precarious. Crops could easily be wiped out by hail, cold, or rain, and transporting food from other areas was impossible. People's diets centered on grain, which was baked into bread, brewed into beer, and especially cooked into gruel. To this were added seasonal vegetables such as peas, cabbage, and onions, and tiny amounts of animal protein, mostly cheese. Clothing and household goods were just as simple, and houses were drafty, smoky, and often shared with animals. Lice, fleas, and other vermin spread disease, and the poor diet led to frequent stomach disorders. Work varied by the season, but at all times of the year it was physically demanding and yielded relatively little. What little there was had to be shared with landowners, who demanded their taxes and rents in the form of crops, animals, or labor.

The Imperial Coronation of Charlemagne

In autumn of the year 800, Charlemagne paid a momentous visit to Rome. Einhard gives this account of what happened:

> His last journey there [to Rome] was due to another factor, namely that the Romans, having inflicted many injuries on Pope Leo—plucking out his eyes and tearing out his tongue, he had been compelled to beg the assistance of the king. Accordingly, coming to Rome in order that he might set in order those things which had exceedingly disturbed the condition of the Church, he remained there the whole winter. It was at the time that he accepted the name of Emperor and Augustus. At first he was so much opposed to this that he insisted that although that day was a great [Christian] feast, he would not have entered the Church if he had known beforehand the pope's intention. But he bore very patiently the jealousy of the Roman Emperors [that is, the Byzantine rulers] who were indignant when he received these titles. He overcame their arrogant haughtiness with magnanimity, . . . by sending frequent ambassadors to them and in his letters addressing them as brothers.[2]

Charlemagne and His Second Wife, Hildegard

This illumination from a ninth-century manuscript portrays Charlemagne with the woman who was his second or third wife, Hildegard of the Vinzgau (ca. 754–783). She had nine

(Imagno/Hulton Archive/Getty Images)

children during her twelve years of marriage, including a set of twins (one of whom was Louis the Pious, Charlemagne's successor), and she died from complications of childbirth. She accompanied Charlemagne on many of his military campaigns and used her position as his wife to gain offices and land for her relatives. She gave extensive financial and political support to the Benedictine Abbey of Kempten in what is today southern Germany. Marriage was an important tool of diplomacy for Charlemagne, and he had a succession of wives, along with concubines during and between his marriages. Whether Hildegard was wife two or three depends on whether Himiltrude, the mother of Charlemagne's first-born son, Pepin the Hunchback, was his wife or his concubine; the sources are unclear. He did briefly marry the daughter of the king of the Lombards (her name is disputed) before he married Hildegard. A few months after Hildegard's death he married again, to Fastrada, the daughter of an East Frankish count who was helping him fight the Saxons, and when she died he married Luitgard, the daughter of another count.

EVALUATE THE EVIDENCE

1. What does Charlemagne appear to be doing? How would you characterize his wife's reaction?
2. Why do you think the artist (whose identity is unknown) portrayed them like this?
3. How does this depiction of a Frankish queen match what you have read about Frankish queens? On what accomplishments did a queen's status rest?

For centuries scholars have debated the reasons for the imperial coronation of Charlemagne. Did Charlemagne plan the ceremony in Saint Peter's on Christmas Day, or did he merely accept the title of emperor? What did he have to gain from it? If, as Einhard implies, the coronation displeased Charlemagne, was that because it put the pope in the superior position of conferring power on the emperor? What were Pope Leo's motives in arranging the coronation?

Though definitive answers will probably never be found, several things seem certain. First, after the coronation Charlemagne considered himself an emperor ruling a Christian people. Through his motto, *Renovatio romani imperi* (Revival of the Roman Empire), Charlemagne was consciously perpetuating old Roman imperial notions while at the same time identifying with the new Rome of the Christian Church. In this sense, Charlemagne might be considered a precursor of the eventual Holy Roman emperor, although that term

didn't come into use for two more centuries. Second, Leo's ideas about gender and rule undoubtedly influenced his decision to crown Charlemagne. In 800 the ruler of the Byzantine Empire was the empress Irene, the first woman to rule Byzantium in her own name, but Leo did not regard her authority as legitimate because she was female. He thus claimed to be placing Charlemagne on a vacant throne. Third, both parties gained: the Carolingian family received official recognition from the leading spiritual power in Europe, and the papacy gained a military protector.

Not surprisingly, the Byzantines regarded the papal acts as rebellious and Charlemagne as a usurper. The imperial coronation thus marks a decisive break between Rome and Constantinople. From Baghdad, however, Harun al-Rashid (r. 786–809), caliph of the Abbasid Empire, congratulated the Frankish ruler with the gift of an elephant. It was named Abu'l Abbas after the founder of the Abbasid Dynasty and may have served as a symbol of the diplomatic link Harun al-Rashid hoped to forge with the Franks against Byzantium. Having plodded its way to Charlemagne's court at Aachen, the elephant survived for nine years, and its death was considered important enough to be mentioned in the Frankish *Royal Annals*, the official chronological record of events, for the year 810. Like everyone else at Aachen, the elephant lived in a city that was far less sophisticated, healthy, and beautiful than the Baghdad of Harun al-Rashid.

The coronation of Charlemagne, whether planned by the Carolingian court or by the papacy, was to have a profound effect on the course of German history and on the later history of Europe. In the centuries that followed, German rulers were eager to gain the imperial title and to associate themselves with the legends of Charlemagne and ancient Rome. Ecclesiastical authorities, on the other hand, continually cited the event as proof that the dignity of the imperial crown could be granted only by the pope.

What were the significant intellectual and cultural developments in Charlemagne's era?

As he built an empire through conquest and strategic alliances, Charlemagne also set in motion a cultural revival that had long-lasting consequences. The stimulus he gave to scholarship and learning may, in fact, be his most enduring legacy, although at the time most people continued to live in a world where knowledge was transmitted orally.

The Carolingian Renaissance

In Roman Gaul through the fifth century, the culture of members of the elite rested on an education that stressed grammar, Greco-Roman works of literature and history, and the legal and medical treatises of the Roman world. Beginning in the seventh and eighth centuries, a new cultural tradition common to Gaul, Italy, the British Isles, and to some extent Spain emerged. This culture was based primarily on Christian sources. Scholars have called the new Christian and ecclesiastical culture of the period from about 760 to 840, and the educational foundation on which it was based, the Carolingian Renaissance because Charlemagne was its major patron.

Charlemagne directed that every monastery in his kingdom should cultivate learning and educate the monks and secular clergy so that they would have a better understanding of the Christian writings. He also urged the establishment of cathedral and monastic schools where boys might learn to read and to pray properly. Thus the main purpose of this rebirth of learning was to promote an understanding of the Scriptures and of Christian writers and to instruct people to pray and praise God in the correct manner.

Women shared with men the work of evangelization and the new Christian learning. Rulers, noblemen, and noblewomen founded monasteries for nuns, each governed by an abbess. The abbess oversaw all aspects of life in the monastery. She handled the business affairs, supervised the copying of manuscripts, and directed the daily round of prayer and worship. Women's monasteries housed women who were unmarried, and also often widows, children being taught to read and recite prayers and chants, elderly people seeking a safe place to live, and travelers

Illuminated Manuscript with Carolingian Minuscule   In the Carolingian period, monks, nuns, and scribes invented a clearer script known as Carolingian minuscule, shown here, which made books more legible and copying more efficient because more words could fit on the page. They also illuminated the manuscripts they were copying, that is, decorated them with colors and small painted scenes, as in this letter C showing Christ being pulled into Heaven by the hand of God.

(Bibliothèque Nationale, Paris, France/akg-images/Newscom)

INDIVIDUALS IN SOCIETY

The Venerable Bede

The finest representative of Northumbrian, and indeed all Anglo-Saxon, scholarship is Bede (ca. 673–735). He was born into a noble family, and when he was seven his parents sent him to a monastery as a sign of their religious devotion. Surrounded by the hundreds of pagan and Christian books Northumbrian abbots had brought from Italy, Bede spent the rest of his life there, studying and writing. He wrote textbooks on grammar and writing designed to help students master the intricacies of Latin, commentaries on the Old and New Testaments, historical works relating the lives of abbots and the development of the church, and scientific works on time. His biblical commentaries survive in hundreds of manuscripts, indicating that they were widely studied throughout the Middle Ages. His doctrinal works led him to be honored after his death with the title *Venerable*, and centuries after his death to be named a "doctor of the church" by the pope.

A manuscript portrait of Bede, from a twelfth-century copy of one of his biographies of important abbots. There are no contemporary descriptions of Bede, so later manuscript illuminators were free to imagine what he looked like. (Album/British Library/Alamy Stock Photo)

Bede's religious writings were actually not that innovative, but his historical writings were, particularly his best-known work, the *Ecclesiastical History of the English People*, written about 720. As the title suggests, Bede's main topic is the growth of Christianity in England. The book begins with a short discussion of Christianity in Roman Britain, then skips to Augustine of Canterbury's mission to the Anglo-Saxons (see "Missionaries' Actions" in Chapter 7). Most of the book tells the story of Christianity's spread from one small kingdom in England to another, with missionaries and the kings who converted as its heroes, and the narrative ends with Bede's own day. Bede searched far and wide for his information, discussed the validity of his evidence, compared various sources, and exercised critical judgment. He includes accounts of miracles, but, like the stories of valiant missionaries, these are primarily related to provide moral lessons, which all medieval writers thought was the chief purpose of history.

One of the lessons that Bede sought to impart with his history is that Christianity should be unified, and one feature of the *Ecclesiastical History of the English People* inadvertently provided a powerful model for this unity. In his history, Bede adopted a way of reckoning time proposed by an earlier monk that would eventually provide a uniform chronology for all Christians. He dated events from the incarnation of Christ, rather than from the foundation of the city of Rome, as the Romans had done, or from the regnal years of kings, as the Germans did. His history was recopied by monks in many parts of Europe, who used this dating method, *anno Domini*, "in the year of the Lord" (later abbreviated A.D.), for their own histories as well. (Though Bede does talk about "before the time of the incarnation of our Lord," the reverse dating system of B.C., "before Christ," does not seem to have been widely used before 1700.) Disputes about whether the year began with the incarnation (that is, the conception) of Christ or his birth, and whether these occurred in 1 B.C. or A.D. 1 (the Christian calendar does not have a year zero), continued after Bede, but his method prevailed.

QUESTIONS FOR ANALYSIS

1. How do the career and accomplishments of Bede fit with the notion of an early medieval "renaissance" of learning?
2. Does Bede's notion that history has a moral purpose still shape the writing of history? Do you agree with him?
3. The Christian calendar dates from a midpoint rather than from a starting point, the way many of the world's calendars do. What advantages does this create in reckoning time? What would you see as the primary reason that the Christian calendar has now been widely adopted worldwide?

needing hospitality. Some female houses were, in fact, double monasteries in which the abbess governed two adjoining establishments, one for women and one for men. Monks provided protection from attack and did the heavy work on the land in double monasteries, but nuns handled everything else.

In monasteries and cathedral schools, monks, nuns, and scribes copied books and manuscripts and built up libraries. They developed the beautifully clear handwriting known as "Carolingian minuscule," with both uppercase and lowercase letters, from which modern Roman type is derived. In this era before printed books, works could survive only if they were copied. Almost all of the works of Roman authors that we are now able to read, both Christian and secular, were preserved by the efforts of Carolingian scribes. Some scholars went beyond copying to develop their own ideas, and by the middle years of the ninth century there was a great outpouring of more sophisticated original works.

The most important scholar at Charlemagne's court was Alcuin (al-KYOO-ihn), who came from Northumbria, one of the kingdoms in England. Alcuin was the leader of a palace school at Aachen, where Charlemagne assembled learned men from all over Europe. From 781 until his death, he was the emperor's chief adviser on religious and educational matters. Alcuin's letters to Charlemagne set forth political theories on the authority, power, and responsibilities of a Christian ruler.

Through monastic and cathedral schools, basic literacy in Latin was established among some of the clergy and even among some of the nobility, a change from Merovingian times. By the tenth century the patterns of thought and the lifestyles of educated western Europeans were those of Rome and Latin Christianity. Most people, however, continued to live in an oral world. They spoke local languages, which did not have a written form. Christian services continued to be conducted in Latin, but not all village priests were able to attend a school, and many simply learned the service by rote. Some Latin words and phrases gradually penetrated the various vernacular languages, but the Carolingian Renaissance did not trickle down to ordinary people.

This division between a learned culture of Latin that built on the knowledge of the ancient world and a vernacular culture of local traditions can also be seen in medicine. The foundation of a medical school at Salerno in southern Italy in the ninth century gave a tremendous impetus to medical study, and the school attracted students from all over the Mediterranean and Europe, including Christians, Jews, and Muslims. Despite the advances at Salerno, however, physicians were few in the early Middle Ages, and only the rich could afford them. Local folk medicine practiced by nonprofessionals provided help for commoners, with treatments made from herbs, bark, and other natural ingredients. Infants and children were especially susceptible to a range of illnesses, and about half of the children born died before age five. Although a few people lived into their seventies, most did not, and a forty-year-old was considered old.

Northumbrian Learning and Writing

Charlemagne's court at Aachen was not the only center of learning in early medieval Christian Europe. Another was the Anglo-Saxon kingdom of Northumbria, situated at the northernmost tip of the old Roman world in what is today northern England. Northumbrian monasteries produced scores of books: missals (used for the celebration of the Mass); psalters (SAL-tuhrs), which contained the 150 psalms and other prayers used by the monks in their devotions; commentaries on the Scriptures; illuminated manuscripts; law codes; and collections of letters and sermons. (See "Individuals in Society: The Venerable Bede," page 215.) The finest product of Northumbrian art is probably the Gospel book produced at Lindisfarne monastery around 700. The book was produced by a single scribe working steadily over a period of several years, with the expenses involved in the production of such a book—for vellum, coloring, and gold leaf—probably supplied by the monastery's aristocratic patrons.

As in Charlemagne's empire, women were important participants in Northumbrian Christian culture. Perhaps the most important abbess of the early medieval period anywhere in Europe was Saint Hilda (d. 680). A noblewoman of considerable learning and administrative ability, she ruled the double monastery of Whitby on the Northumbrian coast, advised kings and princes, and encouraged scholars and poets. Hilda played a key role in the adoption of Roman practices by Anglo-Saxon churches (see "Missionaries' Actions" in Chapter 7).

At about the time the monks at Lindisfarne were producing their Gospel book, another author was probably at work on a nonreligious epic poem, *Beowulf* (BAY-uh-woolf). The poem tells the story of the hero Beowulf's progress from valiant warrior to wise ruler. (See "Evaluating Written Evidence: The Death of Beowulf," page 217.) In contrast to most writings of this era, which were in Latin, *Beowulf* was written in Old English. The identity of its author (or authors) is unknown, and it survives only in a single copy, made about 1000 in England. The poem includes descriptions of real historical events that took place in fifth- and sixth-century Denmark and Sweden that have been confirmed by archaeological excavations. These are mixed in with legends, oral traditions, and material from

The Death of Beowulf

In the long Old English epic poem that bears his name, the hero Beowulf fights and kills the monster Grendel and then Grendel's mother. He becomes the king of the Geats, one of the Germanic groups that lived in western Sweden, and takes arms late in life against a dragon that was threatening his people. As does the entire poem, the story of this final battle sets the hero's words and actions within the context of cultural values that were shared widely across northern Europe. *Beowulf* has been translated hundreds of times into more modern English and other languages; this translation was published in 2020.

Beowulf blasted his last boast:
"I laid my life down on the daily when I was your age.
Now, gray guardian though I am, I'll show you
how it's done. I'll kill this creature if it's the last thing
   I do. . . .
Watch and see who wins—who can suffer more,
who can be worse wounded, who can survive fire.
This is my fight. I don't ask for intervention—
none of you are strong enough to take this thing,
to try to stake your manhood on doing a dragon.
I'll be the one winning the gold, my bravery
the broadest, and if not, boys, this'll be
the battle that breaks your king."
Beowulf stood tall, his iron shield upraised, armored
in his own fame, his helmet, his mail-shirt, his faith
firm only in Fate, a grit-god bearing brute weight,
beneath the rocky ledge. No trembling in his hands, but
a strong salute. He'd survived worse than this, a veteran
of foreign wars, of battle-betrayals, of heartbreak, flung
himself from cliffs over and over, surfaced singing. . . .
He worked his wrath into a roar. The main man of the
Weder-Geats bellowed into the blast zone, calling forth
   his foe. . . .

[Beowulf battles the dragon, alone at first, but then one warrior assists him. Together they kill the dragon, though Beowulf is mortally wounded in the fight.]

The old warrior's wounds wept the dragon's legacy:
Scalding spit set by poisoned fangs, seething into sepsis.
Beowulf knew he was a goner. . . .

Beowulf spoke, mortally wounded. . . .
"I've been ruling here, fearless, for fifty winters.
I was the man. No neighbor came to war—my name
kept enemies at bay, and no one could scare me. I lived
in peace, and released my lease on battle, knowing
I had nothing to prove. I wasn't ambitious, never threw
   shade
never took shit, never spat curses when I felt wronged,
but sat on the throne and weighed my people's woes
and wishes. I have to say, I did okay. Now, as I lie
dying, doomed by dragon, no one can claim I was a
   bad king.
God can't call me a murderer, for I slew none of my kin. . . .
To God, the King, Eternal Throne-Holder
I sing my thanks. . . .
My God, watch over my Geats. I'm going.
These people are your people now. Shout
my last orders—tell my army to build a barrow
before my body blazes, one like the dragon had,
high up on the coast. I want it visible, towering
like a giant's tooth on Whales' Cape, so my people
know I was king, and so seafarers say my name
daily, nightly, call out 'Beowulf's Barrow!'
as they pass in their tall ships, bound here
over wild and misty waters."
Those were the warrior's last words. He had no more
   wisdom,
no more secrets, before he consigned himself to the pyre,
the final battle-fire for a body brutally broken. Beowulf's
   soul
stepped from his breast to see what it could see.

EVALUATE THE EVIDENCE

1. Based on Beowulf's actions and words, what were the qualities of an ideal leader in the early Middle Ages?
2. How do these sections of *Beowulf* provide evidence for the assimilation of Germanic and Christian values discussed in Chapter 7? How do they provide evidence of the distinctive aspects of early medieval culture discussed in this chapter?

Source: Maria Dahvana Headley, *Beowulf: A New Translation* (New York: Farrar, Straus and Giroux, 2020), pp. 108–110, 116–118, 120–121.

the Bible; though it tells a story set in pagan Denmark and Sweden, it was written in Christian England sometime in the seventh to tenth centuries. *Beowulf* provides evidence of the close relationship between England and the northern European continent in the early Middle Ages, for the North Sea was no barrier to regular contact and cultural exchange. The movements of people and ideas that allowed a work like *Beowulf* to be written only increased in the ninth century, when the North Sea became even more of a highway.

How did the ninth-century invasions and migrations shape Europe?

Charlemagne left his vast empire to his sole surviving son, Louis the Pious (r. 814–840), who attempted to keep the empire intact. This proved to be impossible. Members of the nobility engaged in plots and open warfare against the emperor, often allying themselves with one of Louis's three sons, who were in conflict with their father and with one another. In 843, shortly after Louis's death, his sons agreed to the **Treaty of Verdun** (vehr-DUHN), which divided the empire into three parts: Charles the Bald received the western part; Lothair the middle part and the title of emperor; and Louis the eastern part, from which he acquired the title "the German." Though no one knew it at the time, this treaty set the pattern for political boundaries in Europe that has been maintained until today.

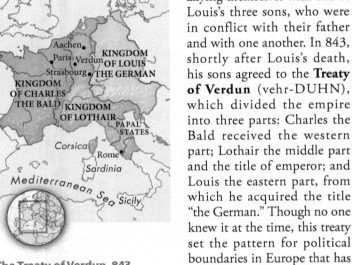

The Treaty of Verdun, 843

After the Treaty of Verdun, continental Europe was fractured politically. All three kingdoms controlled by the sons of Louis the Pious were torn by domestic dissension and disorder. The frontier and coastal defenses erected by Charlemagne and maintained by Louis the Pious were neglected. No European political power was strong enough to put up effective resistance to external attacks. Beginning around 850 three main groups invaded western Europe: Vikings from Scandinavia, representing the final wave of Germanic migrants; Muslims from the Mediterranean; and Magyars from central Europe forced westward by other peoples (Map 8.3).

Vikings in Western Europe

From the moors of Scotland to the mountains of Sicily, there arose in the ninth century the prayer,

"Save us, O God, from the fury of the Northmen." The feared Northmen were Germanic peoples from the area of modern-day Norway, Sweden, and Denmark who originally lived by farming and fishing. They began to make overseas expeditions, which they themselves called *vikings*, a word that probably derives from a unit of maritime distance. *Viking* came to be used both for the activity ("to go a-viking") and for the people who went on such expeditions. Propelled either by oars or by sails, deckless, and about sixty-five feet long, a Viking ship could carry between forty and sixty men — enough to harass an isolated monastery or village. These ships, navigated by experienced and fearless sailors, moved through complicated rivers, estuaries, and waterways in Europe. Their targets were initially often isolated monasteries, as these had gold, silver, and other goods that could be easily plundered, but later the Vikings turned to more substantial targets. The Carolingian Empire, with no navy, was helpless. The Vikings moved swiftly, attacked, and escaped to return again.

Scholars disagree about the reasons for Viking attacks and migrations. A very unstable Danish kingship and disputes over the succession had led to civil war and disorder, which may have driven warriors abroad in search of booty and supporters. The population of Scandinavia may have grown too large for the available land to support, and cities on the coasts of northern Europe offered targets for plunder. Goods plundered could then be sold, and looting raids turned into trading ventures. Some scholars assert that the Vikings were looking for trade and new commercial contacts from the beginning. (See "Thinking Like a Historian: Vikings Tell Their Own Story," page 220.)

Whatever the motivations, Vikings burned, looted, and did extensive property damage, although there is little evidence that they caused long-term physical destruction — perhaps because, arriving in small bands, they lacked the manpower to do so. They seized nobles and high churchmen and held them for ransom; they also demanded tribute from kings. In the Seine and Loire Valleys the frequent presence of Viking war bands seems to have had economic consequences, stimulating the production of food and wine

■ **Treaty of Verdun** Treaty signed in 843 by Charlemagne's grandsons dividing the Carolingian Empire into three parts and setting the pattern for political boundaries in Europe still in use today.

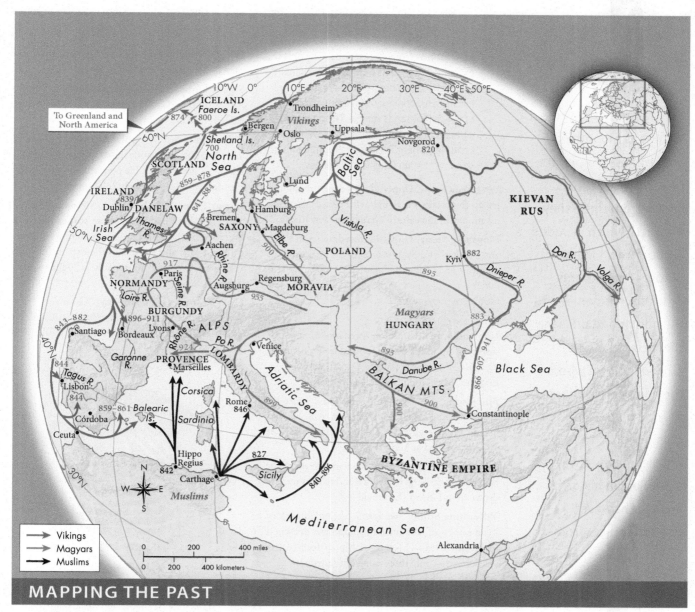

MAP 8.3 Invasions and Migrations of the Ninth and Tenth Centuries

This map shows the Viking, Magyar, and Arab invasions and migrations in the ninth and tenth centuries. Compare it with Map 7.3 (page 187) on the barbarian migrations of late antiquity to answer the following questions.

ANALYZING THE MAP What similarities do you see in the patterns of migration in these two periods? What significant differences?

CONNECTIONS How did the Vikings' expertise in shipbuilding and sailing make their migrations different from those of earlier Germanic tribes? How did this expertise set them apart from the Magyar and Muslim invaders of the ninth century?

Vikings Tell Their Own Story

The traditional view of Vikings as bloodthirsty and ruthless marauders driven by fury comes largely from those they attacked, which included Europe's most literate group — monks and other churchmen — and the nobles and officials the Vikings held for ransom or from whom they demanded tribute. Relying on the views of outsiders, particularly hostile ones, is always a problem in historical analysis, however. How do sources from Scandinavians themselves in this era portray Viking actions, motivations, and values?

1 **Inscriptions from runestones.** The only existing written texts from Scandinavians themselves from before 1050 are runic inscriptions, primarily on memorial stones, of which thousands survive. The ones below come from the tenth and early eleventh centuries, when Christianity was spreading, so some contain Christian references.

Veda Stone, Uppland, Sweden: "Irenmuder set up this stone. He bought this estate and made his money in the east, in Gardar [eastern Russia]."

Lingsberg Stone, Uppland, Sweden: "And Danr and Húskarl and Sveinn had the stone erected in memory of Ulfríkr, their father's father. He had taken two payments in England. May God and God's mother help the souls of the father and son."

Uppland Stone, Uppland, Sweden: "Áli had this stone put up in his own honour. He took Knútr's *danegeld* [the tribute paid to Danish invaders] in England. May God help his soul!"

Fjuckby Stone, Uppland, Sweden: "Liótr set up this stone in memory of his son, Áki. He was master of a freighter, docking in the harbors of Greece. He died at home."

Ada Stone, Sweden: "Hermóðr had (the rock) cut in memory of Bergviðr/Barkviðr, his brother. He drowned in Lífland [Livonia]."

Vallentuna Stone, Sweden: ". . . and Ingibjörg in memory of her husbandman. He drowned in Holmr's sea — his cargo-ship drifted to the sea-bottom — only three came out (alive)."

Gripsholm Stone, Södermanland, Sweden: "Tola set up this stone in memory of her son Haraldt, Ingvarr's brother. Like men they went far to seek gold, and in the east they fed the eagle. Died south, in Serkland ['Saracen land,' or Muslim territory]."

Uppland Stone 1011, Uppland, Sweden: "Vigmund had this stone carved in memory of himself, the cleverest of men. May God help the soul of Vigmund, the ship captain. Vigmund and Åfrid carved this memorial while he lived."

Sigurd Stone, Södermanland, Sweden: "Sigrid, Alrik's mother, Orm's daughter made this bridge for her husband Holmgers, father of Sigoerd."

Odenslunda Stone, Uppland, Sweden: "Véketill and Ôzurr had this stone raised in memory of Eysteinn, . . . good father. He perished abroad with all the seamen. May God help (his) spirit."

Ingvar Stone 778, Uppland, Sweden: "Thjalfi and Holmlaug had all of these stones raised in memory of Banki/Baggi, their son, who alone owned a ship and steered to the east in Ingvarr's retinue. May God help Banki's/Baggi's spirit. Áskell carved."

Dynna Stone, Gran, Norway: "Gunnvor, Thrydrik's daughter, made a bridge in memory of her daughter, Ástrídr. She was the most skillful girl in Hadeland."

2 **Silver coin.** This silver coin, minted in Hedeby in Denmark, was unearthed at Birka, an archaeological site on an island in Lake Mälaren in eastern Sweden, which in Viking times was a trading center handling goods from as far away as Byzantium and the Abbasid caliphate. (De Agostini Picture Library/ Getty Images)

ANALYZING THE EVIDENCE

1. What activities do the runic inscriptions in Source 1 highlight? What personal qualities do they praise? What do they say about people's motivations for what they undertake?
2. How are the activities and qualities described in Source 1 reflected in the scenes shown in Sources 2–5?
3. What information do the runic inscriptions in Source 1 provide about relations among family members?
4. What do the written and visual sources suggest about gender roles in Viking society?
5. Why would memorial inscriptions and burials be good sources for studying social values? For what aspects of life would they *not* be good sources?

4 **Carving from the side of the Oseberg cart.** The Oseberg ship burial (see the photo in "Slavs and Vikings in Eastern Europe"), from early ninth-century Norway, contains a decoratively carved wooden cart, one side of which shows a woman with streaming hair apparently restraining a man striking at a horseman with his sword.

(Werner Forman/Universal Images Group/Getty Images)

3 **Memorial stone.** This memorial stone from Gotland, Sweden, carved and erected in the eighth century, shows scenes common on early Viking memorial stones, with a mounted warrior carrying a shield above, and a ship below. (Ancient Art and Architecture Collection Ltd./Bridgeman Images)

(Bridgeman Images)

5 **Tapestry found with the Oseberg ship.** A tapestry fragment found with the Oseberg ship shows animals pulling carts; other tapestry fragments show groves of trees, battle scenes, women riding horses, houses with dragons on their gables, and ships.

PUTTING IT ALL TOGETHER

Using the sources above, along with what you have learned in class and in this chapter, write a short essay that assesses the traditional view of the Vikings. How do sources from Scandinavians themselves in this era portray Viking actions, motivations, and values? What judgments of outsiders are supported, and which are refuted, in sources from insiders?

Source: (1) English translations from R. I. Paige, *Runes: Reading the Past* (Berkeley: University of California Press, 1987), pp. 46–51.

and possibly the manufacture (for sale) of weapons and the breeding of horses.

The slave trade represented an important part of Viking plunder and commerce. As in other Germanic groups, Viking society was divided into free and unfree persons, the latter known as *thralls*. Thralls' status was the result of capture, debt, or being born to thrall parents. Within Scandinavia, thralls could be bought and sold, and Vikings also took people from the British Isles and territories along the Baltic Sea as part of their booty and sold them in the markets of Magdeburg and Regensburg, at the fairs of Lyons, and in seaports of the Muslim world. Dublin became a center of the Viking slave trade, with hundreds and sometimes thousands of young men and women bought and sold there in any one year.

In 911 Danish Vikings besieged Paris with fleets of more than a hundred highly maneuverable ships, and the Frankish king Charles the Simple bought them off by giving them a large part of northern France. There the Vikings established the province of "Northmanland," or Normandy as it was later known, intermarrying with the local population and creating a distinctive Norman culture. From there they sailed around Spain and into the Mediterranean, eventually seizing Sicily from the Muslim Arabs in 1060–1090, while other Normans crossed the English Channel, defeating Anglo-Saxon forces in 1066. Between 850 and 1000 Viking control of northern Europe reached its zenith. Norwegian Vikings moved farther west than any Europeans had before, establishing permanent settlements on Iceland and short-lived settlements in Greenland and Newfoundland in what is now Canada.

The Vikings made positive contributions to the areas they settled. They carried their unrivaled knowledge of shipbuilding and seamanship everywhere. The northeastern and central parts of England where the Vikings settled became known as the *Danelaw* because Danish, not English, laws and customs prevailed there. Scholars believe that some legal institutions, such as the ancestor of the modern grand jury, originated in the Danelaw. Exports from Ireland included iron tools and weapons manufactured there by Viking metal-smiths.

Slavs and Vikings in Eastern Europe

Vikings also brought change in eastern Europe, which was largely populated by Slavs. In antiquity the Slavs lived in central Europe, farming with iron technology, building fortified towns, and worshipping a variety of deities. With the start of the mass migrations of the late Roman Empire, the Slavs moved in different directions and split into what historians later identified as three groups: West, South, and East Slavs.

The group labeled the West Slavs included the Poles, Czechs, Slovaks, and Wends. The South Slavs, comprising peoples who became the Serbs, Croats, Slovenes, Macedonians, and Bosnians, migrated southward into the Balkans. In the seventh century Slavic peoples of the west and south created the state of Moravia along the banks of the Danube River. By the tenth century Moravia's residents were Roman Christian, along with most of the other West and South Slavs. The pattern of conversion was similar to that of the Germanic tribes: first the ruler was baptized, and then missionaries

Oseberg Ship This well-preserved and elaborately decorated Viking ship, discovered in a large burial mound in southern Norway, could be powered by sail or oars. Boatbuilders recently constructed a full-scale replica using traditional building methods and materials, and sailed it on the open ocean in 2014, reaching a speed of ten knots. The burial mound contained the skeletons of two older women, one wearing a dress made of fine wool and silk, along with a cart, several sleighs, horses, dogs, and many artifacts, suggesting that this was the grave of a powerful and prominent woman, though her identity is unknown.
(Werner Forman Archive/Bridgeman Images)

preached, built churches, and spread Christian teachings among the common people. The ruler of Poland was able to convince the pope to establish an independent archbishopric there in 1000, the beginning of a long-lasting connection between Poland and the Roman Church. In the Balkans the Serbs accepted Orthodox Christianity, while the Croats became Roman Christian, a division with a long-standing impact. This religious division was one of the factors in the civil war that split the large country of Yugoslavia into a number of smaller states in the late twentieth century.

Between the fifth and ninth centuries the eastern Slavs moved into present-day European Russia and Ukraine. This enormous area consisted of an immense virgin forest to the north, where most of the eastern Slavs settled, and an endless prairie grassland to the south. In the tenth century Ibrahim Ibn Jakob, a learned Jew from the Muslim caliphate in Córdoba in Spain, traveled in Slavic areas. He found the Slavs to be "violent and inclined to aggression," but far cleaner than Christians in other parts of Europe in which he had traveled, "who wash only once or twice a year." Such filthy habits were unacceptable to someone raised in Muslim Spain, but the Slavs had an ingenious way of both getting clean and staying healthy: "They have no bathhouses as such, but they do make use of wooden huts [for bathing]. They build a stone stove, on which, when it is heated, they pour water. . . . They hold a bunch of grass in their hands, and waft the steam around. Then their pores open, and all excess matter escapes from their bodies."[3]

In the ninth century the Vikings appeared in the lands of the eastern Slavs. Called "Varangians" in the old Russian chronicles, the Vikings were interested primarily in gaining wealth through plunder and trade, and the opportunities were good. Moving up and down the rivers, they soon linked Scandinavia and northern Europe to the Black Sea and to the Byzantine Empire's capital at Constantinople. They raided and looted the cities along the Caspian Sea several times in the tenth century, taking booty and people, whom they then sold elsewhere. But raiding turned into trading, and the Scandinavians later established settlements, intermarried, and assimilated with Slavic peoples.

To increase and protect their international commerce and growing wealth, the Vikings declared themselves the rulers of the eastern Slavs. According to tradition, the semi-legendary chieftain Ruirik founded

Kievan Rus, ca. 1050

- ▢ Area settled by Varangians, ca. 880
- ▢ Kievan Rus, 1054

a princely dynasty about 860. In any event, the Varangian ruler Oleg (r. 878–912) established his residence at Kyiv in modern-day Ukraine. He and his successors ruled over a loosely united confederation of Slavic territories known as Rus, with its capital at Kyiv, until 1054. (The word *Russia* comes from *Rus*.)

Oleg and his clansmen quickly became assimilated into the Slavic population, taking local wives and emerging as the noble class. Missionaries of the Byzantine Empire converted the Vikings and local Slavs to Eastern Orthodox Christianity, accelerating the unification of the two groups. Thus the rapidly Slavified Vikings left two important legacies for the future: in about 900 they created a loose unification of Slavic territories, **Kievan Rus**, under a single ruling prince and dynasty, and they imposed a basic religious unity by accepting Orthodox Christianity, as opposed to Roman Catholicism, for themselves and the eastern Slavs.

Even at its height under Great Prince Iaroslav (YAHR-uh-slahv) the Wise (r. 1019–1054), the unity of Kievan Rus was extremely tenuous. Trade, not government, was the main concern of the rulers. Moreover, the Slavified Vikings failed to find a way to peacefully transfer power from one generation to the next. In early Rus there were apparently no fixed rules, and much strife accompanied each succession. Possibly to avoid such chaos, Great Prince Iaroslav, before his death in 1054, divided Kievan Rus among his five sons, who in turn divided their properties when they died. Between 1054 and 1237, Kievan Rus disintegrated into more and more competing units, each ruled by a prince claiming to be a descendant of Ruirik. The princes divided their land like private property because they thought of it as private property. A prince owned a certain number of farms or landed estates, farmed primarily by enslaved workers, called *kholops* in Russian. Outside of these estates, which constituted the princely domain, the prince exercised only limited authority in his principality.

Excluding the clergy, two kinds of people lived on these estates: the noble boyars and the commoner peasants. The **boyars** were descendants of the original Viking warriors, and they also held their lands as free and clear private property. The boyars normally fought

---

- ■ **Kievan Rus** A confederation of Slavic territories, with its capital at Kyiv, ruled by descendants of the Vikings.

- ■ **boyars** High-ranking nobles in Russia who were descendants of Viking warriors and held their lands as free and clear private property.

in princely armies, and the customary law declared that they could serve any prince they wished. Ordinary peasants could also move at will if they thought that opportunities would be greater elsewhere. In short, fragmented princely power, private property, and personal freedom all went hand in hand.

Magyars and Muslims

Groups of central European steppe peoples known as Magyars also raided villages in the late ninth century, taking plunder and captives and forcing leaders to pay tribute in an effort to prevent further looting and destruction. Moving westward, small bands of Magyars on horseback reached as far as Spain and the Atlantic coast. They subdued northern Italy, compelled Bavaria and Saxony to pay tribute, and even penetrated into the Rhineland and Burgundy (see Map 8.3). Because of their skill with horses and their Eastern origins, the Magyars were often identified with the earlier Huns by those they conquered, though they are probably unrelated ethnically. This identification, however, may be the origin of the word *Hungarian*.

Magyar forces were defeated by a combined army of Frankish and other Germanic troops at the Battle of Lechfeld near Augsburg in southern Germany in 955, and the Magyars settled in the area that is now Hungary in eastern Europe. Much as Clovis had centuries earlier, the Magyar ruler Géza (GEE-zuh) (r. 970–997), who had been a pagan, became a Roman Christian. This conversion gave him the support of the papacy and offered prospects for alliances with other Roman Christian rulers against the Byzantine Empire, Hungary's southern neighbor. Géza's son Stephen I (r. 997–1038) was officially crowned the king of Hungary by a papal representative on Christmas Day of 1000. He supported the building of churches and monasteries, increased royal power, and encouraged the use of Latin and the Roman alphabet. Hungary's alliance with the papacy shaped the later history of eastern Europe just as

Charlemagne's alliance with the papacy shaped western European history. The Hungarians adopted settled agriculture, wrote law codes, and built towns, and Hungary became an important crossroads of trade for German and Muslim merchants.

The ninth century also saw Muslim invasions into Europe from the south. In many ways these were a continuation of the earlier conquests in the Iberian Peninsula, but now they focused on Sicily and mainland Italy. Muslims sacked Rome in 846 and captured towns along the Adriatic coast almost all the way to Venice. In the tenth century Frankish, papal, and Byzantine forces were able to retake much territory, though the Muslims continued to hold Sicily. Under their rule, agricultural innovations from elsewhere in the Muslim world led to new crops such as cotton and sugar, and fortified cities became centers of Muslim learning. Disputes among the Muslim rulers on the island led one faction to ask the Normans for assistance, and between 1060 and 1090 the Normans gradually conquered all of Sicily.

What was the impact of these invasions? From the perspective of those living in what had been Charlemagne's empire, Viking, Magyar, and Muslim attacks contributed to increasing disorder and violence. Italian, French, and English sources often describe this period as one of terror and chaos: "Save us, O God, from the fury of the Northmen." People in other parts of Europe might have had a different opinion, however. In Muslim Spain scholars worked in thriving cities, and new crops such as rice enhanced ordinary people's lives. In eastern Europe, states such as Moravia and Hungary became strong kingdoms. A Viking point of view might be the most positive, for by 1100 descendants of the Vikings not only ruled their homelands in Denmark, Norway, and Sweden but also ruled Normandy, England, Sicily, Iceland, and Kievan Rus, with an outpost in Greenland and occasional voyages to North America.

How and why did Europe become politically and economically decentralized in this period?

The large-scale division of Charlemagne's empire into three parts in the ninth century led to a decentralization of power at the local level. Civil wars weakened the power and prestige of kings, who could do little about domestic violence. The great invasions, especially those of the Vikings, also weakened royal authority. The western Frankish kings were unable to halt the invaders, and the local

aristocracy had to assume responsibility for defense. Thus, in the ninth and tenth centuries great aristocratic families increased their authority in the regions of their vested interests. They lived in private castles for defense, and they governed virtually independent territories in which distant and weak kings could not interfere. Common people turned for protection to the strongest power, the local counts, whom they considered their rightful rulers, and free peasants sank to the level of serfs.

Decentralization and the Origins of "Feudalism"

The political power of the Carolingian rulers had long rested on the cooperation of the dominant social class, the Frankish aristocracy. Charlemagne and his predecessors relied on the nobles to help wage wars of expansion and suppress rebellions, and in return these families were given a share of the lands and riches confiscated by the rulers. The most powerful nobles were those able to gain the allegiance of warriors, often symbolized in an oath-swearing ceremony in which a warrior (knight) swore his loyalty as a **vassal** — from a Celtic term meaning "servant" — to the more powerful individual, who became his lord. In return for the vassal's loyalty, aid, and military assistance, the lord promised him protection and material support. This support might be a place in the lord's household, but was more likely a piece of land called a *feudum* or **fief** (feef). In the Roman Empire soldiers had been paid for their services with money, but in the cash-poor early Middle Ages their reward was instead a piece of land. Most legal scholars and historians have seen these personal ties of loyalty cemented by grants of land rather than allegiance to an abstract state as a political and social system they term **feudalism**. They have traced its spread from Frankish areas to other parts of Europe.

In the last several decades, increasing numbers of medieval historians have found the idea of a "feudal system" problematic. They note that the word *feudalism* was a later invention and that vassalage ceremonies, military obligations, and the ownership rights attached to fiefs differed widely from place to place and changed considerably in form and pattern over time. Thus, to these historians, "feudalism" is so varied that it doesn't really have a clear meaning, and it would be better not to use the term at all. The problem is that no one has come up with a better term for the loose arrangements of personal and property ties that developed among elites in the ninth century.

Whether one chooses to use the word *feudalism* or not, these relationships provided some degree of cohesiveness in a society that lacked an adequate government bureaucracy or method of taxation. In fact, because vassals owed administrative as well as military service to their lords, vassalage actually functioned as a way to organize political authority. Vassals were expected to serve as advisers to their lord and also to pay him fees for important family events, such as the marriage of the vassal's children.

Along with granting land to knights, lords gave land to the clergy for spiritual services or promises of allegiance. In addition, the church held its own lands, and bishops, archbishops, and abbots and abbesses of monasteries sometimes granted fiefs to their own knightly vassals. Thus the "lord" in a feudal relationship was sometimes an institution. Women other than abbesses were generally not granted fiefs, but in most parts of Europe daughters could inherit them if their fathers had no sons. Occasionally, women did go through ceremonies swearing homage and fealty and swore to send fighters when the lord demanded them. More commonly, women acted as surrogates when their husbands were away, defending the territory from attack and carrying out administrative duties.

Manorialism, Serfdom, and the Slave Trade

In feudal relationships, the "lord" was the individual or institution that had authority over a vassal, but the word *lord* was also used to describe the person or institution that had economic and political authority over peasants who lived in villages and farmed the land. Thus a vassal in one relationship was a slightly different type of lord in another. Most European people in the early Middle Ages were peasants who lived in family groups in villages or small towns and made their living predominantly by raising crops and animals. The village and the land surrounding it were called a manor, from the Latin word for "dwelling" or "homestead." Some fiefs might include only one manor, while great lords or kings might have hundreds of manors under their direct control. Residents of manors worked for the lord in exchange for protection, a system that was later referred to as **manorialism**. Free peasants surrendered themselves and their lands to the lord's jurisdiction. The land was given back, but the peasants became tied to it by various kinds of payments and services. Thus, like vassalage, manorialism involved an exchange. Because the economic power of the warring class rested on landed estates worked by peasants, feudalism and manorialism were linked, but they were not the same system.

■ **vassal** A warrior who swore loyalty and service to a noble in exchange for land, protection, and support.

■ **fief** A piece of land granted by a feudal lord to a vassal in return for service and loyalty.

■ **feudalism** A term devised by later scholars to describe the political system in which a vassal was generally given a piece of land in return for his loyalty.

■ **manorialism** A system in which peasant residents of manors, or farming villages, provided work and goods for their lord in exchange for protection.

Selling a Goose   In this illustration from an eleventh-century manuscript copy of the Carolingian bishop and scholar Rabanus Maurus's (ca. 780–856) encyclopedic *De universo*, a man sells another a goose. Despite the rise of serfdom, small-scale trade continued on many manors, often by barter, though here one of the men appears to be holding a coin. (Gianni Dagli Orti/Shutterstock)

Local custom determined precisely what services villagers would provide to their lord, but certain practices became common throughout Europe. The peasant was obliged to give the lord a percentage of the annual harvest, usually in produce, sometimes in cash. The peasant paid a fee to marry someone from outside the lord's estate. To inherit property, the peasant paid a fine, often the best beast the person owned. Above all, the peasant became part of the lord's permanent labor force. With vast stretches of uncultivated virgin land and a tiny labor population, manorial lords encouraged population growth and immigration. The most profitable form of capital was not land but laborers.

In entering into a relationship with a manorial lord, free farmers lost status. Their position became servile,

and they became **serfs**. That is, they were bound to the land and could not leave it without the lord's permission. Serfdom was not the same as slavery in that lords did not own the person of the serf, but serfs were subject to the jurisdiction of the lord's court in any dispute over property and in any case of suspected criminal behavior.

The transition from freedom to serfdom was slow. In the late eighth century there were still many free peasants. And within the legal category of serfdom there were many economic levels, ranging from the highly prosperous to the desperately poor. Nevertheless, a social and legal revolution was taking place. By the year 800 perhaps 60 percent of the population of western Europe—completely free a century before—had been reduced to serfdom. The ninth-century Viking assaults on Europe created extremely unstable conditions and individual insecurity, increasing the need for protection, accelerating the transition to serfdom, and leading to additional loss of personal freedom.

Though serfdom was not slavery, the Carolingian slave trade was extensive, generally involving persons captured in war or raids. Merchants in early medieval towns paid the suppliers of the luxury goods their noble and clerical customers desired with enslaved persons, most of which came into Europe from the East. The Muslim conquest of Spain produced thousands of enslaved captives, as did Charlemagne's long wars and the Viking raids. When Frankish conquests declined in the tenth century, German and Viking merchants bought and captured people on the empire's eastern border who spoke Slavic languages. Slavs were so numerous among those captured and enslaved, in fact, that the English word *slave* comes from the medieval Latin word for Slavs. Prices were often higher in Muslim lands, so Christian slave traders sold them there. Christian moralists sometimes complained about the sale of Christians to non-Christians, but they did not object to slavery itself.

NOTES

1. Quoted in R. McKitterick, *The Frankish Kingdoms Under the Carolingians, 751–987* (New York: Longman, 1983), p. 77.
2. Quoted in B. D. Hill, ed., *Church and State in the Middle Ages* (New York: John Wiley & Sons, 1970), pp. 46–47.
3. From Charles Melville and Ahmad Ubaydli, eds. and trans., *Christians and Moors in Spain*, vol. 3 (New York: Oxbow Books, 1992), p. 54.

■ **serfs** Peasants bound to the land by a relationship with a manorial lord.

LOOKING BACK LOOKING AHEAD

The culture that emerged in Europe in the early Middle Ages has justifiably been called the first "European" civilization. While it was by no means "civilized" by modern standards, it had definite characteristics that were shared across a wide region. Other than in Muslim Spain and the pagan areas of northern and eastern Europe, almost all people were baptized Christians. Everywhere—including Muslim and pagan areas—most people lived in small villages, supporting themselves and paying their obligations to their superiors by raising crops and animals. These villages were on pieces of land increasingly granted to knights in exchange for loyalty and service to a noble lord. The educated elite was infused with Latin ideas and models, for Latin was the common language—written as well as spoken—of educated people in most of Europe.

In the several centuries after 1000, these characteristics—Christianity, village-based agriculture, vassalage, and Latin culture—would not disappear. Historians conventionally term the era from 1000 to about 1300 the High Middle Ages, but this era built on a foundation that had already been established. The soaring Gothic cathedrals that were the most glorious architectural feature of the High Middle Ages were often constructed on the footings of early medieval churches, and their walls were built of stones that had once been part of Carolingian walls and castles. Similarly, political structures grew out of the institutions established in the Carolingian period, and later literary and cultural flowerings followed the model of the Carolingian Renaissance in looking to the classical past. Less positive developments also had their roots in the early Middle Ages, including hostilities between Christians and Muslims that would motivate the Crusades, as well as the continued expansion of serfdom and other forms of unfree labor.

Make Connections

Think about the larger developments and continuities within and across chapters.

1. In both Christianity and Islam, political leaders played an important role in the expansion of the faith into new territory. How would you compare the actions of Constantine and Clovis (both in Chapter 7) with those of the Muslim leaders and Charlemagne (in this chapter) in promoting, extending, and establishing their chosen religion?

2. Charlemagne considered himself to be the reviver of the Roman Empire. Thinking about Roman and Carolingian government and society, do you believe this is an accurate self-description? Why or why not?

3. How were the ninth-century migrations and invasions of the Vikings, Magyars, and Muslims similar to the earlier barbarian migrations discussed in Chapter 7? How were they different?

8 REVIEW & EXPLORE

Identify Key Terms

Identify and explain the significance of each item below.

Qur'an (p. 202)

Five Pillars of Islam (p. 204)

caliph (p. 205)

al-Andalus (p. 206)

infidel (p. 208)

civitas (p. 209)

comites (p. 209)

Treaty of Verdun (p. 218)

Kievan Rus (p. 223)

boyars (p. 223)

vassal (p. 225)

fief (p. 225)

feudalism (p. 225)

manorialism (p. 225)

serfs (p. 226)

Review the Main Ideas

Answer the section heading questions from the chapter.

1. What were the origins of Islam, and what impact did it have on Europe as it spread? (p. 202)

2. How did the Franks build and govern a European empire? (p. 209)

3. What were the significant intellectual and cultural developments in Charlemagne's era? (p. 214)

4. How did the ninth-century invasions and migrations shape Europe? (p. 218)

5. How and why did Europe become politically and economically decentralized in this period? (p. 224)

Suggested Resources

BOOKS

- Barbero, Allesandro. *Charlemagne: Father of a Continent*. 2004. A wonderful biography of Charlemagne and study of the times in which he lived that argues for the complexity of his legacy.

- Barford, P. M. *The Early Slavs: Culture and Society in Early Medieval Eastern Europe*. 2001. An excellent survey of developments in much of eastern Europe.

- Bitel, Lisa. *Women in Early Medieval Europe, 400–1100*. 2002. Uses literary works and archaeological evidence as well as more traditional sources to trace all aspects of women's lives: social, intellectual, political, and economic.

- Donner, Fred M. *Muhammad and the Believers: At the Origins of Islam*. 2010. Examines the relationship between Jews, Christians, and Muslims in the early history of Islam.

- Esposito, John L. *Islam: The Straight Path*, 5th ed. 2016. An informed and balanced work on Islam based on the best modern scholarship and original sources, designed for students.

- Heather, Peter. *Empires and Barbarians: The Fall of Rome and the Birth of Europe*. 2010. Evaluates the dynamics of migration and the social, economic, and ethnic interactions that created Europe.

- McKitterick, Rosamond. *Charlemagne: The Formation of a European Identity*. 2008. Analyzes Charlemagne's understanding of his role and methods of rule.

- Reynolds, Susan. *Fiefs and Vassals: The Medieval Evidence Reconsidered*. 1996. A comprehensive challenge to traditional conceptions of feudalism, the fief, and vassalage that has led to a rethinking of medieval political relationships.

- Riche, Pierre. *Daily Life in the World of Charlemagne.* Trans. JoAnn McNamara. 1988. A detailed study of many facets of Carolingian society.

- Verhulst, Adriaan. *The Carolingian Economy.* 2002. A brief survey, designed for students, of all aspects of the Carolingian economy, including agrarian production, crafts, and commerce.

- Watt, W. Montgomery, and Pierre Cachea. *A History of Islamic Spain.* 2007. A succinct analysis of Islam's influence on Spain.

- Wells, Peter S. *Barbarians to Angels: The Dark Ages Reconsidered.* 2008. Uses archaeological evidence to examine continuities in social and cultural life during the early Middle Ages.

- Wickham, Chris. *Framing the Early Middle Ages: Europe and the Mediterranean, 400–800.* 2007. A massive, yet accessible, survey of economic and social changes in many regions, with great attention to ordinary people.

- Winroth, Anders. *The Age of the Vikings.* 2014. Insightful look at all aspects of Viking society: raiding, trade, religion, art, poetry, and life at home in early medieval Scandinavia.

MEDIA

- *Beowulf and Grendel* (Sturla Gunnarsson, 2005). A feature-film version of the *Beowulf* story with some new plot elements; loaded with violence and shot in the bleak landscape of Iceland.

- *Cities of Light: The Rise and Fall of Islamic Spain* (PBS, 2007). A documentary focusing on the culture of pluralism in tenth-century Muslim Spain, especially in the city of Córdoba, and its collapse because of internal and external forces. With an accompanying website at **www.islamicspain.tv**.

- *The Dark Ages* (History Channel, 2007). A blood-and-gore-filled documentary of the violence and instability of the early Middle Ages that also looks at Charlemagne and others as heroic creators of new institutions.

- *Internet Medieval Sourcebook.* The definitive online location for primary sources from the Middle Ages. Most of the texts are in English and are organized chronologically and thematically. **www.fordham.edu/halsall/sbook.html**

- *The Labyrinth: Resources for Medieval Studies.* Run by Georgetown University, this website provides free access to electronic resources in medieval studies, which are organized thematically. **labyrinth.georgetown.edu**

- *The Vikings* (*Nova*, 2000). A two-hour special that presents the Vikings as merchants, shipbuilders, artisans, and colonizers and that re-creates Viking voyages in the Atlantic and eastern Europe using replicas of their ships.

9

State and Church in the High Middle Ages

1000–1300

The concept of the state had been one of Rome's great legacies to Western civilization, but for almost five hundred years after the disintegration of the Roman Empire in the West, the state did not exist. Political authority was decentralized, with power spread among many lords, bishops, abbots, and other types of local rulers. The deeply fragmented political units that covered the early medieval European continent did not have the characteristics or provide the services of a modern state.

Beginning in the last half of the tenth century, the invasions and migrations that had contributed to European fragmentation gradually ended, and domestic disorder slowly subsided. Rulers began to develop new institutions of law and government that enabled them to assert their power over lesser lords and the general population. Although nobles remained the dominant class, centralized states slowly crystallized, first in western Europe, and then in eastern and northern Europe. At the same time, energetic popes built their power within the Western Christian Church and tried to assert their superiority over kings and emperors. Monks, nuns, and friars played significant roles in medieval society, both as individuals and as members of institutions. A papal call to retake the holy city of Jerusalem led to nearly two centuries of warfare between Christians and Muslims. Christian warriors, clergy, and settlers moved out from western and central Europe in all directions, so that through conquest and colonization border regions were gradually incorporated into a more uniform Christian realm. ■

ANT·ARMAS· ADNAVES· ETSIC
TRAHVNT: CARRVM
CVMVINO:ETARM IS:

CHAPTER PREVIEW

- How did monarchs try to centralize political power?

- How did the administration of law evolve in this period?

- What were the political and social roles of nobles?

- How did the papacy reform the church, and what were the reactions to these efforts?

- What roles did monks, nuns, and friars play in medieval society?

- What were the causes, course, and consequences of the Crusades and the broader expansion of Christianity?

Hauling Supplies for Battle
In this detail from the Bayeux tapestry, men pull a cart loaded with wine, helmets, and spears to the ships with which Duke William of Normandy crossed the English Channel in his invasion of England in 1066. Medieval chronicles, songs, and stories focus on the heroic glories of battle, but logistics and supply were just as important to a medieval army as they are today. Now on display in Bayeux, France, the Bayeux tapestry is actually not a tapestry, but an embroidery panel measuring 231 feet by 19 inches that records the entire conquest. (funkyfood London — Paul Williams/Alamy Stock Photo)

How did monarchs try to centralize political power?

Beginning in the eleventh century, rulers in some parts of Europe began to manipulate existing institutions to build up their power, becoming kings over growing and slowly centralizing states. As rulers expanded their territories and extended their authority, they developed larger bureaucracies, armies, judicial systems, and other institutions to maintain control and ensure order. Because these institutions cost money, rulers also initiated systems for generating revenue and handling financial matters. Some rulers were more successful than others, and the solutions they found to these problems laid the foundations for modern national states.

England

Throughout the ninth century the Vikings had made a concerted effort to conquer and rule all of Anglo-Saxon England. In 878 Alfred, king of the West Saxons (or Wessex), one of several kingdoms in England, defeated the Vikings, inaugurating a period of recovery and stability in England. Alfred and his immediate successors built a system of local defenses and slowly extended royal rule beyond Wessex to other Anglo-Saxon peoples until one law — royal law — took precedence over local custom. England was divided into local units called shires, or counties, each under the jurisdiction of a shire-reeve (a word that soon evolved into *sheriff*) appointed by the king. Sheriffs were unpaid officials from well-off families who were responsible for collecting taxes, catching and trying criminals, and raising infantry when the king required it.

The Viking invasions of England resumed, however, and the island eventually came under Viking rule. The Viking Canute (r. 1016–1035) made England the center of his empire while promoting a policy of assimilation and reconciliation between Anglo-Saxons and Vikings. When Canute died, his son Harthacnut struggled to maintain this empire, and at his sudden death in 1042 it was broken up, with separate rulers in Denmark, Norway, and England, though all were related by blood or marriage to one another, as was common for medieval rulers. England was ruled by Edward the Confessor (r. 1042–1066), who was in the Wessex dynasty and was also Harthacnut's half brother; they had the same mother, Emma of Normandy, who played an important political role in the reigns of both her sons. Succession troubles continued when Edward died childless, and three claimants to the throne of England arose — the Anglo-Saxon noble Harold Godwinson (ca. 1022–1066), who had been crowned by English nobles; the Norwegian king Harald III (r. 1045–1066), the grandson of Canute;

and Duke William of Normandy, the illegitimate son of Edward's cousin.

In 1066 the forces of Harold Godwinson crushed Harald's invading army in northern England, then quickly marched south when they heard that William had invaded England with his Norman vassals. Harold was decisively defeated by William at the Battle of Hastings — an event now known as the Norman Conquest. In both England and Normandy, William (now called William the Conqueror) limited the power of the nobles and church officials and built a unified monarchy. In England he retained the office of sheriffs but named Normans to the posts. To determine how much wealth there was in his new kingdom and who held what land, he sent royal officials to every part of the country, and in every village local men were put under oath to answer the questions of these officials. In the words of a contemporary chronicler:

> So very narrowly did he have it investigated, that there was no single hide [a hide was a measure of land large enough to support one family], nor yard of land, nor indeed . . . one ox nor one cow nor one pig was there left out, and not put down in his record: and all these records were brought to him afterwards.[1]

The resulting record, called the **Domesday Book** (DOOMZ-day) from the Anglo-Saxon word *doom*, meaning "judgment," helped William and his descendants tax land appropriately. The book still survives and is an invaluable source of social and economic information about medieval England. It also helped William and future English kings regard their country as one unit.

William's son Henry I (r. 1100–1135) established a bureau of finance called the Exchequer that became the first institution of the government bureaucracy of England. In addition to various taxes and annual gifts, Henry's income came from money paid to the Crown for settling disputes and as penalties for crimes, as well as money due to him in his private position as landowner and lord. Officials of the Exchequer began to keep careful records of all of this income.

In 1128 Henry's daughter Matilda was married to Geoffrey of Anjou, a count of a large province in what is now France; their son became Henry II of England and inaugurated the Angevin (AN-juh-vuhn; from Anjou, his father's county) dynasty. Henry II inherited the French provinces of Anjou, Normandy, Maine,

TIMELINE

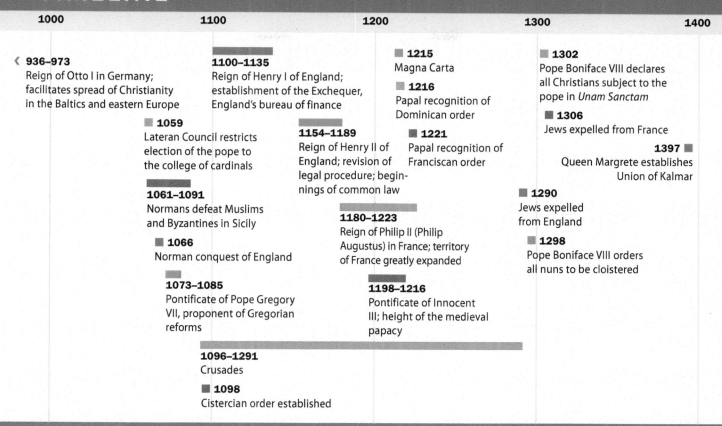

1000   **1100**   **1200**   **1300**   **1400**

936–973
Reign of Otto I in Germany; facilitates spread of Christianity in the Baltics and eastern Europe

1100–1135
Reign of Henry I of England; establishment of the Exchequer, England's bureau of finance

1059
Lateran Council restricts election of the pope to the college of cardinals

1154–1189
Reign of Henry II of England; revision of legal procedure; beginnings of common law

1061–1091
Normans defeat Muslims and Byzantines in Sicily

1066
Norman conquest of England

1073–1085
Pontificate of Pope Gregory VII, proponent of Gregorian reforms

1096–1291
Crusades

1098
Cistercian order established

1180–1223
Reign of Philip II (Philip Augustus) in France; territory of France greatly expanded

1198–1216
Pontificate of Innocent III; height of the medieval papacy

1215
Magna Carta

1216
Papal recognition of Dominican order

1221
Papal recognition of Franciscan order

1302
Pope Boniface VIII declares all Christians subject to the pope in *Unam Sanctam*

1306
Jews expelled from France

1397
Queen Margrete establishes Union of Kalmar

1290
Jews expelled from England

1298
Pope Boniface VIII orders all nuns to be cloistered

---

and Touraine in northwestern France, and in 1152 he married Eleanor of Aquitaine, heir to Aquitaine, Poitou (pwah-TOO), and Gascony in southwestern France. As a result, Henry claimed nearly half of today's France, and the histories of England and France became closely intertwined, leading to disputes and conflicts down to the fifteenth century.

France

French kings overcame the Angevin threat to expand and increasingly unify their realm. Following the death of the last Carolingian ruler in 987, an assembly of nobles selected Hugh Capet (kah-PAY) as his successor. Soon after his own coronation, Hugh crowned his oldest surviving son Robert as king to ensure the succession and prevent disputes after his death. This action broke with the earlier practices of electing kings or dividing a kingdom among one's sons, establishing instead the principle of **primogeniture** (prigh-muh-JEH-nuh-choor), in which the king's eldest son received the Crown as his rightful inheritance. Primogeniture became the standard pattern of succession in medieval western Europe, and it also became an increasingly common pattern of

inheritance for noble titles as well as for land and other forms of wealth among all social classes.

The Capetian (kuh-PEE-shuhn) kings were weak, but they laid the foundation for later political stability. This stability came slowly. In the early twelfth century France still consisted of a number of virtually independent provinces, and the king of France maintained clear jurisdiction over a relatively small area in the center of France, the Île-de-France. Over time medieval French kings worked to increase the royal domain and extend their authority over the provinces.

The work of unifying France began under the Capetian king Philip II (r. 1180–1223), also known as Philip Augustus. Philip took Normandy by force from King John of England in 1204, gained other northern provinces as well, and was able to secure oaths of fealty from nobles in provinces not under his direct rule. (See "Viewpoints: Oaths of Fealty," page 234.) In the thirteenth century Philip Augustus's descendants acquired important holdings in the south. By the end

---

■ **Domesday Book** A manuscript that records the general inquiry about the wealth of his lands ordered by William of Normandy.

■ **primogeniture** An inheritance system in which the oldest son inherits all land and noble titles.

Rulers in the High Middle Ages often required oaths of fealty from nobles in conquered or allied provinces, building on earlier oath-swearing that linked lords and vassals. The first document below, from 1198, is Philip II of France's formal acceptance of the oath of fealty of Count Theobald III of Troyes, who had just become ruling count in Champagne, which bordered France. Theobald died three years later, leaving his wife, Blanche of Navarre, with a young daughter and pregnant with another child. The second document is Blanche's oath of fealty to Philip. She ruled as regent for twenty-one years, surviving a war of succession.

Philip II of France's Acceptance of the Oath of Fealty from Theobald of Troyes, 1198

Philip, by the grace of God king of France. Be it known to all men, present and future, that we have received our beloved nephew, Theobald, count of Troyes, as our liege man, against every creature, living or dead, for all the lands which his father, count Henry, our uncle, held from our father, and which count Henry, the brother of Theobald, held from us. Count Theobald has sworn to us on the most holy body of the Lord and on the holy gospel that he will aid us in good faith, as his liege lord, against every creature, living or dead; at his command the following persons have sworn to us that they approve of this and will support and aid him in keeping this oath: Guy of Dampierre, Gualcher of Chatillon, Geoffroy, marshal of Champagne, etc. [vassals of the count of Champagne]. . . . We have sworn with our own hand that we will aid count Theobald against every creature, living or dead; at our command the following men have sworn that they approve of this and will support and aid us in keeping this oath: Pierre, count of Nevers, Drogo of Mello, William of Galande, etc. [vassals of the king]. . . . We have also agreed that our beloved uncle, William, archbishop of Rheims, and the bishops of Chalons and Meaux, may place those of our lands that are in their dioceses under interdict [a ban of all Christian ceremonies], as often as we fail in our duty to count Theobald, unless we make amends within a month from the time when they learn of it; and count Theobald has agreed that the same archbishop and bishops may place his lands under an interdict as often as he fails in his duty to us, unless he makes amends within a month from the time when they learn of it.

Oath of Fealty of Blanche of Navarre, Countess of Troyes and Champagne, 1201

I, Blanche, countess palatine of Troyes. Be it known to all, present and future, that I have voluntarily sworn to my lord, Philip, king of France, to keep the agreements contained in this charter. . . . I have voluntarily sworn that I will never take a husband without the advice, consent, and wish of my lord, Philip, king of France, and that I will place under his guardianship my daughter and any child of whom I may be pregnant from my late husband, count Theobald. In addition, I will turn over to him the fortresses of Bray and Montereau, and give him control of all the men who dwell there and all the knights who hold fiefs of the castles, so that if I break my promise to keep these agreements, all the aforesaid men shall hold directly of my lord, Philip, king of France; and they shall swear to aid him even against men and against every other man or woman. . . . I will do liege homage to my lord, Philip, king of France, and I will keep faith with him against all creatures, living or dead.

QUESTIONS FOR ANALYSIS

1. Philip is a male ruler accepting an oath of fealty, Blanche a female noble making one. How do these differences shape what is required of them in these oaths?
2. How are others incorporated into these promises? What does this information suggest about links among nobles and between state and church?

Source: Oliver J. Thatcher and Edgar Holmes McNeal, eds., *A Source Book for Medieval History* (New York: Scribners, 1905), pp. 369–370, 371–372.

---

of the thirteenth century most of the provinces of modern France had been added to the royal domain through diplomacy, marriage, war, and inheritance (Map 9.1).

In addition to expanding the royal territory, Philip Augustus devised a method of governing the provinces and providing for communication between the central government in Paris and local communities. Each province retained its own institutions and laws, but royal agents were sent from Paris into the provinces as the king's official representatives with authority to act for him. These agents were never natives of the provinces to which they were assigned, and they could not own land there. This policy reflected the fundamental principle of French administration that officials should gain their power from their connection to the monarchy, not from their own wealth or local alliances. Philip Augustus and his successors were slower and less effective, however, than were English kings at setting up an efficient bureau of finance.

Central Europe

In central Europe the German king Otto I (r. 936–973) defeated many other lords to build his power from his original base in Saxony. Some of our knowledge of Otto derives from *The Deeds of Otto*, a history of his reign in heroic verse written by a nun, Hroswitha of Gandersheim (ca. 935–ca. 1003). Hroswitha viewed Otto's victories as part of God's plan: "As often as he set out for war, there was not a people, though haughty because of its strength, that could harm or conquer him, supported as he was by the consolation of the heavenly King."[2]

Otto garnered financial support from church leaders and also asserted the right to control ecclesiastical appointments. Before receiving religious consecration and being invested with the staff and ring symbolic of their offices, bishops and abbots had to perform feudal homage for the lands that accompanied the church office. This practice, later known as lay investiture, created a grave crisis between the church and the monarchy in the eleventh century (see "Emperor Versus Pope").

In 955 Otto I inflicted a crushing defeat on the Magyars in the Battle of Lechfeld (see "Magyars and Muslims" in Chapter 8), which made Otto a great hero to the Germans. In 962 he used this victory to have himself crowned emperor by the pope in Aachen, which had been the capital of the Carolingian Empire. He chose this site to symbolize his intention to continue the tradition of Charlemagne and to demonstrate papal support for his rule. Though it was not exactly clear what Otto was the emperor of, by the eleventh century people were increasingly using the term **Holy Roman Empire** to refer to a loose confederation of principalities, duchies, cities, bishoprics, and other types of regional governments stretching from Denmark to Rome and from Burgundy to Poland (Map 9.2).

In this large area of central Europe and northern Italy, the Holy Roman emperors shared power with princes, dukes, archbishops, counts, bishops, abbots, and cities. The office of emperor remained an elected one, though the electors numbered seven — four secular rulers of large territories within the empire and three archbishops.

None of Otto's successors were as forceful as he had been, and by the first half of the twelfth century civil wars wracked the empire. The electors decided that the only alternative to continued chaos was the selection of a strong ruler. They chose Frederick Barbarossa of the house of Hohenstaufen (HOH-uhn-shtow-fuhn) (r. 1152–1190). Like William the Conqueror in England and Philip in France, Frederick required vassals to take an oath of allegiance to him as emperor and appointed officials to exercise full imperial authority over local communities.

Between 1154 and 1188 Frederick made six military expeditions into Italy in an effort to assert his imperial

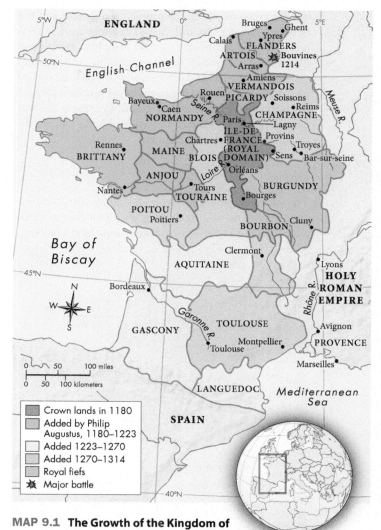

MAP 9.1　The Growth of the Kingdom of France, 1180–1314　The kings of France expanded their holdings through warfare, diplomacy, and strategic marriages, annexing lands that had belonged to independent nobles and taking over territory from the Angevin kings who also ruled England. The province of Toulouse in the south became part of France as a result of the crusade against the Albigensians (see "Criticism and Heresy").

rights over the increasingly wealthy towns of northern Italy. While he initially made significant conquests, the Italian cities formed leagues to oppose him, and also allied with the papacy. In 1176 Frederick suffered a crushing defeat at Legnano, where the league armies took massive amounts of booty and many prisoners (see Map 9.2). This battle marked the first time a cavalry of armed knights was decisively defeated by an army largely made of infantrymen from the cities. Frederick

■ **Holy Roman Empire**　The loose confederation of principalities, duchies, cities, bishoprics, and other types of regional governments stretching from Denmark to Rome and from Burgundy to Poland.

was forced to recognize the municipal autonomy of the northern Italian cities and the pope's sovereignty in central Italy. His campaigns in Italy took him away from the parts of the empire north of the Alps, and regional rulers there reasserted their authority toward the end of Frederick's reign and in the reigns of his successors. Thus, in contrast to France and England, Germany did not become a unified state in the Middle Ages, and would not until the nineteenth century.

Italy

The emperor and the pope also came into conflict over Sicily and southern Italy, disputes that eventually involved the kings of France and Spain as well.

Between 1061 and 1091 a bold Norman knight, Roger de Hauteville, with papal support and a small band of mercenaries, defeated the Muslims and Byzantines who controlled the island of Sicily. Roger then faced the problem of governing Sicily's heterogeneous population of native Sicilians, Italians, Greeks, Jews, Arabs, and Normans. Roger distributed scattered lands to his followers so no vassal would have a centralized power base. He took an inquest of royal property and forbade his followers to engage in war with one another. To these Norman practices, Roger fused Arab and Greek institutions, such as the bureau for record keeping and administration that had been established by the previous Muslim rulers.

In 1137 Roger's son and heir, Count Roger II, took the city of Naples and much of the surrounding territory in southern Italy. The entire area came to be known as the kingdom of Sicily (or sometimes the Kingdom of the Two Sicilies). Roger II's grandson Frederick II (r. 1212–1250) was also the grandson of Frederick Barbarossa of Germany. He was crowned king of the Germans at Aachen (1216) and Holy Roman emperor at Rome (1220), but he concentrated all his attention on the southern parts of the empire. Frederick had grown up in multicultural Sicily, knew six languages, wrote poetry, and supported scientists, scholars, and artists, whatever their religion or background. In 1224 he founded the University of Naples to train officials for his growing bureaucracy, sending them out to govern the towns of the kingdom. He tried to administer justice fairly to all his subjects, declaring, "We cannot in the least permit Jews and Saracens [Muslims] to be defrauded of the power of our protection and to be deprived of all other help, just because the difference of their religious practices makes them hateful to Christians," implying a degree of toleration exceedingly rare at the time.[3]

Because of his broad interests and abilities, Frederick's contemporaries called him the "Wonder of the World." But ruling Sicily required constant attention, and Frederick was often gone, on campaigns in mainland Italy or on the Crusades—holy wars sponsored by the papacy for the recovery of Jerusalem from the Muslims. He did not oversee his officials or the royal bureaucracy well, and shortly after he died, the kingdom fell to pieces. The pope, worried about being encircled by imperial power, called in a French prince

MAP 9.2 The Holy Roman Empire and the Kingdom of Sicily, ca. 1200 Frederick Barbarossa greatly expanded the size of the Holy Roman Empire, but it remained a loose collection of various types of government. The Christian kingdom of Sicily was created when Norman knights overthrew the Muslim rulers, but it was later ruled by Frederick II, who was also the Holy Roman emperor.

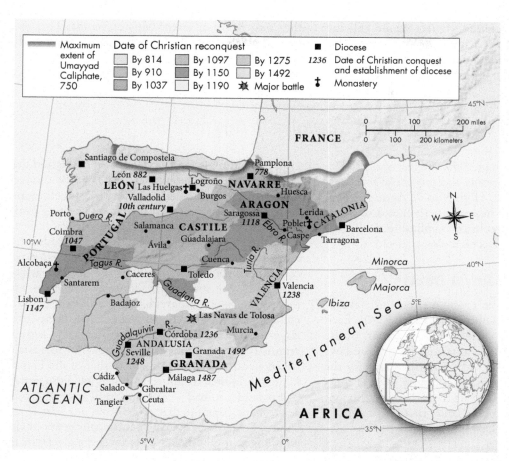

MAP 9.3 **The Reconquista, ca. 750–1492** The Christian conquest of Muslim Spain was followed by ecclesiastical reorganization, with the establishment of dioceses, monasteries, and the Latin liturgy, which gradually tied the peninsula to the heartland of Christian Europe and to the Roman papacy.

to rule the kingdom of Sicily. Like Germany, Italy would remain divided until the nineteenth century.

The Iberian Peninsula

From the eleventh to the thirteenth centuries, power in the Iberian Peninsula shifted from Muslim to Christian rulers. Castile, in the north-central part of the peninsula, became the strongest of the growing Christian kingdoms, and Aragon, in the northeast, the second most powerful. Alfonso VIII (1158–1214) of Castile, aided by the kings of Aragon, Navarre, and Portugal, won a crushing victory over the Muslims in 1212, accelerating the Christian push southward. Over the next several centuries, successive popes gave Christian warriors in the Iberian Peninsula the same spiritual benefits that they gave those who traveled to Jerusalem, such as granting them forgiveness for their sins, transforming this advance into a crusade. Christian troops captured the great Muslim cities of Córdoba in 1236 and Seville in 1248. With this success, Christians controlled nearly the entire Iberian Peninsula, save for the small state of Granada (Map 9.3). The chief mosques in Muslim cities became cathedrals, and Christian rulers recruited immigrants from western and southern Europe. The cities quickly became overwhelmingly Christian, and gradually rural areas did as well.

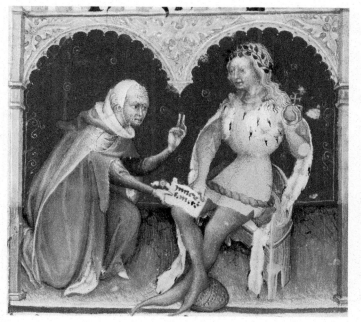

Emperor Frederick II Granting Privileges A young and handsome Frederick II, with a laurel wreath symbolizing his position as emperor, signs a grant of privileges for a merchant of the Italian city of Asti in this thirteenth-century manuscript. Frederick wears the flamboyant and fashionable clothing of a high noble — long-toed shoes, slit sleeves, and a cape of ermine tails — while the merchant seeking his favor is dressed in more sober and less expensive garb. (Miniature from the *Codex of Astensis*, Archivio Municipale, Asti, Italy/Scala/Art Resource, NY)

Fourteenth-century clerical writers would call the movement to expel the Muslims the **reconquista** (reconquest), a sacred and patriotic crusade to wrest the country from "alien" Muslim hands. This idea became part of Spanish political culture and of the national psychology.

How did the administration of law evolve in this period?

Throughout Europe in 1000, the law was a hodge-podge of local customs and provincial practices. Over the course of the High Middle Ages, national rulers tried to blend these elements into a uniform system of rules acceptable and applicable to all their peoples, though their success at doing so varied.

Local Laws and Royal Courts

In France, the effort to create a royal judicial system was launched by Louis IX (r. 1226–1270). Each French province, even after being made part of the kingdom of France, had retained its unique laws and procedures, but Louis IX published laws for the entire kingdom and sent royal judges to hear complaints of injustice. He established the Parlement of Paris, a kind of supreme court that heard appeals

Child and Mother Plead Before the King   In this fourteenth-century manuscript of Justinian's code of civil law, made in France, a mother and her child stand before the king to plead their case. He holds a sword, a symbol of both power and justice. Ordinary people did appear before royal courts, though they often sent legal representatives. (Gianni Dagli Orti/Shutterstock)

from local administrators and regional courts and that also registered (or announced) royal laws. By the very act of appealing the decisions of local courts to the Parlement of Paris, French people in far-flung provinces were recognizing the superiority of royal justice.

In the Holy Roman Empire, justice was administered at multiple levels. The manorial or seigneurial court, presided over by the local lay or ecclesiastical lord, dealt with such matters as damage to crops and fields, trespass, boundary disputes, and debt. Dukes, counts, bishops, and abbots possessed authority over larger regions, and they dispensed justice in serious criminal cases there. The Holy Roman emperors established a court of appeal similar to that of the French kings, but in their disunited empire it had little power.

England also had a variety of local laws with procedures and penalties that varied from one part of the country to another. Henry I occasionally sent out circuit judges, royal officials who traveled a given circuit or district, to hear civil and criminal cases. Henry II (r. 1154–1189) made this way of extending royal justice an annual practice. Every year royal judges left London and set up court in the counties. These courts regularized procedures in civil cases, gradually developing the idea of a **common law**, one that applied throughout the whole country. Over the next two or three centuries common law became a reality as well as a legal theory. Common law relied on precedent: a decision in an important case served as an authority for deciding similar cases. Thus written codes of law played a less important role in England than they did elsewhere. (This practice has continued to today; in contrast to the United States and most other countries, the United Kingdom does not have a written constitution.)

Henry also improved procedure in criminal justice. In 1166 he instructed the sheriffs to summon local juries to conduct inquests and draw up lists of known or suspected criminals, to be presented to the royal judges when they arrived in the community. This accusing jury is the ancestor of the modern grand jury. Gradually, in the course of the thirteenth century, the king's judges adopted the practice of calling on twelve people (other than the accusing jury) to consider the question of innocence or guilt; this was the forerunner of the trial jury.

One aspect of Henry II's judicial reforms encountered stiff resistance from an unexpected source.

In 1164 Henry insisted that everyone, including clerics, be subject to the royal courts. The archbishop of Canterbury Thomas Becket, who was Henry's friend and former chief adviser, vigorously protested that church law required clerics to be subject to church courts.

The disagreement between king and archbishop dragged on for years. Late in December 1170, in a fit of rage, Henry expressed the wish that Becket be destroyed. Four knights took the king at his word. They rode to Canterbury Cathedral and, as the archbishop was leaving evening services, murdered him, slashing off the crown of his head and scattering his brains on the floor of the cathedral. The assassination of an archbishop turned public opinion in England and throughout western Europe against the king, and Henry had to back down. He did public penance for the murder and gave up his attempts to bring clerics under the authority of the royal courts. Miracles were recorded at Becket's tomb; Becket was made a saint; and in a short time Canterbury Cathedral became a major pilgrimage and tourist site.

The Magna Carta

In the later years of Henry's reign, his sons, spurred on by their mother, Eleanor of Aquitaine, fought against their father and one another for power and land. Richard I, known as the Lion-Hearted (r. 1189–1199), won this civil war and acceded to the throne on Henry's death. Soon after, however, he departed on one of the Crusades. Richard was captured on his way back from the Crusades and held by the Holy Roman emperor for a very high ransom, paid primarily through loans and high taxes on the English people. He was freed but died several years later as the result of a wound on yet another military campaign.

John (r. 1199–1216) inherited his father's and brother's heavy debts, and his efforts to squeeze money out of his subjects created an atmosphere of resentment. In July 1214 John's cavalry suffered a severe defeat at the hands of Philip Augustus of France, strengthening the opposition to John back in England. A rebellion begun by northern barons eventually grew to involve many key members of the English nobility. After lengthy negotiations, John met the barons in 1215 at Runnymede and was forced to approve the charter of rights later called **Magna Carta**.

The charter was simply meant to assert traditional rights enjoyed by certain groups, including the barons, the clergy, and the merchants of London, and thus state limits on the king's power. In time, however, it came to signify the broader principle that everyone, including the king and the government, must obey the law. The Magna Carta also contains the germ of the idea of "due process of law," meaning that a person has the right to be heard and defended in court and

is entitled to the protection of the law. Because later generations referred to the Magna Carta as a written statement of English liberties, it gradually came to have an almost sacred symbolic importance.

Law in Everyday Life

Statements of legal principles such as the Magna Carta were not how most people experienced the law in medieval Europe. Instead they were involved in or witnessed something judged to be a crime, and then experienced or watched the determination of guilt and the punishment. Judges determined guilt or innocence in a number of ways. In some cases, particularly those in which there was little clear evidence, they ordered a trial by ordeal. An accused person could be tried by fire or water. In the latter case, the accused was tied hand and foot and dropped in a lake or river. People believed that water was a pure substance and would reject anything foul or unclean. Thus a person who sank was considered innocent; a person who floated was found guilty. Trial by ordeal was a ritual that appealed to the supernatural for judgment. Trials by ordeal are fascinating to modern audiences, but they were relatively rare, and their use declined over the High Middle Ages as judges and courts increasingly favored more rational procedures. Judges heard testimony, sought witnesses, and read written evidence if it was available.

A London case in 1277 provides a good example of how law worked. Around Easter, a man was sent to clean a house that had been abandoned, "but when he came to a dark and narrow place where coals were usually kept, he there found [a] headless body; upon seeing which, he sent word to the chamberlain and sheriffs." These officials went to the house and interviewed the neighbors. The men who lived nearby said that the headless body belonged to Symon de Winten, a tavern owner, whom they had seen quarreling with his servant Roger in early December. That night Roger "seized a knife, and with it cut the throat of Symon quite through, so that the head was entirely severed from the body." He had stuffed the body in the coal room, stolen clothes and a silver cup, and disappeared.[4] The surviving records don't indicate whether Roger was ever caught, but they do indicate that the

---

■ **reconquista** The Christian term for the conquest of Muslim territories in the Iberian Peninsula by Christian forces.

■ **common law** A body of English law established by King Henry II's court that in the next two or three centuries became common to the entire country.

■ **Magna Carta** A peace treaty intended to redress the grievances that particular groups had against King John; it was later viewed as the source of English rights and liberty more generally.

sheriffs took something as "surety" from the neighbors who testified, that is, cash or goods as a pledge that their testimony was true. Taking sureties from witnesses was a common practice, which may be why the neighbors had not come forward on their own even though they seemed to have detailed knowledge of the murder. People were supposed to report crimes, and they could be fined for not doing so, but it is clear from this case that such community involvement in crime fighting did not always happen.

Had Roger been caught and found guilty, his punishment would have been as public as the investigation. Murder was a capital crime, as were a number of other violent acts, and executions took place outdoors on a scaffold. Hanging was the most common method of execution, although nobles might be beheaded because hanging was seen as demeaning. Minor crimes were punished by fines, corporal punishments such as whipping, or banishment from the area.

What were the political and social roles of nobles?

The expansion of centralized royal power and law involved limiting the power of the nobility, but rulers also worked through nobles, who retained their privileged status and cultural importance. In fact, despite political, scientific, and industrial revolutions, the nobility continued to hold real political and social power in Europe into the nineteenth century.

Origins and Status of the Nobility

In the early Middle Ages noble status was generally limited to a very few families who either were descended from officials at the Carolingian court or were leading families among Germanic tribes. Beginning in the eleventh century, knights in the service of higher nobles or kings began to claim noble status. Although nobles were only a small fraction of the total population, the noble class grew larger and more diverse, ranging from poor knights who held tiny pieces of land (or sometimes none at all) to dukes and counts with vast territories.

Originally, most knights focused solely on military skills, but around 1200 there emerged a different ideal of knighthood, usually termed **chivalry** (shih-vuhl-ree). Chivalry was a code of conduct in which fighting to defend the Christian faith and protecting one's countrymen were declared to have a sacred purpose. Other qualities gradually became part of chivalry: bravery, generosity, honor, graciousness, mercy, and eventually gallantry toward women, which came to be called "courtly love." The chivalric ideal created a new standard of masculinity for nobles, in which loyalty and honor remained the most important qualities, but graceful dancing and intelligent conversation were not considered unmanly.

Saint Maurice This sandstone statue of Saint Maurice, made about 1250 for Magdeburg Cathedral in Germany, depicts the legendary third-century Roman soldier — who, according to accounts of saints' lives, refused to attack his fellow Christians — with African features, the first surviving portrayal to do so. Maurice was widely venerated, held up as a model knight and protector of the Holy Roman Empire. He was (and, in some cases, still is) the patron saint of several military orders, including the Order of Saint Maurice of the National Infantry Association in the United States. Images of Saint Maurice as a Black man largely ended in the mid-sixteenth century, at a point when the Atlantic slave trade was expanding. (Markus Hilbich/akg-images)

■ **chivalry** Code of conduct in which fighting to defend the Christian faith and protecting one's countrymen were declared to have a sacred purpose.

Training, Marriage, and Inheritance

At about the age of seven, a boy of the noble class who was not intended for the church was placed in the household of one of his father's friends or relatives. There he became a servant to the lord and received formal training in arms, learning to ride, wield a sword, hurl a lance, and shoot with a bow and arrow. Increasingly, noble youths learned to read and write some Latin. Formal training was concluded around the age of twenty-one, often with the ceremony of knighthood.

The ceremony of knighthood did not necessarily mean attainment of adulthood, power, and responsibility. Sons were completely dependent on their fathers for support. A young man remained a youth until he was in a financial position to marry — that is, until his father died. Increasingly, families adopted primogeniture, with property passing to the oldest son. Younger sons might be forced into the clergy or simply forbidden to marry.

Once knighted, the young man traveled for two to three years, visiting other noble households, engaging in local warfare, and perhaps going on a crusade. He hunted, meddled in local conflicts, and did the tournament circuit. The tournament, in which a number of men competed from horseback (in contrast to the joust, which involved only two competitors), gave the young knight experience in pitched battle and a way to show off his masculinity before an audience. Since the horses and equipment of the vanquished were forfeited to the victors, the knight could also gain a profit. Everywhere they went, young knights stirred up trouble, for chivalric ideals of honorable valor and gallant masculinity rarely served as a check on actual behavior.

While noble girls were also trained in preparation for their future tasks, that training was quite different. They were often taught to read the local language and perhaps some Latin and to write and do enough arithmetic to keep household accounts. They also learned music, dancing, and embroidery and how to ride and hunt, both common noble pursuits. Much of this took place in the girl's own home, but, like boys, noble girls were often sent to the homes of relatives or higher nobles to act as servants or ladies in waiting or to learn how to run a household.

Parents often wanted to settle daughters' futures as soon as possible. Men tended to prefer young brides who would have more years to produce children. Therefore, aristocratic girls in the High Middle Ages were married at around the age of sixteen, often to much older men. In the early Middle Ages the custom was for the groom

Female Donor in Chartres Cathedral Windows   Nobles and other wealthy people who paid for stained-glass windows often had their portraits included. In the south transept of Chartres Cathedral at the foot of the prophet Isaiah is the portrait of Alix of Thouars, hereditary duchess of Brittany. The windows were made in 1221–1230, right after Alix's death in childbirth, and were donated by her husband, who is also shown in one of the windows; the remaining windows show their son and daughter, though as young adults rather than as the small children they would have been at the time the windows were made. (Chartres Cathedral, Chartres, France/Bridgeman Images)

to present a dowry to the bride and her family, but by the late twelfth century the process was reversed because men were in greater demand. Thereafter, the sizes of dowries offered by brides and their families rose higher and higher.

Power and Responsibility

A male member of the nobility became fully adult when he came into the possession of property. He then acquired authority over lands and people, protecting them from attack, maintaining order, and settling disputes. With this authority went responsibility. In the words of Honorius of Autun:

> Soldiers: You are the arm of the Church, because you should defend it against its enemies. Your duty is to aid the oppressed, to restrain yourself from rapine and fornication, to repress those who impugn the Church with evil acts, and to resist those who are rebels against priests. Performing such a service, you will obtain the most splendid of benefices from the greatest of Kings.[5]

Nobles rarely lived up to this ideal, however, and there are countless examples of nobles stealing church lands instead of defending them, tyrannizing the oppressed rather than aiding them, and regularly engaging in "rapine and fornication" rather than resisting them.

Women played a large and important role in the functioning of the estate. They were responsible for the practical management of the household's "inner economy" — cooking, brewing, spinning, weaving, caring for yard animals. When the lord was away for long periods, the women frequently managed the herds, barns, granaries, and outlying fields as well. Often the responsibilities of the estate fell to them permanently, as the number of men slain in medieval warfare ran high.

Throughout the High Middle Ages, fighting remained the dominant feature of the noble lifestyle. The church's preaching and condemnations reduced but did not stop violence, and the military values of the nobles' social class encouraged petty warfare and disorder. The nobility thus represented a constant source of trouble for the monarchy.

How did the papacy reform the church, and what were the reactions to these efforts?

Kings and emperors were not the only rulers consolidating their power in the High Middle Ages; popes did so as well, through a series of measures that made the church more independent of secular control. The popes' efforts were sometimes challenged by medieval kings and emperors, and the wealth of the church came under sharp criticism.

The Gregorian Reforms

During the ninth and tenth centuries the local church had come under the control of kings and feudal lords, who chose priests and bishops in their territories, granting them land and expecting loyalty and service in return. Church offices from village priest to pope were sources of income as well as positions of authority. Officeholders had the right to collect taxes and fees and often the profits from the land under their control. Church offices were thus sometimes sold outright — a practice called **simony** (SIGH-muh-nee). Not surprisingly, clergy at all levels who had bought their positions or had been granted them for political reasons provided little spiritual guidance, and their personal lives were rarely models of high moral standards. Although the Roman Church officially required men to be unmarried in order to be ordained, there were many married priests and others simply living

with women. Popes were chosen by wealthy Roman families from among their members, and after gaining the papal office, they paid more attention to their families' political fortunes than to the health of the church.

Serious efforts to change all this began under Pope Leo IX (pontificate 1049–1054). Leo ordered clergy in Rome to dismiss their wives and invalidated the ordination of church officials who had purchased their offices. Pope Leo and several of his successors believed that secular or lay control over the church was largely responsible for its lack of moral leadership, so in a radical shift they proclaimed the church independent of secular rulers. The Lateran Council of 1059 decreed that the authority and power to elect the pope rested solely in the **college of cardinals**, a special group of priests from the major churches in and around Rome. The college retains that power today, though the membership has grown and become international.

Leo's successor Pope Gregory VII (pontificate 1073–1085) was even more vigorous in his championing of reform and expansion of papal power; for that reason, the eleventh-century movement is frequently called the "Gregorian reform movement." He denounced clerical marriage and simony in harsh language and ordered **excommunication** (being cut off from the sacraments and all Christian worship) for those who disagreed. He believed that the pope, as the successor of Saint Peter, was the vicar of God on earth and that papal orders were thus the orders of God. Gregory was particularly opposed to lay investiture—the selection and appointment of church officials by secular authority. In February 1075 he held a council at Rome that decreed that clerics who accepted investiture from laymen were to be deposed and laymen who invested clerics were to be excommunicated.

In the late eleventh century and throughout the twelfth and thirteenth, the papacy pressed Gregory's campaign for reform of the church. The popes held a series of councils, known as the Lateran Councils, that ratified decisions ending lay investiture, ordered bishops to live less extravagantly, and ordered married priests to give up their wives and children or face dismissal. Most church officials apparently obeyed, though we have little information on what happened to the families. In other reforms, marriage was defined as a sacrament—a ceremony that provided visible evidence of God's grace—and divorce was forbidden.

Gregory's reforms had a profound effect on nuns and other women in religious orders. The movement built a strict hierarchical church structure with bishops and priests higher in status than nuns, who could not be ordained. The double monasteries of the early Middle Ages were placed under the authority of male abbots. Church councils forbade monks and nuns to sing church services together and ordered priests to limit their visits to convents. The reformers' emphasis on clerical celibacy and chastity led them to portray women as impure and lustful. Thus, in 1298 in the papal decree *Periculoso*, Pope Boniface VIII ordered all nuns to be strictly cloistered, that is, to remain permanently inside the walls of the convent, and ordered visits with people from outside the house, including family members, to be limited. *Periculoso* was not enforced everywhere, but it did mean that convents became more cut off from medieval society than monasteries were.

Emperor Versus Pope

Gregory thought that the threat of excommunication would compel rulers to abide by his move against lay investiture. Immediately, however, Henry IV in the Holy Roman Empire, William the Conqueror in England, and Philip I in France protested, as the reform would deprive them not only of church income but also of the right to choose which monks and clerics would help them administer their kingdoms. The strongest reaction came from the Holy Roman Empire. Within the empire, religious and secular leaders took sides to pursue their own advantage. In January 1076 many of the German bishops who had

been invested by Henry withdrew their allegiance from the pope. Gregory promptly suspended them and excommunicated Henry. The pope told German nobles they no longer owed allegiance to Henry, which obviously delighted them. When powerful nobles invited the pope to come to Germany to settle their dispute with Henry, Gregory traveled to the north. Christmas of 1076 thus witnessed an ironic situation in Germany: the clergy supported the emperor while the great nobility favored the pope.

Henry managed to outwit the pope temporarily. In January 1077 he approached the castle where the pope was staying. According to a letter later sent by Gregory to his German noble allies, Henry stood for three days in the snow, imploring the pope to lift the excommunication. Henry's pleas for forgiveness won him public sympathy, and the pope readmitted the emperor to the Christian community. When the sentence of excommunication was lifted, however, Henry regained the emperorship and authority over his rebellious subjects, but continued his moves against papal power. In 1080 Gregory again excommunicated and deposed the emperor. In return, when Gregory died in 1085, Henry invaded Italy and captured Rome. But Henry won no lasting victory. Gregory's successors encouraged Henry's sons to revolt against their father.

Finally, in 1122 at a conference held at Worms, the issue was settled by compromise. Bishops were to be chosen by the clergy. But since lay rulers were permitted to be present at ecclesiastical elections and to accept or refuse homage from the new prelates, they still possessed an effective veto over ecclesiastical appointments. Papal power was enhanced, but neither side won a clear victory.

The long controversy over lay investiture had tremendous social and political consequences in Germany. The lengthy struggle between papacy and emperor allowed emerging noble dynasties to enhance their position. To control their lands, the great lords built castles, symbolizing their increased power and growing independence. When the papal-imperial conflict ended in 1122, the nobility held the balance of power in Germany, and later German kings, such as Frederick Barbarossa, would fail in their efforts to strengthen the monarchy. For these reasons, division and local independence characterized the Holy Roman Empire in the High Middle Ages.

■ **simony** The buying and selling of church offices, a policy that was officially prohibited but often practiced.

■ **college of cardinals** A special group of high clergy with the authority and power to elect the pope and the responsibility to govern the church when the office of the pope is vacant.

■ **excommunication** A penalty used by the Christian Church that meant being cut off from the sacraments and all Christian worship.

Criticism and Heresy

The Gregorian reform movement contributed to dissatisfaction with the church among townspeople as well as monarchs. Papal moves against simony, for example, led to widespread concern about the role of money in the church just as papal tax collectors were becoming more efficient and sophisticated. Papal efforts to improve the sexual morality of the clergy led some laypersons to assume they could, and indeed should, remove priests for any type of immorality.

Criticism of the church emerged in many places but found its largest audience in the cities, where the contrast between wealth and poverty could be seen more acutely. In northern Italian towns, the monk Arnold of Brescia (BREH-shah) (ca. 1090–1155), a vigorous advocate of strict clerical poverty, denounced clerical wealth. In France, Peter Waldo (ca. 1140–ca. 1218), a rich merchant of the city of Lyons, gave his money to the poor and preached that only prayers, not sacraments, were needed for salvation. The Waldensians (wawl-DEHN-shuhnz) — as Peter's followers were called — bitterly attacked the sacraments and church hierarchy, and they carried these ideas across Europe. In the towns and cities of southern France, the Albigensians (al-buh-JEHN-see-uhns), also known as the Cathars, used the teachings of Jesus about the evils of material goods to call for the church to give up its property. They asserted that the material world was created not by the good God of the New Testament, but by a different evil God of the Old Testament. People who rejected worldly things, not wealthy bishops or the papacy, should be the religious leaders.

Critical of the clergy and spiritually unfulfilled, townspeople joined the Waldensians and the Albigensians. The papacy denounced supporters of both movements as heretics and began extensive campaigns to wipe them out. In 1208 Pope Innocent III proclaimed a crusade against the Albigensians, and the French monarchy and northern French knights willingly joined in, eager to gain the lands and wealth of southern French cities. After years of fighting, the leaders agreed to terms of peace, which left the French monarchy the primary beneficiary. Later popes sent inquisitors with the power to seek out and eliminate the remaining heretics.

The Popes and Church Law

Pope Urban II laid the foundations for the papal monarchy by reorganizing the papal *curia* (the central government of the Roman Church) and recognizing the college of cardinals as a definite consultative body. The papal curia had its greatest impact as a court of law. As the highest ecclesiastical tribunal, it formulated church law, termed **canon law**. The church developed a system of courts separate from those of secular rulers that handled disputes over church property and ecclesiastical elections and especially questions of marriage and annulment. Most of the popes in the twelfth and thirteenth centuries were canon lawyers who expanded the authority of church courts.

The most famous of the lawyer-popes was Innocent III (pontificate 1198–1216), who became the most powerful pope in history. During his pontificate the church in Rome declared itself to be supreme, united, and "catholic" (worldwide), responsible for the earthly well-being as well as the eternal salvation of Christians everywhere. Innocent pushed the kings of Europe to do his will, compelling King Philip Augustus of France to take back his wife, Ingeborg of Denmark, and King John of England to accept as archbishop of Canterbury a man John did not want.

Innocent called the Fourth Lateran Council in 1215, which affirmed the idea that ordained priests had the power to transform bread and wine during church ceremonies into the body and blood of Christ (a change termed transubstantiation). According to papal doctrine, priests now had the power to mediate for everyone with God, setting the spiritual hierarchy of the church above the secular hierarchies of kings and other rulers. The council affirmed that Christians should confess their sins to a priest at least once a year, and that marriage was a sacrament, and thus indissoluble. It also ordered Jews and Muslims to wear special clothing that set them apart from Christians.

By the early thirteenth century papal efforts at reform begun more than a century earlier had attained phenomenal success, and the popes ruled a powerful, centralized institution. At the end of the century, however, the papacy again came into a violent dispute with secular rulers. Pope Boniface VIII (pontificate 1294–1303), arguing from precedent, insisted that King Edward I of England and Philip IV of France obtain his consent for taxes they had imposed on the clergy. Edward immediately denied the clergy the protection of the law, and Philip halted the shipment of all ecclesiastical revenue to Rome. Boniface had to back down.

The battle for power between the papacy and the French monarchy became a bitter war of propaganda, with Philip at one point calling the pope a heretic. Finally, in 1302, in a formal written statement known as a papal bull, Boniface insisted that all Christians — including kings — were subject to the pope in all things. (See "Evaluating Written Evidence: Pope Boniface VIII, *Unam Sanctam*," page 246.) In retaliation, French mercenary troops assaulted and arrested the aged pope at Anagni in Italy. Although Boniface was soon freed, he died shortly afterward. The confrontation at Anagni foreshadowed further difficulties in the Christian Church in the fourteenth century.

Bishop Ending a Marriage
In this thirteenth-century illumination from a legal manual, a bishop ends a marriage. Marriage was first declared a sacrament by officials in the Catholic Church in the late eleventh century as part of the condemnation of the Cathars, and confirmed as such at the Fourth Lateran Council. For this reason, divorce was prohibited, although marriages could be annulled — that is, declared never to have been valid in the first place — for a variety of reasons, and annulments did occur, particularly for members of the nobility.
(Archives Charmet/Bridgeman Images)

What roles did monks, nuns, and friars play in medieval society?

While the reforming popes transformed the Christian Church into an institution free of lay control at the highest level, leaders of monasteries and convents asserted their independence from secular control on the local level as well. Monks, nuns, and friars played significant roles in medieval society, both as individuals and as members of institutions. Medieval people believed that monks and nuns performed an important social service when they prayed, for their prayers and chants secured God's blessing for society. The friars worked in the cities, teaching and preaching Christian doctrine, but also investigating heretics.

Monastic Revival

In the early Middle Ages many religious houses followed the Benedictine *Rule*, while others developed their own patterns (see "Monastery Life" in Chapter 7). In the High Middle Ages this diversity became more formalized, and **religious orders**, groups of monastic houses following a particular rule, were established. Historians term the foundation, strengthening, and reform of religious orders in the High Middle Ages the "monastic revival."

In the period of political disorder that followed the disintegration of the Carolingian Empire, many religious houses fell under the control and domination of local lords. Powerful laymen appointed themselves or their relatives as abbots, took the lands and goods of monasteries, and seized monastic revenues. Accordingly, the level of spiritual observance and intellectual activity in monasteries and convents declined. The local lords also compelled abbots from time to time to provide contingents of soldiers, an obligation stemming from the abbots' judicial authority over knights and peasants on monastic lands.

The first sign of reform came in 909, when William the Pious, duke of Aquitaine, established the abbey of Cluny in Burgundy. Duke William declared that the monastery was to be free from any feudal responsibilities to him or any other lord, its members subordinate only to the pope. The monastery at Cluny, which initially held high standards of religious behavior, came to exert vast religious influence. In the eleventh century Cluny was fortunate in having a series of highly able abbots who ruled for a long time. In a disorderly world, Cluny gradually came to represent stability. Therefore, laypersons placed lands under its custody and monastic priories under its jurisdiction (a priory is a religious house, with generally fewer residents than

---

■ **canon law** Church law, which had its own courts and procedures.

■ **religious orders** Groups of monastic houses following a particular rule.

Pope Boniface VIII, *Unam Sanctam*

In late 1302, after several years of bitter conflict with King Philip IV of France over control and taxation of the clergy in France, Pope Boniface VIII issued a papal bull declaring the official church position on the proper relationships between church and state. Throughout, the pope uses the "royal we," that is, the plural "we" instead of "I" when talking about himself.

We are obliged by the faith to believe and hold — and we do firmly believe and sincerely confess — that there is one Holy Catholic and Apostolic Church, and that outside this Church there is neither salvation nor remission of sins. . . . In which Church there is "one Lord, one faith, one baptism." . . . Of this one and only Church there is one body and one head — not two heads, like a monster — namely Christ, and Christ's vicar is Peter, and Peter's successor, for the Lord said to Peter himself, "Feed my sheep." "My sheep" He said in general, not these or those sheep; wherefore He is understood to have committed them all to him. . . .

And we learn from the words of the Gospel that in this Church and in her power are two swords, the spiritual and the temporal. . . . Truly he who denies that the temporal sword is in the power of Peter, misunderstands the words of the Lord, "Put up thy sword into the sheath." Both are in the power of the Church, the spiritual sword and the material. But the latter is to be used for the Church, the former by her; the former by the priest, the latter by kings and captains but at the will and by the permission of the priest. The one sword, then, should be under the other, and temporal authority subject to spiritual. . . .

If, therefore, the earthly power err, it shall be judged by the spiritual power; and if a lesser power err, it shall be judged by a greater. But if the supreme power [the papacy] err, it can only be judged by God, not by man. . . . For this authority, although given to a man and exercised by a man, is not human, but rather divine, given at God's mouth to Peter and established on a rock for him and his successors in Him whom he confessed, the Lord saying to Peter himself, "Whatsoever thou shalt bind," etc. Whoever therefore resists this power thus ordained of God, resists the ordinance of God. . . . Furthermore, we declare, state, define, and pronounce that it is altogether necessary to salvation for every human creature to be subject to the Roman pontiff.

EVALUATE THE EVIDENCE

1. According to Pope Boniface, what is the proper relationship between the authority of the pope and the authority of earthly rulers? What is the basis for that relationship?
2. How might the earlier conflicts between popes and secular rulers traced in this chapter have influenced Boniface's declaration?

Source: Henry Bettenson, ed., *Documents of the Christian Church* (Oxford: Oxford University Press, 1963), pp. 115–116.

an abbey, governed by a prior or prioress). In this way, hundreds of religious houses, primarily in France and Spain, came under Cluny's authority.

Deeply impressed laypeople showered gifts on monasteries with good reputations. Monasteries became richer, owning extensive lands and the exclusive rights to services such as milling flour. Many built large abbey churches and became sites of pilgrimage, where laypeople as well as monks viewed relics, heard Mass, and prayed to saints. (See "Evaluating Visual Evidence: Illustrations from the *Life of St. Edmund*," page 247.) As the monasteries became richer, the lifestyle of the monks grew increasingly luxurious. Monastic observance and spiritual fervor declined. Soon fresh demands for reform were heard, resulting in the founding of new religious orders in the late eleventh and early twelfth centuries.

The Cistercians (sihs-TUHR-shuhnz) best represent the new reforming spirit because of their phenomenal expansion and great economic, political, and spiritual influence. In 1098 a group of monks left the rich abbey of Molesmes in Burgundy and founded a new house in the swampy forest of Cîteaux (see-TOH). The early Cistercians (the word is derived from *Cîteaux*) determined to keep their services simple and their lives austere, returning to work in the fields and other sorts of manual labor. As with Cluny, their high ideals made them a model, and 525 Cistercian monasteries were founded in the course of the twelfth century all over Europe. The Cistercians' influence on European society was profound, for they used new agricultural methods and technology and spread them throughout Europe. Their improvements in farming and animal raising brought wealth, however, and wealth brought power. By the later twelfth century, as with Cluny earlier, economic prosperity and political power had begun to compromise the original Cistercian ideals.

Illustrations from the *Life of St. Edmund*

Edmund was a king of East Anglia (r. 855–869), about whom almost nothing is known for certain other than that he was apparently killed by pagan Danish Viking invaders. Later writers invented stories, transforming him into a model king and Christian martyr and saint. Remains assumed to be his were buried in the church of the abbey of Bury, and various miracles were reported at the shrine. (The abbey and town surrounding it were later renamed Bury St. Edmunds.) An illuminated copy of the Benedictine monk Abbo of Fleury's *Life of St. Edmund,* made at the abbey in around 1130, illustrates several of these stories. Here eight thieves trying to break into Edmund's burial place are miraculously paralyzed. Later illustrations show the thieves tried and hanged.

EVALUATE THE EVIDENCE

1. How are the thieves trying to break into the abbey? What tools are they using, and what do these and the building itself tell you about medieval building techniques?
2. How does the artist use the figures' body position and expression to capture their sudden paralysis?
3. How would stories such as the one shown here about the paralysis of the thieves contribute to Edmund's reputation as a powerful ruler and saint? How could such stories increase the prosperity of the abbey and the town that grew up around it?

(The Morgan Library & Museum/Art Resource, NY)

Life in Convents and Monasteries

Medieval monasteries were religious institutions whose organization and structure fulfilled the social needs of the nobility. The monasteries provided noble boys with education and opportunities for ecclesiastical careers. Beginning in the thirteenth century an increasing number of boys and men from professional and merchant families became monks, seeking to take advantage of the opportunities monasteries offered.

Throughout the Middle Ages social class also defined the kinds of religious life open to women. Kings and nobles usually established convents for their daughters,

sisters, aunts, or aging mothers, and for other women of their class. Like monks, many nuns came into the convent as children, and very often sisters, cousins, aunts, and nieces could all be found in the same place. Thus, though nuns were to some degree cut off from their families by being cloistered, family relationships were maintained within the convent.

The office of abbess or prioress was the most powerful position a woman could hold in medieval society. (See "Individuals in Society: Hildegard of Bingen," page 248.) Abbesses were part of the political structure in the same way that bishops and abbots were, with manors under their financial and legal

INDIVIDUALS IN SOCIETY

Hildegard of Bingen

The tenth child of a lesser noble family, Hildegard (1098–1179) was given as a child to an abbey in the Rhineland when she was eight years old; there she learned Latin and received a good education. She spent most of her life in various women's religious communities, two of which she founded herself. When she was a child, she began having mystical visions, often of light in the sky, but told few people about them. In middle age, however, her visions became more dramatic: "And it came to pass . . . when I was 42 years and 7 months old, that the heavens were opened and a blinding light of exceptional brilliance flowed through my entire brain. And so it kindled my whole heart and breast like a flame, not burning but warming . . . and suddenly I understood of the meaning of expositions of the books."* She wanted the church to approve of her visions and wrote first to Bernard of Clairvaux, who answered her briefly and dismissively, and then to Pope Eugenius, who encouraged her to write them down. Her first work was *Scivias* (Know the ways of the Lord), a record of her mystical visions that incorporates vast theological learning.

Possessed of leadership and administrative talents, Hildegard left her abbey in 1147 to found the convent of Rupertsberg near Bingen. There she produced *Physica* (On the physical elements) and *Causa et Curae* (Causes and cures), scientific works on the curative properties of natural elements, as well as poems, a mystery play, and several more works of mysticism. She carried on a huge correspondence with scholars, prelates, and ordinary people. When she was over fifty, she left her community to preach to audiences of clergy and laity, and she was the only woman of her time whose opinions on religious matters were considered authoritative by the church.

Hildegard's visions have been explored by theologians and also by neurologists, who judge that they may have originated in migraine headaches, as she reports many of the same phenomena that migraine sufferers do: auras of light around objects, areas of blindness, feelings of intense doubt and intense euphoria. The interpretations that she develops come from her theological insight and learning, however, not illness. That same insight also emerges in her music, for which she is best known today. Eighty of her compositions survive — a huge number for a medieval composer — most of them written to be sung by the nuns in her convent, so they have strong lines for female voices. Many of her songs and chants have been recorded and are available on CD, as downloads, and on several websites.

Inspired by heavenly fire, Hildegard begins to dictate her visions to her scribe. The original of this elaborately illustrated twelfth-century copy of *Scivias* disappeared from Hildegard's convent during World War II, but fortunately a facsimile copy had already been made. (Art Images/Hulton Fine Art Collection/Getty Images)

QUESTIONS FOR ANALYSIS

1. Why do you think Hildegard sought church approval for her visions after keeping them secret for so many years?
2. In what ways is Hildegard's life representative of nuns' lives in the High Middle Ages? In what ways were her accomplishments extraordinary?

*From *Scivias*, trans. Mother Columba Hart and Jane Bishop, *The Classics of Western Spirituality* (New York/Mahwah: Paulist Press, 1990), p. 65.

control. They appointed tax collectors, bailiffs, judges, and often priests in their lands. Some abbesses in the Holy Roman Empire even had the right to name bishops and send representatives to imperial assemblies.

Abbesses also opened and supported hospitals, orphanages, and schools and hired builders, sculptors, and painters to construct and decorate residences and churches.

Monasteries for men were headed by an abbot or a prior, who was generally a member of a noble family, often a younger son in a family with several sons. The main body of monks, known as "choir monks" because one of their primary activities was reciting prayers and services while sitting in the part of the church called the choir, were largely of noble or middle-class background, and they did not till the land themselves. Men from peasant families sometimes became choir monks, but more often they served as lay brothers, doing the manual labor essential to running the monastery. The novice master or novice mistress was responsible for the training of recruits.

The pattern of life within individual monasteries varied widely from house to house and from region to region. One central activity, however, was performed everywhere. Daily life centered on the liturgy or Divine Office, psalms and other prayers prescribed by Saint Benedict that monks and nuns prayed seven times a day and once during the night. Prayers were offered for peace, rain, good harvests, the civil authorities, and the monks' families and benefactors. Everything connected with prayer was understood as praise of God, so abbeys spent a large percentage of their income on splendid objects to enhance the service, including sacred vessels of embossed silver or gold, altar cloths of the finest silks or velvets, embroideries, and beautiful reliquaries to house the relics of the patron saint.

In some abbeys monks and nuns spent much of their time copying books and manuscripts and then illuminating them, decorating them with human and animal figures or elaborate designs, often painted in bright colors or gold. A few monasteries and convents became centers of learning where talented residents wrote their own works as well as copying those of others.

Monks and nuns also performed a variety of social services in an age when there was no state and no conception of social welfare as a public responsibility. Monasteries often ran schools that gave primary education to young boys; convents did the same for girls. Monasteries served as hotels and resting places for travelers and frequently operated hospitals and leprosariums, which provided care and attention to the sick, the aged, and the afflicted.

The Friars

Monks and nuns carried out their spiritual and social services largely within the walls of their institutions, but in the thirteenth century new types of religious orders were founded whose members lived out in the world. Members of these new groups were **friars**, not monks. They thought that more contact with ordinary Christians, not less, was a better spiritual path. Friars stressed apostolic poverty, a life based on the teaching

Saint Dominic Rescuing Shipwrecked Fishermen from Drowning   In this detail from an altarpiece in the convent of St. Clare de Vic in present-day northeastern Spain, painted by the Catalan artist Lluís Borrassà in 1415, Saint Dominic miraculously saves fishermen from drowning. Accounts of miracles were an important part of devotion to saints, and often the subject of religious artwork in the Middle Ages. The altarpiece of which this is a part, made for a convent of Poor Clares, shows Saint Francis of Assisi in the center, surrounded by other male and female saints, including Saint Clare, whose followers founded the convent for which it was made. (Museo Episcopal, Vich, Osona, Catalonia, Spain/Bridgeman Images)

of the Gospels in which they would own no property and depend on Christian people for their material needs. Hence they were called mendicants, from the Latin word for begging. The friars' service to the towns and the poor, their ideal of poverty, and their compassion for the human condition made them popular.

One order of friars was started by Domingo de Gúzman (1170?–1221), born in Castile. Domingo (later called Dominic), a well-educated priest, accompanied his bishop in 1206 on an unsuccessful mission to win the Albigensians in southern France back to orthodox teaching. Determined to succeed through ardent preaching, he subsequently returned to France with a few followers. In 1216 the group—officially known as the Preaching Friars, though often called Dominicans—won papal recognition as a new religious order.

■ **friars** Men belonging to certain religious orders who lived not in monasteries but out in the world.

Francesco di Bernardone (1181–1226), son of a wealthy Italian cloth merchant of Assisi, had a religious conversion and decided to live and preach the Gospel in absolute poverty. Francis of Assisi, as he came to be known, emphasized not withdrawal from the world, but joyful devotion. In contrast to the Albigensians, who saw the material world as evil, Francis saw all creation as God-given and good. He was widely reported to perform miracles involving animals and birds, and he wrote hymns to natural objects.

The simplicity, humility, and joyful devotion with which Francis carried out his mission soon attracted others. Although he resisted pressure to establish an order, his followers became so numerous that he was obliged to develop some formal structure. In 1221 the papacy approved the Rule of the Little Brothers of Saint Francis, generally called the Franciscans (frahn-SIHS-kuhnz).

Friars worked among the poor, but they also addressed the spiritual and intellectual needs of the middle classes and the wealthy. The Dominicans preferred that their friars be university graduates so that they could better preach to a sophisticated urban society. Dominicans soon held professorial chairs at leading universities, and the Franciscans followed suit.

Beginning in 1231 the papacy also used friars to investigate heretics, sometimes under the auspices of a new ecclesiastical court, the Inquisition, in which accused people were subjected to lengthy interrogations and torture could be used to extract confessions. It is ironic that groups whose teachings were similar in so many ways to those of heretics were charged with rooting them out. That irony deepened in the case of the Spiritual Franciscans, a group that broke away from the main body of Franciscans to follow Francis's original ideals of absolute poverty. When they denied the pope's right to countermand that ideal, he ordered them tried as heretics.

Women sought to develop similar orders devoted to active service out in the world. Clare of Assisi (1193–1253) became a follower of Francis, who established a place for her to live in a church in Assisi. She was joined by other women, and they attempted to establish a rule that would follow Francis's ideals of absolute poverty and allow them to serve the poor. This rule was accepted by the papacy only after many decades, and then only because she agreed that the order, the Poor Clares, would be cloistered.

In the growing cities of Europe, especially in the Netherlands, groups of laywomen seeking to live religious lives came together as what later came to be known as Beguines (bay-GEENS). They lived communally in small houses called *beguinages*, combining lives of prayer with service to the needy. Beguine spirituality emphasized direct personal communication with God, sometimes through mystical experiences, rather than through the intercession of a saint or official church rituals. Initially some church officials gave guarded approval of the movement, but the church grew increasingly uncomfortable with women who were neither married nor cloistered nuns. By the fourteenth century Beguines were declared heretical, and much of their property was confiscated.

What were the causes, course, and consequences of the Crusades and the broader expansion of Christianity?

The Crusades of the eleventh and twelfth centuries were the most obvious manifestation of the papal claim to the leadership of Christian society. The **Crusades** were wars sponsored by the papacy for the recovery of the holy city of Jerusalem from the Muslims. The enormous popular response to papal calls for crusading reveals the influence of the reformed papacy and the depth of religious fervor among many different types of people. The Crusades also reflected the church's new understanding of the noble warrior class, for whom war against the church's enemies was understood as a religious duty. The word *crusade* was not actually used at the time and did not appear in English until the late sixteenth century. It means literally "taking the cross," from the cross that soldiers sewed on their garments as a Christian symbol. At the time people going off to fight simply said they were taking "the way of the cross" or "the road to Jerusalem."

Background and Motives of the Crusades

The medieval church's attitude toward violence was contradictory. On the one hand, church councils threatened excommunication for anyone who attacked peasants, clerics, or merchants or destroyed crops and unfortified places, a movement termed the Peace of God. Councils also tried to limit the number of days on which fighting was permitted, prohibiting it on Sundays, on special feast days, and in the seasons of Lent and Advent. On the other hand, popes supported armed conflict against kings and emperors if this worked to their advantage, thus encouraging warfare among Christians. After a serious theological disagreement in 1054 split the Orthodox Church of Byzantium and the Roman Church of the West, the pope also contemplated invading the Byzantine

Empire, an idea that subsequent popes considered as well.

Although conflicts in which Christians fought Christians were troubling to many thinkers, war against non-Christians was another matter. By the ninth century popes and other church officials encouraged war in defense of Christianity, promising spiritual benefits to those who died fighting. By the eleventh century these benefits were extended to all those who simply joined a campaign: their sins would be remitted without having to do penance, that is, without having to confess to a priest and carry out some action to make up for the sins. Around this time, Christian thinkers were developing the concept of purgatory, a place where those on their way to Heaven stayed for a while to do any penance they had not completed while alive. (Those on their way to Hell went straight there.) Engaging in holy war could shorten one's time in purgatory, or, as many people understood the promise, allow one to head straight to paradise. Popes signified this by providing **indulgences**, grants with the pope's name on them that lessened earthly penance and postmortem purgatory. Popes promised these spiritual benefits, and also provided financial support, for Christian armies in the reconquista in Spain and the Norman campaign against the Muslims in Sicily. Preachers communicated these ideas widely and told stories about warrior-saints who slew hundreds of enemies.

Religious devotion had long been expressed through pilgrimages to holy places, and these were increasingly described in military terms, as battles against the hardships along the way. Pilgrims to Jerusalem were often armed, so the line between pilgrimage and holy war on this particular route was increasingly blurred. In the midst of these developments came a change in possession of Jerusalem. The Arab Muslims who had ruled Jerusalem and the surrounding territory for centuries had generally allowed Christian pilgrims to travel freely, but in the late eleventh century the Seljuk (SEHL-jook) Turks took over Palestine, defeating both Arab and Byzantine armies and pillaging in Christian and Muslim parts of Asia Minor (Map 9.4). They harassed pilgrims and looted churches, and the emperor at Constantinople appealed to the West for support. The emperor's appeal fit well with papal aims, and in 1095 Pope Urban II called for a great Christian holy war against the infidels—a term Christians and Muslims both used to describe the other. Urban offered indulgences to those who would fight for and regain the holy city of Jerusalem.

The Course of the Crusades

Thousands of Western Christians of all classes joined the First Crusade, which began in 1096. Of all the developments of the High Middle Ages, none better reveals Europeans' religious and emotional fervor and the influence of the reformed papacy than the extraordinary outpouring of support for the First Crusade.

The First Crusade was successful, mostly because of the dynamic enthusiasm of the participants. The Crusaders had little more than religious zeal. They knew nothing about the geography or climate of the Middle East. Although there were several nobles with military experience among them, the Crusaders could never agree on a leader, and the entire expedition was marked by disputes among the great lords. Lines of supply were never set up, and starvation and disease wracked the army. Nevertheless, the army pressed on, defeating the Turks in several land battles and besieging a few larger towns, including Antioch. Finally, in 1099, three years after departing Europe, the Crusaders reached Jerusalem. After a month-long siege they got inside the city, where they slaughtered the Muslim defenders. (See "Thinking Like a Historian: Christian and Muslim Views of the Crusades," page 254.)

In the aftermath of the First Crusade, four small "Crusader kingdoms"—Jerusalem, Edessa, Tripoli, and Antioch—were established. Castles and fortified towns were built to defend against Muslim reconquest (see Map 9.4). Between 1096 and 1270 the crusading ideal was expressed in eight papally approved expeditions, though none after the First Crusade accomplished very much. Despite this lack of success, members of European noble families from nearly every generation took up the cross for roughly two hundred years.

The Crusades inspired the establishment of new religious orders, particularly military orders dedicated to protecting the Christian kingdoms. The most important was the Knights Templars, founded in 1119. Many people going off to the Holy Land put their property in Europe under Templar protection, and by the end of the thirteenth century the order was extremely wealthy, with secret rituals in which members pledged obedience to their leaders. The Templars began serving as moneylenders and bankers, which further increased their wealth. In 1307 King Philip IV of France sought to grab that wealth for himself; he arrested many Templars, accusing them of heresy, blasphemy, and sodomy. They were tortured, a number were burned at the stake, Philip took much of their money, and the Templars were disbanded.

Women from all walks of life participated in the Crusades. When King Louis IX of France was

---

■ **Crusades** Wars sponsored by the papacy for the recovery of Jerusalem and surrounding territories from the Muslims in the late eleventh to the late thirteenth centuries.

■ **indulgences** Grants by the pope that lessened or eliminated the penance that sinners had to pay on earth and in purgatory before ascending to Heaven.

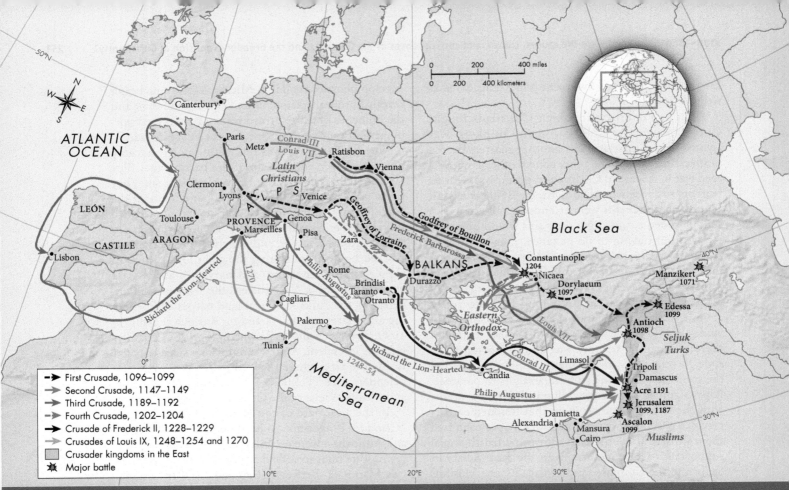

MAPPING THE PAST

MAP 9.4 The Crusades

This map shows the many different routes that Western Christians took over the centuries to reach Jerusalem.

ANALYZING THE MAP How were the results of the various Crusades shaped by the routes that the Crusaders took?

CONNECTIONS How did the routes and Crusader kingdoms offer opportunities for profit?

captured on the Seventh Crusade (1248–1254), his wife, Queen Marguerite, negotiated the surrender of the Egyptian city of Damietta to the Muslims. Some women concealed their sex by donning chain mail and helmets and fought with the knights. Some joined in the besieging of towns and castles. More typically, women provided water to fighting men, worked as washerwomen, foraged for food, and provided sexual services. There were many more European men than women, however, so marriage and sexual relations between Christian men and Muslim women were not unheard of, although marriages between Western Christian men and Orthodox Christian women who lived in the area were more common.

The Muslim states in the Middle East were politically fragmented when the Crusaders first came, and it took about a century for them to reorganize. They did

so dramatically under Saladin (Salah al-Dihn), who first unified Egypt and Syria and then retook Jerusalem in 1187. Christians immediately attempted to take it back in what was later called the Third Crusade (1189–1192), but disputes among the leaders and strategic problems prevented any lasting results. The Crusaders could not retake Jerusalem, though they did keep their hold on port towns, and Saladin allowed pilgrims safe passage to Jerusalem. He also made an agreement with Christian rulers for keeping the peace. From that point on, the Crusader states were more important economically than politically or religiously, giving Italian and French merchants direct access to Eastern products such as perfumes and silk.

In 1202 Innocent III sent out preachers who called on Christian knights to retake Jerusalem. Those who responded — in what would become the Fourth

Crusade—negotiated with the Venetians to take them by boat to Cairo, but Venetian interests combined with a succession struggle over the Byzantine throne led the fleet to go to Constantinople instead. Once there, the Crusaders decided to capture and sack Constantinople, destroying its magnificent library and seizing gold, silver, and relics to send home. The Byzantines reasserted their control over the empire in 1261, but it was much smaller and weaker and soon consisted of little more than the city of Constantinople. The assault by one Christian people on another helped discredit the entire crusading movement.

Nonetheless, there were a few more efforts. The Seventh Crusade in 1248, led by King Louis IX of France (r. 1223–1270), tried unsuccessfully to come in through Egypt. Louis also sent monks to the court of the Mongols in Central Asia, who were at this point led by Chinggis Khan, to forge an alliance that would encircle the Muslims. The monks were unsuccessful, but they brought back geographical knowledge of Asia and the peoples they had encountered. In the end, the Mamluk rulers of Egypt conquered the Crusader states, and in 1291 the last Crusader stronghold, the port of Acre, fell. Some knights continued their crusading efforts by joining the reconquista in Spain.

Consequences of the Crusades

The Crusades gave kings and the pope opportunities to expand their bureaucracies. They also provided kings with the perfect opportunity to get rid of troublemaking knights, particularly restless younger sons for whom the practice of primogeniture meant few prospects. Even some members of the middle class who stayed at home profited from the Crusades. Nobles often had to borrow money from city residents to pay for their expeditions, and they put up part of their land as security. If a noble did not return home or could not pay the interest on the loan, the middle-class creditor took over the land.

The Crusades introduced some Europeans to Eastern luxury goods, but their immediate cultural impact on the West remains debatable. Strong economic and intellectual ties with the East had already been developed by the late eleventh century. The Crusades did greatly benefit Italian merchants, who profited from the outfitting of military expeditions, the opening of new trade routes, and the establishment of trading communities in the Crusader states. Since commerce with the West benefited both Muslims and Europeans, it continued to flourish even after the Crusader states collapsed.

The Crusades proved to be a disaster for Jewish-Christian relations. In many parts of Europe, Jews lent money to peasants, townspeople, and nobles, and indebtedness bred resentment. Inspired by the ideology of holy war and resentment of Jewish economic activities, Christian armies on their way to Jerusalem on the First Crusade joined with local people to attack Jewish families and sometimes entire Jewish communities. In the German cities along the Rhine River, for example, an army of Crusaders under the leadership of a German noble forced Jews to convert through mass baptisms and killed those who resisted; more than eight hundred Jews were killed in Worms and more than a thousand in Mainz. Later Crusades brought similar violence, enhanced by rumors that Jews engaged in the ritual murder of Christians to use their blood in religious rites. As a result of growing hostility, legal restrictions on Jews gradually increased throughout Europe. In 1290 King Edward I of England expelled the Jews from England and confiscated their property and goods; it would be four centuries before they would be allowed back in. King Philip IV of France followed Edward's example in 1306.

The long-term cultural legacy of the Crusades may have been more powerful than their short-term impact. The ideal of a sacred mission to conquer or convert Muslim peoples entered some Europeans' consciousness and was later used in other situations. When Christopher Columbus sailed west in 1492, he hoped to reach India in part to establish a Christian base from which a new crusade against Islam could be launched. Muslims later looked back on the Crusades as expansionist and imperialist, the beginning of a long trajectory of Western attempts to limit or destroy Islam.

The Expansion of Christianity

The Crusades were not the only example of Christian expansion in the High Middle Ages. As we saw earlier, Christian kingdoms were established in the Iberian Peninsula through the reconquista. This gradual Christian advance was replicated in northern and eastern Europe in the centuries after 1000. People and ideas moved from western France and western Germany into Ireland, Scandinavia, the Baltic lands, and eastern Europe, with significant consequences for those territories. Wars of expansion, the establishment of new Christian bishoprics, and the vast migration of colonists, together with the papal emphasis on a unified Christian world, brought about the gradual Christianization of a larger area. By 1350 Roman Catholic Europe was double the size it had been in 950.

Ireland had been Christian since the days of Saint Patrick (see "Missionaries' Actions" in Chapter 7), but in the twelfth century Norman knights crossed from England, defeated Irish lords, and established bishoprics with defined territorial dioceses. Latin Christian influences also entered the Scandinavian and Baltic

Christian and Muslim Views of the Crusades

Both Christians and Muslims wrote accounts of the Crusades as they happened, which circulated among those who could read and served as the basis for later histories and visual depictions. How do Christian and Muslim views differ, and how are they similar?

1 **Peter Tudebode on the fall of Antioch, 1098.** Peter Tudebode was a French priest who accompanied the First Crusade and later wrote an account of it.

There was a Turkish emir [high-ranking army officer], Firuz, who became very friendly with Bohemond [a Norman noble, one of the leaders of the First Crusade]. Often through mutual messengers Bohemond suggested that Firuz admit him to Antioch; and, in turn, the Norman offered him the Christian religion along with great wealth from many possessions. Firuz, in accepting these provisions, replied: "I pledge freely the delivery of three towers of which I am a custodian.". . . The knights took to the plain and the footmen to the mountain, and all night they maneuvered and marched until almost daybreak, when they came to the towers which Firuz guarded. Bohemond immediately dismounted and addressed the group: "Go in dare-devil spirit and great *elan*, and mount the ladder into Antioch, which shall soon be in our hands if God so wills." They then went to a ladder, which was raised and lashed to the walls of the city, and almost sixty of our men scaled the ladder and divided their forces in the towers guarded by Firuz. . . . [W]e crashed down the gate, and poured into Antioch. . . . At sunup the crusaders who were outside Antioch in their tents, upon hearing piercing shrieks arising from the city, raced out and saw the banner of Bohemond flying high on the hill. Thereupon they rushed forth and each one speedily came to his assigned gate and entered Antioch, killing Turks and Saracens whom they found. . . . Yaghi Siyan, commander of Antioch, in great fear of the Franks, took to heel along with many of his retainers. . . . All of the streets of Antioch were choked with corpses so that the stench of rotting bodies was unendurable, and no one could walk the streets without tripping over a cadaver.

2 **Ibn al-Athir on the fall of Antioch.** Ali Ibn al-Athir (1160–1223), a Kurdish scholar and historian who lived in Mosul (today's Iraq), wrote a history of the First Crusade that relied on Arab sources.

Yaghi Siyan, the ruler of Antioch, showed unparalleled courage and wisdom, strength and judgment. If all the Franks who died had survived they would have overrun all the lands of Islam. He protected the families of the Christians in Antioch and would not allow a hair of their heads to be touched. After the siege had been going on for a long time the Franks made a deal with . . . an armor-maker called Ruzbih whom they bribed with a fortune in money and lands. He worked in the tower that stood over the riverbed, where the river flowed out of the city into the valley. The Franks sealed their pact with the armor-maker, God damn him! and made their way to the watergate. They opened it and entered the city. Another gang of them climbed the tower with their ropes. At dawn, when more than 500 of them were in the city and the defenders were worn out after the night watch, they sounded their trumpets. . . . Panic seized Yaghi Siyan and he opened the city gates and fled in terror, with an escort of thirty pages. . . . This was of great help to the Franks, [who] entered the city by the gates and sacked it, slaughtering all the Muslims they found there. . . .

It was the discord between the Muslim princes . . . that enabled the Franks to overrun the country.

3 **Fulcher of Chartres on the fall of Jerusalem to the Crusaders, 1099.** Fulcher was a chaplain to military leaders on the First Crusade and over several decades wrote a long and influential chronicle.

Soon thereafter the Franks gloriously entered the city at noon on the day known as Dies Veneris, the day in which Christ redeemed the whole world on the Cross. [That is, a Friday.]

ANALYZING THE EVIDENCE

1. How do Sources 1 and 2 differ in how they portray Yaghi Siyan and the man who opened the towers of Antioch to Christian forces? How do these and other differences influence the story?
2. In Sources 3 and 4, how is the course of the two battles for Jerusalem different? How is the aftermath different?
3. How does the artist who painted Source 5 convey his ideas about why the battle ended as it did?
4. How do these accounts balance the various aims — religious devotion, military glory, economic gain — of the two sides?

Amid the sound of trumpets and with everything in an uproar they attacked boldly, shouting "God help us!" At once they raised a banner in the city on the top of the wall. . . . They ran with the greatest exultation as fast as they could into the city and joined their companions in pursuing and slaying their wicked enemies without cessation. . . . If you had been there your feet would have been stained to the ankles in the blood of the slain. What shall I say? None of them were left alive. Neither women nor children were spared. How astonishing it would have seemed to you to see our squires and footmen, after they discovered the trickery of the Saracens, split open the bellies of those they had just slain in order to extract from the intestines the bezants [gold coins minted in Byzantium] which the Saracens had gulped down their loathsome throats while still alive! . . . After this great slaughter they entered the houses of the citizens, seizing whatever they found in them. This was done in such a way that whoever first entered a house, whether he was rich or poor, was not challenged by any other Frank. In this way many poor people became wealthy.

4 Al-Isfahani on Saladin's retaking of Jerusalem, 1187.
Imad ad-Din al-Isfahani (1125–1187) was a Persian scholar who served as secretary to Saladin and accompanied him on many of his military campaigns.

Saladin marched forward to take the reins of Jerusalem. . . . [T]he Franks despaired of finding any relief from their situation and decided all to give their lives (in defense of Jerusalem). . . . The Sultan mounted catapults, and by this means milked the udders of slaughter. . . . [I]n every heart on either side burned the fire of longing, faces were exposed to the blade's kiss, hearts were tormented with longing for combat. . . . Every onslaught was energetic and achieved its object, the goal was reached, the enemy wounded. . . . The city became Muslim and the infidel belt around it was

cut. . . . By striking coincidence the date of the conquest of Jerusalem was the anniversary of the Prophet's ascension to heaven. Great joy reigned for the brilliant victory won, and words of prayer and invocation to God were on every tongue. . . . Ibn Barzun [Balian of Ibelin, one of the Crusader leaders] came out to secure a treaty with the Sultan, and asked for an amnesty for his people. . . . [A]n amount was fixed for which they were to ransom themselves and their possessions . . . ten dinar for every man, five for a woman, and two for a boy or girl. . . . Every man who paid left his house in safety, and the rest were to be enslaved. . . . The Franks began selling their possessions and taking their precious things out of safe-keeping. . . . They scavenged in their own churches and stripped them of their ornaments of gold and silver. . . . Then I said to the Sultan, "These are things of great riches; do not allow these rascals to keep this in their grasp." But he replied, "If we interpret the treaty to their disadvantage they will accuse us of breaking faith." So they carried away the most precious and lightest [objects] and shook from their hands the dust of their heritage.

5 Capture of Antioch.
This illustration comes from a 1280 version of William of Tyre's *A History of Deeds Beyond the Sea*, the most widely read account of the Crusades, which drew extensively on earlier histories.

(Bibliothèque Municipale de Lyon, France/Bridgeman Images)

PUTTING IT ALL TOGETHER

Using the sources above, along with what you have learned in class and in this chapter, write a short essay that analyzes Christian and Muslim views of the Crusades. How did they differ, and how were they similar? How did the Crusades help shape the understanding that Christians and Muslims had of each other?

Sources: (1) Peter Tudebode, *Historia de Hierosolymitano Itinere,* trans. and ed. John H. Hill and Laurita L. Hill (Philadelphia: American Philosophical Society, 1974), pp. 56–57; (2) From *Arab Historians of the Crusades,* edited and translated by Francesco Gabrieli. Copyright © 1984 by the Regents of the University of California. Published by the University of California Press. Reprinted by Permission; (3) Fulcher of Chartres, *A History of the Expedition to Jerusalem, 1095–1127,* trans. Frances Rita Ryan and ed. Harold S. Fink (Knoxville: University of Tennessee Press, 1969), pp. 121–122; (4) Gabrieli, *Arab Historians of the Crusades,* pp. 147, 150, 154, 155, 156, 157–158, 162.

Persecution of Jews   This marginal illustration from the *Rochester Chronicle*, a fourteenth-century copy made by a monk in the English city Rochester of an earlier Latin chronicle, shows a man beating Jews with a club. The Jews are wearing badges in the form of two white tablets on their clothes, first ordered by royal mandate in 1218, "so that in this way Jews may be clearly distinguished from Christians." Both royal restrictions and local violence continued, so that by the time this illustration was made, Jews had been expelled from England. They would not be allowed to return until 1657. (British Library/Album/Alamy Stock Photo)

regions primarily through the erection of dioceses. Otto I established the first Scandinavian dioceses in Denmark. In Norway Christianity spread in coastal areas beginning in the tenth century, and King Olaf II (r. 1015–1028) brought in clergy and bishops from England and Germany to establish the church more firmly. From Norway Christianity spread to Iceland; from Denmark it spread to Sweden and Finland. In all of these areas, Christian missionaries preached, baptized, and built churches. Royal power advanced institutional Christianity, and traditional Norse religions practiced by the Vikings were outlawed.

In 1397 Queen Margrete I (1353–1412) united the crowns of Denmark, Sweden-Finland, and Norway in the Union of Kalmar. She continued royal support of bishops and worked toward creating a stronger state by checking the power of the nobility and creating a stronger financial base for the monarchy.

In eastern Europe, the German emperor Otto I planted a string of dioceses along his northern and eastern frontiers, hoping to pacify the newly conquered Slavs. German nobles built castles and ruthlessly crushed revolts by Slavic peoples, sometimes using the language of crusade to describe their actions.

A military order of German knights founded in Palestine, the Teutonic (too-TAH-nihk) Knights, moved their operations to eastern Europe and waged wars against the pagan Prussians in the Baltic region, again terming these "crusades." After 1230, from a base in Poland, they established a new Christian territory, Prussia, and gradually the entire eastern shore of the Baltic came under their hegemony.

The church also moved into central Europe, first in Bohemia in the tenth century and from there into Poland and Hungary in the eleventh. In the twelfth and thirteenth centuries, thousands of settlers poured into eastern Europe. These immigrants were German in descent, name, language, and law. Larger towns such as Kraków and Riga engaged in long-distance trade and gradually grew into large urban centers.

Christendom

Through the actions of the Roman emperors Constantine and Theodosius (see Chapter 7), Christianity became in some ways a state as well as a religion. Early medieval writers began to use the word **Christendom** to refer to this Christian realm. When the pope called for holy war against the Muslims, for example, he spoke not only of the retaking of Jerusalem, but also of the

■ **Christendom** The term used by early medieval writers to refer to the realm of Christianity.

defense of Christendom. When missionaries, officials, and soldiers took Christianity into the Iberian Peninsula, Scandinavia, or the Baltic region, they understood their actions as aimed at the expansion of Christendom.

From the point of view of popes such as Gregory VII and Innocent III, Christendom was a unified hierarchy with the papacy at the top. They pushed for uniformity of religious worship and campaigned continually for use of the same religious service, the Roman liturgy in Latin, in all countries and places. They forbade vernacular Christian rituals or those that differed in their pattern of worship. As we have seen in this chapter, however, not everyone had the same view. Kings and emperors may have accepted the Roman liturgy in their lands, but they had their own ideas of the way power should operate in Christendom, even if this brought them into conflict with the papacy. They remained loyal to Christendom as a concept, but they

had a profoundly different idea about how it should be structured and who could best defend it. The battles in the High Middle Ages between popes and kings and between Christians and Muslims were signs of how deeply religion had replaced tribal, political, and ethnic structures as the essence of Western culture.

NOTES

1. D. C. Douglas and G. E. Greenaway, eds., *English Historical Documents*, vol. 2 (London: Eyre & Spottiswoode, 1961), p. 853.
2. *Hrosvithae Liber Tertius, a Text with Translation*, ed. and trans. Mary Bernardine Bergman (Covington, Ky.: The Sisters of Saint Benedict, 1943), p. 45.
3. J. Johns, *Arabic Administration in Norman Sicily: The Royal Diwān* (New York: Cambridge University Press, 2002), p. 293.
4. H. T. Riley, ed., *Memorials of London* (London: Longmans Green, 1868).
5. Honorius of Autun, "Elucidarium sive Dialogus," vol. 172, col. 1148.

LOOKING BACK LOOKING AHEAD

The High Middle Ages were a time when kings, emperors, and popes expanded their powers and created financial and legal bureaucracies to support those powers. With political expansion and stability came better communication of information, more uniform legal systems, and early financial institutions. Nobles remained the dominant social group, but as monarchs developed new institutions, their kingdoms began to function more like modern states than disorganized territories. Popes made the church more independent of lay control, established the papal curia and a separate system of canon law, approved new religious orders that provided spiritual and social services, and developed new ways of raising revenue. They supported the expansion of Christianity in southern, northern, and eastern Europe and proclaimed a series of Crusades against Muslims to extend still further the boundaries of a Christendom under their control.

Many of the systems of the High Middle Ages expanded in later centuries and are still in existence today: the financial department of the British government remains the Exchequer; the legal systems of Britain and many former British colonies (including the United States) are based on common law; the pope is still elected by the college of cardinals and assisted by the papal curia; the Roman Catholic, Eastern Orthodox, and Anglican Churches still operate law courts that make rulings based on canon law. These systems also contained the seeds of future problems, however, for wealthier nations could sustain longer wars, independent popes could more easily abuse their power, and leaders who espoused crusading ideology could justify the enslavement or extermination of whole peoples.

Despite the long-lived impact of the growth of centralized political and ecclesiastical power — for good or ill — most people who lived during the high medieval period did not have direct experience of centralized institutions. Kings and popes sent tax collectors, judges, and sometimes soldiers, but they themselves remained far away. For most people, what went on closer to home in their families and local communities was far more important.

Make Connections

Think about the larger developments and continuities within and across chapters.

1. What similarities and differences do you see between the institutions and laws established by medieval rulers and those of Roman and Byzantine emperors (Chapters 6 and 7)?

2. What factors over the centuries enabled the Christian Church to become the most powerful and wealthy institution in Europe, and what problems did this create?

3. How would you compare the privileges and roles of medieval nobles with those of earlier hereditary elites, such as those of ancient Mesopotamia and Egypt (Chapter 1) or the patricians of republican Rome (Chapter 5)?

9 REVIEW & EXPLORE

Identify Key Terms

Identify and explain the significance of each item below.

Domesday Book (p. 232)

primogeniture (p. 233)

Holy Roman Empire (p. 235)

reconquista (p. 238)

common law (p. 238)

Magna Carta (p. 239)

chivalry (p. 240)

simony (p. 242)

college of cardinals (p. 242)

excommunication (p. 242)

canon law (p. 244)

religious orders (p. 245)

friars (p. 249)

Crusades (p. 250)

indulgences (p. 251)

Christendom (p. 256)

Review the Main Ideas

Answer the section heading questions from the chapter.

1. How did monarchs try to centralize political power? (p. 232)

2. How did the administration of law evolve in this period? (p. 238)

3. What were the political and social roles of nobles? (p. 240)

4. How did the papacy reform the church, and what were the reactions to these efforts? (p. 242)

5. What roles did monks, nuns, and friars play in medieval society? (p. 245)

6. What were the causes, course, and consequences of the Crusades and the broader expansion of Christianity? (p. 250)

Suggested Resources

BOOKS

- Bartlett, Robert. *England Under the Norman and Angevin Kings, 1075–1225.* 2000. An excellent synthesis of social, cultural, and political history in highly readable prose.

- Deane, Jennifer Kolpacoff. *A History of Medieval Heresy and Inquisition.* 2011. A concise history of the increasingly bitter encounters between dissent and the institutional church.

- Kaeuper, Richard W. *Chivalry and Violence in Medieval Europe.* 2006. Examines the role chivalry played in promoting violent disorder.
- Karras, Ruth M. *From Boys to Men: Formations of Masculinity in Late Medieval Europe.* 2002. Explores the way boys of different social groups were trained in what it meant to be a man; designed for students.
- Lawrence, C. H. *Medieval Monasticism: Forms of Religious Life in Western Europe in the Middle Ages,* 4th ed. 2015. Provides a solid introduction to monastic life as it was practiced.
- Madden, Thomas. *The New Concise History of the Crusades.* 2005. A highly readable brief survey by the pre-eminent American scholar of the Crusades.
- Moore, R. I. *The Formation of a Persecuting Society,* 2d ed. 2007. Sets the Inquisition and medieval heresy within a broad cultural, social, and political context.

- Newman, Barbara. *Voice of the Living Light: Hildegard of Bingen and Her World.* 1998. A book designed for general readers that places the medieval mystic within her social, intellectual, and political contexts.
- O'Callaghan, Joseph. *Reconquest and Crusade in Medieval Spain.* 2004. A broad survey that situates the Spanish reconquista within the context of crusading efforts.
- Rubin, Miri. *Gentile Tales: The Narrative Assault on Late Medieval Jews.* 2004. Explores the way that stories that were spread about Jews contributed to violence against them.
- Starkey, David. *Magna Carta: The Medieval Roots of Modern Politics.* 2015. A lively account for general readers of the document and its impact.
- Tyerman, Christopher. *Fighting for Christendom: Holy War and the Crusades.* 2005. Assesses the impact of the Crusades on modern times.

MEDIA

- *Battle Castle* (Parallax, 2012). A six-part interactive documentary, first shown on Canadian television, with an accompanying website and computer game, that examines sieges and battles involving six formidable castles in Syria, France, Spain, Wales, Poland, and England. Reflects high production values and excellent scholarship.
- *Becket* (Peter Glenville, 1964). Richard Burton stars as Thomas Becket and Peter O'Toole as King Henry II of England in a widely acclaimed film that focuses on the conflict between the two and the growth of royal power.
- *Braveheart* (Mel Gibson, 1995). Loosely based on the story of the thirteenth-century Scottish nobleman William Wallace, this historical epic regularly shows up on lists of best medieval films (for its battle scenes) and worst medieval films (for its historical inaccuracy).
- *De Re Militari.* The official website of the Society for the Study of Medieval Military History, with primary sources, articles, dissertations, and other resources for the study of military actions, technology, and topics from the fall of Rome to the early seventeenth century. **deremilitari.org/**

- *The Lion in Winter* (Anthony Harvey, 1968) (Andrey Konchalovskiy, 2003). Two award-winning film versions of the same play, centering on the intense and hostile relationships among Henry II, his wife Eleanor of Aquitaine, and their sons. The 1968 version stars Katharine Hepburn and Peter O'Toole, and the 2003 version stars Glenn Close and Patrick Stewart.
- *Medievalists.net.* This medieval-oriented blog provides news, articles, videos, reviews, and general information about the Middle Ages and medieval society. **www.medievalists.net**
- *Monastic Matrix.* A database website designed to make available all existing data about nuns and other women in religious communities in Christian Europe between 400 and 1600. Organized thematically and very easy to use. **arts.st-andrews.ac.uk/monasticmatrix/home**
- *Vision: From the Life of Hildegard von Bingen* (Margarethe von Trotta, 2010). A German film, with English subtitles, that focuses on the famed twelfth-century Benedictine nun, mystic, composer, and philosopher. Shot on location in the convent of Bingen and the surrounding countryside.

10

Life in Villages and Cities of the High Middle Ages

1000–1300

Kings, emperors, nobles, and their officials created political and legal institutions that structured many aspects of life in the High Middle Ages, but ordinary people typically worked and lived without paying much attention to the political developments that took place at faraway centers of power. Similarly, the conflicts between popes and secular leaders were dramatic, but for most people religion was primarily a matter of joining with neighbors and family members in rituals to express beliefs, thanks, and hopes.

While the routines of medieval life followed familiar rhythms for centuries, this does not mean that life in the High Middle Ages was unchanging. Agricultural improvements such as better plows and water mills increased the amount and quality of food, and the population grew. Relative security and the increasing food supply allowed for the growth and development of towns and a revival of long-distance trade. Some urban merchants and bankers became as wealthy as great nobles. Trade brought in new ideas as well as merchandise, and cities developed into intellectual and cultural centers. The university, a new type of educational institution, came into being, providing advanced training in theology, medicine, and law. Traditions and values were spread orally and in written form through poems, stories, and songs. Gothic cathedrals, where people saw beautiful stained-glass windows and listened to complex music, were physical manifestations of medieval people's deep faith and pride in their own community. ■

IAM CRISTI · VI TI

CHAPTER PREVIEW

- What was village life like in medieval Europe?

- How did religion shape everyday life in the High Middle Ages?

- What led to Europe's economic growth and reurbanization?

- What was life like in medieval cities?

- How did universities serve the needs of medieval society?

- How did literature and architecture express medieval values?

Mosaic of a Woman Feeding Chickens
In this detail from a magnificent gold mosaic in the ceiling of the Basilica of Saint Clement in Rome, made in the twelfth century, a woman feeds her chickens. Scenes from everyday life often feature in the margins of paintings, mosaics, and books, providing information about the lives of ordinary people that is unavailable elsewhere. (G. Dagli Orti/© NPL — DeA Picture Library/Bridgeman Images)

What was village life like in medieval Europe?

The vast majority of people in medieval Europe were peasants who lived in small villages and rarely traveled very far, but since villagers did not perform what were considered "noble" deeds, the aristocratic monks and clerics who wrote the records that serve as historical sources did not spend time or precious writing materials on the peasantry. When common people were mentioned, it was usually with contempt or in terms of the services and obligations they owed. Today's scholars are far more interested than were their medieval predecessors in the lives of ordinary people, however, and are using archaeological, artistic, and material sources to fill in details that are rarely mentioned in written documents.

Serfdom and Social Mobility

By the eleventh century, slavery was disappearing in rural areas of western Europe, replaced by serfdom, in which peasants could not be bought or sold but were required to stay on the land and provide labor services to the landowner. (For more on this subject, see "Manorialism, Serfdom, and the Slave Trade" in Chapter 8.) Most serfs worked small plots of land; in addition, all serfs were required to provide a certain number of days of labor a week—more in planting and harvest seasons—on a lord's land. Serfs were also often obliged to pay fees on common occurrences, such as marriage or the inheritance of land from one generation to the next.

Serfdom was a hereditary condition. As money became more widely available and widely used, however, some serfs bought their freedom. Some gained it when manorial lords organized groups of villagers to cut down forests or fill in swamps and marshes to make more land available for farming. A serf could clear a patch of fen or forestland, make it productive, and, through prudent saving, buy more land and eventually purchase freedom. Serfs who migrated longer distances, such as German peasants who moved eastward into Slavic lands, were often granted a reduction in labor services or freedom from serfdom as a reward. Thus both internal and external frontier lands in the High Middle Ages provided some opportunities for upward mobility. By 1300, about half of all peasants in England were free; they still often owed labor services on a lord's manor and other sorts of dues and taxes, but they were not bound to the land.

The Manor

Most peasants, free and serf, lived in family groups in small villages. One or more villages and the land surrounding them made up a manor controlled by a noble lord or a church official such as a bishop, abbot, or abbess. Most villages had a church. In some the lord's large residence was right next to the small peasant

Harvesting Hay   A peasant with his socks rolled down to stay cool mows hay with a long scythe, while in the background a mill along a stream stands ready to grind grain or carry out other tasks. This illustration comes from a book of hours made in France in the early fifteenth century, probably for the duke of Bedford. Books of hours were devotional books with psalms, prayers, and calendars of church holidays, sometimes lavishly decorated. They often included cycles of months that linked seasonal rural activities to signs of the zodiac; here Cancer the crab shows that this is June.
(© British Library Board. All Rights Reserved/ Bridgeman Images)

TIMELINE

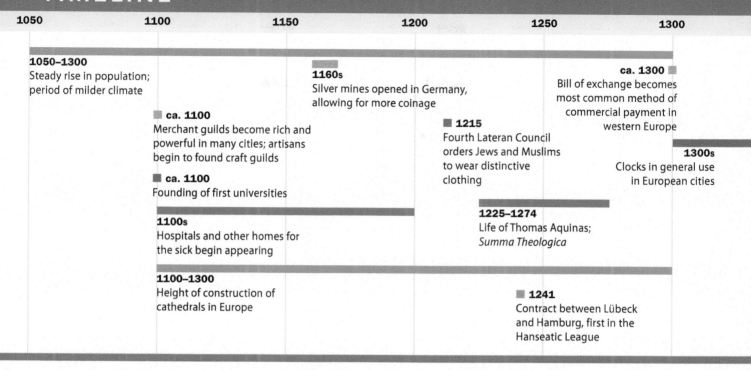

1050 **1100** **1150** **1200** **1250** **1300**

1050–1300
Steady rise in population; period of milder climate

ca. 1100
Merchant guilds become rich and powerful in many cities; artisans begin to found craft guilds

ca. 1100
Founding of first universities

1100s
Hospitals and other homes for the sick begin appearing

1100–1300
Height of construction of cathedrals in Europe

1160s
Silver mines opened in Germany, allowing for more coinage

1215
Fourth Lateran Council orders Jews and Muslims to wear distinctive clothing

1225–1274
Life of Thomas Aquinas; *Summa Theologica*

1241
Contract between Lübeck and Hamburg, first in the Hanseatic League

ca. 1300
Bill of exchange becomes most common method of commercial payment in western Europe

1300s
Clocks in general use in European cities

---

houses, while in others the lord lived in a castle or manor house separate from the village. Manors varied greatly in size; some contained a number of villages, and some were very small.

The arable land of the manor was divided between the lord and the peasantry, with the lord's portion known as the demesne (dih-MAYN), or home farm. The manor usually also held pasture or meadowland for the grazing of livestock, and often had some forest-land as well. Forests were valuable resources, providing wood, ash, and resin for a variety of purposes, and were also used for feeding domestic animals on nuts, roots, and wild berries.

Lords generally appointed officials, such as bailiffs, to oversee the legal and business operations of their manors, collect taxes and fees, and handle disputes. Villages in many parts of Europe also developed institutions of self-government to handle issues such as crop rotation, and villagers themselves chose additional officials such as constables, jurors, and ale-tasters. (See "Thinking Like a Historian: Social and Economic Relations in Medieval English Villages," page 264.) Women had no official voice in running the village, but they did buy, sell, and hold land independently, especially as widows who headed households. In areas of Europe where men left seasonally or more permanently in search of work elsewhere, women played a larger decision-making role, though they generally did not hold official positions.

Manors did not represent the only form of medieval rural economy. In parts of Germany and the Netherlands and in much of southern France, free independent farmers owned land outright, free of rents and service obligations. In Scandinavia the climate was so harsh and the soil was so poor that people tended to live on widely scattered farms rather than in villages, growing what crops they could. They also fished and cut timber, for their own use and to trade.

Work

The peasants' work was typically divided according to gender. Men cleared new land, plowed, and cared for large animals; women cared for small animals, spun yarn, and prepared food. Both sexes planted and harvested.

Once children were able to walk, they helped their parents in the hundreds of chores that had to be done. Small children collected eggs if the family had chickens or gathered twigs and sticks for firewood. As they grew older, children had more responsible tasks, such as weeding the family's vegetable garden, milking the cows, and helping with the planting or harvesting.

In many parts of Europe, medieval farmers employed the **open-field system**, a pattern that differs sharply from modern farming practices. In the open-field system, the arable land of a manor was divided into two or three fields without hedges or fences to mark the individual holdings of the lord, serfs, and free men. The village as a whole decided what would

> **open-field system** System in which the arable land of a manor was divided into two or three fields without hedges or fences to mark individual holdings.

Social and Economic Relations in Medieval English Villages

Medieval villages have often been portrayed as squalid hamlets where downtrodden peasants lived in an unchanging equality of misery under the harsh control of a lord. Do sources about actual rural life support this view of village social and economic relations, do they refute it, or do they make it more complex?

1 **Extent of the village of Alwalton, 1279.** Extents were surveys taken by landholders that listed the land and obligations of each household in a village.

The abbot of Peterborough holds the manor at Alwalton and village from the lord king directly. . . . Hugh Miller holds 1 virgate [about 25–30 acres] of land in villeinage by paying thence to the abbot 3 s. 1 d. [3 shillings, 1 denarius, or pence; there were 12 pence per shilling]. Likewise the same Hugh works through the year except 1 week at Christmas, 1 week at Easter, and 1 at Whitsuntide that is in each week 3 days, each day with 1 man, and in autumn each day with 2 men, performing the said works at the will of the said abbot as in plowing and other work. Likewise he gives 1 bushel of wheat for seed and 18 sheaves of oats for foddercorn. Likewise he gives 3 hens and 1 cock yearly and 5 eggs at Easter. Likewise he does carrying to Peterborough and to Jakele and nowhere else, at the will of the said abbot. Likewise if he sells a brood mare in his courtyard for 6 s. or more, he shall give to the said abbot 4 d., and if for less he shall give nothing. He gives also merchet [a payment when his daughters marry] and heriot [a payment when a family member dies] and is taxed at the feast of St. Michael, at the will of the said abbot. There are also 17 other villeins . . . paying and doing in all things, each for himself, to the said abbot yearly just as the said Hugh Miller. . . .

Henry, son of the miller, holds a cottage with a croft which contains 1 rood [¼ acre, a square about 100 feet on a side], paying thence yearly to the said abbot 2 s. Likewise he works for 3 days in carrying hay and in other works at the will of the abbot, each day with 1 man and in autumn 1 day in cutting grain with 1 man. . . . Likewise William Drake holds a cottage with a croft which contains half a rood [⅛ acre], paying to the abbot 6 d.; and he works just as the said Henry. There are also 18 other crofters . . . doing all things just as the said Henry.

2 **Extent of the manor of Bernehorne, 1307.**

John of Cayworth holds a house and 30 acres of land and owes yearly 2 s., at Easter and Michaelmas; and he owes a cock and two hens at Christmas, of the value of 4 d.

And he ought to harrow for 2 days at the Lenten sowing with one man and his own horse and his own harrow; the value of the work being 4 d.; and he is to receive from the lord on each day 3 meals, of the value of 5 d., and then his food will be at a loss of 1 d. Thus his harrowing is of no value to the service of the lord.

And he ought to carry the manure of the lord for 2 days with one cart, with his own 2 oxen, the value of the work being 8 d.; and he is to receive from the lord each day 3 meals of the price as above. And thus the service is worth 3 d. clear.

And he shall find one man for 2 days of mowing the meadow of the lord, who can mow, by estimation 1 acre and a half, the value of the mowing of an acre being 6 d.: the sum is therefore 9 d. and he is to receive each day 3 meals of the value given above; and thus that mowing is worth 4 d. clear. . . .

And he ought to carry the hay of the lord with a cart and 3 animals of his own . . . and in autumn carry beans and oats for 2 days with a cart . . . and carry wood from the woods of the lord as far as the manor house for two days in summer. . . . And he ought to find 1 man for 2 days to cut heath [for fuel] . . . and carry the heath that he has cut . . . and carry to Battle [a nearby town] twice in the summer season, each time a half a load of grain.

ANALYZING THE EVIDENCE

1. What types of obligations did peasants owe their lord? What types of obligations did they have to each other? How were these enforced?
2. What concerns of the villagers themselves emerge in the bylaws in Source 4? What do these concerns suggest about village society?
3. Are all villagers equal? What social and economic differences do you see among them?
4. What evidence do you see of growing commercialization, such as money, wage labor, market exchange, and considerations of market value?

3 Cart being pulled and pushed up a hill. This marginal illustration comes from the *Luttrell Psalter*, an illuminated devotional book commissioned by Sir Geoffrey Luttrell (1276–1345), the lord of a manor in Lincolnshire, and made by scribes and artists whose identity is unknown.

4 Village bylaws, Great Horwood, 1306 and 1319. Villagers themselves set rules regarding activities that they saw as problems. ("Gleaning" was picking up small bits of grain that had fallen from the stalks, an activity reserved for the elderly, small children, and ill or handicapped people.)

No one shall accept any outsider as a gleaner in autumn nor any man or woman to glean who is able to earn a penny a day for reaping if he finds someone who wishes to hire him.

Nor shall anyone pay in the field with whole sheaves, only handfuls of grain.

Nor shall anyone reap or cart except by day.

Nor shall anyone allow his calves or foals to go into the common fields of grain.

Nor shall anyone gather straw in the fields unless it be each from his own land. . . .

And if anyone is found guilty he shall pay the lord 4 d.

5 Court records from the village of Broughton, 1286. Several times a year villagers gathered for court proceedings during which the legal and financial affairs of both the lord and village were handled; this is a small part of the records from one day in one village.

John Nuncium le Mung [was fined] 12 d. because he did not send to the first day of service for the lord as many men as he had at his own work. . . .

William de Broughton is compelled to answer at the next court for the damage done by his two horses in the lord's peas.

Richard de Broughton [is compelled to answer] because he did not come to work for the lord in ditching. . . .

Alice Robynes is compelled to pay 6 d. for her geese damaging the lord's grain. . . .

Thomas Prat acknowledges that he is in debt to Agnes Gylot for goods to the value of 6 d. Therefore he shall make satisfaction to her for the aforesaid 6 d.

The chief pledges [male villagers responsible to know what was going on] say that the bailiff of the lord abbot made two pits in the town, to its nuisance. Therefore the bailiff is ordered to put them right. . . . And they say that Hugh Knyt harbored a strange woman who is not profitable to the town. Fined 6 d. . . . And they say that Robert Strypling pastured the grass of the neighbors by night. Fined 12 d. . . . And they say that the wife of Thomas le Hund was a gleaner against the common statute of the town. Fined 12 d. . . . And they say that Reginald Gylbert overused the pasture with twenty sheep. Fined 12 d. And they say that William Kepline paid with sheaves in the field in autumn contrary to the common statute of the town. Fined 12 d.

PUTTING IT ALL TOGETHER

Using the sources above, along with what you have learned in class and in this chapter and Chapters 8 and 9, write a short essay that analyzes social and economic relations in an English village in the High Middle Ages. To what extent is the traditional view of village life as uniformly oppressive warranted? If you believe that the traditional view is not accurate, what would be a better description?

Sources: (1, 2) *Translations and Reprints from the Original Sources of European History*, vol. 3, no. 5 (Philadelphia: University of Pennsylvania Department of History, 1897), pp. 4–7, 10–11; (4, 5) Warren O. Ault, *Open Field Farming in Medieval England: A Study of Village By-Laws* (London: George Allen and Unwin, 1972), pp. 86, 89, 155–159.

be planted in each field, rotating the crops according to tradition and need. Some fields would be planted with crops such as wheat, rye, peas, or barley for human consumption, some with oats or other crops for both animals and humans, and some left unworked or fallow to allow the soil to rejuvenate. In addition, legume crops such as peas and beans helped the soil rebuild nutrients and also increased the villagers' protein consumption. In most areas with open-field agriculture, the holdings farmed by any one family did not consist of a whole field but consisted, instead, of strips in many fields. Families worked their own land and the lord's, but also cooperated with other families if they needed help, particularly during harvest time. This meant that all shared in any disaster as well as in any large harvest.

Meteorologists think that a slow but steady retreat of polar ice occurred between the ninth and eleventh centuries, and Europe experienced a significant warming trend from 1050 to 1300. The mild winters and dry summers that resulted helped increase agricultural output throughout Europe, particularly in the north.

The tenth and eleventh centuries also witnessed a number of agricultural improvements, especially in the development of mechanisms that replaced or aided human labor. Mills driven by wind and water power dramatically reduced the time and labor required to grind grain, crush seeds for oil, and carry out other tasks. This change had a significant impact on women's productivity, for grinding was women's work. When water- and wind-driven mills were introduced into an area, women were freed from the task of grinding grain and could turn to other tasks, such as raising animals, working in gardens or vineyards, and raising and preparing flax to make linen. They could also devote more time to spinning yarn, which was the bottleneck in cloth production, as each weaver needed at least six spinners. Thus the spread of wind and water power indirectly contributed to an increase in cloth production in medieval Europe.

Another change, which came in the early twelfth century, was a significant increase in the production of iron. Much of this iron was used for weapons and armor, but it also filled a growing demand in agriculture. Iron was first used for plowshares (the part of the plow that cuts a deep furrow), and then for pitchforks, harrows (dragged tools that raked soil), spades, and axes. Peasants needed money to buy iron implements from village blacksmiths, and they increasingly also needed money to pay their obligations to their lords. To get the cash they needed, they sold whatever surplus they produced in nearby towns, transporting it there in wagons with iron parts.

In central and northern Europe, peasants made increasing use of heavy wheeled iron plows pulled by teams of oxen to break up the rich, clay-filled soil common there, and agricultural productivity increased. Further technological improvements, including padded horse collars and iron horseshoes, allowed horses, as well as oxen, to be used for plowing. The use of horses spread in the twelfth century because their greater speed brought greater efficiency to farming and reduced the amount of human labor involved. Horses were also used to haul goods to markets, where peasants sold any excess vegetables, grain, and animals.

By modern standards, medieval agricultural yields were very low, but there was striking improvement between the fifth and the thirteenth centuries. Increased output had a profound impact on society, improving Europeans' health, commerce, industry, and general lifestyle. More food meant that fewer people suffered from hunger and malnourishment and that devastating famines were rarer. Higher yields brought more food for animals as well as people, and the amount of meat that people ate increased slightly. A better diet had an enormous impact on women's lives in particular. More food meant increased body fat, which increased fertility, and more meat—which provided iron—meant that women were less anemic and less subject to disease. Some researchers believe that it was during the High Middle Ages that Western women began to outlive men. Improved opportunities also encouraged people to marry somewhat earlier, which meant larger families and further population growth. Demographers estimate that in an era before birth control, every three years earlier that a woman married meant she bore one more child, though not all of them reached adulthood.

Home Life

In western and central Europe, villages were generally made up of small houses for individual families. Households generally consisted of a married couple, their children (including stepchildren), and perhaps one or two other relatives. But not everyone married; some households contained only an unmarried person or several unmarried people living together. (See "Individuals in Society: Cecilia Penifader," page 267.) Older widows sometimes lived with their grown children, but they also might live on their own. In southern and eastern Europe, extended families were more likely to live in the same household.

The size and quality of peasants' houses varied according to their relative prosperity, which usually depended on the amount of land held. Poorer peasants lived in windowless one-room cottages. Prosperous peasants added rooms; some wealthy peasants in the early fourteenth century had two-story houses with separate bedrooms for parents and children. For most people, however, living space—especially living

Many medieval records have disintegrated or been destroyed in wars and revolutions, but those for England in the thirteenth and fourteenth centuries have survived especially well. They allow us to learn details about the lives of ordinary people, including Cecilia Penifader (1297?–1344), who lived in Brigstock, a village and royal manor of several hundred people in the English midlands, seventy-five miles north of London.

Cecilia's family was better-off and larger than those of most peasants. Her parents were free landholders, not serfs, and she had three brothers and three sisters who survived into adulthood. She never married, but lived close to or with her siblings for some of her life. When Cecilia was in her late teens, Brigstock and the rest of England suffered a series of poor harvests because of unusually cold and wet weather (see "Climate Change and Famine" in Chapter 11). Both her parents died during the Great Famine from 1315 to 1322, but their deaths, along with difficulties her neighbors experienced during this dismal time, also provided Cecilia with opportunities. She acquired a bit of land, perhaps with money inherited from her parents, and then purchased several more pieces, including a house and farmyard, arable fields, and meadows, along with sheep, oxen, goats, pigs, chickens, and other animals. As an unmarried female landholder, Cecilia was expected to attend the manorial court held every three weeks, where aspects of day-to-day life were managed; the records of that court are how we know about her.

Cecilia most likely did some tasks that were generally understood to be "male" herself, such as reaping, and she also hired men and boys from less prosperous families to help her, especially during labor-intensive times of the agricultural year. Most of her property was meadow or pasture for raising animals, which required less labor than crops. In contrast to her married sisters, she could manage her lands and animals as she saw fit, raising what she thought would sell and purchasing things made by others. But in contrast to her brothers and other male landholders, Cecilia could not hold a manorial office or serve as a pledge for someone else, activities that created networks of mutual obligation and friendship for men in the village; those networks also benefited their wives. If she did business at the court, one of her brothers or a brother-in-law stood pledge for her, guaranteeing that her word on agreements and contracts was good.

When she was in her late thirties, Cecilia and her unmarried brother Robert combined their resources and lands, creating their own household, which lasted until he died. Cecilia fell ill in 1344 and tried to give a long-term lease on her landholdings to three young people, including a niece and nephew. This arrangement disinherited her sister, who would have normally been her primary heir, and after Cecilia died, the sister successfully fought it in court, arguing that Cecilia had been too weak in body and mind to make a valid death-bed bequest. Instead her properties were dispersed among various family members.

QUESTIONS FOR ANALYSIS

1. How is Cecilia Penifader's life like that of her brothers? Her married sisters? How is it different?
2. How is her life shaped by her gender, her marital status, and her family's status as free and relatively prosperous peasants?
3. In what ways does Cecilia Penifader's life seem typical of a medieval peasant? In what ways is it distinctive?

Source: Information about Cecilia Penifader's life from Judith M. Bennett, *A Medieval Life: Cecilia Penifader and the World of English Peasants Before the Plague*. (Philadelphia: University of Pennsylvania Press, 2021).

Women reap grain with sickles while a man binds sheaves, from the *Luttrell Psalter*, created during Cecilia's lifetime for the lord of a manor just thirty miles north of Brigstock.
(Fine Art Images/Heritage Images/Getty Images)

space close enough to a fire to feel some warmth in cold weather—was cramped, dark, smoky, and smelly, with animals and people both sharing tight quarters, sometimes with each other.

The mainstay of the diet for peasants—and for all other classes—was bread. It was a hard, black substance made of barley, millet, and oats, rarely of expensive wheat, which they were more likely to use to pay their taxes and fees to the lord than for their own bread. Most households did not have ovens, which were expensive to build and posed a fire danger; their bread was baked in communal ovens or purchased from households that specialized in bread-baking. The main meal was often bread and a thick soup of vegetables and grains eaten around noon. Peasants ate vegetables not because they appreciated their importance for good health but because there was usually little else available. Animals were too valuable to be used for food on a regular basis, but weaker animals were often slaughtered in the fall so that they did not need to be fed through the winter. Their meat was salted for preservation and eaten on great feast days such as Christmas and Easter.

The diet of people with access to a river, lake, or stream would be supplemented with fish, which could be eaten fresh or preserved by salting. People living close to the sea gathered shellfish. Many places had severe laws against hunting and trapping in the forests. Deer, wild boars, and other game were reserved for the king and nobles. These laws were flagrantly violated, however, and rabbits and wild game often found their way to peasants' tables.

Medieval households were not self-sufficient but bought cloth, metal, leather goods, and even some food in village markets. They also bought ale, the universal drink of the common people in northern Europe. Women dominated in the production of ale. Ale provided needed calories and was safer to drink than the water from many rivers and streams, and it also provided some relief from the difficult, monotonous labor that filled people's lives. Medieval men and women often drank heavily, and brawls and violent fights were frequent at taverns.

The steady rise in population between the mid-eleventh and fourteenth centuries was primarily the result of warmer climate, increased food supply, and a reduction of violence with growing political stability, rather than dramatic changes in health care. Most illnesses were treated with home remedies. Treatments were often mixtures of herbal remedies, sayings, specific foods, prayers, amulets, and ritual healing activities. People suffering from wounds, skin diseases, or broken bones sometimes turned to barber-surgeons. For internal ailments, people consulted apothecaries, who suggested and mixed compounds taken internally or applied as a salve or ointment.

Beginning in the twelfth century in England, France, and Italy, the clergy, noble men and women, and newly rich merchants also established small hospitals and other institutions to care for the sick or for those who could not take care of themselves. Such institutions might be staffed by members of religious orders or by laymen and laywomen who were paid for their work.

Childbirth and Childhood

The most dangerous period of life for any person, peasant or noble, was infancy and early childhood. In normal years perhaps as many as one-third of all children died before age five from illness, malnutrition, and accidents, and this death rate climbed to more than half in years with plagues, droughts, or famines. However, once people reached adulthood, many lived well into their fifties and sixties.

Childbirth was dangerous for mothers as well as infants. Village women helped one another through childbirth, and women who were more capable acquired midwifery skills. In larger towns and cities, such women gradually developed into professional midwives who were paid for their services and who trained younger women as apprentices. For most women, however, childbirth was handled by female friends and family.

Historians used to paint a grim picture of medieval childhood. Childhood, they argued, was not recognized as a distinct stage in life until at least the late eighteenth century, and because so many children died young, they received little parental attention by parents wary about coming to love them too much. These views were derived largely from advice about raising children provided by priests and educators who advocated strict discipline and warned against coddling, from portraits of children that showed them dressed as little adults, and from the fact that parents sometimes abandoned infants or gave them to monasteries as religious acts, donating them to the service of God in the same way they might donate money.

This view has been made less bleak more recently by scholars using sources that reveal how children were actually treated. They have discovered that many parents showed great affection for their children and experienced deep grief when they died young. Parents left children to monasteries not because they were indifferent, but because they hoped thereby to ensure them a better material and spiritual future. Parents made toys for children: balls, dolls, rattles, boats, hobbyhorses, tops, and many other playthings. They tried to protect their children with religious amulets and pilgrimages to special shrines and sang them lullabies. Even practices that to us may seem cruel, such as tight swaddling, were motivated by a concern for the child's safety and health at a time when most households had open fires, domestic animals wandered freely, and mothers and older siblings engaged in labor-intensive work that prevented them from continually watching a toddler.

How did religion shape everyday life in the High Middle Ages?

Apart from the land, the weather, and local legal and social conditions, religion had the greatest impact on the daily lives of ordinary people in the High Middle Ages. Religious practices varied widely from country to country and even from province to province. But nowhere was religion a one-hour-a-week affair. Most people in medieval Europe were Christian, but there were small Jewish communities scattered in many parts of Europe, and Muslims lived in the Iberian Peninsula, Sicily, and other Mediterranean islands.

Christian Life in Medieval Villages

For Christians the village church was the center of community life — social, political, and economic, as well as religious — with the parish priest in charge of a host of activities. Although church law placed the priest under the bishop's authority, the manorial lord appointed the priest. Rural priests were peasants and often worked in the fields with the people during the week. On Sundays and holy days, they put on a robe and celebrated Mass, or the Eucharist, the ceremony in which the priest consecrated bread and wine and distributed it to believers, in a re-enactment of Jesus's Last Supper. They recited the Mass in Latin, a language that few commoners, sometimes including the priest himself, could understand. At least once a year villagers were expected to take part in the ceremony and eat the consecrated bread. This usually happened at Easter, after they had confessed their sins to the priest and been assigned a penance.

In everyday life people engaged in rituals and used language heavy with religious symbolism. Before planting, the village priest customarily went out and sprinkled the fields with water, symbolizing refreshment and life. Everyone participated in village processions to honor the saints and ask their protection. The entire calendar was filled with reference to events in the life of Jesus and his disciples, such as Christmas (celebrating Jesus's birth), Easter (celebrating Jesus's resurrection after death), and Pentecost (commemorating the descent of the Holy Spirit on the disciples). Scriptural references and proverbs dotted everyone's language. The English *good-bye*, the French *adieu*, and the Spanish *adios* all derive from words meaning "God be with you." The signs and symbols of Christianity were visible everywhere, but so, people believed, was the Devil, who lured them to evil deeds. In some medieval images and literature, the Devil is portrayed as black, an identification that shaped Western racial attitudes.

Saints and Sacraments

Along with days marking events in the life of Jesus, the Christian calendar was filled with saints' days. Veneration of the saints had been an important tool of Christian conversion since late antiquity (see "The Process of Conversion" in Chapter 7), and the cult of the saints was a central feature of popular culture in the Middle Ages. In return for the saint's healing and support, peasants offered the saint prayers, loyalty, and gifts. In the later Middle Ages popular hagiographies (ha-gee-AH-gruh-fees) — biographies of saints based on myths, legends, and popular stories — attributed specialized functions to the saints. Every occupation had a patron saint, as did cities and even realms.

The Virgin Mary, Christ's mother, was the most important saint. In the eleventh century theologians began to emphasize Mary's spiritual motherhood of all Christians. Special Masses commemorated her, churches were built in her honor, and hymns and prayers to her multiplied. Villagers listened intently to sermons telling stories about her life and miracles. One favorite story told of a minstrel and acrobat inspired to perform tumbling feats in Mary's honor:

> [He performed] until from head to heel sweat stood upon him, drop by drop, as blood falls from meat turning on a hearth. . . . [Then] there came down from the heavens a Dame so glorious, that certainly no man had seen one so precious, nor so richly crowned. . . . Then the sweet and courteous Queen herself took a white napkin in her hand, and with it gently fanned her minstrel before the altar. . . . She blesses her minstrel with the sign of God.[1]

People reasoned that if Mary would even bless tumbling (a disreputable form of popular entertainment) as long as it was done with a reverent heart, she would certainly bless their lives of hard work and pious devotion even more.

Along with the veneration of saints, sacraments were an important part of religious practice. Twelfth-century

Statue of Saint Anne, the Virgin Mary, and the Christ Child   Nearly every church had at least one image of the Virgin Mary, the most important figure of Christian devotion in medieval Europe. In this thirteenth-century wooden sculpture, she is shown holding the infant Jesus and is herself sitting on the lap of her mother, Anne. Statues such as this reinforced people's sense that the heavenly family was much like theirs, with grandparents who sometimes played important roles. (Museo Nazionale del Bargello, Florence, Italy/Scala/Art Resource, NY)

theologians expanded on Saint Augustine's understanding of sacraments (see "Saint Augustine on Human Nature, Will, and Sin" in Chapter 7) and created an entire sacramental system. In 1215 the Fourth Lateran Council formally accepted seven sacraments (baptism, penance, the Eucharist, confirmation, marriage, priestly ordination, anointment of the dying). Medieval Christians believed that these seven sacraments brought God's grace, the divine assistance or help needed to lead a good Christian life and to merit salvation. Most sacraments had to be dispensed by a priest, although spouses officially administered the sacrament of marriage to each other, and laypeople could baptize a dying infant or anoint a dying person if no priest could be found. In this way, the sacramental system enhanced the authority of priests over people's lives, but did not replace strong personal devotion to the saints.

Muslims and Jews

The centrality of Christian ceremonies to daily life for most Europeans meant that those who did not participate were clearly marked as outsiders. Many Muslims left Spain as the Christian "reconquest" proceeded and left Sicily when this became a Christian realm (see "Italy" and "The Iberian Peninsula" in Chapter 9), but others converted. In more isolated villages, people simply continued their Muslim rituals and practices, though they might hide these from the local priest or visiting officials.

Islam was geographically limited in medieval Europe, but by the late tenth century Jews could be found in many areas, often brought in from other areas as clients of rulers to help with finance. Jewish communities could be found in Italian and French cities and in the cities along the Rhine. Jewish dietary laws require meat to be handled in a specific way, so Jews had their own butchers; there were Jewish artisans in many other trades as well. Jews held weekly religious services on Saturday, the Sabbath, and celebrated their own annual cycle of holidays. Each of these holidays involved special prayers, services, and often foods, and many of them commemorated events from Jewish history, including various times when Jews had been rescued from captivity.

Jews could supply other Jews with goods and services, but rulers and city leaders increasingly restricted their trade with Christians to banking and money-lending. This restriction enhanced Christian resentment, as did the ideology of holy war that accompanied the Crusades (see "Background and Motives of the Crusades" in Chapter 9). Violence against Jews and restrictions on their activities increased further in much of Europe. Jews were expelled from England and later from France. However, Jews continued to live in the independent cities of the Holy Roman Empire and Italy, and some migrated eastward into new towns that were being established in Slavic areas.

Rituals of Marriage and Birth

Increasing suspicion and hostility marked relations between religious groups throughout the Middle Ages, but there were also important similarities in the ways Christians, Jews, and Muslims understood and experienced their religions. In all three traditions, every

Wedding Door of the Cathedral in Strasbourg Medieval cathedrals, such as this one from the thirteenth century, sometimes had a side door depicting a biblical story of ten young women who went to meet a bridegroom. Five of them wisely took extra oil for their lamps, while five foolishly did not (Matthew 25:1–13). In the story, which is a parable about being prepared for the end of the world, the foolish maidens were out of oil when the bridegroom arrived and missed the wedding feast. The "maidens' door" became a popular site for weddings, which were held right in front of it. (akg-images/Paul M.R. Maeyaert/Newscom)

major life transition was marked by a ceremony that included religious elements.

Christian weddings might be held in the village church or at the church door, though among well-to-do families the ceremony took place in the house of the bride or bridegroom. A priest's blessing was often sought, though it was not essential to the marriage. Muslim weddings were also finalized by a contract between the bride and groom and were often overseen by a wedding official. Jewish weddings were guided by statements in Talmudic law that weddings were complete when the bride had entered the *chuppah*, which medieval Jewish authorities interpreted to mean a room in the groom's house.

In all three faiths, the wedding ceremony was followed by a wedding party that often included secular rituals. Some rituals symbolized the proper hierarchical relations between the spouses—such as placing the husband's shoe on the bedstead over the couple, symbolizing his authority—or were meant to ensure the couple's fertility—such as untying all the knots in the household, for it was believed that people possessing magical powers could tie knots to inhibit a man's reproductive power. All this came together in what was often the final event of a wedding: the religious official blessed the couple in their marriage bed, often with family and friends standing around or banging on pans, yelling, or otherwise making as much noise as possible to make fun of the couple's first sexual encounter. (Tying cans on the back of the car in which a couple leaves the wedding is a modern remnant of such rituals.)

Friends and family members had generally been part of the discussions, negotiations, and activities leading up to the marriage; marriage united two families and was far too important to leave up to two people alone. Among serfs, the manorial lord's permission was often required, with a special fee

required to obtain it. (This permission did not, as often alleged, give the lord the right to deflower the bride. Though lords certainly forced sex on female serfs, there is no evidence in any legal sources that lords had the "right of first night," the *jus primae noctis*.) The involvement of family and friends in choosing one's spouse might lead to conflict, but more often the wishes of the couple and their parents, kin, and community were quite similar: all hoped for marriages that provided economic security, honorable standing, and a good number of healthy children. The best marriages offered companionship, emotional support, and even love, but these were understood to grow out of the marriage, not necessarily precede it. Breaking up a marriage meant breaking up the basic production and consumption unit, a very serious matter. The Christian Church forbade divorce, and even among non-Christians marital dissolution by any means other than the death of one spouse was rare.

Most brides hoped to be pregnant soon after the wedding. Christian women hoping for children said special prayers to the Virgin Mary or her mother, Anne. Some wore amulets of amber, bone, or mistletoe, thought to increase fertility. Others repeated charms and verses they had learned from other women, or, in desperate cases, went on pilgrimages to make special supplications. Muslim and Jewish women wore small cases with sacred verses or asked for blessings from religious leaders. Women continued these prayers and rituals throughout pregnancy and childbirth, often combining religious traditions with folk beliefs.

Judaism, Christianity, and Islam all required women to remain separate from the community for a short time after childbirth and often had special ceremonies welcoming them back once this period was over. These rituals often included prayers, such as this one from the Christian ritual of thanksgiving and purification, called churching, which a woman celebrated six weeks after giving birth: "Almighty and everlasting God, who has freed this woman from the danger of bearing a child, consider her to be strengthened from every pollution of the flesh so that with a clean heart and pure mind she may deserve to enter into the bosom of our mother, the church, and make her devoted to Your service."[2]

Religious ceremonies also welcomed children into the community. Among Christian families, infants were baptized soon after they were born to ensure that they could enter Heaven. Midwives who delivered children who looked especially weak and sickly often baptized them in an emergency service. In normal baptisms, the women who had assisted the mother in the birth often carried the baby to church, where godparents vowed their support. Godparents were often close friends or relatives, but parents might also choose prominent villagers or even the local lord in the hope that he might later look favorably on the child and provide for him or her in some way.

Within Judaism, a boy was circumcised by a religious official and given his name in a ceremony on his eighth day of life. This *brit milah*, or "covenant of circumcision," was viewed as a reminder of the Covenant between God and Abraham described in Hebrew Scripture. Muslims also circumcised boys in a special ritual, though the timing varied from a few days after birth to adolescence.

Death and the Afterlife

Death was similarly marked by religious ceremonies, and among Europeans of all faiths death did not sever family obligations and connections. Christians called for a priest to perform the sacrament of extreme unction, with holy water, holy oil, a crucifix, and a censer with incense, when they thought the hour of death was near.

Once the person had died, the body was washed and dressed in special clothing—or a sack of plain cloth—and buried within a day or two. Family and friends joined in a funeral procession. The wealthy were sometimes buried inside the church—in the walls, under the floor, or under the building itself in a crypt—but most people were buried in the church-yard or a cemetery close by. At the graveside, the priest asked for God's grace for the soul of the deceased and also asked that soul to "rest in peace." This final request was made not only for the benefit of the dead, but also for that of the living as the souls of the dead were widely believed to return to earth. Priests were hired to say memorial Masses on anniversaries of family deaths, especially one week, one month, and one year afterward.

During the High Middle Ages, learned theologians increasingly emphasized the idea of purgatory, the place where souls on their way to Heaven went after death to make amends for their earthly sins. Memorial Masses, prayers, and donations made in their names could shorten their time in purgatory. So could indulgences, those papal grants that relieved a person from earthly penance. Indulgences were initially granted for performing meritorious acts, such as going on a pilgrimage or crusade, but later on they could be obtained by paying a small fee (see "Background and Motives of the Crusades" in Chapter 9). With this development, their spiritual benefits became transferable, so indulgences could be purchased to shorten the stay in purgatory of one's deceased relatives, as well as to lessen one's own penance or time in purgatory.

Among Muslims and Jews, the living also had obligations to the dead. In both groups deceased people were buried quickly, and special prayers were said by mourners and family members. Muslims fasted on behalf of the dead and maintained a brief period of official mourning. The Qur'an promises an eternal paradise with flowing rivers to "those who believe and do good deeds" (Qur'an, 4:57) and a Hell of eternal torment to those who do not.

Jews observed specified periods of mourning during which the normal activities of daily life were curtailed. Every day for eleven months after a death and every year after that on the anniversary of the death, a son of the deceased was to recite Kaddish, a special prayer of praise and glorification of God. Judaism emphasized life on earth more than an afterlife, so beliefs about what happens to the soul after death were more varied; the very righteous might go directly to a place of spiritual reward, but most souls went first to a place of punishment and purification generally referred to as *Gehinnom*. After a period that did not exceed twelve months, the soul ascended to the world to come. Those who were completely wicked during their lifetimes might simply go out of existence or continue in an eternal state of remorse.

What led to Europe's economic growth and reurbanization?

Most people continued to live in villages in the High Middle Ages, but the rise of towns and the growth of a new business and commercial class were a central part of Europe's recovery after the disorders of the tenth century. As towns gained legal and political rights, merchant and craft guilds grew more powerful, and towns became centers of production as well as commerce.

The Rise of Towns

Medieval towns began in many different ways. Some were fortifications erected as a response to ninth-century invasions; the peasants from the surrounding countryside moved within the walls when their area was attacked. Other towns grew up around great cathedrals (see "Churches and Cathedrals" at the end of this chapter) and monasteries whose schools drew students from distant areas. Many other towns grew from the sites of Roman army camps or cities, which had shrunk in the early Middle Ages but never entirely disappeared. Still others arose where a trade route crossed a river or a natural harbor allowed ships to moor easily.

Regardless of their origins, medieval towns had a few common characteristics. Each town had a marketplace, and most had a mint for the coining of money. The town also had a court to settle disputes. In addition, medieval towns were enclosed by walls.

The terms *burgher* (BUHR-guhr) and *bourgeois* derive from the Old English and Old German words *burg*, *burgh*, *borg*, and *borough* for "a walled or fortified place." Thus a burgher or bourgeois originally was a person who lived or worked inside the walls. Townspeople supported themselves primarily by exchanging goods and services with one another, becoming artisans, shopkeepers, and merchants. They bought their food from the surrounding countryside and purchased goods from far away brought by traveling merchants.

No matter where people congregated, they settled on someone's land and had to secure permission to live there from the king, count, abbot, or bishop. Aristocratic nobles and churchmen were sometimes hostile to the towns set up on their land, but they soon realized that these could be a source of profits and benefits.

The growing towns of medieval Europe slowly gained legal and political rights, including the rights to hold municipal courts, select the mayor and other municipal officials, and tax residents and visitors. Lords were often reluctant to grant towns self-government, fearing loss of authority and revenue if they gave the residents full independence. When burghers bargained for a town's political independence, however, they offered sizable amounts of ready cash and sometimes promised payments for years to come. Consequently, lords ultimately agreed to self-government.

Walled Town of Carcassonne   The walls of Carcassonne, a hilltop town in southern France, were built over many centuries from the Roman period into the Middle Ages, and restored in the nineteenth century. Linking more than fifty towers, the walls defended the city in a number of sieges. The vineyards in the foreground may have been there in the Middle Ages as well, as southern France was already an important wine-growing area. (Patrick Frilet/Shutterstock)

Urban population
- ○ Over 80,000
- ■ Over 40,000
- ▲ Over 20,000
- • Over 10,000

Population density per square km
- More than 30
- 21–30
- 11–20
- 10 or less

MAP 10.1 European Population Density, ca. 1300

The development of towns and the reinvigoration of trade were directly related in medieval Europe. Using this map, Maps 10.2 and 10.3, and the information in this chapter, answer the following questions.

ANALYZING THE MAP What were the four largest cities in Europe? What part of Europe had the highest density of towns?

CONNECTIONS What role did textile and other sorts of manufacturing play in the growth of towns? How was the development of towns related to that of universities, monastery schools, and cathedral schools?

In addition to working for the independence of the towns, townspeople tried to acquire liberties for themselves. In the Middle Ages the word *liberties* meant special privileges. The most important privilege a medieval townsperson could gain was personal freedom. It gradually developed that an individual who fled his or her manor and lived in a town for a year and a day was free of servile obligations and status. Thus the growth of towns contributed to a slow decline of serfdom in western Europe, although this process took centuries.

Towns developed throughout much of Europe, but the concentration of the textile industry led to the growth of many towns in the Low Countries (present-day Holland, Belgium, and French Flanders). In 1300 Paris was the largest city in western Christian Europe, with a population of about 200,000 (Map 10.1), and Constantinople was larger still, with perhaps 300,000 people. Córdoba, the capital of Muslim Spain, may have been the largest city in the world, with a population that might have been nearly half a million, although this number declined steeply when the city was conquered by Christian forces in 1236 and many people fled southward, swelling the population of Granada.

Merchant and Craft Guilds

The merchants, who were influential in winning towns' independence from feudal lords, also used their power and wealth to control life within the city walls. The merchants of a town joined together to form a **merchant guild** that prohibited nonmembers from trading in the town. Guild members often made up the earliest town government, serving as mayors and members of the city council. By the late eleventh century, especially in the towns of the Low Countries and northern Italy, the leaders of the merchant guilds were rich and politically powerful.

While most towns were initially established as trading centers, they quickly became centers of production as well. Peasants looking for better opportunities moved to towns—either with their lord's approval or without it—providing both workers and mouths to feed. Some townspeople began to specialize in certain types of food and clothing production. Over time some cities specialized in certain items, becoming known for their fine fabrics, their reliable arms and armor, or their elegant gold and silver work.

Like merchants, producers recognized that organizing would bring benefits, and beginning in the twelfth century in many cities they formed **craft guilds** that regulated most aspects of production. Guilds set quality standards for their particular product and regulated the size of workshops and the conduct of members. In most cities individual guilds, such as those of shoemakers or blacksmiths, achieved a monopoly in the production of one particular product, forbidding nonmembers to work. The craft guild then chose some of its members to act as inspectors and set up a court to hear disputes between members, though the city court remained the final arbiter.

Each guild set the pattern by which members were trained and the length of the training period. A boy who wanted to become a weaver, for instance, or whose parents wanted him to, spent four to seven years as an apprentice, often bound by a contract. When the apprenticeship was finished, a young artisan spent several years as a journeyman, working in the shop of a master artisan. He then could make his "masterpiece"—in the case of weavers, a long piece of cloth. If the other masters judged the cloth acceptable, and if they thought the market in their town was large enough to support another weaver, the

journeyman could then become a master and start a shop. If the guild decided there were already enough masters, he would need to leave that town and try elsewhere. Guilds developed in services as well as production, including those for barber-surgeons, notaries, innkeepers, and money-changers. (See "Evaluating Written Evidence: Apprenticeship Contract for a Money-Changer," page 276.)

Many guilds required masters to be married, as they recognized the vital role of the master's wife. She assisted in running the shop, often selling the goods her husband had produced. Their children, both male and female, also worked alongside the apprentices and journeymen. The sons were sometimes formally apprenticed, but the daughters were generally not apprenticed because many guilds limited formal membership to males. Most guilds allowed a master's widow to continue operating a shop for a set period of time after her husband's death, for they recognized that she had the necessary skills and experience. Such widows paid all guild dues, but they were not considered full members and could not vote or hold office in the guild. In a handful of cities there were a few all-female guilds, especially in spinning gold thread or weaving silk ribbons for luxury clothing, trades in which girls were formally apprenticed in the same way boys were.

Both craft and merchant guilds were not only economic organizations, but also systems of social support. They took care of elderly masters who could no longer work, and they often supported masters' widows and orphans. They maintained an altar at a city church and provided for the funerals of members and baptisms of their children. Guild members marched together in city parades and reinforced their feelings of solidarity with one another by special ceremonies and distinctive dress. Merchant guilds in some parts of Europe, such as the German cities of Hamburg, Lübeck, and Bremen, had special buildings for celebrations and ceremonies.

The Revival of Long-Distance Trade

The growth of towns went hand in hand with a revival of trade as artisans and craftsmen manufactured goods for both local and foreign consumption (Map 10.2). Most trade centered in towns and was controlled by professional traders. Long-distance trade was risky and required large investments of capital. Thus, merchants would often pool their resources to finance an expedition to a distant place. When the ship or caravan

---

■ **merchant guild** A band of merchants in a town that prohibited nonmembers from trading in that town.

■ **craft guild** A band of producers in a town that regulated most aspects of production of a good in that town.

Apprenticeship Contract for a Money-Changer

Most medieval cities minted their own money, as did rulers, abbots, and some nobles, so in every city there were money-changers who exchanged money from outside the city for that used in the city itself. They needed to know the value of a huge array of currencies in silver and gold, and keep track of those in which base metals such as tin and lead might have been mixed in, as these were worth less. Money-changing became a guild in many cities, and young men learned through apprenticeship, sealed by a contract, such as this one from the Mediterranean port of Marseilles in 1248.

May twelfth, in the year of the Incarnation of Our Lord 1248. I, John of St. Maximin, lawyer, place with you John Cordier, money-changer, my son William Deodat, as an apprentice, so that you may teach and instruct him in the art of money-changing, for two complete and continuous years from this date. I promise by this agreement that I will take care that my son will serve his apprenticeship with you and that he will be faithful and honest in all his dealings for the whole of the said period, and that he will not depart from you nor take anything away from you. And if it should happen, which God forbid, that the said William should cause you any loss I promise to reimburse you by this agreement, believing in your unsupported word, etc. Also I promise to give by this agreement for the expenses of the said William food, that is bread and wine and meat, fourteen *heminae* [a liquid and dry measure] of good grain and fifty solidi of the money now current in Marseilles, at your request, and to provide the said William with clothing and necessaries, pledging all my goods, etc.; renouncing the benefit of all laws, etc. To this I, the said John Cordier, receive the said William as a pupil and promise you, the said John St. Maximin, to teach your son well and faithfully the business of money-changing, etc., pledging all my goods, etc.; renouncing the benefit of all laws, etc. Witnesses, etc.

EVALUATE THE EVIDENCE

1. What does John of St. Maximin promise to give John Cordier for training his son William, and what does he promise about William's conduct? What does John Cordier promise in return?
2. What is John of St. Maximin's occupation, and what does this suggest about the profession of money-changer in medieval cities?
3. Like modern contracts, medieval contracts were often formulaic, drawn up by notaries, who used standardized language. What evidence do you see for such standardization in this source, and what does this suggest about apprenticeship contracts?

Source: Roy C. Cave and Herbert H. Coulson, eds., *A Source Book for Medieval Economic History* (New York: Biblio and Tannen, 1965), p. 145.

returned and the cargo was sold, these investors would share the profits. If disaster struck the caravan, an investor's loss was limited to the amount of that individual's investment.

In the late eleventh century the Italian cities, especially Venice, led the West in trade in general and completely dominated trade with the East. Venetian ships carried salt from the city's own lagoon, pepper and other spices from India and North Africa, silks and carpets from Central Asia, and enslaved people from many places. In northern Europe, the towns of Bruges, Ghent, and Ypres (EE-pruh) in Flanders built a vast cloth industry, becoming leaders in both the manufacture and trade of textiles. With easy access to high-quality English wool, Flemish clothmakers could produce high-quality cloth, the most important manufactured product handled by merchants and one of the few European products for which there was a market in the East.

From the late eleventh through the thirteenth centuries, Europe enjoyed a steadily expanding volume of international trade. Trade surged markedly with demand for sugar from the Mediterranean islands to replace honey; spices from Asia to season a bland diet; and fine wines from the Rhineland, Burgundy, and Bordeaux to make life more pleasant. Other consumer goods included luxury woolens from Flanders and Tuscany, furs from Ireland and Russia, brocades and tapestries from Flanders, and silks from Constantinople and even China. As the trade volume expanded, the use of cash became more widespread. Beginning in the 1160s the opening of new silver mines in Germany, Bohemia, northern Italy, northern France, and western England led to the minting and circulation of vast quantities of silver coins.

Increased trade also led to a higher standard of living. Contact with Eastern civilizations introduced Europeans to eating utensils, and table manners improved. Nobles learned to eat with forks and knives instead of tearing the meat from a roast with their hands. They began to use napkins instead of wiping

■ **Hanseatic League** A mercantile association of towns begun in northern Europe that allowed for mutual protection and trading rights.

their greasy fingers on their clothes or on the dogs lying under the table.

Business Procedures

The economic surge of the High Middle Ages led merchants to invent new business procedures. Beginning in Italy, merchants formalized their agreements with new types of contracts, including temporary contracts for land and sea trading ventures and permanent partnerships termed *compagnie* (kahm-pah-NYEE; literally "bread together," that is, sharing bread; the root of the word *company*). Many of these agreements were initially between brothers or other relatives and in-laws, but they quickly grew to include people who were not family members. In addition, they began to

involve individuals—including a few women—who invested only their money, leaving the actual running of the business to the active partners. Commercial correspondence, unnecessary when one businessperson oversaw everything and made direct bargains with buyers and sellers, proliferated. Accounting and record keeping became more sophisticated, and credit facilitated business expansion.

The ventures of the German Hanseatic League illustrate these new business procedures. The **Hanseatic League** (often called simply the Hansa) was a mercantile association of towns. It originated in agreements between merchants for mutual security and exclusive trading rights, and it gradually developed into agreements among towns themselves, the first of which was one between Hamburg and Lübeck

MAP 10.2   **Trade and Manufacturing in Thirteenth-Century Europe**   Note the overland and ocean lines of trade and the sources of silver, iron, copper, lead, paper, wool, carpets and rugs, and enslaved captives.

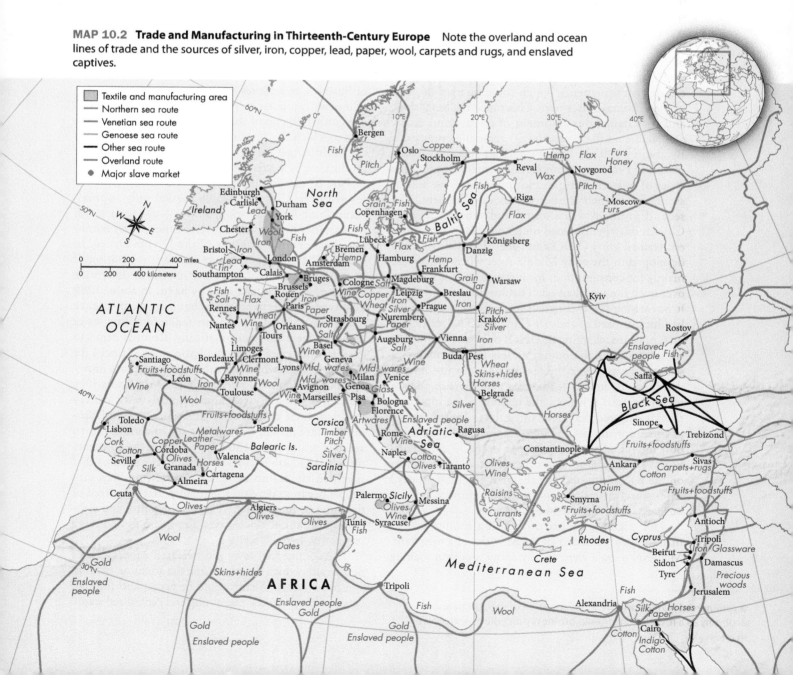

in 1241. At its height, the league included perhaps two hundred cities from Holland to Poland. From the fourteenth to the sixteenth centuries the Hanseatic League controlled the trade of northern Europe. In cities such as Bruges and London, Hansa merchants secured special trading concessions, exempting them from all tolls and allowing them to trade at local fairs.

The dramatic increase in trade ran into two serious difficulties in medieval Europe. One was the problem of minting money. Despite investment in mining operations to increase the production of metals, the amount of gold, silver, and copper available for coins was not adequate for the increased flow of commerce. Merchants developed paper bills of exchange, in which coins or goods in one location were exchanged for a sealed letter (much like a modern deposit statement), which could be used in place of metal coinage elsewhere. This made the long, slow, and very dangerous shipment of coins unnecessary and facilitated the expansion of credit and commerce. By about 1300 the bill of exchange was the normal method of making commercial payments among the cities of western Europe, and it proved to be a decisive factor in their later economic development. The second problem was a moral and theological one. Church doctrine frowned on lending money at interest, termed *usury* (YOO-zhuh-ree). This doctrine was developed in the early Middle Ages when loans were mainly for consumption, for instance, to tide a farmer over until the next harvest. Theologians reasoned that it was wrong for a Christian to take advantage of the bad luck or need of another Christian. This restriction on Christians' charging interest is one reason why Jews were frequently the moneylenders in early medieval society; it was one of the few occupations not forbidden them. As money-lending became more important to commercial ventures, the church relaxed its position. It declared that some interest was legitimate as a payment for the risk the investor was taking, and that only interest above a certain level would be considered usury. (Even today, governments generally set limits on the rate businesses may charge for loaning money.) The church itself then got into the money-lending business, opening pawnshops in cities.

The stigma attached to lending money was in many ways attached to all the activities of a merchant. Medieval people were uneasy about a person making

The Hanseatic League, 1300–1400

a profit merely from the investment of money rather than from labor, skill, and time. Merchants themselves shared these ideas to some degree, so they gave generous donations to the church and to charities, and they took pains not to flaunt their wealth through flashy dress and homes.

The Commercial Revolution

Changes in business procedures, combined with the growth in trade, led to a transformation of the European economy often called the **commercial revolution** by historians, who see it as the beginning of the modern capitalist economy. In using this label, historians point not only to increases in the sheer volume of trade and in the complexity and sophistication of business procedures, but also to the development of a new "capitalist spirit" in which making a profit is regarded as a good thing in itself, regardless of the uses to which that profit is put. Because capitalism in the Middle Ages primarily involved trade rather than production, it is referred to as mercantile capitalism.

Part of this capitalist spirit was a new attitude toward time. Country people needed only approximate times—dawn, noon, sunset—for their work. Monasteries needed more precise times to call monks together for the recitation of the Divine Office. In the early Middle Ages monks used a combination of hourglasses, sundials, and water-clocks to determine the time, and then rang bells by hand. In about 1280 new types of mechanical mechanisms seem to have been devised in which weights replaced falling water and bells were rung automatically. Records begin to use the word *clock* (from the Latin word for bell) for these machines, which sometimes indicated the movement of astronomical bodies as well as the hours. The merchants who ran city councils quickly saw clocks as useful, as these devices allowed the opening and closing of markets and shops to be set to certain hours, and beginning about 1300, they ordered the construction of large public clocks. Through regulations that specified times and bells that marked the day, city people began to develop a mentality that conceived of the universe in quantitative terms. Beautiful and elaborate mechanical clocks were also symbols of a city's prosperity.

The commercial revolution created a great deal of new wealth, which did not escape the attention of kings and other rulers. Wealth could be taxed, and through taxation kings could create strong and centralized states.

■ **commercial revolution** The transformation of the European economy as a result of changes in business procedures and growth in trade.

Astronomical Clock in Prague The central part of this clock, an astronomical dial representing the sun and moon in the sky and the ring of the zodiac, was installed on the town hall of Prague in 1410, and the other parts were added later in the century. It has been renovated several times, including in 2018, so that it still functions. Beautiful and elaborate mechanical clocks, usually installed on the cathedral or town church, were in general use in Italy by the 1320s, in Germany by the 1330s, in England by the 1370s, and in France by the 1380s. (François Pugnet/Getty Images)

The commercial revolution also provided the opportunity for thousands of serfs to improve their social position. The slow but steady transformation of European society from almost completely rural and isolated to urban and relatively more sophisticated constituted the greatest effect of the commercial revolution that began in the eleventh century.

Even so, merchants and business people did not run medieval communities other than in central and northern Italy and in the county of Flanders. Kings and nobles maintained ultimate control over most European cities. Most towns remained small, and urban residents never amounted to more than 10 percent of the total European population. The commercial changes of the eleventh through thirteenth centuries did, however, lay the economic foundations for the development of urban life and culture.

What was life like in medieval cities?

In their backgrounds and abilities, townspeople represented diversity and change. Their occupations and their preoccupations were different from those of nobles and peasants. Cities were crowded and polluted, though people flocked into them because they offered the possibility of economic advancement, social mobility, and improvement in legal status. Some urban residents grew spectacularly rich, but the numbers of poor swelled as well.

City Life

Walls surrounded almost all medieval towns and cities, and constant repair of these walls was usually the town's greatest expense. Gates pierced the walls, and visitors waited at the gates to gain entrance to the town. Most streets in a medieval town were marketplaces as much as passages for transit. Poor people selling soap, candles, wooden dishes, and similar cheap products stood next to farmers from the surrounding countryside selling eggs, chickens, or vegetables. Because there was no way to preserve food easily, people—usually female family members or servants—had to shop every day, and the market was where they met their neighbors, exchanged information, and talked over recent events, as well as purchased needed supplies.

Some selling took place not in the open air but in the craftsman's home. The family lived above the business on the second or third floor. As the business and the family expanded, additional stories were added. Second and third stories jutted out over the ground floor and thus over the street. Because the streets were narrow to begin with, houses lacked fresh air and light. Fire was a constant danger; because houses were built so close to one another, fires spread rapidly.

Most medieval cities developed with little planning. As the population increased, space became increasingly limited. Air and water pollution presented serious problems. Horses and oxen, the chief means of transportation and power, dropped tons of dung on the streets every year. It was universal practice in the early towns to dump household waste, both animal and human, into the road in front of one's house. The stench must have been abominable. In 1298 the citizens of the town of Boutham in Yorkshire, England, received the following order:

> To the bailiffs of the abbot of St. Mary's York, at Boutham. Whereas it is sufficiently evident that the pavement of the said town of Boutham is so very greatly broken up . . . , and in addition the air is so corrupted and infected by the pigsties situated in the king's highways and in the lanes of that town and by the swine feeding and frequently wandering about . . . and by dung and dunghills and many other foul things placed in the streets and lanes, that great repugnance overtakes the king's ministers staying in that town and also others there dwelling and passing through . . . : the king, being unwilling longer to tolerate such great and unbearable defects there, orders the bailiffs to cause the pavement to be suitably repaired . . . before All Saints next, and to cause the pigsties, aforesaid streets and lanes to be cleansed from all dung . . . and to cause them to be kept thus cleansed hereafter.[3]

People of all sorts, from beggars to wealthy merchants, regularly rubbed shoulders in the narrow streets and alleys of crowded medieval cities. This interaction did not mean that people were unaware of social differences, however, for clothing clearly indicated social standing and sometimes occupation. Friars wore black, white, or gray woolen clothing that marked them as members of a particular religious order. Military men and servants who lived in noble households dressed in the nobles' distinctive colors known as livery (LIH-vuh-ree). Wealthier urban residents wore bright colors, imported silk or fine woolen fabrics, and fancy headgear, while poorer ones wore darker clothing made of rough linen or linen and wool blends. In university towns, students wore clothing and headgear that marked their status. University graduates — lawyers, physicians, and professors — often wore dark robes, trimmed with fur if they could afford it.

In the later Middle Ages many cities attempted to make clothing distinctions a matter of law as well

as of habit. City councils passed **sumptuary laws** that regulated the value of clothing and jewelry that people of different social groups could wear; only members of high social groups could wear velvet, satin, pearls, or fur, for example, or wear clothing embroidered with gold thread or dyed in colors that were especially expensive to produce, such as the purple dye that came from mollusk shells. Along with enforcing social differences, sumptuary laws also attempted to impose moral standards by prohibiting plunging necklines on women or doublets (fitted buttoned jackets) that were too short on men. Their limits on imported fabrics or other materials also served to protect local industries.

Some of these laws called for marking certain individuals as members of groups not fully acceptable in urban society. Many cities ordered prostitutes to wear red or yellow bands on their clothes that were supposed to represent the flames of Hell, and the Fourth Lateran Council required Jews and Muslims to dress in ways that distinguished them from their Christian neighbors. (Many Jewish communities also developed their own sumptuary laws prohibiting extravagant or ostentatious dress.) Sumptuary laws were frequently broken and were difficult to enforce, but they provide evidence of the many material goods available to urban dwellers as well as the concern of city leaders about the social mobility and extravagance they saw all around them.

Servants and the Poor

Many urban houses were larger than the tiny village dwellings, so families took in domestic servants. A less wealthy household employed one woman who assisted in all aspects of running the household; a wealthier one employed a large staff of male and female servants with specific duties. In Italian cities, households often included enslaved women and children, generally captives from the Black Sea region or North Africa traded by Genoese, Venetian, Egyptian, and Turkish merchants.

Along with live-in servants, many households hired outside workers to do specific tasks. These workers laundered clothing and household linens, cared for children or invalids, repaired houses and walls, and carried messages or packages around the city or the surrounding countryside. Urban workers had to buy all their food, so they felt any increase in the price of ale or bread immediately. Their wages were generally low, and children from such families sought work at very young ages.

Illegal activities offered another way for people to support themselves. They stole merchandise from houses, wagons, and storage facilities, bringing it to

■ **sumptuary laws** Laws that regulated the value and style of clothing and jewelry that various social groups could wear as well as the amount they could spend on celebrations.

Young Men Playing Stickball With their tunics hitched up in their belts so that they could move around more easily, young men play a game involving hitting a ball with a stick. Games involving bats and balls were popular, for the equipment needed was made from simple, inexpensive materials. (DEA/G. Dagli Orti/Getty Images)

pawnbrokers or taking it to the next town to sell. They stole goods or money directly from people, cutting the strings of their bags or purses. They sold sex for money, standing on street corners or moving into houses that by the fifteenth century became official brothels. They made and sold mixtures of herbs and drugs claimed to heal all sorts of ailments, perhaps combining this venture with a puppet show, trained animals, magic tricks, or music to draw customers. Or they did all these things and also worked as laundresses, day laborers, porters, peddlers, or street vendors when they could. Cities also drew in orphans, blind people, and the elderly, who resorted to begging for food and money.

Popular Entertainment

Games and sports were common forms of entertainment and relaxation. There were wrestling matches and games akin to modern football, rugby, stickball, and soccer in which balls were kicked, hit, and thrown. People played cards, dice, and board games of all types. They trained dogs to fight each other or put them in an enclosure to fight a captured bear. In Spain, Muslim knights confronted and killed bulls from horseback as part of religious feast days, developing a highly ritualized ceremony that would later be further adapted by Spain's Christians. All these sports and games were occasions for wagering and gambling.

Religious and family celebrations also meant dancing. Men and women danced in lines toward a specific object, such as a tree or a maypole, or in circles, groups, or pairs with specific step patterns. They were accompanied by a variety of instruments: reed pipes such as the chalumeau (an ancestor of the clarinet) and shawm (predecessor to the oboe); woodwinds such as flutes, panpipes, and recorders; stringed instruments including dulcimers, harps, lyres, lutes, zithers, and mandolins; brass instruments such as horns and trumpets; and percussion instruments like drums and tambourines. Many of these instruments were simple and were made by their players. Musicians playing string or percussion instruments often sang as well, and people sang without instrumental accompaniment on festive occasions or while working.

How did universities serve the needs of medieval society?

Just as the first strong secular states emerged in the High Middle Ages, so did the first universities. This was no coincidence. The new bureaucratic states and the church needed educated administrators, and universities were a response to this need.

Origins

In the early Middle Ages, monasteries and cathedral schools had offered most of the available formal instruction. Monastery schools were small, but cathedral

MAP 10.3 Intellectual Centers of Medieval Europe Universities provided more sophisticated instruction than did monastery and cathedral schools, but all these institutions educated only males who had the money to attend.

schools, run by the bishop and his clergy in bustling cities, gradually grew larger. In Italian cities like Bologna (boh-LOH-nyuh), wealthy businessmen established municipal schools. Beginning about 1100, cathedral schools in France and municipal schools in Italy developed into educational institutions that attracted students from a wide area (Map 10.3). These schools were often called *universitas magistrorum et scholarium* (universal society of teachers and students), the origin of the English word *university*. The first European universities appeared in Italy in Bologna, where the specialty was law, and Salerno, where the specialty was medicine.

Legal and Medical Training

The growth of the University of Bologna coincided with a revival of interest in Roman law during the investiture controversy. The study of Roman law as

embodied in the Code of Justinian (see "The Law Code of Justinian" in Chapter 7) had never completely died out in the West, but in the late eleventh century a complete manuscript of Justinian's Code was discovered in a library in Pisa. This discovery led scholars in nearby Bologna to study and teach Roman law intently.

Teachers at Bologna taught law as an organic whole related to the society it regulated, an all-inclusive system based on logical principles that could be applied to difficult practical situations. Thus, as social and economic structures changed, law would change with them. Jurists educated at Bologna—and later at other universities—were hired by rulers and city councils to systematize their law codes and write legal treatises. Canon law (see "The Popes and Church Law" in Chapter 9) was also shaped by the reinvigoration of Roman law, and canon lawyers in ever-greater numbers were hired by church officials or became prominent church officials themselves.

Jewish scholars also produced elaborate commentaries on law and religious tradition. Medieval universities were closed to Jews, but in some cities in the eleventh century special rabbinic academies opened that concentrated on the study of the Talmud, a compilation of legal arguments, proverbs, sayings, and folklore that had been produced in the fifth century in Babylon (present-day Iraq). Men seeking to become rabbis — highly respected figures within the Jewish community, with authority over economic and social as well as religious matters — spent long periods of time studying the Talmud, which served as the basis for their decisions affecting all areas of life.

Professional medical training began at Salerno. Individuals there began to translate medical works out of Arabic. These translations included writings by the ancient Greek physicians and Muslim medical writers, a blending of knowledge that later occurred on the nearby island of Sicily as well. (See "Evaluating Visual Evidence: Healthy Living," page 284.) Students of medicine poured into the city.

Medical studies at Salerno were based on classical ideas, particularly those of Hippocrates, Aristotle, and Galen (see "The Flowering of Philosophy" in Chapter 3 and "Medicine" in Chapter 4). Prime among these was the notion of the four bodily humors — blood, phlegm, black bile, and yellow bile — fluids in the body that influenced bodily health. Each individual was thought to have a characteristic temperament or complexion determined by the balance of these humors, just as today we might describe a person as having a "positive outlook" or a "type A" personality. Disease was generally regarded as an imbalance of humors, which could be diagnosed by taking a patient's pulse or examining his or her urine. Treatment was thus an attempt to bring the humors back into balance, which might be accomplished through diet or drugs — mixtures of herbal or mineral substances — or by vomiting, emptying the bowels, or bloodletting. The bodily humors were somewhat gender related — women were regarded as tending toward cold and wet humors and men toward hot and dry — so therapies were also gender distinctive. Men's greater heat, scholars taught, created other gender differences: heat caused men's hair to burn internally so that they went bald, and their shoulders and brains to become larger than those of women (because heat rises and causes things to expand).

These ideas spread throughout Europe from Salerno and became the basis of training for physicians at other universities. University training gave physicians high social status and allowed them to charge high fees. They were generally hired directly by patients as needed, though some had more permanent positions as members of the household staffs of especially wealthy nobles or rulers.

Theology and Philosophy

Law and medicine were important academic disciplines in the Middle Ages, but theology was "the queen of sciences" because it involved the study of God, who made all knowledge possible. Paris became the place to study theology. In the first decades of the twelfth century, students from across Europe crowded into the cathedral school of Notre Dame (NOH-truh DAHM) in Paris.

University professors (a term first used in the fourteenth century) were known as "schoolmen" or **Scholastics**, one of the first of whom was Peter Abelard. They developed a method of thinking, reasoning, and writing in which questions were raised and authorities cited on both sides of a question. The goal of this method was to arrive at definitive answers and to provide rational explanations for what was believed on faith.

The Scholastic approach rested on the recovery of classical philosophical texts. Ancient Greek and Arabic texts entered Europe in the twelfth century by way of Islamic intellectual centers at Baghdad, Córdoba, and Toledo (see "The Teachings and Expansion of Islam" in Chapter 8). The works of Muslim philosophers and commentators, especially those on Aristotle, were translated into Latin, making the ideas of this ancient Greek philosopher available to educated Christian Europeans for the first time in many centuries.

In the thirteenth century Scholastics devoted an enormous amount of time to collecting and organizing knowledge on all topics. Such a collection was published as a *summa* (SOO-muh), or reference book. Saint Thomas Aquinas (1225–1274), a Dominican friar and professor at the University of Paris, produced the most famous of these collections, the *Summa Theologica*, a summation of Christian ideas on a vast number of theological questions, including the nature of God and Christ, moral principles, and the role of the sacraments. In this, and many of his other writings, Aquinas used arguments that drew from ancient Greek philosophers, especially the ideas of Aristotle available in the new translations of works by Muslim scholars, as well as earlier Christian writers.

In all these works, Aquinas stressed the power of human reason to demonstrate many basic Christian principles, including the existence of God. To obtain true Christian understanding, he wrote, one needed both reason and faith. His ideas have been extremely influential in both philosophy and theology: in the former through the philosophical school known as

---

■ **Scholastics** University professors in the Middle Ages who developed a method of thinking, reasoning, and writing in which questions were raised and authorities cited on both sides of a question.

Healthy Living

In this illustration from a very popular fourteenth-century Latin handbook on maintaining health and well-being, women with their sleeves rolled up prepare cloth for medical uses; the woman on the left is trimming small threads off with a one-bladed shear, and the woman on the right is boiling the cloth to bleach it. The men in the background eat a meal and drink wine. The text of this handbook was a translation of an Arabic medical treatise, made in the kingdom of Sicily, the site of much cultural borrowing.

EVALUATE THE EVIDENCE

1. Cleanliness and moderation were recommended as essential to healthy living in this hand-book. How does the artist convey these values in this scene?
2. Given what you have learned about medieval medical care, why might a handbook like this have been popular with literate urban residents?

(PRISMA ARCHIVO/Alamy Stock Photo)

Thomism, and in the latter especially through the Catholic Church, which has affirmed many times that his ideas are foundational to Roman Catholic doctrine.

University Students

The influx of students eager for learning, together with dedicated and imaginative teachers, created the atmosphere in which universities grew. By the end of the fifteenth century there were at least eighty universities in Europe. Some universities also offered younger students training in what were termed the seven liberal arts — grammar, rhetoric, logic, mathematics, geometry, music, and astronomy — that could serve as a foundation for more specialized study in all areas. The curriculum typically consisted of a core of ancient texts that all students had

to master, and the standard method of teaching was a lecture. Lecture courses were augmented by seminars in which students debated key issues in what they were studying. Because books had to be copied by hand, they were extremely expensive, and few students could afford them.

If a candidate passed all exams, he was awarded a license to teach, the earliest form of academic degree. Initially these licenses granted the title of master or doctor, both derived from Latin words meaning "teach." The lower bachelor's degree was developed later.

University students were generally considered to be lower-level members of the clergy — this was termed being in "minor orders" — so any students accused of legal infractions were tried in church, rather than in city, courts. This clerical status, along with widely held ideas about women's lesser intellectual capabilities,

Teaching Grammar   This small illumination from a French manuscript version of *L'image du monde* (The image of the world) by the priest and poet Gautier de Metz, painted in about 1277, shows a teacher holding a switch in one hand and admonishing his anxious students with the other. Students did not normally learn dressed only in their underwear, but Latin grammar was the first subject students were taught, and corporal punishment could be part of the process. Later illustrations in the same book show fully clothed older students learning the other liberal arts, including logic and rhetoric, though still with apprehensive expressions. (Photo © Raffaello Bencini/Bridgeman Images)

meant that university education was restricted to men. (Most European universities did not admit women until after World War I.)

Though university classes were not especially expensive, the many years that a university education required meant that the sons of peasants or artisans could rarely attend, unless they could find wealthy patrons who would pay their expenses. Most students were the sons of urban merchants or lower-level nobles, especially the younger sons who would not inherit family lands. University degrees were initially designed as licenses to teach at the university, but most students staffed the expanding diocesan, royal, and papal administrations as lawyers and officials.

Students did not spend all their time preparing for their degrees. Much information about medieval students concerns what we might call "extracurricular"

activities: university regulations forbidding them to throw rocks at professors; sermons about breaking and entering, raping local women, attacking town residents, and disturbing church services; and court records discussing their drunken brawls, riots, and fights and duels. Student life was described by students in poems, usually anonymous, that celebrated the joys of Venus (the goddess of love) and other gods:

> When we are in the tavern,
> we do not think how we will go to dust,
> but we hurry to gamble,
> which always makes us sweat.
>
> . . .
>
> Here no-one fears death,
> but they throw the dice in the name of Bacchus.
>
> . . .
>
> To the Pope as to the king
> they all drink without restraint.[4]

How did literature and architecture express medieval values?

The High Middle Ages saw the creation of new types of literature, architecture, and music. Technological advances in such areas as papermaking and stone masonry made some of these innovations possible, as did the growing wealth and sophistication of patrons. Artists and artisans flourished in the more secure environment of the High Middle Ages, producing works that celebrated the glories of love, war, and God.

Vernacular Literature and Drama

Latin was the language used in university education, scholarly writing, and works of literature. By the High Middle Ages, however, no one spoke Latin as his or her original mother tongue. The barbarian invasions, the mixture of peoples, and the usual changes in language that occur over time had resulted in a variety of local dialects that blended words and linguistic forms in various ways. As kings increased the size of their holdings, they often ruled people who spoke many different dialects.

In the High Middle Ages, some authors departed from tradition and began to write in their local dialect, that is, in the everyday language of their region, which linguistic historians call the vernacular. This new **vernacular literature** gradually transformed some local dialects into literary languages, such as French, German, Italian, and English, while other local dialects, such as Breton and Bavarian, remained (and remain to this day) means of oral communication.

Facilitating this vernacular writing was a technological advance. By the thirteenth century techniques of making paper from old linen cloth and rags began to spread from Spain, where they had been developed in the Muslim caliphates, providing a much cheaper material on which to write than parchment or vellum. People started to write down the more mundane and the less serious—personal letters, lists, songs, recipes, rules, instructions—in their dialects, using spellings that were often personal and idiosyncratic. These writings included fables, legends, stories, and myths that had circulated orally for generations, adding to the growing body of written vernacular literature.

Stories and songs in the vernacular were composed and performed at the courts of nobles and rulers. In Germany and most of northern Europe, the audiences favored stories and songs recounting the great deeds of warrior heroes. These epics, known as *chansons de geste* (SHAN-suhn duh JEHST; songs of great deeds), celebrate violence, slaughter, revenge, and physical power. In southern Europe, especially in Provence in southern France, poets who called themselves **troubadours** (TROO-buh-dorz) wrote and sang lyric verses celebrating love, desire, beauty, and gallantry. Troubadours included a few women, called *trobairises* (plural of *trobairitz*), most of whose exact identities are not known. (See "Viewpoints: Male and Female Troubadours," page 287.)

The songs of the troubadours were widely imitated in Italy, England, and Germany, so they spurred the development of vernacular literature there as well. At the court of his patron, Marie of Champagne, Chrétien de Troyes (ca. 1135–ca. 1190) used the legends of the fifth-century British king Arthur (see "Celtic and Germanic People in Gaul and Britain" in Chapter 7) as the basis for innovative tales of battle and forbidden love. His most popular story is that of the noble Lancelot, whose love for Guinevere, the wife of King Arthur, his lord, became physical as well as spiritual. Most of the troubadours came from and wrote for the aristocratic classes, and their poetry suggests the interests and values of noble culture. Their influence extended to all social groups, however, for people who could not read heard the poems and stories from people who could, so that what had originally come from oral culture was recycled back into it.

Drama, derived from the church's liturgy, emerged as a distinct art form during the High Middle Ages. Amateurs and later professional actors performed plays based on biblical themes and on the lives of the saints; these dramas were presented in the towns, first in churches and then at the marketplace. By combining comical farce based on ordinary life with serious religious scenes, plays gave ordinary people an opportunity to identify with religious figures and think about their faith.

Churches and Cathedrals

The development of secular vernacular literature focusing on human concerns did not mean any lessening of the importance of religion in medieval people's lives. As we have seen, religious devotion was expressed through daily rituals, holiday ceremonies, and the creation of new institutions such as universities and religious orders. People also wanted permanent visible representations of their piety, and both church and city leaders wanted physical symbols of their wealth and power. These aims found their outlet in the building of tens of thousands of churches, chapels, abbeys, and, most spectacularly, **cathedrals** in the twelfth and thirteenth centuries. A cathedral is the church of a bishop and the administrative headquarters of a diocese. The word comes from the Latin word *cathedra*, meaning chair, because the bishop's throne, a symbol of the office, is located in the cathedral.

Most of the churches in the early Middle Ages had been built primarily of wood, which meant they were susceptible to fire. They were often small, with a flat roof, in a rectangular form with a central aisle; this structure, called a basilica, was based on earlier Roman public buildings. With the increasing political stability of the eleventh century, bishops and abbots supported the construction of larger and more fire-resistant churches made almost completely out of stone. As the size of the church grew horizontally, it also grew vertically. Builders adapted Roman-style rounded barrel vaults made of stone for the ceiling; this use of Roman forms led the style to be labeled **Romanesque**.

The next architectural style was **Gothic**, so named by later Renaissance architects who thought that

---

■ **vernacular literature** Writings in the author's local dialect, that is, in the everyday language of the region.

■ **troubadours** Poets who wrote and sang lyric verses celebrating love, desire, beauty, and gallantry.

■ **cathedral** The church of a bishop and the administrative headquarters of a diocese.

■ **Romanesque** An architectural style with rounded arches and small windows.

■ **Gothic** An architectural style typified by pointed arches and large stained-glass windows.

VIEWPOINTS
Male and Female Troubadours

The troubadour poets celebrated what in English has come to be called "courtly love," in which the writer praises his or her love object, idealizing the beloved and promising loyalty and great deeds. Most poems that have survived were written by men and are from a male perspective, but a few poems by female trobairises (plural of *trobairitz*) have survived. The first poem below was written by Arnaut Daniel, a thirteenth-century troubadour about whom not much is known, and the second by the Countess of Dia, purportedly the wife of a Provençal nobleman.

Poem by Arnaut Daniel

I only know the grief that comes to me,
to my love-ridden heart, out of over-loving,
since my will is so firm and whole
that it never parted or grew distant from her
whom I craved at first sight, and afterwards:
and now, in her absence, I tell her burning words;
then, when I see her, I don't know, so much I have to, what to say.

To the sight of other women I am blind, deaf to hearing them
since her only I see, and hear and heed,
and in that I am surely not a false slanderer,
since heart desires her more than mouth may say;
wherever I may roam through fields and valleys, plains and
    mountains
I shan't find in a single person all those qualities
which God wanted to select and place in her.

I have been in many a good court,
but here by her I find much more to praise:
measure and wit and other good virtues,
beauty and youth, worthy deeds and fair disport;
so well kindness taught and instructed her
that it has rooted every ill manner out of her:
I don't think she lacks anything good. . . .

Joy and merriment from another woman seems false and ill
    to me,
since no worthy one can compare with her,
and her company is above the others'.
Ah me, if I don't have her, alas, so badly she has taken me!
But this grief is amusement, laughter and joy,
since in thinking of her, of her am I gluttonous and greedy:
ah me, God, could I ever enjoy her otherwise!

And never, I swear, I have liked game or ball so much,
or anything has given my heart so much joy
as did the one thing that no false slanderer

made public, which is a treasure for me only.
Do I tell too much? Not I, unless she is displeased:
beautiful one, by God, speech and voice
I'd lose ere I say something to annoy you.

And I pray my song does not displease you
since, if you like the music and lyrics,
little cares Arnaut whether the unpleasant ones like them
    as well.

Poem by the Countess of Dia

I've suffered great distress
From a knight whom I once owned.
Now, for all time, be it known:
I loved him—yes, to excess. His jilting I've regretted,
Yet his love I never really returned. Now for my sin I can only
    burn:
Dressed, or in my bed.

O if I had that knight to caress
Naked all night in my arms,
He'd be ravished by the charm
Of using, for cushion, my breast. His love I more deeply prize
Than Floris did Blancheor's
Take that love, my core, My sense, my life, my eyes!

Lovely lover, gracious, kind,
When will I overcome your fight?
O if I could lie with you one night!
Feel those loving lips on mine! Listen, one thing sets me afire:
Here in my husband's place I want you,
If you'll just keep your promise true: Give me everything I
    desire.

QUESTIONS FOR ANALYSIS

1. Both of these songs focus on a beloved who does not return the lover's affection. What similarities and differences do you see in them?
2. How does courtly love reinforce other aspects of medieval society? Are there aspects of medieval society it contradicts?
3. Can you find examples from current popular music that parallel the sentiments expressed in these two songs?

Sources: "Sol sui qui sai lo sobrafan qu'em sortz" by Arnaut Daniel, translated by Leonardo Malcovati, from *Prosody in England and Elsewhere: A Comparative Approach* (London: Gival Press, 2006); Three verses from lyrics by the Countess of Dia, often called Beatritz, the Sappho of the Rhone, in *Lyrics of the Middle Ages: An Anthology*, edited and translated by James J. Wilhelm (New York: Routledge, 1990).

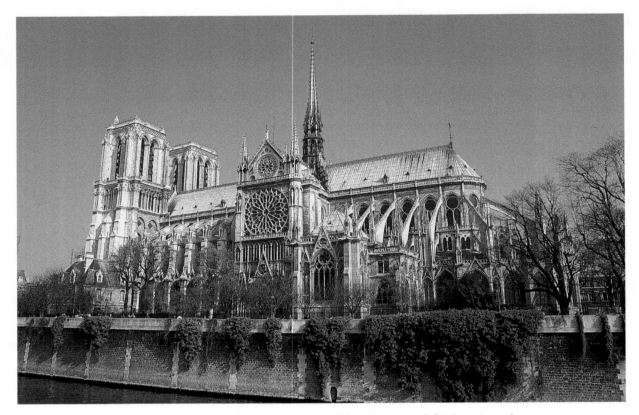

Notre Dame Cathedral, Paris This view offers a fine example of the twin towers (left), the spire and great rose window over the south portal (center), and the flying buttresses that support the walls and the vaults. Like hundreds of other churches in medieval Europe, it was dedicated to the Virgin Mary. With a spire rising more than 300 feet, Notre Dame was the tallest building in Europe. In April 2019, a massive fire destroyed the spire and most of the lead-covered wooden roof, though the stone-vaulted ceiling prevented the fire from reaching the interior. Firefighters were able to save the façade, towers, walls, buttresses, stained-glass windows, and much of the artwork. French president Emmanuel Macron pledged to rebuild the cathedral by 2024 and launched an international fundraising campaign. (David R. Frazier/Science Source)

only the uncouth Goths could have invented such a disunified style. In Gothic churches the solid stone barrel-vaulted roof was replaced by a roof made of stone ribs with plaster in between. Because this ceiling was much lighter, side pillars and walls did not need to carry as much weight. Exterior arched stone supports called flying buttresses also carried some of the weight of the roof, so solid walls could be replaced by windows, which let in great amounts of light. Originating in the Île-de-France in the twelfth century, Gothic architecture spread throughout France with the expansion of royal power. From France the new style spread to England, Germany, Italy, Spain, and eastern Europe.

Extraordinary amounts of money were needed to build these houses of worship. The economic growth of the period meant that merchants, nobles, and the church could afford the costs of this unparalleled building boom. A great number of artisans had to be assembled: quarrymen, sculptors, stonecutters, masons, mortar makers, carpenters, blacksmiths, glassmakers, roofers. Bishops and abbots sketched out what they wanted and set general guidelines, but they left practical needs and aesthetic considerations to the master mason, who held overall responsibility for supervision of the project. Because cathedrals were symbols of civic pride, towns competed to build the largest and most splendid church. In 1163 the citizens of Paris began Notre Dame Cathedral, planning it to reach the height of 114 feet from the floor to the ceiling at the highest point inside. Many other cathedrals well over 100 feet tall on the inside were built as each bishop and town sought to outdo the neighbors. Construction of a large cathedral was rarely completed in a lifetime; many were never finished at all. Because generation after generation added to the buildings, many of these churches show the architectural influences of two or even three centuries.

Stained glass beautifully reflects the creative energy of the High Middle Ages. It is both an integral part of Gothic architecture and a distinct form of visual art. From large sheets of colored glass made by glassblowers, artisans cut small pieces, linked them together with narrow strips of lead, and set them in an iron frame prepared to fit the window opening. Windows showed scenes from the Old and New Testaments and the lives of the saints, designed to teach people doctrines of the Christian faith. They also showed scenes from the lives of the artisans and merchants who paid for them.

Once at least part of a cathedral had been built, the building began to be used for religious services. Town residents gathered for Masses, baptisms, funerals, and saint's day services, and also used it for guild meetings and other secular purposes. Services became increasingly complex to fit with their new surroundings, with music, incense, candles, statuary, tapestry wall hangings, and the building itself all contributing to making services in a Gothic cathedral a rich experience.

The frenzy to create the most magnificent Gothic cathedrals eventually came to an end. Begun in 1247, the cathedral in Beauvais reached a height of 157 feet in the interior, exceeding all others. Unfortunately, the weight imposed on the vaults was too great, and the building collapsed in 1284. The collapse was viewed as an aberration, for countless other cathedrals were in various stages of completion at the same time, and none of them fell. In hindsight, however, it can be viewed as a harbinger. Very few cathedrals not yet completed at the time of its collapse were ever finished, and even fewer were started. In the fourteenth century the church itself splintered, and the cities that had so proudly built cathedrals were decimated by famine and disease.

NOTES

1. Thirteenth-century sermon story, in David Herlihy, ed., *Medieval Culture and Society* (New York: Harper and Row, 1968), pp. 295, 298.
2. Translated and quoted in Susan C. Karant-Nunn, *The Reformation of Ritual: An Interpretation of Early Modern Germany* (London: Routledge, 1997), p. 77.
3. H. Rothwell, ed., *English Historical Documents*, vol. 3 (London: Eyre & Spottiswoode, 1975), p. 854.
4. www.classical.net/music/comp.lst/works/orff-cb/carmlyr.php#track14. This verse is from one of the songs known as the Carmina Burana, which are widely available as recordings, downloadable files, and even cell phone ring tones.

LOOKING BACK LOOKING AHEAD

The High Middle Ages represent one of the most creative periods in the history of Western society. Institutions that are important parts of the modern world, including universities, jury trials, and investment banks, were all developed in this era. Advances were made in the mechanization of labor, business procedures, architectural design, and education. Through the activities of merchants, Europeans again saw products from Africa and Asia in city marketplaces, as they had in Roman times, and wealthier urban residents bought them. Individuals and groups such as craft guilds provided money for building and decorating magnificent Gothic cathedrals, where people heard increasingly complex music and watched plays that celebrated both the lives of the saints and their own daily struggles.

Toward the end of the thirteenth century, however, there were increasing signs of impending problems. The ships and caravans bringing exotic goods also brought new pests. The new vernacular literature created a stronger sense of national identity, which increased hostility toward others. The numbers of poor continued to grow, and efforts to aid their suffering were never enough. As the century ended, villagers and city residents alike continued to gather for worship, but they also wondered whether God was punishing them.

Make Connections

Think about the larger developments and continuities within and across chapters.

1. How was life in a medieval city different from life in a Hellenistic city (Chapter 4), or life in Rome during the time of Augustus (Chapter 6)? In what ways was it similar? What problems did these cities confront that are still issues for cities today?

2. Historians have begun to turn their attention to the history of children and childhood. How were children's lives in the societies you have examined shaped by larger social structures and cultural forces? What commonalities do you see in children's lives across time?

3. Chapter 4 and this chapter both examine ways in which religion and philosophy shaped life for ordinary people and for the educated elite. How would you compare Hellenistic religious practices with those of medieval Europe? How would you compare the ideas of Hellenistic philosophers such as Epicurus or Zeno with those of Scholastic philosophers such as Thomas Aquinas?

10   REVIEW & EXPLORE

Identify Key Terms

Identify and explain the significance of each item below.

open-field system (p. 263)	Scholastics (p. 283)
merchant guild (p. 275)	vernacular literature (p. 286)
craft guild (p. 275)	troubadours (p. 286)
Hanseatic League (p. 277)	cathedral (p. 286)
commercial revolution (p. 278)	Romanesque (p. 286)
sumptuary laws (p. 280)	Gothic (p. 286)

Review the Main Ideas

Answer the section heading questions from the chapter.

1. What was village life like in medieval Europe? (p. 262)

2. How did religion shape everyday life in the High Middle Ages? (p. 269)

3. What led to Europe's economic growth and reurbanization? (p. 273)

4. What was life like in medieval cities? (p. 279)

5. How did universities serve the needs of medieval society? (p. 281)

6. How did literature and architecture express medieval values? (p. 285)

Suggested Resources

BOOKS

- Coldstream, Nicola. *Medieval Architecture*. 2002. A beautifully illustrated discussion of all types of buildings and how they reflect the material and spiritual concerns of the people who built and used them.

- Epstein, Steven A. *An Economic and Social History of Later Medieval Europe, 1000–1500*. 2009. Examines European social and economic history in its cultural setting.

- Gaunt, Simon, and Sarah Kay, eds. *The Troubadours: An Introduction*. 1999. A collection of essays that trace the development of troubadour song and the reception of troubadour poetry.

- Gies, Frances, and Joseph Gies. *Life in a Medieval City*. 2016. A newly reissued classic account of life in medieval cities, using Troyes in 1250 as its example.

- Glick, Leonard B. *Abraham's Heirs: Jews and Christians in Medieval Europe.* 1999. Provides information on many aspects of Jewish life and Jewish-Christian relations.
- Janin, Hunt. *The University in Medieval Life, 1179–1499.* 2008. An overview of medieval universities, designed for general readers.
- Moore, R. I. *The First European Revolution: 970–1215.* 2000. A bold assessment of the long-term significance of the changes discussed in this chapter.
- Shahar, Shulamit. *The Fourth Estate: A History of Women in the Middle Ages,* 2d ed. 2003. Provides information on the lives of women, including nuns, peasants, noblewomen, and townswomen.
- Shinners, John. *Medieval Popular Religion, 1000–1500,* 2d ed. 2006. A wide variety of sources that provide evidence about the beliefs and practices of ordinary Christians.
- Spufford, Peter. *Power and Profit: The Merchant in Medieval Europe.* 2003. A comprehensive history of medieval commerce, designed for general readers.

MEDIA

- *Epistolae: Medieval Women's Letters.* A collection of letters to and from women in the Middle Ages, from the fourth to the thirteenth centuries, on a range of topics including religion, diplomacy, family, and politics. Includes both the original Latin and English translations and, where available, information about the writer and the historical context of the letter. **epistolae.ctl.columbia.edu/**
- *Inside the Medieval Mind* (BBC, 2008). Professor Robert Bartlett of St. Andrew's University in Scotland examines the ways in which medieval people understood the world, including knowledge systems, religious beliefs, and ideas about sexuality.
- *Monty Python and the Holy Grail* (Terry Gilliam and Terry Jones, 1975). A spoof of the King Arthur legend and a send-up of popular views of many aspects of the Middle Ages (chivalry, dirt, disease, witchcraft). The basis for Eric Idle's 2005 Tony Award–winning musical *Spamalot*, and the source of countless pop culture references.
- *Sorceress* (Suzanne Schiffman, 1987). Written by a medieval historian and shot in both French and English, this wonderful film is based on an actual text by a thirteenth-century Dominican friar investigating the cult of Saint Guinefort, the holy greyhound, near Lyons in France. The film addresses issues relating to healing, popular religion, and the role of women.
- *TEAMS Middle English Texts.* Run by the Consortium for Teaching the Middle Ages (TEAMS), this website provides a well-organized portal into the world of medieval English literature through more than 350 poems, prose narratives, sermons, books of advice, and other works. Each text has an introduction giving the cultural context. **www.lib.rochester.edu/camelot/teams/tmsmenu.htm**
- *Terry Jones' Medieval Lives* (BBC, 2004). Award-winning eight-part documentary series that focuses on the real experiences of certain kinds of medieval people often portrayed stereotypically, including the peasant, the damsel, the minstrel, the knight, and the outlaw.

11

The Later Middle Ages

1300–1450

During the later Middle Ages the last book of the New Testament, the book of Revelation, inspired thousands of sermons and hundreds of religious tracts. The book of Revelation deals with visions of the end of the world, with disease, war, famine, and death — often called the "Four Horsemen of the Apocalypse" — triumphing everywhere. It is no wonder this part of the Bible was so popular in this period, for between 1300 and 1450 Europeans experienced a frightful series of shocks. The climate turned colder and wetter, leading to poor harvests and famine. People weakened by hunger were more susceptible to disease, and in the middle of the fourteenth century a new disease, probably the bubonic plague, spread throughout Europe. With no effective treatment, the plague killed millions of people. War devastated the countryside, especially in France, leading to widespread discontent and peasant revolts. Workers in cities also revolted against dismal working conditions, and violent crime and ethnic tensions increased as well. Massive deaths and preoccupation with death make the fourteenth century one of the most wrenching periods of Western civilization. Yet, in spite of the pessimism and crises, important institutions and cultural forms, including representative assemblies and national literatures, emerged. Even institutions that experienced severe crisis, such as the Christian Church, saw new types of vitality. ▰

CHAPTER PREVIEW

- How did climate change shape the late Middle Ages?

- How did the plague affect European society?

- What were the causes, course, and consequences of the Hundred Years' War?

- Why did the church come under increasing criticism?

- What explains the social unrest of the late Middle Ages?

Noble Violence in the Later Middle Ages

In this French manuscript illumination from 1465, armored knights kill peasants while they work in the fields or take refuge in a castle. Aristocratic violence was a common feature of late medieval life, although nobles would generally not have bothered to put on their armor to harass villagers. (© Musée Condé, Chantilly, France/Bridgeman Images)

How did climate change shape the late Middle Ages?

Toward the end of the thirteenth century the expanding European economy began to slow down, and in the first half of the fourteenth century Europe experienced a series of climate changes that led to lower levels of food production, which had dramatic and disastrous ripple effects.

Climate Change and Famine

The period from about 1000 to about 1300 saw a warmer-than-usual climate in Europe, which underlay all the changes and vitality of the High Middle Ages. Around 1300, however, the climate in the Northern Hemisphere changed for the worse, becoming colder and wetter. Historical geographers refer to the period from 1300 to about 1800 as the **Little Ice Age**. Colder and less stable climate led to repeated poor harvests, scarcity, and starvation. Across Europe, an unusual number of storms brought torrential rains, ruining the wheat, oat, and hay crops on which people and animals almost everywhere depended. Almost all of northern Europe suffered a terrible famine between 1315 and 1322. Undernourished people and animals were more vulnerable to disease, including the great cattle plague of the early fourteenth century that killed the majority of European livestock.

With colder and more unstable climate, voyages in northern oceans became more hazardous and fewer. Memories of Norse trips to North America were turned into myths, their reality confirmed only in the late twentieth century through archeological excavations in Newfoundland. By 1450 the small Norse colony on Greenland had shrunk to a remnant.

Death from Famine In this fifteenth-century painting, dead bodies lie in the middle of a path, while a funeral procession at the right includes a man with an adult's coffin and a woman with the coffin of an infant under her arm. People did not simply allow the dead to lie in the street in medieval Europe, though during famines and epidemics it was sometimes difficult to maintain normal burial procedures. (British Library/Album/Alamy Stock Photo)

TIMELINE

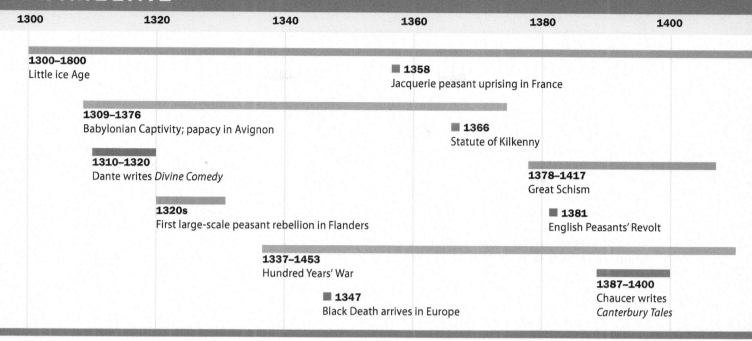

1300	1320	1340	1360	1380	1400

1300–1800
Little Ice Age

1358
Jacquerie peasant uprising in France

1309–1376
Babylonian Captivity; papacy in Avignon

1366
Statute of Kilkenny

1310–1320
Dante writes *Divine Comedy*

1378–1417
Great Schism

1320s
First large-scale peasant rebellion in Flanders

1381
English Peasants' Revolt

1337–1453
Hundred Years' War

1387–1400
Chaucer writes
Canterbury Tales

1347
Black Death arrives in Europe

Evidence for climate change and its impact can be traced through both natural and human records. Evidence from nature emerges through the study of Alpine and polar glaciers, tree rings, and pollen left in bogs. Human-produced sources include written reports of rivers freezing, crops never ripening, and people and animals dying, as well as archaeological evidence such as the collapsed houses and emptied villages.

Increasing prices meant that fewer people could afford to buy food. Workers on reduced diets had less energy, which meant lower productivity, lower output, and higher grain prices. Long-distance transportation of food was expensive and difficult, so most urban areas depended on areas no more than a day's journey away for grain, produce, and meat. Rulers attempted to find solutions and provide famine relief, but government responses to these crises were ineffectual.

Social Consequences

The changing climate and resulting agrarian crisis of the fourteenth century had grave social consequences. Poor harvests and famine led to the abandonment of homesteads. In parts of the Low Countries and in the Scottish-English borderlands, entire villages were deserted, and many people became vagabonds, wandering in search of food and work. In Flanders and eastern England, some peasants were forced to mortgage, sublease, or sell their holdings to richer farmers in order to buy food. Throughout the affected areas, young men and women sought work in the towns, delaying marriage.

As the subsistence crisis deepened, starving people focused their anger on the rich, speculators, and the Jews, who were often portrayed as creditors fleecing the poor through pawnbroking. (As explained in Chapter 10, Jews often became moneylenders because Christian authorities restricted their ownership of land and opportunities to engage in other trades.) Rumors spread of a plot by Jews and their alleged agents, the lepers, to kill Christians by poisoning wells. Based on "evidence" collected by torture, many lepers and Jews were killed, beaten, or heavily fined.

Meanwhile, the international character of trade and commerce meant that a disaster in one country had serious implications elsewhere. For example, the infection that attacked English sheep in 1318 caused a sharp decline in wool exports in the following years. Without wool, Flemish weavers could not work, and thousands were laid off. Without woolen cloth, the businesses of Flemish, Hanseatic, and Italian merchants suffered. Unemployment encouraged people to turn to crime.

> ■ **Little Ice Age** Period of colder and wetter weather that began in the fourteenth century, leading to poor harvests, famine, and other problems.

How did the plague affect European society?

Colder weather, failed harvests, and resulting malnourishment left Europe's population susceptible to disease, and a virulent one appeared in the mid-fourteenth century. Around 1300 improvements in ship design had allowed year-round shipping for the first time. European merchants took advantage of these advances, and ships continually at sea carried all types of cargo. They also carried vermin of all types, especially insects and rats, both of which often harbored pathogens. Just as modern air travel has allowed diseases such as AIDS and COVID to spread quickly over very long distances, medieval shipping allowed the diseases of the time to do the same. The most frightful of these diseases spread to Europe in 1347 and killed as much as one-third of the population when it first reached an area. Contemporaries called it the "great plague" or "great pestilence," though by the nineteenth century this fourteenth-century epidemic became known by the name we generally use today, the **Black Death**.

Pathology

The Black Death was one of several types of plague caused by the bacterium *Yersinia pestis*. The disease normally afflicts rats and is passed through the fleas that live on them. Fleas living on the infected rats drink their blood and then pass the bacteria that cause the plague on to the next rat they bite. Usually the disease is limited to rats and other rodents, but at certain points in history the fleas have jumped from their rodent hosts to humans and other animals. One of these instances appears to have occurred in the Eastern Roman Empire in the sixth century, when what became known as Justinian's plague killed millions of people (see "Byzantine Learning and Science" in Chapter 7). Another was in China and India in the 1890s, when millions again died. Doctors and epidemiologists closely studied this outbreak, identified the bacterium, and learned about the exact cycle of infection for the first time.

The fourteenth-century outbreak showed many similarities to the nineteenth-century one, but also some differences, which led a few historians to speculate that the Black Death was not *Yersinia pestis*. In the 2010s, however, microbiologists studying human tooth pulp in mass graves associated with the Black Death in several parts of Europe found the DNA of *Yersinia pestis*. Those studying a grave in London were able to sequence the bacterium's whole genome,

Burial of Plague Victims   In this manuscript illumination from the Flemish city of Tournai in 1349, men and women bury the dead in plain wooden coffins. The death rate overwhelmed the ability of people to carry out normal funeral ceremonies, and in some places the dead were simply dumped in mass graves, with no coffins at all. (Bibliothèque Royale de Belgique, Brussels, Belgium/Bridgeman Images)

showing that it differed little from the *Yersinia pestis* that is still in the world today. The causes of the very high mortality rate of the fourteenth-century outbreak may have included a high level of direct person-to-person infection through coughing and sneezing (what epidemiologists term *pneumonic plague*), as well as other factors that we don't yet fully understand. Research into the plague is a thriving interdisciplinary field of study, with new findings coming every year from various outbreaks around the world that occurred in different eras of the past or are happening today.

There is no dispute about the plague's dreadful effects on the body. Whether it gets into the body from a cough or a flea bite, *Yersinia pestis* enters the lymph system, creating the classic symptom of the bubonic plague, a growth the size of a nut or an apple in the lymph nodes of the armpit, groin, or neck. This was the boil, or *bubo*, that gave the disease its name and caused agonizing pain. If the bubo was lanced and the pus thoroughly drained, the victim had a chance of recovery. If the boil was not lanced, however—and in the fourteenth century, it rarely was—the next stage was the appearance of black spots or blotches caused by bleeding under the skin as *Yersinia pestis* moved into the bloodstream. Finally, the victim began to cough violently and spit blood. This stage, indicating the presence of millions of bacilli in the bloodstream, signaled the end, and death followed in two or three days. The coughing also released those pathogens into the air, infecting others when they were breathed in and beginning the deadly cycle again on new victims.

Spread of the Disease

The newest genetic research on the plague finds that it originated in western China and then spread throughout multiple radiations into Europe, Africa, and elsewhere in Asia. Several new strains developed in the thirteenth or early fourteenth century that spread from western China along the trade routes of the Mongol Empire, for caravans carrying silk, spices, and gold across Central Asia were accompanied by rats and other vermin. Rats and humans carried the disease onto ships, especially in the ports of the Black Sea. One Italian chronicler told of a more dramatic means of spreading the disease as well: Mongol armies besieging the city of Kaffa on the shores of the Black Sea catapulted plague-infected corpses over the walls to infect those inside, a type of early biological warfare. The chronicler was not an eyewitness, but modern epidemiologists find his account plausible, though the plague most likely spread from many Black Sea ports, not just Kaffa.

In October 1347 Genoese ships brought the plague from the Black Sea to Messina, from which it spread across Sicily and then to Italy and over the Alps to Germany. Frightened French authorities chased a galley bearing plague victims away from the port of Marseilles, but not before plague had infected the city, from which it spread to southern France and Spain. In June 1348 two ships entered the Bristol Channel and introduced it into England, and from there it traveled northeast into Scandinavia. The plague seems to have entered Poland through the Baltic seaports and spread eastward from there (Map 11.1).

Medieval urban conditions were ideal for the spread of disease. Narrow streets were filled with refuse, human excrement, and dead animals. Houses whose upper stories projected over the lower ones blocked light and air. In addition, people were already weakened by famine, standards of personal hygiene remained frightfully low, and the urban populace was crowded together. Fleas and body lice were universal afflictions: everyone from peasants to archbishops had them. One more bite did not cause much alarm, and the association between rats, fleas, and the plague was unknown.

Mortality rates can be only educated guesses because population figures for the period before and after the arrival of the plague do not exist for most countries and cities. Densely populated Italian cities endured incredible losses. Florence lost between one-half and two-thirds of its population when the plague visited in 1348. Of a total English population of perhaps 4.2 million, probably 1.4 million died in the Black Death, but the number may actually have been higher. Archaeologists studying the amounts of pottery shards left at various sites in eastern England conclude that the pottery-using population—which would have included all social classes—in the period after the Black Death was 45 percent lower than it had been before. Islamic parts of Europe were not spared, nor was the rest of the Muslim world. The most widely accepted estimate for western Europe and the Mediterranean is that the plague killed about one-third of the population in the first wave of infection. (Some areas, including such cities as Milan, Liège, and Nuremberg, were largely spared, primarily because city authorities closed the gates to all outsiders when plague was in the area and enough food had been stored to sustain the city until the danger had passed.)

Nor did central and eastern Europe escape the ravages of the disease. One chronicler records that, in the summer and autumn of 1349, between five hundred and six hundred died every day in Vienna. As the plague took its toll on the Holy Roman Empire, waves of emigrants fled to Poland, Bohemia, and Hungary, taking the plague with them. In the Byzantine Empire the plague ravaged the population. The youngest son

■ **Black Death** Plague that first struck Europe in 1347 and killed perhaps one-third of the population.

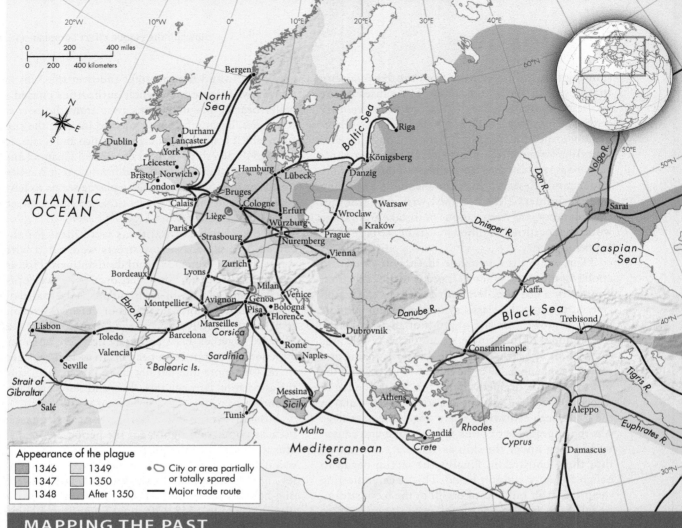

MAP 11.1 The Course of the Black Death in Fourteenth-Century Europe

The bubonic plague spread across Europe after beginning in the mid-1340s, with the first cases of disease reported in Black Sea ports.

ANALYZING THE MAP When did the plague reach Paris? How much time passed before it spread to the rest of northern France and southern Germany? Which cities and regions were spared?

CONNECTIONS How did the expansion of trade contribute to the spread of the Black Death?

---

of Emperor John VI Kantakouzenos died just as his father took over the throne in 1347. "So incurable was the evil," wrote John later in his history of the Byzantine Empire, "that neither any regularity of life, nor any bodily strength could resist it. Strong and weak bodies were all similarly carried away, and those best cared for died in the same manner as the poor."[1]

Across Europe, a second wave of the plague occurred in 1359–1363, and then it recurred intermittently for centuries, though never with the same virulence because by then Europeans had some resistance. Improved standards of hygiene and strictly enforced quarantine measures also lessened the plague's toll, but only in 1721 did it make its last appearance in Europe, in the French port of Marseilles. And only in 1947,

six centuries after the arrival of the plague in Europe, did the American microbiologist Selman Waksman discover an effective treatment, streptomycin. Plague continues to infect rodent and human populations sporadically today.

Care of the Sick

Fourteenth-century medical literature indicates that physicians tried many different methods to prevent and treat the plague, basing treatments on their understanding of how the body worked, as do doctors in any era. People understood that plague and other diseases could be transmitted person to person, and they observed that crowded cities had high death rates, especially when the weather was warm and moist. We now understand that warm, moist conditions make it easier for germs to grow and spread, but fourteenth-century people thought in terms of "poisons" in the air or "corrupted air" coming from swamps, unburied animals, or the positions of the stars. These poisons caused the fluids in the body to become unbalanced, which led to illness, an idea that had been the core of Western ideas about the primary cause of disease since the ancient Greeks. Certain symptoms of the plague, such as boils that oozed and blood-filled coughing, were believed to be the body's natural reaction to too much fluid. Doctors thus recommended preventive measures that would block the poisoned air from entering the body, such as burning incense or holding strong-smelling herbs or other substances, like rosemary, juniper, or sulfur, in front of the nose. Other treatments focused on ridding the air and the body of these poisons and on rebalancing bodily fluids through vomiting, sweating, or letting blood, which was also thought to rid the body of poisons.

In their fear and dread, people tried anything they thought might help. Perhaps loud sounds like ringing church bells or firing the newly invented cannon would clean poisoned air. Medicines made from plants that were bumpy or that oozed liquid might work, keeping the more dangerous swelling and oozing of the plague away. Magical letter and number combinations, called cryptograms, were especially popular in Muslim areas. They were often the first letters of words in prayers or religious sayings, and they gave people a sense of order when faced with the randomness with which the plague seemed to strike.

To avoid contagion, wealthier people often fled cities for the countryside, though sometimes this simply spread the plague faster. (See "Viewpoints: Italian and English Views of the Plague," page 300.) Some cities tried shutting their gates to prevent infected people and animals from coming in, which worked in a few cities. They also walled up houses in which there was plague, trying to isolate those who were sick from those who were still healthy. Though some members of the clergy took flight, many cared for the sick and buried the dead, which meant they had a high mortality rate.

Economic, Religious, and Cultural Effects

Economic historians and demographers dispute the impact of the plague on the economy in the late fourteenth century, and this impact clearly was different in different parts of Europe. Some places never recovered their economic standing, while in others, those people who survived may have had a higher standard of living. By the mid-1300s the population

of Europe had grown somewhat beyond what could easily be supported by available agricultural technology, particularly in the worsening climate of the Little Ice Age. The dramatic drop in population allowed less fertile land to be abandoned, making yields per acre somewhat better. People also turned to less labor-intensive types of agriculture, such as raising sheep or wine grapes, which in the long run proved to be a better use of the land.

The Black Death did bring on a general European inflation. High mortality produced a fall in production, shortages of goods, and a general rise in prices. The price of wheat in most of Europe increased, as did the costs of meat, sausage, and cheese. This inflation continued to the end of the fourteenth century. But labor shortages resulting from the high mortality caused by the plague meant that workers could demand better wages. The greater demand for labor also meant greater mobility for peasants in rural areas and for artisans in towns and cities.

The plague also had effects on religious practices. Not surprisingly, some people sought release from the devastation through wild living, but more became more deeply pious. Rather than seeing the plague as a medical issue, they interpreted it as the result of an evil within themselves. God must be punishing them for terrible sins, they thought, so the best remedies were religious ones: asking for forgiveness, praying, trusting in God, making donations to churches, and trying to live better lives. In Muslim areas, religious leaders urged virtuous living in the face of death: give to the poor, reconcile with your enemies, free your slaves, and say a proper good-bye to your friends and family.

Believing that the Black Death was God's punishment for humanity's wickedness, some Christians turned to the severest forms of asceticism and frenzied religious fervor, joining groups of **flagellants** (FLA-juh-luhnts), who whipped and scourged themselves as penance for their own and society's sins. Groups of flagellants traveled from town to town, often growing into unruly mobs. Officials, worried that they would provoke violence and riots, ordered groups to disband or forbade them to enter cities.

Along with seeing the plague as a call to reform their own behavior, however, people also searched for scapegoats, and savage cruelty sometimes resulted. As in the decades before the plague, many people believed that the Jews had poisoned the wells of Christian communities and thereby infected the drinking water. Others thought that killing Jews would prevent the plague from spreading to their town, a belief encouraged by flagellant groups. These charges led to the murder of thousands of Jews across Europe, especially in the cities

---

■ **flagellants** People who believed that the plague was God's punishment for sin and sought to do penance by flagellating (whipping) themselves.

VIEWPOINTS

Italian and English Views of the Plague

Eyewitness commentators on the plague include the Italian writer Giovanni Boccaccio (1313–1375), who portrayed the course of the disease in Florence in the preface to his book of tales, *The Decameron*, and the English monastic chronicler Henry Knighton (d. 1396), who described the effects of the plague on English towns and villages in his four-volume chronicle of English history.

Giovanni Boccaccio

⟋ Against this pestilence no human wisdom or foresight was of any avail. . . . Men and women in great numbers abandoned their city, their houses, their farms, their relatives, and their possessions and sought other places, going at least as far away as the Florentine countryside—as if the wrath of God could not pursue them with this pestilence wherever they went but would only strike those it found within the walls of the city! . . . Almost no one cared for his neighbor, and relatives hardly ever visited one another—they stayed far apart. This disaster had struck such fear into the hearts of men and women that brother abandoned brother, uncle abandoned nephew, sister left brother, and very often wife abandoned husband, and—even worse, almost unbelievable—fathers and mothers neglected to tend and care for their children as if they were not their own. . . . So many corpses would arrive in front of a church every day and at every hour that the amount of holy ground for burials was certainly insufficient for the ancient custom of giving each body its individual place; when all the graves were full, huge trenches were dug in all the cemeteries of the churches and into them the new arrivals were dumped by the hundreds; and they were packed in there with dirt, one on top of another, like a ship's cargo, until the trench was filled. . . . Oh how many great palaces, beautiful homes and noble dwellings, once filled with families, gentlemen, and ladies, were now emptied, down to the last servant!

Henry Knighton

⟋ Then that most grievous pestilence penetrated the coastal regions [of England] by way of Southampton, and came to Bristol, and people died as if the whole strength of the city were seized by sudden death. For there were few who lay in their beds more than three days or two and half days; then that savage death snatched them about the second day. In Leicester, in the little parish of St. Leonard, more than three hundred and eighty died; in the parish of Holy Cross, more than four hundred. . . . And so in each parish, they died in great numbers. . . . At the same time, there was so great a lack of priests everywhere that many churches had no divine services. . . . One could hardly hire a chaplain to minister to the church for less than ten marks, whereas before the pestilence, when there were plenty of priests, one could hire a chaplain for five or four marks. . . . Meanwhile, the king ordered that in every county of the kingdom, reapers and other labourers should not receive more than they were accustomed to receive, under the penalty provided in the statute, and he renewed the statute at this time. The labourers, however, were so arrogant and hostile that they did not heed the king's command, but if anyone wished to hire them, he had to pay them what they wanted, and either lose his fruits and crops or satisfy the arrogant and greedy desire of the labourers as they wished. . . . Similarly, those who received day-work from their tenants throughout the year, as is usual from serfs, had to release them and to remit such service. They either had to excuse them entirely or had to fix them in a laxer manner at a small rent, lest very great and irreparable damage be done to the buildings and the land everywhere remain uncultivated.

QUESTIONS FOR ANALYSIS

1. How did the residents of Florence respond to the plague, as described by Boccaccio?
2. What were some of the effects of the plague in England, as described by Knighton?
3. How might the fact that Boccaccio was writing in an urban setting and Knighton was writing from a rural monastery that owned a large amount of land have shaped their perspectives?

Sources: Giovanni Boccaccio, *The Decameron*, trans. Mark Musa and Peter Bondanella (New York: W. W. Norton, 1982), pp. 7, 9, 12; Henry Knighton, *Chronicon Henrici Knighton*, in *The Portable Medieval Reader*, ed. James Bruce Ross and Mary Martin McLaughlin (London: Penguin Books, 1949).

of France and Germany. In Strasbourg, for example, several hundred Jews were publicly burned alive. Their houses were looted, their property was confiscated, and the remaining Jews were expelled from the city.

The literature and art of the late Middle Ages reveal a people gripped by morbid concern with death. One highly popular literary and artistic motif, the Dance of Death, depicted a dancing skeleton leading away living people, often in order of their rank. (See "Evaluating Visual Evidence: Dance of Death," page 301.)

The years of the Black Death witnessed the foundation of new colleges at old universities and of

Dance of Death

In this allegorical fresco from the Holy Trinity Church in the village of Hrastovlje, Slovenia, skeletons lead people of all social classes in a procession. One of them carries a scythe for reaping grain, long a symbol of death cutting off human life. In the late fifteenth century the Croatian artist John of Kastav painted the entire church in frescoes, which were discovered in 1949 under layers of plaster. The Dance of Death became a common theme in late medieval painting, especially on the walls of cemeteries, churches, and chapels, and in engravings and woodcuts. Designed as *memento mori* (in Latin: "Remember that you have to die"), symbolic reminders of mortality, they encouraged viewers to think about the fleetingness of human life.

(Church of the Holy Trinity, Hrastovlje, Slovenia/Bridgeman Images)

EVALUATE THE EVIDENCE

1. Based on their clothing and the objects they are carrying, who are the people shown in the fresco? What does this suggest about the artist's message about death?
2. Paintings such as this clearly provide evidence of the preoccupation with death in this era, but does this work highlight other social issues as well? Is so, what are they?

entirely new universities. The foundation charters give the shortage of priests and the decay of learning as the reasons for their establishment. Whereas older universities such as those at Bologna and Paris had international student bodies, these new institutions established in the wake of the Black Death had more national or local constituencies. Thus the international character of medieval culture weakened, paving the way for schism (SKIH-zuhm) in the Catholic Church even before the Reformation.

As is often true with devastating events, the plague highlighted central qualities of medieval society: deep religious feeling, suspicion of those who were different, and a view of the world shaped largely by oral tradition, with a bit of classical knowledge mixed in among the educated elite.

What were the causes, course, and consequences of the Hundred Years' War?

A long international war that began a decade or so before the plague struck and lasted well into the next century added further misery to a disease-ravaged population. England and France had engaged in sporadic military hostilities from the time of the Norman Conquest in 1066, and in the middle of the fourteenth century these became more intense. From 1337 to 1453 the two countries intermittently fought one another in what was the longest war in European history, ultimately dubbed the **Hundred Years' War**, though it actually lasted 116 years.

Causes

The Hundred Years' War had a number of causes, including disagreements over rights to land, a dispute over the succession to the French throne, and economic conflicts. Many of these revolved around the duchy of Aquitaine, a province in southern France that became part of the holdings of the English Crown when Eleanor of Aquitaine married King Henry II of England in 1152 (see "England" in Chapter 9; a duchy is a territory ruled by a duke). In 1259 Henry III of England had signed the Treaty of Paris with Louis IX of France, affirming English claims to Aquitaine in return for becoming a vassal of the French Crown. French policy in the fourteenth century was strongly expansionist, however, and the French kings resolved to absorb the duchy into the kingdom of France. Aquitaine therefore became a disputed territory.

The immediate political cause of the war was a disagreement over who would inherit the French throne after Charles IV of France, the last surviving son of Philip the Fair, died childless in 1328. With him

Isabella of France and Her Son Edward Invade England   Isabella, the sister of Charles IV of France and the wife of Edward II of England, and her son Edward III are welcomed by clergy into the city of Oxford in 1326, in this illustration for the chronicles of the counts of Flanders, made in 1477. Isabella and Edward, who was only fourteen at the time, had just invaded England with a small army to overthrow her husband. Isabella ruled as regent for her son for three years before he assumed personal rule by force. She lived another twenty-eight years in high style as a wealthy woman, watching her son lead successful military ventures in France in the first decades of the Hundred Years' War. (By kind permission of Lord Leicester and the Trustees of Holkham Estate, Norfolk/Bridgeman Images)

ended the male line of the Capetian dynasty of France. Charles IV had a sister, Isabella, married to Edward II, the king of England, and just two years earlier she and her lover Roger Mortimer had invaded England with a small army to overthrow her husband and end the influence of his male favorite, Hugh le Despenser. They captured and imprisoned both men, executed Despenser, deposed the king (and may have ordered his murder), and put her teenage son Edward III on the throne. Seeking to keep Isabella and Edward from the French throne, an assembly of French high nobles proclaimed that "no woman nor her son could succeed to the [French] monarchy." French lawyers defended the position with the claim that the exclusion of women from ruling or passing down the right to rule was part of Salic law, a sixth-century law code of the Franks (see "Customary and Written Law" in Chapter 7), and that Salic law itself was part of the fundamental law of France. They used this invented tradition to argue that Edward should be barred from the French throne. (The ban on female succession became part of French legal tradition until the end of the monarchy in 1789.) The nobles passed the Crown to Philip VI of Valois (r. 1328–1350), a nephew of Philip the Fair.

In 1329 Edward III formally recognized his status as a vassal to Philip VI for Aquitaine, as required by the 1259 Treaty of Paris. Eight years later, in 1337, Philip, eager to exercise full French jurisdiction there, confiscated the duchy. Edward III interpreted this action as a gross violation of the treaty and as a cause for war. Moreover, Edward argued, as the eldest directly surviving male descendant of Philip the Fair, he deserved the title of king of France. To increase their independent power, many French nobles abandoned Philip VI, using the excuse that they accepted Edward's claims to the throne. One reason the war lasted so long was that it became a French civil war, with some French nobles, especially the dukes of Burgundy, supporting English monarchs in order to thwart the centralizing goals of the French kings. On the other side, Scotland—resisting English efforts of assimilation—often allied with France; the French supported Scottish raids in northern England, and Scottish troops joined with French armies on the continent.

The governments of both England and France manipulated public opinion to support the war. Kings in both countries instructed the clergy to deliver sermons filled with patriotic sentiment. Royal propaganda on both sides fostered a kind of early nationalism, and both sides developed a deep hatred of the other.

Economic factors involving the wool trade and the control of Flemish towns were linked to these political issues. The wool trade between England and Flanders served as the cornerstone of both countries' economies; they were closely interdependent. Flanders technically belonged to the French Crown,

THE HUNDRED YEARS' WAR

1337	Philip VI of France confiscates Aquitaine; war begins
1346	English longbowmen defeat French knights at Crécy
1356	English defeat French at Poitiers
1370s–1380s	French recover some territory
1415	English defeat the French at Agincourt
1429	French victory at Orléans; Charles VII crowned king
1431	Joan of Arc declared a heretic and burned at the stake
1440s	French reconquer Normandy and Aquitaine
1453	War ends
1456	Joan cleared of charges of heresy and declared a martyr

and the Flemish aristocracy was highly sympathetic to that monarchy. But the wealth of Flemish merchants and cloth manufacturers depended on English wool, and Flemish burghers strongly supported the claims of Edward III. The disruption of commerce with England threatened their prosperity.

The war also presented opportunities for wealth and advancement. Poor and idle knights were promised regular wages. Criminals who enlisted were granted pardons. The great nobles expected to be rewarded with estates. Royal exhortations to the troops before battles repeatedly stressed that, if victorious, the men might keep whatever they seized.

English Successes

The war began with a series of French sea raids on English coastal towns in 1337, but the French fleet was almost completely destroyed when it attempted to land soldiers on English soil, and from that point on the war was fought almost entirely in France and the Low Countries (Map 11.2). It consisted mainly of a series of random sieges and cavalry raids, fought in fits and starts, with treaties along the way to halt hostilities.

During the war's early stages, England was highly successful. At Crécy in northern France in 1346, English longbowmen scored a great victory over French knights and crossbowmen. Although the aim of longbowmen was not very accurate, the weapon allowed

■ **Hundred Years' War** A war between England and France from 1337 to 1453, with political and economic causes and consequences.

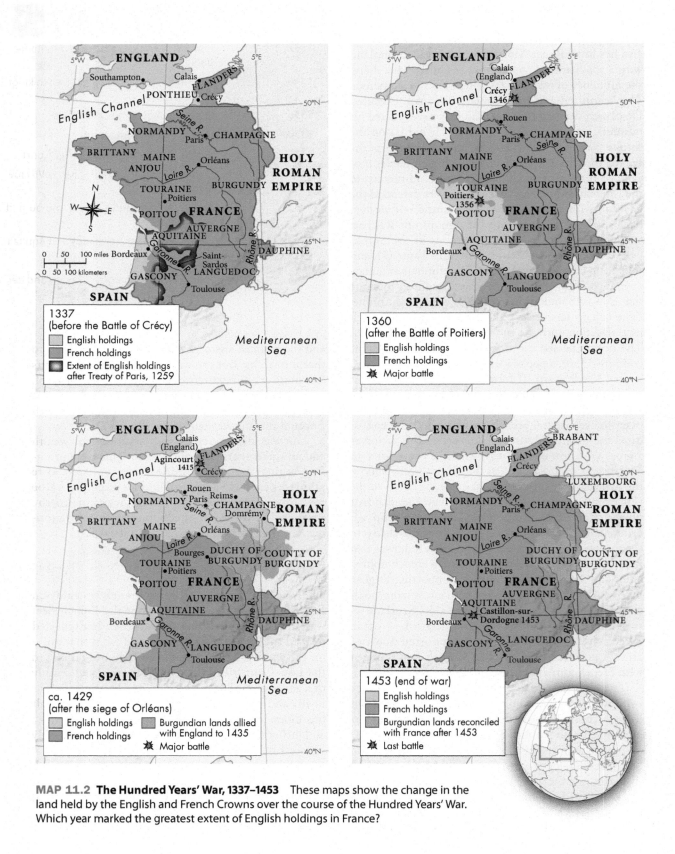

MAP 11.2 The Hundred Years' War, 1337–1453 These maps show the change in the land held by the English and French Crowns over the course of the Hundred Years' War. Which year marked the greatest extent of English holdings in France?

for rapid reloading, and an English archer could send off three arrows to the French crossbowman's one. The result was a blinding shower of arrows that unhorsed the French knights and caused mass confusion. The roar of English cannon — probably the first use of artillery in the Western world — created further panic. Edward's son, Edward the Black Prince, used the same tactics ten years later to smash the French at Poitiers, where he captured the French king and held him for ransom. Edward was not able to take all of France, but the English held Aquitaine and other provinces, and allied themselves with many of France's nobles. After a brief peace, the French fought back and recovered some territory during the 1370s and 1380s, and then a treaty again halted hostilities as both sides concentrated on conflicts over power at home.

War began again in 1415 when the able English soldier-king Henry V (r. 1413–1422) invaded France. At Agincourt (AH-jihn-kort), Henry's army defeated a much larger French force, again primarily through the skill of English longbowmen. Henry followed up his triumph at Agincourt with the reconquest of Normandy, and by 1419 the English had advanced to the walls of Paris (see Map 11.2). Henry married the daughter of the French king, and a treaty made Henry and any sons the couple would have heir to the French throne. It appeared that Henry would indeed rule both England and France, but he died unexpectedly

in 1422, leaving an infant son as heir. The English continued their victories, however, and besieged the city of Orléans (or-lay-AHN), the only major city in northern France not under their control. But the French cause was not lost.

Joan of Arc and France's Victory

The ultimate French success rests heavily on the actions of Joan, an obscure French peasant girl whose vision and military leadership revived French fortunes and led to victory. (Over the centuries, she acquired the name "of Arc" — *d'Arc* in French — based on her father's name; she never used this name for herself, but called herself "the maiden" — *la Pucelle* in French.) Born in 1412 to well-to-do peasants in the village of Domrémy in Champagne, Joan grew up in a religious household. During adolescence she began to hear voices, which she later said belonged to Saint Michael, Saint Catherine, and Saint Margaret. In 1428 these voices spoke to her with great urgency, telling her that the dauphin (DOH-fehn), the uncrowned King Charles VII, had to be crowned and the English expelled from France. Joan traveled to the French court wearing male clothing. She had an audience with Charles, who had her questioned about her angelic visions and examined to make sure she was the virgin she said she was. She secured his support to travel with the French army to Orléans dressed as a knight — with

Battle of Poitiers, 1356   This fifteenth-century manuscript highlights the role of English longbowmen in defeating French armies. Though the scene is fanciful, the artist accurately depicts a standard tactic, shooting unarmored horses rather than the heavily armored knights, who were killed or captured when they fell from horseback. Commentators at the time and military historians since judge this tactic to have been especially important in the English victory. (Photo 12/Universal Images Group/ Getty Images)

borrowed armor and sword. There she dictated a letter to the English ordering them to surrender:

> King of England . . . , do right in the King of Heaven's sight. Surrender to The Maid sent hither by God the King of Heaven, the keys of all the good towns you have taken and laid waste in France. She comes in God's name to establish the Blood Royal, ready to make peace if you agree to abandon France and repay what you have taken. And you, archers, comrades in arms, gentles and others, who are before the town of Orléans, retire in God's name to your own country.[2]

Such words coming from a teenage girl—even one inspired by God—were laughable given the recent course of the conflict, but Joan was amazingly successful. She inspired and led French attacks, forcing the English to retreat from Orléans. The king made Joan co-commander of the entire army, and she led it to a string of victories; other cities simply surrendered without a fight and returned their allegiance to France. In July 1429, two months after the end of the siege of Orléans, Charles VII was crowned king at Reims.

Joan and the French army continued their fight against the English and their Burgundian allies. In 1430 the Burgundians captured Joan. Charles refused to ransom her, and she was sold to the English. A church court headed by a pro-English bishop tried her for heresy, and though nothing she had done was heretical by church doctrine, she was found guilty and burned at the stake in the marketplace at Rouen. (See "Evaluating Written Evidence: The Trial of Joan of Arc," page 307.)

The French army continued its victories without her. Sensing a shift in the balance of power, the Burgundians switched their allegiance to the French, who reconquered Normandy and, finally, ejected the English from Aquitaine in the 1440s. As the war dragged on, loss of life mounted, and money appeared to be flowing into a bottomless pit, demands for an end increased in England. Parliamentary opposition to additional war grants stiffened, fewer soldiers were sent, and more territory passed into French hands. At the war's end in 1453, only the town of Calais (KA-lay) remained in English hands.

What of Joan? A new trial in 1456—requested by Charles VII, who either had second thoughts about his abandonment of Joan or did not wish to be associated with a condemned heretic—was held by the pope. It cleared her of all charges and declared her a martyr.

She became a political symbol of France from that point on, and sometimes also a symbol of the Catholic Church in opposition to the government of France. In 1920, for example, she was canonized as a saint shortly after the French government declared separation of church and state in France. Similarly, Joan has been (and continues to be) a symbol of deep religious piety to some, of conservative nationalism to others, and of gender-bending cross-dressing to others. Beneath the pious and popular legends is a teenage girl who saved the French monarchy, the embodiment of France.

Aftermath

In France thousands of soldiers and civilians had been slaughtered and hundreds of thousands of acres of rich farmland ruined, leaving the rural economy of many areas a shambles. These losses exacerbated the dreadful losses caused by the plague. The war had disrupted trade and the great trade fairs, resulting in the drastic reduction of French participation in international commerce. Defeat in battle and heavy taxation contributed to widespread dissatisfaction and aggravated peasant grievances.

The war had wreaked havoc in England as well, even though only the southern coastal ports saw actual battle. England spent the huge sum of over £5 million on the war effort, and despite the money raised by some victories, the net result was an enormous financial loss. The government attempted to finance the war by raising taxes on the wool crop, which priced wool out of the export market.

In both England and France, men of all social classes had volunteered to serve in the war in the hope of acquiring booty and becoming rich, and some were successful in the early years of the war. As time went on, however, most fortunes seem to have been squandered as fast as they were made. In addition, the social order was disrupted because the knights who ordinarily served as sheriffs, coroners, jurymen, and justices of the peace were abroad.

The war stimulated technological experimentation, especially with artillery. Cannon revolutionized warfare, making the stone castle no longer impregnable. Because only central governments, not private nobles, could afford cannon, their use strengthened the military power of national states.

The long war also had a profound impact on the political and cultural lives of the two countries. Most notably, it stimulated the development of the English Parliament. Between 1250 and 1450 **representative assemblies** flourished in many European countries. In the English Parliament, German *diets*, and Spanish *cortes*, deliberative practices developed that laid the foundations for the representative institutions of modern democratic nations. While

■ **representative assemblies** Deliberative meetings of lords and wealthy urban residents that flourished in many European countries between 1250 and 1450.

The Trial of Joan of Arc

Joan's interrogation was organized and led by Bishop Pierre Cauchon, one of many French clergy who supported the English. In a number of sessions that took place over several months, she was repeatedly asked about her voices, her decision to wear men's clothing, and other issues. This extract is from the fourth session, on Tuesday, February 27, 1431; Joan is here referred to with the French spelling of her name, Jeanne.

In their presence Jeanne was required by my lord the Bishop of Beauvais to swear and take the oath concerning what touched her trial. To which she answered that she would willingly swear as to what touched her trial, but not as to everything she knew. . . .

Asked whether she had heard her voice since Saturday, she answered: "Yes, indeed, many times." . . . Asked what it said to her when she was back in her room, she replied: "That I should answer boldly." . . . Questioned as to whether it were the voice of an angel, or of a saint, or directly from God, she answered that the voices were those of Saint Catherine and of Saint Margaret. And their heads are crowned with beautiful crowns, most richly and preciously. And [she said] for [telling you] this I have leave from our Lord. . . .

Asked if the voice ordered her to wear a man's dress, she answered that the dress is but a small matter; and that she had not taken it by the advice of any living man; and that she did not take this dress nor do anything at all save by the command of Our Lord and the angels.

Questioned as to whether it seemed to her that this command to take male dress was a lawful one, she answered that everything she had done was at Our Lord's command, and if He had ordered Jeanne to take a different dress, she would have done so, since it would have been at God's command. . . .

Asked if she had her sword when she was taken prisoner, she said no, but that she had one which was taken from a Burgundian. . . . Asked whether, when she was before the city of Orleans, she had a standard, and of what colour it was, she replied that it had a field sown with fleurs-de-lis, and showed a world with an angel on either side, white in colour, of linen or *boucassin* [a type of fabric], and she thought that the names JESUS MARIA were written on it; and it had a silk fringe. . . . Asked which she preferred, her sword or her standard, she replied that she was forty times fonder of her standard than she was of her sword. . . . She said moreover that she herself bore her standard during an attack, in order to avoid killing anyone. And she added that she had never killed anyone at all. . . .

She also said that during the attack on the fort at the bridge she was wounded in the neck by an arrow, but she was greatly comforted by Saint Catherine, and was well again in a fortnight. . . . Asked whether she knew beforehand that she would be wounded, she said that she well knew it, and had informed her king of it; but that notwithstanding she would not give up her work.

EVALUATE THE EVIDENCE

1. How does Joan explain the way that she chose to answer the interrogators' questions, and her decisions about clothing and actions in battle?
2. Thinking about the structures of power and authority in fifteenth-century France, how do you believe the interrogators would have regarded Joan's answers?

Source: *The Trial of Joan of Arc*, translated with an introduction by W. S. Scott (Westport, Conn.: Associated Booksellers, 1956), pp76, 77, 79–80, 82, 83.

representative assemblies declined in most countries after the fifteenth century, the English Parliament endured. Edward III's constant need for money to pay for the war compelled him to summon not only the great barons and bishops, but knights of the shires and citizens from the towns as well. Parliament met in thirty-seven of the fifty years of Edward's reign.

The frequency of the meetings is significant. Representative assemblies were becoming a habit in England. Knights and wealthy urban residents — or the "Commons," as they came to be called — recognized their mutual interests and began to meet

apart from the great lords. The Commons gradually realized that they held the country's purse strings, and a parliamentary statute of 1341 required parliamentary approval of most new taxes. By signing the law, Edward III acknowledged that the king of England could not tax without Parliament's consent. In France, by contrast, there was no single national assembly, and regional or provincial assemblies never gained much power over taxation.

In both countries, the war promoted the growth of nationalism — the feeling of unity and identity that binds together a people. After victories, each country experienced a surge of pride in its military strength. Just as English patriotism ran strong after Crécy and Poitiers, so French national confidence rose after Orléans. French national feeling demanded the expulsion of the enemy not merely from Normandy and Aquitaine but from all French soil. Perhaps no one expressed this national consciousness better than Joan when she exulted that the enemy had been "driven out of *France.*"

Why did the church come under increasing criticism?

In times of crisis or disaster, people of all faiths have sought the consolation of religion. In the fourteenth century, however, the official Christian Church offered little solace. Many priests and friars helped the sick and the hungry, but others paid more attention to worldly matters, and the leaders of the church added to the sorrow and misery of the times. In response to this lack of leadership, members of the clergy challenged the power of the pope, and laypeople challenged the authority of the church itself. Women and men increasingly relied on direct approaches to God, often through mystical encounters, rather than on the institutional church.

The Babylonian Captivity and Great Schism

Conflicts between the secular rulers of Europe and the popes were common throughout the High Middle Ages, and in the early fourteenth century the dispute between King Philip the Fair of France and Pope Boniface VIII became particularly bitter (see "The Popes and Church Law" in Chapter 9). After Boniface's death, Philip pressured the new pope, Clement V, to settle permanently in Avignon in southeastern France, so that he, Philip, could control the church and its policies. The popes lived in Avignon from 1309 to 1376, a period in church history often called the **Babylonian Captivity** (referring to the seventy years the ancient Hebrews were held captive in Mesopotamian Babylon).

The Babylonian Captivity badly damaged papal prestige. The leadership of the church was cut off from its historic roots and the source of its ancient authority, the city of Rome. The seven popes at Avignon concentrated on bureaucratic and financial matters to the exclusion of spiritual objectives, and the general atmosphere was one of luxury and extravagance, which was also the case at many bishops' courts. Raimon de Cornet, a troubadour poet from southern France who was himself a priest, was only one among many criticizing the church. He wrote:

I see the pope his sacred trust betray,
For while the rich his grace can gain alway,
His favors from the poor are aye withholden.
He strives to gather wealth as best he may,
Forcing Christ's people blindly to obey,
So that he may repose in garments golden.

. . .

Our bishops, too, are plunged in similar sin,
For pitilessly they flay the very skin
From all their priests who chance to have fat
    livings.
For gold their seal official you can win
To any writ, no matter what's therein.
Sure God alone can make them stop their thievings.[3]

In 1377 Pope Gregory XI brought the papal court back to Rome but died shortly afterward. Roman citizens pressured the cardinals to elect an Italian, and they chose a distinguished administrator, the archbishop of Bari, Bartolomeo Prignano, who took the name Urban VI.

Urban VI (pontificate 1378–1389) had excellent intentions for church reform, but he went about it in a tactless manner. He attacked clerical luxury, denouncing individual cardinals and bishops by name, and even threatened to excommunicate some of them. The cardinals slipped away from Rome and met at Anagni. They declared Urban's election invalid because it had come about under threats from the Roman mob, and excommunicated the pope. The cardinals then elected Cardinal Robert of Geneva, the cousin of King Charles V of France, as pope. Cardinal Robert took the name Clement VII. There were thus two popes in 1378 — Urban at Rome and Clement VII (pontificate 1378–1394) at Avignon. So began the **Great Schism**, which divided Western Christendom until 1417.

The powers of Europe aligned themselves with Urban or Clement along strictly political lines. France naturally recognized the French pope, Clement. England, France's long-time enemy, recognized the

Avignon

Rome

■ Allegiance to Rome
■ Allegiance to Avignon
□ Official allegiance to Rome but with shifting local allegiances

The Great Schism, 1378–1417

Italian pope, Urban. Scotland, an ally of France, supported Clement. Aragon, Castile, and Portugal hesitated before deciding for Clement as well. The German emperor, hostile to France, recognized Urban. At first the Italian city-states recognized Urban; later they opted for Clement. The schism weakened the religious faith of many Christians and brought church leadership into serious disrepute.

The Hussite Revolution, 1415–1436

Area under Hussite control

Critiques, Divisions, and Councils

Criticism of the church during the Avignon papacy and the Great Schism often came from the ranks of highly learned clergy and lay professionals. One of these was William of Occam (1289?–1347?), a Franciscan friar and philosopher who saw the papal court at Avignon during the Babylonian Captivity. Occam argued vigorously against the papacy and also wrote philosophical works in which he questioned the connection between reason and faith that had been developed by Thomas Aquinas (see "Theology and Philosophy" in Chapter 10). All governments should have limited powers and be accountable to those they govern, according to Occam, and church and state should be separate.

The Italian lawyer and university official Marsiglio of Padua (ca. 1275–1342) agreed with Occam. In his *Defensor Pacis* (The defender of the peace), Marsiglio argued against the medieval idea of a society governed by both church and state, with church supreme. Instead, Marsiglio claimed, the state was the great unifying power in society, and the church should be subordinate to it. Church leadership should rest in a general council that is made up of laymen as well as priests and that is superior to the pope. Marsiglio was excommunicated for these radical ideas, and his work was condemned as heresy—as was Occam's—but in the later part of the fourteenth century many thinkers agreed with these two critics of the papacy. They believed that reform of the church could best be achieved through periodic assemblies, or councils, representing all the Christian people. Those who argued this position were called **conciliarists**.

The English scholar and theologian John Wyclif (WIH-klihf) (ca. 1330–1384) went further than the conciliarists in his argument against medieval church structure. He wrote that the Scriptures alone should be the standard of Christian belief and practice and that papal claims of secular power had no foundation in the Scriptures. He urged that the church be stripped of its property. He also wanted Christians to read the Bible for themselves and produced the first complete translation of the Bible into English. Wyclif's followers, dubbed Lollards, from a Dutch word for "mumble," by those who ridiculed them, spread his ideas and made many copies of his Bible. Lollard teaching allowed women to preach, and women played a significant role in the movement. Lollards were persecuted in the fifteenth century; some were executed, some recanted, and others continued to meet secretly in houses, barns, and fields to read and discuss the Bible and other religious texts in English.

Bohemian students returning from study at the University of Oxford around 1400 brought Wyclif's ideas with them to Prague, the capital of what was then Bohemia and is now the Czech Republic. There another university theologian, Jan Hus (ca. 1372–1415), built on these ideas. He also denied papal authority, called for translations of the Bible into the local Czech language, and declared indulgences—papal offers of remission of penance—useless. Hus gained many followers, who linked his theological ideas with their opposition to the church's wealth and power and with a growing sense of Czech nationalism in opposition to the pope's international power. Hus's followers were successful at defeating the combined armies of the pope and the emperor many times. In the 1430s the emperor finally agreed to recognize the Hussite Church in Bohemia, which survived into the Reformation and then merged with other Protestant churches.

The ongoing schism threatened the church, and in response to continued calls throughout Europe for a council, the cardinals of Rome and Avignon summoned a council at Pisa in 1409. That gathering of prelates and theologians deposed both popes and selected another. Neither the Avignon pope nor the Roman pope would resign, however, and the appalling result was the creation of a threefold schism.

Finally, under pressure from the German emperor Sigismund, a great council met at the imperial city of Constance (1414–1418). It had three objectives: to

---

■ **Babylonian Captivity** The period from 1309 to 1376 when the popes resided in Avignon rather than in Rome. The phrase refers to the seventy years when the Hebrews were held captive in Babylon.

■ **Great Schism** The division, or split, in church leadership from 1378 to 1417 when there were two, then three, popes.

■ **conciliarists** People who believed that the authority in the Roman Church should rest in a general council composed of clergy, theologians, and laypeople, rather than in the pope alone.

The Arrest and Execution of Jan Hus   In this woodcut from Ulrich of Richental's chronicle of the Council of Constance, Hus is arrested by bishops, led away by soldiers while wearing a hat of shame with the word *arch-heretic* on it, and burned at the stake. The final panel shows executioners shoveling his ashes and burned bones into the Rhine. Ulrich of Richental was a merchant in Constance and an eyewitness to Hus's execution and many of the other events of the council. He wrote his chronicle in German shortly after the council ended and paid for it to be illustrated. The original is lost, but many copies were made later in the fifteenth century, and the volume was printed in 1483 with many woodcuts, including this one. Hus became an important symbol of Czech independence, and in 1990 the Czech Republic declared July 6, the date of his execution in 1415, a national holiday. (© Archives Charmet/Bridgeman Images)

wipe out heresy, to end the schism, and to reform the church. Members included cardinals, bishops, abbots, and professors of theology and canon law from across Europe. The council moved first on the first point: despite being granted a safe-conduct to go to Constance by the emperor, Jan Hus was tried, condemned, and burned at the stake as a heretic in 1415. The council also eventually healed the schism. It deposed both the Roman pope and the successor of the pope chosen at Pisa, and it isolated the Avignon pope. A conclave elected a new leader, the Roman cardinal Colonna, who took the name Martin V (pontificate 1417–1431).

Martin proceeded to dissolve the council, and nothing was done about reform, the third objective of the council. In the later part of the fifteenth century the papacy concentrated on Italian problems to the exclusion of universal Christian interests. But the schism and the conciliar movement had exposed the crying need

for ecclesiastical reform, thus laying the foundation for the great reform efforts of the sixteenth century.

Lay Piety and Mysticism

The failings of the Avignon papacy followed by the scandal of the Great Schism did much to weaken the spiritual mystique of the clergy in the popular mind. Laypeople had already begun to develop their own forms of piety somewhat separate from the authority of priests and bishops, and these forms of piety became more prominent in the fourteenth century.

In the thirteenth century lay Christian men and women had formed **confraternities**, voluntary lay groups organized by occupation, devotional preference, neighborhood, or charitable activity. Some confraternities specialized in praying for souls in purgatory, or held collections to raise money to clean and repair church buildings and to supply churches with candles and other liturgical objects. Like craft guilds, most

■ **confraternities** Voluntary lay groups organized by occupation, devotional preference, neighborhood, or charitable activity.

Mysticism — the direct experience of the divine — is an aspect of many world religions and has been part of Christianity throughout its history. During the late Middle Ages, however, the pursuit of mystical union became an important part of the piety of many laypeople, especially in the Rhineland area of Germany. In this they were guided by the sermons of the churchman generally known as Meister Eckhart. Born into a German noble family, Eckhart (1260–1329?) joined the Dominican order and studied theology at Paris and Cologne, attaining the academic title of *master* (*Meister* in German). The leaders of the Dominican order appointed him to a series of administrative and teaching positions, and he wrote learned treatises in Latin that reflected his Scholastic training and deep understanding of classical philosophy.

He also began to preach in German, attracting many listeners through his beautiful language and mystical insights. God, he said, was "an oversoaring being and an over-being nothingness," whose essence was beyond the ability of humans to express: "if the soul is to know God, it must know Him outside time and place, since God is neither in this or that, but One and above them." Only through "unknowing," emptying oneself, could one come to experience the divine. Yet God was also present in individual human souls, and to a degree in every creature, all of which God had called into being before the beginning of time. Within each human soul there was what Eckhart called a "little spark," an innermost essence that allows the soul — with God's grace and Christ's redemptive action — to come to God. "Our salvation depends upon our knowing and recognizing the Chief Good which is God Himself," preached Eckhart; "the Eye with which I see God is the same Eye with which God sees me." "I have a capacity in my soul for taking in God entirely," he went on, a capacity that was shared by all humans, not only members of the clergy or those with special spiritual gifts. Although Eckhart did not reject church sacraments or the hierarchy, he frequently stressed that union with God was best accomplished through quiet detachment and simple prayer rather than pilgrimages, extensive fasts, or other activities: "If the only prayer you said in your whole life was 'thank you,' that would suffice."*

Eckhart's unusual teachings led to charges of heresy in 1327, which he denied. The pope — who was at this point in Avignon — presided over a trial condemning him, but Eckhart appears to have died during the course of the proceedings or shortly thereafter. His writings were ordered destroyed, but his followers preserved many and spread his teachings.

A sixteenth-century woodcut of Meister Eckhart teaching.
(Visual Connection Archive)

In the last few decades, Meister Eckhart's ideas have been explored and utilized by philosophers and mystics in Buddhism, Hinduism, and neo-paganism, as well as by Christians. His writings sell widely for their spiritual insights, and quotations from them — including the one above about thank-you prayers — can be found on coffee mugs, tote bags, and T-shirts.

QUESTIONS FOR ANALYSIS

1. Why might Meister Eckhart's preaching have been viewed as threatening by the leaders of the church?
2. Given the situation of the church in the late Middle Ages, why might mysticism have been attractive to pious Christians?

*Meister Eckhart's Sermons, trans. Claud Field (London: n.p., 1909).

confraternities were groups of men, but separate women's confraternities were formed in some towns, often to oversee the production of vestments, altar cloths, and other items made of fabric. All confraternities carried out special devotional practices such as prayers or processions, often without the leadership of a priest. Famine, plague, war, and other crises led to an expansion of confraternities in larger cities and many villages.

In Holland beginning in the late fourteenth century, a group of pious laypeople called the Brethren and Sisters of the Common Life lived in stark simplicity while daily carrying out the Gospel teaching of feeding the hungry, clothing the naked, and visiting the sick. They sought to both ease social problems and make religion a personal inner experience. The spirituality of the Brethren and Sisters of the Common Life found its finest expression in the classic *The Imitation of Christ* by the Dutch monk Thomas à Kempis (1380?–1471), which gained wide appeal among laypeople. It urges Christians to take Christ as their model, seek perfection in a simple way of life, and look to the Scriptures for guidance in living a spiritual life. In the mid-fifteenth century the movement had founded houses in the Netherlands, in central Germany, and in the Rhineland.

For some individuals, both laypeople and clerics, religious devotion included mystical experiences. (See "Individuals in Society: Meister Eckhart," page 311.) Bridget of Sweden (1303–1373) was a noblewoman who journeyed to Rome after her husband's death. She began to see visions and gave advice based on these visions to both laypeople and church officials. At the end of her life Bridget made a pilgrimage to Jerusalem, where she saw visions of the Virgin Mary, who described to her exactly how she was standing "with [her] knees bent" when she gave birth to Jesus, and how she "showed to the shepherds the nature and male sex of the child."[4] Bridget's visions provide evidence of the ways in which laypeople used their own experiences to enhance their religious understanding; her own experiences of childbirth shaped the way she viewed the birth of Jesus, and she related to the Virgin Mary in part as one mother to another.

The confraternities and mystics were generally not considered heretical unless they began to challenge the authority of the papacy the way Wyclif, Hus, and some conciliarists did. However, the movement of lay piety did alter many people's perceptions of their own spiritual power.

What explains the social unrest of the late Middle Ages?

At the beginning of the fourteenth century famine and disease profoundly affected the lives of European peoples. As the century wore on, decades of slaughter and destruction, punctuated by the decimating visits of the Black Death, added further woes. In many parts of France and the Low Countries, fields lay in ruin or untilled for lack of labor. In England, as taxes increased, criticisms of government policy and mismanagement multiplied. Crime and new forms of business organization aggravated economic troubles, and throughout Europe the frustrations of the common people erupted into widespread revolts.

Peasant Revolts

Nobles and clergy lived on the food produced by peasant labor, thinking little of adding taxes to the burden of peasant life. While peasants had endured centuries of exploitation, the difficult conditions of the fourteenth and fifteenth centuries spurred a wave of peasant revolts across Europe. Peasants were sometimes joined by those low on the urban social ladder, resulting in a wider revolution of poor against rich. (See "Thinking Like a Historian: Popular Revolts in the Late Middle Ages," page 314.)

The first large-scale rebellion was in the Flanders region of present-day Belgium in the 1320s (Map 11.3). In order to satisfy peace agreements, Flemish peasants were forced to pay taxes to the French. Monasteries also pressed peasants for additional money above their customary tithes. In retaliation, peasants burned and pillaged castles and aristocratic country houses. A French army crushed the peasant forces, however, and savage repression and the confiscation of peasant property followed in the 1330s.

In the following decades, revolts broke out in many other places. In 1358, when French taxation for the Hundred Years' War fell heavily on the poor, the frustrations of the French peasantry exploded in a massive uprising called the **Jacquerie** (zhah-kuh-REE), after a mythical agricultural laborer, Jacques Bonhomme (Good Fellow). Peasants blamed the nobility for oppressive taxes, for the criminal banditry of the countryside, for losses on the battlefield, and for the general misery. Artisans and small merchants in cities and parish priests joined the peasants. Rebels committed terrible destruction, killing nobles and burning castles, and for several weeks the nobles were on the defensive. Then the upper class united to repress the revolt with merciless ferocity. That forcible

MAP 11.3 Fourteenth-Century Revolts In the later Middle Ages peasant and urban uprisings were endemic, as common as factory strikes in the industrial world. The threat of insurrection served to check unlimited exploitation.

suppression of social rebellion, without any effort to alleviate its underlying causes, served to drive protest underground.

In England the Black Death drastically cut the labor supply, and as a result peasants demanded higher wages and fewer manorial obligations. Their lords countered in 1351 with the Statute of Laborers, a law issued by the king that froze wages and bound workers to their manors. This attempt to freeze wages could not be enforced, but a huge gap remained between peasants and their lords, and the peasants sought release for their economic frustrations in revolt. Other factors combined with these economic grievances to fuel the rebellion. The south of England, where the revolt broke out, had been subjected to destructive French raids during the Hundred Years' War. The English government did little to protect the region, and villagers grew increasingly frightened and insecure. Moreover, decades of aristocratic violence against the weak

peasantry had bred hostility and bitterness. Social and religious agitation by the popular preacher John Ball fanned the embers of discontent.

The English revolt was ignited by the reimposition of a tax on all adult males to pay for the war with France. Despite widespread opposition to the tax, the royal council ordered sheriffs to collect unpaid taxes by force in 1381. This led to a major uprising later termed the **English Peasants' Revolt**, which involved thousands of people, including artisans and the poor in cities as well as rural residents. Many nobles, including the archbishop of Canterbury, who had ordered the collection of the tax, were murdered. The center of the revolt lay in the highly populated and

■ **Jacquerie** A massive uprising by French peasants in 1358 protesting heavy taxation.

■ **English Peasants' Revolt** Revolt by English peasants in 1381 in response to changing economic conditions.

Popular Revolts in the Late Middle Ages

Famine, plague, and war led to population decline and economic problems in the fourteenth century, which fueled both resentment and fear. How did such crises, and the response of those in power to these crises, spur calls for reform and revolts among peasants and workers?

1 **The Statute of Laborers, 1351.** After the English population declined by one-third because of the Black Death, rural and urban workers demanded higher wages and better working conditions, which led the English Parliament and King Edward III to pass the following law.

Because a great part of the people and especially of the workmen and servants has now died in that pestilence, some, seeing the straights of the masters and the scarcity of servants, are not willing to serve unless they receive excessive wages, and others, rather than through labour to gain their living, prefer to beg in idleness: We, considering the grave inconveniences which might come from the lack especially of ploughmen and such labourers . . . have seen fit to ordain: that every man and woman of our kingdom of England, of whatever condition, whether bond or free, who is able bodied and below the age of sixty years, . . . shall be bound to serve him who has seen fit so to seek after him; and he shall take only the wages . . . or salary which, in the places where he sought to serve, were accustomed to be paid in the twentieth year of our reign of England [1346], . . . and if any man or woman, being thus sought after in service, will not do this, the fact being proven by two faithful men before the sheriffs or the bailiffs of our lord the king, or the constables of the town where this happens . . . shall be taken and sent to the next jail, and there he shall remain in strict custody until he shall find surety for serving in the aforesaid form. . . .

Likewise saddlers, skinners, white-tawers, cordwainers, tailors, smiths, carpenters, masons, tilers, shipwrights, carters and all other artisans and labourers shall not take for their labour and handiwork more than what, in the places where they happen to labour, was customarily paid to such persons in [1346]; and if any man take more, he shall be committed to the nearest jail in the manner aforesaid.

2 **John Ball preaches to the peasants.** Beginning in the 1360s, the priest John Ball traveled around England delivering radical sermons, such as this one, reported in a fourteenth-century chronicle by Jean Froissart. In the aftermath of the 1381 English Peasants' Revolt, Ball was arrested, imprisoned, and executed; his body was drawn and quartered; and his head was stuck on a pike on London Bridge.

John Ball was accustomed to assemble a crowd around him in the marketplace and preach to them. On such occasions he would say: "My good friends, matters cannot go on well in England until all things shall be in common; where there shall be neither vassals nor lords; when the lords shall be no more masters than ourselves. How ill they behave to us! For what reasons do they thus hold us in bondage? Are we not all descended from the same parents, Adam and Eve? When Adam delved and Eve span, who was then the gentleman? What reason can they give, why they should be more masters than ourselves? They are clothed in velvet and rich stuffs, ornamented with ermine and other furs, while we are forced to wear poor clothing. They have wines, spices, and fine bread, while we have only rye and the refuse of straw, and when we drink it must be water. They have handsome seats and manors, while we must brave the wind and rain in our labors in the field; and it is by our labor they have wherewith to support their pomp. We are called slaves, and if we do not perform our service we are beaten, and we have no sovereign to whom we can complain or who would be willing to hear us. Let us go to the King and remonstrate with him; he is young, and from him we may obtain a favorable answer, and if not we must ourselves seek to amend our condition."

ANALYZING THE EVIDENCE

1. In Source 1, what does the law require laborers to do, and what penalties does it provide if they do not do so? How did laws such as this contribute to growing social tensions?
2. What do John Ball in Source 2 and the peasants mentioned in Source 3 view as wrong in English society, and what do they want done about it?
3. In Sources 4 and 5, what do the wool workers in Florence want? How do the authors of these sources differ in their opinions about these demands?
4. What was the response of those in power to the demands of peasants and workers?

3 **English peasants meet with the king.** In 1381 peasants angered by taxes imposed to pay for the war with France seized the city of London and forced the young king Richard II to meet with them, as reported in this contemporary chronicle by Henry Knighton, an Augustinian priest.

〰 The King advanced to the assigned place, while many of the wicked mob kept following him. . . . They complained that they had been seriously oppressed by many hardships and that their condition of servitude was unbearable, and that they neither could nor would endure it longer. The King, for the sake of peace, and on account of the violence of the times, yielding to their petition, granted to them a charter with the great seal, to the effect that all men in the kingdom of England should be free and of free condition, and should remain both for themselves and their heirs free from all kinds of servitude and villeinage forever. . . . [But] the charter was rejected and decided to be null and void by the King and the great men of the kingdom in the Parliament held at Westminster [later] in the same year.

4 **Judicial inquiry of a labor organizer in Florence, 1345.** The rulers of Florence investigated the actions of a man seeking to organize a guild of carders and combers, the lowest-paid workers in the cloth industry; he was arrested and executed by hanging.

〰 This is the inquisition which the lord captain and his judge . . . have conducted . . . against Ciuto Brandini, of the parish of S. Piero Maggiore, a man of low condition and evil reputation. . . . Together with many others who were seduced by him, he planned to organize an association . . . of carders, combers, and other laborers in the woolen cloth industry, in the largest number possible. In order that they might have the means to congregate and to elect consuls and leaders of their association . . . he organized meetings on several occasions and on various days of many persons of lowly condition. . . . Moving from bad to worse, he sought . . . to accomplish similar and even worse things, seeking always [to incite] noxious disorders, to the harm, opprobrium, danger, and destruction of the citizens of Florence, their persons and property, and of the stable regime of that city.

5 **Chronicle of the Ciompi Revolt, 1378.** An anonymous chronicle describes the 1378 revolt of the *ciompi*, the lowest-paid workers in the wool trade in Florence, against the Lana guild of wool merchants, which controlled all aspects of cloth production and dominated the city government. The changes described lasted four years, until an army organized by the wool merchants overthrew the new government.

〰 When the *popolo* [common people, that is, the *ciompi*] and the guildsmen had seized the palace, they sent a message . . . that they wished to make certain demands by means of petitions, which were just and reasonable. . . . They said that, for the peace and repose of the city, they wanted certain things which they had decided among themselves. . . . The first chapter [of the petition] stated that the Lana guild would no longer have a [police] official of the guild. Another was that the combers, carders, trimmers, washers, and other cloth workers would have their own [guild]. . . . Moreover, all penalties involving a loss of a limb would be cancelled, and those who were condemned would pay a money fine instead. . . . Furthermore, for two years none of the poor people could be prosecuted for debts of 50 florins or less.

The *popolo* entered the palace and the podestà [the highest official in Florence] departed, without any harm being done to him. . . . Then the banners of the other guilds were unfurled from the windows . . . and also the standard of justice [the city's official banner]. Those inside the palace threw out and burned . . . every document that they found . . . and they entered all the rooms and they found many ropes which [the authorities] had bought to hang the poor people. . . . Several young men climbed the bell tower and rang the bells to signal the victory which they had won in seizing the palace, in God's honor. . . . Then [the *popolo*] decided to call priors who would be good comrades . . . and these priors called together the colleges and consuls of the guilds. . . . And this was done to give a part to more people, and so that each would be content, and each would have a share of the offices, and so that all of the citizens would be united. Thus poor men would have their due, for they have always borne the expenses [of government] and only the rich have profited. . . . And they deliberated to expand the lower guilds, and where there had been fourteen, there would now be seventeen, and thus they would be stronger, and this was done. . . . So all together, the lower guilds increased by some thirteen thousand men.

PUTTING IT ALL TOGETHER

Using the sources above, along with what you have learned in class and in this chapter and Chapters 9 and 10, write a short essay that analyzes popular revolts in the late Middle Ages. How did population decline and economic crisis, and the response of those in power to these challenges, spur calls for reform and revolts among peasants and workers? Why do you think the response to these revolts by those in power was so brutal?

Sources: (1) Ernest F. Henderson, trans. and ed., *Select Historical Documents of the Middle Ages* (London: George Bell and Sons, 1892), pp. 165–167; (2) Sir John Froissart, *The Chronicles of England, France, Spain, etc.* (London: Everyman's Library, 1911), pp. 207–208; (3) Edward P. Cheyney, *Readings in English History Drawn from the Original Sources* (Boston: Ginn, 1935), p. 263; (4, 5) Gene Brucker, ed., *The Society of Renaissance Florence: A Documentary Study* (New York: Harper Torchbooks, 1971), pp. 235, 237–239.

Beheading of a Leader of the Jacquerie in 1358   A leader of the Jacquerie is beheaded, while knights and Charles II, the king of Navarre, look on. Charles led the nobles' suppression of the revolt and the subsequent massacre, and was also a major player in the Hundred Years' War, frequently switching sides to further his own aims. This illustration comes from a lavishly illuminated copy of the *Grandes Chroniques de France*, produced in the last quarter of the fourteenth century for a French royal patron. It made its way to England, where it was owned by the man who became King Richard III (r. 1483–1485), as his name is inscribed on one of the pages. (Album/British Library/Newscom)

economically advanced south and east, but sections of the north also witnessed rebellions (see Map 11.3).

The boy-king Richard II (r. 1377–1399) met the leaders of the revolt, agreed to charters ensuring peasants' freedom, tricked them with false promises, and then crushed the uprising with terrible ferocity. In the aftermath of the revolt, the nobility tried to restore the labor obligations of serfdom, but they were not successful, and the conversion to money rents continued. The English Peasants' Revolt did not bring social equality to England, but rural serfdom continued to decline, disappearing in England by 1550.

Urban Conflicts

In Flanders, France, and England, peasant revolts often blended with conflicts involving workers in cities. Unrest also occurred in Italian, Spanish, and German cities. The urban revolts had their roots in the changing conditions of work. In the thirteenth century craft guilds had organized the production of most goods, with masters, journeymen, and apprentices working side by side. In the fourteenth century a new system evolved to make products on a larger scale. Capitalist investors hired many households, with each household performing only one step of the process. Initially these investors were wealthy bankers and merchants, but eventually shop masters themselves embraced the system. This change promoted a greater division within guilds between wealthier masters and the poorer masters and journeymen they hired.

While capitalism provided opportunities for some artisans to become investors and entrepreneurs, especially in cloth production, for many it led to a decrease in income and status. Guilds sometimes responded to crises by opening up membership, as they did in some places immediately after the Black Death, but they more often responded to competition by limiting membership to existing guild families, which meant that journeymen who were not master's sons or who could not find a master's widow or daughter to marry could never become masters themselves. Remaining journeymen their entire lives, they lost their sense of solidarity with the masters of their craft. Resentment led to rebellion.

Urban uprisings were also sparked by issues involving honor, as when employers required workers to do tasks they regarded as beneath them. As their actual status and economic prospects declined and their work became basically wage labor, journeymen and poorer masters emphasized skill and honor as qualities that set them apart from less skilled workers. Guilds increasingly came to view the honor of their work as tied to an all-male workplace, and they passed regulations excluding women. These tended to be overlooked when more workers were needed, however, especially as the practice of paying women less than men meant they could be hired more cheaply.

Sex in the City

Peasant and urban revolts and riots had clear economic bases, but some historians have suggested that late medieval marital patterns may have also played a role. In northwestern Europe, people believed that couples should be economically independent before they married. Thus not only during times of crisis such as the Great Famine, but also in more general circumstances, men and women spent long periods as servants or workers in other households, saving money for married life and learning skills, or they waited until their own parents had died and the family property was distributed.

The most unusual feature of this pattern was the late age of marriage for women. Unlike in earlier time periods and in most other parts of the world, a woman in late medieval northern and western Europe generally entered marriage as an adult in her twenties and took charge of running a household immediately. Because she was older, she had skills she had already developed, and was often not as dependent on her husband or mother-in-law as was a woman who married at a younger age. She also had fewer pregnancies than a woman who married earlier, though not necessarily fewer surviving children.

Men of all social groups had long tended to be older than women when they married. In general, men were in their middle or late twenties at first marriage, with wealthier urban merchants often much older. Journeymen and apprentices were often explicitly prohibited from marrying, as were the students at universities, who were understood to be in "minor orders" and thus like clergy, even if they were not intending to have careers in the church.

The prohibitions on marriage for certain groups of men and the late age of marriage for most men meant that cities and villages were filled with large numbers of young adult men with no family responsibilities who often formed the core of riots and unrest. Not surprisingly, this situation also contributed to a steady market for sexual services outside of marriage, services that in later centuries were termed prostitution. In many cities, municipal authorities set up brothels or districts for prostitution either outside the city walls or away from respectable neighborhoods. Selling and buying sex thus passed from being a private concern to being a social matter requiring public supervision.

Public Bath   In this fanciful scene of a medieval public bath from a 1470 illuminated manuscript, men and women soak in tubs while they eat and drink, entertained by a musician, and a king and church official look on. At the left is a couple about to hop in a bed for sex in what might be a brothel. Normal public baths were far less elaborate, and while they did sometimes offer food, wine, and sex, their main attraction was hot water. This painting is not meant to be realistic but a commentary on declining morals. (Staatsbibliothek Preussischer Kulturbesitz, Berlin, Germany/ AKG Images)

Young men associated visiting brothels with achieving manhood; for the women themselves, of course, their activities were work. Some women had no choice, for they had been traded to the brothel manager by their parents or some other person as payment for debt, or had quickly become indebted to the manager (most managers were men) for the clothes and other finery regarded as essential to their occupation. Poor women—and men—also sold sex illegally outside of city brothels, combining this with other sorts of part-time work such as laundering or sewing. Prostitution was an urban phenomenon because only populous towns had large numbers of unmarried young men, communities of transient merchants, and a culture accustomed to a cash exchange.

Though selling sex for money was legal in the Middle Ages, the position of women who did so was always marginal. In the late fifteenth century cities began to limit brothel residents' freedom of movement and choice of clothing, requiring them to wear distinctive head coverings or bands on their clothing so that they would not be mistaken for "honorable" women. Cities also began to impose harsher penalties on women who did not live in the designated house or section of town. A few women who sold sex did earn enough to donate money to charity or buy property, but most were very poor.

Along with buying sex, young men also took it by force. Unmarried women often found it difficult to avoid sexual contact. Many worked as domestic servants, where their employers or employers' sons or male relatives could easily coerce them, or they worked in proximity to men. Notions of female honor kept upper-class women secluded in their homes, particularly in southern and eastern Europe, but there was little attempt anywhere to protect female servants or day laborers from the risk of seduction or rape. Rape was a capital crime in many parts of Europe, but the actual sentences handed out were more likely to be fines and brief imprisonment, with the severity of the sentence dependent on the social status of the victim and the perpetrator.

According to laws regarding rape in most parts of Europe, the victim had to prove that she had cried out and had attempted to repel the attacker, and she had to bring the charge within a short period of time after the attack had happened. Women bringing rape charges were often more interested in getting their own honorable reputations back than in punishing the perpetrators. For this reason, they sometimes asked the judge to force their rapists to marry them.

Same-sex relations—what in the late nineteenth century would be termed "homosexuality"—were another feature of medieval urban life (and of village life, though there are very few sources relating to sexual relations of any type in the rural context). Same-sex relations were of relatively little concern to church or state authorities in the early Middle Ages, but this attitude changed beginning in the late twelfth century. By 1300 most areas had defined such actions as "crimes against nature," with authorities seeing them as particularly reprehensible because they thought they did not occur anywhere else in creation. Same-sex relations, usually termed "sodomy," became a capital crime in most of Europe, with adult offenders threatened with execution by fire. The Italian cities of Venice, Florence, and Lucca created special courts to deal with sodomy, which saw thousands of investigations.

How prevalent were same-sex relations? This is difficult to answer, even in modern society, but the city of Florence provides a provocative case study. In 1432 Florence set up a special board of adult men, the Office of the Night, in an attempt to end sodomy. Between 1432 and the abolition of the board in 1502, about seventeen thousand men came to its attention, which, even over a seventy-year period, represents a great number in a population of about forty thousand. The men came from all classes of society, but almost all cases involved an adult man and an adolescent boy; they ranged from sex exchanged for money or gifts to long-term affectionate relationships. Like the ancient Romans, late medieval Florentines believed in a generational model in which different roles were appropriate to different stages in life. In a socially and sexually hierarchical world, the boy in the passive role was identified as subordinate, dependent, and mercenary, words usually applied to women. Florentines, however, never described the dominant partner in feminine terms, for he had not compromised his masculine identity or violated a gender ideal; in fact, the adult partner might be married or have female sexual partners as well as male. Only if an adult male assumed the passive role was his masculinity jeopardized.

Thus in Florence, and no doubt elsewhere in Europe, sodomy was not a marginal practice, which may account for the fact that, despite harsh laws and special courts, actual executions for sodomy were rare. Same-sex relations often developed within the context of all-male environments, such as the army, the craft shop, and the artistic workshop, and were part of the collective male experience. Homoerotic relationships played important roles in defining stages of life, expressing distinctions of status, and shaping masculine gender identity. Same-sex relations involving women almost never came to the attention of legal authorities, so it is difficult to find out how common they were. However, female-female desire was expressed in songs, plays, and stories, as was male-male desire, offering evidence of the way people understood same-sex relations.

Fur-Collar Crime

The fourteenth and fifteenth centuries witnessed a great deal of what we might term "fur-collar crime," a medieval version of today's white-collar crime in which those higher up the social scale prey on those who are less well-off. The Hundred Years' War had provided employment and opportunity for thousands of idle and fortune-seeking knights. But during periods of truce and after the war finally ended, many nobles once again had little to do. Inflation hurt them. Although many were living on fixed incomes, their chivalric code demanded lavish generosity and an aristocratic lifestyle. Many nobles thus turned to crime as a way of raising money.

This "fur-collar crime" involved both violence and fraud. Groups of noble bandits roamed the English countryside, stealing from both rich and poor. Operating like modern urban racketeers, knightly gangs demanded that peasants pay protection money or else have their hovels burned and their fields destroyed. They seized wealthy travelers and held them for ransom. Corrupt landowners, including some churchmen, pushed peasants to pay higher taxes and extra fees. When accused of wrongdoing, fur-collar criminals intimidated witnesses, threatened jurors, and used their influence to persuade judges to support them—or used cash to bribe them outright.

Aristocratic violence led to revolt, and it also shaped popular culture. The ballads of Robin Hood, a collection of folk legends from late medieval England, describe the adventures of the outlaw hero and his merry men as they avenge the common people against fur-collar criminals—grasping landlords, wicked sheriffs, and mercenary churchmen. Robin Hood was a popular figure because he symbolized the deep resentment of aristocratic corruption and abuse; he represented the struggle against tyranny and oppression.

Ethnic Tensions and Restrictions

Large numbers of people in the twelfth and thirteenth centuries migrated from one part of Europe to another in search of land, food, and work: the English into Scotland and Ireland; Germans, French, and Flemings into Poland, Bohemia, and Hungary; Christians into Muslim Spain. Everywhere in Europe, towns recruited people from the countryside as well (see "The Rise of Towns" in Chapter 10). In frontier regions, townspeople were usually long-distance immigrants and, in eastern Europe, Ireland, and Scotland, ethnically different from the surrounding rural population. In eastern Europe, German was the language of the towns; in Irish towns, French, the tongue of Norman or English settlers, predominated. As a result of this colonization and movement to towns, peoples of different ethnic backgrounds lived side by side.

In the early periods of conquest and colonization, and in all regions with extensive migrations, a legal dualism existed: native peoples remained subject to their traditional laws; newcomers brought and

were subject to the laws of the countries from which they came. The great exception to this broad pattern of legal pluralism was Ireland. From the start, the English practiced an extreme form of discrimination toward the native Irish. The English distinguished between the free and the unfree, and the entire Irish population, simply by the fact of Irish birth, was unfree. When English legal structures were established beginning in 1210, the Irish were denied access to the common-law courts. In civil (property) disputes, an English defendant did not need to respond to an Irish plaintiff; no Irish person could make a will. In criminal procedures, the murder of an Irishman was not considered a felony.

The later Middle Ages witnessed a movement away from legal pluralism or dualism and toward legal homogeneity and an emphasis on blood descent. The dominant ethnic group in an area tried to bar others from positions of church leadership and guild membership. Marriage laws were instituted that attempted to maintain ethnic purity by prohibiting intermarriage, and some church leaders actively promoted ethnic discrimination. As Germans moved eastward, for example, German bishops refused to appoint non-Germans to any church office, while Czech bishops closed monasteries to Germans.

The most extensive attempt to prevent intermarriage and protect ethnic purity is embodied in the **Statute of Kilkenny** (1366), a law the ruling English imposed on Ireland that states that "there were to be no marriages between those of immigrant and native stock; that the English inhabitants of Ireland must employ the English language and bear English names; that they must ride in the English way [that is, with saddles] and have English apparel; that no Irishmen were to be granted ecclesiastical benefices or admitted to monasteries in the English parts of Ireland."[5]

Late medieval chroniclers used words such as *gens* (race or clan) and *natio* (NAH-tee-oh; species, stock, or kind) to refer to different groups. They held that peoples differed according to language, traditions, customs, and laws. None of these were unchangeable, however, and commentators increasingly also described ethnic differences in terms of "blood," which made ethnicity heritable. As national consciousness grew with the Hundred Years' War, for example, people began to speak of "French blood" and "English blood." Religious beliefs came to be conceptualized in terms of blood as well, with people regarded as having Jewish blood, Muslim blood, or Christian blood. The most dramatic expression of this was in Spain, where "purity of blood" — having no Muslim or Jewish

---

■ **Statute of Kilkenny** Law issued in 1366 that discriminated against the Irish, forbidding marriage between the English and the Irish, requiring the use of the English language, and denying the Irish access to ecclesiastical offices.

ancestors—became an obsession. Blood also came to be used as a way to talk about social differences, especially for nobles. Just as the Irish and English were prohibited from marrying each other, those of "noble blood" were prohibited from marrying commoners in many parts of Europe. As Europeans increasingly came into contact with people from Africa and Asia, and particularly as they developed colonial empires, these notions of blood also became a way of conceptualizing racial categories.

Literacy and Vernacular Literature

The development of ethnic identities had many negative consequences, but a more positive effect was the increasing use of the vernacular, that is, the local language that people actually spoke, rather than Latin (see "Vernacular Literature and Drama" in Chapter 10). Two masterpieces of European culture, Dante's *Divine Comedy* (1310–1320) and Chaucer's *Canterbury Tales* (1387–1400), illustrate a sophisticated use of the rhythms and rhymes of the vernacular.

The *Divine Comedy* of Dante Alighieri (DAHN-tay ah-luh-GYEHR-ee) (1265–1321) is an epic poem of one hundred cantos (verses), each of whose three equal parts describes one of the realms of the next world: Hell, Purgatory, and Paradise. The Roman poet Virgil, representing reason, leads Dante through Hell, where Dante observes the torments of the damned and denounces the disorders of his own time. Passing up into Purgatory, Virgil shows the poet how souls are purified of their disordered inclinations. From Purgatory, Beatrice, a woman Dante once loved and who serves as the symbol of divine revelation in the poem, leads him to Paradise.

The *Divine Comedy* portrays contemporary and historical figures, comments on secular and ecclesiastical affairs, and draws on the Scholastic philosophy of uniting faith and reason. Within the framework of a symbolic pilgrimage, the *Divine Comedy* embodies the psychological tensions of the age. A profoundly Christian poem, it also contains bitter criticism of some church authorities. In its symmetrical structure and use of figures from the ancient world such as Virgil, the poem perpetuates the classical tradition, but as the first major work of literature in the Italian vernacular, it is distinctly modern.

Geoffrey Chaucer (1342–1400) was an official in the administrations of the English kings Edward III and Richard II and wrote poetry as an avocation. His *Canterbury Tales* is a collection of stories in lengthy rhymed narrative. On a pilgrimage to the shrine of Saint Thomas Becket at Canterbury (see "Local Laws and Royal Courts" in Chapter 9), thirty people of various social backgrounds tell tales. In depicting the interests and behavior of all types of people, Chaucer

Chaucer's Wife of Bath Chaucer's *Canterbury Tales* were filled with memorable characters, including the often-married Wife of Bath, shown here in a fifteenth-century manuscript. In the prologue that details her life, she denies the value of virginity and criticizes her young and handsome fifth husband for reading a book about "wicked wives." "By God, if women had but written stories . . . ," she comments, "They would have written of men more wickedness / Than all the race of Adam could redress." (Private Collection/Bridgeman Images)

presents a rich panorama of English social life in the fourteenth century. Like the *Divine Comedy*, the *Canterbury Tales* reflects the cultural tensions of the times. Ostensibly Christian, many of the pilgrims are also materialistic, sensual, and worldly, suggesting the ambivalence of the broader society's concern for the next world and frank enjoyment of this one.

Beginning in the fourteenth century, a variety of evidence attests to the increasing literacy of laypeople. Wills and inventories reveal that many people, not just nobles, possessed books—mainly devotional texts, but also romances, manuals on manners and etiquette, histories, and sometimes legal and philosophical texts. In England the number of schools in the diocese of York quadrupled between 1350 and 1500. Information from Flemish and German towns is similar: children were sent to schools and were taught the fundamentals of reading, writing, and arithmetic. Laymen increasingly served as managers or stewards of estates and as clerks to guilds and town governments; such positions obviously required the ability to keep administrative and financial records.

The penetration of laymen into the higher positions of governmental administration, long the preserve of clerics, also illustrates rising lay literacy. With growing frequency, the upper classes sent their daughters to convent schools, where, in addition to instruction in singing, religion, needlework, deportment, and household management, they gained the rudiments of reading and sometimes writing.

The spread of literacy represents a response to the needs of an increasingly complex society. Trade, commerce, and expanding government bureaucracies required an increasing number of literate people. Late medieval culture remained a decidedly oral culture. But by the fifteenth century the evolution toward a more literate culture was already perceptible, and

craftsmen would develop the new technology of the printing press in response to the increased demand for reading materials.

NOTES

1. Christos S. Bartsocas, "Two Fourteenth Century Descriptions of the 'Black Death,'" *Journal of the History of Medicine* (October 1966): 395.
2. W. P. Barrett, trans., *The Trial of Jeanne d'Arc* (London: George Routledge, 1931), pp. 165–166.
3. James Harvey Robinson, *Readings in European History*, vol. 1 (Boston: Ginn and Company, 1904), pp. 375–376.
4. Quoted in Katharina M. Wilson, ed., *Medieval Women Writers* (Athens: University of Georgia Press, 1984), p. 245.
5. Quoted in R. Bartlett, *The Making of Europe: Conquest, Colonization and Cultural Change, 950–1350* (Princeton, N.J.: Princeton University Press, 1993), p. 239.

LOOKING BACK LOOKING AHEAD

The fourteenth and early fifteenth centuries were certainly times of crisis in western Europe, meriting the label *calamitous* given to them by one popular historian. Famine, disease, and war decimated the European population, and traditional institutions, including secular governments and the church, did little or nothing or, in some cases, made things worse. Trading connections that had been reinvigorated in the High Middle Ages spread the most deadly epidemic ever experienced through western Asia, North Africa, and almost all of Europe. No wonder survivors experienced a sort of shell shock and a fascination with death.

The plague did not destroy the prosperity of the medieval population, however, and it may in fact have indirectly improved the European economy. Wealthy merchants had plenty of money to spend on luxuries and talent. In the century after the plague, Italian artists began to create new styles of painting, writers to pen new literary forms, educators to found new types of schools, and philosophers to develop new ideas about the purpose of human life. These cultural changes eventually spread to the rest of Europe, following many of the same paths that the plague had traveled.

Make Connections

Think about the larger developments and continuities within and across chapters.

1. The Black Death has often been compared with later pandemics, including the COVID-19 pandemic. It is easy to note differences between these two, but what similarities do you see in the course and responses to these two diseases? In their social and cultural consequences?

2. Beginning with Chapter 7, every chapter in this book has discussed the development of the papacy and relations between popes and secular rulers. How were the problems facing the papacy in the fourteenth century the outgrowth of long-term issues? Why had attempts to solve these issues not been successful?

3. In Chapter 3 you learned about the Bronze Age Collapse, and in Chapter 7 about the end of the Roman Empire in the West, both of which have also been seen as "calamitous." What similarities and differences do you see in these earlier times of turmoil and those of the late Middle Ages?

11 REVIEW & EXPLORE

Identify Key Terms

Identify and explain the significance of each item below.

Little Ice Age (p. 294)

Black Death (p. 296)

flagellants (p. 299)

Hundred Years' War (p. 302)

representative assemblies (p. 306)

Babylonian Captivity (p. 308)

Great Schism (p. 308)

conciliarists (p. 309)

confraternities (p. 310)

Jacquerie (p. 312)

English Peasants' Revolt (p. 313)

Statute of Kilkenny (p. 319)

Review the Main Ideas

Answer the section heading questions from the chapter.

1. How did climate change shape the late Middle Ages? (p. 294)

2. How did the plague affect European society? (p. 296)

3. What were the causes, course, and consequences of the Hundred Years' War? (p. 302)

4. Why did the church come under increasing criticism? (p. 308)

5. What explains the social unrest of the late Middle Ages? (p. 312)

Suggested Resources

BOOKS

- Allmand, Christopher. *The Hundred Years War: England and France at War, ca. 1300–1450*, rev. ed. 2005. Designed for students; examines the war from political, military, social, and economic perspectives, and compares the way England and France reacted to the conflict.

- Campbell, Bruce M. S. *The Great Transition: Climate, Disease, and Society in the Late Medieval World*. 2016. Brings together economic and environmental history.

- Cohn, Samuel K. *Lust for Liberty: The Politics of Social Revolt in Medieval Europe*. 2006. Analyzes a number of revolts from across Europe in terms of the aims of their leaders and participants.

- Dunn, Alastair. *The Peasants' Revolt: England's Failed Revolution of 1381*. 2004. Offers new interpretations of the causes and consequences of the English Peasants' Revolt.

- Epstein, Steven A. *An Economic and Social History of Later Medieval Europe, 1000–1500*. 2009. Examines economic realities and social conditions.

- Fagan, Brian. *The Little Ice Age: How Climate Made History 1300–1850*. 2019. A broad overview of climate change in this era, written for general readers.

- Green, Monica. *Pandemic Disease in the Medieval World: Rethinking the Black Death*. 2015. Collection of essays by historians and scientists that contains the newest research on the plague and its impact.

- Harrington, Joel. *Dangerous Mystic: Meister Eckhart's Path to the God Within*. 2018. An illuminating biography and study of Eckhart's spiritual ideas.

- Karras, Ruth M. *Sexuality in Medieval Europe: Doing unto Others*, 3d ed. 2017. A brief overview designed for undergraduates that incorporates the newest scholarship.

* McGinn, Bernard. *The Varieties of Vernacular Mysticism, 1350–1550*. 2012. A comprehensive survey that demonstrates how this period gave rise to mystical writers who remain influential even today.

* Swanson, R. N. *Religion and Devotion in Europe, c. 1215–c. 1515*. 2004. Explores many aspects of spirituality.

* Tanner, Norman. *The Church in the Later Middle Ages*. 2008. A concise survey of institutional and intellectual issues and developments.

* Tuchman, Barbara. *A Distant Mirror: The Calamitous Fourteenth Century*. 1978. Written for a general audience, it remains a vivid description of this tumultuous time.

MEDIA

* *Henry V* (Kenneth Branagh, 1989). A widely acclaimed film adaptation of Shakespeare's play about the English king and the Battle of Agincourt, with nearly every well-known English actor.

* *The Hundred Years' War* (BBC, 2012). This three-part series examines the military, political, and cultural aspects of the Hundred Years' War.

* *Michael Wood's Story of England* (BBC, 2010). This series focuses on the village of Kibworth in central England, for which extensive archives survive that give insight into daily life. Episode 3 examines the Great Famine and the Black Death, and episode 4 the Hundred Years' War and economic change.

* *The Name of the Rose* (Jean-Jacques Annaud, 1986). Based on the novel by Umberto Eco about a fourteenth-century monk (played by Sean Connery), this feature film is both a murder mystery and a commentary on issues facing the church.

* *The Plague* (History Channel, 2005). A documentary examining the path and impact of the plague in Europe, with firsthand accounts taken from diaries and journals.

* *The Reckoning* (Paul McGuigan, 2003). The story of a troupe of actors who perform a morality play for the villagers of a fourteenth-century English town, combined with a murder mystery about the death of a child.

12

European Society in the Age of the Renaissance

1350–1550

While the Hundred Years' War gripped northern Europe, a new culture emerged in southern Europe. The fourteenth century witnessed remarkable changes in Italian intellectual, artistic, and cultural life. Artists and writers thought that they were living in a new golden age, but not until the sixteenth century was this change given the label we use today—the *Renaissance*, derived from the French word for "rebirth." That word was first used by art historian Giorgio Vasari (1511–1574) to describe the art of "rare men of genius" such as his contemporary Michelangelo. Through their works, Vasari judged, the glory of the classical past had been reborn after centuries of darkness. Over time, the word's meaning was broadened to include many aspects of life during that period. The new attitude had a slow diffusion out of Italy, so that the Renaissance "happened" at different times in different parts of Europe. The Renaissance was a movement, not a time period.

Later scholars increasingly saw the cultural and political changes of the Renaissance, along with the religious changes of the Reformation (see Chapter 13) and the European voyages of exploration (see Chapter 14), as ushering in the "modern" world. Some historians view the Renaissance as a bridge between the medieval and modern eras because it corresponded chronologically with the late medieval period and because there were many continuities with that period along with the changes that suggested aspects of the modern world. Others have questioned whether the word *Renaissance* should be used at all to describe an era in which many social groups saw decline rather than improvement. The debates remind us that these labels—*medieval, Renaissance, modern*—are intellectual constructs devised after the fact, and all contain value judgments. ■

CHAPTER PREVIEW

- How did political and economic developments in Italy shape the Renaissance?

- What new ideas were associated with the Renaissance?

- How did art reflect new Renaissance ideals?

- What were the key social hierarchies in Renaissance Europe?

- How did nation-states develop in this period?

Birth in the Renaissance

In this detail from a fresco of the birth of the Virgin Mary in the Church of San Michele al Pozzo Bianco in Bergamo, Italian painter Lorenzo Lotto depicts a birth scene that would have been common among upper-class urban residents in Renaissance Italy. The birth occurs at home, with lots of women bustling about, including servants, dressed simply, and female relatives, in fancier clothing. A professional midwife sits by the side of the bed, and the mother looks quite content, a sign that this has been a successful and fairly easy childbirth, which was not always the case. (Photo © Mauro Ranzani/Bridgeman Images)

How did political and economic developments in Italy shape the Renaissance?

The magnificent art and new ways of thinking in the **Renaissance** rested on economic and political developments in the city-states of northern Italy. Economic growth laid the material basis for the Italian Renaissance, and ambitious merchants gained political power to match their economic power. They then used their money and power to buy luxuries and hire talent in a system of **patronage**, through which cities, groups, and individuals commissioned writers and artists to produce specific works. Political leaders in Italian cities admired the traditions and power of ancient Rome, and this esteem shaped their commissions. Thus economics, politics, and culture were interconnected.

Trade and Prosperity

Northern Italian cities led the way in the great commercial revival of the eleventh century (see "What led to Europe's economic growth and reurbanization?" in Chapter 10). By the middle of the twelfth century Venice, supported by a huge merchant marine, had grown enormously rich through overseas trade, as had Genoa and Milan, which had their own sizable fleets. These cities made important strides in shipbuilding that allowed their ships to sail all year long at accelerated speeds and to carry more and more merchandise.

Another commercial leader, and the city where the Renaissance began, was Florence, situated on fertile soil along the Arno River. Its favorable location on the main road northward from Rome made Florence a commercial hub, and the city grew wealthy buying and selling all types of goods throughout Europe and the Mediterranean — grain, cloth, wool, weapons, armor, spices, glass, and wine.

Florentine merchants also loaned and invested money, and toward the end of the thirteenth century

they acquired control of papal banking. Florentine mercantile families began to dominate European banking on both sides of the Alps, setting up offices in major European and North African cities. The profits from loans, investments, and money exchanges that poured back to Florence were pumped into urban industries such as clothmaking, and by the early fourteenth century the city had about eighty thousand people, about twice the population of London at that time. Profits contributed to the city's economic vitality and allowed banking families to control the city's politics and culture.

By the first quarter of the fourteenth century, the economic foundations of Florence were so strong that even severe crises could not destroy the city. In 1344 King Edward III of England repudiated his huge debts to Florentine bankers, forcing some of them into bankruptcy. Soon after, Florence suffered frightfully from the Black Death, losing at least half its population, and serious labor unrest shook the political establishment (see "How did the plague affect European society?" in Chapter 11). Nevertheless, the basic Florentine economic structure remained stable, and the city grew again.

In Florence, Venice, and other thriving Italian cities, wealth allowed many people greater material pleasures, a more comfortable life, imported luxuries, and leisure time to appreciate and patronize the arts. Merchants and bankers commissioned public and private buildings from architects and hired sculptors and painters to decorate their homes and churches. Despite the massive loss of life in the plague, the rich, social-climbing residents of Venice, Florence, Genoa, and Rome came to see life more as an opportunity to be enjoyed than as a painful pilgrimage to the City of God.

Communes and Republics of Northern Italy

The northern Italian cities were **communes**, sworn associations of free men led by members of merchant guilds. Like merchants elsewhere, merchants in Italy began in the twelfth century to seek political and economic independence from the nobles who owned the land (see "The Rise of Towns" in Chapter 10). In contrast to nobles elsewhere who maintained their social distinction from merchants, those in Italy frequently moved into the cities, marrying the daughters of rich commercial families and starting their own businesses, often with money they had gained through the dowries provided by their wives. This merger of the northern

■ **Renaissance** A French word meaning "rebirth," used to describe the rebirth of the culture of classical antiquity in Italy during the fourteenth to sixteenth centuries.

■ **patronage** Financial support of writers and artists by cities, groups, and individuals, often to produce specific works or works in specific styles.

■ **communes** Sworn associations of free men in Italian cities led by merchant guilds.

■ **popolo** Disenfranchised common people in Italian cities who resented their exclusion from power.

■ **signori** Government by one-man rule in Italian cities such as Milan; also refers to these rulers.

■ **courts** Magnificent households and palaces where signori and other rulers lived, conducted business, and supported the arts.

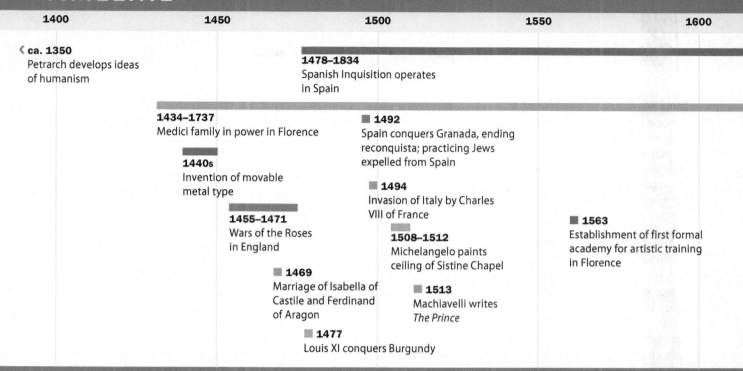

‹ ca. 1350
Petrarch develops ideas
of humanism

1478–1834
Spanish Inquisition operates
in Spain

1434–1737
Medici family in power in Florence

1440s
Invention of movable
metal type

1455–1471
Wars of the Roses
in England

1469
Marriage of Isabella of
Castile and Ferdinand
of Aragon

1477
Louis XI conquers Burgundy

1492
Spain conquers Granada, ending
reconquista; practicing Jews
expelled from Spain

1494
Invasion of Italy by Charles
VIII of France

1508–1512
Michelangelo paints
ceiling of Sistine Chapel

1513
Machiavelli writes
The Prince

1563
Establishment of first formal
academy for artistic training
in Florence

Italian nobility and the commercial elite created a powerful oligarchy, a small group that ruled the city and surrounding countryside. Yet because of rivalries among competing powerful families within this oligarchy, Italian communes were often politically unstable.

Unrest from below exacerbated the instability. Merchant elites made citizenship in the communes dependent on a property qualification, years of residence within the city, and social connections. Only a tiny percentage of the male population possessed these qualifications and thus could hold political office. The common people, called the **popolo**, were disenfranchised and heavily taxed, and they bitterly resented their exclusion from power. Throughout most of the thirteenth century, in city after city, the popolo used armed force to take over the city governments. Republican government—in which political power theoretically resides in the people and is exercised by their chosen representatives—was sometimes established in numerous Italian cities. These victories of the popolo proved temporary, however, because they could not establish civil order within their cities. Merchant oligarchies reasserted their power and sometimes brought in powerful military leaders to establish order. These military leaders, called *condottieri* (kahn-duh-TYER-ee; singular *condottiero*), had their own mercenary armies and sometimes took over political power once they had supplanted the existing government.

Many cities in Italy became **signori** (seen-YOHR-ee), in which one man—whether condottiero, merchant, or noble—ruled and handed down the right to rule to his son. Some signori (the word is plural in Italian and is used for both persons and forms of government) kept the institutions of communal government in place, but these had no actual power. As a practical matter, there wasn't much difference between oligarchic regimes and signori.

In the fifteenth and sixteenth centuries the signori in many cities and the most powerful merchant oligarchs in others transformed their households into **courts**. Courtly culture afforded signori and oligarchs the opportunity to display and assert their wealth and power. They built magnificent palaces in the centers of cities and required all political business to be done there. Ceremonies connected with family births, baptisms, marriages, and funerals offered occasions for magnificent pageantry and elaborate ritual. Cities welcomed rulers who were visiting with magnificent entrance parades that often included fireworks, colorful banners, mock naval battles, decorated wagons filled with people in costume, and temporary triumphal arches modeled on those of ancient Rome. Rulers of nation-states later copied and adapted all these aspects of Italian courts.

City-States and the Balance of Power

Renaissance Italians had a passionate attachment to their individual city-states: they were politically loyal and felt centered on the city. This intensity of local feeling perpetuated the dozens of small states and hindered the development of one unified state. (See "Viewpoints: Venice Versus Florence," page 328.)

VIEWPOINTS

Venice Versus Florence

Praise of one's own city, a form of written work that developed in ancient Rome, was revived and expanded in Renaissance Italy. In the first selection below, written in 1493, the Venetian patrician Marin Sanudo (1466–1536) praises Venice in a work of praise, which was a common genre at the time, and in the second selection the Florentine merchant and historian Benedetto Dei (DAY-ee) (1418–1492) praises his own city in a letter to an acquaintance from Venice.

Marin Sanudo on Venice, 1493

The city of Venice is a free city, a common home to all men, and it has never been subjugated by anyone, as have all other cities. . . . Moreover it was founded not by shepherds as Rome was, but by rich and powerful people, such as have ever been since that time, with their faith in Christ, an obstacle to barbarians and attackers. . . . For it takes pride of place before all others, if I may say so, in prudence, fortitude, magnificence, benignity and clemency; everyone throughout the world testifies to this. . . . It is, then, a very big and beautiful city, excelling over all others, with houses and piazze [public squares] founded upon salt water, and it has a Grand Canal. . . . On either side are houses of patricians and others; they are very beautiful, costing from 20,000 ducats downwards. . . . The Venetians, just as they were merchants in the beginning, continue to trade every year; they send galleys to Flanders, the Barbary Coast, Beirut, Alexandria, the Greek Lands, and Auiges-Mortes [a city in southern France]. . . . Here, on the Canal, there are embankments where on one side there are barges for timber, and on the other side wine; they are rented as though they were shops. There is a very large butchery, which is full every day of good meat, and there is another one at St. Mark's. The Fishmarket overlooks the Grand Canal; here are the most beautiful fish, high in price and of good quality. . . . And in the city nothing grows, yet whatever you want can be found in abundance. And this is because of the great turnover in merchandise; everything comes here, especially things to eat, from every city and every part of the world, and money is made very quickly. This is because everyone is well-off for money.

Benedetto Dei on Florence, 1472

Florence is more beautiful and five hundred forty years older than your Venice. We spring from triply noble blood. We are one-third Roman, one-third Frankish, and one-third Fiesolan [three different groups that were all viewed as honorable]. . . . We have round about us thirty thousand estates, owned by noblemen and merchants, citizens and craftsmen, yielding us yearly bread and meat, wine and oil, vegetables and cheese, hay and wood, to the value of nine hundred thousand ducats in cash, as you Venetians, Genoese, and Rhodians who come to buy them know well enough. We have two trades greater than any four of yours in Venice put together — the trades of wool and silk. . . .

Our beautiful Florence contains within the city in this present year two hundred seventy shops belonging to the wool merchants' guild. . . . It contains also eighty-three rich and splendid warehouses of the silk merchants' guild, and furnishes gold and silver stuffs, velvet, brocade, damask, taffeta, and satin to Rome, Naples, Catalonia, and the whole of Spain, especially Seville, and to Turkey and Barbary. . . . The number of banks amounts to thirty-three; the shops of the cabinetmakers, whose business is carving and inlaid work, to eighty-four; and the workshops of the stonecutters and marble workers in the city and its immediate neighborhood, to fifty-four. There are forty-four goldsmiths' and jewelers' shops, thirty goldbeaters, silver wire-drawers, and a wax-figure maker. . . . Sixty-six is the number of the apothecaries' and grocer shops; seventy that of the butchers, besides eight large shops in which are sold fowls of all kinds, as well as game and also the native wine called Trebbiano, from San Giovanni in the upper Arno Valley; it would awaken the dead in its praise.

QUESTIONS FOR ANALYSIS

1. What qualities do the two men choose to highlight in praising their hometowns?
2. How do these praises of Florence and Venice represent new values that emerged in the Renaissance?

Sources: David Chambers, Brian Pullan, and Jennifer Fletcher, eds., *Venice: A Documentary History, 1450–1630* (Oxford: Basil Blackwell, 1992), pp. 4–5, 11, 13; Gertrude R. B. Richards, ed., *Florentine Merchants in the Age of the Medici* (Cambridge, Mass.: Harvard University Press, 1932).

In the fifteenth century five powers dominated the Italian peninsula: Venice, Milan, Florence, the Papal States, and the kingdom of Naples (Map 12.1). The major Italian powers controlled the smaller city-states, such as Siena, Mantua, Ferrara, and Modena, and competed furiously among themselves for territory. While the states of northern Europe were moving toward centralization and consolidation, the world of Italian politics resembled a jungle where the powerful dominated the weak. Venice, with its enormous trade empire, was a republic in name, but an oligarchy of merchant-aristocrats actually ran the city. Milan was also called a

MAP 12.1 The Italian City-States, ca. 1494   In the fifteenth century the Italian city-states represented great wealth and cultural sophistication, though the many political divisions throughout the peninsula invited foreign intervention.

republic, but the condottieri-turned-signori of the Sforza (SFORT-sah) family ruled harshly and dominated Milan. Likewise, in Florence the form of government was republican, with authority vested in several councils of state, but the city was effectively ruled by the great Medici (MEH-duh-chee) banking family for three centuries, beginning in 1434. Though not public officials, Cosimo (1389–1464), his son Piero, and his grandson Lorenzo (1449–1492), called Lorenzo the Magnificent by his contemporaries, ruled from behind the scenes from 1434 to 1492. The Medici were then in and out of power for several decades, and in 1569 Florence became no longer a republic but the hereditary Grand Duchy of Tuscany,

with the Medici as the Grand Dukes until 1737. The Medici family produced three popes, and most other Renaissance popes were also members of powerful Italian families, selected for their political skills, not their piety. Along with the Italians was one Spaniard, Pope Alexander VI (pontificate 1492–1503), who was the most ruthless; aided militarily and politically by his illegitimate son Cesare Borgia, he reasserted papal authority in the papal lands. South of the Papal States, the kingdom of Naples was under the control of the king of Aragon.

In one significant respect, however, the Italian city-states anticipated future relations among competing European states after 1500. Whenever one Italian

Savonarola Preaching   With vigorous gestures, Savonarola preaches to a crowd of Florentines, the women separated from the men and surrounded by a curtain, reflecting Savonarola's views of the moral changes needed in Florence. This woodcut appeared in a printed version of his sermons published in 1496, when he was at the height of his power. (World History Archive/Alamy)

state appeared to gain a predominant position within the peninsula, other states combined against it to establish a balance of power. In the formation of these alliances, Renaissance Italians invented the machinery of modern diplomacy: permanent embassies with resident ambassadors in capitals where political relations and commercial ties needed continual monitoring.

At the end of the fifteenth century Venice, Florence, Milan, and the papacy possessed great wealth and represented high cultural achievement. Wealthy and divided, however, they were also an inviting target for invasion. When Florence and Naples entered into an agreement to acquire Milanese territories, Milan called on France for support, and the French king Charles VIII (r. 1483–1498) invaded Italy in 1494.

Prior to this invasion, the Dominican friar Girolamo Savonarola (1452–1498) had preached to large crowds in Florence a number of fiery sermons predicting that God would punish Italy for its moral vice and corrupt leadership. Florentines interpreted the French invasion as the fulfillment of this prophecy and expelled the Medici dynasty. Savonarola became the political and religious leader of a new Florentine republic and promised Florentines even greater glory in the future if they would reform their ways. He reorganized the government; convinced it to pass laws against same-sex relations, adultery, and drunkenness; and organized groups of young men to patrol the streets looking for immoral dress and behavior. He held religious processions and what became known as "bonfires of the vanities," huge fires on the main square of Florence in which fancy clothing, cosmetics, pagan books, musical instruments, paintings, and poetry that celebrated human beauty were gathered together and burned.

For a time Savonarola was wildly popular, but eventually people tired of his moral denunciations, and he was excommunicated by the pope, tortured, and burned at the very spot where he had overseen the bonfires. The Medici returned as the rulers of Florence.

The French invasion inaugurated a new period in Italian and European power politics. Italy became the focus of international ambitions and the battleground of foreign armies, particularly those of the Holy Roman Empire and France in a series of conflicts called the Habsburg-Valois wars (named for the German and French dynasties). The Italian cities suffered severely from continual warfare, especially in the frightful sack of Rome in 1527 by imperial forces under the emperor Charles V. Thus the failure of the city-states to consolidate, or at least to establish a common foreign policy, led to centuries of subjection by outside invaders. Italy was not to achieve unification until 1870.

What new ideas were associated with the Renaissance?

The Renaissance was characterized by a self-conscious conviction among educated Italians that they were living in a new era. Somewhat ironically, this idea rested on a deep interest in ancient Latin and Greek literature and philosophy. Through reflecting on the classics, Renaissance thinkers developed new notions of human nature, new plans for education, and new concepts of political rule. The advent of the printing press with movable type would greatly accelerate the spread of these ideas throughout Europe.

Humanism

Giorgio Vasari was the first to use the word *Renaissance* in print, but he was not the first to feel that something was being reborn. Two centuries earlier the Florentine poet and scholar Francesco Petrarch (1304–1374) spent long hours searching for classical Latin manuscripts in dusty monastery libraries and wandering around the many ruins of the Roman Empire remaining in Italy. He became obsessed with the classical past and felt that the writers and artists of ancient Rome had reached a level of perfection in their work that had not since been duplicated. Petrarch believed that the recovery of classical texts and their use as models would bring about a new golden age of intellectual achievement, an idea that many others came to share.

Petrarch clearly thought he was witnessing the dawning of a new era in which writers and artists would recapture the glory of the Roman Republic. Around 1350 he proposed a new kind of education to help them do this, in which young men would study the works of ancient Roman authors, using them as models of how to write clearly, argue effectively, and speak persuasively. The study of Latin classics became known as the *studia humanitates* (STOO-dee-uh oo-mahn-ee-TAH-tayz), usually translated as "liberal studies" or the "liberal arts." People who advocated it were known as *humanists* and their program as **humanism**. Humanism was the main intellectual component of the Renaissance. Like all programs of study, it contained an implicit philosophy: that human nature and human achievements, evident in the classics, were worthy of contemplation.

Many humanists saw Julius Caesar's transformation of Rome from a republic into an empire as a betrayal of the great society, marking the beginning of a long period of decay that the barbarian migrations then accelerated. In his history of Florence written in 1436, the humanist historian and Florentine city official Leonardo Bruni (1374–1444) closely linked the decline of the Latin language to the decline of the Roman Republic: "After the liberty of the Roman people had been lost through the rule of the emperors . . . the flourishing condition of studies and of letters perished, together with the welfare of the city of Rome."[1] In this same book, Bruni was also very clear that by the time of his writing, the period of decay had ended and a new era had begun. He was the first to divide history into three eras—ancient, medieval, and modern—though it was another humanist historian who actually invented the term *Middle Ages*.

In the fifteenth century Florentine humanists became increasingly interested in Greek philosophy as well as Roman literature, especially in the ideas of Plato. Under the patronage of the Medici, the scholar Marsilio Ficino (1433–1499) began to lecture to an informal group of Florence's cultural elite; his lectures became known as the Platonic Academy, but they were not really a school. Ficino regarded Plato as a divinely inspired precursor to Christ. He translated Plato's dialogues into Latin and wrote commentaries attempting to synthesize Christian and Platonic teachings. Plato's emphasis on the spiritual and eternal over the material and transient fit well with Christian teachings about the immortality of the soul. The Platonic idea that the highest form of love was spiritual desire for pure, perfect beauty uncorrupted by bodily desires could easily be interpreted as the Christian desire for the perfection of God.

For Ficino and his most gifted student, Giovanni Pico della Mirandola (1463–1494), both Christian and classical texts taught that the universe was a hierarchy of beings from God down through spiritual beings to material beings, with humanity, right in the middle, as the crucial link that possessed both material and spiritual natures. Pico developed his ideas in a series of nine hundred theses, or points of argumentation, and offered to defend them against anyone who wanted to come to Rome. The pope declared some of the ideas heretical and arrested Pico, though he was freed through the influence of Lorenzo de' Medici. At Lorenzo's death, Pico became a follower of Savonarola, renounced his former ideas and writings, and died of arsenic poisoning, perhaps at the hands of the recently ousted Medici family.

Along with Greek and Roman writings, Renaissance thinkers were also interested in individual excellence. Families, religious brotherhoods, neighborhoods, workers' organizations, and other groups continued to have meaning in people's lives, but Renaissance thinkers increasingly viewed these groups as springboards to far greater individual achievement. They were especially interested in individuals who had risen above their background to become brilliant, powerful, or unique. (See "Individuals in Society: Leonardo da Vinci," page 332.) Such individuals had the admirable quality of **virtù** (vihr-TOO), which is not virtue in the sense of moral goodness, but instead the ability to shape the world around according to one's will. Bruni and other historians included biographies of individuals with virtù in their histories of cities and nations, describing ways in which these people had affected the course of history. Through the quality of their works and their influence on others, artists could also exhibit virtù, an idea that Vasari captures in the title of his major work, *The Lives of the Most Excellent Painters, Sculptors, and Architects*. His subjects had achieved not simply excellence but the pinnacle of excellence.

■ **humanism** A program of study designed by Italians that emphasized the critical study of Latin and Greek literature with the goal of understanding human nature.

■ **virtù** The quality of being able to shape the world according to one's own will.

INDIVIDUALS IN SOCIETY

Leonardo da Vinci

What makes a genius? A deep curiosity about an extensive variety of subjects? A divine spark that emerges in talents that far exceed the norm? Or is it just "one percent inspiration and ninety-nine percent perspiration," as Thomas Edison said? However it is defined, Leonardo da Vinci counts as a genius. In fact, Leonardo was one of the individuals whom the Renaissance label *genius* was designed to describe: a special kind of human being with exceptional creative powers. Leonardo (who, despite the title of a popular novel and film, is always called by his first name) was born in Vinci, near Florence, the illegitimate son of Caterina, a local peasant girl, and Ser Piero da Vinci, a notary public. When Ser Piero's marriage to Donna Albrussia produced no children, he and his wife took in Leonardo, whose mother had married another man. Ser Piero secured Leonardo an apprenticeship with the painter and sculptor Andrea del Verrocchio in Florence. In 1472, when Leonardo was just twenty years old, he was already listed as a master in Florence's "Company of Artists."

Leonardo's most famous portrait, *Mona Lisa*, shows a woman with an enigmatic smile that Giorgio Vasari described as "so pleasing that it seemed divine rather than human." The portrait, probably of the young wife of a rich Florentine merchant (her exact identity is hotly debated), may be the best-known painting in the history of art. One of its competitors for that designation would be another work of Leonardo, *The Last Supper*, which has been called "the most revered painting in the world."

Leonardo's reputation as a genius does not rest on his paintings, however, which are actually few in number, but rather on the breadth of his abilities and interests. He is considered by many the first "Renaissance man," a phrase still used for a multitalented individual. Hoping to reproduce what the eye can see, he drew everything he saw around him, including executed criminals hanging on gallows as well as the beauties of nature. Trying to understand how the human body worked, Leonardo studied live and dead bodies, doing autopsies and dissections to investigate muscles and circulation. He carefully analyzed the effects of light, and he experimented with perspective.

Leonardo used his drawings not only as the basis for his paintings but also as a tool of scientific investigation. He drew plans for hundreds of inventions, many of which would become reality centuries later, such as the helicopter, tank, machine gun, and parachute. He was hired by one of the powerful new rulers in Italy, Duke Ludovico Sforza of Milan, to design weapons, fortresses, and water systems, as well as to produce works of art. When Sforza was overthrown, Leonardo left Milan and spent the last years of his life painting, drawing, and designing for the pope and the French king.

Leonardo experimented with new materials for painting and sculpture, not all of which worked. The experimental method he used to paint *The Last Supper* caused the picture to deteriorate rapidly, and it began to flake off the wall as soon

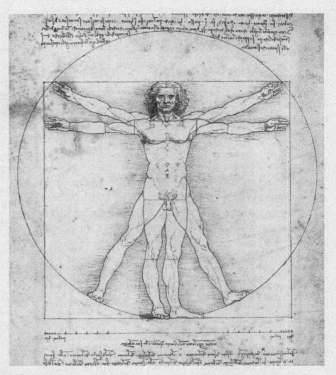

Vitruvian Man, **a drawing by Leonardo showing correlations between the ideal human proportions and the geometric shapes of the circle and square, is based on the ideas of the ancient Roman architect Vitruvius, whose works Leonardo read.** (The Picture Art Collection/Alamy Stock Photo)

as it was finished. Leonardo regarded it as never quite completed, for he could not find a model for the face of Christ who would evoke the spiritual depth he felt the figure deserved. His gigantic equestrian statue in honor of Ludovico's father, Duke Francesco Sforza, was never made, and the clay model collapsed. He planned to write books on many subjects but never finished any of them, leaving only notebooks. Leonardo once said that "a painter is not admirable unless he is universal." The patrons who supported him — and he was supported very well — perhaps wished that his inspirations would have been a bit less universal in scope, or at least accompanied by more perspiration.

QUESTIONS FOR ANALYSIS

1. In what ways do the notions of a "genius" and of a "Renaissance man" both support and contradict each other? Which better fits Leonardo?

2. Has the idea of artistic genius changed since the Renaissance? How?

Sources: Giorgio Vasari, *Lives of the Artists*, vol. 1, trans. G. Bull (London: Penguin Books, 1965); S. B. Nuland, *Leonardo da Vinci* (New York: Lipper/Viking, 2000).

The last artist included in Vasari's book is Vasari himself, for Renaissance thinkers did not exclude themselves when they searched for models of talent and achievement. Vasari begins his discussion of his own works modestly, saying that these might "not lay claim to excellence and perfection" when compared with those of other artists, but he then goes on for more than thirty pages, clearly feeling he has achieved some level of excellence.

Leon Battista Alberti (1404–1472) had similar views of his own achievements. He had much to be proud of: he wrote novels, plays, legal treatises, a study of the family, and the first scientific analysis of perspective; he designed churches, palaces, and fortifications effective against cannon; he invented codes for sending messages secretly and a machine that could cipher and decipher them. In his autobiography—written late in his life, and in the third person, so that he calls himself "he" instead of "I"—Alberti described his personal qualities and accomplishments, noting that he excelled in many sports and "was devoted to the knowledge of the most strange and difficult things. . . learned music without teachers . . . then turned to physics and the mathematical arts. . . . When his favorite dog died he wrote a funeral oration for him."[2] His achievements in many fields did make Alberti a "Renaissance man," as we use the term, though it may be hard to believe his assertion later in the autobiography that "ambition was alien to him."

Biographies and autobiographies presented individuals that humanist authors thought were worthy models, but sometimes people needed more direct instruction. The ancient Greek philosopher Plato, whom humanists greatly admired, taught that the best way to learn something was to think about its perfect, ideal form. If you wanted to learn about justice, for example, you should imagine what ideal justice would be, rather than look at actual examples of justice in the world around you, for these would never be perfect. Following Plato's ideas, Renaissance authors speculated about perfect examples of many things. Alberti wrote about the ideal country house, which was to be useful, convenient, and elegant. The English humanist Thomas More described a perfect society, which he called Utopia.

Education

Humanists thought that their recommended course of study in the classics would provide essential skills for future politicians, diplomats, lawyers, military leaders, and businessmen, as well as writers and artists. It would provide a much broader and more practical type of training than that offered at universities, which at the time focused on theology and philosophy or on theoretical training for lawyers and physicians. Humanists poured out treatises, often in the form of letters, on the structure and goals of education and the training of rulers and leaders. (See "Thinking Like a Historian: Humanist Learning," page 334.)

Humanists put their ideas into practice. Beginning in the early fifteenth century, they opened schools and academies in Italian cities and courts in which pupils began with Latin grammar and rhetoric, went on to study Roman history and political philosophy, and then learned Greek in order to study Greek literature and philosophy. Gradually, humanist education became the basis for intermediate and advanced education for well-to-do urban boys and men. Humanist schools were established in Florence, Venice, and other Italian cities, and by the early sixteenth century across the Alps in Germany, France, and England.

Humanists disagreed about education for women. Many saw the value of exposing women to classical models of moral behavior and reasoning, but they also wondered whether a program of study that emphasized eloquence and action was proper for women, whose sphere was generally understood to be private and domestic. In his book on the family, Alberti stressed that a wife's role should be restricted to the orderliness of the household, food preparation and the serving of meals, the education of children, and the supervision of servants. (Alberti never married, so he never put his ideas into practice in his own household.) Women themselves were bolder in their claims about the value of the new learning. Although humanist academies were not open to women, a few women did become educated in the classics, and they wrote and published poetry, fiction, and essays in Latin and vernacular languages.

No book on education had broader influence than Baldassare Castiglione's *The Courtier* (1528). This treatise sought to train, discipline, and fashion the young man into the courtly ideal, the gentleman. According to Castiglione (kahs-teel-YOH-nay), himself a courtier serving several different rulers, the educated man should have a broad background in many academic subjects and should train his spiritual and physical faculties as well as his intellect. Castiglione envisioned a man who could compose a sonnet, wrestle, sing a song while accompanying himself on an instrument, ride expertly, solve difficult mathematical problems, and, above all, speak and write eloquently. Castiglione also discussed the perfect court lady, who, like the courtier, was to be well educated and able to paint, dance, and play a musical instrument. Physical beauty, delicacy,

Humanist Learning

Renaissance humanists wrote often and forcefully about education, and learning was also a subject of artistic works shaped by humanist ideas. What did humanists see as the best course of study and the purpose of education, and how were these different for men and women?

1 Peter Paul Vergerius, letter to Ubertinus of Padua, 1392. The Venetian scholar and church official Vergerius (1370–1445) advises the son of the ruler of Padua about the proper education for men.

~ We call those studies liberal which are worthy of a free man; those studies by which we attain and practise virtue and wisdom; that education which calls forth, trains and develops those highest gifts of body and of mind which ennoble men, and which are rightly judged to rank next in dignity to virtue only. . . . Amongst these I accord the first place to History, on grounds both of its attractiveness and of its utility, qualities which appeal equally to the scholar and to the statesman. Next in importance ranks Moral Philosophy, which indeed is, in a peculiar sense, a "Liberal Art," in that its purpose is to teach men the secret of true freedom. History, then, gives us the concrete examples of the precepts inculcated by philosophy. The one shews what men should do, the other what men have said and done in the past, and what practical lessons we may draw therefrom for the present day. I would indicate as the third main branch of study, Eloquence, which indeed holds a place of distinction amongst the refined Arts. By philosophy we learn the essential truth of things, which by eloquence we so exhibit in orderly adornment as to bring conviction to differing minds. And history provides the light of experience — a cumulative wisdom fit to supplement the force of reason and the persuasion of eloquence. For we allow that soundness of judgment, wisdom of speech, integrity of conduct are the marks of a truly liberal temper.

2 Leonardo Bruni, letter to Lady Baptista Malatesta, ca. 1405. The Florentine humanist and city official Leonardo Bruni advises the daughter of the duke of Urbino about the proper education for women.

~ There are certain subjects in which, whilst a modest proficiency is on all accounts to be desired, a minute knowledge and excessive devotion seem to be a vain display. For instance, subtleties of Arithmetic and Geometry are not worthy to absorb a cultivated mind, and the same must be said of Astrology. You will be surprised to find me suggesting (though with much more hesitation) that the great and complex art of Rhetoric should be placed in the same category. My chief reason is the obvious one, that I have in view the cultivation most fitting to a woman. To her neither the intricacies of debate nor the oratorical artifices of action and delivery are of the least practical use, if indeed they are not positively unbecoming. Rhetoric in all its forms — public discussion, forensic argument, logical fence, and the like — lies absolutely outside the province of woman. What Disciplines then are properly open to her? In the first place she has before her, as a subject peculiarly her own, the whole field of religion and morals. The literature of the Church will thus claim her earnest study. . . . Moreover, the cultivated Christian lady has no need in the study of this weighty subject to confine herself to ecclesiastical writers. Morals, indeed, have been treated of by the noblest intellects of Greece and Rome. [Then] I place History: a subject which must not on any account be neglected by one who aspires to true cultivation. For it is our duty to understand the origins of our own history and its development; and the achievements of Peoples and of Kings.

ANALYZING THE EVIDENCE

1. According to these sources, what should people learn? Why should they learn?
2. Renaissance humanism has sometimes been viewed as opposed to religion, especially to the teachings of the Catholic Church at the time. Do these sources support this idea?
3. How are the programs of study recommended for men and women similar? How and why are they different?
4. How does the gender of the author shape his or her ideas about the human capacity for reason and learning?

3 **Luca della Robbia, Grammar, 1437–1439.** In this hexagonal panel made for the bell tower of the cathedral of Florence, Luca della Robbia conveys ideas about the course and goals of learning with the open classical door in the background.

(Museo Opera del Duomo, Florence, Italy/De Agostini/Getty Images)

4 **Giovanni Pico della Mirandola, "Oration on the Dignity of Man," 1486.** Pico, the brilliant son of an Italian count and protégé of Lorenzo de' Medici, wrote an impassioned summary of human capacities for learning that ends with this selection.

Oh unsurpassed generosity of God the Father, Oh wondrous and unsurpassable felicity of man, to whom it is granted to have what he chooses, to be what he wills to be! The brutes, from the moment of their birth, bring with them, as Lucilius [a classical Roman author] says, "from their mother's womb" all that they will ever possess. The highest spiritual beings were, from the very moment of creation, or soon thereafter, fixed in the mode of being which would be theirs through measureless eternities. But upon man, at the moment of his creation, God bestowed seeds pregnant with all possibilities, the germs of every form of life. Whichever of these a man shall cultivate, the same will mature and bear fruit in him. If vegetative, he will become a plant; if sensual, he will become brutish; if rational, he will reveal himself a heavenly being; if intellectual, he will be an angel and the son of God. And if, dissatisfied with the lot of all creatures, he should recollect himself into the center of his own unity, he will there become one spirit with God, in the solitary darkness of the Father, Who is set above all things, himself transcend all creatures. Who then will not look with awe upon this our chameleon, or who, at least, will look with greater admiration on any other being?

5 **Cassandra Fedele, "Oration on Learning," 1487.** The Venetian Cassandra Fedele (1465–1558), the best-known female scholar of her time, gave an oration in Latin at the University of Padua in honor of her (male) cousin's graduation.

I shall speak very briefly on the study of the liberal arts, which for humans is useful and honorable, pleasurable and enlightening since everyone, not only philosophers but also the most ignorant man, knows and admits that it is by reason that man is separated from beasts. For what is it that so greatly helps both the learned and the ignorant? What so enlarges and enlightens men's minds the way that an education in and knowledge of literature and the liberal arts do? . . . But erudite men who are filled with the knowledge of divine and human things turn all their thoughts and considerations toward reason as though toward a target, and free their minds from all pain, though plagued by many anxieties. These men are scarcely subjected to fortune's innumerable arrows and they prepare themselves to live well and in happiness. They follow reason as their leader in all things; nor do they consider themselves only, but they are also accustomed to assisting others with their energy and advice in matters public and private. . . . The study of literature refines men's minds, forms and makes bright the power of reason, and washes away all stains from the mind, or at any rate, greatly cleanses it. . . . States, however, and their princes who foster and cultivate these studies become more humane, more gracious, and more noble. . . . But enough on the utility of literature since it produces not only an outcome that is rich, precious, and sublime, but also provides one with advantages that are extremely pleasurable, fruitful, and lasting—benefits that I myself have enjoyed. And when I meditate on the idea of marching forth in life with the lowly and execrable weapons of the little woman—the needle and the distaff [the rod onto which yarn is wound after spinning]—even if the study of literature offers women no rewards or honors, I believe women must nonetheless pursue and embrace such studies alone for the pleasure and enjoyment they contain.

PUTTING IT ALL TOGETHER

Using the sources above, along with what you have learned in class and in this chapter, write a short essay that analyzes humanist learning. What were the goals and purposes of humanist education, and how were these different for men and women? How did these differences reflect Renaissance society more generally?

Sources: (1, 2) W. H. Woodward, ed. and trans., *Vittorino da Feltre and Other Humanist Educators* (London: Cambridge University Press, 1897), pp. 102, 106–107, 126–127; (4) ebooks, University of Adelaide, https://ebooks.adelaide.edu.au/p/pico_della_mirandola/giovanni/dignity/; (5) Cassandra Fedele, *Letters and Orations*, ed. and trans. Diana Robin (Chicago: University of Chicago Press, 2000).

Portrait of Baldassare Castiglione   In this portrait by Raphael, the most sought-after portrait painter of the Renaissance, Castiglione is shown dressed exactly as he advised courtiers to dress, in elegant but subdued clothing that would enhance the splendor of the court but never outshine the ruler. (Art Media/Print Collector/Getty Images)

affability, and modesty were also important qualities for court ladies.

In the sixteenth and seventeenth centuries *The Courtier* was translated into most European languages and widely read. It influenced the social mores and patterns of conduct of elite groups in Renaissance and early modern Europe and became a how-to manual for people seeking to improve themselves and rise in the social hierarchy. Echoes of its ideal for women have perhaps had an even longer life.

Political Thought

Ideal courtiers should preferably serve an ideal ruler, and biographies written by humanists often described rulers who were just, wise, pious, dignified, learned, brave, kind, and distinguished. In return for such flattering portraits of living rulers or their ancestors, authors sometimes received positions at court, or at

least substantial payments. Particularly in Italian cities, however, which often were divided by political factions, taken over by homegrown or regional despots, and attacked by foreign armies, such ideal rulers were hard to find. Humanists thus looked to the classical past for their models. Some, such as Bruni, argued that republicanism was the best form of government. Others used the model of Plato's philosopher-king in the *Republic* to argue that rule by an enlightened individual might be best. Both sides agreed that educated men should be active in the political affairs of their city, a position historians have since termed "civic humanism."

The most famous (or infamous) civic humanist, and ultimately the best-known political theorist of this era, was Niccolò Machiavelli (1469–1527). After the ouster of the Medici with the French invasion of 1494, Machiavelli was secretary to one of the governing bodies in the city of Florence; he was responsible for diplomatic missions and organizing a citizen army. Almost two decades later, power struggles in Florence between rival factions brought the Medici family back to power, and Machiavelli was arrested, tortured, and imprisoned on suspicion of plotting against them. He was released but had no government position, and he spent the rest of his life writing—political theory, poetry, prose works, plays, and a multivolume history of Florence—and making fruitless attempts to regain employment.

The first work Machiavelli finished—though not the first to be published—is his most famous: *The Prince* (1513), which uses the examples of classical and contemporary rulers to argue that the function of a ruler (or any government) is to preserve order and security. Weakness only leads to disorder, which might end in civil war or conquest by an outsider, situations clearly detrimental to any people's well-being. To preserve the state, a ruler should use whatever means he needs—brutality, lying, manipulation—but should not do anything that would make the populace turn against him; stealing or cruel actions done for a ruler's own pleasure would lead to resentment and destroy the popular support needed for a strong, stable realm. "It is much safer for the prince to be feared than loved," Machiavelli advised, "but he ought to avoid making himself hated."[3]

Like the good humanist he was, Machiavelli knew that effective rulers exhibited the quality of virtù. He presented examples from the classical past of just the type of ruler he was describing, but also wrote about contemporary leaders. Cesare Borgia (1475?–1507), Machiavelli's primary example, was the son of Rodrigo Borgia, a Spanish nobleman who later became Pope Alexander VI. Cesare Borgia combined his father's power and his own ruthlessness to build up a state of his own in central Italy. He made good use of new military equipment and tactics, hiring Leonardo da Vinci (1452–1519) as a military engineer, and murdered his political enemies, including the second husband of his sister, Lucrezia. Despite Borgia's efforts, his state fell apart after his father's death, which Machiavelli ascribed not to weakness, but to the operations of fate (*fortuna*, for-TOO-nah, in Italian), whose power even the best-prepared and most merciless ruler could not fully escape, though he should try. Fortuna was personified and portrayed as a goddess in ancient Rome and Renaissance Italy, and Machiavelli's last words about fortune are expressed in gendered terms: "It is better to be impetuous than cautious, for fortune is a woman, and if one wishes to keep her down, it is necessary to beat her and knock her down."[4]

The Prince is often seen as the first modern guide to politics, though Machiavelli was denounced for writing it, and people later came to use the word *Machiavellian* to mean cunning and ruthless. Medieval political philosophers had debated the proper relation between church and state, but they regarded the standards by which all governments were to be judged as emanating from moral principles established by God. Machiavelli argued that governments should instead be judged by how well they provided security, order, and safety to their populace. A ruler's moral code in maintaining these was not the same as a private individual's, for a leader could — indeed, should — use any means necessary. Machiavelli put a new spin on the Renaissance search for perfection, arguing that ideals needed to be measured in the cold light of the real world. This more pragmatic view of the purposes of government, along with Machiavelli's discussion of the role of force and cruelty, was unacceptable to many.

Even today, when Machiavelli's more secular view of the purposes of government is widely shared, scholars debate whether Machiavelli actually meant what he wrote. Most regard him as realistic or even cynical, but some suggest that he was being ironic or satirical, showing princely government in the worst possible light to contrast it with republicanism, which he favored, and also wrote about at length in the *Discourses on Livy*. He dedicated *The Prince* to the new Medici ruler of Florence, however, so any criticism was deeply buried within what was, in that era of patronage, essentially a job application.

Christian Humanism

In the last quarter of the fifteenth century, students from the Low Countries, France, Germany, and England flocked to Italy, absorbed the "new learning," and carried it back to their own countries. Northern humanists shared the ideas of Ficino and Pico about the wisdom of ancient texts, but they went beyond Italian efforts to synthesize the Christian and classical traditions to see humanist learning as a way to bring about reform of the church and deepen people's spiritual lives. These **Christian humanists**, as they were later called, thought that the best elements of classical and Christian cultures should be combined. For example, the classical ideals of calmness, stoical patience, and broad-mindedness should be joined in human conduct with the Christian virtues of love, faith, and hope.

The English humanist Thomas More (1478–1535) began life as a lawyer, studied the classics, and entered government service. Despite his official duties, he had time to write, and he became most famous for his controversial dialogue *Utopia* (1516), a word More invented from the Greek words for "nowhere." *Utopia* describes a community on an island somewhere beyond Europe where all children receive a good education, primarily in the Greco-Roman classics, and adults divide their days between manual labor or business pursuits and intellectual activities. The problems that plagued More's fellow citizens, such as poverty and hunger, have been solved by a beneficent government. There is religious toleration, and order and reason prevail. Because Utopian institutions are perfect, however, dissent and disagreement are not acceptable.

More's purposes in writing *Utopia* have been debated just as much as have Machiavelli's in penning *The Prince*. Some view it as a revolutionary critique of More's own hierarchical and violent society, some as a call for an even firmer hierarchy, and others as part of the humanist tradition of satire. It was widely read by learned Europeans in the Latin in which More wrote it, and later in vernacular translations, and its title quickly became the standard word for any imaginary society.

Better known by contemporaries than Thomas More was the Dutch humanist Desiderius Erasmus (dehz-ih-DARE-ee-us ih-RAZ-muhs) (1466?–1536) of Rotterdam. Erasmus's long list of publications includes *The Education of a Christian Prince* (1504), a book combining idealistic and practical suggestions for the formation of a ruler's character through the careful study of the Bible and classical authors; *The Praise of Folly* (1509), a witty satire poking fun at political, social, and especially religious institutions;

■ **Christian humanists** Northern humanists who interpreted Italian ideas about and attitudes toward classical antiquity and humanism in terms of their own religious traditions.

and, most important, a new Latin translation of the New Testament alongside the first printed edition of the Greek text (1516). In the preface to the New Testament, Erasmus expressed his ideas about Bible translations: "I wish that even the weakest woman should read the Gospel—should read the epistles of Paul. And I wish these were translated into all languages, so that they might be read and understood, not only by Scots and Irishmen, but also by Turks and Saracens."[5]

Two fundamental themes run through all of Erasmus's work. First, education in the Bible and the classics is the means to reform, the key to moral and intellectual improvement. Erasmus called for a renaissance of the ideals of the early church to accompany the renaissance in classical education that was already going on, and criticized the church of his day for having strayed from these ideals. Second, renewal should be based on what he termed "the philosophy of Christ," an emphasis on inner spirituality and personal morality rather than Scholastic theology or outward observances such as pilgrimages or the veneration of relics. His ideas, and Christian humanism in general, were important roots of the Protestant Reformation, although Erasmus himself denied this and never became a follower of Luther (see "Martin Luther" in Chapter 13).

The Printed Word

The fourteenth-century humanist Petrarch and the sixteenth-century humanist Erasmus had similar ideas

on many topics, but the immediate impact of their ideas was very different because of one thing: the invention of the printing press with movable metal type. The ideas of Petrarch were spread slowly from person to person by hand copying. The ideas of Erasmus were spread quickly through print, allowing hundreds or thousands of identical copies to be made in a short time.

Printing with movable metal type developed in Germany in the 1440s as a combination of existing technologies. Several metalsmiths, most prominently Johann Gutenberg, recognized that the metal stamps used to mark signs on jewelry could be covered with ink and used to mark symbols onto a surface in the same way that other craftsmen were using carved wood stamps to print books. (This woodblock printing technique originated in China and Korea centuries earlier.) Gutenberg and his assistants made metal stamps—later called *type*—for every letter of the alphabet and built racks that held the type in rows. This type could be rearranged for every page and so used over and over.

The printing revolution was also made possible by the ready availability of paper, which was also produced using techniques that had originated in China. Unlike the printing press, this technology had been brought into Europe through Muslim Spain rather than developing independently.

By the fifteenth century the increase in urban literacy, the development of primary schools, and the opening of more universities had created an expanding market for reading materials. When Gutenberg developed movable type printing as a faster way to

Printer's Shop   This engraving from a late-sixteenth-century book captures the many tasks and mix of individuals in a print shop. On the far left three compositors assemble pieces of type into a framework, while in the left foreground another checks a frame and a proofreader, wearing glasses, checks printed proof. At the back a woman, perhaps the printer's wife, inks type, while in front of her the printer pulls a lever to operate the press. In the front a young apprentice hangs sheets to dry, and the well-dressed man at the right may be the patron or official who ordered the print job. (INTERFOTO/Alamy)

MAP 12.2 The Growth of Printing in Europe, 1448–1554

The speed with which artisans spread printing technology across Europe provides strong evidence for the growing demand for reading material. Presses in the Ottoman Empire were first established by Jewish immigrants who printed works in Hebrew, Greek, and Spanish.

ANALYZING THE MAP What part of Europe had the greatest number of printing presses by 1554? What explains this?

CONNECTIONS Printing was developed in response to a market for reading materials. Use Maps 10.2 and 10.3 (pages 277 and 282) to help explain why printing spread the way it did.

---

copy, professional copyists writing by hand and wood-block printers, along with monks and nuns, were already churning out reading materials on paper as fast as they could for the growing number of people who could read.

Gutenberg was not the only one to recognize the huge market for books, and his invention was quickly copied. Other craftsmen made their own type, built their own presses, and bought their own paper, setting themselves up in business (Map 12.2). Historians estimate that, within a half century of the publication of Gutenberg's Bible in 1456, somewhere between 8 million and 20 million books were printed in Europe. Whatever the actual figure, the number is far greater than the number of books produced in all of Western history up to that point.

The effects of the invention of movable-type printing were not felt overnight. Nevertheless, movable type radically transformed both the private and the public lives of Europeans by the dawn of the sixteenth century. Print shops became gathering places for people interested in new ideas. Though printers were trained through apprenticeships just as blacksmiths or butchers were, they had connections to the world of politics, art, and scholarship that other craftsmen did not.

Printing gave hundreds or even thousands of people identical books, allowing them to more easily discuss the ideas that the books contained with one another in person or through letters. Printed materials reached an invisible public, allowing silent individuals to join causes and groups of individuals widely separated by geography to form a common identity; this new group consciousness could compete with and transcend older, localized loyalties.

Government and church leaders both used and worried about printing. They printed laws, declarations of war, battle accounts, and propaganda, and they also attempted to censor books and authors whose ideas they thought challenged their authority or were incorrect. Officials developed lists of prohibited books and authors, enforcing their prohibitions by confiscating books, arresting printers and booksellers, or destroying the presses of printers who disobeyed. None of this was very effective, and books were printed secretly, with fake title pages, authors, and places of publication, and smuggled all over Europe.

Printing also stimulated the literacy of laypeople and eventually came to have a deep effect on their private lives. Although most of the earliest books and pamphlets dealt with religious subjects, printers produced anything that would sell. They printed professional reference sets for lawyers, doctors, and students, and historical romances, biographies, and how-to manuals for the general public. They discovered that illustrations increased a book's sales, so they published books on a wide range of topics — from history to pornography — full of woodcuts and engravings. Single-page broadsides and fly sheets allowed great public events and "wonders" such as comets and two-headed calves to be experienced vicariously by a stay-at-home readership. Since books and other printed materials were read aloud to illiterate listeners, print also bridged the gap between the written and oral cultures.

How did art reflect new Renaissance ideals?

No feature of the Renaissance evokes greater admiration than its artistic masterpieces. The 1400s (*quattrocento*) and 1500s (*cinquecento*) bore witness to dazzling creativity in painting, architecture, and sculpture. In all the arts, the city of Florence led the way. But Florence was not the only artistic center, for Rome and Venice also became important, and northern Europeans perfected their own styles.

Patronage and Power

In early Renaissance Italy, powerful urban groups often flaunted their wealth by commissioning works of art. In the late fifteenth century, wealthy individuals and rulers, rather than corporate groups, sponsored works of art. Patrician merchants and bankers, popes, and princes spent vast sums on the arts to glorify themselves and their families. Writing in about 1470, Florentine ruler Lorenzo de' Medici declared that his family had spent hundreds of thousands of gold florins for artistic and architectural commissions, but commented, "I think it casts a brilliant light on our estate [public reputation] and it seems to me that the monies were well spent and I am very pleased with this."[6]

Patrons varied in their level of involvement as a work progressed; some simply ordered a specific subject or scene, while others oversaw the work of the artist or architect very closely, suggesting themes and styles and demanding changes while the work was in progress. For example, Pope Julius II (pontificate 1503–1513), who commissioned Michelangelo to paint the ceiling of the Vatican's Sistine Chapel in 1508, demanded that the artist work as fast as he could and frequently visited him at his work with suggestions and criticisms. Michelangelo, a Florentine who had spent his young adulthood at the court of Lorenzo de' Medici, complained in person and by letter about the pope's meddling, but his reputation did not match the power of the pope, and he kept working until the chapel was finished in 1512.

In addition to power, art reveals changing patterns of consumption among the wealthy elite in European society. In the rural world of the Middle Ages, society had been organized for war, and men of wealth spent their money on military gear. As Italian nobles settled in towns, they adjusted to an urban culture (see "What led to Europe's economic growth and reurbanization?" in Chapter 10). Rather than employing knights for warfare, cities hired mercenaries. Accordingly,

Plate Showing the Abduction of Helen of Troy　Filled with well-muscled men, curvaceous women, and exotic landscapes, this colorful plate with a gold rim depicts a well-known scene from Greek mythology, the abduction of Helen, which sparked the Trojan War. Such tin-glazed pottery, known as maiolica and made in many places in Italy beginning in the late fifteenth century, was sold throughout Europe to wealthy consumers, who favored designs with family crests or legendary or historical scenes, known as istoriato ("painted with stories"). (Museo Nazionale del Bargello, Florence, Italy/Bridgeman Images)

expenditures on military hardware by nobles declined. For the noble recently arrived from the countryside or the rich merchant of the city, a grand urban palace represented the greatest outlay of cash. Wealthy individuals and families ordered gold dishes, embroidered tablecloths, wall tapestries, paintings on canvas (an innovation), and sculptural decorations to adorn these homes. Expanded trade brought in silks, pearls, gemstones, feathers, dyes, and furs, which tailors, goldsmiths, seamstresses, furriers, and hatmakers turned into magnificent clothing and jewelry. Men and women wore clothing that displayed many layers of expensive fabrics, with golden rings, earrings, pins, and necklaces to provide additional glamour.

Changing Artistic Styles

Both the content and style of Renaissance art often differed from those of the Middle Ages. Religious topics remained popular among both patrons and artists, but frequently the patron had himself and his family portrayed in the scene. As the fifteenth century advanced and humanist ideas spread more widely, classical themes and motifs figured increasingly in painting and sculpture, with the facial features of the gods sometimes modeled on living people.

The individual portrait emerged as a distinct artistic genre in this movement. Rather than reflecting a spiritual ideal, as medieval painting and sculpture tended to do, Renaissance portraits showed human ideals, often portrayed in the more realistic style increasingly favored by both artists and patrons. The Florentine painter Giotto (JAH-toh) (1276–1337) led the way in the use of realism; his treatment of the human body and face replaced the formal stiffness and artificiality that had long characterized representation of the human body. Piero della Francesca (frahn-CHAY-skah) (1420–1492) and Andrea Mantegna (mahn-TEHN-yuh) (1430/31–1506) pioneered perspective, the linear representation of distance and space on a flat surface, which enhanced the realism of paintings and differentiated them from the flatter and more stylized images of medieval art. (See "Evaluating Visual Evidence: Andrea Mantegna, *Adoration of the Magi*, ca. 1495–1505," page 343.) The sculptor Donatello (1386–1466) revived the classical figure, with its balance and self-awareness. In architecture, Filippo Brunelleschi (1377–1446) looked to the classical past for inspiration, designing a hospital for orphans and foundlings in which all proportions — of the windows, height, floor plan, and covered walkway with a series of rounded arches — were carefully thought out to achieve a sense of balance and harmony.

Art produced in northern Europe tended to be more religious in orientation than that produced in Italy. Some Flemish painters, notably Rogier van der Weyden (1399/1400–1464) and Jan van Eyck (1366–1441), were considered the artistic equals of Italian painters and were much admired in Italy. Van Eyck

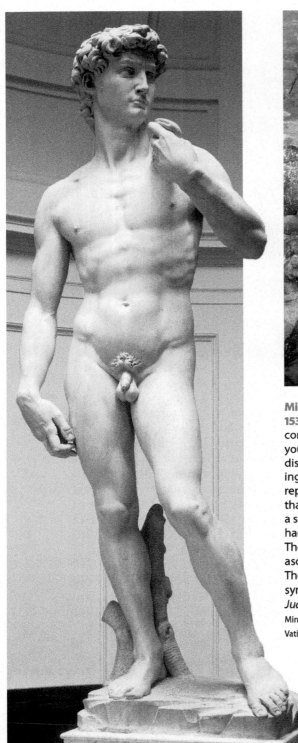

Michelangelo's *David* (1501–1504) and the *Last Judgment* (detail, 1537–1541)   Like all Renaissance artists, Michelangelo worked largely on commissions from patrons. Officials of the city of Florence contracted the young sculptor to produce a statue of the Old Testament hero David (left) to be displayed on the city's main square. Michelangelo portrayed David anticipating his fight against the giant Goliath, and the statue came to symbolize the republic of Florence standing up to its larger and more powerful enemies. More than thirty years later, Michelangelo was commissioned by the pope to paint a scene of the Last Judgment on the altar wall of the Sistine Chapel, where he had earlier spent four years covering the ceiling with magnificent frescoes. The massive work shows a powerful Christ standing in judgment, with souls ascending into Heaven while others are dragged by demons into Hell (above). The *David* captures ideals of human perfection and has come to be an iconic symbol of Renaissance artistic brilliance, while the dramatic and violent *Last Judgment* conveys both terror and divine power. (sculpture: Accademia, Florence, Italy/ Ministero per i Beni e le Attività Culturali/Scala/Art Resource, NY; painting: Vatican Museums and Galleries, Vatican State/Alinari/Bridgeman Images)

was one of the earliest artists to use oil-based paints successfully, and his religious scenes and portraits all show great realism and remarkable attention to human personality. Albrecht Dürer (1471–1528), from the German city of Nuremberg, studied with artists in Italy and produced woodcuts, engravings, and etchings that rendered the human form and the natural world in amazing detail. Fascinated with the theoretical and practical problems of perspective, he designed mechanical devices that could assist artists in solving these

Andrea Mantegna, *Adoration of the Magi*, ca. 1495–1505

Applying his study of ancient Roman relief sculpture to compress figures into a shallow space, Mantegna painted this scene of the three wise men coming to visit the infant Christ. The three wise men represent the entire world — that is, the three continents known to medieval and Renaissance Europeans: Europe, Asia, and Africa. They also symbolize the three stages of life: old age, middle age, and youth. As in most depictions, Melchior, the oldest, his large cranium symbolizing wisdom, represents Europe. He offers gold in a Chinese porcelain cup. Balthazar, with a dark beard and Turkish turbaned hat, represents Asia and middle age, and holds a bronze vessel with frankincense. Caspar, representing Africa and youth, gives myrrh in a covered cup made of agate. The three wise men were a common subject in Renaissance art, as they allowed artists to show figures from a variety of cultures wearing sumptuous clothing.

(Fine Art Images/Heritage Images/Getty Images)

EVALUATE THE EVIDENCE

1. How does Mantegna use shadowing, foreshortening, and other artistic techniques to show a three-dimensional scene on a two-dimensional surface?
2. How does Mantegna use clothing, headgear, and jewelry to depict Caspar (right) as distinctively African and — to European eyes — unfamiliar and mysterious? How does this portrayal of him relate to Europeans' changing attitudes about race during this era?

problems. Like many Renaissance artists, Dürer was open to new ideas, no matter what their source. Late in his life he saw the first pieces of Aztec art shipped back to Europe from the New World and commented in his diary about how amazing they were.

In the early sixteenth century, the center of the new art shifted from Florence to Rome, where wealthy cardinals and popes wanted visual expression of the church's and their own families' power and piety. Renaissance popes expended enormous enthusiasm

The Madonna of Chancellor Rolin, ca. 1435   This exquisitely detailed oil painting by Jan van Eyck, commissioned by Nicolas Rolin, the chancellor of the duchy of Burgundy, shows the Virgin Mary presenting the infant Jesus to Rolin, whose portrait in a brocade fur-lined robe takes up the entire left side. The foreground is an Italian-style loggia with an inlaid floor, while the background shows Rolin's hometown of Autun, where he was a major landowner and where the painting was displayed in his parish church. Renaissance paintings from southern and northern Europe often show their patrons together with biblical figures and highlight exactly the qualities the patron wanted: wealth, learning, piety, and power. (Josse/Leemage/Corbis Historical/Getty Images)

and huge sums of money to beautify the city. Pope Julius II tore down the old Saint Peter's Basilica and began work on the present structure in 1506. Michelangelo went to Rome from Florence in about 1500 and began the series of statues, paintings, and architectural projects from which he gained an international reputation: the *Pietà*, *Moses*, the redesigning of the plaza and surrounding palaces on the Capitoline Hill in central Rome, and, most famously, the dome for Saint Peter's and the ceiling and altar wall of the nearby Sistine Chapel.

Raphael Sanzio (1483–1520), another Florentine, got the commission for frescoes in the papal apartments, and in his relatively short life he painted hundreds of portraits and devotional images, becoming the most sought-after artist in Europe. Raphael also oversaw a large workshop with many collaborators and apprentices — who assisted on the less difficult sections of some paintings — and wrote treatises on his philosophy of art in which he emphasized the importance of imitating nature and developing an orderly sequence of design and proportion.

Venice became another artistic center in the sixteenth century. Titian (TIH-shuhn) (1490–1576) produced portraits, religious subjects, and mythological scenes; he developed techniques of painting in oil without doing elaborate drawings first, which speeded up the process and pleased patrons eager to display their acquisitions. Titian and other sixteenth-century painters developed an artistic style known in English as "mannerism" (from *maniera* or "style" in Italian) in which artists sometimes distorted figures, exaggerated musculature, and heightened color to express emotion and drama more intently. (See the Titian paintings *Laura de Dianti* on page 348 and *Philip II* on page 412; this is also the style in which Michelangelo painted the *Last Judgment* in the Sistine Chapel, shown on page 342.)

The Renaissance Artist

Some patrons rewarded certain artists very well, and some artists gained great public acclaim as, in Vasari's words, "rare men of genius." This adulation of the

Villa Capra   Architecture as well as literature and art aimed to re-create classical styles. The Venetian architect Andrea Palladio modeled this country villa, constructed for a papal official in 1566, on the Pantheon of ancient Rome (see "The Nerva-Antonine Dynasty" in Chapter 6). Surrounded by statues of classical deities, it is completely symmetrical, capturing humanist ideals of perfection and balance. This villa and other buildings that Palladio designed influenced later buildings all over the world, including the U.S. Capitol in Washington, D.C., and countless state capitol buildings. (DEA/W. BUSS//De Agostini/ Getty Images)

artist has led many historians to view the Renaissance as the beginning of the concept of the artist as having a special talent. In the Middle Ages people believed that only God created, albeit through individuals; the medieval conception recognized no particular value in artistic originality. Renaissance artists and humanists came to think that a work of art was the deliberate creation of a unique personality who transcended traditions, rules, and theories. A genius had a peculiar gift that ordinary laws should not inhibit. (See "Individuals in Society: Leonardo da Vinci," page 332.)

However, it is important not to overemphasize the Renaissance notion of genius. As certain artists became popular and well known, they could assert their own artistic styles and pay less attention to the wishes of patrons, but even major artists like Raphael generally worked according to the patron's specific guidelines. Whether in Italy or northern Europe, most Renaissance artists trained in the workshops of older artists; Botticelli, Raphael, Titian, and at times even Michelangelo were known for their large, well-run, and prolific workshops. Though they might be men of genius, artists were still expected to be well trained in proper artistic techniques and stylistic conventions;

the notion that artistic genius could show up in the work of an untrained artist did not emerge until the twentieth century. Beginning artists spent years mastering their craft by copying drawings and paintings; learning how to prepare paint and other artistic materials; and, by the sixteenth century, reading books about design and composition. Younger artists gathered together in the evenings for further drawing practice; by the later sixteenth century some of these informal groups had turned into more formal artistic "academies," the first of which was begun in 1563 in Florence by Vasari under the patronage of the Medici.

As Vasari's phrase indicates, the notion of artistic genius that developed in the Renaissance was gendered. All the most famous and most prolific Renaissance artists were male. The types of art in which more women were active, such as textiles, needlework, and painting on porcelain, were regarded not as "major arts," but only as "minor" or "decorative" arts. (The division between "major" and "minor" arts begun in the Renaissance continues to influence the way museums and collections are organized today.) Like painting, embroidery changed in the Renaissance to become more naturalistic, more visually complex, and more classical in its subject matter. Embroiderers were not trained to view

Botticelli, *Primavera* (Spring), ca. 1482   Framed by a grove of orange trees, Venus, goddess of love, is flanked on the right by Flora, goddess of flowers and fertility, and on the left by the Three Graces, goddesses of banquets, dance, and social occasions. Above, Venus's son Cupid, the god of love, shoots darts of desire, while at the far right the wind-god Zephyrus chases the nymph Chloris. The entire scene rests on classical mythology, though some art historians claim that Venus is an allegory for the Virgin Mary. Botticelli captured the ideal for female beauty in the Renaissance: slender, with pale skin, a high forehead, red-blond hair, and sloping shoulders. (Galleria degli Uffizi, Florence, Italy/Bridgeman Images)

their work as products of individual genius, however, so they rarely included their names on the works, and there is no way to discover their identities.

There are no female architects whose names are known and only one female sculptor, though several women did become well known as painters in their day. Stylistically, their works are different from one another, but their careers show many similarities. Most female painters were the daughters of painters or of minor noblemen with ties to artistic circles. Many were eldest daughters or came from families in which there were no sons, so their fathers took unusual interest in their careers. Many women painters began their careers before they were twenty and either produced far fewer paintings after they married or stopped painting entirely. Women were not allowed to study the male nude, a study that was viewed as essential if one wanted to paint large history or biblical paintings with many figures. Women also could not learn the technique of fresco, in which colors are applied directly to wet plaster walls, because such work had to be done in public, which was judged

inappropriate for women. Joining a group of male artists for informal practice was also seen as improper, so women had no access to the newly established artistic academies. Like universities, humanist academies, and most craft guild shops, artistic workshops were male-only settings in which men of different ages came together for training and created bonds of friendship, influence, patronage, and sometimes intimacy.

Women were not alone in being excluded from the institutions of Renaissance culture. Though a few rare men of genius such as Leonardo and Michelangelo emerged from artisanal backgrounds, most scholars and artists came from families with at least some money. The ideas of the highly educated humanists did not influence the lives of most people in cities and did not affect life in the villages at all. For rural people and for less well-off town residents, work and play continued much as they had in the High Middle Ages: religious festivals and family celebrations provided people's main amusements, and learning came from one's parents, not through formal schooling.

The Chess Game, 1555   In this oil painting, the Italian artist Sofonisba Anguissola (1532–1625) shows her three younger sisters playing chess, a game that was growing in popularity in the sixteenth century. Each sister looks at the one immediately older than herself, with the girl on the left looking out at her sister, the artist. Anguissola's father, a minor nobleman, recognized his daughter's talent and arranged for her to study with several painters. She became a court painter at the Spanish royal court, where she painted many portraits. Returning to Italy, she continued to be active, painting her last portrait when she was over eighty. (Museum Narodowe, Poznan, Poland/ Bridgeman Images)

What were the key social hierarchies in Renaissance Europe?

The division between educated and uneducated people was only one of many social hierarchies evident in the Renaissance. Every society has social hierarchies; in ancient Rome, for example, there were patricians and plebeians (see "The Roman State" in Chapter 5). Such hierarchies are to some degree descriptions of social reality, but they are also idealizations — that is, they describe how people imagined their society to be, without all the messy reality of social-climbing plebeians or groups that did not fit the standard categories. Social hierarchies in the Renaissance were built on those of the Middle Ages that divided nobles from commoners, but new concepts were also developed that contributed to modern social hierarchies, such as those of race, class, and gender.

Race and Slavery

Renaissance people did not use the word *race* the way we do, but often used *race, people,* and *nation* interchangeably for ethnic, national, religious, or other groups — the French race, the Jewish nation, the Irish people, "the race of learned gentlemen," and so on. They made distinctions between groups based on language, religion, culture, geographic location, real or perceived kinship, and other characteristics. Differences between groups were (and are) sometimes evident in the body, and were (and are) often conceptualized as blood, a substance with deep meaning. People spoke of "French blood," "noble blood," "Jewish blood," and so on, and thought of difference as heritable.

In some parts of Europe, urban residents included Black Africans, small numbers of whom had lived in Europe since Roman times, but whose numbers increased in the fifteenth century as Portuguese ships brought enslaved Africans to the markets of Seville, Barcelona, Marseilles, and Genoa. In Portugal and Spain, enslaved people, mostly from Africa, supplemented the labor force in virtually all occupations — as servants, laborers, artisans, and sailors. By the mid-sixteenth century enslaved, freed, and free people of African descent made up about 10 percent of the Portuguese city of Lisbon and perhaps 3 percent of the Portuguese population overall. Cities such as Lisbon also had significant numbers of people of mixed African and European descent, as Africans intermingled with the people they lived among and sometimes intermarried.

Africans lived in other parts of Europe as well, especially in port cities. Some were enslaved, but others were free servants, musicians, mariners, and artisans. There were free Black gondoliers in Venice and Black weavers in London. John Blanke was a Black trumpeter at King Henry VIII's court in London, and a diver from West Africa worked to salvage Henry VIII's flagship, the *Mary Rose,* when it sank in the English Channel. For wealthy Europeans, a Black servant — especially a child — was a sought-after commodity, akin to other imported luxury goods. Portraits of aristocrats and courtiers contrasted white and black skin (as in the painting on page 348, which depicts a Black child gazing up at a richly dressed central figure).

As contacts between Black Africans and Europeans increased in the later Middle Ages and Renaissance, Europeans increasingly focused on skin color as a marker of

Laura de Dianti, 1523   The Venetian artist Titian portrays a young Italian woman with a gorgeous blue dress and an elaborate pearl and feather headdress, accompanied by a young Black page with a gold earring. Enslaved servants from Africa and the Ottoman Empire were common in wealthy Venetian households. (Private Collection/© Human Bios International AG)

difference, beginning to define, and in visual art to portray, themselves as "white." (In Greek and Roman art and texts, heroes are ruddy or dark-skinned from their active life outdoors while women, sick people, and cowards are white.) European Christians associated the color black with sin, evil, and the Devil, and increasingly applied this to people, viewing Black Africans as inferior, barbaric, or even demonic—attitudes that allowed them to buy and sell enslaved Africans without any concern. By linking whiteness with freedom and blackness with slavery, the slave trade strengthened these ideas. Distinctions based on skin color, facial features, and continent of origin would later mix with those based on religion, kinship, and other characteristics to coalesce into modern notions of race.

Wealth and the Nobility

The word *class*—as in *working class, middle class,* and *upper class*—was not used in the Renaissance to describe social divisions, but by the thirteenth century, and even more so by the fifteenth, the idea of a hierarchy based on wealth was emerging. This was particularly true in cities, where wealthy merchants who oversaw vast trading empires lived in splendor that rivaled the richest nobles. As we saw earlier, in many cities these merchants had gained political power to match their economic might, becoming merchant oligarchs who ruled through city councils. This hierarchy of wealth was more fluid than the older divisions into noble and commoner, allowing individuals and families to rise—and fall—within one generation.

The development of a hierarchy of wealth did not mean an end to the prominence of nobles, however, and even poorer nobility still had higher status than wealthy commoners. Thus wealthy Italian merchants enthusiastically bought noble titles and country villas in the fifteenth century, and wealthy English or Spanish merchants eagerly married their daughters and sons into often-impoverished noble families. The nobility maintained its status in most parts of Europe not by maintaining rigid boundaries, but by taking in and integrating the new social elite of wealth.

Along with being tied to hierarchies of wealth and family standing, social status was linked to considerations of honor. Among the nobility, for example, certain weapons and battle tactics were favored because they were viewed as more honorable. Among urban dwellers, certain occupations, such as city executioner or manager of the municipal brothel, might be well paid but were understood to be dishonorable and so of low status. In cities, sumptuary laws reflected both wealth and honor (see "City Life" in Chapter 10); merchants were specifically allowed fur and jewels, while prostitutes were ordered to wear yellow bands that would remind potential customers of the flames of Hell.

Gender Roles

Renaissance people would not have understood the word *gender* to refer to categories of people, but they would have easily grasped the concept. Toward the end of the fourteenth century, learned men (and a few women) began what was termed the **debate about women** (*querelle des femmes*), a debate about women's character and nature that would last for centuries. Misogynist (muh-SAH-juh-nihst) critiques of women from both clerical and secular authors denounced females as devious, domineering, and demanding. In answer, several authors compiled long lists of famous and praiseworthy women exemplary for their loyalty, bravery, and morality. Christine de Pizan (1364?–1430), an Italian woman who became the first woman in Europe to make her living as a writer, was among the writers who not only defended women, but also explored the reasons behind women's secondary status—that is, why the great philosophers, statesmen, and poets had generally been men. In this they were anticipating discussions about the social construction of gender by six hundred years. Christine also wrote histories, biographies, a book of military tactics, and an advice book for women of all social classes (see "Evaluating Written Evidence: Christine de Pizan, *The Treasure of the City of Ladies,*" page 349).

Christine de Pizan, *The Treasure of the City of Ladies*

Christine de Pizan's *The Treasure of the City of Ladies* (1405) provides moral suggestions and practical advice on behavior and household management for women of all social classes. Most of the book is directed toward princesses and court ladies (who would have been able to read it), but Christine also includes shorter sections for the wives of merchants and artisans, serving-women, female peasants, and even prostitutes. Excerpted here is her advice to the wives of artisans, such as blacksmiths, bakers, or shoemakers.

All wives of artisans should be very painstaking and diligent if they wish to have the necessities of life. They should encourage their husbands or their workmen to get to work early in the morning and work until late, for mark our words, there is no trade so good that if you neglect your work you will not have difficulty putting bread on the table. And besides encouraging the others, the wife herself should be involved in the work to the extent that she knows all about it, so that she may know how to oversee his workers if her husband is absent, and to reprove them if they do not do well. She ought to oversee them to keep them from idleness, for through careless workers the master is sometimes ruined. And when customers come to her husband and try to drive a hard bargain, she ought to warn him solicitously to take care that he does not make a bad deal. She should advise him to be chary of giving too much credit if he does not know precisely where and to whom it is going, for in this way many come to poverty, although sometimes the greed to earn more or to accept a tempting proposition makes them do it.

In addition, she ought to keep her husband's love as much as she can, to this end: that he will stay at home more willingly and that he may not have any reason to join the foolish crowds of other young men in taverns and indulge in unnecessary and extravagant expense, as many tradesmen do, especially in Paris. By treating him kindly she should protect him as well as she can from this. It is said that three things drive a man from his home: a quarrelsome wife, a smoking fireplace and a leaking roof. She too ought to stay at home gladly and not go every day traipsing hither and yon gossiping with the neighbours and visiting her chums to find out what everyone is doing. That is done by slovenly housewives roaming about the town in groups. Nor should she go off on these pilgrimages got up for no good reason and involving a lot of needless expense. Furthermore, she ought to remind her husband that they should live so frugally that their expenditure does not exceed their income, so that at the end of the year they do not find themselves in debt.

If she has children, she should have them instructed and taught first at school by educated people so that they may know how better to serve God. Afterwards they may be put to some trade by which they may earn a living, for whoever gives a trade or business training to her child gives a great possession. The children should be kept from wantonness and from voluptuousness above all else, for truly it is something that most shames the children of good towns and is a great sin of mothers and fathers, who ought to be the cause of the virtue and good behavior of their children, but they are sometimes the reason (because of bringing them up to be finicky and indulging them too much) for their wickedness and ruin.

EVALUATE THE EVIDENCE

1. How would you describe Christine's view of the ideal artisan's wife? The ideal family and household?
2. How are economic and moral virtues linked for Christine?

Source: Christine de Pizan, *The Treasure of the City of Ladies,* translated with an introduction by Sarah Lawson (London: Penguin Classics, 1985).

With the development of the printing press, popular interest in the debate about women grew, and works were translated, reprinted, and shared around Europe. Prints that juxtaposed female virtues and vices were also very popular, with the virtuous women depicted as those of the classical or biblical past and the vice-ridden dressed in contemporary clothes. The favorite metaphor for the virtuous wife was either the snail or the tortoise, both animals that never leave their "houses" and are totally silent, although such images were never as widespread as those depicting wives beating their husbands or hiding their lovers from them.

Beginning in the sixteenth century, the debate about women also became a debate about female rulers, sparked primarily by dynastic accidents in many countries, including Spain, England, Scotland, and France, that led to women's ruling in their own right or serving as advisers to child-kings. The questions were vigorously and at times viciously argued. They directly concerned the social construction of gender: Could a woman's being born into a royal family and educated to rule allow her to overcome the limitations of her sex? Should it? Or stated another way: Which was (or should be) the stronger determinant of character and

■ **debate about women** Debate among writers and thinkers in the Renaissance about women's qualities and proper role in society.

social role, gender or rank? Despite a prevailing sentiment that women were not as fit to rule as men, there were no successful rebellions against female rulers. In part this might have been because female rulers, especially Queen Elizabeth I of England, emphasized qualities regarded as masculine—physical bravery, stamina, wisdom, duty—whenever they appeared in public.

Ideas about women's and men's proper roles determined the actions of ordinary men and women even more forcefully. The dominant notion of the "true" man was that of the married head of household, so men whose social status and age would have normally conferred political power but who remained unmarried did not participate in politics at the same level as their married brothers. Unmarried men in Venice, for example, could not be part of the ruling council.

Women were also understood as either "married or to be married," even if the actual marriage patterns in Europe left many women (and men) unmarried until quite late in life (see "Sex in the City" in Chapter 11). This meant that women's work was not viewed as financially supporting a family—even if it did—and was valued less than men's. If they worked for wages, and many women did, women earned about half to two-thirds of what men did, even for the same work. Regulations for vineyard workers in the early sixteenth century, for example, specified:

> Men who work in the vineyards, doing work that is skilled, are to be paid 16 pence per day; in addition, they are to receive soup and wine in the morning, at midday beer, vegetables and meat, and in the evening soup, vegetables and wine. Young boys are to be paid 10 pence per day. Women who work as haymakers are to be given 6 pence a day. If the employer wants to have them doing other work, he may make an agreement with them to pay them 7 or 8 pence. He may also give them soup and vegetables to eat in the morning—but no wine—milk and bread at midday, but nothing in the evening.[7]

The maintenance of appropriate power relationships between men and women, with men dominant and women subordinate, served as a symbol of the proper functioning of society as a whole. Disorder in the proper gender hierarchy was linked with social upheaval and was viewed as threatening. Of all the ways in which Renaissance society was hierarchically arranged—social rank, age, level of education, race, occupation—gender was regarded as the most "natural" and therefore the most important to defend.

How did nation-states develop in this period?

The High Middle Ages had witnessed the origins of many of the basic institutions of the modern state. Sheriffs, inquests, juries, circuit judges, professional bureaucracies, and representative assemblies all trace their origins to the twelfth and thirteenth centuries. The linchpin for the development of states, however, was strong monarchy, and during the period of the Hundred Years' War no ruler in western Europe was able to provide effective leadership. The resurgent power of feudal nobilities weakened the centralizing work begun earlier.

Beginning in the fifteenth century, however, rulers utilized aggressive methods to rebuild their governments. First in the regional states of Italy, then in the expanding monarchies of France, England, and Spain, rulers began the work of reducing violence, curbing unruly nobles, and establishing domestic order. They attempted to secure their borders and enhanced the methods of raising revenue.

France

The Black Death and the Hundred Years' War left France drastically depopulated, commercially ruined, and agriculturally weak. Nonetheless, the ruler whom Joan of Arc had seen crowned at Reims, Charles VII (r. 1422–1461), revived the monarchy and France. Charles reconciled the Burgundians and Armagnacs (ahr-muhn-YAKZ), who had been waging civil war for thirty years. By 1453 French armies had expelled the English from French soil except in Calais.

Charles reorganized the royal council, giving increased influence to lawyers and bankers, and strengthened royal finances through taxes on certain products and on land, which remained the Crown's chief sources of income until the Revolution of 1789.

By establishing regular companies of cavalry and archers—recruited, paid, and inspected by the state—Charles created the first permanent royal army anywhere in

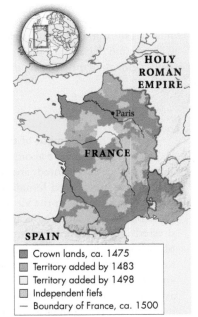

The Expansion of France, 1475–1500

Crown lands, ca. 1475
Territory added by 1483
Territory added by 1498
Independent fiefs
— Boundary of France, ca. 1500

A Gold Coin of Ferdinand and Isabella   This large gold coin, known as the "double excelente," was issued by the Seville mint in 1475, one year after Isabella had become queen in her own right of Castile and Ferdinand had become king because he was her husband. (Ferdinand would become king of Aragon in 1479 when his father died.) The front (right) shows the royal couple both seated on thrones, wearing crowns and holding scepters, conveying the idea that the marriage was the union of two equal rulers. The back (below) depicts an eagle with a halo and their coats of arms, more symbols of power. Minting coins provided a way for Renaissance monarchs to enhance their economies and also to show royal might and communicate other messages.
(© Fitzwilliam Museum/Bridgeman Images)

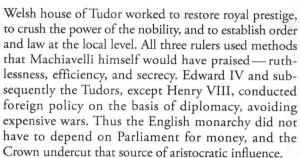

Europe. His son Louis XI (r. 1461–1483) improved upon Charles's army and used it to control the nobles' separate militias and to curb urban independence. The army was also employed in 1477 when Louis conquered Burgundy upon the death of its ruler Charles the Bold. Three years later, the extinction of the house of Anjou with the death of its last legitimate male heir brought Louis the counties of Anjou, Bar, Maine, and Provence.

Two further developments strengthened the French monarchy. The marriage of Louis XII (r. 1498–1515) and Anne of Brittany added the large western duchy of Brittany to the state. Then King Francis I and Pope Leo X reached a mutually satisfactory agreement about church and state powers in 1516. The new treaty, the Concordat of Bologna, approved the pope's right to receive the first year's income of newly named bishops and abbots in France. In return, Leo X recognized the French ruler's right to select French bishops and abbots. French kings thereafter effectively controlled the appointment and thus the policies of church officials in the kingdom.

England

English society also suffered severely from the disorders of the fifteenth century. The aristocracy dominated the government of Henry IV (r. 1399–1413) and indulged in disruptive violence at the local level, fighting one another, seizing wealthy travelers for ransom, and plundering merchant caravans (see "Fur-Collar Crime" in Chapter 11). Population continued to decline. Between 1455 and 1471 adherents of the ducal houses of York and Lancaster contended for control of the Crown in a civil war, commonly called the Wars of the Roses because the symbol of the Yorkists was a white rose and that of the Lancastrians a red one. The chronic disorder hurt trade, agriculture, and domestic industry. Under the pious but mentally disturbed Henry VI (r. 1422–1461), the authority of the monarchy sank lower than it had been in centuries.

The Yorkist Edward IV (r. 1461–1483) began establishing domestic tranquility. He succeeded in defeating the Lancastrian forces and after 1471 began to reconstruct the monarchy. Edward, his brother Richard III (r. 1483–1485), and Henry VII (r. 1485–1509) of the

Welsh house of Tudor worked to restore royal prestige, to crush the power of the nobility, and to establish order and law at the local level. All three rulers used methods that Machiavelli himself would have praised — ruthlessness, efficiency, and secrecy. Edward IV and subsequently the Tudors, except Henry VIII, conducted foreign policy on the basis of diplomacy, avoiding expensive wars. Thus the English monarchy did not have to depend on Parliament for money, and the Crown undercut that source of aristocratic influence.

Henry VII did summon several meetings of Parliament in the early years of his reign, primarily to confirm laws, but the center of royal authority was the royal council, which governed at the national level. Henry VII revealed his distrust of the nobility through his appointments to the council: though not completely excluded, very few great lords were among the king's closest advisers. Instead he chose men from among the smaller landowners and urban residents trained in law. The council conducted negotiations with foreign governments and secured international recognition of the Tudor dynasty through the marriage in 1501 of Henry VII's eldest son, Arthur, to Catherine of Aragon, the daughter of Ferdinand and Isabella of Spain. The council dealt with real or potential aristocratic threats through a judicial offshoot, the Court of Star Chamber, so called because of the stars painted on the ceiling of the room. The court applied methods that were sometimes terrifying: accused persons were not entitled to see evidence against them, sessions were secret, juries were not called, and torture could be applied to extract confessions. These procedures ran directly counter to English common-law precedents, but they effectively reduced aristocratic troublemaking. When Henry VII died in 1509, he left a country at peace both domestically and internationally, a substantially

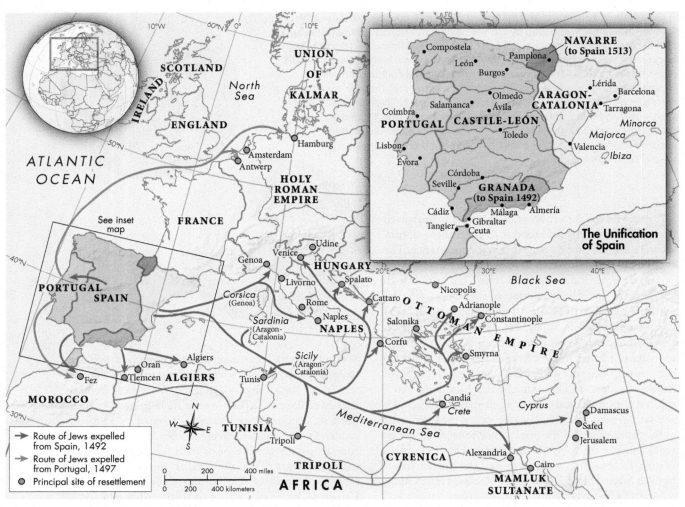

MAP 12.3 **The Unification of Spain and the Expulsion of the Jews, Fifteenth Century** The marriage of Ferdinand of Aragon and Isabella of Castile in 1469 brought most of the Iberian Peninsula under one monarchy, although different parts of Spain retained distinct cultures, languages, and legal systems. In 1492 Ferdinand and Isabella conquered Granada, where most people were Muslim, and expelled the Jews from all of Spain. Spanish Jews resettled in cities of Europe and the Mediterranean that allowed them in, including Muslim states such as the Ottoman Empire. Muslims were also expelled from Spain over the course of the sixteenth and early seventeenth centuries.

augmented treasury, an expanding wool trade, and a Crown with its dignity and role much enhanced.

Spain

While England and France laid the foundations of unified nation-states during the Middle Ages, Spain remained a conglomerate of independent kingdoms. By the middle of the fifteenth century, the kingdoms of Castile and Aragon dominated the weaker Navarre, Portugal, and Granada; and the Iberian Peninsula, with the exception of Granada, had been won for Christianity (Map 12.3). But even the wedding in 1469 of the dynamic and aggressive Isabella of Castile (r. 1474–1504) and the crafty and persistent Ferdinand of Aragon (r. 1479–1516) did not

bring about administrative unity, as each state maintained its own *cortes* (parliament), laws, courts, and systems of coinage and taxation until about 1700. But the two rulers pursued a common foreign policy, and under their heirs Spain became a more unified realm.

Ferdinand and Isabella were able to exert their authority in ways similar to the rulers of France and England. They curbed aristocratic power by excluding high nobles from the royal council, which had full executive, judicial, and legislative powers under the monarchy, instead appointing lesser landowners. The council and various government boards recruited men trained in Roman law, which exalted the power of the Crown. They also secured from the Spanish Borgia pope Alexander VI — Cesare Borgia's father — the right to appoint bishops in Spain and in the Hispanic territories in America, enabling them to establish the equivalent of a national church. With the revenues from ecclesiastical estates, they were able to expand their territories

■ **New Christians** A term for Jews and Muslims in the Iberian Peninsula who accepted Christianity; in many cases they included Christians whose families had converted centuries earlier.

to include the remaining land held by Arabs in southern Spain. The victorious entry of Ferdinand and Isabella into Granada on January 6, 1492, signaled the conclusion of the reconquista (see Map 9.3, page 237). Granada was incorporated into the Spanish kingdom, and after Isabella's death Ferdinand conquered Navarre in the north.

There still remained a sizable and — in the view of the majority of the Spanish people — potentially dangerous minority, the Jews. When the kings of France and England had expelled the Jews from their kingdoms (see "Consequences of the Crusades" in Chapter 9), many had sought refuge in Spain. During the long centuries of the reconquista, Christian kings had recognized Jewish rights and privileges; in fact, Jewish industry, intelligence, and money had supported royal power. While Christians borrowed from Jewish moneylenders and while all who could afford them sought Jewish physicians, a strong undercurrent of resentment of Jewish influence and wealth festered.

In the fourteenth century anti-Semitism in Spain was aggravated by fiery anti-Jewish preaching, by economic dislocation, and by the search for a scapegoat during the Black Death. Anti-Semitic pogroms swept the towns of Spain, and perhaps 40 percent of the Jewish population was killed or forced to convert. Those converted were called *conversos* or **New Christians**. Conversos were often well educated and held prominent positions in government, the church, medicine, law, and business. Numbering perhaps 200,000 in a total Spanish population of about 7.5 million, New Christians and Jews in fifteenth-century Spain exercised influence disproportionate to their numbers.

Such successes bred resentment. Aristocratic grandees resented the conversos' financial independence, the poor hated the converso tax collectors, and churchmen doubted the sincerity of their conversions. Queen Isabella shared these suspicions, and she and Ferdinand had received permission from Pope Sixtus IV in 1478 to establish their own Inquisition to "search out and punish converts from Judaism who had transgressed against Christianity by secretly adhering to Jewish beliefs and performing rites of the Jews."[8] Investigations and trials began immediately, as officials of the Inquisition looked for conversos who showed any sign of incomplete conversion, such as not eating pork, a dietary practice followed by Jews and Muslims.

Recent scholarship has carefully analyzed documents of the Inquisition. Most conversos identified themselves as sincere Christians; many came from families that had received baptism generations before. In response to conversos' statements, officials of the Inquisition developed a new type of anti-Semitism. A person's status as a Jew, they argued, could not be changed by religious conversion, but was in the person's blood and was heritable, so Jews could never be true Christians. In what were known as "purity of blood" laws, having pure Christian blood became a requirement for noble status. Ideas about Jews developed in Spain were important components in European concepts of race, and discussions of "Jewish blood" later expanded into notions of the "Jewish race."

In 1492, shortly after the conquest of Granada, Isabella and Ferdinand issued an edict expelling all practicing Jews from Spain. Of the community of perhaps 200,000 Jews, 150,000 fled. Many Muslims in Granada were forcibly baptized and became another type of New Christian investigated by the Inquisition. Absolute religious orthodoxy and purity of blood served as the theoretical foundation of the Spanish national state.

The Spanish national state rested on marital politics as well as military victories and religious courts. Following their own example, the royal couple made astute marriages for their children with every country that could assist them against France, their most powerful neighbor. In 1496 Ferdinand and Isabella married their second daughter, Joanna, heiress to Castile, to the archduke Philip, heir to the Burgundian Netherlands and the Holy Roman Empire. Philip and Joanna's son Charles V (r. 1519–1556) thus succeeded to a vast inheritance. When Charles's son Philip II joined Portugal to the Spanish Crown in 1580, the Iberian Peninsula was at last politically united.

NOTES

1. James B. Ross and Mary Martin McLaughlin, eds., *The Portable Renaissance Reader* (London: Penguin Books, 1953), p. 27.
2. Ross and McLaughlin, *The Portable Renaissance Reader*, pp. 480–481, 482, 492.
3. Niccolò Machiavelli, *The Prince*, trans. Leo Paul S. de Alvarez (Prospect Heights, Ill.: Waveland Press, 1980), p. 101.
4. Machiavelli, *The Prince*, p. 149.
5. Quoted in F. Seebohm, *The Oxford Reformers* (London: J. M. Dent & Sons, 1867), p. 256.
6. Quoted in Lauro Martines, *Power and Imagination: City-States in Renaissance Italy* (New York: Vintage Books, 1980), p. 253.
7. Stuttgart, Württembergische Hauptstaatsarchiv, Generalreskripta, A38, Bü. 2, 1550; trans. Merry Wiesner-Hanks.
8. Quoted in Benzion Netanyahu, *The Origins of the Inquisition in Fifteenth Century Spain* (New York: Random House, 1995), p. 921.

 ## LOOKING BACK LOOKING AHEAD

The art historian Giorgio Vasari, who first called this era the Renaissance, thought that his contemporaries had both revived the classical past and gone beyond it. Vasari's judgment was echoed for centuries as historians sharply contrasted the art, architecture, educational ideas, social structures, and attitude toward life of the Renaissance with those of the Middle Ages: in this view, whereas the Middle Ages were corporate and religious, the Renaissance was individualistic and secular. More recently, historians and other scholars have stressed continuity as well as change. Families, kin networks, guilds, and other corporate groups remained important in the Renaissance, and religious belief remained firm. This re-evaluation changes our view of the relationship between the Middle Ages and the Renaissance.

It may also change our view of the relationship between the Renaissance and the dramatic changes in religion that occurred in Europe in the sixteenth century. Those religious changes, the Reformation, used to be viewed as a rejection of the values of the Renaissance and a return to the intense concern with religion of the Middle Ages. This idea of the Reformation as a sort of counter-Renaissance may be true to some degree, but there are powerful continuities as well. Both movements looked back to a time that people regarded as purer and better than their own, and both offered opportunities for strong individuals to shape their world in unexpected ways.

Make Connections

Think about the larger developments and continuities within and across chapters.

1. The word *Renaissance*, invented to describe the cultural flowering in Italy that began in the fifteenth century, has often been used for other periods of advances in learning and the arts, such as the "Carolingian Renaissance" that you read about in Chapter 8. Can you think of other, more recent "Renaissances"? How else is the word used today?

2. Many artists in the Renaissance consciously modeled their works on those of ancient Greece (Chapters 3 and 4) and Rome (Chapters 5 and 6). Comparing the art and architecture shown in those chapters with those in this chapter, what similarities do you see? Are there aspects of classical art and architecture that were *not* emulated in the Renaissance? Why do you think this might be?

3. The Renaissance was clearly a period of cultural change for educated men. Given what you have read about women's lives and ideas about women in this and earlier chapters, did women have a Renaissance? (This question was posed first by the historian Joan Kelly in 1977 and remains a topic of great debate.) Why or why not?

12 REVIEW & EXPLORE

Identify Key Terms

Identify and explain the significance of each item below.

Renaissance (p. 326)
patronage (p. 326)
communes (p. 326)
popolo (p. 327)
signori (p. 327)
courts (p. 327)

humanism (p. 331)
virtù (p. 331)
Christian humanists (p. 337)
debate about women (p. 348)
New Christians (p. 353)

Review the Main Ideas

Answer the section heading questions from the chapter.

1. How did political and economic developments in Italy shape the Renaissance? (p. 326)

2. What new ideas were associated with the Renaissance? (p. 330)

3. How did art reflect new Renaissance ideals? (p. 340)

4. What were the key social hierarchies in Renaissance Europe? (p. 347)

5. How did nation-states develop in this period? (p. 350)

Suggested Resources

BOOKS

- Earle, T. F., and K. J. P. Lowe, eds. *Black Africans in Renaissance Europe*. 2005. Includes essays discussing many aspects of ideas about race and the experience of Africans in Europe.

- Eisenstein, Elizabeth. *The Printing Press as an Agent of Change: Communications and Cultural Transformations in Early Modern Europe*. 1979. The definitive study of the impact of printing.

- Ertman, Thomas. *The Birth of Leviathan: Building States and Regimes in Medieval and Early Modern Europe*. 1997. A good introduction to the creation of nation-states.

- Hartt, Frederick, and David Wilkins. *History of Italian Renaissance Art*, 7th ed. 2010. A comprehensive survey of painting, sculpture, and architecture in Italy.

- Heng, Geraldine. *The Invention of Race in the European Middle Ages*. 2018. A survey of medieval ideas about difference.

- Jardine, Lisa. *Worldly Goods: A New History of the Renaissance*. 1998. Discusses changing notions of social status, artistic patronage, and consumer goods.

- Johnson, Geraldine. *Renaissance Art: A Very Short Introduction*. 2005. An excellent brief survey that includes male and female artists, and sets the art in its cultural and historical context.

- King, Ross. *Machiavelli: Philosopher of Power*. 2006. A brief biography that explores Machiavelli's thought in its social and political context.

- Man, John. *Gutenberg Revolution: The Story of a Genius and an Invention That Changed the World*. 2002. Presents a rather idealized view of Gutenberg, but has good discussions of his milieu and excellent illustrations.

- Najemy, John M. *A History of Florence, 1200–1575*. 2008. A comprehensive survey of cultural, political, and social developments, based on the newest research.

- Nauert, Charles. *Humanism and the Culture of Renaissance Europe*, 2d ed. 2006. A thorough introduction to humanism throughout Europe.

- Rummel, Erica. *Desiderius Erasmus*. 2006. An excellent short introduction to Erasmus as a scholar and Christian thinker.

- Waley, Daniel, and Trevor Dean. *The Italian City-Republics*, 4th ed. 2009. Analyzes the rise of independent city-states in northern Italy, including discussion of the artistic and social lives of their inhabitants.

- Wiesner-Hanks, Merry E. *Women and Gender in Early Modern Europe*, 4th ed. 2019. Discusses all aspects of women's lives and ideas about gender.

MEDIA

- *The Agony and the Ecstasy* (Carol Reed, 1965). A classic film highlighting the conflict between Michelangelo and Pope Julius II over the painting of the Sistine Chapel, with Charlton Heston as the artist and Rex Harrison as the pope.

- *The Borgias* (Showtime, 2011). A fictionalized docudrama of the rise of the Borgia family to power in the church and in Italy, with Jeremy Irons as Pope Alexander VI.

- *Dangerous Beauty* (Marshall Herskovitz, 1998). A biographical drama about the life of Veronica Franco, a well-educated courtesan in sixteenth-century Venice, based on the biography of Franco written by Margaret Rosenthal.

- *Heilbrunn Timeline of Art History*. An online chronological, geographical, and thematic exploration of the history of art from around the world, run by the Metropolitan Museum of Art. It includes numerous special topics sections on nearly every aspect of Renaissance art, and also on book production, musical instruments, clothing, household furnishings, and political and economic developments. **www.metmuseum.org/toah/**

- *Leonardo da Vinci* (BBC, 2004). A three-part documentary telling the life story of Leonardo as an artist, inventor, and engineer. Features tests of his designs for the parachute, tank, diving suit, and glider, and an investigation of the *Mona Lisa*.

- *Medici Archive Project*. An online database for researching the nearly 3 million letters held by the archives on the Medici Grand Dukes of Tuscany, who ruled Florence from 1537 to 1743. Includes topical "document highlights" in English and Italian, accompanied by illustrations. **www.medici.org/**

- *The Medici: Godfathers of the Renaissance* (PBS, 2004). A four-part documentary examining the power and patronage of the Medici family, shot on location, with extensive coverage of art and architecture.

13

Reformations and Religious Wars

1500–1600

Calls for reform of the Christian Church began very early in its history. Throughout the centuries, many Christians believed that the early Christian Church represented a golden age, akin to the golden age of the classical past celebrated by Renaissance humanists. When Christianity became the official religion of the Roman Empire in the fourth century, many believers thought that the church had abandoned its original mission, and they called for a return to a church that was not linked to the state. Throughout the Middle Ages, individuals and groups argued that the church had become too wealthy and powerful and urged monasteries, convents, bishoprics, and the papacy to give up their property and focus on service to the poor. Some asserted that basic teachings of the church were not truly Christian and that changes were needed in theology as well as in institutional structures and practices. The Christian humanists of the late fifteenth and early sixteenth centuries such as Erasmus urged reform, primarily through educational and social change. What was new in the sixteenth century was the breadth of acceptance and the ultimate impact of the calls for reform. This acceptance was due not only to religious issues and problems within the church, but also to political and social factors. In 1500 there was one Christian Church in western Europe to which all Christians at least nominally belonged. One hundred years later there were many, a situation that continues today. ■

CHAPTER PREVIEW

- ■ What were the central ideas of the reformers, and why were they appealing to different social groups?

- ■ How did the political situation in Germany shape the course of the Reformation?

- ■ How did Protestant ideas and institutions spread beyond German-speaking lands?

- ■ What reforms did the Catholic Church make, and how did it respond to Protestant reform movements?

- ■ What were the causes and consequences of religious violence, including riots, wars, and witch-hunts?

Religious Violence in the Reformation

This 1590 painting shows Catholic military forces, including friars in their robes, parading through one of the many towns affected by the French religious wars that followed the Reformation. (Musée des Beaux-Arts, Valenciennes, France/Bridgeman Images)

What were the central ideas of the reformers, and why were they appealing to different social groups?

In early-sixteenth-century Europe a wide range of people had grievances with the church. Educated laypeople such as Christian humanists and urban residents, villagers and artisans, and church officials themselves called for reform. This widespread dissatisfaction helps explain why the ideas of Martin Luther, an obscure professor from a new and not very prestigious German university, found a ready audience. Within a decade of his first publishing his ideas (using the new technology of the printing press), much of central Europe and Scandinavia had broken with the Catholic Church, and even more radical concepts of the Christian message were being developed and linked to calls for social change.

The Christian Church in the Early Sixteenth Century

If external religious observances are an indication of conviction, Europeans in the early sixteenth century were deeply pious. People participated in processions, made pilgrimages to the great shrines, and devoted an enormous amount of their time and income to religious causes and organizations. Despite—or perhaps because of—the depth of their piety, many people were also highly critical of the Roman Catholic Church and its clergy. The papal conflict with the German emperor Frederick II in the thirteenth century, followed by the Babylonian Captivity and the Great Schism, badly damaged the prestige of church leaders, and the fifteenth-century popes' concentration on artistic patronage and building up family power did not help matters. Papal tax collection methods were attacked orally and in print. Some criticized the papacy itself as an institution, and even the great wealth and powerful courts of the entire church hierarchy. Some groups and individuals argued that certain doctrines taught by the church, such as the veneration of saints and the centrality of the sacraments, were incorrect. They suggested measures to reform institutions, improve clerical education and behavior, and alter basic doctrines. Occasionally these reform efforts had some success, and in at least one area, Bohemia (the modern-day Czech Republic), they led to the formation of a church independent of Rome a century before Luther (see "Critiques, Divisions, and Councils" in Chapter 11).

In the early sixteenth century court records, bishops' visitations of parishes, and popular songs and printed images show widespread **anticlericalism**, or opposition to the clergy. The critics concentrated primarily on three problems: clerical immorality, clerical ignorance, and clerical pluralism (the practice of holding more than one church office at a time), with the related problem of absenteeism. Many priests, monks, and nuns lived pious lives of devotion, learning, and service and had strong support from the laypeople in their areas, but everyone also knew (and repeated) stories about lecherous monks, lustful nuns, and greedy priests.

In regard to absenteeism and pluralism, many clerics held several benefices, or offices, simultaneously, but they seldom visited the benefices, let alone performed the spiritual responsibilities those offices entailed. Instead, they collected revenues from all of them and hired a poor priest, paying him just a fraction of the income to fulfill the spiritual duties of a particular local church. Many Italian officials in the papal curia, the pope's court in Rome, held benefices in England, Spain, and Germany. Revenues from those countries paid the Italian clerics' salaries, provoking not only charges of absenteeism but also nationalistic resentment aimed at the upper levels of the church hierarchy, which was increasingly viewed as foreign. This was particularly the case in Germany, where the lack of a strong central government to negotiate with the papacy meant that church demands for revenue were especially high.

There was also local resentment of clerical privileges and immunities. Priests, monks, and nuns were exempt from civic responsibilities, such as defending the city and paying taxes. Yet religious orders frequently held large amounts of urban property, in some cities as much as one-third. City governments were increasingly determined to integrate the clergy into civic life by reducing their privileges and giving them public responsibilities. Urban leaders wanted some say in who would be appointed to high church offices, rather than having this decided far away in Rome. This brought city leaders into opposition with bishops and the papacy, which for centuries had stressed the independence of the church from lay control and the distinction between members of the clergy and laypeople.

Martin Luther

By itself, widespread criticism of the church did not lead to the dramatic changes of the sixteenth century. Instead, the personal religious struggle of a

■ **anticlericalism** Opposition to the clergy.

■ **indulgence** A document issued by the Catholic Church lessening penance or time in purgatory, widely believed to bring forgiveness of all sins.

TIMELINE

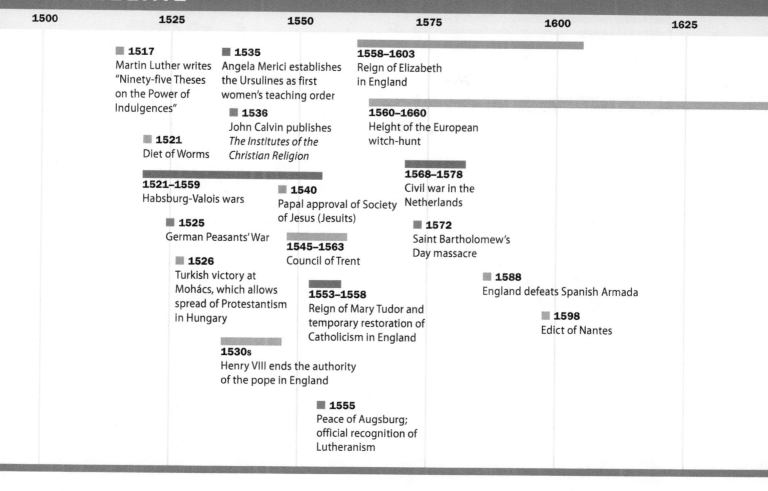

1500   1525   1550   1575   1600   1625

1517
Martin Luther writes "Ninety-five Theses on the Power of Indulgences"

1521
Diet of Worms

1521–1559
Habsburg-Valois wars

1525
German Peasants' War

1526
Turkish victory at Mohács, which allows spread of Protestantism in Hungary

1530s
Henry VIII ends the authority of the pope in England

1535
Angela Merici establishes the Ursulines as first women's teaching order

1536
John Calvin publishes *The Institutes of the Christian Religion*

1540
Papal approval of Society of Jesus (Jesuits)

1545–1563
Council of Trent

1553–1558
Reign of Mary Tudor and temporary restoration of Catholicism in England

1555
Peace of Augsburg; official recognition of Lutheranism

1558–1603
Reign of Elizabeth in England

1560–1660
Height of the European witch-hunt

1568–1578
Civil war in the Netherlands

1572
Saint Bartholomew's Day massacre

1588
England defeats Spanish Armada

1598
Edict of Nantes

German university professor and priest, Martin Luther (1483–1546), propelled the wave of movements we now call the Reformation. Luther's education was intended to prepare him for a legal career. Instead, however, a sense of religious calling led him to join the Augustinian friars, a religious order whose members often preached to, taught, and assisted the poor. (Religious orders were groups whose members took vows and followed a particular set of rules.) Luther was ordained a priest in 1507 and after additional study earned a doctorate of theology. From 1512 until his death in 1546, he served as professor of the Scriptures at the new University of Wittenberg.

Martin Luther was a very conscientious friar, but he was plagued with anxieties about sin and his ability to meet God's demands. Through his study of Saint Paul's letters in the New Testament, he gradually arrived at a new understanding of Christian doctrine. His understanding is often summarized as "faith alone, grace alone, Scripture alone." He believed that salvation and justification come through faith. Faith is a free gift of God's grace, not the result of human effort. God's word is revealed only in the Scriptures, not in the traditions of the church.

At the same time that Luther was engaged in scholarly reflections and professorial lecturing, Pope Leo X authorized the sale of a special Saint Peter's indulgence to finance his building plans in Rome. The archbishop who controlled the area in which Wittenberg was located, Albert of Mainz, was an enthusiastic promoter of this indulgence sale, from which he received a share of the profits.

What exactly was an **indulgence**? According to Catholic theology, individuals who sin could be reconciled to God by confessing their sins to a priest and by doing an assigned penance, such as praying or fasting. But beginning in the twelfth century learned theologians increasingly emphasized the idea of purgatory, a place where souls on their way to Heaven went to make further amends for their earthly sins. Both earthly penance and time in purgatory could be shortened by drawing on what was termed the "treasury of merits," which was a collection of all the virtuous acts that Christ, the apostles, and the saints had done during their lives. People thought of it as a sort of strongbox, like those in which merchants carried coins. An indulgence was a piece of parchment (later, paper), signed by the pope or another church official,

Selling Indulgences   A German single-page pamphlet shows a monk offering an indulgence, with the official seals of the pope attached, as people run to put their money in the box in exchange for his promise of heavenly bliss, symbolized by the dove above his head. Indulgences were sold widely in Germany and became the first Catholic practice that Luther criticized openly. This pamphlet also attacks the sale of indulgences, calling this practice devilish and deceitful, a point of view expressed in the woodcut by the peddler's riding on a donkey, an animal that had long been used as a symbol of ignorance. Indulgences were often printed fill-in-the-blank forms. This indulgence (upper left), purchased in 1521, has space for the indulgence seller's name at the top, the buyer's name in the middle, and the date at the bottom. (pamphlet: ullstein bild/Getty Images; indulgence: bpk, Bildagentur/Art Resource, NY)

that substituted a virtuous act from the treasury of merits for penance or time in purgatory.

Archbishop Albert's indulgence sale, run by a Dominican friar named Johann Tetzel who mounted an advertising blitz, promised that the purchase of indulgences would bring full forgiveness for one's own sins or release from purgatory for a loved one. One of the slogans — "As soon as coin in coffer rings, the soul from purgatory springs" — brought phenomenal success, and people traveled from miles around to buy indulgences.

Luther was severely troubled that many people believed they had no further need for repentance once they had purchased indulgences. In 1517 he wrote a letter to Archbishop Albert on the subject and enclosed in Latin his "Ninety-five Theses on the Power of Indulgences." His argument was that indulgences undermined the seriousness of the sacrament of penance, competed with the preaching of the Gospel, and downplayed the importance of charity in Christian life. After Luther's death, biographies reported that the theses were also nailed to the door of the church at Wittenberg Castle on October 31, 1517. Such an act would have been very strange — they were in Latin and written for those learned in theology, not for ordinary churchgoers — but it has become a standard part of Luther lore.

Whether the theses were posted or not, they were quickly printed, first in Latin and then in German translation. Luther was ordered to come to Rome, although because of the political situation in the empire, he was able instead to engage in formal scholarly debate with a representative of the church, Johann Eck, at Leipzig in 1519. He refused to take back his ideas and continued to develop his calls for reform, publicizing them in a series of pamphlets in which he moved further and further away from Catholic theology. Both popes and church councils could err, he wrote, and secular leaders should reform the church if the pope and clerical hierarchy did not. There was no distinction between clergy and laypeople, and requiring clergy to be celibate was a fruitless attempt to control a natural human drive. Luther clearly understood the power of the new medium of print, so he authorized the publication of his works.

The papacy responded with a letter condemning some of Luther's propositions, ordering that his books be burned, and giving him two months to recant or be excommunicated. Luther retaliated by publicly burning the letter. By 1521, when the excommunication was supposed to become final, Luther's theological issues had become interwoven with public controversies about the church's wealth, power, and basic structure. In this highly charged atmosphere, the twenty-one-year-old emperor Charles V held his first diet (assembly of representatives of the nobility, clergy, and cities of the Holy Roman Empire) in the German city of Worms and summoned Luther to appear. Luther refused to give in to demands that he take back his ideas. "Unless I am convinced by the evidence of Scripture or by plain reason," he said, "I cannot and will not recant anything, for it is neither safe nor right to go against conscience."[1] His appearance at the Diet of Worms in 1521 created an even broader audience for reform ideas, and throughout central Europe other individuals began to preach and publish against the existing doctrines and practices of the church, drawing on the long tradition of calls for change as well as on Luther's teachings.

Protestant Thought

The most important early reformer other than Luther was the Swiss humanist, priest, and admirer of Erasmus, Ulrich Zwingli (ZWIHNG-lee) (1484–1531). Zwingli was convinced that Christian life rested on the Scriptures, which were the pure words of God and the sole basis of religious truth. He went on to attack indulgences, the Mass, the institution of monasticism, and clerical celibacy. In his gradual reform of the church in Zurich, which began in 1519, he had the strong support of the city authorities, who had long resented the privileges of the clergy.

The followers of Luther, Zwingli, and others who called for a break with Rome came to be called Protestants. The word **Protestant** derives from the protest drawn up by a small group of reforming German princes at the Diet of Speyer in 1529. The princes "protested" the decisions of the Catholic majority, and the word gradually became a general term applied to all non-Catholic western European Christians.

Luther, Zwingli, and other early Protestants agreed on many things. First, how is a person to be saved? Traditional Catholic teaching held that salvation is achieved by both faith and good works. Protestants held that salvation comes by faith alone, irrespective of good works or the sacraments. God, not people, initiates salvation. (See "Evaluating Written Evidence: Martin Luther, *On Christian Liberty*," page 362.) Second, where does religious authority reside? Christian doctrine had long maintained that authority rests both in the Bible and in the traditional teaching of the church. For Protestants, authority rested in the Bible alone. For a doctrine or issue to be valid, it had to have a scriptural basis. For this reason, most Protestants rejected Catholic teachings about the sacraments—the rituals that the church had defined as imparting God's benefits on the believer (see "Saints and Sacraments" in Chapter 10)—holding that only baptism and the Eucharist have scriptural support.

Third, what is the church? Protestants held that the church is a spiritual priesthood of all believers, an invisible fellowship not fixed in any place or person, which differed markedly from the Roman Catholic practice of a hierarchical clerical institution headed by the pope in Rome. Fourth, what is the highest form of Christian life? The medieval church had stressed the superiority of the monastic and religious life over the secular. Protestants disagreed and argued that every person should serve God in his or her individual calling.

Protestants did not agree on everything, and one important area of dispute was the ritual of the Eucharist (also called communion, the Lord's Supper, and, in Catholicism, the Mass). Catholicism holds the dogma of transubstantiation: by the consecrating words of the priest during the Mass, the bread and wine become the actual body and blood of Christ. Luther also believed that Christ was really present in the consecrated bread and wine, but he held that this is the result of God's mystery, not the actions of a priest. Zwingli understood the Eucharist as a memorial in which Christ was present in spirit among the faithful, but not in the bread and wine. The Colloquy of Marburg, summoned in 1529 to unite Protestants, failed to resolve these differences, though Protestants reached agreement on almost everything else.

■ **Protestant** The name originally given to followers of Luther, which came to mean all non-Catholic Western Christian groups.

Martin Luther, *On Christian Liberty*

The idea of liberty has a religious as well as political dimension, and the reformer Martin Luther formulated a classic interpretation of liberty in his treatise *On Christian Liberty* (sometimes translated as *On the Freedom of a Christian*), arguably his finest piece. Written in Latin for the pope but translated immediately into German and published widely, it contains the main themes of Luther's theology: the importance of faith, the relationship between Christian faith and good works, the dual nature of human beings, and the fundamental importance of the Scriptures.

∽

A Christian man is the most free lord of all, and subject to none; a Christian man is the most dutiful servant of all, and subject to everyone. Although these statements appear contradictory, yet, when they are found to agree together, they will do excellently for my purpose. They are both the statements of Paul himself, who says, "Though I be free from all men, yet have I made myself a servant unto all" (I Corinthians 9:19) and "Owe no man anything but to love one another" (Romans 13:8). Now love is by its own nature dutiful and obedient to the beloved object. Thus even Christ, though Lord of all things, was yet made of a woman; made under the law; at once free and a servant; at once in the form of God and in the form of a servant.

Let us examine the subject on a deeper and less simple principle. Man is composed of a twofold nature, a spiritual and a bodily. As regards the spiritual nature, which they name the soul, he is called the spiritual, inward, new man; as regards the bodily nature, which they name the flesh, he is called the fleshly, outward, old man. . . .

We first approach the subject of the inward man, that we may see by what means a man becomes justified, free, and a true Christian; that is, a spiritual, new, and inward man. It is certain that absolutely none among outward things, under whatever name they may be reckoned, has any influence in producing Christian righteousness or liberty, nor, on the other hand, unrighteousness or slavery. This can be shown by an easy argument. What can it profit to the soul that the body should be in good condition, free, and full of life, that it should eat, drink, and act according to its pleasure, when even the most impious slaves of every kind of vice are prosperous in these matters? Again, what harm can ill health, bondage, hunger, thirst, or any other outward evil, do to the soul, when even the most pious of men, and the freest in the purity of their conscience, are harassed by these things? Neither of these states of things has to do with the liberty or the slavery of the soul. . . .

One thing, and one alone, is necessary for life, justification, and Christian liberty; and that is the most Holy Word of God, the Gospel of Christ, as He says, "I am the resurrection and the life; he that believeth in me shall not die eternally" (John 9:25), and also, "If the Son shall make you free, ye shall be free indeed" (John 8:36), and "Man shall not live by bread alone, but by every word that proceedeth out of the mouth of God" (Matthew 4:4).

Let us therefore hold it for certain and firmly established that the soul can do without everything except the Word of God, without which none at all of its wants is provided for. But, having the Word, it is rich and wants for nothing, since that is the Word of life, of truth, of light, of peace, of justification, of salvation, of joy, of liberty, of wisdom, of virtue, of grace, of glory, and of every good thing. . . .

But you will ask, "What is this Word, and by what means is it to be used, since there are so many words of God?" I answer, "The Apostle Paul (Romans 1) explains what it is, namely the Gospel of God, concerning His Son, incarnate, suffering, risen, and glorified through the Spirit, the Sanctifier." To preach Christ is to feed the soul, to justify it, to set it free, and to save it, if it believes the preaching. For faith alone, and the efficacious use of the Word of God, bring salvation. "If thou shalt confess with thy mouth the Lord Jesus, and shalt believe in thine heart that God hath raised Him from the dead, thou shalt be saved" (Romans 9:9); . . . and "The just shall live by faith" (Romans 1:17). . . .

And since it [faith] alone justifies, it is evident that by no outward work or labour can the inward man be at all justified, made free, and saved; and that no works whatever have any relation to him. . . . Therefore the first care of every Christian ought to be to lay aside all reliance on works, and strengthen his faith alone more and more, and by it grow in knowledge, not of works, but of Christ Jesus, who has suffered and risen again for him, as Peter teaches (I Peter 5).

EVALUATE THE EVIDENCE

1. What did Luther mean by liberty?
2. Why, for Luther, were the Scriptures basic to Christian life?
3. For Luther, how were Christians made free?

Source: *Luther's Primary Works*, ed. H. Wace and C. A. Buchheim (London: Hodder and Stoughton, 1896), pp. 256–259.

The Appeal of Protestant Ideas

Pulpits and printing presses spread the Protestant message all over Germany, and by the middle of the sixteenth century people of all social classes had rejected Catholic teachings and had become Protestant. What was the immense appeal of Luther's religious ideas and those of other Protestants?

Educated people and many humanists were much attracted by Luther's teachings. He advocated a simpler personal religion based on faith, a return to the spirit of the early church, the centrality of the Scriptures in the liturgy and in Christian life, and the abolition of elaborate ceremonies — precisely the reforms the Christian humanists had been calling for. The Protestant insistence that everyone should read and reflect on the Scriptures attracted literate and thoughtful city residents. This included many priests and monks who left the Catholic Church to become clergy in the new Protestant churches. In addition, townspeople who envied the church's wealth and resented paying for it were attracted by the notion that the clergy should also pay taxes and should not have special legal privileges.

Scholars in many disciplines have attributed Luther's fame and success to the invention of the printing press, which rapidly reproduced and made known his ideas. Many printed works included woodcuts and other illustrations, so that even those who could not read could grasp the main ideas. Equally important was Luther's incredible skill with language, as seen in his two catechisms (compendiums of basic religious knowledge) and in hymns that he wrote for congregations to sing. Luther's linguistic skill, together with his translation of the New Testament into German in 1523, led to the acceptance of his dialect of German as the standard written version of the German language.

Both Luther and Zwingli recognized that for reforms to be permanent, political authorities as well as concerned individuals and religious leaders would have to accept them. Zwingli worked closely with the city council of Zurich, and city councils themselves took the lead in other cities and towns of Switzerland and south Germany. They appointed pastors who they knew had accepted Protestant ideas, required them to swear an oath of loyalty to the council, and oversaw their preaching and teaching.

Luther lived in a territory ruled by a noble — the elector of Saxony — and he also worked closely with political authorities, viewing them as fully justified in asserting control over the church in their territories.

The Four Apostles   Albrecht Dürer, the most prominent artist north of the Alps, painted these panels of the four apostles (John, Peter, Paul, and Mark) in 1526 and gave them to the city of Nuremberg, where he lived and worked. Like many cities in Germany, Nuremberg had become officially Protestant, and paintings such as this that emphasized biblical figures and books rather than saints and miracles were appealing to city leaders. Whether Dürer himself had officially left the Catholic Church is not clear, but his letters indicate that he had Protestant sympathies, and he had contacts with many Christian humanists and reformers. (PHAS/Universal Images Group/Getty Images)

Indeed, he demanded that German rulers reform the papacy and its institutions, and he instructed all Christians to obey their secular rulers, whom he saw as divinely ordained to maintain order. Individuals may have been convinced of the truth of Protestant teachings by hearing sermons, listening to hymns, or reading pamphlets, but a territory became Protestant when its ruler, whether a noble or a city council, brought in a reformer or two to re-educate the territory's clergy, sponsored public sermons, and confiscated church property. This happened in many of the states of the Holy Roman Empire during the 1520s.

The Radical Reformation and the German Peasants' War

While Luther and Zwingli worked with political authorities, some individuals and groups rejected the idea that church and state needed to be united. Beginning in the 1520s groups in Switzerland, Germany, and the Netherlands sought instead to create a voluntary community of believers separate from the state, as they understood it to have existed in New Testament times. In terms of theology and spiritual practices, these individuals and groups varied widely, though they are generally termed "radicals" for their insistence on a more extensive break with prevailing ideas. Some adopted the baptism of adult believers, for which they were called by their enemies "Anabaptists," which means "rebaptizers." (Early Christians had practiced adult baptism, but infant baptism became the norm, which meant that adults undergoing baptism were repeating the ritual.) Some groups attempted communal ownership of property, living very simply and rejecting anything they thought unbiblical. Some reacted harshly to members who deviated, but others argued for complete religious toleration and individualism.

The radicals' unwillingness to accept a state church marked them as societal outcasts and invited hatred and persecution, for both Protestant and Catholic authorities saw a state church as key to maintaining order. Anabaptists and other radicals were banished or cruelly executed by burning, beating, or drowning. (See "Individuals in Society: Anna Jansz of Rotterdam," page 365.) Their community spirit and heroism in the face of martyrdom, however, contributed to the survival of radical ideas. The opposition to the "establishment of religion" (state churches) in the U.S. Constitution is, in part, an outgrowth of the ideas of the radicals of the sixteenth century.

Radical reformers sometimes called for social as well as religious change, a message that resonated with the increasingly struggling German peasantry. In the early sixteenth century the economic condition of the peasantry varied from place to place but was generally worse than it had been in the fifteenth century and was deteriorating. Crop failures in 1523 and 1524 aggravated an explosive situation. Nobles had aggrieved peasants by seizing village common lands, by imposing new rents and requiring additional services, and by taking the peasants' best horses or cows whenever a head of household died. The peasants made demands that they believed conformed to the Scriptures, and they cited radical thinkers as well as Luther as proof that they did.

Initially Luther sided with the peasants, blasting the lords for robbing their subjects. But when rebellion broke out, peasants who expected Luther's support were soon disillusioned. Freedom for Luther meant independence from the authority of the Roman Church; it did not mean opposition to legally established secular powers. He maintained that the Scriptures had nothing to do with earthly justice or material gain, a position that Zwingli supported. Firmly convinced that rebellion would hasten the end of civilized society, Luther wrote the tract *Against the Murderous, Thieving Hordes of the Peasants*: "Let everyone who can smite, slay, and stab [the peasants], secretly and openly, remembering that nothing can be more poisonous, hurtful or devilish than a rebel."[2] The nobility ferociously crushed the revolt. Historians estimate that more than seventy-five thousand peasants were killed in 1525.

The German Peasants' War of 1525 greatly strengthened the authority of lay rulers. Not surprisingly, the Reformation lost much of its popular appeal after 1525, though peasants and urban rebels sometimes found a place for their social and religious ideas in radical groups. Peasants' economic conditions did moderately improve, however. For example, in many parts of Germany, enclosed fields, meadows, and forests were returned to common use.

Marriage, Sexuality, and the Role of Women

Luther and Zwingli both believed that a priest's or nun's vows of celibacy went against human nature and God's commandments, and that marriage brought spiritual advantages and so was the ideal state for nearly all human beings. Luther married a former nun, Katharina von Bora (1499–1532), and Zwingli married a Zurich widow, Anna Reinhart (1491–1538). Both women quickly had several children. Most other Protestant reformers also married, and their wives had to create a new and respectable role for themselves — pastor's wife — to overcome being viewed as simply a new type of priest's concubine. They were living demonstrations of their husband's convictions about the superiority of marriage to celibacy, and they were expected to be models of wifely obedience and Christian charity.

Anna Jansz (1509–1539) was born into a well-to-do family in the small city of Briel in the Netherlands. She married, and when she was in her early twenties she and her husband came to accept Anabaptism after listening to a traveling preacher. They were baptized in 1534 and became part of a group who believed that God would soon come to bring judgment on the wicked and deliver his true followers. Jansz wrote a hymn conveying these apocalyptic beliefs and foretelling vengeance on those who persecuted Anabaptists: "I hear the Trumpet sounding, From far off I hear her blast! . . . O murderous seed, what will you do? Offspring of Cain, you put to death The lambs of the Lord, without just cause — It will be doubly repaid to you! Death now comes riding on horseback, We have seen your fate! The sword is passing over the land, With which you will be killed and slain, And you will not escape from Hell!"

An etching of Anna Jansz on the way to her execution, from a 1685 Anabaptist martyrology. (Used by permission of the Mennonite Historical Library, Goshen College, Indiana)

designed to inspire deeper faith. One of the most widely read of these describes Jansz on her way to the execution. She offered a certain amount of money to anyone who would care for her son; a poor baker with six children agreed, and she passed the child to him. The martyrology reports that the baker later became quite wealthy, and that her son, Isaiah, became mayor of the city of Rotterdam. As such, he would have easily been able to read the court records of his mother's trial.

Anna Jansz was one of thousands of people executed for their religious beliefs in sixteenth-century Europe. A few of these were high-profile individuals such as Thomas More, the Catholic former chancellor of England executed by King Henry VIII, but most were quite ordinary people. Many were women. Women's and men's experiences of martyrdom were similar in many ways, but women

Jansz and her husband traveled to England, where she had a child, but in November 1538 she and her infant son, Isaiah, returned to the Netherlands, along with another woman. As the story was later told, the two women were recognized as Anabaptists by another traveler because of songs they were singing, perhaps her "Trumpet Song" among them. They were arrested and interrogated in the city of Rotterdam, and sentenced to death by drowning. The day she was executed — January 24, 1539 — Anna Jansz wrote a long testament to her son, providing him with spiritual advice: "My son, hear the instruction of your mother, and open your ears to hear the words of my mouth. Watch, today I am travelling the path of the Prophets, Apostles, and Martyrs, and drink from the cup from which they have all tasted. . . . But if you hear of the existence of a poor, lowly, cast-out little company, that has been despised and rejected by the World, go join it. . . . Honor the Lord through the works of your hands. Let the light of Scripture shine in you. Love your Neighbor; with an effusive, passionate heart deal your bread to the hungry."

Anabaptists later compiled accounts of trials and executions, along with letters and other records, into martyrologies

also confronted additional challenges. Some were pregnant while in prison — execution was delayed until the baby was born — or, like Jansz, had infants with them. They faced procedures of questioning, torture, and execution that brought dishonor as well as pain. Eventually many Anabaptists, as well as others whose religion put them in opposition to their rulers, migrated to parts of Europe that were more tolerant. By the seventeenth century the Netherlands had become one of the most tolerant places in Europe, and Rotterdam was no longer the site of executions for religious reasons.

QUESTIONS FOR ANALYSIS

1. How did religion, gender, and social class all shape Jansz's experiences and the writings that she left behind?
2. Why might Jansz's hymn and her Anabaptist beliefs have seemed threatening to those who did not share her beliefs?

Source: Quotations from *Elisabeth's Manly Courage: Testimonials and Songs of Martyred Anabaptist Women in the Low Countries*, ed. and trans. Hermina Joldersma and Louis Peter Grijp (Milwaukee: Marquette University Press, 2001).

Martin Luther and Katharina von Bora   Lucas Cranach the Elder painted this double marriage portrait to celebrate Luther's wedding in 1525 to Katharina von Bora, a former nun. The artist was one of the witnesses at the wedding and, in fact, had presented Luther's marriage proposal to Katharina. Using a go-between for proposals was very common, as was having a double wedding portrait painted. This particular couple quickly became a model of the ideal marriage, and many churches wanted their portraits. More than sixty similar paintings, with slight variations, were produced by Cranach's workshop and hung in churches and wealthy homes. (Galleria degli Uffizi, Florence, Italy/Bridgeman Images)

Though they denied that marriage was a sacrament, Protestant reformers stressed that it had been ordained by God when he presented Eve to Adam, served as a "remedy" for the unavoidable sin of lust, provided a site for the pious rearing of the next generation of God-fearing Christians, and offered husbands and wives companionship and consolation. A proper marriage was one that reflected both the spiritual equality of men and women and the proper social hierarchy of husbandly authority and wifely obedience.

Protestants did not break with medieval Scholastic theologians in their idea that women were to be subject to men. Women were advised to be cheerful rather than grudging in their obedience, for in doing so they demonstrated their willingness to follow God's plan. Men were urged to treat their wives kindly and considerately, but also to enforce their authority, through physical coercion if necessary. European marriage manuals used the metaphor of breaking a horse for teaching a wife obedience, though laws did set limits on the husband's power to do so.

Most Protestants came to allow divorce and remarriage for marriages that were irretrievably broken.

Protestant allowance of divorce differed markedly from Catholic doctrine, which viewed marriage as a sacramental union that, if validly entered into, could not be dissolved (Catholic canon law allowed only separation with no remarriage). Although permitting divorce was a dramatic legal change, it did not have a dramatic impact on newly Protestant areas. Because marriage was the cornerstone of society socially and economically, divorce was a desperate last resort. In many Protestant jurisdictions the annual divorce rate hovered around 0.02 to 0.06 per thousand people. (By contrast, in 2016 the U.S. divorce rate was 3.2 per thousand people.)

As Protestants believed marriage was the only proper remedy for lust, they uniformly condemned prostitution. The licensed brothels that were a common feature of late medieval urban life (see "Sex in the City" in Chapter 11) were closed in Protestant cities, and harsh punishments were set for prostitution. Many Catholic cities soon closed their brothels as well, although Italian cities favored stricter regulations rather than closure. Selling sex was couched in moral rather than economic terms, as simply one type of "whoredom," a term that also included premarital sex, adultery, and other unacceptable sexual activities. *Whore* was also a term that reformers used for their theological opponents; Protestants compared the pope to the biblical whore of Babylon, a symbol of the end of the world, while Catholics called Luther's wife a whore because she had first been married to Christ as a nun before her marriage to Luther. Closing brothels did not end the exchange of sex for money, of course, but simply reshaped it. Smaller illegal brothels were established, or women selling sex moved to areas right outside city walls.

The Protestant Reformation raised the status of marriage in people's minds, but its impact on women was more mixed. Many nuns were in convents not out of a strong sense of religious calling, but because their parents placed them there. Convents nevertheless provided women of the upper classes with an opportunity to use their literary, artistic, medical, or administrative talents if they could not or would not marry. The Reformation generally brought the closing of monasteries and convents, and marriage became virtually the only occupation for upper-class Protestant women. Women

in some convents recognized this and fought the Reformation, or argued that they could still be pious Protestants within convent walls. Most nuns left, however, and we do not know what happened to them. The Protestant emphasis on marriage made unmarried women (and men) suspect, for they did not belong to the type of household regarded as the cornerstone of a proper, godly society.

A few women took Luther's idea about the priesthood of all believers to heart and wrote religious works. Argula von Grumbach, a German noblewoman, supported Protestant ideas in print, asserting, "I am not unfamiliar with Paul's words that women should be silent in church but when I see that no man will or can speak, I am driven by the word of God when he said, he who confesses me on earth, him will I confess, and he who denies me, him will I deny."[3] No sixteenth-century Protestants allowed women to be members of the clergy, however, though monarchs such as Elizabeth I of England and female territorial rulers of the states of the Holy Roman Empire did determine religious policies just as male rulers did.

How did the political situation in Germany shape the course of the Reformation?

Although criticism of the church was widespread in Europe in the early sixteenth century, reform movements could be more easily squelched by the strong central governments that had evolved in Spain and France. England, too, had a strong monarchy, but the king broke from the Catholic Church for other reasons (see "Henry VIII and the Reformation in England" later in this chapter). The Holy Roman Empire, in contrast, included hundreds of largely independent states. Against this background of decentralization and strong local power, Martin Luther had launched a movement to reform the church. Two years after he published the "Ninety-five Theses," the electors of the Holy Roman Empire chose as emperor a nineteen-year-old Habsburg prince who ruled as Charles V (r. 1519–1556). The course of the Reformation was shaped by this election and by the political relationships surrounding it.

The Rise of the Habsburg Dynasty

War and diplomacy were important ways that states increased their power in sixteenth-century Europe, but so was marriage. Royal and noble sons and daughters were important tools of state policy. The

benefits of an advantageous marriage stretched across generations, a process that can be seen most dramatically with the Habsburgs. The Holy Roman emperor Frederick III, a Habsburg who was the ruler of most of Austria, acquired only a small amount of territory—but a great deal of money—with his marriage to Princess Eleonore of Portugal in 1452. He arranged for his son Maximilian to marry Europe's most prominent heiress, Mary of Burgundy, in 1477; she inherited the Netherlands, Luxembourg, and the County of Burgundy in what is now eastern France. Through this union with the rich and powerful duchy of Burgundy, the Austrian house of Habsburg, already the strongest ruling family in the empire, became an international power. The marriage of Maximilian and Mary angered the French, however, who considered Burgundy French territory, and inaugurated centuries of conflict between the Austrian house of Habsburg and the kings of France.

Maximilian learned the lesson of marital politics well, marrying his son and daughter to the children of Ferdinand and Isabella, the rulers of Spain, much of southern Italy, and eventually the Spanish New World empire. His grandson Charles V fell heir to a vast and incredibly diverse collection of states and peoples, each governed in a different manner and held together only by the person of the emperor (Map 13.1). Charles, raised in the Netherlands but spending much of his later life in Spain, remained a Catholic and was convinced that it was his duty to maintain the political and religious unity of Western Christendom.

Religious Wars in Switzerland and Germany

In the sixteenth century the practice of religion remained a public matter. The ruler determined the official form of religious practice in his (or occasionally her) jurisdiction. Almost everyone believed that the presence of a faith different from that of the majority represented a political threat to the security of the state, and few believed in religious liberty.

Luther's ideas appealed to German rulers for a variety of reasons. Though Germany was not a nation, people did have an understanding of being German because of their language and traditions. Luther frequently used the phrase "we Germans" in his attacks on the papacy. Luther's appeal to national feeling influenced many rulers otherwise confused by or indifferent to the complexities of the religious matters of the time. Some German rulers were sincerely attracted to Lutheran ideas, but material considerations swayed many others to embrace the new faith. The rejection of Roman Catholicism and adoption of Protestantism would mean the legal confiscation of lush farmlands, rich monasteries, and wealthy shrines. Thus many political authorities in the empire became Protestant in part to extend their financial and political power and to enhance their independence from the emperor.

MAP 13.1 The Global Empire of Charles V, ca. 1556 Charles V exercised theoretical jurisdiction over more European territory than anyone since Charlemagne. He also claimed authority over large parts of North and South America, though actual Spanish control was weak in much of the area.

Charles V was a vigorous defender of Catholicism, so it is not surprising that the Reformation led to religious wars. The first battleground was Switzerland, which was officially part of the Holy Roman Empire, though it was really a loose confederation of thirteen largely autonomous territories called cantons. Some cantons remained Catholic, and some became Protestant, and in the late 1520s the two sides went to war. Zwingli was killed on the battlefield in 1531, and both sides quickly decided that a treaty was preferable to further fighting. The treaty basically allowed each canton to determine its own religion and ordered each side to give up its foreign alliances, a policy of neutrality that has been characteristic of modern Switzerland.

Trying to halt the spread of religious division, Charles V called an Imperial Diet in 1530, to meet at Augsburg. The Lutherans developed a statement of faith, later called the Augsburg Confession, and the Protestant princes presented this to the emperor. (The Augsburg Confession remains an authoritative statement of belief for many Lutheran churches.) Charles refused to accept it and ordered all Protestants to return to the Catholic Church and give up any confiscated church property. This demand backfired, and Protestant territories in the empire—mostly northern German principalities and southern German cities—formed a military alliance. The emperor could not respond militarily, as he

was in the midst of a series of wars with the French: the Habsburg-Valois wars (1521–1559). The Ottoman Turks had also taken much of Hungary and in 1529 were besieging Vienna.

The 1530s and early 1540s saw complicated political maneuvering among many of the powers of Europe. Various attempts were made to heal the religious split with a church council, but stubbornness on both sides made it increasingly clear that this would not be possible and that war was inevitable. Charles V realized that he was fighting not only for religious unity, but also for a more unified state, against territorial rulers who wanted to maintain their independence. He was thus defending both church and empire.

Fighting began in Germany in 1546, and initially the emperor was very successful. This success alarmed both France and the pope, however, who did not want Charles to become even more powerful. The pope withdrew papal troops, and the Catholic king of France sent money and troops to the Lutheran princes. Finally, in 1555 Charles and a military league of German princes and cities agreed to the Peace of Augsburg, which officially recognized Lutheranism. The political authority in each territory within the Holy Roman Empire was permitted to decide whether the territory would be Catholic or Lutheran. Most of northern and central Germany became Lutheran, while the south remained

Swiss and German Mercenary Soldiers in Combat   In this engraving from the 1520s by Hans Holbein the Younger, foot soldiers wield pikes, swords, and halberds in a disorganized way in fierce hand-to-hand combat that contemporaries called "bad war." Holbein, who would later become famous as a portrait painter of English royalty and nobles, was living in Switzerland at the time and was an eyewitness to religious violence. Units of trained Swiss pikemen, organized by their cantons, were hired by all sides in the political and religious wars of the sixteenth century because they were fearless and effective. Switzerland continued to export mercenaries until the nineteenth century. (De Agostini Picture Library/Getty Images)

Roman Catholic. There was no freedom of religion within the territories, however. Princes or town councils established state churches to which all subjects of the area had to belong, and those who disagreed had to convert or leave. Religious refugees became a common feature on the roads of the empire, and eventually in other parts of Europe as well. Every political authority in Christian Europe developed a policy of religious uniformity, although there were also examples of coexistence and toleration. Particularly where those

of different confessions lived fairly close to one another, ordinary people developed pragmatic arrangements for getting along, maintaining existing social and economic ties despite religious differences.

The Peace of Augsburg ended religious war in Germany for many decades. His hope of uniting his empire under a single church dashed, Charles V abdicated in 1556 and moved to a monastery, transferring power over his holdings in Spain and the Netherlands to his son Philip and his imperial power to his brother Ferdinand.

How did Protestant ideas and institutions spread beyond German-speaking lands?

States within the Holy Roman Empire were the earliest territories to accept the Protestant Reformation, but by the later 1520s and 1530s religious change came to Denmark-Norway, Sweden, England, France, and eastern Europe. In most of these areas, a second generation of reformers, the most important of whom was John Calvin, built on Lutheran and Zwinglian ideas to develop their own theology and plans for institutional change.

Scandinavia

The first area outside the empire to officially accept the Reformation was the kingdom of Denmark-Norway under King Christian III (r. 1536–1559). Danish scholars studied at the University of Wittenberg, and Lutheran ideas spread into Denmark very quickly. In the 1530s the king officially broke with the Catholic Church, and most clergy followed. The process went smoothly in Denmark, but in northern Norway and Iceland (which Christian also ruled) there were violent reactions, and Lutheranism was only gradually imposed on a largely unwilling populace.

In Sweden, Gustavus Vasa (r. 1523–1560), who came to the throne during a civil war with Denmark, also took over control of church personnel and income. Protestant ideas spread, though the Swedish Church did not officially accept Lutheran theology until later in the century.

Henry VIII and the Reformation in England

As on the continent, the Reformation in England had economic and political as well as religious causes. The impetus for England's break with Rome was the desire of King Henry VIII (r. 1509–1547) for a new wife, though his own motives also included political, social, and economic elements.

Henry VIII was married to Catherine of Aragon, the daughter of Ferdinand and Isabella and widow of

Henry's older brother, Arthur. Marriage to a brother's widow went against canon law, and Henry had been required to obtain a special papal dispensation to marry Catherine. The marriage had produced only one living heir, a daughter, Mary. By 1527 Henry decided that God was showing his displeasure with the marriage by denying him a son, and he appealed to the pope to have the marriage annulled. He was also in love with a court lady in waiting, Anne Boleyn, and assumed that she would give him the son he wanted. Normally an annulment would not have been a problem, but the troops of Emperor Charles V were in Rome at that point, and Pope Clement VII was essentially their prisoner. Charles V was the nephew of Catherine of Aragon and thus was vigorously opposed to an annulment.

With Rome thwarting his matrimonial plans, Henry decided to remove the English Church from papal jurisdiction. In a series of measures during the 1530s, Henry used Parliament to end the authority of the pope and make himself the supreme head of the church in England. Some opposed the king and were beheaded, among them Thomas More, the king's chancellor and author of *Utopia* (see "Christian Humanism" in Chapter 12). When Anne Boleyn failed twice to produce a male child, Henry VIII charged her with adulterous incest and in 1536 had her beheaded. His third wife, Jane Seymour, gave Henry the desired son, Edward, but she died a few days after childbirth. Henry went on to three more wives.

Theologically, Henry was conservative, and the English Church retained such traditional Catholic practices and doctrines as confession, clerical celibacy, and transubstantiation. Under the influence of his chief minister, Thomas Cromwell, and the man he had appointed archbishop of Canterbury, Thomas Cranmer, he did agree to place an English Bible in every church. He also decided to dissolve the English monasteries, primarily because he wanted their wealth. Working through Parliament, between 1535 and 1539 the king ended nine hundred years of English monastic life, dispersing the monks and nuns and confiscating their lands. Hundreds of properties went first into the royal treasury and then were sold to the middle and upper classes, which tied them to both the Tudor dynasty and the new Protestant Church.

The nationalization of the church and the dissolution of the monasteries led to important changes in government administration. Vast tracts of formerly monastic land came temporarily under the Crown's jurisdiction, and new bureaucratic machinery had to be developed to manage those properties. Cromwell reformed and centralized the king's household, the council, the secretariats, and the Exchequer. New departments of state were set up. Surplus funds from all departments went into a liquid fund to be applied to areas where there were deficits. This balancing resulted in greater efficiency and economy, and Henry VIII's reign saw the growth of the modern centralized bureaucratic state.

Did the religious changes under Henry VIII have broad popular support? Historians disagree about this. Some English people had been dissatisfied with the existing Christian Church before Henry's measures, and Protestant literature circulated. Traditional Catholicism exerted an enormously strong and vigorous hold over the imagination and loyalty of the people, however. Most clergy and officials accepted Henry's moves, but all did not quietly acquiesce. In 1536 popular opposition in the north to the religious changes led to the Pilgrimage of Grace, a massive rebellion that proved the most serious uprising in Tudor history. The "pilgrims" accepted a truce, but their leaders were arrested, tried, and executed. Recent scholarship points out that people rarely "converted" from Catholicism to Protestantism overnight. People responded to an action of the Crown that was played out in their own neighborhood — the closing of a monastery, the ending of Masses for the dead — with a combination of resistance, acceptance, and collaboration. Some enthusiastically changed to Protestant forms of prayer, for example, while others recited Protestant prayers in church while keeping pictures of the Catholic saints at home.

Loyalty to the Catholic Church was particularly strong in Ireland. Ireland had been claimed by English kings since the twelfth century, but in reality the English had firm control of only the area around Dublin, known as the Pale. In 1536, on orders from London, the Irish Parliament, which represented only the English landlords and the people of the Pale, approved the English laws severing the church from Rome. The Church of Ireland was established on the English pattern, and the (English) ruling class adopted the new reformed faith. Most of the Irish people remained Roman Catholic, thus adding religious antagonism to the ethnic hostility that had been a feature of English policy toward Ireland for centuries (see "Ethnic Tensions and Restrictions" in Chapter 11). The Roman Church was essentially driven underground, and the Catholic clergy acted as national as well as religious leaders.

Upholding Protestantism in England

In the short reign of Henry's sickly son, Edward VI (r. 1547–1553), Protestant ideas exerted a significant influence on the religious life of the country. Archbishop Thomas Cranmer simplified the liturgy, invited Protestant theologians to England, and prepared the first *Book of Common Prayer* (1549), a book of services and prayers, which was later approved by Parliament.

The equally brief reign of Mary Tudor (r. 1553–1558) witnessed a sharp move back to Catholicism. The devoutly Catholic daughter of Catherine of Aragon, Mary rescinded the Reformation legislation of her father's reign and restored Roman Catholicism. Mary's marriage to her cousin Philip II of Spain (r. 1556–1598), son of the emperor Charles V, proved highly unpopular in England, and her execution of several hundred Protestants further alienated her subjects. During her reign, about a thousand Protestants fled to the continent. Mary's death raised to the throne her half-sister Elizabeth, Henry's daughter with Anne Boleyn, who had been raised a Protestant. Elizabeth's reign from 1558 to 1603 inaugurated the beginnings of religious stability.

At the start of Elizabeth's reign, sharp religious differences existed in England. On the one hand, Catholics wanted a Roman Catholic ruler. On the other hand, a vocal number of returning exiles wanted all Catholic elements in the Church of England eliminated. The latter, because they wanted to "purify" the church, were called "Puritans."

Shrewdly, Elizabeth chose a middle course between Catholic and Puritan extremes. Working through Parliament, she ordered church and government officials to swear that she was supreme in matters of religion as well as politics, required her subjects to attend services in the Church of England or risk a fine, and called for frequent preaching and promotion of Protestant ideas. (See "Evaluating Visual Evidence: Lucas de Heere, *Allegory of the Tudor Succession*, 1572," page 373.) She did not interfere with people's privately held beliefs, however. As she put it, she did not "want to make windows into men's souls." The Anglican Church, as the Church of England was called, moved in a moderately Protestant direction. Services were conducted in English, monasteries were not re-established, and clergymen were allowed to marry. But the church remained hierarchical, with archbishops and bishops, and services continued to be elaborate, with the clergy in distinctive robes, in contrast to the simpler services favored by many continental Protestants and English Puritans.

Toward the end of the sixteenth century Elizabeth's reign was threatened by European powers attempting to re-establish Catholicism. Philip II of Spain had hoped that his marriage to Mary Tudor would reunite England with Catholic Europe, but Mary's death ended those plans. Another Mary — Mary, Queen of Scots (r. 1560–1567) — provided a new opportunity. Mary was Elizabeth's cousin, but she was Catholic. Mary was next in

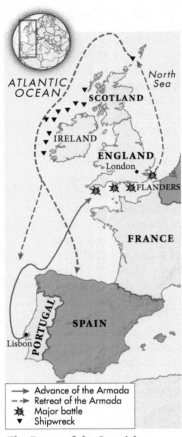

The Route of the Spanish Armada, 1588

→ Advance of the Armada
--→ Retreat of the Armada
✸ Major battle
▼ Shipwreck

line to the English throne, and Elizabeth imprisoned her because she worried — quite rightly — that Mary would become the center of Catholic plots to overthrow her. In 1587 Mary became implicated in a plot to assassinate Elizabeth, a conspiracy that had Philip II's full backing. When the English executed Mary, the Catholic pope urged Philip to retaliate.

Philip prepared a vast fleet to sail from Lisbon to Flanders, where a large army of Spanish troops was stationed because of religious wars in the Netherlands (see "The Netherlands Under Charles V" later in this chapter). The Spanish ships were to escort barges carrying some of the troops across the English Channel to attack England. On May 9, 1588, the **Spanish Armada,** composed of more than 130 vessels, sailed from Lisbon harbor. It met an English fleet in the Channel before it reached Flanders. A combination of storms and squalls, spoiled food and rank water, inadequate Spanish ammunition, and, to a lesser extent, English fire ships that caused the Spanish to scatter gave England the victory. On the journey home many Spanish ships went down in the rough seas around Ireland; perhaps sixty-five ships managed to reach home ports.

The battle in the English Channel has frequently been described as one of the decisive battles in world history. In fact, it had mixed consequences. Spain soon rebuilt its navy, and after 1588 the quality of the Spanish fleet improved. The war between England and Spain dragged on for years. Yet the defeat of the Spanish Armada prevented Philip II from reimposing

Catholicism on England by force. In England the victory contributed to a David and Goliath legend that enhanced English national sentiment.

Calvinism

In 1509, while Luther was preparing for a doctorate at Wittenberg, John Calvin (1509–1564) was born in Noyon in northwestern France. As a young man he studied law, which had a decisive impact on his mind and later his thought. In 1533 he experienced a religious crisis, as a result of which he converted to Protestantism.

Calvin believed that God had specifically selected him to reform the church. Accordingly, he accepted an invitation to assist in the reformation of the city of Geneva. There, beginning in 1541, Calvin worked assiduously to establish a well-disciplined Christian society in which church and state acted together.

To understand Calvin's Geneva, it is necessary to understand Calvin's ideas. These he embodied in ***The Institutes of the Christian Religion***, published first in 1536 and in its final form in 1559. The cornerstone of Calvin's theology was his belief in the absolute sovereignty and omnipotence of God and the total weakness of humanity. Before the infinite power of God, he asserted, men and women are as insignificant as grains of sand.

Calvin did not ascribe free will to human beings because that would detract from the sovereignty of God. Men and women cannot actively work to achieve salvation; rather, God in his infinite wisdom decided at the beginning of time who would be saved and who damned. This viewpoint constitutes the theological principle called **predestination**. Calvin explained his view:

> Predestination we call the eternal decree of God, by which he has determined in himself, what he would have become of every individual. . . . For they are not all created with a similar destiny; but eternal life is foreordained for some, and eternal damnation for others. . . . To those whom he devotes to condemnation, the gate of life is closed by a just and irreprehensible, but incomprehensible, judgment. How exceedingly presumptuous it is only to inquire into the causes of the Divine will; which is in fact, and is justly entitled to be, the cause of everything that exists. . . . For the will of God is the highest justice; so that what he wills must be considered just, for this very reason, because he wills it.[4]

Many people consider the doctrine of predestination, which dates back to Saint Augustine and Saint

■ **Spanish Armada** The fleet sent by Philip II of Spain in 1588 against England as a religious crusade against Protestantism. Weather and the English fleet defeated it.

■ ***The Institutes of the Christian Religion*** Calvin's formulation of Christian doctrine, which became a systematic theology for Protestantism.

■ **predestination** The teaching that God has determined the salvation or damnation of individuals based on his will and purpose, not on their merit or works.

Lucas de Heere, *Allegory of the Tudor Succession*, 1572

In this painting by the Dutch artist Lucas de Heere, King Henry VIII (seated) hands the sword of justice to his Protestant son Edward VI. The Catholic queen Mary and her husband, King Philip of Spain, stand at the left, followed by Mars, the god of war. At the right, the Protestant Elizabeth I holds the hand of the goddess of Peace, followed by Plenty, carrying a cornucopia of fruit. The painting was commissioned in 1572 by Queen Elizabeth as a gift for Francis Walsingham, her secretary of state and the head of her spy network. Both Elizabeth and Edward are shown standing on a carpet, symbolizing the Protestant Church of England, whereas Philip and Mary are adjacent to the carpet. All of the figures are shown in clothing that was in style during the time that they reigned and that appears in other portraits. Lucas de Heere could have seen these portraits in Whitehall Palace, the main residence of English monarchs at that time, as he was in England when he painted this, after fleeing the Netherlands when Philip II tried to suppress Protestantism there.

(VCG Wilson/Corbis/Getty Images)

EVALUATE THE EVIDENCE

1. How does the artist suggest that by returning to Catholicism and an alliance with Spain, there will be troubles and possibly even war for England? How does he suggest that things will be good if England follows the Protestant Elizabeth?
2. How does the painting highlight the connection between Henry and Elizabeth? Why might Elizabeth have wanted to emphasize this connection?
3. Lucas de Heere was a Protestant refugee. Why might Elizabeth have chosen him for this painting?

Paul, to be a pessimistic view of the nature of God. But "this terrible decree," as even Calvin called it, did not lead to pessimism or fatalism. Instead, many Calvinists came to believe that although one's own actions could do nothing to change one's fate, hard work, thrift, and proper moral conduct could serve as signs that one was among the "elect" chosen for salvation.

Calvin transformed Geneva into a community based on his religious principles. The most powerful organization in the city became the Consistory, a group of laymen and pastors charged with investigating and disciplining deviations from proper doctrine and conduct. (See "Thinking Like a Historian: Social Discipline in the Reformation," page 374.)

Social Discipline in the Reformation

Both Protestant and Catholic leaders thought it important that people understand the basics of their particular version of Christianity, and they also wanted people to lead proper, godly lives. How and why did religious and secular authorities try to shape people's behavior?

1 Ordinances in Calvin's Geneva, 1547.

⌒ **Blasphemy:** Whoever shall have blasphemed, swearing by the body or by the blood of our Lord, or in similar manner, he shall be made to kiss the earth for the first offence; for the second to pay 5 sous, and for the third 6 sous, and for the last offence be put in the pillory [a wooden frame set up in a public place, in which a person's head and hands could be locked] for one hour.

Drunkenness: No one shall invite another to drink under penalty of 3 sous. Taverns shall be closed during the sermon, under penalty that the tavern-keeper shall pay 3 sous, and whoever may be found therein shall pay the same amount. If anyone be found intoxicated he shall pay for the first offence 3 sous and shall be remanded to the consistory; for the second offence he shall be held to pay the sum of 6 sous, and for the third 10 sous and be put in prison.

Songs and Dances: If anyone sing immoral, dissolute or outrageous songs, or dance the *virollet* or other dance, he shall be put in prison for three days and then sent to the consistory.

Usury: No one shall take upon interest or profit [on a loan] more than five percent, upon penalty of confiscation of the principal and of being condemned to make restitution as the case may demand.

Games: No one shall play at any dissolute game or at any game whatsoever it may be, neither for gold nor silver nor for any excessive stake, upon penalty of 5 sous and forfeiture of the stake played for.

2 Ordinances of the (Lutheran) city of Malmø, Denmark, 1540.

⌒ No one should be sitting and drinking alcohol during the sermon on Sundays or other holy days, nor should anyone wander around in the street or in the chapel behind the choir during the sermon. Nor should any [wine] cellar be opened on aforesaid days before the noonday sermon is over, unless it is done for the sake of strangers and travelers who arrive and want to leave at once. Whoever breaks this rule will be punished accordingly.

All single men and unemployed manservants should at once appear at the City Hall and swear an oath to the Mayors and the Council acting on behalf of His Royal Majesty and the city of Malmø [that they will try to find a position as a servant or journeyman] or they should at once be expelled from the city. Similarly, all girls who are self-supporting should enter into service again or be expelled from the city.

3 School ordinance from the (Lutheran) duchy of Württemberg, 1559.

⌒ Each pastor shall make in his sermons serious admonitions to parishioners that they must be diligent in sending their children to school. And let him stress the great benefit bound to come from this, schools being necessary not only for learning the liberal arts, but also the fear of God, virtue, and discipline. Where the young are neglected and kept out of school, permanent harm, both eternal and temporal, must result, as children grow up without fear and knowledge of God, like dumb beasts of the field, learning nothing about what is needed for their salvation, nor what is useful to them and their neighbors in worldly life. And the pastor shall inform them, furthermore, that school-mastering is a troublesome office and laborious, thankless work for which teachers should be honored and respected, and their hard-earned pay given to them willingly and without grudge. . . . In addition, all parents are obliged on the danger

ANALYZING THE EVIDENCE

1. Given the actions prohibited or required in the ordinances, how would you describe ideal Christian behavior, in the eyes of religious and political authorities?
2. What would an ideal Christian household look and sound like? An ideal community?
3. Are there differences between Protestant and Catholic visions of ideal households and communities, and if so, how do these distinctions relate to differences in theology or institutional structures?
4. Judging by the two visitation reports in Sources 5 and 6, did measures like those in Sources 1–3 work? What other sources would allow you to better answer this question?

of losing their souls to teach the catechism to their children and domestic servants. Ask them also what they remember from last Sunday's sermon, and, if they remember nothing, admonish them to pay closer attention. And if kind words don't help, take the stick to them or give them nothing to eat and drink for supper until they have repeated something from the sermon.

4 Decrees of the Council of Trent, 1563.
Like Protestant authorities, the Roman Catholic Council of Trent (see "Papal Reform and the Council of Trent") also issued decrees about teaching and behavior.

~ That the faithful may approach the sacraments with greater reverence and devotion of mind, the holy Council commands all bishops that not only when they themselves are about to administer them to the people, they shall first, in a manner adapted to the mental ability of those who receive them, explain their efficacy and use, but also that they shall see to it that the same is done piously and prudently by every parish priest, and in the vernacular tongue. . . . In like manner shall they explain on all festivals and solemnities during the solemnization of the Mass or the celebration of divine office, in the vernacular tongue, the divine commands and the maxims of salvation, and leaving aside useless questions, let them strive to engraft these things on the hearts of all and instruct them in the law of the Lord. . . .

When therefore anyone has publicly and in the sight of many committed a crime by which there is no doubt that others have been offended and scandalized, it is proper that a penance commensurate with his guilt be publicly imposed on him, so that those whom he by his example has led to evil morals, he may bring back to an upright life by the evidence of his correction.

5 Visitation report from (Catholic) Ourense, Spain, 1566.
Visitations were inspection tours by religious and secular officials in which they traveled from village to village, trying to assess how well ordinances were actually being followed.

~ His majesty is informed that on past visits Gregorio Gomez and Alonso Galente, inhabitants of Dacon, Juan de Mondian and Juan Bernáldez, inhabitants of Toscana, and Gabriel de Dacon, all tavern owners, were admonished not to open the taverns nor sell wine, bread or meat to the parishioners on Sundays and holidays before High Mass. They have not wanted to comply, opening the taverns and selling wine and meat so that the parishioners quit coming to Mass in order to be there playing and drinking. Being compassionate with them he fines each one of them three reales [a very small amount] for the fabric of the church for this first time, except Alonso Galente, who is fined only one and a half reales on account of his poverty. Henceforth, they will be fined one ducat for each time that they open during the Mass.

6 Visitation report from (Lutheran) Nassau-Wiesbaden, Germany, 1594.

~ First, gruesome cursing and blaspheming, as for instance "by God," "by God's Holy Cross," "by God's Passion, death, flesh, blood, heart, hand, etc.," "A Thousand Sacraments," "thunder and hail," "earth." Also dreadful swearing by various fears, epidemics, and injuries. These oaths are very common among young and old, women as well as men. People cannot carry on a friendly chat, or even address their children, without the use of these words. And none of them considers it a sin to swear.

Everyone is very lax about going to church, both young and old. Many have not been seen by their pastor in a year or more. . . . Those who come to service are usually drunk. As soon as they sit down they lean their heads on their arms and sleep through the whole sermon, except that sometimes they fall off the benches, making a great clatter, or women drop their babies on the floor. . . . At times the wailing of babies is so loud the preacher cannot make himself heard in the church. And the moment that the sermon ends, everyone runs out. No one stays for the hymn, prayer, or blessing. They behave as if they were at a dance, not a divine service. . . . On Sunday afternoons, hardly ten or fifteen of the 150 householders come to catechism practice, nor do they oblige their children and servants to attend. Instead they loaf at home, or sit about gossiping.

PUTTING IT ALL TOGETHER

Using the sources above, along with what you have learned in class and in this chapter, write a short essay that analyzes social discipline in the Reformation. How and why did religious and secular authorities try to shape people's behavior and instill morality and piety? Were they successful?

Sources: (1) Merrick Whitcomb, ed., *Translations and Reprints from the Original Sources of European History*, vol. 3 (Philadelphia: University of Pennsylvania, 1897), no. 3, pp. 10–11; (2) *Malmø standsbog 1549–1559* (Copenhagen: Selskabet for Udgivelse af Kilder til dansk Historie, 1952), p. 35. Trans. Grethe Jacobsen and Pernille Arenfeldt; (3) Gerald Strauss, *Luther's House of Learning: Indoctrination of the Young in the German Reformation* (Baltimore, Md.: Johns Hopkins University Press, 1978), pp. 45–46; (4) H. J. Schroeder, *Canons and Decrees of the Council of Trent* (St. Louis, Mo.: B. Herder, 1941), pp. 197–198; (5) *Libro de Visitas*, Santa Maria Amarante, Archivo Histórico Diocesano de Ourense, 24.1.13, fols. 9–10, 1566. Trans. Allyson Poska; (6) Strauss, *Luther's House of Learning*, pp. 283–284.

Drawing of Calvin This informal drawing of Calvin lecturing, doodled by one of his students, captures the sense of reserve that comes out in Calvin's writings as well. (Bibliothèque Publique et Universitaire/DEA/G. DAGLI ORTI/De Agostini/Getty Images)

Serious crimes and heresy were handled by the civil authorities, which, with the Consistory's approval, sometimes used torture to extract confessions. Between 1542 and 1546 alone seventy-six persons were banished from Geneva, and fifty-eight were executed for heresy, adultery, blasphemy, and witchcraft (see "The Great European Witch-Hunt" at the end of this chapter).

Geneva became the model of a Christian community for many Protestant reformers. Religious refugees from France, England, Spain, Scotland, and Italy visited Calvin's Geneva, and many of the most prominent exiles from Mary Tudor's England stayed. Subsequently, the church of Calvin — often termed "Reformed" — served as the model for the Presbyterian Church in Scotland, the Huguenot Church in France (see "French Religious Wars" later in this chapter), and the Puritan churches in England and New England.

Calvinism became the compelling force in international Protestantism in the sixteenth and seventeenth centuries. Calvinists believed that any occupation could be a God-given "calling" and should be carried out with diligence and dedication. This doctrine encouraged an aggressive, vigorous activism in both work and religious life. Consistories, boards of elders and ministers, were established in Calvinist congregations, with regional elected bodies usually called presbyteries having authority over some issues. Church services became simpler but longer, with a focus on the sermon, and art and ornamentation were removed from churches, with the pulpit rather than an elaborate altar in the middle of the church. (See "Viewpoints: Catholic and Calvinist Churches," page 377.)

Calvinism spread on the continent of Europe, and it also found a ready audience in Scotland. There, as elsewhere, political authority was the decisive influence in reform. King James V and his daughter Mary, Queen of Scots, staunch Catholics and close allies of Catholic France, opposed reform, but the Scottish nobles supported it. One man, John Knox (1505?–1572), dominated the reform movement, which led to the establishment of a state church. Knox was determined to structure the Scottish Church after the model of Geneva, where he had studied and worked with Calvin. In 1560 Knox persuaded the Scottish Parliament, which was dominated by reform-minded barons, to end papal authority and rule by bishops, substituting governance by presbyteries. The Presbyterian Church of Scotland was strictly Calvinist in doctrine, and, as with Calvinists everywhere, adopted a simple and dignified service of worship, with great emphasis on preaching.

The Reformation in Eastern Europe

While political and economic issues determined the course of the Reformation in western and northern Europe, ethnic factors often proved decisive in eastern Europe, where people of diverse backgrounds had settled in the later Middle Ages. In Bohemia in the fifteenth century, a Czech majority was ruled by Germans. Most Czechs had adopted the ideas of Jan Hus, and the emperor had been forced to recognize a separate Hussite Church (see "Critiques, Divisions, and Councils" in Chapter 11). Yet Lutheranism appealed to Germans in Bohemia in the 1520s and 1530s, and the nobility embraced Lutheranism in opposition to the Catholic Habsburgs. The forces of the Catholic Reformation (see "Papal Reform and the Council of Trent" later in the chapter) promoted a Catholic spiritual revival in Bohemia, and some areas reconverted. This complicated situation would be one of the causes of the Thirty Years' War in the early seventeenth century.

In 1500, the Kingdom of Poland and the Grand Duchy of Lithuania were jointly ruled by a common monarch, and after 1569 also united under a single parliament, but the two territories retained separate officials, judicial systems, armies, and forms of citizenship. The population of Poland-Lithuania was also very diverse; Germans, Italians, Tartars, and Jews lived among Poles and Lithuanians. Such peoples had come as merchants, invited by medieval rulers because of their wealth or to make agricultural improvements. Each group spoke its native language, though all educated people spoke Latin. Luther's ideas took root in Germanized towns but were opposed by King Sigismund I (r. 1506–1548) as well as by ordinary Poles, who held strong anti-German feeling. The Reformed tradition of John Calvin, with its stress on the power of church elders, appealed to the Polish nobility, however. The fact that Calvinism originated in France, not in Germany, also made it

Old Church, Delft (built 13th century). (Johnny van Haeften Gallery, London, UK/ Bridgeman Images)

Church of St. Ignatius, Rome (built 1626–1650). (Adam Eastland/Alamy)

Protestant and Catholic ideas were expressed orally and in writing, and also in the churches in which services were held. The church on the left is a painting made by Hendrik Cornelisz van Vliet (ca. 1611–1675) of the Old Church in Delft in the Netherlands, where the painter himself would be buried. Built originally in the thirteenth century, in the 1560s the church was the scene of iconoclasm that removed or destroyed much of the artwork. It was then renovated to fit with the Calvinist principles of the Dutch Reformed Church, with the pulpit for the preacher in the middle of the church. The Catholic church on the right is the Church of St. Ignatius at Campius Martius in Rome, built between 1626 and 1650 and dedicated to the founder of the Jesuits. The interior was designed by Orazio Grazzi (1583–1684), himself a Jesuit, in the powerful new style later labeled "baroque," with elaborate Corinthian pillars, colored marble, many stucco figures, paintings on the walls and ceiling, and a gilded high altar.

QUESTIONS FOR ANALYSIS

1. Imagine yourself a worshipper or visitor to each of these churches. How would you describe their interiors and the mood they convey?
2. How do these interiors reflect and express Calvinist and Catholic ideas?

more attractive than Lutheranism. But doctrinal differences among Calvinists, Lutherans, and other groups prevented united opposition to Catholicism, and a Catholic Counter-Reformation gained momentum. By 1650, due largely to the efforts of the Jesuits (see "New and Reformed Religious Orders" later in this chapter), Poland was again staunchly Roman Catholic.

Hungary's experience with the Reformation was even more complex. Lutheranism was spread by Hungarian students who had studied at Wittenberg, and sympathy for it developed at the royal court of King Louis II in Buda. But concern about "the German heresy" by the Catholic hierarchy and among the high nobles found expression in a decree of the Hungarian Diet in 1523 that Lutherans and those who favored them should be executed and their property confiscated.

Before such measures could be acted on, a military event on August 26, 1526, had profound consequences for both the Hungarian state and the Protestant Reformation there. On the plain of Mohács

in southern Hungary, the Ottoman sultan Suleiman the Magnificent inflicted a crushing defeat on the Hungarians, killing King Louis II, many of the nobles, and more than sixteen thousand ordinary soldiers. The Hungarian kingdom was then divided into three parts: the Ottoman Turks absorbed the great plains, including the capital, Buda; the Habsburgs ruled the north and west; and Ottoman-supported Janos Zapolya held eastern Hungary and Transylvania.

The Turks were indifferent to the religious conflicts of Christians, whom they regarded as infidels. Christians of all types paid extra taxes to the sultan, but they kept their faith. Many Magyar (Hungarian) nobles accepted Lutheranism; Lutheran schools and parishes headed by men educated at Wittenberg multiplied; and peasants welcomed the new faith. The majority of Hungarian people were Protestant until the late seventeenth century, when Hungarian nobles recognized Habsburg (Catholic) rule and Ottoman Turkish withdrawal in 1699 led to Catholic restoration.

What reforms did the Catholic Church make, and how did it respond to Protestant reform movements?

Between 1517 and 1547 Protestantism made remarkable advances. Nevertheless, the Roman Catholic Church made a significant comeback. After about 1540 no new large areas of Europe, other than the Netherlands, accepted Protestant beliefs (Map 13.2). Many historians see the developments within the Catholic Church after the Protestant Reformation as two interrelated movements: one a drive for internal reform linked to earlier reform efforts, the other a Counter-Reformation that opposed Protestants intellectually, politically, militarily, and institutionally. In both movements, the papacy, new religious orders, and the Council of Trent that met from 1545 to 1563 were important agents.

Papal Reform and the Council of Trent

Renaissance popes and their advisers were not blind to the need for church reforms, but they resisted calls for a general council representing the entire church and feared that any transformation would mean a loss of power, revenue, and prestige. This attitude changed beginning with Pope Paul III (pontificate 1534–1549), when the papal court became the center of the reform movement rather than its chief opponent. The lives of the pope and his reform-minded cardinals, abbots, and bishops were models of decorum and

piety, in contrast to Renaissance popes, who concentrated on building churches and enhancing the power of their own families. Paul III and his successors supported improvements in education for the clergy, the end of simony (the selling of church offices), and stricter control of clerical life.

In 1542 Pope Paul III established the Supreme Sacred Congregation of the Roman and Universal Inquisition, often called the **Holy Office**, with jurisdiction over the Roman Inquisition, a powerful instrument of the Catholic Reformation. The Roman Inquisition was a committee of six cardinals with judicial authority over all Catholics and the power to arrest, imprison, and execute suspected heretics. The Holy Office published the *Index of Prohibited Books*, a catalogue of forbidden reading that included works by Christian humanists such as Erasmus as well as by Protestants. Within the Papal States the Inquisition effectively destroyed heresy, but outside the papal territories its influence was slight.

Pope Paul III also called a general council that met intermittently from 1545 to 1563 at Trent, an imperial city close to Italy. The council was called to reform the Catholic Church and to secure reconciliation with the Protestants, though the latter proved impossible. Nonetheless, the decrees of the Council of Trent laid a solid basis for the spiritual renewal of the Catholic Church. They gave equal validity to the Scriptures and to tradition as sources of religious truth and authority.

■ **Holy Office** The official Roman Catholic agency founded in 1542 to combat international doctrinal heresy.

MAP 13.2 Religious Divisions in Europe, ca. 1555

The Reformations shattered the religious unity of Western Christendom. The situation was even more complicated than a map of this scale can show. Many cities within the Holy Roman Empire, for example, accepted a different faith than the surrounding countryside; Augsburg, Basel, and Strasbourg were all Protestant, though surrounded by territory ruled by Catholic nobles.

ANALYZING THE MAP Which countries were the most religiously diverse in Europe? Which were the least diverse?

CONNECTIONS Where was the first arena of religious conflict in sixteenth-century Europe, and why did it develop there and not elsewhere? To what degree can nonreligious factors be used to explain the religious divisions in sixteenth-century Europe?

They also reaffirmed the seven sacraments and the traditional Catholic teaching on transubstantiation. They tackled the disciplinary matters that had disillusioned the faithful, including absenteeism, pluralism, priests having sex with local women or keeping concubines, and the selling of church offices. Bishops were given greater authority and ordered to establish a seminary in their diocese for the education and training of the clergy. Seminary professors were to determine whether candidates for ordination had vocations, or genuine callings to the priesthood. This was a novel idea, since from the time of the early church, parents

Pasquale Cati, *The Council of Trent*, 1588 Cati's imagined depiction of the Council of Trent, painted for a church in Rome twenty-five years after the council ended, shows the representatives seated in rows, with the cardinals in front. Cati includes allegorical female figures in the foreground, and at their center the Church Triumphant, wearing the papal tiara and the splendid white robe of doctrinal clarity and trampling a figure representing the enemies of Catholicism. (Magite Historic/Alamy Stock Photo)

had determined their sons' (and daughters') religious careers. For the first time, great emphasis was laid on preaching and instructing the laity, especially the uneducated. (See "Thinking Like a Historian: Social Discipline in the Reformation," page 374.)

One decision had especially important social consequences for laypeople. The Council of Trent stipulated that for a marriage to be valid, the marriage vows had to be made publicly before a priest and witnesses. Trent thereby ended the widespread practice of private marriages in Catholic countries, curtailing the number of denials and conflicts that inevitably resulted from marriages that took place in secret.

Although it did not achieve all of its goals, the Council of Trent composed decrees that laid a solid basis for the spiritual renewal of the church. The doctrinal and disciplinary legislation of Trent served as the basis for Roman Catholic faith, organization, and practice through the middle of the twentieth century.

New and Reformed Religious Orders

Just as seminaries provided education, so did religious orders, which aimed at raising the moral and intellectual level of the clergy and people. The monasteries and convents of many existing religious orders were

reformed so that they followed more rigorous standards. In Spain, for example, the Carmelite nun Teresa of Ávila (1515–1582) traveled around the country reforming her Carmelite order to bring it back to stricter standards of asceticism and poverty, a task she understood God had set for her in mystical visions, which she described in her own writings. Some officials in the church criticized her as a "restless gadabout, a disobedient and obstinate woman" who had gone against Saint Paul's commands that women were not to teach. At one point she was even investigated by the Spanish Inquisition in an effort to make sure her inspiration came from God and not the Devil. The process was dropped, however, and she founded many new convents, which she saw as answers to the Protestant takeover of Catholic churches elsewhere in Europe. "We shall fight for Him [God]," she wrote, "even though we are very cloistered."[5]

New religious orders were founded, some of which focused on education. The Ursuline order of nuns, for example, founded in 1535 by Angela Merici (1474–1540), focused on the education of women. The Ursulines concentrated on teaching young girls, with the goal of re-Christianizing society by training future wives and mothers. After receiving papal approval in 1565, the Ursulines rapidly spread to France and the New World.

The most significant new order was the Society of Jesus, or **Jesuits.** Founded by Ignatius Loyola (1491–1556), the Jesuits played a powerful international role in strengthening Catholicism in Europe and spreading the faith around the world. While recuperating from a

■ **Jesuits** Members of the Society of Jesus, founded by Ignatius Loyola, whose goal was the spread of the Roman Catholic faith.

severe battle wound in his legs, Loyola studied books about Christ and the saints and decided to give up his military career and become a soldier of Christ. During a year spent in seclusion, prayer, and asceticism, he gained insights that went into his great classic, *Spiritual Exercises* (1548). This work, intended for study during a four-week period of retreat, set out a training program of structured meditation designed to develop spiritual discipline and allow one to meld one's will with that of God:

> By the term "Spiritual Exercises" is meant every method of examination of conscience, of meditation, of contemplation, of vocal and mental prayer, and of other spiritual activities. For just as taking a walk, journeying on foot, and running are bodily exercises, so we call Spiritual Exercises every way of preparing and disposing the soul to rid itself of all inordinate attachments, and, after their removal, of seeking and finding the will of God in the disposition of our life for the salvation of our soul.[6]

Like today's physical trainers, Loyola provided daily exercises that build in intensity over the four weeks of the program, as well as charts on which the exerciser can track his progress.

Loyola was a man of considerable personal magnetism. After studying at universities in Salamanca and Paris, he gathered a group of six companions and in 1540 secured papal approval of the new Society of Jesus. The first Jesuits, recruited primarily from wealthy merchant and professional families, saw their mission as improving people's spiritual condition rather than altering doctrine. Their goal was not to reform the church, but "to help souls."

The Society of Jesus developed into a highly centralized, tightly knit organization. In addition to the traditional vows of poverty, chastity, and obedience, professed members vowed special obedience to the pope. Flexibility and the willingness to respond to the needs of time and circumstance formed the Jesuit tradition, which proved attractive to many young men. The Jesuits achieved phenomenal success for the papacy and the reformed Catholic Church, carrying Christianity to India and Japan before 1550 and to Brazil, North America, and the Congo in the seventeenth century. Within Europe the Jesuits brought southern Germany and much of eastern Europe back to Catholicism. Jesuit schools adopted the modern humanist curricula and methods, educating the sons of the nobility as well as the poor. As confessors and spiritual directors to kings, Jesuits exerted great political influence.

Revitalization of the Catholic Church was not simply a matter of the church hierarchy and new religious orders, but also of devotional life at the local level. Confraternities of laypeople were established or expanded in many parishes, which held processions and feasts, handed out charity, and supported the church financially. The papacy, the Jesuits, and other patrons built and renovated churches and chapels, often filling them with objects and paintings, as they thought dramatic art would glorify the reformed and reinvigorated Catholic Church, appealing to the senses and proclaiming the power of the church to all who looked at paintings or sculpture or worshipped in churches. (See "Viewpoints: Catholic and Calvinist Churches," page 377.)

What were the causes and consequences of religious violence, including riots, wars, and witch-hunts?

In 1559, France and Spain signed the Treaty of Cateau-Cambrésis (CAH-toh kam-BRAY-sees), which ended the long conflict known as the Habsburg-Valois wars. Spain was the victor. France, exhausted by the struggle, had to acknowledge Spanish dominance in Italy, where much of the fighting had taken place. However, true peace was elusive, and over the next century religious differences led to riots, civil wars, and international conflicts. Especially in France and the Netherlands, Protestants and Catholics used violent actions as well as preaching and teaching against each other, for each side regarded the other as a poison in the community that would provoke the wrath of God. Catholics continued to believe that Calvinists and Lutherans could be reconverted; Protestants persisted in thinking that the Roman Church should be destroyed. Catholics and Protestants alike feared people of other faiths, whom they often saw as agents of Satan. Even more, they feared those who were explicitly identified with Satan: witches living in their midst. This era was the time of the most virulent witch persecutions in European history, as both Protestants and Catholics tried to make their cities and states more godly.

French Religious Wars

The costs of the Habsburg-Valois wars, waged intermittently through the first half of the sixteenth century, forced the French to increase taxes and borrow heavily. King Francis I (r. 1515–1547) also tried two new devices to raise revenue: the sale of public offices and a treaty with the papacy. The former proved to be only a temporary source of money: once a man bought an office, he and his heirs were exempt from taxation.

Spanish Soldiers Killing Protestants in Haarlem
In this engraving by the Calvinist artist Franz Hogenberg, Spanish soldiers accompanied by priests kill residents of the Dutch city of Haarlem by hanging or beheading, and then dump their bodies in the river. Haarlem had withstood a seven-month siege by Spanish troops in 1572–1573, and after the starving city surrendered, the garrison of troops and forty citizens judged guilty of sedition were executed. Images such as this were part of the propaganda battle that accompanied the wars of religion, but in many cases there were actual atrocities, on both sides. (Private Collection/Bridgeman Images)

But the latter, known as the Concordat of Bologna (see "France" in Chapter 12), gave the French Crown the right to appoint all French bishops and abbots and require them to pay taxes to the Crown. Because French rulers possessed control over the personnel of the church and had a vested financial interest in Catholicism, they had no need to revolt against Rome.

Significant numbers of those ruled, however, were attracted to the Reformed religion of Calvinism. Initially, Calvinism drew converts from among reform-minded members of the Catholic clergy, industrious city dwellers, and artisan groups. Most French Calvinists, called **Huguenots**, lived in major cities, such as Paris, Lyons, and Rouen. By the time King Henry II (r. 1547–1559) died in 1559 — accidentally shot in the face at a tournament celebrating the Treaty of Cateau-Cambrésis — perhaps one-tenth of the population had become Calvinist.

Strong religious fervor combined with a weak French monarchy led to civil violence. Both Calvinists and Catholics believed that the other's books, services, and ministers polluted the community, and preachers incited violence. The three weak sons of Henry II who occupied the throne could not provide the necessary leadership, and they were often dominated by their mother, Catherine de' Medici. The French nobility took advantage of this monarchical weakness. Just as German princes

in the Holy Roman Empire had adopted Lutheranism as a means of opposing Emperor Charles V, so French nobles frequently adopted Protestantism as a religious cloak for their independence. Armed clashes between the forces of Catholic royalist lords and Calvinist antimonarchical lords occurred in many parts of France, beginning a series of religious wars that lasted for decades.

Calvinist teachings called the power of sacred images into question, and mobs in many cities took down and smashed statues, stained-glass windows, and paintings, viewing this as a way to purify the church. Though it was often inspired by fiery Protestant sermons, this iconoclasm, or destruction of religious images, is an example of ordinary men and women carrying out the Reformation themselves. Catholic mobs responded by defending images, and crowds on both sides killed their opponents, often in gruesome ways.

A savage Catholic attack on Calvinists in Paris on Saint Bartholomew's Day, August 24, 1572, followed the usual pattern. This happened a few days after the marriage ceremony of the king's sister Margaret of Valois to the Protestant Henry of Navarre, which was intended to help reconcile Catholics and Huguenots. Instead, Huguenot leaders who had come to Paris to attend the wedding were massacred by the king's soldiers. Other Protestants were slaughtered by mobs and their houses looted. Traditionally Catherine de' Medici was blamed for instigating this violence, but more recently historians have pointed to other members of the royal family and to Catholic fears of a Protestant takeover. The massacre spread to the provinces, where thousands of Protestants were killed by Catholic mobs who thought they were doing God's and the king's will. The Saint Bartholomew's Day massacre led to a renewal of the wars of religion, which dragged on for decades.

What ultimately saved France was a small group of moderates of both faiths, called **politiques**, who believed that only the restoration of a strong monarchy

■ **Huguenots** French Calvinists.

■ **politiques** Catholic and Protestant moderates who held that only a strong monarchy could save France from total collapse.

■ **Edict of Nantes** A document issued by Henry IV of France in 1598, granting liberty of conscience and of public worship to Calvinists, which helped restore peace in France.

■ **Union of Utrecht** The alliance of seven northern provinces (led by Holland) that declared its independence from Spain and formed the United Provinces of the Netherlands.

could reverse the trend toward collapse. The politiques also favored accepting the Huguenots as an officially recognized and organized group. The death of Catherine de' Medici, followed by the assassination of King Henry III, paved the way for the accession of Henry of Navarre (the unfortunate bridegroom of the Saint Bartholomew's Day massacre), a politique who became Henry IV (r. 1589–1610).

Henry's willingness to sacrifice religious principles to political necessity saved France. He converted to Catholicism but also issued the **Edict of Nantes** in 1598, which granted liberty of conscience and liberty of public worship to Huguenots in 150 fortified towns. The reign of Henry IV and the Edict of Nantes prepared the way for French absolutism in the seventeenth century by helping restore internal peace in France.

The Netherlands, 1609

between the seventeen provinces and Spain. Eventually the ten southern provinces, the Spanish Netherlands (the future Belgium), came under the control of the Spanish Habsburg forces. The seven northern provinces, led by Holland, formed the **Union of Utrecht** and in 1581 declared their independence from Spain. The north was Protestant; the south remained Catholic. Philip did not accept this situation, and war continued. England was even drawn into the conflict, supplying money and troops to the northern United Provinces. (Spain launched an unsuccessful invasion of England in response; see "Upholding Protestantism in England" in this chapter.) Hostilities ended in 1609 when Spain agreed to a truce that recognized the independence of the United Provinces.

The Netherlands Under Charles V

In the Netherlands, what began as a movement for the reformation of the church developed into a struggle for independence. Emperor Charles V had inherited the seventeen provinces that compose present-day Belgium and the Netherlands. In the Low Countries, as elsewhere, corruption in the Roman Church and the critical spirit of the Renaissance provoked pressure for reform, and Lutheran ideas took root. Charles V had grown up in the Netherlands, however, and he was able to limit the impact of Protestant ideas. But Charles V abdicated in 1556 and transferred power over the Netherlands to his son Philip II, who had grown up in Spain.

Protestant ideas spread, and by the 1560s Protestants in the Netherlands were primarily Calvinists. Calvinism's intellectual seriousness, moral gravity, and emphasis on any form of labor well done appealed to urban merchants, financiers, and artisans. Whereas Lutherans taught respect for the powers that be, Calvinists tended to encourage opposition to political authorities who were judged to be ungodly. Thus when Spanish authorities attempted to suppress Calvinist worship and raised taxes in the 1560s, rioting ensued. Calvinists sacked thirty Catholic churches in Antwerp, destroying the religious images in them in a wave of iconoclasm. From Antwerp the destruction spread. Philip II sent twenty thousand Spanish troops under the duke of Alva to pacify the Low Countries. Alva interpreted "pacification" to mean ruthless extermination of religious and political dissidents. To Calvinists, all this was clear indication that Spanish rule was ungodly and should be overthrown.

Between 1568 and 1578 civil war raged in the Netherlands between Catholics and Protestants and

The Great European Witch-Hunt

The relationship between the Reformation and the upsurge in trials for witchcraft that occurred at roughly the same time is complex. Increasing persecution for witchcraft actually began before the Reformation in the 1480s, but it became especially common about 1560, and the mania continued until roughly 1660. Both Protestants and Catholics tried and executed witches, with church officials and secular authorities acting together.

The heightened sense of God's and the Devil's power in the Reformation era was an important factor in the witch-hunts, but so was a change in the idea of what a witch was. In the later Middle Ages, many educated Christian theologians, canon lawyers, and officials added a demonological component to the common notion of witches as people who use magic. For them, the essence of witchcraft was making a pact with the Devil. Witches were no longer simply people who used magical power to get what they wanted, but rather people used by the Devil to do what he wanted. Witches were thought to engage in wild sexual orgies with the Devil, fly through the night to meetings called sabbats that parodied Christian services, and steal communion wafers and unbaptized babies to use in their rituals. Some demonological theorists also claimed that witches were organized in an international conspiracy to overthrow Christianity. Witchcraft was thus spiritualized, and witches became the ultimate heretics, enemies of God.

Scholars estimate that during the sixteenth and seventeenth centuries between 100,000 and 200,000 people were officially tried for witchcraft and between 40,000 and 60,000 were executed. Though the gender balance varied widely in different parts of Europe, between 75 and 85 percent of those tried and executed were women. Ideas about women and the roles women actually played in society were thus important factors shaping the witch-hunts. Some demonologists expressed virulent misogyny, or hatred of women, and particularly emphasized women's powerful sexual desire, which could be satisfied only by a demonic lover. Most people viewed women as weaker than men and so more likely to give in to an offer by the Devil. In both classical and Christian traditions, women were associated with nature, disorder, and the body, all of which were linked with the demonic. Women's actual lack of power in society and gender norms about the use of violence meant that they were more likely to use scolding and cursing to get what they wanted instead of taking people to court or beating them up. Curses were generally expressed (as they often are today) in religious terms; "go to Hell" was calling on the powers of Satan.

Legal changes also played a role in causing, or at least allowing for, massive witch trials. One of these was a change from an accusatorial legal procedure to an inquisitorial procedure. In the former, a suspect knew the accusers and the charges they had brought, and an accuser could in turn be liable for trial if the charges were not proven. In the latter, legal authorities themselves brought the case. This change made people much more willing to accuse others, for they never had to take personal responsibility for the accusation or face the accused person's relatives. Inquisitorial procedure involved intense questioning of the suspect, often with torture.

The use of inquisitorial procedure did not always lead to witch-hunts. The most famous inquisitions in early modern Europe, those in Spain, Portugal, and Italy, were in fact very lenient in their treatment of people accused of witchcraft. The Inquisition in Spain executed only a handful of witches, the Portuguese Inquisition only one, and the Roman Inquisition none, though in each of these there were hundreds of cases. Inquisitors believed in the power of the Devil and were no less misogynist than other judges, but they doubted very much whether the people accused of witchcraft had actually made pacts with the Devil that gave them special powers. They viewed such people not as diabolical Devil worshippers but as superstitious and ignorant peasants who should be educated rather than executed. Thus most people brought up before the Inquisition for witchcraft were sent home with a warning and a penance.

Most witch trials began with a single accusation in a village or town. Individuals accused someone they knew of using magic to spoil food, make children ill, kill animals, raise a hailstorm, or do other types of harm. Tensions within families, households, and neighborhoods often played a role in these accusations. Women number very prominently among accusers and witnesses as well as among those accused of witchcraft because the actions witches were initially charged with, such as harming children or curdling milk, were generally part of women's sphere. A woman also gained economic and social security by conforming to the standard of the good wife and mother and by confronting women who deviated from it.

Once a charge was made, the suspect was brought in for questioning. One German witch pamphlet from 1587 described a typical case:

> Walpurga Hausmännin . . . upon kindly questioning and also torture . . . confessed . . . that the Evil One indulged in fornication with her . . . and made her many promises to help her in her poverty and need. . . . She promised herself body and soul to him and disowned God in heaven. . . . She destroyed a number of cattle, pigs, and geese . . . and dug up [the bodies] of one or two innocent children. With her devil-paramour and other playfellows she has eaten these and used their hair and their little bones for witchcraft.

Confession was generally followed by execution. In this case, Hausmännin was "dispatched from life to death by burning at the stake . . . her body first to be torn five times with red-hot irons."[7]

Detailed records of witch trials survive for many parts of Europe. They have been used by historians to study many aspects of witchcraft, but they cannot directly answer what seems to us an important question: did people really practice witchcraft and think they were witches? They certainly confessed to evil deeds and demonic practices, sometimes without torture, but where would we draw the line between reality and fantasy? Clearly people were not riding through the air on pitchforks, but did they think they did? Did they actually invoke the Devil when they were angry at a neighbor, or was this simply in the minds of their accusers? Trial records cannot tell us, and historians have answered these questions very differently, often using insights from psychoanalysis or the study of more recent victims of torture in their explanations.

After the initial suspect had been questioned, and particularly if he or she had been tortured, the people who had been implicated were brought in for questioning. This might lead to a small hunt, involving from five to ten suspects, and it sometimes grew into a much larger hunt, which historians have called a "witch panic." Panics were most common in the part of Europe that saw the most witch accusations in general: the Holy Roman Empire, Switzerland, and parts of France. Most of this area consisted of very small governmental units that were jealous of one another and, after the Reformation, were divided by religion. The rulers of these small territories often felt more threatened than did the monarchs of western Europe, and they saw persecuting witches as a way to demonstrate their piety and concern for order. Moreover, witch panics often occurred after some type of climatic disaster, such as an unusually cold and wet summer, and they came in waves.

In large-scale panics a wider variety of suspects were taken in — wealthier people, children, a greater

The ende and last confession of mother Waterhouse at her death, whiche was the xxix. daye of Iuly.

Anno. 1566.

Mother wa=terhouse.

IF first (beinge redi prepared to receiue her death) she confessed earnestly that shee had bene a wytche and vsed suche execrable sorserye the space of. xv. yeres, and had don many abhominable dede, the which she repented earnestly & vnfaynedly, and desyred almyghty God forgeuenes in that she had abused hys most holy name by her

Witch Pamphlet This printed pamphlet presents the confession of "Mother Waterhouse," a woman convicted of witchcraft in England in 1566, who describes her "many abominable deeds" and "execrable sorcery" committed over fifteen years, and asks for forgiveness right before her execution. Enterprising printers often produced cheap, short pamphlets during witch trials, knowing they would sell, sometimes based on the actual trial proceedings and sometimes just made up. They both reflected and helped create stereotypes about what witches were and did. (Private Collection/Bridgeman Images)

proportion of men. Mass panics tended to end when it became clear to legal authorities, or to the community itself, that the people being questioned or executed were not what they understood witches to be, or that the scope of accusations was beyond belief.

As the seventeenth century ushered in new ideas about science and reason, many began to question whether witches could make pacts with the Devil or engage in the wild activities attributed to them. Doubts about whether secret denunciations were valid or whether torture would ever yield truthful confessions gradually spread among the same types of religious and legal authorities who had so vigorously persecuted witches. Prosecutions for witchcraft became less common and were gradually outlawed. The last official execution for witchcraft in England was in 1682, though the last one in the Holy Roman Empire was not until 1775.

NOTES

1. Quoted in E. H. Harbison, *The Age of Reformation* (Ithaca, N.Y.: Cornell University Press, 1963), p. 52.
2. Quoted in S. E. Ozment, *The Age of Reform, 1250–1550: An Intellectual and Religious History of Late Medieval and Reformation Europe* (New Haven, Conn.: Yale University Press, 1980), p. 284.
3. Ludwig Rabus, *Historien der heyligen Außerwolten Gottes Zeugen, Bekennern und Martyrern* (n.p., 1557), fol. 41. Trans. Merry Wiesner-Hanks.
4. J. Allen, trans., *John Calvin: The Institutes of the Christian Religion* (Philadelphia: Westminster Press, 1930), bk. 3, chap. 21, para. 5, 7.
5. Teresa of Avila, *The Way of Perfection*, translated and quoted in Jodi Bilinkoff, *The Avila of St. Teresa: Religious Reform in a Sixteenth-Century City* (Ithaca, N.Y.: Cornell University Press, 1989), p. 136.
6. *The Spiritual Exercises of St. Ignatius of Loyola*, trans. Louis J. Puhl, S. J. (Chicago: Loyola University, 1951), p. 1.
7. From *The Fugger News-Letters*, ed. Victor von Klarwell, trans. P. de Chary (London: John Lane, The Bodley Head Ltd., 1924), quoted in James Bruce Ross and Mary Martin McLaughlin, eds., *The Portable Renaissance Reader* (New York: Penguin, 1953), pp. 258, 260, 262.

LOOKING BACK   LOOKING AHEAD

The Renaissance and the Reformation are often seen as two of the key elements in the creation of the "modern" world. The radical changes brought by the Reformation contained many aspects of continuity, however. Sixteenth-century reformers looked back to the early Christian Church for their inspiration, and many of their reforming ideas had been advocated for centuries. Most Protestant reformers worked with political leaders to make religious changes, just as early church officials had worked with Emperor Constantine and his successors as Christianity became the official religion of the Roman Empire in the fourth century. The

spread of Christianity and the spread of Protestantism were accomplished not only by preaching, persuasion, and teaching, but also by force and violence. The Catholic Reformation was carried out by activist popes, a church council, and new religious orders, as earlier reforms of the church had been.

Just as they linked with earlier developments, the events of the Reformation were also closely connected with what is often seen as the third element in the "modern" world: European exploration and colonization. Only a week after Martin Luther stood in front of Charles V at the Diet of Worms declaring his independence in matters of religion, Ferdinand

Magellan, a Portuguese sea captain with Spanish ships, was killed in a group of islands off the coast of Southeast Asia. Charles V had provided the backing for Magellan's voyage, the first to circumnavigate the globe. Magellan viewed the spread of Christianity as one of the purposes of his trip, and later in the sixteenth century institutions created as part of the Catholic Reformation, including the Jesuit order and the Inquisition, would operate in European colonies overseas as well as in Europe itself. The islands where Magellan was killed were later named the Philippines, in honor of Charles's son Philip, who sent the ill-fated Spanish Armada against England. Philip's opponent Queen Elizabeth was similarly honored when English explorers named a huge chunk of territory in North America "Virginia" as a tribute to their "Virgin Queen." The desire for wealth and power was an important motivation in the European voyages and colonial ventures, but so was religious zeal.

Make Connections

Think about the larger developments and continuities within and across chapters.

1. Martin Luther is always on every list of the one hundred most influential people of all time. Should he be? Why or why not? Who else from this chapter should be on such a list, and why?

2. How did Protestant ideas about gender, marriage, and the role of women break with those developed earlier in the history of the Christian Church (Chapters 6, 7, 9)? What continuities do you see? What factors account for the pattern that you have found?

3. In what ways was the Catholic Reformation of the sixteenth century similar to earlier efforts to reform the church, including the Gregorian reforms of the twelfth century (Chapter 9) and late medieval reform efforts (Chapter 11)? In what ways was it different?

13 REVIEW & EXPLORE

Identify Key Terms

Identify and explain the significance of each item below.

anticlericalism (p. 358)

indulgence (p. 359)

Protestant (p. 361)

Spanish Armada (p. 372)

The Institutes of the Christian Religion (p. 372)

predestination (p. 372)

Holy Office (p. 378)

Jesuits (p. 380)

Huguenots (p. 382)

politiques (p. 382)

Edict of Nantes (p. 383)

Union of Utrecht (p. 383)

Review the Main Ideas

Answer the section heading questions from the chapter.

1. What were the central ideas of the reformers, and why were they appealing to different social groups? (p. 358)

2. How did the political situation in Germany shape the course of the Reformation? (p. 367)

3. How did Protestant ideas and institutions spread beyond German-speaking lands? (p. 370)

4. What reforms did the Catholic Church make, and how did it respond to Protestant reform movements? (p. 378)

5. What were the causes and consequences of religious violence, including riots, wars, and witch-hunts? (p. 381)

Suggested Resources

BOOKS

- Gordon, Bruce. *John Calvin.* 2009. Situates Calvin's theology and life within the context of his relationships and the historical events of his time.
- Holt, Mack P. *The French Wars of Religion, 1562–1629*, 2d ed. 2005. A thorough survey designed for students.
- Hsia, R. Po-Chia. *The World of Catholic Renewal, 1540–1770*, 2d ed. 2005. Situates the Catholic Reformation in a global context and provides coverage of colonial Catholicism.
- Levack, Brian. *The Witch-Hunt in Early Modern Europe*, 4th ed. 2015. A good introduction to the witch-hunts, with helpful bibliographies of the vast literature on witchcraft.
- Levi, Anthony. *Renaissance and Reformation: The Intellectual Genesis.* 2002. Surveys the ideas of major Reformation figures against the background of important political issues.
- Matheson, Peter, ed. *Reformation Christianity.* 2004. This volume in A People's History of Christianity series explores social issues and popular religion.

- O'Malley, John W. *Trent and All That: Renaming Catholicism in the Early Modern Era.* 2000. Provides an excellent historiographical review of the literature and explains why and how early modern Catholicism influenced early modern European history.
- Roper, Lyndal. *Martin Luther: Renegade and Prophet.* 2017. Provides a thorough grounding in Luther's life and thought.
- Rublack, Ulinka. *Reformation Europe*, 2d ed. 2017. A solid analysis of the Protestant and Catholic reformations, designed for students.
- Terpstra, Nicolas. *Religious Refugees in the Early Modern World: An Alternative History of the Reformation.* 2015. Traces the rise of religious refugees as a mass phenomenon in the Reformation era.
- Wallace, Peter. *The Long European Reformation: Religion, Political Conflict, and the Search for Conformity, 1350–1750*, 2d ed. 2012. Examines the political and cultural impact of the Reformation.

MEDIA

- *H. Henry Meeter Center for Calvin Studies.* Resources, including audio and video recordings, on John Calvin and Calvinism, collected by the Meeter Center at Calvin College in Michigan. **https://calvin.edu/centers-institutes/meeter-center/**
- *A Man for All Seasons* (Fred Zinnemann, 1966). A classic Academy Award–winning film on Thomas More's confrontation with Henry VIII over the king's efforts to obtain a divorce; portrays More as a heroic figure who followed his principles.
- *Martin Luther: The Idea That Changed the World* (PBS, 2017). A well-received documentary produced for the 500th anniversary of the Reformation.
- *Project Wittenberg.* Concordia Theological Seminary's website devoted to the life and works of Martin Luther, with the largest online collection of Luther's writings in English, and many of his works in the original German or Latin. **projectwittenberg.org**

- *The Protestant Revolution* (BBC, 2007). A four-part documentary series that examines the religious roots and the scientific, cultural, social, economic, and political impact of Protestantism, viewing these as wide ranging and global in scope.
- *The Tudors* (Showtime, 2007–2010). A four-season historical fiction extravaganza centering on Henry VIII and his wives, full of sex and intrigue. Great fun, but not-so-great history.
- *Witchcraze* (BBC, 2003). A docudrama examining the Scottish witch trials of 1590–1591, when thirty women and one man were arrested, tortured, and eventually hanged or burned at the stake; based on original documents from the period, including court records.
- *Wolf Hall* (BBC, 2015). A miniseries based on the award-winning historical novels by Hilary Mantel that focuses on Thomas Cromwell, Henry VIII's chief minister. Praised for its acting and staging, but criticized for its harsh treatment of Thomas More.

14

European Exploration and Conquest

1450–1650

In 1450 Europeans were relatively marginal players in a centuries-old trading system that linked Africa, Asia, and Europe. In this vibrant cosmopolitan Afro-Eurasian trading world centered on the Indian Ocean, Arab, Persian, Turkish, Indian, African, Chinese, and European merchants and adventurers competed for trade in spices, silks, and other goods.

A century later, by 1550, the Portuguese search for better access to African gold and Asian trade goods had led to a new overseas empire, and Spanish explorers had accidentally discovered the Western Hemisphere. Through violent conquest, the Iberian powers established large-scale colonies in the Americas, and northern European powers sought to establish colonies of their own. The era of European expansion had begun, creating new political systems and forms of economic exchange—including the transatlantic slave trade—as well as cultural assimilation, conversion, and resistance. The age of exploration (1450–1650), as the time of these encounters is known, helped lay the foundations for the modern world. ■

CHAPTER PREVIEW

■ **What was the Afro-Eurasian trading world before Columbus?**

■ **How and why did Europeans undertake ambitious voyages of expansion?**

■ **What was the impact of European conquest on the New World?**

■ **How did Europe and the world change after Columbus?**

■ **How did expansion change European attitudes and beliefs?**

Life in the Age of Exploration
The arrival of the Portuguese in Japan in 1543 inspired a series of artworks depicting the *namban-jin*, "southern barbarians," as the Japanese called them. This detail from an early-seventeenth-century painted screen shows a Portuguese merchant with three enslaved South Asian men unloading trade goods from a merchant ship. (De Agostini/Getty Images)

What was the Afro-Eurasian trading world before Columbus?

Columbus did not sail west on a whim. To understand his and other Europeans' voyages of exploration, we must first understand late medieval trade networks. Historians now recognize that a type of world economy, known as the Afro-Eurasian trade world, linked the products, people, and ideas of Africa, Europe, and Asia during the Middle Ages. The West was not the dominant player before Columbus, and the voyages derived from a desire to gain direct access to the goods of overseas trade. European monarchs and explorers also wished to spread Christianity. Their projects for exploration and conquest received support from the papacy in Rome.

The Trade World of the Indian Ocean

Covering 20 percent of the earth's total ocean area, the Indian Ocean is the globe's third-largest waterway (after the Pacific and Atlantic). Moderate and predictable monsoon winds blow from the northwest or northeast between November and January and from the south and southwest between April and August. These wind patterns enabled cross-oceanic travel and shaped its rhythms, creating a vibrant trade world in which goods, people, and ideas circulated among China, India, the Middle East, Southeast Asia, and Africa (Map 14.1). From the seventh through the fourteenth centuries, the volume and integration of Indian Ocean trade steadily increased, favored by two parallel movements: political unification and economic growth in China and the spread of Islam through much of the Indian Ocean world.

Merchants congregated in a series of cosmopolitan port cities strung around the Indian Ocean. Most of these cities had some form of autonomous self-government, and no one state or region dominated. Ethnic, religious, and family ties encouraged trust among traders and limited violence.

Located at the northeastern edge of the Indian Ocean trade world, China exercised a powerful economic and cultural influence. In addition to safeguarding the famous Silk Road overland trade routes through Central Asia and the Middle East, the Mongols also increased connections with Indian Ocean trade. The Venetian trader Marco Polo's tales of his travels from 1271 to 1295, including his encounter with the Great Khan, fueled Western fantasies about the wealth and sophistication of Asian empires. Polo vividly recounted the splendors of the khan's court and the city of Hangzhou, which he described as "the finest and noblest in the world" in which "the number and wealth of the merchants, and the amount of goods that passed through their hands, was so enormous that no man could form a just estimate thereof."[1]

After the Mongols fell to the Ming Dynasty in 1368, China entered a new period of economic expansion, population growth, and urbanization. China's huge cities hungered for luxury products of the Indian Ocean world, and its artisans produced goods highly prized in export markets, especially porcelain and silk. The Ming emperor dispatched Admiral Zheng He (jehng huh) on a remarkable series of naval expeditions that traveled the oceanic web as far west as Egypt. From 1405 to 1433 each of his seven expeditions involved hundreds of ships and tens of thousands of men. In one voyage alone, Zheng He sailed more than 12,000 miles.[2] Although the ships brought back many wonders, such as giraffes and zebras, the purpose of the voyages was primarily diplomatic: to enhance China's prestige and seek tribute-paying alliances. After the deaths of Zheng He and the emperor, the voyages ceased, but Chinese overseas traders continued vigorous activity in the South China Sea and throughout the Indian Ocean.

India was the central hinge of Indian Ocean trade. Muslim Arab and Persian merchants who circumnavigated India on their way to trade in the South China Sea established trading posts along the southern coasts of east and west India. Cities such as Calicut and Quilon became thriving commercial centers. India was also an important contributor of goods to the world trading system. Most of the world's pepper was grown in India, and Indian cotton and silk textiles, mainly from the Gujarat region, were also highly prized.

On the east coast of Africa, Swahili-speaking city-states engaged directly in the Indian Ocean trade, exchanging ivory, rhinoceros horn, tortoise shells, and enslaved people for textiles, spices, cowrie shells, porcelain, and other goods. Cities such as Kilwa, Malindi, Mogadishu, and Mombasa, dominated by Muslim merchants, were known for their prosperity and culture.

Southeast Asia maintained an active trade with China across the South China Sea and with ports on the Coromandel Coast of southeast India. In the fifteenth century the strategically located port of Malacca became a great commercial entrepôt (AHN-truh-poh), a trading post to which goods were shipped for storage while awaiting redistribution. To Malacca came porcelains, silks, and camphor (used in the manufacture of many medications) from China; pepper, cloves, nutmeg, and raw materials such as sandalwood from the Moluccas; and textiles, copper weapons, incense, and dyes from India.

TIMELINE

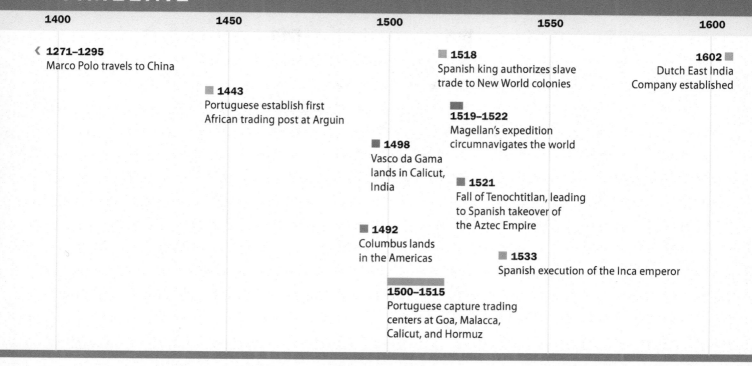

1400　　　　**1450**　　　　**1500**　　　　**1550**　　　　**1600**

1271–1295
Marco Polo travels to China

1443
Portuguese establish first
African trading post at Arguin

1498
Vasco da Gama
lands in Calicut,
India

1492
Columbus lands
in the Americas

1500–1515
Portuguese capture trading
centers at Goa, Malacca,
Calicut, and Hormuz

1518
Spanish king authorizes slave
trade to New World colonies

1519–1522
Magellan's expedition
circumnavigates the world

1521
Fall of Tenochtitlan, leading
to Spanish takeover of
the Aztec Empire

1533
Spanish execution of the Inca emperor

1602
Dutch East India
Company established

The Trading States of Africa

In addition to the Swahili city-states, by 1450 Africa had a few large empires along with hundreds of smaller states. After the Mongol invasion of Baghdad in 1258, the Mamluk rulers of Egypt proclaimed a new Abbasid caliphate. Until its defeat by the Ottomans in 1517, the Mamluk empire was one of the most powerful on the continent. Its capital, Cairo, was a center of Islamic learning and religious authority as well as a major hub for goods moving between the Indian Ocean trade world and the Mediterranean.

In the fifteenth century most of the gold that reached Europe came from the western part of the Sudan region in West Africa and from the Akan (AH-kahn) peoples living near present-day Ghana. Transported across the Sahara by Arab and African traders on camels, the gold was sold in the ports of North Africa. Other trading routes led to the Egyptian cities of Alexandria and Cairo, where the Venetians held commercial privileges.

Inland nations that sat astride the north-south caravan routes grew wealthy from this trade. In the mid-thirteenth century the kingdom of Mali emerged as an important player on the overland trade route, gaining prestige from its ruler Mansa Musa's fabulous pilgrimage to Mecca in 1324/25. Desire to gain direct access to African gold motivated the initial Portuguese voyages into northern and western Africa.

Gold was one important object of trade; enslaved people were another. Slavery was practiced in Africa, as it was virtually everywhere else in the world, long before the arrival of Europeans. Arab and North African merchants took enslaved people from West Africa to the Mediterranean to be sold in European, Egyptian, and Middle Eastern markets. In addition, Indian and Arab merchants traded enslaved people in the coastal regions of East Africa.

The Middle East

From its capital in Baghdad, the Abbasid caliphate (750–1258) controlled an enormous region from Spain to the western borders of China, including the Red Sea and the Persian Gulf, the two major waterways linking the Indian Ocean trade world to the West. The political stability enshrined by the caliphate, along with the shared language, legal system, and culture of Islam, fostered economic prosperity and commercial activity. During this period, Muslim Arab traders, who had spread through eastern Africa and western India in the early Middle Ages, reached even further across the trade routes of the Indian Ocean to obtain spices, porcelain, and other goods for the bustling cities of the caliphate.

After the Abbasids fell to Mongol invasions, two great rival Muslim empires, the Persian Safavids (sah-FAH-vidz) and the Turkish Ottomans, dominated the region and competed for control of east-west trade. Like Arabs, Persian merchants could be found in trading communities in India and throughout the Afro-Eurasian trade world. Persia was also a major producer and exporter of silk cloth.

Under Sultan Mohammed II (r. 1451–1481), the Ottomans captured Europe's largest city, Constantinople, in May 1453. The city became the capital of the

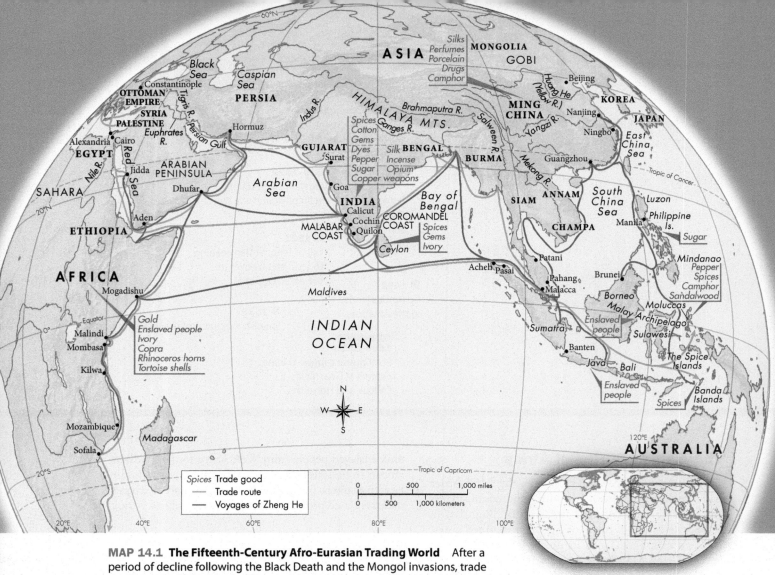

MAP 14.1 The Fifteenth-Century Afro-Eurasian Trading World After a period of decline following the Black Death and the Mongol invasions, trade revived in the fifteenth century. Muslim merchants dominated trade, linking ports in East Africa and the Red Sea with those in India and the Malay Archipelago. Chinese admiral Zheng He's voyages (1405–1433) followed the most important Indian Ocean trade routes.

Ottoman Empire. By the mid-sixteenth century the Ottomans had established control over the maritime trade in the eastern Mediterranean and their power extended into Europe as far west as Vienna. The extension of Ottoman control provided impetus for European traders to seek direct access to Eastern trade goods.

Genoese and Venetian Middlemen

In the late Middle Ages, the Italian city-states of Venice and Genoa controlled the European luxury trade with the East. In 1304 Venice established formal relations with the sultan of Mamluk Egypt, opening operations in Cairo, a major outlet for Asian trade goods brought through the Red Sea. Venetian merchants purchased goods such as spices, silks, and carpets in Cairo for re-export throughout Europe. Venetians funded these purchases through trade in European woolen cloth and metal goods, as well as through shipping and trade in firearms and enslaved people.

Venice's ancient rival was Genoa. In the wake of the Crusades, Genoa dominated the northern route to Asia through the Black Sea. Expansion in the thirteenth and fourteenth centuries took the Genoese as far as Persia and the Far East. In 1291 they sponsored an expedition into the Atlantic in search of India. The ships were lost, and their exact destination and motivations remain unknown. This voyage reveals the long roots of Genoese interest in Atlantic exploration.

In the fifteenth century, with Venice claiming victory in the spice trade, the Genoese shifted their focus from trade to finance and from the Black Sea to the western Mediterranean. When Spanish and Portuguese voyages began to explore the western Atlantic, Genoese merchants, navigators, and financiers provided their skills and capital to the Iberian monarchs, whose own subjects had less commercial experience. Genoese merchants would eventually help finance Spanish colonization of the New World.

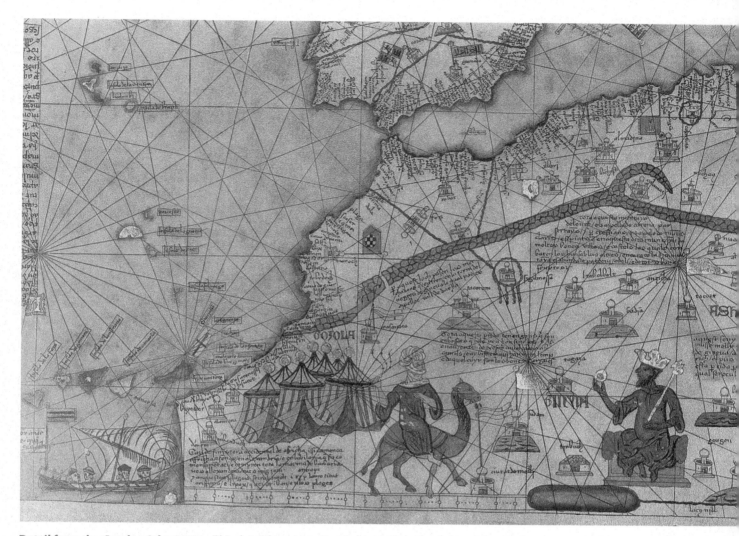

Detail from the *Catalan Atlas*, 1375   This detail from a medieval map depicts Mansa Musa (lower right), who ruled the powerful West African empire of Mali from 1312 to 1337. Musa's golden crown and scepter, and the gold ingot he holds in his hand, represent the empire's wealth. The map also depicts Catalan sailors heading from the Balearic Islands out to the Atlantic Ocean. (From *The Catalan Atlas*, 1375, by Abraham Cresques/Bibliothèque Nationale, Paris, France/Getty Images)

A major element of Italian trade was slavery. Merchants purchased enslaved people, many of whom were fellow Christians, in the Balkans and the Black Sea region. The men were sold to Egypt for the sultan's army or sent to work as agricultural laborers in the Mediterranean. Young girls, who constituted the majority of the trade, were sold in western Mediterranean ports as servants and concubines. After the loss of the Black Sea — and thus the source of enslaved people — to the Ottomans, the Genoese sought new supplies of enslaved people in the West, taking the Guanches (Indigenous peoples from the Canary Islands), Muslim prisoners, Jewish refugees from Spain, and by the early 1500s both sub-Saharan and Berber Africans. With the growth of Spanish colonies in the New World in the sixteenth century, Genoese and Venetian merchants would become important players in the transatlantic slave trade.

How and why did Europeans undertake ambitious voyages of expansion?

As we have seen, Europe was by no means isolated before the voyages of exploration and the "discovery" of the New World. Italian merchants traded actively in North Africa for gold and in eastern Mediterranean depots for Indian Ocean luxury goods, but trade through intermediaries was slow and expensive. In the first decades of the fifteenth century, new players entered the scene with novel technology, eager to obtain direct access to trade and to spread Christianity. First Portuguese and then Spanish expeditions undertook long-distance voyages that helped create the modern world, with tremendous consequences for their own continent and the rest of the planet.

Causes of European Expansion

European expansion had multiple causes. The first was economic. The Portuguese and Spanish, the first to undertake voyages of exploration, sought new sources of gold and silver as well as a direct route to the Asian trade in spices and other luxury goods. Financial incentives became even more important in the mid-fifteenth century as the revival of population after the Black Death increased demand and Ottoman control of eastern trade routes reduced the flow of trade.

Why were spices so desirable? Introduced into western Europe by the Crusaders in the twelfth century, pepper, ginger, mace, cinnamon, nutmeg, and cloves added flavor and variety to the monotonous European diet. Not only did spices serve as flavorings for food, but they were also used in anointing oil, as incense for religious rituals, and as perfumes, medicines, and dyes in daily life. Apart from their utility, the expense and exotic origins of spices meant that they were a high-status good that European elites could use to demonstrate their social standing.

Religious fervor and the crusading spirit were another cause of expansion. From the eleventh through the thirteenth centuries, the Christian kingdoms of the Iberian Peninsula emerged through warfare against Muslim states, a process that became known as the *reconquista*. Portugal's expansion across the Mediterranean to North Africa in 1415 and Christopher Columbus's voyage in 1492 thus represented overseas extensions of the crusading spirit. Only seven months separated Isabella and Ferdinand's conquest of the emirate of Granada, the last remaining Muslim state on the Iberian Peninsula, and Columbus's departure across the Atlantic in 1492. As they conquered Indigenous empires in the Americas, Iberians brought attitudes and administrative practices developed during the reconquista to the New World. **Conquistadors** (kohn-KEES-tuh-dorz) (Spanish for "conquerors") fully expected to be rewarded with land,

titles, and power over conquered peoples, just as the leaders of the reconquista had been.

To gain authorization and financial support for their expeditions, explorers sought official sponsorship from the state. Competition among European monarchs for the prestige and profit of overseas exploration was thus another crucial factor in encouraging the steady stream of expeditions that began in the late fifteenth century.

Like other men of the Renaissance era, explorers demonstrated a genuine passion for expanding human knowledge. The European discoveries thus constituted one manifestation of Renaissance curiosity about the physical universe. The detailed journals many voyagers kept attest to their wonder and fascination with the new peoples and places they visited, albeit usually framed by their Christian beliefs and assumptions about European superiority.

The small number of Europeans who could read provided a rapt audience for tales of faraway places and unknown peoples. Cosmography, natural history, and geography aroused enormous interest among educated people in the fifteenth and sixteenth centuries. One of the most popular books of the time was the fourteenth-century text *The Travels of Sir John Mandeville*, which purported to be a firsthand account of the author's travels in the Middle East, India, and China.

Technology and the Rise of Exploration

The Portuguese were pioneers in seeking technological improvements in shipbuilding, weaponry, and navigation in order to undertake successful voyages of exploration and trade. Medieval European seagoing vessels consisted of single-masted sailing ships or narrow, open galleys propelled by oars, which were common in Mediterranean trade. Though adequate for short journeys that hugged the shoreline, such vessels were incapable of long-distance journeys or high-volume trade. In the fifteenth century, the Portuguese developed the **caravel**, a two- or three-masted sailing ship. Its multiple sails and sternpost rudder made the caravel a highly maneuverable vessel that required fewer crewmen to operate. The Portuguese were also the first to fit their ships with cannon, which produced immense advantages for naval warfare and bombardment of port cities, both of which were to play a crucial role in their expansion into Asia.[3]

This period also saw great strides in cartography and navigational aids. Around 1410 Arab scholars reintroduced Europeans to **Ptolemy's** *Geography*. Written in the second century C.E., the work synthesized the geographical knowledge of the classical world. It represented a major improvement over

---

■ **conquistadors** Spanish for "conquerors"; armed Spaniards such as Hernán Cortés and Francisco Pizarro, who sought to conquer people and territories in the New World for the Spanish Crown.

■ **caravel** A small, maneuverable, two- or three-masted sailing ship developed by the Portuguese in the fifteenth century that gave them a distinct advantage in exploration and trade.

■ **Ptolemy's** *Geography* A second-century-C.E. work that synthesized the classical knowledge of geography and introduced the concepts of longitude and latitude. Reintroduced to Europeans about 1410 by Arab scholars, its ideas allowed cartographers to create more accurate maps.

medieval cartography by depicting the world as round and introducing the idea of latitude and longitude markings, but it also contained crucial errors. Unaware of the Americas, Ptolemy showed the world as much smaller than it is, so that Asia appeared not very much to the west of Europe.

Originating in China, the compass was brought to the West in the late Middle Ages. By using the compass to determine their direction and estimating their speed of travel over a set length of time, mariners could determine the course of a ship's voyage, a system of navigation known as "dead reckoning." In the late fifteenth century Portuguese scholars devised the new technique of "celestial reckoning," which involved using the astrolabe, an instrument invented by the ancient Greeks to determine the position of the stars and other celestial bodies. Commissioned by Portuguese king John II, a group of astronomers in the 1480s showed that mariners could determine their latitude at sea by using a specially designed astrolabe to determine the altitude of the polestar or the sun, and by consulting tables of

these bodies' movements. This was a crucial step forward in maritime navigational techniques.

Much of the new technology that Europeans used on their voyages originated in the East. Gunpowder, the compass, and the sternpost rudder were Chinese inventions. The triangular lateen sail, which allowed caravels to tack against the wind, was a product of the Indian Ocean trade world. Advances in navigational techniques and cartography, including the maritime astrolabe, drew on the rich tradition of Judeo-Arabic mathematical and astronomical learning in Iberia. In exploring new territories, European sailors thus called on techniques and knowledge developed over centuries in China, the Muslim world, and the Indian Ocean.

Despite technological improvements, life at sea meant danger, overcrowding, and hunger. For months at a time, 100 to 120 poorly paid crew members lived and worked in a space of 1,600 to 2,000 square feet. A lucky sailor would find enough space on deck to unroll his sleeping mat. Horses, cows, pigs, chickens, rats, and lice accompanied sailors on the voyages.

Ptolemy's *Geography*   The recovery of Ptolemy's *Geography* in the early fifteenth century gave Europeans new access to ancient geographical knowledge. This 1486 world map, based on Ptolemy, is a great advance over medieval maps but contains errors that had significant consequences for future exploration. It shows a single continent watered by a single ocean, with land covering three-quarters of the world's surface. Africa and Asia are joined with Europe, making the Indian Ocean a landlocked sea and rendering the circumnavigation of Africa impossible. Australia and the Americas are nonexistent, and the continent of Asia is stretched far to the east, greatly shortening the distance from Europe to Asia via the Atlantic. (Bibliothèque Nationale, Paris, France/Bridgeman Images)

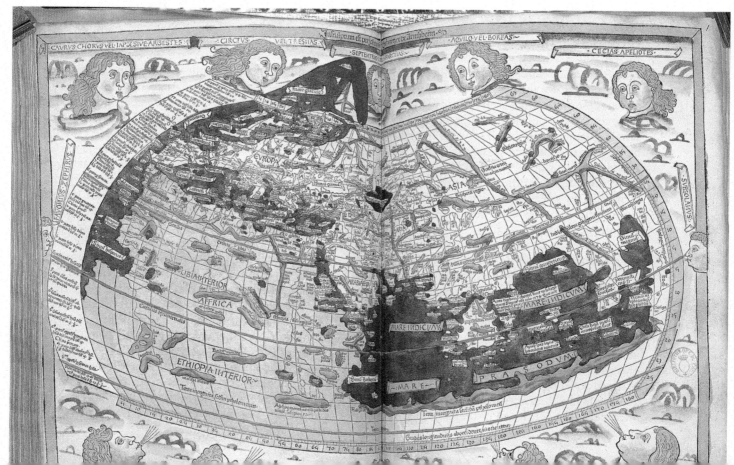

The Caravel This illustration from a sixteenth-century manuscript depicts a caravel, a type of ship developed in Portugal in the fifteenth century. The caravel was highly maneuverable because of its "lateen" sails — a type of triangular sail that allowed the ship to sail against the wind — and its sternpost rudder. (JEAN-LOUIS JOSSE/Bridgeman Images)

The Portuguese Overseas Empire

Established during the reconquista in the mid-thirteenth century, the kingdom of Portugal had a long Atlantic coastline that favored fishing and maritime trading. By the end of the thirteenth century Portuguese merchants were trading fish, salt, and wine to ports in northern England and the Mediterranean. Nature favored the Portuguese: winds blowing along their coast offered passage to Africa, its Atlantic islands, and, ultimately, Brazil. Once they had mastered the secret to sailing against the wind to return to Europe (by sailing further west to catch winds from the southwest), they were ideally poised to pioneer Atlantic exploration.

In the early phases of Portuguese exploration, Prince Henry (1394–1460), a younger son of the king, played a leading role. A nineteenth-century scholar dubbed Henry "the Navigator" because of his support for Portuguese voyages of discovery. Henry participated in Portugal's conquest of Ceuta, an Arab city in northern Morocco in 1415, an event that marked the beginning of European overseas expansion. In the 1420s, under Henry's direction, the Portuguese claimed sovereignty over islands in the Atlantic off the northwest coast of Africa, Madeira (ca. 1420) and the Azores (1427). In 1443 they founded their first

African commercial settlement at Arguin in modern-day Mauretania.

By the time of Henry's death in 1460, his support for exploration was vindicated—from the Portuguese point of view—by thriving sugar plantations on the Atlantic islands, the first arrival of enslaved Africans in Portugal, and new access to African gold. It was also authorized and legitimized by the Catholic Church. In 1454, Pope Nicholas V issued a bull reiterating the rights of the Portuguese Crown to conquer and enslave non-Christians and recognizing Portuguese possession of territories in West Africa. Such papal proclamations legitimized Portuguese—and later Spanish—seizure of land and people in their own eyes, but of course it meant nothing to the people whom the Europeans invaded and conquered.

The Portuguese next established fortified trading posts, called factories, on the gold-rich Guinea coast (Map 14.2). By 1500 Portugal controlled the flow of African gold to Europe. In contrast to the Spanish conquest of the Americas, the Portuguese did not seek to establish large settlements in West Africa or to control the political or cultural lives of those with whom they traded. Instead, they pursued easier and faster profits by inserting themselves into pre-existing trading systems. For the first century of their relations, African rulers were equal partners with the Portuguese, benefiting from their experienced armies and European vulnerability to tropical diseases.

The Portuguese then pushed farther south down the west coast of Africa. In 1488 Bartholomeu Dias rounded the Cape of Good Hope at the southern tip of Africa, but poor conditions forced him to turn back. A decade later Vasco da Gama succeeded in rounding the Cape while commanding a fleet of four ships in search of a sea route to India. With the help of an Arab guide, da Gama reached the port of Calicut in India in 1498. He returned to Lisbon loaded with spices and samples of Indian cloth, having proved the possibility of lucrative trade with the East via the Cape route. Thereafter, a Portuguese convoy set out for passage around the Cape every year in March or April.

Lisbon became the major entrance port for Asian goods into Europe, but this was not accomplished without a fight. Muslim-controlled port city-states had long controlled the rich trade of the Indian Ocean, and they did not surrender their dominance willingly. From 1500 to 1515 the Portuguese used a combination of bombardment and diplomatic treaties to establish trading forts at Calicut, Goa, Malacca, and Hormuz, thereby laying the foundation for a Portuguese trading empire in the sixteenth and seventeenth centuries. The acquisition of port cities and their trade routes allowed Portugal to dominate trade in the Indian Ocean, but, as in Africa, the Portuguese did not seek to transform the lives and religious faith of peoples beyond their coastal holdings.

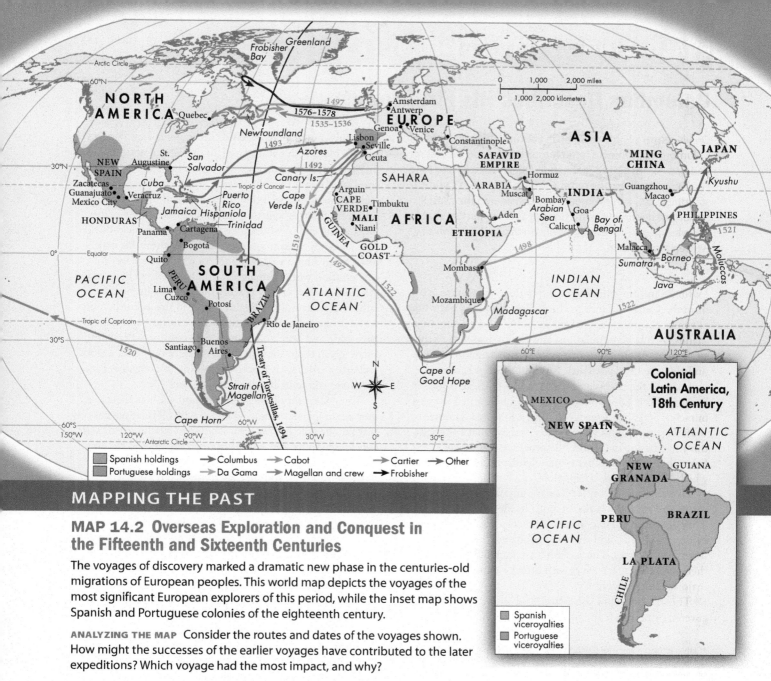

MAPPING THE PAST

MAP 14.2 Overseas Exploration and Conquest in the Fifteenth and Sixteenth Centuries

The voyages of discovery marked a dramatic new phase in the centuries-old migrations of European peoples. This world map depicts the voyages of the most significant European explorers of this period, while the inset map shows Spanish and Portuguese colonies of the eighteenth century.

ANALYZING THE MAP Consider the routes and dates of the voyages shown. How might the successes of the earlier voyages have contributed to the later expeditions? Which voyage had the most impact, and why?

CONNECTIONS How would you compare Spanish and Portuguese New World holdings in the sixteenth century with those of the eighteenth century? How would you explain the differences and continuities over time?

Inspired by the Portuguese, the Spanish had also begun to seek direct access to the wealth of Asian trade. Theirs was to be a second, entirely different, mode of colonization, leading to the conquest of existing empires, large-scale settlement, and the assimilation of a subjugated Indigenous population.

Spain's Voyages to the Americas

Christopher Columbus was not the first to explore the Atlantic. Ninth-century Vikings established short-lived settlements in Newfoundland, and it is probable that others made the voyage, either on purpose or accidentally, carried by westward currents off the coast of Africa. In the late fifteenth century, however, the achievements of Portugal's decades of exploration made the moment right for Christopher Columbus's attempt to find a westward route across the Atlantic to Asia.

Christopher Columbus, a native of Genoa, was an experienced seaman and navigator, with close ties to the world of Portuguese seafaring. He had worked as a mapmaker in Lisbon and spent time on Madeira, where his wife's father led the Portuguese colony. He was familiar with *portolans*—written descriptions of the courses along which ships sailed—and the use of the compass for dead reckoning. (He carried an astrolabe on his first voyage, but did not use it for navigation.)

Columbus Describes His First Voyage

On his return voyage to Spain in February 1493, Christopher Columbus composed a letter intended for wide circulation and had copies of it sent ahead to Queen Isabella and King Ferdinand. Because the letter sums up Columbus's understanding of his achievements, it is considered the most important document of his first voyage. Remember that his knowledge of Asia rested heavily on Marco Polo's *Travels*, written around 1298.

I write to inform you how in thirty-three days I crossed from the Canary Islands to the Indies, with the fleet which our most illustrious sovereigns gave me. I found very many islands with large populations and took possession of them all for their Highnesses; this I did by proclamation and unfurled the royal standard. No opposition was offered.

I named the first island that I found "San Salvador," in honour of our Lord and Saviour who has granted me this miracle. . . . When I reached Cuba, I followed its north coast westwards, and found it so extensive that I thought this must be the mainland, the province of Cathay. . . .* From there I saw another island eighteen leagues eastwards which I then named "Hispaniola." . . .†

Hispaniola is a wonder. The mountains and hills, the plains and meadow lands are both fertile and beautiful. They are most suitable for planting crops and for raising cattle of all kinds, and there are good sites for building towns and villages. The harbours are incredibly fine and there are many great rivers with broad channels and the majority contain gold.‡

The inhabitants of this island, and all the rest that I discovered or heard of, go naked, as their mothers bore them,

*Cathay is the old name for China. In the logbook and later in this letter, Columbus accepts the native story that Cuba is an island that can be circumnavigated in something more than twenty-one days, yet he insists here and during the second voyage that it is part of the Asiatic mainland.

†Hispaniola is the second-largest island of the West Indies. Today Haiti occupies the western third of the island, the Dominican Republic the rest.

‡This did not prove to be true.

men and women alike. A few of the women, however, cover a single place with a leaf of a plant or piece of cotton which they weave for the purpose. They have no iron or steel or arms and are not capable of using them, not because they are not strong and well built but because they are amazingly timid. All the weapons they have are canes cut at seeding time, at the end of which they fix a sharpened stick, but they have not the courage to make use of these, for very often when I have sent two or three men to a village to have conversation with them a great number of them have come out. But as soon as they saw my men all fled immediately, a father not even waiting for his son. And this is not because we have harmed any of them; on the contrary, wherever I have gone and been able to have conversation with them, I have given them some of the various things I had, a cloth and other articles, and received nothing in exchange. But they have still remained incurably timid.

True, when they have been reassured and lost their fear, they are so ingenuous and so liberal with all their possessions that no one who has not seen them would believe it. If one asks for anything they have they never say no. On the contrary, they offer a share to anyone with demonstrations of heartfelt affection, and they are immediately content with any small thing, valuable or valueless, that is given them. I forbade the men to give them bits of broken crockery, fragments of glass or tags of laces, though if they could get them they fancied them the finest jewels in the world. . . .

I hoped to win them to the love and service of their Highnesses and of the whole Spanish nation and to persuade them to collect and give us of the things which they possessed in abundance and which we needed. They have no religion and are not idolaters; but all believe that power and goodness dwell in the sky and they are firmly convinced that I have come from the sky with these ships and people. In this belief they gave me a good reception everywhere, once they had overcome their fear; and this is not because they are stupid — far from it, they are men of great intelligence, for they navigate all those seas, and give a marvellously good account of every thing — but because

Columbus was also a deeply religious man. He had witnessed the Spanish conquest of Granada and shared fully in the religious fervor surrounding that event. Like the Spanish rulers and most Europeans of his age, Columbus understood Christianity as a missionary religion that should be carried to all places of the earth.

Given Portugal's leading role in Atlantic exploration and his personal connections, Columbus first appealed to the Portuguese rulers for support for a voyage to find a westward passage to the Indies in

1483. When they refused, he turned, unsuccessfully, to Ferdinand and Isabella in 1486 and then finally won the backing of the Spanish monarchy in 1492. Buoyed by the success of the reconquista and eager to earn profits from trade, the Spanish Crown named Columbus viceroy over any territory he might discover and promised him one-tenth of the material rewards of the journey.

Columbus and his small fleet left Spain on August 3, 1492. Inspired by the stories of Mandeville and Marco

they have never before seen men clothed or ships like these. . . .

In all these islands the men are seemingly content with one woman, but their chief or king is allowed more than twenty. The women appear to work more than the men and I have not been able to find out if they have private property. As far as I could see whatever a man had was shared among all the rest and this particularly applies to food. . . . In another island, which I am told is larger than Hispaniola, the people have no hair. Here there is a vast quantity of gold, and from here and the other islands I bring Indians as evidence.

In conclusion, to speak only of the results of this very hasty voyage, their Highnesses can see that I will give them as much gold as they require, if they will render me some very slight assistance; also I will give them all the spices and cotton they want. . . . I will also bring them as much aloes as they ask and as many slaves, who will be taken from the idolaters.§

EVALUATE THE EVIDENCE

1. What was Columbus's view of the Native Americans he met, and what does he want the Spanish rulers to know about them?
2. Columbus describes the wealth of the Caribbean islands in gold, cotton, and spices and also says that the Native Americans were eager to share their possessions with the Spanish. How trustworthy do you think Columbus is on these points? Why would he exaggerate these elements of his voyage?
3. How does Columbus describe his treatment of the people he encountered? What impression does he seem to want to convey? What does his description show about Europeans' attitudes to the peoples they encountered in the New World?

Source: *The Four Voyages of Christopher Columbus*, ed. and trans. J. M. Cohen (London: Penguin Books, 1992), pp. 115–123.

§ This contradicts his earlier statement that the Indigenous people were not "idolaters"; elsewhere in the letter he comments that the inhabitants of the Caribbean could be easily enslaved.

Polo, Columbus dreamed of reaching the court of the Great Khan (not realizing that the Ming Dynasty had overthrown the Mongols in 1368). Based on Ptolemy's *Geography* and other texts, he expected to pass the islands of Japan and then land on the east coast of China.

On October 12, 1492, he landed in the Bahamas, which he christened San Salvador and claimed for the Spanish Crown. In a letter submitted to Ferdinand and Isabella on his return to Spain, Columbus described the Indigenous population as handsome,

peaceful, and "timid." Their body painting reminded him of that of the Canary Islands people. Believing he was somewhere off the east coast of Japan, in what he considered the Indies, he called them "Indians," a name later applied by Europeans to all Indigenous inhabitants of the Americas. Columbus concluded that he could easily enslave them and convert them to Christianity. (See "Evaluating Written Evidence: Columbus Describes His First Voyage," page 398.)

Columbus's First Voyage to the New World, 1492–1493

Scholars have identified the inhabitants of the islands as the Taino people, who inhabited Hispaniola (modern-day Haiti and Dominican Republic) and other islands in the Caribbean. From San Salvador, Columbus sailed southwest, landing on Cuba on October 28. Deciding that he must be on the mainland near the coastal city of Quinsay (now Hangzhou), described by Marco Polo, he sent a small embassy inland with letters from Ferdinand and Isabella and instructions to locate the grand city. Although they found no large settlement or any evidence of a great kingdom, the sight of Taino people wearing gold ornaments on Hispaniola suggested that gold was available in the region. In January, confident that its source would soon be found, Columbus headed back to Spain to report on his discovery.[4]

On his second voyage in 1493, Columbus brought with him settlers for the new Spanish territories, along with agricultural seed and livestock. Columbus and his followers forcibly took control of the island of Hispaniola and established a new town, which they named Isabella, as a base for mining gold. Columbus himself, however, had limited skills in governing. His harsh discipline and labor requirements led to great resentment among Spanish settlers and revolt among the Indigenous population. He responded with military force, imposing tribute payments on Indigenous villages and enslaving Indigenous people. In March 1496, Columbus returned to Spain to defend himself against his critics, leaving his brother in charge of Hispaniola. During his two-year absence, a group of rebel Spanish settlers created a breakaway colony. To appease the rebels, Columbus granted them control over Indigenous labor. A royal expedition sent to investigate Columbus's leadership returned him and his brother to Spain in chains, and a royal governor assumed control of Hispaniola.

To the end of his life in 1506, Columbus incorrectly believed that he had found small islands off the coast of Asia. He could not know that the scale of his discoveries would revolutionize world power and set in motion a new era of trade, conquest, and empire. The brutal exploitation of Indigenous people that he initiated would set the pattern for European conquest and settlement.

Spain "Discovers" the Pacific

The Florentine navigator Amerigo Vespucci (veh-SPOO-chee) (1454–1512) was one of the first to begin to perceive what Columbus had not. Writing about his discoveries on the coast of modern-day Venezuela, Vespucci stated: "Those new regions which we found and explored with the fleet . . . we may rightly call a New World." This letter, titled *Mundus Novus* (The New World), was the first document to describe America as a continent separate from Asia. In recognition of Amerigo's bold claim, a German mapmaker named the new continent for him in 1507.

As soon as Columbus returned from his first voyage, Isabella and Ferdinand sought to establish their claims to the new territories and forestall potential opposition from Portugal, which had previously dominated Atlantic exploration. Spanish-born Pope Alexander VI, to whom they appealed for support, proposed drawing an imaginary line down the Atlantic, giving Spain possession of all lands discovered to the west and Portugal everything to the east. The pope enjoined both powers to carry the Christian faith to these newly discovered lands and their peoples. The **Treaty of Tordesillas** (tor-duh-SEE-yuhs) negotiated between Spain and Portugal in 1494 retained the pope's idea, but moved the line further west as a concession to the Portuguese. This arbitrary division worked in Portugal's favor when in 1500 an expedition led by Pedro Álvares Cabral, en route to India, landed on the coast of Brazil, which Cabral claimed as Portuguese territory. (Because the line was also imagined to extend around the globe, it meant that the Philippine Islands would eventually end up in Spanish control.)

The search for profits determined the direction of Spanish exploration. Because its revenue from Hispaniola and other Caribbean islands was insignificant compared to the enormous riches that the Portuguese were reaping in Asia, Spain renewed the search for a western passage to Asia. In 1519 Charles I of Spain (who was also Holy Roman emperor Charles V) sent the Portuguese mariner Ferdinand Magellan (1480–1521) to find a sea route to the spices of Southeast Asia. Magellan sailed southwest across the Atlantic to Brazil, and after a long search along the coast he located the treacherous straits that now bear his name (see Map 14.2). The new ocean he sailed into after a rough passage through the straits seemed so calm that Magellan dubbed it the Pacific, from the Latin

word for peaceful. His fleet sailed north up the west coast of South America and then headed west into the immense expanse of the Pacific in 1520 toward the Malay Archipelago, which includes modern-day Indonesia and other island nations.

Magellan's first impressions of the Pacific were terribly mistaken. Terrible storms, disease, starvation, and violence devastated the expedition. Magellan himself died in a skirmish in the Malay Archipelago, and only one of the five ships that began the expedition made it back to Spain. The ship returned home in 1522 with only 18 of the approximately 270 men who originally set out, having traveled from the east by way of the Indian Ocean, the Cape of Good Hope, and the Atlantic. The voyage — the first to circumnavigate the globe — had taken close to three years.

Despite the losses, this voyage revolutionized Europeans' understanding of the world by demonstrating the vastness of the Pacific. The earth was clearly much larger than Ptolemy's map had shown. Although the voyage made a small profit in spices, it also demonstrated that the westward passage to the Indies was too long and dangerous for commercial purposes. Spain's rulers soon abandoned the attempt to oust Portugal from the Eastern spice trade and concentrated on exploiting their New World territories.

Early Exploration by Northern European Powers

Shortly following Columbus's voyages, northern European nations entered the competition for a northwest passage to the Indies. In 1497 John Cabot, a Venetian merchant living in London, obtained support from English king Henry VII for such a voyage. Following a northern route that he believed would provide shorter passage to Asia, Cabot and his crew landed on Newfoundland. In subsequent years, Cabot made two additional voyages to explore the northeast coast of Canada. These forays did not reveal a passage to the Indies, and Cabot made no attempt to establish settlements in the coastal areas he explored.

News of the riches of Mexico and Peru later inspired the English to renew their efforts to find a westward passage, this time in the extreme north. Between 1576 and 1578 Martin Frobisher made three voyages in and around the Canadian bay that now bears his name. Frobisher brought a quantity of ore back to England with him, hoping he had found a new source of gold or silver, but it proved to be worthless.

The French Crown also sponsored efforts to find a westward passage to Asia. Between 1534 and 1541 Frenchman Jacques Cartier made several voyages and explored the St. Lawrence River of Canada. His exploration of the St. Lawrence was halted at the great rapids west of the present-day island of

Montreal; he named the rapids "La Chine" in the optimistic belief that China lay just beyond. When this hope proved in vain, the French turned to a new source of profit within Canada itself: trade in beavers and other furs. As had the Portuguese in Asia, French traders bartered with local people, who maintained autonomous control of their trade goods during this period.

French fishermen also competed with Portuguese and Spanish, and later English, ships for the teeming schools of cod they found in the Atlantic waters around Newfoundland, one of the richest fish stocks in the world. Fishing vessels salted the catch on board and brought it back to Europe, where a thriving market for fish was created by the Catholic prohibition on eating meat on Fridays and during Lent.

What was the impact of European conquest on the New World?

Before Columbus's arrival, the Americas were inhabited by thousands of groups of Indigenous peoples with different languages and cultures. These groups ranged from hunter-gatherers organized into confederations to settled agriculturalists to large-scale empires containing bustling cities and towns. The best estimate is that the peoples of the Americas numbered between 35 and 50 million in 1492. Their lives were radically transformed by the arrival of Europeans.

The growing European presence in the New World transformed its land and its peoples forever. While Iberian powers conquered enormous territories in Central and South America, incorporating pre-existing peoples and empires, the northern European powers came later to colonization and, at first, established scattered settlements hugging the North American Atlantic coastline. Over time, the expansion of northern European settlers led to large-scale displacement of Indigenous peoples and severe population loss, and their Caribbean colonies would be among the most important destinations of the transatlantic slave trade.

Conquest of the Aztec Empire

The first two decades after Columbus's arrival in the New World saw Spanish settlement of Hispaniola, Cuba, Puerto Rico, and other Caribbean islands. Based on rumors of a wealthy mainland civilization, the Spanish governor in Cuba sponsored expeditions to the Yucatán coast of the Gulf of Mexico, including one in 1519 under the command of Hernán Cortés (1485–1547), a minor Spanish nobleman who had spent fifteen years in the Caribbean as an imperial administrator. Alarmed by Cortés's ambition, the governor decided to withdraw his support, but Cortés quickly set sail before being removed from command. Cortés, accompanied by several hundred fellow conquistadors as well as enslaved Taino people and Africans, landed on the Mexican coast on April 21, 1519. His camp soon received visits by delegations from the Aztec emperor bearing gifts and news of their great emperor.

The **Aztec Empire** was formed in the early fifteenth century through an alliance of the Mexica people of

Tenochtitlan (tay-nawch-teet-LAHN) with other city-states in the Valley of Mexico. Over the next decades, the empire expanded rapidly through conquest. At the time of the Spanish arrival, emperor Moctezuma II (r. 1502–1520) ruled an empire of several million inhabitants from the capital at Tenochtitlan, now Mexico City. The Aztec Empire had a highly developed culture with advanced mathematics, astronomy, and engineering as well as oral poetry and written record keeping. Aztec society was highly hierarchical. A hereditary nobility dominated the army, the priesthood, and the state bureaucracy and lived from tribute collected from conquered states and ordinary people, who composed the vast majority of the population. At the bottom of the social scale were landless serfs and people enslaved for crimes or as prisoners of war. Women were excluded from public life and expected to devote their lives to marriage, child rearing, and domestic tasks. The Aztec state waged war against neighboring peoples to secure captives for religious sacrifices and laborers for agricultural and building projects.

After arriving on the mainland, Cortés took steps to establish authority independent of Cuba and the Spanish governor. He formally declared the establishment of a new town called Vera Cruz, naming his leading followers as town councilors and himself as military commander. He then sent letters to the Spanish Crown requesting authorization to conquer and govern new lands.

The brutal nature of the Aztec Empire provided an opening for Cortés to obtain local assistance, a necessity for conquistadors throughout the Americas given their small numbers and ignorance of local conditions. Within weeks of his arrival, Cortés acquired translators who provided vital information on the empire and its weaknesses. In September 1519, after initial hostilities in which many Spaniards died, Cortés formed an

---

■ **Treaty of Tordesillas** A 1494 treaty that settled competing claims to newly discovered Atlantic territories by giving Spain everything to the west of an imaginary line drawn down the Atlantic and giving Portugal everything to the east.

■ **Aztec Empire** A large and complex Native American civilization in modern Mexico and Central America that possessed advanced mathematical, astronomical, and engineering technology.

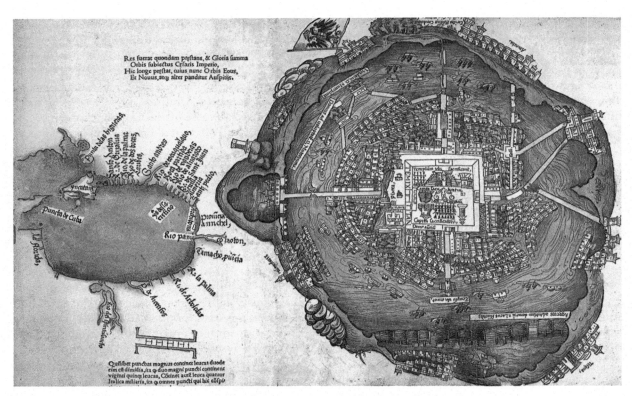

The Mexica Capital of Tenochtitlan   This woodcut map was published in 1524 along with Cortés's letters describing the conquest of the Aztec Empire. As it shows, Tenochtitlan occupied an island and was laid out in concentric circles. The administrative and religious buildings were at the heart of the city, which was surrounded by residential quarters. Cortés marveled at the city in his letters: "The city is as large as Seville or Cordoba. . . . There are bridges, very large, strong, and well constructed, so that, over many, ten horsemen can ride abreast. . . . The city has many squares where markets are held. . . . There is one square . . . where there are daily more than sixty thousand souls, buying and selling. In the service and manners of its people, their fashion of living was almost the same as in Spain, with just as much harmony and order." (FLHC A17/Alamy Stock Photo)

alliance with Tlaxcala (tlah-SKAH-lah), an independent city-state that had successfully resisted incorporation into the Aztec Empire.

In October a combined Spanish-Tlaxcalan force marched to the city of Cholula, which had recently switched loyalties from Tlaxcala to the Aztec Empire, and massacred many thousands of inhabitants, including women and children. Impressed by this display of ruthless power, other Indigenous states joined Cortés's alliance against Aztec rule. In November 1519, these combined forces marched on Tenochtitlan.

Historians have long debated Moctezuma's response to the arrival of the Spanish. Despite the fact that Cortés was allied with enemies of the empire, Moctezuma refrained from attacking the Spaniards and instead welcomed Cortés and approximately 250 Spanish followers into

Invasion of Tenochtitlan, 1519–1521

Tenochtitlan. Cortés later claimed that at this meeting the emperor, inspired by prophecies of the Spaniards' arrival, agreed to become a vassal of the Spanish king. Although impossible for historians to verify, Cortés and later Spanish colonists used this claim to legitimate violence against any who resisted their rule.

After spending more than seven months in the city, in an ambiguous position that combined the status of honored guests, occupiers, and detainees, the Spanish seized Moctezuma as a hostage. During the ensuing attacks and counterattacks, Moctezuma was killed. The city's population rose up against the Spaniards, who fled with heavy losses. In May 1521 the Spanish-Tlaxcalan alliance assaulted Tenochtitlan a second time with an army of approximately one thousand Spanish and seventy-five thousand Indigenous warriors.[5]

The fall of the Aztec capital in late summer 1521 was hard-won and greatly facilitated by the fact that small-pox, brought to the Americas by the Spanish, devastated the besieged population of the city. After establishing a new capital in the ruins of Tenochtitlan, Cortés and other conquistadors began the systematic conquest of Mexico. Major campaigns continued in Mesoamerica for at least two decades against ongoing resistance.

The Fall of the Incas

More surprising than the defeat of the Aztecs was the fall of the remote **Inca Empire**. With their seat of power located in what are now the Andes Mountains in Peru, the Incas were isolated from North American Indigenous cultures and knew nothing of the Aztec Empire or its collapse. In 1438 the hereditary ruler of the Incas had himself crowned emperor and embarked on a successful campaign of conquest. At its greatest extent, the empire extended to the frontier of present-day Ecuador and Colombia in the north and to present-day Chile in the south, an area containing some 16 million people and 350,000 square miles.

Ruled from the capital city of Cuzco, the empire was divided into four major regions containing eighty provinces and twice as many districts. Officials at each level used an extensive network of roads to transmit information and orders back and forth through the empire. While the Aztecs used a system of glyphs for writing, the Incas had devised a complex system of colored and knotted cords, called *khipus*, for administrative bookkeeping. The empire also benefited from the use of llamas as pack animals (by contrast, no beasts of burden existed in Mesoamerica). The Incas integrated regions they conquered by spreading their religion and imposing their language, Quechua, as the official language of the empire.

By the time of the Spanish invasion, however, the Inca Empire had been weakened by a civil war over succession and an epidemic of disease, possibly small-pox, which may have spread through trade with groups in contact with Europeans. Francisco Pizarro (ca. 1475–1541), a conquistador of modest Spanish origins, landed on the northern coast of Peru on May 13, 1532, the very day the Inca leader Atahualpa (ah-tuh-WAHL-puh) won control of the empire after five years of fighting. As Pizarro advanced across the steep Andes toward Cuzco, the capital of the Inca Empire, Atahualpa was also heading there for his coronation.

Like Moctezuma in Mexico, Atahualpa was aware of the Spaniards' movements. He sent envoys to invite the Spanish to meet him in the provincial town of Cajamarca. His plan was to lure the Spanish into a trap, seize their horses and ablest men for his army, and execute the rest. With an army of some forty thousand men stationed nearby, Atahualpa felt he had little

to fear. Instead, the Spaniards ambushed and captured him, collected an enormous ransom in gold, and then executed him in 1533 on trumped-up charges. The Spanish then marched on to Cuzco, profiting once again from internal conflicts to form alliances with local peoples. When Cuzco fell in 1533, the Spanish plundered the empire's wealth in gold and silver.

As with the Aztec Empire, the fall of the imperial capital did not end hostilities. Warfare between Spanish and Inca forces continued to the 1570s. During this period, civil war broke out among Spanish settlers vying for power.

For centuries students have wondered how it was possible for several hundred Spanish conquistadors to defeat powerful empires commanding large armies, vast wealth, and millions of inhabitants. This question is based on a mistaken understanding of the conquest as the rapid work of Spaniards acting alone, ideas that were spread in the aftermath by the conquistadors themselves. Instead, the defeat of the Aztec and Inca Empires was a long process enabled by divisions within the empires that produced political weakness and many skilled and motivated Indigenous allies who fought alongside the Spanish. Spanish steel swords, guns, horses, and dogs produced military advantages, but these tools of war were limited in number and effectiveness. Very few of the conquistadors were experienced soldiers. Probably the most important factor was the devastating impact of contagious diseases among the Indigenous population, which swept through the Aztec and Inca Empires at the time of the conquest.

Portuguese Brazil

Unlike Mesoamerica or the Andes, the territory of Brazil contained no urban empires, but instead roughly 2.5 million nomadic and settled people divided into small communities and many different language groups. In 1500 the Portuguese Crown named Pedro Álvares Cabral commander of a fleet headed for the spice trade of the Indies. En route the fleet sailed far to the west, accidentally landing on the coast of Brazil, which Cabral claimed for Portugal under the terms of the Treaty of Tordesillas. The Portuguese soon undertook a profitable trade with local people in brazil-wood, a valued source of red dye.

Portuguese settlers began arriving in the 1530s, with numbers rising after 1550. In the early years of settlement, the Portuguese brought sugarcane production to Brazil. They initially used enslaved Indigenous laborers on sugar plantations, but the rapid decline in the Indigenous population soon led to the use of forcibly transported Africans. In Brazil the Portuguese thus created a new form of colonization in the Americas:

■ **Inca Empire** The vast and sophisticated Peruvian empire centered at the capital city of Cuzco that was at its peak from 1438 until 1533.

large plantations worked by enslaved people. This model would spread throughout the Caribbean along with sugar production in the seventeenth century.

Colonial Empires of England and France

For almost a century after the fall of the Aztec capital of Tenochtitlan, the Spanish and Portuguese dominated European overseas trade and colonization. In the early seventeenth century, however, northern European powers began to challenge the Iberian monopoly. They eventually succeeded in creating multisited overseas empires, consisting of settler colonies in North America and the Caribbean as well as scattered trading

The Chief of the Powhatan People   In the first years of the seventeenth century, Wahunsenacawh, known as Chief Powhatan of the Powhatan people, ruled some thirty tribal groups in the Chesapeake Bay region. After initially assisting the Jamestown colony, in 1609 Chief Powhatan began to resent English demands and became hostile to them. After his daughter Pocahontas married an English settler (after having been captured and converted to Christianity), peaceful relations returned. This image, which shows the ruler in a traditional Powhatan wooden house, is a detail from a map of the Chesapeake Bay based on an original by John Smith, who spent several weeks as a captive of Powhatan. (Archives Charmet/Bridgeman Images)

posts in West Africa and Asia. Competition among European states for colonies was encouraged by mercantilist economic doctrine, which dictated that foreign trade was a zero-sum game in which one country's gains necessarily entailed another's losses.

Unlike the Iberian powers, whose royal governments financed exploration and directly ruled the colonies, England, France, and the Netherlands conducted the initial phase of colonization via chartered companies endowed with government monopolies over settlement and trade in a given area. These corporate bodies were granted extensive powers over faraway colonies, including exclusive rights to conduct trade, wage war, raise taxes, and administer justice.

The colony of Virginia, founded at Jamestown in 1607, initially struggled to grow sufficient food and faced hostility from the Powhatan Confederacy, a military alliance composed of around thirty Algonquian-speaking Native American groups. Eventually it thrived by producing tobacco for a growing European market. Indentured servants obtained free passage to the colony in exchange for several years of work and the promise of greater opportunity for economic and social advancement than in England. In the 1670s English colonists from the Caribbean island of Barbados settled Carolina, where conditions were suitable for large rice plantations. During the late seventeenth century, following the Portuguese model in Brazil, enslaved Africans replaced indentured servants as laborers on tobacco and rice plantations, and a harsh racial divide was imposed.

Settlement on the coast of New England was undertaken for different reasons. There, radical Protestants sought to escape Anglican repression in England and begin new lives. The small and struggling outpost of Plymouth Colony (1620), founded by the Pilgrims who arrived on the *Mayflower*, was followed by Massachusetts Bay Colony (1630), which grew into a prosperous settlement. Because New England lacked the conditions for plantation agriculture, slavery was always a minor element of life there.

French navigator and explorer Samuel de Champlain founded the first permanent French settlement, at Quebec, in 1608. Ville-Marie, later named Montreal, was founded in 1642. Following the waterways of the St. Lawrence, the Great Lakes, and the Mississippi, the French ventured into much of modern-day Canada and at least thirty-five of the fifty states of the United States. French traders forged relations with the Huron Confederacy, a league of four Indigenous nations that dominated a large region north of Lake Erie, as a means of gaining access to hunting grounds and trade routes for beaver and other animals. In 1682, French explorer René-Robert Cavelier LaSalle descended the Mississippi to the Gulf of Mexico, opening the way for French occupation of Louisiana.

Spanish expansion shared many similarities with that of other European powers, including the use of violence against Indigenous populations and efforts toward Christian conversion, but there were important differences. Whereas the Spanish conquered Indigenous empires, forcing large population groups to render tribute and enter state labor systems, English settlements hugged the Atlantic coastline and did not seek to incorporate the Indigenous population. The English disinterest in full-scale conquest did not prevent conflict with Indigenous groups over land and resources, however. At Jamestown, for example, English expansion led to war with the Powhatan Confederacy, which, along with disease, led to drastic population losses among the Powhatans.

In the first decades of the seventeenth century, English and French naval captains also defied Spain's hold over the Caribbean Sea (see Map 14.2). The English seized control of Bermuda (1612), Barbados (1627), Jamaica (1655), and a succession of other islands. The French took Cayenne (1604), St. Christophe (1625), Martinique and Guadeloupe (1635), and, finally, Saint-Domingue (1697) on the western half of Spanish-occupied Hispaniola. These islands acquired new importance after 1640, when the Portuguese brought sugar plantations to Brazil. Sugar and enslaved people quickly followed in the West Indies (see "Sugar and Slavery"), making the Caribbean plantations the most lucrative of all colonial possessions.

Northern European expansion also occurred in West Africa. In the seventeenth century France and England—along with Denmark and other northern European powers—established fortified trading posts in West Africa as bases for purchasing enslaved people and in India and the Indian Ocean as bases for purchasing spices and other luxury goods. Thus, by the end of the seventeenth century, a handful of European powers possessed overseas empires that truly spanned the globe.

Colonial Administration

In 1482, King John II of Portugal established a royal trading house in Lisbon to handle gold and other goods (including enslaved people) being extracted from Africa. After Portuguese trade expanded into the Indian Ocean spice trade, it was named the *Casa da India* (House of the Indies). Through the Casa, the Crown exercised a monopoly over the export of European goods and the import and distribution of spices and precious metals. It charged taxes on all other incoming goods. The Casa also established a viceroy in the Indian city of Goa to administer Portuguese trading posts and naval forces in Africa and Asia.

To secure the vast expanse of Brazil, in the 1530s the Portuguese implemented the system of captaincies, hereditary grants of land given to nobles and loyal officials who were to bear the costs of settling and administering their territories. The failure of this system led the Crown to bring the captaincies under state control by appointing royal governors to act as administrators. The captaincy of Bahia was the site of the capital, Salvador, home to the governor general and other royal officials.

Spain adopted a similar system for overseas trade. In 1503 the Spanish granted the port of Seville a monopoly over all traffic to the New World and established the *Casa de la Contratación* (House of Trade) to oversee economic matters. In 1524 Spain created the Royal and Supreme Council of the Indies, with authority over all colonial affairs, subject to approval by the king.

By the end of the sixteenth century, European-spread disease and warfare had devastated the Indigenous populations throughout modern-day Mexico, the southwestern United States, and Central and South America (with the exception of Portuguese Brazil), allowing the Spanish to consolidate their power in these regions. In Mesoamerica and the Andes, the Spanish had taken over the cities and tribute systems of the Aztecs and the Incas, leaving in place well-established Indigenous cities and towns but redirecting tribute payments toward the Crown.

The Spanish Crown divided its New World possessions initially into two **viceroyalties**, or administrative divisions: New Spain, created in 1535, with its capital at Mexico City, and Peru, created in 1542, with its capital at Lima. In the eighteenth century two additional viceroyalties were added: New Granada, with Bogotá as its administrative center, and La Plata, with Buenos Aires as its capital (see Map 14.2).

Within each territory the viceroy, or imperial governor, exercised broad military and civil authority as the direct representative of Spain. The viceroy presided over the *audiencia* (ow-dee-EHN-see-ah), a board of twelve to fifteen judges that served as his advisory council and the highest judicial body. As in Spain, settlement in the Americas was centered on cities and towns. Spanish settlers and enslaved Africans congregated in a small number of urban centers, but the vast majority of towns were still populated almost entirely by Indigenous people. By Spanish law, Indigenous communities were permitted to follow traditional rules and customs, unless Spanish administrators determined that they violated royal edicts or Christian doctrine. Conflicts over these determinations, both in law courts and in armed resistance and revolt, continued throughout the colonial period. Women throughout New Spain were denied participation in public life, a familiar pattern from both European and precolonial Indigenous society.

By the end of the seventeenth century the French Crown had followed the Iberian example and imposed

---

■ **viceroyalties** The name for the four administrative units of Spanish possessions in the Americas: New Spain, Peru, New Granada, and La Plata.

direct rule over its North American colonies. The king appointed military governors to rule alongside intendants, royal officials possessed of broad administrative and financial authority within their intendancies. In the mid-eighteenth century reform-minded Spanish king Charles III (r. 1759–1788) adopted the intendant system for the Spanish colonies.

England's colonies followed a distinctive path. Drawing on English traditions of representative government, its colonists established their own proudly autonomous assemblies to regulate local affairs. Wealthy merchants and landowners dominated the assemblies, yet common men had more say in politics than was the case in England.

How did Europe and the world change after Columbus?

The New and Old Worlds were brought into contact and forever changed by the European voyages of discovery and their aftermath. For the first time, a global economy emerged in the sixteenth and seventeenth centuries, and it forged new links among far-flung peoples, cultures, and societies. The ancient civilizations of Europe, Africa, the Americas, and Asia confronted one another in new and rapidly evolving ways. Those confrontations led to conquest, voluntary and forced migration, devastating population losses, and brutal exploitation. The exchange of goods and people between Europe and the New World brought highly destructive diseases to the Americas, but it also gave both the New and Old Worlds new crops that eventually altered consumption patterns across the globe.

Economic Exploitation of the Indigenous Population

From the first decades of settlement, the Spanish made use of the **encomienda system**, by which the Crown granted the conquerors the right to employ groups of Native Americans as laborers or to demand tribute from them in exchange for providing food and shelter. The encomiendas were also intended as a means to organize Indigenous people for missionary work and Christian conversion. This system was first used in Hispaniola to work goldfields, then in Mexico for agricultural labor, and, when silver was discovered in the 1540s, for silver mining.

A 1512 Spanish law authorizing the use of encomiendas called for Indigenous people to be treated fairly, but in practice the system led to terrible abuses, including overwork, beatings, and sexual violence. Spanish missionaries publicized these abuses, leading to debates in Spain about the nature and proper treatment of Indigenous people (see "Religious Conversion" ahead in this chapter). King Charles I

responded to complaints in 1542 with the New Laws, which set limits on the authority of encomienda holders, including their ability to transmit their privileges to heirs. The New Laws recognized Indigenous people who accepted Christianity and Spanish rule as free subjects of the Spanish Crown and prohibited the enslavement of Indigenous people, while leaving intact the system of slavery for people of African descent. According to these laws, Indigenous people had voluntarily accepted to be vassals of the Spanish king and thereby gained personal liberty and the right to form their own communities.

The New Laws provoked a revolt in Peru among encomienda holders, and they were little enforced throughout Spanish territories. For example, although the laws forbade enslavement of Indigenous people, the practice did not end completely. To respond to persistent abuses in the encomiendas and a growing shortage of Indigenous workers, royal officials established a new government-run system of forced labor, called *repartimiento* in New Spain and *mita* in Peru. Administrators assigned a certain percentage of the inhabitants of Indigenous communities to labor for a set period each year in public works, mining, agriculture, and other tasks. Laborers received modest wages in exchange, which they could use to fulfill tribute obligations. In the seventeenth century, as land became a more important source of wealth than labor, elite settlers purchased *haciendas*, large tracts of farmland worked by dependent Indigenous laborers and enslaved Africans.

Spanish systems for exploiting the labor of Indigenous peoples were both a cause of and a response to the disastrous decline in their numbers that began soon after the arrival of Europeans. Some Indigenous people died as a direct result of the violence of conquest and the disruption of agriculture and trade caused by warfare, but the most important cause of death was infectious disease. (See "Population Loss and the Ecological Impacts of Contact" ahead in this chapter.)

Colonial administrators responded to this population decline by forcibly combining dwindling Indigenous communities into new settlements and imposing the rigors of the encomienda and the repartimiento. By the end of the sixteenth century the search for fresh

■ **encomienda system** A system whereby the Spanish Crown granted the conquerors the right to forcibly employ groups of Native Americans in exchange for providing food, shelter, and Christian teaching.

■ **Columbian exchange** The exchange of diseases, animals, and plants between the Old and the New Worlds, named after Christopher Columbus, who initiated this contact.

sources of labor had given birth to the new tragedy of the transatlantic slave trade (see "Sugar and Slavery").

Society in the Colonies

Many factors helped shape life in European colonies, including geographical location, pre-existing Indigenous cultures, patterns of settlement, and the policies and cultural values of the different nations that claimed the colonies as empire. Throughout the New World, colonial settlements were hedged by immense borderlands where European power was weak and Europeans and non-Europeans interacted on a more equal basis.

Women played a crucial role in the emergence of colonial societies. As European men conquered and colonized the Americas, one way in which they acquired and exercised power was through relations with Indigenous women. These women acted as intermediaries between cultures, such as by serving as translators and guides (see "Thinking Like a Historian: Who Was Doña Marina?" on page 408). Some acquired status and privileges in the emerging colonial society, especially those from elite Indigenous families who could bring advantageous alliances. The more common pattern in these relations was coerced labor and rape. Many young Indigenous women were taken by force or given as "gifts" to conquering Europeans.

As colonization proceeded, European and Indigenous women played a crucial role in the new societies. In some areas, European men adapted to local cultures through their ties to women; this occurred, for example, among European merchants in Southeast Asia and French fur traders in North America. European governments, eager to populate colonies with families of European descent, adopted various measures, both punitive and positive, to encourage settlers to bring their families. Over time these measures had some success, especially in New Spain and British North America, where new settlements took on European languages, religion, and ways of life that have endured, with strong input from local cultures, to this day. Women also played an important part in Christian conversion efforts as nuns and Protestant teachers and missionaries.

Most women who crossed the Atlantic were captive Africans, constituting four-fifths of the female newcomers before 1800.[6] Wherever slavery existed, enslavers used their power to coerce sexual relations with enslaved women. One important difference among European colonies was in the status of children born from these relations. In some colonies, mostly those dominated by the Portuguese, Spanish, or French, substantial populations of free people of color descended from the freed children of enslaved women of African descent and free European fathers. In English colonies, enslavers were less likely to free children they fathered with enslaved women. The multiracial children of Indigenous people, Europeans, and Africans created whole new populations and ethnicities and complex forms of identity (see "New Ideas About Race").

Population Loss and the Ecological Impacts of Contact

Contact between the Old and New Worlds had profound human and ecological ramifications. In particular, the migration of people to the New World led to an exchange of diseases, animals, and plants, a complex process known to historians as the **Columbian exchange**, since it was inaugurated by the voyages of Christopher Columbus. The most important element of the exchange was the introduction of European pathogens to the New World, which had a disastrous impact on the Indigenous population. In Europe, infectious diseases like smallpox, measles, and influenza—originally passed on from domestic animals living among the population—killed many people each year. Given the size of the population and the frequency of outbreaks, in most of Europe these diseases were experienced in childhood, and survivors carried immunity or resistance. Over centuries of dealing with these diseases, the European population had had time to adapt. Prior to contact with Europeans, Indigenous peoples of the New World suffered from insect-borne diseases and some infectious ones, but they lacked the domestic

A Multiracial Procession　The Incas used drinking vessels, known as *keros*, for the ritual consumption of maize beer at feasts. This kero from the early colonial period depicts a multiracial procession: an Inca dignitary is preceded by a Spanish trumpet player and an African drummer. This is believed to be one of the earliest visual representations of an African in the Americas. (British Museum, London, UK/Werner Forman/Universal Images Group/Getty Images)

Who Was Doña Marina?

In April 1519 a young woman named Malintzin was among twenty enslaved women given to Cortés as a peace offering. Fluent in Nahuatl and Yucatec Maya (spoken by a Spanish priest with Cortés), she acted as an interpreter and diplomatic guide for the Spanish. Malintzin took the name Doña Marina after her conversion to Christianity and bore a son to Cortés in 1522. No writings by Doña Marina survive, but she figures prominently in both Spanish and Indigenous sources on the conquest. Her situation as both an unfree woman and a central figure in the conquest renders her a complex and compelling historical figure.

1 Cortés's letter to Charles V, 1522. This letter to Charles V contains one of only two written references to Doña Marina found in Cortés's correspondence with the emperor. He describes her as his "interpreter."

During the three days I remained in that city they fed us worse each day, and the lords and principal persons of the city came only rarely to see and speak with me. And being somewhat disturbed by this, my interpreter, who is an Indian woman from Putunchan, which is the great river of which I spoke to Your Majesty in the first letter, was told by another Indian woman and a native of this city that very close by many of Mutezuma's men were gathered, and that the people of the city had sent away their women and children and all their belongings, and were about to fall on us and kill us all; and that if she wished to escape she should go with her and she would shelter her. All this she told to Gerónimo de Aguilar, an interpreter whom I acquired in Yucatán, of whom I have also written to Your Highness; and he informed me.

2 Díaz's account of the conquest of the Aztecs. Bernal Díaz del Castillo participated in the conquest of the Aztecs alongside Cortés. His historical account of the conquest, written much later in life, provides the lengthiest descriptions of Doña Marina.

Early the next morning many Caciques and chiefs of Tabasco and the neighbouring towns arrived and paid great respect to us all, and they brought a present of gold, . . . and some other things of little value. . . . This present, however, was worth nothing in comparison with the twenty women that were given us, among them one very excellent woman called Doña Marina, for so she was named when she became a Christian.

. . . Cortés allotted one of the women to each of his captains and Doña Marina, as she was good looking and intelligent and without embarrassment, he gave to Alonzo Hernández Puertocarrero. When Puertocarrero went to Spain, Doña Marina lived with Cortés, and bore him a son named Don Martin Cortés.

. . . Her father and mother were chiefs and Caciques of a town called Paynala. . . . Her father died while she was still a little child, and her mother married another Cacique, a young man, and bore him a son. It seems that the father and mother had a great affection for this son and it was agreed between them that he should succeed to their honours when their days were done. So that there should be no impediment to this, they gave the little girl, Doña Marina, to some Indians from Xicalango, and this they did by night so as to escape observation, and they then spread the report that she had died, and as it happened at this time that a child of one of their Indian slaves died they gave out that it was their daughter and the heiress who was dead.

The Indians of Xicalango gave the child to the people of Tabasco and the Tabasco people gave her to Cortés.

. . . As Doña Marina proved herself such an excellent woman and good interpreter throughout the wars in New Spain, Tlaxcala and Mexico (as I shall show later on) Cortés always took her with him, and during that expedition she was married to a gentleman named Juan Jaramillo at the town of Orizaba.

Doña Marina was a person of the greatest importance and was obeyed without question by the Indians throughout New Spain.

ANALYZING THE EVIDENCE

1. How would you compare the attitudes toward Doña Marina displayed in Cortés's letter to the Spanish Crown (Source 1) and Díaz's account of the conquest (Source 2)? Why would Cortés downplay his reliance on Doña Marina in correspondence with the Spanish emperor?
2. What skills and experience enabled Doña Marina to act as an intermediary between the Spanish and the Aztecs? Based on the evidence, what role did she play in these interactions?
3. According to Díaz (Source 2), how did Doña Marina feel about her relationship with Cortés and the Spanish? How do you interpret this passage? Is there any evidence in the other sources that supports or undermines the sentiments he attributed to her?
4. Overall, how reliable are these sources for understanding Doña Marina, her relations with the Spanish, and her role in the conquest? What can the sources tell us, and what can they not? How would you compare the sources to one another?

3 **Doña Marina translating for Hernán Cortés during his meeting with Moctezuma.** This image was created by Tlaxcalan artists approximately six decades after the conquest of Mexico and represents one Indigenous perspective on the events.

(The Granger Collection)

Marina . . . said that God had been very gracious to her in freeing her from the worship of idols and making her a Christian, and letting her bear a son to her lord and master Cortés and in marrying her to such a gentleman as Juan Jaramillo, who was now her husband. That she would rather serve her husband and Cortés than anything else in the world, and would not exchange her place to be Cacica of all the provinces in New Spain.

Doña Marina knew the language of Coatzacoalcos, which is that common to Mexico, and she knew the language of Tabasco, as did also Jerónimo de Aguilar, who spoke the language of Yucatan and Tabasco, which is one and the same. So that these two could understand one another clearly, and Aguilar translated into Castilian for Cortés.

This was the great beginning of our conquests and thus, thanks be to God, things prospered with us. I have made a point of explaining this matter, because without the help of Doña Marina we could not have understood the language of New Spain and Mexico.

PUTTING IT ALL TOGETHER

4 **The *Florentine Codex*.** In the decades following the conquest, a Franciscan monk, Bernardino de Sahagún, worked with Indigenous partners to compile a history of Aztec society. Known today as the *Florentine Codex*, it contains images and text written in both Nahuatl and Spanish. The following excerpt describes the entry of the victorious Spanish into Tenochtitlan.

Next they went to Motecuhzoma's storehouse, in the place called Totocalco, where his personal treasures were kept. The Spaniards grinned like little beasts and patted each other with delight.

When they entered the hall of treasures, it was as if they had arrived in Paradise. They searched everywhere and coveted everything; they were slaves to their own greed. . . .

They seized these treasures as they were their own, as if this plunder were merely a stroke of good luck. And when they had taken all the gold, they heaped up everything else in the middle of the patio.

La Malinche [Doña Marina] called all the nobles together. She climbed up to the palace roof and cried: "Mexicanos, come forward! The Spaniards need your help! Bring them food and pure water. They are tired and hungry; they are almost fainting from exhaustion! Why do you not come forward? Are you angry with them?"

The Mexicas were too frightened to approach. They were crushed by terror and would not risk coming forward. They shied away as if the Spaniards were wild beasts, as if the hour were midnight on the blackest night of the year. Yet they did not abandon the Spaniards to hunger and thirst. They brought them whatever they needed, but shook with fear as they did so. They delivered the supplies to the Spaniards with trembling hands, then turned and hurried away.

Using the sources above, along with what you have learned in class and in this chapter, imagine the events and experiences described in these sources from Doña Marina's point of view. Reflect on the various aspects of Doña Marina described in the sources — betrayed daughter, enslaved woman, mother, wife, interpreter, and commander — and write an essay that uses her experience to explore the interaction among Spanish, Aztec, and other Indigenous groups during the conquest period.

Sources: (1) Hernán Cortés to Emperor Carlos V, 1522, in *Hernán Cortés: Letters from Mexico*, trans. and ed. Anthony Pagden (New Haven: Yale University Press, 1986), pp. 72–74; (2) Bernal Díaz del Castillo, *The Discovery and Conquest of Mexico, 1517–1521*, trans. A. P. Maudslay (New York: Noonday Press, 1965), pp. 62–63, 64, 66–67; (4) Miguel León-Portilla, ed., *The Broken Spears: The Aztec Account of the Conquest of Mexico* (Boston: Beacon Press, 1992), pp. 68–69.

livestock that hosted the highly infectious diseases known in the Old World. The arrival of Europeans spread these microbes among a completely unprepared population, and they fell victim in vast numbers.

While the major cause of death was disease, another factor was the brutal exploitation of Indigenous people. Indigenous workers died in staggering numbers amid the extremely harsh and dangerous conditions of cane fields and mines. Moreover, forced labor diverted local people from agricultural work, leading to malnutrition, reduced fertility rates, and starvation. Women's capacity to nurse their babies was greatly reduced, leading to high infant mortality rates in a population with no livestock to supply alternatives to breastmilk. Malnutrition and hunger in turn lowered resistance to disease. Finally, many Indigenous people also died through outright violence in warfare. Overall, the Indigenous population declined by as much as 90 percent or more, but with important regional variations. In general, densely populated urban centers were worse hit than rural areas, and tropical, low-lying regions suffered more than cooler, higher-altitude ones.

Another element of the Columbian exchange was the movement of new crops and animals across the Atlantic. Everywhere they settled, the Spanish and Portuguese brought and raised wheat with labor provided by the encomienda system. Grapes and olives brought over from Spain did well in parts of Peru and Chile. Perhaps the most significant introduction to the diet of Native Americans came via the meat and milk of the livestock that the early conquistadors brought with them, including cattle, sheep, and goats. The horse allowed for faster travel and easier transport of heavy loads.

In turn, Europeans returned home with many food crops that became central elements of their diet and eventually many parts of the world. Crops originating in the Americas included tomatoes, squash, pumpkins, peppers, and many varieties of beans, as well as tobacco. One of the most important of such crops was maize (corn). By the late seventeenth century maize had become a staple in Spain, Portugal, southern France, and Italy, and in the eighteenth century it became one of the chief foods of southeastern Europe and southern China. Even more valuable was the nutritious white potato, which slowly spread from west to east, contributing everywhere to a rise in population.

Sugar and Slavery

Throughout the Middle Ages slavery was deeply entrenched in the Mediterranean. The constant warfare of the reconquista had supplied captive Muslims for domestic slavery in Iberia, but the success of these wars meant that the number of enslaved workers had greatly dwindled by the mid-fifteenth century.

As Portuguese explorers began their voyages along the western coast of Africa, one of the first commodities they sought was enslaved human beings. In 1444 the first ship returned to Portugal with a cargo of enslaved Africans. While the first enslaved people were seized by small raiding parties, Portuguese merchants soon found that it was easier to trade with local leaders, who dealt in captives acquired through warfare with neighboring powers. In 1483 the Portuguese established an alliance with the kingdom of Kongo. The royal family eventually converted to Christianity and Kongolese women intermarried with Portuguese merchants, creating a permanent Afro-Portuguese community. From 1490 to 1530 Portuguese traders brought hundreds of enslaved Africans to Portugal each year (Map 14.3).

In this stage of European expansion, the history of slavery became intertwined with that of sugar. Originally sugar was an expensive luxury, but population increases and economic expansion in the fifteenth century led to increasing demand. Native to the South Pacific, sugar was taken in ancient times to India, where farmers learned to preserve cane juice as granules that could be stored and shipped. From there, sugar crops traveled to China and the Mediterranean, where islands like Crete and Sicily had the warm and humid climate needed for growing sugarcane. When Genoese and other Italians colonized the Canary Islands and the Portuguese settled on the Madeira Islands, which possessed the requisite climate conditions, sugar plantations came to the Atlantic.

Sugar was a difficult and demanding crop to produce for profit. Seed-stems were planted by hand, thousands to the acre. When mature, the cane had to be harvested and processed rapidly to avoid spoiling. Moreover, sugar has a virtually constant growing season, meaning that there was no fallow period when workers could recuperate from the arduous labor. The invention of roller mills to crush the cane more efficiently meant that yields could be significantly augmented, but only if a sufficient labor force supplied the mills. Europeans addressed this labor problem by forcing first Indigenous islanders and then enslaved Africans to provide the backbreaking work.

The transatlantic slave trade began in 1518 when Spanish king Charles I authorized traders to bring enslaved Africans to the Americas. The Portuguese brought the first enslaved people to Brazil around 1550; by 1600, four thousand were being imported annually. After its founding in 1621, the Dutch West India Company forcibly transported thousands of Africans to Brazil and the Caribbean, mostly to work on sugar plantations. In the mid-seventeenth century the English entered the slave trade.

Before 1700, when slavers decided it was better business to improve conditions, some 20 percent of captives died on the voyage across the Atlantic.[7] The most common cause of death was dysentery induced by poor-quality food and water, crowding, and lack of

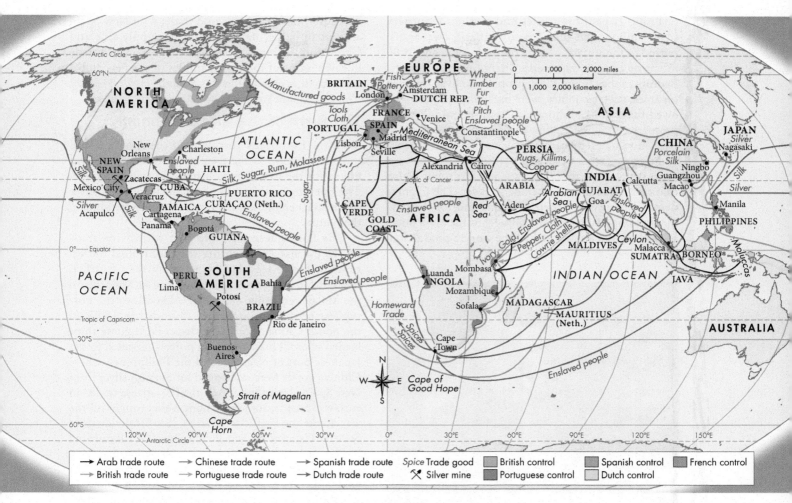

MAP 14.3 **Seaborne Trading Empires in the Sixteenth and Seventeenth Centuries**   By the mid-seventeenth century trade linked all parts of the world except for Australia. Notice that trade in enslaved people was not confined to the Atlantic but involved almost all parts of the world.

sanitation. Men were often kept in irons during the passage, while women and girls suffered sexual violence from sailors. On sugar plantations, death rates from the brutal pace of labor were extremely high, leading to demand among plantation owners for a constant stream of new shipments from Africa.

Spanish Silver and Its Economic Effects

In 1545, at an altitude of fifteen thousand feet, the Spanish discovered an extraordinary source of silver at Potosí (poh-toh-SEE) (in present-day Bolivia) in territory conquered from the Inca Empire. By 1550 Potosí yielded perhaps 60 percent of all the silver mined in the world. From Potosí and the mines at Zacatecas (za-kuh-TAY-kuhhs) and Guanajuato (gwah-nah-HWAH-toh) in Mexico, huge quantities of precious metals poured forth.

Mining became the most important industry in the colonies. Millions of Indigenous laborers died as a result of brutal conditions in the silver mines. Demand for new sources of labor for the mines also contributed to the intensification of the African slave trade. Profits for the Spanish Crown were immense. The Crown claimed the quinto, one-fifth of all precious metals mined in South America, which represented 25 percent of its total income. Between 1503 and 1650, 35 million pounds of silver and over 600,000 pounds of gold entered Seville's port.

Spain's immense profits from silver paid for the tremendous expansion of its empire and for the large armies that defended it. However, the easy flow of money also dampened economic innovation. It exacerbated the rising inflation Spain was already experiencing in the mid-sixteenth century due to population growth and stagnant production. Several times between 1557 and 1647, King Philip II and his successors wrote off the state debt, thereby undermining confidence in the government and damaging the economy. Only after 1600, when the population declined, did prices gradually stabilize.

Philip II paid his armies and foreign debts with silver bullion, and thus Spanish inflation was transmitted to the rest of Europe. Between 1560 and 1600 much of Europe experienced large price increases. Because money bought less, people who lived on fixed incomes, such as nobles, were badly hurt. Those who owed fixed sums of money, such as the middle class, prospered because in a time of rising prices, debts lessened in value each year. Food costs rose most sharply, and the poor fared worst of all.

In many ways, though, it was not Spain but China that controlled the world trade in silver. The Chinese demanded silver for their products and for the payment of imperial taxes. China was thus the main buyer of world silver, absorbing half the world's production.

The silver market drove world trade, with New Spain and Japan being mainstays on the supply side and China dominating the demand side. The world trade in silver is one of the best examples of the new global economy that emerged in this period.

The Birth of the Global Economy

With the Europeans' discovery of the Americas and their exploration of the Pacific, the entire world was linked for the first time in history by seaborne trade. The opening of that trade brought into being three commercial empires: the Portuguese, the Spanish, and the Dutch.

The Portuguese were the first worldwide traders. In the sixteenth century they controlled the sea route to India (see Map 14.3). From their fortified bases at Goa on the Arabian Sea and at Malacca on the Malay Peninsula, ships carried goods to the Portuguese settlement at Macao, founded in 1557, in the South China Sea. From Macao Portuguese ships loaded with Chinese silks and porcelains sailed to the Japanese port of Nagasaki and the Philippines, where Chinese goods were exchanged for Spanish silver from New Spain. Throughout Asia the Portuguese traded in enslaved people, some of whom were brought all the way across the Pacific to Mexico. (See "Individuals in Society: Catarina de San Juan," page 414.) Returning to Portugal, they brought Asian spices that had been purchased with textiles produced in India and with gold and ivory from East Africa. From their colony in Brazil, they shipped sugar produced by enslaved Africans whom they had forcibly transported across the Atlantic.

Coming to empire a few decades later than the Portuguese, the Spanish were determined to claim their place in world trade. The Spanish Empire in the New World was basically a land empire, but across the Pacific the Spaniards built a seaborne empire centered at Manila in the Philippines. Established in 1571, the city of Manila served as the transpacific link between Spanish America and China. In Manila, Spanish traders used silver from American mines to purchase Chinese silk for European markets (see Map 14.3).

In the final years of the sixteenth century the Dutch challenged the Spanish and Portuguese Empires. During this period the Protestant Dutch were engaged in a long war of independence from their Spanish Catholic overlords. The joining of the Portuguese Crown to Spain in 1580 meant that the Dutch had both strategic and commercial reasons to attack Portugal's commercial empire. In 1599 a Dutch fleet returned to Amsterdam carrying 600,000 pounds of pepper and 250,000 pounds of cloves and nutmeg. Those who had invested in the expedition received a 100 percent profit. The voyage led to the establishment in 1602 of the Dutch East India Company,

Philip II, ca. 1533 This portrait of Philip II as a young man and crown prince of Spain is by the celebrated artist Titian, court painter to Philip's father, Charles V. After taking the throne, Philip became another great patron of the artist.
(IanDagnall Computing/Alamy Stock Photo)

Goods from the Global Economy   Spices from Southeast Asia were a driving force behind the new global economy and among the most treasured European luxury goods. They were used not only for cooking but also as medicines and health tonics. This fresco (below) shows a fifteenth-century Italian pharmacist measuring out spices for a customer. After the discovery of the Americas, a wave of new items entered European markets, silver foremost among them. The incredibly rich silver mines at Potosí (in modern-day Bolivia) were the source of this eight-reale coin (left) struck at the mine during the reign of Charles II. Such coins were the original "pieces of eight" prized by pirates and adventurers. Soon Asian and American goods were mixed together by enterprising tradesmen. This mid-seventeenth-century Chinese teapot (below right) was made of porcelain with the traditional Chinese design prized in the West, but with a silver handle added to suit European tastes. (teapot: Paul Freeman/ Bridgeman Images; spice shop: Alfredo Dagli Orti/Shutterstock; coin: Hoberman Collection/SuperStock)

founded with the stated intention of capturing the Asian spice trade from the Portuguese.

In return for assisting Indonesian princes in local conflicts and disputes with the Portuguese, the Dutch won broad commercial concessions and forged military alliances. With Indonesian assistance, they captured the strategically located fort of Malacca in 1641, gaining western access to the Malay Archipelago. Gradually, they acquired political domination over the archipelago itself. The Dutch were willing to use force more ruthlessly than the Portuguese and had superior organizational efficiency. These factors allowed them to expel the Portuguese from Sri Lanka in 1660 and henceforth control the immensely lucrative production and trade of spices. The company

also established the colony of Cape Town on the southern tip of Africa as a provisioning point for its Asian fleets.

Not content with challenging the Portuguese in the Indian Ocean, the Dutch also aspired to a role in the Americas. Founded in 1621, during their war with Spain, the Dutch West India Company aggressively sought to open trade with North and South America and capture Spanish territories there. The company captured or destroyed hundreds of Spanish ships, seized the Spanish silver fleet in 1628, and captured portions of Brazil and the Caribbean. The Dutch also successfully interceded in the transatlantic slave trade, establishing a large number of trading stations on the west coast of Africa.

INDIVIDUALS IN SOCIETY

Catarina de San Juan

A long journey led Catarina de San Juan from enslavement in South Asia to adulation as a popular saint in Mexico. Her journey began on the west coast of India around 1610 when Portuguese traders captured a group of children, including the small girl who would become Catarina. Their ship continued around the southern tip of India, across the Bay of Bengal, through the Strait of Malacca, and across the South China Sea. It docked at Manila, a Spanish city in the Philippines, where the girl was sold at a slave auction. In 1619 Catarina boarded a ship that was part of the Manila Galleon, the annual convoy of Spanish ships that crossed the Pacific between Manila and the Mexican port of Acapulco. After a six-month voyage, Catarina arrived in Acapulco; she then walked to Mexico City and continued on to the city of Puebla.

In Puebla, Catarina became the property of a Portuguese merchant and worked as a domestic servant. She was one of thousands of *chinos*, a term for people of the East Indies who were brought via the Philippines to Spanish America. Many were enslaved people, transported as part of a transoceanic trade that reached from the Indian Ocean to the South China Sea and across the Pacific to the Atlantic world. They constituted a small but significant portion of people forcibly transported by Europeans to the Americas in the late sixteenth and early seventeenth centuries to replace dwindling numbers of Indigenous laborers. *Chinos* were considered particularly apt for domestic labor, and many wealthy Spanish Americans bought them in Manila.

Before crossing the Pacific, Catarina converted to Catholicism and chose her Christian name. In Puebla her enslaver encouraged Catarina's faith and allowed her to attend Mass every day. He also drafted a will emancipating her after his death, which occurred in 1619. With no money of her own, Catarina became the servant of a local priest. On his advice, Catarina reluctantly gave up her dream of becoming a lay sister and married a fellow *chino* named Domingo. The marriage was unhappy; Catarina reportedly refused to enter sexual relations with her husband and suffered from his debts, infidelity, and hostility to her faith. She found solace in renewed religious devotion, winning the admiration of priests and neighbors who flocked to her for spiritual comfort and to hear about her ecstatic visions. After fourteen years of marriage, Catarina became a widow and lived out her life in the home of wealthy supporters.

Catarina's funeral in 1688 drew large crowds. Her followers revered her as an unofficial saint, and soon the leaders of Puebla began a campaign to have Catarina beatified (officially recognized by the Catholic Church as a saint). Her former confessors published accounts of her life emphasizing her piety, beauty, and what they perceived as her exotic Asian origins. Her followers also marveled at what they saw as the miraculous preservation of her virginity through the perils of enslavement

Nineteenth-century painting of Puebla women in traditional clothing. (De Agostini/Getty Images)

and marriage. Much of what we know about Catarina derives from these sources and must be viewed as idealized and based on cultural stereotypes, rather than as strictly historically accurate. The Spanish Inquisition, which oversaw the process of beatification, rejected Catarina's candidacy and, fearing that popular adulation might detract from the authority of the church, forbade the circulation of images of and texts about her. Despite this ban, popular reverence for Catarina de San Juan continued, and continues to this day in Mexico.

QUESTIONS FOR ANALYSIS

1. What does Catarina's story reveal about the global nature of the Spanish Empire and the slave trade in this period? What does it reveal about divisions within the Catholic Church?
2. Compare the experience of Catarina to that of Doña Marina (see "Thinking Like a Historian: Who Was Doña Marina?" on page 408). In what ways were their experiences similar? How did they differ? How do you think the sources available about Catarina shape our understanding of her story?

Sources: Tatiana Seijas, *Asian Slaves in Colonial Mexico: From Chinos to Indians* (New York: Cambridge University Press, 2014), pp. 8–26; Ronald J. Morgan, *Spanish American Saints and the Rhetoric of Identity, 1600–1810* (Tucson: University of Arizona Press, 2002), pp. 119–142.

How did expansion change European attitudes and beliefs?

The age of overseas expansion heightened Europeans' contacts with the rest of the world. Religion was one of the most important arenas of cultural contact, as European missionaries aimed to spread Christianity throughout the territories they acquired, with mixed results. While Christianity was embraced in parts of the New World, it was met largely with suspicion in places such as China and Japan. However, East-West contacts did lead to exchanges of influential cultural and scientific ideas. These contacts also gave birth to new ideas about the inherent superiority or inferiority of different races, sparking vociferous debate about the status of Africans and Indigenous peoples of the Americas. The essays of Michel de Montaigne epitomized a new spirit of skepticism and cultural relativism, while the plays of William Shakespeare reflected the efforts of one great writer to come to terms with the cultural complexity of his day.

Religious Conversion

Christian conversion was one of the most important justifications for European expansion. Jesuit missionaries were active in Japan and China in the sixteenth and seventeenth centuries, until authorities banned their teachings. The first missionaries to the New World accompanied Columbus on his second voyage, and more than 2,500 priests and friars of the Franciscan, Dominican, Jesuit, and other Catholic orders crossed the Atlantic in the following century. Later French explorers were also accompanied by missionaries who preached to the Native Americans with whom the French traded. Protestants also led missionary efforts, but in much smaller numbers than Catholics. Colonial powers built convents, churches, and cathedrals for converted Indigenous people and European settlers, and they established religious courts to enforce correct beliefs and morals.

To stamp out old beliefs and encourage sincere conversions, colonial authorities destroyed shrines and objects of religious worship and harshly persecuted men and women who continued to participate in traditional religious practices. They also imposed European Christian norms of family life, especially monogamous marriage. While many resisted these efforts, over time a large number accepted Christianity. (See "Viewpoints: Aztec and Spanish Views on Christian Conversion in New Spain," page 416.) It is estimated that missionaries had baptized between 4 and 9 million Indigenous people in New Spain by the mid-1530s.[8]

Christian conversion was a complex and ambiguous process involving cultural exchanges that impacted both sides. Catholic friars were among the first Europeans to seek an understanding of Indigenous cultures and languages as part of their effort to render Christianity comprehensible to Indigenous people. In Mexico they not only learned the Nahuatl language but also taught it to non-Nahuatl-speaking groups to create a shared language for Christian teaching. In translating Christianity, missionaries, working in partnership with Indigenous converts, adapted it to the symbols and ritual objects of pre-existing cultures and beliefs, thereby creating distinctive forms of Catholicism.

European Debates About Indigenous Peoples

Iberian exploitation of the Indigenous population of the Americas began from the moment of Columbus's arrival in 1492. Denunciations of this abuse by Catholic missionaries, however, quickly followed, inspiring debates both in Europe and in the colonies about the nature of Indigenous peoples and how they should be treated. Bartolomé de Las Casas (1474–1566), a Dominican friar and former encomienda holder, was

Franciscan Monks Burning Indigenous Temples　In the late sixteenth century, Diego Muñoz Camargo, an educated man of Spanish and Indigenous descent, produced a history of the Tlaxcala people — one of the first and most important Spanish allies against the Aztecs — starting from the time of conquest. An important theme of the text and its accompanying images was the efforts made by Franciscan missionaries to stamp out polytheistic Indigenous religions in favor of Catholicism. This included, as shown here, burning temples, as well as destroying religious texts and punishing lapsed converts. (University of Glasgow Library/Bridgeman Images)

In justifying their violent conquest of the Aztec and Inca empires, Spanish conquistadors emphasized the need to bring Christianity to peoples they regarded as heathen. For the conquered, the imposition of Christianity and the repression of their pre-existing religions were often experienced as yet another form of loss. The first document recounts the response of vanquished Aztec leaders of Tenochtitlan to Franciscan missionaries. It was written forty years after the events described by the Spanish missionary and scholar Bernardino de Sahagún based on what he learned from Spanish chroniclers and surviving Aztec leaders. Despite resistance, missionaries eventually succeeded in converting much of the Indigenous population to Catholicism. In the second document, an account of the Spanish conquest and its aftermath written in the 1560s by a man who had participated in the conquest, Bernal Díaz del Castillo professes great satisfaction at the Catholic piety of converted Indigenous communities and their assimilation into European culture. As you read, ask yourself what motivations Díaz may have had to present such a positive picture.

Aztec Response to the Franciscans' 1524 Explanation of Mission, 1564

You have told us that we do not know the One who gives us life and being, who is Lord of the heavens and of the earth. You also say that those we worship are not gods. This way of speaking is entirely new to us, and very scandalous. We are frightened by this way of speaking because our forebears who engendered and governed us never said anything like this. On the contrary, they left us this our custom of worshiping our gods, in which they believed and which they worshiped all the time that they lived here on earth. They taught us how to honor them. And they taught us all the ceremonies and sacrifices that we make. They told us that through them [our gods] we live and are, and that we were beholden to them, to be theirs and to serve countless centuries before the sun began to shine and before there was daytime. They said that these gods that we worship give us everything we need for our physical existence: maize, beans, chia seeds, etc. . . .

All of us together feel that it is enough to have lost, enough that the power and royal jurisdiction have been taken from us. As for our gods, we will die before giving up serving and worshiping them.

Bernal Díaz del Castillo on the Spread of Christianity in New Spain, 1560s

It is a thing to be grateful for to God, and for profound consideration, to see how the natives assist in celebrating a holy Mass. . . . There is another good thing they do [namely] that both men, women and children, who are of the age to learn them, know all the holy prayers in their own languages and are obliged to know them. They have other good customs about their holy Christianity, that when they pass near a sacred altar or Cross they bow their heads with humility, bend their knees, and say the prayer "Our Father," which we Conquistadores have taught them, and they place lighted wax candles before the holy altars and crosses. . . . In addition to what I have said, we taught them to show great reverence and obedience to all the monks and priests. . . . Beside the good customs reported by me they have others both holy and good, for when the day of Corpus Christ comes, or that of Our Lady, or other solemn festivals when among us we form processions, most of the pueblos in the neighbourhood of this city of Guatemala come out in procession with their crosses and lighted wax tapers, and carry on their shoulders, on a litter, the image of the saint who is the patron of the pueblo.

QUESTIONS FOR ANALYSIS

1. What reasons do the leaders of Tenochtitlan offer for rejecting the teachings of Franciscan missionaries? What importance do they accord their own religious traditions?
2. What evidence does Díaz provide for the conversion of the Indigenous people in the city of Guatemala?
3. How and why do you think the attitudes of Indigenous peoples might have evolved from those described in the first document to those praised in the second? Why do you think Díaz may have exaggerated the Christian fervor of Indigenous people?

Sources: "The Lords and Holy Men of Tenochtitlan Reply to the Franciscans Bernardino de Sahagún, Coloquios y doctrina Cristiana," ed. Miguel León-Portilla, in Kenneth Mills and William B. Taylor, eds., *Colonial Spanish America: A Documentary History* (Lanham, Md.: Rowman & Littlefield, 2002), pp. 20–21; Bernal Díaz, *The True History of the Conquest of New Spain*, in Stuart B. Schwartz, *Victors and Vanquished: Spanish and Nahua Views of the Conquest of Mexico* (Boston: Bedford/St. Martin's, 2000), pp. 218–219.

one of the earliest and most outspoken critics of the brutal treatment inflicted on Indigenous peoples.

Mounting criticism in Spain led King Charles I to assemble a group of churchmen and lawyers to debate the issue in 1550 in the city of Valladolid. One side, led by Juan Ginés de Sepúlveda, argued that conquest and forcible conversion were both necessary and justified to save Indigenous people from what he described as the horrors of human sacrifice, cannibalism, and idolatry. He depicted them as barbarians who belonged to a category of inferior beings identified by the ancient Greek philosopher Aristotle as naturally destined for slavery. Against these arguments, Las Casas and his supporters portrayed Indigenous people as rational and innocent children, who deserved protection and tutelage from more advanced civilizations. Although Las Casas was more sympathetic to Indigenous people, both sides in this debate agreed on the superiority of European culture and the need for Indigenous people to adapt to the European model.

While the debate did not end exploitation of Indigenous people, the Crown did use it to justify limiting the rights of settlers in favor of the Catholic Church and royal authorities and to increase legal protections for their communities. In 1573, Philip II issued detailed laws regulating how new towns should be formed and administered, and how Spanish settlers should interact with Indigenous populations. The impact of these laws can still be seen in Mexico's colonial towns, which are laid out as grids around a central plaza. They had only limited impact, however, on the treatment of Indigenous people, who continued to experience abuse and exploitation.

New Ideas About Race

European conquest and settlement led to the emergence of new ideas about "race" as a form of biological difference among humans. In medieval Spain and Portugal, sharp distinctions were drawn between, on the one hand, supposedly "pure-blooded" Christians and, on the other hand, Jews and *conversos*, people of Jewish origins who had converted to Christianity. In the fifteenth century Iberian rulers issued discriminatory laws against conversos as well as against Muslims and their descendants. Feeling that conversion could not erase the taint of heretical belief, they came to see Christian faith as a type of inherited identity that was passed through the blood.

The idea of "purity of blood" changed through experiences in the colonies. There the transatlantic slave trade initiated in the sixteenth century meant that the colonial population included people of European, Indigenous, and African descent. Spanish colonizers came to believe that the Indigenous people of the Americas were free from the taint of unbelief because they had never been exposed to Christianity. Accordingly, the ideology of "purity of blood" they brought from Iberia could more easily incorporate Indigenous populations. By contrast, the Spanish regarded Africans—whom they believed had refused the message of Christ that was preached in the Old World—as impure.

Sexual relations between Europeans, Native Americans, and people of African descent—most often through the sexual coercion of women—were relatively common in the Spanish colonies. A complex system of racial classification, known as *castas* in Spanish America, emerged to describe different proportions of European, Indigenous, and African parentage. Spanish concerns about religious purity were thus transformed

Depictions of Africans in European Portraiture
Starting in the Italian Renaissance, with the emergence of portraiture as a new genre, European elites began to commission images of themselves accompanied by enslaved people of African descent as a way to display their wealth and power. In this painting by the Flemish painter Anthony Van Dyke, noblewoman Marchesa Elena Grimaldi Cattaneo gazes confidently at the viewer, while her attendant, a young boy of African descent (probably enslaved), holds a parasol to protect her pale skin from the sun. By drawing visual attention to her skin tone and situating the subservient dark-skinned boy as a foil, the painting valorizes whiteness as an attribute of supposed European superiority. (By Anthony Van Dyck [1599–1641], 1623 [oil on canvas]/Widener Collection, 1942.9.92/Image courtesy National Gallery of Art, Washington)

in the colonial context into concerns about racial bloodlines, with "pure" Spanish blood occupying the summit of the racial hierarchy and Indigenous and African descent ranked in descending order. These concerns heightened scrutiny of European women's sexual activity, so as to preserve the racial purity of the colonial

Portrait of Don Francisco de Arobe and His Sons, 1599

This painting depicts a fifty-six-year-old man, Don Francisco de Arobe (center), and two young men, Don Pedro and Don Domingo, believed to be his sons. De Arobe was the leader of a settlement in the province of Esmeraldas on the north coast of modern-day Ecuador. In this tropical, coastal region, Africans who escaped from slavery in the 1550s joined, intermarried with, and eventually became the majority in some Indigenous communities suffering population loss due to Spanish-spread disease. The men in this painting are probably of African and Indigenous descent. Their fine clothing displays a mixture of European and Indigenous styles: they wear imported Spanish silk cloaks and lace collars and cuffs, combined with gold nose- and earplugs and seashell necklaces, adornments that had been worn by Indigenous people since before contact with the Spanish. A Spanish official commissioned the painting in 1599 for the king of Spain to commemorate de Arobe's conversion to Christianity and his declaration of loyalty to Spain. The painter, Andrés Sánchez Gallque, was himself an Indigenous artist, trained to paint in the European style.

(Album/Alamy)

EVALUATE THE EVIDENCE

1. What impression of Don Francisco de Arobe and his sons do you get from this painting, and what elements of the painting convey this impression? What do we learn from the clothing and decorations they are wearing?
2. Why would a Spanish official have commissioned this painting for the king of Spain? What message is he sending to the king with this image?

family. Meanwhile, the stereotype that Indigenous women and women of African descent were naturally promiscuous and incapable of sexual honor was used to justify their exploitation at the hands of European men.

All European colonies in the New World relied on racial distinctions drawn between Europeans and Indigenous people and those of African descent, including later French and English settlements. (See "Evaluating Visual Evidence: Portrait of Don Francisco de Arobe and His Sons, 1599.") With its immense plantation agriculture system based on enslaved labor, large Indigenous population, and relatively low Portuguese immigration, Brazil developed a particularly complex racial and ethnic mosaic.

After 1700 the emergence of new methods of observing and describing nature led to the use of scientific frameworks to define race. Although it originally referred to a nation or an ethnic group, henceforth the term *race* would be used to describe supposedly biologically distinct groups of people, whose physical differences were believed to produce differences in culture, character, and intelligence. This change occurred at the same time as a shift to defining gender differences as inherent in the biological differences between male and female bodies (see "Women and the Enlightenment" in Chapter 16). Science thus served to justify and naturalize existing inequalities between Europeans and non-Europeans and between men and women.

Montaigne and Cultural Curiosity

Decades of religious fanaticism and civil war led some Catholics and Protestants to doubt that any one faith contained absolute truth. Added to these doubts was the discovery of peoples in the New World who had radically different ways of life. These shocks helped produce ideas of skepticism and cultural relativism. Skepticism is a school of thought founded on doubt that total certainty or definitive knowledge is ever attainable. Cultural relativism suggests that one culture is not necessarily superior to another, just different. Both notions found expression in the work of Frenchman Michel de Montaigne (duh mahn-TAYN) (1533–1592).

Montaigne developed a new literary genre, the essay, to express his ideas. Intending his works to be accessible, he wrote in French rather than Latin and in an engaging conversational style. His essays were quickly translated into other European languages and became some of the most widely read texts of the early modern period. Montaigne's essay "Of Cannibals" reveals the impact of overseas discoveries on one thoughtful European. In contrast to the prevailing views of his day, he rejected the notion that one culture is superior to another. Speaking of Indigenous Brazilians, he wrote: "I find that there is nothing barbarous and savage in this nation [Brazil], . . . except, that everyone gives the title of barbarism to everything that is not according to his usage."[9]

In his own time, few Europeans would have agreed with Montaigne's challenge to ideas of European superiority or his even more radical questioning of the superiority of humans over animals. Nevertheless, his popular essays contributed to a long-term evolution in attitudes. "Wonder," he said, "is the foundation of all philosophy, research is the means of all learning, and ignorance is the end."[10] Montaigne thus inaugurated an era of doubt.

Shakespeare and His Influence

In addition to the essay as a literary genre, the period fostered remarkable creativity in other branches of literature that also reflected the impact of European expansion and changing ideas about race. England—especially in the latter part of Queen Elizabeth I's reign and in the first years of her successor, James I (r. 1603–1625)—witnessed remarkable developments in theater and poetry. The undisputed master of the period was the dramatist William Shakespeare. Born in 1564 to a successful glove manufacturer in Stratford-upon-Avon, his genius lay in the originality of his characterizations, the diversity of his plots, his understanding of human psychology, and his unsurpassed gift for language. Although he wrote sparkling comedies and stirring historical plays, his greatest masterpieces were his later tragedies, including *Hamlet*, *Othello*, and *Macbeth*, which explore an enormous range of human problems and are open to an almost infinite variety of interpretations.

Like Montaigne's essays, Shakespeare's work reveals the impact of the new discoveries and contacts of his day on Europeans. The title character of *Othello* is described as a "Moor," a term that in Shakespeare's day referred to Muslims of North African origin, including those who had migrated to the Iberian Peninsula. It could also be applied, though, to people originating in the Iberian Peninsula who converted to Islam or to non-Muslim Berbers in North Africa. To complicate things even more, references in the play to Othello as "black" in skin color have led many to believe that Shakespeare intended him to be a sub-Saharan African.

This confusion in the play aptly reflects the important links in this period between racial and religious classifications. In contrast to the prevailing view of Moors as inferior, a view echoed by the Venetian characters in the play, Shakespeare presents Othello as a complex human figure, capable of great courage and nobility, but flawed by jealousy and suspicion.

The play also exposes women's suffering at the hands of the patriarchal family. In the society depicted in *Othello*, fathers treat unmarried daughters as property and husbands murder wives they suspect of infidelity. Revealing anxieties about racial purity, several characters assert that Othello's "blackness" has tainted his Venetian wife, Desdemona. By wrongly believing that Desdemona has betrayed him with another man, Othello himself seems to have internalized these negative attitudes. The play thus shows how racial ideologies very similar to those developed in the Spanish Empire existed in Elizabethan England.

NOTES

1. Marco Polo, *The Book of Ser Marco Polo, the Venetian: Concerning the Kingdoms and Marvels of the East*, vol. 2, trans. and ed. Colonel Sir Henry Yule (London: John Murray, 1903), pp. 185–186.
2. Thomas Benjamin, *The Atlantic World: Europeans, Africans, Indians and Their Shared History, 1400–1900* (Cambridge: Cambridge University Press, 2009), p. 56.
3. John Law, "On the Methods of Long Distance Control: Vessels, Navigation, and the Portuguese Route to India," in *Power, Action and Belief: A New Sociology of Knowledge?* ed. John Law, Sociological Review Monograph 32 (London: Routledge & Kegan Paul, 1986), pp. 234–263.
4. Peter Hulme, *Colonial Encounters: Europe and the Native Caribbean, 1492–1797* (London: Methuen, 1986), pp. 22–31.
5. Benjamin, *The Atlantic World*, p. 141.
6. Geoffrey Vaughn Scammell, *The First Imperial Age: European Overseas Expansion, c. 1400–1715* (London: Routledge, 2002), p. 432.
7. Herbert S. Klein, "Profits and the Causes of Mortality," in *The Atlantic Slave Trade*, ed. David Northrup (Lexington, Mass.: D. C. Heath and Co., 1994), p. 116.
8. David Carrasco, *The Oxford Encyclopedia of Mesoamerican Cultures* (Oxford: Oxford University Press, 2001), p. 208.
9. C. Cotton, trans., *The Essays of Michel de Montaigne* (New York: A. L. Burt, 1893), pp. 207, 210.
10. Cotton, *The Essays*, p. 523.

LOOKING BACK LOOKING AHEAD

In 1517 Martin Luther issued his "Ninety-five Theses," launching the Protestant Reformation; just five years later, Ferdinand Magellan's expedition sailed around the globe, shattering European notions of terrestrial geography. Within a few short years, old medieval certainties about Heaven and earth began to collapse. In the ensuing decades, Europeans struggled to come to terms with religious difference at home and the multitudes of new peoples and places they encountered abroad. While some Europeans were fascinated and inspired by this new diversity, much more often the result was hostility and violence. Europeans endured decades of civil war between Protestants and Catholics, and Indigenous peoples suffered massive population losses as a result of European disease, exploitation, and warfare. Tragically, both Catholic and Protestant religious leaders condoned the African slave trade that brought suffering and death to millions of people as well as the conquest of Native American land and the subjugation of Indigenous people.

Even as the voyages of discovery coincided with the fragmentation of European culture, they also played a role in longer-term processes of state centralization and consolidation. The new monarchies of the Renaissance produced stronger and wealthier governments capable of financing the huge expenses of exploration and colonization. Competition to gain overseas colonies became an integral part of European politics. Spain's investment in conquest proved spectacularly profitable, and yet, as we will see in Chapter 15, the ultimate result was a weakening of its power. Over time the Netherlands, England, and France also reaped tremendous profits from colonial trade, which helped them build modernized, centralized states. The path from medieval Christendom to modern nation-states led through religious warfare and global conquest.

Make Connections

Think about the larger developments and continuities within and across chapters.

1. Michel de Montaigne argued that people's assessments of what was "barbaric" merely drew on their own habits and customs; based on the earlier sections of this chapter, how widespread was this openness to cultural difference among Europeans? Was he alone, or did other Europeans share this view?

2. To what extent did the European voyages of expansion and conquest inaugurate an era of global history? Is it correct to date the beginning of "globalization" from the late fifteenth century? Why or why not?

14 REVIEW & EXPLORE

Identify Key Terms

Identify and explain the significance of each item below.

conquistadors (p. 394)	Treaty of Tordesillas (p. 400)	viceroyalties (p. 405)
caravel (p. 394)	Aztec Empire (p. 401)	encomienda system (p. 406)
Ptolemy's *Geography* (p. 394)	Inca Empire (p. 403)	Columbian exchange (p. 407)

Review the Main Ideas

Answer the section heading questions from the chapter.

1. What was the Afro-Eurasian trading world before Columbus? (p. 390)

2. How and why did Europeans undertake ambitious voyages of expansion? (p. 393)

3. What was the impact of European conquest on the New World? (p. 401)

4. How did Europe and the world change after Columbus? (p. 406)

5. How did expansion change European attitudes and beliefs? (p. 415)

Suggested Resources

BOOKS

* Brosseder, Claudia. *The Power of Huacas: Change and Resistance in the Andean World of Colonial Peru*. 2014. A fascinating study of Indigenous religious practitioners in the Andes and their encounter with the colonial Spanish world; tells the story of religion from the Indigenous perspective.

* Crosby, Alfred W. *The Columbian Exchange: Biological and Cultural Consequences of 1492*, 30th anniversary ed. 2003. An innovative and highly influential account of the environmental impact of the transatlantic movement of animals, plants, and microbes inaugurated by Columbus.

* Mangan, Jane E. *Transatlantic Obligations: Creating the Bonds of Family in Conquest-Era Peru and Spain*. 2016. A study of the impact of Spanish expansion into Peru on the formation of families among Spanish, Indigenous, and multiracial people.

* Mann, Charles C. *1491: New Revelations on the Americas Before Columbus*, 2d ed. 2011. A highly readable account of the peoples and societies of the Americas before the arrival of Europeans.

* Martinez, Maria Elena. *Genealogical Fictions: Limpieza de Sangre, Religion and Gender in Colonial Mexico*. 2008. A fascinating study of the relationship between Spanish ideas of religious purity developed during the reconquista and the emergence of racial hierarchies in colonial Mexico.

* Parker, Charles H. *Global Interactions in the Early Modern Age, 1400–1800*. 2010. An examination of the rise of global connections in the early modern period that situates the European experience in relation to the world's other empires and peoples.

* Restall, Matthew. *Seven Myths of Spanish Conquest*. 2003. A re-examination of common misconceptions about why and how the Spanish conquered Indigenous civilizations in the New World.

* Subrahmanyam, Sanjay. *The Portuguese Empire in Asia, 1500–1700: A Political and Economic History*, 2d ed. 2012. A masterful study of the Portuguese overseas empire in Asia that draws on both European and Asian sources.

* Wiesner-Hanks, Merry, ed. *Christianity and Sexuality in the Early Modern World: Regulating Desire, Reforming Practice*. 2000. Organized by global regions, a book that examines the interaction of Christian ideas and institutions with sexuality, with coverage of issues such as marriage, same-sex and interracial relations, and witchcraft.

MEDIA

* *America Before Columbus* (National Geographic, 2010). Explores the complex societies and cultures of North America before contact with Europeans and the impact of the Columbian exchange.

* *Black Robe* (Bruce Beresford, 1991). A classic film about French Jesuit missionaries among Algonquin and Huron Indians in New France in the seventeenth century.

* *Conquistadors* (PBS, 2000). Traveling in the footsteps of the Spanish conquistadors, the narrator tells their story while following the paths and rivers they used. Includes discussion of the perspectives and participation of Indigenous peoples.

* *The Globalization of Food and Plants*. Hosted by the Yale University Center for the Study of Globalization, this website provides information on how various foods and plants—such as spices, coffee, and tomatoes—traveled the world in the Columbian exchange. **https://archive-yaleglobal.yale.edu/globalization-food-plants**

* *Historic Jamestowne*. Showcasing archaeological work at the Jamestown settlement, the first permanent English settlement in America, this site provides details of the latest digs along with biographical information about settlers, historical background, and resources for teachers and students. **www.historicjamestowne.org**

* *The New World* (Terrence Malick, 2005). Set in 1607 at the founding of Jamestown, this film retells the story of John Smith and Pocahontas.

* *Plymouth Colony Archive Project*. A site hosted by the University of Illinois anthropology department that contains a collection of searchable primary and secondary sources relating to the Plymouth colony, including court records, laws, seventeenth-century journals and memoirs, wills, maps, and biographies of colonists. **www.histarch.uiuc.edu/Plymouth/index.html**

* *Silence* (Martin Scorsese, 2016). Based on a 1966 Japanese novel, the film depicts the travels of two seventeenth-century Jesuits from Portugal to Japan during a time of Japanese persecution of Christians.

15

Absolutism and Constitutionalism

ca. 1589–1725

The seventeenth century was a period of crisis and transformation in Europe. Agricultural and manufacturing slumps led to food shortages and shrinking population rates. Religious and dynastic conflicts led to almost constant war, visiting violence and destruction on ordinary people and reshaping European states. To consolidate their authority and compete with rival states, European rulers greatly increased the size of their armies. This change required taxing subjects more heavily and implementing bureaucratic forms of government. By the end of the seventeenth century, a more powerful centralized state had emerged, which historians have termed the fiscal-military state.

The growth of state power within Europe raised a series of questions for rulers and subjects: Who held supreme power? What made it legitimate? Conflicts over these questions led to rebellions and, in some areas, outright civil war. The result was a wide variety of political systems across Europe, ranging from absolutism to republicanism and, by the end of the seventeenth century, constitutional monarchy. ■

CHAPTER PREVIEW

- What were the crises and achievements of seventeenth-century European states?

- What was absolutism, and how did it evolve in western and central Europe?

- What explains the rise of absolutism in Prussia and Austria?

- What were the distinctive features of Russian and Ottoman absolutism?

- What were alternatives to absolutism in early modern Europe?

Life at the French Royal Court
This painting shows King Louis XIV receiving foreign ambassadors to celebrate a peace treaty. The king grandly occupied the center of his court, which in turn served as the pinnacle for the French people and, at the height of his glory, for all of Europe. (Charles Le Brun [1619–1690], 1678/ Museum of Fine Arts, Budapest, Hungary/Erich Lessing/Art Resource, NY)

What were the crises and achievements of seventeenth-century European states?

Historians often refer to the seventeenth century as an "age of crisis" because Europe was challenged by population losses, economic decline, and social and political unrest. These difficulties were partially due to climate changes that reduced agricultural productivity, but they also resulted from bitter religious divides, war, and increased governmental pressures. Peasants and the urban poor were especially hard hit by the economic problems, and they frequently rioted against high food prices.

The atmosphere of crisis encouraged governments to take emergency measures to restore order, measures that they successfully turned into long-term reforms that strengthened the power of the state. In the long run, European states proved increasingly able to impose their will on the populace. This period also saw the flourishing of art and music with the drama and emotional intensity of the baroque style.

The Social Order and Peasant Life

In the seventeenth century, society was organized in hierarchical levels. In much of Europe, the monarch occupied the summit and was celebrated as a semidivine being, chosen by God to embody the state. The clergy constituted the first order of society, due to its sacred role in interceding with God on behalf of its flocks. Next came nobles, whose privileged status derived from their ancient bloodlines and centuries of leadership in battle. Many prosperous mercantile families succeeded in buying their way into the nobility through service to the monarchy in the fifteenth and sixteenth centuries. Those lower on the social scale, the peasants and artisans who constituted the vast majority of the population, were expected to show deference to their betters. This was the "Great Chain of Being" that linked God to his creation in a series of ranked social groups.

In addition to being rigidly hierarchical, European societies were patriarchal. The father ruled over his wife, children, and servants just as a king ruled over his domains. Fathers were legally entitled to use physical violence, imprisonment, and other forceful measures to impose their authority. These powers were somewhat balanced by expectations that a good father would provide and care for his dependents.

In the seventeenth century most Europeans lived in the countryside. In western Europe, a small number of peasants in each village owned enough land to feed themselves and possessed the livestock and plows necessary to work their land. These independent farmers were leaders of the peasant village. Below them were small landowners and tenant farmers who did not have enough land to be self-sufficient. At the bottom were villagers who worked as dependent laborers and servants. In central and eastern Europe, the vast majority of peasants toiled as serfs for noble landowners.

Environmental, Economic, and Social Crisis

In the seventeenth century a period of colder and wetter climate throughout Europe, dubbed a Little Ice Age by historians, meant a shorter farming season with lower yields. A bad harvest created food shortages; a series of bad harvests could lead to famine. Recurrent famines significantly reduced the population of early modern Europe, reducing fertility and increasing susceptibility to disease, as well as causing outright starvation.

Industry also suffered. The output of woolen textiles, one of the most important European manufactures, declined sharply in the first half of the seventeenth century. Food prices were high, wages stagnated, and unemployment soared. This economic crisis was not universal: it struck various regions at different times and to different degrees. In the middle decades of the century, for example, Spain, France, Germany, and the British Isles all experienced great economic difficulties, as did the Ottoman Empire and China, but these years were the golden age of the Netherlands because of wealth derived from foreign trade.

The urban poor and peasants were the hardest hit. When the price of bread rose beyond their capacity to pay, they frequently expressed their anger by rioting. Women often led these actions, since their role as mothers gave them some impunity in authorities' eyes. Historians have used the term *moral economy* for this vision of a world in which community needs predominate over competition and profit.

During the middle years of the seventeenth century, harsh conditions transformed neighborhood bread riots into armed uprisings across much of Europe. Popular revolts were common in England, France, and throughout the Spanish Empire, particularly during the 1640s. At the same time that he struggled to put down an uprising in Catalonia, the economic center of the realm, Spanish king Philip IV faced revolt in Portugal and in Spanish-held territories in the northern Netherlands and Sicily. France suffered an uprising in the same period that won enthusiastic support from both nobles and peasants, while the English monarch was tried and executed by his subjects and Russia experienced an explosive rebellion.

Municipal and royal authorities struggled to overcome popular revolt. They feared that stern repressive measures, such as sending in troops to fire on crowds,

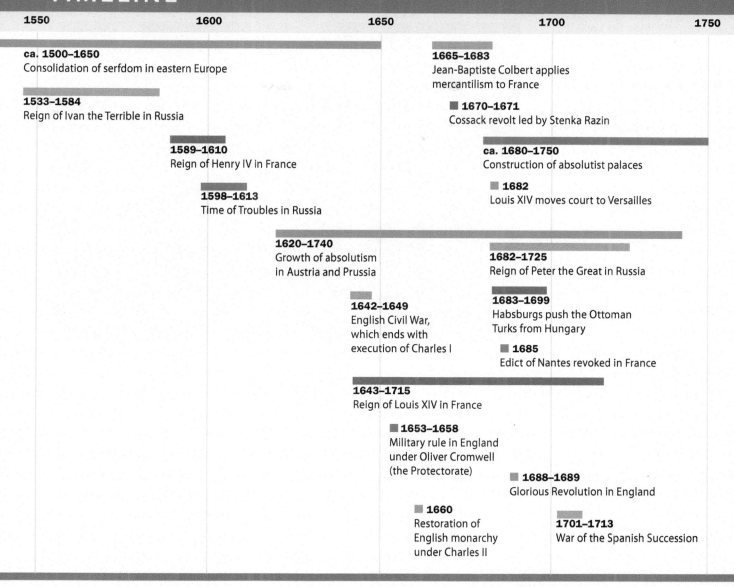

1550 **1600** **1650** **1700** **1750**

ca. 1500–1650
Consolidation of serfdom in eastern Europe

1533–1584
Reign of Ivan the Terrible in Russia

1589–1610
Reign of Henry IV in France

1598–1613
Time of Troubles in Russia

1620–1740
Growth of absolutism
in Austria and Prussia

1642–1649
English Civil War,
which ends with
execution of Charles I

1643–1715
Reign of Louis XIV in France

1653–1658
Military rule in England
under Oliver Cromwell
(the Protectorate)

1660
Restoration of
English monarchy
under Charles II

1665–1683
Jean-Baptiste Colbert applies
mercantilism to France

1670–1671
Cossack revolt led by Stenka Razin

ca. 1680–1750
Construction of absolutist palaces

1682
Louis XIV moves court to Versailles

1682–1725
Reign of Peter the Great in Russia

1683–1699
Habsburgs push the Ottoman
Turks from Hungary

1685
Edict of Nantes revoked in France

1688–1689
Glorious Revolution in England

1701–1713
War of the Spanish Succession

would further inflame the situation, while full-scale occupation of a city would be expensive and detract from military efforts elsewhere. The limitations of royal authority gave some leverage to rebels. To quell riots, royal edicts were sometimes suspended, prisoners released, and discussions initiated. By the beginning of the eighteenth century rulers had gained much greater control over their populations as a result of various achievements in state-building (see "State-Building and the Growth of Armies" later in this chapter).

The Thirty Years' War

Harsh economic conditions were greatly exacerbated by the decades-long conflict known as the Thirty Years' War (1618–1648), the first military conflict on a European scale. The Holy Roman Empire was a confederation of hundreds of principalities, independent cities, duchies, and other polities loosely united under an elected emperor. The uneasy truce between Catholics and Protestants created by the Peace of Augsburg in 1555 (see "Religious Wars in Switzerland and Germany" in Chapter 13) deteriorated as the faiths of various areas shifted. Lutheran princes felt compelled to form the Protestant Union (1608), and Catholics retaliated with the Catholic League (1609). Each alliance was determined that the other should make no religious or territorial advance. Dynastic interests were also involved; the Spanish Habsburgs strongly supported the goals of their Austrian relatives, which was to preserve the unity of the empire and Catholicism within it.

Peasants Working the Land
Working the land was harsh toil for seventeenth-century peasants, but strong family and community bonds gave life meaning and made survival possible. The rich and colorful clothing of the peasants shown here reflects an idealized vision of the peasants' material circumstances.
(Sotheby's/akg-images)

The war began with a conflict in Bohemia between the Catholic League and the Protestant Union but soon spread through the Holy Roman Empire, drawing in combatants from across Europe. After a series of initial Catholic victories, the tide of the conflict turned because of the intervention of Sweden, under its brilliant young king Gustavus Adolphus (r. 1594–1632), and then France, whose chief minister, Cardinal Richelieu (REESH-uh-lyuh), intervened on the side of the Protestants to undermine Habsburg power.

The 1648 **Peace of Westphalia** that ended the Thirty Years' War marked a turning point in European history. The treaties that established the peace not only ended major conflicts fought over religious faith but also recognized the independent authority of more than three hundred German princes (Map 15.1), reconfirming the emperor's severely limited authority. The Augsburg agreement of 1555 became permanent, adding Calvinism to Catholicism and Lutheranism as legally permissible creeds. The United Provinces of the Netherlands, known as the Dutch Republic, won official freedom from Spain.

The Thirty Years' War was the most destructive event in central Europe prior to the world wars of the twentieth century. Perhaps one-third of urban residents and two-fifths of the rural population died,

and agriculture and industry withered. Across Europe, states increased taxes to meet the cost of war, further increasing the suffering of a traumatized population.

State-Building and the Growth of Armies

In the context of warfare, economic crisis, and demographic decline, rulers took urgent measures to restore order and rebuild their states. Despite differences in political systems, all these states shared common projects of protecting and expanding their frontiers, raising new taxes, consolidating central control, and competing for the new colonies opening up in the New and Old Worlds.

Rulers who wished to increase their authority encountered formidable obstacles, including poor communications, entrenched local power structures, and ethnic and linguistic diversity. Nonetheless, over the course of the seventeenth century both absolutist and constitutional governments achieved new levels of power and national unity. They did so by transforming emergency measures of wartime into permanent structures of government and by subduing privileged groups through the use of force and through economic and social incentives. Increased state authority could be seen in four areas in particular: greater taxation, growth in armed forces, larger and more efficient bureaucracies, and territorial expansion, both within Europe and overseas. Historians have used the term **fiscal-military state** to describe these increasingly centralized and bureaucratic states, which harnessed domestic resources to maintain large armies

■ **Peace of Westphalia** The name of a series of treaties that concluded the Thirty Years' War in 1648 and marked the end of large-scale religious violence in Europe.

■ **fiscal-military state** Centralized bureaucratic states that appeared in Europe in the seventeenth century and that harnessed domestic resources to maintain large armies.

MAP 15.1 Europe After the Thirty Years' War This map shows the political division of Europe after the Peace of Westphalia (1648) ended the war. France expanded its borders to the east and Sweden gained territory on the northern German coastline. The Dutch Republic formally won its independence after a long struggle against Spain, but Spain retained territory in the southern Netherlands and Italy.

Legend:
- Austrian Habsburg lands
- Spanish Habsburg lands
- Other German states
- Swedish lands by 1648
- Ottoman Empire and tributary states
- Boundary of the Holy Roman Empire

for internal order and to compete for territory within Europe and overseas.

Over time, centralized power added up to something close to sovereignty. A state may be termed sovereign when it possesses a monopoly over the instruments of justice and the use of force within clearly defined boundaries. In a sovereign state, no system of courts, such as church tribunals, competes with state courts in the dispensation of justice; and private armies, such as those of feudal lords, present no threat to central authority. While seventeenth-century states did not acquire total sovereignty, they made important strides toward that goal.

The driving force of seventeenth-century state-building was warfare. In medieval times, feudal lords had raised armies only for particular wars or campaigns; now monarchs began to recruit their own forces and maintain permanent standing armies. Instead of serving their own interests, army officers were required to be loyal and obedient to state officials. New techniques for training and deploying soldiers meant a rise in the professional standards of the army.

Along with professionalization came an explosive growth in army size. The French took the lead, with the army growing from roughly 125,000 men in the Thirty Years' War to 340,000 at the end of

Seventeenth-Century Artillery   Mobile light artillery, consisting of bronze or iron cannon mounted on wheeled carriages, played a crucial role in seventeenth-century warfare. In contrast to earlier heavy artillery used in siege operations to breach fortifications, light artillery could be deployed to support troops during battle. This image is from an early-seventeenth-century military manual. (Science History Images/Alamy)

the seventeenth century.[1] Other European powers were quick to follow the French example. The rise of absolutism in central and eastern Europe led to a vast expansion in the size of armies. England followed a similar, albeit distinctive pattern. Instead of building a land army, the island nation focused on naval forces and eventually built the largest navy in the world.

Baroque Art and Music

State-building and the growth of armies were not the only achievements of the seventeenth century; the arts flourished as well. Rome and the revitalized Catholic Church of the late sixteenth century spurred the early development of the **baroque style** in art and music. The papacy and the Jesuits encouraged the growth of an intensely emotional, exuberant art. They wanted artists to appeal to the senses and thereby touch the souls and kindle the faith of ordinary churchgoers while proclaiming the power and confidence of the reformed Catholic Church. In addition to this underlying religious emotionalism, the baroque drew its sense of drama, motion, and ceaseless striving from the Catholic Reformation.

■ **baroque style**   A style in art and music lasting from roughly 1600 to 1750 characterized by the use of drama and motion to create heightened emotion, especially prevalent in Catholic countries.

Taking definite shape in Italy after 1600, the baroque style in the visual arts developed with exceptional vigor in Catholic countries — in Spain and Latin America, Austria, southern Germany, and Poland. Yet baroque art was more than just "Catholic art" in the seventeenth century and the first half of the eighteenth. It had broad appeal, and Protestants accounted for some of the finest examples of baroque style, especially in music. The baroque style spread partly because its tension and bombast spoke to an agitated age that was experiencing great violence and controversy in politics and religion.

In painting, the baroque reached maturity early with Peter Paul Rubens (1577–1640), the most outstanding and most representative of baroque painters. Studying in his native Flanders and in Italy, where he was influenced by masters of the High Renaissance such as Michelangelo, Rubens developed his own rich, sensuous, colorful style, which was characterized by animated figures, melodramatic contrasts, and monumental size.

Gian Lorenzo Bernini, *The Ecstasy of Saint Teresa of Avila*, 1647–1652   In 1647, Italian sculptor Gian Lorenzo Bernini accepted a commission to build a chapel in honor of the family of a Catholic cardinal and the newly canonized Spanish Carmelite nun and mystic, Teresa of Avila. Bernini's sculpture depicts the saint at the moment of her rapturous union with the divine, symbolized by an angel standing poised to pierce her heart with a golden arrow. In its heightened emotionalism and the drama of its composition, the sculpture is one of the masterpieces of baroque art. (G. NIMATALLAH/De Agostini/Getty Images)

In music, the baroque style reached its culmination almost a century later in the dynamic, soaring lines of the endlessly inventive Johann Sebastian Bach (1685–1750). Organist and choirmaster of several Lutheran churches across Germany, Bach was equally at home writing secular concertos and sublime religious cantatas. Bach's organ music combined the baroque spirit of invention, tension, and emotion in an unforgettable striving toward the infinite. Unlike Rubens, Bach was not fully appreciated in his lifetime, but since the early nineteenth century his reputation has grown steadily.

What was absolutism, and how did it evolve in western and central Europe?

Rulers in absolutist states asserted that, because they were chosen by God, they were responsible to God alone. They claimed exclusive, or absolute, power to make and enforce laws, denying any other institution or group the authority to check their power. In France the founder of the Bourbon monarchy, Henry IV, established foundations upon which his successors Louis XIII and Louis XIV built a stronger, more centralized French state. Louis XIV is often seen as the epitome of an "absolute" monarch, with his endless wars, increased taxes and economic regulation, and glorious palace at Versailles. In truth, his success relied on collaboration with nobles, and thus his example illustrates both the achievements and the compromises of absolutist rule.

As French power rose in the seventeenth century, the glory of Spain faded. Once the fabulous revenue from American silver declined, Spain's economic stagnation could no longer be disguised, and the country faltered under weak leadership.

The Decline of Absolutist Spain in the Seventeenth Century

The discovery of silver at Potosí in 1545 produced momentous wealth for Spain, allowing the Habsburg dynasty to dominate other European states and maintain its global empire (see "Spanish Silver and Its Economic Effects" in Chapter 14). Yet Spain had inherent weaknesses that the wealth of empire had hidden. When Philip IV took power in 1621, he inherited a Spanish throne that encompassed different kingdoms with their own traditions and loyalties as well as a vast and overstretched overseas empire. Spanish silver had generated great wealth, but also dependency. While Creoles — people of European ancestry born in the colonies — undertook new industries and European nations targeted Spanish colonial trade, industry and finance in Spain itself did not develop.

Spain's challenges mounted during the first half of the seventeenth century. Between 1610 and 1650, Spanish trade with the colonies in the New World fell 60 percent because of competition from local industries in the colonies and from Dutch and English traders. To make matters worse, in 1609 the Crown expelled some three hundred thousand Moriscos, or former Muslims, significantly reducing the pool of skilled workers and merchants. At the same time epidemic disease decimated the enslaved workforce in the South American silver mines. Moreover, the mines themselves started to run dry, and the quantity of metal produced steadily declined after 1620.

Within Spain itself, the effects of the Little Ice Age greatly reduced the productivity of land. In order to stay afloat, Spanish aristocrats increased their land rents, but this increase encouraged peasants to leave the land and thus led to a decline in agricultural productivity. In cities, the high price of food diminished demand for industrial goods, meaning low wages and unemployment for city dwellers. Steep inflation forced textile manufacturers out of business by increasing their production costs to the point where they could not compete in colonial and international markets.[2]

In Madrid, the expenses of war and imperial rule constantly exceeded income. Despite the efforts of Philip's able chief minister, Gaspar de Guzmán, Count-Duke of Olivares, it proved impossible to force the distinct kingdoms of the empire to shoulder the cost of its defense. To meet mountainous state debt, the Crown repeatedly devalued the coinage and declared bankruptcy, which resulted in the collapse of state credit and increased inflation.

Spain's situation worsened with internal rebellions and military defeats during the Thirty Years' War and through the remainder of the seventeenth century. In 1640 Spain faced serious revolts in Catalonia and Portugal. In 1643 the French inflicted a crushing defeat on a Spanish army at Rocroi in what is now Belgium. The Peace of Westphalia, which ended the Thirty Years' War, compelled Spain to recognize the independence of the Dutch Republic, and another treaty in 1659 granted extensive territories to France. Finally, in 1688 the Spanish Crown reluctantly recognized the independence of Portugal. With these losses, the era of Spanish dominance in Europe ended.

The Foundations of French Absolutism

Although France was the largest and most populous state in western Europe, its position at the beginning of the seventeenth century appeared extremely weak. Struggling to recover from decades of religious civil war, France posed little threat to Spain's empire or its powerful army. Yet by the end of the century their positions were reversed, and France had attained European dominance.

Henry IV (r. 1589–1610) inaugurated the Bourbon dynasty, defused religious tensions, and rebuilt France's economy. He issued the Edict of Nantes in 1598, allowing Huguenots (French Protestants) the right to worship in 150 traditionally Protestant towns throughout France. He also improved the infrastructure of the country, building new roads and canals and repairing the ravages of years of civil war. Despite his efforts at peace, Henry was murdered in 1610 by a Catholic zealot.

Cardinal Richelieu (1585–1642) became first minister of the French Crown on behalf of Henry's young son, Louis XIII (r. 1610–1643). Richelieu designed his domestic policies to strengthen royal control. He extended the use of intendants, commissioners for each of France's thirty-two districts who were appointed directly by the monarch. By using the intendants to gather information, collect taxes, and ensure that royal edicts were enforced, Richelieu reduced the power of provincial nobles.

Richelieu also viewed France's Huguenots as potential rebels, and he laid siege to La Rochelle, a Protestant stronghold, to preserve control within France. Richelieu's anti-Protestant measures took second place, however, to his most important policy goal, which was to secure French pre-eminence in European power politics. This meant doing everything within his means to weaken the Habsburgs and prevent them from controlling territories that surrounded France. Consequently, Richelieu supported Habsburg enemies, including the Protestant nation of Sweden, during the Thirty Years' War.

Cardinal Jules Mazarin (1602–1661) succeeded Richelieu as chief minister for the next child-king, the four-year-old Louis XIV, who inherited the throne from his father in 1643. Mazarin's struggle to increase royal revenues to meet the costs of the Thirty Years' War led to the uprisings of 1648–1653 known as **the Fronde**. Much of the rebellion died away, however, when Louis XIV was declared king in his own right in 1651, ending the regency of his mother, Anne of Austria. The French people were desperate for peace and stability after the disorders of the Fronde and were willing to accept a strong monarch who could restore order.

Louis XIV and Absolutism

In the reign of Louis XIV (r. 1643–1715), France overcame weakness and division to become the most powerful nation in western Europe. Louis based his authority on the divine right of kings: God had established kings as his rulers on earth, and they were answerable ultimately to him alone. However, Louis also recognized that kings could not simply do as they pleased. They had to obey God's laws and rule for the good of the people.

Louis worked very hard at the business of governing, refusing to delegate power to a first minister. He ruled his realm through several councils of state and insisted on taking a personal role in many of their decisions. Despite increasing financial problems, Louis never called a meeting of the Estates General, the traditional French representative assembly composed of the three estates of clergy, nobility, and commoners. The nobility, therefore, had no means of united expression or action. To further restrict nobles' political power, Louis chose his ministers from capable men of modest origins.

Louis also moved to impose religious unity on France, which he viewed as essential to the security of the state. He thus pursued the policy of Protestant repression launched by Richelieu. In 1685 Louis revoked the Edict of Nantes. The new law ordered the Catholic baptism of Huguenots (French Calvinists), the destruction of Huguenot churches, the closing of schools, and the exile of Huguenot pastors who refused to renounce their faith. Around two hundred thousand Protestants, including some of the king's most highly skilled artisans, fled into exile.

Despite his claims to absolute authority, multiple constraints existed on Louis's power. As a representative of divine power, he was obliged to rule in a manner consistent with virtue and benevolence. (See "Thinking Like a Historian: What Was Absolutism?" on page 432.) He had to uphold the laws issued by his royal predecessors. He also relied on the collaboration of nobles, who maintained tremendous prestige and authority in their ancestral lands. Without their cooperation, it would have been impossible to extend his power throughout France or wage his many foreign wars. Louis's efforts to elicit noble cooperation led him to revolutionize court life at his spectacular palace at Versailles.

Life at Versailles

In 1682 Louis moved his court and government to the newly renovated palace at Versailles, a former hunting lodge. He then required all great nobles to spend at least part of the year in attendance on him there, so he could keep an eye on their activities. Because Louis controlled the distribution of state power and wealth,

■ **the Fronde** A series of violent uprisings during the early reign of Louis XIV triggered by growing royal control and increased taxation.

View of the Palace and Gardens of Versailles, 1668　Located ten miles southwest of Paris, Versailles began as a modest hunting lodge. Louis XIV spent decades enlarging and decorating the structure with the help of architect Louis Le Vau and gardener André Le Nôtre. In 1682, the new palace became the official residence of the Sun King and his court and an inspiration to absolutist palace builders across Europe. (Leemage/Corbis Historical/Getty Images)

nobles had no choice but to obey and compete for his favor at Versailles. The glorious palace was a mirror to the world of French glory and was soon copied by would-be absolutist monarchs across Europe.

Louis further revolutionized court life by establishing an elaborate set of etiquette rituals to mark every moment of his day, from waking up and dressing in the morning to removing his clothing and retiring at night. Courtiers vied for the honor of participating in these ceremonies, with the highest in rank claiming the privilege of handing the king his shirt. These rituals may seem absurd, but they were far from trivial. The king controlled immense resources and privileges; access to him meant favored treatment for government offices, military and religious posts, state pensions, honorary titles, and a host of other benefits. Courtiers sought these rewards for themselves and their family members and followers. A system of patronage—in which a higher-ranked individual protected a lower-ranked one in return for loyalty and services—flowed from the court to the provinces. Through this mechanism Louis gained cooperation from powerful nobles.

Although they could not hold public offices or posts, women played a central role in the patronage system. At court the king's wife, mistresses, and other female relatives recommended individuals for honors, advocated policy decisions, and brokered alliances between factions. Noblewomen played a similar role, bringing their family connections to marriage to form powerful social networks.

Louis XIV was also an enthusiastic patron of the arts, commissioning many sculptures and paintings for Versailles as well as performances of dance and music. He also loved the stage, and in the plays of Molière and Jean Racine his court witnessed the finest achievements in the history of French theater. Some of Molière's targets in this period were aristocratic ladies who wrote literature and held receptions, called salons, in their Parisian mansions, where they engaged in witty and cultured discussions of poetry, art, theater, and the latest worldly events. Their refined conversational style led Molière and other observers to mock them as "*précieuses*" (PREH-see-ooz; literally "precious"), or affected and pretentious. Despite this

What Was Absolutism?

Historians have long debated the nature of "absolutism" in seventeenth-century Europe. While many historians have emphasized the growth of state power in this period, especially under Louis XIV of France, others have questioned whether such a thing as "absolutism" ever existed. The following documents will allow you to draw your own conclusions about absolutism.

1 Jacques-Bénigne Bossuet, political treatise, 1709. In 1670 Louis XIV appointed Bishop Bossuet tutor to his son and heir, known as the dauphin. In *Politics Drawn from the Very Words of Holy Scripture*, Bossuet argued that royal power was divine and absolute, but not without limits.

It appears from all this that the person of the king is sacred, and that to attack him in any way is sacrilege. God has the kings anointed by his prophets with the holy unction in like manner as he has bishops and altars anointed. But even without the external application in thus being anointed, they are by their very office the representatives of the divine majesty deputed by Providence for the execution of his purposes. Accordingly God calls Cyrus his anointed. "Thus saith the Lord to his anointed, to Cyrus, whose right hand I have holden, to subdue nations before him." Kings should be guarded as holy things, and whosoever neglects to protect them is worthy of death. . . . There is something religious in the respect accorded to a prince. The service of God and the respect for kings are bound together. St. Peter unites these two duties when he says, "Fear God. Honour the king.". . . But kings, although their power comes from on high, as has been said, should not regard themselves as masters of that power to use it at their pleasure; . . . they must employ it with fear and self-restraint, as a thing coming from God and of which God will demand an account.

2 Letter of the prince of Condé, royal governor of the province of Burgundy, to Controller General Jean-Baptiste Colbert, June 18, 1662. In this letter, the king's representative in the province of Burgundy reports on his efforts to compel the leaders of the province to pay taxes levied by the royal government. The Estates of Burgundy comprised representatives of the three orders, or estates, of society: the clergy, the nobility, and the commoners.

Since then the Estates have deliberated every day, persuaded that the extreme misery in this province—caused by the great levies it has suffered, the sterility [of the land] in recent years, and the disorders that have recently occurred—would induce the king to give them some relief. That is why they offered only 500,000 for the free gift. Then, after I had protested this in the appropriate manner, they raised it to 600,000, then 800,000, and finally 900,000 livres. Until then I had stood firm at 1.5 million, but when I saw that they were on the verge of deciding not to give any more . . . I finally came down to the 1.2 million livres contained in my instructions and invited them to deliberate again, declaring that I could not agree to present any other proposition to the king and that I believed that there was no better way to serve their interests than to obey the king blindly. They agreed with good grace and came this morning to offer me a million. They begged me to leave it at that and not to demand more from them for the free gift; and since I told them they would have to do a little better to satisfy the king completely on this occasion, they again exaggerated their poverty and begged me to inform the king of it, but said that, rather than not please him, they preferred to make a new effort, and they would leave it up to me to declare what they had to do. I told them that I believed His Majesty would have the goodness to be satisfied with 1.05 million livres for the free gift, and they agreed. . . . So Monsieur, there is the deed done.

ANALYZING THE EVIDENCE

1. What elements of royal authority does the portrait of Louis XIV in Source 4 present to viewers? How would you compare this depiction of political power with images from modern-day politicians? How would you explain the differences?
2. What justification do the sources offer for Louis's claim to exercise "absolute" political authority? Based on his own words in Source 3, how do you think Louis would have viewed the constitutional governments of England and the Dutch Republic?
3. Compare and contrast the evidence for Louis's power given in these sources with evidence for limitations on it. What resources would a king have to muster to enlarge his army drastically (Source 5)? What insight do the negotiations over taxation (Source 2) give you into the ways the royal government acquired those resources?

3 **Louis XIV, memoir for the *Instruction of the Dauphin.*** In 1670 Louis XIV finished a memoir he had compiled for the education of his son and heir. Presented in the king's voice — although cowritten with several royal aides — the memoir recounts the early years of Louis's reign and explains his approach to absolute rule.

〜 For however it be held as a maxim that in every thing a Prince should employ the most mild measures and first, and that it is more to his advantage to govern his subjects by persuasive than coercive means, it is nevertheless certain that whenever he meets with impediments or rebellion, the interest of his crown and the welfare of his people demand that he should cause himself to be indispensably obeyed; for it must be acknowledged there is nothing can so securely establish the happiness and tranquility of a country as the perfect combination of all authority in the single person of the Sovereign. The least division in this respect often produces the greatest calamities; and whether it be detached into the hands of individuals or those of corporate bodies, it always is there in a state of fermentation.

. . . [B]esides the insurrections and the intestine commotions which the ambition of power infallibly produces when it is not repressed, there are still a thousand other evils created by the inactivity of the Sovereign. Those who are nearest his person are the first to observe his weakness, and are also the first who are desirous of profiting by it. Every one of those persons have necessarily others who are subservient to their avaricious views, and to whom they at the same time give the privilege of imitating them. Thus, from the highest to the lowest is a systematic corruption communicated, and it becomes general in all classes.

(Art Images/Hulton Fine Art Collection/Getty Images)

4 **Hyacinthe Rigaud, portrait of Louis XIV, 1701.** This was one of Louis XIV's favorite portraits of himself. He liked it so much that he had many copies of the portrait made; his successors had their own portraits painted in the same posture with the same clothing and accoutrements.

5 **Growth of the French Army.**

Time Period	Size of Army
Middle Ages	10,000 men
1635 (Louis XIII and Richelieu enter Thirty Years' War)	125,000 men
1670s (Louis XIV wages Dutch War)	280,000 men
1690s (Louis XIV wages Nine Years' War)	340,000 men

PUTTING IT ALL TOGETHER

Using the sources above, along with what you have learned in class and in this chapter, what was "absolutism"? Write a brief essay explaining what contemporaries thought absolute power entailed and the extent to which Louis XIV achieved such power.

Sources: (1) J. H. Robinson, ed., *Readings in European History*, vol. 2 (Boston: Ginn, 1906), p. 274; (2) William Beik, ed., *Louis XIV and Absolutism: A Brief Study with Documents* (Boston: Bedford/St. Martin's, 2000), pp. 127–128; (3) *Memoirs of Lewis the Fourteenth, Written by Himself, and Addressed to His Son*, vol. 1 (London: Longman, Hurst, Rees and Orme, 1806), pp. 13–14; (5) Based on information from John A. Lynn, *The Wars of Louis XIV, 1667–1714* (London: Routledge, 2013), pp. 5–51.

mockery, the précieuses represented an important cultural force ruled by elite women.

With Versailles as the center of European politics, French culture grew in international prestige. French became the language of polite society and international diplomacy, gradually replacing Latin as the language of scholarship and learning. Royal courts across Europe spoke French, and the great aristocrats of Russia, Sweden, Germany, and elsewhere were often more fluent in French than in the tongues of their homelands. France inspired a cosmopolitan European culture in the late seventeenth century that looked to Versailles as its center.

Louis XIV's Wars

In pursuit of dynastic glory, Louis kept France at war for thirty-three of the fifty-four years of his personal rule. During his reign, the French army almost tripled in size, and its professionalism greatly increased. Uniforms and weapons were standardized, and a system of training and promotion was devised. These developments were part of a European-wide phenomenon scholars have dubbed a "military revolution." Military competition among early modern European states was a key catalyst for the development of the fiscal-military state.

The results of Louis's military aggression were decidedly mixed. During the 1660s and 1670s, French armies won a number of important victories and managed to extend French borders to include commercial centers in the Spanish Netherlands and Flanders as well as the province of Franche-Comté, formerly held by Spain. In 1681 Louis seized the city of Strasbourg, and three years later his armies entered the province of Lorraine. This was the height of his achievement.

The wars of the 1680s and 1690s, however, brought no additional territories and placed unbearable strain on French resources. Louis's last war, the War of the Spanish Succession (1701–1713), was endured by a French people suffering high taxes, crop failure, and widespread malnutrition and death. This war was the result of Louis's unwillingness to abide by a previous agreement to divide Spanish possessions

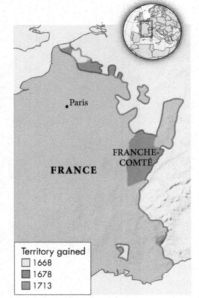

The Acquisitions of Louis XIV, 1668–1713

Territory gained
1668
1678
1713

between France and the Holy Roman emperor upon the death of the childless Spanish king Charles II (r. 1665–1700). In 1701 the English, Dutch, Austrians, and Prussians formed the Grand Alliance against Louis XIV. War dragged on until 1713.

The **Peace of Utrecht**, which ended the war, allowed Louis's grandson Philip to remain king of Spain on the understanding that the French and Spanish Crowns would never be united in order to protect the "balance of power" in Europe. (This was the first time this phrase occurred in a peace treaty.) France surrendered Nova Scotia, Newfoundland, and the Hudson Bay territory to England, which also acquired Gibraltar, Minorca, and control of the African slave trade from Spain (Map 15.2). At the time of Louis's death in 1715, an exhausted France hovered on the brink of bankruptcy.

The French Economic Policy of Mercantilism

France's ability to build armies and fight wars depended on a strong economy. Fortunately for Louis, his controller general, Jean-Baptiste Colbert (1619–1683), proved to be a financial and administrative genius. Colbert's central principle was that the wealth and the economy of France should serve the state. To this end, from 1665 to his death in 1683, Colbert rigorously applied mercantilist policies to France.

Mercantilism was a collection of governmental policies for the regulation of economic activities by and for the state. It derived from the idea that a state's international power is based on its wealth, specifically its supply of gold and silver. To accumulate wealth, a country always had to sell more goods abroad than it bought.

To increase exports, Colbert supported old industries and created new ones, focusing especially on textiles, which were the most important sector of manufacturing. He enacted new production regulations, created guilds to boost quality standards, and encouraged foreign craftsmen to immigrate to France. To encourage the purchase of French goods, he abolished many domestic tariffs and raised tariffs on foreign products. In 1664 Colbert founded the Company of the East Indies with (unfulfilled) hopes of competing with the Dutch for Asian trade.

■ **Peace of Utrecht** A series of treaties, from 1713 to 1715, that ended the War of the Spanish Succession, ended French expansion in Europe, and marked the rise of the British Empire.

■ **mercantilism** A system of economic regulations aimed at increasing the power of the state based on the belief that a nation's international power was based on its wealth, specifically its supply of gold and silver.

Inset map: **North America, 1714**
HUDSON'S BAY COMPANY
Newfoundland
QUEBEC
NEW FRANCE
NOVA SCOTIA
LOUISIANA
THIRTEEN COLONIES
SP. FLORIDA

Claims
British
French
Spanish

Legend:
French Bourbon lands
Spanish Bourbon lands
Austrian Habsburg lands
Prussian lands
Great Britain
Russian Empire
— Boundary of the Holy Roman Empire

MAPPING THE PAST

MAP 15.2 Europe After the Peace of Utrecht, 1715

The series of treaties commonly called the Peace of Utrecht ended the War of the Spanish Succession and redrew the map of Europe. A French Bourbon king succeeded to the Spanish throne. France surrendered the Spanish Netherlands (later Belgium), then in French hands, to Austria, and recognized the Hohenzollern rulers as kings in Prussia. Spain ceded Gibraltar to Great Britain, for which it has been a strategic naval station ever since. Spain also granted Britain the *asiento*, the contract for supplying enslaved Africans to the Americas.

ANALYZING THE MAP Comparing this map to Map 15.1, identify the areas on the map that changed hands between the Peace of Westphalia and the Peace of Utrecht. How did these changes affect the balance of power in Europe?

CONNECTIONS How and why did so many European countries possess scattered or noncontiguous territories? What does this suggest about European politics in this period? Does this map suggest potential for future conflict?

Colbert also hoped to make Canada — rich in untapped minerals and some of the best agricultural land in the world — part of a vast French empire. He sent four thousand colonists to Quebec, whose capital had been founded in 1608 under Henry IV. Subsequently, the Jesuit Jacques Marquette and the merchant Louis Joliet sailed down the Mississippi River, which they named Colbert in honor of their sponsor (the name soon reverted to the original Native American one). Marquette and Joliet claimed

possession of the land on both sides of the river as far south as present-day Arkansas. In 1684 French explorers continued down the Mississippi to its mouth and claimed vast territories for Louis XIV. They called the area, naturally, Louisiana.

During Colbert's tenure as controller general, Louis was able to pursue his goals without massive tax increases and without creating a stream of new offices. The constant pressure of warfare after Colbert's death, however, undid many of his economic achievements.

What explains the rise of absolutism in Prussia and Austria?

Absolutism was also the dominant form of monarchical rule among the more than one thousand states that composed the Holy Roman Empire. The most successful states were Austria and Prussia, which witnessed the rise of absolutism between 1620 and 1740. Their rulers built on social and economic foundations far different from those in western Europe, namely, serfdom and the strong nobility who benefited from it. The constant warfare of the seventeenth century allowed them to increase their power by building large armies, increasing taxation, and suppressing representative institutions. In exchange for their growing political authority, monarchs allowed nobles to retain unchallenged control over their peasants, a deal that appeased both king and nobility but left serfs at the mercy of the lords.

The Return of Serfdom

While economic and social hardship was common across Europe, important differences existed between east and west. In the west the demographic losses of the Black Death allowed peasants to escape from serfdom as they acquired enough land to feed themselves. In central and eastern Europe, noble lords dealt with the labor shortages caused by the Black Death by restricting the right of their peasants to move to take advantage of better opportunities elsewhere.

As economic expansion and population growth resumed after 1500, only noble landowners had the capacity to organize large-scale agricultural production for foreign markets. Benefiting from the captive labor of the peasantry, between 1500 and 1650, lords increased the production of their estates. Selling their surpluses through foreign merchants, they became the foremost suppliers of grain to feed the growing cities of western Europe.

Declining productivity during the wars and other crises of the seventeenth century led to worsening conditions for serfs. Regulations in many central and eastern European territories required that runaway serfs be hunted down and returned to their lords. Moreover, lords steadily took more and more of their peasants' land and arbitrarily imposed heavier labor obligations. Not only was their freedom of movement restricted, but they also required permission to marry. Lords could reallocate the lands worked by their serfs or sell serfs apart from their families.

It was not only the peasants who suffered. With the approval of kings, landlords systematically undermined the medieval privileges of the towns and the power of the urban classes. Instead of selling products to local merchants, landlords sold directly to foreigners, bypassing local towns. Eastern towns also lost their medieval right of refuge and were compelled to return

runaways to their lords. The population of the towns and the urban middle classes declined significantly.

The Austrian Habsburgs

Like all of central Europe, the Habsburgs emerged from the Thirty Years' War impoverished and exhausted. Their efforts to destroy Protestantism in the German lands and to turn the weak Holy Roman Empire into a real state had failed. The Habsburg dynasty occupied the elected imperial throne between 1438 and 1740, but real power lay in the hands of a bewildering variety of separate political jurisdictions. Defeat in central Europe encouraged the Habsburgs to turn away from a quest for imperial dominance and to focus inward and eastward in an attempt to unify their diverse holdings.

Habsburg victory over Bohemia during the Thirty Years' War was an important step in this direction. Ferdinand II (r. 1619–1637) drastically reduced the power of the Bohemian Estates, the largely Protestant representative assembly. He also confiscated the landholdings of Protestant nobles and gave them to loyal Catholic nobles and to the foreign aristocratic mercenaries who led his armies. After 1650 a large portion of the Bohemian nobility was of recent origin and owed its success to the Habsburgs.

With the support of this new nobility, the Habsburgs established direct rule over Bohemia. Under their rule the condition of the enserfed peasantry worsened substantially: three days per week of unpaid labor became the norm. Protestantism was also stamped out. These changes were significant advances in creating absolutist rule in Bohemia.

Ferdinand III (r. 1637–1657) continued to build state power. He centralized the government in the empire's German-speaking provinces, which formed the core Habsburg holdings. For the first time, a permanent standing army was ready to put down any internal opposition. The Habsburg monarchy then turned east toward the plains of Hungary, which had been divided between the Ottomans and the Habsburgs in the early sixteenth century. Between 1683 and 1699 the Habsburgs pushed the Ottomans from most of Hungary and Transylvania. The recovery of all of the former kingdom of Hungary was completed in 1718.

The Hungarian nobility, despite its reduced strength, effectively thwarted the full development of Habsburg absolutism. Throughout the seventeenth century Hungarian nobles rose in revolt against attempts to impose absolute rule. They never triumphed decisively, but neither were they crushed the way the nobility had been in Bohemia. In 1703, with the Habsburgs bogged down in the War of the Spanish

MAP 15.3 The Growth of Austria and Brandenburg-Prussia to 1748 Austria expanded to the southwest into Hungary and Transylvania at the expense of the Ottoman Empire. It was unable to hold the rich German province of Silesia, however, which was conquered by Brandenburg-Prussia.

Succession, the Hungarians rose in one last patriotic rebellion under Prince Francis Rákóczy. The prince and his forces were eventually defeated, but the Habsburgs agreed to restore many of the traditional privileges of the aristocracy in return for Hungarian acceptance of hereditary Habsburg rule. Thus Hungary, unlike Austria and Bohemia, was never fully integrated into a centralized, absolute Habsburg state.

Despite checks on their ambitions in Hungary, the Habsburgs made significant achievements in state-building elsewhere by forging consensus with the church and the nobility. A sense of common identity and loyalty to the monarchy grew among elites in Habsburg lands, even to a certain extent in Hungary. Vienna became the political and cultural center of the empire. By 1700 it was a thriving city with a population of one hundred thousand and its own version of Versailles, the royal palace of Schönbrunn.

Prussia in the Seventeenth Century

Originating in the eastern portions of Charlemagne's Frankish empire, the Hohenzollern dynasty rose to prominence in the fifteenth and sixteenth centuries. In 1415, the Holy Roman emperor made Frederick I of the Hohenzollern family elector of Brandenburg. The title of *elector* gave its holder the privilege of being one of only seven princes or archbishops entitled to elect the Holy Roman emperor, but the electors had little real power. The title continued to be held by the Hohenzollern family, including by Frederick William, who came to power in 1640. Later known as the Great Elector, Frederick William was determined to unify his three provinces and enlarge his holdings. These provinces were Brandenburg; Prussia, inherited in 1618; and scattered territories along the Rhine inherited in 1614 (Map 15.3). Each had its own estates. Although the estates had not met regularly during the chaotic Thirty Years' War, taxes could not be levied without their consent. The estates of Brandenburg and Prussia were dominated by the nobility and the landowning classes, known as the **Junkers**.

■ **Junkers** The nobility of Brandenburg and Prussia, who were reluctant allies of Frederick William in his consolidation of the Prussian state.

A Prussian Giant Grenadier Frederick William I wanted tall, handsome soldiers. He dressed them in tight, bright uniforms to distinguish them from the peasant population from which most soldiers came. He also ordered several portraits of his favorites, such as this one, from his court painter, J. C. Merk. Grenadiers (greh-nuh-DEERZ) wore the miter cap instead of an ordinary hat so that they could hurl their heavy grenades unimpeded by a broad brim. (Deutsches Historisches Museum/© DHM/Bridgeman Images)

in return for aiding the Habsburgs during the War of the Spanish Succession, received permission from the Holy Roman emperor to crown himself *king in Prussia* (not king *of* Prussia, which would have threatened the supremacy of the emperor); he retained the title of elector of Brandenburg.

The Consolidation of Prussian Absolutism

Frederick William I, "the Soldiers' King" (r. 1713–1740), completed his grandfather's work, eliminating the last traces of parliamentary estates and local self-government. It was he who truly established Prussian absolutism and transformed Prussia into a military state. Frederick William was intensely attached to military life. He always wore an army uniform, and he lived the highly disciplined life of the professional soldier. Years later he followed the family tradition by leaving his own written instructions to his son: "A formidable army and a war chest large enough to make this army mobile in times of need can create great respect for you in the world, so that you can speak a word like the other powers."[3]

Penny-pinching, ruthless, and hard-working, Frederick William achieved results. The king and his ministers built an exceptionally efficient bureaucracy to administer the country and foster economic development. Twelfth in Europe in population, Prussia had the fourth-largest army by 1740. The Prussian army was considered one of the best in Europe, astonishing foreign observers with its precision, skill, and discipline.

Nevertheless, Prussians paid a heavy and lasting price for the obsessions of their royal drillmaster. Army expansion was achieved in part through forced conscription, which was declared lifelong in 1713. Desperate draftees fled the country or injured themselves to avoid service. Finally, in 1733 Frederick William I ordered that all Prussian men undergo military training and serve as reservists in the army, allowing him to preserve both agricultural production and army size. To appease the Junkers, the king enlisted them to lead his growing army. The proud nobility thus commanded the peasantry in the army as well as on the estates.

With all men harnessed to the war machine, Prussian civil society became rigid and highly disciplined. An observation attributed to the French philosophe Mirabeau held that Prussia was not a state in possession of an army but an army in possession of a state. Thus the policies of Frederick William I, combined with harsh peasant bondage and Junker tyranny, laid the foundations for a highly militaristic country.

Frederick William profited from ongoing European war and the threat of invasion from Sweden when he argued for the need for a permanent standing army. In 1660 he persuaded Junkers in the estates to accept taxation without consent in order to fund an army. They agreed to do so in exchange for reconfirmation of their own privileges, including authority over the serfs. Having won over the Junkers, the king crushed potential opposition to his power from the towns. One by one, Prussian cities were eliminated from the estates and subjected to new taxes on goods and services. Thereafter, the estates' power declined rapidly, for the Great Elector had both financial independence and superior force. During his reign, Frederick William tripled state revenue and expanded the army drastically. In 1688 a population of 1 million supported a peacetime standing army of 30,000. In 1701 the elector's son, Frederick I,

What were the distinctive features of Russian and Ottoman absolutism?

Russia occupied a unique position among Eurasian states. With borders straddling eastern Europe and northwestern Asia, its development into a strong imperial state drew on elements from both continents. Like the growth of the Muslim empires in Central and South Asia and the Ming Dynasty in China, the expansion of Russia eastward was a result of the weakening of the great Mongol Empire. After gaining independence from the Mongols, the rulers of the Grand Duchy of Moscow were able to create a vast empire, extending through North Asia all the way to the Pacific Ocean. State-building and territorial expansion culminated during the reign of Peter the Great, who forcibly introduced elements of Western culture and society.

Great debate existed, and continues to exist, both within and outside Russia on the question of whether or not Russia was a Western society. On the other hand, there was no question in contemporary western European minds that the Ottomans were outsiders. Even absolutist rulers depicted Ottoman sultans as tyrannical despots. Despite these stereotypes, the Ottoman Empire was in many ways more tolerant than its Western counterparts, providing protection and security to other religions while maintaining the Muslim faith. Flexibility and openness to other ideas and practices were sources of strength for the empire.

Mongol Rule in Russia and the Rise of Moscow

The two-hundred-year period of rule by the Mongol khan (king) set the stage for the rise of absolutist Russia. The Mongols, a group of nomadic tribes from present-day Mongolia, established an empire that, at its height, stretched from Korea to eastern Europe. In the thirteenth century the Mongols had conquered Kievan Rus, the medieval Slavic state that included most of present-day Ukraine, Belarus, and part of northwest Russia. For two hundred years the Mongols forced the Slavic princes to submit to their rule. The Mongols showed favor to the princes of the Grand Duchy of Moscow, a principality that emerged in the territory of the former Kievan Rus. The wealth and power they accrued from Mongol patronage allowed the prince of Moscow to surpass rival local rulers. Ivan III (r. 1462–1505), known as Ivan the Great, successfully expanded the principality of Moscow westward toward the Baltic Sea and eastward to the Ural Mountains and the Siberian frontier (see Map 15.4).

By 1480 Ivan III was strong enough to declare the autonomy of Moscow. To legitimize their new position, Ivan and his successors borrowed elements of Mongol rule. They forced weaker Slavic principalities to render tribute and borrowed Mongol institutions such as the tax system, postal routes, and census. Loyalty from the highest-ranking nobles, or **boyars**, helped the Muscovite princes consolidate their power.

Another source of legitimacy for Moscow was its claim to the political and religious legacy of the Byzantine Empire. After the fall of Constantinople to the Turks in 1453, the princes of Moscow saw themselves as the heirs of the Byzantine caesars (or emperors) and guardians of the Orthodox Christian Church. The marriage of Ivan III to the niece of the last Byzantine emperor further enhanced Moscow's assertion of imperial authority.

By the time of Ivan's death, a system of autocracy was already well developed in Muscovy. The ruler's power was believed to be derived from God and was limited only by religious precepts, not by laws or assemblies. The Russian tsar thus fulfilled claims to absolute power to a much greater extent than western European monarchs, who had to compromise and collaborate with elites in assemblies and other institutions.

Building the Russian Empire

Developments in Russia took a chaotic turn with the reign of Ivan IV (r. 1533–1584), the famous "Ivan the Terrible," who ascended to the throne at age three. His mother died when he was eight, leaving Ivan to suffer insults and neglect from the boyars at court. At age sixteen Ivan pushed aside his advisers and had crowned himself "tsar of all Russia" in 1547, the first Muscovite ruler to claim the title of *tsar*, the Russian term for the Roman and Byzantine caesars. After the sudden death of his wife, Ivan began a campaign of persecution against those he suspected of opposing him. He executed members of leading boyar families, along with their families, friends, and servants. To replace them, Ivan created a new service nobility of several thousand men whom he rewarded with land to ensure their loyalty.

As landlords demanded more from the serfs who survived the persecutions, growing numbers of peasants fled toward recently conquered territories to the east and south. There they joined free groups and warrior bands known as **Cossacks**. Ivan responded

---

■ **boyars** The highest-ranking members of the Russian nobility.

■ **Cossacks** Free groups and outlaw armies originally comprising runaway peasants living on the borders of Russian territory from the fourteenth century onward. By the end of the sixteenth century they had formed an alliance with the Russian state.

The Shuysky Tribute This painting depicts the Shuysky Tribute, in which the Russian tsar Vasily Shuysky and his brothers swore allegiance to the Polish-Lithuanian Commonwealth and its king in the Senate Hall of the Royal Palace in Warsaw. This event occurred in 1611, after the invasion of Russia by Polish-Lithuanian forces. By 1613, Russian armies had reclaimed Moscow, leading to the election of Michael Romanov as tsar and the creation of the Romanov dynasty. (ART Collection/Alamy Stock Photo)

by tying peasants ever more firmly to the land. Simultaneously, so that he could tax them more heavily, he ordered that urban dwellers be bound to their towns and jobs. These restrictions checked the growth of the Russian middle classes and stood in sharp contrast to economic and social developments in western Europe.

Ivan's reign was successful in defeating the remnants of Mongol power and in laying the foundations for the huge, multiethnic Russian Empire. In the 1550s, Ivan conquered the Muslim khanates of Kazan and Astrakhan and brought the fertile steppe region around the Volga River under Russian control. Ivan's efforts to expand to the west were less successful. His bid to secure control of Livonia, as a means of gaining access to the Baltic Sea, led to war with Sweden and the Grand Duchy of Lithuania. These conflicts encouraged Lithuania to formalize its ties to Poland with the Union of Lublin in 1569.

In the 1580s Cossacks fighting for the Russian state crossed the Ural Mountains and began the long conquest of Siberia. Because of the size of the new territories and their distance from Moscow, the Russian state did not initially seek to impose the Orthodox religion and maintained local elites in positions of honor and leadership, buying their loyalty with grants of land.

Following Ivan's death, Russia entered a chaotic period known as the Time of Troubles (1598–1613), triggered by a breakdown in dynastic succession and a severe famine, in which up to one-third of the population perished. Political and social crisis led to civil war and an uprising of Cossacks and other groups supporting various contenders for the throne. This breakdown in order allowed Polish-Lithuanian armies to occupy Moscow between 1610 and 1612. These threats brought the fractious Russian nobles together. An assembly of nobles elected the grandnephew of Ivan's wife, Michael Romanov (r. 1613–1645), the new hereditary tsar. They presented the election as an act of God, ensuring that the new tsar carried the same divine legitimacy as his predecessors.

With their legitimacy assured, the Romanov tsars, like their Western counterparts, made several important achievements in territorial expansion and state-building. After a long war, Russia gained land to the west in Ukraine in 1667. By the end of the century,

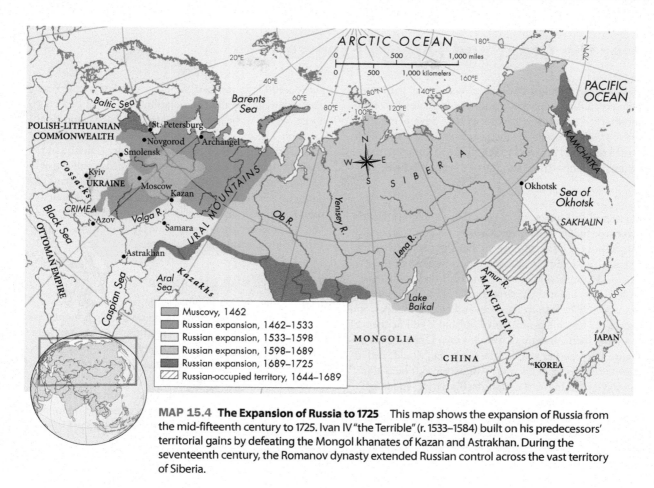

MAP 15.4 The Expansion of Russia to 1725   This map shows the expansion of Russia from the mid-fifteenth century to 1725. Ivan IV "the Terrible" (r. 1533–1584) built on his predecessors' territorial gains by defeating the Mongol khanates of Kazan and Astrakhan. During the seventeenth century, the Romanov dynasty extended Russian control across the vast territory of Siberia.

it had completed the conquest of Siberia (Map 15.4) and its people. This vast territorial expansion brought Russian power to the Sea of Okhotsk in the Pacific Ocean and was only checked by the powerful Qing Dynasty of China. Like the French in Canada, the basis of Russian wealth in Siberia was furs, which the state collected by forced annual tribute payments from local people. Profits from furs and other natural resources, especially mining in the eighteenth century, funded expansion of the Russian imperial bureaucracy and the army.

The growth of state power did nothing to improve the lot of the common people. In 1649 a new law code extended serfdom to all peasants in the realm, giving lords unrestricted rights over their serfs and establishing penalties for harboring runaways. Henceforth, Moscow maintained strict control of trade and administration throughout the empire.

The peace imposed by harsh Russian rule was disrupted in 1670 by a failed rebellion led by the Cossack Stenka Razin, who attracted a great army of urban poor and peasants. The ease with which Moscow crushed the rebellion testifies to the success of the Russian state in unifying and consolidating its empire.

The Reforms of Peter the Great

Heir to the Romanovs, Peter the Great (r. 1682–1725) successfully created the Russian fiscal-military state. Peter built on the service obligations of Ivan the Terrible and his successors and continued their tradition of territorial expansion. In particular, he was determined to gain access to the sea for his virtually landlocked state, by extending Russia's borders first to the Black Sea (controlled by the Ottomans) and then to the Baltic Sea (dominated by Sweden).

Peter moved toward the first goal by conquering the Ottoman fort of Azov near the Black Sea in 1696, and quickly built Russia's first navy base. In 1697 the tsar embarked on an eighteen-month tour of western European capitals. Peter was fascinated by foreign technology, and he hoped to forge an anti-Ottoman alliance to strengthen his claims on the Black Sea. Peter failed to secure a military alliance, but he did learn his lessons from the growing power of the Dutch and the English. He also engaged more than a hundred foreign experts to return with him to Russia to help build the navy and improve Russian infrastructure. (See "Evaluating Written Evidence: Peter the Great and Foreign Experts," page 442.)

Peter the Great and Foreign Experts

John Deane, an eminent shipbuilder, was one of the many foreign artisans and experts brought to Russia by Peter the Great after the latter's foreign tour of 1697. Several months after his arrival in Russia, Deane sent a glowing account of the tsar's technical prowess to his patron in England, the marquess of Carmarthen, admiral of the English fleet.

At my arrival in Moscow, I fell very ill of the Bloody-Flux, which made me be in Moscow when his Majesty came home: About the latter end of October I was somewhat recovered, his Majesty then carried me down to Voronize* with him. Voronize is about 400 English Miles South-East from Moscow. There the Czar immediately set up a ship of 60 guns, where he is both Foreman and Master-Builder; and not to flatter him, I'll assure your Lordship it will be the best ship among them, and 'tis all from his own Draught; How he fram'd her together and how he made the Mould, and in so short a time as he did is really wonderful: But he is able at this day to put his own notions into practice, and laugh at his Dutch and Italian builders for their ignorance. There are several pieces of workmanship, as in the keel, stem, and post, which are all purely his own invention, and sound good work, and would be approved of by all the shipwrights of England if they saw it. . . .

After some time [I] fell sick again; and at Christmas, when his Majesty came to Moscow, he brought me back again for recovery of my health, where I am at present. . . . The whole place is inhabited by the Dutch; I believe there may be 400 families. Last Sunday and Monday the strangers were invited to the consecration of General La Fort's house, which is the noblest building in Russia, and finely furnisht. There were all the envoys, and as near as I could guess 200 gentlemen, English, French, and Dutch, and about as many ladies; each day were dancing and musick. All the envoys, and all the lords (but three in Moscow) are going to Voronize to see the fleet, I suppose. His majesty went last Sunday to Voronize with Prince Alexander and I am to go down (being something recovered) with the Vice-Admiral about six days hence.

EVALUATE THE EVIDENCE

1. According to Deane, what evidence did Peter give of his skills in shipbuilding? Based on this document, how would you characterize the relationship between Peter the Great and his foreign experts?
2. What other evidence does Deane provide of the impact of foreigners on life in Russia?
3. How trustworthy do you think this source is? What impression does the author seem to be aiming for in his account of Peter and his relations with the foreign shipbuilders?

Source: John Deane, *A Letter from Moscow to the Marquess of Carmarthen, Relating to the Czar of Muscovy's Forwardness in His Great Navy, & c. Since His Return Home*, London, 1699.

*Site of the naval shipyard, today's city of Voronezh.

To gain access to the Baltic Sea, Peter allied with Denmark and the Polish-Lithuanian Commonwealth to wage a sudden war of aggression against Sweden. Eighteen-year-old Charles XII of Sweden (1697–1718), however, surprised Peter. He defeated Denmark quickly in 1700 and then turned on Russia. His well-trained professional army attacked and routed unsuspecting Russians besieging the Swedish fortress of Narva on the Baltic coast. It was, for the Russians, a grim beginning to the long and brutal Great Northern War, which lasted from 1700 to 1721.

Peter responded to this defeat with new measures to increase state power, strengthen his military forces, and gain victory. He required all nobles to serve in the army or in the civil administration—for life. Peter also created schools of navigation and mathematics, medicine, engineering, and finance to produce skilled technicians and experts. He established an interlocking military-civilian bureaucracy with fourteen ranks, and he decreed that everyone had to start at the bottom and work toward the top. These measures gradually combined to make the army and government more powerful and efficient.

Peter also greatly increased the service requirements of commoners. In the wake of the Narva disaster, he established a regular standing army of more than two hundred thousand peasant-soldiers, drafted for life and commanded by noble officers. He added an additional hundred thousand men in special regiments of Cossacks and foreign mercenaries. To fund the army, taxes on peasants increased threefold during Peter's reign. Serfs were also arbitrarily assigned to work in the growing number of factories and mines that supplied the military.

In 1709 Peter's new war machine was able to crush the much smaller army of Sweden in Ukraine at Poltava, one of the most significant battles in Russian history. Russia's victory against Sweden was conclusive in 1721, and Estonia and present-day Latvia came under Russian rule. The cost was high: warfare consumed 80 to 85 percent of all revenues. But Russia became the dominant power in the Baltic and very much a great European power.

After his victory at Poltava, Peter channeled enormous resources into building a new Western-style capital on the Baltic. Each summer, 25,000 to 40,000 peasants were sent to provide construction labor in St. Petersburg without pay. Many of these laborers died from hunger, sickness, and accidents. To populate his new capital, Peter ordered nobles to build costly palaces in St. Petersburg and required merchants and artisans to settle in the new capital. The building of St. Petersburg was, in truth, an enormous direct tax levied on the wealthy, with the peasantry forced to do the work.

There were other important consequences of Peter's reign. For Peter, modernization meant westernization, and he encouraged the spread of Western culture along with technology and urban planning. Peter required nobles to shave their heavy beards and wear Western clothing, previously banned in Russia. He also ordered them to attend parties where young men and women would mix together and freely choose their own spouses. From these efforts a new elite class of Western-oriented Russians began to emerge.

Peter's reforms were unpopular with many Russians. For nobles, one of Peter's most detested reforms was the imposition of unigeniture — inheritance of land by one son alone — cutting daughters and other sons from family property. For peasants, the reign of the tsar saw a significant increase in the bonds of serfdom. Despite the unpopularity of Peter's reforms, his modernizing and westernizing of Russia paved the way for it to move somewhat closer to the European mainstream in its thought and institutions during the Enlightenment, especially under Catherine the Great.

The Ottoman Empire

The Ottomans came out of Central Asia as conquering warriors, settled in Anatolia (present-day Turkey), and, at their peak in the mid-sixteenth century, ruled one of the most powerful empires in the world. Their possessions stretched from western Persia across North Africa and into the heart of central Europe (Map 15.5).

The Ottoman Empire was built on a unique model of state and society. Much of the agricultural land was the personal hereditary property of the **sultan**, and peasants paid taxes to use the land. Thus there was an

Peter the Great Cutting a Boyar's Beard   As part of his westernization program, Peter the Great obliged Russian men to shave their long beards, a shock to traditional Orthodox notions of masculinity. Like many of his reforms, these were aimed primarily at the noble boyars; many peasants continued to wear beards in the countryside. (Universal Images Group/Getty Images)

almost complete absence of private landed property and no hereditary nobility.

The Ottomans also employed a distinctive form of government administration. The top ranks of the bureaucracy were staffed by the sultan's corps of enslaved men. Because Muslim law prohibited enslaving other Muslims, the sultan's agents obtained captives along the borders of the empire. Within the realm, the sultan levied a "tax" of one thousand to three thousand male children on the conquered Christian populations in the Balkans every year. These enslaved youths were raised in Turkey as Muslims and were trained as soldiers and government administrators. The most talented rose to the top of the bureaucracy, where they might acquire wealth and power. The less fortunate formed the core of the sultan's army, the **janissary corps**. These highly organized

---

■ **sultan** The ruler of the Ottoman Empire; he owned all the agricultural land of the empire and was served by an army and bureaucracy composed of highly trained enslaved people.

■ **janissary corps** The core of the sultan's army, composed of enslaved conscripts from non-Muslim parts of the empire; after 1683 it became a volunteer force.

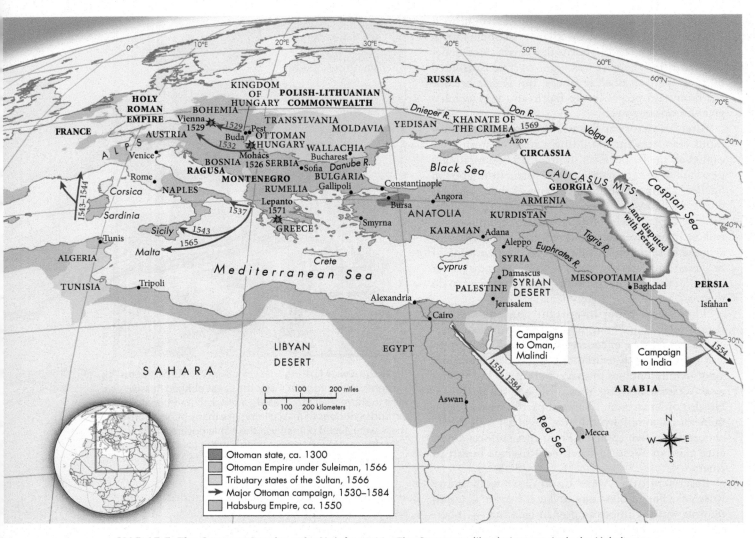

MAP 15.5 The Ottoman Empire at Its Height, 1566 The Ottomans, like their great rivals the Habsburgs, rose to rule a vast dynastic empire encompassing many different peoples and ethnic groups. The army and the bureaucracy served to unite the disparate territories into a single state under an absolutist ruler.

and efficient troops gave the Ottomans a formidable advantage in war with western Europeans. By the first half of the seventeenth century, service in the janissary corps had become so prestigious that the sultan ceased recruitment by force, and it became a volunteer army open to Christians and Muslims.

The Ottoman sultan claimed to be the leader of all Muslims, and the empire waged war in the name of Islam. Yet the Ottomans also practiced a higher degree of religious tolerance than most European states of the time. The Ottomans divided their subjects into religious communities, and each *millet*, or "nation," enjoyed a degree of religious and social autonomy. The Ottoman Empire recognized Orthodox Christians,

Jews, and Armenian Christians as distinct millets. The **millet system** created a powerful bond between the Ottoman ruling class and religious leaders, who supported the sultan's rule in return for relative autonomy for their communities. Each millet collected taxes for the state, regulated collective behavior, and maintained law courts, schools, houses of worship, and hospitals for its people.

Constantinople (today's Istanbul) was the capital of the empire. The "old palace" was for the sultan's female family members, who lived in isolation under the care of eunuchs, men who were castrated to prevent sexual relations with women. The newer Topkapi palace was where officials worked and enslaved youths were trained for future administrative or military careers. Sultans married women of the highest social standing, while keeping many concubines of low rank. To prevent the elite families into which they married

■ **millet system** A system used by the Ottomans whereby subjects were divided into religious communities, with each millet (nation) enjoying autonomous self-government under its religious leaders.

INDIVIDUALS IN SOCIETY
Hürrem

I n Muslim culture, *harem* means a sacred place or a sanctuary. The term was applied to the part of the household occupied by women and children and forbidden to men outside the family. The most famous harem member in Ottoman history was Hürrem, wife of Suleiman the Magnificent.

Like many of the sultan's concubines, Hürrem (1505?–1558) was of foreign birth. Tradition holds that she was born Aleksandra Lisowska in the Polish-Lithuanian Commonwealth (present-day Ukraine). Captured during a Tatar raid and enslaved, she entered the imperial harem between 1517 and 1520, when she was about fifteen years old. Reports from Venetian visitors claimed that she was not outstandingly beautiful, but was possessed of wonderful grace, charm, and good humor, earning her the Turkish nickname Hürrem, or "joyful one." Soon after her arrival, Hürrem became the imperial favorite.

Suleiman's love for Hürrem led him to set aside all precedents for the role of a concubine, including the rule that concubines must cease having children once they gave birth to a male heir. By 1531 Hürrem had given Suleiman one daughter and five sons. In 1533 or 1534 Suleiman entered formal marriage with his consort—an unprecedented and scandalous honor for a concubine. Suleiman reportedly lavished attention on his wife and defied convention by allowing her to remain in the palace throughout her life instead of accompanying her son to a provincial governorship.

Contemporaries were shocked by Hürrem's influence over the sultan and resentful of the apparent role she played in politics and diplomacy. The Venetian ambassador Bassano wrote that "the Janissaries and the entire court hate her and her children likewise, but because the Sultan loves her, no one dares to speak."* Court rumors circulated that Hürrem used witchcraft to control the sultan and ordered the sultan's execution of his first-born son by another mother.

The correspondence between Suleiman and Hürrem, unavailable until the nineteenth century, along with Suleiman's own diaries, confirms her status as the sultan's most trusted confidant and adviser. During his frequent absences, the pair exchanged passionate love letters. Hürrem included political information and warned of potential uprisings. She also intervened in affairs between the empire and her former home, apparently helping Poland attain its privileged diplomatic status. She brought a feminine touch to diplomatic relations, sending personally embroidered articles to foreign leaders.

Hürrem used her enormous pension to contribute a mosque, two schools, a hospital, a fountain, and two public baths to Istanbul. In Jerusalem, Mecca, and Istanbul, she provided soup kitchens and hospices for pilgrims and the poor. She died in 1558, eight years before her husband. Her son Selim II (r. 1566–1574) inherited the throne.

Hürrem journeyed from enslaved woman to harem favorite to wife of the sultan and mother of his successor. (Pictures From History/CPA Media Pte Ltd./Alamy Stock Photo)

Relying on Western observers' reports, historians traditionally depicted Hürrem as a manipulative and power-hungry social climber. They portrayed her career as the beginning of a "sultanate of women" in which strong imperial leadership gave way to court intrigue and debauchery. More recent historians have emphasized the intelligence and courage Hürrem demonstrated in navigating the ruthlessly competitive world of the harem.

Hürrem's journey from Ukrainian maiden to concubine to sultan's wife captured enormous public attention. She is the subject of numerous paintings, plays, and novels, as well as an opera, a ballet, and a symphony by the composer Haydn. Interest in and suspicion of Hürrem continues. In 2003 a Turkish miniseries once more depicted her as a scheming intriguer.

QUESTIONS FOR ANALYSIS

1. What types of power did Hürrem exercise during her lifetime? How did her gender enable her to attain certain kinds of power and also constrain her ability to exercise it?
2. What can an exceptional woman like Hürrem reveal about the broader political and social world in which she lived?

*Quoted in Galina Yermolenko, "Roxolana: The Greatest Empresse of the East," *The Muslim World* 95 (2005): 235.

Source: Leslie P. Pierce, *The Imperial Harem: Women and Sovereignty in the Ottoman Empire* (New York: Oxford University Press, 1993).

Entertainment at the Court of Ottoman Sultan Ahmet III   Imitating the palace building of French monarchs, Sultan Ahmet III (r. 1703–1730) built a summer palace with extensive gardens, where he hosted extravagant parties featuring music, dancing, poetry recitations, and fine food. His courtiers quickly followed his example and built their own pleasure palaces nearby. (Bridgeman Images)

from acquiring influence over the government, sultans had children only with their concubines and not with official wives. They also adopted a policy of allowing each concubine to produce only one male heir. At a young age, each son went to govern a province of the empire accompanied by his mother. These practices were intended to stabilize power and prevent a recurrence of the civil wars of the late fourteenth and early fifteenth centuries.

Sultan Suleiman I, known as Suleiman the Magnificent (1520–1566), undid these policies when he boldly married his concubine, a formerly enslaved woman from Ruthenia (today's Ukraine) named Hürrem, and had several children with her. (See "Individuals in Society: Hürrem," page 445.) Starting with Suleiman, imperial wives began to take on more power. Marriages were arranged between sultans' daughters and high-ranking servants, creating powerful new members of the imperial household. Over time, the sultan's exclusive authority waned in favor of a more bureaucratic administration.

Like European states, the Ottoman Empire suffered significant crises in the late sixteenth and early seventeenth centuries. Raised in the harem rather than taking on provincial governorships, the sultans who followed Suleiman were inexperienced and faced numerous political revolts. Ottoman finances suffered from the loss of international trade to the Portuguese and the Dutch, and the empire—like Spain—suffered from rising prices and a shrinking population. While the Bourbon monarchy was modernizing and enlarging the French army, the Ottomans failed to adopt new military technologies and training methods. As a result, the empire's military strength, long feared throughout Europe, declined, leading ultimately to the ceding of Hungary and Transylvania to the Austrian Habsburgs in 1699. The Ottoman state adapted to these challenges with some measure of success, but it did not recover the glory it held under Suleiman.

What were alternatives to absolutism in early modern Europe?

While most European nations emerged from the crises of the seventeenth century with absolutist forms of government, other alternatives existed. **Constitutionalism** is the limitation of government by law, implying a balance between the authority and power of the government, on the one hand, and the rights and liberties of the subjects. It could take the form of **republicanism**, a form of government in which there is no monarch and power rests in the hands of the people as exercised through elected representatives. The Dutch Republic, one of the most important republican states in Europe, experienced a golden age in the seventeenth century. Some states, like the Polish-Lithuanian Commonwealth and England, evolved instead toward forms of constitutional monarchy, in

which a monarchy (hereditary or elected) ruled but within legal limitations.

The Polish-Lithuanian Commonwealth

After a marriage between their rulers in the Middle Ages, the kingdom of Poland and the Grand Duchy of Lithuania were governed as separate polities ruled by a common monarch. In 1569, the Union of Lublin formally joined the two territories in a confederation. The terms of the union submitted the monarch to oversight by a noble-dominated parliament known as the *Sejm*, composed of a Senate appointed by the king and an elected Chamber of Deputies. The Polish-Lithuanian Commonwealth thus was one of

The Synagogue of Gwoździec The substantial Jewish communities of the Polish-Lithuanian Commonwealth developed a unique style of wooden synagogues during the mid-sixteenth century that continued through the eighteenth century. This reconstruction of the elaborately decorated ceiling of the synagogue in the town of Gwoździec is exhibited today in the POLIN Museum of the History of Polish Jews in Warsaw. The reconstruction is based on early-twentieth-century photographs, since all of the original wooden synagogues were destroyed in the Holocaust during the Second World War. (Endless Travel/Alamy Stock Photo)

the earliest examples of a constitutional monarchy in Europe. Moreover, in contrast to almost all other European monarchies, the ruler was not hereditary but elected by a vote of all male members of the nobility. (The other important example of an elected ruler was the Holy Roman emperor, who in practice was almost always the head of the Austrian Habsburg dynasty.)

The Polish-Lithuanian Commonwealth was a majority Catholic state. In 1573, to appease fears over the potential election as king of a prince who had participated in the massacre of Protestants, the parliament adopted the Compact of Warsaw. This compact guaranteed religious freedom to all non-Catholics in the commonwealth, which became one of the most ethnically and religiously diverse European states, inhabited by Jews and Muslims as well as by Catholic, Protestant, and Orthodox Christians. In particular, it was the state with the largest Jewish population in the world at that time: historians estimate that Jews constituted up to 10 percent of the population by the eighteenth century.

In the first half of the seventeenth century, the Polish-Lithuanian Commonwealth vied with Sweden and Russia for territory, and its forces occupied Moscow from 1610 to 1612 (see "Building the Russian Empire"). The commonwealth remained neutral during the Thirty Years' War and thereby avoided the destruction that ravaged other central European states. However, its political stability declined in the second half of the seventeenth century, and it fell under the influence of an increasingly powerful Russian Empire.

The Failure of Absolutism in England

Rather than being achieved through a treaty of confederation, the road to constitutional monarchy in England ran through civil war against a would-be absolute monarch, a brief experiment with republicanism, and two efforts to restore monarchical rule. In 1603 beloved

Queen Elizabeth was succeeded by her Scottish cousin James Stuart. A rare female monarch, Elizabeth had succeeded as queen in part because she refused to marry and submit to the control of a husband. Yet the cost of the decision was that she died without heirs, leaving her cousin to rule England as James I (r. 1603–1625). Like Louis XIV, James believed in the absolute and divine rule of monarchs. James went so far as to lecture the House of Commons: "There are no privileges and immunities which can stand against a divinely appointed King." Such a view ran directly counter to English traditions that a person's property could not be taken away without due process of law. James I and his son Charles I (r. 1625–1649) considered any legislative constraint a threat to their divine-right prerogative. The expenses of England's intervention in the Thirty Years' War only exacerbated tensions. (See "Viewpoints: Stuart Claims to Absolutism and the Parliamentary Response," page 448.)

Religious issues also embittered relations between the king and the House of Commons. In the early seventeenth century many English people felt dissatisfied with the Church of England established by Henry VIII (r. 1509–1547). Calvinist **Puritans** wanted to take the Reformation further by "purifying"

■ **constitutionalism** A form of government in which power is limited by law and balanced between the authority and power of the government, on the one hand, and the rights and liberties of the subjects or citizens on the other hand; could include constitutional monarchies or republics.

■ **republicanism** A form of government in which there is no monarch and power rests in the hands of the people as exercised through elected representatives.

■ **Puritans** Members of a sixteenth- and seventeenth-century reform movement within the Church of England that advocated purifying it of Roman Catholic elements such as bishops, elaborate ceremonials, and wedding rings.

James I (r. 1603–1625), king of England, fervently believed in the divine right of kings, a doctrine he expounded in a speech to Parliament in 1609. The efforts of James I and his son and successor Charles I (r. 1625–1649) to impose absolute rule in England led to conflict with Parliament. In the 1628 Petition of Right, Parliament rebuked Charles I for disregarding the existing laws of the kingdom, which limited royal power.

James I, Address to Parliament, 1609

Kings are justly called Gods, for that they exercise a manner or resemblance of Divine power upon earth: For if you will consider the Attributes to God, you shall see how they agree in the person of a King. God hath power to create, or destroy, or unmake at his pleasure, to give life, or send death, to judge all, and to be judged nor accountable to none: To raise low things, and to make high things low at his pleasure, and to God are both soul and body due. And the like power have Kings: they make and unmake their subjects: they have power of raising, and casting down: of life, and of death: Judges over all their subjects, and in all causes, and yet accountable to none but God only. They have power to exalt low things, and abase high things, . . . and to cry up, or down [praise or criticize] any of their subjects, as they do their money. And to the King is due both the affection of the soul and the service of the body of his subjects. . . .

. . . So is it sedition in Subjects, to dispute what a King may do in the height of his power: But just Kings will ever be willing to declare what they will do, if they will not incur the curse of God. I will not be content that my power be disputed upon: but I shall ever be willing to make the reason appear of all my doings, and rule my actions according to my Laws.

Petition of Right, 1628

By . . . the good laws and statutes of this realm, your subjects have inherited this freedom, that they should not be compelled to contribute to any tax, tallage,* aid, or other like charge nor set by common consent, in parliament.

*Tallage was a tax formerly imposed by kings on town citizens.

. . . Yet nevertheless, of late . . . your people have been in divers places assembled, and required to lend certain sums of money unto your Majesty, and many of them, upon their refusal so to do . . . have been therefore imprisoned, confined, and sundry other ways molested and disquieted. . . .

. . . And whereas also, by the statute called, *The Great Charter of the Liberties of England* [i.e., Magna Carta], it is declared and enacted, That no freeman may be taken or imprisoned, or be disseized [dispossessed] of his freehold or liberties, or of his free customs, or be outlawed or exiled, or in any manner destroyed, but by the lawful judgment of his peers, or by the law of the land. . . .

. . . Nevertheless, against the tenor of . . . the good laws and statutes of your realm . . . divers of your subjects have of late been imprisoned without any cause showed. . . .

. . . They do therefore humbly pray your most excellent Majesty; that no man hereafter be compelled to make or yield any gift, loan, benevolence, tax, or such like charge, without common consent, by Act of Parliament: . . . And that no freemen, in any such manner as is before mentioned, be imprisoned or detained. . . .

. . . All which they most humbly pray of your most excellent Majesty as their rights and liberties, according to the laws and statutes of this realm. . . .

QUESTIONS FOR ANALYSIS

1. In what ways does James I believe royal power resembles divine power? Why does he believe kings possess such extensive powers? Does he see any limits to his powers?
2. What rights and liberties do English subjects believe they possess, and how has Charles violated them? Why do they believe it is Parliament's role to defend these freedoms?
3. Do you see any common ground and possibility for compromise between James's understanding of royal power and the rights of English subjects outlined by Parliament?

Sources: *The Political Works of James I*, ed. Charles Howard McIlwain (Cambridge, Mass.: Harvard University Press, 1918), pp. 307–308, 310. Spellings have been modernized; *Magna Charta, The Bill of Rights; with the Petition of Right, Presented to Charles I* (London: J. Bailey, 1820), pp. 18–20.

the Anglican Church of Roman Catholic elements, including Crown-appointed bishops.

James's son and successor, Charles I, further antagonized religious sentiments by marrying a French Catholic princess and supporting the heavy-handed policies of the archbishop of Canterbury William Laud (1573–1645). Political and religious conflict in this period was exacerbated by economic distress caused by plague and by the severe weather conditions of the Little Ice Age.

Charles avoided direct confrontation with his subjects by refusing to call Parliament into session from 1629 to 1640. Instead, he financed his government through extraordinary stopgap levies considered illegal by most English people. However, when Scottish Calvinists revolted against his religious policies, Charles was forced to summon Parliament to obtain funds for an army to put down the revolt. Angry with his behavior and sympathetic with the Scots'

Van Dyck, *Charles I at the Hunt*, ca. 1635
Anthony Van Dyck was the greatest of Rubens's many students. In 1633 he became court painter to Charles I. This portrait of Charles just dismounted from a horse emphasizes the aristocratic bearing, elegance, and innate authority of the king. Van Dyck's success led to innumerable commissions by members of the court and aristocratic society. He had a profound influence on portraiture in England and beyond; some scholars believe that this portrait influenced Rigaud's 1701 portrayal of Louis XIV (see "Thinking Like a Historian: What Was Absolutism?" on page 432). (Leemage/Corbis/Getty Images)

religious beliefs, in 1641 the House of Commons passed the Triennial Act, which compelled the king to summon Parliament every three years. The Commons also impeached Archbishop Laud and threatened to abolish bishops. King Charles, fearful of a Scottish invasion, reluctantly accepted these measures. The next act in the conflict was precipitated by the outbreak of rebellion in Ireland, where English governors and landlords had long exploited the people. In 1641 the Catholic gentry of Ireland led an uprising in response to a feared invasion by English anti-Catholic forces.

Without an army, Charles I could neither come to terms with the Scots nor respond to the Irish rebellion. After a failed attempt to arrest parliamentary leaders, Charles left London for the north of England and began to raise an army. In response, Parliament formed its own army, the New Model Army, composed of the militia of the city of London and country squires with business connections.

The English Civil War (1642–1649) that erupted pitted the power of the king against that of Parliament. After three years of fighting, Parliament's army defeated the king's forces at the Battles of Naseby and Langport in the summer of 1645. Charles refused to concede defeat, and both sides waited for a decisive event. This arrived in the form of the army under the leadership of Oliver Cromwell, a member of the House of Commons and a devout Puritan. In 1648 Cromwell's forces captured the king and dismissed anti-Cromwell members of the Parliament. In 1649 the remaining representatives, known as the Rump Parliament, put Charles on trial for high treason. Charles was found guilty and beheaded on January 30, 1649, an act that sent shock waves around Europe.

The English Civil War, 1642–1649

a confectioner   a Smith   a Sho=maker   a Taylor

a Sadler   a Porter   a Box-maker   a Sope-boyler

a Glover   a Meal-man   a Chick en-man   a Button-maker

Puritan Occupations
These twelve engravings depict typical Puritan occupations and show that the Puritans came primarily from the artisan and lower middle classes. The governing classes and peasants made up a much smaller percentage of the Puritans and generally adhered to the traditions of the Church of England. (Private Collection/Look and Learn/Peter Jackson Collection/Bridgeman Images)

The Puritan Protectorate

With the execution of Charles, kingship was abolished. The question remained of how the country would be governed. One answer was provided by philosopher Thomas Hobbes (1588–1679). Hobbes held a pessimistic view of human nature and believed that, left to themselves, humans would compete violently for power and wealth. The only solution, as he outlined in his 1651 treatise *Leviathan*, was a social contract in which all members of society placed themselves under the absolute rule of the sovereign, who would maintain peace and order. Hobbes imagined society as a human body in which the monarch served as head and individual subjects together made up the body.

Just as the body cannot sever its own head, so Hobbes believed that society could not, having accepted the contract, rise up against its king.

Hobbes's longing for a benevolent absolute monarch was not widely shared in England. Instead, Oliver Cromwell and his supporters enshrined a commonwealth, or republican government, known as the **Protectorate**. Theoretically, legislative power rested in the surviving members of Parliament, and executive power was lodged in a council of state. In fact, the army controlled the government, and Oliver Cromwell controlled the army. Though called the Protectorate, the rule of Cromwell (1653–1658) was a form of military dictatorship.

The fiction of republican government was maintained until 1655, when, after repeated disputes, Cromwell dismissed Parliament. Cromwell continued the standing army and proclaimed quasi-martial law. Reflecting Puritan ideas of morality, Cromwell's state forbade sports, closed the theaters, and rigorously censored the press.

■ **Protectorate** The English military dictatorship (1653–1658) established by Oliver Cromwell following the execution of Charles I.

■ **Test Act** Legislation passed by the English Parliament in 1673 to secure the position of the Anglican Church by stripping Puritans, Catholics, and other dissenters of the right to vote, preach, assemble, hold public office, and teach at or attend the universities.

On the issue of religion, Cromwell favored some degree of toleration, and all Christians except Roman Catholics held the right to practice their faiths. Cromwell had long associated Catholicism in Ireland with sedition and heresy, and he led an army there to reconquer the country in August 1649. One month later, his forces crushed a rebellion at Drogheda and massacred the garrison. After Cromwell's departure for England, atrocities worsened. The English banned Catholicism in Ireland, executed priests, and confiscated land from Catholics for English and Scottish settlers.

Cromwell adopted mercantilist policies similar to those of absolutist France. He enforced a Navigation Act (1651) requiring that English goods be transported on English ships or on the ship of the country where the goods were produced. The act was a great boost to the development of an English merchant marine and brought about a short but successful war with the commercially threatened Dutch over trade with the Atlantic colonies. While mercantilist legislation ultimately benefited English commerce, for ordinary people the turmoil of foreign war only added to the harsh conditions of life induced by years of civil war. Cromwell also welcomed the immigration of Jews because of their experience in finance and trade, and they began to return to England four centuries after the expulsion of Jews by King Edward I in 1290.

The Protectorate collapsed when Cromwell died in 1658 and his ineffectual son succeeded him. Fed up with military rule, the English longed for a return to civilian government and, with it, common law and social stability. By 1660 they were ready to abandon their experiment with republicanism.

The Restoration of the English Monarchy

The Restoration of 1660 brought to the throne Charles II (r. 1660–1685), eldest son of Charles I, who had been living on the continent. Both houses of Parliament were also restored, together with the established Anglican Church. The Restoration failed to resolve two serious problems, however. What was to be the attitude of the state toward Puritans, Catholics, and dissenters from the established church? And what was to be the relationship between the king and Parliament?

To answer the first question, Parliament enacted the **Test Act** of 1673 against those outside the Church of England, denying them the right to vote, hold public office, preach, teach, attend universities, or even assemble for meetings. But these restrictions could not be enforced. When the Quaker William Penn held a meeting of his Friends and was arrested, the jury refused to convict him.

In politics, Charles II's initial determination to work well with Parliament did not last long. Finding that Parliament did not grant him an adequate income, Charles entered into a secret agreement with his cousin Louis XIV in 1679. The French king would give Charles £200,000 annually, and in return Charles would relax the laws against Catholics, gradually

***The Family of Henry Chorley, Haberdasher of Preston,* ca. 1680**
This painting celebrates the Puritan family values of order, discipline, and self-restraint. The wife is surrounded by her young children, emphasizing her motherly duties, while her husband is flanked by their grown sons. Nevertheless, the woman's expression suggests she is a strong-minded partner to her husband, not meekly subservient. The couple probably worked side by side in the family business of selling men's clothing and accessories. (Harris Museum and Art Gallery/Bridgeman Images)

re-Catholicize England, and convert to Catholicism himself. When the details of this treaty leaked out, a great wave of anti-Catholic sentiment swept England.

When Charles died and his Catholic brother James became king, the worst English anti-Catholic fears were realized. In violation of the Test Act, James II (r. 1685–1688) appointed Roman Catholics to positions in the army, the universities, and local government. He also supported the opening of new Catholic churches and schools.

James's opponents, a powerful coalition of eminent persons in Parliament and the Church of England, wrote to James's Protestant daughter Mary and her Dutch husband, Prince William of Orange, asking them to restore English liberties by taking the throne of England. In November 1688 William arrived on the English coast with five hundred ships and over twenty thousand soldiers. Early in 1689 William and Mary were jointly crowned as king and queen of England.

The English call the events of 1688 and 1689 the Glorious Revolution because they believe it replaced one king with another with barely any bloodshed. In truth, William's arrival sparked revolutionary riots and violence across the British Isles and in North American cities such as Boston and New York. Uprisings by supporters of James, known as Jacobites, occurred in 1689 in Scotland. In Ireland, the two sides waged outright war from 1689 to 1691. But William's victory at the Battle of the Boyne (1690) and the subsequent Treaty of Limerick (1691) sealed his accession to power.

Constitutional Monarchy

In England, the Glorious Revolution represented the final destruction of the idea of divine-right monarchy. The men who brought about the revolution framed their intentions in the Bill of Rights of 1689, which was formulated in direct response to Stuart absolutism. Law was to be made in Parliament; once made, it could not be suspended by the Crown. Parliament had to be called at least once every three years. The independence of the judiciary was established, and there was to be no standing army in peacetime. Protestants could possess arms, but the Catholic minority could not. A Catholic could not inherit the throne. Additional legislation granted freedom of worship to Protestant dissenters, but not to Catholics. William and Mary accepted these principles when they took the throne, and the House of Parliament passed the Bill of Rights in December 1689. The Bill of Rights, along with other pieces of legislation, formed an informal constitution, one that persisted through the Act of Union creating Great Britain in 1707 (see Chapter 17) and remains in effect today.

The concept of a constitutional monarchy responsible to representatives of the people found its best defense in political philosopher John Locke's *Two Treatises of Government* (1690). Locke (1632–1704) maintained that a government that oversteps its proper function — protecting the natural rights of life, liberty, and property — becomes a tyranny. Under a tyrannical government, the people have the natural right to rebellion.

Although the events of 1688 and 1689 brought England closer to Locke's ideal, they did not constitute a democratic revolution. The revolution placed sovereignty in Parliament, and Parliament represented the upper classes.

The Dutch Republic in the Seventeenth Century

In the late sixteenth century the seven northern provinces of the Netherlands fought for and won their independence from Spain. The independence of the Republic of the United Provinces of the Netherlands was formally recognized in 1648 in the treaty that ended the Thirty Years' War. In this period, often called the golden age of the Netherlands, Dutch ideas and attitudes played a profound role in shaping a new and modern worldview. At the same time, the United Provinces developed its own distinctive model of a constitutional state.

Rejecting the rule of a monarch, the Dutch established a republic, a state in which power was exercised through elected representatives rather than hereditary rulers. Other examples of republics in early modern Europe included the Swiss Confederation and several autonomous city-states of Italy and the Holy Roman Empire. Among the Dutch, an oligarchy of wealthy businessmen called regents handled domestic affairs in each province's Estates (assemblies). The provincial Estates held virtually all the power. A federal assembly, or States General, handled foreign affairs and war, but it did not possess sovereign authority. All issues had to be referred back to the local Estates for approval, and each of the seven provinces could veto any proposed legislation. Holland, the province with the largest navy and the most wealth, usually dominated the republic and the States General.

In each province, the Estates appointed an executive officer, known as the **stadholder**, who carried out ceremonial functions and was responsible for military defense. Although in theory the stadholder was freely chosen by the Estates and was answerable to them, in practice the strong and influential House of Orange usually held the office of stadholder in several of the seven provinces of the republic. Tensions persisted between supporters of the House of Orange and those of the staunchly republican Estates, who suspected that the princes of Orange harbored monarchical ambitions.

■ **stadholder** The executive officer in each of the United Provinces of the Netherlands, a position often held by the princes of Orange.

Gonzales Coques, *The Young Scholar and His Wife*, 1640

During the seventeenth century much of Europe was gripped by economic, social, and political crisis. A long period of cold, wet weather destroyed crops, while religious divides contributed to the outbreak of the highly destructive Thirty Years' War. A shining exception to this grim picture was the Netherlands, which saw increased agricultural productivity, growing involvement in world trade, and a thriving urban culture. The bustling cities of the Dutch Republic and Flanders gave birth in this period to a new style of painting, now known as "genre painting," that celebrated the virtues of everyday life, family, and the domestic sphere.

Whereas earlier generations of artists had reserved their highest praise for paintings that imaginatively re-created great historical and mythological events, genre painters depicted realistic scenes set in family homes, taverns, and other prosaic locales. They eschewed idealized heroes and dramatic imagery in favor of the earthly pleasures of eating, drinking, socializing, and spending time with friends and family in cozy interiors, often furnished with the exotic wares pouring in from the East. Genre paintings thus reflected the values and pastimes of the wealthy bourgeois merchants and other urban elites who commissioned them. This

painting style of the Dutch golden age became extremely popular and spread to the rest of northern Europe.

Gonzales Coques, the painter of this image, was born in Antwerp (part of modern Belgium) around 1615. He apprenticed with the Flemish artist Pieter Brueghel the Younger and became a master of the Antwerp painters' guild in 1640. Specializing in portraits of individuals and families—such as this fine rendition of an affluent young scholar and his wife—Coques contributed to the development of genre painting.

EVALUATE THE EVIDENCE

1. What social and cultural values does this painting seem to celebrate? List the details in the painting that provide evidence for your answer.
2. What insight does the painter offer into the roles of men and women in this society and the attributes of masculinity and femininity? Why do you think the husband and wife are standing separately and not together, as they probably would in a modern family portrait?
3. How does the artist's use of color help convey meaning in the painting?

(Gemaeldegalerie Alte Meister, Kassel, Germany/© Museumslandschaft Hessen Kassel/Bridgeman Images)

Jan Steen, *The Merry Family*, 1668 In this painting from the Dutch golden age, a happy family enjoys a bois-terous song while seated around the dining table. Despite its carefree appearance, the painting was intended to teach a moral lesson. The children are shown drinking wine and smoking, bad habits they have learned from their parents. The inscription hanging over the mantelpiece (upper right) spells out the message clearly: "As the Old Sing, so Pipe the Young." (Universal Images Group/Getty Images)

(See "Evaluating Visual Evidence: Gonzales Coques, *The Young Scholar and His Wife,* 1640," page 453.)

The political success of the Dutch rested on their phenomenal commercial prosperity. The Dutch orig-inally came to dominate European shipping by put-ting profits from their original industry — herring fishing — into shipbuilding. They boasted the lowest shipping rates and largest merchant marine in Europe, which allowed them to undersell foreign competitors. In the seventeenth century global trade and commerce brought the Dutch the highest standard of living in Europe, perhaps in the world. Salaries were high, and all classes of society ate well. A scholar has described the Netherlands as "an island of plenty in a sea of want." Consequently, the Netherlands experienced very few of the food riots that characterized the rest of Europe.[4]

The moral and ethical bases of Dutch commer-cial wealth were thrift, social discipline, and reli-gious toleration. Although there is scattered evidence of anti-Semitism, Jews enjoyed a level of acceptance

and assimilation in business and general culture that was highly unusual in early modern Europe (another example was the Polish-Lithuanian Commonwealth; see "The Polish-Lithuanian Commonwealth"). Anti-Catholic laws existed through the eighteenth cen-tury, but they were only partly enforced. In the Dutch Republic, toleration paid off: it attracted a great deal of foreign capital and investment. After Louis XIV revoked the Edict of Nantes, many Huguenots fled France for the Dutch Republic. They brought with them a high level of artisanal skill and business expe-rience as well as a loathing for state repression that would inspire the political views of the Enlightenment (see "The Early Enlightenment" in Chapter 16).

NOTES

1. John A. Lynn, "Recalculating French Army Growth," in *The Mil-itary Revolution Debate: Readings on the Military Transformation of Early Modern Europe*, ed. Clifford J. Rogers (Boulder, Colo.: West-view Press, 1995), p. 125.

2. J. H. Elliott, *Imperial Spain, 1469–1716* (New York: Mentor Books, 1963), pp. 306–308.

3. Quoted in H. Rosenberg, *Bureaucracy, Aristocracy, and Autocracy: The Prussian Experience, 1660–1815* (Boston: Beacon Press, 1966), p. 43.

4. S. Schama, *The Embarrassment of Riches: An Interpretation of Dutch Culture in the Golden Age* (New York: Alfred A. Knopf, 1987), pp. 165–170; quotation is on p. 167.

LOOKING BACK LOOKING AHEAD

The seventeenth century represented a difficult passage between two centuries of dynamism and growth in Europe. On one side lay the sixteenth century's religious enthusiasm and strife, overseas discoveries, rising populations, and vigorous commerce. On the other side stretched the eighteenth century's renewed population growth, economic development, and cultural flourishing. The first half of the seventeenth century was marked by harsh climate conditions and violent conflict across Europe. Recurring crop failure, famine, and epidemic disease contributed to a stagnant economy and population loss. In the middle decades of the seventeenth century, the very survival of the European monarchies established in the Renaissance appeared in doubt.

With the re-establishment of order in the second half of the century, maintaining stability was of paramount importance to European rulers. While a few nations placed their trust in constitutionally limited governments, many more were ruled by monarchs proclaiming their absolute and God-given authority. Despite their political differences, most European states emerged from the period of crisis with shared achievements in state power, territorial expansion, and long-distance trade.

The eighteenth century was to see these power politics thrown into question by new Enlightenment aspirations for human society that derived from the inquisitive and self-confident spirit of the Scientific Revolution. These movements are explored in the next chapter. By the end of the eighteenth century demands for real popular sovereignty, colonial self-rule, and slave emancipation challenged the very bases of order so painfully achieved in the seventeenth century.

Make Connections

Think about the larger developments and continuities within and across chapters.

1. This chapter has argued that, despite their political differences, rulers in absolutist and constitutionalist nations faced similar obstacles in the mid-seventeenth century and achieved many of the same goals. Based on the evidence presented here, do you agree with this argument? Why or why not?

2. Proponents of absolutism in western Europe believed that their form of monarchical rule was fundamentally different from and superior to what they saw as the "despotism" of Russia and the Ottoman Empire. What was the basis of this belief, and how accurate do you think it was?

3. What evidence does this chapter provide for the impact on European states of the discoveries and conquests discussed in Chapter 14?

15 REVIEW & EXPLORE

Identify Key Terms

Identify and explain the significance of each item below.

Peace of Westphalia (p. 426)

fiscal-military state (p. 426)

baroque style (p. 428)

the Fronde (p. 430)

Peace of Utrecht (p. 434)

mercantilism (p. 434)

Junkers (p. 437)

boyars (p. 439)

Cossacks (p. 439)

sultan (p. 443)

janissary corps (p. 443)

millet system (p. 444)

constitutionalism (p. 446)

republicanism (p. 446)

Puritans (p. 447)

Protectorate (p. 450)

Test Act (p. 451)

stadholder (p. 452)

Review the Main Ideas

Answer the section heading questions from the chapter.

1. What were the crises and achievements of seventeenth-century European states? (p. 424)

2. What was absolutism, and how did it evolve in western and central Europe? (p. 429)

3. What explains the rise of absolutism in Prussia and Austria? (p. 436)

4. What were the distinctive features of Russian and Ottoman absolutism? (p. 439)

5. What were alternatives to absolutism in early modern Europe? (p. 446)

Suggested Resources

BOOKS

- Beik, William. *A Social and Cultural History of Early Modern France.* 2009. An overview of early modern French history, by one of the leading authorities on the period.

- Clark, Christopher. *Iron Kingdom: The Rise and Downfall of Prussia, 1600–1947.* 2007. A sweeping survey of Prussian history from the birth of the Prussian state through the horrors of World War II.

- Elliott, John H. *Imperial Spain, 1469–1716,* 2d ed. 2002. An authoritative account of Spain's rise to imperial greatness and its slow decline.

- Engel, Barbara, and Janet Martin. *Russia in World History.* 2015. A brief but nuanced account of the rise of the Russian Empire and its role in world history.

- Gaunt, Peter, ed. *The English Civil War: The Essential Readings.* 2000. A collection showcasing leading historians' interpretations of the civil war.

- Goldgard, Anne. *Tulipmania: Money, Honor, and Knowledge in the Dutch Golden Age.* 2007. A fresh look at the speculative fever for tulip bulbs in the early-seventeenth-century Dutch Republic.

- Ingrao, Charles W. *The Habsburg Monarchy, 1618–1815,* 2d ed. 2000. An excellent synthesis of the political and social development of the Habsburg empire in the early modern period.

- Parker, Geoffrey. *Global Crisis: War, Climate Change and Catastrophe in the Seventeenth Century.* 2013. A sweeping account of the worldwide crisis of the seventeenth century, which the author argues was largely caused by climatic changes known as the Little Ice Age.

- Pincus, Steven. *1688: The First Modern Revolution.* 2009. Revisionary account of the Glorious Revolution, emphasizing its toll in bloodshed and destruction of property and its global repercussions.

- Romaniello, Matthew P. *The Elusive Empire: Kazan and the Creation of Russia, 1552–1671*. 2012. A study of the conquest of Kazan by Ivan the Terrible in 1552 and the Russian Empire built in its aftermath.
- Snyder, Timothy. *The Reconstruction of Nations: Poland, Ukraine, Lithuania, Belarus, 1569–1999*. 2003. A sweeping examination of the emergence of nations in northeastern Europe from the early modern period to contemporary times.
- Wilson, Peter H. *The Thirty Years War: Europe's Tragedy*. 2009. An overview of the origins and outcomes of the Thirty Years' War, focusing on political and economic issues in addition to religious conflicts.

MEDIA

- *A Little Chaos* (Alan Rickman, 2014). Directed by Alan Rickman, with Rickman (in his last role) as Louis XIV and Kate Winslet as a female landscaper, a film about the construction of the gardens at the palace of Versailles.
- *Alastriste* (Agustín Díaz Yanes, 2006). Set in the declining years of Spain's imperial glory, this film follows the violent adventures of an army captain who takes the son of a fallen comrade under his care.
- *The Art of Baroque Dance* (Dancetime Publications, 2006). An introduction to baroque dance that incorporates images of the architecture and art of the period alongside dance performances and information on major elements of the style.
- *Charles II: The Power and the Passion* (BBC, 2003). An award-winning television miniseries about the son of executed English king Charles I and the Restoration that brought him to the throne in 1660.
- *Cromwell* (Ken Hughes, 1970). The English Civil War from its origin to Oliver Cromwell's victory, with battle scenes as well as personal stories of Cromwell and other central figures.
- *Girl with a Pearl Earring* (Peter Webber, 2003). The life and career of painter Johannes Vermeer told through the eyes of a fictional servant girl who becomes his assistant and model.
- *Molière* (Laurent Tirard, 2007). A film about the French playwright Molière, a favorite of King Louis XIV, that fancifully incorporates characters and plotlines from some of the writer's most celebrated plays.
- *Rubens: Passion, Faith, Sensuality and the Art of the Baroque* (Kultur Studio, 2011). A documentary introducing viewers to the work of Peter Paul Rubens, one of the greatest artists of the baroque style.
- *Tour of Restoration London*. A website offering information on the places, food, and people of Restoration London, inspired by the novel *Invitation to a Funeral* by Molly Brown (1999). **www.okima.com/**
- *Versailles* (television series 2015–2018). A three-season Franco-Canadian television series follows Louis XIV as he oversees the building of the palace of Versailles amidst the scheming of his courtiers.

16

Toward a New Worldview

1540–1789

From the mid-sixteenth century on, age-old patterns of knowledge and daily life were disrupted by a series of transformative developments. In this period, scholars challenged, and eventually discarded, ancient frameworks for understanding the heavens. The resulting conception of the universe and its laws remained in force until Albert Einstein's discoveries at the beginning of the twentieth century. Along with new discoveries in botany, zoology, chemistry, electricity, and other domains, these developments constituted a fundamental shift in the basic framework for understanding the natural world and the methods for examining it, known collectively as the Scientific Revolution.

In the eighteenth century philosophers extended the use of reason from the study of nature to human society. They sought to bring the light of reason to bear on the darkness of prejudice, long-standing traditions, and general ignorance. Self-proclaimed members of an "Enlightenment" movement, they wished to bring the same progress to human affairs as their predecessors had brought to understanding of the natural world. The Enlightenment created concepts of human rights, equality, progress, universalism, and tolerance that still guide Western societies today. At the same time, some Europeans used their new understanding of nature and reason to proclaim their own superiority, thus rationalizing attitudes now regarded as racist and sexist. Despite these biases, European intellectual change in fact profited from contact and exchange with non-European peoples, ideas, and natural organisms. ■

CHAPTER PREVIEW

- What revolutionary discoveries were made in the sixteenth and seventeenth centuries?

- What intellectual and social changes occurred as a result of the Scientific Revolution?

- How did the Enlightenment emerge, and what were major currents of Enlightenment thought?

- How did the Enlightenment change cultural ideas and social practices?

- What impact did new ways of thinking have on politics?

Life During the Scientific Revolution

This 1768 painting by Joseph Wright captures the popularization of science and experimentation during the Enlightenment. Here, a scientist demonstrates the creation of a vacuum by withdrawing air from a flask, with the suffocating cockatoo serving as shocking proof of the experiment. (Photo 12/Universal Images Group/Getty Images)

What revolutionary discoveries were made in the sixteenth and seventeenth centuries?

Until the middle of the sixteenth century, Europeans relied on an understanding of motion and matter drawn from the ancient Greek philosopher Aristotle and adapted to Christian theology. The rise of the university, along with the intellectual vitality of the Renaissance and technological advancements, inspired European scholars to seek better explanations. From the work of Nicolaus Copernicus to the work of Isaac Newton, a revolutionary new understanding of the universe had emerged by the end of the seventeenth century. Collectively known as the Scientific Revolution, the work of these scientists constituted significant milestones in the creation of modern science.

The major figures of the Scientific Revolution (ca. 1540–1700) were for the most part devout Christians who saw their work as heralding the glory of creation and who combined older traditions of magic, astrology, and alchemy with their pathbreaking experimentation. Their discoveries took place in a broader context of international trade, imperial expansion, and cultural exchange. Alongside developments in modern science and natural philosophy, the growth of natural history in this period is now recognized by historians as a major achievement of the Scientific Revolution.

Contributions from the Muslim World

In 1500 scientific activity flourished in many parts of the world. Between 750 and 950, scholars in the expanding Muslim world began translating the legacy of ancient Greek science and philosophy into Arabic, with the help of Christian and Jewish translators. The peaceful conditions and religious tolerance established by the Abbasid caliphate (750–1258) gave rise to a period of cultural exchange and flourishing known as the golden age of Islam, which was highly favorable to advances in learning. During this period, Muslim scholars thrived in cultural centers such as Baghdad, capital of the caliphate; and Córdoba, capital of Muslim Spain. They established the world's first institutions of higher learning, called *madrasas*, in Constantinople, Fez (Morocco), and Cairo, which were devoted to Islamic theology and law. In this fertile atmosphere, scholars surpassed the texts they had inherited from the classical world in areas such as mathematics, physics, astronomy, and medicine. Arab and Persian mathematicians, for example, invented algebra, the concept of the algorithm, and decimal point notation. Arab astronomers built observatories to collect celestial observations, and an Egyptian scholar, Ibn al-Haytham (d. 1042), revolutionized optics by demonstrating mathematically that light travels in straight lines.

Given the scientific and philosophical knowledge possessed by Arab and Muslim scholars in the tenth and eleventh centuries, one might have expected that modern science would have emerged in the Muslim world first. However, the madrasas excluded study of the natural sciences, and Muslim scholars did not benefit from institutions dedicated to the creation and dissemination of scientific knowledge. Thus there was no cadre of scholars to carry on the work of the great scientific scholars patronized by Muslim rulers.

The re-establishment of stronger monarchies and the growth of trade in the High Middle Ages contributed to a renewal of learning in western Europe. As European scholars became aware of advances in knowledge made in Muslim territories, they traveled to Islamic territories in Iberia, Sicily, and the eastern Mediterranean to gain access to this knowledge. In the twelfth century, these scholars translated many

Astronomy Lecture in the Ottoman Empire   Like other Muslim states, the Ottoman Empire was an early center for scientific research, particularly in the fields of astronomy, medicine, and geography. This early-fifteenth-century image depicts a master providing a lecture in astronomy to four students. (Leemage/Universal Images Group/Universal Images Group/Newscom)

■ **natural philosophy** An early modern term for the study of the nature of the universe, its purpose, and how it functioned; it encompassed what we would call "science" today.

TIMELINE

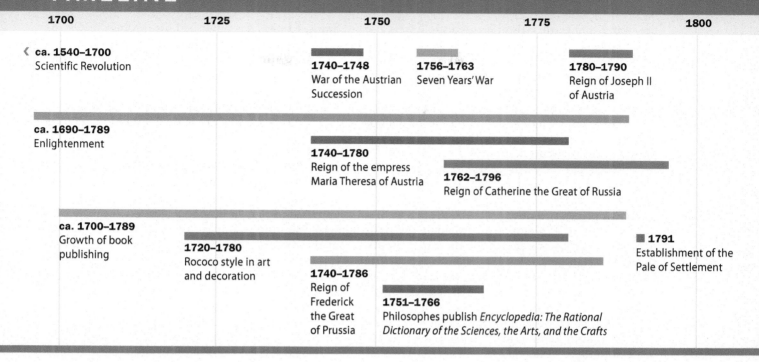

1700   **1725**   **1750**   **1775**   **1800**

ca. 1540–1700
Scientific Revolution

1740–1748
War of the Austrian Succession

1756–1763
Seven Years' War

1780–1790
Reign of Joseph II of Austria

ca. 1690–1789
Enlightenment

1740–1780
Reign of the empress Maria Theresa of Austria

1762–1796
Reign of Catherine the Great of Russia

ca. 1700–1789
Growth of book publishing

1720–1780
Rococo style in art and decoration

1740–1786
Reign of Frederick the Great of Prussia

1751–1766
Philosophes publish *Encyclopedia: The Rational Dictionary of the Sciences, the Arts, and the Crafts*

1791
Establishment of the Pale of Settlement

Greek texts—including works of Aristotle, Ptolemy, Galen, and Euclid previously lost to the West—into Latin, along with the commentaries of Arab scholars. With the patronage of kings and religious institutions, groups of scholars created universities in which these translated works, especially those of the ancient Greek philosopher Aristotle, dominated the curriculum.

As Europe recovered from the ravages of the Black Death in the late fourteenth and fifteenth centuries, the intellectual and cultural movement known as the Renaissance provided a crucial foundation for the Scientific Revolution. Scholars called humanists working in the wealthy city-states of Italy emphasized the value of classical education for creating a virtuous and civic-minded elite. The quest to restore the glories of the ancient past led to a new period of rediscovery of classical texts, including Ptolemy's *Geography*, which was translated into Latin around 1410. An encyclopedic treatise on botany by Theophrastus was rediscovered in the 1450s moldering on the shelves of the Vatican library. The fall of Constantinople to the Ottomans in 1453 resulted in a great influx of little-known Greek works, as Christian scholars fled to Italy with their precious texts.

In this period, western European universities established new professorships of mathematics, astronomy, and natural philosophy. The prestige of the new fields was low, especially of mathematics, which was reserved for practical problems such as accounting, surveying, and computing planetary tables, but not used to understand the functioning of the physical world itself. Nevertheless, these professorships eventually enabled

the union of mathematics with natural philosophy that was to be a hallmark of the Scientific Revolution.

Scientific Thought to 1500

The term *science* as we use it today came into use only in the nineteenth century. For medieval scholars, philosophy was the path to true knowledge about the world, and its proofs consisted of the authority of ancients (as interpreted by Muslim and Christian theologians) and their techniques of logical argumentation. Questions about the physical nature of the universe and how it functioned belonged to a minor branch of philosophy, called **natural philosophy**. Drawing on scholarship in the Muslim world, natural philosophy was based primarily on the ideas of Aristotle. Medieval theologians such as Thomas Aquinas brought Aristotelian philosophy into harmony with Christian doctrines. According to the Christianized view of Aristotle, a motionless earth stood at the center of the universe and was encompassed by ten separate concentric crystal spheres in which were embedded the moon, the sun, planets, and stars. Beyond the spheres was Heaven, with the throne of God and the souls of the saved. Angels kept the spheres moving in perfect circles.

Aristotle's views also dominated thinking about physics and motion on earth. Aristotle had distinguished between the world of the celestial spheres and that of the earth—the sublunar world. The spheres consisted of a perfect, incorruptible "quintessence," or fifth essence. The sublunar world, however, was made up of four imperfect, changeable elements: air,

461

fire, water, and earth. Aristotle and his followers also believed that a uniform force moved an object at a constant speed and that the object would stop as soon as that force was removed. The great second-century-C.E. Greek scholar Ptolemy amended Aristotle's physics by positing that the planets moved in small circles, called epicycles, each of which moved in turn along a larger circle, or deferent. This theory accounted for the apparent backward motion of the planets (which in fact occurs as the earth passes the slower-moving outer planets or is passed by the faster-moving inner ones) and provided a surprisingly accurate model for predicting planetary motion.

The work of Ptolemy also provided the basic foundation of knowledge about the earth. Rediscovered in Europe and translated from Arabic into Latin around 1410, his *Geography* presented crucial advances on medieval cartography by representing a round earth divided into 360 degrees with the major latitude marks. However, Ptolemy's map reflected the limits of ancient knowledge, showing only the continents of Europe, Africa, and Asia, with land covering three-quarters of the world.

These two frameworks reveal the strengths and limitations of European knowledge on the eve of the Scientific Revolution. Overcoming the authority of the ancients to develop a new understanding of the natural world, derived from precise techniques of observation and experimentation, was the Scientific Revolution's monumental achievement. Europeans were not the first to use experimental methods — of which there was a long tradition in the Muslim world and elsewhere — but they were the first to separate scientific knowledge decisively from philosophical and religious beliefs and to accord mathematics a fundamental role in understanding the natural world.

The Copernican Hypothesis

The first great departure from the medieval system was the work of the German-Polish cleric Nicolaus Copernicus (1473–1543). Copernicus studied astronomy, medicine, and church law at the famed universities of Cracow, Bologna, Padua, and Ferrara before taking up a church position in Prussia. Copernicus came to believe that Ptolemy's cumbersome rules detracted from the majesty of a perfect creator. He preferred an idea espoused by some ancient Greek scholars: that the sun, rather than the earth, was at the center of the universe. Without questioning the Aristotelian belief in crystal spheres or the idea that circular motion was divine, Copernicus theorized that the stars and planets, including the earth, revolved around a fixed sun. In 1543, the year of his

death, Copernicus published his findings in *On the Revolutions of the Heavenly Spheres*.

The **Copernican hypothesis** had enormous scientific and religious implications, many of which the conservative Copernicus did not anticipate. First, it put the stars at rest, their apparent nightly movement simply a result of the earth's rotation. Thus it destroyed the main reason for believing in crystal spheres capable of moving the stars around the earth. Second, Copernicus's theory suggested a universe of staggering size. If in the course of a year the earth moved around the sun and yet the stars appeared to remain in the same place, then the universe was unthinkably large. Third, by using mathematics, instead of philosophy, to justify his theories, Copernicus challenged the traditional hierarchy of the disciplines. Finally, by characterizing the earth as just another planet, Copernicus destroyed the basic idea of Aristotelian physics — that the earthly sphere was quite different from the heavenly one. Where then were Heaven and the throne of God?

Religious leaders varied in their response to Copernicus's theories. A few Protestant scholars became avid Copernicans, while others accepted some elements of his criticism of Ptolemy but firmly rejected the notion that the earth moved, a doctrine that contradicted the literal reading of some passages of the Bible. Because the Catholic Church had never insisted on literal interpretations of the Bible, it did not officially declare the Copernican hypothesis false until provoked by the publications of Galileo Galilei in 1616 (see "Science and Religion" later in this chapter).

Brahe, Kepler, and Galileo: Proving Copernicus Right

One astronomer who partially agreed with the Copernican hypothesis was the Danish astronomer Tycho Brahe (TEE-koh BRAH-hee) (1546–1601). Brahe established himself as Europe's leading astronomer with his detailed observations of a new star that appeared suddenly in 1572 and shone very brightly for almost two years. The new star, which was actually a distant exploding star, challenged the idea that the heavenly spheres were unchanging and therefore perfect. Impressed by his work, the king of Denmark provided funds for Brahe to build the most sophisticated observatory of his day.

Upon the king's death, Brahe acquired a new patron in the Holy Roman emperor Rudolph II and built a new observatory in Prague. For twenty years Brahe and his assistants observed the stars and planets with the naked eye in order to create new and improved tables of planetary motion, dubbed the *Rudolphine Tables* in honor of his patron. Part Ptolemaic, part Copernican, Brahe believed that all the planets except

■ **Copernican hypothesis** The idea that the sun, not the earth, is the center of the universe.

the earth revolved around the sun and that the entire group of sun and planets revolved in turn around the earth-moon system.

Brahe's assistant, Johannes Kepler (1571–1630), carefully re-examined his predecessor's notations and came to believe that they could not be explained by Ptolemy's astronomy. Abandoning the notion of the circular paths of epicycles and deferents, Kepler used Brahe's data to develop three revolutionary laws of planetary motion. First, largely through observations of the planet Mars, he demonstrated that the orbits of the planets around the sun are elliptical rather than circular. Second, he demonstrated that the planets do not move at a uniform speed in their orbits. When a planet is close to the sun, it accelerates, and it slows as it moves farther away from the sun. Finally, Kepler's third law stated that the time a planet takes to make its complete orbit is precisely related to its distance from the sun.

Kepler's contribution was monumental. Whereas Copernicus had used mathematics to describe planetary movement, Kepler proved mathematically the precise relations of a sun-centered (solar) system. He thus united for the first time the theoretical cosmology of natural philosophy with mathematics. His work demolished the old system of Aristotle and Ptolemy, and with his third law he came close to formulating the idea of universal gravitation. In 1627 he also published the *Rudolphine Tables*. Based on his observations and those of Tycho Brahe, it listed more than one thousand stars as well as tables of the positions of the sun, moon, and planets.

While Kepler was unraveling planetary motion, a Florentine named Galileo Galilei (1564–1642) was challenging Aristotelian ideas about motion on earth. He measured the movement of a rolling ball across a surface, repeating the action again and again to verify his results. In his famous acceleration experiment, he showed that a uniform force—in this case, gravity—produced a uniform acceleration. He also achieved new insight into the principle of inertia by hypothesizing that an object would continue in motion forever unless stopped by some external force.

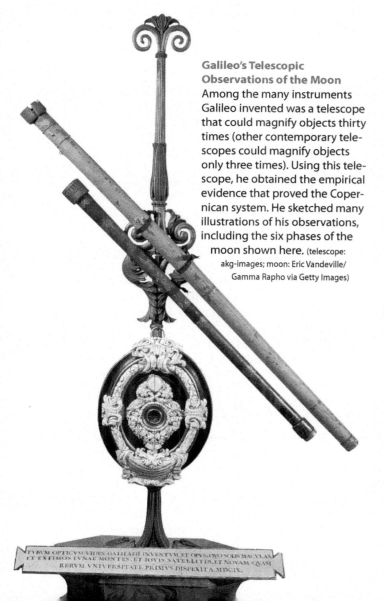

Galileo's Telescopic Observations of the Moon
Among the many instruments Galileo invented was a telescope that could magnify objects thirty times (other contemporary telescopes could magnify objects only three times). Using this telescope, he obtained the empirical evidence that proved the Copernican system. He sketched many illustrations of his observations, including the six phases of the moon shown here. (telescope: akg-images; moon: Eric Vandeville/ Gamma Rapho via Getty Images)

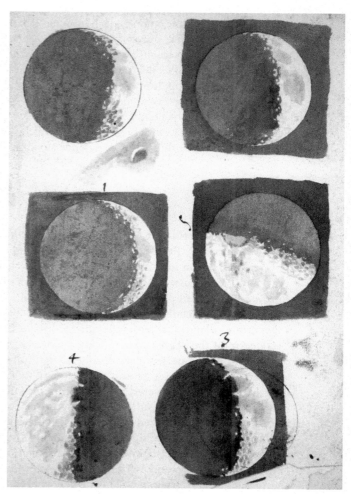

Galileo Galilei, *The Sidereal Messenger*

In this passage from *The Sidereal Messenger* (1610), Galileo Galilei recounts his experiments to build a telescope and his observations of the moon. By discovering the irregularity of the moon's surface, Galileo disproved a central tenet of medieval cosmography: that the heavens were composed of perfect, unblemished spheres essentially different from the base matter of earth.

~

About ten months ago a report reached my ears that a Dutchman had constructed a telescope, by the aid of which visible objects, although at a great distance from the eye of the observer, were seen distinctly as if near. . . . A few days after, I received confirmation of the report in a letter written from Paris . . . , which finally determined me to give myself up first to inquire into the principle of the telescope, and then to consider the means by which I might compass [achieve] the invention of a similar instrument, which a little while after I succeeded in doing, through deep study of the theory of refraction; and I prepared a tube, at first of lead, in the ends of which I fitted two glass lenses, both plane on one side, but on the other side one spherically convex, and the other concave. . . . At length, by sparing neither labour nor expense, I succeeded in constructing for myself an instrument so superior that objects seen through it appear magnified nearly a thousand times, and more than thirty times nearer than if viewed by the natural powers of sight alone. . . .

Let me speak first of the surface of the moon, which is turned towards us. For the sake of being understood more easily, I distinguish two parts in it, which I call respectively the brighter and the darker. The brighter part seems to surround and pervade the whole hemisphere, but the darker part, like a sort of cloud, discolours the moon's surface and makes it appear covered with spots. Now these spots . . . are plain to every one, and every age has seen them, wherefore I shall call them *great* or *ancient* spots, to distinguish them from other spots, smaller in size, but so thickly scattered that they sprinkle the whole surface of the moon, but especially the brighter portion of it. These spots have never been observed by any one before me, and from my observations of them, often repeated, I have been led to that opinion which I have expressed, namely, that I feel sure that the surface of the moon is not perfectly smooth, free from inequalities and exactly spherical, as a large school of philosophers considers with regard to the moon and the other heavenly bodies, but that, on the contrary, it is full of inequalities, uneven, full of hollows and protuberances, just like the surface of the earth itself, which is varied everywhere by lofty mountains and deep valleys.

EVALUATE THE EVIDENCE

1. What did the telescope permit Galileo to see on the moon that was not visible to the naked eye, and how did he interpret his observations?
2. Why were Galileo's observations so important to the destruction of the Ptolemaic universe?

Source: Galileo Galilei, *The Sidereal Messenger* (London: Rivingtons, 1880), pp. 10–11, 14–15.

The **law of inertia** was formulated explicitly after Galileo's death by René Descartes (see "The Methods of Science: Bacon and Descartes" later in this chapter) and Pierre Gassendi. Galileo's work on mechanics proved Aristotelian physics wrong.

On hearing details about the invention of the telescope in Holland, Galileo made one for himself and trained it on the heavens. He quickly discovered that, far from being a perfect crystal sphere, the moon is cratered with mountains and valleys, just like the earth. He then discovered the first four moons of Jupiter, which clearly suggested that Jupiter could not possibly be embedded in an impenetrable crystal sphere as Aristotle and Ptolemy maintained. This discovery provided concrete evidence for the Copernican theory. Galileo wrote in 1610 in *The Sidereal Messenger*: "By the aid of a telescope anyone may behold [the Milky Way] in a manner which so distinctly appeals to the senses that all the disputes which have tormented philosophers through so many ages are exploded by the irrefutable evidence of our eyes, and we are freed from wordy disputes upon the subject."[1] (See "Evaluating Written Evidence: Galileo Galilei, *The Sidereal Messenger*.")

Newton's Synthesis

By about 1640 the work of Brahe, Kepler, and Galileo had been largely accepted by the scientific community despite opposition from religious leaders. The old Aristotelian astronomy and physics were in ruins, and several fundamental breakthroughs had been made. But the new findings failed to explain what forces controlled the movement of the planets and objects on earth. That challenge was taken up by English scientist Isaac Newton (1642–1727), a genius who spectacularly united the experimental and theoretical-mathematical sides of modern science.

Newton was born into the lower English gentry, and he enrolled at Cambridge University in 1661. He arrived at some of his most basic ideas about physics in 1666 at age twenty-four but was unable to prove them mathematically. In 1684, after years of studying optics, Newton returned to mechanics for eighteen intensive months. The result was his towering accomplishment, a single explanatory system that could integrate the astronomy of Copernicus, as corrected by Kepler's laws, with the physics of Galileo and his predecessors. Newton did this through a set of mathematical laws that explain motion and mechanics. These laws were published in 1687 in Newton's *Mathematical Principles of Natural Philosophy* (also known as the *Principia Mathematica*). Because of their complexity, it took scientists and engineers two hundred years to work out all their implications.

The key feature of the Newtonian synthesis was the **law of universal gravitation**. According to this law, every body in the universe attracts every other body in the universe in a precise mathematical relationship, whereby the force of attraction is proportional to the quantity of matter of the objects and inversely proportional to the square of the distance between them. The whole universe—from Kepler's elliptical orbits to Galileo's rolling balls—was unified in one majestic system. Newton's synthesis of mathematics with physics and astronomy established him as one of the most important figures in the history of science; it prevailed until Albert Einstein's formulation of the general theory of relativity in 1915. Yet, near the end of his life, he declared: "I do not know what I may appear to the world; but to myself I seem to have been only like a boy, playing on the seashore, and diverting myself, in now and then finding a smoother pebble or a prettier shell than ordinary, whilst the great ocean of truth lay all undiscovered before me."[2]

Natural History and Empire

At the same time that they made advances in astronomy and physics, Europeans embarked on the pursuit of knowledge about unknown geographical regions and the useful and valuable resources they contained. Because they were the first to acquire a large overseas empire, the Spanish pioneered these efforts. Following the conquest of the Aztec and Inca Empires (see "Conquest of the Aztec Empire" and "The Fall of the Incas" in Chapter 14), they sought to learn about and profit from their New World holdings. The Spanish Crown sponsored many scientific expeditions to gather information and specimens, out of which emerged new

discoveries that reshaped the fields of botany, zoology, cartography, and metallurgy, among others. These accomplishments have attracted less attention from historians in part because the strict policy of secrecy imposed on scientific discoveries by the Spanish Crown limited the documents circulating about them.

Plants were a particular source of interest because they offered potential for tremendous profits in the form of spices, medicines, dyes, and cash crops. King Philip II of Spain sent his personal physician, Francisco Hernández, to New Spain for seven years in the 1560s. Hernández filled fifteen volumes with illustrations of three thousand plants previously unknown in Europe. He extensively interviewed local healers about the plants' medicinal properties, thereby benefiting from centuries of Mesoamerican and South American botanical knowledge. In the seventeenth century, for example, the Spanish obtained a monopoly on the world's supply of cinchona bark, which comes from a tree native to the high altitudes of the Andes and was the first effective treatment for malaria.

Other countries followed the Spanish example as their global empires expanded, relying on both official expeditions and the private initiative of merchants, missionaries, and settlers. Royal botanical gardens served as living laboratories for cultivating valuable foreign plants. Over time, the stream of new information about plant and animal species overwhelmed existing European intellectual frameworks. Carl Linnaeus (1707–1778) of Sweden sent his students on exploratory voyages around the world and, based on their observations and the specimens they collected, devised a formal system of naming and classifying living organisms still used today (with substantial revisions).

New encyclopedias of natural history popularized this knowledge with realistic drawings and descriptions emphasizing the usefulness of animals and plants. Audiences at home eagerly read the accounts of naturalists, who braved the heat, insects, and diseases of tropical jungles to bring home foreign animal, vegetable, and mineral specimens. Indigenous people also journeyed to Europe, some as captives, some voluntarily. Audiences heard little about the labor and expertise of the many local guides, translators, and practitioners of medicine and science who made these expeditions possible and who contributed a great deal of knowledge about the natural world.

■ **law of inertia** A law hypothesized by Galileo that states that motion, not rest, is the natural state of an object, and that an object continues in motion forever unless stopped by some external force.

■ **law of universal gravitation** Newton's law that all objects are attracted to one another and that the force of attraction is proportional to the objects' quantity of matter and inversely proportional to the square of the distance between them.

Magic and Alchemy

Recent historical research on the Scientific Revolution has focused on the contribution of ideas and practices we no longer recognize as science, such as astrology and alchemy. For most of human history, interest in astronomy was inspired by the belief that the movement of heavenly bodies influenced events on earth. Many of the most celebrated astronomers also worked as astrologers. Used as a diagnostic tool in medicine, astrology formed a regular part of the curriculum of medical schools.

Centuries-old practices of magic and alchemy also remained important traditions for natural philosophers. Early modern practitioners of magic strove to understand and control hidden connections they perceived among different elements of the natural world, such as that between a magnet and iron. The idea that objects possessed hidden or "occult" qualities that allowed them to affect objects at a distance was a particularly important legacy of the magical tradition. Belief in occult qualities—or numerology or cosmic harmony—was not antithetical to belief in God. On the contrary, adherents believed that only a divine creator could infuse the universe with such meaningful mystery.

Johannes Kepler exemplifies the interaction among these different strands of interest. His duties as court mathematician included casting horoscopes for the royal family, and he guided his own life by astrological principles. He also wrote at length on cosmic harmonies and explained elliptical motion through ideas about the beautiful music created by the combined motion of the planets. Kepler's fictional account of travel to the moon, written partly to illustrate the idea of a non-earth-centered universe, caused controversy and may have contributed to the arrest and trial of his mother as a witch in 1620. Kepler also suffered because of his unorthodox brand of Lutheranism, which led to his condemnation by both Lutherans and Catholics.

Another example of the interweaving of ideas and beliefs is Sir Isaac Newton, who was both intensely religious and fascinated by alchemy, whose practitioners believed (among other things) that base metals could be turned into gold. Critics complained that his idea of universal gravitation was merely a restatement of old magical ideas about the innate sympathies between bodies; Newton himself believed that the attraction of gravity resulted from God's actions in the universe.

What intellectual and social changes occurred as a result of the Scientific Revolution?

The Scientific Revolution was not accomplished by a handful of brilliant individuals working alone. Advancements occurred in many fields—medicine, chemistry, and botany, among others—as scholars developed new methods to seek answers to long-standing problems. They did so in collaboration with skilled craftsmen who invented new instruments and helped conduct experiments. These results circulated in an intellectual community from which women were usually excluded.

The Methods of Science: Bacon and Descartes

One of the keys to the achievement of a new worldview in the seventeenth century was the development of better ways of obtaining knowledge. Two important thinkers, Francis Bacon (1561–1626) and René Descartes (day-KAHRT) (1596–1650), were influential in describing and advocating for improved scientific methods based, respectively, on empirical observation and on mathematical reasoning.

The English politician and writer Francis Bacon was the greatest early propagandist for the experimental method. Rejecting the Aristotelian and medieval method of using speculative reasoning to build general theories, Bacon called for a new approach to scientific inquiry based on direct observation, free from the preconceptions and prejudices of the past. The researcher who wants to learn more about leaves or rocks, for example, should not speculate about the subject but rather collect a multitude of specimens and then compare and analyze them to derive general principles. This technique of producing knowledge is known as inductive reasoning, which works from specific observations up to broader generalizations and theories. Bacon's work, and his prestige as lord chancellor under James I, led to the widespread adoption of what was called "experimental philosophy" in Britain after his death. In 1660 followers of Bacon created the Royal Society (still in existence), which met weekly to conduct experiments and discuss the latest findings of scholars across Europe.

On the continent, more speculative methods gained support. In 1619, as a twenty-three-year-old soldier serving in the Thirty Years' War, the French philosopher René Descartes experienced a

■ **Cartesian dualism** Descartes's view that all of reality could ultimately be reduced to mind and matter.

life-changing intellectual vision. Descartes saw that there was a perfect correspondence between geometry and algebra and that geometrical spatial figures could be expressed as algebraic equations and vice versa. A major step forward in the history of mathematics, Descartes's discovery of analytic geometry provided scientists with an important new tool.

Descartes used mathematics to elaborate a new vision of the workings of the cosmos. Accepting Galileo's claim that all elements of the universe are composed of the same matter, Descartes began to investigate the basic nature of matter. Drawing on ancient Greek atomist philosophies, he developed the idea that matter was made up of "corpuscles" (tiny particles) that collided together in an endless series of motions, akin to the workings of a machine. All occurrences in nature could be analyzed as matter in motion, and the total "quantity of motion" in the universe was constant. Descartes's mechanistic view of the universe depended on the idea that space was identical to matter and that empty space — a vacuum — was therefore impossible.

Although Descartes's hypothesis about the vacuum was proved wrong, his notion of a mechanistic universe intelligible through the physics of motion proved inspirational. Decades later, Newton rejected Descartes's idea of a full universe and several of his other ideas, but retained the notion of a mechanistic universe as a key element of his own system.

Descartes's greatest achievement was to develop his initial vision into a whole philosophy of knowledge and science. The Aristotelian cosmos was appealing in part because it corresponded with the evidence of the human senses. When experiments proved that sensory impressions could be wrong, Descartes decided it was necessary to doubt them and everything that could reasonably be doubted, and to then, as in geometry, use deductive reasoning from self-evident truths, which he called "first principles," to ascertain scientific laws. For Descartes these innate ideas included the existence of God and mathematical principles.

Descartes's reasoning ultimately reduced all substances to "matter" and "mind" — that is, to the physical and the mental. The devout Descartes believed that God had endowed man with reason for a purpose and that rational speculation could provide a path to the truths of creation. His view of the world as

consisting of these two fundamental entities is known as **Cartesian dualism**. Descartes's thought was highly influential in France and the Netherlands, but less so in England, where experimental philosophy won the day.

Both Bacon's inductive experimentalism and Descartes's deductive mathematical reasoning had flaws. Bacon's inability to appreciate the importance of mathematics and his obsession with practical results clearly showed the limitations of antitheoretical empiricism. Likewise, some of Descartes's positions demonstrated the inadequacy of rigid, dogmatic rationalism. For example, he believed that it was possible to deduce the whole science of medicine from first principles. Although insufficient on their own, Bacon's and Descartes's extreme approaches are combined in the modern scientific method, which began to crystallize in the late seventeenth century.

MAJOR CONTRIBUTORS TO THE SCIENTIFIC REVOLUTION

Nicolaus Copernicus (1473–1543)	Wrote *On the Revolutions of the Heavenly Spheres* (1543); theorized that the sun, rather than the earth, was the center of the universe
Paracelsus (1493–1541)	Swiss physician and alchemist who pioneered the use of chemicals to address illness
Andreas Vesalius (1514–1564)	Wrote *On the Structure of the Human Body* (1543)
Tycho Brahe (1546–1601)	Built observatory and recorded data on planetary motions
Francis Bacon (1561–1626)	Advocated experimental method, formalizing theory of inductive reasoning known as empiricism
Galileo Galilei (1564–1642)	Used telescopic observation to provide evidence for Copernican hypothesis
Johannes Kepler (1571–1630)	Used Brahe's data to provide mathematical support for the Copernican hypothesis; his new laws of planetary motion united for the first time natural philosophy and mathematics; completed the *Rudolphine Tables* in 1627
William Harvey (1578–1657)	Discovered the circulation of the blood (1628)
René Descartes (1596–1650)	Used deductive reasoning to formulate the theory of Cartesian dualism
Robert Boyle (1627–1691)	Formulated Boyle's law (1662) governing the pressure of gases
Isaac Newton (1642–1727)	Published *Principia Mathematica* (1687); set forth the law of universal gravitation, synthesizing previous theories of motion and matter

Medicine, the Body, and Chemistry

The Scientific Revolution, which began with the study of the cosmos, soon transformed the understanding of the microcosm of the human body. For many centuries the ancient Greek physician Galen's explanation of the body carried the same authority as Aristotle's account of the universe. According to Galen, the body contained four humors: blood, phlegm, black bile, and yellow bile. Illness was believed to result from an imbalance of humors, which is why doctors frequently prescribed bloodletting to expel excess blood.

Swiss physician and alchemist Paracelsus (1493–1541) was an early proponent of the experimental method in medicine and pioneered the use of chemicals to address what he saw as chemical, rather than humoral, imbalances. Another experimentalist, Flemish physician Andreas Vesalius (1514–1564), studied anatomy by dissecting human bodies, often those of executed criminals. In 1543, the same year Copernicus published *On the Revolutions*, Vesalius issued his masterpiece, *On the Structure of the Human Body*. Its two hundred precise drawings revolutionized the understanding of human anatomy, disproving Galen, just as Copernicus and his successors had disproved Aristotle and Ptolemy. The experimental approach also led English royal physician William Harvey (1578–1657) to discover the circulation of blood through the veins and arteries in 1628. Harvey was the first to explain that the heart worked like a pump and to explain the function of its muscles and valves.

Robert Boyle (1627–1691), a key figure in the victory of experimental methods in England, helped create the Royal Society in 1660. Among the first scientists to perform controlled experiments and publish details of them, he helped improve a number of scientific instruments. For example, he built and experimented with an air pump, which he used to investigate the properties of air and create a vacuum, thus disproving Descartes's belief that a vacuum could not exist in nature. Based on these experiments, he formulated a new law in 1662, now known as Boyle's law, that states that the pressure of a gas varies inversely with volume. Boyle also hypothesized that chemical substances were composed of tiny mechanical particles, out of which all other matter was formed.

Science and Religion

It is sometimes assumed that the relationship between science and religion is fundamentally hostile and that the pursuit of knowledge based on reason and proof is incompatible with faith. Yet during the Scientific Revolution most practitioners were devoutly religious and saw their work as contributing to the celebration of God's glory rather than undermining it. However, the concept of heliocentrism, which displaced the

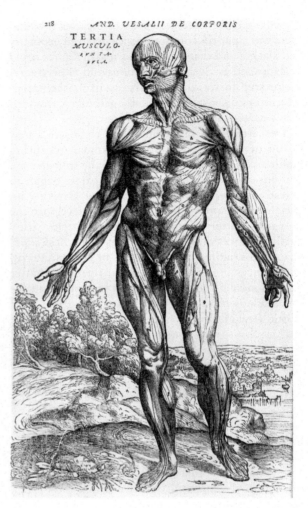

Vesalius's *De Humani Corporis Fabrica*   This illustration from Andreas Vesalius's pioneering 1543 work *De humani corporis fabrica* (On the Structure of the Human Body) depicts human musculature. Rather than relying on ancient Greek theories, Vesalius based his observations on dissections he conducted himself on human cadavers, thereby deriving a much more accurate account of the structure and functions of the body. (Bibliothèque de la Faculté de Médecine, Paris, France/Bridgeman Images)

earth from the center of the universe, threatened the understanding of the place of mankind in creation as stated in Genesis. Religious traditions that traced their origins to the Hebrew Bible — Catholic, Protestant, Jewish, and Muslim — thus faced difficulties accepting the Copernican system. Catholic Church leaders were initially less hostile than Protestant and Jewish religious leaders, but in the first decades of the sixteenth century the Catholic attitude changed. In 1616, alarmed by research findings by Galileo Galilei and other astronomers that undermined traditional astronomy, the Holy Office placed the works of Copernicus and his supporters on a list of books Catholics were forbidden to read. It also warned Galileo not to espouse heliocentrism or face the consequences.

Out of caution, Galileo silenced his views for several years, until 1623 saw the ascension of Pope Urban VIII, a man sympathetic to the new science. However, Galileo's 1632 *Dialogue on the Two Chief Systems of the World* went too far. Published in Italian and widely read, it openly lampooned the Aristotelian view and defended Copernicus. In 1633 the papal Inquisition placed Galileo on trial for heresy. Imprisoned and threatened with torture, the aging Galileo recanted, "renouncing and cursing" his Copernican errors.

Thereafter, the Catholic Church became more hostile to science, a change that helped account for the decline of science in Italy (but not in Catholic France, where there was no Inquisition and the papacy held less sway). At the same time, some Protestant countries, including the Netherlands, Denmark, and England, became quite pro-science. This was especially true in countries without a strong religious authority capable of imposing religious orthodoxy on scientific questions.

Science and Society

The rise of modern science had many consequences. First, it created a new social group — the international scientific community. Members of this community were linked together by common interests and values as well as by scholarly journals and associations. The personal success of scientists and scholars depended on making new discoveries, and science became competitive. Second, as governments intervened to support and sometimes direct research, the new scientific community became closely tied to the state and its agendas. National academies of science were created under state sponsorship in London in 1660, Paris in 1666, Berlin in 1700, and later across Europe.

It was long believed that the Scientific Revolution had little relationship to practical concerns and the life of the masses until the late-eighteenth-century Industrial Revolution (see Chapter 20). More recently, historians have emphasized the importance of skilled craftsmen in the rise of science, particularly in the development of the experimental method. Many artisans developed a strong interest in emerging scientific ideas, and, in turn, the practice of science in the seventeenth century often relied on artisans' expertise in making instruments and conducting precise experiments.

Some things did not change in the Scientific Revolution. For example, scholars willing to challenge received ideas about the natural universe did not question the seemingly natural inequalities between the sexes. Instead, the emergence of professional science may have worsened them in some ways. When Renaissance courts served as centers of learning,

talented noblewomen could find niches in study and research. But the rise of a scientific community raised new barriers for women because the universities and academies that furnished professional credentials did not admit women.

There were, however, a number of noteworthy exceptions. In Italy, universities and academies did offer posts to women. Across Europe, women worked as makers of wax anatomical models and as botanical and zoological illustrators, like Maria Sibylla Merian. They were also very much involved in informal scientific communities, attending salons (see "Women and the Enlightenment" later in this chapter), participating in scientific experiments, and writing learned treatises. Some female intellectuals

Metamorphoses of the Caterpillar and Moth Maria Sibylla Merian (1647–1717), the stepdaughter of a Dutch painter, became a celebrated scientific illustrator in her own right. Her finely observed pictures of insects in the South American colony of Suriname introduced many new species. For Merian, science was intimately tied with art: she not only painted but also bred caterpillars and performed experiments on them. Her two-year stay in Suriname, accompanied by a teenage daughter, was a daring feat for a seventeenth-century woman. (akg-images/Newscom)

became full-fledged members of the philosophical dialogue. In England, Margaret Cavendish, Anne Conway, and Mary Astell all contributed to debates about Descartes's mind-body dualism, among other issues. Descartes himself conducted an intellectual correspondence with the princess Elizabeth of Bohemia, of whom he stated: "I attach more weight to her judgment than to those messieurs the Doctors, who take for a rule of truth the opinions of Aristotle rather than the evidence of reason."[3]

How did the Enlightenment emerge, and what were major currents of Enlightenment thought?

The political, intellectual, and religious developments of the early modern period that gave rise to the Scientific Revolution further contributed to a series of debates about key issues in late-seventeenth- and eighteenth-century Europe and the wider world that came to be known as the **Enlightenment**. By shattering the unity of Western Christendom, the conflicts of the Reformation brought old religious certainties into question; the strong states that emerged to quell the disorder soon inspired questions about political sovereignty and its limits. Increased movement of peoples, goods, and ideas within and among the continents of Asia, Africa, Europe, and America offered examples of surprisingly different ways of life and patterns of thought. Finally, the tremendous achievements of the Scientific Revolution inspired intellectuals to believe that true answers to all the questions being asked could be found through the use of reason and critical thinking. Nothing was to be accepted on faith; everything was to be submitted to **rationalism**, a secular, critical way of thinking. In a characteristically optimistic spirit, Enlightenment thinkers embraced the belief that fundamental progress could be made in human society as well as science.

The Early Enlightenment

Loosely united by certain key ideas, the European Enlightenment (ca. 1690–1789) was a broad intellectual and cultural movement that gained strength gradually and did not reach its maturity until about 1750. Its origins in the late seventeenth century lie in a combination of developments, including political opposition to absolutist rule; religious conflicts between Protestants and Catholics and within Protestantism; European contacts with other cultures; and the attempt to apply principles and practices from the Scientific Revolution to improve living conditions in human society.

A key crucible for Enlightenment thought was the Dutch Republic, with its traditions of religious tolerance and republican rule. When Louis XIV demanded that all Protestants convert to Catholicism, around two hundred thousand French Protestants, or Huguenots, fled France, many destined for the Dutch Republic. From this haven of tolerance, Huguenots and their supporters began to publish tracts denouncing religious intolerance and suggesting that only a despotic monarch, not a legitimate ruler, would deny religious freedom. Their challenge to authority thus combined religious and political issues.

These dual concerns drove the career of one important early Enlightenment writer, Pierre Bayle (1647–1706), a Huguenot who took refuge in the Dutch Republic. Bayle critically examined the religious beliefs and persecutions of the past in his *Historical and Critical Dictionary* (1697). Demonstrating that human beliefs had been extremely varied and very often mistaken, he concluded that nothing can ever be known beyond all doubt, a view known as skepticism. His influential *Dictionary* was found in more private libraries of eighteenth-century France than any other book.

The Dutch Jewish philosopher Baruch Spinoza (1632–1677) was another key figure in the transition from the Scientific Revolution to the Enlightenment. Deeply inspired by advances in science—in particular by debates about Descartes's thought—Spinoza sought to apply natural philosophy to thinking about human society. He borrowed Descartes's emphasis on rationalism and his methods of deductive reasoning, but he rejected the French thinker's mind-body dualism. Instead, Spinoza came to espouse monism, the idea that mind and body were united in one substance and that God and nature were merely two names for the same thing. He envisioned a deterministic universe in which good and evil were merely relative values and

■ **Enlightenment** The influential intellectual and cultural movement of the late seventeenth and eighteenth centuries that introduced a new worldview based on the use of reason, the scientific method, and progress.

■ **rationalism** A secular, critical way of thinking in which nothing was to be accepted on faith and everything was to be submitted to reason.

■ **sensationalism** The idea that all human ideas and thoughts are produced as a result of sensory impressions.

■ **philosophes** A group of French intellectuals who proclaimed that they were bringing the light of knowledge to their fellow humans in the Age of Enlightenment.

human actions were shaped by outside circumstances, not free will. Spinoza was excommunicated by the Jewish community of Amsterdam for his controversial religious ideas, but he was heralded by his Enlightenment successors as a model of personal virtue and courageous intellectual autonomy.

The German philosopher and mathematician Gottfried Wilhelm von Leibniz (1646–1716), who had developed calculus independently of Isaac Newton, refuted both Cartesian dualism and Spinoza's monism. Instead, he adopted the idea of an infinite number of substances, or "monads," from which all matter is composed. His *Theodicy* (1710) declared that ours must be "the best of all possible worlds" because it was created by an omnipotent and benevolent God. Leibniz's optimism was later ridiculed by the French philosopher Voltaire in *Candide or Optimism* (1759).

Out of this period of intellectual turmoil came John Locke's *Essay Concerning Human Understanding* (1690), perhaps the most important text of the early Enlightenment. In this work Locke (1632–1704), a physician and member of the Royal Society, set forth a new theory about how human beings learn and form their ideas. Whereas Descartes based his deductive logic on the conviction that certain first principles, or innate ideas, are imbued in humans by God, Locke insisted that all ideas are derived from experience. The human mind at birth is like a blank tablet, or *tabula rasa*, on which understanding and beliefs are inscribed by experience. Human development is therefore determined by external forces, like education and social institutions, not innate characteristics. Locke's essay contributed to the theory of **sensationalism**, the idea that all human ideas and thoughts are produced as a result of sensory impressions.

Along with Newton's *Principia*, the *Essay Concerning Human Understanding* was one of the great intellectual inspirations of the Enlightenment. Locke's equally important contribution to political theory, *Two Treatises of Government* (1690), insisted on the sovereignty of the Parliament against the authority of the Crown (see "Constitutional Monarchy" in Chapter 15).

The Influence of the Philosophes

Divergences among the early thinkers of the Enlightenment show that, while they shared many of the same premises and questions, the answers they found differed widely. The spread of this spirit of inquiry owed a great deal to the work of the **philosophes** (fee-luh-ZAWFZ) (French for "philosopher"), a group of French intellectuals who proudly proclaimed that they were bringing the light of reason to their ignorant fellow humans.

In the mid-eighteenth century France became a hub of Enlightenment thought, for at least three reasons. First, French was the international language of the educated classes, and France was the wealthiest and most populous country in Europe. Second, the rising unpopularity of the French monarchy generated growing discontent and calls for reform among the educated elite. Third, the French philosophes made it their goal to reach a larger audience of elites, many of whom were joined together in a concept inherited from the Renaissance known as the Republic of Letters—an imagined transnational realm in which critical thinkers and writers participated.

To appeal to the public and get around the censors, the philosophes wrote novels and plays, histories and philosophies, and dictionaries and encyclopedias, all filled with satire and double meanings to spread their message. One of the greatest philosophes, the baron de Montesquieu (mahn-tuhs-KYOO) (1689–1755), pioneered this approach in *The Persian Letters*, published in 1721. This work consists of letters written by two fictional Persian travelers, who as outsiders see European customs in unique ways and thereby allow Montesquieu a vantage point for criticizing existing practices and beliefs.

Disturbed by the growth in absolutism under Louis XIV and inspired by the example of the physical sciences, Montesquieu set out to apply the critical method to the problem of government in *The Spirit of Laws* (1748). Arguing that forms of government were shaped by history and geography, Montesquieu identified three main types: monarchies, republics, and despotisms. A great admirer of the English parliamentary system, he argued for a separation of powers, with political power divided among different classes and legal estates holding unequal rights and privileges. Montesquieu was no democrat; he was apprehensive about the uneducated poor and did not question the sovereignty of the French monarchy. But he was concerned that absolutism in France was drifting into tyranny and believed that strengthening the influence of intermediary powers was the best way to prevent it. Decades later, his theory of separation of powers had a great impact on the constitutions of the young United States in 1789 and of France in 1791.

The most famous philosophe was François Marie Arouet, known by the pen name Voltaire (vohl-TAIR) (1694–1778). In his long career, Voltaire wrote more than seventy witty volumes, hobnobbed with royalty, and died a millionaire through shrewd speculations. His early career, however, was turbulent, and he was twice arrested for insulting noblemen. To avoid a prison term, Voltaire moved to England for three years, and there he came to share Montesquieu's enthusiasm for English liberties and institutions.

Philosophes' Dinner Party This engraving depicts one of the famous dinners hosted by Voltaire at Ferney, the estate on the French-Swiss border where he spent the last twenty years of his life. A visit to the great philosophe (pictured in the center with arm raised) became a cherished pilgrimage for Enlightenment writers. (Album/Alamy)

Returning to France, Voltaire met Gabrielle-Emilie Le Tonnelier de Breteuil, marquise du Châtelet (SHAH-tuh-lay) (1706–1749), a gifted noblewoman. Madame du Châtelet invited Voltaire to live in her country house at Cirey in Lorraine and became his long-time companion, under the eyes of her tolerant husband. Passionate about science, she studied physics and mathematics and published scientific articles and translations, including the first translation of Newton's *Principia* into French, still in use today. Excluded from the Royal Academy of Sciences because she was a woman, Madame du Châtelet had no doubt that women's limited role in science was due to their unequal education. Discussing what she would do if she were a ruler, she wrote, "I would reform an abuse which cuts off, so to speak, half the human race. I would make women participate in all the rights of humankind, and above all in those of the intellect."[4]

While living at Cirey, Voltaire wrote works praising England and popularizing English science. Yet, like almost all of the philosophes, Voltaire was a reformer, not a revolutionary, in politics. He pessimistically concluded that the best one could hope for in the way of government was a good monarch, since human beings "are very rarely worthy to govern themselves." Nor did Voltaire believe in social and economic equality. The only realizable equality, Voltaire thought, was that "by which the citizen only depends on the laws which protect the freedom of the feeble against the ambitions of the strong."[5]

Voltaire's philosophical and religious positions were much more radical. He believed in God, but he rejected Catholicism in favor of **deism**, belief in a distant noninterventionist deity. Drawing on mechanistic philosophy, he envisioned a universe in which God acted like a great clockmaker who built an orderly system and then stepped aside to let it run. Above all, Voltaire and most of the philosophes hated all forms of religious intolerance, which they believed led to fanaticism and cruelty. (See "Thinking Like a Historian: The Enlightenment Debate on Religious Tolerance," page 474.)

The strength of the philosophes lay in their dedication and organization. Their greatest achievement was a group effort — the seventeen-volume *Encyclopedia: The Rational Dictionary of the Sciences, the Arts, and the Crafts*, edited by Denis Diderot (DEE-duh-roh) (1713–1784) and Jean le Rond d'Alembert (dah-luhm-BEHR) (1717–1783). Completed in 1766 despite opposition from the French state and the Catholic Church, the *Encyclopedia* contained seventy-two thousand articles by leading scientists, writers, skilled workers, and progressive priests. Science and the industrial arts were exalted, religion and immortality questioned. Intolerance, legal injustice, and out-of-date social institutions were openly criticized. The *Encyclopedia* also included many articles describing non-European cultures and societies, and it acknowledged Muslim scholars' contribution to Western science. Summing up the new worldview of the Enlightenment, the *Encyclopedia* was widely read, especially in less expensive reprint editions, and it was extremely influential.

After about 1770 a number of thinkers and writers began to attack the philosophes' faith in reason and progress. The most famous of these was Jean-Jacques Rousseau (1712–1778). The son of a poor Swiss watchmaker, Rousseau made his way into the

■ **deism** Belief in a distant, noninterventionist deity; common among Enlightenment thinkers.

Parisian Enlightenment through his brilliant intellect. Like other Enlightenment thinkers, he was passionately committed to individual freedom. Unlike them, however, he attacked rationalism and civilization as destroying, rather than liberating, the individual. Warm, spontaneous feeling, Rousseau believed, had to complement and correct cold intellect. Moreover, he asserted, the basic goodness of the individual and the unspoiled child had to be protected from the cruel refinements of civilization. Rousseau's ideals greatly influenced the early Romantic movement, which rebelled against the culture of the Enlightenment in the late eighteenth century.

Rousseau's contribution to political theory in *The Social Contract* (1762) was based on two fundamental concepts: the general will and popular sovereignty. According to Rousseau, the general will is sacred and absolute, reflecting the common interests of all the people, who have displaced the monarch as the holder of sovereign power (and thus exercise popular sovereignty). The general will is not necessarily the will of the majority, however. At times the general will may be the authentic, long-term needs of the people as correctly interpreted by a farsighted minority. Little noticed before the French Revolution, Rousseau's concept of the general will appealed greatly to democrats and nationalists after 1789.

Enlightenment Movements Across Europe

The Enlightenment was a movement of international dimensions, with thinkers traversing borders in a constant exchange of visits, letters, and printed materials. Voltaire alone wrote almost eighteen thousand letters to correspondents in France and across Europe. The Republic of Letters, as this international group of scholars and writers was called, was a truly cosmopolitan set of networks stretching from western Europe to its colonies in the Americas, to Russia and eastern Europe, and along the routes of trade and empire to Africa and Asia.

Within this broad international conversation, scholars have identified numerous regional and national particularities. Outside of France, many strains of Enlightenment — Protestant, Catholic, and Jewish — sought to reconcile reason with faith, rather than emphasizing the errors of religious fanaticism and intolerance. Some scholars point to a distinctive "Catholic Enlightenment" that aimed to renew and reform the church from within, looking to divine grace rather than human will as the source of progress.

The Scottish Enlightenment, which was centered in Edinburgh, was marked by an emphasis on common sense and scientific reasoning. After the Act of Union with England in 1707, Scotland was freed

MAJOR FIGURES OF THE ENLIGHTENMENT	
Baruch Spinoza (1632–1677)	Early Enlightenment thinker excommunicated from the Jewish religion for his concept of a deterministic universe
John Locke (1632–1704)	*Essay Concerning Human Understanding* (1690)
Gottfried Wilhelm von Leibniz (1646–1716)	German philosopher and mathematician known for his optimistic view of the universe
Pierre Bayle (1647–1706)	*Historical and Critical Dictionary* (1697)
Montesquieu (1689–1755)	*The Persian Letters* (1721); *The Spirit of Laws* (1748)
Voltaire (1694–1778)	Renowned French philosophe and author of more than seventy works
David Hume (1711–1776)	Central figure of the Scottish Enlightenment; *Of Natural Characters* (1748)
Jean-Jacques Rousseau (1712–1778)	*The Social Contract* (1762)
Denis Diderot (1713–1784) and Jean le Rond d'Alembert (1717–1783)	Editors of *Encyclopedia: The Rational Dictionary of the Sciences, the Arts, and the Crafts* (1751–1766)
Adam Smith (1723–1790)	*An Inquiry into the Nature and Causes of the Wealth of Nations* (1776)
Immanuel Kant (1724–1804)	*What Is Enlightenment?* (1784); *On the Different Races of Man* (1775)
Moses Mendelssohn (1729–1786)	Major philosopher of the Haskalah, or Jewish Enlightenment
Cesare Beccaria (1738–1794)	*On Crimes and Punishments* (1764)

from political crisis to experience a vigorous period of intellectual growth. Advances in philosophy were also stimulated by the creation of the first public educational system in Europe.

A central figure in Edinburgh was David Hume (1711–1776), whose emphasis on civic morality and religious skepticism had a powerful impact at home and abroad. Hume strove to apply Newton's experimental methods to what he called the "science of man." Building on Locke's writings on learning, Hume argued that the human mind is really nothing but a bundle of impressions that originate only in sensory

The Enlightenment Debate on Religious Tolerance

Enlightenment philosophers questioned many aspects of European society, including political authority, social inequality, and imperialism. A major focus of their criticism was the dominance of the established church and the persecution of minority faiths. While many philosophers defended religious tolerance, they differed widely in their approaches to the issue.

1 **Moses Mendelssohn, "Reply to Lavater," 1769.** In 1769 Johann Caspar Lavater, a Swiss clergyman, called on Moses Mendelssohn to either refute proofs of Christianity publicly or submit to baptism. Mendelssohn's reply is both a call for toleration and an affirmation of his Judaism.

It is, of course, the natural obligation of every mortal to diffuse knowledge and virtue among his fellow men, and to do his best to extirpate their prejudices and errors. One might think, in this regard, that it was the duty of every man publicly to oppose the religious opinions that he considers mistaken. But not all prejudices are equally harmful, and hence the prejudices we may think we perceive among our fellow men must not all be treated in the same way. Some are directly contrary to the happiness of the human race. . . . These must be attacked outright by every friend of humanity. . . . Of this kind are all people's errors and prejudices that disturb their own or their fellows' peace and contentment and kill every seed of the true and the good in man before it can germinate. On the one hand, fanaticism, misanthropy, and the spirit of persecution, and on the other, frivolity, luxury, and libertinism.

Sometimes, however, the opinions of my fellow men, which in my belief are errors, belong to the higher theoretical principles which are too remote from practical life to do any direct harm; but, precisely because of their generality, they form the basis on which the nation that upholds them has built its moral and social system, and thus happen to be of great importance to this part of the human race. To oppose such doctrines in public, because we consider them prejudices, is to dig up the ground to see whether it is solid and secure, without providing any other support for the building that stands on it. Anyone who cares more for the good of humanity than for his own fame will be slow to voice his opinion about such prejudices, and will take care not to attack them outright without extreme caution.

2 **Voltaire, *Treatise on Toleration*, 1763.** Voltaire, the prominent French philosophe, began his *Treatise on Toleration* by recounting the infamous trial of Jean Calas. Although all the evidence pointed toward suicide, the judges concluded that Calas had killed his son to prevent him from converting to Catholicism, and Calas was brutally executed in 1762. For Voltaire, the Calas affair was a battle between fanaticism and reason, extremism and moderation.

Some fanatic in the crowd cried out that Jean Calas had hanged his son Marc Antoine. The cry was soon repeated on all sides; some adding that the deceased was to have abjured Protestantism on the following day, and that the family and young Lavaisse had strangled him out of hatred of the Catholic religion. In a moment all doubt had disappeared. The whole town was persuaded that it is a point of religion with the Protestants for a father and mother to kill their children when they wish to change their faith.

. . . There was not, and could not be, any evidence against the family; but a deluded religion took the place of proof. . . . [The judges] were confounded when the old man, expiring on the wheel, prayed God to witness his innocence, and begged him to pardon his judges.

The daughters were taken from the mother and put in a convent. The mother, almost sprinkled with the blood of her husband, her eldest son dead, the younger banished, deprived of her daughters and all her property, was alone in the world, without bread, without hope, dying of the intolerable misery. Certain persons, having carefully examined the circumstances of this horrible adventure, were so impressed that they urged the widow, who had retired into solitude, to go and demand justice at the feet of the throne. . . . She reached Paris almost at the point of death. She was astonished at her reception, at the help and the tears that were given to her.

At Paris reason dominates fanaticism, however powerful it be; in the provinces fanaticism almost always overcomes reason.

ANALYZING THE EVIDENCE

1. Based on these sources, what attitudes did eighteenth-century Europeans manifest toward religions other than their own? Were such attitudes always negative?
2. What justifications did Enlightenment philosophers use to argue in favor of religious tolerance? Were these arguments necessarily antireligious?
3. Why did Judaism figure so prominently in debates about religious tolerance in eighteenth-century Europe? In what ways do you think Mendelssohn's experience as a Jew (Source 1) shaped his views on religious tolerance?

3 **Bernard Picart, "Jewish Meal During the Feast of the Tabernacles," from** *Ceremonies and Customs of All the Peoples of the World,* **1724.** Eighteenth-century travel literature provided eager audiences with images and descriptions of religious practices from around the world. This image emphasizes the prosperity and warm family relations of a Jewish family enjoying a holiday meal, echoing the tolerant mind-set of the author.

(Jewish Chronicle/Heritage Images/Getty Images)

4 **Gotthold Ephraim Lessing,** *Nathan the Wise,* **1779.** In this excerpt from *Nathan the Wise,* a play by German writer Gotthold Ephraim Lessing, the sultan Saladin asks a Jewish merchant named Nathan to tell him which is the true religion: Islam, Christianity, or Judaism. Nathan responds with a parable about a man who promised to leave the same opal ring, a guarantor of divine favor, to each of his three beloved sons. He then had two exact replicas of the ring made so that each son would believe he had inherited the precious relic.

NATHAN: Scarce was the father dead,
When each one with his ring appears
Claiming each the headship of the house.
Inspections, quarrelling, and complaints ensue;
But all in vain, the veritable ring
Was not distinguishable —
(*After a pause, during which he expects the Sultan's answer*)
Almost as indistinguishable as to us,
Is now — the true religion.

SALADIN: What? Is that meant as answer to my question?

NATHAN: 'Tis meant but to excuse myself, because
I lack the boldness to discriminate between the rings,
Which the father by express intent had made
So that they might not be distinguished.

SALADIN: The rings! Don't play with me.
I thought the faiths which I have named

Were easily distinguishable,
Even to their raiment, even to meat and drink.

NATHAN: But yet not as regards their proofs:
For do not all rest upon history, written or traditional?
And history can also be accepted
Only on faith and trust. Is it not so?
Now, whose faith and confidence do we least misdoubt?
That of our relatives? Of those whose flesh and blood we are,
Of those who from our childhood
Have lavished on us proofs of love,
Who ne'er deceived us, unless 'twere wholesome for us so?
How can I place less faith in my forefathers
Than you in yours? or the reverse?
Can I desire of you to load your ancestors with lies,
So that you contradict not mine? Or the reverse?
And to the Christian the same applies.
Is that not so?

PUTTING IT ALL TOGETHER

Using the sources above, along with what you have learned in class and in this chapter, compare and contrast the views on religious toleration presented in the sources. On what would the authors of these works have agreed? How did their arguments in favor of toleration differ? What explanation can you offer for the differences you note?

Sources: (1) Ritchie Robertson, ed., *The German-Jewish Dialogue: An Anthology of Literary Texts, 1749–1993* (New York: Oxford University Press, 1999), pp. 41–42; (2) Voltaire, *A Treatise on Toleration and Other Essays,* trans. Joseph McCabe (Amherst, N.Y.: Prometheus Books, 1994), pp. 147–149, 152–153; (4) Crane Brinton, ed., *The Portable Age of Reason Reader* (New York: Viking Press, 1956), pp. 383–389.

experiences and our habits of mentally joining these experiences together. Therefore, reason cannot tell us anything about questions that cannot be verified by sensory experience (in the form of controlled experiments or mathematics), such as the origin of the universe or the existence of God. Hume further argued, in opposition to Descartes, that reason alone could not supply moral principles and that they derived instead from emotions and desires, such as feelings of approval or shame. Hume's rationalistic inquiry thus ended up undermining the Enlightenment's faith in the power of reason by emphasizing the superiority of the senses and the passions over reason in driving human thought and behavior.

Hume's emphasis on human experience, rather than abstract principle, had a formative influence on another major figure of the Scottish Enlightenment, Adam Smith (1723–1790). Smith argued that social interaction produced feelings of mutual sympathy that led people to behave in ethical ways, despite inherent tendencies toward self-interest. By observing others and witnessing their feelings, individuals imaginatively experienced such feelings and learned to act in ways that would elicit positive sentiments and avoid negative ones. Smith believed that the thriving commercial life of the eighteenth century was likely to produce civic virtue through the values of competition, fair play, and individual autonomy. In *An Inquiry into the Nature and Causes of the Wealth of Nations* (1776), Smith attacked the laws and regulations created by mercantilist governments that, he argued, prevented commerce from reaching its full capacity (see "Adam Smith and Economic Liberalism" in Chapter 17).

Inspired by philosophers of moral sentiments like Hume and Smith, as well as by physiological studies of the role of the nervous system in human perception, the celebration of sensibility became an important element of eighteenth-century culture. *Sensibility* referred to an acute sensitivity of the nerves and brains to outside stimuli, which produced strong emotional and physical reactions. Novels, plays, and other literary genres depicted moral and aesthetic sensibility as a particular characteristic of women and the upper classes. The proper relationship between reason and the emotions (or between *Sense and Sensibility*, as Jane Austen put it in the title of her 1811 novel) became a key question.

After 1760 Enlightenment ideas were hotly debated in the German-speaking states, often in dialogue with Christian theology. Immanuel Kant (1724–1804), a professor in East Prussia, was the greatest German philosopher of his day. Kant posed the question of the age when he published a pamphlet in 1784 titled *What Is Enlightenment?* He answered, "*Sapere Aude* [dare to know]! 'Have the courage to use your own understanding' is therefore the motto of enlightenment." He argued that if intellectuals were granted the freedom to exercise their reason publicly in print, enlightenment would almost surely follow. Kant was no revolutionary; he also insisted that in their private lives individuals must obey all laws, no matter how unreasonable, and should be punished for "impertinent" criticism. Like other Enlightenment figures in central and east-central Europe, Kant thus tried to reconcile absolute monarchical authority and religious faith with a critical public sphere.

Along with other German intellectuals, such as Johann Gottlieb Fichte, Kant introduced a new strain of philosophy that became known as German idealism. Inspired by the work of David Hume, Kant argued that, since our senses provide access only to the appearance of things and not to "things in themselves," a gap exists between reality and perception. However, Kant did not accept the religious skepticism and moral relativism that these ideas

Beccaria's *On Crimes and Punishments* An Italian nobleman, the marquis de Beccaria brought the Enlightenment spirit of rationalism and tolerance to bear on the justice system. In his 1764 work *On Crimes and Punishments*, from which this illustration is taken, he argued for the abolition of torture and capital punishment as being ineffectual deterrents to crime and unethical actions on the part of the state. (Bibliothèque Nationale, Paris, France/Bridgeman Images)

produced in Hume. Instead, he came to believe that humans possessed a shared framework for understanding sensory impressions that did correspond to empirical reality. For Kant, these realities included the existence of God and universal moral law. Kant thus attempted to reconcile rationalism and empiricism, on the one hand, with faith and ethics on the other. Fichte and other German philosophers after Kant took his idealism even further, arguing that objects have no independent existence outside of people's consciousness of them. By placing severe constraints on the capacity of human reason to generate knowledge, German idealism represented a sharp blow to the optimistic rationalism of earlier Enlightenment thinkers.

Important developments in Enlightenment thought also took place in the Italian peninsula. After achieving independence from Habsburg rule (1734), the kingdom of Naples entered a period of intellectual flourishing as reformers struggled to lift the heavy weight of church and noble power. In northern Italy a central figure was Cesare Beccaria (1738–1794), a nobleman educated at Jesuit schools and the University of Pavia. His *On Crimes and Punishments* (1764) was a passionate plea for reform of the penal system that decried the use of torture, arbitrary imprisonment, and capital punishment, and advocated the prevention of crime over the reliance on punishment. The text was quickly translated into French and English and made an impact throughout Europe and its colonies.

How did the Enlightenment change cultural ideas and social practices?

Europeans' increased interactions with non-European peoples and cultures also helped produce the Enlightenment spirit. Enlightenment thinkers struggled to assess differences between Western and non-Western cultures, often adopting Eurocentric views, but sometimes expressing admiration for other cultures. These same thinkers focused a great deal of attention on other forms of cultural and social difference, developing new ideas about race, gender, and political power. Although new "scientific" ways of thinking often served to justify inequality, the Enlightenment did see a rise in religious tolerance, a particularly crucial issue for Europe's persecuted Jewish population. As literacy rates rose and print culture flourished, Enlightenment ideas spread in a new "public sphere" composed of coffeeshops, literary salons, lending libraries, and other social institutions.

Global Contacts

In the wake of European expansion in the fifteenth and sixteenth centuries, a rapidly growing travel literature taught Europeans that the peoples of China, India, Africa, and the Americas had very different beliefs and customs. Educated Europeans began to look at truth and morality in relative, rather than absolute, terms. If anything was possible, who could say what was right or wrong?

The powerful and advanced nations of Asia were obvious sources of comparison with the West. Seventeenth-century Jesuit missionaries brought knowledge to the West about Chinese history and culture. Leibniz corresponded with Jesuits stationed in China, coming to believe that Chinese ethics and political philosophy were superior, but that Europeans had equaled China in science and

technology; some scholars believe his concept of monads was influenced by Confucian teaching on the harmony between the cosmic order and human society.[6]

During the Enlightenment, European opinion on China was divided. Voltaire and some other philosophes revered China as an ancient culture replete with wisdom and learning, ruled by benevolent absolutist monarchs. They enthusiastically embraced Confucianism as a natural religion in which universal moral truths were uncovered by reason. By contrast, Montesquieu and Diderot criticized China as a despotic land ruled by fear. Attitudes toward Islam and the Muslim world were similarly mixed. As the Ottoman military threat receded at the end of the seventeenth century, some Enlightenment thinkers assessed Islam favorably. Some deists praised Islam as superior to Christianity and valued Judaism for its rationality, compassion, and tolerance. Others, including Spinoza, saw Islamic culture as superstitious and favorable to despotism. In most cases, European writing about Islam and Muslim cultures served primarily as a means to reflect on European values and practices. Thus Montesquieu's *Persian Letters* used the Persian harem as a symbol of despotic rule that he feared his own country was adopting. Voltaire's play about the life of the Prophet portrayed Muhammad as the epitome of the religious fanaticism the philosophes opposed.

One writer with considerable personal experience in a Muslim country was Lady Mary Wortley Montagu, wife of the English ambassador to the Ottoman Empire. Her letters challenged prevailing ideas by depicting Turkish people as sympathetic and civilized. Montagu also disputed the notion that women were oppressed in Ottoman society compared to their European counterparts.

Apart from debates about Asian and Muslim lands, the "discovery" of the New World and subsequent

Portrait of Lady Mary Wortley Montagu Lady Mary Wortley Montagu accompanied her husband to the Ottoman Empire after he was named British ambassador to the empire. Her lively letters home, published after her death, question the supposedly inferior social status of Ottoman women compared to that of European women and other European assumptions about Ottoman society and culture. After her return home she publicized Ottoman practices of smallpox inoculation (as yet unknown in the West) and commissioned portraits of herself in Ottoman dress. (Photo © Christie's Images/Bridgeman Images)

explorations in the Pacific Ocean also challenged existing norms and values in Europe. One popular idea, among Rousseau and others, was that Indigenous peoples of the Americas were living examples of "natural man," who embodied the essential goodness of humanity uncorrupted by decadent society. Others depicted as utopian natural men were the Pacific Island societies explored by Captain James Cook and others from the 1770s on.

Enlightenment Debates About Race

As scientists developed taxonomies of plant and animal species in response to discoveries in the Americas, they also began to classify humans into hierarchically ordered "races" and to speculate on the origins of such races. In *The System of Nature* (1735), Swedish botanist

Carl Linnaeus argued that nature was organized into a God-given hierarchy. The comte de Buffon (komt duh buh-FOHN) argued that humans originated with one species that then developed into distinct races due largely to climatic conditions. Although the notion of a single origin of human beings opened the door to arguments for equality, Buffon and others who espoused this idea wrongly maintained that white Europeans represented the human norm, while other groups had degenerated from this norm over time.

Enlightenment thinkers such as David Hume and Immanuel Kant ascribed to and helped popularize ideas about racial difference and inequality. In *Of Natural Characters* (1748), Hume wrote: "I am apt to suspect the negroes and in general all other species of men (for there are four or five different kinds) to be naturally inferior to the whites. There never was a civilized nation of any other complexion than white, nor even any individual eminent amongst them, no arts, no sciences."[7] Kant taught and wrote as much about anthropology and geography as he did about standard philosophical themes such as logic, metaphysics, and moral philosophy. He elaborated his views about race in *On the Different Races of Man* (1775), claiming that there were four human races, each of which had derived from an original race. The closest descendants of the original race, which he believed was the most superior, were the white inhabitants of northern Germany. Scientists now know the human race originated in Africa.

Using the word *race* to designate biologically distinct groups of humans, akin to distinct animal species, was new. Previously, Europeans had grouped other peoples into "nations" based on their historical, political, and cultural affiliations, rather than on supposedly innate physical differences. When European thinkers drew up a hierarchical classification of human species, they placed their own "race" at the top. Europeans had long believed they were culturally superior to supposedly "barbaric" peoples in Africa and, since 1492, the New World. Now they used emerging ideas about racial difference to claim that they were biologically superior as well. Europeans thus drew on scientific racism to legitimate and justify the enormous expansion of the slave trade and exploitation of enslaved labor that they undertook during the eighteenth century. By depicting one "race" of humans as fundamentally different and inferior, white Europeans claimed that such people were particularly fit for enslavement and liable to benefit from tutelage by the so-called "superior" race.

Such racist and Eurocentric ideas did not go unchallenged. Formerly enslaved people, like Olaudah Equiano and Ottobah Cugoana, published eloquent memoirs testifying to the horrors of slavery and the innate equality of all humans. Some white European authors voiced similar views. The abbé Raynal's *History of the Two Indies* (1770) fiercely attacked slavery and the abuses of European colonization. *Encyclopedia* editor Denis Diderot adopted Montesquieu's technique of criticizing European attitudes through the voice of outsiders in "Supplement to Bougainville's Voyage," which contains an imaginary dialogue between Tahitian villagers and their European visitors. Scottish philosopher James Beattie (1735–1803) responded directly to claims of white superiority by pointing out that many non-European peoples in the Americas, Asia, and Africa had achieved high levels of civilization.

These challenges to racism, however, were relatively few. Many more Enlightenment thinkers supported racial inequality, including Thomas Jefferson and other prominent Americans among them. Thus, one of the major outcomes of Enlightenment thought was the production of theories of race that propagated ideals of freedom, liberty, and equality for white Europeans while legitimizing the conquest, eradication, and enslavement of other people.

Women and the Enlightenment

Dating back to the Renaissance *querelle des dames*, the debate over women's proper role in society and the nature of gender differences continued to fascinate Enlightenment thinkers. Most philosophers believed that women were inferior to men intellectually as well as physically. They sought moderate reform at best, particularly in the arena of female education, and had no desire to upend men's traditional dominance over women. Some thinkers, however, did champion greater rights and expanded education for women.[8] The French philosopher René Descartes believed that women had the same capacity for rational thought as men, because "reason operates independently of the body." This idea inspired François Poulain de la Barre to publish "On the Equality of the Sexes" in 1673 and other works championing women's equality. In the late eighteenth century, one of the most vocal proponents of this position was the marquis de Condorcet, a celebrated mathematician and contributor to the *Encyclopedia*. Condorcet advocated for women's right to plan their pregnancies and called for girls to be educated alongside boys in coeducational schools. A separate strand of thought that became increasingly important over the eighteenth century postulated for women's rights on the grounds that they made unique contributions to society—for example, through their role as mothers.

From the first years of the Enlightenment, women writers made crucial contributions both to debates about women's rights and to the broader Enlightenment conversations. In 1694 Mary Astell published

A Serious Proposal to the Ladies, which encouraged women to aspire to the life of the mind and proposed the creation of a college for women. Astell also harshly criticized the institution of marriage. Echoing arguments made against the absolute authority of kings during the Glorious Revolution (see "Constitutional Monarchy" in Chapter 15), she argued that husbands should not exercise absolute control over their wives in marriage. Yet Astell, like most female authors of the period, was careful to acknowledge women's God-given duties to be good wives and mothers.

The explosion of printed literature during the eighteenth century (see the next section) brought significant numbers of women writers into print, but they remained a small proportion of published authors. In the second half of the eighteenth century, women produced some 15 percent of published novels, the genre in which they enjoyed the greatest success. They constituted a much tinier proportion of nonfiction authors.[9]

If they remained marginal in the world of publishing, women played a much more active role in the informal dimensions of the Enlightenment: conversation, letter writing, travel, and patronage. A key element of their informal participation was as salon hostesses, or *salonnières* (sah-lahn-ee-EHRZ). **Salons** were weekly meetings held in wealthy households that brought together writers, aristocrats, financiers, and noteworthy foreigners for meals and witty discussions of the latest trends in literature, science, and philosophy. One prominent salonnière was Madame du Deffand, whose weekly Parisian salon included such guests as Montesquieu, d'Alembert, and Benjamin Franklin, then serving as the first U.S. ambassador to France. Invitations to salons were highly coveted; introductions to the rich and powerful could make the career of an ambitious writer, and, in turn, the social elite found amusement and cultural prestige in their ties to up-and-coming artists and men of letters.

Elite women also exercised great influence on artistic taste. Rather than liking the somber and grandiose character of Baroque art, they favored a style of art and architecture that focused on themes of pleasure and sensuality, expressed in soft pastels, ornamental decoration, and asymmetrical patterns. This style, known as **rococo** (ruh-KOH-koh), was popular throughout Europe from 1720 to 1780. It was particularly associated with the mistress of Louis XV, Madame de Pompadour, who used her position to commission

---

■ **salon** Regular social gathering held by talented and rich Parisians in their homes, where philosophes and their followers met to discuss literature, science, and philosophy.

■ **rococo** A style of art and architecture in Europe in the eighteenth century, known for its soft pastels, ornamental decoration, asymmetrical patterns, and its thematic focus on pleasure and sensuality.

Madame de Pompadour, Mistress to French King Louis XV　Madame de Pompadour used the wealth at her command to patronize many highly skilled artists and craftsmen. She helped popularize the ornate, lightly colored, and highly decorative rococo style, epitomized by the sumptuous trimmings of her dress. (National Galleries of Scotland/Bridgeman Images)

paintings, furniture, and other luxury objects in the rococo style.

Women's prominent role as society hostesses and patrons of the arts and letters outraged some Enlightenment thinkers. According to Jean-Jacques Rousseau, women and men were radically different by nature and should play diametrically opposed roles in life. In his view, men were destined by nature to assume the active role in sexual relations and were naturally suited for the rough-and-tumble of politics and public life. Women's role was to attract male sexual desire in order to marry and create families and then to care for their homes and children in private. For Rousseau, wealthy Parisian women's love for attending social gatherings and pulling the strings of power was unnatural and had a corrupting effect on both politics and society. Some women eagerly accepted Rousseau's idealized view of their domestic role, but others—such as the English writer Mary Wollstonecraft—vigorously rejected his notion of women's limitations. (See "Viewpoints: Rousseau and Wollstonecraft Debate Women's Equality," page 481.)

Rousseau's emphasis on the natural laws governing women echoed a wider shift in ideas about gender during this period, as doctors, scientists, and philosophers increasingly agreed that women's essential characteristics were determined by their sexual organs and reproductive functions. This turn to nature, rather than tradition or biblical scripture, as a means to understand human society had parallels in contemporary views on racial difference. Just as writers like Rousseau used women's allegedly "natural" passivity to argue for their subordinate role in society, so Kant and others used wrong ideas about non-Europeans' "natural" inferiority to defend slavery and colonial domination. The new powers of science and reason were thus marshaled to imbue traditional stereotypes with the force of natural law. Scholars continue to debate the stark paradox between Enlightenment thinkers' ideals of universalism, progress, and reason and their support for racial and gender inequality.

Urban Culture and Life in the Public Sphere

Enlightenment ideas did not float on thin air. A series of new institutions and practices encouraged the spread of enlightened ideas. From about 1700 to 1789, the production and consumption of books grew significantly and the types of books people read

Enlightenment philosophers fervently debated the essential characteristics of the female sex and the appropriate education and social roles for women. Two of the most vociferous participants in this debate were Jean-Jacques Rousseau and Mary Wollstonecraft. Looking to nature as a guiding principle, Rousseau reasoned that women's role in the process of reproduction meant they were intended to be subordinate to men and to devote themselves to motherhood and home life. Wollstonecraft responded that virtue was a universal human attribute created by God that could not be differentiated by gender. While acknowledging that women were weaker in some ways than men, she insisted that they should strive to honor their God-given human dignity through education and duty, just like men.

Jean-Jacques Rousseau, *Emile, or on Education*

In the union of the sexes, both pursue one common object, but not in the same manner. From their diversity in this particular, arises the first determinate difference between the moral relations of each. The one should be active and strong, the other passive and weak: it is necessary the one should have both the power and the will, and that the other should make little resistance. . . .

Woman and man are made for each other; but their mutual dependence is not the same. The men depend on the women only on account of their desires; the women on the men both on account of their desires and their necessities: we could subsist better without them than they without us. Their very subsistence and rank in life depend on us, and the estimation in which we hold them, their charms and their merit. By the law of nature itself, both women and children lie at the mercy of the men. . . .

To please, to be useful to us, to make us love and esteem them, to educate us when young, and take care of us when grown up, to advise, to console us, to render our lives easy and agreeable; these are the duties of women at all times, and what they should be taught in their infancy.

Mary Wollstonecraft, *A Vindication of the Rights of Woman*

Rousseau declares that a woman should never, for a moment, feel herself independent, that she should be governed by fear to exercise her *natural* cunning, and made a coquettish slave in order to render her a more alluring object of desire, a *sweeter* companion to man, whenever he chooses to relax himself. . . .

What nonsense! When will a great man arise with sufficient strength of mind to puff away the fumes which pride and sensuality have thus spread over the subject! If women are by nature inferior to men, their virtues must be the same in quality, if not in degree, or virtue is a relative idea; consequently, their conduct should be founded on the same principles, and have the same aim. . . .

. . . [C]ultivate their minds, give them the salutary, sublime curb of principle, and let them attain conscious dignity by feeling themselves only dependent on God. Teach them, in common with man, to submit to necessity instead of giving, to render them more pleasing, a sex to morals. . . . Further, should experience prove that they cannot attain the same degree of strength of mind, perseverance, and fortitude, let their virtues be the same in kind, though they may vainly struggle for the same degree.

QUESTIONS FOR ANALYSIS

1. How does Rousseau derive his ideas about women's proper relationship to men from his view of "nature"?
2. What does Wollstonecraft mean when she criticizes writers like Rousseau for giving "a sex to morals"? What arguments does she use to oppose such views?
3. Rousseau and Wollstonecraft differed greatly in their ideas on the essential characteristics of men and women, but do you see any areas where they agree?

Sources: Jean-Jacques Rousseau, *Emilius and Sophia: or, a new system of education*, trans. William Kenrick (London: T. Becket and P.A. de Hondt, 1763), vol. 4, pp. 3–4, 18–20; Mary Wollstonecraft, *A Vindication of the Rights of Woman* (London: Johnson, 1792), pp. 47–48, 71.

changed dramatically. For example, the proportion of religious and devotional books published in Paris declined after 1750; history and law held constant; the arts and sciences surged.

Reading more books on many more subjects, the educated public approached reading in a new way. The old style of reading in Europe had been centered on a core of sacred texts read aloud by the father to his assembled family. Now reading involved a broader field of books that constantly changed. Reading became individual and silent, and texts could be questioned.

For those who could not afford to purchase books, lending libraries offered access to the new ideas of the Enlightenment. Coffeehouses, which first appeared in the late seventeenth century, became meccas of philosophical discussion. In addition to these institutions, book clubs, debating societies, Masonic lodges (groups of Freemasons, a secret society based on egalitarian principles that accepted craftsmen and shopkeepers as well as middle-class men and nobles), salons, and newspapers all played roles in the creation of a new **public sphere** that celebrated open debate informed by critical reason. The public sphere was an idealized space where members of society came together as individuals to discuss issues relevant to the society, economics, and politics of the day. (See "Evaluating Visual Evidence: Léonard Defrance and the Public Sphere," page 483.)

What of the common people? Did they participate in the Enlightenment? Enlightenment philosophes did not direct their message to peasants or urban laborers. They believed that the masses had no time or talent for philosophical speculation and that elevating them would be a long and potentially dangerous process. Deluded by superstitions and driven by violent passions, the people, they thought, were like children in need of firm parental guidance. D'Alembert characteristically made a sharp distinction between "the truly enlightened public" and "the blind and noisy multitude."[10]

Despite these prejudices, the ideas of the philosophes did find an audience among some members of the working classes. At a time of rising literacy, book prices were dropping, and many philosophical ideas were popularized in cheap pamphlets and through public reading. Although they were barred from salons and academies, working people were not immune to the new ideas in circulation. Some of them made vital contributions to the debate, like Englishman Thomas Paine, born and apprenticed to a corset-maker, who wrote *Common Sense*, a foundational text of the American Revolution.

What impact did new ways of thinking have on politics?

Enlightenment thinkers' insistence on questioning long-standing traditions and norms inevitably led to issues of power and politics. Most Enlightenment thinkers outside of Britain and the Netherlands, especially in central and eastern Europe, believed that political change could best come from above — from the ruler — rather than from below. Royal absolutism was a fact of life, and the monarchs of Europe's leading states clearly had no intention of giving up their great power. Therefore, the philosophes and their sympathizers realistically concluded that a benevolent absolutism offered the best opportunities for improving society.

Many government officials were interested in philosophical ideas. They were among the best-educated members of society, and their daily involvement in complex affairs of state made them naturally attracted to ideas for improving human society. Encouraged and instructed by these officials, some absolutist rulers tried to reform their governments in accordance with Enlightenment ideals — what historians have called the **enlightened absolutism** of the later eighteenth century. In both Catholic and Protestant lands, rulers typically fused Enlightenment principles with religion, drawing support for their innovations from reform-minded religious thinkers. The most influential of the new-style monarchs were in Prussia, Russia, and Austria, and their example illustrates both the achievements and the great limitations of enlightened absolutism. France experienced its own brand of enlightened absolutism in the contentious decades prior to the French Revolution.

Frederick the Great of Prussia

Frederick II (r. 1740–1786) of Prussia, commonly known as Frederick the Great, built masterfully on the work of his father, Frederick William I (see "The Consolidation of Prussian Absolutism" in Chapter 15). Although in his youth he embraced culture and literature rather than the militarism championed by his father, by the time he came to the throne Frederick was determined to use the splendid army he had inherited.

Therefore, when Maria Theresa inherited the Habsburg dominions upon the death of her father, Holy Roman emperor Charles VI, Frederick pounced. He invaded the rich province of Silesia (sigh-LEE-zhuh), which bordered the Prussian territory of Brandenburg, thereby defying solemn Prussian promises to respect the Pragmatic Sanction, a diplomatic agreement that had guaranteed Maria Theresa's succession. In 1742, as other powers vied for Habsburg lands in the European War of the Austrian Succession (1740–1748), Maria Theresa was forced to cede almost all of Silesia to Prussia. In one stroke Prussia had doubled its population to 6 million people and now stood as a major European power.

Though successful in 1742, Frederick had to fight against great odds to save Prussia from destruction

■ **public sphere** An idealized intellectual space that emerged in Europe during the Enlightenment, where the public came together to discuss important issues relating to society, economics, and politics.

■ **enlightened absolutism** Term coined by historians to describe the rule of eighteenth-century monarchs who, without renouncing their own absolute authority, adopted Enlightenment ideals of rationalism, progress, and tolerance.

Léonard Defrance and the Public Sphere

Born in the city of Liège (in modern-day Belgium), Léonard Defrance (1735–1805) was apprenticed to a painter as an adolescent and at the age of eighteen traveled across Italy and France, meeting fellow artists and absorbing new ideas and cultural impressions. He returned to Liège and began a professional career as a painter, specializing in scenes of everyday life, especially the interior of artisanal workshops and manufactures. His success led to a role as director of the city's Academy of Painting and Sculpture from 1778 to 1784.

Defrance passionately supported the Enlightenment ideas spreading across western Europe in this period. This painting, *A l'égide de Minerve* (Under the Protection of Minerva), depicts a bustling bookshop named in honor of Minerva, the Roman goddess of reason and wisdom. The painting was inspired by the 1781 Edict of Toleration issued by Habsburg emperor Joseph II in 1781, a copy of which is pasted to the wall on the left of the entrance to the shop.

In the foreground, a Protestant pastor and a Catholic priest shake hands, signifying peaceful coexistence among members of different faiths, while a shopgirl chats with a monk. In the foreground on the lower right, a public writer sits on a stack of religious treatises as he pens a document for a female client.

EVALUATE THE EVIDENCE

1. What attitude toward religion does Defrance convey in this painting?
2. What evidence does the painting provide that Defrance viewed Enlightenment ideas as universal and applicable to all people? Are there any significant groups of people excluded from this vision of the Enlightenment?
3. Judging by the elements in this painting, how did cultural ideas and information circulate in this period? How did people acquire and share information? How is that similar to or different from our own information culture?

(DEA/G. DAGLI ORTI/Getty Images)

after competition between Britain and France for colonial empire brought another great conflict in 1756. Maria Theresa, seeking to regain Silesia, formed an alliance with the leaders of France and Russia. The aim of the alliance during the resulting Seven Years' War (1756–1763) was to conquer Prussia and divide up its territory. Despite invasions from all sides, Frederick fought on. In the end he was unexpectedly saved when Peter III came to the Russian throne in 1762 and called off the attack against Frederick, whom he greatly admired.

The terrible struggle of the Seven Years' War tempered Frederick's interest in territorial expansion and brought him to consider how more humane policies for his subjects might also strengthen the state. He tolerantly allowed his subjects to believe as they wished in religious and philosophical matters. He promoted the advancement of knowledge, improving his country's schools and permitting scholars to publish their findings. Moreover, Frederick tried to improve the lives of his subjects more directly. As he wrote to his friend Voltaire in 1770, "[I have to] enlighten mind, cultivate morality, and make the people as happy as it suits human nature, and as the means at my disposal permit."[11]

The legal system and the bureaucracy were Frederick's primary tools. Prussia's laws were simplified, torture was abolished, and judges decided cases quickly and impartially. After the Seven Years' War ended in 1763, Frederick's government energetically promoted the reconstruction of agriculture and industry. In 1763, Prussia also became the first country in the world to introduce compulsory public education at the elementary level. Frederick himself set a good example. He worked hard and lived modestly, claiming that he was "only the first servant of the state." Thus Frederick justified monarchy in terms of practical results and said nothing of the divine right of kings.

Frederick's dedication to high-minded government went only so far, however. While he condemned serfdom in the abstract, he accepted it in practice and did not free the serfs on his own estates. He accepted and extended the privileges of the nobility, who remained

☐ Prussia, 1740
■ Prussian gains, 1742
▨ Austria, 1740
— Boundary of the Holy Roman Empire

Königsberg

Berlin

POLISH-LITHUANIAN COMMONWEALTH

SILESIA

Prague

Vienna

AUSTRIA

HUNGARY

The War of the Austrian Succession, 1740–1748

the backbone of the army and the entire Prussian state.

In reforming Prussia's bureaucracy, Frederick drew on the principles of **cameralism**, the German science of public administration that emerged in the decades following the Thirty Years' War and came to occupy a central place in the university curriculum of the German lands. Cameralism held that monarchy was the best of all forms of government, that all elements of society should be placed at the service of the state, and that, in turn, the state should make use of its resources and authority to improve society. Predating the Enlightenment, cameralist interest in the public good was usually inspired by the needs of war. Cameralism shared with the Enlightenment an emphasis on rationality, progress, and utilitarianism.

Catherine the Great of Russia

Catherine the Great of Russia (r. 1762–1796) was one of the most remarkable rulers of her age, and the French philosophes adored her. Catherine was a German princess from Anhalt-Zerbst, a small principality sandwiched between Prussia and Saxony. Her father commanded a regiment of the Prussian army, but her mother was related to the Romanovs of Russia, and that proved to be Catherine's opening to power.

Catherine's Romanov connection made her a suitable bride at the age of fifteen for the heir to the Russian throne. It was a mismatch from the beginning, but her *Memoirs* made her ambitions clear: "I did not care about Peter, but I did care about the crown." When her husband, Peter III, came to power during the Seven Years' War, his decision to withdraw Russian troops from the coalition against Prussia alienated the army. Catherine profited from his unpopularity to form a conspiracy to depose her husband. In 1762 Catherine's lover Gregory Orlov and his three brothers, all army officers, murdered Peter, and the German princess became empress of Russia.

Catherine had drunk deeply at the Enlightenment well. Never questioning that absolute monarchy was the best form of government, she set out to rule in an enlightened manner. She had three main goals. First, she worked hard to continue Peter the Great's effort to bring the culture of western Europe to Russia (see "The Reforms of Peter the Great" in Chapter 15). To do so, she imported Western architects, musicians, and intellectuals. She bought masterpieces of Western

■ **cameralism** View that monarchy was the best form of government, that all elements of society should serve the monarch, and that, in turn, the state should use its resources and authority to increase the public good.

Catherine the Great and Denis Diderot   Self-proclaimed adherent of Enlightenment ideals, Russian empress Catherine the Great enthusiastically corresponded with philosophes like Voltaire and Denis Diderot. When Diderot put his library on sale to raise much-needed funds, Catherine sent him the money but allowed him to keep his books. Historians have long debated the "enlightened despotism" represented by Catherine and other absolutist rulers. (Catherine: Museum of Art, Serpukhov, Russia/Bridgeman Images; Diderot: Heritage Images/Getty Images)

art and patronized the philosophes. An enthusiastic letter writer, she corresponded extensively with Voltaire and praised him as the "champion of the human race." When the French government banned the *Encyclopedia*, she offered to publish it in St. Petersburg, and she sent money to Diderot when he needed it. With these actions, Catherine won good press in the West for herself and for her country. Moreover, this intellectual ruler, who wrote plays and loved good talk, set the tone for the entire Russian nobility. Peter the Great westernized Russian armies, but it was Catherine who westernized the imagination of the Russian nobility.

Catherine's second goal was domestic reform, and she began her reign with sincere and ambitious projects. In 1767 she appointed a legislative commission to prepare a new law code. This project was never completed, but Catherine did restrict the practice of torture and allowed limited religious toleration. She also tried to improve education and strengthen local government. The philosophes applauded these measures and hoped more would follow.

Such was not the case. In 1773 a Cossack soldier named Emelian Pugachev sparked a gigantic uprising of serfs, very much as Stenka Razin had done a century earlier (see "Building the Russian Empire" in Chapter 15). Proclaiming himself the true tsar, Pugachev issued orders abolishing serfdom, taxes, and army service. Thousands joined his cause, slaughtering landlords and officials over a vast area of southwestern Russia. Pugachev's untrained forces eventually proved no match for Catherine's professional army. Betrayed by his own company, Pugachev was captured and brutally executed.

Pugachev's rebellion put an end to any intentions Catherine had about reforming the system and improving the lot of the peasantry. After 1775 Catherine gave the nobles absolute control of their serfs, and she extended serfdom into new areas, such as Ukraine. In 1785 she freed nobles from taxes and state service. Under Catherine the Russian nobility attained its most exalted position, and serfdom entered its most oppressive phase.

Catherine's third goal was territorial expansion, and in this respect she was extremely successful. Her armies subjugated the last descendants of the Mongols and the Crimean Tatars and began the conquest of the Caucasus (KAW-kuh-suhs), the region between the

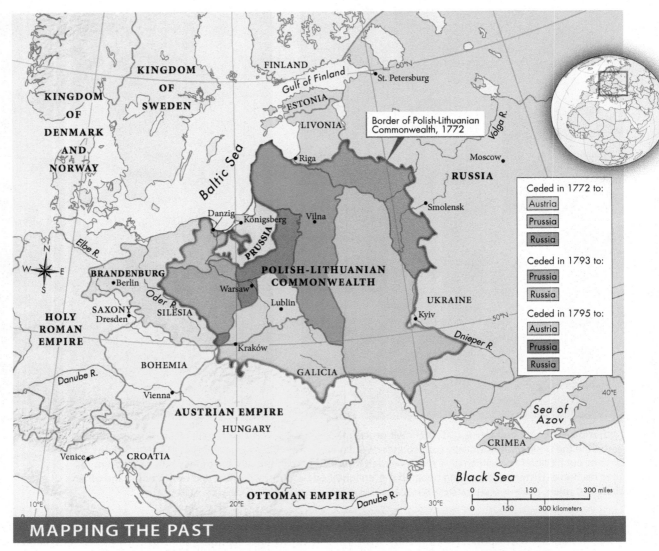

MAPPING THE PAST

MAP 16.1 The Partition of the Polish-Lithuanian Commonwealth, 1772–1795

In 1772 war between Russia and Austria threatened due to Russian gains from the Ottoman Empire. To satisfy desires for expansion without fighting, Prussia's Frederick the Great proposed that parts of the Polish-Lithuanian Commonwealth be divided among Austria, Prussia, and Russia. In 1793 and 1795 the three powers partitioned the remainder.

ANALYZING THE MAP Of the three powers that divided the Polish-Lithuanian Commonwealth, which gained the most territory? How did the partition affect the geographical boundaries of each state, and what was the significance? What border with the former commonwealth remained unchanged? Why do you think this was the case?

CONNECTIONS Look at the map of the Pale of Settlement (page 489). How do the borders of the Pale of Settlement compare to those of the Polish-Lithuanian Commonwealth? Based on what you have read in the text, why might Russia have created a vast territory for Jewish settlement in this area?

Black Sea and the Caspian Sea. Her greatest coup by far was the partition of the Polish-Lithuanian Commonwealth (Map 16.1). When, between 1768 and 1772, Catherine's armies scored unprecedented victories against the Ottomans and thereby threatened to disturb the balance of power between Russia and

Austria in eastern Europe, Frederick of Prussia obligingly came forward with a deal. He proposed that the Ottomans be let off easily and that Prussia, Austria, and Russia each compensate itself by taking a gigantic slice of the weakly ruled Polish territory. Catherine jumped at the chance. The first partition of the

Polish-Lithuanian Commonwealth took place in 1772. Subsequent partitions in 1793 and 1795 gave away the rest of Polish territory. Poland did not regain its independence until the twentieth century.

The Austrian Habsburgs

Another female monarch, Maria Theresa (r. 1740–1780) of Austria, set out to reform her nation, although traditional dynastic power politics was a more important motivation for her than were Enlightenment teachings. A devoutly Catholic mother and wife who inherited power from her father, Charles VI, Maria Theresa was a remarkable but old-fashioned absolutist. Her more radical son, Joseph II (r. 1780–1790), drew on Enlightenment ideals, earning the title of "revolutionary emperor."

Emerging from the long War of the Austrian Succession in 1748 with the serious loss of Silesia, Maria Theresa was determined to introduce reforms that would make the state stronger and more efficient. First, she initiated church reform, with measures aimed at limiting the papacy's influence, eliminating many religious holidays, and reducing the number of monasteries. Second, a whole series of administrative renovations strengthened the central bureaucracy, smoothed out some provincial differences, and revamped the tax system, taxing even the lands of nobles, previously exempt from taxation. Third, the government sought to improve the conditions of the agricultural population, cautiously reducing the power of lords over their hereditary serfs and their partially free peasant tenants.

Joseph II, coregent with his mother from 1765 onward and a strong supporter of change from above, implemented reform rapidly when he came to the throne in 1780. Most notably, Joseph issued an edict of religious toleration in 1781. In the same year he abolished serfdom, and in 1789 he decreed that peasants could pay landlords in cash rather than through labor on their land. This measure was violently rejected not only by the nobility but also by the peasants it was intended to help, because they lacked the necessary cash. When a disillusioned Joseph died prematurely at forty-nine, the entire Habsburg empire was in turmoil. His brother Leopold II (r. 1790–1792) canceled Joseph's radical edicts in order to re-establish order. Peasants once again were required to do forced labor for their lords.

Despite differences in their policies, Joseph II and the other absolutists of the later eighteenth century combined old-fashioned state-building with the culture and critical thinking of the Enlightenment. In doing so, they succeeded in expanding the role of the state in the life of society. They perfected bureaucratic machines that were to prove surprisingly adaptive and enduring. Their failure to implement policies we would recognize as humane and enlightened—such as abolishing serfdom—probably reveal inherent limitations in Enlightenment thinking about equality and social justice, rather than deficiencies in their execution of Enlightenment programs. The fact that leading philosophes supported rather than criticized absolutist rulers' policies thus exposes the blind spots of the era.

Jewish Life and the Limits of Enlightened Absolutism

Perhaps the best example of the limitations of enlightened absolutism is the debates surrounding the emancipation of the Jews. Europe's small Jewish populations lived under highly discriminatory laws. For the most part, Jews were confined to tiny, overcrowded neighborhoods called *ghettoes,* a term that may have originated in the Jewish quarter of Venice with the Italian word *borghetto,* meaning "little town." In most European countries, Jews were excluded by law from many professions and could be ordered out of a kingdom at a moment's notice. For example, Catherine I, the widow and successor of Peter the Great, expelled all Jews from Russia in 1727, an order that her daughter Elizabeth repeated when she took the throne in 1742. The Dutch Republic and the Polish-Lithuanian Commonwealth were notable exceptions to this norm.

Despite these obstacles, a very few Jewish groups did manage to succeed and to obtain the right of permanent settlement, usually by performing some special service for the state. Many rulers relied on Jewish bankers for loans to raise armies and run their kingdoms. Jewish merchants prospered in international trade because they could rely on contacts with colleagues in Jewish communities scattered across Europe.

In the eighteenth century an Enlightenment movement known as the **Haskalah** emerged from within the European Jewish community, led by the Prussian philosopher Moses Mendelssohn (1729–1786). (See "Individuals in Society: Moses Mendelssohn and the Jewish Enlightenment," page 488.) Christian and Jewish Enlightenment philosophers, including Mendelssohn, began to advocate for freedom and civil rights for European Jews. In an era of reason and progress, they argued, restrictions on religious grounds could not stand. The Haskalah accompanied a period of controversial social change within Jewish communities in which rabbinic controls loosened and interaction with Christians increased.

■ **Haskalah** The Jewish Enlightenment of the second half of the eighteenth century, led by the Prussian philosopher Moses Mendelssohn.

Moses Mendelssohn and the Jewish Enlightenment

In 1743 a small, humpbacked Jewish boy with a stammer left his poor parents in Dessau in central Germany and walked eighty miles to Berlin, the capital of Frederick the Great's Prussia. According to one story, when the boy reached the Rosenthaler (ROH-zuhn-taw-lehr) Gate, the only one through which Jews could pass, he told the inquiring watchman that his name was Moses and that he had come to Berlin "to learn." The watchman laughed and waved him through. "Go Moses, the sea has opened before you."[*]

In Berlin the young Mendelssohn studied Jewish law and eked out a living copying Hebrew manuscripts in a beautiful hand. But he was soon fascinated by an intellectual world that had been closed to him in the Dessau ghetto. There, like most Jews throughout central Europe, he had spoken Yiddish — a mixture of German, Polish, and Hebrew. Now, working mainly on his own, he mastered German; learned Latin, Greek, French, and English; and studied mathematics and Enlightenment philosophy. Word of his exceptional abilities spread in Berlin's Jewish community (the dwelling of 1,500 of the city's 100,000 inhabitants). He began tutoring the children of a wealthy Jewish silk merchant, and he soon became the merchant's clerk and later his partner. But his great passion remained the life of the mind and the spirit, which he avidly pursued in his off-hours.

Gentle and unassuming in his personal life, Mendelssohn was a bold thinker. Reading eagerly in Western philosophy since antiquity, he was, as a pious Jew, soon convinced that Enlightenment teachings need not be opposed to Jewish thought and religion. He concluded that reason could complement and strengthen religion, although each would retain its integrity as a separate sphere.[†] Developing his idea in his first great work, *On the Immortality of the Soul* (1767), Mendelssohn used the neutral setting of a philosophical dialogue between Socrates and his followers in ancient Greece to argue that the human soul lived forever. In refusing to bring religion and critical thinking into conflict, he was strongly influenced by contemporary German philosophers who argued similarly on behalf of Christianity. He reflected the way the German Enlightenment generally supported established religion, in contrast to the French Enlightenment, which attacked it.

Mendelssohn's treatise on the human soul captivated the educated German public, which marveled that a Jew could have written a philosophical masterpiece. In the excitement, a Christian zealot named Johann Casper Lavater challenged

Lavater (right) attempts to convert Mendelssohn, in a painting by Moritz Oppenheim of an imaginary encounter. (akg-images/Newscom)

Mendelssohn in a pamphlet to demonstrate how the Christian faith was not "reasonable" or to accept Christianity. Replying politely but passionately, the Jewish philosopher affirmed that his studies had only strengthened him in his faith, although he did not seek to convert anyone not born into Judaism. Rather, he urged toleration in religious matters and spoke up courageously against Jewish oppression.

Orthodox Jew and German philosophe, Moses Mendelssohn serenely combined two very different worlds. He built a bridge from the ghetto to the dominant culture over which many Jews would pass, including his novelist daughter Dorothea and his famous grandson, the composer Felix Mendelssohn.

QUESTIONS FOR ANALYSIS

1. How did Mendelssohn seek to influence Jewish religious thought in his time?
2. How do Mendelssohn's ideas compare with those of the French Enlightenment?

[*]H. Kupferberg, *The Mendelssohns: Three Generations of Genius* (New York: Charles Scribner's Sons, 1972), p. 3.

[†]David Sorkin, *Moses Mendelssohn and the Religious Enlightenment* (Berkeley: University of California Press, 1996), pp. 8ff.

The Pale of Settlement, 1791

Arguments for tolerance won some ground. The British Parliament passed a law allowing naturalization of Jews in 1753, but it later repealed the law due to public opposition. The most progressive reforms took place under Austrian emperor Joseph II. Among his liberal edicts of the 1780s were measures intended to integrate Jews more fully into society, including eligibility for military service, admission to higher education and artisanal trades, and removal of requirements for special clothing or emblems. Welcomed by many Jews, these reforms raised fears among traditionalists about the possibility of assimilation into the general population.

Many monarchs rejected all ideas of emancipation. Although he permitted freedom of religion to his Christian subjects, Frederick the Great of Prussia firmly opposed any general emancipation for the Jews, as he did for the serfs. In Russia, the partition of the Polish-Lithuanian Commonwealth in the last decades of the eighteenth century brought a large number of Jewish subjects into the empire. In 1791 Catherine the Great established the Pale of Settlement in land formerly belonging to the commonwealth. She forbade Jews to live outside of the Pale of Settlement, a requirement that only ended with the Russian Revolution of 1917.

The first European state to remove all restrictions on the Jews was France during the French Revolution. Over the next hundred years, Jews gradually won full legal and civil rights throughout the rest of western Europe. Emancipation in eastern Europe took even longer and aroused more conflict and violence.

NOTES

1. Quoted in H. Butterfield, *The Origins of Modern Science* (New York: Macmillan, 1951), p. 120.
2. Quoted in John Freely, *Aladdin's Lamp: How Greek Science Came to Europe Through the Islamic World* (New York: Knopf, 2009), p. 225.
3. Quoted in Jacqueline Broad, *Women Philosophers of the Seventeenth Century* (Cambridge: Cambridge University Press, 2003), p. 17.
4. Quoted in L. Schiebinger, *The Mind Has No Sex? Women in the Origins of Modern Science* (Cambridge, Mass.: Harvard University Press, 1989), p. 64.
5. Quoted in G. L. Mosse et al., eds., *Europe in Review* (Chicago: Rand McNally, 1964), p. 156.
6. D. E. Mungello, *The Great Encounter of China and the West, 1500–1800*, 2d ed. (Lanham, Md.: Rowman & Littlefield, 2005), p. 98.
7. Quoted in Emmanuel Chukwudi Eze, ed., *Race and the Enlightenment: A Reader* (Oxford: Blackwell, 1997), p. 33.
8. See E. Fox-Genovese, "Women in the Enlightenment," in *Becoming Visible: Women in European History*, 2d ed., ed. R. Bridenthal, C. Koonz, and S. Stuard (Boston: Houghton Mifflin, 1987), esp. pp. 252–259, 263–265.
9. Aurora Wolfgang, *Gender and Voice in the French Novel, 1730–1782* (Aldershot, U.K.: Ashgate, 2004), p. 8.
10. Jean Le Rond d'Alembert, *Eloges lus dans les séances publiques de l'Académie française* (Paris, 1779), p. ix, quoted in Mona Ozouf, "'Public Opinion' at the End of the Old Regime," *The Journal of Modern History* 60, Supplement: Rethinking French Politics in 1788 (September 1988): S9.
11. Cited in Giles McDonough, *Frederick the Great: A Life in Deed and Letters* (New York: St. Martin's Griffin, 2001), 341.

◀▶ LOOKING BACK LOOKING AHEAD

Hailed as the origin of modern thought, the Scientific Revolution must also be seen as a product of its past and of the interaction between Europeans and non-Europeans. Medieval translations of ancient Greek texts from Arabic into Latin spurred the advance of scholarship in western Europe, giving rise to universities that produced and disseminated knowledge of the natural world. Natural philosophers following Copernicus pioneered new methods of observing and explaining nature while drawing on centuries-old traditions of Christian faith as well as astrology, alchemy, and magic. In expanding their knowledge about the natural world, Europeans drew on traditions of observation and practice among Indigenous peoples of the New World.

The Enlightenment ideas of the eighteenth century were a similar blend of past and present, European and non-European; they could serve as much to bolster absolutist monarchical regimes as to inspire revolutionaries to fight for individual rights and liberties. Although the Enlightenment fostered critical thinking about everything from science to religion, the majority of Europeans, including many prominent thinkers, remained devout Christians. Enlightenment ideas were inspired by contact and exchange with non-Europeans in Asia, Africa, and the Americas.

The achievements of the Scientific Revolution and the Enlightenment are undeniable. Key Western values of rationalism, human rights, and tolerance were born from these movements. With their new notions of progress and social improvement, Europeans would embark on important revolutions in industry and politics in the centuries that followed.

Nonetheless, there is a darker side to these developments. Mastery over nature permitted by the Scientific Revolution today threatens to overwhelm the earth's fragile equilibrium. The Enlightenment also fostered scientific racism and sexism, and the idea that Europeans had identified universal rational truths that could be imposed on other cultures and peoples. Modern-day debates about the legacy of these intellectual and scientific developments testify to their continuing importance in today's world.

Make Connections

Think about the larger developments and continuities within and across chapters.

1. How did the era of European exploration and discovery (Chapter 14) affect the ideas of the scientists and philosophers discussed in this chapter? In what ways did contact with new peoples and places stimulate new forms of thought among Europeans?

2. What was the relationship between the Scientific Revolution and the Enlightenment? How did new ways of understanding the natural world influence thinking about human society?

3. Compare the policies and actions of seventeenth-century absolutist rulers (Chapter 15) with their "enlightened" descendants described in this chapter. How accurate is the term *enlightened absolutism*?

16   REVIEW & EXPLORE

Identify Key Terms

Identify and explain the significance of each item below.

natural philosophy (p. 461)

Copernican hypothesis (p. 462)

law of inertia (p. 464)

law of universal gravitation (p. 465)

Cartesian dualism (p. 467)

Enlightenment (p. 470)

rationalism (p. 470)

sensationalism (p. 471)

philosophes (p. 471)

deism (p. 472)

salon (p. 479)

rococo (p. 479)

public sphere (p. 482)

enlightened absolutism (p. 482)

cameralism (p. 484)

Haskalah (p. 487)

Review the Main Ideas

Answer the section heading questions from the chapter.

1. What revolutionary discoveries were made in the sixteenth and seventeenth centuries? (p. 460)

2. What intellectual and social changes occurred as a result of the Scientific Revolution? (p. 466)

3. How did the Enlightenment emerge, and what were major currents of Enlightenment thought? (p. 470)

4. How did the Enlightenment change cultural ideas and social practices? (p. 477)

5. What impact did new ways of thinking have on politics? (p. 482)

Suggested Resources

BOOKS

- Bevilacqua, Alexander. 2018. *The Republic of Arabic Letters: Islam and the European Enlightenment.* An engaging study of the origins of scholarship on Islam in the West and the central role of this scholarship in inspiring the Enlightenment.

- Blanning, T. C. W. *Joseph II.* 2013. A biography of the would-be enlightened reformer, Habsburg emperor Joseph II.

- Curran, Andrew S. *The Anatomy of Blackness: Science and Slavery in an Age of Enlightenment.* 2013. Examines how Enlightenment thinkers transformed traditional thinking about people of African descent into ideas about biological racial difference.

- Delbourgo, James, and Nicholas Dew, eds. *Science and Empire in the Atlantic World.* 2008. A collection of essays examining the relationship between the Scientific Revolution and the imperial expansion of European powers across the Atlantic.

- Ellis, Markman. *The Coffee House: A Cultural History.* 2004. An engaging study of the rise of the coffeehouse and its impact on European cultural and social life.

- Jardine, Lisa. *Ingenious Pursuits: Building the Scientific Revolution.* 1999. A lively and accessible account of how the Scientific Revolution emerged from intellectual exchange and competition among scholars.

- Massie, Robert K. *Catherine the Great: Portrait of a Woman.* 2012. Recounts the life story of Catherine, from obscure German princess to enlightened ruler of Russia.

- McMahon, Darrin M. *Happiness: A History.* 2006. Discusses how worldly pleasure became valued as a duty of individuals and societies in the Enlightenment.

- Portuondo, María. *Secret Science: Spanish Cosmography and the New World.* 2009. Examines the role of natural scientists in providing useful knowledge for Spanish imperial expansion in the Americas and the impact of their work on the overall development of science.

- Robertson, John. *The Case for the Enlightenment: Scotland and Naples, 1680–1760.* 2005. A comparative study of Enlightenment movements in Scotland and Naples, emphasizing commonalities between these two small kingdoms on the edges of Europe.

- Sutcliffe, Adam. *Judaism and Enlightenment.* 2003. Traces Enlightenment thinkers' fascination with Judaism, which included both negative and positive attitudes.

MEDIA

- *Catherine the Great* (A&E, 1995). A made-for-television movie starring Catherine Zeta-Jones as the German princess who becomes Catherine the Great.

- *Dangerous Liaisons* (Stephen Frears, 1988). Based on a 1782 novel, the story of two aristocrats who cynically manipulate others, until one of them falls in love with a chaste widow chosen as his victim.

- *The Encyclopedia of Diderot & d'Alembert Collaborative Translation Project.* A collaborative project to translate the *Encyclopedia* edited by Denis Diderot and Jean le Rond d'Alembert into English, with searchable entries submitted by students and scholars and vetted by experts. **quod.lib.umich.edu/d/did/**

- *Galileo's Battle for the Heavens* (PBS, 2002). Recounts the story of Galileo's struggle with the Catholic Church over his astronomical discoveries, featuring re-enactments of key episodes in his life.

- *The Hermitage Museum.* The website of the Russian Hermitage Museum founded by Catherine the Great in the Winter Palace in St. Petersburg, with virtual tours of the museum's rich collections. **http://www.hermitagemuseum.org/wps/portal/hermitage**

- *Longitude* (A&E, 2000). A television miniseries that follows the parallel stories of an eighteenth-century clockmaker striving to find a means to measure longitude at sea and a modern-day veteran who restores the earlier man's clocks.

- *Mapping the Republic of Letters.* A site hosted by Stanford University showcasing projects using mapping software to create spatial visualizations based on the correspondence and travel of members of the eighteenth-century Republic of Letters. **republicofletters.stanford.edu/**

- *Newton's Dark Secrets* (PBS, 2005). Explores Isaac Newton's fundamental scientific discoveries alongside his religious faith and practice of alchemy.

- *Ridicule* (Patrice Leconte, 1996). When a provincial nobleman travels to the French court in the 1780s to present a project to drain a malarial swamp in his district, his naïve Enlightenment ideals incur the ridicule of decadent courtiers.

17

The Expansion of Europe

1650–1800

Absolutism and aristocracy, a combination of raw power and elegant refinement, were a world apart from the common people of the eighteenth century. For most people, life remained a struggle with poverty and uncertainty, with the landlord and the tax collector. In 1700 peasants on the land and artisans in their shops lived little better than had their ancestors in the Middle Ages, primarily because European societies still could not produce very much as measured by modern standards. Despite the hard work of ordinary men, women, and children, there was seldom enough good food, warm clothing, and decent housing. The idea of progress, of substantial improvement in the lives of great numbers of people, was still the dream of only a small elite in fashionable salons.

Yet the economic basis of European life was beginning to change. In the course of the eighteenth century, the European economy emerged from the long crisis of the seventeenth century, responded to challenges, and began to expand once again. Population resumed its growth, while colonial empires were extended and developed. Some areas were more fortunate than others. The rising Atlantic powers—the Dutch Republic, France, and above all England—and their colonies led the way. The expansion of agriculture, industry, trade, and population marked the beginning of a surge comparable to that of the eleventh- and twelfth-century springtime of European civilization. But this time, broadly based expansion was not cut short by plague and famine. This time the response to new challenges led toward one of the most influential developments in human history, the Industrial Revolution, considered in Chapter 20. ■

CHAPTER PREVIEW

■ **Why did European agriculture grow between 1650 and 1800?**

■ **Why did the European population rise dramatically in the eighteenth century?**

■ **How and why did rural industry intensify in the eighteenth century?**

■ **What important changes occurred in economic thought and practice in the eighteenth century?**

■ **How did empire and trade shape new economic, cultural, and social developments?**

The Port of Bristol
Starting in the late seventeenth century, the English port of Bristol prospered through colonial trade with the West Indies and North America. In the eighteenth century it became a major hub of the slave trade, shipping finished goods to Africa to purchase captives, who were in turn transported to the Americas in exchange for sugar, rum, and tobacco for English markets. (Bristol Museums, Galleries & Archives/Bridgeman Images)

Why did European agriculture grow between 1650 and 1800?

At the end of the seventeenth century the economy of Europe was agrarian. With the exception of the Dutch Republic and England, at least 80 percent of the people of western Europe drew their livelihoods from agriculture. In eastern Europe the percentage was considerably higher. Men and women were tied to the land, plowing fields and sowing seed, reaping harvests and storing grain. Yet even in a rich agricultural region such as the Po Valley in northern Italy, every bushel of wheat seed sown yielded on average only five or six bushels of grain at harvest. By modern standards, output was distressingly low.

In most regions of Europe, climatic conditions produced poor or disastrous harvests every eight or nine years. In famine years the number of deaths soared far above normal. A third of a village's population might disappear in a year or two. But new developments in agricultural technology and methods gradually brought an end to the ravages of hunger in western Europe.

The Legacy of the Open-Field System

Why, in the late seventeenth century, did many areas of Europe produce barely enough food to survive? The answer lies in patterns of farming inherited from the Middle Ages, which sustained fairly large numbers of people but did not produce material abundance. From the Middle Ages up to the seventeenth century, much of Europe was farmed through the open-field system. The land to be cultivated was divided into several large fields, which were in turn cut up into long, narrow strips. The fields were open, and the strips were not enclosed into small plots by fences or hedges. The whole peasant village followed the same pattern of plowing, sowing, and harvesting in accordance with long-standing traditions.

The ever-present problem was soil exhaustion. Wheat planted year after year in a field will deplete nitrogen in the soil. Since the supply of manure for fertilizer was limited, the only way for the land to recover was to lie fallow for a period of time. Clover and other annual grasses that sprang up in unplanted fields restored nutrients to the soil and provided food for livestock. In the early Middle Ages a year of fallow was alternated with a year of cropping; then three-year rotations were introduced. On each strip of land, a year of wheat or rye was followed by a year of oats or beans and only then by a year of fallow. The three-year system was an important achievement because cash crops could be grown two years out of three, rather than only one year in two.

Traditional village rights reinforced communal patterns of farming. In addition to rotating field crops in a uniform way, villages maintained open meadows for hay and natural pasture. After the harvest villagers also pastured their animals on the wheat or rye stubble. In many places such pasturing followed a brief period, also established by tradition, for the gleaning of grain. In this process, poor women would go through the fields picking up the few single grains that had fallen to the ground in the course of the harvest. Many villages were surrounded by woodlands, also held in common, which provided essential firewood, building materials, and nutritional roots and berries.

The state and landlords continued to levy heavy taxes and high rents, thereby stripping peasants of their meager earnings. The level of exploitation varied. Generally speaking, the peasants of eastern Europe were worst off. As we saw in Chapter 15, they were serfs bound to their lords in hereditary service. In much of eastern Europe, working several days per week on the lord's land was not uncommon. Well into the nineteenth century, individual Russian serfs and serf families were regularly bought and sold.

Social conditions were better in western Europe, where peasants were generally free from serfdom. In France, western Germany, England, and the Low Countries (modern-day Belgium and the Netherlands), peasants could own land and could pass it on to their children. Even in these regions, however, life in the village was hard, and poverty was the reality for most people.

New Methods of Agriculture

The seventeenth century saw important gains in productivity in some regions that slowly extended to the rest of Europe. By 1700 less than half of the population of Britain and the Dutch Republic worked in agriculture, producing enough to feed the remainder of the population. Many elements combined in this production growth, but the key was new ways of rotating crops that allowed farmers to forgo the unproductive fallow period altogether and maintain their land in continuous cultivation. The secret to eliminating the fallow lay in deliberately alternating grain with crops that restored nutrients to the soil, such as peas and beans, root crops like turnips and potatoes, and clover and other grasses.

Clover was one of the most important crops, because it restores nitrogen directly to the soil through its roots. Other crops produced additional benefits.

■ **enclosure** The movement to fence in fields in order to farm more effectively, at the expense of poor peasants, who relied on common fields for farming and pasture.

TIMELINE

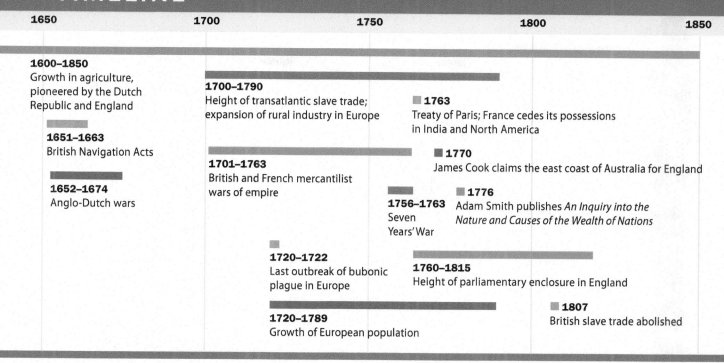

| 1650 | 1700 | 1750 | 1800 | 1850 |

1600–1850
Growth in agriculture, pioneered by the Dutch Republic and England

1651–1663
British Navigation Acts

1652–1674
Anglo-Dutch wars

1700–1790
Height of transatlantic slave trade; expansion of rural industry in Europe

1701–1763
British and French mercantilist wars of empire

1720–1722
Last outbreak of bubonic plague in Europe

1720–1789
Growth of European population

1763
Treaty of Paris; France cedes its possessions in India and North America

1770
James Cook claims the east coast of Australia for England

1776
Adam Smith publishes *An Inquiry into the Nature and Causes of the Wealth of Nations*

1756–1763
Seven Years' War

1760–1815
Height of parliamentary enclosure in England

1807
British slave trade abolished

Potatoes and many types of beans came to Europe as part of the sixteenth-century Columbian exchange between the New and the Old Worlds (see "Population Loss and the Ecological Impacts of Contact" in Chapter 14). These crops were widely adopted, starting in Spain and Italy in the early seventeenth century, and spread across the continent by the end of the eighteenth century. Rich in nutrients, they provided a welcome supplement to the peasant's meager diet. With more fodder, hay, and root vegetables for the winter months, peasants and larger farmers could build up their herds of cattle and sheep. More animals meant more manure to fertilize and restore the soil. More animals also meant more meat and dairy products as well as more power to pull plows in the fields and bring carts to market.

Over time, crop rotation spread to other parts of Europe, and farmers developed increasingly specialized patterns of rotation to suit different kinds of soils. For example, in the late eighteenth century farmers in French Flanders near Lille alternated a number of grain, root, and hay crops in a given field on a ten-year schedule. Ongoing experimentation, fueled by developments in the Scientific Revolution, led to more methodical farming.

Advocates of the new crop rotations, who included an emerging group of experimental scientists, some government officials, and a few big landowners, believed that new methods were scarcely possible within the traditional framework of open fields and common rights. A farmer who wanted to experiment with new methods would have to get all the landholders in the village to agree. Advocates of improvement argued that innovating agriculturalists needed to enclose and consolidate their scattered holdings into compact, fenced-in fields in order to farm more effectively. In doing so, the innovators also needed to enclose the village's natural pastureland, or common, into individual shares. According to proponents of this movement, known as **enclosure**, the upheaval of village life was the necessary price of technical progress.

That price seemed too high to many rural people who had small, inadequate holdings or very little land at all. Traditional rights were precious to these poor peasants, who used commonly held pastureland to graze livestock, and marshlands or forest outside the village as a source for foraged goods. Thus, when the small landholders and the village poor could effectively oppose the enclosure of the open fields and the common lands, they did so. In many countries they found allies among larger, predominantly noble landowners who were also wary of enclosure because it required large investments in purchasing and fencing land.

The old system of unenclosed open fields and the new system of continuous rotation coexisted in Europe for a long time. Open fields could still be found in much of France and Germany as late as the nineteenth century because peasants there had successfully opposed eighteenth-century efforts to introduce the new techniques. Through the end of the eighteenth century, the new system of enclosure was extensively adopted only in the Low Countries and England.

The Leadership of the Low Countries and England

The seventeenth-century Dutch Republic, already the most advanced country in Europe in many areas of human endeavor (see "The Dutch Republic in the Seventeenth Century" in Chapter 15), pioneered advancements in agriculture. By the middle of the seventeenth century intensive farming was well established, and the innovations of enclosed fields, continuous rotation, heavy manuring, and a wide variety of crops were all present. Agriculture was highly specialized and commercialized, especially in the province of Holland.

One reason for early Dutch leadership in farming was that the area was one of the most densely populated in Europe. To feed themselves, the Dutch were forced at an early date to seek maximum yields from their land and to increase the cultivated area through the steady draining of marshes and swamps. The pressure of population was connected with the second cause: the growth of towns and cities. Stimulated by commerce and overseas trade, Amsterdam grew from thirty thousand to two hundred thousand inhabitants in its golden seventeenth century. The growing urban population provided Dutch peasants with markets for all they could produce and allowed each region to specialize in what it did best. Thus the Dutch could develop their potential, and the Low Countries became, as one historian wrote, "the Mecca of foreign agricultural experts who came . . . to see Flemish agriculture with their own eyes, to write about it and to propagate its methods in their home lands."[1]

The English were among their best students. In the mid-seventeenth century English farmers borrowed the system of continuous crop rotation from the Dutch. They also drew on Dutch expertise in drainage and water control. Large parts of seventeenth-century Holland had once been sea and sea marsh, and the efforts of centuries had made the Dutch the world's leaders in drainage. In the first half of the seventeenth century, Dutch experts also helped to drain the extensive marshes of wet and rainy England and turn swampy wilderness into thousands of acres of productive land.

Based on the seventeenth-century achievements, English agriculture continued to progress during the eighteenth century, growing enough food to satisfy a rapidly growing population. Jethro Tull (1674–1741) was an important English innovator. A true son of the early Enlightenment, Tull adopted a critical attitude toward accepted ideas about farming and tried to develop better methods through empirical research. He was especially enthusiastic about using horses, rather than slower-moving oxen, for plowing. He also advocated sowing seed with drilling equipment rather than scattering it by hand. Drilling distributed seed in an even manner and at the proper depth. There were also improvements in livestock, inspired in part by the earlier successes of English country gentlemen in breeding ever-faster horses for the races and fox hunts that were their passions. Selective breeding of ordinary livestock was a marked improvement over the haphazard breeding of the past.

The Seed Drill   The seed drill had a metal plow in front (depicted behind the horse's back feet) to dig channels in the earth and a container behind it that distributed seed evenly into the channels. The drill allowed farmers to plant seeds at consistent depths and in straight lines, a much more efficient system than the old method of simply scattering seed across the field. (Universal Images Group/Getty Images)

One of the most important—and bitterly contested—aspects of English agricultural development was the enclosure of open fields and commons. Much of the farmland in England was enclosed through private initiatives prior to 1700; Parliament completed this work in the eighteenth century. From the 1760s to 1815 a series of acts of Parliament enclosed most of the remaining common land. Arthur Young, another agricultural experimentalist, celebrated large-scale enclosure as a necessary means to achieve progress. Many of his contemporaries, as well as the historians that followed him, echoed that conviction. More recent research, however, has shown that regions that maintained open-field farming were still able to adopt crop rotation and other innovations, suggesting that enclosures were not a prerequisite for increased production.

By eliminating common rights and greatly reducing the access of poor men and women to the land, the eighteenth-century enclosure movement marked the completion of two major historical developments in England—the rise of capitalist market-oriented estate agriculture and the emergence of a landless rural proletariat. By the early nineteenth century a tiny minority of wealthy English and Scottish landowners held most of the land and pursued profits aggressively, leasing their holdings through agents at competitive prices to middle-size farmers, who relied on landless laborers for their workforce. These landless laborers worked very long hours, usually following a dawn-to-dusk schedule six days a week all year long. Not only was the small landholder deprived of land, but improvements in technology meant that fewer laborers were needed to work the large farms, and unemployment spread throughout the countryside. As one observer commented:

> It is no uncommon thing for four or five wealthy graziers to engross a large inclosed lordship, which was before in the hands of twenty or thirty farmers, and as many smaller tenants or proprietors. All these are thereby thrown out of their livings, and many other families, who were chiefly employed and supported by them, such as blacksmiths, carpenters, wheelwrights and other artificers and tradesmen, besides their own labourers and servants.[2]

In no other European country had this **proletarianization**—this transformation of large numbers of small peasant farmers into landless rural wage earners—gone so far. England's village poor found the cost of change heavy and unjust.

Why did the European population rise dramatically in the eighteenth century?

Another factor that affected the existing order of life and drove economic changes in the eighteenth century was the beginning of the population explosion. Explosive growth continued in Europe until the twentieth century, by which time it was affecting non-Western areas of the globe. In this section we examine the background and causes of the population growth; the following section considers how the challenge of more mouths to feed and more hands to employ affected the European economy.

Long-Standing Obstacles to Population Growth

Until 1700 the total population of Europe grew slowly much of the time, and it followed an irregular cyclical pattern (Figure 17.1). This cyclical pattern had a great influence on many aspects of social and economic life. The terrible ravages of the Black Death of 1348–1350 caused a sharp drop in population and food prices after 1350. The resulting labor shortage throughout Europe meant that workers and peasants could demand better wages and working conditions, and food was more affordable for all. Some economic historians calculate that for those common people in western Europe who managed to steer clear of warfare and power struggles within the ruling class, the later Middle Ages was an era of exceptional well-being.

But this well-being eroded in the course of the sixteenth century. The second great surge of population growth outstripped the growth of agricultural production after about 1500. There was less food per person, and food prices rose more rapidly than wages, a development intensified by the inflow of precious metals from the Americas and a general, if uneven, European price revolution. The result was a substantial decline in living standards throughout Europe. By 1600 the pressure of population on resources was severe in much of Europe, and widespread poverty was an undeniable reality.

■ **proletarianization** The transformation of large numbers of small peasant farmers into landless rural wage earners.

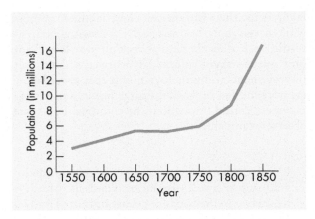

FIGURE 17.1 The Growth of Population in England, 1550–1850 England is a good example of both the uneven increase of European population before 1700 and the third great surge of growth that began in the eighteenth century. (Source: Data from E. A. Wrigley et al., *English Population History from Family Reconstitution, 1580–1837* [Cambridge: Cambridge University Press, 1997], p. 614.)

For this reason, population growth slowed and stopped in seventeenth-century Europe. Births and deaths, fertility and mortality, were in a crude but effective balance. The population grew modestly in normal years at a rate of perhaps 0.5 to 1 percent, or enough to double the population in 70 to 140 years. This is, of course, a generalization encompassing many different patterns. In areas such as Russia and colonial New England, where there was a great deal of frontier to be settled, the annual rate of natural increase, not counting immigration, might well have exceeded 1 percent. (The New England increase did not include Native Americans, whose numbers diminished sharply in the seventeenth century as a result of European diseases and, to a lesser extent, warfare.) In a country such as France, where the land had long been densely settled, the rate of increase might have been less than 0.5 percent.

Although a population growth of even 1 percent per year seems fairly modest, it will produce a very large increase over a long period: in three hundred years it will result in sixteen times as many people. Yet such significant increases did not occur in agrarian Europe. In certain abnormal years and tragic periods — the Black Death was only the most extreme example — many more people died than were born, and total population fell sharply, even catastrophically. A number of years of modest growth would then be necessary to make up for those who had died in an abnormal year. Such increases in deaths occurred periodically in the seventeenth century on a local and regional scale, and these demographic

crises combined to check the growth of population until after 1700.

The grim reapers of demographic crisis were famine, epidemic disease, and war. Episodes of famine were inevitable in all eras of premodern Europe, given low crop yields and unpredictable climatic conditions. In the seventeenth century much of Europe experienced unusually cold and wet weather, which produced even more severe harvest failures and food shortages than usual. Contagious diseases, like typhus, smallpox, syphilis, and the ever-recurring bubonic plague, also continued to ravage Europe's population on a periodic basis and to inflict grievous losses on Indigenous populations in European colonies, which are estimated to have reached their lowest numbers by the end of the seventeenth century. War was another scourge, and its indirect effects were even more harmful than the purposeful killing during military campaigns. Soldiers and camp followers passed all manner of contagious diseases throughout the countryside. Armies requisitioned scarce food supplies and disrupted the agricultural cycle while battles destroyed precious crops, livestock, and farmlands. The Thirty Years' War (1618–1648) witnessed all possible combinations of distress (see "The Thirty Years' War" in Chapter 15). The number of inhabitants in the German states alone declined by more than two-thirds in some large areas and by at least one-third almost everywhere else.

The New Pattern of the Eighteenth Century

In the eighteenth century the traditional demographic pattern of Europe was transformed. Growth took place unevenly, with Russia growing very quickly after 1700 and France much more slowly. Nonetheless, the explosion of population was a major phenomenon in all European countries. Europeans grew in numbers steadily from 1720 to 1789, with especially dramatic increases after about 1750 (Figure 17.2). Between 1700 and 1835 the population of Europe doubled in size.

What caused this population growth? In some areas, especially England, women had more babies than before because new opportunities for employment in rural industry (see "The Industrious Revolution" later in this chapter) allowed them to marry at an earlier age. But the basic cause of European population increase as a whole was a decline in mortality — fewer deaths.

One of the primary reasons behind this decline was the still-unexplained disappearance of the bubonic plague. Following the Black Death in the fourteenth century, plague had remained part of the European

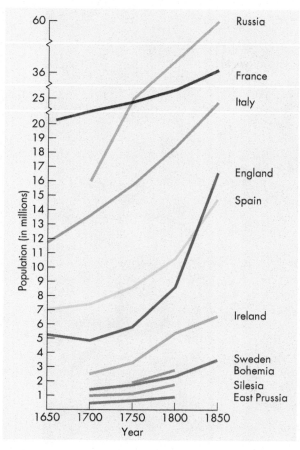

FIGURE 17.2 The Increase of Population in Europe, 1650–1850 Population grew across Europe in the eighteenth century, though the most dramatic increases occurred after 1750. Russia experienced the largest increase and emerged as Europe's most populous state, as natural increase was complemented by growth from territorial expansion. (Source: Data from Massimo Livi Bacci, *The Population of Europe* [Wiley-Blackwell, 2000], p. 8.)

Advances in medical knowledge did not contribute much to reducing the death rate in the eighteenth century. The most important advance in preventive medicine in this period was inoculation against smallpox, a disease that killed approximately four hundred thousand people each year in Europe. Widely practiced in the Ottoman Empire, inoculation was popularized in England in the 1720s by the wife of the former English ambassador to the empire, but it did not spread to the rest of the continent for decades. Improvements in the water supply and sewage did contribute to somewhat better public health and helped reduce such diseases as typhoid and typhus in urban areas of western Europe. Improvements in water supply and the drainage of swamps also reduced Europe's large insect population. Flies and mosquitoes played a major role in spreading diseases, especially those striking children and young adults. Thus early public health measures contributed to the decline in mortality that began with the disappearance of plague and continued into the early nineteenth century.

Human beings also became more successful in safeguarding the supply of food. The eighteenth century was a time of considerable canal and road building in western Europe. These advances in transportation lessened the impact of local crop failure and famine. Emergency supplies could be brought in, and localized starvation became less frequent.

A final significant factor in preventing deaths in the eighteenth century was that wars became less destructive than in the previous century. Fewer people died in warfare and, even more important, there were fewer armies on the move to spread epidemic disease.

None of the population growth would have been possible if not for the advances in agricultural production in the seventeenth and eighteenth centuries, which increased the food supply and contributed nutritious new foods, particularly the potato from South America. In short, population grew in the eighteenth century primarily because years of higher-than-average death rates were less catastrophic. Famines, epidemics, and wars continued to occur and to affect population growth, but their severity moderated.

Inspired by these developments, economist Thomas Malthus developed his famous theory on human population, warning that population would always tend to expand beyond the available food supply, leading to famine and other forms of misery. (See "Evaluating Written Evidence: Thomas Malthus on the Limitations of Population Growth," page 501.) By the end of the eighteenth century, population growth had intensified the imbalance between the number of people and the economic opportunities available to them. Deprived of land by the enclosure movement, the rural poor were forced to look for new ways to make a living.

experience, striking again and again, particularly in towns. In 1720 a ship from Syria and the Levant brought the disease to Marseilles. As a contemporary account described it, "The Porters employ'd in unloading the Vessel, were immediately seiz'd with violent Pains in the Head . . . soon after they broke out in Blotches and Buboes, and died in three Days."[3] Plague quickly spread within and beyond Marseilles, killing up to one hundred thousand. By 1722 the epidemic had passed, and that was the last time plague fell on western and central Europe. Exactly why plague disappeared is unknown. Stricter measures of quarantine in Mediterranean ports and along the Austrian border with the Ottoman Empire helped by carefully isolating human carriers of plague. Chance and plain good luck were probably just as important.

Eighteenth-Century Road Construction   Eighteenth-century European states undertook important projects to improve and extend infrastructure, drawing on coerced labor from local peasants to build a network of new roads, bridges, and canals across their territories. (Gianni Dagli Orti/Shutterstock)

How and why did rural industry intensify in the eighteenth century?

The growth of population increased the number of rural workers with little or no land, and this in turn contributed to the development of industry in rural areas. The poor in the countryside increasingly needed to supplement their agricultural earnings with other types of work, and urban capitalists were eager to employ them, often at lower wages than urban workers received. **Cottage industry**, which consisted of manufacturing with hand tools in peasant cottages and work sheds, grew markedly in the eighteenth century and became a crucial feature of the European economy. The growth of rural industry led to far-reaching changes in daily life in the countryside.

The Putting-Out System

Cottage industry was often organized through the **putting-out system**. The two main participants in this system were the merchant capitalist and the rural worker. The merchant loaned, or "put out," raw materials to cottage workers, who processed the raw materials in their own homes and returned the finished products to the merchant. The relative importance of earnings from the land and from industry varied greatly for handicraft workers, although industrial wages usually became more important for a given family with time.

As industries grew in scale and complexity, production was often broken into many stages. For example, a merchant would provide raw wool to one group of workers for spinning into thread. He would then pass the thread to another group of workers to be bleached, to another for dyeing, and to another for weaving into

■ **cottage industry** A stage of industrial development in which rural workers used hand tools in their homes to manufacture goods on a large scale for sale in a market.

■ **putting-out system** The eighteenth-century system of rural industry in which a merchant loaned raw materials to cottage workers, who processed them and returned the finished products to the merchant.

Thomas Malthus on the Limitations of Population Growth

Thomas Malthus (1766–1834) was an English economist whose father was a friend of the Scottish Enlightenment philosopher David Hume. After studying at Cambridge University, Malthus was appointed at the East India Company's college as Britain's first professor of the new field of "political economy." He is known for his theory on population, which argued that human population would naturally outgrow the supply of food, unless reduced either by people choosing to abstain from sexual relations (what he called "preventative checks") or by increased mortality rates caused by a variety of factors, including famine (what he called "positive checks"). Malthus's theory played a key role in convincing English legislators to eliminate social welfare, which he believed only encouraged the poor to have more children, and to keep working people's wages at the bare subsistence level. His pessimistic view of the inevitability of human suffering was a sharp contrast to the optimism and belief in progress characteristic of the Enlightenment thought of his father's generation.

~

The principal object of the present essay is to examine the effects of one great cause intimately united with the very nature of man . . . the constant tendency in all animated life to increase beyond the nourishment prepared for it. . . .

It may safely be pronounced, therefore, that population, when unchecked, goes on doubling itself every twenty-five years, or increases in a geometrical ratio.

The rate according to which the productions of the earth may be supposed to increase, it will not be so easy to determine. Of this, however, we may be perfectly certain, that the ratio of their increase in a limited territory must be of a totally different nature from the ratio of the increase of population. . . . It may fairly be pronounced, therefore, that considering the present average state of the earth, the means of subsistence, under circumstances the most favorable to human industry, could not possibly be made to increase faster than in an arithmetical ratio. . . . The ultimate check to population appears then to be want of food, arising necessarily from the different ratios according to which population and food increase. But this ultimate check is never the immediate check, except in the cases of actual famine.

The immediate check may be stated to consist in all those customs and diseases, which seem to be generated by a scarcity of the means of subsistence; and all those causes, independent of this scarcity, whether of a moral or physical nature, which tend prematurely to weaken and destroy the human frame.

These checks to population which are constantly operating with more or less force in every society, and keep down the number to the level of the means of subsistence, may be classed under two general heads—the preventative and positive checks.

The preventative check, as far as it is voluntary, is peculiar to man, and arises from that distinctive superiority in his reasoning faculties which enables him to calculate distant consequences. . . . These considerations are calculated to prevent, and certainly do prevent, a great number of persons in all civilized nations from pursuing the dictate of nature in an early attachment to one woman. . . .

The positive checks to population are extremely various, and include every cause, whether arising from vice or misery, which in any degree contributes to shorten the natural duration of human life. Under this head, therefore, may be enumerated all unwholesome occupations, severe labor and exposure to the seasons, extreme poverty, bad nursing of children, great towns, excesses of all kinds, the whole train of common diseases, and epidemics, wars, plague, and famine.

EVALUATE THE EVIDENCE

1. What does Malthus mean when he says that population will increase in a geometrical ratio and food production in an arithmetical ratio? What conclusion does he draw from this discrepancy?

2. What is the difference between "preventative" and "positive" checks on population, according to Malthus? Do they have the same effects on population growth?

3. Based on your reading in this chapter, what developments occurring in agriculture during his lifetime might have challenged Malthus's assumptions about the consequences of population growth? Are there any other changes in human society since he wrote this text that seem relevant to a reconsideration of his arguments?

Source: Thomas Robert Malthus, *Essay on the Principle of Population* (1798; London: John Murray, 1826), pp. 1–2, 6–7, 10, 12–15.

cloth. The merchant paid outworkers by the piece and sold the finished product to regional, national, or international markets.

The putting-out system grew because it had competitive advantages. Underemployed labor was abundant, and poor peasants and landless laborers would work for low wages. Since production in the countryside was unregulated, workers and merchants could change procedures and experiment as they saw fit. Because workers did not need to meet rigid guild standards, cottage industry became capable of producing many kinds of goods. Textiles; all manner of knives,

MAP 17.1 Industry and Population in Eighteenth-Century Europe

The growth of cottage manufacturing in rural areas helped country people increase their income and contributed to population growth. The putting-out system began in England, and much of the work was in the textile industry. Cottage industry was also strong in the Low Countries — modern-day Belgium and the Netherlands.

ANALYZING THE MAP What does this map suggest about the relationship between population density and the growth of textile production? What geographical characteristics seem to have played a role in encouraging this industry?

CONNECTIONS How would you account for the distribution of each type of cloth across Europe? Did metal production draw on different demographic and geographical conditions? Why do you think this was the case?

forks, and housewares; buttons and gloves; and clocks could be produced quite satisfactorily in the countryside. Although luxury goods for the rich, such as exquisite tapestries and fine porcelain, demanded special training, close supervision, and centralized workshops, the limited skills of rural industry were sufficient for everyday articles.

Rural manufacturing did not spread across Europe at an even rate. It developed most successfully in England, particularly for the spinning and weaving of woolen cloth. By 1500 half of England's textiles were produced in the countryside. By 1700 English industry was generally more rural than urban and heavily reliant on the putting-out system. Most continental countries, with the exception of Flanders and the Dutch Republic, developed rural industry more slowly. The latter part of the eighteenth century witnessed a remarkable expansion of rural industry in certain densely populated regions of continental Europe. This was in contrast to metal production, which usually occurred in areas of less dense population (Map 17.1).

The Lives of Rural Textile Workers

Until the nineteenth century the industry that employed the most people in Europe was textiles. The making of linen, woolen, and eventually cotton cloth was the typical activity of cottage workers engaged in the putting-out system. A look inside the cottage of the English weaver illustrates a way of life as well as an economic system. The rural worker lived in a small cottage with tiny windows and little space. The cottage was often a single room that served as workshop, kitchen, and bedroom. There were only a few pieces of furniture, of which the weaver's loom was by far the largest and most important. That loom changed somewhat in the early eighteenth century when John Kay's invention of the flying shuttle enabled the weaver to throw the shuttle back and forth between the threads with one hand. Aside from that improvement, however, the loom was as it had been for much of history and as it would remain until the arrival of mechanized looms in the first decades of the nineteenth century.

Handloom weaving was a family enterprise. All members of the family helped in the work, so that "every person from seven to eighty (who retained their sight and who could move their hands) could earn their bread," as one eighteenth-century English observer put it.[4] Operating the loom was usually considered a man's job, reserved for the male head of the family. Women and children worked at auxiliary tasks; they prepared the warp (vertical) threads and mounted them on the loom, wound threads on bobbins for the weft (horizontal) threads, and sometimes operated the warp frame while the father passed the shuttle.

The work of four or five spinners was needed to keep one weaver steadily employed. Since the weaver's family usually could not produce enough thread, merchants hired the wives and daughters of agricultural workers, who took on spinning work in their spare time. In England, many widows and single women also became spinners or "spinsters," so many in fact that the word became a synonym for an unmarried woman.

Relations between workers and employers were often marked by sharp conflict. (See "Thinking Like a Historian: Rural Industry: Progress or Exploitation?" on page 504.) There were constant disputes over the weights of materials and the quality of finished work. Merchants accused workers of stealing raw materials, and weavers complained that merchants delivered underweight bales.

Conditions were particularly hard for female workers. While men could earn decent wages through long hours of arduous labor, women's wages were usually much lower because they were not considered the family's primary wage earner. In England's Yorkshire wool industry, a male wool comber earned a good wage of 12 shillings or more a week, while a female spinner could hope for only 3½ shillings.[5] A single or widowed spinner faced a desperate struggle with poverty. Any period of illness or unemployment could spell disaster for her and any children she might have.

From the merchant capitalist's point of view, the problem was not low wages but maintaining control over the labor force. Cottage workers were scattered across the countryside, and their work depended on the agricultural calendar. In spring and late summer, planting and haymaking occupied all hands in the rural village, leading to shortages in the supply of thread. Merchants bitterly resented their lack of control over rural labor because their own livelihood depended on their ability to meet orders on time. They accused workers—especially female spinners—of laziness, drunkenness, and immorality. If workers failed to produce enough thread, they reasoned, it must be because their wages were too high and they had little incentive to work.

Merchants thus insisted on maintaining the lowest possible wages to force the "idle" poor into productive labor. They also lobbied for, and obtained, new police powers over workers. Imprisonment and public whipping became common punishments for pilfering small amounts of yarn or cloth. For poor workers, their right to hold on to the bits and pieces left over in the production process was akin to the traditional peasant right of gleaning in common lands. With industrial progress came the loss of traditional safeguards for the poor.

The Industrious Revolution

One scholar has used the term **industrious revolution** to summarize the social and economic changes taking place in northwestern Europe in the late seventeenth and early eighteenth centuries.[6] This occurred as households reduced leisure time, stepped up the pace of work, and, most important, redirected the labor of women and children away from the production of goods for household consumption and toward wagework. In the countryside the spread of cottage industry was one manifestation of the industrious revolution, while in the cities there was a rise in female employment outside the home. By working harder and increasing the number of wageworkers, rural and urban households could purchase more goods, even in a time of stagnant or falling real wages.

The effect of these changes is still debated. While some scholars lament the encroachment of longer work hours and stricter discipline on traditional family life, others

■ **industrious revolution** The shift that occurred as families in northwestern Europe focused on earning wages instead of producing goods for household consumption; this reduced their economic self-sufficiency but increased their ability to purchase consumer goods.

Rural Industry: Progress or Exploitation?

Eighteenth-century commentators noted the effects of the growth of rural industry on families and daily life. Some were greatly impressed by the rise in living standards made possible by the putting-out system, while others criticized the rising economic inequality between merchants and workers and the power the former acquired over the latter.

1 **Daniel Defoe's observations of English industry.** Novelist and economic writer Daniel Defoe claimed that the labor of women and children in spinning and weaving brought in as much income as or more income than the man's agricultural work, allowing the family to eat well and be warmly clothed.

～ *Being a compleat prospect of the trade of this nation, as well the home trade as the foreign*, 1728.

[A] poor labouring man that goes abroad to his Day Work, and Husbandry, Hedging, Ditching, Threshing, Carting, &c. and brings home his Week's Wages, suppose at eight Pence to twelve Pence a Day, or in some Counties less; if he has a Wife and three or four Children to feed, and who get little or nothing for themselves, must fare hard, and live poorly; 'tis easy to suppose it must be so.

But if this Man's Wife and Children can at the same Time get Employment, if at next Door, or at the next Village there lives a Clothier, or a Bay Maker, or a stuff or Drugget Weaver;* the Manufacturer sends the poor Woman combed Wool, or carded Wool every Week to spin, and she gets eight Pence or nine Pence a day at home; the Weaver sends for her two little Children, and they work by the Loom, winding, filling quills, &c. and the two bigger Girls spin at home with their Mother, and these earn three Pence or four Pence a Day each: So that put it together, the Family at Home gets as much as the Father gets Abroad, and generally more.

This alters the Case extremely, the Family feels it, they all feed better, are cloth'd warmer, and do not so easily nor so often fall into Misery and Distress; the Father gets them Food, and the Mother gets them Clothes; and as they grow, they do not run away to be Footmen and Soldiers, Thieves and Beggars or sell themselves to the Plantations to avoid the Gaol and the Gallows, but have a Trade at their Hands, and every one can get their Bread.

*Bay, stuff, and drugget were types of coarse woolen cloth typical of the inexpensive products of rural weaving.

2 **Anonymous, "The Clothier's Delight."** Couched in the voice of the ruthless cloth merchant, this song from around 1700 expresses the bitterness and resentment textile workers felt against the low wages paid by employers. One can imagine a group of weavers gathered at the local tavern singing their protest on a rare break from work.

～ Of all sorts of callings that in England be
There is none that liveth so gallant as we;
Our trading maintains us as brave as a knight,
We live at our pleasure and take our delight;
We heapeth up richest treasure great store
Which we get by griping and grinding the poor.
　And this is a way for to fill up our purse
　Although we do get it with many a curse.

Throughout the whole kingdom, in country and
　　　town,
There is no danger of our trade going down,
So long as the Comber can work with his comb,
And also the Weaver weave with his lomb;
The Tucker and Spinner that spins all the year,
We will make them to earn their wages full dear.
　And this is a way, etc.

3 **Late-eighteenth-century diary.** This diary entry from 1788 illustrates the dangers of bringing textile manufacture into the family home.

～ Fire at Isaac Hardy's, which burnt 6 lbs. of cotton, 5 pairs of stockings and set the cradle on fire, with a child in which was much burnt. It happened through the wife improvidently holding the candle under the cotton as it was drying.

ANALYZING THE EVIDENCE

1. What impression of cottage industry does the painting of the Irish linen industry in Source 4 present? How does this contrast with the impressions from the written sources?
2. Do you think the personal accounts of a diary (Source 3) or a memoir (Source 5) are more reliable sources on rural industry than a social commentator's opinion (Source 1) or a song (Source 2)? Why or why not?
3. Who was involved in the work of rural textile manufacture, and what tasks did these workers perform? How does this division of labor resemble or differ from the household in which you grew up?

4 **The linen industry in Ireland.** Many steps went into making textiles. Here the women and girls are beating away the woody part of the flax plant so that the man can comb out the soft part. The combed fibers will then be spun into thread and woven into cloth by this family enterprise. (The Stapleton Collection/ Bridgeman Images)

5 **Samuel Crompton's memories of childhood labor.** In his memoir, Samuel Crompton recalled his childhood labor in the cotton industry of the mid-eighteenth century. When he grew up, he invented the spinning mule, which greatly improved the efficiency of the process (see Chapter 20).

I recollect that soon after I was able to walk I was employed in the cotton manufacture. My mother used to bat the cotton wool on a wire riddle. It was then put into a deep brown mug with a strong ley of soap suds. My mother then tucked up my petticoats about my waist, and put me into the tub to tread upon the cotton at the bottom. When a second riddleful was batted I was lifted out, it was placed in the mug, and I again trod it down. This process was continued untill the mug became so full that I could no longer safely stand in it, when a chair was placed beside it, and I held on by the back. When the mug was quite full the soapsuds were poured off, and each separate dollop [i.e., lump] of wool well squeezed to free it from moisture. They were then placed on the bread-rack under the beams of the kitchen-loft to dry. My mother and my grand-mother carded the cotton wool by hand, taking one of the dollops at a time, on the simple hand cards. When carded they were put aside in separate parcels ready for spinning.

PUTTING IT ALL TOGETHER

Using the sources above, along with what you have learned in class and in this chapter, write an essay assessing the impact of the putting-out industry on rural families and their way of life. Make sure to consider the experiences of all members of the household.

Sources: (1) Daniel Defoe, *A Plan of the English Commerce: Being a compleat prospect of the trade of this nation, as well the home trade as the foreign* (London, 1728), pp. 90–91; (2) Paul Mantoux and Marjorie Vernon, eds., *The Industrial Revolution in the Eighteenth Century: An Outline of the Beginnings of the Modern Factory System in England* (1928; Abingdon, U.K.: Taylor and Francis, 2006), pp. 75–76; (3, 5) Ivy Pinchbeck, *Women Workers and the Industrial Revolution, 1750–1850* (1930; Abingdon, U.K.: Frank Cass, 1977), p. 114.

insist that poor families made decisions based on their own self-interest. With more finished goods becoming available at lower prices, households sought cash income to participate in an emerging consumer economy.

The role of women and girls in this new economy is particularly controversial. When women entered the labor market, they almost always worked at menial, tedious jobs for very low wages. Yet when women earned their own wages, they also seem to have exercised more independence in marriage choices and household decision making. Most of their scant earnings went for household necessities, items of food and clothing they could no longer produce now that they worked full-time, but sometimes a few shillings were left for a ribbon or a new pair of stockings. Women's use of their surplus income thus helped spur the rapid growth of the textile industries in which they labored so hard.

These new sources and patterns of labor established important foundations for the Industrial Revolution of the late eighteenth and nineteenth centuries (see Chapter 20). They created households in which all members worked for wages rather than in a family business and in which consumption relied on market-produced rather than homemade goods. It was not until the mid-nineteenth century, with rising industrial wages, that a new model emerged in which the male "breadwinner" was expected to earn enough to support the whole family and women and children were relegated back to the domestic sphere. With women estimated to compose more than 40 percent of the global workforce, today's world is experiencing a second industrious revolution in a similar climate of stagnant wages and increased demand for consumer goods.[7]

What important changes occurred in economic thought and practice in the eighteenth century?

Late-seventeenth- and eighteenth-century Europe also experienced revolutionary developments in finance and economic thought. Up to the mid-eighteenth century, governments heavily controlled the circulation of grain and the price of bread, fearing the social turmoil and political instability that would arise from food shortages. In urban areas, the **guild system** dominated production of artisanal goods, providing their masters with economic privileges as well as a proud social identity.

In the second half of the eighteenth century, political economy emerged as a new mode of thought influenced by the Enlightenment. Economic thinkers, like Adam Smith, attacked government regulations as a hindrance to innovation and competition, developing a doctrine known as economic liberalism (see "Adam Smith and Economic Liberalism" later in the chapter).

Economic Regulation and the Guilds

Given the precariousness of survival for most people, European governments believed that it was essential to regulate economic production and exchange. They feared that shortages of bread could lead to social turmoil and political upheaval, as they did many times in the hard conditions of the seventeenth century (see "Environmental, Economic, and Social Crisis" in Chapter 15). Moreover, mercantilist doctrine dictated that maintaining a trade surplus was crucial to obtain the funds necessary to build a strong state. Thus rulers believed they must impose strict production standards on industry and control access to trade to ensure that craftsmen and manufacturers produced goods of high quality, especially for export markets.

Based on these ideas, the guild system, which had emerged during the economic boom of the Middle Ages, reached its peak in most of Europe in the seventeenth and eighteenth centuries. During this period, the number of urban guilds increased dramatically in cities and towns across Europe. Authorities granted each guild a detailed set of privileges, including exclusive rights to produce and sell certain goods, access to restricted markets in raw materials, and the rights to train apprentices, hire workers, and open shops. Guilds also served social and religious functions, providing a locus of sociability and group identity to the middling classes of European cities.

To ensure there was enough work to go around, guilds restricted their membership to men who were Christians, had several years of work experience, paid membership fees, and successfully completed a masterpiece. Masters' sons enjoyed automatic access to their fathers' guilds, while outsiders—including Jews and Protestants in Catholic countries—were barred from entering. Most urban men and women worked in non-guild trades as domestic servants, manual laborers, and vendors of food, used clothing, and other goods.

While most were hostile to women, a small number of guilds did accept women. Most involved needlework and textile production, occupations that

■ **guild system** The organization of artisanal production into trade-based associations, or guilds, each of which received a monopoly over its trade and the right to train apprentices and hire workers.

were considered appropriate for women. In 1675 seamstresses gained a new all-female guild in Paris, and soon seamstresses joined tailors' guilds in parts of France, England, and the Dutch Republic. By the mid-eighteenth century male masters began to hire more female workers, often in defiance of their own guild statutes.

The Financial Revolution

Changes in overseas trade and rural industry, combined with the militaristic ambitions of European rulers, helped bring about crucial changes in economic life. In the early seventeenth century, Dutch prosperity in agriculture and overseas trade encouraged the development of new financial innovations, including short-term bonds for public credit and a maritime insurance industry. The Bank of Amsterdam (founded in 1609) issued paper money and traded bills of exchange, which facilitated merchant ventures at home and abroad. Dutch financial methods came to England when William of Orange and his wife Mary Stuart took control of the English throne in the Glorious Revolution (see "The Restoration of the English Monarchy" in Chapter 15). The Bank of England was founded in 1694 as a government-chartered joint stock company, and William used the bank as a source of credit to pursue war against the French. In subsequent decades, hundreds of new private banks were created in London and across the country to provide credit to private individuals. These innovations laid the foundations of modern banking and finance systems, a development described by historians as a "financial revolution."

Another element of this revolution was the emergence of financial speculation, enabled by the creation of stock exchanges in Amsterdam, London, and other European capitals. Speculative bubbles occurred in the Netherlands as early as the 1630s based on trading in tulip bulbs. In 1720, both England and France experienced catastrophic financial crises caused by the collapse of shares in colonial trading companies. The shock of this experience dissuaded the French from creating a national bank until the reign of Napoleon (see Chapter 20).

Adam Smith and Economic Liberalism

At the same time that cottage industry began to infringe on the livelihoods of urban artisans and new financial institutions encouraged the circulation of credit, philosophers and administrators began to develop new ways of thinking about economic production and exchange. The notion of the "economy" as a discrete entity, subject to natural laws that could be discovered by rational thought, constituted an important element of Enlightenment thought. The

Receipt from the Painters' Guild   The Guild of Saint Luke (after the patron saint of artists) was the most common name for a guild of painters and other artists in early modern Europe. This receipt to a glazier named James Cip, signed by guild officers in 1729, displays the arms of the guild and common painters' tools, including a model human head. The bull was the symbol of Saint Luke, which meant that he was often the patron saint of butchers' guilds as well. (Rijksmuseum, Amsterdam, The Netherlands/Bridgeman Images)

first university position devoted to "political economy," as the formal study of production and exchange came to be called, was occupied by Thomas Malthus in 1805, and others soon followed. In France, the Physiocrats, a distinctive group of economic thinkers, established the first large-scale explanation of the economy, what we now call a "macro-economic" model, based on land as the sole source of economic value.

Many economic thinkers in this period came to believe that the economy could best function when unimpeded by government laws. They attacked tariffs and other forms of government regulation and ridiculed guilds as outmoded and exclusionary institutions that obstructed technical innovation and progress. One of the best-known critics of government regulation of trade and industry was Adam Smith (1723–1790), a leading figure of the Scottish Enlightenment (see "Enlightenment Movements Across Europe" in Chapter 16). Smith developed the general idea of freedom of enterprise and established the basis for modern economics in his groundbreaking work *Inquiry into the Nature and Causes of the Wealth of Nations* (1776). Smith criticized guilds for their stifling restrictions, a critique he extended to all state monopolies and privileged companies. Far preferable, in his view, was free competition, which would protect consumers from price gouging and give all citizens an equal right to do what they did best. Smith advocated a more highly developed "division of labor" that entailed separating craft production into individual tasks to increase workers' speed and efficiency.

In keeping with his fear of political oppression and with the "system of natural liberty" that he championed, Smith argued that government should limit itself to "only three duties": it should provide a defense against foreign invasion, maintain civil order with courts and police protection, and sponsor certain indispensable public works and institutions that could never adequately profit private investors. He believed that the pursuit of self-interest in a competitive market would be sufficient to improve the living conditions of citizens, a view that quickly emerged as the classic argument for **economic liberalism**.

However, Smith did not advocate unbridled capitalism. Unlike many disgruntled merchant capitalists, he applauded the modest rise in real wages of British workers in the eighteenth century, stating: "No society can surely be flourishing and happy, of which the far greater part of the members are poor and miserable." Smith also acknowledged that employers were "always and everywhere in a sort of tacit, but constant and uniform combination, not to raise the wages of labor above their

actual rate" and sometimes entered "into particular combinations to sink the wages even below this rate." While he celebrated the rise in productivity allowed by the division of labor, he also acknowledged its demoralizing effects on workers and called for government intervention to raise workers' living standards.[8]

Many educated people in France, including Physiocrats and some government officials, shared Smith's ideas. In 1774, the reform-minded economics minister Anne-Robert-Jacques Turgot issued a law in the name of Louis XV, ordering the grain trade to be freed from state regulation. Two years later, another edict abolished all French guilds. Vociferous popular protest against these measures led to Turgot's disgrace shortly afterward and the cancellation of his reforms (see "Viewpoints: Opposing Views on Guilds and Economic Regulation," page 509). But the legislators of the French Revolution (see "The Thermidorian Reaction and the Directory" in Chapter 19) returned to a liberal economic agenda in 1789. The National Assembly definitively abolished guilds in 1791. Other European countries followed suit more slowly, with guilds surviving in central Europe and Italy into the second half of the nineteenth century. By the middle of the nineteenth century economic liberalism was championed by most European governments and elites.

How did empire and trade shape new economic, cultural, and social developments?

In addition to agricultural improvement, population pressure, and a growing cottage industry, the expansion of Europe in the eighteenth century was characterized by an increase in world trade. Adam Smith declared that "the discovery of America and that of a passage to the East Indies by the Cape of Good Hope, are the two greatest and most important events recorded in the history of mankind."[9] In the eighteenth century Spain and Portugal revitalized their empires and began drawing more wealth from renewed colonial development. Yet once again the countries of northwestern Europe—the Dutch Republic, France, and above all Great Britain—benefited most.

The Atlantic economy that these countries developed from 1650 to 1790 would prove crucial in the building of a global economy. Great Britain, which was formed in 1707 by the union of England and Scotland into a single kingdom, gradually became the

leading maritime power. Thus the British played the critical role in building a fairly unified Atlantic economy that provided remarkable opportunities for them and their colonists. They also competed ruthlessly with France and the Netherlands for trade and territory in the Americas and Asia.

Mercantilism and Colonial Competition

Britain's commercial leadership had its origins in mercantilist doctrine. Eventually eliciting criticism from Enlightenment thinker Adam Smith and other proponents of free trade in the late eighteenth century, European mercantilism was a system of economic regulations aimed at increasing the power of the state. As practiced by a leading figure such as Colbert under Louis XIV, mercantilism aimed particularly at creating a favorable balance of foreign trade in order to increase a country's stock of gold. A country's gold holdings

■ **economic liberalism** A belief in free trade and competition based on Adam Smith's argument that the invisible hand of free competition would benefit all individuals, rich and poor.

Influenced by Enlightenment ideas about individual liberty, some mid-eighteenth-century thinkers argued that all people should be free to practice whatever economic activity they wanted, how they wanted, subject only to the law of supply and demand. When a proponent of these views, Anne-Robert-Jacques Turgot, became controller general of France, he prevailed on the king to issue a series of edicts dismantling economic regulations and abolishing the guilds. Arguing against Turgot, the magistrates of the Parlement of Paris asserted that guilds were necessary to impose high quality standards and protect consumers from fraud.

Anne-Robert-Jacques Turgot, Royal Edict Abolishing the French Guilds, February 1776

God, by giving to men needs and making them dependent upon the resource of labor, has made the right of labor the property of all men, and that property is primary, the most sacred and the most imprescriptible of all.

We regard it as one of the first obligations of our justice . . . to emancipate our subjects from all the restraints which have been laid upon that inalienable right of humanity. Wherefore we will to abolish the arbitrary institutions which do not permit the indigent to live by their labor; which exclude the sex whose weakness implies greatest needs and fewest resources, and which seem, by condemning it to inevitable misery, to encourage seduction and debauchery; which stifle emulation and industry and make useless the talents of those whom circumstances exclude from admission to the guilds; which deprive the State and art of all the advantages which foreigners might furnish; which retard the progress of the arts by the difficulties which inventors find multiplied by the guilds . . . ; which, by means of the inordinate expenses artisans are compelled to incur in order to acquire the liberty of labor, by the exactions of all kinds they must meet, by the multiplied penalties for so-called infractions, . . . by the endless litigations which arise between the different guilds . . . , surcharge industry with an enormous tax, grievous to the subjects and with no corresponding advantage to the State; which, in short, by the facility they afford to members of the guilds to combine among themselves and to compel the poorer members of the unions to submit to the rule of the wealthy, become an instrument of monopoly

and give rise to schemes whose effect is to increase beyond all natural proportion the price of commodities which are indispensable to the subsistence of the people.

Parlement of Paris, Argument Against the Edict Suppressing the Guilds, March 1776

The law has wished to prevent fraud of all kinds and to remedy all abuses; the law watches equally over the interest of the buyer and the seller; it maintains mutual confidence between the two. . . . The guilds can be considered so many small republics occupied solely with the general interest of all the members that compose them; and if it is true that the general interest results from the union of the interests of each particular individual, it is equally true that each member, in working for his own personal advantage, works necessarily, even without wishing to, for the true advantage of the whole community. To unloose the springs that move this multitude of different bodies, to annihilate the guilds, to abolish the regulations . . . is to destroy all the various means which commerce itself must desire for its own preservation. Every manufacturer, every skilled artisan, every worker will see himself as an isolated being dependent on himself alone and free to indulge all the flights of an often disordered imagination. All subordination will be destroyed . . . thirst for gain will dominate all the workshops; and since honesty is not always the surest way to fortune, the entire public, . . . will be the constant dupes of artful methods secretly prepared to blind and seduce them.

QUESTIONS FOR ANALYSIS

1. On what grounds does Turgot criticize the guilds? Why would considering labor as a form of property support these criticisms?
2. Why did the magistrates of the Parlement think guilds were a necessary social institution?
3. Based on these passages, what was the most important value that each side defended?

Sources: Robert Perry Shepherd, *Turgot and the Six Edicts* (New York: Columbia University Press, 1903), pp. 121–122; Keith Michael Baker, ed., *University of Chicago Readings in Western Civilization*, vol. 7: *The Old Regime and the French Revolution* (Chicago: University of Chicago Press, 1987).

served as an all-important treasure chest that could be opened periodically to pay for war in a violent age.

The desire to increase both military power and private wealth led England's rulers to impose the mercantile system of the **Navigation Acts**. Oliver Cromwell established the first of these laws in 1651, and the restored monarchy of Charles II extended them in 1660 and 1663. The acts required that most goods imported from Europe into England and Scotland (Great Britain after 1707) be carried on British-owned ships with British crews or on ships of the country producing the articles. Moreover, these laws gave British merchants and shipowners a virtual monopoly on trade with British colonies. The colonists were required to ship their products on British (or U.S.) ships and to buy almost all European goods from Britain. It was believed that these economic regulations would eliminate foreign competition, thereby helping British merchants and workers as well as colonial plantation owners and farmers. It was hoped, too, that the emerging British Empire would develop a shipping industry with a large number of experienced seamen who could serve during wartime in the Royal Navy.

The Navigation Acts were a form of economic warfare. Their initial target was the Dutch, who were far ahead of the English in shipping and foreign trade in the mid-seventeenth century (see "The Dutch Republic in the Seventeenth Century" in Chapter 15). In conjunction with three Anglo-Dutch wars between 1652 and 1674, the Navigation Acts seriously damaged Dutch shipping and commerce. The British seized the thriving Dutch colony of New Amsterdam in 1664 and renamed it New York. By the late seventeenth century, the Dutch Republic was falling behind England in shipping, trade, and colonies.

Thereafter France stood clearly as England's most serious rival in the competition for overseas empire. Rich in natural resources, with a population three or four times that of England, and allied with Spain, continental Europe's leading military power was already building a powerful fleet and a worldwide system of rigidly monopolized colonial trade. Thus from 1701 to 1763 Britain and France were locked in a series of wars to decide, in part, which nation would become the leading maritime power and claim the profits of Europe's overseas expansion (Map 17.2).

The first round was the War of the Spanish Succession (see "Louis XIV's Wars" in Chapter 15), which started in 1701 when Louis XIV accepted the Spanish Crown willed to his grandson. Besides upsetting the

continental balance of power, a union of France and Spain threatened to encircle and destroy the British colonies in North America (see Map 17.2). Defeated by a great coalition of states after twelve years of fighting, Louis XIV was forced in the Peace of Utrecht (YOO-trehkt) in 1713 to cede his North American holdings in Newfoundland, Nova Scotia, and the Hudson Bay territory to Britain. Spain was compelled to give Britain control of its West African slave trade — the so-called *asiento* (ah-SYEHN-toh) — and to let Britain send one ship of merchandise into the Spanish colonies annually.

Conflict continued among the European powers over both domestic and colonial affairs. The War of the Austrian Succession (1740–1748), which started when Frederick the Great of Prussia seized Silesia from Austria's Maria Theresa (see "Frederick the Great of Prussia" in Chapter 16), gradually became a world war that included Anglo-French conflicts in India and North America. The war ended with no change in the territorial situation in North America. This inconclusive standoff helped set the stage for the Seven Years' War (1756–1763; see Chapter 19). In central Europe, France aided Austria's Maria Theresa in her quest to win back Silesia from the Prussians, who had formed an alliance with England. In North America, French and British settlers engaged in territorial skirmishes that eventually resulted in an all-out war that drew in Native American allies on both sides of the conflict (see Map 19.1). By 1763 Prussia had held off the Austrians, and British victory on all colonial fronts was ratified in the **Treaty of Paris**. British naval power, built in large part on the rapid growth of the British shipping industry after the passage of the Navigation Acts, had triumphed decisively: Britain had realized its goal of monopolizing a vast trading and colonial empire.

The Atlantic Economy

As the volume of transatlantic trade increased, the regions bordering the ocean were increasingly drawn into an integrated economic system. Commercial exchange in the Atlantic has often been referred to as the "triangle trade," designating a three-way transport of goods: European commodities, like guns and textiles, to Africa; enslaved Africans to the colonies; and colonial goods, such as cotton, tobacco, and sugar, back to Europe (see Map 17.2).

Over the course of the eighteenth century, the economies of European nations bordering the Atlantic Ocean, especially England, relied more and more on colonial exports. In England, sales to the mainland colonies of North America and the West Indian

■ **Navigation Acts** A series of English laws that controlled the import of goods to Britain and British colonies.

■ **Treaty of Paris** The treaty that ended the Seven Years' War in Europe and the colonies in 1763 and that ratified British victory on all colonial fronts.

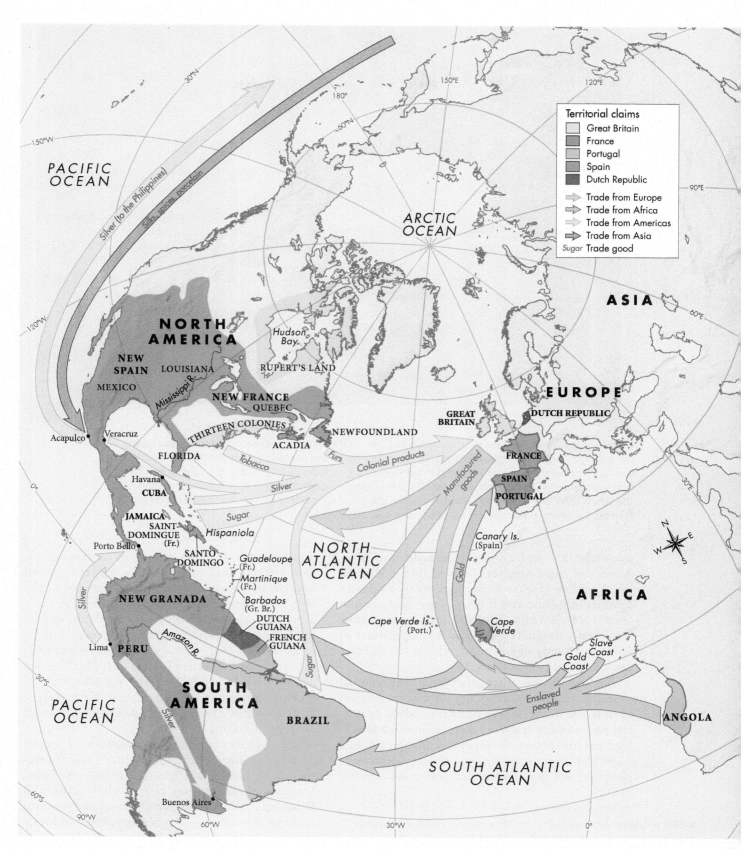

MAP 17.2 The Atlantic Economy in 1701   The growth of trade encouraged both economic development and military conflict in the Atlantic basin. Four continents were linked together by the exchange of goods and people.

Siege of the French Fortress of Louisbourg in 1745   In the eighteenth century, European wars were increasingly waged in overseas theaters. The so-called War of the Austrian Succession (1740–1748) saw hostilities between France and England in North America, including a British assault on the French fort of Louisbourg (on Cape Breton Island) in 1745. French-English rivalry in North America culminated in the Seven Years' War (1756–1763), which led to the loss of most French territory, with the exception of France's Caribbean holdings. (Peter Newark American Pictures/Bridgeman Images)

sugar islands — with an important assist from West Africa and Latin America — soared from £500,000 to £4 million (Figure 17.3). Exports to England's colonies in Ireland and India also rose substantially from 1700 to 1800. By 1800 sales to European countries — England's traditional trading partners — represented only one-third of exports, down from two-thirds a century earlier.

England also benefited from importing colonial products. Colonial monopolies allowed the English to obtain a steady supply of such goods at beneficial prices and to re-export them to other nations at high profits. Moreover, many colonial goods, like sugar and tobacco, required processing before consumption and thus contributed new manufacturing

jobs in England. In the eighteenth century, stimulated by trade and empire building, England's capital city, London, grew into the West's largest and richest city. Thus the mercantilist system of foreign trade achieved remarkable success for England, and by the 1770s the country stood on the threshold of the epoch-making changes that would become known as the Industrial Revolution (see Chapter 20). This was also the period when Adam Smith and other political economists began to criticize mercantilism and argue for free trade as a means to increase prosperity for all people and nations.

Although they lost many possessions to the English in the Seven Years' War, the French still profited enormously from colonial trade. The colonies of Saint-Domingue (modern-day Haiti), Martinique, and Guadeloupe remained in French hands and provided immense fortunes in plantation agriculture and trading in enslaved people during the second half of the eighteenth century. By 1789 the population of Saint-Domingue included five hundred thousand enslaved people whose labor had allowed the colony to become the world's leading producer of coffee and sugar and the

■ **debt peonage**   A form of serfdom that allowed a planter or rancher to keep workers in perpetual debt bondage by periodically advancing food, shelter, and a little money.

■ **transatlantic slave trade**   The forced migration of Africans across the Atlantic for enslaved labor on plantations and in other industries; the trade reached its peak in the eighteenth century and ultimately involved more than 12 million Africans.

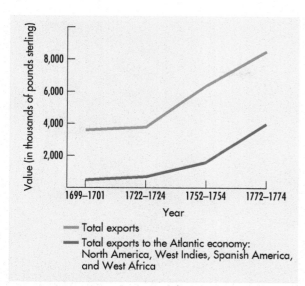

FIGURE 17.3 Exports of English Manufactured Goods, 1700–1774   While trade between England and Europe stagnated after 1700, English exports to Africa and the Americas boomed and greatly stimulated English economic development.
(Source: Data from R. Davis, "English Foreign Trade, 1700–1774," *Economic History Review*, 2d ser., 15 [1962]: 302–303.)

most profitable plantation colony in the New World.[10] The wealth generated from colonial trade fostered the confidence of the merchant classes in Paris, Bordeaux, and other large cities, and merchants soon joined other elite groups clamoring for political reforms.

The third major player in the Atlantic economy, Spain, also saw its colonial fortunes improve during the eighteenth century under the leadership of the new Bourbon dynasty. Not only did it gain Louisiana from France in 1763, but its influence expanded westward all the way to northern California through the efforts of Spanish missionaries and ranchers. Shipping and trade grew rapidly within the empire, reaching a peak in the 1780s. The policies of the Bourbon administrators, including tax incentives, increased investments, and the application of scientific methods, contributed to a boom in silver production, which had dropped significantly in the seventeenth century.

Silver mining also stimulated food production for the mining camps, and wealthy Spanish landowners developed a system of **debt peonage** to keep Indigenous workers on their estates to grow food for this market. Under this system, which was similar to serfdom, a planter or rancher would keep workers in perpetual debt bondage by advancing them food, shelter, and a little money.

Although the "triangle trade" model highlights some of the most important flows of commerce across the Atlantic, it significantly oversimplifies the picture. For example, a brisk intercolonial trade also existed, with the Caribbean colonies importing food in the form of fish, flour, and livestock from the northern

colonies and rice from the south, in exchange for sugar and enslaved people (see Map 17.2). Many colonial traders also violated imperial monopolies to trade with the most profitable partners, regardless of nationality. Moreover, the Atlantic economy was inextricably linked to trade with the Indian and Pacific Oceans (see "Trade and Empire in Asia and the Pacific" at the end of this chapter).

The Transatlantic Slave Trade

At the core of the Atlantic world were the misery and profit of the **transatlantic slave trade**. The forced migration and enslavement of millions of Africans was a key element in the Atlantic system and in western European economic expansion throughout the eighteenth century. The brutal practice intensified dramatically after 1700 and especially after 1750 with the growth of trade and demand for goods like sugar and cotton that were produced by enslaved men, women, and children. According to the most authoritative source, European traders purchased and shipped 6.5 million enslaved Africans across the Atlantic between 1701 and 1800 — more than half of the estimated total of 12.5 million Africans forcibly transported between 1450 and 1900, of whom 15 percent died in the wretched conditions of capture and transport.[11]

The rise of plantation agriculture was responsible for the tremendous growth of the slave trade. Among all European colonies, the plantations of Portuguese Brazil received by far the largest number of enslaved Africans over the entire period of the slave trade — 45 percent of the total. Another 45 percent were divided among the many Caribbean colonies. The colonies of mainland North America took only 3 percent of enslaved people arriving from Africa, a little under four hundred thousand.

Eighteenth-century intensification of the slave trade resulted in fundamental changes in its organization. After 1700, as Britain became the undisputed leader in shipping enslaved people across the Atlantic, European governments and ship captains cut back on fighting among themselves and concentrated on commerce. They generally adopted the shore method of trading, which was less expensive than maintaining fortified trading posts. Under this system, European ships sent boats ashore to trade with African dealers or invited dealers

Plantation Zones, ca. 1700

The Transatlantic Slave Trade This eighteenth-century French engraving depicts the brutal treatment of enslaved people in transit across the Atlantic and upon arrival in the colonies. The image on the bottom reproduces a famous engraving, *Description of a Slave Ship*, published in 1789 by the British Society for Effecting the Abolition of the Slave Trade. At the top, a small child in the foreground is surrounded by slave drivers, while a large crowd of captives, newly embarked from the ship at harbor on the right, is led toward the plantation. This image testifies to the international circulation of imagery among abolition activists. (Musée des Arts d'Afrique et d'Océanie, Paris, France/Bridgeman Images)

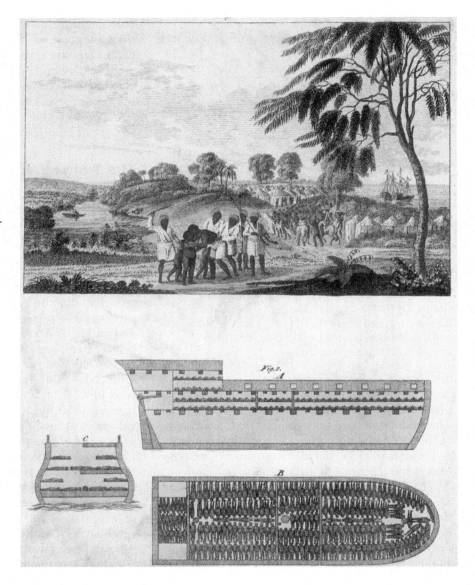

to bring traders and the enslaved out to their ships. This method was advantageous for traders because it allowed ships to move easily along the coast from market to market and to depart more quickly for the Americas.

Some African merchants and rulers who controlled exports profited from the greater demand for captive laborers. With their newfound wealth, they gained access to European and colonial goods, including firearms. But generally such economic returns did not spread very far, and the negative consequences of the expanding slave trade predominated. Wars among African states to obtain salable captives increased, and leaders used profits to purchase more arms than textiles and consumer goods. While the populations of Europe and Asia grew substantially in the eighteenth century, the population of Africa stagnated or possibly declined. As one contemporary critic observed:

I do not know if coffee and sugar are essential to the happiness of Europe, but I know that these two products have accounted for the unhappiness of two great regions of the world: America has been depopulated so as to have land on which to plant them; Africa has been depopulated so as to have the people to cultivate them.[12]

Most Europeans did not personally witness the horrors of the slave trade between Africa and the Americas, and until the early part of the eighteenth century they considered it to be a legitimate business. But as details of the plight of enslaved people became known, a campaign to abolish slavery developed in Britain. In the late 1780s the abolition campaign grew into a mass movement of public opinion, the first in British history. British women were prominent in this movement, denouncing the immorality of human bondage and stressing the cruel and sadistic treatment of enslaved women and families. These attacks put the defenders of slavery on the defensive. In 1807 Parliament abolished the British slave trade, although slavery continued in British colonies and the Americas for decades.

Identities and Communities of the Atlantic World

As contacts between the Atlantic coasts of the Americas, Africa, and Europe became more frequent, and as European settlements grew into well-established colonies, new identities and communities emerged. The term *Creole* referred to people of Spanish ancestry born in the Americas. Wealthy Creoles and their counterparts throughout the Atlantic colonies prided themselves on following European ways of life. In addition to their lavish plantation estates, they maintained townhouses in colonial cities built on the European model, with theaters, central squares, churches, and coffeehouses. They purchased luxury goods made in Europe, and their children were often sent to be educated in the home country.

Over time, however, the colonial elite came to feel that their circumstances gave them different interests and characteristics from those of their home population. As one observer explained, "A turn of mind peculiar to the planter, occasioned by a physical difference of constitution, climate, customs, and education, tends . . . to repress the remains of his former attachment to his native soil."[13] Colonial elites became "Americanized" by adopting native foods, like chocolate and potatoes, and sought relief from tropical disease in native remedies. Creole traders and planters, along with their counterparts in English colonies, increasingly resented the regulations and taxes imposed by colonial bureaucrats. Such resentment would eventually lead to revolution against colonial powers (see Chapter 19).

Not all Europeans in the colonies were wealthy; indeed, many arrived as indentured servants and had to labor for several years before acquiring freedom. Numerous poor or middling whites worked as clerks, shopkeepers, craftsmen, and, in North America, farmers and laborers. With the exception of British North America, white Europeans made up a minority of the population; they were outnumbered in Spanish America by Indigenous people and in the Caribbean and Brazil by the growing numbers of enslaved people of African descent. Since European migrants were disproportionately male, much of the population of the Atlantic world descended from unions — often forced — of European men and Indigenous or African women (see "Evaluating Visual Evidence: New

Ideas About Race and Identity," page 516). Colonial attempts to identify and control racial categories greatly influenced developing Enlightenment thought on racial difference (see "Enlightenment Debates About Race" in Chapter 16).

Multiracial people sometimes rose to the colonial elite. The Spanish conquistadors often consolidated their power through marriage to the daughters of local rulers, and their descendants were among the most powerful inhabitants of Spanish America. In the Spanish and French Caribbean, as in Brazil, many enslavers acknowledged and freed their biracial children, leading to sizable populations of free people of color. Advantaged by their fathers, some became wealthy in their own right. In the second half of the eighteenth century, the prosperity of some free people of color motivated the white population of Saint-Domingue to pass new race laws prohibiting people of color from marrying white people and forcing them to adopt distinctive attire.

British colonies followed a distinctive pattern. There, whole families, rather than individual men, migrated, resulting in a rapid increase in the white population. This development was favored by British colonial law, which forbade marriage between English men and women and Africans or Native Americans. In the British colonies of the Caribbean and the southern mainland, enslavers tended to leave their biracial progeny in slavery rather than freeing them, maintaining a stark discrepancy between free whites and enslaved people of color.[14] The identities inspired by the Atlantic world were equally complex. In some ways, the colonial encounter helped create new and more fixed forms of identity. Europeans whose loyalties had been to their towns and regions came to see themselves as "Spanish" or "English" when they crossed the Atlantic; similarly, their colonial governments imposed the identity of "Indian" and "African" on peoples with vastly different linguistic, cultural, and political origins. The result was the creation of new multiracial groups and communities that melded cultural and social elements of many different Indigenous and African groups with the new European cultures.

Spanish administrators applied "purity of blood" (*limpieza de sangre*) laws — originally used to exclude Jews and Muslims during the *reconquista* (Christian reconquest of Spain) — to Indigenous and African people.[15] The status of multiracial people in the Spanish colonies was ambiguous. Some people of European and Indigenous descent sought to enter Creole society and obtain its many official and unofficial privileges by passing as white. Over time, free people of color came to constitute a significant portion of the population and were intimately connected with the dominant society both in the colonies and

New Ideas About Race and Identity

When Spanish settlers came to the Americas, they brought with them the religious and racial prejudices of the old country. One of the most important of these was the doctrine of *limpieza de sangre*, or purity of blood. It was originally adopted during the reconquista to refer to Spaniards whose ancestors had always been Christian and were therefore not tainted (in their eyes) by the blood of Jewish or Muslim converts. After the conquest, the Spanish applied this notion in the Americas; because they had never been exposed to Christianity, the Spanish reasoned, Indigenous people could not be considered impure like Jews and Muslims. By contrast, the Spanish considered Africans to be heretics because they — like Muslims and Jews — had refused the word of Christ in the Old World. These distinctions help explain why the Spanish officially banned the enslavement of Indigenous people in 1542, a prohibition that did not prevent the ongoing exploitation of Indigenous people throughout the Spanish Empire.

Despite these obsessions with racial purity, male conquistadors formed unions with women of high-ranking Indigenous families as soon as Spanish colonization began. During the sixteenth century, the Spanish brought 35,000 enslaved Africans to Mexico, and some of them had children with Spanish or Indigenous people, creating additional racial categories. Many of these unions were coerced, with Spanish men forcibly taking concubines among Indigenous women and enslaved women of African descent. In addition, the fact that children inherited their legal status from their mothers encouraged enslaved African men to seek wives among Indigenous and mestiza women. Defying the neat boundaries that were supposed to exist between racial categories, the children born of these unions were viewed with suspicion by state and religious officials, and they suffered from a range of discriminatory laws.

An elaborate terminology emerged to describe the many possible combinations of Native American, African, and European ancestry, which were known collectively as *castas*. This painting belongs to a genre, known as casta paintings, that emerged in the late seventeenth century in Mexico

De Chino cambujoy dIndia ; Loba

(Index Fototeca/Bridgeman Images)

depicting multiracial couples and their children. This genre reflects the ambivalent fascination inspired by the new categories of race and identity that arose in Spanish America.

EVALUATE THE EVIDENCE

1. What does this image suggest about the interaction of people of different races in Spanish America, and the new ideas about race that emerged as a result of this interaction?

2. Who do you think the audience might have been for such images, and why would viewers find them fascinating?

3. What elements of this chapter might suggest that this is a romanticized or idealized depiction of relations among different racial and ethnic groups?

in Europe through ties of family, work, and property ownership.

Converting Indigenous people to Christianity was an important goal for European powers in the New World. Galvanized by the Protestant Reformation and the perceived need to protect and spread Catholicism, Catholic powers actively sponsored missionary efforts. Jesuits, Franciscans, Dominicans, and other religious orders established missions throughout Spanish, Portuguese, and French colonies (see "Religious Conversion" in Chapter 14). In Central and South America, large-scale conversion forged enduring Catholic cultures in Portuguese and Spanish colonies. Conversion efforts in North America were less effective because Indigenous settlements were more scattered and Indigenous people were less integrated into colonial communities. On the whole, Protestants were less active as missionaries in this period, although some dissenters, like Moravians, Quakers, and Methodists, sought converts among Indigenous and enslaved people. (See "Individuals in Society: Rebecca Protten," page 518.)

The practice of slavery reveals important limitations on efforts to spread Christianity. Enslavers often refused baptism, fearing that enslaved people would use Christian status to claim additional rights. In some areas — particularly in the Caribbean, where the majority of enslaved people were born in Africa — African religious beliefs and practices endured, often incorporated with Christian traditions.

Restricted from owning land and holding many occupations in Europe, Jews were eager participants in the new Atlantic economy and established a network of mercantile communities along its trade routes. As in the Old World, Jews in European colonies faced discrimination; for example, restrictions existed on the number of enslaved people they could own in Barbados in the early eighteenth century.[16] Jews were considered to be white Europeans and thus ineligible to be enslaved, but they did not enjoy equal status with Christians.

The Atlantic Enlightenment

Enlightenment ideas crisscrossed the Atlantic and were developed in a process of exchange that included thinkers of European, Indigenous, and African ancestry (see Chapter 16). Enlightenment ideas of liberty, for example, drew on Europeans' observation of the personal freedom enjoyed by Indigenous people and their communitarian forms of governance. One example was Roger Williams, founder of Rhode Island and an early advocate for religious toleration and the separation of church and state, whose ideas directly influenced John Locke. After spending time with the Narragansett

and Wampanoag near Massachusetts Bay Colony, Williams returned to London in 1643, where he published a book explaining Narragansett language and culture and using the example of consensus building among their leaders to argue in favor of participatory governance. In another example, French missionaries recorded the criticisms they heard from Indigenous people about the selfishness, overly rigid legal and religious rules, and drive to dominate other people that they witnessed among the French. Missionaries' letters and memoirs discussing these criticisms became bestsellers in Europe and were cited by philosophers such as Montesquieu and Voltaire. A third example is Ottobah Cugoano. Alongside other formerly enslaved writers, Cugoano drew on Locke's idea of personal freedom to draw the conclusion that Locke himself had denied: that freedom applied to all people, including those of African descent. Such arguments formed the basis of the antislavery movement that emerged in the late eighteenth century.

Colonists in British North America were also influenced by the Scottish Enlightenment, with its emphasis on pragmatic approaches to the problems of life. Echoing the Scottish model, leaders in the colonies adopted a moderate, "commonsense" version of the Enlightenment that emphasized self-improvement and ethical conduct. In most cases, this version of the Enlightenment was perfectly compatible with religion and was chiefly spread through the growing colleges and universities of the colonies, which remained church-based institutions.

The Bourbon dynasty that took power in Spain in the early eighteenth century followed its own course of enlightened absolutism, just like its counterparts in the rest of Europe (see "What impact did new ways of thinking have on politics?" in Chapter 16). Under King Carlos III (r. 1759–1788) and his son Carlos IV (r. 1788–1808), Spanish administrators attempted to strengthen colonial rule by posting a standing army in the colonies and increasing royal taxes. They also ordered officials to gather more accurate information about the colonies as a basis for improving the government. Administrators debated the status of Indigenous peoples and whether it would be better for these people (and for the prosperity of Spanish America) if they maintained their distinct legal status or were integrated into Spanish society. Indigenous people actively participated in debates about their rights and standing through petitions, lawsuits, and published texts.

Educated Creoles avidly followed new currents of thought, and the universities, newspapers, and salons of Spanish America produced their own reform ideas. The establishment of a mining school in Mexico City in 1792, the first in the Spanish colonies, illuminates

INDIVIDUALS IN SOCIETY

Rebecca Protten

In the mid-1720s a young English-speaking girl who came to be known as Rebecca traveled by ship from Antigua to the small Danish sugar colony of St. Thomas, today part of the U.S. Virgin Islands. Eighty-five percent of St. Thomas's four thousand inhabitants were of African descent, almost all enslaved. Sugar plantations demanded backbreaking work, and enslavers used extremely brutal methods to maintain control, including amputations and beheadings for runaways.

Surviving documents indicate that Rebecca was of European and African ancestry. A wealthy Dutch planter named van Beverhout purchased the girl for his household staff, sparing her a position in the grueling and deadly sugar fields. Rebecca won the family's favor, and they taught her to read, write, and speak Dutch. They also shared with her their Protestant faith and took the unusual step of emancipating her from slavery.

As a free woman, Rebecca continued to work as a servant for the van Beverhouts and to study the Bible and spread its message of spiritual freedom. In 1736 she met some missionaries for the Moravian Church, a German-Protestant sect that emphasized emotion and communal worship and devoted its mission work to the enslaved peoples of the Caribbean. The missionaries were struck by Rebecca's piety and her potential to assist their work. As one wrote: "She researches diligently in the Scriptures, loves the Savior, and does much good for other Negro women because she does not simply walk alone with her good ways but instructs them in the Scriptures as well." A letter Rebecca sent to Moravian women in Germany declared: "Oh how good is the Lord. My heart melts when I think of it. His name is wonderful. Oh! Help me to praise him, who has pulled me out of the darkness. I will take up his cross with all my heart and follow the example of his poor life."*

Rebecca soon took charge of the Moravians' female missionary work. Every Sunday and every evening after work, she would walk for miles to lead meetings with enslaved and free Black women. The meetings consisted of reading and writing lessons, prayers, hymns, a sermon, and individual discussions in which she encouraged her new sisters in their spiritual growth.

In 1738 Rebecca married a German Moravian missionary, Matthaus Freundlich, a rare but not illegal case of biracial marriage. The same year, her husband bought a plantation, with enslaved laborers, to serve as the headquarters of their mission work. The Moravians — and presumably Rebecca herself — wished to spread Christian faith among enslaved people and improve their treatment, but did not oppose the institution of slavery itself.

Authorities nonetheless feared that enslaved people who were baptized and literate would agitate for freedom, and

A portrait of Rebecca Protten with her second husband and their daughter, Anna-Maria. (Courtesy of Jon F. Sensbach. Used by permission of the Moravian Archives [Unity Archives, Herrnhut, Germany], GS-393)

they imprisoned Rebecca and Matthaus and tried to shut down the mission. Only the unexpected arrival on St. Thomas of German aristocrat and Moravian leader Count Zinzendorf saved the couple. Exhausted by their ordeal, they left for Germany in 1741 accompanied by their small daughter, but both father and daughter died soon after their arrival.

In Marienborn, a German center of the Moravian faith, Rebecca encountered other Moravians of African descent, who lived in equality alongside their European brethren. In 1746 she married another missionary, Christian Jacob Protten, son of a Danish sailor and, on his mother's side, grandson of a West African king. She and another female missionary from St. Thomas were ordained as deaconesses, probably making them the first women of color to be ordained in the Western Christian Church.

In 1763 Rebecca and her husband set out for her husband's birthplace, the Danish slave trade fort at Christiansborg (in what is now Accra, Ghana), to establish a school for multiracial children. Her husband died in 1769, leaving Rebecca a widow once more. After declining the offer of passage back to the West Indies in 1776, she died in obscurity near Christiansborg in 1780.

QUESTIONS FOR ANALYSIS

1. Why did Moravian missionaries assign such an important leadership role to Rebecca? What particular attributes did she offer?
2. Why did Moravians, including Rebecca, accept the institution of slavery instead of fighting to end it?
3. What does Rebecca's story teach us about the Atlantic world of the mid-eighteenth century?

*Quotations from Jon F. Sensbach, *Rebecca's Revival: Creating Black Christianity in the Atlantic World* (Cambridge, Mass.: Harvard University Press, 2006), pp. 61, 63.

Colonel James Tod of the East India Company Traveling by Elephant Through Rajasthan, India
By the end of the eighteenth century agents of the British East India Company exercised growing military and political authority in India, in addition to monopolizing Britain's lucrative economic trade with the subcontinent. (Victoria & Albert Museum, London, UK/Bridgeman Images)

the practical achievements of reformers. As in other European colonies, one effect of Enlightenment thought was to encourage Creoles to criticize the policies of the mother country and aspire toward greater autonomy. Thus efforts to administer, control, and resist empire played a key role in the development of Enlightenment thought.

Trade and Empire in Asia and the Pacific

As the Atlantic economy took shape, Europeans continued to vie for dominance in the Asian trade. Between 1500 and 1600 the Portuguese had become major players in the Indian Ocean trading world, eliminating Venice as Europe's chief supplier of spices and other Asian luxury goods. The Portuguese dominated but did not fundamentally alter the age-old pattern of Indian Ocean trade, which involved merchants from many areas as more or less autonomous players. This situation changed radically with the intervention of the Dutch and then the English.

Formed in 1602, the Dutch East India Company had taken control of the Portuguese spice trade in the Indian Ocean, with the port of Batavia (Jakarta) in Java as its center of operations. Within a few decades the Dutch had expelled the Portuguese from Ceylon and other East Indian islands. Unlike the Portuguese, the Dutch transformed the Indian Ocean trading world. Whereas East Indian states and peoples maintained independence under the Portuguese, who treated them as autonomous business partners, the Dutch established outright control over local people.

After these successes, the Dutch hold in Asia faltered in the eighteenth century because the company failed to diversify to meet changing consumption patterns. Spices continued to compose much of its shipping, despite their declining importance in the European diet, probably due to changing fashions in food and luxury consumption. Fierce competition from its main rival, the British East India Company (established 1600), also severely undercut Dutch trade.

Britain initially struggled for a foothold in Asia. With the Dutch monopolizing maritime trade in the Indian Ocean, the British sought to establish trading relations with rulers on the subcontinent of India, the source of lucrative trade in silks, textiles,

India, 1805

and pepper. Throughout the seventeenth century the British East India Company relied on trade concessions from the powerful Mughal emperor, who granted only piecemeal access to the subcontinent. Finally, in 1716 the Mughals conceded empire-wide trading privileges. As Mughal power waned, British East India Company agents increasingly intervened in local affairs and made alliances or waged war against Indian princes.

Britain's great rival for influence in India was France. During the War of the Austrian Succession, British and French forces in India supported opposing rulers in local power struggles. In 1757 East India Company forces under Robert Clive conquered the rich northeastern province of Bengal at the Battle of Plassey. French-English rivalry was finally resolved by the Treaty of Paris, which granted all of France's possessions in India to the British with the exception of Pondicherry, an Indian Ocean port city. With the elimination of their rival, British ascendancy in India accelerated. In 1765 the Mughal ruler granted the East India Company *diwani*, the right to civil administration and tax collection, in Bengal and neighboring provinces. By the early nineteenth century the company had overcome vigorous Indian resistance to gain economic and political dominance of much of the subcontinent; direct administration by the British government replaced East India Company rule after a large-scale rebellion in 1857.

The late eighteenth century also witnessed the beginning of British settlement of the continent of Australia. The continent was first sighted by Europeans in the early seventeenth century, and thereafter parts of the coast were charted by European ships. Captain James Cook, who charted much of the Pacific Ocean for the first time, claimed the east coast of Australia for England in 1770, naming it New South Wales. The first colony was established there in the late 1780s, relying on the labor of convicted prisoners forcibly transported from Britain. Settlement of the western portion of the continent followed in the 1790s. The first colonies struggled for survival and, after an initial period of friendly relations, soon aroused the hostility and resistance of Aboriginal people. Cook himself was killed by Indigenous people in Hawaii in 1779.

The rising economic and political power of Europeans in this period drew on the connections they established between the Asian and Atlantic trade worlds. An outstanding example is the trade in cowrie shells. These seashells, originating in the Maldive Islands in the Indian Ocean, were used as a form of currency in West Africa. European traders obtained them in Asia and packed them alongside porcelains, spices, and silks for the journey home. The cowries were then brought from European ports to the West African coast to be traded for enslaved people. Indian textiles were also prized in Africa and played a similar role in exchange. Thus the trade of the Atlantic was inseparable from Asian commerce, and Europeans played an increasingly central role in commerce in both worlds.

NOTES

1. B. H. Slicher van Bath, *The Agrarian History of Western Europe, A.D. 500–1850* (New York: St. Martin's Press, 1963), p. 240.
2. Quoted in Paul Mantoux, *The Industrial Revolution in the Eighteenth Century: An Outline of the Beginnings of the Modern Factory System* (1961; Abingdon, U.K.: Routledge, 2005), p. 175.
3. Thomas Salmon, *Modern History: Or the Present State of All Nations* (London, 1730), p. 406.
4. Quoted in I. Pinchbeck, *Women Workers and the Industrial Revolution, 1750–1850* (1930; Abingdon, U.K.: Frank Cass, 1977), p. 113.
5. Richard J. Soderlund, "'Intended as a Terror to the Idle and Profligate': Embezzlement and the Origins of Policing in the Yorkshire Worsted Industry, c. 1750–1777," *Journal of Social History* 31 (Spring 1998): 658.
6. Jan de Vries, *The Industrious Revolution: Consumer Behavior and the Household Economy, 1650 to the Present* (Cambridge: Cambridge University Press, 2008).
7. Jan de Vries, "The Industrial Revolution and the Industrious Revolution," *Journal of Economic History* 54, no. 2 (June 1994): 249–270; discusses the industrious revolution of the second half of the twentieth century.
8. R. Heilbroner, *The Essential Adam Smith* (New York: W. W. Norton, 1986), p. 196.
9. S. Pollard and C. Holmes, eds., *Documents of European Economic History*, vol. 1: *The Process of Industrialization, 1750–1870* (New York: St. Martin's Press, 1968), p. 281.
10. Laurent Dubois and John D. Garrigus, *Slave Revolution in the Caribbean, 1789–1904* (New York: Palgrave, 2006), p. 8.
11. Figures obtained from Voyages: The Trans-Atlantic Slave Trade Database, http://www.slavevoyages.org/assessment/estimates (accessed January 17, 2016).
12. Quoted in Thomas Benjamin, *The Atlantic World: Europeans, Africans, Indians and Their Shared History, 1400–1900* (Cambridge: Cambridge University Press, 2009), p. 211.
13. Pierre Marie François Paget, *Travels Round the World in the Years 1767, 1768, 1769, 1770, 1771*, vol. 1 (London, 1793), p. 262.
14. Orlando Patterson, *Slavery and Social Death* (Cambridge, Mass.: Harvard University Press, 1982), p. 255.
15. Tamar Herzog, "Identities and Processes of Identification in the Atlantic World," in *The Oxford Handbook of the Atlantic World, 1450–1850*, ed. Nicholas Canny and Philip Morgan (Oxford: Oxford University Press, 2011), pp. 480–491.
16. Erik R. Seeman, "Jews in the Early Modern Atlantic: Crossing Boundaries, Keeping Faith," in *The Atlantic in Global History, 1500–2000*, ed. Jorge Cañizares-Esguerra and Erik R. Seeman (Upper Saddle River, N.J.: Pearson Prentice Hall, 2007), p. 43.

LOOKING BACK LOOKING AHEAD

By the turn of the eighteenth century, western Europe had begun to shake off the effects of a century of famine, disease, warfare, economic depression, and demographic stagnation. The eighteenth century witnessed a breakthrough in agricultural production that, along with improved infrastructure and the retreat of epidemic disease, contributed to a substantial increase in population. One crucial catalyst for agricultural innovation was the Scientific Revolution, which provided new tools of empirical observation and experimentation. The Enlightenment as well, with its emphasis on progress and public welfare, convinced government officials, scientists, and informed landowners to seek better solutions to old problems. By the end of the century, industry and trade had also attracted enlightened commentators who advocated free markets and less government control. Modern ideas of political economy thus constitute one more legacy of the Enlightenment, but—like the Enlightenment itself—they drew criticism at the time and from later generations.

As the era of European exploration and conquest gave way to colonial empire building, the eighteenth century witnessed increased consolidation of global markets and bitter competition among Europeans for the spoils of empire. From its slow inception in the mid-fifteenth century, the African slave trade reached appalling heights in the second half of the eighteenth century. The eighteenth-century Atlantic world tied the shores of Europe, the Americas, and Africa in a web of commercial, human and cultural exchange that also had strong ties with the Pacific and the Indian Oceans.

The new dynamics of the eighteenth century prepared the way for world-shaking changes. Population growth and rural industry began to undermine long-standing traditions of daily life in western Europe. The transformed families of the industrious revolution developed not only new habits of work, but also a new sense of confidence in their abilities. By the 1770s England was approaching an economic transformation fully as significant as the great political upheaval destined to develop shortly in neighboring France. In the same period, the first wave of resistance to European domination rose up in the colonies. The great revolutions of the late eighteenth century would change the world forever.

Make Connections

Think about the larger developments and continuities within and across chapters.

1. How did agriculture, industry, and population affect each other in the eighteenth century? How and why did developments in one area affect the other areas?

2. Compare the economic and social situation of western Europe in the mid-eighteenth century with that of the seventeenth century (Chapter 15). What were the achievements of the eighteenth century, and what factors allowed for such progress to be made?

3. The eighteenth century was the period of the European Enlightenment, which celebrated tolerance and human liberty (Chapter 16). Paradoxically, it was also the era of a tremendous increase in slavery, which brought suffering and death to millions. How can you explain this paradox?

17   REVIEW & EXPLORE

Identify Key Terms

Identify and explain the significance of each item below.

enclosure (p. 495)

proletarianization (p. 497)

cottage industry (p. 500)

putting-out system (p. 500)

industrious revolution (p. 503)

guild system (p. 506)

economic liberalism (p. 508)

Navigation Acts (p. 510)

Treaty of Paris (p. 510)

debt peonage (p. 513)

transatlantic slave trade (p. 513)

Review the Main Ideas

Answer the section heading questions from the chapter.

1. Why did European agriculture grow between 1650 and 1800? (p. 494)

2. Why did the European population rise dramatically in the eighteenth century? (p. 497)

3. How and why did rural industry intensify in the eighteenth century? (p. 500)

4. What important changes occurred in economic thought and practice in the eighteenth century? (p. 506)

5. How did empire and trade shape new economic, cultural, and social developments? (p. 508)

Suggested Resources

BOOKS

+ Allen, Robert, et al., eds. *Living Standards in the Past: New Perspectives on Well-Being in Asia and Europe.* 2004. Offers rich comparative perspectives on population growth and living standards among common people.

+ Anderson, Virginia DeJohn. *Creatures of Empire: How Domestic Animals Transformed Early America.* 2004. Explores the importance of domestic animals in the colonization of North America and the conflicting attitudes of English settlers and Native Americans toward animals.

+ Bell, Dean Phillip. *Jews in the Early Modern World.* 2008. A broad examination of Jewish life and relations with non-Jews in the early modern period.

+ Farr, James R. *Artisans in Europe, 1300–1914.* 2000. An overview of guilds and artisanal labor in early modern Europe.

+ Kwass, Michael. *Contraband: Louis Mandrin and the Making of a Global Underworld.* 2014. Through the story of a bandit leader, explores the role of smuggling in bringing the goods of the Atlantic world to European consumers.

+ Morgan, Jennifer Lyle. *Laboring Women: Reproduction and Gender in New World Slavery.* 2004. Focuses on the role of women's labor in the evolution of slavery in Britain's North American colonies.

+ Ormrod, David. *The Rise of Commercial Empires: England and the Netherlands in the Age of Mercantilism, 1650–1770.* 2003. Examines the battle for commercial and maritime supremacy in the North Sea.

+ Palmer, Jennifer. *Intimate Bonds: Family and Slavery in the French Atlantic.* 2016. An examination of the role of women and family in building the French colonial empire and the plantation system.

+ Rediker, Marcus. *The Slave Ship: A Human History.* 2007. The horrors of the transatlantic slave trade from the perspective of the captains, sailors, and captives of the ships that crossed the ocean.

◆ Winterer, Caroline. *American Enlightenments: Pursuing Happiness in the Age of Reason.* 2016. An examination of enlightened thought in the eighteenth-century Americas, emphasizing the impact of the colonial context on American thought and the contribution Americans made to European ideas.

MEDIA

◆ *Amazing Grace* (Michael Apted, 2006). An idealistic Briton's struggle to end his country's involvement in the slave trade alongside allies Olaudah Equiano and a repentant former slave-ship captain.

◆ *Blackbeard: Terror at Sea* (National Geographic, 2006). A documentary recounting the exploits of the most famous eighteenth-century pirate.

◆ *Common-place: The Interactive Journal of Early American Life.* Aimed at a diverse audience of scholars, teachers, students, and history buffs, with articles, blogs, and other resources on early America. **www.common-place.org**

◆ *The Last of the Mohicans* (Michael Mann, 1992). Set among the battles of the Seven Years' War (known as the French and Indian War in the colonies), a man raised as a Mohican saves the daughter of an English officer.

◆ *Olaudah Equiano, or, Gustavus Vassa, the African.* A website featuring material on the movement to abolish slavery and the career of Olaudah Equiano, a formerly enslaved person who published an autobiography in which he discussed his experience in bondage. **www.brycchancarey.com/equiano**

◆ *Rob Roy* (Michael Caton-Jones, 1995). A Scottish Highlander's effort to better his village by borrowing money to raise and sell cattle is challenged by the treachery of a noble lord and greedy bankers.

◆ *Tales from the Green Valley* (BBC, 2005). A television series exploring life on a British farm in the seventeenth century.

◆ *The Trans-Atlantic Slave Trade Database.* Presents the results of decades of research into the voyages of the transatlantic slave trade, interpretive articles, and an interactive database including ships, ports of arrival and departure, captains, and information on individuals taken in slavery. **www.slavevoyages.org**

◆ *Word and Utopia* (Manoel de Oliveira, 2000). A Portuguese missionary struggles to improve the treatment of Indigenous people in seventeenth-century Brazil.

18

Life in the Era of Expansion

1650–1800

The discussion of agriculture and industry in the last chapter showed the common people at work, straining to make ends meet within the larger context of population growth, economic expansion, and ferocious competition at home and overseas. This chapter shows how that world of work was embedded in a rich complex of family organization, community practices, everyday experiences, and collective attitudes. As with the economy, traditional habits of daily life changed considerably over the eighteenth century. Change was particularly dramatic in the growing cities of northwestern Europe, where traditional social controls were undermined by the anonymity and increased social interaction of the urban setting.

Historians have studied many aspects of popular life, including marriage patterns and family size, childhood and education, nutrition, health care, and religious worship. While common people left few written records, imaginative research has resulted in major findings and much greater knowledge. It is now possible to follow the common people into their homes, workshops, churches, and taverns and to ask, "What were the everyday experiences and attitudes of ordinary people, and how did they change over the eighteenth century?" ■

CHAPTER PREVIEW

- How did marriage and family life change in the eighteenth century?

- What was life like for children, and how did attitudes toward childhood evolve?

- How did increasing literacy and new patterns of consumption affect people's lives?

- What role did religion play in eighteenth-century society?

- How did the practice of medicine evolve in the eighteenth century?

How did marriage and family life change in the eighteenth century?

The family is an institution that has evolved and changed throughout history, assuming different forms in different times and places. The eighteenth century was an important moment of change in family life, as patterns of marriage shifted and individuals adapted and conformed to the new and changing realities of the family unit.

Late Marriage and Nuclear Families

The three-generation extended family was a rarity in western and central Europe. When young European couples married, they normally established their own households and lived apart from their parents, much like the nuclear families (a family group consisting of parents and their children with no other relatives) common in the United States today. If a three-generation household came into existence, it was usually because a widowed parent moved into the home of a married child.

Most people did not marry young in the seventeenth and eighteenth centuries. The average person married many years after reaching adulthood and many more after beginning to work. Studies of western Europe in the seventeenth and eighteenth centuries show that both men and women married for the first time at an average age of twenty-five to twenty-seven. Furthermore, 10 to 20 percent of men and women in western Europe never married at all. Matters were different in parts of eastern and southern Europe, where the multigeneration household was the norm, marriage occurred around age twenty, and permanent celibacy was much less common.

Why did young people in western Europe delay marriage? The main reason was that couples normally did not marry until they could start an independent household and support themselves and future children. Peasants often needed to wait until their father's death to inherit land and marry. In the towns, men and women worked to accumulate enough savings to start a small business and establish their own home.

Laws and tradition also discouraged early marriage. In some areas couples needed permission from the local lord or landowner in order to marry. Poor couples had particular difficulty securing the approval of local officials, who believed that freedom to marry for the lower classes would result in more landless paupers, more abandoned children, and more money for welfare. Village elders often agreed.

The custom of late marriage combined with the nuclear family household distinguished western European society from other areas of the world. Historians have argued that this late-marriage pattern was responsible for at least part of the economic advantage western Europeans acquired relative to other world regions. Late marriage joined a mature man and a mature woman—two adults who had already accumulated social and economic capital and could transmit self-reliance and skills to the next generation. The relative closeness in age between husband and wife favored a greater degree of gender equality than existed in areas where older men married much younger women.

Work Away from Home

Many young people worked within their families until they could start their own households. Boys plowed and wove; girls spun and tended the cows. The growth in population in eighteenth-century Europe was accompanied by a strong rise in urbanization, as young men and women migrated from the countryside to the cities in search of work and new opportunities. In cities and towns, teenaged boys were apprenticed to learn a trade. If a boy were lucky and had connections, he might eventually be admitted to a guild and establish his economic independence. Many poor families could not afford apprenticeships for their sons. Without craft skills, these youths drifted from one tough job to another: wage laborer on a new road, carrier of water, or domestic servant.

Many adolescent girls also left their families to work. Indeed, in northwestern Europe, the majority of migrants from the country to the city were young women. The range of opportunities open to them was more limited, however. Apprenticeship was sometimes available with mistresses in traditionally female occupations like seamstress, linen draper, or midwife. With the growth in production of finished goods for the emerging consumer economy during the eighteenth century, demand rose for skilled female labor, and a wider range of jobs became available for women. Nevertheless, women still continued to earn much lower wages for their work than men.

Service in another family's household was by far the most common job for girls, and even middle-class families often sent their daughters into service. The legions of young servant girls worked hard but had little independence. Constantly under the eye of her mistress, the servant girl had many tasks—cleaning, shopping, cooking, and child care. Often the work was endless, for there were few laws to limit exploitation. Court records are full of servant girls' complaints of physical mistreatment by their mistresses. There were many like the fifteen-year-old English girl in the early eighteenth century who told the judge that her mistress had not only called her "very opprobrious

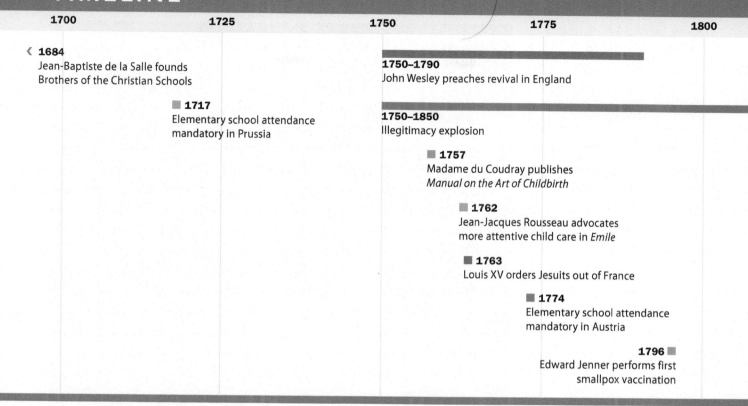

TIMELINE

| 1700 | 1725 | 1750 | 1775 | 1800 |

‹ 1684
Jean-Baptiste de la Salle founds
Brothers of the Christian Schools

■ 1717
Elementary school attendance
mandatory in Prussia

1750–1790
John Wesley preaches revival in England

1750–1850
Illegitimacy explosion

■ 1757
Madame du Coudray publishes
Manual on the Art of Childbirth

■ 1762
Jean-Jacques Rousseau advocates
more attentive child care in *Emile*

■ 1763
Louis XV orders Jesuits out of France

■ 1774
Elementary school attendance
mandatory in Austria

1796 ■
Edward Jenner performs first
smallpox vaccination

names, as Bitch, Whore and the like," but also "beat her without provocation and beyond measure."[1]

In theory, domestic service offered a girl security in a new family. But in practice, she was often the easy prey of a lecherous master or his sons or friends. If the girl became pregnant, she could be thrown out in disgrace and her family might refuse to take her back. Forced to make their own way, these girls had no choice but to turn to a harsh life of prostitution and petty thievery. "What are we?" exclaimed a bitter Parisian prostitute. "Most of us are unfortunate women, without origins, without education, servants and maids for the most part."[2] Adult women who remained in service, at least in large towns and cities, could gain more autonomy and distressed their employers by changing jobs frequently.

Contraception and Community Controls

Ten years between puberty and marriage was a long time for sexually mature young people to wait. Many unmarried couples satisfied their sexual desires with fondling and petting. Others went further and engaged in premarital intercourse. Those who did so risked pregnancy and the stigma of illegitimate birth.

Sexually active men and women sought to control when and with whom they had children. They drew on a variety of methods, some more effective than others. Washing after intercourse, wearing amulets, and burying the afterbirth from a previous birth were among the folk methods that we now know were useless in preventing pregnancy. Condoms, made from sheep intestines, became available in the mid-seventeenth century, replacing uncomfortable earlier versions made from cloth. They were expensive and mainly used by aristocratic libertines and prostitutes. Apart from abstinence, the most common and somewhat effective method of contraception was coitus interruptus—withdrawal by the male before ejaculation. This method appears to have been widespread in Europe by the end of the eighteenth century.

Women also sought to end unwanted pregnancies through a variety of means, including physical exertion and bleedings, magical spells, and consumption of herbs known to induce miscarriage. Using such methods to produce early-term miscarriage was often considered legitimate across Protestant, Catholic, and Muslim regions as a means to restore the "normal" flow of menstrual blood; however, they were often unsuccessful. The term *abortion* usually only applied to the termination of pregnancies past the fourth month, when the fetus was developed enough to move perceptibly in the womb. Such abortions were capital crimes in most parts of Europe.

Despite the lack of reliable contraception, premarital sex did not result in a large proportion of illegitimate births in most parts of Europe until 1750.

Young Serving Girl Increased migration to urban areas in the eighteenth century contributed to a loosening of traditional morals and soaring illegitimacy rates. Young women who worked as servants or shopgirls could not be supervised as closely as those who lived at home. The themes of seduction, fallen virtue, and familial conflict were popular in eighteenth-century art. (Musée Cognacq-Jay, Paris, France/Bridgeman Images)

Where collective control over sexual behavior among youths failed, community pressure to marry often prevailed. A comparison of marriage and birth dates of seven representative parishes in seventeenth-century England shows that around 20 percent of children must have been conceived before the couple was married, but only 2 percent were born out of wedlock.[3] Figures for the French village of Auffay in Normandy in the eighteenth century were remarkably similar.

The combination of low rates of illegitimate birth with large numbers of pregnant brides reflects the powerful **community controls** of the traditional village, particularly the open-field village, with its pattern of cooperation and common action. An unwed mother with an illegitimate child was viewed as a grave threat to the economic, social, and moral stability of the community. Irate parents, anxious

village elders, indignant priests, and stern landlords all combined to pressure young people who wavered about marriage in the face of unexpected pregnancies. In the countryside these controls meant that premarital sex was not entered into lightly and that it was generally limited to those contemplating marriage.

The concerns of the village and the family weighed heavily on couples' lives after marriage as well. Whereas uninvolved individuals today often try to stay out of the domestic disputes of their neighbors, peasant communities gave such affairs loud and unfavorable publicity either at the time or during the carnival season (see "Leisure and Recreation" later in this chapter). Relying on degrading public rituals, known as **charivari**, the young men of the village would typically gang up on their victim and force him or her to sit astride a donkey facing backward and holding up the donkey's tail. They would parade the overly brutal spouse-beater or the adulterous couple around the village, loudly proclaiming the offenders' misdeeds. Such punishments epitomized the community's effort to police personal behavior and maintain moral standards.

New Patterns of Marriage and Illegitimacy

In the second half of the eighteenth century, long-standing patterns of marriage and illegitimacy shifted dramatically. One important change was an increased ability for young people to make decisions about marriage for themselves, rather than following the interests of their families. This change occurred because social and economic transformations made it harder for families and communities to supervise their behavior. More youths in the countryside worked for their own wages as agricultural laborers, rather than on a family farm, and their economic autonomy translated into increased freedom of action. The many youths who joined the flood of migrants to the cities enjoyed more social contacts and less social control than their friends who stayed at home.

A less positive outcome of loosening social control was an **illegitimacy explosion**, concentrated in England, France, Germany, and Scandinavia. In Frankfurt, Germany, for example, births out of wedlock rose steadily from about 2 percent of all births in the early eighteenth century to a peak of about 25 percent around 1850. In Bordeaux, France, 36 percent of all babies were being born out of wedlock by 1840. Given the meager economic opportunities open to single mothers, their circumstances were desperate.

Why did the number of illegitimate births skyrocket? One reason was a rise in sexual activity among young people. The loosened social controls that gave young people more choice in marriage also provided them with more opportunities to yield to sexual desire. As in previous generations, many of the young couples who engaged in sexual activity intended to marry. In one medium-size French city in 1787–1788, the great majority of unwed mothers stated that sexual intimacy had followed promises of marriage. Their sisters in rural Normandy frequently reported that they had been "seduced in anticipation of marriage."[4]

The problem for young women who became pregnant was that fewer men followed through on their promises. The second half of the eighteenth century witnessed sharply rising prices for food, homes, and other necessities of life. Many soldiers, day laborers, and male servants were no doubt sincere in their proposals, but their lives were insecure, and they were unwilling or unable to take on the burden of a wife and child.

The romantic yet practical dreams and aspirations of young people were thus frustrated by low wages, inequality, and changing economic and social conditions. Old patterns of marriage and family were breaking down. Only in the late nineteenth century would more stable patterns reappear.

Sex on the Margins of Society

Not all sex acts took place between men and women hopeful of marriage. Prostitution offered both single and married men an outlet for sexual desire. After a long period of relative tolerance, prostitutes encountered increasingly harsh and repressive laws in the sixteenth and early seventeenth centuries as officials across Europe closed licensed brothels and declared prostitution illegal.

Despite this repression, prostitution continued to flourish, especially when economic times were harsh. Most prostitutes were working women who turned to the sex trade when confronted with paltry wages and unemployment. Such women did not become social pariahs, but retained ties with the communities of laboring poor to which they belonged. If caught by the police, however, they were liable to imprisonment or banishment. Venereal disease was also a constant threat. Prostitutes were subjected to humiliating police examinations for disease, although medical treatments were at best rudimentary. Farther up the social scale were courtesans whose wealthy protectors provided apartments, servants, fashionable clothing, and cash allowances. After a brilliant but brief career, an aging courtesan faced with the loss of her wealthy client could descend once more to streetwalking.

Relations between individuals of the same sex attracted even more condemnation than did prostitution, since they defied the Bible's limitation of sex to the purposes of procreation. Male same-sex relations, described as "sodomy" or "buggery," were prohibited by law in most European states, theoretically under pain of death. Such laws, however, were enforced unevenly, most strictly in Spain and far less so in the Scandinavian countries and Russia.[5]

Protected by their status, nobles and royals sometimes openly indulged their same-sex desires, which were accepted as long as they married and produced legitimate heirs. It was common knowledge that

> ■ **community controls** A pattern of cooperation and common action in a traditional village that sought to uphold the economic, social, and moral stability of the closely knit community.
>
> ■ **charivari** Degrading public rituals used by village communities to police personal behavior and maintain moral standards.
>
> ■ **illegitimacy explosion** The sharp increase in out-of-wedlock births that occurred in Europe between 1750 and 1850, caused by low wages and the breakdown of community controls.

Eighteenth-Century Lesbianism The late eighteenth century saw the emergence of the first lesbian subculture in urban areas of western Europe. Political opponents of the French monarchy circulated attacks on the French queen as a sexually licentious libertine, including pornographic images such as this engraving depicting her in a lesbian relationship with one of her female courtiers. (Bridgeman Images)

King James I, sponsor of the first translation of the Bible into English, had male lovers. These relationships were tolerated because they did not prevent

him from having seven children with his wife, Anne of Denmark. The duchess of Orléans, sister-in-law of French king Louis XIV, complained in her letters about her husband's male lovers, one of whom was appointed tutor to the couple's son. She also repeated rumors about the homosexual inclinations of King William of England, hero of the Glorious Revolution (see "The Restoration of the English Monarchy" in Chapter 15).

In the late seventeenth century male homosexual subcultures began to emerge in Paris, Amsterdam, and London, with their own slang, meeting places, and styles of dress. Unlike men who took both wives and male lovers, these groups included men exclusively oriented toward other men. In London, they called themselves "mollies," a term originally applied to prostitutes, and some began to wear women's clothing and adopt effeminate behavior. A new self-identity began to form among homosexual men: a belief that their same-sex desire made them fundamentally different from other men. As a character in one late-eighteenth-century fiction declared, he was in "a category of men different from the other, a class Nature has created in order to diminish or minimize propagation."[6]

Same-sex relations existed among women as well, but they attracted less attention and condemnation than those among men. Some women were prosecuted for "unnatural" relations; others attempted to escape the narrow confines imposed on them by dressing as men. Cross-dressing women occasionally snuck into the armed forces, such as Ulrika Elenora Stålhammar, who served as a man in the Swedish army for thirteen years and married a woman. After confessing her transgressions, she was sentenced to a lenient one-month imprisonment.[7] The beginnings of a distinctive lesbian subculture appeared in London and other large cities at the end of the eighteenth century.

What was life like for children, and how did attitudes toward childhood evolve?

On the whole, western European women married late but then began bearing children rapidly. If a woman married before she was thirty, and if both she and her husband lived to fifty, she would most likely give birth to six or more children. Infant mortality varied across Europe, but it was very high by modern standards, and many women died in childbirth due to limited medical knowledge and technology.

For those children who did survive, Enlightenment ideals that emerged in the latter half of the century stressed the importance of parental nurturing. The new worldview also led to an increase in elementary

schools throughout Europe. Despite the efforts of enlightened absolutists and religious institutions, however, formal education reached only a minority of ordinary children.

Child Care and Nursing

Newborns entered a dangerous world. They were vulnerable to infectious diseases, and many babies died of dehydration brought about by bad bouts of ordinary diarrhea. Of those who survived infancy, many more died in childhood. Even in a rich family, little could be done for an ailing child. Childbirth was also dangerous. Women who bore six children faced a cumulative risk of dying in childbirth of 5 to 10 percent, a thousand times as great as the risk in Europe today.[8] They died from blood loss and shock during delivery and from infections caused by unsanitary conditions. The joy of pregnancy was thus shadowed by fear of loss of the mother or her child.

In the countryside, women of the lower classes generally breast-fed their infants for two years or more. Although not a foolproof means of birth control, breast-feeding decreases the likelihood of pregnancy by delaying the resumption of ovulation. By nursing their babies, women spaced their children two or three years apart. Nursing also saved lives: breast-fed infants received precious immunity-producing substances and were more likely to survive than those who were fed other food.

Areas with lower rates of breast-feeding—typically in northern France, Scandinavia, and central and eastern Europe—experienced the highest infant mortality rates.[9] In these areas, many people believed that breast-feeding was bad for a woman's health or appearance. Across Europe, women of the aristocracy and upper middle class seldom nursed their own children because they found breast-feeding undignified and it interfered with their social responsibilities. The alternatives to breast-feeding were feeding babies cow's or goat's milk or paying lactating women to provide their milk.

Wealthy women hired live-in wet nurses to suckle their babies (which usually meant sending the nurse's own infant away to be nursed by someone else). Working women in the cities also relied on the cheaper services of wet nurses in the countryside because they needed to earn a living. In the eighteenth century rural **wet-nursing** was a widespread business, conducted within the framework of the putting-out system. The traffic was in babies rather than in yarn or cloth, and two or three years often passed before the wet-nurse worker in the countryside finished her task.

Wet-nursing was particularly common in northern France. Toward the end of the century, roughly twenty thousand babies were born in Paris each year. Almost half were placed with rural wet nurses through a government-supervised distribution network; 20 to 25 percent were placed in the homes of Parisian nurses personally selected by their parents; and another 20 to 25 percent were abandoned to foundling hospitals, which would send them to wet nurses in the countryside. The remainder (perhaps 10 percent) were nursed at home by their mothers or live-in nurses.[10]

Reliance on wet nurses raised levels of infant mortality because of the dangers of travel, the lack of supervision of conditions in wet nurses' homes, and the need to share milk between a wet nurse's own baby and the one or more babies she was hired to feed. A study of mortality rates in mid-eighteenth-century France shows that 25 percent of babies died before their first birthday, and another 30 percent before age ten.[11] In England, where more mothers nursed, only some 30 percent of children did not reach their tenth birthday.

Within each country and across Europe, tremendous regional variation existed. Mortality rates were higher in overcrowded and dirty cities; in low-lying, marshy regions; and during summer months when rural women were busy in agricultural work and had less time to tend to infants. The corollary of high infant mortality was high fertility. Women who did not breast-feed their babies or whose children died in infancy became pregnant more quickly and bore more children. Thus, on balance, the number of children who survived to adulthood tended to be the same across Europe, with higher births balancing the greater loss of life in areas that relied on wet-nursing.

In the second half of the eighteenth century, critics mounted a harsh attack against wet-nursing. Enlightenment thinkers proclaimed that wet-nursing was preventing European society from reaching its full potential. They were convinced, incorrectly, that the population was declining (in fact it was rising, but they lacked accurate population data) and blamed this decline on women's failure to nurture their children properly. Some also railed against practices of contraception and masturbation, which they believed were lowering the birthrate. Despite these complaints, many women continued to rely on wet nurses for convenience or from necessity.

Foundlings and Infanticide

The young woman who could not provide for an unwanted child had few choices, especially if she had no prospect of marriage. In desperation, some women, particularly in the countryside, hid unwanted pregnancies, delivered in secret, and smothered their newborn infants. The punishment for infanticide was death. Yet across Europe, convictions for infanticide dropped in the second half of the eighteenth century, perhaps due to growing social awareness of the crushing pressures caused by unwanted pregnancies.

Another sign of this awareness was the spread of homes for abandoned children. Homes for abandoned children first took hold in Italy, Spain, and Portugal in the sixteenth century, spreading to France in 1670 and the rest of Europe thereafter. By the end of the eighteenth century, European foundling hospitals were admitting annually about one hundred thousand abandoned children, nearly all of them infants.

■ **wet-nursing** A widespread and flourishing business in the eighteenth century in which women were paid to breast-feed other women's babies.

One-third of all babies born in Paris in the 1770s were immediately abandoned to foundling homes. There appears to have been no differentiation by sex in the numbers of children sent to foundling hospitals. Many of the children were the offspring of single women, the result of the illegitimacy explosion of the second half of the eighteenth century. But fully one-third of all the foundlings were abandoned by married couples too poor to feed another child.[12]

At their best, foundling homes were a good example of Christian charity and social concern in an age of great poverty and inequality. They provided the rudiments of an education and sought to place the children in apprenticeship or domestic service once they reached an appropriate age. Yet the foundling system was no panacea. Even in the best of these institutions, 50 percent of the babies normally died within a year. In the worst, fully 90 percent did not survive, falling victim to infectious disease, malnutrition, and neglect.[13] Because raising foundling children was a significant financial burden, many small towns and even some major cities sent babies to hospitals in large cities, like Paris and London, which had the policy of accepting all children.

Attitudes Toward Children

Parents were well aware of the dangers of infancy and childhood. The great eighteenth-century English historian Edward Gibbon (1737–1794) wrote, with some exaggeration, that "the death of a newborn child before that of its parents may seem unnatural but it is a strictly probable event, since of any given number the greater part are extinguished before the ninth year, before they possess the faculties of the mind and the body." Gibbon's father named all his boys Edward after himself, hoping that at least one of them would survive to carry his name. His prudence was not misplaced. Edward the future historian and eldest survived. Five brothers and sisters who followed him all died in infancy.

Emotional prudence could lead to emotional distance. The French essayist Michel de Montaigne, who lost five of his six daughters in infancy, wrote, "I cannot abide that passion for caressing new-born children, which have neither mental activities nor recognizable bodily shape by which to make themselves loveable and I have never willingly suffered them to be fed in my presence."[14] In contrast to this harsh picture, however, historians have drawn ample evidence from diaries, letters, and family portraits that parents of all social classes cherished their children and experienced great emotional distress when they died. This was equally true of mothers and fathers and of attitudes toward both sons and daughters. The English poet

Ben Jonson wrote movingly in "On My First Son" of the death of his son Benjamin, which occurred during a London plague outbreak in 1603:

> Farewell, thou child of my right hand, and joy;
> My sin was too much hope of thee, loved boy.
> Seven years thou wert lent to me, and I thee pay,
> Exacted by thy fate, on the just day.

Parental love was often expressed through harsh discipline. The axiom "Spare the rod and spoil the child" seems to have been coined in the mid-seventeenth century. Susannah Wesley (1669–1742), mother of John Wesley, the founder of Methodism (see "Protestant Revival" later in this chapter), agreed. According to her, the first task of a parent toward her children was "to conquer the will, and bring them to an obedient temper." She reported that her babies were "taught to fear the rod, and to cry softly; by which means they escaped the abundance of correction they might otherwise have had, and that most odious noise of the crying of children was rarely heard in the house."[15] They were beaten for lying, stealing, disobeying, and quarreling, and forbidden from playing with other children. Susannah's methods of disciplining her children were probably extreme even in her own day, but they do reflect a broad consensus that children were born with an innately sinful will that parents must overcome.

The Enlightenment produced an enthusiastic new discourse about childhood and child rearing. Starting around 1760 critics called for greater tenderness toward children and proposed imaginative new teaching methods. In addition to supporting foundling homes and urging women to nurse their babies, these new voices ridiculed the practices of swaddling babies and dressing children in miniature versions of adult clothing. They called instead for children to wear comfortable garments allowing freedom of movement. Rather than emphasizing original sin, these enlightened voices celebrated the child as an innocent product of nature. Since they viewed nature as inherently positive, Enlightenment educators advocated safeguarding and developing children's innate qualities rather than thwarting and suppressing them. Accordingly, they believed the best hopes for a new society lay in a radical reform of child-rearing techniques.

One of the century's most influential works on child rearing was Jean-Jacques Rousseau's *Emile, or On Education* (1762), inspired in part, Rousseau claimed, by remorse for the abandonment of his own children. In *Emile*, Rousseau argued that boys' education should include plenty of fresh air and exercise and that boys should be taught practical craft skills in addition to book learning. Reacting to what he perceived as the vanity

The First Step of Childhood
This tender snapshot of a baby's first steps toward an adoring mother exemplifies new attitudes toward children and raising them ushered in by the Enlightenment. Authors like Jean-Jacques Rousseau encouraged elite mothers like the one pictured here to take a more personal interest in raising their children, instead of leaving them in the hands of indifferent wet nurses and nannies. Many women responded eagerly to this call, and the period saw a more sentimentalized view of childhood and family life. (Erich Lessing/Art Resource, NY)

and frivolity of upper-class Parisian women, Rousseau insisted that girls' education focus on their future domestic responsibilities. For Rousseau, women's "nature" destined them solely for a life of marriage and child rearing. The sentimental ideas of Rousseau and other reformers were enthusiastically adopted by elite women, some of whom began to nurse their own children.

The Spread of Elementary Schools

The availability of education outside the home gradually increased over the early modern period. The wealthy led the way in the sixteenth century with special colleges, often run by Jesuits in Catholic areas. Schools charged specifically with educating children of the common people began to appear in the second half of the seventeenth century. They taught six- to twelve-year-old children basic literacy, religion, and perhaps some arithmetic for the boys and needlework for the girls. The number of such schools expanded in the eighteenth century, although they were never sufficient to educate the majority of the population.

Religion played an important role in the spread of education. From the middle of the seventeenth century, Presbyterian Scotland was convinced that the path to salvation lay in careful study of the Scriptures, and it established an effective network of parish schools for rich and poor alike. The first proponents of universal education, in Prussia, were inspired by the Protestant idea that every believer should be able to read the Bible and by the new idea of raising a population capable of effectively serving the state. As early as 1717 Prussia made attendance at elementary schools compulsory for boys and girls in areas where schools existed.[16] More Protestant German states followed suit in the eighteenth century.

Catholic states pursued their own programs of popular education. In the 1660s France began setting up charity schools to teach poor children their catechism and prayers as well as reading and writing. These were run by parish priests or by new educational teaching orders. One of the most famous orders was Jean-Baptiste de la Salle's Brothers of the Christian Schools. Founded in 1684, the schools had thirty-five thousand students across France by the 1780s. Enthusiasm for popular education was even greater in the Habsburg empire. Inspired by the expansion of schools in rival Protestant German states, Maria Theresa issued her own compulsory education edict in 1774, imposing five hours of school, five days a week, for all children aged six to twelve.[17] Across Europe some elementary education was becoming a reality, and schools became increasingly significant in the life of the child.

How did increasing literacy and new patterns of consumption affect people's lives?

Because of the new efforts in education, basic literacy expanded among the popular classes, whose reading habits centered primarily on religious material, but who also began to incorporate more practical and entertaining literature. In addition to reading, people of all classes enjoyed a range of leisure activities, including storytelling, fairs, festivals, and sports.

One of the most important developments in European society in the eighteenth century was the emergence of a fledgling consumer culture. Much of the expansion took place among the upper and upper-middle classes, but a boom in cheap reproductions of luxury items also opened doors for people of modest means. From food to ribbons and from coal stoves to umbrellas, the material worlds of city dwellers grew richer and more diverse. This "consumer revolution," as it has been called, created new expectations for comfort, hygiene, and self-expression, thus dramatically changing European daily life in the eighteenth century.

Popular Literature

The surge in childhood education in the eighteenth century led to a remarkable growth in literacy between

1600 and 1800. Whereas in 1600 only one male in six was barely literate in France and Scotland, and one in four in England, by 1800 almost nine out of ten Scottish males, two out of three French males (Map 18.1), and more than half of English males were literate. In all three countries, most of the gains occurred in the eighteenth century. Women were also increasingly literate, although they lagged behind men.

The growth in literacy promoted growth in reading, and historians have carefully examined what the common people read. While the Bible remained the overwhelming favorite, especially in Protestant countries, short pamphlets known as chapbooks were the staple of popular literature. Printed on the cheapest paper, many chapbooks featured Bible stories, prayers, and the lives of saints and exemplary Christians. This pious literature gave believers moral teachings and a faith that helped them endure their daily struggles.

Entertaining, often humorous stories formed a second element of popular literature. Fairy tales, romances, true crime stories, and fantastic adventures were some of the delights that filled the peddler's pack as he approached a village. These tales presented a world of danger and magic, of supernatural powers, fairy godmothers, and evil trolls that provided a temporary escape from harsh everyday reality. They also contained nuggets of ancient folk wisdom, counseling prudence in a world full of danger and injustice, where wolves dress like grandmothers and eat Little Red Riding Hoods.

Finally, some popular literature was highly practical, dealing with rural crafts, household repairs, useful plants, and similar matters. Much lore was stored in almanacs, where calendars listing secular, religious, and astrological events were mixed with agricultural schedules, arcane facts, and jokes. The almanac was highly appreciated even by many in the comfortable classes. In this way, elites shared some elements of a common culture with the masses.

While it is safe to say that the vast majority of ordinary people did not read the great works of the Enlightenment, they were not cut off entirely from the new ideas. Urban working people were exposed to Enlightenment thought through the news and gossip that spread across city streets, workshops, markets, and taverns. They also had access to cheap pamphlets that helped translate Enlightenment critiques into ordinary language. Servants, who usually came from rural areas and traveled home periodically, were well situated to transmit ideas from educated employers to the village.

The Commercialization of Sports   Sports events became popular commercial spectacles during the eighteenth century. In this early-eighteenth-century painting, two men spar in a boxing match staged in London for the entertainment of the gathered crowd. (bpk Bildagentur/ Gemaeldegalerie Alte Meiser, Museumslandschaft Hessen, Kassel, Germany/Art Resource, NY)

Leisure and Recreation

Despite the spread of literacy, the culture of the village remained largely oral rather than written. In the cold, dark winter months, peasant families gathered around the fireplace to sing, tell stories, do craftwork, and keep warm. In some parts of Europe, women would gather in someone's cottage to chat, sew, spin, and laugh. Sometimes a few young men would be invited so that the daughters (and mothers) could size up potential suitors in a supervised atmosphere. A favorite recreation of men was drinking and talking with buddies in public places, and it was a sorry village that had no tavern. In addition to old favorites such as beer and wine, the common people turned with gusto to cheap and potent hard liquor, which fell in price because of improved techniques for distilling grain in the eighteenth century.

Towns and cities offered a wider range of amusements, including public parks, theaters, and lending libraries. Urban fairs featured prepared foods, acrobats, and conjuring acts. Leisure activities were another form of consumption marked by growing commercialization. For example, commercialized spectator sports emerged in this period, including horse races, boxing matches, and bullfights. Modern sports heroes, such as brawny heavyweight champions and elegant bullfighting matadors, made their appearance on the historical scene.

Blood sports, such as bullbaiting and cockfighting, also remained popular, reflecting a society in which violence was commonplace and cruelty to animals had not yet attracted widespread condemnation. In bullbaiting, the bull, usually staked on a chain in the courtyard of an inn, was attacked by dogs for the amusement of the innkeeper's clients. Eventually the maimed and tortured animal was slaughtered by a butcher and sold as meat. In cockfighting, two roosters, carefully trained by their owners and armed with razor-sharp steel spurs, slashed and clawed each other in a small ring until the victor won—and the loser died. An added attraction of cockfighting was that spectators could bet on the lightning-fast combat.

Popular recreation merged with religious celebration in a variety of festivals and processions throughout the year. The most striking display of these religiously inspired events was **carnival**, a time of reveling and excess in Catholic Europe, especially in Mediterranean countries. Carnival preceded Lent—the forty days of fasting and penitence before Easter—and for a few exceptional days in February or March, a wild release of drinking, masquerading, and dancing reigned. Moreover, a combination of plays, processions, and raucous spectacles turned the established order upside down. Peasants dressed as nobles and men as women, and wealthy elites waited on their servants at

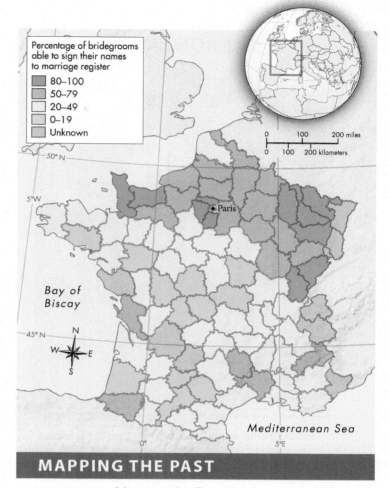

MAPPING THE PAST

MAP 18.1 Literacy in France, ca. 1789

Literacy rates increased but still varied widely between and within states in eighteenth-century Europe.

ANALYZING THE MAP What trends in French literacy rates does this map reveal? Which regions seem to be ahead? How would you explain the regional variations?

CONNECTIONS Note the highly variable nature of literacy rates across the country. Why might the rate of literacy be higher closer to the capital city of Paris? Why would some areas have low rates?

the table. This annual holiday gave people a much-appreciated chance to release their pent-up frustrations and aggressions before life returned to the usual pattern of hierarchy and hard work.

■ **blood sports** Events such as bullbaiting and cockfighting that involved inflicting violence and bloodshed on animals and that were popular with the eighteenth-century European masses.

■ **carnival** The few days of revelry in Catholic countries that preceded Lent and that included drinking, masquerading, dancing, and rowdy spectacles that upset the established order.

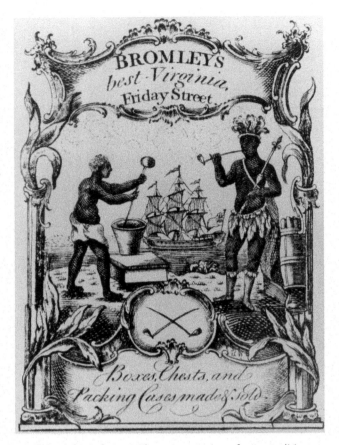

Colonial Products The consumption of commodities imported from the colonies, including coffee, sugar, and tobacco, grew dramatically across the eighteenth century. Merchants emphasized the origins of such goods in their advertising, as seen in this image featuring stereotypical images of Native Americans to promote the "best Virginia" tobacco. (Fotosearch/Getty Images)

The rowdy pastimes of the populace attracted criticism from clerical and lay elites in the second half of the eighteenth century. In 1772 the Spanish Crown banned dragons and giants from the Corpus Christi parade, and the vibrant carnival of Venice was outlawed under Napoleon's rule in 1797. In the same period English newspapers publicly denounced boxing, gambling, blood sports, and other uncouth activities; one described bullbaiting in 1791 as "a disgrace to a civilized people."[18] Anti-cruelty activism would lead to the establishment of the Royal Society for the Protection of Animals in England and Wales in 1824.

Despite elite criticism of the pastimes of the populace, many wealthy and educated Europeans continued to enjoy the folktales of the chapbooks, and they shared the love of gambling, theater, and sport. Moreover, both peasants and patricians—even most enlightened thinkers—shared a deep religiosity. In turn, as we have seen, common people were by no means cut off from the new currents of thought. Thus cultural beliefs and practices continued to be shared across social divides.

New Foods and Appetites

At the beginning of the eighteenth century, ordinary men and women depended on grain as fully as they had in the past. Bread was quite literally the staff of life. Peasants in the Beauvais region of France ate two pounds of bread a day, washing it down with water, wine, or beer. Their dark bread was made from roughly ground wheat and rye—the standard flour of the common people. Even peasants normally needed to buy some grain for food, and, in full accord with landless laborers and urban workers, they believed in the moral economy and the **just price**. That is, they believed that prices should be fair, protecting both consumers and producers, and that just prices should be imposed by government decree if necessary. When prices rose above this level, they often took action in the form of bread riots.

The rural poor also ate a quantity of vegetables. Peas and beans were probably the most common. Grown as field crops in much of Europe since the Middle Ages, they were eaten fresh in late spring and summer. Dried, they became the basic ingredients in the soups and stews of the long winter months. In most regions other vegetables appeared on the tables of the poor in season, primarily cabbages, carrots, and wild greens. Fruit was mostly limited to the summer months. Too precious to drink, milk was used to make cheese and butter, which peasants sold in the market to earn cash for taxes and land rents.

The common people of Europe ate less meat in 1700 than in 1500 because their general standard of living had declined and meat was more expensive. Moreover, harsh laws in most European countries reserved the right to hunt and eat game, such as rabbits, deer, and partridges, to nobles and large landowners. Few laws were more bitterly resented—or more frequently broken—by ordinary people than those governing hunting.

The diet of small traders and artisans—the people of the towns and cities—was less monotonous than that of the peasantry. Bustling markets provided a substantial variety of meats, vegetables, and fruits, although bread and beans still formed the bulk of such families' diets. Not surprisingly, the diet of the rich was quite different from that of the poor. The upper classes were rapacious carnivores, and a truly elegant dinner consisted of an abundance of rich meat and fish dishes laced with piquant sauces and complemented

■ **just price** The idea that prices should be fair, protecting both consumers and producers, and that they should be imposed by government decree if necessary.

■ **consumer revolution** The wide-ranging growth in consumption and new attitudes toward consumer goods that emerged in the cities of northwestern Europe in the second half of the eighteenth century.

with sweets, cheeses, and wine in great quantities. During such dinners, it was common to spend five or more hours at table, eating and drinking and enjoying the witty banter of polite society.

Patterns of food consumption changed markedly as the century progressed. Because of a growth of market-oriented gardening, a greater variety of vegetables appeared in towns and cities. This was particularly the case in the Low Countries and England, which pioneered new methods of farming. Introduced into Europe from the Americas — along with corn, squash, tomatoes, and many other useful plants — the humble potato provided an excellent new food source. Containing a good supply of carbohydrates, calories, and vitamins A and C, the potato offset the lack of vitamins in the poor person's winter and early-spring diet, and it provided a much higher caloric yield than grain for a given piece of land. After initial resistance, the potato became an important dietary supplement in much of Europe by the end of the century.

The most remarkable dietary change in the eighteenth century was in the consumption of commodities imported from abroad. Originally expensive and rare luxury items, goods like tea, sugar, coffee, chocolate, and tobacco became staples for people of all social classes. With the exception of tea — which originated in China — most of the new consumables were produced in European colonies in the Americas. In many cases, the labor of enslaved peoples enabled the expansion in production and drop in prices that allowed such items to spread to the masses.

Part of the motivation for consuming colonial products was a desire to emulate the luxurious lifestyles of the elite that people witnessed as domestic servants and in public spaces. In addition, the quickened pace of work in the eighteenth century created new needs for stimulants among working people. (See "Evaluating Written Evidence: A Day in the Life of Paris," page 538.) Whereas the gentry took tea as a leisurely and genteel ritual, the lower classes drank tea or coffee at work to fight monotony and fatigue. With the widespread adoption of these products (which turned out to be mildly to extremely addictive), working people in Europe became increasingly dependent on faraway colonial economies and enslaved labor. Their understanding of daily necessities and how to procure those necessities shifted definitively, linking them to global trade networks they could not comprehend or control.

Toward a Consumer Society

Along with foodstuffs, all manner of other goods increased in variety and number in the eighteenth century. This proliferation led to a growth in consumption and new attitudes toward consumer goods

Café Society   Italian merchants introduced coffee to Europe around 1600, and the first European coffee shop opened in Venice in 1645, soon followed by ones in Oxford, England, in 1650, London in 1652, and Paris in 1672. Open to all social classes, they provided a new public space for urban Europeans to learn about and debate the issues of the day. Within a few years, each political party, philosophical sect, scientific society, and literary circle had its own coffeehouse. (Guildhall Library & Art Gallery/Heritage ImagesHulton Archive/Getty Images)

so wide-ranging that some historians have referred to an eighteenth-century **consumer revolution**.[19] The result of this revolution was the birth of a new type of society in which people derived their self-identity as much from their consuming practices as from their working lives and place in the production process. As people gained the opportunity to pick and choose among a wide variety of consumer goods, new notions of individuality and self-expression developed. A shopgirl could stand out from her peers by her choice of a striped jacket, a colored parasol, or simply a new ribbon for her hair. The full emergence of a consumer society did not take place until much later, but its roots lie in the eighteenth century.

Increased demand for consumer goods was not merely an innate response to increased supply. Eighteenth-century merchants cleverly pioneered new

A Day in the Life of Paris

Louis-Sébastien Mercier (1740–1814) was the best chronicler of everyday life in eighteenth-century Paris. His masterpiece was the *Tableau de Paris* (1781–1788), a multivolume work composed of 1,049 chapters that covered subjects ranging from convents to cafés, bankruptcy to booksellers, the latest fashions to royal laws. As this excerpt demonstrates, he aimed to convey the infinite diversity of people, places, and things he saw around him, and in so doing he left future generations a precious record of the changing dynamics of Parisian society in the second half of the eighteenth century.

Mercier's family belonged to the respectable artisan classes. This middling position ideally situated Mercier to observe the extremes of wealth and poverty around him. Although these volumes contain many wonderful glimpses of daily life, they should not be taken for an objective account. Mercier brought his own moral and political sensibilities, influenced by Jean-Jacques Rousseau, to the task of description.

Chapter 39: How the Day Goes

It is curious to see how, amid what seems perpetual life and movement, certain hours keep their own characteristics, whether of bustle or of leisure. Every round of the clock-hand sets another scene in motion, each different from the last, though all about equal in length. Seven o'clock in the morning sees all the gardeners, mounted on their nags and with their baskets empty, heading back out of town again. No carriages are about, and not a presentable soul, except a few neat clerks hurrying to their offices. Nine o'clock sets all the barbers in motion, covered from head to foot with flour — hence their soubriquet of "whitings"* — wig in one hand, tongs in

the other. Waiters from the lemonade-shops are busy with trays of coffee and rolls, breakfast for those who live in furnished rooms. . . . An hour later the Law comes into action; a black cloud of legal practitioners and hangers-on descend upon the Châtelet,[†] and the other courts; a procession of wigs and gowns and briefbags, with plaintiffs and defendants at their heels. Midday is the stockbrokers' hour, and the idlers'; the former hurry off to the Exchange, the latter to the Palais-Royal.[‡] The Saint-Honoré[§] quarter, where all the financiers live, is at its busiest now, its streets are crowded with the customers and clients of the great.

At two o'clock those who have invitations to dine set out, dressed in their best, powdered, adjusted, and walking on tiptoe not to soil their stockings. All the cabs are engaged, not one is to be found on the rank; there is a good deal of competition for these vehicles, and you may see two would-be passengers jumping into a cab together from different sides, and furiously disputing which was first. . . .

Three o'clock and the streets are not so full; everyone is at dinner; there is a momentary calm, soon to be broken, for at five fifteen the din is as though the gates of hell were opened, the streets are impassable with traffic going all ways at once, towards the playhouses or the public gardens. Cafés are at their busiest.

Towards seven the din dies down, everywhere and all at once. You can hear the cab-horses' hoofs pawing the stones as they wait — in vain. It is as though the whole town were gagged and bound, suddenly, by an invisible hand. This is the most dangerous time of the whole day for thieves and such, especially towards autumn when the days begin to draw in; for the watch is not yet about, and violence takes its opportunity.

Night falls; and, while scene-shifters set to work at the playhouses, swarms of other workmen, carpenters, masons

*Small fish typically rolled in flour and fried.

[†]The main criminal court of Paris.

[‡]A garden surrounded by arcades with shops and cafés.

[§]A fashionable quarter for the wealthy.

techniques to incite demand: they initiated marketing campaigns, opened fancy boutiques with large windows, and advertised the patronage of royal princes and princesses. By diversifying their product lines and greatly accelerating the turnover of styles, they seized the reins of fashion from the courtiers who had earlier controlled it. Instead of setting new styles, duchesses and marquises now bowed to the dictates of fashion merchants. (See "Individuals in Society: Rose Bertin, 'Minister of Fashion,'" page 540.) Fashion also extended beyond court circles to influence many more items and social groups.

Clothing was one of the chief indicators of the growth of consumerism. Shrewd entrepreneurs made fashionable clothing seem more desirable, while legions of women entering the textile and needle trades made it ever cheaper. As a result, eighteenth-century western Europe witnessed a dramatic rise in the consumption of clothing, particularly in large cities. Colonial economies again played an important role in lowering the cost of materials, such as cotton cloth and vegetable dyes, largely due to the unpaid toil of enslaved Africans. Cheaper copies of elite styles made it possible for working people to aspire to follow fashion for the first time.

and the like, make their way towards the poorer quarters. They leave white footprints from the plaster on their shoes, a trail that any eye can follow. They are off home, and to bed, at the hour which finds elegant ladies sitting down to their dressing-tables to prepare for the business of the night.

At nine this begins; they all set off for the play. Houses tremble as the coaches rattle by, but soon the noise ceases; all the fine ladies are making their evening visits, short ones, before supper. Now the prostitutes begin their night parade, breasts uncovered, heads tossing, colour high on their cheeks, and eyes as bold as their hands. These creatures, careless of the light from shop-windows and street lamps, follow and accost you, trailing through the mud in their silk stockings and low shoes, with words and gestures well matched for obscenity. . . .

By eleven, renewed silence. People are at supper, private people, that is; for the cafés begin at this hour to turn out their patrons, and to send the various idlers and workless and poets back to their garrets for the night. A few prostitutes still linger, but they have to use more circumspection, for the watch is about, patrolling the streets, and this is the hour when they "gather 'em in"; that is the traditional expression.

A quarter after midnight, a few carriages make their way home, taking the non–card players back to bed. These lend the town a sort of transitory life; the tradesman wakes out of his first sleep at the sound of them, and turns to his wife, by no means unwilling. More than one young Parisian must owe his existence to this sudden passing rattle of wheels. . . .

At one in the morning six thousand peasants arrive, bringing the town's provision of vegetables and fruits and flowers, and make straight for the Halles.** . . . As for the market itself, it never sleeps. . . . Perpetual noise, perpetual motion, the curtain never rings down on the enormous stage; first come the fishmongers, and after these the egg-dealers, and after these the retail buyers; for the Halles keep all the other markets of Paris going; they are the warehouses whence these draw their supplies. The food of the whole city is shifted and sorted in high-piled baskets; you may see eggs, pyramids of eggs, moved here and there, up steps and down, in and out of the throngs, miraculous; not one is ever broken. . . .

This impenetrable din contrasts oddly with the sleeping streets, for at that hour none but thieves and poets are awake.

Twice a week, at six, those distributors of the staff of life, the bakers of Gonesse,†† bring in an enormous quantity of loaves to the town, and may take none back through the barriers. And at this same hour workmen take up their tools, and trudge off to their day's labour. Coffee with milk is, unbelievably, the favoured drink among these stalwarts nowadays. . . .

So coffee-drinking has become a habit, and one so deep-rooted that the working classes will start the day on nothing else. It is not costly, and has more flavour to it, and more nourishment too, than anything else they can afford to drink; so they consume immense quantities, and say that if a man can only have coffee for breakfast it will keep him going till nightfall.

EVALUATE THE EVIDENCE

1. What different social groups does Mercier describe? Does he approve or disapprove of Parisian society as he describes it?
2. How do the social classes described by Mercier differ in their use of time, and why? Do you think the same distinctions exist today?
3. What evidence of the consumer revolution can you find in Mercier's account? How do the goods used by eighteenth-century Parisians compare to the ones you use in your life today?

Source: *Panorama of Paris: Selections from "Le Tableau de Paris,"* by Louis-Sébastien Mercier, based on the translation by Helen Simpson, edited with a new preface and translations by Jeremy D. Popkin (University Park: Pennsylvania State University Press, 1999).

**The city's central wholesale food market.

††A suburb of Paris, famous for the excellent bread baked there.

Elite onlookers were sometimes shocked by the sight of lower-class people in stylish outfits. In 1784 Mrs. Fanny Cradock described encountering her milkman during an evening stroll "dressed in a fashionable suit, with an embroidered waistcoat, silk knee-breeches and lace cuffs."[20] The spread of fashion challenged the traditional social order of Europe by blurring the boundaries between social groups and making it harder to distinguish between noble and commoner on the bustling city streets.

Mrs. Cradock's milkman notwithstanding, women took the lead in the spread of fashion. Parisian women significantly out-consumed men, acquiring larger and more expensive wardrobes than those of their husbands, brothers, and fathers. This was true across the social spectrum; in ribbons, shoes, gloves, and lace, European working women reaped in the consumer revolution what they had sown in the industrious revolution (see "The Industrious Revolution" in Chapter 17). There were also new gender distinctions in dress. Previously, noblemen had vied with noblewomen in the magnificence of their apparel; by the end of the eighteenth century men had renounced brilliant colors and voluptuous

One day in 1779, as the French royal family rode in a carriage through the streets of Paris, Queen Marie Antoinette noticed her fashion merchant, Rose Bertin, observing the royal procession. "Ah! there is mademoiselle Bertin," the queen exclaimed, waving her hand. Bertin responded with a curtsy. The king then stood and greeted Bertin, followed by the royal family and their entourage.* The incident shocked the public, for no common merchant had ever received such homage from royalty.

Bertin had come a long way from her humble beginnings. Born in 1747 to a poor family in northern France, she moved to Paris in the 1760s to work as a shop assistant and eventually opened her own boutique on the fashionable Rue Saint-Honoré. In 1775 Bertin received the highest honor of her profession when she was selected by Marie Antoinette as one of her official purveyors.

Based on the queen's patronage, and riding the wave of the new consumer revolution, Bertin became one of the most successful entrepreneurs in Europe, establishing not only a large clientele, but also a reputation for pride and arrogance. She refused to work for non-noble customers, claiming that the orders of the queen and the court required all her attention. Bertin astounded courtiers by referring to her "work" with the queen, as though the two were collaborators rather than absolute monarch and lowly subject. Her close relationship with Marie Antoinette and the fortune the queen spent on her wardrobe hurt the royal family's image. One journalist derided Bertin as a "minister of fashion," whose influence outstripped that of all the others in royal government.

In January 1787 rumors spread through Paris that Bertin had filed for bankruptcy with debts of 2 to 3 million livres (a garment worker's annual salary was around 200 livres). Despite her notoriously high prices and rich clients, this news did not shock Parisians, because the nobility's reluctance to pay its debts was equally well known. Bertin somehow held on to her business. Some said she had spread the bankruptcy rumors herself to shame the court into paying her bills.

Bertin remained loyal to the Crown during the tumult of the French Revolution (see Chapter 19) and sent dresses to the queen even after the arrest of the royal family. Fearing for her life, she left France for Germany in 1792 and continued to ply her profession in exile. She returned to France in 1800 and died in 1813, one year before the restoration of the Bourbon monarchy might have renewed her acclaim.[†]

Rose Bertin scandalized public opinion with her self-aggrandizement and ambition, yet history was on her side.

In this 1746 painting by François Boucher, a leisured lady has just been coiffed by her hairdresser. Wearing the cape she donned to protect her clothing from the hair powder, she receives a fashion merchant, who displays an array of ribbons and other finery. (DeAgostini/DEA PICTURE LIBRARY/Getty Images)

She was the first celebrity fashion stylist and one of the first self-made career women to rise from obscurity to fame and fortune based on her talent, taste, and hard work. Her legacy remains in the exalted status of today's top fashion designers and in the dreams of small-town girls to make it in the big city.

QUESTIONS FOR ANALYSIS

1. Why was the relationship between Queen Marie Antoinette and Rose Bertin so troubling to the public? Why would relations between a queen and a fashion merchant have political implications?

2. Why would someone who sold fashionable clothing and accessories rise to such a prominent position in business and society? What makes fashion so important in the social world?

*Mémoires secrets pour servir à l'histoire de la république des lettres en France, vol. 13, 299, 5 mars 1779 (London: John Adamson, 1785).

[†]On Rose Bertin, see Clare Haru Crowston, "The Queen and Her 'Minister of Fashion': Gender, Credit and Politics in Pre-Revolutionary France," Gender and History 14, no. 1 (April 2002): 92–116.

fabrics to don early versions of the plain dark suit that remains standard male formal wear in the West. This was one more aspect of the increasingly rigid boundaries drawn between appropriate male and female behavior.

Changes in outward appearances were reflected in inner spaces, as new attitudes about privacy, individualism, and intimate life also emerged. In 1700 the cramped home of a modest family consisted of a few rooms, each of which had multiple functions. The same room was used for sleeping, receiving friends, and working. In the eighteenth century rents rose sharply, making it impossible to gain more space, but families began attributing specific functions to specific rooms. They also began to partition space within the home to provide small niches in which individuals could seek privacy. (See "Thinking Like a Historian: A New Subjectivity," page 542.)

New levels of comfort and convenience accompanied this trend toward more individualized ways of life. In 1700 a meal might be served in a common dish, with each person dipping his or her spoon into the pot. By the end of the eighteenth century even humble households contained a much greater variety of cutlery and dishes, making it possible for each person to eat from his or her own plate. More books and prints, which also proliferated at lower prices, decorated the shelves and walls. Improvements in glassmaking provided more transparent glass, which allowed daylight to penetrate into gloomy rooms. Cold and smoky hearths were increasingly replaced by more efficient and cleaner coal stoves, which also eliminated the backache of cooking over an open fire. Rooms were warmer, better lit, more comfortable, and more personalized, and the spread of street lighting made it safer to travel in cities at night.

New standards of bodily and public hygiene also emerged. Public bathhouses, popular across Europe in the Middle Ages, had gradually closed in the early modern period due to concerns over sexual promiscuity and infectious disease. Many Europeans came to fear that immersing the body in hot water would allow harmful elements to enter the skin. Carefully watched by his physician, Louis XIII of France took his first bath at age seven, while James I of England refused to wash more than his hands. Personal cleanliness consisted of wearing fresh linen and using perfume to mask odors, both expensive practices that bespoke wealth and social status. From the mid-eighteenth century on, enlightened doctors revised their views and began to urge more frequent bathing. Spa towns, like Bath, England, became popular sites for the wealthy to see each other and be seen. Officials also took measures to improve the cleaning of city streets in which trash, human soil, and animal carcasses were often left to rot.

Wedgwood Portland Vase   After serving as an apprentice in his family's small pottery business, Josiah Wedgwood (1730–1795) struck off on his own. Studying chemistry and determined to succeed, he spent his evenings experimenting with chemicals and firing conditions to produce new glazes and other innovative products. He achieved success by gaining patronage from royalty and aristocrats and then expanding beyond the luxury market with cheaper goods for the ordinary consumer. Among his inventions was jasperware, in which pieces of unglazed stoneware in pale colors were decorated with molded reliefs in contrasting colors. The vase shown here is an example of jasperware. (Heritage Images/ Hulton Archive/Getty Images)

The scope of the new consumer economy should not be exaggerated. These developments were concentrated in large cities in northwestern Europe and North America. Even in these centers the elite benefited the most from new modes of life. This was not yet the society of mass consumption that emerged toward the end of the nineteenth century with the full expansion of the Industrial Revolution. The eighteenth century did, however, lay the foundations for one of the most distinctive features of modern Western life: societies based on the consumption of goods and services obtained through the market in which individuals form their identities and self-worth through the goods they consume.

A New Subjectivity

Traditional European society was organized into groups that shared common values: families, parishes, guilds, and social ranks. Most people's time was spent working and socializing alongside people in the same group. But the eighteenth century introduced a new, more private and individualized sense of self. Artisans and merchants created a host of material goods that allowed men and women to pursue this new subjectivity in comfort and style.

1 Jean-Jacques Rousseau, *The Confessions*, 1782. Swiss philosopher Jean-Jacques Rousseau felt driven to understand and express his inner feelings. His autobiography, *The Confessions*, had an enormous impact on European culture, stirring generations of Europeans to strive for greater self-knowledge.

I have resolved on an enterprise which has no precedent, and which, once complete, will have no imitator. My purpose is to display to my kind a portrait in every way true to nature, and the man I shall portray will be myself.

Simply myself. I know my own heart and understand my fellow man. But I am made unlike any one I have ever met; I will even venture to say that I am like no one in the whole world. I may be no better, but at least I am different. Whether Nature did well or ill in breaking the mould in which she formed me, is a question which can only be resolved after the reading of my book. . . .

I have displayed myself as I was, as vile and despicable when my behavior was such, as good, generous, and noble when I was so. I have bared my secret soul as Thou thyself hast seen it, Eternal Being! So let the numberless legion of my fellow men gather round me, and hear my confessions.

2 Pierre Choderlos de Laclos, *Les Liaisons Dangereuses*, 1782. Like other elite young women of her day, the fictional heroine of this novel found privacy in a small room, or cabinet, of her own where she could read, write, and reflect. It contained a locked desk where she hid her love letters.

You see, my good friend, [that] I am keeping my word to you, and that bonnets and pompons do not take up all my time; there is some left for you. . . . Mama has consulted me about everything; she treats me much less like a schoolgirl than she used to. I have my own chambermaid; I have a bedroom and a cabinet to myself, and I am writing to you on a very pretty Secretary, to which I have been given the key, and in which I can hide whatever I wish.

3 The dressing gown. Dressing gowns became popular in the eighteenth century as a warm and comfortable garment for reading, writing, and relaxing in the privacy of the home, before putting on formal wear to go out to dinner or the theater.

(Musée du Louvre, Paris, France/Bridgeman Images)

ANALYZING THE EVIDENCE

1. What did Rousseau think was new and important about the autobiography he was writing (Source 1)?
2. What do the material objects displayed in Sources 3, 4, and 5 tell us about the new subjectivity? Why would historians turn to material objects to understand shifts in the understanding of the self? Do you see advantages or limitations to this approach?
3. Think about how different groups of people might have experienced subjectivity in distinctive ways. Why might a private room and a locked desk be particularly important for a young woman (Source 2)? What challenges would the poor face in following the path traced by Rousseau (Source 1)?

4 **The bedroom.** Architects helped create private spaces where the new subjectivity could develop. As Louis-Sébastien Mercier declared, "Wise and ingenious divisions economize the property, multiply it and give it new and precious comforts." This alcove bedchamber provided a cozy nook for receiving intimate friends and engaging in private self-reflection.

(Bridgeman Images)

(Photo © Christie's Images/Bridgeman Images)

5 **Dressing table.** This dressing table could double as a writing desk when its cleverly constructed drawers were folded away. Probate inventories show a strong rise in the number of mirrors, writing desks, and toilette items owned by men and women over the course of the eighteenth century.

PUTTING IT ALL TOGETHER

Using the sources above, along with what you have learned in class and in this chapter, write an essay that explores the connection in the eighteenth century between social relationships, the changing material circumstances of life, and developing ideas of the individual and the self.

Sources: (1) Jean-Jacques Rousseau, *The Confessions* (London: Penguin, 1953), p. 17; (2) Dena Goodman, *Becoming a Woman in the Age of Letters* (Ithaca, N.Y.: Cornell University Press, 2009), p. 243.

What role did religion play in eighteenth-century society?

Though the critical spirit of the Enlightenment made great inroads in the eighteenth century, the majority of ordinary men and women, especially those in rural areas, retained strong religious faith. The church promised salvation, and it gave comfort in the face of sorrow and death. Religion also remained strong because it was embedded in local traditions and everyday social experience.

Yet the popular religion of village Europe was also enmeshed in a larger world of church hierarchies and state power. These powerful outside forces sought to regulate religious life at the local level. Their efforts created tensions that helped set the scene for vigorous religious revivals in Protestant Germany and England as well as in Catholic France.

Church Hierarchy

In the eighteenth century religious faith not only endured, but grew more fervent in many parts of Europe. The local parish church remained the focal point of religious devotion and community cohesion. Congregants gossiped and swapped stories after services, and neighbors came together in church for baptisms, marriages, and funerals. Priests and parsons kept the community records of births, deaths, and marriages; distributed charity; and provided primary education to the common people. Thus the parish church was woven into the very fabric of community life.

While the parish church remained central to the community, it was also subject to greater control from the state. In Protestant areas, princes and monarchs headed the official church, and they regulated their "territorial churches" strictly, selecting personnel and imposing detailed rules. Clergy of the official church dominated education, and followers of other faiths suffered religious and civil discrimination. By the eighteenth century the radical ideas of the Reformation had resulted in another version of church bureaucracy.

Catholic monarchs in this period also took greater control of religious matters in their kingdoms, weakening papal authority. In both Spain and Portugal, the Catholic Church was closely associated with the state, a legacy of the long internal reconquista and sixteenth-century imperial conquests overseas. In the eighteenth century the Spanish Crown took firm control of ecclesiastical appointments. Papal proclamations could not even be read in Spanish churches without prior approval from the government. In Portugal, religious enthusiasm led to a burst of new churches and monasteries in the early eighteenth century.

France went even further in establishing a national Catholic Church, known as the Gallican Church.

Louis XIV's expulsion of Protestants in 1685 was accompanied by an insistence on the king's prerogative to choose and control bishops and issue laws regarding church affairs. Catholicism gained new ground in the Holy Roman Empire with the conversion of a number of Protestant princes and successful missionary work by Catholic orders among the populace. While it could not eradicate Protestantism altogether, the Habsburg monarchy successfully consolidated Catholicism as a pillar of its political control.

The Jesuit order played a key role in fostering the Catholic faith, providing extraordinary teachers, missionaries, and agents of the papacy. In many Catholic countries they exercised tremendous political influence, holding high government positions and educating the nobility in their colleges. By playing politics so effectively, however, the Jesuits elicited a broad coalition of enemies. Bitter controversies led Louis XV to order the Jesuits out of France in 1763 and to confiscate their property. France and Spain then pressured Rome to dissolve the Jesuits completely. In 1773 a reluctant pope caved in, although the order was revived after the French Revolution.

The Jesuit order was not the only Christian group to come under attack in the middle of the eighteenth century. The dominance of the larger Catholic Church and established Protestant churches was also challenged, both by enlightened reformers from above and by the faithful from below. Influenced by Enlightenment ideals, some Catholic rulers believed that the clergy in monasteries and convents should make a more practical contribution to social and religious life. Austria, a leader in controlling the church and promoting primary education, showed how far the process could go. Maria Theresa began by sharply restricting entry into what she termed "unproductive" orders. In his Edict on Idle Institutions, her successor, Joseph II, abolished contemplative orders, henceforth permitting only orders that were engaged in teaching, nursing, or other practical work. The state expropriated the dissolved monasteries and convents and used their wealth to create more parishes throughout Austria. This edict had a disproportionate effect on women because most of their orders were cloistered from the outside world and thus were not seen as "useful." Joseph II also issued edicts of religious tolerance, including for Jews, making Austria one of the first European states to lift centuries-old restrictions on its Jewish population.

Protestant Revival

By the late seventeenth century the vast transformations of the Protestant Reformation were complete and had been widely adopted in most Protestant churches.

Medieval practices of idolatry, saint worship, and pageantry were abolished; stained-glass windows were smashed and murals whitewashed. Yet many official Protestant churches had settled into a smug complacency. This, along with the growth of state power and bureaucracy in local parishes, threatened to eclipse one of the Reformation's main goals—to bring all believers closer to God.

In the Reformation heartland, one concerned German minister wrote that the Lutheran Church "had become paralyzed in forms of dead doctrinal conformity" and badly needed a return to its original inspiration.[21] His voice was one of many that prepared and then guided a Protestant revival that succeeded because it answered the intense but increasingly unsatisfied needs of common people.

The Protestant revival began in Germany in the late seventeenth century. It was known as **Pietism** (PIGH-uh-tih-zum), and three aspects helped explain its powerful appeal. First, Pietism called for a warm, emotional religion that everyone could experience. Enthusiasm—in prayer, in worship, in preaching, in life itself—was the key concept. "Just as a drunkard becomes full of wine, so must the congregation become filled with spirit," declared one exuberant writer.[22]

Second, Pietism reasserted the earlier radical stress on the priesthood of all believers, thereby reducing the gulf between official clergy and Lutheran laity. Bible reading and study were enthusiastically extended to all classes, providing a powerful spur for popular literacy as well as individual religious development. Pietists were largely responsible for the educational reforms implemented by Prussia in the early eighteenth century. Third and finally, Pietists believed in the practical power of Christian rebirth in everyday affairs. Reborn Christians were expected to lead good, moral lives and to come from all social classes.

Pietism soon spread through the German-speaking lands and to Scandinavia. It also had a major impact on John Wesley (1703–1791), who served as the catalyst for popular religious revival in England. Wesley came from a long line of ministers, and when he went to Oxford University to prepare for the clergy, he mapped a fanatically earnest "scheme of religion." After becoming a teaching fellow at Oxford, Wesley organized a Holy Club for similarly minded students, who were soon known contemptuously as **Methodists** because they were so methodical in their devotion. (See "Evaluating Visual Evidence: Hogarth's Satirical View of the Church," page 546.) Yet like the young Martin Luther, Wesley remained intensely troubled about his own salvation even after his ordination as an Anglican priest in 1728.

Wesley's anxieties related to grave problems of the faith in England. The government used the Church of England to provide favorites with high-paying jobs. Both church and state officials failed to respond to the spiritual needs of the people, and services and sermons had settled into an uninspiring routine. Moreover, Enlightenment skepticism was making inroads among the educated classes, and deism—a belief in God but not in organized religion—was becoming popular. Some bishops and church leaders seemed to believe that doctrines such as the virgin birth were little more than elegant superstitions.

Wesley's inner search in the 1730s was deeply affected by his encounter with Moravian Pietists, whom he first met on a ship as he traveled across the Atlantic to take up a position in Savannah, Georgia. The small Moravian community in Georgia impressed him as a productive, peaceful, and pious world, reflecting the values of the first apostles. (For more on the Moravian Church, see "Individuals in Society: Rebecca Protten" in Chapter 17.) After returning to London, following a disastrous failed engagement and the disappointment of his hopes to convert Native Americans, he sought spiritual counseling from a Pietist minister from Germany. Their conversations prepared Wesley for a mystical, emotional "conversion" in 1738. He described this critical turning point in his *Journal*:

> In the evening I went to a [Christian] society in Aldersgate Street where one was reading Luther's preface to the Epistle to the Romans. About a quarter before nine, while he was describing the change which God works in the heart through faith in Christ, I felt my heart strangely warmed. I felt I did trust in Christ, Christ alone for salvation; and an assurance was given me that he had taken away my sins, even mine, and saved me from the law of sin and death.[23]

Wesley's emotional experience resolved his intellectual doubts about the possibility of his own salvation. Moreover, he was convinced that any person, no matter how poor or uneducated, might have a similarly heartfelt conversion and gain the same blessed assurance. He took the good news to the people, traveling some 225,000 miles by horseback and preaching more than forty thousand sermons between 1750 and 1790. Since existing churches were often overcrowded and the church-state establishment was hostile, Wesley preached in open fields. People came in large numbers. Of critical importance was Wesley's rejection of Calvinist predestination—the doctrine of salvation granted to only a select few. Instead, he

■ **Pietism** A Protestant revival movement in early-eighteenth-century Germany and Scandinavia that emphasized a warm and emotional religion, the priesthood of all believers, and the power of Christian rebirth in everyday affairs.

■ **Methodists** Members of a Protestant revival movement started by John Wesley, so called because they were so methodical in their devotion.

Hogarth's Satirical View of the Church

Eighteenth-century London was a thriving, bustling city in which members of the landed gentry crossed paths with educated professionals, middling shopkeepers, and ordinary working people. In this rising commercial society, gossip and scandal circulated freely among salons, coffee shops, and tea houses and in printed newspapers and magazines. This was the great era of satire, in which writers and visual artists used humor to expose the failures of human society and institutions.

William Hogarth (1697–1764) was one of the foremost satirical artists of his day. This image, entitled "Credulity, Superstition, and Fanaticism," mocks a London Methodist meeting, where the congregation swoons in enthusiasm over the preacher's sermon. The woman in the foreground giving birth to rabbits is an allusion to a public scandal of 1726 involving a servant named Mary Tofts who claimed she gave birth to rabbits (she later confessed she had herself inserted the rabbits into her vagina). In this image the gullibility of those who believed Tofts is likened to that of the Methodist congregation. The preacher, whose robe falls open to reveal a Harlequin's costume,* is reading the Bible passage "I speak as a fool" (2 Corinthians 11:23). On the right, a religious thermometer measures the emotional state of the congregation, ranging from raving, madness, and convulsion fits at the top of the scale through sorrow, despair, and suicide at the bottom.

(The Stapleton Collection/Bridgeman Images)

EVALUATE THE EVIDENCE

1. What elements of this image convey the "Credulity, Superstition, and Fanaticism" of the title of the engraving?

2. To whom do you think Hogarth's image was addressed? What impact do you think he hoped it would have on his audience?

3. In your view, is this an effective satire of religious enthusiasm? Why or why not?

*Harlequin was the traditional character of a fool or trickster in Italian comic theater.

preached that all men and women who earnestly sought salvation might be saved. It was a message of hope and joy, of free will and universal salvation.

Wesley's ministry used lay preachers to reach new converts, formed Methodist cells, and eventually resulted in a new denomination. And just as Wesley had been inspired by the Pietist revival in Germany, so evangelicals in the Church of England and the old dissenting groups now followed Wesley's example of preaching to all people, giving impetus to an even broader awakening among the lower classes. Thus in Protestant countries religion continued to be a vital force in the lives of the people.

Catholic Piety

Religion also flourished in Catholic Europe around 1700, but there were important differences from Protestant practice. First, the visual contrast was striking; baroque art still lavished rich and emotionally exhilarating figures and images on Catholic churches, whereas most Protestant churches had removed their art during the Reformation. Moreover, people in Catholic Europe on the whole participated more actively in formal worship than did Protestants. More than 95 percent of the population probably attended church for Easter communion, the climax of the religious year.

The tremendous popular strength of religion in Catholic countries can in part be explained by the church's integral role in community life and popular culture. Thus, although Catholics reluctantly confessed their sins to priests, they enthusiastically came together in religious festivals to celebrate the passage of the liturgical year. In addition to the great processional days—such as Palm Sunday, the joyful re-enactment of Jesus's triumphal entry into Jerusalem—each parish had its own saints' days, processions, and pilgrimages. Led by its priest, a congregation might march around the village or across the countryside to a local shrine. Millions of Catholic men and women also joined religious associations, known as confraternities, where they participated in prayer and religious services and collected funds for poor relief and members' funerals. The Reformation had largely eliminated such activities in Protestant areas.

Catholicism had its own version of the Pietist revivals that shook Protestant Europe in the form of **Jansenism**. It originated with Cornelius Jansen (1585–1638), bishop of Ypres in the Spanish Netherlands, who called for a return to the austere early Christianity of Saint Augustine. In contrast to the worldly Jesuits, Jansen emphasized the heavy weight of original sin and accepted the doctrine of predestination. Although outlawed by papal and royal edicts as Calvinist heresy, Jansenism attracted Catholic followers eager for religious renewal, particularly among the French. Many members of France's

The Repression of Jansenism In 1710, the French royal government ordered the destruction of the convent of Port-Royal des Champs and the expulsion of the nuns living there, accusing the convent of being a hotbed of Jansenist subversion. Despite royal oppression, Jansenism—a movement within Catholicism emphasizing human sinfulness that was condemned by the papacy—continued to thrive in France among educated elites and the common people. (Tallandier/Bridgeman Images)

urban elite, especially judicial nobles and some parish priests, became known for their Jansenist piety and spiritual devotion. Such stern religious values encouraged the judiciary's increasing opposition to the French monarchy in the second half of the eighteenth century.

Among the urban poor, a different strain of Jansenism took hold. Prayer meetings brought men and women together in ecstatic worship, and some participants fell into convulsions and spoke in tongues. The police of Paris posted spies to report on such gatherings and conducted mass raids and arrests.

■ **Jansenism** A sect of Catholicism originating with Cornelius Jansen that emphasized the heavy weight of original sin and accepted the doctrine of predestination; it was outlawed as heresy by the pope.

Marginal Beliefs and Practices

In the countryside, many peasants continued to hold religious beliefs that were marginal to the Christian faith altogether, often of obscure or even pagan origin. On the Feast of Saint Anthony, for example, priests were expected to bless salt and bread for farm animals to protect them from disease. Catholics believed that saints' relics could bring fortune or attract lovers, and there were healing springs for many ailments. In 1796 the Lutheran villagers of Beutelsbach in southern Germany incurred the ire of local officials when they buried a live bull at a crossroads to ward off an epidemic of hoof-and-mouth disease.[24] The ordinary person combined strong Christian faith with a wealth of time-honored superstitions.

Inspired initially by the fervor of the Reformation era, then by the critical rationalism of the Enlightenment, religious and secular authorities sought increasingly to "purify" popular spirituality. Thus one parish priest in France lashed out at his parishioners, claiming that they were "more superstitious than devout . . . and sometimes appear as baptized idolators."[25]

French priests particularly denounced the "various remnants of paganism" found in popular bonfire ceremonies during Lent, in which young men, "yelling and screaming like madmen," tried to jump over the bonfires in order to help the crops grow and to protect themselves from illness. One priest saw rational Christians regressing into pagan animals — "the triumph of Hell and the shame of Christianity."[26]

The severity of the attack on popular belief varied widely by country and region. Where authorities pursued purification vigorously, as in Austria under Joseph II, pious peasants saw only an incomprehensible attack on age-old faith and drew back in anger. It was in this era of rationalism and disdain for superstition that the persecution of witches slowly came to an end across Europe. Common people in the countryside continued to fear the Devil and his helpers, but the elite increasingly dismissed such fears and refused to prosecute suspected witches. The last witch was executed in England in 1682, the same year France prohibited witchcraft trials. By the late eighteenth century the witchcraft hunts had ended across Europe.

How did the practice of medicine evolve in the eighteenth century?

Although significant breakthroughs in medical science would not come until the middle and late nineteenth century, the Enlightenment's optimism and its focus on improving human life through understanding of the laws of nature produced a great deal of research and experimentation in the eighteenth century. Medical practitioners greatly increased in number, although their techniques did not differ much from those of previous generations. Care of the sick in this era was the domain of several competing groups: traditional healers, apothecaries (pharmacists), physicians, surgeons, and midwives. From the Middle Ages through the seventeenth century, both men and women were medical practitioners. However, since women were generally denied admission to medical colleges and lacked the diplomas necessary to practice, the range of medical activities open to them was restricted. In the eighteenth century women's traditional roles as midwives and healers eroded even further.

Faith Healing and General Practice

In the course of the eighteenth century, traditional healers remained active, drawing on centuries of folk knowledge about the curative properties of roots, herbs, and other plants. Faith healing also remained popular, especially in the countryside. Faith healers and their patients believed that evil spirits caused illness by lodging in people and that the proper treatment was to exorcise, or drive out, the offending devil. Religious and secular officials did their best to stamp out such practices, but with little success.

In the larger towns and cities, apothecaries sold a vast number of herbs, drugs, and patent medicines for every conceivable "temperament and distemper." By the eighteenth century many of these medicines were derived from imported plants. The Asian spices prized since medieval times often had medicinal uses; from the sixteenth century onward, the Portuguese and then the Dutch dominated the Indian Ocean trade in these spices. As Europeans expanded to the New World, they brought a keen interest in potentially effective and highly profitable medicinal plants. Botanists accompanied European administrators and explorers to the Americas, where they profited from the healing traditions of Indigenous peoples and, in the plantation societies of the Caribbean, enslaved Africans. They returned to Europe with a host of medicinal plants such as ipecacuanha, sarsaparilla, opium, and cinchona, the first effective treatment for fever. Over the course of the seventeenth century, imports of medicinal plants boomed. By the late eighteenth century, England was importing annually £100,000 worth of drugs, compared to only £1,000 or £2,000 in 1600.[27]

Like all varieties of medical practitioners, apothecaries advertised their wares, their high-class customers, and their miraculous cures in newspapers and

VIEWPOINTS

The Case for and Against Female Midwives

Until the middle of the seventeenth century, mothers delivered babies with the assistance of female relatives and friends and, for difficult births, female midwives. During the late seventeenth century, male medical practitioners, so-called man-midwives, began to move into the realm of childbirth, seeking to eliminate female competition by arguing that women were incapable of acquiring medical skill and that female midwives were ignorant and dangerous. One such male practitioner was Louis Lapeyre, author of the first excerpt, below. In response to this criticism, female midwives, including Angélique du Coudray in France, began to develop training programs for women. Du Coudray traveled all over France using a life-size model of the female torso and fetus to help teach illiterate women.

A Man-Midwife Criticizes Female Midwives, 1772

⟋ A midwife is usually a creature of the lowest class of human beings, and of course utterly destitute of education, who from indigence, and that she is incapable of everything else, has been compelled to follow, as the last and sole resource a profession which people fondly imagine no very difficult one, never dreaming that the least glimpse of previous instruction is required for that purpose. . . . Midwives are universally ignorant. For where or how should she come by any thing deserving the name of knowledge[?] It could not possibly be whilst she was a girl, since, even had she been daughter of the first man-midwife in Europe, I will venture to say, that no father would be rash enough to communicate to a young creature . . . such instructions as are indispensably necessary to accomplish her in the art he professed. . . .

In a word, a midwife is an animal, who has nothing of the woman left, but the weakness of her understanding, the wretched prejudices of old doting women, the perpetual prating of a superannuated gossip, the *routine* of ignorance, and that unfeeling heart, which renders female old age almost always callous to the misery and sufferings of those, whose youth excites her jealousy; and lastly, a mean and sordid avarice, which makes her precipitate the delivery at all events, that the business may be the sooner over.

Madame du Coudray, *Manual on the Art of Childbirth*, 1757

⟋ The infinite calamities caused by ignorance in the countryside and which my profession has given me occasion to witness moved me to compassion and animated my zeal to procure more secure relief for humanity. Drawn to Auvergne, I invented there a machine for demonstrating delivery. . . . The advantages of this invention are immediately apparent. The academy [of Surgery] approved it and the king accorded me a certificate permitting me to teach throughout the realm. . . . In three months of lessons a woman free of prejudice, and who has never had the remotest knowledge of childbirth, will be sufficiently trained. We have the advantage of students practicing on the machine and performing all the deliveries imaginable. Therein lies the principal merit of this invention. A surgeon or a woman who takes the sort of course available until now will learn only theory [and will expect] the situations encountered in practice to be uniform. . . . But when difficulties arise they are absolutely unskilled and until long experience instructs them they are the witness or the cause of many misfortunes.

QUESTIONS FOR ANALYSIS

1. According to Lapeyre (the author of the first text above), why are female midwives incompetent? Why would a father refuse to impart obstetric knowledge to his daughter?
2. How does du Coudray propose to solve the deficiencies of training among midwives criticized by Lapeyre? To what extent does she share Lapeyre's negative attitude regarding female midwives?
3. What does a comparison between these two documents reveal about attitudes toward gender and medical practice in this period?

Sources: Louis Lapeyre, *An Enquiry into the Merits of These Two Important Questions: I. Whether Women with Child Ought to Prefer the Assistance of Their Own Sex to That of Men-Midwives? II. Whether the Assistance of Men-Midwives Is Contrary to Decency?* (London: S. Bladon, 1772), pp. 29, 31, 35, 37, 39, 41; "The National Midwife's Mission Statement," cited in Nina Gelbart, *The King's Midwife: A History and Mystery of Madame du Coudray* (Berkeley and Los Angeles: University of California Press, 2002), pp. 16–17.

commercial circulars. Medicine, like food and fashionable clothing, thus joined the era's new and loosely regulated commercial culture.

Physicians, who were almost always men, were apprenticed in their teens to practicing physicians for several years of on-the-job training. This training was then rounded out with hospital work or some university courses. Seen as gentlemen who did not labor with their hands, many physicians diagnosed and treated patients by correspondence or through oral dialogue,

without conducting a physical examination. Because their training was expensive, physicians came mainly from prosperous families and usually concentrated on urban patients from similar social backgrounds. Nevertheless, even poor people spent hard-won resources to seek treatment for their loved ones.

Physicians in the eighteenth century were increasingly willing to experiment with new methods, but time-honored practices lay heavily on them. They laid great stress on purging, and bloodletting was still

The Cow Pock, or the Wonderful Effects of the New Inoculation Artist James Gillray created this satirical print in 1802, four years after Edward Jenner published a book describing his success in vaccinating patients against smallpox, a disease that at the time killed approximately 400,000 people per year in Europe. As the print suggests, controversy quickly arose about the practice, in part generated by the vaccine's origins in cowpox. Gillray mocks critics' opposition by showing cows erupting from patients' bodies and one woman growing horns. With successful public education efforts and government mandates, vaccination against smallpox and other infectious diseases spread across the world in the nineteenth and twentieth centuries, saving untold millions of lives. (James Gillray (1757–1815)/Private Collection/Bridgeman Images)

considered a medical cure-all. It was the way "bad blood," the cause of illness, was removed and the balance of humors necessary for good health was restored.

Improvements in Surgery

Long considered to be craftsmen comparable to butchers and barbers, surgeons began studying anatomy seriously and improved their art in the eighteenth century. With endless opportunities to practice, army surgeons on gory battlefields led the way. They learned that the life of a soldier with an extensive wound, such as a shattered leg or arm, could perhaps be saved if the surgeon could apply a flat surface above the wound that could be cauterized with fire. Thus, if a soldier had a broken limb and the bone stuck out, the surgeon amputated so that the remaining stump could be cauterized and the likelihood of death reduced.

The eighteenth-century surgeon (and patient) labored in the face of incredible difficulties. Almost all operations were performed without painkillers, for the anesthesia of the day was hard to control and too dangerous for general use. Many patients died from the agony and shock of such operations. Surgery was also performed in utterly unsanitary conditions, for there was no knowledge of bacteriology and the nature of infection. The simplest wound treated by a surgeon could fester and lead to death.

Midwifery

Midwives continued to deliver the overwhelming majority of babies throughout the eighteenth century.

Trained initially by another woman practitioner — and regulated by a guild in some cities — the midwife primarily assisted in labor and delivering babies. She also ministered to small children and treated female problems, such as irregular menstrual cycles, breast-feeding difficulties, infertility, and venereal disease.

The midwife orchestrated labor and birth in a woman's world, where friends and relatives assisted the pregnant woman in the familiar surroundings of her own home. The male surgeon (and the husband) rarely entered this female world, because most births, then as now, were normal and spontaneous. After the invention of forceps became publicized in 1734, surgeon-physicians used their monopoly over this and other instruments to seek lucrative new business. Attacking midwives as ignorant and dangerous, they sought to undermine faith in midwives and persuaded growing numbers of wealthy women of the superiority of their services (see "Viewpoints: The Case for and Against Female Midwives," page 549). Despite criticism, it appears that midwives generally lost no more babies than did male doctors, who were still summoned to treat non-elite women only when life-threatening situations required surgery.

Women also continued to perform almost all nursing. Female religious orders ran many hospitals, and at-home nursing was almost exclusively the province of women. Thus, although they were excluded from the growing ranks of formally trained and authorized practitioners, women continued to perform the bulk of informal medical care. Nursing as a secular profession did not emerge until the nineteenth century.

Smallpox and the Birth of Vaccination

Experimentation and the intensified search for solutions to human problems led to some real advances in medicine after 1750. The eighteenth century's greatest medical triumph was the eradication of smallpox. With the progressive decline of bubonic plague, smallpox became the most terrible of the infectious diseases, and it is estimated that 60 million Europeans died of it in the eighteenth century.

The first step in the conquest of this killer in Europe came in the early eighteenth century. An English aristocrat whose beauty had been marred by the pox, Lady Mary Wortley Montagu, learned about the long-established practice of smallpox inoculation in the Muslim lands of western Asia while her husband was serving as British ambassador to the Ottoman Empire. Determined to use the most advanced scientific practices to protect her son from a potentially lethal disease, she had him successfully inoculated with the pus from a smallpox victim. Montagu was then instrumental in spreading the practice in England after her return in 1722. But inoculation was risky and was widely condemned because about one person in fifty died from it. In addition, people who had been inoculated were infectious and often spread the disease.

While the practice of inoculation with the smallpox virus was refined over the century, the crucial breakthrough was made by Edward Jenner (1749–1823), a talented country doctor. His starting point was the countryside belief that dairymaids who had contracted cowpox did not get smallpox. Cowpox produces sores that resemble those of smallpox, but the disease is mild and is not contagious.

For eighteen years Jenner practiced a kind of Baconian science, carefully collecting data. Finally, in 1796 he performed his first vaccination on a young boy using matter taken from a milkmaid with cowpox. After performing more successful vaccinations, Jenner published his findings in 1798. The new method of treatment—which effectively protected against smallpox and did not carry the same risks as inoculating with live smallpox virus—spread rapidly. Smallpox soon declined to the point of disappearance in Europe and then throughout the world. As the creator of the world's first vaccine, Jenner is credited with saving more lives than perhaps any other individual in history.

NOTES

1. Quoted in J. M. Beattie, "The Criminality of Women in Eighteenth-Century England," *Journal of Social History* 8 (Summer 1975): 86.

2. Quoted in Richard Cobb, *The Police and the People: French Popular Protest, 1789–1820* (Oxford: Clarendon Press, 1970), p. 238.

3. Peter Laslett, *Family Life and Illicit Love: Essays in Historical Sociology* (Cambridge: Cambridge University Press, 1977).

4. Gay Gullickson, *Spinners and Weavers of Auffay: Rural Industry and the Sexual Division of Labor in a French Village, 1750–1850* (Cambridge: Cambridge University Press, 1986), p. 186.

5. Louis Crompton, *Homosexuality and Civilization* (Cambridge, Mass.: Belknap Press, 2003), p. 321.

6. D. S. Neff, "Bitches, Mollies, and Tommies: Byron, Masculinity and the History of Sexualities," *Journal of the History of Sexuality* 11, no. 3 (July 2002): 404.

7. George E. Haggerty, ed., *Encyclopedia of Gay Histories and Cultures* (New York: Garland Publishing, 2000), pp. 1311–1312.

8. Pier Paolo Viazzo, "Mortality, Fertility, and Family," in *Family Life in Early Modern Times, 1500–1789*, ed. David I. Kertzer and Marzio Barbagli (New Haven, Conn.: Yale University Press, 2001), p. 180.

9. Viazzo, "Mortality, Fertility, and Family," p. 166.

10. George Sussman, *Selling Mother's Milk: The Wet-Nursing Business in France, 1715–1914* (Urbana: University of Illinois Press, 1982), p. 22.

11. Yves Blayo, "La Mortalité en France de 1740 à 1820," *Population*, special issue 30 (1975): 135.

12. Viazzo, "Mortality, Fertility, and Family," pp. 176–178.

13. Alysa Levene, "The Estimation of Mortality at the London Foundling Hospital, 1741–99," *Population Studies* 59, no. 1 (2005): 87–97.

14. Quoted in Robert Woods, "Did Montaigne Love His Children? Demography and the Hypothesis of Parental Indifference," *Journal of Interdisciplinary History* 33, no. 3 (2003): 421.

15. Quoted in Gay Ochiltree and Don Edgar, *The Changing Face of Childhood* (Melbourne: Institute of Family Studies, 1981), p. 11.

16. James Van Horn Melton, *Absolutism and the Eighteenth-Century Origins of Compulsory Schooling in Prussia and Austria* (Cambridge: Cambridge University Press, 2003), p. 46.

17. James Van Horn Melton, "The Theresian School Reform of 1774," in *Early Modern Europe*, ed. James B. Collins and Karen L. Taylor (Oxford: Blackwell, 2006).

18. Jeremy Black, *The English Press in the Eighteenth Century* (Philadelphia: University of Pennsylvania Press, 1987), p. 262.

19. Neil McKendrik, John Brewer, and J. H. Plumb, *The Birth of a Consumer Society: The Commercialization of Eighteenth-Century England* (Bloomington: Indiana University Press, 1982).

20. Quoted in Cissie Fairchilds, "The Production and Marketing of Populuxe Goods in Eighteenth-Century Paris," in *Consumption and the World of Goods*, ed. John Brewer and Roy Porter (London: Routledge, 1993), p. 228.

21. Quoted in Koppel Pinson, *Pietism as a Factor in the Rise of German Nationalism* (New York: Columbia University Press, 1934), p. 13.

22. Pinson, *Pietism as a Factor*, pp. 43–44.

23. Quoted in Stuart Andrews, *Methodism and Society* (London: Longmans, Green, 1970), p. 327.

24. David Sabean, *The Power in the Blood: Popular Culture and Village Discourse in Early Modern Germany* (Cambridge: Cambridge University Press, 1984), p. 174.

25. Quoted in Isser Woloch, *Eighteenth-Century Europe: Tradition and Progress, 1715–1789* (New York: W. W. Norton, 1982), p. 292.

26. Quoted in Timothy Tackett, *Priest and Parish in Eighteenth-Century France* (Princeton, N.J.: Princeton University Press, 1977), p. 214.

27. Patrick Wallis, "Exotic Drugs and English Medicine: England's Drug Trade, c. 1550–c. 1800," *Social History of Medicine* 2, no. 1 (2012): 26.

LOOKING BACK LOOKING AHEAD

The fundamental patterns of life in early modern Europe remained very much the same up to the eighteenth century. The vast majority of people lived in the countryside and followed age-old rhythms of seasonal labor in the fields and farmyard. Community ties were close in small villages, where the struggle to prevail over harsh conditions called on all hands to work together and to pray together. The daily life of a peasant in 1700 would have been familiar to his ancestors in the fifteenth century. Indeed, the three orders of society enshrined in the medieval social hierarchy—clergy, nobility, peasantry—were binding legal categories in France up to 1789.

And yet, the economic changes inaugurated in the late seventeenth century—intensive agriculture, cottage industry, the industrious revolution, and colonial expansion—contributed to the profound social and cultural transformation of daily life in eighteenth-century Europe. Men and women of the laboring classes, especially in the cities, experienced change in many facets of their daily lives: in loosened community controls over sex and marriage, rising literacy rates, new goods and new forms of self-expression, and a wave of religious piety that challenged traditional orthodoxies. Lay and secular elites attacked some forms of popular life, but considerable overlap continued between popular and elite culture.

Economic, social, and cultural change would culminate in the late eighteenth century with the outbreak of revolution in the Americas and Europe. Initially led by the elite, political upheavals relied on the enthusiastic participation of the poor and their desire for greater inclusion in the life of the nation. Such movements also encountered resistance from the common people when revolutionaries trampled on their religious faith. For many observers, contemporaries and historians alike, the transformations of the eighteenth century constituted a fulcrum between the old world of hierarchy and tradition and the modern world with its claims to equality and freedom.

Make Connections

Think about the larger developments and continuities within and across chapters.

1. How did the expansion of agriculture and trade (Chapter 17) contribute to changes in daily life in the eighteenth century?

2. What were the main areas of improvement in the lives of the common people in the eighteenth century, and what aspects of life remained unchanged or even deteriorated?

3. How did Enlightenment thought (Chapter 16) affect education, child care, medicine, and religion in the eighteenth century?

18 REVIEW & EXPLORE

Identify Key Terms

Identify and explain the significance of each item below.

community controls (p. 528)

charivari (p. 528)

illegitimacy explosion (p. 529)

wet-nursing (p. 531)

blood sports (p. 535)

carnival (p. 535)

just price (p. 536)

consumer revolution (p. 537)

Pietism (p. 545)

Methodists (p. 545)

Jansenism (p. 547)

Review the Main Ideas

Answer the section heading questions from the chapter.

1. How did marriage and family life change in the eighteenth century? (p. 526)
2. What was life like for children, and how did attitudes toward childhood evolve? (p. 530)
3. How did increasing literacy and new patterns of consumption affect people's lives? (p. 534)
4. What role did religion play in eighteenth-century society? (p. 544)
5. How did the practice of medicine evolve in the eighteenth century? (p. 548)

Suggested Resources

BOOKS

- Bennet, Michael. *War Against Smallpox: Edward Jenner and the Global Spread of Vaccination.* 2020. A study of the development of a vaccine against smallpox and the expansion of the vaccine across the globe.
- Bongie, Laurence L. *From Rogue to Everyman: A Foundling's Journey to the Bastille.* 2005. The story of an eighteenth-century orphan and, through his eyes, the Parisian underworld of gamblers, prostitutes, and police spies.
- Burke, Peter. *Popular Culture in Early Modern Europe*, 3d ed. 2009. An updated version of a classic introduction to everyday life, mentalities, and leisure pursuits.
- Gatrell, Vic. *City of Laughter: Sex and Satire in Eighteenth-Century London.* 2007. A study of eighteenth-century visual satire as a window into the new sensibilities and sexual attitudes of the day.
- Gawthrop, Richard. *Pietism and the Making of Eighteenth-Century Prussia.* 2006. An examination of the importance of Pietist morality and institutions in the making of the Prussian state.
- Gelbart, Nina. *The King's Midwife: A History and Mystery of Madame du Coudray.* 2002. A vivid and accessible biography of the most famous midwife of eighteenth-century France.

- Goodman, Dena. *Becoming a Woman in the Age of Letters.* 2009. An exploration of women as writers in the eighteenth century, delving into their use of writing as a form of self-expression and the material culture of desks, pens, and rooms that enabled them to write.
- Hardwick, Julie. *Sex in an Old Regime City: Young Workers and Intimacy in France, 1660–1789.* 2020. A lively and engaging study of love and sex among young men and women of the working classes in eighteenth-century France.
- Kertzer, David I., and Marzio Barbagli, eds. *Family Life in Early Modern Times, 1500–1789.* 2001. A rich collection of essays on the history of the family, women, and children in early modern Europe.
- Kushner, Nina. *Erotic Exchanges: The World of Elite Prostitution in Eighteenth-Century Paris.* 2013. A study of the lives and careers of courtesans in the French capital.
- Merritt, Jane T. *The Trouble with Tea: The Politics of Consumption in the Eighteenth-Century Global Economy.* 2017. An examination of how tea shifted from a luxury good to an everyday necessity and the impact of its consumption on global trade and politics.

MEDIA

- *At Home with the Georgians* (BBC, 2011). A documentary examining the new domestic ideals of the eighteenth century, with re-enactments of daily life in British homes in all ranks of society.
- *Becoming Jane* (Julian Jarrold, 2007). The early life of famous novelist Jane Austen; mixes fact with fiction to make her the protagonist of a romance in the spirit of her own novels.
- *City of Vice* (Channel 4, 2008). A British crime series focusing on Henry Fielding, the eighteenth-century writer and magistrate who founded the first police force of London, the Bow Street Runners.
- *Colonial Williamsburg.* The website for Colonial Williamsburg offers many resources for exploring everyday life in the eighteenth century, including an online tour of the historic site, descriptions of the eighteenth-century people and trades, and short videos illustrating many aspects of daily life. **http://www.history.org/**

- *The Fortunes and Misfortunes of Moll Flanders* (PBS, 1996). A lively Masterpiece Theater adaptation of Daniel Defoe's famous novel recounting an orphaned girl's struggle to survive in eighteenth-century London.
- *The Freedom of the Streets: Gender and Urban Space in Eurasia, 1600–1850.* The website of a research group dedicated to analyzing the ways in which early modern cities in Europe and Asia were shaped by gender.
- *A History of Private Life* (BBC Radio 4, 2009). A radio documentary series, available on CD, that examines four hundred years of domestic life, drawn from letters and diaries.
- *London Lives.* A collection of almost 250,000 searchable digitized primary sources about ordinary people in eighteenth-century London, including criminal trials, hospital records, and other documents. **www.londonlives.org/static/Project.jsp**

19

Revolutions in Politics

1775–1815

A great wave of revolution rocked both sides of the Atlantic Ocean in the last decades of the eighteenth century. With trade goods, individuals, and ideas circulating in ever-greater numbers across the Atlantic Ocean, debates and events in one locale soon influenced those in another. Changing social realities challenged the old order of life, and Enlightenment ideals of freedom and equality flourished, leading reformers in many places to demand fundamental changes in politics and government. At the same time, wars fought for dominance of the Atlantic economy left European states weakened by crushing debts, making them vulnerable to calls for reform.

The revolutionary era began in North America in 1775, and the United States of America won freedom from Britain in 1783. Then in 1789, France, the most populous country in western Europe and a center of culture and intellectual life, became the leading revolutionary nation. It established first a constitutional monarchy, then a radical republic, and finally a new European empire under Napoleon that would last until 1815. Inspired both by the ideals of the Revolution on the continent and by their own experiences and desires, enslaved people in the French colony of Saint-Domingue rose up in 1791. Their rebellion would eventually lead to the creation of the new independent nation of Haiti in 1804. In Europe and its colonies abroad, the age of modern politics was born. ■

CHAPTER PREVIEW

- What were the factors behind the revolutions of the late eighteenth century?

- Why and how did American colonists forge a new, independent nation?

- How did the events of 1789 result in a constitutional monarchy in France?

- Why and how did the French Revolution take a radical turn?

- How did Napoleon Bonaparte create a French empire, and why did it fail?

- How did revolt by enslaved people on colonial Saint-Domingue lead to the independent nation of Haiti?

The Taking of the Bastille, July 14, 1789
The French Revolution began on July 14, 1789, when a group of angry Parisians attacked a royal prison on the east side of the city, known as the Bastille. Although only seven prisoners were being held at the time, the prison had become a symbol of despotic rule. (Art Images/Hulton Fine Art Collection/Getty Images)

What were the factors behind the revolutions of the late eighteenth century?

The origins of the late-eighteenth-century revolutions in British North America, France, and Haiti were complex. No one cause lay behind them, nor was revolution inevitable or certain of success. However, a set of shared factors helped set the stage for revolt. Among them were fundamental social and economic changes and political crises that eroded state authority. Another significant cause of revolutionary fervor was the impact of political ideas derived from the Enlightenment. Even though most Enlightenment writers were cautious about political reform, their confidence in reason and progress helped inspire a new generation to fight for greater freedom from repressive governments. Perhaps most important, financial crises generated by the expenses of imperial warfare brought European states to their knees and allowed abstract discussions of reform to become pressing realities.

Social Change

Eighteenth-century European society was legally divided into groups with special privileges, such as the nobility and the clergy, and groups with special burdens, such as the peasantry. Nobles were the largest landowners, possessing one-quarter of the agricultural land of France, while constituting less than 2 percent of the population. In many parts of Europe, nobles enjoyed exemption from direct taxation as well as exclusive rights to hunt game, bear swords, and use gold thread in their clothing. Various middle-class groups — professionals, merchants, and guild masters — enjoyed privileges that allowed them to monopolize all sorts of economic activity. Poor peasants and urban laborers, who constituted the vast majority of the population, bore the brunt of taxation and were excluded from the world of privilege.

Traditional prerogatives persisted in societies undergoing dramatic and destabilizing change. Europe's population rose rapidly after 1750, and its cities and towns swelled in size. Inflation kept pace with population growth, making it ever more difficult to find affordable food and living space. One way the poor kept up, and even managed to participate in the new consumer revolution (see "How did increasing literacy and new patterns of consumption affect people's lives?" in Chapter 18), was by working harder and for longer hours. More women and children entered the paid labor force, challenging the traditional hierarchies and customs of village life.

Economic growth created new inequalities between rich and poor. While the poor struggled with rising prices, investors grew rich from the spread of rural manufacture and overseas trade, including the trade in enslaved people and in goods created by their labor. Old distinctions between landed aristocracy and city merchants began to fade as enterprising nobles put money into trade and rising middle-class bureaucrats and merchants purchased landed estates and noble titles. Marriages between proud nobles and wealthy, educated commoners (called the *bourgeoisie* [boor-ZHWAH-zee] in France) served both groups' interests, and a mixed elite began to take shape. In the context of these changes, ancient privileges seemed to pose an intolerable burden to many observers.

Another social change involved the racial regimes established in European colonies to legitimize and protect slavery. By the late eighteenth century European law accepted that only Africans and people of African descent were subject to slavery. Even free people of color — a term for people of African or African-European descent who were not enslaved — were subject to special laws restricting the property they could own, whom they could marry, and what clothes they could wear. Racial privilege conferred a new dimension of entitlement on European settlers in the colonies, and they used extremely brutal methods to enforce it. The contradiction between slavery and the Enlightenment ideals of liberty and equality was all too evident to enslaved and free people of color.

Growing Demands for Liberty and Equality

In addition to destabilizing social changes, the ideals of liberty and equality helped fuel revolutions in the Atlantic world. The call for liberty was first of all a call for individual human rights. Supporters of the cause of individual liberty (who became known as "liberals" in the early nineteenth century) demanded freedom to worship according to the dictates of their consciences, an end to censorship, and freedom from arbitrary laws and from judges who simply obeyed orders from the government. The Declaration of the Rights of Man and of the Citizen, issued at the beginning of the French Revolution, proclaimed that "liberty consists in being able to do anything that does not harm another person." In the context of the monarchical and absolutist forms of government then dominating Europe, this was a truly radical idea.

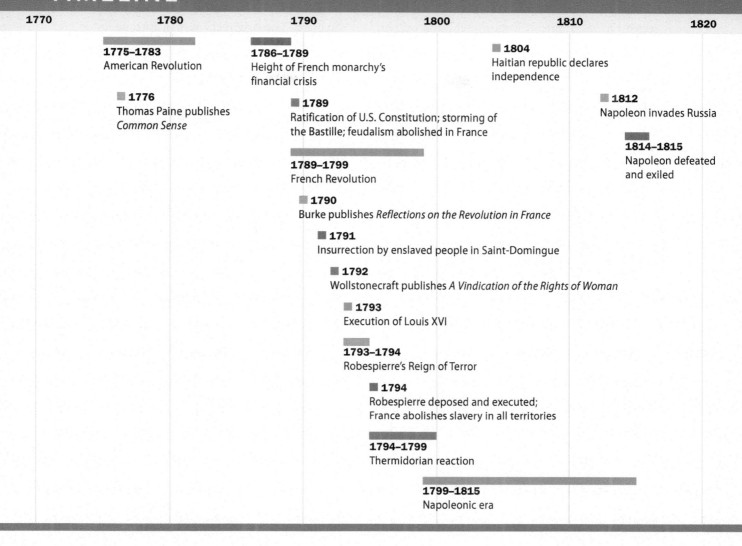

1770   1780   1790   1800   1810   1820

1775–1783
American Revolution

1786–1789
Height of French monarchy's
financial crisis

1804
Haitian republic declares
independence

1776
Thomas Paine publishes
Common Sense

1789
Ratification of U.S. Constitution; storming of
the Bastille; feudalism abolished in France

1812
Napoleon invades Russia

1789–1799
French Revolution

1814–1815
Napoleon defeated
and exiled

1790
Burke publishes *Reflections on the Revolution in France*

1791
Insurrection by enslaved people in Saint-Domingue

1792
Wollstonecraft publishes *A Vindication of the Rights of Woman*

1793
Execution of Louis XVI

1793–1794
Robespierre's Reign of Terror

1794
Robespierre deposed and executed;
France abolishes slavery in all territories

1794–1799
Thermidorian reaction

1799–1815
Napoleonic era

The call for liberty was also a call for a new kind of government. Reformers believed that the people had sovereignty — that is, that the people alone had the authority to make laws limiting an individual's freedom of action. In practice, this system of government meant choosing legislators who represented the people and were accountable to them. Monarchs might retain their thrones, but their rule should be constrained by the will of the people.

Equality was a more ambiguous idea. Eighteenth-century liberals argued that, in theory, all citizens should have identical rights and liberties and that the nobility had no right to special privileges based on birth. However, they accepted a number of distinctions. First, most eighteenth-century liberals were men of their times, and they generally believed that equality between men and women was neither practical nor desirable. Women played an important political role in the revolutionary movements at several points, but the men who wrote constitutions for the new republics limited formal political rights — the right to vote, to run for office, and to participate in government — to men. Second, few liberals questioned the superiority of people of European descent over those of Indigenous or African origin. Even those who believed that the slave trade was unjust and should be abolished, such as Thomas Jefferson (who himself owned hundreds of enslaved people), usually felt that emancipation was so dangerous that it must be undertaken slowly and gradually, if at all.

Third, liberals never believed that everyone should be equal economically. Great differences in fortune between rich and poor were perfectly acceptable. The essential point was that every free white male should have a legally equal chance at economic gain. However limited they appear to modern eyes, these demands for liberty and equality were revolutionary in the eighteenth-century context.

The two most important Enlightenment references for late-eighteenth-century liberals were John Locke and the baron de Montesquieu (see Chapter 16). Locke maintained that England's long political tradition rested on "the rights of Englishmen" and on representative government through Parliament. He argued that if a government oversteps its proper function of protecting the natural rights of life, liberty, and private property, it becomes a tyranny. Montesquieu was also inspired by English constitutional history and the Glorious Revolution of 1688–1689, which placed sovereignty in Parliament. He, too, believed that powerful "intermediary groups" — such as the judicial nobility of which he was a proud member — offered the best defense of liberty against despotism.

The belief that representative institutions could defend their liberty and interests appealed powerfully to the educated middle classes. Yet liberal ideas about individual rights and political freedom also appealed to members of the hereditary nobility, at least in western Europe and as formulated by Montesquieu. Representative government did not mean democracy, which liberal thinkers tended to equate with mob rule. Rather, they envisioned voting for representatives who owned property — those with "a stake in society." The blurring of practical distinctions between landed aristocrats and wealthy commoners meant that there was no clear-cut opposition between nobles and non-nobles on political issues.

Revolutions thus began with aspirations for equality and liberty among the social elite. Soon, however, dissenting voices emerged as some revolutionaries became frustrated with the limitations of liberal notions of equality and liberty and clamored for a fuller realization of these concepts. Depending on location, their demands included universal male suffrage, political rights for women and free people of color, the emancipation of enslaved people, and government regulations to reduce economic inequality. The age of revolution was thus marked by bitter conflicts over how far reform should go and to whom it should apply. (See "Thinking Like a Historian: The Rights of Which Men?" on page 568.)

The Seven Years' War

The roots of revolutionary ideas could be found in Enlightenment texts, but it was by no means inevitable that such ideas would result in revolution. Instead, events — political, economic, and military — created crises that opened the door for the development of radical thought and action. One of the most important was the global conflict known as the Seven Years' War (1756–1763).

The war's battlefields stretched from central Europe to India, West Africa, the Philippines, and North America (where the conflict was known as the French and Indian War), pitting a new alliance of England and Prussia against the French, Austrians, and, later, Spanish. The origins of war in Europe lay in conflicts left unresolved at the end of the War of the Austrian Succession in 1748 (see "Frederick the Great of Prussia" in Chapter 16), during which Prussia seized the Austrian territory of Silesia. In central Europe, Austria's empress Maria Theresa vowed to win back Silesia and to crush Prussia, thereby re-establishing the Habsburgs' traditional leadership in German affairs. By the end of the Seven Years' War, Austria had almost succeeded, but Prussia survived with its boundaries intact.

Inconclusive in Europe, the Seven Years' War was the decisive round in the Franco-British competition for colonial empire. In North America, hostilities resulted from unresolved tensions regarding the border between the French and British colonies. The population of New France was centered in Quebec and along the St. Lawrence River, but French soldiers and Canadian fur traders had also built forts and trading posts along the Great Lakes, through the Ohio country, and down the Mississippi to New Orleans. Allied with Indigenous nations, the French built more forts in 1753 in what is now western Pennsylvania to protect their claims. The following year a Virginia force attacked a small group of French soldiers; thus war began in North America prior to the formal outbreak of hostilities between France and Britain on the European continent.

Although the inhabitants of New France were greatly outnumbered — Canada counted 55,000 inhabitants, compared to 1.2 million in the thirteen English colonies — French forces achieved major victories until 1758. Both sides relied on the participation of Indigenous groups with whom they had long-standing trading contacts and actively sought new Indigenous allies during the conflict. The tide of the conflict turned when the British diverted resources from the war in Europe, using superior sea power to destroy France's fleet and choke its commerce around the world. In 1759 the British laid siege to Quebec for four long months, finally defeating the French in a battle that sealed the nation's fate in North America.

British victory on all colonial fronts was ratified in the 1763 Treaty of Paris. Canada and all French territory east of the Mississippi River passed to Britain, and France ceded Louisiana to Spain as compensation for Spain's loss of Florida to Britain. France also gave up most of its holdings in India, opening the way to British dominance on the subcontinent (Map 19.1).

By 1763 Britain had realized its goal of monopolizing a vast trading and colonial empire, but at a tremendous cost in war debt. France emerged from the conflict humiliated and broke, but with its profitable Caribbean colonies intact. In the aftermath of war, both British and French governments had to raise

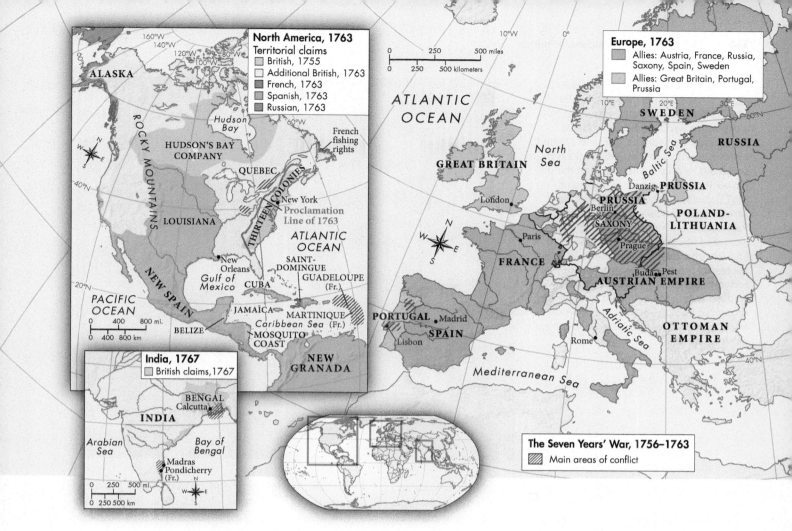

MAP 19.1 The Seven Years' War in Europe, North America, and India, 1756–1763 As a result of the war, France lost its vast territories in North America and India. In an effort to avoid costly conflicts with Native Americans living in the newly conquered territory, the British government in 1763 prohibited colonists from settling west of the Appalachian Mountains. One of the few remaining French colonies in the Americas, Saint-Domingue (on the island of Hispaniola) was the most profitable plantation colony in the New World.

taxes to repay loans, raising a storm of protest that led to demands for fundamental reform. Since the Caribbean colony of Saint-Domingue remained French, political turmoil in France would directly affect its population. The seeds of revolutionary conflict in the Atlantic world were thus sown.

Why and how did American colonists forge a new, independent nation?

Increased taxes and increased government control were crucial factors behind colonial protests in the New World, where the era of liberal political revolution began. After revolting against their home country, the thirteen mainland colonies of British North America succeeded in establishing a new unified government. Participants in the revolution believed they were demanding only the traditional rights of English men and women. Those traditional rights were liberal rights, and in the American context they had strong democratic and popular overtones. Yet in challenging and recasting authority in the colonies, the revolution did not resolve the question of social and political equality, which continued to elude enslaved people, free people of color, Indigenous people, and women.

The Origins of the Revolution

The high cost of the Seven Years' War doubled the British national debt. Anticipating further expenses to defend the half a billion acres in new territory granted by the Treaty of Paris, the government in London imposed bold new administrative measures. Breaking with a tradition of loose colonial oversight, the British announced that

Paul Revere, *The Bloody Massacre in King-Street,* 1770   In May 1770, 4,000 British soldiers were stationed in Boston, a city with a population of only 15,000. After a crowd of workers and sailors pelted a group of British soldiers with rocks and snowballs, several soldiers fired on the crowd. Five civilians were killed, including Crispus Attucks, a formerly enslaved African American sailor. Three weeks later, Paul Revere, a silversmith and engraver, produced this image of what came to be known as the Boston Massacre. In a highly successful propaganda effort, Revere distorted the events by making the British soldiers appear to be firing in a deliberate, organized fashion and without provocation. (Library of Congress Prints and Photographs Division Washington, D.C. 20540)

they would maintain a large army in North America and tax the colonies directly. In 1765 Parliament passed the Stamp Act, which levied taxes on a long list of commercial and legal documents, diplomas, newspapers, almanacs, and playing cards. A stamp glued to each article indicated that the tax had been paid.

These measures seemed perfectly reasonable to the British, for a much heavier stamp tax already existed in Britain, and proceeds from the tax were to fund the defense of the colonies. Nonetheless, the colonists vigorously protested the Stamp Act by rioting and by boycotting British goods. Thus Parliament reluctantly repealed it.

Another area of contention was settlement of the new territory acquired by the Treaty of Paris. At the end of the Seven Years' War, land-squeezed settlers quickly moved west across the Appalachian Mountains into the Ohio Valley, sparking conflict with the Ottawa and other Indigenous groups already present in the region, as well as with remaining French settlers. To prevent costly wars in distant territory, the British government in 1763 issued a royal proclamation prohibiting colonists from settling west of the Appalachian Mountains. The so-called Proclamation Line did little to stem land speculation and the flow of migrants, but it did exacerbate suspicion and tensions between Britain and its colonies.

These disputes raised important political questions. To what extent could the British government reassert its power while limiting the authority of elected colonial bodies? Who had the right to make laws for Americans?

The British government replied that Americans were represented in Parliament, albeit indirectly (like most British people), and that Parliament ruled throughout the empire. Many Americans felt otherwise. In the words of John Adams, a major proponent of colonial independence, "A Parliament of Great Britain can have no more rights to tax the colonies than a Parliament of Paris." Thus British colonial administration and parliamentary supremacy came to appear as unacceptable threats to existing American liberties.

Americans' resistance to these threats was fed by the great degree of independence they had long enjoyed. In British North America, unlike in England and the rest of Europe, no powerful established church existed, and religious freedom was taken for granted. Colonial assemblies made the important laws, which were seldom overturned by the British government. Also, the right to vote was much more widespread than in England. In many parts of colonial Massachusetts, for example, as many as 95 percent of adult males could vote.

Moreover, greater political equality was matched by greater social and economic equality, at least for the free white population. No hereditary nobility exercised privileges over peasants and other social groups. Instead, independent farmers dominated colonial society. This was particularly true in the northern colonies, where the revolution originated.

In 1770, the so-called Boston Massacre, in which British troops occupying Boston fired on a rebellious crowd, inflamed anti-British feelings. In 1773 disputes over taxes and representation flared up again. Under the Tea Act of that year, the British government permitted the financially struggling East India Company to ship tea from China directly to its agents in the colonies, rather than through London middlemen, who sold to independent merchants in the colonies. Thus the company secured a profitable monopoly on the tea trade, and colonial merchants were excluded. The price on tea was actually lowered for colonists, but the act generated a great deal of opposition because of its impact on local merchants.

In protest, Boston men disguised as Native Americans staged a raucous protest (later called the "Tea Party") by boarding East India Company ships and throwing tea from them into the harbor. The British responded with the so-called Coercive Acts of 1774, which closed the port of Boston, curtailed local elections, and expanded the royal governor's power. County conventions in Massachusetts urged that the acts be "rejected as the attempts of a wicked administration to enslave America." Other colonial assemblies joined in the denunciations. In September 1774 the First Continental Congress—consisting of colonial delegates who sought at first to peacefully resolve conflicts with Britain—met in Philadelphia. The more radical members of this assembly argued successfully against concessions to the English Crown. The British Parliament also rejected compromise, and in April 1775 fighting between colonial and British troops began at Lexington and Concord.

Independence from Britain

As fighting spread, the colonists moved slowly toward open calls for independence. The uncompromising attitude of the British government and its use of German mercenaries did much to dissolve loyalties to the home country and to unite the separate colonies. *Common Sense* (1775), a brilliant attack by the recently arrived English radical Thomas Paine (1737–1809), also mobilized public opinion in favor of independence.

On July 4, 1776, the Second Continental Congress adopted the Declaration of Independence. Written by Thomas Jefferson and others, this document boldly listed the tyrannical acts committed by George III (r. 1760–1820) and confidently proclaimed the natural rights of mankind and the sovereignty of the American states. The Declaration of Independence in effect universalized the traditional rights of English people and made them the individual rights of all men. It stated that "all Men are created equal, that they are endowed by their Creator with certain unalienable Rights, that among these are Life, Liberty, and the Pursuit of Happiness." The purpose of the state was to protect these individual rights, not the interests of privileged groups. No other American political document has ever caused such excitement, either at home or abroad.

After the Declaration of Independence, the conflict often took the form of a civil war pitting patriots against Loyalists, those who maintained an allegiance to the Crown. The Loyalists, who numbered up to 20 percent of the total settler population, tended to be wealthy and politically moderate. They were small in number in New England and Virginia, but more common in the Deep South and on the western frontier. British commanders also recruited Loyalists among enslaved people by promising freedom to those who left their masters to fight for the mother country.

Many wealthy patriots—such as John Hancock and George Washington—willingly allied themselves with farmers and artisans in a broad coalition. This coalition harassed the Loyalists and confiscated their property to help pay for the war, causing 60,000 to 80,000 of them to flee, mostly to Canada. The broad social base of the revolutionaries tended to make the revolution democratic. State governments extended the right to vote to many more men, including free African American men in many cases, but not to women.

On the international scene, the French wanted revenge against the British for the humiliating defeats of the Seven Years' War. Thus they sympathized with the rebels and supplied guns and gunpowder from the beginning of the conflict. By 1777 French volunteers were arriving in Virginia, and a dashing young nobleman, the marquis de Lafayette (1757–1834), quickly became one of the most trusted generals of George Washington, who was commanding American troops. In 1778 the French government offered a formal alliance to the American ambassador in Paris, Benjamin Franklin, and in 1779 and 1780 the Spanish and Dutch declared war on Britain. Catherine the Great of Russia helped organize the League of Armed Neutrality to protect neutral shipping rights and succeeded in hampering Britain's naval power.

Thus by 1780 Britain was engaged in a war against most of Europe as well as the thirteen colonies. In these circumstances, and in the face of severe reverses in India, in the West Indies, and at Yorktown in Virginia, a new British government decided to cut its losses and end the war. American officials in Paris were receptive to negotiating a deal with England alone, for they feared that France wanted a treaty that would bottle up the new nation east of the Appalachian Mountains and give British holdings west of the Appalachians to France's ally, Spain. Thus the American negotiators deserted their French allies and accepted the extraordinarily favorable terms Britain offered.

Under the Treaty of Paris of 1783, Britain recognized the independence of the thirteen colonies and ceded all its territory between the Allegheny Mountains and the Mississippi River to the Americans. Out of the bitter rivalries of the Old World, the Americans snatched dominion over a vast territory.

THE AMERICAN REVOLUTION

1765	Britain passes the Stamp Act
1773	Britain passes the Tea Act
1774	Britain passes the Coercive Acts in response to the Tea Party in the colonies; the First Continental Congress refuses concessions to the English Crown
April 1775	Fighting begins between colonial and British troops
July 4, 1776	Second Continental Congress adopts the Declaration of Independence
1777–1780	The French, Spanish, and Dutch side with the colonists against Britain
1783	Treaty of Paris recognizes the independence of the American colonies
1787	U.S. Constitution is signed
1791	The first ten amendments to the Constitution (the Bill of Rights) are ratified

Framing the Constitution

The liberal program of the American Revolution was consolidated by the federal Constitution, the Bill of Rights, and the creation of a national republic. Assembling in Philadelphia in the summer of 1787, the delegates to the Constitutional Convention were determined to end the period of economic depression, social uncertainty, and leadership under a weak central government that had followed independence. The delegates thus decided to grant the federal, or central, government important powers: regulation of domestic and foreign trade, the right to tax, and the means to enforce its laws.

Strong rule would be placed squarely in the context of representative self-government. Senators and congressmen would be the lawmaking delegates of the voters, and the president of the republic would be an elected official. The central government would operate in Montesquieu's framework of checks and balances, under which authority was distributed across three different branches—the executive, legislative, and judicial branches—to prevent one interest from gaining too much power. The power of the federal government would in turn be checked by that of the individual states.

In addition to European Enlightenment thinkers, Indigenous nations were another intellectual influence on the framers of the Constitution. John Adams produced a lengthy handbook describing different types of governments and political theories that referenced the Iroquois Confederacy and other Indigenous nations as well as Montesquieu and John Locke. Both George Washington and Benjamin Franklin expressed admiration for

the political system of the Iroquois Confederacy, which united six nations in a federal government with aspects of representative democracy, while preserving autonomous governance for each nation. (In 1988 the U.S. Senate passed a resolution acknowledging the influence of the Iroquois Confederacy on the U.S. Constitution.)

When the results of the Constitutional Convention were presented to the states for ratification, a great public debate began. The opponents of the proposed Constitution—the Antifederalists—charged that the framers of the new document had taken too much power from the individual states and made the federal government too strong. Moreover, many Antifederalists feared for the individual freedoms for which they had fought. To overcome these objections, the Federalists promised to spell out these basic freedoms as soon as the new Constitution was adopted. The result was the first ten amendments to the Constitution, which the first Congress passed shortly after it met in New York in March 1789. These amendments, ratified in 1791, formed an effective Bill of Rights to safeguard the individual. Most of them—trial by jury, due process of law, the right to assemble, freedom from unreasonable search—had their origins in English law and the English Bill of Rights of 1689. Other rights—the freedoms of speech, the press, and religion—reflected natural-law theory and the strong value colonists had placed on independence from the start.

Limitations of Liberty and Equality

The U.S. Constitution and the Bill of Rights exemplified the strengths and the limits of what came to be called classical liberalism. Liberty meant individual freedoms and political safeguards. Liberty also meant representative government, but it did not mean democracy, with its principle of one person, one vote. Equality meant equality before the law, not equality of political participation or wealth. It did not mean equal rights for the enslaved, free people of color, Indigenous people, or women.

A vigorous abolitionist movement during the 1780s led to the passage of emancipation laws in all northern states, but slavery remained prevalent in the South, and discord between pro- and antislavery delegates roiled the Constitutional Convention of 1787. The result was a compromise stipulating that an enslaved person would count as three-fifths of a person in tallying population numbers for taxation and proportional representation in the House of Representatives. This solution levied higher taxes on the South, but it also guaranteed slaveholding states greater representation in Congress, which they used to oppose emancipation. Congress did ban slavery in federal territory in 1789, then the export of enslaved people from any state, and finally, in 1808, the import of enslaved people to any state.

Anishinaabe Outfit Collected by Andrew Foster, ca. 1790　　Lieutenant Andrew Foster, a British officer serving on frontier forts near Detroit in the late eighteenth century, collected Native American clothing and ceremonial items, including this outfit. It combines garments and objects seemingly made by members of different Great Lakes nations, including the Anishinaabe, Huron-Wendat, and eastern Sioux. It contains traditional materials — such as hide, porcupine quills, and feathers — as well as goods acquired through trade with Europeans. Foster probably acquired the outfit as a diplomatic gift from Anishinaabe leaders, who reinforced their alliance with the British and other nations through such gift giving. (National Museum of the American Indian, Smithsonian Institution [24/2001]. Photo by NMAI Photo Services.)

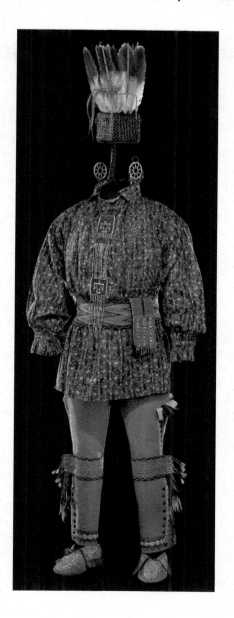

The new republic also failed to protect the Indigenous groups whose lands fell within or alongside the territory ceded by Britain at the Treaty of Paris. The 1787 Constitution promised protection to Indigenous people and guaranteed that their land would not be taken without consent. Nonetheless, the federal government forced them to concede their land for meager returns. State governments and the rapidly expanding U.S. population paid even less heed to the Constitution and often simply seized Native American land for new settlements.

Although lacking the voting rights enjoyed by so many of their husbands and fathers in the relatively democratic colonial assemblies, women played a vital role in the American Revolution. As household provisioners, women were essential participants in boycotts of British goods, like tea, which squeezed profits from British merchants and fostered the revolutionary spirit. After the outbreak of war, women raised funds for the Continental Army and took care of homesteads, workshops, and other businesses when their men went off to fight. Yet despite Abigail Adams's plea to her husband, John Adams, that the framers of the Declaration of Independence should "remember the ladies," women did not receive the right to vote in the new Constitution, an omission confirmed by an explicit clause denying women the vote that was added in 1844. (See "Evaluating Written Evidence: Abigail Adams, 'Remember the Ladies,'" page 564.)

How did the events of 1789 result in a constitutional monarchy in France?

No country felt the consequences of the American Revolution more deeply than France. Hundreds of French officers served in America and were inspired by the experience. The most famous of these, the marquis de Lafayette, left home as a proud young aristocrat determined to fight France's traditional foe, England. He returned with a love of liberty and firm republican convictions. French intellectuals engaged in passionate analysis of the federal Constitution as well as the constitutions of the various states of the new United States. The American Revolution undeniably fueled dissatisfaction with the old monarchical order in France. Yet the French Revolution did not mirror the American example. It was more radical and more complex, more influential and more controversial, more loved and more hated. For Europeans and most of the rest of the world, it was the momentous revolution that opened the modern era in politics.

Abigail Adams, "Remember the Ladies"

Abigail Adams wrote many letters to her husband, John Adams, during the long years of separation imposed by his political career. In March 1776 he was serving in the Continental Congress in Philadelphia as Abigail and their children experienced the British siege of Boston and a smallpox epidemic. This letter, written from the family farm in Braintree, Massachusetts, combines news from home with pressing questions about the military and political situation, and a call to "Remember the Ladies" when drafting a new constitution.

March 31, 1776

I wish you would ever write me a Letter half as long as I write you; and tell me if you may where your Fleet are gone? What sort of Defence Virginia can make against our common Enemy? Whether it is so situated as to make an able Defence? . . .

Do not you want to see Boston; I am fearful of the smallpox, or I should have been in before this time. I got Mr. Crane to go to our House and see what state it was in. I find it has been occupied by one of the Doctors of a Regiment, very dirty, but no other damage has been done to it. The few things which were left in it are all gone. . . .

I feel very differently at the approach of spring to what I did a month ago. We knew not then whether we could plant or sow with safety, whether when we had toiled we could reap the fruits of our own industry, whether we could rest in our own Cottages, or whether we should not be driven from the sea coasts to seek shelter in the wilderness, but now we feel as if we might sit under our own vine and eat the good of the land. . . .

I long to hear that you have declared an independency— and by the way in the new Code of Laws which I suppose it will be necessary for you to make I desire you would Remember the Ladies, and be more generous and favorable to them than your ancestors. Do not put such unlimited power in the hands of the Husbands. Remember all men would be tyrants if they could. If particular care and attention is not paid to the Ladies we are determined to foment a Rebellion, and will not hold ourselves bound by any Laws in which we have no voice, or Representation.

That your Sex are Naturally Tyrannical is a Truth so thoroughly established as to admit of no dispute, but such of you as wish to be happy willingly give up the harsh title of Master for the more tender and endearing one of Friend. Why then, not put it out of the power of the vicious and the Lawless to use us with cruelty and indignity with impunity. Men of Sense in all Ages abhor those customs which treat us only as the vassals of your Sex. Regard us then as beings placed by providence under your protection and in imitation of the Supreme Being make use of that power only for our happiness.

EVALUATE THE EVIDENCE

1. What does Adams's letter suggest about her relationship with her husband and the role of women in the family in this period?
2. What does Adams's letter tell us about what it was like to live through the American Revolution and how a woman might perceive the new liberties demanded by colonists?

Source: Letter from Abigail Adams to John Adams, 31 March–5 April 1776. *Adams Family Correspondence, Volume 1 and 2: December 1761–March 1778*, edited by L. H. Butterfield (Cambridge, Mass.: The Belknap Press of Harvard University Press, 1963).

Breakdown of the Old Order

As did the American Revolution, the French Revolution had its immediate origins in the government's financial difficulties. The ministers of King Louis XV (r. 1715–1774) sought to raise taxes to meet the expenses of the War of the Austrian Succession and the Seven Years' War and to make nobles pay direct taxes for the first time. These efforts were thwarted by the high courts, known as the parlements. The noble judges of the parlements resented the Crown's threat to their exemption from taxation and decried the government's actions as a form of royal despotism.

When renewed efforts to reform the tax system similarly failed in 1776, the government was forced to finance its enormous expenditures during the American war with borrowed money. As a result, the national debt soared. Fully 50 percent of France's annual budget went to interest payments on the ever-increasing debt. By 1786 the nation was on the verge of bankruptcy.

Financial crisis struck a monarchy whose royal authority was badly tarnished. Louis XV had scandalized the country with a series of mistresses of low social origins. To make things worse, he refused to take communion because his adultery placed him in a state of sin. The king was being stripped of the sacred aura of God's anointed on earth (a process called desacralization) and was being reinvented in the popular imagination as a degenerate.

Despite the progressive desacralization of the monarchy, Louis XV would probably have prevailed had he lived longer, but he died in 1774. The new king, Louis XVI (r. 1774–1792), was a shy twenty-year-old with good intentions. Taking the throne, he is reported to have said, "What I should like most is to be loved."[1] Louis waffled on political reform and the economy and proved unable to quell the rising storm of opposition.

The Formation of the National Assembly

Spurred by a depressed economy and falling tax receipts, Louis XVI's minister of finance revived old proposals to impose a general tax on all landed property as well as to form provincial assemblies to help administer the tax, and he convinced the king to call an assembly of notables in 1787 to gain support for the idea. The assembled notables, mainly aristocrats and high-ranking clergy, declared that such sweeping tax changes required the approval of the **Estates General**, the representative body of all three estates, which had not met since 1614. Louis XVI's efforts to reject their demands failed, and in July 1788 he reluctantly called the Estates General into session.

As its name indicates, the Estates General was a consultative body with representatives from the three orders, or **estates**, of society: the clergy, the nobility, and everyone else. Following centuries-old tradition, each estate met separately to elect delegates, first at a local and then at a regional level. Results of the elections reveal the mind-set of each estate on the eve of the Revolution. The local assemblies of the clergy, representing the first estate, elected mostly parish priests rather than church leaders, demonstrating their dissatisfaction with the church hierarchy. The nobility, or second estate, voted in a majority of conservatives, primarily from the provinces, where nobles were less wealthy, more devout, and more numerous. Nonetheless, fully one-third of noble representatives were liberals committed to major changes. Commoners of the third estate, who constituted over 95 percent of the population, elected primarily lawyers and government officials to represent them, with few delegates representing business and the poor.

The petitions for change drafted by the assemblies showed a surprising degree of consensus about the key issues confronting the realm. In all three estates, voices spoke in favor of replacing absolutism with a constitutional monarchy in which laws and taxes would require the consent of the Estates General in regular meetings. There was also a strong feeling that individual liberties would have to be guaranteed by law and that economic regulations should be loosened.

On May 5, 1789, the twelve hundred delegates of the three estates gathered in Versailles for the opening session of the Estates General. Despite widespread hopes for serious reform, the Estates General quickly deadlocked over voting procedures. Controversy had begun during the electoral process itself, when the government confirmed that, following precedent, each estate should meet and vote separately. This meant that the two privileged estates could always outvote the third.

During the lead-up to the Estates General, critics had demanded a single assembly dominated by the third estate. In his famous pamphlet *What Is the Third Estate?* Emmanuel Joseph Sieyès (himself a member of the first estate) argued that the nobility was a tiny, overprivileged minority and that the third estate constituted the true strength of the French nation.

The issue came to a crisis in June 1789 when delegates of the third estate refused to meet until the king ordered the clergy and nobility to sit with them in a single body. On June 17 the third estate, which had been joined by a few parish priests, voted to call itself the **National Assembly**. On June 20, excluded from their hall because of "repairs," the delegates moved to a large indoor tennis court, where they swore the famous Tennis Court Oath, pledging not to disband until they had been recognized as a national assembly and had written a new constitution.

The king's response was disastrously ambivalent. Although he made conciliatory gestures in favor of the Assembly's demands, he called an army of eighteen thousand troops toward the capital to bring the delegates under control, and on July 11 he dismissed his finance minister and other liberal ministers. It appeared that the monarchy was prepared to use violence to restore its control.

Popular Uprising and the Rights of Man

While delegates at Versailles were pressing for political rights, economic hardship gripped the common people. Conditions were already tough because of the government's disastrous financial situation. Then a poor grain harvest in 1788 had caused the price of bread to soar, and inflation spread quickly through the economy. As a result, demand for manufactured goods collapsed, and many artisans and small traders lost work. In Paris perhaps 150,000 of the city's 600,000 people were unemployed by July 1789.

■ **Estates General** A legislative body in prerevolutionary France made up of representatives of each of the three classes, or estates. It was called into session in 1789 for the first time since 1614.

■ **estates** The three legal categories, or orders, of France's inhabitants: the clergy, the nobility, and everyone else.

■ **National Assembly** The first French revolutionary legislature, made up primarily of representatives of the third estate and a few from the nobility and clergy, in session from 1789 to 1791.

The Awakening of the Third Estate
This cartoon from July 1789 represents the third estate as a common man throwing off his chains and rising up against his oppression, as the first estate (the clergy) and the second estate (the nobility) look on in fear. (Bridgeman Images)

Against this background of poverty and political crisis, the people of Paris entered decisively onto the revolutionary stage. They believed that, to survive, they should have steady work and enough bread at fair prices. They also feared that the dismissal of the king's liberal finance minister would put them at the mercy of aristocratic landowners and grain speculators. At the beginning of July, knowledge spread that troops were massing near Paris. On July 14, 1789, several hundred people stormed the Bastille (ba-STEEL), a royal prison, to obtain weapons for the city's defense. Faced with popular violence, Louis soon announced the reinstatement of his finance minister and the withdrawal of troops from Paris. The National Assembly was free to continue its work.

Just as the laboring poor of Paris had decisively intervened in the Revolution, the struggling French peasantry also took matters into their own hands. Peasants bore the brunt of state taxation, church tithes, and noble privileges. Since most did not own enough land to be self-sufficient, they were hard-hit by the rising price of bread. In the summer of 1789, throughout France peasants began to rise in insurrection against their lords, ransacking manor houses and burning feudal documents that recorded their obligations. In some areas peasants reoccupied common lands enclosed by landowners and seized forests. Fear of retaliation from the state and noble landowners against these actions — called the **Great Fear** by contemporaries — seized the rural poor and fanned the flames of rebellion.

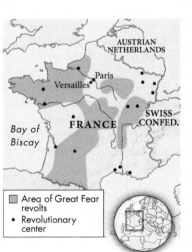

The Great Fear, 1789

Faced with chaos, the National Assembly responded to the swell of popular uprising with a surprise maneuver on the night of August 4, 1789. By a decree of the Assembly, all the old noble privileges — peasant serfdom where it still existed, exclusive hunting rights, fees for having legal cases judged in the lord's court, the right to make peasants work on the roads, and a host of other dues — were abolished along with the tithes paid to the church. On August 27, 1789, the Assembly further issued the Declaration of the Rights of Man and of the Citizen. This clarion call of the liberal revolutionary ideal guaranteed equality before the law, representative government for a sovereign people, and individual freedom. It was quickly disseminated throughout France and the rest of Europe and around the world. (See "Thinking Like a Historian: The Rights of Which Men?" on page 568.)

The National Assembly's declaration had little practical effect for the poor and hungry people of France. The economic crisis worsened after the fall of the Bastille, as aristocrats fled the country and the luxury market collapsed. Foreign markets also shrank, and unemployment among the urban working classes grew. In addition, women — the traditional managers of food and resources in poor homes — could no longer look to the church, which had been stripped of its tithes, for aid.

On October 5 some seven thousand women marched the twelve miles from Paris to Versailles to demand action. This great crowd, "armed with scythes, sticks and pikes," invaded the National Assembly. Interrupting a delegate's speech, an

The Tennis Court Oath, June 20, 1789   Painted two years after the event shown, this dramatic painting by Jacques-Louis David depicts a crucial turning point in the early days of the Revolution. On June 20 delegates of the third estate arrived at their meeting hall in the Versailles palace to find the doors closed and guarded. Fearing the king was about to dissolve their meeting by force, the deputies reassembled at a nearby indoor tennis court and swore a solemn oath not to disperse until they had been recognized as the National Assembly. (Josse/Leemage/Corbis/Getty Images)

old woman defiantly shouted into the debate, "Who's that talking down there? Make the chatterbox shut up. That's not the point: the point is that we want bread."[2] The women invaded the royal apartments, killed some of the royal bodyguards, and searched for the queen, Marie Antoinette, who was widely despised for her frivolous and supposedly immoral behavior. It seems likely that only the intervention of Lafayette and the National Guard saved the royal family. But the crowd demanded that the king live closer to his people in Paris, and that seemed the only way to calm the disorder.

A Constitutional Monarchy and Its Challenges

The next two years, until September 1791, saw the consolidation of the liberal revolution. In June 1790 the National Assembly abolished the nobility, and in July the king swore to uphold the as-yet-unwritten constitution, effectively enshrining a constitutional monarchy. The king remained the head of state, but

all lawmaking power now resided in the National Assembly, elected by French males who possessed a set amount of property, comprising roughly half the male population. The constitution passed in September 1791 was the first in French history. It legalized divorce and broadened women's rights to inherit property and to obtain financial support for illegitimate children from fathers, but excluded women from political office and voting.

This decision was attacked by a small number of men and women who believed that the rights of man should be extended to all French citizens. Politically active women wrote pamphlets, formed clubs, and petitioned the Assembly on behalf of women's right to participate in the life of the nation. Olympe de Gouges (1748–1793), a self-taught writer and woman of the people, protested the evils of slavery as well as the injustices done to women. In September 1791 she published her

■ **Great Fear** The fear of noble reprisals against peasant uprisings that seized the French countryside and led to further revolt.

The Rights of Which Men?

In August 1789 the legislators of the French Revolution adopted the Declaration of the Rights of Man and of the Citizen, enshrining full legal equality under the law for French citizens. Who exactly could become a citizen and what rights they might enjoy quickly became contentious issues.

1 **Robespierre on the distinction between active and passive citizenship.** In a November 1789 letter, Maximilien Robespierre denounced the decision to limit political participation to those with a certain amount of wealth. In 1792 a new law installed universal suffrage, but wealth restrictions returned under the Directory in 1795.

No doubt you know that a specific sum of money is being demanded of citizens for them to exercise the rights of citizens; that they must pay a tax equivalent to three days' work in order to participate in the primary assemblies; ten days' to be a member of the secondary assemblies which are called departments; finally 54 livres tax and possession of landed property to be eligible for the national assembly. These provisions are the work of the aristocratic party in the Assembly which has not even permitted the others to defend the rights of the people and has constantly shouted them down; so that the most important of all our deliberations was taken without discussion, carried off in tumult. . . .

[I]t seems to me that a representation founded on the bases I have just indicated could easily raise up an aristocracy of riches on the ruins of the feudal aristocracy; and I do not see that the people which should be the aim of every political institution will gain much from this kind of arrangement. Moreover I fail to see how representatives who derive their power from their constituents, that is to say from all the citizens without distinction of wealth, have the right to despoil the major part of these constituents of the power which they have confided to them.

2 **Petition of the French Jews.** After granting civil rights to Protestants in December 1789, the National Assembly began to consider the smaller but more controversial population of French Jews. Eager to become citizens in their own right, the Jews of Paris, Alsace, and Lorraine presented a joint petition to the National Assembly in January 1790.

A great question is pending before the supreme tribunal of France. *Will the Jews be citizens or not?* . . .

In general, civil rights are entirely independent from religious principles. And all men of whatever religion, whatever sect they belong to, whatever creed they practice, provided that their creed, their sect, their religion does not offend the principles of a pure and severe morality, all these men, we say, equally able to serve the fatherland, defend its interests, contribute to its splendor, should all equally have the title and the rights of citizen. . . .

Reflect, then, on the condition of the Jews. Excluded from all the professions, ineligible for all the positions, deprived even of the capacity to acquire property, not daring and not being able to sell openly the merchandise of their commerce, to what extremity are you reducing them? You do not want them to die, and yet you refuse them the means to live: you refuse them the means, and you crush them with taxes. You leave them therefore really no other resource than usury [lending money with interest]. . . .

Everything is changing; the lot of the Jews must change at the same time; and the people will not be more surprised by this particular change than by all those which they see around them every day.

ANALYZING THE EVIDENCE

1. Both the active-passive citizenship distinction discussed by Robespierre in Source 1 and the petition by the Jews of France in Source 2 raise the issue of the relationship between economic status and citizenship rights. Why was a man's wealth so important for possessing political rights? Are these two texts making the same arguments about this relationship?
2. Compare the claims made by the free men of color in Source 3 and by Etta Palm d'Aelders in Source 5. Why did the free men of color insist on the strong contributions they had already made while d'Aelders emphasized women's weakness and humiliation? What do these rhetorical strategies tell you about contemporary ideas about masculinity and femininity?
3. In Source 4, what arguments does the Colonial Committee advance in favor of legal autonomy of the colonies? Why would autonomy favor the position of colonial landowners?

3 **Free men of color address the National Assembly.** In the first years of the Revolution, debate raged over the question of political equality in Saint-Domingue. In October 1789 a group of free men of color appeared before the National Assembly to present an appeal for political rights for themselves (but not for the enslaved).

〜 [C]itizens of all classes have been called to the great work of public regeneration; all have contributed to writing complaints and nominating deputies to defend their rights and set forth their interests.

The call of liberty has echoed in the other hemisphere.

It should certainly have erased even the memory of these outrageous distinctions between citizens of the same land; instead, it has brought forth even more appalling ones. . . . In this strange system, the citizens of color find themselves represented by the white colonists' deputies, although they have still never been included in their partial assemblies and they have not entrusted any power to these deputies. Their opposition interests, which sadly are only too obvious, make such representation absurd and contradictory. . . . The citizens of color are clearly as qualified as the whites to demand this representation.

Like them they are all citizens, free and French; the edict of March 1685 accords them all such rights and guarantees them all such privileges. . . . Like them they are property owners and farmers; like them they contribute to the relief of the state by paying the levies and bearing all expenses that they and the whites share. Like them they have already shed their blood and are prepared to spill it again for the defense of the fatherland. Like them, finally, though with less encouragement and means, they have proven their patriotism again and again.

4 **The Colonial Committee defends colonists' autonomy.** In March 1790 the Colonial Committee — dominated by slaveholding plantation owners — recommended that colonial assemblies be given the right to make their own laws. This meant that any laws passed in France on the abolition of slavery or the enfranchisement of people of color would not affect the colonies. A member of the committee summarized its views.

〜 It would be a mistake as dangerous as it is unforgivable to envisage the colonies as provinces, and to want to subject them to the same regime. . . . [A] land so different from ours in every way, inhabited by different classes of people, distinguished from each other by characteristics unfamiliar to us, and for whom our social distinctions offer no analogy . . . needs laws which might be called indigenous. . . . [I]t belongs only to the inhabitants of our colonies, convened in the colonies themselves, to gather to elect the body of representatives to work in virtue of its powers and without leaving its territory, to create the constitution, that is to say the form of the internal regime and local administration which is most suited to assure colonials of the advantages of civil society.

5 **Etta Palm d'Aelders on the rights of women.** During the Revolution, Dutch-born Etta Palm d'Aelders became one of the most outspoken advocates for women's rights. In her Address of French Citizenesses to the National Assembly in 1791, she addresses the National Assembly in opposition to a proposed law reserving for husbands the capacity to seek legal redress for adultery.

〜 It is a question of your duty, your honor, your interest, to destroy down to their roots these gothic laws which abandon the weakest but [also] the most worthy half of humanity to a humiliating existence, to an eternal slavery.

You have restored to man the dignity of his being in recognizing his rights; you will no longer allow woman to groan beneath an arbitrary authority; that would be to overturn the fundamental principles on which rests the stately edifice you are raising by your untiring labors for the happiness of Frenchmen. It is too late to equivocate. Philosophy has drawn truth from the darkness; the time has come; justice, sister of liberty, calls all individuals to the equality of rights, without discrimination of sex; the laws of a free people must be equal for all beings, like the air and the sun. . . .

[T]he powers of husband and wife must be equal and separate. The law cannot establish any difference between these two authorities; they must give equal protection and maintain a perpetual balance between the two married people. . . .

You will complete your work by giving girls a moral education equal to that of their brothers; for education is for the soul what watering is for plants; it makes it fertile, causes it to bloom, fortifies it, and carries the germ productive of virtue and talents to a perfect maturity.

PUTTING IT ALL TOGETHER

Using the sources above, along with what you have learned in class and in this chapter, write a short essay exploring how different groups drew on the events, language, and principles of the French Revolution to make claims for additional rights. Keep in mind both differences and similarities in their rhetorical strategies as well as any additional sources of legitimation they employed.

Sources: (1) John Hardman, *The French Revolution Sourcebook* (London: Arnold, 2002), pp. 120–121; (2) *The French Revolution and Human Rights: A Brief Documentary History*, edited, translated, and with an introduction by Lynn Hunt (Boston: Bedford/St. Martin's, 1996), pp. 93, 95–97; (3) Laurent Dubois and John D. Garrigus, *Slave Revolution in the Caribbean, 1789–1804: A Brief History with Documents* (Boston: Bedford/St. Martin's, 2006), pp. 68–69; (4) Frédéric Régent, "Slavery and the Colonies," in Peter McPhee, *A Companion to the French Revolution* (Chichester: Wiley Blackwell, 2015), p. 401; (5) Darline Gay Levy, Harriet Branson Applewhite, and Mary Durham Johnson, eds., *Women in Revolutionary Paris, 1789–1795* (Champaign-Urbana: University of Illinois Press, 1981), pp. 75–77.

The Women of Paris March to Versailles On October 5, 1789, thousands of poor Parisian women marched to Versailles to protest the price of bread. For the common people, the king was the baker of last resort, responsible for feeding his people during times of scarcity. The image of a set of scales one woman holds aloft (along with a loaf of bread stuck on the tip of her pike) symbolizes the crowd's desire for justice and for bread to be sold at the same price per pound as it always had been. The women forced the royal family to return with them to live in Paris, rather than remain isolated from their subjects at court. (Fine Art Images/Heritage Images/HultonArchive/Getty Images)

Declaration of the Rights of Woman, which echoed its famous predecessor, the Declaration of the Rights of Man and of the Citizen, proclaiming, "Woman is born free and remains equal to man in rights." De Gouges's position found little sympathy among leaders of the Revolution, however.

In addition to expanding women's legal rights, the National Assembly replaced the complicated patchwork of historic provinces with eighty-three departments of approximately equal size, a move toward more rational and systematic methods of administration. In the name of economic liberty, the deputies prohibited guilds and workers' associations and abolished internal customs fees. Thus the National Assembly applied the spirit of the Enlightenment in a thorough reform of France's laws and institutions.

The National Assembly also imposed a radical reorganization on religious life. The Assembly granted religious freedom to the small minority of French Protestants and Jews. In November 1789 it nationalized the property of the Catholic Church and abolished monasteries. The government used all former church property as collateral to guarantee a new paper currency, the assignats (A-sihg-nat), and then sold the property in an attempt to put the state's finances on a solid footing.

Imbued with the rationalism and skepticism of the eighteenth-century Enlightenment, many delegates distrusted popular piety and "superstitious religion." Thus in July 1790, with the Civil Constitution of the Clergy, they established a national church with priests chosen by voters. The National Assembly then forced the Catholic clergy to take an oath of loyalty to the new government. The pope formally condemned this measure, and only half the priests of France swore the oath. Many sincere Christians, especially those in the countryside, were appalled by these changes in the religious order.

Why and how did the French Revolution take a radical turn?

When Louis XVI accepted the National Assembly's constitution in September 1791, a young provincial lawyer and delegate named Maximilien Robespierre (1758–1794) concluded that "the Revolution is over." Robespierre was right in the sense that the most constructive and lasting reforms were in place. Yet he was wrong in suggesting that turmoil had ended, for a much more radical stage lay ahead, one that would bring war with foreign powers, the declaration of terror at home, and a transformation in France's government.

THE FRENCH REVOLUTION

National Assembly (1789–1791)

May 5, 1789	Estates General meets at Versailles
June 17, 1789	Third estate declares itself the National Assembly
June 20, 1789	Tennis Court Oath
July 14, 1789	Storming of the Bastille
July–August 1789	Great Fear
August 4, 1789	Abolishment of feudal privileges
August 27, 1789	Declaration of the Rights of Man and of the Citizen
October 5, 1789	Women march on Versailles; royal family returns to Paris
November 1789	National Assembly confiscates church land
July 1790	Civil Constitution of the Clergy establishes a national church; Louis XVI agrees to constitutional monarchy
June 1791	Royal family arrested while fleeing France
August 1791	Declaration of Pillnitz

Legislative Assembly (1791–1792)

April 1792	France declares war on Austria
August 1792	Mob attacks the palace, and Legislative Assembly takes Louis XVI prisoner

National Convention (1792–1795)

September 1792	September Massacres; National Convention abolishes monarchy and declares France a republic
January 1793	Louis XVI executed
February 1793	France declares war on Britain, the Dutch Republic, and Spain; revolts take place in some provinces
March 1793	Struggle between Girondists and the Mountain
April 1793	Creation of the Committee of Public Safety
September 1793	Price controls instituted
October 1793	National Convention bans women's political societies
1793–1794	Reign of Terror
Spring 1794	French armies victorious on all fronts
July 1794	Robespierre executed; Thermidorian reaction begins

The Directory (1795–1799)

1795	Economic controls abolished; suppression of the sans-culottes begins
1799	Napoleon seizes power

The International Response

The outbreak of revolution in France produced great excitement and a sharp division of opinion in Europe and the United States. On the one hand, liberals and radicals saw a mighty triumph of liberty over despotism. On the other hand, conservative leaders such as British statesman Edmund Burke (1729–1797) were intensely troubled. In 1790 Burke published *Reflections on the Revolution in France*, one of the great expressions of European conservatism. He derided abstract principles of "liberty" and "rights" and insisted on the importance of inherited traditions and privileges as a bastion of social stability.

One passionate rebuttal came from a young writer in London, Mary Wollstonecraft (1759–1797). Incensed by Burke's book, Wollstonecraft (WOOL-stuhn-kraft) wrote a blistering attack, *A Vindication of the Rights of Man* (1790). Two years later, she published her masterpiece, *A Vindication of the Rights of Woman* (1792). Like de Gouges in France, Wollstonecraft demanded equal rights for women. She also advocated coeducation out of the belief that it would make women better wives and mothers, good citizens, and economically independent. Considered very radical for the time, the book became a founding text of later feminist movements.

The kings and nobles of continental Europe, who had at first welcomed the Revolution in France as weakening a competing power, now feared its impact. In June 1791 the royal family was arrested after a failed attempt to escape France. To supporters of the Revolution, the attempted flight was proof that the king was treacherously seeking foreign support for an invasion of France. To the monarchs of Austria and Prussia, the arrest of a crowned monarch was an unacceptable outrage. Two months later they issued the Declaration of Pillnitz, proclaiming their willingness to intervene in France to restore Louis XVI's rule if necessary.

But the crowned heads of Europe misjudged the situation. The new French representative body, called the Legislative Assembly, had new delegates and a different character. Although the delegates were still prosperous, well-educated middle-class men, they were younger and less cautious than their predecessors. Since the National Assembly had declared sitting deputies ineligible for re-election, none of them had previously served as national representatives. Many of them belonged to the political **Jacobin Club**, one of the many political clubs that had formed to debate the political issues of the day.

Jacobins and other deputies reacted with patriotic fury to the Declaration of Pillnitz. In a speech to the Assembly, one deputy declared that if the kings of Europe were attempting to incite war against France, then "we will incite a war of people against kings. . . . Ten million Frenchmen, kindled by the fire of liberty, armed with the sword, with reason, with eloquence would be able to change the face of the world and make the tyrants tremble on their thrones."[3] In April 1792 France declared war on Francis II, the Habsburg ruler of the Holy Roman Empire.

France's crusade against tyranny went poorly at first. Prussia joined Austria against the French forces, who broke and fled at their first military encounter with this First Coalition of antirevolutionary foreign powers. On behalf of the Crowns of Austria and

Prussia, the duke of Brunswick, commander of the coalition armies, issued a declaration threatening to destroy Paris if harm came to the royal family. The Legislative Assembly declared the country in danger, and volunteers rallied to the capital. The Brunswick manifesto heightened suspicions of treason on the part of the French king and queen. On August 10, 1792, a revolutionary crowd attacked the royal palace at the Tuileries (TWEE-luh-reez), while the royal family fled to the Legislative Assembly. Rather than offering refuge, the Assembly suspended the king from all his functions, imprisoned him, and called for a constitutional assembly to be elected by universal male suffrage.

The Second Revolution and the New Republic

The fall of the monarchy marked a radicalization of the Revolution, a phase that historians often call the **second revolution**. Louis's imprisonment was followed by the September Massacres. Fearing invasion by the Prussians and riled up by rumors that counter-revolutionaries would aid the invaders, angry crowds stormed the prisons and killed jailed priests and aristocrats. In late September 1792 the new, popularly elected National Convention, which replaced the Legislative Assembly, proclaimed France a republic, a nation in which the people, instead of a monarch, held sovereign power.

As with the Legislative Assembly, many members of the new National Convention belonged to the Jacobin Club of Paris. But the Jacobins themselves were increasingly divided into two bitterly opposed groups—the **Girondists** (juh-RAHN-dihsts) and **the Mountain**, led by Robespierre and another young lawyer, Georges Jacques Danton.

This division emerged clearly after the National Convention overwhelmingly convicted Louis XVI of treason. The Girondists accepted his guilt but did not wish to put the king to death. By a narrow majority, the Mountain carried the day, and Louis was executed on January 21, 1793, by guillotine, which the French had recently perfected. Marie Antoinette suffered the same fate later that year. But both the Girondists and the Mountain were determined to continue the "war against tyranny." The Prussians had been stopped at the Battle of Valmy on September 20, 1792, one day before the republic was proclaimed. French armies then invaded Savoy and captured Nice, moved into the German Rhineland, and by November 1792 were occupying the entire Austrian Netherlands (modern Belgium).

Everywhere they went, French armies of occupation chased princes, abolished feudalism, and found support among some peasants and middle-class people. But French armies also lived off the land,

---

■ **Jacobin Club** A political club in revolutionary France whose members were well-educated radical republicans.

■ **second revolution** From 1792 to 1795, the second phase of the French Revolution, during which the fall of the French monarchy introduced a rapid radicalization of politics.

■ **Girondists** A moderate group that fought for control of the French National Convention in 1793.

■ **the Mountain** Led by Robespierre, the French National Convention's radical faction, which seized legislative power in 1793.

■ **sans-culottes** The laboring poor of Paris, so called because the men wore trousers instead of the knee breeches of the aristocracy and middle class; the word came to refer to the militant radicals of the city.

The Guillotine

Prior to the French Revolution, methods of execution included hanging and being broken at the wheel. Only nobles enjoyed the privilege of a relatively swift and painless death by decapitation, delivered by an executioner's ax. The guillotine, a model of which is shown here, was devised by a French revolutionary doctor named Guillotin as a humane and egalitarian form of execution. Ironically, because of the mass executions under the Terror, it is now seen instead as a symbol of revolutionary cruelty. (Art Images/Hulton Fine Art Collection/Getty Images)

With the middle-class delegates so bitterly divided, the people of Paris once again emerged as the decisive political factor. The laboring poor and the petty traders were often known as the **sans-culottes** because their men wore trousers instead of the knee breeches of the aristocracy and the solid middle class. (See "Viewpoints: Contrasting Visions of the Sans-Culottes," page 574.) They demanded radical political action to defend the Revolution. The Mountain, sensing an opportunity to outmaneuver the Girondists, joined with sans-culottes activists to engineer a popular uprising. On June 2, 1793, armed sans-culottes invaded the Convention and forced its deputies to arrest twenty-nine Girondist deputies for treason. All power passed to the Mountain.

The Convention also formed the Committee of Public Safety in April 1793 to deal with threats from within and outside France. The Committee, led by Robespierre, held dictatorial power and was allowed to use whatever force necessary to defend the Revolution. Moderates in leading provincial cities revolted against the Committee's power and demanded a decentralized government. Counter-revolutionary forces in the Vendée won significant victories, and the republic's armies were driven back on all fronts. By July 1793 only the areas around Paris and on the eastern frontier were firmly held by the central government. Defeat seemed imminent.

requisitioning food and supplies and plundering local treasures. The liberators therefore looked increasingly like foreign invaders. Meanwhile, international tensions mounted. In February 1793 the National Convention, at war with Austria and Prussia, declared war on Britain, the Dutch Republic, and Spain as well. Republican France was now at war with almost all of Europe.

Groups within France added to the turmoil. Peasants in western France revolted against being drafted into the army, with the Vendée region emerging as the epicenter of revolt. Devout Catholics, royalists, and foreign agents encouraged their rebellion, and the counter-revolutionaries recruited veritable armies to fight for their cause.

In March 1793 the National Convention was locked in a life-and-death political struggle between members of the Mountain and the more moderate Girondists.

Caen • Paris
BRITTANY
VENDÉE
FRANCE • Lyons
• Bordeaux
• Marseilles
SPAIN
Mediterranean Sea

■ Vendée Rebellion
▨ Counter-revolutionary insurrections

Areas of Insurrection, 1793

Total War and the Terror

A year later, in July 1794, the central government had reasserted control over the provinces, and the Austrian Netherlands and the Rhineland were once again in French hands. This remarkable change of fortune was due to the revolutionary government's success in harnessing the explosive forces of a planned economy, revolutionary terror, and modern nationalism in a total war effort.

Robespierre and the Committee of Public Safety advanced on several fronts in 1793 and 1794, seeking to impose republican unity across the nation. First, they collaborated with the sans-culottes, who continued pressing the common people's case for fair prices and a moral economic order. Thus in September 1793 Robespierre and his coworkers established a planned economy with egalitarian social overtones. Rather than let supply and demand determine prices, the government set maximum prices for key products. Though the state was

VIEWPOINTS

Contrasting Visions of the Sans-Culottes

These two images offer profoundly different representations of a sans-culotte woman. The image on the left was created by a French artist, while the image on the right is English. The French words above the image on the right read in part, "Heads! Blood! Death! . . . I am the Goddess of Liberty! . . . Long Live the Guillotine!" These images demonstrate the importance of gendered imagery in the conflicts of the French Revolution. Although women were denied active participation in the political life of the new republic, representations of women featured prominently in the way both supporters and opponents of the Revolution depicted the events that unfolded after 1789. Proponents of the traditional social order and hierarchy used images of bloodthirsty radical women to suggest that the Revolution had turned the "world upside down" and perverted women's naturally docile and domestic character. By contrast, those who supported the Revolution were eager to emphasize the down-to-earth virtue of the mothers and wives of the male citizens of the republic.

As these images suggest, both sides agreed on certain elements of femininity. Women were associated with their outward appearances. At the time, the love of fashion and appearance was seen in Europe as both a particularly feminine and French characteristic. These associations were strengthened by the fact that France had dominated the luxury trades in clothing and accessories since the late seventeenth century and that many working women earned their living in these trades.

French Illustration of Sans-Culotte Woman. (Fine Art Images/ Heritage Images/Getty Images)

British Illustration of Sans-Culotte Woman. (Courtesy of the Warden and Scholars of New College, Oxford, UK/Bridgeman Images)

QUESTIONS FOR ANALYSIS

1. How would you describe the woman on the left? What qualities does the artist seem to ascribe to her, and how do you think these qualities relate to the sans-culottes and the Revolution?
2. How would you characterize the facial expression and attire of the woman on the right? How do the words accompanying the image contribute to your impression of her?
3. What does the contrast between these two images suggest about differences between supporters and opponents of the sans-culottes and of the French Revolution? Do you think the use of women to represent the Revolution is effective in these images?

too weak to enforce all its price regulations, it did fix the price of bread in Paris at levels the poor could afford.

The people were also put to work producing arms, munitions, uniforms, boots, saddles, and other necessary supplies for the war effort. The government told craftsmen what to produce, nationalized many small workshops, and requisitioned raw materials and grain. These reforms amounted to an emergency form of socialism, which thoroughly frightened Europe's propertied classes and greatly influenced the subsequent development of socialist ideology.

Second, while radical economic measures furnished the poor with bread and the armies with supplies, the **Reign of Terror** (1793–1794) enforced compliance with republican beliefs and practices. The constitution, which had been completed in June 1793 and approved by a national referendum, was indefinitely suspended in favor of a "revolutionary government." Special courts responsible only to Robespierre's Committee of Public Safety tried "enemies of the nation" for political crimes. Some forty thousand French men and women were executed or died in prison, and around three hundred thousand were arrested, making the Reign of Terror one of the most controversial phases of the Revolution. Presented as a necessary measure to save the republic, the Terror was a weapon directed against all suspected of opposing the revolutionary government.

In their efforts to impose unity, the Jacobins also took actions to suppress women's participation in political debate, which they perceived as disorderly and a distraction from women's proper place in the home. On October 30, 1793, the National Convention declared that "the clubs and popular societies of women, under whatever denomination are prohibited." Among those convicted of sedition was writer Olympe de Gouges, who was sent to the guillotine in November 1793.

The third element of the Committee's program was to bring about a cultural revolution that would transform former royal subjects into republican citizens. The government sponsored revolutionary art and songs as well as a new series of secular festivals to celebrate republican virtue and patriotism. It also attempted to rationalize French daily life by adopting the decimal system for weights and measures and a new calendar based on ten-day weeks. Another important element of this cultural revolution was the campaign of de-Christianization, which aimed to eliminate Catholic symbols and beliefs. Fearful of the hostility aroused in rural France, however, Robespierre called for a halt to de-Christianization measures in mid-1794.

The final element in the program of the Committee of Public Safety was its appeal to a new sense of national identity and patriotism. With a common language and a common tradition newly reinforced by the revolutionary ideals of popular sovereignty and democracy, many French people developed an intense emotional commitment to the defense of the nation, and they saw the war against foreign opponents as a life-and-death struggle between good and evil. This was the birth of modern nationalism, which would have a profound effect on subsequent European history.

The all-out mobilization of French resources under the Terror combined with the fervor of nationalism to create an awesome fighting machine. A decree of August 1793 imposed the draft on all unmarried young men, and by January 1794 French armed forces outnumbered those of their enemies almost four to one.[4] Well trained, well equipped, and constantly indoctrinated, the enormous armies of the republic were led by young, impetuous generals who often had risen from the ranks and who personified the opportunities the Revolution offered gifted sons of the people. To gain new recruits for colonial warfare, the Convention abolished slavery in all French colonies in February 1794. By spring 1794 French armies were victorious on all fronts and domestic revolt was largely suppressed. The republic was saved.

The Thermidorian Reaction and the Directory

The success of French armies led the Committee of Public Safety to relax the emergency economic controls, but the Committee extended the political Reign of Terror. In March 1794 the revolutionary tribunal sentenced many of its critics to death. Two weeks later Robespierre sent long-standing collaborators whom he believed had turned against him, including Danton, to the guillotine. In June 1794 a new law removed defendants' right of legal counsel and criminalized criticism of the Revolution.

A group of radicals and moderates in the Convention, knowing that they might be next, organized a conspiracy. They howled down Robespierre when he tried to speak to the National Convention on July 27, 1794 — a date known as 9 Thermidor according to France's newly adopted republican calendar. The next day it was Robespierre's turn to be guillotined.

As Robespierre's closest supporters followed their leader to the guillotine, the respectable middle-class lawyers and professionals who had led the liberal Revolution of 1789 reasserted their authority. This period of **Thermidorian reaction**, as it was called, hearkened back to the ideals of the early Revolution; the new leaders of government proclaimed an end to the revolutionary expediency of the Terror and the return of representative

■ **Reign of Terror** The period from 1793 to 1794 during which Robespierre's Committee of Public Safety tried and executed thousands suspected of treason and a new revolutionary culture was imposed.

■ **Thermidorian reaction** A reaction to the violence of the Reign of Terror in 1794, resulting in the execution of Robespierre and the loosening of economic controls.

Plate Showing a Festival of the Cult of the Supreme Being   During the French Revolution, a series of festivals with patriotic themes replaced traditional Catholic feast days. One of the most important was the festival of the Cult of the Supreme Being, a form of deism promoted by Robespierre and the Jacobins as a rational state religion. This commemorative plate was issued to mark the 1796 festival. (Musée de la Ville de Paris, Musée Carnavalet, Paris, France/Erich Lessing/Art Resource, NY)

government, the rule of law, and liberal economic policies. In 1795 the National Convention abolished many economic controls, let prices rise sharply, and severely restricted the local political organizations through which the sans-culottes exerted their strength.

In the same year, members of the National Convention wrote a new constitution to guarantee their economic position and political supremacy. As in previous elections, the mass of the population could vote only for electors, who would in turn elect the legislators, but the new constitution greatly reduced the number of men eligible to become electors by instating a substantial property requirement. It also inaugurated a bicameral legislative system for the first time in the Revolution, with a Council of 500 serving as the lower house that initiated legislation and a Council of Elders (composed of about 250 members aged forty

years or older) acting as the upper house that approved new laws. To prevent a new Robespierre from monopolizing power, the constitution granted executive power to a five-man body, called the Directory.

The Directory continued to support French military expansion abroad. War was no longer so much a crusade as a response to economic problems. Large, victorious French armies reduced unemployment at home. However, the French people quickly grew weary of the corruption and ineffectiveness that characterized the Directory. The trauma of years of military and political violence had alienated the public, and the Directory's heavy-handed and opportunistic policies did not reverse the situation. This general dissatisfaction revealed itself clearly in the national elections of 1797, which returned a large number of conservative and even monarchist deputies who favored peace at almost any price. Two years later Napoleon Bonaparte ended the Directory in a coup d'état (koo day-TAH; violent overthrow of government by a small number of people) and substituted a strong dictatorship for a weak one.

■ **Napoleonic Code**   French civil code promulgated in 1804 that reasserted the 1789 principles of the equality of all male citizens before the law and the absolute security of wealth and private property, as well as restricting rights accorded to women by previous revolutionary laws.

How did Napoleon Bonaparte create a French empire, and why did it fail?

For almost fifteen years, from 1799 to 1814, France was in the hands of a keen-minded military dictator of exceptional ability. One of history's most fascinating leaders, Napoleon Bonaparte (1769–1821) realized that he needed to put an end to civil strife in France in order to create unity and consolidate his rule. And he did. But Napoleon saw himself as a man of destiny, and the glory of war and the dream of universal empire proved irresistible. For years he triumphed from victory to victory, but in the end he was destroyed by a mighty coalition united in fear of his relentless ambition.

Napoleon's Rule of France

Born in Corsica into an impoverished noble family in 1769, Napoleon left home and became a lieutenant in the French artillery in 1785. Converted to the revolutionary cause and rising rapidly in the republican army, Napoleon gained command of French forces in Italy and won brilliant victories there in 1796 and 1797. His next campaign, in Egypt, was a failure, but Napoleon returned to France before the fiasco was generally known, and his reputation remained intact. French aggression in Egypt and elsewhere provoked the British to organize a new alliance in 1798, the Second Coalition, that also included Austria and Russia.

Napoleon soon learned that prominent members of the legislature were plotting against the Directory. The plotters' dissatisfaction stemmed not so much from the Directory's dictatorial rule as from the fact that it was an ineffective dictatorship. Ten years of upheaval and uncertainty had made firm rule much more appealing than liberty and popular politics to these disillusioned revolutionaries. The abbé Sieyès personified this evolution in thinking. In 1789 he had written that the nobility was grossly overprivileged and that the entire people should rule the French nation. Now Sieyès's motto was "Confidence from below, authority from above."

The flamboyant thirty-year-old Napoleon, nationally revered for his military exploits, was an ideal figure of authority. On November 9, 1799, Napoleon and his conspirators ousted the Directors, and the following day soldiers disbanded the legislature at bayonet point. Napoleon was named first consul of the republic, and a new constitution consolidating his position was overwhelmingly approved by a nationwide vote in December 1799. Republican appearances were maintained, but Napoleon became the real ruler of France.

Napoleon worked to maintain order and end civil strife by appeasing powerful groups in France, offering them favors in return for loyal service. Napoleon's bargain with the middle class was codified in the Civil Code of March 1804, also known as the **Napoleonic Code**, which reasserted two of the fundamental principles of the Revolution of 1789: equality of all male citizens before the law, and security of wealth and private property. Napoleon and the leading bankers of

THE NAPOLEONIC ERA	
November 1799	Napoleon overthrows the Directory
December 1799	Napoleon's new constitution approved
1800	Foundation of the Bank of France
1801	France defeats Austria and acquires Italian and German territories in the Treaty of Lunéville; Napoleon signs papal Concordat
1802	Treaty of Amiens
March 1804	Napoleonic Code
December 1804	Napoleon crowned emperor
October 1805	Britain defeats the French fleet at the Battle of Trafalgar
December 1805	Napoleon defeats Austria and Russia at the Battle of Austerlitz
1807	Napoleon redraws map of Europe in the treaties of Tilsit
1808	Spanish revolt against French occupation
1810	Height of the Grand Empire
June 1812	Napoleon invades Russia
Fall–Winter 1812	Napoleon makes a disastrous retreat from Russia
March 1814	Russia, Prussia, Austria, and Britain sign the Treaty of Chaumont, pledging alliance to defeat Napoleon
April 1814	Napoleon abdicates and is exiled to Elba; Louis XVIII restored to constitutional monarchy
February–June 1815	Napoleon escapes from Elba but is defeated at the Battle of Waterloo; Louis XVIII restored to throne for second time

Paris established the privately owned Bank of France in 1800, which served the interests of both the state and the financial oligarchy. Napoleon won over peasants by defending the gains in land and status they had won during the Revolution.

At the same time, Napoleon consolidated his rule by recruiting disillusioned revolutionaries to form a network of ministers, prefects, and centrally appointed mayors. Nor were members of the old nobility slighted. In 1800 and again in 1802 Napoleon granted amnesty to one hundred thousand émigrés on the condition that they return to France and take a loyalty oath. Members of this returning elite soon occupied many high posts in the expanding centralized state. Napoleon also created a new imperial nobility to reward his most talented generals and officials.

Furthermore, Napoleon sought to restore the Catholic Church in France so that it could serve as a bulwark of social stability. After arduous negotiations, Napoleon and Pope Pius VII (pontificate 1800–1823) signed the Concordat (kuhn-KOHR-dat) of 1801. The pope obtained the right for French Catholics to practice their religion freely, but Napoleon's government now nominated bishops, paid the clergy, and exerted great influence over the church.

The reforms of Napoleon's early years were his greatest achievement. Much of his legal and administrative reorganization has survived in France to this day, but order and unity had a price: authoritarian rule with little regard for the advances in human rights accomplished by revolutionaries. In 1802, Napoleon re-established slavery in the colonies, hoping to profit from a revival of plantation agriculture. Women also lost many of the gains they had made in the 1790s. Under the Napoleonic Code, women became dependents of either their fathers or their husbands, and they could not make contracts or have bank accounts in their own names. Napoleon and his advisers aimed at re-establishing a family monarchy, where the power of the husband and father was as absolute over the wife and the children as that of Napoleon was over his subjects. He also curtailed free speech and freedom of the press and manipulated voting in the occasional elections. After 1810 political suspects were held in state prisons, as they had been during the Terror.

Napoleon's Expansion in Europe

After coming to power in 1799, Napoleon sent peace feelers to Austria and Great Britain, the dominant members of the Second Coalition. When these overtures were rejected, Napoleon's armies decisively defeated the Austrians. In the Treaty of Lunéville (1801), Austria accepted the loss of almost all its Italian possessions, and German territory on the west bank of the Rhine was incorporated into France. The British agreed to the Treaty of Amiens in 1802, allowing France to control the former Dutch Republic (known

as the Batavian Republic since 1795), the Austrian Netherlands, the west bank of the Rhine, and most of the Italian peninsula. The Treaty of Amiens was a diplomatic triumph for Napoleon, and peace with honor and profit increased his popularity at home.

In 1802 Napoleon was secure but still driven to expand his power. Aggressively redrawing the map of German-speaking lands so as to weaken Austria and encourage the secondary states of southwestern Germany to side with France, Napoleon tried to restrict British trade with all of Europe. He then plotted to attack Great Britain, but his Mediterranean fleet was

Portrait of Napoleon Bonaparte on the Imperial Throne   On December 2, 1804, in Notre-Dame Cathedral in Paris, Napoleon Bonaparte was handed the crown by Pope Pius VII and placed it on his own head, proclaiming himself emperor of France. As shown in this portrait by Jean-Auguste-Dominique Ingres, Napoleon wore crimson velvet robes decorated with golden bees, the emblem he chose to replace the fleur-de-lis, the traditional symbol of the French monarchy. To proclaim his legitimacy as emperor, he wears a laurel crown (as did ancient Roman emperors) and holds in his right hand a scepter topped with a statue of Charlemagne and in his left the rod of justice. A sword inspired by the one carried by Charlemagne stands on his left side. (Josse/Leemage/Corbis/Getty Images)

The Battle of the Pyramids   After leading French armies to victory in Italy, Napoleon proposed a campaign against Egypt to gain control of the Mediterranean and block British access to the Red Sea, a major route to India. On July 1, 1798, Napoleon and his army—accompanied by 160 scholars and artists—landed in Egypt, then part of the Ottoman Empire ruled by the Mamluks. After initial victory, the campaign ended with French defeat, but the work of French scholars constituted the beginning of Western scholarly knowledge about the ancient civilization of Egypt. (Watteau, Francois Louis Joseph/Musée des Beaux-Arts, Valenciennes, France/Bridgeman Images)

destroyed by Lord Nelson at the Battle of Trafalgar on October 21, 1805. Invasion of England was henceforth impossible. Renewed fighting had its advantages, however, for the first consul used the wartime atmosphere to have himself proclaimed emperor in late 1804.

Austria, Russia, and Sweden joined with Britain to form the Third Coalition against France shortly before the Battle of Trafalgar. Actions such as Napoleon's assumption of the Italian Crown had convinced both Alexander I of Russia and Francis II of Austria that Napoleon was a threat to the European balance of power. Yet they were no match for Napoleon, who scored a brilliant victory over them at the Battle of Austerlitz in December 1805. Alexander I decided to pull back, and Austria accepted large territorial losses in return for peace as the Third Coalition collapsed.

German Confederation of the Rhine, 1806

Napoleon then reorganized the German states to his liking. In 1806 he abolished many of the tiny German states as well as the centuries-old Holy Roman Empire. In their place he established by decree the German Confederation of the Rhine, a union of fifteen German states minus Austria, Prussia, and Saxony. Naming himself "protector" of the confederation, Napoleon firmly controlled western Germany.

Napoleon's intervention in German affairs alarmed the Prussians, who mobilized their armies after more than a decade of peace with France. Napoleon attacked and won two more brilliant victories in October 1806 at Jena and Auerstädt, where the French were outnumbered two to one. The war with Prussia, now joined by Russia, continued into the following spring. After Napoleon's larger armies won another victory,

Alexander I of Russia was ready to negotiate the peace. In the subsequent treaties of Tilsit in 1807, Prussia lost half of its population through land concessions. These included former Polish territories (acquired at the time of the partition of the Polish-Lithuanian Commonwealth), which Napoleon established as a French protectorate named the Grand Duchy of Warsaw. Russia accepted Napoleon's reorganization of western and central Europe and promised to enforce Napoleon's economic blockade against British goods.

The Grand Empire and Its End

Increasingly, Napoleon saw himself as the emperor of Europe, not just of France. The so-called **Grand Empire** he built had three parts. The core, or first part, was an ever-expanding France, which by 1810 included today's Belgium and the Netherlands, parts of northern Italy, and German territories on the west bank of the Rhine. The second part consisted of a number of dependent satellite kingdoms, on the thrones of which Napoleon placed members of his large family. The third part comprised the independent but allied states of Austria, Prussia, and Russia. After 1806 Napoleon expected both satellites and allies to support his **Continental System**, a blockade in which no ship coming from Britain or her colonies could dock at a port controlled by the French. It was intended to halt all trade between Britain and continental Europe, thereby destroying the British economy and its military force.

The impact of the Grand Empire on the peoples of Europe was considerable. In the areas incorporated into France and in the satellites (Map 19.2), Napoleon followed revolutionary principles by abolishing feudal dues and serfdom, to the benefit of the peasants and middle class. Yet Napoleon had to put the prosperity and special interests of France first in order to safeguard his power base. Levying heavy taxes in money and men for his armies, he came to be regarded more as a conquering tyrant than as an enlightened liberator. Thus French rule sparked patriotic upheavals and encouraged the growth of reactive nationalism, for individuals in different lands learned to identify emotionally with their own embattled national families as the French had done earlier.

The first great revolt occurred in Spain. In 1808 Napoleon deposed Spanish king Ferdinand VII and placed his own brother Joseph on the throne. However, a coalition of Catholics, monarchists, and patriots rebelled against Napoleon's attempts to make Spain

a French satellite. French armies occupied Madrid, but the foes of Napoleon fled to the hills and waged uncompromising guerrilla warfare. (See "Evaluating Visual Evidence: Francisco Goya, *The Third of May 1808*," page 582.) Spain was a clear warning: resistance to French imperialism was growing.

Yet Napoleon pushed on. In 1810, when the Grand Empire was at its height, Britain still remained at war with France, helping the guerrillas in Spain and Portugal. The Continental System was a failure. Instead of harming Britain, the system provoked the British to set up a counter-blockade, which created hard times in France. Perhaps looking for a scapegoat, Napoleon turned on Alexander I of Russia, who had opened Russian ports to British goods in December 1810.

Napoleon's invasion of Russia began in June 1812 with a force that eventually numbered 600,000, probably the largest force yet assembled in a single army. Only one-third of this army was French, however; nationals of all the satellites and allies were drafted into the operation. Hoping for a decisive victory followed by peace negotiations, Napoleon pressed on toward Moscow. The great Battle of Borodino that followed was a draw. Alexander ordered the evacuation of Moscow, which the Russians then burned in part, and he refused to negotiate. Finally, after five weeks in the scorched and abandoned city, Napoleon ordered a retreat, one of the greatest military disasters in history. The Russian army, the Russian winter, and starvation cut Napoleon's army to pieces. When the frozen remnants staggered into Poland and Prussia in December, 370,000 men had died and another 200,000 had been taken prisoner.[5]

Leaving his troops to their fate, Napoleon raced to Paris to raise yet another army. Possibly he might still have saved his throne if he had been willing to accept a France reduced to its historical size — the proposal offered by Austria's foreign minister, Prince Klemens von Metternich. But Napoleon refused. Austria and Prussia deserted Napoleon and joined Russia and Great Britain in the Treaty of Chaumont in March 1814, by which the four powers formed the Quadruple Alliance to defeat the French emperor.

All across Europe patriots called for a "war of liberation" against Napoleon's oppression. Less than a month later, on April 4, 1814, a defeated Napoleon abdicated his throne. After this unconditional abdication, the victorious allies granted Napoleon the island of Elba off the coast of Italy as his own tiny state. Napoleon was allowed to keep his imperial title, and France was required to pay him a yearly income of 2 million francs.

The allies also agreed to the restoration of the Bourbon dynasty under Louis XVIII (r. 1814–1824) and promised to treat France with leniency in a peace settlement. The new monarch sought support among the people by issuing the Constitutional Charter, which accepted many of France's revolutionary changes and guaranteed civil liberties.

■ **Grand Empire** The empire over which Napoleon and his allies ruled, encompassing virtually all of Europe except Great Britain and Russia.

■ **Continental System** A blockade imposed by Napoleon to halt all trade between continental Europe and Britain, thereby weakening the British economy and military.

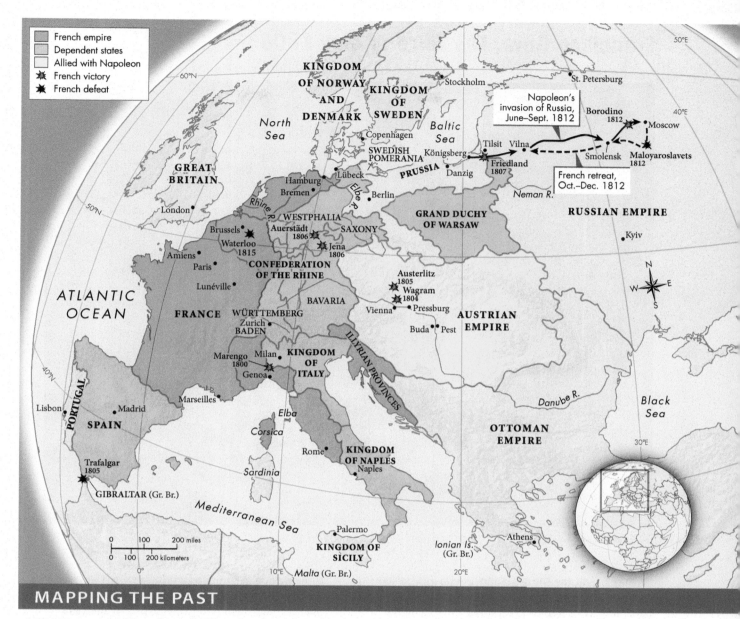

MAPPING THE PAST

MAP 19.2   Napoleonic Europe in 1812

At the height of the Grand Empire in 1810, Napoleon had conquered or allied with every major European power except Britain. But in 1812, angered by Russian repudiation of his ban on trade with Britain, Napoleon invaded Russia with disastrous results. Compare this map with Map 15.2 (page 435), which shows the division of Europe in 1715.

ANALYZING THE MAP   How had the balance of power shifted in Europe from 1715 to 1812? What changed, and what remained the same? What was the impact of Napoleon's wars on Germany and the Italian peninsula?

CONNECTIONS   Why did Napoleon succeed in achieving vast territorial gains where Louis XIV did not?

Yet Louis XVIII lacked the magnetism of Napoleon. Hearing of political unrest in France and diplomatic tensions in Vienna, Napoleon staged a daring escape from Elba in February 1815 and marched on Paris with a small band of followers. French officers and soldiers who had fought so long for their emperor responded to the call. Louis XVIII fled, and once more Napoleon took command. But Napoleon's gamble was a desperate long shot, for the allies were united against him. At the end of a frantic period known as the Hundred Days, they crushed his forces at Waterloo on June 18, 1815, and imprisoned him on the rocky island of St. Helena, off the western coast of Africa. Louis XVIII returned to the throne, and the allies dealt more harshly with the French.

Francisco Goya, *The Third of May 1808*

(PHAS/Getty Images)

On May 2, 1808, the city of Madrid rose up in rebellion against the occupying forces of French emperor Napoleon Bonaparte. French soldiers captured and executed hundreds of rebels the following day in a brutal show of repression. On May 5, Napoleon deposed the Spanish king and placed his own brother Joseph on the throne.

After the French were expelled in 1814, the great Spanish painter Francisco Goya commemorated the uprising with a pair of paintings: the first depicted Spanish fighters battling the French, while the second (pictured here) was a haunting portrayal of the execution of captured Spaniards.

In this painting, Goya broke with a hallowed artistic tradition of depicting war as glorious and soldiers as brave heroes. Instead, Goya portrayed the Spanish rebels as frightened men weeping for their lives before a ruthless French firing squad, thus implicitly denouncing the atrocities of war. Goya's painting represented an important turning point in European attitudes toward violence and warfare. Its initial reception, however, was mixed, and the Spanish national museum did not display the painting until the late nineteenth century. Now it is considered one of the masterpieces of modern art.

EVALUATE THE EVIDENCE

1. Many viewers have noted the way the central figure of the painting evokes the crucified Christ. What elements of the figure echo Christ, and what do you think Goya was trying to suggest with this association?
2. Why did Goya choose to show the faces of the Spanish victims but not the French executioners? What impact does this artistic choice have on the viewer?
3. How did Goya use light and shadow to convey meaning in this painting?

How did revolt by enslaved people on colonial Saint-Domingue lead to the independent nation of Haiti?

The events that led to the creation of the independent nation of Haiti constitute the third, and most extraordinary, chapter of the revolutionary era in the late eighteenth century. Prior to 1789 Saint-Domingue, the French colony that was to become the independent nation of Haiti, reaped huge profits for merchants and the French state through a ruthless system of plantation agriculture based on enslaved labor. News of revolution in France lit a powder keg of contradictory aspirations among French planters, free people of color, and enslaved people. While revolutionary authorities debated how far to extend the rights of man on Saint-Domingue, first free people of color and then enslaved people took matters into their own hands, rising up to demand their rights. As they did so, they drew on elements of African religious and military experience and visions of freedom they created in defiance of the brutality of slavery. Their revolution succeeded despite invasion by the British and Spanish and Napoleon Bonaparte's bid to reimpose French control. In 1804 Haiti became the only nation in history to claim its freedom through revolt by enslaved people.

Revolutionary Aspirations in Saint-Domingue

On the eve of the French Revolution, Saint-Domingue — the most profitable of all Caribbean colonies — was even more rife with social tensions than France itself. The colony, which occupied the western third of the island of Hispaniola, was inhabited by a variety of social groups who resented and mistrusted one another. The European population included French colonial officials, wealthy plantation owners and merchants, and poor artisans and clerks. Individuals of French or European descent born in the colonies were called Creoles, and over time they had developed their own interests, at times distinct from those of metropolitan France. Vastly outnumbering the white population were the colony's five hundred thousand enslaved people, alongside a sizable population of some forty thousand free people of African and mixed African and European descent. Members of this last group referred to themselves as free people of color.

Legal and economic conditions on Saint-Domingue vastly favored the white population. Most of the island's enslaved population performed grueling toil in the island's sugar plantations, with a smaller number working in coffee and indigo plantations or as urban artisans and servants. The highly outnumbered planters used extremely brutal methods, such as beating, maiming, and executing enslaved people, to maintain their control. The 1685 Code Noir (Black Code) that legally regulated slavery was intended to provide minimal standards of humane treatment, but its tenets were rarely enforced. Enslavers calculated that they could earn more by working their human captives ruthlessly and purchasing new ones when they died, than by providing the food, rest, and medical care needed to allow the enslaved population to reproduce naturally. This meant that a constant inflow of newly enslaved people from Africa was necessary to work the plantations. Some people found freedom by escaping into the mountains to join groups of fugitives from enslavement, known as "maroons."

Despite their brutality, enslavers on Saint-Domingue granted freedom to a small number of individuals, mostly their own biracial children, thereby contributing to one of the largest populations of free people of color

THE HAITIAN REVOLUTION	
May 1791	French National Assembly enfranchises free men of color born of two free parents
August 1791	Insurrections among enslaved people in Saint-Domingue
April 1792	French National Assembly grants full citizenship rights to free people of color, including the right to vote for men
September 1793	British troops invade Saint-Domingue
February 1794	Abolition of slavery in all French territories
1796	France regains control of Saint-Domingue under Toussaint L'Ouverture
1803	Death of Toussaint L'Ouverture in France
January 1804	Declaration of Haitian independence
May 1805	First Haitian constitution

Life on Saint-Domingue Although the brutal conditions of plantation slavery left little time or energy for leisure, enslaved people on Saint-Domingue took advantage of their day of rest on Sunday to engage in social and religious activities. The law officially prohibited enslaved people belonging to different owners from mingling together, but such gatherings were often tolerated if they remained peaceful. This image depicts a fight between two enslaved men, precisely the type of unrest and violence feared by authorities. (Yale Center for British Art, Paul Mellon Collection, USA/Bridgeman Images)

in any slaveholding colony. The Code Noir had originally granted free people of color the same legal status as whites: they could own property, live where they wished, and pursue any education or career they desired. From the 1760s on, however, the rising prosperity and visibility of this group provoked resentment from the white population. In response, colonial administrators began rescinding the rights of free people of color, and by the time of the French Revolution free people of color were subject to many discriminatory laws.

The political and intellectual turmoil of the 1780s, with its growing rhetoric of liberty, equality, and fraternity, raised new challenges and possibilities for each of Saint-Domingue's social groups. For enslaved people, who constituted approximately 90 percent of the population, news of abolitionist movements in France led to hopes that the mother country might grant them freedom. Free people of color looked to reforms in Paris as a means of gaining political enfranchisement and reasserting equal status with whites. The Creole elite, however, was determined to protect its way of life, including slaveholding. They looked to revolutionary ideals of representative government for

the chance to gain control of their own affairs, as had the North American colonists before them.

The National Assembly frustrated the hopes of all these groups. Cowed by colonial representatives who claimed that support for free people of color would result in insurrection among enslaved people and the loss of the colony for France, the Assembly refused to extend French constitutional safeguards to the colonies. At the same time, however, the Assembly also reaffirmed French monopolies over colonial trade, thereby angering Creole planters as well.

In July 1790 Vincent Ogé (aw-ZHAY) (ca. 1750–1791), a free man of color, returned to Saint-Domingue from Paris determined to win rights for his people. He raised an army of several hundred and sent letters to the new Provincial Assembly of Saint-Domingue demanding political rights for all free citizens. When Ogé's demands were refused and he was threatened with violence, he and his followers turned to armed insurrection. After initial victories, his army was defeated, and Ogé was tortured and executed by colonial officials. (See "Individuals in Society: Vincent Ogé, Free Man of Color and Revolutionary," page 585.) Revolutionary

INDIVIDUALS IN SOCIETY

Vincent Ogé, Free Man of Color and Revolutionary

Vincent Ogé was born in 1757 in a rural parish of the French colony of Saint-Domingue. He belonged to a social group known as "free people of color," people of African descent who acquired freedom from slavery. Many free people of color had biracial ancestry, being descended from unions between French men and enslaved or free African women. According to Ogé, his father was French and his mother was a free woman, born from a legal marriage between a French man and an African woman. Free people of color like Ogé constituted a significant minority within the colony, about the same size as the French colonial population, but both groups were vastly outnumbered by the enslaved.

Coffee had arrived in Saint-Domingue in the 1730s, bringing plantations and prosperity. Like many free people of color, Ogé's family had inherited property from French relatives. The family's thriving coffee plantation allowed Vincent and his siblings to pursue educational opportunities in France. In 1768, Vincent was apprenticed as a goldsmith in the city of Bordeaux, the most important French port for Atlantic trade, and his younger sisters were educated there as well. Upon his return to Saint-Domingue in 1775, Vincent successfully embarked on his own business career. He brokered coffee and other commodities, was part owner of a schooner, and made lucrative real estate deals. By the 1780s, he was the wealthiest merchant of African descent in the city of Cap Français.*

When the French Revolution broke out in the summer of 1789, Ogé was in Paris overseeing his family's affairs. He quickly emerged as a leader of the small group of free men of color residing there. The burning issue for these men was whether the Declaration of the Rights of Man and of the Citizen applied to them as well. The declaration's language of liberty and equality was universal, but a powerful lobby of absentee plantation owners in Paris was determined to prevent men of African descent from enjoying full citizenship rights. Ogé led efforts to convince the National Assembly to pass laws ensuring the equality of all free men. As a slave-owning planter, he did not advocate abolishing slavery, but argued instead that giving rights to free men of color would win the loyalty of the enslaved and thus help preserve slavery.

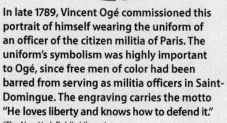

In late 1789, Vincent Ogé commissioned this portrait of himself wearing the uniform of an officer of the citizen militia of Paris. The uniform's symbolism was highly important to Ogé, since free men of color had been barred from serving as militia officers in Saint-Domingue. The engraving carries the motto "He loves liberty and knows how to defend it." (The New York Public Library)

In March 1790, the National Assembly compromised with a vaguely worded law restricting the vote to men who possessed a minimum amount of property. Upon his return to Saint-Domingue in October, Ogé pressed provincial authorities to interpret the law literally, meaning that wealthy free men of color could vote. The white planters who controlled the colony's assembly were outraged by these demands and ordered his arrest. In response, Ogé and his ally Jean-Baptiste Chavannes, a militia officer and veteran of the American Revolution, raised a force of around three hundred men, most of whom had served in the free colored militia.

This small force successfully held out against an initial assault by colonial troops, but a second larger attack forced them to disperse. Ogé escaped to Spanish territory with about two dozen comrades, but Spanish authorities arrested them and extradited them to Saint-Domingue. To prevent any further acts of rebellion, officials in Saint-Domingue ordered Ogé, Chavannes, and other leaders of the revolt to be brutally executed in the cathedral square of Cap Français. The executioner strapped them to the wheel, broke all their bones, and left them to die. Afterward, their heads were displayed on pikes.

Although Ogé's uprising failed, only ten months later an uprising by enslaved people spread across the island. This revolt helped bring about the end of slavery and, ultimately, led to the creation of the independent nation of Haiti in 1804.

QUESTIONS FOR ANALYSIS

1. How important was race as a factor in Vincent Ogé's life? In the lives of other inhabitants of the island? What does his life up to 1789 tell you about the nature of racial identity in Saint-Domingue?

2. What was Ogé's motivation in taking up political activism in 1789? How do you think he justified demanding equality for property-owning free men of color, while continuing to support the system of slavery?

3. Do you see Ogé as a radical or a defender of the status quo? Should his uprising be seen as part of the Haitian Revolution?

*John D. Garrigus, "'Thy Coming Fame, Ogé! Is Sure': New Evidence on Ogé's 1790 Revolt and the Beginnings of the Haitian Revolution," in *Assumed Identities: The Meanings of Race in the Atlantic World*, ed. John D. Garrigus and Christopher Morris (Arlington: University of Texas Press, 2010), p. 24.

leaders in Paris were more sympathetic to Ogé's cause. In May 1791, responding to what it perceived as partly justified grievances, the National Assembly granted political rights to free people of color born to two free parents who possessed sufficient property. When news of this legislation arrived in Saint-Domingue, the colonial governor refused to enact it. Violence then erupted between groups of Creoles and free people of color in parts of the colony.

The Outbreak of Revolt

Just as the sans-culottes helped push forward more radical reforms in France, decisive action from below brought about the second stage of revolution in Saint-Domingue. In August 1791 enslaved people, who had witnessed the confrontation between French settlers and free people of color for over a year, took events into their own hands. A series of nighttime meetings occurred in which groups of enslaved people planned a mass insurrection. In doing so, they drew on their own experience with

African politics, warfare, and society. The majority of enslaved people had been born in Africa, and perhaps a quarter had only been in Saint-Domingue for a short period. They had lived in a range of different African states with distinctive political systems, social institutions, and cultural forms. Many had served in the civil wars of the kingdom of Kongo and other conflicts before being taken into captivity, and they drew on these experiences in planning and executing the insurrection.[6] They also drew on a long tradition of resistance prior to 1791, which had included work slowdowns and running away.[7] According to some sources, the August 1791 pact to take up arms was sealed by a ritual that was part of the African-derived religious rituals and dances known as *vodou* (or voodoo).

Revolts began on a few plantations on the night of August 22. Within a few days the uprising had swept much of the northern plain, creating an army of enslaved rebels estimated at around 2,000 individuals. By August 27 it was described by one observer as "10,000 strong, divided into 3 armies, of whom

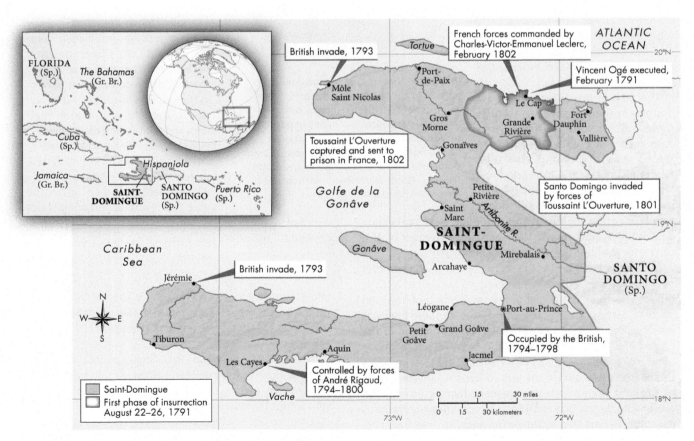

MAP 19.3 The War of Haitian Independence, 1791–1804 Neighbored by the Spanish colony of Santo Domingo, Saint-Domingue was the most profitable European colony in the Caribbean. In 1770 the French transferred the capital from Le Cap to Port-au-Prince. Revolts among enslaved people erupted in the north near Le Cap in 1791. Port-au-Prince became the capital of the newly independent Haiti in 1804.

700 or 800 are on horseback, and tolerably well-armed."[8] During the next month enslaved combatants attacked and destroyed hundreds of sugar and coffee plantations.

On April 4, 1792, as war loomed with the European states, the National Assembly issued a decree extending full citizenship rights to free people of color, including the right to vote. As in France, voting rights and the ability to hold public office applied to men only. The Assembly hoped this measure would win the loyalty of free people of color and their aid in defeating the uprising.

Warfare in Europe soon spread to Saint-Domingue (Map 19.3). Since the beginning of the insurrection, the Spanish colony of Santo Domingo, on the eastern side of the island of Hispaniola, had supported the rebels. In early 1793 the Spanish began to bring leaders of the uprising and their soldiers into the Spanish army. Toussaint L'Ouverture (TOO-sahn LOO-vair-toor) (1743–1803), a formerly enslaved man who had joined the revolt, was named a Spanish officer. In September the British navy blockaded Saint-Domingue, and invading British troops captured French territory on the island. For the Spanish and British, revolutionary chaos provided a tempting opportunity to capture a profitable colony.

Desperate for forces to oppose France's enemies, commissioners sent by the newly elected National Convention promised freedom to enslaved people who fought for France. By October 1793 they had abolished slavery throughout the colony. On February 4, 1794, the Convention ratified the abolition of slavery and extended it to all French territories. In some ways this act merely acknowledged the achievements already won by the insurrection itself.

The tide of battle began to turn when Toussaint L'Ouverture switched sides, bringing his military and political skills, along with four thousand well-trained soldiers, to support the French war effort. By 1796 the French had regained control of the colony, and L'Ouverture had emerged as a key military leader. In May 1796 he was named commander of the western province of Saint-Domingue (see Map 19.3). The increasingly conservative nature of the French government during the Thermidorian reaction, however, threatened to undo the gains made by the formerly enslaved and free people of color.

The War of Haitian Independence

With Toussaint L'Ouverture acting increasingly as an independent ruler of the western province of Saint-Domingue, another general, André Rigaud (1761–1811), set up his own government in the southern peninsula. Tensions mounted between L'Ouverture and Rigaud. While L'Ouverture was a freed man of African descent, Rigaud belonged to the elite among the free people of color. This elite resented

The Abolition of Slavery, 1794   The French government's abolition of slavery in 1794 inspired images of the formerly enslaved enjoying their new freedom. With the caption "I am Free," this engraving shows an individual wearing the red, white, and blue of the French flag and sporting a Phrygian cap, a garment worn in ancient Rome by freed people and adopted by French revolutionaries on the mainland as a symbol of the freedoms provided by the Revolution. This positive image downplays the suffering and oppression caused by slavery prior to abolition and the struggles of enslaved people to win their freedom that began in 1791. (Archives Charmet/Bridgeman Images)

the growing power of formerly enslaved people like L'Ouverture, who in turn accused them of adopting the prejudices of French colonizers. Civil war broke out between the two sides in 1799, when L'Ouverture's forces, led by his lieutenant, Jean Jacques Dessalines (1758–1806), invaded the south. Victory over Rigaud in 1800 gave L'Ouverture control of the entire colony.

This victory was soon challenged by Napoleon, who had his own plans for using the profits from plantation agriculture as a basis for expanding French power. In 1802, Napoleon re-established slavery throughout the French colonies, an act that was not reversed until 1848, when the French government permanently abolished slavery in its remaining colonies. French forces under the command of Napoleon's brother-in-law, General Charles-Victor-Emmanuel Leclerc, invaded Saint-Domingue and arrested Toussaint L'Ouverture. The rebel leader, along with his family, was deported to France, where he died in 1803.

It was left to L'Ouverture's lieutenant, Jean Jacques Dessalines, to unite the resistance, and he led it to a crushing victory over French forces. On January 1, 1804, Dessalines formally declared the independence of Saint-Domingue and the creation of the new sovereign nation of Haiti, the name used by the pre-Columbian inhabitants of the island. The Haitian constitution was ratified in 1805.

Haiti, the second independent state in the Americas and the first in Latin America, was born from the first successful large-scale revolt of enslaved people in history. The claims of formerly enslaved people to have not only the right to freedom, but also the right to govern themselves according to their own laws, was the most radical development of the entire revolutionary era. Occurring in the most profitable plantation colony in the world, the Haitian Revolution spread shock and fear through slaveholding societies in the Caribbean and the United States, bringing to life their worst nightmares of the utter reversal of their power and privilege. Fearing the spread of rebellion to the United States, President Thomas Jefferson refused to recognize Haiti as an independent nation. The liberal proponents of the American Revolution thus chose to protect slavery at the expense of revolutionary ideals of universal human rights. The French government imposed crushing indemnity charges on Haiti to recompense the loss of French property, dealing a harsh blow to the fledgling nation's economy.

Yet Haitian independence had fundamental repercussions for world history, helping spread the idea that liberty, equality, and fraternity must apply to all people and that no one should be enslaved. The next phase of Atlantic revolution soon opened in the Spanish American colonies.

NOTES

1. Quoted in G. Wright, *France in Modern Times*, 4th ed. (New York: W. W. Norton, 1987), p. 34.
2. Quoted in G. Pernoud and S. Flaisser, eds., *The French Revolution* (Greenwich, Conn.: Fawcett, 1960), p. 61.
3. Quoted in L. Gershoy, *The Era of the French Revolution, 1789–1799* (New York: Van Nostrand, 1957), p. 150.
4. T. Blanning, *The French Revolutionary Wars, 1787–1802* (London: Arnold, 1996), pp. 116–128.
5. D. Sutherland, *France, 1789–1815: Revolution and Counterrevolution* (New York: Oxford University Press, 1986), p. 420.
6. John K. Thornton, "'I Am the Subject of the King of Congo': African Political Ideology and the Haitian Revolution," *Journal of World History* 4, no. 2 (Fall 1993): 181–214.
7. Laurent Dubois, *Avengers of the New World: The Story of the Haitian Revolution* (Cambridge, Mass.: Belknap Press, 2004), pp. 43–45, 99–100.
8. Quoted in Dubois, *Avengers of the New World*, p. 97.

LOOKING BACK LOOKING AHEAD

A great revolutionary wave swept both sides of the Atlantic Ocean in the late eighteenth century. The revolutions in British North America, France, and Haiti were individual and unique, but they had common origins and consequences for Western and, indeed, world history. The eighteenth century had witnessed monumental social and economic changes, as populations grew, urbanization spread, and literacy increased. Enlightenment ideals influenced all orders of society, and reformers increasingly championed limiting monarchical authority in the name of popular sovereignty. In the newly independent United States, the political systems of Indigenous nations provided an inspirational model, and in Saint-Domingue the African military, political, and religious inheritance, as well as the experience of resisting slavery, was a vital source of the uprising against the colonial regime.

The Atlantic world was the essential context for this age of revolutions. The movement of peoples, commodities, and ideas across the Atlantic Ocean in the eighteenth century created a world of common debates, conflicts, and aspirations. Moreover, the high stakes of colonial empire heightened competition among European states, leading to a series of wars that generated crushing costs for overburdened treasuries. For both the British in their North American colonies and the French at home, the desperate need for new taxes weakened government authority and opened the door to revolution. In turn, the ideals of the French Revolution inspired enslaved people and free people of color in Saint-Domingue, thus opening the promise of liberty, equality, and fraternity to people of all races.

The chain reaction did not end with the birth of an independent Haiti in 1804. On the European continent throughout the nineteenth and early twentieth centuries, periodic convulsions occurred as successive generations struggled over political rights first proclaimed by the generation of 1789. Meanwhile, as dramatic political events unfolded, a parallel economic revolution was gathering steam. This was the Industrial Revolution, originating around 1780 and accelerating through the end of the eighteenth century (see Chapter 20). After 1815 the twin forces of industrialization and democratization would combine to transform Europe and the world.

Make Connections

Think about the larger developments and continuities within and across chapters.

1. Which do you think was more important: the achievements of the American, French, and Haitian revolutions in terms of liberty and equality, or the limitations imposed on these principles?

2. How did the increased circulation of goods, people, and ideas across the Atlantic in the eighteenth century (Chapter 17) contribute to the outbreak of revolution on both sides of the ocean?

3. To what extent would you characterize the revolutions discussed in this chapter as Enlightenment movements (Chapter 16)?

19   REVIEW & EXPLORE

Identify Key Terms

Identify and explain the significance of each item below.

Estates General (p. 565)

estates (p. 565)

National Assembly (p. 565)

Great Fear (p. 566)

Jacobin Club (p. 572)

second revolution (p. 572)

Girondists (p. 572)

the Mountain (p. 572)

sans-culottes (p. 573)

Reign of Terror (p. 575)

Thermidorian reaction (p. 575)

Napoleonic Code (p. 577)

Grand Empire (p. 580)

Continental System (p. 580)

Review the Main Ideas

Answer the section heading questions from the chapter.

1. What were the factors behind the revolutions of the late eighteenth century? (p. 556)

2. Why and how did American colonists forge a new, independent nation? (p. 559)

3. How did the events of 1789 result in a constitutional monarchy in France? (p. 563)

4. Why and how did the French Revolution take a radical turn? (p. 570)

5. How did Napoleon Bonaparte create a French empire, and why did it fail? (p. 577)

6. How did revolt by enslaved people on colonial Saint-Domingue lead to the independent nation of Haiti? (p. 583)

Suggested Resources

BOOKS

- Armitage, David, and Sanjay Subrahmanyam, eds. *The Age of Revolutions in Global Context, c. 1760–1840.* 2009. Presents the international causes and consequences of the age of revolutions.

- Bell, David A. *The First Total War: Napoleon's War and the Birth of Warfare as We Know It.* 2007. Argues that the French Revolution created a new form of "total" war that prefigured the world wars of the twentieth century.

- Calloway, Colin G. *The Indian World of George Washington: The First President, the First Americans and the Birth of the Nation.* 2018. A study of the first president that examines the long-lasting and complex relations between Washington and Indigenous leaders and nations, revealing the central role they played in his life and, by extension, that of the new nation.

- Chernow, Ron. *Alexander Hamilton.* 2004. A sweeping biography of a previously overlooked Founding Father, which served as the inspiration for the Broadway hit *Hamilton.*

- Desan, Suzanne. *The Family on Trial in Revolutionary France.* 2004. Studies the effects of revolutionary law on the family, including the legalization of divorce.

- Dubois, Laurent. *Avengers of the New World: The Story of the Haitian Revolution.* 2004. An excellent and highly readable account of the revolution that transformed the French colony of Saint-Domingue into the independent state of Haiti.

- Garrioch, David. *The Making of Revolutionary Paris.* 2004. A study of how social and economic changes impacted the city of Paris in the eighteenth century, creating the conditions for the outbreak of revolution.

- Klooster, Wim. *Revolutions in the Atlantic World: A Comparative History.* 2009. An accessible and engaging comparison of the revolutions in North America, France, Haiti, and Spanish America.

- McPhee, Peter, ed. *A Companion to the French Revolution.* 2013. A wide-ranging collection of essays on the French Revolution, written by outstanding experts in the field.

- Schechter, Ronald. *Obstinate Hebrews: Representations of Jews in France, 1715–1815.* 2003. An illuminating study of Jews and attitudes toward them in France, from the Enlightenment to emancipation.

- Scott, Julius. *The Common Wind: Afro-American Currents in the Age of the French Revolution.* 2020. A vivid account of the intercontinental networks that developed among enslaved and free people of color across the Atlantic colonies and that inspired the Haitian Revolution.

- Wood, Gordon S. *The American Revolution: A History.* 2003. A concise introduction to the American Revolution by a Pulitzer Prize–winning historian.

MEDIA

- *Colonel Chabert* (Yves Angelo, 1994). A Napoleonic cavalryman severely wounded in battle and left for dead recovers and returns home to find that his wife has remarried an ambitious politician.

- *Égalité for All: Toussaint Louverture and the Haitian Revolution* (PBS, 2009). Uses music, interviews, voodoo rituals, and dramatic re-enactments to explore the Haitian Revolution and its fascinating leader, Toussaint L'Ouverture.

- *Farewell, My Queen* (Benoît Jacquot, 2012). A fictional view of the final days of the French monarchy, from the perspective of a female servant whose job is to read to Queen Marie Antoinette.

- *French Revolution Digital Archive.* A website hosted by Stanford University that includes fourteen thousand digital images from the French Revolution. **http://frda.stanford.edu/**

- *Haiti Digital Library.* A guide to online primary sources, articles, and websites related to Haitian history, from the revolution to modern times; sponsored by the Haiti Laboratory at Duke University. **sites.duke.edu/haitilab/english/**

- *John Adams* (HBO, 2008). An award-winning miniseries on the life of one of the Founding Fathers of the United States.

- *Liberty, Equality, Fraternity: Exploring the French Revolution.* Features a large image and document collection from the era of the French Revolution, as well as songs, maps, and thematic essays written by expert scholars in the field. **chnm.gmu.edu/revolution/**

- *Liberty! The American Revolution* (PBS, 1997). A dramatic documentary about the American Revolution, consisting of six hour-long episodes that cover events from 1763 to 1788.

- *Master and Commander: The Far Side of the World* (Peter Weir, 2003). A British navy captain pursues a French vessel along the coast of South America during the Napoleonic Wars.

- *The Papers of George Washington.* A site with online versions of many documents pertaining to and written by George Washington, accompanied by articles on themes related to Washington's life and views. **gwpapers.virginia.edu/**

- *The War That Made America* (PBS, 2006). A miniseries about the French and Indian War that focuses on alliances between Native Americans and the French and British, including George Washington's role in the conflict as a young officer.

20

The Revolution in Energy and Industry

ca. 1780–1850

While revolutions in France and across the Atlantic were opening a new political era, another revolution was beginning to transform economic and social life. The Industrial Revolution took off around 1780 in Great Britain and soon began to influence continental Europe and the United States. Non-European nations began to industrialize after 1860.

Industrialization profoundly modified much of human experience. It changed patterns of work and daily life, transformed the social class structure and the way people thought about class, and eventually altered the international balance of political power. Quite possibly only the development of agriculture during Neolithic times had a comparable impact and significance.

What was revolutionary about the Industrial Revolution was not its pace or that it represented a sharp break with the previous period. On the contrary, the Industrial Revolution built on earlier developments, and the rate of progress was slow. What was remarkable about the Industrial Revolution was that it inaugurated a period of sustained economic and demographic growth that has continued to the present day. Although it took time, the Industrial Revolution eventually helped ordinary people in the West gain a higher standard of living as the widespread poverty of preindustrial Europe gradually receded.

Such fundamental transitions did not occur overnight. National wealth rose much more quickly than improvements in the European standard of living until about 1850. This was because, even in Britain, only a few key industries experienced a technological revolution. Many more industries continued to use old methods. In addition, wage increases were modest until the mid-nineteenth century, and the gradual withdrawal of children and married women from paid work meant that the household as a whole earned the same or less. ▪

CHAPTER PREVIEW

- Why and how did the Industrial Revolution emerge in Britain?

- How did countries outside Britain respond to the challenge of industrialization?

- How did work and daily life evolve during the Industrial Revolution?

- What were the social consequences of industrialization?

Life in the Industrial Revolution
Daily life for industrial workers was harsh, especially for the many child laborers who worked in the new factories and in other industries, like the coal-sorting workshop pictured here. Long hours of work, strict discipline, and low wages were the lot of most industrial workers, whose living standards did not improve until the 1840s. (Archives Charmet/Bridgeman Images)

Why and how did the Industrial Revolution emerge in Britain?

The Industrial Revolution began in Great Britain, the nation created in 1707 by the formal union of Scotland, Wales, and England. The transformation in industry was something new in history, and it was unplanned. With no models to copy and no idea of what to expect, Britain pioneered not only in industrial technology but also in social relations and urban living. Just as France was a trailblazer in political change, Britain was the leader in economic development, and it must therefore command special attention.

Why Britain?

Perhaps the most important debate in economic history focuses on why the Industrial Revolution originated in western Europe, and Britain in particular, rather than in other parts of the world, such as Asia. Historians continue to debate this issue, but the best answer seems to be that Britain possessed a unique set of possibilities and constraints—abundant coal deposits, high wages, a relatively peaceful and centralized government, well-developed financial systems, an innovative culture, highly skilled craftsmen, and a strong position in empire and global trade—that spurred its people to adopt a capital-intensive, machine-powered system of production. The long-term economic advantages of this system were not immediately apparent, and its adoption by the British was more a matter of circumstance than a planned strategy.

Thus a number of factors came together over the long term to give rise to the Industrial Revolution in Britain. The Scientific Revolution and the Enlightenment fostered a new worldview that embraced progress and the role of research and experimentation in understanding and mastering the natural world. Britain's intellectual culture extended across many institutions: scientific societies, universities, museums, and workers' associations. The institutions constituted a network for the public sharing of knowledge, including the work of scientists and technicians from other countries. The British Royal Society of Arts, for example, sponsored prizes for innovations in machinery and agriculture and played a pivotal part in the circulation of "useful knowledge."

In the economic realm, the seventeenth-century expansion of rural industry produced a surplus of English woolen cloth. Exported throughout Europe, English cloth brought commercial profits and high wages to the detriment of traditional producers in Flanders and Italy. By the eighteenth century the expanding Atlantic economy and trade with India and China were also serving Britain well. The mercantilist colonial empire Britain aggressively built, augmented by a strong position in Latin America and in the transatlantic slave trade, provided raw materials like cotton and a growing market for British manufactured goods. Strong demand for British manufacturing meant that British workers earned high wages compared to the rest of Europe and that capital was available for investment in new industrial development.

Agriculture also played an important role in bringing about the Industrial Revolution in Britain. English farmers were second only to the Dutch in productivity in 1700, and they were continually adopting new methods of farming. The result, especially before 1760, was a period of bountiful crops and low food prices. Because of increasing efficiency, landowners were able to produce more food with a smaller workforce. The enclosure movement had deprived many small landowners of their land, leaving the landless poor to work as hired agricultural laborers or in cottage industry. By the 1760s, on the eve of the Industrial Revolution, less than 40 percent of Britain's population worked in agriculture (as compared to 60 percent in 1700), while fully one-third worked in the manufacturing sectors, weaving textiles and producing other craft goods.

Abundant food and high wages in turn meant that many English families no longer had to spend almost everything they earned just to buy bread. Thus the family could spend more on manufactured goods—a razor for the man or a shawl for the woman. They could also pay to send their children to school. Britain's populace enjoyed high levels of literacy and numeracy (knowledge of mathematics) compared to the rest of Europe. Moreover, in the eighteenth century the members of the average British family were redirecting their labor away from unpaid work for household consumption and toward work for wages that they could spend on goods, a trend reflecting the increasing commercialization of the entire European economy.

Britain also benefited from rich natural resources and a well-developed infrastructure. In an age when it was much cheaper to ship goods by water than by land, no part of England was more than fifty miles from navigable water. Beginning in the 1770s a canal-building boom enhanced this advantage. Rivers and canals provided easy movement of England's and Wales's enormous deposits of iron and coal, resources that would be critical raw materials in Europe's early industrial age. The abundance of coal combined with high wages in manufacturing placed Britain in a unique position among European nations:

■ **Industrial Revolution** A term first coined in 1799 to describe the burst of major inventions and economic expansion that began in Britain in the late eighteenth century.

TIMELINE

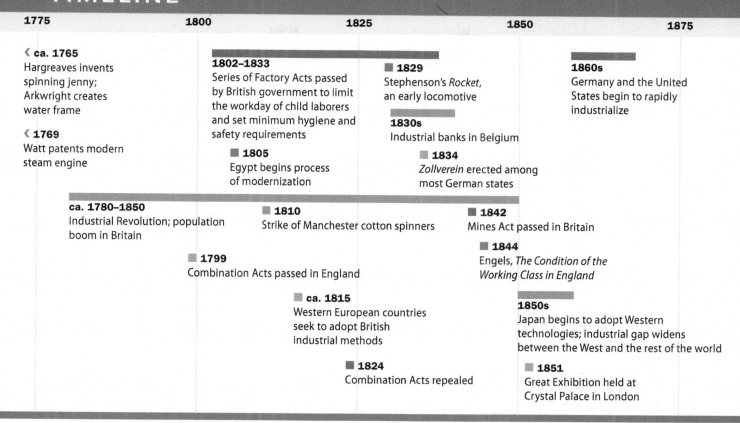

| 1775 | 1800 | 1825 | 1850 | 1875 |

❮ ca. 1765
Hargreaves invents spinning jenny; Arkwright creates water frame

❮ 1769
Watt patents modern steam engine

ca. 1780–1850
Industrial Revolution; population boom in Britain

■ 1799
Combination Acts passed in England

1802–1833
Series of Factory Acts passed by British government to limit the workday of child laborers and set minimum hygiene and safety requirements

■ 1805
Egypt begins process of modernization

■ 1810
Strike of Manchester cotton spinners

■ ca. 1815
Western European countries seek to adopt British industrial methods

■ 1824
Combination Acts repealed

■ 1829
Stephenson's *Rocket*, an early locomotive

1830s
Industrial banks in Belgium

■ 1834
Zollverein erected among most German states

■ 1842
Mines Act passed in Britain

■ 1844
Engels, *The Condition of the Working Class in England*

1850s
Japan begins to adopt Western technologies; industrial gap widens between the West and the rest of the world

■ 1851
Great Exhibition held at Crystal Palace in London

1860s
Germany and the United States begin to rapidly industrialize

---

its manufacturers had strong incentives to develop technologies to draw on the power of coal to increase workmen's productivity. In parts of the world with lower wages, such as India and China, the costs of mechanization at first outweighed potential gains in productivity.

A final factor favoring British industrialization was the heavy hand of the British state and its policies, especially in the formative decades of industrial change. Despite its rhetoric in favor of "liberty," Britain's parliamentary system taxed its population aggressively. The British state collected twice as much per capita as the supposedly "absolutist" French monarchy and spent the money on a navy to protect imperial commerce and on an army that could be used to quell uprisings by disgruntled workers. Starting with the Navigation Acts under Oliver Cromwell (see "The Puritan Protectorate" in Chapter 15), the British state also adopted aggressive tariffs, or duties, on imported goods to protect its industries.

Cottage Industry and Transportation in Eighteenth-Century Great Britain

All these factors combined to initiate the **Industrial Revolution,** a term first coined by contemporaries in 1799 to describe the burst of major inventions and technical changes under way. This technical revolution contributed to an impressive quickening in the annual rate of industrial growth in Britain. Whereas industry had grown at only 0.7 percent between 1700 and 1760 (before the Industrial Revolution), it grew at almost 3 percent between 1801 and 1831 (when industrial transformation was in full swing).[1]

Technological Innovations and Early Factories

The pressure to produce more goods for a growing market and to reduce the labor costs of manufacturing was directly related to the first decisive breakthrough of the Industrial Revolution: the creation of the world's first machine-powered factories in the British cotton textile industry. Technological innovations in the manufacture of cotton cloth led to a new system of production and social relationships. This was not the first time in European history that large numbers of people were systematically put to work in a single locale; the military arsenals of late medieval Venice are one example of a much older form of "factory." The crucial innovation in Britain was the introduction of machine power into the factory and the organization of labor around the functioning of highly productive machines.

The putting-out system that developed in the seventeenth-century textile industry involved a merchant who loaned, or "put out," raw materials to cottage workers who processed the raw materials in their own homes and returned the finished products to the merchant. There was always a serious imbalance in textile production based on cottage industry: the work of four or five spinners was needed to keep one weaver steadily employed. Cloth weavers constantly had to find more thread and more spinners. During the eighteenth century the putting-out system grew across Europe, but most extensively in Britain. There, pressured by growing demand, the system's limitations began to outweigh its advantages around 1760.

Many a tinkering worker knew that a better spinning wheel promised rich rewards. It proved hard to spin the traditional raw materials — wool and flax — with improved machines, but cotton was different. Cotton textiles had first been imported into Britain from India by the East India Company as a rare and delicate luxury for the upper classes. In the eighteenth century, as the transatlantic slave trade reached its peak, a lively market for cotton cloth emerged in West Africa, where the English and other Europeans traded it for human captives. By 1760 a tiny domestic cotton industry had emerged in northern England, but it could not compete with cloth produced in India and other parts of Asia. At this time, Indian cotton textiles dominated the world market because of their workers' mastery over design and dyeing techniques, easy access to raw materials, and relatively low wages. International competition thus drove English entrepreneurs to invent new technologies to bring down labor costs.

After many experiments over a generation, a gifted carpenter and jack-of-all-trades, James Hargreaves, invented his cotton-spinning jenny about 1765. At almost the same moment, a barber-turned-manufacturer named Richard Arkwright invented (or possibly pirated) another kind of spinning machine,

the water frame. These breakthroughs produced an explosion in the infant cotton textile industry in the 1780s, when it was increasing the value of its output at an unprecedented rate of about 13 percent each year. In 1793, Eli Whitney's invention of the cotton gin, a machine for separating cotton fibers from seeds, vastly increased the productivity of cotton fields in the United States, leading to an expansion of slavery and an influx of raw materials for British manufacturers. In the 1790s, the new machines were producing ten times as much cotton yarn as had been made in 1770.

Hargreaves's **spinning jenny** was simple, inexpensive, and powered by hand. In early models from six to twenty-four spindles were mounted on a sliding carriage, and each spindle spun a fine, slender thread. The machines were usually worked by women, who moved the carriage back and forth with one hand and turned a wheel to supply power with the other. Now it was the male weaver who could not keep up with the vastly more efficient female spinner.

Arkwright's spinning frame employed a different principle, using a series of rollers to stretch the yarn. It quickly acquired a capacity of several hundred spindles and demanded much more power than a single operator could provide. A solution was found in waterpower. The **water frame** required large specialized mills located beside rivers in factories that employed as many as one thousand workers. The water frame did not completely replace cottage industry, however, for it could spin only a coarse, strong thread, which was then put out for respinning on hand-operated cottage jennies. Around 1780 a hybrid machine — called a mule — invented by Samuel Crompton proved capable of spinning very fine and strong thread in large quantities. (See "Individuals in Society: Samuel Crompton," page 597.) Gradually, all cotton spinning was concentrated in large-scale water-powered factories.

These revolutionary developments in the textile industry allowed British manufacturers to compete successfully in international markets in both fine and coarse cotton thread. At first, the machines were too expensive to build and did not provide enough savings in labor to be adopted in continental Europe or elsewhere. Where wages were low and investment capital was scarce, there was little point in adopting mechanized production until significant increases in the machines' productivity, and a drop in the cost of manufacturing them, occurred in the first decades of the nineteenth century.[2]

As a result of these developments, families using cotton in cottage industry were freed from their constant search for adequate yarn from scattered part-time spinners, since all the thread needed could be spun in the cottage on the jenny or obtained from a nearby

■ **spinning jenny** A simple, inexpensive, hand-powered spinning machine created by James Hargreaves in 1765.

■ **water frame** A spinning machine created by Richard Arkwright that had a capacity of several hundred spindles and used waterpower; it therefore required a larger and more specialized mill — a factory.

INDIVIDUALS IN SOCIETY

Samuel Crompton

Samuel Crompton's life story illustrates the remarkable ingenuity and determination of the first generation of inventors of the Industrial Revolution as well as the struggles they faced in controlling and profiting from their inventions. Crompton was born in 1753 in Bolton-in-the-Moors, a Lancashire village active in the domestic production of cotton thread and cloth. Crompton descended from small landowners and weavers, but his grandfather had lost the family land and his father died shortly after his birth.

Crompton's mother was a pious and energetic woman who supported the family by tenant farming and spinning and weaving cotton. Crompton spent years spinning in childhood until he was old enough to begin weaving. His mother ensured that he was well educated at the local school, and as a teenager he attended night classes, studying algebra, mathematics, and trigonometry.

This was the period when John Kay's invention of the flying shuttle doubled the speed of handloom weaving, leading to a drastic increase in the demand for thread (see "The Lives of Rural Textile Workers" in Chapter 17). Crompton's family acquired one of the new spinning jennies — invented by James Hargreaves — and he saw for himself how they advanced production. He was also acquainted with Richard Arkwright, inventor of the water frame, who then operated a barbershop in Bolton.

In 1774 Crompton began work on the spinning machine that would consume what little free time, and spare money, he possessed over the next five years. Solitary by nature, and fearful of competition and the violence of machine breakers, Crompton worked alone and in secret. He earned a little extra money playing violin in the Bolton theater orchestra, and he possessed a set of tools left over from his father's mechanical experiments.

The result of all this effort was the spinning mule, so called because it combined the rollers of Arkwright's water frame with the moving carriage of Hargreaves's spinning jenny. With the mule, spinners could produce very fine and strong thread in large quantities, something no previous machine had permitted. The mule effectively ended England's reliance on India for the finest muslin cloth.

In 1780, possessed of a spectacular technological breakthrough and a beloved bride, Crompton seemed poised for a prosperous and happy life. Demand surged for the products of his machine, and manufacturers were desperate to learn its secrets. Too poor and naïve to purchase a patent for his invention, Crompton shared it with manufacturers through a subscription agreement. Unfortunately, he received little of the promised money in return.

Samuel Crompton, inventor of the spinning mule.
(Science & Society Picture Library/Getty Images)

Replica of the spinning mule, a hybrid machine that combined features from Hargreaves's spinning jenny and Arkwright's water frame. (Science & Society Picture Library/Getty Images)

Once exposed to the public, the spinning mule quickly spread across Great Britain. Crompton continued to make high-quality yarn, but he had to compete with all the other workshops using his machine. Moreover, he could not keep skilled workers, since they were constantly lured away by his competitors' higher wages.

As others earned great wealth with the mule, Crompton grew frustrated by his relative poverty. In 1811 he toured Great Britain to document his invention's impact. He estimated that 4,600,000 mules were then in operation that directly employed 70,000 people. Crompton's supporters took these figures to Parliament, which granted him a modest reward of £5,000. However, this boost did little to improve his fortunes, and his subsequent business ventures failed. In 1824 local benefactors took up a small subscription to provide for his needs, but he died in poverty in 1827 at the age of seventy-four.

QUESTIONS FOR ANALYSIS

1. What factors in Crompton's life enabled him to succeed as an inventor?
2. Why did Crompton fail to profit from his inventions?
3. What does the contrast between Richard Arkwright's fantastic success and Crompton's relative failure tell us about innovation and commercial enterprise in the Industrial Revolution?

Source: Gilbert James France, *The Life and Times of Samuel Crompton, Inventor of the Spinning Machine Called the Mule* (London: Simpkin Marshall, 1859).

Woman Working a Spinning Jenny
The loose cotton strands on the slanted
bobbins shown in this illustration of Hargreaves's
spinning jenny passed up to the sliding carriage and then on to
the spindles (inset) in back for fine spinning. The worker, almost always
a woman, regulated the sliding carriage with one hand, and with the
other she turned the crank on the wheel to supply power. By 1783 one
woman could spin by hand a hundred threads at a time. (spinning jenny:
Chronicle/Alamy Stock Photo; spindle: Picture Research Consultants & Archives)

factory. The income of weavers, now hard-pressed to
keep up with the spinners, rose markedly until about
1792. They were among the highest-earning workers
in England. As a result, large numbers of agricultural
laborers became handloom weavers, while mechanics
and capitalists sought to invent a power loom to save on
labor costs. This Edmund Cartwright achieved in 1785.

The power looms of the factories worked poorly at
first and did not replace handlooms until the 1820s.
By 1831 the largely mechanized cotton textile industry accounted for fully 22 percent of the country's
entire industrial production. British cotton textiles
cost half as much as Indian ones.

The Steam Engine Breakthrough

Well into the eighteenth century Europe, like other
areas of the world, continued to rely mainly on wood
for energy, and human beings and animals continued
to perform most work. This dependence meant that
Europe and the rest of the world remained poor in
energy and power.

By the eighteenth century, wood was in ever-shorter
supply in Britain. Processed wood (charcoal) was the
fuel that was mixed with iron ore in the blast furnace
to produce pig iron, which was further processed into
steel, cast iron, or wrought iron. The iron industry's
appetite for wood was enormous, and by 1740 the
British iron industry was stagnating due to the depleted
supply of fuel. Vast forests enabled Russia in the eighteenth century to become the world's leading producer
of iron, much of which was exported to Britain. As
wood became ever more scarce, the British looked to
coal (combustible rock composed of fossilized organic
matter) as an alternative. They had first used coal in
the late Middle Ages as a source of heat. By 1640 most
homes in London were heated with coal, and it was
also used in industry to provide heat for making beer,
glass, soap, and other products. The breakthrough

James Nasmyth's Mighty Steam Hammer In 1842, Scottish engineer James Nasmyth obtained a patent for his new steam-driven industrial hammer, a forerunner of the modern pile driver. In this painting by the inventor himself, workers manipulate a massive iron shaft being hammered into shape at Nasmyth's foundry near Manchester. The successful introduction of the steam hammer epitomized the rapid development of steam-power technology in Britain. (Ann Ronan Picture Library/Heritage-Images/The Print Collector/Alamy Stock Photo)

came when industrialists began to use coal to produce mechanical energy and to power machinery.

To produce more coal, mines had to be dug deeper and deeper and, as a result, were constantly filling with water. Mechanical pumps, usually powered by animals walking in circles at the surface, had to be installed. But animal power was expensive and inconvenient. In an attempt to overcome these disadvantages, Thomas Savery in 1698 and Thomas Newcomen in 1705 invented the first primitive **steam engines**. Both engines burned coal to produce steam, which was then used to operate a pump. Although both models were extremely inefficient, by the early 1770s many of the Savery engines and hundreds of the Newcomen engines were operating successfully in English and Scottish mines.

In 1763 a gifted young Scot named James Watt (1736–1819) was drawn to a critical study of the steam engine. Watt was employed at the time by the University of Glasgow as a skilled craftsman making scientific instruments. Scotland's Enlightenment emphasis on practicality and social progress had caused its universities to become pioneers in technical education. In 1763 Watt was called on to repair a Newcomen engine being used in a physics course. After a series of observations, Watt saw that the Newcomen engine's waste of energy could be reduced by adding a separate condenser. This splendid invention, patented in 1769, greatly increased the efficiency of the steam engine.

To invent something is one thing; to make it a practical success is quite another. Watt needed skilled workers, precision parts, and capital, and the relatively advanced nature of the British economy proved essential. A partnership in 1775 with Matthew Boulton, a wealthy English industrialist, provided Watt with adequate capital and exceptional skills in salesmanship. Among Britain's highly skilled locksmiths, tinsmiths, and millwrights, Watt found mechanics who could install, regulate, and repair his sophisticated engines. This support allowed him to create an effective vacuum in the condenser and regulate a complex engine. In more than twenty years of constant effort, Watt made many further improvements. By the late 1780s the firm of Boulton and Watt had made the steam engine a practical and commercial success in Britain.

The coal-burning steam engine of Watt and his followers was the Industrial Revolution's most fundamental advance in technology. For the first time, inventors and engineers could devise and implement all kinds of power equipment to aid people in their work. The steam-power plant began to replace waterpower in cotton-spinning factories during the 1780s, contributing to that industry's phenomenal rise. Steam also gradually took the place of waterpower in flour mills, in the malt mills used in breweries, in the flint mills supplying the pottery industry, and in the mills exported by Britain to the West Indies to crush sugarcane.

■ **steam engines** A breakthrough invention by Thomas Savery in 1698 and Thomas Newcomen in 1705 that burned coal to produce steam, which was then used to operate a pump; the early models were superseded by James Watt's more efficient steam engine, patented in 1769.

The British iron industry was radically transformed. Originally, the smoke and fumes resulting from coal burning meant that coal could not be substituted for charcoal in smelting iron. Starting around 1710, ironmakers began to use coke — a smokeless and hot-burning fuel produced by heating coal to rid it of water and other impurities — to smelt pig iron. After 1770 the adoption of steam-driven bellows in blast furnaces allowed for great increases in the quantity of pig iron produced by British ironmakers.

In the 1780s Henry Cort developed the coke-fired puddling furnace, which allowed for brittle pig iron to be refined into malleable wrought iron. Strong, skilled ironworkers — the puddlers — "cooked" molten pig iron in a great vat, raking off globs of refined iron for further processing. Cort also developed steam-powered rolling mills, which quickly and efficiently pressed the molten iron into bars, further purifying them in the process. These technical innovations fostered a great boom in the British iron industry. In 1740 annual British iron production was only 17,000 tons. With the spread of coke smelting and the impact of Cort's inventions, production had reached 250,000 tons by 1806. In 1844 Britain produced 3 million tons of iron. Once expensive, iron became the cheap, basic, indispensable building block of the British economy, used to manufacture railway tracks, textile machines, bridges, iron frames for factories and warehouses, weapons, pipes, gears, and steam engines themselves, among other goods.

Steam-Powered Transportation

Steam power also revolutionized transportation. The coal industry had long used plank roads and rails to move coal wagons within mines and at the surface. Rails reduced friction and allowed a horse or a human being to pull a much heavier load. Thus, once a rail capable of supporting a heavy locomotive was developed in 1816, all sorts of experiments with steam engines on rails went forward.

The first steam locomotive was built by Richard Trevithick after much experimentation. George Stephenson acquired glory for his locomotive named **Rocket**, which sped down the track of the just-completed Liverpool and Manchester Railway at a maximum speed of 35 miles per hour, without a load, in 1829. The line from Liverpool to Manchester was the first modern railroad, using steam-powered locomotives to carry customers to the new industrial cities. It was a financial as well as a technical success, and many private companies quickly began to build more rail lines. Within twenty years they had completed the main trunk lines of Great Britain (Map 20.1). Other countries were quick to follow, with the first steam-powered trains operating in the United States in the 1830s and in Brazil, Chile, Argentina, and the British colonies of Canada, Australia, and India in the 1850s.

The arrival of the railroad had many significant consequences. It dramatically reduced the cost and uncertainty of shipping freight over land. Previously, markets had tended to be small and local; as the barrier of high transportation costs was lowered, markets became larger and even nationwide. Larger markets encouraged manufacturers to build larger

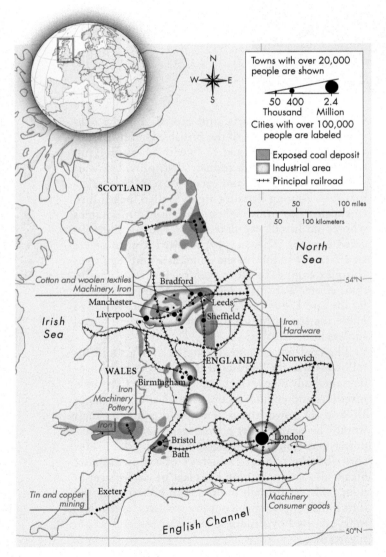

MAP 20.1   The Industrial Revolution in Great Britain, ca. 1850
Industry concentrated in the rapidly growing cities of the north and the center of England, where rich coal and iron deposits were close to one another.

Rain, Steam, and Speed—the Great Western Railway   Steam power created a revolution in human transportation, allowing a constant, rapid rate of travel with no limits on its duration. Time and space suddenly and drastically contracted, as faraway places could be reached in one-third the time or less. Some great painters, notably Joseph M. W. Turner (1775–1851), succeeded in expressing the sense of power and awe inspired by the speed of steam-powered trains. This 1844 painting by Turner depicts a train on the newly laid Great Western Railway line in England crossing the Thames River on the Maidenhead bridge. (Fine Art Images/Heritage Images/GettyImages)

factories with more sophisticated machinery in a growing number of industries. Such factories could make goods more cheaply and gradually subjected most cottage workers and many urban artisans to severe competitive pressures. In all countries, the construction of railroads created a strong demand for unskilled labor and contributed to the growth of a class of urban workers.

The steam engine also transformed water travel. French engineers completed the first steamships in the 1770s, and the first commercial steamships came into use in North America several decades later. The *Clermont* began to travel the waters of the Hudson River in New York State in 1807, shortly followed by ships belonging to brewer John Molson on the St. Lawrence River. The steamship brought the advantages of the railroad—speed, reliability, efficiency—to water travel.

Industry and Population

In 1851 Great Britain celebrated the new era of industrial technology and its role as a world economic leader through an industrial fair in London called the Great Exhibition. Sponsored by the British royal family and situated in the newly built **Crystal Palace**, the fair drew more than 6 million visitors from all over Europe who marveled at the gigantic new exhibition hall set in the middle of a large, centrally located park. The building was made entirely of glass and iron, both of which were now cheap and abundant.

Britain's claim to be the "workshop of the world" was no idle boast, for it produced two-thirds of the

■ *Rocket* The name given to George Stephenson's effective locomotive that was first tested in 1829 on the Liverpool and Manchester Railway at 35 miles per hour.

■ **Crystal Palace** The location of the Great Exhibition in 1851 in London; an architectural masterpiece made entirely of glass and iron.

Interior View of the Crystal Palace   Built for the Great Exhibition of 1851, the Crystal Palace was a spectacular achievement in engineering, prefabricated from 300,000 sheets of glass. With almost 15,000 exhibitors, the event constituted the first international industrial exhibition, showcasing manufactured products from Britain, its empire, and the rest of the world. Later, the building was disassembled and moved to another site in London, where it stood until destroyed by fire in 1936. (Engraving by William Simpson/London Metropolitan Archives/Bridgeman Images)

world's coal and more than half of all iron and cotton cloth. More generally, in 1860 Britain produced a remarkable 20 percent of the entire world's output of industrial goods, whereas it had produced only about 2 percent of the total in 1750.[3] As the British economy significantly increased its production of manufactured goods, the gross national product (GNP) rose roughly fourfold at constant prices between 1780 and 1851. At the same time, the population of Britain boomed, growing from about 9 million in 1780 to almost 21 million in 1851. Thus growing numbers consumed much of the increase in total production.

Rapid population growth in Britain was key to industrial development. More people meant a more mobile labor force, with many young workers in need of employment and ready to go where the jobs were. The dramatic increase in population, in turn, was only sustained through advances in production in agriculture and industry. Based on the lessons of history, many contemporaries feared that the rapid growth in population would inevitably lead to disaster. In his *Essay on the Principle of Population* (1798), Thomas Malthus (1766–1834) argued that

population constantly tended to expand beyond the food available to support it, leading to misery and starvation.[4] Malthus concluded that the only hope of warding off such a catastrophe was for young men and women to limit the growth of population by marrying late in life. (See "Evaluating Written Evidence: Thomas Malthus on the Limitations of Population Growth" in Chapter 17.)

Economist David Ricardo (1772–1823) spelled out the pessimistic implications of Malthus's thought. Ricardo's depressing **iron law of wages** posited that over an extended period of time, because of the pressure of population growth, wages would always sink to subsistence level. That is, wages would be just high enough to keep workers from starving.

Malthus, Ricardo, and their followers were proved wrong by the second half of the nineteenth century, largely because industrialization improved productivity beyond what they could imagine. However, until the 1820s, or even the 1840s, contemporary observers might reasonably have concluded that the economy and the total population were racing neck and neck, with the outcome very much in doubt. There was another problem as well.

Perhaps workers, farmers, and ordinary people did not get their rightful share of the new wealth. Perhaps only the rich got richer, while the poor got poorer or made no progress. We will turn to this great issue after situating the process of industrialization in its European and global context (see "Living Standards for the Working Class" later in this chapter).

How did countries outside Britain respond to the challenge of industrialization?

As new technologies and a new organization of labor began to revolutionize production in Britain, other countries took notice and began to emulate its example. With the end of the Napoleonic Wars, the nations of the European continent quickly adopted British inventions and achieved their own pattern of technological innovation and economic growth. By the last decades of the nineteenth century, western European countries as well as the United States and Japan had industrialized their economies to a considerable, albeit variable, degree.

Industrialization in other parts of the world proceeded more gradually, with uneven advances and great national and regional variations. Scholars are still struggling to explain these variations as well as the dramatic gap that emerged for the first time in history between Western and non-Western levels of economic production. These questions are especially important because they may offer valuable lessons for poor countries that today are seeking to improve their material condition through industrialization and economic development. The latest findings on the nineteenth-century experience are encouraging. They suggest that there were alternative paths to the industrial world and that there was and is no need to follow a rigid, predetermined British model.

National and International Variations

Comparative data on industrial production in different countries over time help give us an overview of what happened. One set of data, the work of a Swiss scholar, compares the level of industrialization on a per capita basis in several countries from 1750 to 1913. These data are far from perfect, but they reflect basic trends and are presented in Table 20.1 for closer study.

Table 20.1 presents a comparison of how much industrial product was produced, on average, for each person in a given country in a given year. All the numbers are expressed in terms of a single index number of 100, which equals the per capita level of industrial goods in Great Britain in 1900. Every number in the table is thus a percentage of the 1900

level in Britain and is directly comparable with other numbers. The countries are listed in roughly the order that they began to use large-scale, power-driven technology.

What does this overview tell us? First, one sees in the first column that in 1750 all countries were fairly close together, including non-Western areas such as China and India. Both China and India had been extremely important players in early modern world trade; both were sophisticated, technologically advanced, and economically powerful up to 1800. However, the column headed 1800 shows that Britain had opened up a noticeable lead over all countries by 1800, and that gap progressively widened as the Industrial Revolution accelerated through 1830 and reached full maturity by 1860.

Second, the table shows that western European countries began to emulate the British model successfully over the course of the nineteenth century, with significant variations in the timing and in the extent of industrialization. Belgium, achieving independence from the Netherlands in 1831 and rich in iron and coal, led in adopting Britain's new technology, and it experienced a great surge between 1830 and 1860. France developed factory production more gradually and did not experience "revolutionary" growth in overall industrial output.

Slow but steady growth in France was overshadowed by the spectacular rise of the German lands and the United States after 1860 in what has been termed the "Second Industrial Revolution." In general, eastern and southern Europe began the process of modern industrialization later than northwestern and central Europe. Nevertheless, these regions made real progress in the late nineteenth century, as growth after 1880 in Austria-Hungary, Italy, and Russia suggests. This meant that all European states as well as the United States managed to raise per capita industrial levels in the nineteenth century.

These increases stood in stark contrast to the decreases that occurred at the same time in many non-Western countries, most notably in China and

---

■ **iron law of wages** Theory proposed by English economist David Ricardo suggesting that the pressure of population growth prevents wages from rising above the subsistence level.

TABLE 20.1 **Per Capita Levels of Industrialization, 1750–1913**

	1750	1800	1830	1860	1880	1900	1913
Great Britain	10	16	25	64	87	100	115
Belgium	9	10	14	28	43	56	88
United States	4	9	14	21	38	69	126
France	9	9	12	20	28	39	59
Germany	8	8	9	15	25	52	85
Austria-Hungary	7	7	8	11	15	23	32
Italy	8	8	8	10	12	17	26
Russia	6	6	7	8	10	15	20
China	8	6	6	4	4	3	3
India	7	6	6	3	2	1	2

Note: All entries are based on an index value of 100, equal to the per capita level of industrialization in Great Britain in 1900. Data for Great Britain includes Ireland, England, Wales, and Scotland.

Source: P. Bairoch, "International Industrialization Levels from 1750 to 1980," *Journal of European Economic History* 11 (Spring 1982): 294, U.S. Journals at Cambridge University Press.

India, as Table 20.1 shows. European countries industrialized to a greater or lesser extent even as most of the non-Western world stagnated. Japan, which is not included in this table, stands out as an exceptional area of non-Western industrial growth in the second half of the nineteenth century. After the forced opening of the country to the West in the 1850s, Japanese entrepreneurs began to adopt Western technology and manufacturing methods, resulting in a production boom by the late nineteenth century. Different rates of wealth- and power-creating industrial development, which heightened disparities within Europe, also greatly magnified existing inequalities between Europe and the rest of the world.

Industrialization in Continental Europe

Throughout Europe the eighteenth century was an era of agricultural improvement, population increase, expanding foreign trade, and growing cottage industry. Thus, when the pace of British industry began to accelerate in the 1780s, continental businesses began to emulate the new methods. British industry enjoyed clear superiority, but the European continent was close behind. During the period of the revolutionary and Napoleonic wars, from 1793 to 1815, however, western Europe experienced tremendous political and social upheaval that temporarily halted economic development. With the return of peace in 1815, western European countries again began to play catch-up.

They faced significant challenges. In the newly mechanized industries, British goods were being produced very efficiently, and these goods had come to dominate world markets. In addition, British

technology had become so advanced that few engineers or skilled technicians outside England understood it. Moreover, the technology of steam power had grown much more expensive. It involved large investments in the iron and coal industries and, after 1830, in railroads. Continental business people had difficulty amassing the large sums of money the new methods demanded, and laborers bitterly resisted the move to working in factories. All these factors slowed the spread of machine-powered industry (Map 20.2).

Nevertheless, western European nations possessed a number of advantages that helped them respond to these challenges. First, most had rich traditions of putting-out enterprise, merchant capitalists, and skilled urban artisans. These assets gave their firms the ability to adapt and survive in the face of new market conditions. Second, continental capitalists did not need to develop their own advanced technology. Instead, they could simply "borrow" the new methods developed in Great Britain. European countries also had a third asset that many non-Western areas lacked in the nineteenth century: they had strong, independent governments that did not fall under foreign political control. These governments would use the power of the state to promote industry and catch up with Britain.

Most continental businesses adopted factory technology slowly, and handicraft methods lived on. Indeed, for a time continental industrialization usually brought substantial but uneven expansion of handicraft industry in both rural and urban areas. Artisan production of luxury items grew in France as the rising income of the international middle class created increased foreign demand for silk scarves, embroidered needlework, perfumes, and fine wines. Focusing on artisanal luxury production made sense for French entrepreneurs given their long history of dominance in that sector. Rather than being a "backward" refusal to modernize, it represented a sound strategic choice that allowed the French to capitalize on their know-how and international reputation for high-quality goods.

Agents of Industrialization

Western European success in adopting British methods took place despite the best efforts of the British to prevent it. The British realized the great value of their technical discoveries and tried to keep their secrets to themselves. Until 1825 it was illegal for artisans and skilled mechanics to leave Britain; until 1843 the export of textile machinery and other equipment was forbidden. Many talented, ambitious workers, however, slipped out of the country illegally and introduced the new methods abroad.

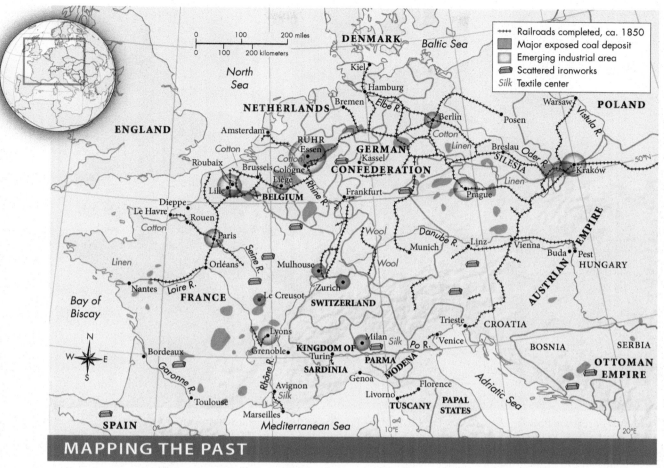

MAPPING THE PAST

MAP 20.2 Continental Industrialization, ca. 1850

Although continental countries were beginning to make progress by 1850, they still lagged far behind Great Britain. For example, continental railroad building was still in an early stage, whereas the British rail system was essentially complete (see Map 20.1). Coal played a critical role in nineteenth-century industrialization, both as a power source for steam engines and as a raw material for making iron and steel.

ANALYZING THE MAP Locate the major exposed (that is, known) coal deposits in 1850. Which countries and areas appear rich in coal resources, and which appear poor? Is there a difference between northern and southern Europe?

CONNECTIONS What is the relationship between known coal deposits and emerging industrial areas in continental Europe? In Great Britain (see Map 20.1)?

One such man was William Cockerill, a Lancashire carpenter. He and his sons began building cotton-spinning equipment in French-occupied Belgium in 1799. In 1817 the most famous son, John Cockerill, built a large industrial enterprise in Liège in southern Belgium, which produced machinery, steam engines, and then railway locomotives. He also established modern ironworks and coal mines. Cockerill's plants in the Liège area became a center for the gathering and transmitting of industrial information across Europe. Many skilled British workers came to work for Cockerill,

and some went on to found their own companies throughout Europe.

Thus British technicians and skilled workers were a powerful force in the spread of early industrialization. A second agent of industrialization consisted of talented entrepreneurs such as Fritz Harkort (1793–1880), a pioneer in the German machinery industry. Serving in England as a Prussian army officer during the Napoleonic Wars, Harkort was impressed with what he saw. He set up shop building steam engines in the Ruhr Valley, on the western border with France. In spite of problems obtaining skilled workers and

The Circle of the Rue Royale, Paris, 1868 The Circle of the Rue Royale was an exclusive club of aristocrats, bankers, railway owners, and other members of Parisian high society. This group portrait exemplifies the consolidation of social and economic power that took place in the second half of the nineteenth century. (Heritage Images/Getty Images)

machinery, Harkort succeeded in building and selling engines. However, his ambitious efforts also resulted in large financial losses for himself and his partners. His career illustrates both the great efforts of a few important business leaders to duplicate the British achievement and the difficulty of the task.

National governments played an even more important role in supporting industrialization in continental Europe than in Britain. **Tariff protection** was one such support, and it proved to be important. The French, for example, responded to a flood of cheap British goods in 1815 after the Napoleonic Wars by laying high taxes on imported goods. Customs agreements emerged among some German states starting in 1818, and in 1834 a number of states signed a treaty creating a customs union, or *Zollverein*. The treaty allowed goods to move between member states without tariffs, while erecting a single uniform tariff against other nations.

After 1815 continental governments also bore the cost of building roads, canals, and railroads to improve transportation. Belgium led the way in the 1830s and 1840s. Built rapidly as a unified network, Belgium's

state-owned railroads stimulated the development of heavy industry and made the country an early industrial leader. In France, the state shouldered all the expense of acquiring and laying roadbed, including bridges and tunnels. In short, governments helped pay for railroads, the all-important leading sector in continental industrialization.

Finally, banks also played a larger and more creative role on the continent than in Britain. Previously, almost all banks in Europe had been private. Because of the possibility of unlimited financial loss, the partners of private banks tended to be conservative and were content to deal with a few rich clients and a few big merchants. They generally avoided industrial investment as being too risky.

In the 1830s, however, two important Belgian banks pioneered in a new direction. They received permission from the growth-oriented government to establish themselves as corporations enjoying limited liability. That is, if the bank went bankrupt, stockholders could now lose only their original investments in the bank's common stock, and they could not be forced by the courts to pay for any additional losses out of other property they owned. Limited liability helped these Belgian banks attract investors. They mobilized impressive resources for investment in big companies, became industrial banks, and successfully promoted industrial development.

Similar corporate banks became important in France and the German lands in the 1850s and 1860s. Usually working in collaboration with governments, corporate banks established and developed many railroads and many companies working in heavy industry, which were also increasingly organized as limited liability corporations.

The combined efforts of governments, skilled workers, entrepreneurs, and industrial banks meshed successfully after 1850 and the financial crash of 1873. In Belgium, France, and the German states, key indicators of modern industrial development—such as railway mileage, iron and coal production, and steam engine capacity—increased at average annual rates of 5 to 10 percent. As a result, rail networks were completed in western and much of central Europe, and the leading continental countries mastered the industrial technologies that had first been developed by the British. In the early 1870s Britain was still Europe's most industrial nation, but a select handful of nations had closed the gap.

The Global Picture

The Industrial Revolution did not have a transformative impact beyond Europe prior to the 1860s, with the exception of the United States and Japan, both early adopters of British practices. In many countries, national governments and pioneering entrepreneurs did make efforts to adopt the technologies and methods of production that had proved so successful in Britain, but they did not fully transition to an industrial economy. For example, in Russia the imperial government brought steamships to the Volga River and a railroad to the capital, St. Petersburg, in the first decades of the nineteenth century. By midcentury ambitious entrepreneurs had established steam-powered cotton factories using imported British machines. However, these advances did not lead to overall industrialization of the country, most of whose people remained mired in rural servitude. Instead, Russia confirmed its role as provider of raw materials, especially timber and grain, to the hungry West.

Egypt, a territory of the Ottoman Empire, similarly began an ambitious program of modernization after a reform-minded viceroy took power in 1805. This program included the use of imported British technology and experts in textile manufacture and other industries. These industries, however, could not compete with lower-priced European imports. Like Russia,

Egypt fell back on agricultural exports to European markets, like sugar and cotton.

Such examples of faltering efforts at industrialization could be found in many other regions of the Middle East, Asia, and Latin America. Where European governments maintained direct or indirect political control, they aggressively acted to monopolize colonial markets as sources of raw materials and as consumers for their own products, rather than encouraging the spread of industrialization. Such regions could not respond to low-cost imports by raising tariffs, as the United States and western European nations had done, because they were controlled by imperial powers that did not allow them to do so. In India, for example, which was a British colony, millions of poor textile workers lost their livelihood and experienced dire poverty because they could not compete with industrially produced British cottons, which were manufactured using raw cotton from India. The British charged stiff import duties on Indian cotton cloth entering the kingdom but prohibited the Indians from doing the same to imported British cloth. As a British trade encyclopedia boasted in 1844:

> The British manufacturer brings the cotton of India from a distance of 12,000 miles, commits it to his spinning jennies and power-looms, carries back their products to the East, making them again to travel 12,000 miles; and in spite of the loss of time, and of the enormous expense incurred by this voyage of 24,000 miles, the cotton manufactured by his machinery becomes less costly than the cotton of India spun and woven by the hand near the field that produced it.[5]

Latin American economies were disrupted by the early-nineteenth-century wars of independence. As these countries' economies recovered in the midnineteenth century, they increasingly adopted steam power for sugar and coffee processing and for transportation. Like elsewhere, this technology first supported increased agricultural production for export and only later drove domestic industrial production. As in India, the arrival of cheap British cottons destroyed the pre-existing textile industry that had employed many people.

The rise of industrialization in Britain, western Europe, and the United States thus caused other regions of the world to become increasingly

■ **tariff protection** A government's way of supporting and aiding its own economy by laying high taxes on imported goods from other countries, as when the French responded to cheaper British goods flooding their country by imposing high tariffs on some imported products.

economically dependent. Instead of industrializing, many territories underwent a process of deindustrialization due to formal and informal European imperialism and economic competition. In turn, relative economic weakness made them vulnerable to the new wave of imperialism undertaken by industrialized nations in the second half of the nineteenth century (see Chapter 24).

As for China, it did not adopt mechanized production until the end of the nineteenth century, but continued as a market-based, commercial society with a massive rural sector and industrial production based on traditional methods. Some regions of China experienced slow economic growth, while others did not. In the 1860s and 1870s, when Japan was successfully adopting industrial methods, the Chinese government showed similar interest in Western technology and science. However, China faced widespread uprisings in the mid-nineteenth century, which drained attention and resources to the military. Moreover, after the Boxer Uprising of 1899–1901, Western powers forced China to pay massive indemnities, further reducing its capacity to promote industrialization.

How did work and daily life evolve during the Industrial Revolution?

Having first emerged in the British countryside in the late eighteenth century, factories and industrial labor began migrating to cities by the early nineteenth century. As factories moved from rural to urban areas, their workforce evolved as well, from pauper children to families to men and women uprooted from their traditional rural communities. Many women, especially young single women and poor women, continued to work, but married women began to limit their participation in the workforce when possible. For some people, the Industrial Revolution brought improvements, but living and working conditions for the poor stagnated or even deteriorated until around 1850, especially in overcrowded industrial cities.

Work in Early Factories

The first factories of the Industrial Revolution were cotton mills, which began functioning in the 1770s along fast-running rivers and streams and were often located in sparsely populated areas. Cottage workers, accustomed to the putting-out system, were reluctant to work in the new factories even when they received relatively good wages. In a factory, workers had to keep up with the machine and follow its relentless tempo. Moreover, they had to show up every day, on time, and work long, monotonous hours under the constant supervision of demanding overseers, and they were punished systematically if they broke the work rules. For example, if a worker was late to work, or accidentally spoiled material, the employer deducted fines from the weekly pay. Employers frequently beat children and adolescents for their infractions.

Cottage workers were not used to that way of life. All members of the family worked hard and long, but in spurts, setting their own pace. They could interrupt their work when they wished. Women and children could break up their long hours of spinning with other tasks. On Saturday afternoon the head of the family delivered the week's work to the merchant manufacturer and got paid. Saturday night was a time of relaxation and drinking, especially for the men.

Also, early factories resembled English poorhouses, where destitute people went to live at public expense. Some poorhouses were industrial prisons, where the inmates had to work in order to receive food and lodging. The similarity between large brick factories and large stone poorhouses increased the cottage workers' fear of factories and their hatred of factory discipline. It was cottage workers' reluctance to work in factories that prompted early cotton mill owners to turn to pauper children. Mill owners contracted with local officials to take on large numbers of such children as "apprentices," boys and girls as young as five or six years of age who had no say in the matter.

Housed, fed, and locked up nightly in factory dormitories, the young workers labored thirteen or fourteen hours a day for little or no pay and for periods up to fourteen years. Harsh physical punishment maintained brutal discipline. Attitudes began to change in the last decade of the eighteenth century, as middle-class reformers publicized the brutal toil imposed on society's most vulnerable members.

Working Families and Children

By the 1790s the early pattern had begun to change. The use of pauper apprentices was in decline, and in 1802 it was forbidden by Parliament. Many more textile factories were being built, mainly in urban areas, where they could use steam power rather than waterpower and attract a workforce more easily than in the countryside. People came from near and far to work in the cities, as factory workers and as porters, builders, and domestic servants. Collectively, these wage laborers came to be known as the "working class," a term first used in the late 1830s.

In some cases, workers accommodated to the system by carrying over familiar working traditions. Some came to the mills and the mines in the family units in which they had labored on farms and in the putting-out system. The mill or mine owner bargained with the head of the family and paid him or her for the efforts of the whole family. In the cotton mills, children worked for their mothers or fathers, collecting scraps and "piecing" broken threads together. In the mines, children sorted coal and worked the ventilation equipment. Their mothers hauled coal in the tunnels below the surface, while their fathers hewed with pick and shovel at the face of the seam.

Ties of kinship were particularly important for newcomers, who often traveled great distances to find work. Many urban workers in Great Britain migrated from Ireland, either on a seasonal or a permanent basis. They were forced out of rural Ireland by population growth and deteriorating economic conditions from 1817 on, and their numbers increased dramatically in the desperate years of the potato famine, from 1845 to 1851 (see "Ireland and the Great Famine" in Chapter 21). As early as 1824 most of the workers in the Glasgow cotton mills were Irish; in 1851 one-sixth of the population of Liverpool was Irish. Like many other immigrant groups held together by ethnic and religious ties, the Irish worked together, formed their own neighborhoods, and preserved their cultural traditions.

In the early decades of the nineteenth century, however, family labor gradually disappeared from the factories. As control and discipline passed into the hands of impersonal managers and overseers, adult workers began to protest against inhuman conditions on behalf of their children. Some enlightened employers and social reformers in Parliament argued that more humane standards were necessary, and they used widely circulated parliamentary reports to influence public opinion. For example, Robert Owen (1771–1858), a successful manufacturer in Scotland, testified in 1816 before an investigating committee. He argued that employing children under ten years of age as factory workers was "injurious to the children, and not beneficial to the proprietors."[6] Workers also provided graphic testimony at such hearings as reformers pressed Parliament to pass corrective laws. (See "Viewpoints: The Experience of Child Labor," page 610.)

These efforts resulted in a series of British **Factory Acts** from 1802 to 1833 that progressively limited the workday of child laborers and set minimum hygiene and safety requirements. The Factory Act of 1833 installed a system of full-time professional inspectors to enforce the provisions of previous acts. Children between ages nine and thirteen could work a maximum of eight hours per day, not including two hours for education. Teenagers aged fourteen to eighteen could work up to twelve hours, while those under nine were banned from employment. The Factory Acts constituted significant progress in preventing the exploitation of children. One unintended drawback of restrictions on child labor, however, was that they broke the pattern of whole families working together in the factory because efficiency required standardized shifts for all workers. After 1833 the number of children employed in industry declined rapidly. The **Mines Act of 1842** prohibited underground work for all women and girls as well as for boys under ten.

The New Sexual Division of Labor

With the restriction of child labor and the collapse of the family work pattern in the 1830s came a new sexual division of labor. By 1850 the man was emerging as the family's primary wage earner, while the married woman found only limited job opportunities. Generally denied good jobs at high wages in the growing urban economy, wives were expected to concentrate on their duties at home.

This new pattern of **separate spheres** had several aspects. First, all studies agree that married women from the working classes were much less likely to work full-time for wages outside the house after the first child arrived, although they often earned small amounts doing putting-out handicrafts at home and taking in boarders. Second, when married women did work for wages outside the house, they usually came from the poorest families, where the husbands were poorly paid, sick, unemployed, or missing. Third, these poor married or widowed women were joined by legions of young unmarried women, who worked full-time but only in certain jobs, of which textile factory work, laundering, and domestic service were particularly important. Fourth, all women were generally confined to low-paying, dead-end jobs. Evolving gradually, but largely in place by 1850, the new sexual division of labor constituted a major development in the history of women and of the family.

Several factors combined to create this new sexual division of labor. First, the new and unfamiliar discipline of the clock and the machine was especially hard on married women of the laboring classes. Relentless factory discipline conflicted with child care in a way that labor on the farm or in the cottage had not. A woman operating earsplitting spinning machinery

---

■ **Factory Acts** English laws passed from 1802 to 1833 that limited the workday of child laborers and set minimum hygiene and safety requirements.

■ **Mines Act of 1842** English law prohibiting underground work for all women and girls as well as for boys under ten.

■ **separate spheres** A gender division of labor with the wife at home as mother and homemaker and the husband as wage earner.

VIEWPOINTS

The Experience of Child Labor

In the first decades of the nineteenth century, the use of child labor in British industrialization attracted the attention of doctors and social reformers. This interest led to investigations by parliamentary commissions, which resulted in laws limiting the hours and the ages of children working in large factories. The moving passages that follow are taken from testimony gathered in 1841 and 1842 by the Ashley Mines Commission. Interviewing employers and many male and female workers, the commissioners focused on the physical condition of the youth and on the sexual behavior of workers far underground. Their work helped bring about the Mines Act of 1842 that prohibited underground work for all women and girls (and for boys younger than ten).

Mr. Payne, coal master

∾ That children are employed generally at nine years old in the coal pits and sometimes at eight. In fact, the smaller the vein of coal is in height, the younger and smaller are the children required; the work occupies from six to seven hours per day in the pits; they are not ill-used or worked beyond their strength; a good deal of depravity exists but they are certainly not worse in morals than in other branches of the Sheffield trade, but upon the whole superior; the morals of this district are materially improving; Mr. Bruce, the clergyman, has been zealous and active in endeavoring to ameliorate their moral and religious education.

Ann Eggley, hurrier, 18 years old

∾ We go at four in the morning, and sometimes at half-past four. We begin to work as soon as we get down. We get out after four, sometimes at five, in the evening. We work the whole time except an hour for dinner, and sometimes we haven't time to eat. I hurry [move coal wagons underground] by myself, and have done so for long. I know the corves [small coal wagons] are very heavy, they are the biggest corves anywhere about. The work is far too hard for me; the sweat runs off me all over sometimes. I am very tired at night. Sometimes when we get home at night we have not power to wash us, and then we go to bed. Sometimes we fall asleep in the chair. Father said last night it was both a shame and a disgrace for girls to work as we do, but there was naught else for us to do. I began

to hurry when I was seven and I have been hurrying ever since. I have been 11 years in the pits. The girls are always tired.

Patience Kershaw, aged 17

∾ My father has been dead about a year; my mother is living and has ten children, five lads and five lasses; . . .

All my sisters have been hurriers, but three went to the mill. Alice went because her legs swelled from hurrying in cold water when she was hot. I never went to day-school; I go to Sunday-school, but I cannot read or write; I go to pit at five o'clock in the morning and come out at five in the evening; I get my breakfast of porridge and milk first; I take my dinner with me, a cake, and eat it as I go; I do not stop or rest any time for the purpose; I get nothing else until I get home, and then have potatoes and meat, not every day meat. I hurry in the clothes I have now got on, trousers and ragged jacket; the bald place upon my head is made by thrusting the corves; . . . I wear a belt and chain at the workings to get the corves out; the putters [miners] that I work for are naked except their caps; they pull off all their clothes; I see them at work when I go up; sometimes they beat me, if I am not quick enough, with their hands; they strike me upon my back; the boys take liberties with me, sometimes, they pull me about; I am the only girl in the pit; there are about 20 boys and 15 men; all the men are naked; I would rather work in mill than in coal-pit.

QUESTIONS FOR ANALYSIS

1. How does Payne's testimony compare with that of Ann Eggley and Patience Kershaw?
2. Describe how the young women perform in the mines. What strikes you most about the testimonies of these workers?
3. The witnesses were responding to questions from middle-class commissioners. What elements of the workers' testimony seemed most interesting to the commissioners? Why?

Source: *Voices of the Industrial Revolution: Selected Readings from the Liberal Economists and Their Critics*, ed. J. Bowditch and C. Ramsland (Ann Arbor: University of Michigan Press, 1961), pp. 87–90.

could mind a child of seven or eight working beside her (until such work was outlawed), but she could no longer pace herself through pregnancy or breast-feed her baby on the job. Thus a working-class woman had strong incentives to stay home, if she could afford it.

Second, running a home in conditions of urban poverty was an extremely demanding job in its own right. There were no supermarkets, public transportation, or modern household appliances. Shopping, washing clothes, and feeding the family constituted a never-ending challenge. Taking on a brutal job outside the house—a "second shift"—had limited appeal for the average married woman from the working class. Thus many women might well have accepted the emerging division of labor as the best available strategy for family survival in the industrializing society.[7]

Child Labor in Coal Mines　Public sentiment against child labor in coal mines was provoked by the publication of dramatic images of the harsh working conditions children endured. The Mines Act of 1842 prohibited the employment underground of women and girls and of boys under the age of ten. (akg-images/Newscom)

Third, to a large degree the young, generally unmarried women who did work for wages outside the home were segregated from men and confined to certain "women's jobs" because the new sexual division of labor replicated long-standing patterns of gender segregation and inequality. In the preindustrial economy, a small sector of the labor market had always been defined as "women's work," especially tasks involving needlework, spinning, food preparation, child care, and nursing. This traditional sexual division of labor took on new overtones, however, in response to the factory system. The growth of factories and mines brought new opportunities for girls and boys to mix on the job, free of familial supervision. (See "Evaluating Visual Evidence: *The Dinner Hour, Wigan*" on page 612.) Such opportunities led to more unplanned pregnancies and fueled the illegitimacy explosion that had begun in the late eighteenth century and that gathered force until at least 1850. Thus the segregation of jobs by gender was partly an effort by older people to control the sexuality of working-class youths.

Some women who had to support themselves protested against being excluded from coal mining, which paid higher wages than most other jobs open to working-class women. But provided they were part of families that could manage economically, the girls and the women who had worked underground were generally pleased with the law. In explaining her satisfaction in 1844, one mother of four provided real insight into why many married working women accepted the emerging sexual division of labor:

While working in the pit I was worth to my [miner] husband seven shillings a week, out of which we had to pay 2½ shillings to a woman for looking after the younger children. I used to take them to her house at 4 o'clock in the morning, out of their own beds, to put them into hers. Then there was one shilling a week for washing; besides, there was mending to pay for, and other things. The house was not guided. The other children broke things; they did not go to school when they were sent; they would be playing about, and get ill-used by other children, and their clothes torn. Then when I came home in the evening,

The Dinner Hour, Wigan

(Manchester Art Gallery UK/Bridgeman Images)

In this painting, artist Eyre Crowe depicts the lunch break of female workers at a cotton mill in Wigan, an industrial city in the north of England. While the group of women in the foreground enjoy a moment of rest and relaxation in their long working day, another group in the background on the right rush back to their factory shift. The women in the foreground are engaged in a variety of activities: some eat, others chat, and one is absorbed in reading. Overall, the image paints a rosy picture of working-class life, depicting healthy, attractive, and well-fed young women who have time to relax over lunch. Reminders of the harsher elements of their lives are suggested by the bottle of alcohol held up by a woman seated behind the reader, and by a baby in the lap of one of the workers — presumably the child's mother — behind the lamppost to the right.

EVALUATE THE EVIDENCE

1. What impression does this painting give you of the relationships among the mill workers?
2. The police officer standing in the distance is one of the only men shown in the painting. What do you think the painter intended to convey by including him?
3. Based on what you have learned in this chapter, do you think this painting is a realistic depiction of the lives of mill workers? In addition to the details discussed above, what elements of the painting support your view?

everything was to do after the day's labor, and I was so tired I had no heart for it; no fire lit, nothing cooked, no water fetched, the house dirty, and nothing comfortable for my husband. It is all far better now, and I wouldn't go down again.[8]

A final factor encouraging working-class women to withdraw from paid labor was the domestic ideals emanating from middle-class women, who had largely embraced the "separate spheres" ideology. Middle-class reformers published tracts and formed societies to urge poor women to devote more care and attention to their homes and families.

Living Standards for the Working Class

Although the evidence is complex and sometimes contradictory, most historians of the Industrial Revolution now agree that overall living standards for the working class did not rise substantially until the 1840s. Factory wages began to rise after 1815, but these gains were modest and were offset by a decline in the labor of children and married women, meaning that many households had less total income than before. Moreover, many people still worked outside the factories as cottage workers or rural laborers, and in those sectors wages declined. Thus the increase in the productivity of industry did not lead to an increase in the purchasing power of the British working classes. Only after 1830, and especially after the mid-1840s, did real wages rise substantially, so that the average worker earned roughly 30 percent more in real terms in 1850 than in 1770.[9]

Up to that point, the demands of labor in the new industries probably outweighed their benefits as far as working people were concerned. Many landless poor people in the late eighteenth century were self-employed cottage workers living in close-knit rural communities; with industrialization they worked longer and harder at jobs that were often more grueling and more dangerous. In England nonagricultural workers labored about 250 days per year in 1760 as compared to 300 days per year in 1830, while the normal workday remained an exhausting eleven hours throughout the entire period. In 1760 nonagricultural workers still observed many religious and public holidays by not working, and many workers took Monday off. These days of leisure and relaxation declined rapidly after 1760, and by 1830 nonagricultural workers had joined landless agricultural laborers in toiling six rather than five days a week.[10]

As the factories moved to urban areas, workers followed them in large numbers, leading to an explosion in the size of cities, especially in the north of England. Life in the new industrial cities, such as Manchester and Glasgow, was grim. Migrants to the booming cities found expensive, hastily constructed, overcrowded apartments and inadequate sanitary systems. Infant mortality, disease, malnutrition, and accidents took such a high toll in human life that average life expectancy was only around twenty-five to twenty-seven years, some fifteen years less than the national average.[11] Perhaps the most shocking evidence of the impact of the Industrial Revolution on living standards is the finding that child mortality levels rose in the first half of the nineteenth century, especially in industrial areas.

Another way to consider the workers' standard of living is to look at the goods they purchased, which also suggest stagnant or declining living standards until the middle of the nineteenth century. One important area of improvement was in the consumption of cotton goods, which became much cheaper and could be enjoyed by all classes. However, in other areas, food in particular, the modest growth in factory wages was not enough to compensate for rising prices.

From the 1850s onward, matters improved considerably as wages made substantial gains and the prices of many goods dropped. A greater variety of foods became available, including the first canned goods. Some of the most important advances were in medicine. Smallpox vaccination became routine, and surgeons began to use anesthesia in the late 1840s. By 1850 trains had revolutionized transportation for the masses, while the telegraph made instant communication possible for the first time in human history. Gaslights greatly expanded the possibilities of nighttime activity.

More difficult to measure than real wages or life expectancy was the impact of the Industrial Revolution on community and social values. As young men and women migrated away from their villages to seek employment in urban factories, many close-knit rural communities were destroyed. Village social and cultural traditions disappeared without new generations to carry them on. Although many young people formed new friendships and appreciated the freedoms of urban life, they also suffered from the loneliness of life in the anonymous city. The loss of skills and work autonomy, along with the loss of community, must be included in the assessment of the Industrial Revolution's effect on the living conditions of workers.

Environmental Impacts of Industrialization

By the mid-seventeenth century, coal had replaced wood as the major fuel for domestic usage. The energy revolution brought about a massive rise in the use of coal to power steam engines in factories and trains as well as to heat blast furnaces, coke ovens, and pottery kilns. The consumption of coal in Britain rose from 10 million tons in 1800 to 60 million in 1856 and to 167 million by 1900.[12] Coal-fueled power transformed living conditions, conveying previously unimaginable levels of comfort, hygiene, and consumer choice on citizens of Western industrialized countries. It also allowed them to use their industrial might to build empires and dominate other countries.

However, coal burning had harsh environmental consequences. Soot and smoke from the chimneys of open coal fires pervaded London and other large cities.

Flames Above an Iron-Smelting Village   Flames from a coke-fired blast furnace light up the night sky in the village of Coalbrookdale, an early center of the English iron ore smelting industry. With smoke billowing from the furnace and broken machinery scattered in the foreground, this painting highlights the environmental degradation that accompanied industrialization. (Universal History Archive/ Universal Images Group/Getty Images)

Burning coal produces toxic ash and emits smoke, soot, heavy metals like mercury and lead, and acidic gases, including sulfur dioxide and carbon dioxide (a greenhouse gas). Hydrochloric acid, a byproduct of the industrial production of goods such as soap, salt, and salt-glazed pottery, was also released into the atmosphere. Together, these gases created the phenomenon of "acid rain," a term coined by a chemist in 1859.

In addition to atmospheric pollution, industrialization created many other environmental hazards. Running water and sewage systems were not widespread until the middle of the nineteenth century, meaning that rapidly expanding industrial cities lacked clean water and relied on outhouses and cesspools for handling human excrement. Garbage collection was haphazard, and rivers provided convenient dumping grounds for industrial and domestic waste, including sewage and dead animals. In the countryside, coal mines contaminated water and soil systems.

Contemporary writers and artists testified to the acrid and impenetrable smog that pervaded industrial cities. Describing London, one writer in the 1830s noted the "dense canopy of smoke that spread itself over her

countless streets and squares, enveloping a million and a half beings in murky vapour."[13] Until the last decades of the nineteenth century, however, most British people viewed smoke belching from factory chimneys as a welcome symbol of economic prosperity. Rather than seeing it as harmful, they believed that acidic smoke purified the air of dangerous gases from decomposing organic waste. Coal smoke smelled bad, but not as bad as putrefying animal corpses and human sewage.

In the 1880s, middle-class reformers presented evidence that smoke had increased the incidence of respiratory diseases and rickets (caused by lack of exposure to the sun) and demanded antipollution laws. But they faced resistance from factory owners, workers fearful of unemployment, and a government committed to laissez-faire economic policies (see "Liberalism and the Middle Class" in Chapter 21). Atmospheric pollution peaked in the late nineteenth century. Around 1900, electric power began to replace steam in industry, leading to substantial improvements in urban air quality over time. At the same time, the British government began to investigate atmospheric pollution, but regulation remained limited.

What were the social consequences of industrialization?

In Great Britain, industrial development led to the creation of new social groups and intensified long-standing conflicts between capital and labor. A new class of factory owners and industrial capitalists arose. These men and women and their families strengthened the wealth and size of the middle class, which had previously been made up mainly of merchants and professional people. The demands of modern industry regularly brought the interests of the middle-class industrialists into conflict with those of the people who worked for them — the working class. (See "Thinking Like a Historian: Making the Industrialized Worker," page 616.) As observers took notice of these changes, they raised new questions about how industrialization affected social relationships. Meanwhile, the forced labor of enslaved people in European colonies contributed to the industrialization process in multiple ways (see "The Impact of Slavery" at the end of this chapter).

The New Class of Factory Owners

Early industrialists operated in a highly competitive economic system. As the careers of James Watt and Fritz Harkort illustrate, there were countless production problems, and success and large profits were by no means certain. Manufacturers therefore waged a constant battle to cut their production costs and stay afloat. Much of the profit had to go back into the business for new and better machinery.

Most early industrialists drew upon their families and friends for labor and capital, but they came from a variety of backgrounds. Many, such as Harkort, were from well-established families with rich networks of contacts and support. Others, such as Watt and Cockerill, were of modest means, especially in the early days. Artisans and skilled workers of exceptional ability had unparalleled opportunities. Members of ethnic and religious groups who had been discriminated against jumped at the new chances and often helped one another.

As factories and firms grew larger, opportunities declined, at least in well-developed industries. It became considerably harder for a poor young mechanic to start a small enterprise and end up as a wealthy manufacturer. Formal education became more important for young men as a means of success and advancement, but studies at the advanced level were expensive. In Britain by 1830 and in France and Germany by 1860, leading industrialists were more likely to have inherited their well-established enterprises, and they were financially much more secure than their struggling parents had been.

Just like working-class women, the wives and daughters of successful businessmen found fewer opportunities for active participation in Europe's increasingly complex business world. Rather than contributing as vital partners in a family-owned enterprise, as so many middle-class women had done, these women were increasingly valued for their ladylike gentility. By 1850 some influential women writers and most businessmen assumed that middle-class wives and daughters should avoid work in offices and factories. Rather, a middle-class lady was expected to concentrate on her proper role as wife and mother, preferably in an elegant residential area far removed from ruthless commerce and the volatile working class. (See "Evaluating Written Evidence: Advice for Middle-Class Women," page 618.)

Responses to Industrialization

From the beginning, the British Industrial Revolution had its critics. Among the first were the Romantic poets. William Blake (1757–1827) called the early factories "satanic mills" and protested against the hard life of the London poor. William Wordsworth (1770–1850) lamented the destruction of the rural way of life and the pollution of the land and water. Some handicraft workers — notably the **Luddites**, members of a secret textile workers organization who attacked factories in northern England in 1811 and later — smashed the new machines, which they believed were putting them out of work. Doctors and reformers wrote of problems in the factories and new towns, while Malthus and Ricardo concluded that workers would earn only enough to stay alive.

This pessimistic view was accepted and reinforced by Friedrich Engels (1820–1895), the future revolutionary and colleague of Karl Marx (see Chapter 21). After studying conditions in northern England, this young son of a wealthy Prussian cotton manufacturer published in 1844 *The Condition of the Working Class in England*, a blistering indictment of the capitalist classes. "At the bar of world opinion," he wrote, "I charge the English middle classes with mass murder, wholesale robbery, and all the other crimes in the calendar." The new poverty of industrial workers was worse than the old poverty of cottage workers and agricultural laborers, according to Engels. The culprit was industrial capitalism, with its relentless competition and constant technical change. Engels's extremely influential charge of capitalist exploitation

> **Luddites** Group of handicraft workers who attacked factories in northern England in 1811 and later, smashing the new machines that they believed were putting them out of work.

Making the Industrialized Worker

Looking back from the vantage point of the 1820s and 1830s, contemporary observers saw in early industrialization a process that was as much about social transformation as it was about technological transformation — a process in which changes in work conditions were closely tied to changes in workers' family lives, values, and mental habits.

1 **Peter Gaskell, *The Manufacturing Population of England: Its Moral, Social, and Physical Conditions, and the Changes Which Have Arisen from the Use of Steam Machinery*, 1833.** In this excerpt, Peter Gaskell sketches the moral, social, and physical conditions of English workers before industrialization took hold, linking these characteristics to preindustrial work conditions.

Prior to the year 1760, manufactures were in a great measure confined to the demands of the home market. At this period, and down to 1800 . . . the majority of the artisans engaged in them had laboured in their own houses, and in the bosoms of their families. . . .

These were, undoubtedly, the golden times of manufactures, considered in reference to the character of the labourers. By all the processes being carried on under a man's own roof, he retained his individual respectability; he was kept apart from associations that might injure his moral worth, whilst he generally earned wages which were sufficient not only to live comfortably upon, but which enabled him to rent a few acres of land; thus joining in his own person two classes, that are now daily becoming more and more distinct. . . .

Thus, removed from many of those causes which universally operate to the deterioration of the moral character of the labouring man, when brought into large towns . . . the small farmer, spinner, or hand-loom weaver presents as orderly and respectable an appearance as could be wished. It is true that the amount of labour gone through was but small; that the quantity of cloth or yarn produced was but limited — for he worked by the rule of his strength and convenience. They were, however, sufficient to clothe and feed himself and family decently, and according to their station; to lay by a penny for an evil day, and to enjoy those amusements and bodily recreations then in being. He was a respectable member of society; a good father, a good husband, and a good son.

2 **Richard Guest, *A Compendious History of the Cotton-Manufacture*, 1823.** Like Peter Gaskell, Richard Guest, one of the earliest historians of the English textile industry, believed that industrialization had "introduced great changes into the manners and habits of the people." Unlike Gaskell, however, Guest was convinced that these changes had been for the better. Where Gaskell saw moral decline, Guest saw moral awakening.

The progress of the Cotton Manufacture introduced great changes into the manners and habits of the people. The operative workmen being thrown together in great numbers had their faculties sharpened and improved by constant communication. Conversation wandered over a variety of topics not before essayed; the questions of Peace and War, which interested them importantly, inasmuch as they might produce a rise or fall of wages, became highly interesting, and this brought them into the vast field of politics and discussions on the character of their Government, and the men who composed it. They took a greater interest in the defeats and victories of their country's arms, and from being only a few degrees above their cattle in the scale of intellect, they became Political Citizens. . . .

The facility with which the Weavers changed their masters, the constant effort to find out and obtain the largest remuneration for their labour, the excitement to ingenuity which the higher wages for fine manufactures and skillful

ANALYZING THE EVIDENCE

1. How does Richard Guest's characterization of preindustrial workers and conditions in Source 2 compare to Peter Gaskell's in Source 1? Why did Gaskell think industrialization would harm workers' morals while Guest saw it as a force for moral improvement?
2. Early-nineteenth-century artists produced many images of the new factories. How would you describe the textile mill shown in Source 4?
3. According to the German doctor in Source 3, what challenges confronted working-class women in their daily lives? To what extent does he seem to blame the women themselves for their situation? How might observations like these have affected the new sexual division of labor discussed in the text?
4. In what ways were Robert Owen's innovations (Source 5) a response to the negative impacts of industrialization highlighted by the German doctor (Source 3)?

workmanship produced, and a conviction that they depended mainly on their own exertions, produced in them that invaluable feeling, a spirit of freedom and independence, and that guarantee for good conduct and improvement of manners, a consciousness of the value of character and of their own weight and importance.

3 **Living conditions of the working class, 1845.** As middle-class reformers began to investigate working-class living conditions, they were shocked at what they found. This excerpt comes from an 1845 interview of doctors in a German industrial city.

~ **Question**: What is your usual experience regarding the cleanliness of these classes?

Dr. Bluemner: Bad! Mother has to go out to work, and can therefore pay little attention to the domestic economy, and even if she makes an effort, she lacks time and means. A typical woman of this kind has four children, of whom she is still suckling one, she has to look after the whole household, to take food to her husband at work, perhaps a quarter of a mile away on a building site; she therefore has no time for cleaning and then it is such a small hole inhabited by so many people. The children are left to themselves, crawl about the floor or in the streets, and are always dirty; they lack the necessary clothing to change more often, and there is no time or money to wash these frequently. There are, of course, gradations; if the mother is healthy, active and clean, and if the poverty is not too great, then things are better.

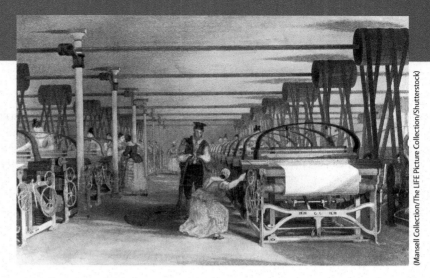

(Mansell Collection/The LIFE Picture Collection/Shutterstock)

4 **Power loom weaving, 1834.** This engraving shows adult women operating power looms under the supervision of a male foreman, and it accurately reflects both the decline of family employment and the emergence of a gender-based division of labor in many British factories. The jungle of belts and shafts connecting the noisy looms to the giant steam engine on the ground floor created a constant din.

5 **Robert Owen, *A New View of Society*, 1831.** Manufacturer and social reformer Robert Owen was also interested in the lessons of the early years of industrialization. He wished not to defend or decry industrialization, but to apply those lessons to the design and operation of his textile factory at New Lanark, Scotland.

~ The system of receiving apprentices from public charities was abolished; permanent settlers with large families were encouraged, and comfortable houses built for their accommodation. The practice of employing children in the mills, of six, seven, and eight years of age, was discontinued, and their parents advised to allow them to acquire health and education until they were ten years old. . . . The children were taught reading, writing, and arithmetic during five years, that is, from five to ten, in the village school, without expense to their parents. . . .

[A]ttention was given to the domestic arrangements of the community. Their houses were rendered more comfortable, their streets were improved, the best provisions were purchased, and sold to them at low rates. . . . They were taught to be rational, and they acted rationally. Thus both parties experienced the incalculable advantages of the system which had been adopted. Those employed became industrious, temperate, healthy, faithful to their employers, and kind to each other; while the proprietors were deriving services . . . far beyond those which could be obtained by any other means than those of mutual confidence and kindness.

PUTTING IT ALL TOGETHER

Using the sources above, along with what you have learned in class and in this chapter, create a comparison of industrial and preindustrial conditions, written from the perspective of a nineteenth-century observer. Your observer can come from any social background: he or she could be a scholar like Peter Gaskell or Richard Guest, a factory owner like Robert Owen, or an actual factory worker. As you write, be sure to consider the influence of your observer's background on his or her characterization of the changes brought by industrialization. What differences would your observer highlight? Why?

Sources: (1) Peter Gaskell, *The Manufacturing Population of England: Its Moral, Social, and Physical Conditions, and the Changes Which Have Arisen from the Use of Steam Machinery* (London: Baldwin and Cradock, 1833), pp. 15–16, 18; (2) E. Royston Pike, *Human Documents of the Industrial Revolution in Britain* (London: George Allen & Unwin, 1970), pp. 26–28; (3) Laura L. Frader, ed., *The Industrial Revolution: A History in Documents* (Oxford: Oxford University Press, 2006), pp. 85–86; (5) Pike, *Human Documents of the Industrial Revolution in Britain*, pp. 37–42.

Advice for Middle-Class Women

The adoption of steam-powered machines generated tremendous profits during the Industrial Revolution. Factory owners and managers enjoyed new wealth, and skilled male workers eventually began to hope for wages high enough to keep their wives and children at home. These social changes encouraged the nineteenth-century "separate spheres" ideology, which emphasized the importance of women's role as caretakers of the domestic realm. Sarah Stickney Ellis's *The Women of England: Their Social Duties and Domestic Habits,* excerpted below, was one of a flood of publications offering middle-class women advice on shopping, housekeeping, and supervising servants.

"What shall I do to gratify myself—to be admired—or to vary the tenor of my existence?" are not the questions which a woman of right feelings asks awaking to the avocations of the day. Much more congenial to the highest attributes of woman's character, are inquiries such as these: "How shall I endeavor through this day to turn the time, the health, and the means permitted me to enjoy, to the best account? Is any one sick, I must visit their chamber without delay, and try to give their apartment an air of comfort, by arranging such things as the wearied nurse may not have thought of. Is any one about to set off on a journey, I must see that the early meal is spread, to prepare it with my own hands,

in order that the servant, who was working late last night, may profit by unbroken rest. Did I fail in what was kind or considerate to any of the family yesterday; I will meet her this morning with a cordial welcome, and show, in the most delicate way I can, that I am anxious to atone for the past. Was any one exhausted by the last day's exertion, I will be an hour before them this morning, and let them see that their labor is so much in advance. Or, if nothing extraordinary occurs to claim my attention, I will meet the family with a consciousness that, being the least engaged of any member of it, I am consequently the most at liberty to devote myself to the general good of the whole, by cultivating cheerful conversation, adapting myself to the prevailing tone of feeling, and leading those who are least happy, to think and speak of what will make them more so."

EVALUATE THE EVIDENCE

1. What daily tasks and duties does Sarah Stickney Ellis prescribe for the mother of the family?
2. How does this document exemplify the changes in the sexual division of labor and ideals of domesticity described in the text?

Source: Sarah Stickney Ellis, "The Women of England: Their Social Duties and Domestic Habits," in *The Past Speaks,* 2d ed., ed. Walter Arnstein (Lexington, Mass.: D. C. Heath, 1993), 2:173.

and increasing worker poverty was embellished by Marx and later socialists (see "The Rise of Marxist Socialism" in Chapter 21).

Analysis of industrial capitalism, often combined with reflections on the French Revolution, led to the development of a new overarching interpretation — a new paradigm — regarding social relationships. Briefly, this paradigm argued that individuals were members of separate classes based on their relationship to the means of production, that is, the machines and factories that dominated the new economy. As owners of expensive industrial machinery and as dependent laborers in their factories, the two main groups of society had separate and conflicting interests. Accordingly, the comfortable, well-educated "public" of the eighteenth century came increasingly to be defined as the middle class ("middle" because they were beneath the small group of aristocracy at the top of society who claimed to be above industrial activity), and the "people" gradually began to perceive themselves as composing a modern

working class. And if the new class interpretation was more of a simplification than a fundamental truth for some critics, it appealed to many because it seemed to explain the dramatic social changes wrought by industrialization. Therefore, conflicting classes existed, in part, because many individuals came to believe they existed and developed an awareness that they belonged to a particular social class — what Karl Marx called **class-consciousness**.

The Early British Labor Movement

Not everyone worked in large factories and coal mines during the Industrial Revolution. In 1850 more British people still worked on farms than in any other single occupation, although rural communities were suffering from outward migration. The second-largest occupation was domestic service, with more than 1 million household servants, 90 percent of whom were women. Thus many old, familiar jobs outside industry lived on and provided alternatives to industrial labor.

Uprising of French Silk Weavers, 1831   In the first decades of the nineteenth century, half of the inhabitants of Lyon, the second-largest city in France, earned a living in the silk industry. The industry was controlled by large-scale merchants, who distributed orders to weavers toiling fifteen to eighteen hours a day on handlooms in their cramped lodgings. In 1831, with a depressed economy causing a drastic fall in silk prices and workers' wages, the silk weavers rose in revolt, briefly seizing control of the city before an army arrived to restore order. (akg-images/Newscom)

Within industry itself, the pattern of artisans working with hand tools in small shops remained unchanged in many trades, even as others were revolutionized by technological change. For example, the British iron industry was completely dominated by large-scale capitalist firms by 1850. Many large ironworks had more than one thousand people on their payrolls. Yet the firms that fashioned iron into small metal goods, such as tools, tableware, and toys, employed on average fewer than ten wage workers who used handicraft skills. The survival of small workshops gave many workers an alternative to factory employment.

Working-class solidarity and class-consciousness developed both in small workshops and in large factories. In the northern factory districts, anticapitalist sentiments were frequent by the 1820s. Commenting in 1825 on a strike in the woolen center of Bradford and the support it had gathered from other regions, one newspaper claimed with pride that "it is all the workers of England against a few masters of Bradford."[14] Even in trades that did not undergo mechanization, unemployment and stagnant wages contributed to class awareness.

Such sentiments ran contrary to the liberal tenets of economic freedom championed by eighteenth-century thinkers like Adam Smith (see "Adam Smith and Economic Liberalism" in Chapter 17). Liberal economic principles were embraced by statesmen and middle-class business owners in the late eighteenth century and continued to gather strength in the early nineteenth century. In 1799 Parliament passed the **Combination Acts**, which outlawed unions and strikes. In 1813 and 1814 Parliament repealed an old law regulating the wages of artisans and the conditions of apprenticeship. As a result of these and other measures, certain skilled artisan workers, such as bootmakers and high-quality tailors, found aggressive capitalists ignoring traditional work rules and trying to flood their trades with unorganized women workers and children to beat down wages.

■ **class-consciousness** Awareness of belonging to a distinct social and economic class whose interests might conflict with those of other classes.

The capitalist attack on artisan guilds and work rules was bitterly resented by many craftworkers, who subsequently played an important part in Great Britain and in other countries in gradually building a modern labor movement. The Combination Acts were widely disregarded by workers. Printers, papermakers, carpenters, tailors, and other such craftsmen continued to take collective action, and societies of skilled factory workers also organized unions in defiance of the law. Unions sought to control the number of skilled workers, to limit apprenticeship to members' own children, and to bargain with owners over wages.

They were not afraid to strike; there was, for example, a general strike of adult cotton spinners in Manchester in 1810. In the face of widespread union activity, Parliament repealed the Combination Acts in 1824, and unions were tolerated, though not fully accepted, after 1825. The next stage in the development of the British trade-union movement was the attempt to create a single large national union. This effort was led not so much by working people as by social reformers such as Robert Owen. Owen, a self-made cotton manufacturer, had pioneered in industrial relations by combining strict discipline with paternalistic concern for the health, safety, and work hours of his employees. After 1815 he experimented with cooperative and socialist communities, including one at New Harmony, Indiana. Then in 1834 Owen was involved in the organization of one of the largest and most visionary of the early national unions, the Grand National Consolidated Trades Union. When Owen's and other ambitious labor organizing schemes collapsed, the British labor movement moved once again after 1851 in the direction of craft unions. The most famous of these was the Amalgamated Society of Engineers, which represented skilled machinists. These unions won real benefits for members by fairly conservative means and thus became an accepted part of the industrial scene.

British workers also engaged in direct political activity in defense of their interests. After the collapse of Owen's national trade union, many working people went into the Chartist movement, which sought political democracy. The key Chartist demand—that all men be given the right to vote—became the great hope of millions of common people. Workers were also active in campaigns to limit the workday in factories to ten hours and to permit duty-free importation of wheat into Great Britain to secure cheap bread.

Thus working people developed a sense of their own identity and played an active role in shaping the new industrial system. They were neither helpless victims nor passive beneficiaries.

The Impact of Slavery

Another mass labor force of the Industrial Revolution was composed of the millions of enslaved men, women, and children who toiled in European colonies in the Caribbean and in North and South America. Historians have long debated the extent to which revenue from slavery contributed to Britain's achievements in the Industrial Revolution. Most now agree that profits from colonial plantations and slave trading were a small portion of British national income in the eighteenth century and were probably more often invested in land than in industry. Nevertheless, the impact of slavery on Britain's economy was much greater than its direct profits alone. In the mid-eighteenth century the need for items to exchange for colonial cotton, sugar, tobacco, and enslaved people stimulated demand for British manufactured goods in the Caribbean, North America, and West Africa. Britain's dominance in the slave trade also led to the development of finance and credit institutions that helped early industrialists obtain capital for their businesses. Investments in canals, roads, and railroads made possible by profits from colonial trade provided the necessary infrastructure to move raw materials and products of the factory system.

The British Parliament abolished the slave trade in 1807 and freed all enslaved people in British territories in 1833, but by 1850 most of the cotton processed by British mills was supplied by the labor of enslaved people in the southern United States. Thus the Industrial Revolution was deeply entangled with the Atlantic world and the brutal exploitation of enslaved people.

NOTES

1. Nicholas Crafts, "Productivity Growth During the British Industrial Revolution: Revisionism Revisited," Working Paper, Department of Economics, University of Warwick, September 2014.

2. Robert C. Allen, *The British Industrial Revolution in Global Perspective* (Cambridge: Cambridge University Press, 2009), pp. 1–2.

3. P. Bairoch, "International Industrialization Levels from 1750 to 1980," *Journal of European Economic History* 11 (Spring 1982): 269–333.

4. J. Bowditch and C. Ramsland, eds., *Voices of the Industrial Revolution* (Ann Arbor: University of Michigan Press, 1961), p. 55, from the fourth edition of Thomas Malthus, *Essay on the Principle of Population* (1807).

■ **Combination Acts** British laws passed in 1799 that outlawed unions and strikes, favoring capitalist business people over skilled artisans. Bitterly resented and widely disregarded by many craft guilds, the acts were repealed by Parliament in 1824.

5. Quoted in Emma Griffin, *A Short History of the British Industrial Revolution* (Basingstoke, U.K.: Palgrave Macmillan, 2010), p. 126.

6. Quoted in E. R. Pike, *"Hard Times": Human Documents of the Industrial Revolution* (New York: Praeger, 1966), p. 109.

7. See especially J. Brenner and M. Rama, "Rethinking Women's Oppression," *New Left Review* 144 (March–April 1984): 33–71, and sources cited there.

8. Quoted in Pike, *"Hard Times,"* p. 208.

9. Joel Mokyr, *The Enlightened Economy: An Economic History of Britain, 1700–1850* (New Haven, Conn.: Yale University Press, 2009), pp. 460–461.

10. Hans-Joachim Voth, *Time and Work in England, 1750–1830* (Oxford: Oxford University Press, 2000), pp. 118–133, 268–270.

11. Mokyr, *The Enlightened Economy*, p. 455.

12. B. W. Clapp, *An Environmental History of Britain* (Abingdon: Routledge, 2013), p. 16.

13. Quoted in Peter Thorsheim, *Inventing Pollution: Coal, Smoke, and Culture in Britain Since 1800* (Athens: Ohio University Press, 2006), p. 5.

14. Quoted in D. Geary, ed., *Labour and Socialist Movements in Europe Before 1914* (Oxford: Berg, 1989), p. 29.

LOOKING BACK LOOKING AHEAD

The Industrial Revolution was a long process of economic innovation and growth originating in Britain around 1780 and spreading to the European continent after 1815. The development of manufacturing machines powered first by water and then by steam allowed for a tremendous growth in productivity that enabled Britain to assume the lead in the world's production of industrial goods. Industrialization fundamentally changed the social landscape of European countries, creating a new elite of wealthy manufacturers and a vast working class of urban wage laborers whose living conditions remained grim until the mid-nineteenth century.

One popular idea in the 1830s, first developed by a French economist, was that Britain's late-eighteenth-century "industrial revolution" paralleled the political events in France during the French Revolution. One revolution was economic, while the other was political; the first was ongoing and successful, while the second had failed and come to a definite end in 1815, when Europe's conservative monarchs defeated Napoleon and restored the French kings of the Old Regime.

In fact, in 1815 the French Revolution, like the Industrial Revolution, was an unfinished work-in-progress. Just as Britain was still in the midst of its economic transformation and the states of northwestern Europe had only begun industrialization, so too after 1815 were the political conflicts and ideologies of revolutionary France still very much alive. The French Revolution had opened the era of modern political life not just in France but also across Europe. It had brought into existence many of the political ideologies that would interact with the social and economic forces of industrialization to refashion Europe and create a new urban society. Moreover, in 1815 the unfinished French Revolution carried the very real possibility of renewed political upheaval. This possibility, which conservatives feared and radicals longed for, would become dramatic reality briefly in 1830 and then again in 1848, when political revolutions swept across Europe like a whirlwind.

Make Connections

Think about the larger developments and continuities within and across chapters.

1. Why did Great Britain take the lead in industrialization, and when and how were other countries able to adopt the new techniques and organization of production?

2. How did the achievements in agriculture and rural industry of the late seventeenth and eighteenth centuries (Chapter 17) pave the way for the Industrial Revolution of the late eighteenth century?

3. How would you compare the legacy of the political revolutions of the late eighteenth century (Chapter 19) with that of the Industrial Revolution? Which seems to you to have created the most important changes, and why?

20 REVIEW & EXPLORE

Identify Key Terms

Identify and explain the significance of each item below.

Industrial Revolution (p. 595)

spinning jenny (p. 596)

water frame (p. 596)

steam engines (p. 599)

Rocket (p. 600)

Crystal Palace (p. 601)

iron law of wages (p. 602)

tariff protection (p. 606)

Factory Acts (p. 609)

Mines Act of 1842 (p. 609)

separate spheres (p. 609)

Luddites (p. 615)

class-consciousness (p. 618)

Combination Acts (p. 619)

Review the Main Ideas

Answer the section heading questions from the chapter.

1. Why and how did the Industrial Revolution emerge in Britain? (p. 594)

2. How did countries outside Britain respond to the challenge of industrialization? (p. 603)

3. How did work and daily life evolve during the Industrial Revolution? (p. 608)

4. What were the social consequences of industrialization? (p. 615)

Suggested Reading and Media Resources

BOOKS

- Allen, Robert C. *The British Industrial Revolution in Global Perspective.* 2009. Explains the origins of the Industrial Revolution and why it took place in Britain and not elsewhere.

- Davidoff, Leonore, and Catherine Hall. *Family Fortunes: Men and Women of the English Middle Class, 1750–1850,* rev. ed. 2003. Examines both economic activities and cultural beliefs with great skill.

- Griffin, Emma. *A Short History of the British Industrial Revolution.* 2010. An accessible and lively introduction to the subject.

- Humphries, Jane. *Childhood and Child Labour in the British Industrial Revolution.* 2010. A moving account of the experience of children during

the Industrial Revolution, based on numerous autobiographies.

- James, Harold. *Family Capitalism.* 2006. A study of the entrepreneurial dynasties of the British Industrial Revolution.

- Morris, Charles R. *The Dawn of Innovation: The First American Industrial Revolution.* 2012. Tells the story of the individuals, inventions, and trade networks that transformed the United States from a rural economy to a global industrial power.

- Prados de la Escosura, Leandro, ed. *Exceptionalism and Industrialisation: Britain and Its European Rivals, 1688–1815.* 2004. Compares the path toward economic development in Britain and the rest of Europe.

- Rosenthal, Jean-Laurent, and R. Bin Wong. *Before and Beyond Divergence: The Politics of Economic Change in China and Europe.* 2011. A study of the similarities and differences between Europe and China that led to the origins and growth of industrialization in Europe.

- Thorsheim, Peter. *Inventing Pollution: Coal, Smoke, and Culture in Britain Since 1800.* Recounts the rise of concerns about atmospheric pollution in Britain during the Industrial Revolution.
- Wrigley, E. A. *Energy and the English Industrial Revolution.* 2010. Explores the vital role of coal-derived steam power in the Industrial Revolution.

MEDIA

- *The Children Who Built Victorian Britain* (BBC, 2011). An account of the role of child labor in the Industrial Revolution, based on written testimonies from children of that era.
- *Germinal* (Claude Berri, 1993). In a European coal-mining town during the Industrial Revolution, exploited workers go on strike and encounter brutal repression from the authorities.
- *Great Victorian Railway Journeys: How Modern Britain Was Built by Victorian Steam Power* (BBC, 2012). A popular British television series re-creates five journeys by train from the Victorian era, showing the impact of rail travel on English culture and society.
- *Hard Times* (Granada TV, 1977). A four-hour miniseries adaptation of Charles Dickens's famous novel about the bitter life of mill workers in England during the Industrial Revolution.
- *Mill Times* (PBS, 2006). A combination of documentary video and animated re-enactments that tells the story of the mechanization of the cotton industry in Britain and the United States.
- *Spinning the Web.* A website offering comprehensive information on the people, places, industrial processes, and products involved in the mechanization of the British cotton industry. **www.spinningtheweb.org.uk/industry**
- *Women Working, 1800–1930.* A digital collection of the Harvard University Library, with sources and links related to women's labor in the nineteenth and early twentieth centuries. **ocp.hul.harvard.edu/ww**

21

Ideologies and Upheavals

1815–1850

The momentous economic and political transformation of modern times that began in the late eighteenth century with the "unfinished" revolutions—the Industrial Revolution in England and the political revolution in France—would play out with unpredictable consequences in the first half of the nineteenth century. Attempts to halt the spread of the progressive forces associated with the French Revolution led first to a reassertion of conservative political control in continental Europe. Following the leadership of Austrian foreign minister Klemens von Metternich, the aristocratic leaders of the Great Powers sought to stamp out the spread of liberal and democratic reforms.

The political and cultural innovations made possible by the unfinished revolutions, however, proved difficult to contain. In politics, powerful new ideologies—liberalism, nationalism, and socialism—emerged to challenge conservative government. In literature, art, and music, Romanticism—an intellectual and artistic movement that challenged the certainties of the Enlightenment and fed the growth of popular nationalism—captured the intensity of the era. A successful revolution in Greece, liberal reform in Great Britain, and popular unrest in France gave voice to ordinary people's desire for political and social change. All these movements helped launch the great wave of revolutions that swept across Europe in 1848. The dramatic results would have a lasting impact on politics and political culture across Western society. ∎

CHAPTER PREVIEW

- **How was peace restored and maintained after the Napoleonic Wars?**

- **What new ideologies emerged to challenge conservative government?**

- **What were the characteristics of the Romantic movement?**

- **How did reforms and revolutions challenge conservatism after 1815?**

- **What were the main causes and consequences of the revolutions of 1848?**

High Passions in the Revolutionary Era

In 1830 and then again in 1848, ordinary people forced political change in many parts of Europe. In this dramatic scene from the revolutions of 1848 in Düsseldorf, Prussia, a group of workers submit a petition to elite members of the city council demanding the restoration of a popular public works program. In the public square visible through the window, an orator harangues a revolutionary crowd beneath a black, red, and gold flag representing unified Germany. The artist presents a sympathetic view of the goals of the revolution. (akg-images/Newscom)

How was peace restored and maintained after the Napoleonic Wars?

The eruption of revolutionary political forces in 1848 was by no means predictable at the end of the Napoleonic era. Quite the contrary. After finally defeating Napoleon, the monarchies of Russia, Prussia, Austria, and Great Britain — known as the Quadruple Alliance — reaffirmed their determination to hold France in line. Even before Napoleon's final defeat, the allies had agreed to fashion a general peace accord in 1814 at the Congress of Vienna, where they faced a great challenge: how could they construct a lasting settlement that would not sow the seeds of another war? By carefully managing the balance of power, redrawing the boundaries of formerly French-held territories, and embracing conservative restoration, they brokered an agreement that contributed to fifty years of peace in Europe (Map 21.1).

The European Balance of Power

Leading representatives of the Quadruple Alliance (plus a representative of the restored Bourbon monarch of France) — including Tsar Alexander I of Russia, King Friedrich Wilhelm III of Prussia, Emperor Franz II of Austria, and their foreign ministers — met to fashion the peace at the **Congress of Vienna** from September 1814 to June 1815. A host of delegates from the smaller European states also attended the conference.

Such a face-to-face meeting of kings and emperors was very rare. Professional ambassadors and court representatives typically conducted state-to-state negotiations; now leaders engaged, for one of the first times, in what we would today call "summit diplomacy." Beyond formal discussions, congress

Congress of Vienna The Congress of Vienna was renowned for its intense diplomatic deal making, resulting in the Treaty of Vienna, the last page of which was signed and sealed in 1815 by the representatives of the various European states attending the conference. The congress won notoriety for its ostentatious parades, parties, and dance balls. The painting here portrays a mounted group of European royalty, led by the Prussian emperor and the Russian tsar, in a flamboyant parade designed to celebrate Napoleon's defeat the year before. Onlookers toast the victorious monarchs. The display of flags, weapons, and heraldic emblems symbolizes the unity of Europe's Great Powers, while the long tables in the background suggest the extent of the festivities. Such images were widely distributed to engender popular support for the conservative program. (akg-images/Newscom)

TIMELINE

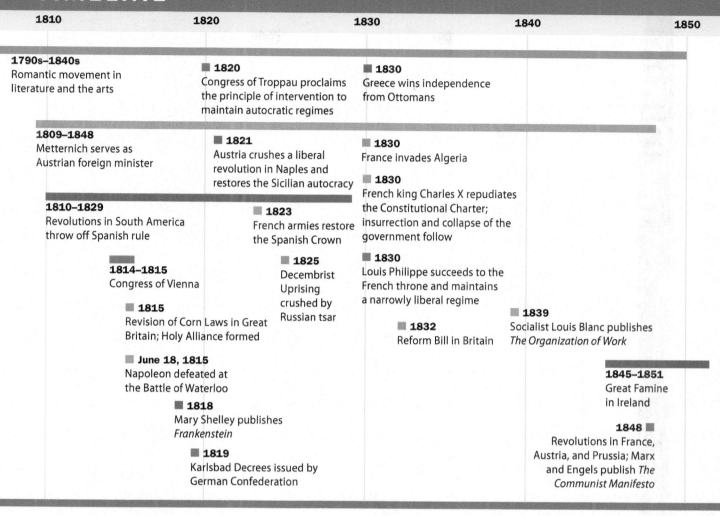

1810	1820	1830	1840	1850

1790s–1840s
Romantic movement in literature and the arts

■ **1820**
Congress of Troppau proclaims the principle of intervention to maintain autocratic regimes

■ **1830**
Greece wins independence from Ottomans

1809–1848
Metternich serves as Austrian foreign minister

■ **1821**
Austria crushes a liberal revolution in Naples and restores the Sicilian autocracy

■ **1830**
France invades Algeria

■ **1830**
French king Charles X repudiates the Constitutional Charter; insurrection and collapse of the government follow

1810–1829
Revolutions in South America throw off Spanish rule

■ **1823**
French armies restore the Spanish Crown

■ **1830**
Louis Philippe succeeds to the French throne and maintains a narrowly liberal regime

1814–1815
Congress of Vienna

■ **1825**
Decembrist Uprising crushed by Russian tsar

■ **1832**
Reform Bill in Britain

■ **1839**
Socialist Louis Blanc publishes *The Organization of Work*

■ **1815**
Revision of Corn Laws in Great Britain; Holy Alliance formed

■ **June 18, 1815**
Napoleon defeated at the Battle of Waterloo

1845–1851
Great Famine in Ireland

■ **1818**
Mary Shelley publishes *Frankenstein*

1848 ■
Revolutions in France, Austria, and Prussia; Marx and Engels publish *The Communist Manifesto*

■ **1819**
Karlsbad Decrees issued by German Confederation

---

participants enjoyed festivities associated with aristocratic court culture, including receptions, military parades, sumptuous dinner parties, ballroom dances, fireworks displays, salon visits, opera, and theater. All were opportunities to socialize, discuss current affairs, and make informal deals that could be confirmed at the conference table. Newspapers, pamphlets, periodicals, and satiric cartoons kept readers across Europe up-to-date on social events and the latest political developments. The conference thus marked an important transitional moment in Western history. The salon society and public sphere of the eighteenth-century Enlightenment (see "How did the Enlightenment change cultural ideas and social practices?" in Chapter 16) gradually shifted toward nineteenth-century cultures of publicity and public opinion informed by more modern mass-media campaigns.[1]

The Quadruple Alliance was first concerned with the defeated enemy, France. Motivated by self-interest and traditional ideas about the balance of power, its members practiced moderation toward the former foe. To Klemens von Metternich (MEH-tuhr-nihk) and Robert Castlereagh (KA-suhl-ray), the foreign ministers of

Austria and Great Britain, the balance of power meant an international equilibrium of political and military forces that would discourage aggression by any combination of states or, worse, the domination of Europe by any single state. Their French negotiating partner, the skillful and cynical diplomat Charles Talleyrand, concurred.

The allies offered France lenient terms after Napoleon's abdication. They agreed to restore the Bourbon king to the French throne. The first Treaty of Paris, signed before the conference (and before Napoleon escaped from Elba and attacked the Bourbon regime), gave France the boundaries it had possessed in 1792. In addition, France did not have to pay war reparations. Thus the victorious powers avoided provoking a spirit of victimization and desire for revenge in the defeated country.

The treaty terms combined leniency with strong defensive measures designed to raise barriers against the possibility of renewed French aggression. Belgium

■ **Congress of Vienna** A meeting of the Quadruple Alliance (Russia, Prussia, Austria, and Great Britain), restoration France, and smaller European states to fashion a general peace settlement that began after the defeat of Napoleon's France in 1814.

Great Powers

- Great Britain
- France
- Kingdom of Prussia
- Austrian Empire
- Russian Empire
- Prussian territorial gains
- Austrian territorial gains
- Boundary of the German Confederation

MAPPING THE PAST

MAP 21.1 Europe in 1815

In 1815 Europe contained many different states, but after the defeat of Napoleon international politics was dominated by the five Great Powers: Russia, Prussia, Austria, Great Britain, and France. (The number rises to six if one includes the Ottoman Empire.) At the Congress of Vienna, the Great Powers redrew the map of Europe.

ANALYZING THE MAP Trace the political boundaries of each Great Power. What are their geographical strengths and weaknesses? Compare these boundaries to those established at the height of Napoleonic power (see Map 19.2). What are the most important changes? What countries lost or gained territory?

CONNECTIONS How did Prussia's and Austria's territorial gains contribute to the balance of power established at the Congress of Vienna? What other factors enabled the Great Powers to achieve such a long-lasting peace?

and Holland—incorporated into the French empire under Napoleon—were united under an enlarged and independent "Kingdom of the Netherlands" capable of opposing French expansion to the north. The German-speaking lands on France's eastern border, also taken by Napoleon, were returned to Prussia. As a famous German anthem put it, the expanded Prussia would now stand as the "watch on the Rhine" against French attack. In addition, the allies reorganized the German-speaking territories of central Europe. A new German Confederation, a loose association of German-speaking states based on Napoleon's reorganization of the territory dominated by Prussia and Austria, replaced the roughly three hundred principalities, free cities, and dynastic states of the Holy Roman Empire with just thirty-eight German states (see Map 21.1).

Austria, Britain, Prussia, and Russia used the notion of the balance of power to settle their own potentially dangerous disputes. The victors generally agreed that they should receive territory for their victory over the French, and they made land swaps without concern for the wishes or allegiances of their inhabitants. Great Britain had already won colonies and strategic outposts during the long wars. Austria gave up territories in Belgium and southern Germany but gained the rich provinces of Venetia and Lombardy in northern Italy, as well as former Polish possessions and new lands on the eastern coast of the Adriatic.

Russian and Prussian claims for territorial expansion were more contentious, particularly in Poland. When Russia had pushed Napoleon out of central Europe, its armies had expanded Russian control over Polish territories. Tsar Alexander I wished to make Russian rule permanent. When France, Austria, and Great Britain all argued for limits on Russian gains, the tsar ceded some western Polish territories back to Prussia. But he kept the bulk of the former Duchy of Warsaw, now renamed the Kingdom of Poland, and set up as a semi-autonomous state ruled by the tsar. About two-thirds of the former Polish-Lithuanian Commonwealth remained under Russian control.

Prussian claims on the state of Saxony, a wealthy kingdom in the German Confederation, were also divisive. The Saxon king had supported Napoleon until his decisive defeat at the 1813 Battle of Leipzig; now Wilhelm III wanted to incorporate Saxony into Prussia. Under pressure, he agreed to partition the state, leaving an independent Saxony in place, a change that posed no real threat to its Great Power neighbors but soothed their fears of Prussian expansionism. These territorial changes and compromises fell very much within the framework of balance-of-power ideology.

In February 1815 Napoleon escaped from his imprisonment on the island of Elba and briefly reignited his wars of expansion in the so-called Hundred Days

(see "The Grand Empire and Its End" in Chapter 19). Yet the second Treaty of Paris, concluded in November 1815 after Napoleon's final defeat at Waterloo, was still relatively moderate toward France. The elderly Louis XVIII was restored to his throne for a second time. France lost only a little territory, had to pay an indemnity of 700 million francs, and was required to support a large army of occupation for five years. The rest of the settlement concluded at the Congress of Vienna was left intact. The members of the Quadruple Alliance, however, did agree to meet periodically to discuss their common interests and to consider appropriate measures for the maintenance of peace in Europe. This agreement marked the beginning of the European "Congress System," which lasted long into the nineteenth century and settled many international crises peacefully.

Metternich and Conservatism

The political ideals of conservatism, often associated with Austrian foreign minister Prince Klemens von Metternich (1773–1859), dominated Great Power discussions at the Congress of Vienna. Metternich's

Prince Klemens von Metternich   This portrait by Sir Thomas Lawrence reveals much about Metternich, the foreign minister of the Austrian Empire. Handsome, refined, and intelligent, this grand aristocrat passionately defended his class and its interests. (The Picture Art Collection/Alamy)

reactionary defense of the monarchical status quo made him a villain in the eyes of most progressive, liberal thinkers of the nineteenth century. Yet rather than denounce his politics, we can try to understand the political ideals he represented. Metternich was an internationally oriented aristocrat who made a brilliant diplomatic career. Austrian foreign minister from 1809 to 1848, his conservatism derived from his pessimistic view of human nature, which he believed was prone to error, excess, and self-serving behavior. The disruptive events of the French Revolution and the Napoleonic Wars confirmed these views, and Metternich's conservatism would emerge as a powerful new political ideology, an attempt to manage the many crises of the revolutionary age.

Metternich firmly believed that liberalism, as embodied in the revolutionary United States and France, bore the responsibility for the suffering caused by twenty-five years of war. Like Edmund Burke and other conservatives, Metternich blamed liberal middle-class revolutionaries for stirring up the lower classes. A strong, authoritarian monarchy, he concluded, was necessary to protect society from the baser elements of human behavior, which were easily released in a parliamentary system. Organized religion was another pillar of strong government. Metternich despised the anticlericalism of the Enlightenment and the French Revolution and maintained that Christian morality was a vital bulwark against radical change.

Born into the landed nobility, Metternich defended his elite class and its rights and privileges. The church and nobility were among Europe's most ancient and valuable institutions, and conservatives regarded tradition as the basic foundation of human society. The threat of liberalism appeared doubly dangerous to Metternich because it generally went with aspirations for national independence. Liberals believed that each people, each national group, had a right to establish its own independent government and fulfill its own destiny; this system threatened to revolutionize central Europe and destroy the Austrian Empire.

After centuries of war, royal intermarriage, and territorial expansion, the vast Austrian Empire of the Habsburgs included many regions and peoples (Map 21.2). The numerous kingdoms, duchies, and principalities under Habsburg rule included the lands of the Austrian Crown, the Kingdom of Hungary, the Kingdom of Bohemia, and the Kingdom of

Lombardy-Venetia. Noble houses in these territories maintained some control, but ultimate authority rested with the Habsburg emperor. The peoples of the Austrian Empire spoke at least eleven different languages and observed vastly different customs; an astonishing variety of different ethnic groups mingled in the same provinces and the same villages. They included about 8 million Germans, almost one-fourth of the population. Some 5.5 million Magyars (Hungarians), 5 million Italians, 4 million Czechs, and 2 million Poles lived alongside one another in the imperial state, as did smaller groups of Ukrainians, Slovaks, Croats, Serbs, Romanians, Jews, and Armenians.[2] The various Slavic groups, together with the Italians and the Romanians, lived in widely scattered regions, yet they outnumbered the politically dominant Germans and Hungarians.

The multiethnic empire Metternich served had strengths and weaknesses. A large population and vast territories gave the empire economic and military clout, but its potentially dissatisfied ethnicities and nationalities undermined political unity. Under these circumstances, Metternich and the Habsburg dynasty had to oppose liberalism and nationalism—if Austria was to remain intact and powerful, it could hardly accommodate ideologies that demanded national independence.

On the Austrian Empire's borders, the Russian Empire and, to a lesser extent, the Ottoman Empire supported and echoed Metternich's efforts to hold back liberalism and nationalism. Bitter enemies, the enormous Russian and Ottoman Empires were both absolutist states with powerful armies and long traditions of expansion and conquest. Because of those conquests, both were also multinational empires with many peoples, languages, and religions, but most of the ruling elite came from the dominant ethnic group—the Orthodox Christian Russians of central and northern Russia and the Muslim Ottoman Turks of Anatolia (modern Turkey). After 1815 these multinational absolutist states worked to preserve their respective conservative orders. Only after 1840 did each in turn experience a profound crisis and embark on a program of fundamental reform and modernization, as we shall see in Chapter 23.

Repressing the Revolutionary Spirit

Conservative political ideologies had important practical consequences. With Metternich's guidance, Austria, Prussia, and Russia embarked on a decades-long crusade against the liberties and civil rights associated with the French and American Revolutions. The first step was the formation in September 1815 of the **Holy Alliance** by Austria, Prussia, and Russia. First proposed by Russia's

---

■ **Holy Alliance** An alliance formed by the conservative rulers of Austria, Prussia, and Russia in September 1815 that became a symbol of the repression of liberal and revolutionary movements all over Europe.

■ **Karlsbad Decrees** Issued in 1819, these repressive regulations were designed to uphold Metternich's conservatism, requiring the German states to root out subversive ideas and suppress any liberal organizations.

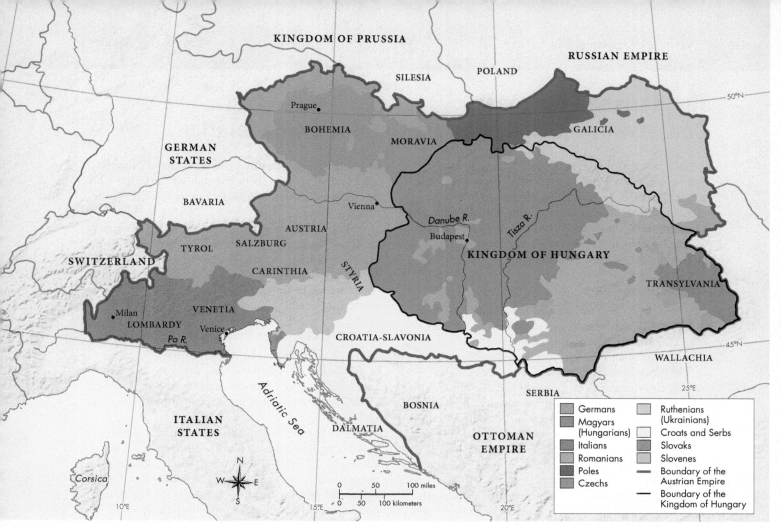

MAP 21.2 Peoples of the Habsburg Monarchy, 1815 The old dynastic state ruled by the Habsburg monarchy was a patchwork of nationalities and ethnic groups, in which territorial borders barely reflected the diversity of where different peoples actually lived. Note especially the widely scattered pockets of Germans and Hungarians. How do you think this ethnic diversity might have led to the rise of national independence movements in the Austrian Empire?

Alexander I, the alliance worked to repress reformist and revolutionary movements and stifle desires for national independence across Europe.

The conservative restoration first brought its collective power to bear in Austria, Prussia, and the entire German Confederation — the German-speaking lands of central Europe. The states in the German Confederation retained independence, and though ambassadors from each met in the Confederation Diet, or federal assembly, it had little real power. When liberal reformers and university students began to protest for the national unification of the German states, the Austrian and Prussian leadership used the assembly to issue and enforce the infamous **Karlsbad Decrees** in 1819. These decrees required the German states to outlaw liberal political organizations, police their universities and newspapers, and establish a permanent committee with spies and informers to clamp down on liberal or radical reformers. (See "Evaluating Written Evidence: The Karlsbad

Decrees: Conservative Reaction in the German Confederation," page 632.)

The conservative policies of Metternich and the Holy Alliance limited reform not only in central Europe but also in Spain and the Italian peninsula. In 1820 revolutionaries successfully forced the kings of Spain and the southern Italian Kingdom of the Two Sicilies to establish constitutional monarchies with press freedoms, universal male suffrage, and other liberal reforms. Metternich was horrified; revolution was rising once again. Calling a conference at Troppau in Austria, he and Alexander I proclaimed the principle of active intervention to maintain all autocratic regimes whenever they were threatened. Austrian forces then marched into Naples in 1821 and restored the autocratic power of Ferdinand I in the Two Sicilies. A French invasion of Spain in 1823 likewise returned power to the king there.

The forces of reaction squelched reform in Russia as well, in the Decembrist Uprising of 1825. In

The Karlsbad Decrees:
Conservative Reaction in the German Confederation

In 1819 a member of a radical student fraternity at the German University of Jena assassinated the conservative author and diplomat August von Kotzebue. Metternich used the murder as an excuse to promulgate the repressive Karlsbad Decrees, excerpted below, which clamped down on liberal nationalists in the universities and the press throughout the German Confederation.

Law on Universities

∼ 1. A special representative of the ruler of each state shall be appointed for each university, with appropriate instructions and extended powers, and shall reside in the place where the university is situated. . . .

The function of this agent shall be to see to the strictest enforcement of existing laws and disciplinary regulations; to observe carefully the spirit which is shown by the instructors in the university in their public lectures and regular courses, and, without directly interfering in scientific matters or in the methods of teaching, to give a salutary direction to the instruction, having in view the future attitude of the students. . . .

2. The confederated governments mutually pledge themselves to remove from the universities or other public educational institutions all teachers who, by obvious deviation from their duty, or by exceeding the limits of their functions, or by the abuse of their legitimate influence over the youthful minds, or by propagating harmful doctrines hostile to public order or subversive of existing governmental institutions, shall have unmistakably proved their unfitness for the important office intrusted to them. . . .

[Articles 3 and 4 ordered the universities to enforce laws against secret student societies.]

Press Law

∼ 1. So long as this decree shall remain in force no publication which appears in the form of daily issues, or as a serial not exceeding twenty sheets of printed matter, shall go to press in any state of the union without the previous knowledge and approval of the state officials. . . .

6. The Diet shall have the right, moreover, to suppress on its own authority . . . [publications that] in the opinion of a commission appointed by it, are inimical to the honor of the union, the safety of individual states, or the maintenance of peace and quiet in Germany. There shall be no appeal from such decisions. . . .

Establishment of an Investigative Committee

∼ 1. Within a fortnight, reckoned from the passage of this decree, there shall convene, under the auspices of the Confederation . . . an extraordinary commission of investigation to consist of seven members, including the chairman.

2. The object of the commission shall be a joint investigation, as thorough and extensive as possible, of the facts relating to the origin and manifold ramifications of the revolutionary plots and demagogical associations directed against the existing constitution and the internal peace both of the union and of the individual states.

EVALUATE THE EVIDENCE

1. How do these regulations express the spirit of reactionary politics after the Napoleonic Wars? Why were university professors and students singled out as special targets?
2. The Karlsbad Decrees were periodically renewed until finally overturned during the revolutions of 1848. Do you think they were effective in checking the growth of liberal politics?

Source: James Harvey Robinson, *Readings in European History*, vol. 2 (Boston: Ginn and Company, 1906), pp. 547–550.

St. Petersburg in December that year, a group of about three thousand army officers inspired by liberal ideals staged a protest against the new tsar, Nicholas I. Troops loyal to Nicholas I surrounded and assaulted the group with gunfire, cavalry, and cannon, leaving some sixty men dead; the surviving leaders were publicly hanged, and the rest sent to exile in Siberia. Through censorship, military might, secret police, imprisonment, and execution, conservative regimes in central Europe used the powers of the state to repress liberal reform wherever possible.

Limits to Conservative Power and Revolution in South America

Metternich liked to call himself "the chief Minister of Police in Europe."[3] His system proved fairly effective in central Europe, at least until 1848, although the monarchists failed to stop dynastic change in France in 1830 or to prevent Belgium from winning independence from the Netherlands in 1831. Yet the most dramatic challenge to conservative power occurred not in Europe, but overseas in South America.

In the 1810s South American elites broke away from the Spanish Crown and established a number of new republics based at first on liberal Enlightenment ideals. The leaders of the revolutions were primarily wealthy Creoles, direct descendants of Spanish parents born in the Americas. The well-established and powerful Creoles—only about 5 percent of the population—resented the political and economic control of an even smaller elite minority of *peninsulares*, people born in Spain who lived in and ruled the colonies. The vast majority of the population, including enslaved and freed Africans, Indigenous peoples, and multiracial people, languished at the bottom of the social pyramid.

By the late 1700s the Creoles had begun to question Spanish policy and the necessity of colonial rule. The spark for revolt came during the Napoleonic Wars, when the French occupation of Spain in 1808 weakened the power of the autocratic Spanish Crown and the Napoleonic rhetoric of rights inspired local revolutionaries. Yet the Creoles hesitated, worried that open revolt might upend the social pyramid or even lead to a slave revolution as in Haiti (see "How did revolt by enslaved people on colonial Saint-Domingue lead to the independent nation of Haiti?" in Chapter 19).

The South American revolutions thus began from below, with spontaneous uprisings by people of color. Creole leaders then took control of a struggle that would be more prolonged and violent than the American Revolution, with outcomes less clear. In the north, the competent general Simón Bolívar defeated Spanish forces and established a short-lived "Gran Colombia," which lasted from 1819 to 1830. Bolívar, the "people's liberator," dreamed of establishing a federation of South American states, modeled on the United States. To the south, José de San Martín, a liberal-minded military commander, successfully threw off Spanish control by 1825.

Dreams of South American federation and unity proved difficult to realize. By 1830 the large northern state established by Bolívar had fractured, leading the disillusioned general to famously remark that trying to unite the region through revolutionary means was like "plowing the sea." By 1840 the borders of the new nations looked much like the map of Latin America today. Most of the new states initially received liberal constitutions, but these were difficult to implement in lands where the vast majority of people had no experience with constitutional rule. Women and the great underclass of non-Creoles were not allowed to vote,

Simón Bolívar's Triumph in Caracas   The military and political expertise of General Simón Bolívar helped liberate Venezuela, Ecuador, Colombia, and other states from Spanish rule in the first decades of the 1800s. Here he leads a triumphal parade through Caracas, Venezuela. Bolívar's vision of a united South America fell apart by 1830, leading the disillusioned general to famously remark that trying to unite the region through revolutionary means was like "plowing the sea." (akg-images/Newscom)

and experiments with liberal constitutions soon gave way to a new political system controlled by *caudillos* (cow-DEE-yohs), or strongmen, sometimes labeled warlords. Often Creoles, the caudillos ruled limited territories on the basis of military strength, family patronage, and populist politics. The South American revolutions had failed to establish lasting constitutional republics, but they did demonstrate the revolutionary potential of liberal ideals and the limits on conservative control.

What new ideologies emerged to challenge conservative government?

In the years following the peace settlement of 1815, intellectuals and social observers sought to harness the radical ideas of the revolutionary age to new political movements. Many rejected conservatism, with its stress on tradition, a hereditary monarchy, a privileged landowning aristocracy, and an official state church. Often inspired by liberties championed during the French Revolution, radical thinkers developed alternative ideologies and tried to convince people to follow them. In so doing, they helped articulate the basic political ideals that continue to shape Western society today.

Liberalism and the Middle Class

The principal ideas of **liberalism**—liberty and legal equality—were by no means defeated in 1815. First realized in the American Revolution and then achieved in part in the French Revolution, liberalism demanded representative government as opposed to autocratic monarchy, and equality before the law for all as opposed to separate classes with separate legal rights. Liberty also meant specific individual freedoms: freedom of the press, freedom of speech, freedom of assembly, freedom of worship, and freedom from arbitrary arrest. Such ideas are still the guiding beliefs in modern democratic states. In Europe after 1815, however, only Louis XVIII's Constitutional Charter in France, the parliamentary monarchy in Great Britain, and the short-lived Polish Constitution of 1815 to 1831 had successfully implemented any of the liberal program. Even in those countries, liberalism had only begun to succeed and did not extend full rights to wide segments of the population, including women and—in many cases—men who did not own land.

Although conservatives still saw liberalism as a profound threat, it had gained a group of powerful adherents: the new upper classes made wealthy through growing industrialization and global commerce. This group promoted the liberal economic doctrine of **laissez faire** (lay-say FEHR), which called for free trade (including relaxation of import/export duties), unrestricted private enterprise, and no government interference in the economy.

As we saw in Chapter 17, Adam Smith posited the idea of economic liberalism and free-market capitalism in 1776 in opposition to mercantilism and its attempt to regulate trade. Smith argued that freely competitive private enterprise would give all citizens a fair and equal opportunity to do what they did best and would result in greater income for everyone, not just the rich. (Smith's form of liberalism is often called "classical liberalism" in the United States, to distinguish it sharply from modern U.S. liberalism, which generally favors government intervention to address social inequality and regulate the economy.)

In the first half of the nineteenth century, liberal political ideals became closely associated with narrow class interests. Starting in the 1820s in Britain, business elites enthusiastically embraced laissez-faire policies because they proved immensely profitable. Labor unions were outlawed because, these elites argued, unions restricted free competition and the individual's "right to work." Early-nineteenth-century liberals favored representative government, but not social equality, and they generally wanted strict property qualifications attached to the right to vote. In practice, this meant limiting the vote to very small numbers of the well-to-do. Workers, peasants, and women, as well as middle-class shopkeepers, clerks, and artisans, did not own the necessary property and thus could not participate in the political process.

As liberalism became increasingly identified with upper-class business interests, some opponents of conservatism felt that liberalism did not go nearly far enough. Inspired by memories of the French Revolution, this group embraced **republicanism**: an expanded liberal ideology that endorsed universal democratic voting rights, at least for men, and radical equality for all. Republicans were more willing than most liberals to endorse violent upheaval to achieve goals. In addition, republicans might advocate government action to create jobs, redistribute income, and level social differences. As the results of the revolutions of 1830 and 1848 would suggest, liberals and radical republicans might join forces against conservatives only up to a point. And although a small minority of European republicans—including the U.S. revolutionary war hero the Marquis de Lafayette—were abolitionists who favored the eventual extension of liberal rights to formerly enslaved people, most believed that republicanism was the exclusive privilege of the white race. (See "Thinking Like a Historian: The Republican Spirit in 1848," page 636.)

The Growing Appeal of Nationalism

Nationalism was another radical idea that gained popularity after 1815. Its power was revealed in the French Revolution and the Napoleonic Wars, when soldiers inspired by patriotic loyalty to the French nation achieved victory after victory. Early nationalists found inspiration in the vision of a people united by a common language, a common history and culture, and a common territory. In German-speaking central Europe, defeat by Napoleon's armies had made the vision of a national people united in defense of their "fatherland" particularly attractive.

In the early nineteenth century such national unity was more a dream than a reality for most ethnic groups or nationalities. Local dialects abounded, even in relatively cohesive countries like France, where peasants from nearby villages often failed to understand each other. Moreover, a variety of ethnic groups shared the territory of most states, not just the Austrian, Russian, and Ottoman Empires discussed earlier. During the nineteenth century, nationalism nonetheless gathered force as a political philosophy. Advancing literacy rates, new mass-circulation newspapers, larger state bureaucracies, compulsory education, and conscription armies all created a common culture that encouraged ordinary people to take pride in their national heritage.

Recognizing the power of the "national idea," European nationalists—generally educated, middle-class liberals and intellectuals—sought to turn the cultural unity that they desired into political reality. They believed that every nation, like every citizen, had the right to exist in freedom and to develop its unique character and spirit, and they hoped to make the territory of each people coincide with well-defined borders in an independent nation-state.

This political goal made nationalism explosive, particularly in central and eastern Europe, where different peoples overlapped and intermingled. As discussed, the Austrian, Russian, and Ottoman central states refused to allow national minorities independence. This suppression fomented widespread discontent among nationalists who wanted freedom from oppressive imperial rule. In the many different principalities of the Italian peninsula and the German Confederation, to the contrary, nationalists yearned for unification across what they saw as divisive and obsolete state borders. Whether they sought independence or unification, before 1850 nationalist movements were fresh, idealistic, and progressive, if not revolutionary.

Historians have tried to understand why the nationalist vision, which typically fit poorly with existing conditions and promised much upheaval, was so successful in the long run. Of fundamental importance was the development of a complex industrial and urban society, which required more sophisticated forms of communication between individuals and groups.[4] The need for improved communication promoted the use of a standardized national language in many areas, creating at least a superficial cultural unity as a standard tongue spread through mass education and the emergence of the popular press. When a minority population was large and concentrated, the nationalist campaign for a standardized language often led the minority group to push for a separate nation-state.

Scholars generally argue that nations are recent creations, the product of a new, self-conscious nationalist ideology. Thus nation-states emerged in the nineteenth century as "imagined communities" that sought to bind millions of strangers together around the abstract concept of an all-embracing national identity. This meant bringing citizens together with emotionally charged symbols and ceremonies, such as independence holidays and patriotic parades. On these occasions the imagined nation of equals might celebrate its most hallowed traditions, which were often relatively recent inventions.[5]

Between 1815 and 1850 most people who believed in nationalism also believed in either liberalism or radical republicanism. They typically shared a deep belief in the creativity and nobility of "the people." Liberals and especially republicans, for example, saw the people as the ultimate source of all government. Yet nationally minded liberals and republicans agreed that the benefits of self-government would be possible only if individuals were bonded together by common traditions that transcended local interests and class differences.

Despite some confidence that a world system based on independent nation-states would promote global harmony, early nationalists eagerly emphasized the differences between peoples and developed a strong sense of "us" versus "them." To this "us-them" outlook, nationalists could all too easily add two highly volatile ingredients: a sense of mission and a sense of national superiority. As Europe entered an age of increased global interaction, these ideas would lead to conflict, as powerful nation-states backed by patriotic citizens competed with one another on the international stage.

The First Socialists

More radical than liberalism, republicanism, or nationalism was **socialism**. Early socialist thinkers were a diverse group with wide-ranging ideas. Yet they shared a sense that the political revolution in France, the growth of industrialization in Britain, and the rise of laissez faire had created a profound spiritual and moral crisis. Modern capitalism, they believed, fomented a selfish individualism that encouraged inequality and split the community into isolated fragments. Society urgently required fundamental change to re-establish a sense of community.

■ **liberalism** The principal ideas of this movement were equality and liberty; liberals demanded representative government and equality before the law as well as individual freedoms such as freedom of the press, freedom of speech, freedom of assembly, freedom of worship, and freedom from arbitrary arrest.

■ **laissez faire** A doctrine of economic liberalism that calls for unrestricted private enterprise and no government interference in the economy.

■ **republicanism** An expanded liberal ideology that endorsed universal democratic voting rights, at least for men, and radical equality for all.

■ **nationalism** The idea that each people had its own genius and specific identity that manifested itself especially in a common language and history, which often led to the desire for an independent political state.

■ **socialism** A backlash against the emergence of individualism and the fragmentation of industrial society, and a move toward cooperation and a sense of community; the key ideas were economic planning, greater social equality, and state regulation of property.

The Republican Spirit in 1848

Political leaders, prominent intellectuals, and ordinary citizens were all inspired by powerful reformist ideologies in the revolutions of 1848: liberalism and especially republicanism. Though the revolutions were crushed, the political ideals articulated by the revolutionaries lived on. How do the various ideas and policies embodied in the "republican spirit" continue to influence politics today?

1 Decrees of the provisional republican government in Paris, February 1848. After a revolutionary mob overturned the bourgeois monarchy of Louis Philippe, the provisional republican government issued the following decrees.

The Overthrow of the Orléanist Monarchy
In the name of the French people:

A reactionary and oligarchical government has just been overthrown by the heroism of the people of Paris. That government has fled, leaving behind it a trail of blood that forbids it ever to retrace its steps.

The blood of the people has flowed as in July [1830]; but this time this noble people shall not be deceived. It has won a national and popular government in accord with the rights, the progress, and the will of this great and generous nation.

A provisional government, the result of pressing necessity and ratified by the voice of the people and of the deputies of the departments, in the session of February 24, is for the moment invested with the task of assuring and organizing the national victory. . . .

The provisional government wishes to establish a republic, — subject, however, to ratification by the people, who shall be immediately consulted.

The unity of the nation (formed henceforth of all the classes of citizens who compose it); the government of the nation by itself; liberty, equality, and fraternity, for fundamental principles, and "the people" for our emblem and watchword: these constitute the democratic government which France owes to itself, and which our efforts shall secure for it. . . .

Decrees Relating to the Workingmen
The provisional government of the French republic pledges itself to guarantee the means of subsistence of the workingman by labor.

It pledges itself to guarantee labor to all citizens.

It recognizes that workingmen ought to enter into associations among themselves in order to enjoy the advantage of their labor. . . .

The provisional government of the French republic decrees that all articles pledged at the pawn shops since the first of February, consisting of linen, garments, or clothes, etc., upon which the loan does not exceed ten francs, shall be given back to those who pledged them. . . .

The provisional government of the republic decrees the immediate establishment of national workshops.

2 *Demands of the German People* (political pamphlet from Mannheim, Germany), 1848. In small towns and communities across German-speaking lands, citizens inspired by republicanism met and confronted autocratic governments with lists of demands in pamphlets and petitions.

A German parliament, freely elected by the people.
Every German man of 21 years of age and above should have the right to vote in a parliamentary election. . . .
Unconditional freedom of the press.
Complete freedom of religion, conscience and teaching.
Administration of justice before a jury.
General granting of citizen's rights for German citizens.
A just system of taxation based on income.
Prosperity, training, and teaching for all.
Protection and security of jobs.
Balancing out of disparities between capital and labor.
Popular and just State administration.
Responsibility of Ministers and civil servants.
Removal of all prejudices.

ANALYZING THE EVIDENCE

1. Why would republican ideologies appeal to ordinary people in 1848? What groups might oppose or be indifferent to republicanism? Why did reformists present liberal-republican ideals in visual formats, as in Source 3?
2. Review the sections on liberalism and republicanism and on tensions within the revolutionary coalition of 1848 in this chapter. Which aspects of the evidence presented in Sources 1–4 appear more liberal, and which appear more republican? Does a close reading of the sources reveal conflicts between liberal and republican ideals?
3. In Source 4, how does Carl Schurz explain the benefits of radical republicanism but also its potential costs?

(Musée de la Ville de Paris, Musée Carnavalet, Paris, France/Bridgeman Images)

3 **Frederic Sorrieu, *Universal Democratic and Social Republic: The Pact*, 1848.** The subtitle of this French lithograph, which celebrates the revolutionary breakthroughs of 1848, reads, "People, Forge a Holy Alliance and Hold Hands." An embodiment of the republican ethos, it portrays the peoples of Europe holding their respective national flags. A heavenly host blesses the gathering, and the shattered symbols of Europe's monarchies litter the foreground.

4 **Carl Schurz, *The Reminiscences of Carl Schurz*, 1913.** In his 1913 memoirs Carl Schurz explains how the threat of autocratic "reaction" (or political repression) led to radical republicanism in the years before 1848.

[T]he visible development of the reaction had the effect of producing among many of those who stood earnestly for national unity and constitutional government a state of mind more open to radical tendencies. The rapid progress of these developments was clearly perceptible in my own surroundings. Our democratic club was composed in almost equal parts of students and citizens, among whom there were many of excellent character, of some fortune and good standing, and of moderate views, while a few others had worked themselves into a state of mind resembling that of the terrorists in the French Revolution. . . .

At first the establishment of a constitutional monarchy with universal suffrage and well-secured civil rights would have been quite satisfactory to us. But the reaction, the threatened rise of which we were observing, gradually made many of us believe that there was no safety for popular liberty except in a republic. . . .

The idealism which saw in the republican citizen the highest embodiment of human dignity we had imbibed from the study of classic antiquity; and the history of the French Revolution satisfied us that a republic could be created in Germany and could maintain its existence in the European system of states. In that history we found striking examples of the possibility of accomplishing the seemingly impossible, if only the whole energy existing in a great nation were awakened and directed with unflinching boldness.

Most of us, indeed, recoiled from the wild excesses which had stained with streams of innocent blood the national uprising in France during the Reign of Terror; but we hoped to stir up the national energies without such terrorism. At any rate, the history of the French Revolution furnished to us models in plenty that mightily excited our imagination. How dangerously seductive such a play of the imagination is we were, of course, then unaware.

PUTTING IT ALL TOGETHER

Using the sources above, along with what you have learned in class and in this chapter, write a short essay that evaluates the appeal of republicanism in 1848. How would a typical republican leader in 1848 have understood the relationship between "the people" or "the citizen" and the state? How did that understanding challenge the conservative viewpoints?

Sources: (1) James Harvey Robinson, *Readings in European History,* vol. 2 (Boston: Ginn and Company, 1906), pp. 559–561; (2) *Questions on German History: Ideas, Forces, Decisions from 1800 to the Present* (Bonn: German Bundestag, Press and Information Centre, Publications' Section, 1984), p. 119 (punctuation has been updated); (4) Carl Schurz, *The Reminiscences of Carl Schurz,* vol. 1 (Garden City, N.Y.: Doubleday, Page & Co., 1913), pp. 136–137 (punctuation updated).

Early socialists felt an intense desire to help the poor, and they preached that the rich and the poor should be more nearly equal economically. They believed that private property should be strictly regulated by the government or abolished outright and replaced by state or community ownership. Economic planning, greater social equality, and state regulation of property were the key ideas of early socialism—and have remained central to socialism since.

One influential group of early socialist advocates became known as the "utopian socialists" because their grand schemes for social improvement ultimately proved unworkable. The Frenchmen Count Henri de Saint-Simon (san-see-MOHN) (1760–1825) and Charles Fourier (FAWR-ee-ay) (1772–1837), as well as the British industrialist Robert Owen, all founded movements intended to establish model communities that would usher in a new age of happiness and equality.

Saint-Simon's "positivism" optimistically proclaimed the possibilities of industrial development: "The golden age of the human species," he wrote, "is before us!"[6] The key to progress was proper social organization that required the "parasites"—the court, the aristocracy, lawyers, and churchmen—to give way to the "doers"—highly trained scientists, engineers, and industrialists. These doers would abolish poverty and war by leading society through a process he called "industrialization," based on scientific principles. Government administrators would carefully plan the economy and guide it forward by establishing investment banks and undertaking vast public works projects that promised employment for all. Saint-Simon also stressed in highly moralistic terms that every social institution ought to have as its main goal human brotherhood and improved conditions for the poor.

Charles Fourier, a follower of Saint-Simon, likewise condemned the inequality and poverty he saw at the base of contemporary capitalism and called for a society based on cooperation. To heal social ills, Fourier called for the construction of mathematically precise, self-sufficient communities called "phalanxes," each made up of 1,620 people. In the phalanx, all property was owned by the community and used for the common good. Fourier was also an early proponent of the total

emancipation of women. According to Fourier, under capitalism young single women were shamelessly "sold" to their future husbands for dowries and other financial considerations. Therefore, he called for the abolition of marriage and for sexual freedom and free unions based only on love. The British factory owner and reformer Robert Owen, an early promoter of labor unions, also envisaged a society organized into socialistic industrial-agricultural communities. Saint-Simon, Fourier, and Owen all had followers who tried to put their ideas into practice. Though these attempts had mostly collapsed by the 1850s, utopian socialist ideas remained an inspiration for future reformers and revolutionaries.

Some socialist thinkers embraced the even more radical ideas of anarchism. In his 1840 pamphlet *What Is Property?* Pierre-Joseph Proudhon (1809–1865), a self-educated printer, famously argued that "property is theft!" Property, he claimed, was profit that was stolen from the worker, the source of all wealth. Distrustful of all authority and political systems, Proudhon believed that states should be abolished and that society should be organized in loose associations of working people.

Other early socialists, like Louis Blanc (1811–1882), a sharp-eyed, intelligent journalist, focused on more practical reforms. In his *Organization of Work* (1839), he urged workers to agitate for universal voting rights and take control of the state peacefully. Blanc believed that the government should provide aid to the sick and elderly and should set up publicly funded workshops and factories to guarantee full employment. Karl Marx would later adopt Blanc's guiding principle, "From each according to his abilities, to each according to his needs."

As industrialization advanced in European cities, working people began to embrace the socialist message. This happened first in France, where workers cherished the memory of the radical phase of the French Revolution and became violently opposed to laissez-faire laws that denied their right to organize in guilds and unions. Developing a sense of class in the process of their protests, workers favored collective action and government intervention in economic life. Thus the aspirations of workers and radical theorists reinforced each other, and a genuine socialist movement emerged in Paris in the 1830s and 1840s.

The Rise of Marxist Socialism

In the 1840s France was the center of socialism, but in the following decades the German intellectual Karl Marx (1818–1883) would weave the diffuse strands of socialist thought into a distinctly modern ideology. Marxist socialism—or **Marxism**—would have a lasting impact on political thought and practice.

The son of a Jewish lawyer who had converted to Lutheranism, the young Marx was a brilliant student.

■ **Marxism** An influential political program based on the socialist ideas of German radical Karl Marx, which called for a working-class revolution to overthrow capitalist society and establish a Communist state.

■ **bourgeoisie** The upper-class minority who owned the means of production and, according to Marx, exploited the working-class proletariat.

■ **proletariat** The industrial working class who, according to Marx, were unfairly exploited by the profit-seeking bourgeoisie.

■ **Romanticism** An artistic movement at its height from about 1790 to the 1840s that was in part a revolt against classicism and the Enlightenment, characterized by a belief in emotional exuberance, unrestrained imagination, and spontaneity in both art and personal life.

After earning a Ph.D. in philosophy at Friedrich Wilhelm (now Humboldt) University in Berlin in 1841, he turned to journalism, and his critical articles about the plight of the laboring poor caught the attention of the Prussian police. Forced to flee Prussia in 1843, Marx traveled around Europe, promoting socialism and avoiding the authorities. He lived a modest, middle-class life with his wife, Jenny, and their children, often relying on his friend and colleague Friedrich Engels for financial support. After the revolutions of 1848, Marx settled in London, where he spent the rest of his life as an advocate of working-class revolution. *Capital*, his magnum opus, appeared in 1867.

Marx was a dedicated scholar, and his work united sociology, economics, philosophy, and history in an impressive synthesis. From Scottish and English political economists like Adam Smith and David Ricardo, Marx learned to apply social-scientific analysis to economic problems, though he pushed these liberal ideas in radical directions. Influenced by the utopian socialists, Marx championed ideals of social equality and community. He criticized his socialist predecessors, however, for their fanciful utopian schemes, claiming that his version of "scientific" socialism was rooted in historic law, and therefore realistic. Deeply influenced by the German philosopher Georg Hegel (1770–1831), Marx came to believe that history had patterns and purpose and moved forward in stages toward an ultimate goal.

Bringing these ideas together, Marx argued that class struggle over economic wealth was the great engine of human history. In his view, one class had always exploited the other, and with the advent of modern industry, society was split more clearly than ever before: between the **bourgeoisie** (boor-ZHWAH-zee), or the upper class, and the **proletariat**, the working class. The bourgeoisie, a tiny minority, owned factories, land, and farms (what Marx called the means of production) and grew rich by exploiting the labor of workers.

Over time, Marx argued, the proletariat would grow ever larger and ever poorer, and their increasing alienation would lead them to develop a sense of revolutionary class-consciousness. Then, just as the bourgeoisie had triumphed over the feudal aristocracy in the French Revolution, the proletariat would overthrow the bourgeoisie in violent revolution. The result would be the end of class struggle and the arrival of communism, a system of radical equality.

Fascinated by the rapid expansion of modern capitalism, Marx based his revolutionary program on an insightful yet critical analysis of economic history. Under feudalism, he wrote, labor had been organized according to long-term contracts of rights and privileges. Under capitalism, to the contrary, labor was a commodity like any other, bought and sold for wages in the free market. The goods workers produced were always worth more than what those workers were paid, and the difference — "surplus value," in Marx's terms — was pocketed by the bourgeoisie in the form of profit.

According to Marx, capitalism was immensely productive but highly exploitative. In a never-ending search for profit, the bourgeoisie would squeeze workers dry and then expand across the globe, until all parts of the world were trapped in capitalist relations of production. Contemporary ideals, such as free trade, private property, and even marriage and Christian morality, were myths that masked and legitimized class exploitation. To some, Marx's argument that the contradictions inherent in this unequal system would eventually be overcome in a working-class revolution appeared to be the irrefutable capstone of a brilliant interpretation of historical trends.

When Marx and Engels published *The Communist Manifesto* on the eve of the revolutions of 1848, their opening claim that "a spectre is haunting Europe — the spectre of Communism" was highly exaggerated. The Communist movement was in its infancy. Scattered groups of socialists, anarchists, and labor leaders were hardly united around Marxist ideas. But by the time Marx died in 1883, Marxist socialism had profoundly reshaped left-wing radicalism in ways that would continue to inspire revolutionaries around the world.

What were the characteristics of the Romantic movement?

Even as intellectuals in the early nineteenth century transformed political ideas, they also embraced radical changes in literature and the arts. Followers of the new Romantic movement (or Romanticism) revolted against the emphasis on rationality, order, and restraint that characterized the Enlightenment and the controlled style of classicism. Forerunners appeared from about 1750 on, but the movement crystallized fully in the 1790s, primarily in England and Germany. Romanticism gained strength and swept across Europe until the 1840s, when it gradually gave way to Realism.

The Romantic Worldview

Although **Romanticism** was characterized by intellectual diversity, it had some common parameters. Artists inspired by Romanticism repudiated the emphasis on reason associated with well-known Enlightenment philosophes like Voltaire and Montesquieu (see "The Influence of the

Philosophes" in Chapter 16). Romantics championed instead emotional exuberance, unrestrained imagination, and spontaneity in both art and personal life.

Where Enlightenment thinkers applied the scientific method to social issues and cast rosy predictions for future progress, Romantics valued intuition and nostalgia for the past. Where Enlightenment thinkers embraced secularization, Romantics sought the inspiration of religious ecstasy. Where Enlightenment thinkers valued public life and civic affairs, Romantics delved into the supernatural and turned inward, pondering the power of love and desire, and hatred and despair, all found in the hidden recesses of the self. As the Austrian composer Franz Schubert exclaimed in 1824: "Oh imagination, thou supreme jewel of mankind, thou inexhaustible source from which artists and scholars drink! Oh, rest with us—despite the fact that thou art recognized only by a few—so as to preserve us from that so-called Enlightenment, that ugly skeleton without flesh or blood!"[7]

Nowhere was the break with Enlightenment classicism more apparent than in Romanticism's conception of nature. Classicists were not particularly interested in the natural world. The Romantics, in contrast, were enchanted by stormy seas, untouched forests, and icy wastelands. Nature could be a source of beauty or spiritual inspiration. Most Romantics saw the growth of modern industry as an ugly, brutal attack on nature and on venerable traditions. They sought escape—whether in the unspoiled Lake District of northern England or in an imaginary and idealized Middle Ages.

The study of history became a Romantic obsession. History held the key to a universe now perceived to be organic and dynamic, not mechanical and static, as Enlightenment thinkers had believed. Historical novels like Sir Walter Scott's *Ivanhoe* (1820), a passionate romance set in twelfth-century England, found eager readers among the literate middle classes. Professional historians influenced by Romanticism, such as Jules Michelet, went beyond the standard accounts of great men or famous battles. Michelet's many books on the history of France encouraged the French people to search the past for their special national destiny.

Romanticism was a lifestyle as well as an intellectual movement. Many early-nineteenth-century Romantics lived lives of tremendous emotional intensity. Obsessive love affairs, duels to the death, madness, strange illnesses, and suicide were not uncommon. Romantic artists typically led bohemian lives, wearing their hair long and uncombed in preference to donning powdered wigs, and rejecting the manners and morals of refined society. Romantics believed that the full development of one's unique human potential was the supreme purpose in life.

Romantic Literature

Romanticism found its distinctive voice in poetry, as the Enlightenment had in prose. Though Romantic poetry had important forerunners in the German "Storm and Stress" movement of the 1770s and 1780s, its first great poets were English: William Blake, William Wordsworth, Samuel Taylor Coleridge, and Sir Walter Scott were all active by 1800, followed shortly by Lord Byron, Percy Bysshe Shelley, and John Keats.

A towering leader of English Romanticism, William Wordsworth was deeply influenced by Rousseau and the liberal spirit of the early French Revolution. Wordsworth settled in the rural Lake District of England with his sister, Dorothy, and Samuel Taylor Coleridge (1772–1834). In 1798 Wordsworth and Coleridge published their *Lyrical Ballads*, which abandoned flowery classical conventions for the language of ordinary speech and endowed simple subjects with the loftiest majesty. Wordsworth believed that all natural things were sacred, and his poetry often expressed a mystical appreciation of nature:

> To every natural form, rock, fruit or flower
> Even the loose stones that cover the high-way
> I gave a moral life, I saw them feel,
> Or link'd them to some feeling: the great mass
> Lay bedded in a quickening soul, and all
> That I beheld, respired with inward meaning.[8]

Here Wordsworth expressed his love of nature in commonplace forms that a variety of readers could appreciate. The short stanza well illustrates his famous conception of poetry as the "spontaneous overflow of powerful feeling [which] takes its origin from emotion recollected in tranquility."[9]

Literature and lifestyle came together in the experience of the writers, friends, and lovers who gathered around Percy Shelley and Lord Byron in the years after the Napoleonic Wars. The circle included Mary Godwin, who eventually married the Romantic poet Percy Shelley. On vacation with Percy, Lord Byron, and others in Switzerland in 1816, Mary Shelley wrote *Frankenstein*, one of the best-known Romantic works, a genre-bending novel that tells the tragic story of a scientist who is able to invent a living, almost-human creature. (See "Individuals in Society: Mary Shelley," page 641.)

In France under Napoleon, classicism remained strong and at first inhibited the growth of Romanticism. Between 1820 and 1850, however, the Romantic impulse broke through in the poetry and prose of Alphonse de Lamartine, Victor Hugo, and George Sand (pseudonym of the woman writer Amandine-Aurore-Lucile Dudevant). Of these, Victor Hugo (1802–1885) achieved the most renown with novels that exemplified the Romantic fascination with fantastic characters, exotic historical settings, and extreme emotions. The hero of Hugo's famous *The Hunchback of Notre Dame* (1831) is the great cathedral's deformed bell-ringer, a "human gargoyle"

INDIVIDUALS IN SOCIETY

Mary Shelley

"I saw — with shut eyes, but acute mental vision — I saw the pale student of unhallowed arts kneeling beside the thing he had put together. I saw the hideous phantasm of a man stretched out, and then, on the working of some powerful engine, show signs of life and stir with an uneasy, half-vital motion."* Thus did Mary Shelley (1797–1851) describe, in feverish terms, the nightmare that inspired her most famous work: *Frankenstein, Or, The Modern Prometheus*. Shelley's horror story remains a classic of early-nineteenth-century Romanticism, while her tempestuous personal experiences capture the emotional intensity of the Romantic lifestyle.

Shelley was born in 1797 in London. Her father was the political radical and freethinker William Godwin; her mother was the protofeminist Mary Wollstonecraft, whose renowned book *A Vindication of the Rights of Woman*, written in 1792 at the height of the French Revolution, made a forceful argument for women's equality.

Strong passions and heartbreaking tragedy coursed through Shelley's life. Her mother died of an infection contracted during childbirth, just eleven days after Shelley was born. In 1812, when she was fifteen, Mary Shelley (then Mary Godwin) met the Romantic poet Percy Bysshe Shelley, a frequent visitor to the Godwin home. Although Percy Shelley was married with a child, the couple fell passionately in love and eloped in 1814, leaving London for France; they married in 1816. During the eight years of their relationship Mary Shelley was almost constantly pregnant. Only one of her four children survived to adulthood.

The young couple traveled around Europe, often meeting other Romantic authors. In 1816 Mary and Percy Shelley, along with the poet Lord Byron and his mistress, spent several months at Lake Geneva, in Switzerland, where they hoped to enjoy the mountainous countryside. Rainy weather, however, kept the group indoors. One evening Lord Byron suggested, as means of entertainment, that each member of the company invent a ghost story to share with the group.

Frankenstein was the result. The novel is about the torment of Dr. Frankenstein, a young scientist who stitches together a rough human form out of pieces of cadavers stolen from graveyards. Using an electrical current, Frankenstein brings his creature to life but flees when he sees the horrible monster he created. The unnamed and unwanted creature stumbles out into the countryside, where he learns to read and speak by secretly listening to a peasant family. Seeking affection, he accidentally kills a young boy. He then seeks revenge for the callousness of Frankenstein, his creator. The creature stalks Frankenstein, killing his brother, best friend, and bride. Unlike the monster portrayed by Boris Karloff in the famous 1931 movie, Shelley's creature is emotional, intelligent, and articulate. He confronts Frankenstein several times, and the two passionately discuss human suffering and happiness, guilt, and responsibility.

Once published in 1818, Shelley's story soon found and continues to fascinate a wide audience. Readers ponder its central themes. What are the ethical limits on science in

Mary Shelley. (Heritage Images/Getty Images)

the modern world? Did Frankenstein violate the contract between God and man? Does the creature represent the failures of the Enlightenment? Or does he symbolize modern humanity, lost and forsaken by an absent God? Is the book a referendum on the French Revolution?

Misfortune continued to trouble Shelley in the years after she published her famous book. Percy Shelley died in a boating accident in 1822, and Lord Byron died in Greece in 1824. Shelley continued to write, but she never remarried, writing that she was "the last relic of a beloved race, my companions extinct before me."[†]

QUESTIONS FOR ANALYSIS

1. Shelley wrote her famous novel in a period defined by momentous political and social changes, embodied in the transatlantic revolutions, the Napoleonic War, the emergence of new political ideologies, and early industrialization. Does this context help explain her story?

2. In what ways does the personal life of Mary Shelley and her associates reflect the Romantic passion for alternative lifestyles?

*Mary Shelley, "Author's Introduction," in *Frankenstein by Mary Shelley* (New York: Bantam Books, 1991), p. xxv.

†Quoted in Jill Lapore, "It's Still Alive: Two Hundred Years of 'Frankenstein,'" *The New Yorker*, February 12 and 19, 2018, p. 91.

overlooking the teeming life of fifteenth-century Paris. Renouncing his early conservatism, Hugo equated freedom in literature with liberty in politics and society. His political evolution was thus exactly the opposite of Wordsworth's, in whom youthful radicalism gave way to middle-aged caution. Thus Romanticism was compatible with many political beliefs.

In German lands, literary Romanticism and nationalism were particularly interconnected, and this Romantic nationalism also inspired the diverse ethnic groups that lived in central and eastern Europe. Well-educated Romantics championed their own people's histories, cultures, and unique greatness. Like modern anthropologists, they studied peasant life and transcribed the folk songs, tales, and proverbs that the cosmopolitan Enlightenment had disdained. The brothers Jacob and Wilhelm Grimm were particularly successful at rescuing German folktales from oblivion. Determined to preserve what Wilhelm called "a world of magic" in a time of rapid social change, the Grimms viewed folktales as a reservoir of "long neglected treasures" that testified to the

deep roots of the German national character. Wilhelm's assumption that folktales persisted "only in places where there is a warm openness to poetry or where there are imaginations not yet deformed by the perversities of modern life" voiced the typical Romantic idealization of past times.[10]

In the Slavic lands, Romantics converted spoken peasant languages into modern written languages, building regional national identities. In the vast Austrian, Russian, and Ottoman Empires, with their many ethnic minorities, the combination of Romanticism and nationalism was particularly potent. Ethnic groups dreaming of independence could find revolutionary inspiration in Romantic visions of a historic national destiny.

Romanticism in Art and Music

Romantic concerns with nature, history, and the imagination extended well beyond literature, into the realms of art and music. France's Eugène Delacroix

Caspar David Friedrich, *Two Men Contemplating the Moon*, 1820   Friedrich's reverence for the mysterious powers of nature radiates from this masterpiece of Romantic art, which he painted in 1820. It shows two relatively small, anonymous figures mesmerized by the sublime beauty of the full moon. Viewers of the painting, positioned by the artist to look over the shoulders of the men, are likewise compelled to experience nature's wonder. In a subtle expression of the connection between Romanticism and political reform, Friedrich has clothed the men in traditional German dress, which radical students had adopted as a form of protest against the repressive conservatism of the post-Napoleonic era. Why might Romantic artists and intellectuals like Friedrich have been drawn to revolutionary reforms? (Universal History Archive/Shutterstock)

(deh-luh-KWAH) (1798–1863), one of Romanticism's great artists, painted dramatic, colorful scenes that stirred the emotions. Delacroix was fascinated with remote and (to his European viewers) exotic subjects, whether lion hunts in Morocco or languishing, sensuous women in a sultan's harem. The famous German painter Caspar David Friedrich (1774–1840) preferred somber landscapes of ruined churches or remote shipwrecks frozen in ice, which captured the divine presence in natural forces.

In England the Romantic painters Joseph M. W. Turner (1775–1851) and John Constable (1776–1837) were fascinated by nature, but their interpretations of it contrasted sharply, aptly symbolizing the tremendous emotional range of the Romantic movement. Turner depicted nature's power and terror; wild storms and sinking ships were favorite subjects. Constable painted gentle Wordsworthian landscapes in which human beings lived peacefully with their environment, the comforting countryside of unspoiled rural England.

Musicians and composers likewise explored the Romantic sensibility. Abandoning well-defined musical structures, the great Romantic composers used a wide range of forms to create musical landscapes that evoked powerful emotions. They transformed the small classical orchestra, tripling its size by adding wind instruments, percussion, and more brass and strings. The crashing chords evoking the surge of the masses in Chopin's

Revolutionary Etude and the bottomless despair of the funeral march in Beethoven's Third Symphony—such were the modern orchestra's musical paintings that plumbed the depths of human feeling.

This range and intensity gave music and musicians much greater prestige and publicity than in the past. Music no longer simply complemented a church service or helped a nobleman digest his dinner. It became a sublime end in itself, most perfectly realizing the endless yearning of the soul. The great virtuoso who could transport the listener to ecstasy and hysteria—such as pianist Franz Liszt (1811–1886)—became a cultural hero, the rock star of the classical age.

The most famous and prolific of Romantic composers, Ludwig van Beethoven (1770–1827), used contrasting themes and tones to produce dramatic conflict and inspiring resolutions. As one contemporary admirer wrote, "Beethoven's music sets in motion the lever of fear, of awe, of horror, of suffering, and awakens just that infinite longing which is the essence of Romanticism."[11] Beethoven's own life embodied these emotional extremes, as he struggled to accept the loss of hearing that began at the peak of his fame. In true Romantic fashion he declared, "I will take fate by the throat; it will not bend me completely to its will."[12] Beethoven continued to pour out immortal music, although his last years were silent, spent in total deafness.

How did reforms and revolutions challenge conservatism after 1815?

While the Romantics enacted a revolution in the arts, liberal, national, and socialist forces battered against the conservative restoration of 1815. Political change could result from gradual and peaceful reform or from violent insurrection, but everywhere it took the determination of ordinary people standing up to the powerful. Between 1815 and 1848 three important countries—Greece, Great Britain, and France—experienced variations on this basic theme.

The Greek War of Independence

Though conservative statesmen had maintained the autocratic status quo despite revolts in Spain and the Two Sicilies, a national revolution succeeded in Greece in the 1820s. Since the fifteenth century, Greek territories had been part of the Ottoman Empire, ruled for the most part by ethnic Turks. Despite centuries of foreign rule, the Greeks had survived as a people, united by language and the Greek Orthodox religion, and they were inspired by nationalist ideas of self-determination. This emerging national movement led to a failed uprising against the Ottoman Turks in

1820. In 1821, a second revolt, led by Greek peasants, began the Greek War of Independence, which lasted nine years.

At first Metternich and the Holy Alliance opposed the revolution, primarily because they sought a stable Ottoman Empire as a bulwark against interests in southeast Europe. Yet the Greeks had powerful defenders. Educated Europeans cherished the culture of classical Greece, which they viewed as a key source of Western civilization; Russians admired the piety of their Orthodox brethren. Writers and artists, moved by the Romantic impulse, responded enthusiastically to the national struggle. The English Romantic poet Lord Byron even joined the Greek revolutionaries to fight (as he wrote in a famous poem) "that Greece might yet be free."

Greek Independence, 1830

Delacroix, *Massacre at Chios*, 1824 This masterpiece by Romantic artist Eugène Delacroix portrays the Ottoman massacre of ethnic Greeks, including women and children, on the island of Chios in 1822, during the struggle for national independence in Greece. The Greek revolt won the enthusiastic support of European liberals, nationalists, and Romantics, and this massive oil painting (about 13 feet by 11 feet) reflects contemporary European attitudes by portraying the Ottomans as cruel and violent oppressors holding back the course of history. (Musée du Louvre, Paris, France/Bridgeman Images)

The Greeks, though often quarreling among themselves, battled the Ottomans while hoping for the support of European governments. The fighting was inconclusive, and ongoing negotiations among the Greeks, the Ottomans, and the European powers yielded little result. During the war both Greeks and Ottomans undertook large-scale massacres of civilians. Greek insurgents killed many ethnic Turks living in their midst. In response, Ottoman soldiers ransacked Orthodox churches and massacred Greek civilians. The murder by the Ottomans of thousands of non-combatants at the Greek port of Chios (KAI-ass) in 1822 inflamed European public opinion, encouraged intervention, and helped spread European stereotypes of the Ottomans as non-Christian barbarians.

In 1827 Britain, France, and Russia yielded to popular pressure at home and directed Ottoman leaders to accept an armistice. When they refused, the navies of these three powers annihilated the Ottoman fleet at the Battle of Navarino. In 1828, Russia invaded Turkey, the Ottoman heartland, and the sultan agreed to withdraw his troops from Greek territories. Great Britain, France, and Russia finally declared Greece independent in 1830 and installed a German prince as king of the new country in 1833. The Greeks resented this imposed regime, and the war had devastated the country. But they had won their independence, and Greek "liberation" inspired grassroots nationalist movements among other ethnic minorities in the Ottoman Empire and in Europe. The war was also an early sign of the Ottoman Empire's territorial decline across the nineteenth century.

Liberal Reform in Great Britain

Pressure from below also reshaped politics in Great Britain, but through a process of gradual reform rather than revolution. Eighteenth-century Britain had been

■ **Corn Laws** British laws governing the import and export of grain, which were revised in 1815 to place high tariffs on imported grain, thus benefiting the aristocracy but making food prices high for working people.

remarkably stable. The landowning aristocracy dominated society, but that class was neither closed nor rigidly defined. Successful business and professional people could buy land and become gentlefolk, while the common people enjoyed limited civil rights. Yet the constitutional monarchy was hardly democratic. With only about 8 percent of the population allowed to vote, the British Parliament, easily manipulated by the king, remained in the hands of the upper classes. The two main political parties—the Tories, which later evolved into the modern British Conservative Party, and the slightly more liberal Whigs—were both led by titled aristocrats, leaving ordinary folk little opportunity to use the formal political process to advance reform. Indeed, government policies consistently supported the aristocracy and the new industrial capitalists at the expense of the laboring classes. Workers fought back with grassroots organizing and public protest.

By the 1780s there was growing interest in political reform, yet the radical example of the French Revolution made the British aristocracy hostile to any attempts to change the status quo. In 1815 open conflict emerged when the aristocracy rammed far-reaching changes in the **Corn Laws** through Parliament. Britain had been unable to import inexpensive grain from eastern Europe

during the war years, leading to high prices and large profits for the landed aristocracy. With the war over, grain (which the British generically called "corn") could be imported again, allowing the price of wheat and bread to go down and benefiting almost everyone—except aristocratic landlords. The new Corn Laws placed high tariffs (or fees) on imported grain. Its cost rose to improbable levels, ensuring artificially high bread prices for working people and handsome revenues for aristocrats. Seldom has a class legislated more selfishly for its own narrow economic advantage or done more to promote a class-based view of political action.

The change in the Corn Laws, coming as it did at a time of postwar economic distress, triggered protests and demonstrations by urban laborers, supported by radical intellectuals. In 1817 the Tory government, controlled completely by the landed aristocracy, responded by temporarily suspending the traditional rights of peaceable assembly and habeas corpus, which gives a person under arrest the right to a trial. Two years later, in August 1819, at least 60,000 lower-class citizens gathered at Saint Peter's Fields in Manchester to demand parliamentary reform. Eighteen demonstrators were killed and over 600 wounded by a government cavalry assault.

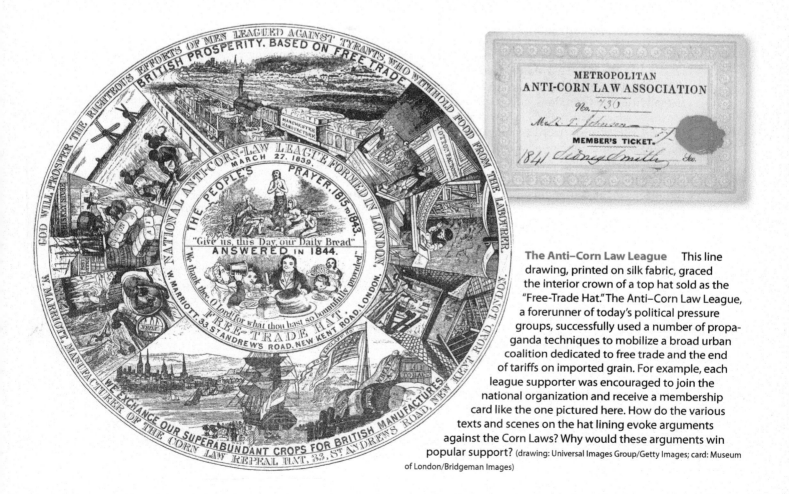

The Anti–Corn Law League This line drawing, printed on silk fabric, graced the interior crown of a top hat sold as the "Free-Trade Hat." The Anti–Corn Law League, a forerunner of today's political pressure groups, successfully used a number of propaganda techniques to mobilize a broad urban coalition dedicated to free trade and the end of tariffs on imported grain. For example, each league supporter was encouraged to join the national organization and receive a membership card like the one pictured here. How do the various texts and scenes on the hat lining evoke arguments against the Corn Laws? Why would these arguments win popular support? (drawing: Universal Images Group/Getty Images; card: Museum of London/Bridgeman Images)

Nicknamed the **Peterloo Massacre**, in scornful reference to the British victory at Waterloo, this incident demonstrated the government's determination to repress dissenters. Parliament then passed the infamous Six Acts, which placed controls on a heavily taxed press and practically eliminated all mass meetings.

Strengthened by ongoing industrial development, emerging manufacturing and commercial groups insisted on a place in the framework of political power and social prestige for their new wealth, alongside the "landed wealth" (based on long-term land ownership) of the aristocracy. They called for many kinds of liberal reform: changes in town government, organization of a new police force, more rights for Catholics and dissenters, and reform of the Poor Laws to provide aid to some low-paid workers. In the 1820s a more secure Tory government moved in the direction of better urban administration, greater economic liberalism, civil equality for Catholics, and limited imports of foreign grain. These actions encouraged the middle classes to press on for reform of Parliament so they could have a larger say in government.

The Whig Party, though led like the Tories by elite aristocrats, had by tradition been more responsive to middle-class commercial and manufacturing interests. After a series of setbacks, the Whigs' **Reform Bill of 1832** was propelled into law by a mighty surge of popular support. The bill moved British politics in a democratic direction and allowed the House of Commons to emerge as the all-important legislative body, at the expense of the aristocrat-dominated House of Lords. The new industrial areas of the country gained representation in the Commons, and many old "rotten boroughs"—electoral districts that had very few voters and that the landed aristocracy had bought and sold—were eliminated. The number of voters increased by about 50 percent, to include about 12 percent of adult men in Britain and Ireland. Comfortable middle-class groups in the urban population, as well as some substantial farmers who leased their land, received the vote. Thus the conflicts building in Great Britain were successfully—though only temporarily—resolved. Continued peaceful reform within the system appeared difficult but not impossible.

The "People's Charter" of 1838 and the Chartist movement it inspired pressed British elites for yet more radical reform. Dismayed by the economic distress of the working class in the 1830s and 1840s, the Chartists demanded universal male (but not female) suffrage. They saw complete political democracy and rule by the common people as the means to a good and just society. Hundreds of thousands of people signed gigantic petitions calling on Parliament to grant all men the right to vote, first in 1839, again in 1842, and yet again in 1848. Parliament rejected all three petitions. In the short run, the working poor failed with their Chartist demands, but they learned a valuable lesson in mass politics.

While calling for universal male suffrage, many working-class people joined with middle-class manufacturers in the Anti–Corn Law League, founded in Manchester in 1839. Mass participation made possible a popular crusade led by liberal intellectuals and politicians, who argued that lower food prices and more jobs in industry depended on repeal of the Corn Laws. Much of the working class agreed. When Ireland's potato crop failed in 1845 and famine prices for food seemed likely in England, Tory prime minister Robert Peel joined with the Whigs and a minority of his own party to repeal the Corn Laws in 1846 and allow free imports of grain. England escaped famine. Thereafter the liberal doctrine of free trade became almost sacred dogma in Great Britain.

The following year, the Tories passed a bill designed to help the working classes, but in a different way. The Ten Hours Act of 1847 limited the workday for women and young people in factories to ten hours. In competition with the middle class for the support of the working class, Tory legislators continued to support legislation regulating factory conditions. This competition between a still-powerful aristocracy and a strong middle class was a crucial factor in Great Britain's peaceful political evolution. The working classes could make temporary alliances with either competitor to better their own conditions.

Ireland and the Great Famine

The people of Ireland did not benefit from the political competition in England. In the mid-nineteenth century, Ireland was an agricultural nation under British rule, and the great majority of the rural population (outside of the northern counties of Ulster, which were partly Presbyterian) were Catholics. They typically rented their land from a tiny minority of Church of England Protestant landowners, who often resided in England. Using a middleman system, these absentee landlords leased land for short periods only, set rents at will, and easily evicted their tenants.

■ **Peterloo Massacre** The British army's violent suppression in 1819 of a protest that took place at Saint Peter's Fields in Manchester in reaction to the revision of the Corn Laws.

■ **Reform Bill of 1832** A major British political reform that increased the number of male voters by about 50 percent and gave political representation to new industrial areas.

■ **Great Famine** The result of four years of potato crop failure in the late 1840s in Ireland, a country that had grown dependent on potatoes as a dietary staple.

In short, landlords used their power to grab as much profit as possible.

Irish peasants, trapped in an exploitative tenant system, lived in abominable conditions. Hundreds of contemporary accounts described hopeless poverty. A compassionate French traveler wrote that Ireland was "pure misery, naked and hungry. . . . I saw the American Indian in his forests and the black slave in his chains, and I believed that I was seeing the most extreme form of human misery; but that was before I knew the lot of poor Ireland."[13]

Despite the terrible conditions, population growth sped upward, part of Europe's general trend begun in the early eighteenth century (see "The New Pattern of the Eighteenth Century" in Chapter 17). Between 1780 and 1840 the Irish population doubled from 4 million to 8 million. Extensive cultivation of the humble potato was largely responsible for this rapid rise. A single acre of land planted with potatoes could feed a family of six for a year, and the hardy tuber thrived on Ireland's boggy wastelands. About one-half of the Irish population subsisted almost exclusively on potatoes, supplemented perhaps with a bit of grain or milk and little else. Needing only a potato patch to survive, the rural poor married early. A young couple faced a life of extreme poverty, yet the decision to marry and have large families made sense. A couple could manage rural poverty better than someone living alone, and children meant extra hands in the fields.

As population and potato dependency grew, however, conditions became more precarious. From 1820 onward, deficiencies and diseases in the potato crop occurred with disturbing frequency. Then in 1845 and 1846, and again in 1848 and 1851, the potato crop failed in Ireland. Blight attacked the young plants, and leaves and tubers rotted. Unmitigated disaster — the **Great Famine** — followed, as already impoverished peasants experienced widespread sickness and starvation.

The British government reacted slowly. Its rigid commitment to free-trade ideology meant that relief efforts were avoided lest they interfere with the sacrosanct free market or contribute to Irish "indolence." Though the British did eventually provide aid, their relief efforts were tragically inadequate. Moreover, the government continued to collect taxes, landlords demanded their rents, and tenants who could not pay were evicted and their homes destroyed. Famine or no, foreign landowners continued to dominate the Irish people and their economy.

The Great Famine shattered the pattern of Irish population growth. One million emigrants fled the famine between 1845 and 1851, mostly to the United States and Canada, and up to 1.5 million people died. The elderly and the very young were hardest hit. Alone among the countries of Europe, Ireland experienced a declining population in the second half of the nineteenth century, as it became a land of continuous out-migration, early death, late marriage, and widespread celibacy.

The Great Famine intensified anti-British feeling and promoted Irish nationalism, for the bitter memory of starvation, exile, and British inaction burned deeply into the popular consciousness. Patriots of the later nineteenth and early twentieth centuries would call on powerful collective emotions in their campaigns for land reform, home rule, and, eventually, Irish independence.

The Revolution of 1830 in France

Like Greece and the British Isles, France experienced dramatic political change in the first half of the nineteenth century, and the French experience especially illustrates the disruptive potential of politics from below. The Constitutional Charter granted by Louis XVIII in the Bourbon restoration of 1814 was a limited liberal constitution. The charter protected economic and social gains made by sections of the middle class and the peasantry in the French Revolution, permitted some intellectual and artistic freedom, and created a parliament with upper and lower houses. Immediately after Napoleon's abortive Hundred Days, the moderate, worldly king refused to bow to the wishes of die-hard aristocrats who wanted to sweep away all the revolutionary changes. Instead, Louis appointed as his ministers moderate royalists, who sought and obtained the support of a majority of the representatives elected to the lower Chamber of Deputies between 1816 and Louis's death in 1824.

Louis XVIII's charter was liberal but hardly democratic. Only about 100,000 of the wealthiest men out of a total population of 30 million had the right to vote for the deputies who, with the king and his ministers, made the laws of the nation. Nonetheless, the "notable people" who did vote came from very different backgrounds. There were wealthy businessmen, war profiteers, successful professionals, ex-revolutionaries, large landowners from the old aristocracy and the middle class, Bourbons, and Bonapartists. The old aristocracy, with its pre-1789 mentality, was a minority within the voting population.

Louis's conservative successor, Charles X (r. 1824–1830), a true reactionary, wanted to re-establish the old order in France. Increasingly blocked by the opposition of the deputies, Charles's government turned in 1830 to military adventure in an effort to rally French nationalism and gain popular support. A long-standing economic and diplomatic dispute with Muslim Algeria, a vassal state of the Ottoman Empire, provided the opportunity.

In June 1830 a French force of thirty-seven thousand crossed the Mediterranean, landed to the west of

Algiers, and took the capital city in three short weeks. Victory seemed complete, but in 1831 Algerians in the interior revolted and waged war until 1847, when French armies finally subdued the country. The conquest of Algeria marked the rebirth of French imperial expansion, and the colonial government encouraged French, Spanish, and Italian immigrants to move to Algeria and settle on large tracts of land expropriated from the region's Muslim inhabitants.

Emboldened by the news from Algeria, Charles repudiated the Constitutional Charter in an attempted coup in July 1830. He censored the press and issued decrees stripping much of the wealthy middle class of its voting rights. The immediate reaction, encouraged by liberal lawyers, journalists, and middle-class businessmen, was an insurrection in the capital. Printers, other artisans, and small traders fired up by popular republicanism rioted in the streets of Paris, and three days of vicious street fighting brought down the government. Charles fled. Then the upper middle class, which had fomented the revolt, abandoned the more radical workers and skillfully seated Charles's cousin, Louis Philippe, duke of Orléans, on the vacant throne.

Events in Paris reverberated across Europe. In the Netherlands, Belgian Catholics revolted against the Dutch king and established the independent kingdom of Belgium. In Switzerland, regional liberal assemblies forced cantonal governments to amend their constitutions, leading to two decades of political conflict. And in the Kingdom of Poland, an armed nationalist rebellion against the tsarist government was crushed by the Russian Imperial Army.

Despite the abdication of Charles X, in France the political situation remained more or less unchanged. The new king, Louis Philippe (r. 1830–1848), accepted the Constitutional Charter of 1814 and adopted the red, white, and blue flag of the French Revolution. Beyond these symbolic actions, however, popular demands for thorough reform went unanswered. The upper middle class had effected a change in dynasty that maintained the status quo and the narrowly liberal institutions of 1815. Republicans, democrats, social reformers, and the poor of Paris were bitterly disappointed. They had made a revolution, but it seemed for naught.

Scenes from the Revolution of 1830 in Paris   Titled "Game of the Heroes of the Memorable Days of July," these hand-colored playing cards portray incidents from the uprising in Paris in July 1830. The captions at the bottom read, from left to right: "Making the Bullets of Patriotism"; "Aid to the Ill-Fated Brave One"; and "The Amazon of 1830." These fanciful yet moving scenes idealize the revolutionary zeal of the ordinary men and women who fought government troops and helped overthrow the rule of King Charles X. In reality, their efforts replaced the king but not the system. (Musée de la Ville de Paris, Musée Carnavalet, Paris, France/Bridgeman Images)

What were the main causes and consequences of the revolutions of 1848?

In the late 1840s Europe entered a period of crisis. Bad harvests across the continent threatened widespread starvation. Uneven industrial development failed to provide jobs or raise incomes, while widespread poverty boosted the popularity of the radical ideologies that emerged in the wake of the French Revolution. As a result, limited revolts broke out across Europe: the "Kraków Uprising" against the Austrian Empire in 1846, a popular insurrection in Portugal in 1846–1847, a civil war in Switzerland in 1847, and an uprising in Sicily in January 1848.

Full-scale revolution broke out in France in February 1848 and then ripped across the continent. The events are sometimes called the "Springtime of Nations" or the "Springtime of the Peoples" because ordinary men and women demanded new political and national rights from authoritarian and imperial governments. Only the most developed countries—Great Britain, Belgium, and the Netherlands—and the least developed—the Ottoman and Russian Empires—escaped untouched. Elsewhere conservative governments toppled, as monarchs and ministers bowed or fled. National independence, democratic constitutions, and social reform: the lofty aspirations of a generation of liberal reformers seemed at hand. By the end of 1849 a wave of violent suppression had restored monarchical rule in most lands, but the momentum of the revolutions nonetheless encouraged the spread of new political ideals.

A Democratic Republic in France

By the late 1840s revolution in Europe was almost universally expected, but it took events in Paris—once again—to turn expectations into realities. For eighteen years Louis Philippe's reign, labeled the "bourgeois monarchy" because its policies served the selfish interests of France's wealthy elites, had been characterized by inaction and complacency. While the king paid himself a lavish salary, corrupt politicians refused to consider legislation or electoral reform that might extend benefits to the middle and lower classes, the vast majority of the population. (See "Evaluating Visual Evidence: Honoré Daumier, *Gargantua*, 1831," page 650.) Frustrated desires for change, high-level financial scandals, and a general sense of stagnation dovetailed with a severe depression that began with crop failures in 1846 to 1847. The government did little to prevent the agrarian crisis from dragging down the entire economy.

The government's failures united a diverse group of opponents against the king. Bourgeois merchants, opposition deputies, and liberal intellectuals shared a sense of outrage with middle-class shopkeepers, skilled artisans, and unskilled working people. Widespread discontent eventually touched off a popular revolt in Paris. On the night of February 22, 1848, workers and some students, armed with guns, began building barricades and demanding a new government. On February 24 the National Guard broke ranks and joined the revolutionaries. Louis Philippe refused to call in the army and abdicated in favor of his grandson. But the common people in arms would tolerate no more monarchy. This refusal led to the proclamation of a provisional republic, headed by a ten-man executive committee and certified by cries of approval from the revolutionary crowd.

The revolutionaries immediately set about drafting a democratic, republican constitution for France's Second Republic and set up a National Assembly. They gave the right to vote to every adult male and issued bold decrees that called for liberty, fraternity, and equality. The revolutionary government guaranteed workplace reforms, freed all enslaved people in French colonies, and abolished the death penalty. In the "spring days" of 1848, revolutionary movements set up parliaments and agitated for similar reforms across the European continent (Map 21.3).

Yet there were profound differences within the various revolutionary coalitions. On the one hand, the moderate liberal republicans of the middle class typically viewed universal male suffrage as the ultimate concession to dangerous popular forces, and they strongly opposed any further social measures. On the other hand, radical republicans, influenced by a generation of utopian socialists and appalled by the poverty and misery of the urban poor, were committed to some kind of socialism. Hard-pressed urban artisans, who hated the unrestrained competition of cutthroat capitalism, advocated a combination of strong craft unions and worker-owned businesses. Such divisions undermined revolutionary unity in Paris but also in Vienna, Berlin, and other revolutionary hotspots.

Worsening depression and rising unemployment exacerbated these conflicting goals in Paris. Socialist journalist Louis Blanc and Alexandre Martin—the first member of the industrial working class to enter the French government—represented the republican socialists in the National Assembly. Blanc and Martin pressed for official recognition of the "right to work." Blanc urged the creation of the permanent government-sponsored cooperative workshops he had advocated in *The Organization of Work*. Such workshops would be an alternative to capitalist employment and a decisive step toward a new, noncompetitive social order.

Honoré Daumier, *Gargantua*, 1831

(akg-images)

In this satirical lithograph from 1831, French artist and caricaturist Honoré Daumier mocked the greed of King Louis Philippe and the corruption of his government. The monstrous king — the "gargantua" — gobbles down baskets of tax money extorted by government clerks from impoverished men and women. Louis Philippe's throne is pictured as a commode or toilet, and his fat ministers and cronies wait beneath him to catch the titles, awards, and medals that represent the waste from the king's meal. *Gargantua* was one of Daumier's early works; alongside his paintings and sculpture, the artist would continue to produce cartoons that criticized the monarchy, the church, and the upper classes until his death in 1879.

EVALUATE THE EVIDENCE

1. How does this cartoon exemplify new political ideologies that were hostile to conservative government? Given the contrast between the king and the people, Daumier most obviously sympathized with which political ideology?
2. Political cartoons such as *Gargantua* are typically loaded with critical symbolism. How does Daumier use satiric, humorous, or ironic imagery in this cartoon to score political points against King Louis Philippe and the French elite?

The moderate republicans, willing to provide only temporary relief, wanted no such thing. The resulting compromise set up National Workshops — soon to become little more than a vast program of pick-and-shovel public works — and established a special commission under Blanc to "study the question." This satisfied no one. The National Workshops were, however, better than nothing. An army of desperate poor from the French provinces and even from foreign countries streamed into Paris to sign up for the workshops. As the economic crisis worsened, the number enrolled in the workshops soared from 10,000 in March to 120,000 by June, and another 80,000 tried unsuccessfully to join.

While the Paris workshops grew, the French people went to the election polls in late April. The result was a bitter loss for the republicans. Voting in most

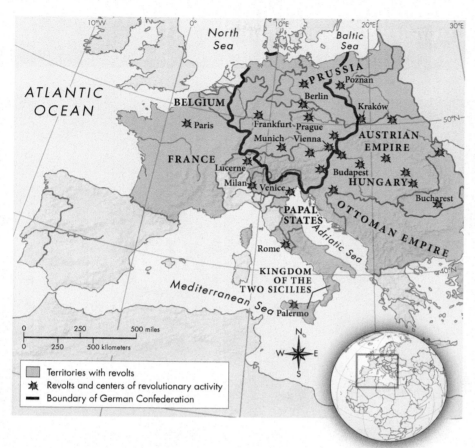

MAP 21.3 The Revolutions of 1848 In February and March 1848, revolutions broke out in the European heartlands: France, the Austrian Empire, and the German Confederation. In contrast, relative stability reigned in Great Britain, Belgium, the Netherlands, and the Russian and Ottoman Empires. Why did some regions descend into revolution, and not others? Can a study of geography help explain the difference?

Territories with revolts
Revolts and centers of revolutionary activity
Boundary of German Confederation

cases for the first time, the people of France elected to the new 900-person Constituent Assembly 500 monarchists and conservatives, only about 270 moderate republicans, and just 80 radicals or socialists.

One of the moderate republicans elected to the Assembly was the author of *Democracy in America*, Alexis de Tocqueville (1805–1859), who had predicted the overthrow of Louis Philippe's government. He explained the election results by observing that the socialist movement in Paris aroused the fierce hostility of France's peasants as well as the middle and upper classes. The French peasants owned land, and according to Tocqueville, "private property had become with all those who owned it a sort of bond of fraternity."[14] Tocqueville saw that a majority of the Constituent Assembly was firmly committed to centrist moderation and strongly opposed to the socialists and their artisan allies, a view he shared.

This clash of ideologies—between moderate liberalism and radical socialism—became a clash of classes and arms after the elections. The new government's executive committee dropped Blanc and thereafter included no representative of the Parisian working class. Fearing that their socialist hopes were about to be dashed, artisans and unskilled workers invaded the Constituent Assembly on May 15 and tried to proclaim a new revolutionary state. The government used

the middle-class National Guard to squelch this uprising. As the workshops continued to fill and grow more radical, the fearful but powerful propertied classes in the Assembly took the offensive. On June 22 the government dissolved the workshops in Paris, giving the workers the choice of joining the army or going to workshops in the provinces.

A spontaneous and violent uprising followed. Frustrated in their thwarted attempt to create a socialist society, masses of desperate people were now losing even their life-sustaining relief. Barricades sprang up again in the narrow streets of Paris, and a terrible class war began. This time the government had the army and the support of peasant France. After three terrible "June Days" of street fighting and the death or injury of more than ten thousand insurgents, the republican army under General Louis Cavaignac stood triumphant. (See "Viewpoints: Picturing Revolutionary Violence in 1848," page 652.)

The February coalition of the middle and working classes had in four short months become locked in mortal combat, and the revolution in France ended in a bloodbath. Yet some reforms endured. While the Assembly failed to craft a generous democratic republic, it did complete a constitution that maintained universal male suffrage and established a strong executive instead of a monarchy. This allowed Louis Napoleon,

Ernest Meissonier, *Memory of the Civil War* (The Barricades). (Fine Art Images/Heritage Images/Hulton Archive/Getty Images)

The Murder of Count Baillet of Latour. (akg-images/Newscom)

The striking similarities between the different national revolutions in 1848 suggest that Europeans lived through common experiences that shaped a generation. The revolutions began with riots and street fighting, and a tremendous surge in political participation and civic activity overthrew rulers or forced them to make major concessions. State officials responded to the uprisings with deadly force. Field artillery bombarded the insurgents and infantrymen overran the barricades in hand-to-hand combat. Fleeing radicals were often hunted down and shot, and the rule of order was restored.

Newspaper publishing exploded as censorship relaxed and interest in public affairs soared, and ordinary people followed the revolutionary carnage in newspapers and printed illustrations. In Vienna, after an angry crowd lynched the Minister of War Count Latour, this lithograph of the murder (right), sold through the post by a German company, shocked viewers with its image of popular violence. Ernest Meissonier's painting *Memory of the Civil War* (1849, left), which portrays the bodies of rebels on a destroyed barricade in Paris, brought home the human cost of rebellion.

QUESTIONS FOR ANALYSIS

1. The 1848 revolutions increased political activity, yet they were crushed. How do the images here help explain this outcome?
2. Do these pictures promote a political message, or do they seem to be more neutral observations of exciting events? How would you react to these depictions of street violence if you were a contemporary urban worker or a prosperous city business owner?

nephew of Napoleon Bonaparte, to win a landslide victory in the election of December 1848. The appeal of his famous name as well as the desire of the propertied classes for order at any cost had led to what would become a centrist, semi-authoritarian regime with some liberal elements in place (see "Napoleon III's Second Empire" in Chapter 23).

Revolution and Reaction in the Austrian Empire

Throughout continental Europe, the first news of the upheaval in France evoked feverish excitement and then popular revolution, lending credence to Metternich's famous quip "When France sneezes, all Europe catches cold." Revolutionary insurrections broke out in Sweden, Denmark, Spain, the Italian states, and elsewhere. The Europe-wide revolts raised popular political awareness. They gave countless people firsthand experience with the alternative political ideologies that had emerged after the Napoleonic Wars and spread the basic idea that the state was responsible for the well-being of its citizens.

The "Springtime of Nations" had a particularly powerful impact in the Austrian Empire and Prussia, both members of the German Confederation. In central Europe, as in France, the revolution went through three phases. First, liberals demanded written constitutions, representative government, and greater civil liberties from authoritarian regimes. When governments hesitated, popular revolts broke out. Urban workers and students served as the shock troops, but they were allied with middle-class liberals and peasants seeking land reforms. In the face of this united front, monarchs made quick concessions. Second, the revolutionary coalition, having secured great and easy victories, broke down as it had in France. Third, the traditional forces — the monarchy, the aristocracy, and the regular army — reasserted their authority and revoked many, though not all, of the reforms.

The revolution in the Austrian Empire began in Hungary in March 1848, when nationalistic reformers demanded national autonomy, freedom of the press, full civil liberties, and universal suffrage. Anti-imperial insurrection broke out in the northern Italian territories of Lombardy-Venetia the same month, and Austrian forces retreated after five days of street fighting. As the monarchy in Vienna hesitated, radicalized Viennese students and workers took to the streets of the imperial capital and raised barricades in defiance of the government. Meanwhile, peasant disturbances broke out across the empire. The Habsburg emperor Ferdinand I (r. 1835–1848) capitulated and promised reforms and a liberal constitution. When Metternich refused to compromise, the aging conservative was forced to resign and fled to London. The old absolutist order seemed to be collapsing with unbelievable rapidity.

Yet the revolutionary coalition lacked stability. Responding to the revolutionary crisis, the monarchy had abolished serfdom with its degrading forced labor and feudal services, and the newly free peasants lost interest in the political and social questions agitating the cities. Meanwhile, urban revolutionaries were increasingly divided along class lines over the issue of socialist workshops and universal voting rights for men.

Conflicting national aspirations further weakened and ultimately destroyed the revolutionary coalition. In March the Hungarian revolutionary leaders pushed through an extremely liberal constitution for the Kingdom of Hungary. But the Hungarian revolutionaries also sought to transform the mosaic of provinces and peoples in their territories into a unified, centralized Hungarian nation. The minority groups that formed half of the population rejected such unification (see Map 21.2). Each group wanted political autonomy and cultural independence. In a similar way, Czech nationalists based in Prague and other parts of Bohemia came into conflict with German nationalists living in the same region. Thus desires for national autonomy within the Austrian Empire enabled the monarchy to maintain power by playing off one ethnic group against the other.

Finally, conservative aristocratic forces rallied under the leadership of the archduchess Sophia, a Bavarian princess married to the Habsburg emperor's brother. Deeply ashamed of the emperor's collapse before a "mess of students," she insisted that Ferdinand I, who had no heir, abdicate in favor of her son, Franz Joseph.[15] Powerful nobles organized around Sophia in a secret conspiracy to reverse and crush the revolution.

The first conservative breakthrough came when the army bombarded Prague and crushed a working-class revolt there on June 17, 1848. By August the Austrians had crushed the Italian insurrection. At the end of October, the well-equipped, predominantly peasant troops of the regular Austrian army bombarded the student and working-class radicals dug in behind barricades in Vienna with heavy artillery. They retook the city at the cost of more than four thousand casualties. The determination of the Austrian aristocracy and the loyalty of its army sealed the triumph of reaction and the defeat of revolution.

When Franz Joseph (r. 1848–1916) was crowned emperor of Austria immediately after his eighteenth birthday in December 1848, only the Hungarians had yet to be brought under control. Another determined conservative, Nicholas I of Russia (r. 1825–1855), obligingly lent his iron hand. On June 6, 1849, 130,000 Russian troops poured into Hungary and subdued the country after bitter fighting. For a number of years, the Habsburgs ruled the Kingdom of Hungary as a conquered territory.

The Frankfurt Assembly in Session   The Frankfurt National Assembly opened to great fanfare in May 1848, but its calls for liberal reforms and German unification were quashed by the revival of authoritarianism under the king of Prussia. The black, red, and gold banners draped around the hall symbolized unity, and the tricolor was later adopted as the national flag of Germany. Although many of the liberal concessions granted by conservative monarchs in response to the revolutions of 1848 were quickly rescinded, the demands for more democratic and participatory governments would continue to inspire reformers and revolutionaries in the following decades. (Unknown Artist [19th century]/LEEMAGE/Private Collection/Bridgeman Images)

Prussia, the German Confederation, and the Frankfurt National Assembly

After Austria, Prussia was the largest and most influential kingdom in the German Confederation. Since the Napoleonic Wars, liberal German reformers had sought to transform absolutist Prussia into a constitutional monarchy, hoping it would then lead the thirty-eight states of the German Confederation into a unified nation-state. The agitation that followed the fall of Louis Philippe, on top of several years of crop failure and economic crises, encouraged liberals to press their demands. In March 1848 excited crowds in urban centers across the German Confederation called for liberal reforms and a national parliament, and many regional rulers quickly gave in to their demands.

When artisans and factory workers rioted in Berlin, the capital of Prussia, and joined temporarily with the middle-class liberals in the struggle against the monarchy, the autocratic yet compassionate Prussian king, Friedrich Wilhelm IV (r. 1840–1861), vacillated and then caved in. On March 21 he promised to grant Prussia a liberal constitution and to merge Prussia into a new national German state.

But urban workers wanted much more — and the Prussian aristocracy wanted much less — than the moderate constitutional liberalism conceded by the king. The workers issued a series of democratic and vaguely socialist demands that troubled their middle-class allies. An elected Prussian Constituent Assembly met in Berlin to write a constitution for the Prussian state, and a conservative clique gathered around the king to urge counter-revolution.

Elections were also held across the German Confederation for a parliament or National Assembly, which convened to write a federal constitution that would lead to national unification. When they met in Frankfurt that May, the state officials, lawyers, professors, and businessmen elected to the Assembly represented the interests of the social elite. Their calls for constitutional monarchy, free speech, religious tolerance, and abolition of aristocratic privilege were typical of moderate national liberalism. The deputies ignored calls for more radical action from industrial workers, peasants, republicans, and socialists.

In October 1848 the National Assembly turned to the question of national unification and borders. At first, the deputies proposed unification around a **Greater Germany** that would include the German-speaking lands of the Austrian Empire in a national state — but not non-German territories in Italy and central Europe. This proposal foundered on Austrian determination to maintain its empire, and some parliamentarians advocated the development of a Lesser Germany that would unify Prussia and other German states without Austria. Even as the deputies debated Germany's future in the autumn of 1848, the forces of counter-revolution pushed back reformists and revolutionaries in Prussia and the other German states.

Despite Austrian intransigence, in March 1849 the deputies in Frankfurt completed a draft of a liberal

■ **Greater Germany**   A liberal plan for German national unification that included the German-speaking parts of the Austrian Empire, put forth at the National Assembly in 1848 but rejected by Austrian rulers.

constitution and requested Friedrich Wilhelm IV of Prussia to serve as emperor of a "lesser" German national state (minus Austria). By early 1849, however, reaction had rolled back liberal reforms across the German Confederation. Prussian troops had already crushed popular movements across the German Confederation, and Friedrich Wilhelm had reasserted his royal authority and disbanded the Prussian Constituent Assembly. He contemptuously refused to accept the "crown from the gutter" offered by the National Assembly in Frankfurt. Bogged down by their preoccupation with nationalist issues, the reluctant revolutionaries in Frankfurt had waited too long and acted too timidly. By May 1849 all but the most radical deputies had resigned from the National Assembly, and in June Prussian troops forcibly dissolved what remained.

Friedrich Wilhelm in fact wanted to be emperor of a unified Germany, but only on his own authoritarian terms. With the liberal threat successfully squelched, he tried to get the small monarchies of Germany to elect him emperor. Austria balked. Supported by Russia, the Austrians forced Prussia to renounce all schemes of unification in late 1850. The German Confederation was re-established in 1851, and a decade of reaction followed. In an echo of the Karlsbad Decrees, state security forces monitored universities, civic organizations, and the press throughout the confederation. Former revolutionaries fled into exile, and German liberals gave up demands for national unification.

At the same time, increasingly moderate monarchs, aided by ever-growing state bureaucracies in the various German states, granted their subjects conservative constitutions and weak parliaments that offered some measure of popular representation within the boundaries of aristocratic control. Attempts to unite the Germans — first in a liberal national state and then in a conservative Prussian empire — had failed.

Yet the revolutionary experience had reframed political debates in Germany and across Europe, giving rise to new ideologies — liberalism, socialism, and nationalism — that had growing popular appeal.

NOTES

1. See B. E. Vick, *The Congress of Vienna: Power and Politics After Napoleon* (Cambridge, Mass.: Harvard University Press, 2014), pp. 11–14.
2. A. Sked, *The Decline and Fall of the Habsburg Empire, 1815–1918* (London: Longman, 1989), pp. 1–2.
3. Quoted in D. Blackbourn, *The Long Nineteenth Century: A History of Germany, 1780–1918* (New York: Oxford University Press, 1998), p. 122.
4. E. Gellner, *Nations and Nationalism* (Oxford: Basil Blackwell, 1983), especially pp. 19–39.
5. This paragraph draws on the influential views of B. Anderson, *Imagined Communities: Reflections on the Origins and Spread of Nationalism*, rev. ed. (London: Verso, 1991), and E. J. Hobsbawm and T. Ranger, eds., *The Invention of Tradition* (Cambridge: Cambridge University Press, 1983).
6. Quoted in F. E. Manuel and F. P. Manuel, *Utopian Thought in the Western World* (Cambridge, Mass.: Harvard University Press, 1979), p. 589.
7. Quoted in H. G. Schenk, *The Mind of the European Romantics* (New York: Oxford University Press, 1979), p. 5.
8. Quoted in Schenk, p. 169.
9. Quoted in O. Frey, *Emotions Recollected in Tranquility — Wordsworth's Concept of Poetry in "I Wandered Lonely as a Cloud"* (Munich: GRIN Verlag, 2008), p. 5.
10. Quoted in Maria Tartar, ed., *The Annotated Brothers Grimm*, bicentennial ed. (New York: Norton, 2012), pp. 436, 443.
11. Quoted in A. Comini, *The Changing Image of Beethoven: A Study in Mythmaking* (Santa Fe, N.M.: Sunstone Press, 2008), p. 79.
12. Quoted in F. B. Artz, *From the Renaissance to Romanticism: Trends in Style in Art, Literature, and Music, 1300–1830* (Chicago: University of Chicago Press, 1962), pp. 276, 278.
13. Quoted in G. O'Brien, *The Economic History of Ireland from the Union to the Famine* (London: Longmans, Green, 1921), pp. 23–24.
14. A. de Tocqueville, *Recollections* (New York: Columbia University Press, 1949), p. 94.
15. W. L. Langer, *Political and Social Upheaval, 1832–1852* (New York: Harper & Row, 1969), p. 361.

LOOKING BACK LOOKING AHEAD

Viewed from a broad historical perspective, Europe's economic and social foundations in 1750 remained agricultural and rural. Although Enlightenment thought was beginning to question the status quo, authoritarian absolutism dominated political life. One hundred years later, the unfinished effects of the Industrial and French Revolutions had brought fundamental changes to the social fabric of daily life and politics across Europe. The liberal ideals of representative government and legal equality realized briefly in revolutionary France inspired intellectuals and social reformers, who adopted ideologies

of liberalism, nationalism, Romanticism, and socialism to challenge the conservative order. The uneven spread of industrial technologies and factory organization into developed areas across Europe spurred the growth of an urban working class but did little to raise the living standards of most workers, peasants, and artisans. Living on the edge of subsistence, the laboring poor in rural and urban areas alike remained subject to economic misfortune, mass unemployment, and food shortages, and they turned repeatedly to protest, riots, and violent insurrection in pursuit of economic and political rights.

In 1848 the poor joined middle- and upper-class reformers in a great wave of revolution that forced conservative monarchs across the continent to grant liberal and national concessions—at least for a moment. Divisions in the revolutionary coalition and the power of the autocratic state forced back the wave of reform, and the revolutions ended in failure. Conservative monarchies revived, nationalist movements collapsed, and hopes for German unification withered. Yet protest on the barricades and debate in liberal parliaments had given a generation a wealth of experience with new forms of participatory politics, and the ideologies associated with the French Revolution would continue to invigorate reformers and revolutionaries after 1850. Nationalism, with its commitment to the imagined community of a great national family and the nation-state, would become a dominant political force, particularly as European empires extended their reach after 1875. At the same time, as agriculture and rural life gradually declined in economic importance, the spread of industrialization would raise living standards, sustain a growing urban society, and reshape family and class relationships. Diverse, complicated, and fascinating, pockets of this new urban society already existed in 1850. By 1900 it dominated northwestern Europe and was making steady inroads to the east and south.

Make Connections

Think about the larger developments and continuities within and across chapters.

1. How did the spread of radical ideas and the movements for reform and revolution explored in this chapter draw on the "unfinished" political and industrial revolutions (Chapters 19 and 20) of the late eighteenth century? Why did the conservative policies put in place by Metternich and the leaders of the Holy Alliance fail to halt the spread of such ideas?

2. Why did the ideas of the Romantic movement so easily support reformist and radical political ideas, including liberalism, republicanism, and nationalism? What does this reveal about the general connections between art and politics?

3. The years between 1815 and 1850 witnessed the invention of a number of new political ideologies. To what extent do the ideas advanced by conservatives, liberals, nationalists, and socialists in the first half of the nineteenth century continue to shape our political debates?

21 REVIEW & EXPLORE

Identify Key Terms

Identify and explain the significance of each item below.

Congress of Vienna (p. 626)

Holy Alliance (p. 630)

Karlsbad Decrees (p. 631)

liberalism (p. 634)

laissez faire (p. 634)

republicanism (p. 634)

nationalism (p. 634)

socialism (p. 635)

Marxism (p. 638)

bourgeoisie (p. 639)

proletariat (p. 639)

Romanticism (p. 639)

Corn Laws (p. 645)

Peterloo Massacre (p. 646)

Reform Bill of 1832 (p. 646)

Great Famine (p. 647)

Greater Germany (p. 654)

Review the Main Ideas

Answer the section heading questions from the chapter.

1. How was peace restored and maintained after the Napoleonic Wars? (p. 626)

2. What new ideologies emerged to challenge conservative government? (p. 634)

3. What were the characteristics of the Romantic movement? (p. 639)

4. How did reforms and revolutions challenge conservatism after 1815? (p. 643)

5. What were the main causes and consequences of the revolutions of 1848? (p. 649)

Suggested Resources

BOOKS

- Brewer, David. *The Greek War of Independence: The Struggle for Freedom and from Ottoman Oppression.* 2001. A compelling narrative history that places nation building at the center of the Greek Revolution.

- Evans, Robert J. W. *Austria, Hungary, and the Habsburgs: Central Europe c. 1683–1867.* 2008. A collection of essays by a prominent historian of Germany and central Europe that places special emphasis on nationalism, ethnic diversity, and the revolutions of 1848.

- Hamilton, Paul, ed. *The Oxford Handbook of European Romanticism.* 2016. The forty-one chapters in this anthology cover Romanticism from the French Revolution to 1848 in numerous European lands.

- Hobsbawm, Eric. *The Age of Revolution, 1789–1848.* 1996. An engaging survey of the transformative effects of the Industrial and French Revolutions.

- Kelly, John. *The Graves Are Walking: The Great Famine and the Saga of the Irish People.* 2012. A well-received, moving history of the Irish potato famine and its social and political causes and consequences.

- Kołakowski, Leszek. *Main Currents of Marxism: The Founders, the Golden Age, the Breakdown.* 1978. In over one thousand pages, this famous masterpiece offers a critical view of the history of Marxist thought.

- Lazarski, Christopher. *Power Tends to Corrupt: Lord Acton's Study of Liberty.* 2012. A compelling intellectual history that explores the political thought of a seminal British theorist of liberty and its development in Western history.

- Rapport, Mike. *1848: Year of Revolution.* 2008. A stimulating, well-written account that examines all of Europe.

- Riding, Jacqueline. *Peterloo: The Story of the Manchester Massacre.* 2019. An accessible history of the Peterloo Massacre that inspired director Mike Leigh's film *Peterloo.*

- Sked, Alan. *Metternich and Austria: An Evaluation.* 2008. Explores Metternich's role in domestic and foreign affairs in the first half of the nineteenth century.

- Sperber, Jonathan. *Karl Marx: A Nineteenth-Century Life.* 2013. An evenhanded cradle-to-grave biography of the famous revolutionary theorist.

- Vick, Brian E. *The Congress of Vienna: Power and Politics After Napoleon.* 2014. An original analysis of political culture at the Congress of Vienna and the celebratory spectacles that accompanied Napoleon's defeat and the return of European peace.

MEDIA

- *Bright Star* (Jane Campion, 2009). A romantic drama about the British Romantic poet John Keats and Fanny Brawne, whose relationship was cut short by Keats's early death.

- *Heaven on Earth: The Rise and Fall of Socialism* (PBS, 2005). A three-part series, this documentary explores the history of the socialist movement.

- *The History Place: Irish Potato Famine.* Information about the background to, events during, and results of the Irish famine, with a bibliography of key scholarly works. **www .historyplace.com/worldhistory/famine/index.html**

- *Landmarks of Western Art: Romanticism* (Kultur Video, 2003). A documentary about the Romantic movement in painting, highlighting artists such as Turner, Constable, Goya, and Géricault.

- *Marxists Internet Archive.* This archive offers a vast amount of material and sources related to Karl Marx, communism, and Communist revolutions. **marxists .org/index.htm**

- *Peterloo* (Mike Leigh, 2018). This feature film, which chronicles the events leading up to the massacre of protesters marching for electoral reform in England in 1819, offers sympathetic commentary on the inequalities that defined social life in early-nineteenth-century Britain.

22

Life in the Emerging Urban Society

1840–1914

When Londoners gathered in 1860 at the Grand Fete in the Crystal Palace (pictured here), they enjoyed the pleasures of an established urban society that would have been unthinkable just sixty years earlier. Across the nineteenth century, as industrialization expanded exponentially, Europeans left their farms and country villages to find work in the ever-growing towns and cities. By 1900, in developed northwestern Europe, more than half the population lived in urban settings. In much of eastern and southern Europe — in Poland and Russia; in southern Italy and Spain; in Greece and the Balkan lands to the southeast — urbanization and industrialization moved more slowly. Nonetheless, rural-to-urban migration spread across Europe and continued into the twentieth century.

Despite the happy faces in the London crowd pictured here, the emerging urban society brought costs as well as benefits. Although living standards rose in the nineteenth century, wages and living conditions varied greatly, and many city dwellers were still poor. Advances in public health and urban planning brought some relief to squalid working-class slums, yet vast differences in income, education, and occupation divided people into socially stratified groups. Major changes in family life and gender roles accompanied this diversified class system. Dramatic breakthroughs in chemistry, medicine, and electrical engineering further transformed urban society after 1880, and a new generation of artists, writers, and professional social scientists worked to understand and portray the changes wrought by urbanization. ■

CHAPTER PREVIEW

- ■ **What were the main changes in urban life in the nineteenth century?**

- ■ **How did class and gender reinforce social difference in the nineteenth century?**

- ■ **How did urbanization affect family life and gender roles?**

- ■ **What were the most important changes in science and culture?**

Everyday Amusements in the Nineteenth-Century City
The excitement and variety of urban life sparkle in this depiction of a public entertainment gala in 1860, sponsored by London's Royal Dramatic College and held in the city's fabulous Crystal Palace. (Fine Art Photographic/Getty Images)

What were the main changes in urban life in the nineteenth century?

Since the Middle Ages, European cities had been centers of government, culture, and commerce. They had also been congested, dirty, and unhealthy. Beginning in the early nineteenth century, the Industrial Revolution pushed these unfortunate realities of urban life to unprecedented levels. Rapid city growth worsened overcrowding, increased environmental pollution, and spread disease. Taming the city posed a major challenge. Only the full-scale efforts of government leaders, city planners, reformers, scientists, and civic-minded citizens would eventually ameliorate the ferocious savagery of the industrial metropolis.

Industry and the Growth of Cities

The main causes of the poor quality of urban life — dense overcrowding, pervasive poverty, and lack of medical knowledge — had existed for centuries. Because the typical city had always been a "walking city," with no public transportation, great masses of people needed to live in close proximity to shops, markets, and workplaces. Packed together almost as tightly as possible, people in cities suffered and died from the spread of infectious disease in far greater numbers than their rural counterparts. In the larger towns, more people died each year than were born, on average, and urban populations maintained their numbers only because newcomers continually arrived from rural areas.

The Industrial Revolution exacerbated these deplorable conditions. The steam engine freed industrialists from dependence on the energy of fast-flowing streams and rivers, so that by 1800 there was every incentive to build new factories in urban areas, which had many advantages. Cities had better transportation facilities than the countryside and thus better supplies of coal and raw materials. Cities had many hands wanting work, for they drew people like a magnet, and as a result concentrated the demand for manufactured goods. And it was a great advantage for a producer to have other factories nearby to supply the business's needs and buy its products. Therefore, as industry grew, already overcrowded and unhealthy cities expanded rapidly.

"What Torrents of Filth Come from That Walbrook Sewer!!"   This 1832 cartoon by satirist George Cruikshank shows the director of the Southwark Water Works, a main source of London's drinking water, enthroned on an intake valve in the midst of a heavily polluted River Thames. Wearing a chamber pot for a hat and holding a trident with an impaled dog, cat, and rat, he raises a glass of foul liquid to cries of "Give Us Clean Water!" and "It Makes Me Sick!" (Science & Society Picture Library/Getty Images)

TIMELINE

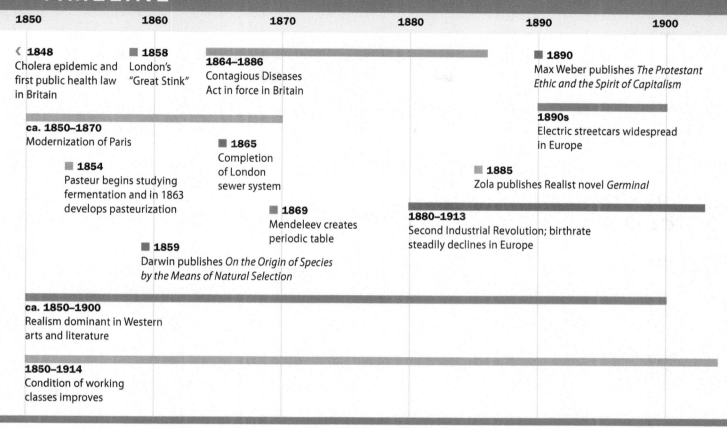

1850	1860	1870	1880	1890	1900

‹ 1848
Cholera epidemic and first public health law in Britain

■ 1858
London's "Great Stink"

1864–1886
Contagious Diseases Act in force in Britain

■ 1890
Max Weber publishes *The Protestant Ethic and the Spirit of Capitalism*

ca. 1850–1870
Modernization of Paris

■ 1854
Pasteur begins studying fermentation and in 1863 develops pasteurization

■ 1865
Completion of London sewer system

1890s
Electric streetcars widespread in Europe

■ 1885
Zola publishes Realist novel *Germinal*

■ 1869
Mendeleev creates periodic table

1880–1913
Second Industrial Revolution; birthrate steadily declines in Europe

■ 1859
Darwin publishes *On the Origin of Species by the Means of Natural Selection*

ca. 1850–1900
Realism dominant in Western arts and literature

1850–1914
Condition of working classes improves

Great Britain, the first country to go through the early stages of the Industrial Revolution, faced the challenges of a changing urban environment early on. In the 1820s and 1830s the populations of a number of British cities increased by 40 to 70 percent each decade. The number of people living in cities of 20,000 or more in England and Wales jumped from 1.5 million in 1801 to 6.3 million in 1851 and reached 15.6 million in 1891. Such cities accounted for 17 percent of the total English population in 1801, 35 percent as early as 1851, and fully 54 percent in 1891. Other countries followed the English pattern as they industrialized (Map 22.1). And as we will see in Chapter 24, rapid growth drew migrants from the countryside and across national borders, creating centers of ethnic and religious diversity in ever-growing European cities.

Except on the outskirts, cities in early-nineteenth-century Britain used every scrap of available land. Parks and open areas were almost nonexistent. Developers erected buildings on the smallest possible lots in order to pack the maximum number of people into a given space. Narrow houses were built attached to one another in long rows. These row houses had neither front nor back yards, and only a narrow alley in back separated one row from the next. Other buildings were built around courtyards completely enclosed on all four sides. Many people lived in tiny apartments or small, overcrowded cellars or attics;

entire families often shared a single room — if they were lucky. In London and Europe's other big cities, extensive poverty often meant homelessness. People with temporary or no employment, including women and children, sometimes lived on the streets or relied on workhouses — state- or church-run shelters for the "tramping poor" where vagrants traded menial labor for a meal and a temporary place to sleep.

These highly concentrated urban populations lived in extremely unsanitary and unhealthy conditions. The sad state of urban sewage systems in London and elsewhere epitomized the problem. Before the mid-nineteenth century, human waste was typically deposited in chamber pots and tossed into the street with a warning shout, where rainwater carried it through open canals into local rivers. In densely populated urban areas, open drains and sewers flowed alongside or down the middle of unpaved streets. Waste was also collected in latrines that led to cesspools, underground pits located beneath living quarters. Cesspool cleaners, or "nightsoilmen," periodically emptied the pits, carting waste to designated dumpsites where it might be turned into fertilizer.

The rapid growth of cities across the nineteenth century overwhelmed these methods of sewage disposal. In an ironic twist, the popularization of a sanitation improvement — the flush toilet — spelled disaster for the cesspool. With each flush, a large volume of water

ATLANTIC OCEAN

North Sea

Black Sea

Mediterranean Sea

1800	1900
• City of 100,000 or more	•
● City of 500,000 or more	●
● City of 1,000,000 or more	●

MAPPING THE PAST

MAP 22.1 European Cities of 100,000 or More, 1800–1900

Urbanization proceeded rapidly in the nineteenth century. There were more large cities in Great Britain in 1900 than in all of Europe in 1800.

ANALYZING THE MAP Compare the spatial distribution of cities in 1800 with the distribution in 1900. Where in 1900 are large cities concentrated in clusters? What does their distribution tell us about the scale and location of industrialization in nineteenth-century Europe?

CONNECTIONS In 1800, what spatial characteristics typified large European cities? How many big cities, for example, were capitals or leading ports? Were these characteristics still shared by the large cities in 1900? What does the pattern of growth suggest about the reasons behind changes in urban topographies?

accompanied a small amount of waste, rapidly filling cesspools with liquid. Cesspool pits then leaked, spilling untreated sewage into waterways. As one historian put it, by the 1840s the better-off classes had come to the "shocking realization that millions of English men, women, and children were living in shit."[1] The results—unbearably odorous—were also deadly. Water polluted with the bacteria that cause cholera and typhoid seeped into drinking supplies, causing mass epidemics across Europe.

London, the largest city in the world at the time, was a perfect example. (See "Evaluating Written Evidence: First Impressions of the World's Biggest City," page 663.) As the population more than tripled from about 1.3 million in 1825 to 4.2 million in 1875, the sewage problem became catastrophic. Cesspools overflowed, and flush toilets installed in new buildings drained directly into the River Thames, the main source of drinking water for London residents. Over twenty thousand died in the cholera epidemics of

First Impressions of the World's Biggest City

In this anonymous, tongue-in-cheek passage, first published as a humorous sketch around 1870, a man from the country describes his first impressions of urban life. At that time London, with over 4 million inhabitants, was the largest city in the world.

A man's first residence in London is a revolution in his life and feelings. He loses at once no small part of his individuality. He was a man before, now he is a "party." No longer known as Mr. Brown, but as (say) No. XXI., he feels as one of many cogs in one of the many wheels of an incessantly wearing, tearing, grinding, system of machinery. His country notions must be modified, and all his life-long ways and takings-for-granted prove crude and questionable. He is hourly reminded "This is not the way in London; that this won't work here," or, "people always expect," and "you'll soon find the difference." . . .

Competition in London is very rife. The cheap five-shilling hatter was soon surprised by a four-and-nine-penny shop opposite. Few London men could live but by a degree of energy which the country dealer little knows. The wear and tear of nerve-power and the discharge of brain-power in London are enormous. The London man lives fast. . . .

Many other things contribute to make our new Londoner feel smaller in his own eyes. The living stream flows by him in the streets; he never saw so many utter strangers to him and to each other before; their very pace and destination are different; there is a walk and business determination distinctly London. In other towns men saunter they know not whither, but nearly every passer-by in London has his point, and is making so resolutely

towards it that it seems not more his way than his destination as he is carried on with the current; and of street currents there are two, to the City and from the City, so distinct and persistent, that our friend can't get out of one without being jostled by the other. . . .

Self-dependence is another habit peculiarly of London growth. Men soon discover they have no longer the friend, the relative or the neighbour of their own small town to fall back upon. . . .

No doubt there are warm friendships and intimacies in London as well as in the country, but few and far between. People associate more at arm's length, and give their hand more readily than their heart, and hug themselves within their own domestic circles. You know too little of people to be deeply interested either in them or their fortunes, so you expect nothing and are surprised at nothing. An acquaintance may depart London life, and even this life, or be sold up and disappear, without the same surprise or making the same gap as in a village circle.

EVALUATE THE EVIDENCE

1. What are the main differences, according to the author, between everyday life in the country and everyday life in the city?
2. Does this account of modern city life support or contradict the arguments of the new sociologists, discussed later in the chapter?
3. How would you describe the tone of this portrait of city life? How does the author use humor to engage the reader?

Source: Henry Mayhew et al., "Life in London," in *London Characters and the Humorous Side of London Life* (London: Chatto and Windus, 1881), pp. 277–281.

1832 and 1848–1849, and another eleven thousand perished of the same disease in 1854. Outbreaks of cholera swept across Europe and the globe with stunning frequency in the nineteenth century, killing hundreds of thousands. So many died in Poland that the word *cholera* became an obscene term, still used today as a curse word. As late as 1892, over 8,500 people died of the disease in the German port city of Hamburg.

The environmental costs of rapid urbanization and industrialization were enormous as well, and London again is a good example. Black soot from coal-fired factories and train engines fouled city air. The city experienced frequent and severe fogs, driven by industrial pollution, that could bring economic activity to

a complete halt. By 1850 the River Thames, which courses through London, was so polluted that it was biologically dead.

Who or what bore responsibility for these awful conditions? The crucial factors included the tremendous pressure of more people and the total absence of public transportation. People simply had to jam themselves together to get to shops and factories on foot. In addition, governments across Europe, both local and national, only slowly established sanitary facilities and adequate building codes. Finally, most people knew little about germs and basic hygiene. Ordinary folk rarely washed and took dirt for granted, habits that encouraged the spread of infectious disease.

The Public Health Movement

Around the middle of the nineteenth century, people's fatalistic acceptance of their overcrowded, unsanitary surroundings began to give way to a growing interest in reform and improvement. Events in London were again exemplary. British reformers such as Edwin Chadwick, John Snow, and Joseph Bazalgette engaged in a process of collaborative problem solving that helped initiate the public health movement. Chadwick, one of the commissioners charged with the administration of relief to paupers under Britain's revised Poor Law of 1834, emerged as a powerful voice for reform. Chadwick found inspiration in the ideas of radical philosopher Jeremy Bentham (1748–1832), whose approach to social issues, called **utilitarianism**, taught that public problems ought to be dealt with on a rational, scientific basis to advance the "greatest good for the greatest number." Applying these principles, Chadwick soon became convinced that disease and death actually caused poverty, because a sick worker was an unemployed worker and orphaned children were poor children. Most important, Chadwick believed that government should help prevent disease by cleaning up the urban environment.

Chadwick collected detailed reports from local Poor Law officials on the "sanitary conditions of the laboring population" and published his hard-hitting findings in 1842. Early reformers, including Chadwick, were seriously handicapped by their adherence to the prevailing miasmatic theory of disease—the belief that people contracted disease when they inhaled the bad odors of decay and putrefying excrement. Nonetheless, the mass of widely publicized evidence gathered in his report suggested that disease was related to filthy environmental conditions, which were in turn caused largely by lack of drainage, sewers, and garbage collection. In 1848, with the public health cause strengthened by a cholera epidemic that raged across Britain, Chadwick's report became the basis of Great Britain's first public health law, which created a national health board and gave cities broad authority to build modern sanitation systems.

The English physician John Snow encouraged further reform. Snow had doubts about the miasma theory, which were confirmed in his famous study of the 1854 Broad Street cholera outbreak that killed over six hundred people in central London. After interviewing local residents, Snow determined that the initial victims had all drunk water from a single well pump built next to an aging cesspool and that the disease had spread from this point. Although he was unaware of germ theory (see "The Bacterial Revolution" ahead), Snow did correctly identify putrid water as the cause and called on urban authorities to take action.

The work of Snow, Chadwick, and other early public health reformers was controversial. Many scientists clung to the miasma theory, and the London city government moved haltingly to implement reforms. The famous **"Great Stink"** of the summer of 1858, when noxious fumes from the River Thames closed Parliament and threatened to shut down the city, underscored the urgent need for change.

In response, between 1858 and 1865 the London Metropolitan Board of Works, led by engineer Joseph Bazalgette, built a massive network of new sewers. Bazalgette and his construction crews enclosed open waste canals and drained private toilets into underground channels that combined flows of rainwater and human waste. London's massive interception sewers now emptied sewage into irrigation fields and treatment plants rather than directly into the Thames. Inspired by London's example, urban engineers across Europe and North America built their own sewers and treatment plants, which limited the dumping of raw waste into local rivers, lakes, or seas.

Efforts to improve public health also targeted smallpox, a common, painful, and deadly disease that killed up to one-third of the people who developed the illness. Smallpox had been carried by European settlers to North America in the sixteenth century, where a devastating epidemic killed hundreds of thousands of Native Americans. The main weapon against smallpox was vaccination, pioneered in China in the 1500s. In the 1790s, English physician Edward Jenner developed an effective vaccine using cowpox, a relatively harmless disease in cattle. The government of the United Kingdom recognized his efforts and implemented a series of Vaccination Acts mandating that every child be vaccinated within four months of birth. The U.S. Congress likewise passed a Vaccine Act in 1813. The **U.K. Vaccination Acts**, however, proved divisive. In Britain, some people distrusted the efficacy of the vaccines; others rejected them for religious reasons. The Vaccine Act of 1898 allowed exemptions to conscientious objectors, but the widespread acceptance of smallpox vaccines eventually led to the near-eradication of the disease around the globe.

As the case of smallpox suggests, the public health movement won dedicated supporters in the United States, France, and Germany from the 1850s on. Governments accepted at least limited responsibility for the health of all citizens, and their reforms broke decisively with the age-old fatalism of urban leaders.

■ **utilitarianism** The idea of Jeremy Bentham that social policies should promote the "greatest good for the greatest number."

■ **"Great Stink"** In the summer of 1858 appalling fumes from the polluted River Thames threatened to shut down London, providing a boost to the emerging public health movement.

■ **U.K. Vaccination Acts** Legislation introduced in the United Kingdom during the nineteenth century requiring that all children be vaccinated against smallpox.

■ **germ theory** The idea that disease was caused by the spread of living organisms that could be controlled.

By the 1860s and 1870s European cities were making real progress toward adequate water supplies and sewer systems. Though factories and coal stoves continued to pump black smoke into the air and pollution remained a serious problem, death rates began to decline as city dwellers began to reap the rewards of government-supported health programs (Figure 22.1).

The Bacterial Revolution

Improved sanitation in cities promoted a better quality of life and some improvements in health care, but effective control of communicable disease required a great leap forward in medical knowledge and biological theory. Although keen observation by doctors and public health officials pinpointed the role of filth and bad drinking water in the transmission of disease, thus weakening the miasmatic idea, they had little idea of how the process actually made people sick.

The breakthrough arrived when the French chemist Louis Pasteur developed the **germ theory** of disease, which finally convinced city officials to institute thorough public sanitation programs. Pasteur (pas-TUHR) (1822–1895), who began studying alcoholic fermentation in 1854, used a microscope to develop a simple test that beer and wine brewers could use to monitor the fermentation process and avoid spoilage. He found that fermentation depended on the growth of living organisms and that the activity of these organisms could be suppressed by heating the beverage—a process that came to be called pasteurization, which he first implemented in the early 1860s. The breathtaking implication of this discovery was that specific diseases were caused by specific living organisms—germs—and that those organisms could be controlled.

By 1870 the microbiological work of Pasteur and others had demonstrated the general connection between germs and disease. When, in the middle of the 1870s, German country doctor Robert Koch (kawkh) and his coworkers developed pure cultures of harmful bacteria and described their life cycles, the dam broke. Over the next twenty years, researchers—mainly Germans—identified the organisms responsible for disease after disease. These discoveries led to the development of effective vaccines, though some infections resisted treatment until scientists developed antibiotics in the middle of the next century.

Acceptance of germ theory brought about dramatic improvements in the deadly environment of hospitals and operating rooms. In 1865, when Pasteur showed that the air was full of bacteria, English surgeon Joseph Lister (1827–1912) immediately grasped the connection between aerial bacteria and the problem of wound infection. He reasoned that a chemical disinfectant applied to a wound dressing would "destroy the life of the floating particles" (or germs). Lister's antiseptic

TRIUMPH OF DE-JENNER-ATION.

[The Bill for the encouragement of Small Pox was passed.]

The Fight over Smallpox Vaccines Effective vaccines against smallpox, once a deadly killer, were introduced in Europe and North America in the early nineteenth century. In the United Kingdom, a series of Vaccination Acts made vaccines against the disease mandatory, which led to a popular backlash. The 1898 Vaccination Act included an exception clause for conscientious objectors, and some 250,000 people pursued that option in the first year alone. This 1898 cartoon from *Punch*, an English magazine famous for its satirical approach to current issues, criticized what it called the "De-Jenner-ation" campaign of those who opposed the vaccine—a play on the name of Dr. Edward Jenner, who pioneered the smallpox vaccine. (Historical Images Archive/Alamy)

principle worked wonders. In the 1880s German surgeons developed the more sophisticated practice of sterilizing not only the wound but also everything—hands, instruments, clothing—that entered the operating room. The simple practice of washing hands before birthing procedures saved the lives of countless mothers.

The professionalization of public health and the spread of Western medical knowledge around the world went hand in hand, in a process that often overlapped with colonialism and Christian missions. By the close of the nineteenth century, medicine had become a key tool for Protestant missionaries, as well as a way that Western nations like Britain

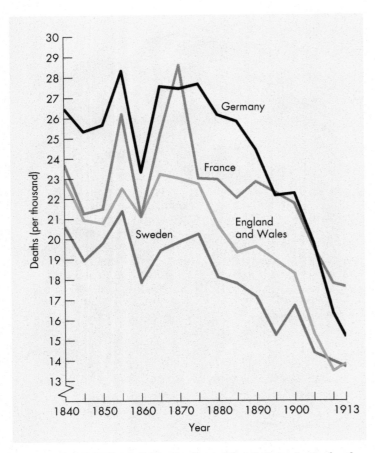

FIGURE 22.1 The Decline of Death Rates in England and Wales, Germany, France, and Sweden, 1840–1913 A rising standard of living, improvements in public health, and better medical knowledge all contributed to the dramatic decline of death rates in the nineteenth century.

could demonstrate that they took care of their colonial subjects. Providing much of the energy for these trends were the growing ranks of educated women who sought career and service opportunities abroad. As medical education opened for women in both England and India, medical work provided British women with fulfilling careers in networks of like-minded individuals.

The bacterial revolution and the public health movement saved millions of lives, particularly after about 1880. Mortality rates began to decline dramatically in European countries (see Figure 22.1) as the awful death sentences of the past—cholera, diphtheria, typhoid, typhus, yellow fever—became vanishing diseases. City dwellers in Europe especially benefited from these developments. By 1910 a great silent revolution had occurred: the death rates for people of all ages in Western urban areas were generally no greater than those for people in rural areas, and sometimes they were lower.

Improvements in Urban Planning

More effective planning was also an important key to unlocking a better quality of urban life. France took the lead during the rule of Napoleon III (r. 1848–1870), who used government action to promote the welfare of his subjects. Napoleon III believed that rebuilding much of Paris would provide employment, improve living conditions, limit the outbreak of cholera epidemics—and testify to the power and glory of his empire. He hired Baron Georges Haussmann (HOWS-muhn) (1809–1884), an aggressive, impatient Alsatian, to modernize the city. An authoritarian manager and capable city planner, Haussmann bulldozed both buildings and opposition. In twenty years Paris was completely transformed (Map 22.2).

The Paris of 1850 was a labyrinth of narrow, dark streets, the results of desperate overcrowding and a lack of effective planning. More than one-third of the city's 1 million inhabitants lived in a central district not twice the size of New York's Central Park. Residents suffered terrible conditions and extremely high death rates. The entire metropolis had few open spaces and only two public parks.

For two decades Haussmann and his fellow planners proceeded on many fronts. With a bold energy that often shocked their contemporaries, they razed old buildings in order to cut broad, straight, tree-lined boulevards through the center of the city as well as in new quarters rising on the outskirts (see Map 22.2). These boulevards, designed in part to prevent revolutionary crowds from throwing up defensive barricades, permitted traffic to flow freely and afforded impressive vistas. Their creation demolished some of the worst slums and stimulated the construction of better housing. In what would become a familiar process, urban renewal forced poorer Parisians from their homes and made way for fashionable apartment buildings for upper-class residents. Planners created small neighborhood parks and open spaces throughout the city and developed two very large parks suitable for all kinds of holiday activities—one on the affluent west side and one on the poor east side. The city improved its sewers, and a system of aqueducts more than doubled the city's supply of clean, fresh water.

Urban planners in cities such as Vienna and Cologne followed the Parisian example of tearing down old walled fortifications and replacing them with broad, circular boulevards on which they erected office buildings, town halls, theaters, opera houses, and museums. These ring roads and the new boulevards that radiated outward from the city center eased movement and encouraged urban expansion (see Map 22.2).

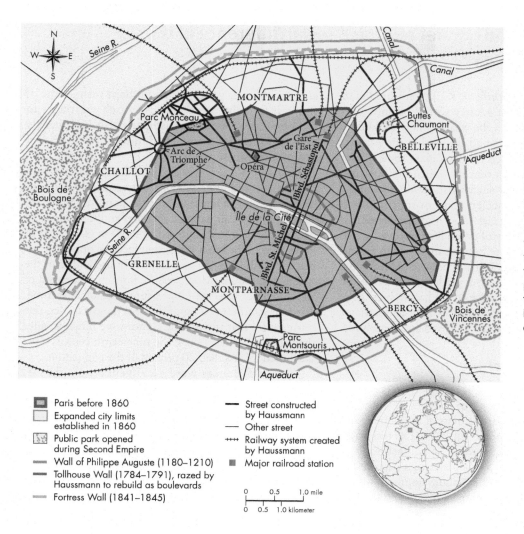

MAP 22.2 The Modernization of Paris, ca. 1850–1870 The addition of broad boulevards, large parks, and grand train stations transformed Paris. The cutting of the new north-south axis — known as the Boulevard Saint-Michel — was one of Haussmann's most controversial projects. His plan razed much of Paris's medieval core and filled the Île de la Cité with massive government buildings. Note the addition of new streets and light rail systems (the basis of the current Parisian subway system, the "metro") that encircle the city core, emblematic of the public transportation revolution that enhanced living conditions in nineteenth-century European cities.

Paris before 1860

Expanded city limits established in 1860

Public park opened during Second Empire

Wall of Philippe Auguste (1180–1210)

Tollhouse Wall (1784–1791), razed by Haussmann to rebuild as boulevards

Fortress Wall (1841–1845)

Street constructed by Haussmann

Other street

Railway system created by Haussmann

Major railroad station

Public Transportation

The development of mass public transportation often accompanied urban planning. In the 1870s many European cities authorized private companies to operate horse-drawn streetcars, which had been developed in the United States, to carry riders along the growing number of major thoroughfares. The world's first electric-powered streetcar, running on iron tracks, opened for use in Berlin in 1881; by the 1890s these streetcars were commonplace in Europe and North America.

Electric streetcars were cheaper, faster, more dependable, cleaner, and more comfortable than their horse-drawn counterparts. Workers, shoppers, and schoolchildren hopped on board during the work-week. On weekends and holidays, streetcars carried urban dwellers on happy outings to parks and the countryside, to racetracks and music halls. In 1886 the horse-drawn streetcars of Austria-Hungary, France, Germany, and Great Britain carried about 900 million riders per year. By 1910 electric streetcar systems in those four countries were carrying 6.7 billion riders annually.[2]

Mass transit encouraged the development of decent housing. The new boulevards and horse-drawn streetcars facilitated a middle-class move to better and more spacious housing in the 1860s and 1870s; after 1890 electric streetcars meant people of even modest means could access new, improved housing. Though still densely populated, cities expanded and became less congested. In England in 1901, only 9 percent of the urban population was overcrowded in terms of the official definition of more than two persons per room. On the continent, many city governments in the early twentieth century built electric streetcar and light rail systems to provide transportation for the growing number of workers who lived in the new public and private housing developments built beyond the city limits. Suburban commuting was born.

How did class and gender reinforce social difference in the nineteenth century?

In *The Communist Manifesto*, Karl Marx predicted that modern capitalist society would be split into "two great hostile camps": the wealthy, powerful bourgeoisie and the impoverished, miserable proletariat. Like Marx, historians see modern class society as a product of the nineteenth century, which built on, but also transformed, earlier social distinctions based on orders and estates. But society did not split into two sharply defined opposing classes, as Marx predicted. To the contrary, as the quality of urban life improved across Europe, the class structure became more complex and diverse. The gap between rich and poor remained enormous, but there were numerous gradations between the extremes. And all along these social hierarchies, gender differences between men and women had a major impact on the way class status was lived and perceived.

The Distribution of Income

By 1850 at the latest, real wages—that is, wages received by workers adjusted for changes in the prices they paid—were rising for the mass of the population, and they continued to do so until 1914. The real wages of British male workers, for example, almost doubled between 1850 and 1906. Similar increases occurred in continental countries as industrial development quickened after 1850. This represented a major step forward in the centuries-old battle against poverty, reinforcing efforts to improve many aspects of human existence. At the same time, as women (and children) entered the industrial workforce, a lasting income gap emerged. Women worked in less desirable, poorly paid jobs, rarely held supervisory positions, and received less pay than men even when they did the same work.

Greater economic rewards for the average person hardly eliminated hardship and poverty, nor did it shrink the gap between the rich and the poor. The aristocracy—with imposing family wealth, unrivaled social prestige, and substantial political influence—retained its position at the very top of the ladder, followed closely by a new rich elite composed mainly of the most successful business families from banking, industry, and large-scale commerce. In fact, the prominent families of the commercial elite tended to marry into the old aristocracy, to form a new upper class of at most 5 percent of the population.

Much of the aristocracy welcomed this development. Having experienced a sharp decline in its relative income in the course of industrialization, the landed aristocracy eagerly allied with big business and was often delighted to trade titles, country homes,

and snobbish elegance for good, hard cash. Some of the best bargains were made through marriages to U.S. heiresses. Wealthy aristocrats also increasingly exploited their agricultural and mineral resources as if they were business people.

Income inequality was closely linked to social status. In almost every advanced country around 1900, the richest 5 percent of all households in the population received about a third of all national income, and the richest 20 percent of households received from 50 to 60 percent of it. As a result, the lower 80 percent received only 40 to 50 percent of all income—far less per household than the two richest groups. Moreover, the bottom 30 percent of all households received 10 percent or less of all income. To understand the full significance of these statistics, one must realize that the middle classes were much smaller than they are today. Across the nineteenth century they accounted for less than 20 percent of the population.

Class differences were also "gendered"; that is, being a man or a woman had a significant impact on earnings and employment. In wealthy families, women rarely had to seek paid employment. As the nineteenth century progressed, women in the middle classes fought for and increasingly found work in professions such as teaching, social work, and nursing. Poorer women took a variety of jobs, ranging from factory labor to domestic service; single poor women were generally at the bottom of all income earners.

The great gap between rich and poor endured, in part, because industrial and urban development made society more diverse and classes less unified. There developed an almost unlimited range of jobs, skills, and earnings; one group blended into another in a complex, confusing hierarchy. Between the tiny elite of the very rich and the sizable mass of the dreadfully poor lived a range of subclasses, each filled with individuals struggling to rise or at least to hold their own in the social order. (See "Evaluating Visual Evidence: Apartment Living in Paris," page 669.) In this atmosphere of competition and hierarchy, neither the "middle class" nor the "working class" actually acted as a single unified force. It makes more sense to speak of the "middle classes" and "working classes."

The People and Occupations of the Middle Classes

The variations within the urban middle classes were striking. Below the top tier whose riches were based on land and title, the larger, much less wealthy, and increasingly diversified middle classes engaged in

Apartment Living in Paris

Marx had predicted that modern society would lead to the development of two great, unequal classes. By 1850, however, although the gap between rich and poor was firmly in place, subtle distinctions of income and status had split Europeans into a number of new social groups. This satirical cartoon shows a cutaway view of a city apartment in Paris around 1850. The artist has taken great care to present detailed if stereotypical portrayals of the various residents, and his drawing captures the characteristic organization of apartment living space in modern cities across the continent. On the ground floor lived servants and the building supervisor. Moving up the stairs, floor by floor, we travel the distance between extreme wealth and wretched poverty. In a striking contrast to our own time, in mid-nineteenth-century Paris rich and poor lived in the same building.

EVALUATE THE EVIDENCE

1. Take a close look at the inhabitants of each floor, at their possessions and behaviors. Can you determine the class and/or status of the residents? How does gender play a role in constructing class?
2. Who owns what? Can an analysis of household goods help reveal the class status of the various residents?
3. How is social status coded in living space? Who, for example, lives on the top two floors, and why do you think they would be up there?

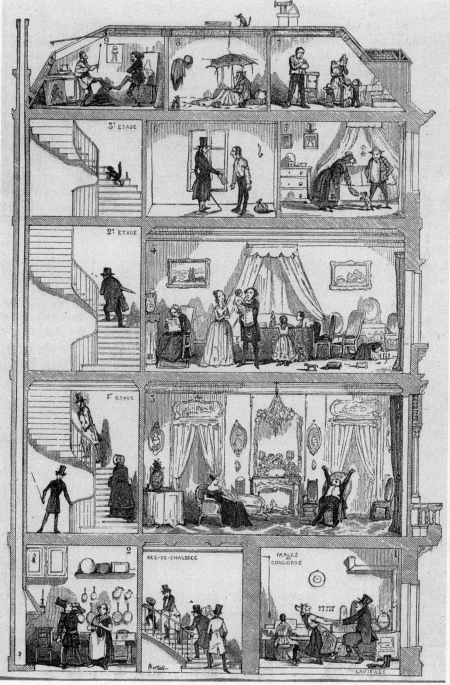

(akg-images)

occupations requiring mental, rather than physical, skill. This group engaged in a wide range of occupations.

As industry and technology expanded, a number of skilled trades and occupations underwent a process historians call **professionalization**. Attorneys, professors, architects, chemists, accountants, and surveyors, to name only a few, established criteria for training and certification, including advanced degrees, and banded together in organizations to promote and defend their interests. The new professions were almost entirely dominated by men, and their specialized knowledge—and professional credentials—bolstered their wages and social standing. Professionalization limited the ability of amateurs and outsiders, and in most cases women, who lacked access to higher education, from working in the field. Engineering and medicine, for example, emerged as full-fledged professions with considerable power, prestige, and privilege. Dentistry was taken out of the hands of working-class barbers and placed in the hands of highly trained middle-class professionals. As governments grew and provided more services, and very large corporations (such as railroads or arms manufacturers) controlled ever-larger numbers of human and physical resources, middle-class male professionals also found jobs as managers in large public and private institutions.

Industrialization expanded and diversified the lower middle class as well, and opportunities grew for women as well as men in the service sector—the proliferating jobs in commerce, government, and business that were neither strictly agricultural nor industrial. The number of independent, property-owning male shopkeepers and small business people grew, as did the number of white-collar employees—a mixed group of traveling salesmen, bookkeepers, store managers, and clerks who staffed the offices and branch stores of large corporations. Women took jobs as shop assistants, department store sales staff, and low-level typists and clerical workers in fast-growing businesses.

Both male and female white-collar employees owned little property and often earned no more than better-paid skilled or semiskilled workers. Yet white-collar workers were fiercely committed to the middle-class ideal of upward social mobility. The business clothes and the soft clean hands that accompanied low-level retail and managerial work became important status symbols that set this group above those who made a living through manual labor. For women, white-collar positions offered a way to earn both money and independence outside the home, loosening former restrictions on employment and social mobility.

Many middle-class women accepted the ideologies of "separate spheres" (see "Separate Spheres and the Importance of Homemaking" later in this chapter) and preferred to expend their energies shaping a comfortable home life, but some struggled to break into the world of professional training and employment. In the second half of the nineteenth century they made important although limited gains. Charity and social work allowed women to break into the professional world. Privileged women increasingly found volunteer and paid employment in public workhouses, prisons, schools, and hospitals, where their supposedly "natural" inclinations for motherly nurturing might help alleviate the plight of the poor.

Women also sought access to higher education. With the great expansion of public education and health systems, many entered teaching or nursing schools, and women came to predominate in these low-paid professions. By 1911 in England, for example, 77,000 women worked as nurses and 183,298 women were employed as teachers, about 73 percent of the total.[3] Nursing and teaching, like social work, were considered appropriate for women.

The battle to enter new, modern universities and earn professional degrees was more difficult, but by 1900 most major European universities had accepted at least a handful of female students. Women such as the Polish-French scientist Marie Curie, whose pathbreaking work on radioactivity earned a Nobel Prize, or the German physician Franziska Tiburtius, who opened a clinic for women factory workers in Berlin, made pioneering inroads into professions previously reserved for men. (See "Individuals in Society: Franziska Tiburtius," page 671.)

The People and Occupations of the Working Classes

At the beginning of the twentieth century, about four out of five people belonged to the working classes—that is, people whose livelihoods depended primarily on physical labor and who did not employ domestic servants. Many of them were still small landowning peasants and hired farm hands, especially in eastern Europe. In western and central Europe, however, the typical worker had left the land. By 1900 less than 8 percent of the people in Great Britain worked in agriculture, and in rapidly industrializing Germany only 25 percent were employed in agriculture and forestry. Even in less industrialized France, under 50 percent of the population worked the land.

Urban workers were as heterogeneous as the middle classes. Economic development and increased specialization expanded the traditional range of working-class skills, earnings, and experiences. Meanwhile, the sharp distinction between skilled artisans and unskilled manual workers gradually broke down. To be sure, highly

■ **professionalization** The process in which members of skilled trades and occupations established criteria for training and certification and banded together in professional organizations to defend their interests.

INDIVIDUALS IN SOCIETY

Franziska Tiburtius

Why did a small number of women in the late nineteenth century brave great odds and embark on professional careers? And how did a few of them manage to reach their objectives? The career and personal reflections of Franziska Tiburtius (tigh-bur-TEE-uhs), a pioneer in German medicine, suggest that talent, determination, and economic necessity were critical ingredients to both the attempt and the success.*

Like many women of her time who studied and pursued professional careers, Franziska Tiburtius (1843–1927) was born into a property-owning family of modest means. The youngest of nine children growing up on a small estate in northeastern Germany, the sensitive child wilted under a harsh governess but flowered with a caring teacher and became an excellent student. Graduating at sixteen and needing to support herself, Tiburtius had few opportunities. A young woman from a "proper" background could work as a governess or teacher without losing her respectability and spoiling her matrimonial prospects, but that was about it. She tried both avenues. Working for six years as a governess in a noble family and no doubt learning that poverty was often one's fate in this genteel profession, she then turned to teaching. Called home from her studies in Britain in 1871 to care for her brother, who had contracted typhus as a field doctor in the Franco-Prussian War, she found her calling. She decided to become a physician.

Supported by her family, Tiburtius's decision was truly audacious. In all Europe, only the University of Zurich accepted female students to advanced degree programs. Moreover, if it became known that she had studied medicine and failed, she would probably never get a job as a teacher. No parent would entrust a daughter to an emancipated radical who had carved up dead bodies. Although the male students at the university sometimes harassed the female ones with crude pranks, Tiburtius thrived. The revolution of the microscope and the discovery of microorganisms thrilled Tiburtius, and she was fascinated by her studies. She became close friends with a fellow female student from Germany, Emilie Lehmus, with whom she would form a lifelong partnership in medicine.

Graduating at age thirty-three in 1876, Tiburtius went to stay with her doctor brother in Berlin. Though well qualified to practice, she was blocked by pervasive discrimination. Not permitted to take the state medical exams, she could practice only as an unregulated (and formally nonprofessional) "natural healer." But after persistent fighting with city bureaucrats, she was able to display her diploma and practice as "Franziska Tiburtius, M.D., University of Zurich."

Franziska Tiburtius, pioneering woman physician in Berlin. (akg-images/Newscom)

Soon Tiburtius and Lehmus realized their dream and opened a clinic. Subsidized by a wealthy industrialist, they focused on treating women factory workers. The clinic filled a great need and was soon treating many patients. A room with beds for extremely sick women was later expanded into a second clinic.

Tiburtius and Lehmus became famous. For fifteen years, they were the only female doctors in all of Berlin and inspired a new generation of women. Though they added wealthy patients to their thriving practice, they always concentrated on the poor, providing them with subsidized and up-to-date treatment. Talented, determined, and working with her partner, Tiburtius experienced fully the joys of personal achievement and useful service. Above all, she overcame the tremendous barriers raised up against women seeking higher education and professional careers, providing an inspiring model for those who dared to follow.

QUESTIONS FOR ANALYSIS

1. Analyze Franziska Tiburtius's life. What lessons do you draw from it? How do you account for her bold action and success?
2. In what ways was Tiburtius's career related to improvements in health in urban society and to the expansion of the professions?

*Information from Conradine Lück, *Frauen: Neun Lebensschicksale* (Reutlingen: Ensslin & Laiblin, n.d.), pp. 153–185.

skilled printers and masons as well as unskilled dock-workers and common laborers continued to exist. But between these extremes there appeared ever more semi-skilled groups, including trained factory workers. Skilled, semiskilled, and unskilled workers developed divergent lifestyles and cultural values, and unlike the homemak-ers in middle-class families, many working-class women had to find paid employment to keep their families afloat, furthering the great diversity at the lower levels of society. These differences contributed to a keen sense of social status and hierarchy within the working classes, undermining the class unity predicted by Marx.

Highly skilled male workers—about 15 percent of the working classes—were later labeled the **labor aristocracy**. They earned only about two-thirds of the income of the bottom ranks of the servant-keeping classes, but that was fully double the earnings of unskilled workers. The most "aristocratic" of these highly skilled workers were construction bosses and factory foremen, who had risen from the ranks and were fiercely proud of their achievement. The labor aristocracy included mem-bers of the traditional highly skilled handicraft trades that had not been mechanized or placed in factories, like cabinetmakers, jewelers, and printers.

While the labor aristocracy enjoyed its exalted position, maintaining that status was by no means certain. Gradually, as factory production eliminated more and more crafts, lower-paid, semiskilled factory workers replaced many skilled artisans. Traditional wood-carvers and watchmakers virtually disappeared, for example, as the making of furniture and time-pieces now took place in factories. At the same time, industrialization opened new opportunities for new kinds of highly skilled workers, such as shipbuilders and railway locomotive engineers. Thus the labor elite remained in a state of flux, as individuals and whole crafts moved up and down the social scale.

To maintain their precarious standing, the upper working class adopted distinctive values and strait-laced, almost puritanical behavior. Like the middle classes, many members of the labor aristocracy believed firmly in Christian morality and economic improve-ment. They saved money regularly, worried about their children's education, and valued good housing. Wives seldom sought employment outside the home. They practiced stern self-discipline and generally frowned on heavy drinking and sexual permissiveness, believing that they set a model for the rest of the working classes. As one German skilled worker somberly warned, "The path to the brothel leads through the tavern" and from there to drastic decline or total ruin.[4]

Below the labor aristocracy stood the enormously complex world of hard work, composed of both semiskilled and unskilled workers, men and women. Established male construction workers—carpenters, bricklayers, pipe fitters—stood near the top of the semiskilled hierarchy, often flirting with (or sliding back from) the labor elite. A large number of the semi-skilled were factory workers, who earned highly vari-able but relatively good wages. These workers included substantial numbers of unmarried women, who began to play an increasingly important role in the industrial labor force.

Below the semiskilled workers, a larger group of unskilled workers included day laborers, mostly men, such as longshoremen, wagon-driving teamsters, and "helpers" of all kinds. Many of these people had real skills and performed valuable services, but they were unorganized and divided, united only by the common fate of meager earnings and poor living conditions. The same lack of unity characterized male and female street vendors and market people—these self-em-ployed members of the lower working classes com-peted savagely with each other and with established shopkeepers of the lower middle class.

Working-class women labored in factories and as street vendors, but by far the largest number of unskilled women worked as domestic servants, whose numbers grew steadily in the nineteenth century. In Great Britain, for example, one out of every seven employed persons in 1911 was a domestic servant. The great majority were women; indeed, one out of every three girls in Britain between the ages of fifteen and twenty worked as a domestic servant. Through-out Europe, many female domestics in the cities were recent migrants from rural areas. As in earlier times, domestic service meant hard work at low pay with limited personal independence and the danger of sex-ual exploitation. For the full-time general maid in a lower-middle-class family, an unending routine of babysitting, shopping, cooking, and cleaning defined a lengthy working day. In the wealthiest households, the serving girl was at the bottom of a rigid hierarchy of status-conscious butlers and housekeepers.

Nonetheless, domestic service had real attractions for young women from rural areas who had few spe-cialized skills. Marriage prospects were better, or at least more varied, in the city than back home. And though wages were low, they were higher and more regular than in hard agricultural work—which was being replaced by mechanization, at any rate. Finally, as one London observer noted, young girls and other migrants from the countryside were drawn to the city by "the contagion of numbers, the sense of something going on, the theaters and the music halls, the brightly lighted streets and busy crowds—all, in short, that makes the difference between the Mile End fair on a

■ **labor aristocracy** The highly skilled workers, such as factory foremen and construction bosses, who made up about 15 percent of the working classes from about 1850 to 1914.

■ **sweated industries** Poorly paid handicraft production, often carried out by married women paid by the piece and working at home.

Saturday night, and a dark and muddy country lane, with no glimmer of gas and with nothing to do."[5]

Some young domestics made the successful transition to working-class wife and mother. Yet with an unskilled or unemployed husband, a growing family, and limited household income, many working-class wives had to join the broad ranks of working women in the **sweated industries**. These industries expanded rapidly after 1850 and resembled the old putting-out and cottage industries of earlier times. The women normally worked at home and were paid by the piece, not by the hour. They and their young children who helped them earned pitiful wages and lacked any job security. Women decorated dishes or embroidered linens, took in laundry for washing and ironing, or made clothing, especially after the popularization of the sewing machine in the 1860s. An army of poor women, usually working at home, accounted for many of the inexpensive ready-made clothes displayed on department store racks and in tiny shops.

Prostitution

In the late nineteenth century prostitution was legal in much of Europe, offering another means of employment for lower-class women hard-pressed to find better-paying jobs in domestic service or factories. In Italy, France, Great Britain, and much of Germany, the state licensed brothels and registered individual prostitutes, and they were a ubiquitous public presence. In Paris, 155,000 women were registered as prostitutes between 1871 and 1903, and 750,000 others were suspected of prostitution in the same years. In Berlin, in 1909 alone, the authorities registered over 40,000 prostitutes. The totals are probably low, since most women in the sex trade tried to avoid government regulation.

In streets, dance halls, and pubs across Europe, working-class women used prostitution as a source of second income or as a way to weather a period of joblessness, in a working environment with few other options. Their clients were generally lower-class men, soldiers, and sailors, though middle- and upper-class men also paid for sexual encounters. In some places, particularly Germany, visits to prostitutes were rites of passage formalized in the culture of student fraternities. Prostitution offered women some measure of financial independence, but the work was dangerous. Violence and rape, police harassment, and venereal disease were commonplace hazards.

Prostitutes clearly transgressed middle-class ideals of feminine respectability, but among the working classes prostitution was tolerated as more or less acceptable work of a temporary nature. Like domestic service, prostitution was a stage of life, not permanent employment. After working as prostitutes in their youth, many women went on to marry and build homes and families.

As middle-class family values became increasingly prominent after the 1860s, prostitution generated great concern among social reformers. The prostitute—perceived as immoral, lascivious, and unhealthy—served as the dark mirror image of the respectable middle-class woman. Authorities blamed prostitutes for spreading crime and disease, particularly syphilis. Before the discovery of penicillin, syphilis was indeed a widespread and terrifying affliction. Its painful symptoms led to physical and mental disorder and often death. Medical treatment was expensive, painful, and slow. It required access to regular health care and was, for the most part, ineffective.

As general concerns with public health gained recognition, state and city authorities across Europe subjected prostitutes to increased surveillance. Under the British Contagious Diseases Acts, in force between 1864 and 1886, special plainclothes policemen required women identified as "common prostitutes" to undergo biweekly medical exams. If they showed signs of venereal disease, they were interned in a "lock hospital" and forced to undergo treatment; when the outward signs of disease went away, they were released.

The Contagious Diseases Acts were controversial from the start. A determined middle-class feminist campaign against the policy, led by feminist Josephine Butler and the Ladies National Association, loudly proclaimed that the acts physically abused poor women, violated their constitutional rights, and legitimized male vice. Under pressure, Parliament repealed the laws in 1886. Yet heavy-handed government regulation had devastated the informality of working-class prostitution. Now branded as "registered girls," prostitutes experienced new forms of public humiliation. Once registered, it was difficult to return to respectable employment, and the trade was increasingly controlled by male pimps rather than by the women themselves. Prostitution had never been safe, but it had been more or less accepted, at least among the working classes. Prostitutes were now stigmatized as social and sexual outsiders.

The Leisure Pursuits of the Working Classes

Notwithstanding hard physical labor and lack of wealth, the urban working classes sought fun and recreation, and they found both. Across Europe, drinking remained the favorite leisure-time activity of working-class men. For many middle-class moralists, as well as moralizing historians since, love of drink was the curse of the modern age—a sign of social dislocation and popular suffering.

Generally, however, heavy problem drinking declined in the late nineteenth century as it became

La Goulue at the Moulin Rouge   Industrialization and urban development made leisure time available to more and more people of all classes, and nighttime entertainment such as dance balls, theater performance, and dining out became increasingly popular. This famous advertising poster (left) by the French artist Henri de Toulouse-Lautrec from 1891 shows "La Goulue" (la GO-luh) and her partner dancing the cancan at the Moulin Rouge (right), a famous Parisian cabaret (nightclub) in the seedy neighborhood of Montmartre. The cancan was a fast and provocative dance that involved rapid dips and turns, as well as high kicks that revealed the performers' stockings and frilly underwear. La Goulue — "the glutton" — was the stage name of local star Louise Weber, who enjoyed grabbing and guzzling down customers' drinks during her performances. (poster: The Picture Art Collection/ Alamy; photo: PRISMATIC PICTURES/Private Collection/Bridgeman Images)

less socially acceptable. This decline reflected in part the moral leadership of the labor aristocracy. Drinking also became more publicly acceptable. Cafés and pubs became increasingly bright, friendly places. Working-class political activities, both moderate and radical, were also concentrated in taverns and pubs. Moreover, social drinking in public places by married couples and sweethearts became an accepted and widespread practice for the first time. This greater participation by women undoubtedly helped civilize the world of drink and hard liquor.

Workers passionately embraced sports and music halls. "Cruel sports," such as bullbaiting and cockfighting, still popular in the middle of the century, had greatly declined throughout Europe by the 1880s. Commercialized spectator sports filled their place; horse racing and soccer were the most

popular. Working people gambled on sports events, and a desire to decipher racing forms provided a powerful incentive toward literacy. Music halls and vaudeville theaters were enormously popular throughout Europe. In 1900 London had more than fifty such halls and theaters. Music hall audiences included men and women, which may account for the fact that drunkenness, premarital sex, marital difficulties, and mothers-in-law were all favorite themes of coarse jokes and bittersweet songs.

Faith and Religion

In more serious moments, religion continued to provide working people with solace and meaning. The eighteenth-century vitality of popular religion in Catholic countries and the Protestant

Rat Catching at the Blue Anchor Tavern   Although antivivisectionist reform groups successfully pressured city and state authorities to ban many forms of cruelty to animals, the sport of "ratting" continued to attract working- and middle-class crowds in England well into the nineteenth century. In this 1852 painting, an all-male crowd at the Blue Anchor Tavern lays bets on Tiny, a trained Manchester terrier, as he tries to kill two hundred rats in a single hour. Because they saw rats as verminous pests that brought filth and disease into Europe's rapidly growing cities, the authorities tolerated rat killing for sport, a pastime that was a throw-back to the inhumane bullbaiting and cockfighting popular in the early modern era (see "Leisure and Recreation" in Chapter 18). (Museum of London/Heritage Images/Hulton Archive/Getty Images)

rejuvenation exemplified by German Pietism and English Methodism (see "What role did religion play in eighteenth-century society?" in Chapter 18) carried over into the nineteenth century. Indeed, many historians see the early nineteenth century as an age of religious revival. The second half of the century likewise saw an upswing in popular faith, embodied in the new religions and institutions that emerged: Theosophy, Seventh-Day Adventism, spiritualism, Christian Science, the Salvation Army. Religious revivals were a working-class sensation, and many grew attached to the fervid Marian devotions, in which prayers called on Jesus's mother Mary to intercede with God on behalf of the believer. In addition, the first mosques were being built in Britain and western Europe, and Jewish migration from eastern Europe was fast diversifying established Jewish populations.

Yet historians also recognize that by the last few decades of the nineteenth century, both church attendance and church donations had declined in most European countries, particularly in big cities. And it seems clear that this decline was greater for the urban working classes than for their rural counterparts or for the middle classes.

Why did working-class church attendance decline? On one hand, the construction of churches failed to keep up with the rapid growth of the urban population, especially in new working-class neighborhoods. On the other, throughout the nineteenth century workers saw Catholic and Protestant churches as conservative institutions that defended status quo politics, hierarchical social order, and middle-class morality. Socialist political parties, in particular, attacked organized religion as a pillar of bourgeois society; as workers became more politically conscious, they tended to see established churches as allied with their political opponents. In addition, religion underwent a process historians call "feminization": in the working and middle classes alike, women were more pious and attended service more regularly than men. Urban workingmen in particular developed vaguely antichurch attitudes, even though they might remain neutral or positive toward God and religion itself.

The pattern was different in the United States, where most nineteenth-century churches also preached social conservatism. But because church and state had always been separate and because a host of denominations and even different religions competed for members, working people identified churches much less with the political and social status quo. Instead, individual churches in the United States were often closely identified with an ethnic group rather than a social class, and churches thrived, in part, as a means of asserting ethnic identity. This same process occurred in Europe if the church or synagogue had never been linked to the state and served as a focus for ethnic cohesion. Irish Catholic churches in Protestant Britain, Catholic churches in partitioned Polish lands, and Jewish synagogues in Russia were prominent examples.

How did urbanization affect family life and gender roles?

Buffeted by the results of industrialization and urbanization, the nineteenth-century middle classes invented a distinctive middle-class lifestyle that set them off from peasants, workers, and the aristocracy. New ideas about marriage, family, home-making, and child rearing would have a profound impact on family life in the century to come. Leading a middle-class lifestyle was prohibitively expensive for workers and peasants, and middle-class family values at first had little relevance for their lives. Yet as the nineteenth century drew to a close, the middle-class lifestyle increasingly became the norm for all classes.

Lifestyles of the Middle Classes

Despite growing occupational diversity and conflicting interests, lifestyle preferences loosely united the European middle classes. Shared tastes for food, housing, clothes, and behavior helped define the middle classes as a group apart from the average worker, who could hardly afford such delicacies. The employment of at least one full-time maid to cook and clean was the clearest sign that a family had crossed the cultural divide separating the working classes from the "servant-keeping classes." The greater a family's income, the greater the number of servants it employed.

Unlike workers, middle-class men and women had the money to eat well, and they spent a substantial portion of their household budget on food and entertainment. They consumed meat in abundance: a well-off family might spend 10 percent of its annual income on meat and fully 25 percent on food and drink. The dinner party—a favored social occasion—boosted spending.

Well fed and well served, by 1900 the middle classes were also well housed. And, just as the aristocracy had long divided the year between palatial country estates and lavish townhouses during "the season," so the upper middle class purchased country homes or built beach houses for weekend and summer use.

The middle classes paid great attention to outward appearances, especially their clothes. The factory, the sewing machine, and the department store had all helped reduce the cost and expand the variety of clothing. Private coaches and carriages, expensive items in the city, further testified to rising social status. Middle-class families could devote more time to "culture" and leisure pursuits than less wealthy or well-established families could, including books,

music, and travel. The long Realist novel, the heroic operas of Wagner and Verdi, the diligent striving of the dutiful daughter at the piano, and the packaged tour to a foreign country were all sources of middle-class pleasure.

In addition to their material tastes, the middle classes generally agreed upon a strict code of manners and morality. They stressed hard work, self-discipline, and personal achievement. Reformers denounced drunkenness and gambling as vices and celebrated sexual purity and fidelity as virtues, especially for women. A stern sense of Christian morals, preached tirelessly by religious leaders, educators, and politicians, reaffirmed these values. Those who fell into vice, crime, or poverty were held responsible for their own circumstances. The middle-class individual was supposed to know right from wrong and act accordingly.

Middle-Class Marriage and Courtship Rituals

Rather than marry for convenience, or for economic or social reasons—as was still common among workers, peasants, and aristocrats—by the 1850s the middle-class couple was supposed to follow an idealized model: they met, courted, fell deeply in love, and joined for life because of a shared emotional bond. Of course, economic considerations in marriage by no means disappeared. But an entire culture of romantic love—popularized in advice manuals, novels and stories, and art, and practiced in courtship rituals, weddings, and married life—now surrounded middle-class couples. The growing popularity among all classes toward the end of the nineteenth century of what historians call **companionate marriage** underscores the impact of historical change on human emotions and behaviors.

Strict guidelines for courtship and engagement enshrined in the concept of falling in love ensured that middle-class individuals would make an appropriate match. Young couples were seldom alone before they became engaged, and individuals rarely paired off with someone from an inappropriate class background. In the straight-laced "Victorian Era"—named for the long reign of the British queen Victoria (1837–1901)—premarital sex was taboo for women, though men might experiment, a double standard that revealed the value the middle classes placed on sexual morality and especially women's virginity before marriage.

Engagement also followed a complicated set of norms and rituals. Secret engagements led to public announcements, and then the couple could appear together, though with chaperones in potentially

■ **companionate marriage** Marriage based on romantic love and middle-class family values that became increasingly dominant in the second half of the nineteenth century.

A Corner of the Table (1904)   With photographic precision, the French artist Paul-Émile Chabas (1869–1937) captured the elegance and intimacy of a sumptuous dinner party. Throughout Europe, members of the upper middle class and aristocracy enjoyed dinners like this with eight or nine separate courses, beginning with appetizers and ending with coffee and liqueurs. (Artepics/Alamy)

delicate situations. The betrothed might walk arm in arm, but custom placed strict limits on physical intimacy.

Marriage had its own set of informal rules. Usually a middle-class man could marry only if he could support a wife, children, and a servant, which meant he had to be well established in his career and fairly prosperous. Some middle-class men never married because they could not afford it. These customs created special difficulties for young middle-class women, who could rarely pursue an independent career or acquire a home without a husband. The system encouraged mixed-age marriages. A new husband was typically much older than his young wife, who usually had no career and entered marriage directly out of her parents' home or perhaps a girl's finishing school. She would have had little experience with the realities of adult life.

Cultural codes of the day insisted that love meant something different to men and women. Trained to fall passionately in love with "Mr. Right," young women equated marriage with emotional intensity. Men, on the other hand, were supposed to "find a wife": they took a more active but dispassionate role in courtship. Since women generally married when they were quite young, the man was encouraged to see himself as the protector of a young and fragile creature, and the typical middle-class marriage was more similar to a child-parent relationship than a partnership of equals, a situation expertly portrayed in Henrik Ibsen's famous Realist play *A Doll's House* (1879). The inequality of marriage was codified in European legal systems that, with rare exceptions, placed property ownership in the hands of the husband.

Middle- and Working-Class Sexuality

A double standard in sexual relations paralleled the gender inequalities built into middle-class standards of love and marriage. Middle-class moralists of all stripes cast men as aggressively sexual creatures, while

Courtship and Marriage Around 1900 The emotional bonds of companionate marriage that crystallized across the nineteenth century were reflected and reinforced in any number of contemporary images, from elegant paintings to common advertisements. This advertising postcard (left) for a jeweler's "Lucky Wedding Ring" captured the pomp and circumstance of the modern wedding, with the bride in her white dress and groom in formal wear. Flower girls and guests parade behind the couple as they pass through a fanciful enlargement of the ring that represents their special bond, while Cupid up above blesses the couple's union. The stereoscopic card from 1902 (right) captures the gender roles played by men and women at the key moment of the marriage proposal. Both sources testify to the ongoing commercialization of love and affection around 1900. (postcard: Amoret Tanner Collection/Shutterstock; stereoscopic card: Library of Congress, Prints and Photographs Division, Washington, D.C./LC-USZ62-63305)

women — the "angels in the house" — were supposed to be pure and chaste and act as a brake on male desire. Contemporary science legitimized this double standard. According to late-nineteenth-century physicians, men, easily aroused by the sight of a wrist or ankle, fell prey to their raging biological drives, while respectable women were supposedly uninterested in sex by nature.

Middle-class moralists assumed that men would enter marriage with some sexual experience, though this was unthinkable for a middle-class woman. When middle-class men did seek premarital sex, middle-class women were off limits. Instead, bourgeois men took advantage of their class status and sought lower-class women, domestic servants, or prostitutes. If a young middle-class woman had experimented with or even was suspected of having had premarital sex, her chances for an acceptable marriage fell dramatically.

The sexual standards of the working classes stood in marked contrast to these norms in the early nineteenth century, but that changed over time. Premarital sex for both men and women was common and more acceptable among workers. In the first half of the nineteenth century, among the lower classes, about one-third of the births in many large European cities occurred outside of wedlock.

The second half of the century saw the reversal of this high rate of illegitimacy: in western, northern, and central Europe, more babies were born to married mothers. Young, unmarried workers were probably engaging in just as much sexual activity as their parents and grandparents, who had created the illegitimacy explosion of 1750 to 1850 (see "New Patterns of Marriage and Illegitimacy" in Chapter 18). But in the later part of the nineteenth century, pregnancy for a young single woman, which a couple might see as the natural consequence of a serious relationship, led increasingly to marriage and the establishment of a two-parent household. Indeed,

■ **separate spheres** The nineteenth-century gendered division of labor and lifestyles that cast men as breadwinners and women as homemakers.

one in three working-class women was pregnant when she married.

This important development reflected the spread of middle-class ideals of family respectability among the working classes, as well as their gradual economic improvement. Romantic love held working-class families together, and marriage was less of an economic challenge. The urban working-class couple of the late nineteenth century thus became more stable, and that stability strengthened the family as an institution.

Separate Spheres and the Importance of Homemaking

After 1850 the work of wives became increasingly distinct and separate from that of their husbands in all classes. The preindustrial pattern among both peasants and cottage workers, in which husbands and wives both worked and shared basic household duties, became less and less common. In wealthier homes, this change was particularly dramatic. The good middle-class family man earned the wages to support the household; the public world of work, education, and politics was male space. Respectable middle-class women did not work outside the home and rarely even traveled alone in public. Working-class women, including servants and prostitutes, were more visible in public places, but if a middle-class woman went out without a male escort, she might be accused of low morals or character. Thus many historians have stressed that the societal ideal in nineteenth-century Europe became a strict division of labor by gender within rigidly constructed **separate spheres**: the "private sphere," where the woman acted as wife, mother, and homemaker, and the "public sphere," where the "breadwinner" husband acted as wage earner and family provider.

Christmas and the Sentimental Pleasures of the Middle-Class Home   A prosperous and productive German couple celebrate Christmas with their many children around a tree decorated with lit candles, something of a new fad in wealthy households in 1875. As this print suggests, holiday rituals evoked the familial feelings of love and affection that grounded private life in the late nineteenth century. How do the children's gifts reflect the notions of separate spheres that organized family life? (bpk Bildagentur/Photo: Dietmar Katz/Art Resource, NY)

For the middle classes, the private single-family home, a symbol of middle-class status and a sanctuary from the callous outside world of competitive capitalism, was central to the notion of separate spheres. At the heart of the middle-class home stood the woman: notions of femininity, motherhood, and family life came together in the ideal of domestic space. Well-furnished middle-class homes grew to include separate sleeping rooms for parents and each family member — unheard of among the lower classes — as well as a special drawing room (or parlor), used to entertain guests. Lower-class servants ensured that middle-class women had free time to turn the private sphere into a domestic refuge of love and privacy, with "a restful and refreshing atmosphere" (as one Swedish housekeeping manual from 1889 put it) far removed from the more masculine burdens of the public sphere.[6]

By 1900 lower-class families had adopted many middle-class values, but they did not have the means to fully realize the ideal of separate spheres. Women were the primary homemakers, and, as in the upper classes, men did little or no domestic labor. But as we have seen, many working-class women also worked, to contribute to family income. While middle-class family life centered on an ample daily meal, working-class women struggled to put sufficient food on the table. Working women could create a homelike environment that at least resembled that of the middle class — cleaning house, collecting trinkets, and decorating domestic interiors — but working men often preferred to spend time in the local pub with workmates, rather than come home for dinner. Indeed, alcoholism and domestic violence afflicted many working-class families, even as they struggled to build relationships based on romantic love.

Historians have often criticized the middle-class ideal of separate spheres because it restricted women's educational and employment opportunities, and the women's rights movement that emerged in the late nineteenth century certainly challenged the way that this social norm limited possibilities for women's self-expression and independence. In recent years, however, some scholars have been rethinking gender roles within the long-term development of consumer behavior and household economies. In the era of industrialization, these scholars suggest, the "breadwinner-homemaker" household that developed from about 1850 onward was rational consumer behavior that improved the lives of all family members, especially in the working classes.[7]

According to this view, the all-too-real limits on women's activity enforced by the notion of separate spheres had some benefits as well. When husbands specialized in earning an adequate cash income — the "family wage" that labor unions demanded — and wives specialized in managing the home, the working-class wife could produce desirable benefits that could not be bought in a market, such as improved health and better eating habits. For example, higher wages from the breadwinner could buy more raw food, but only the homemaker's careful selection, processing, and cooking would allow the family to benefit from increased spending on food. Although it was unpaid, running an urban household was a complicated, demanding, and valuable task. Twice-a-day food shopping, careful economizing, and fighting the growing crusade against dirt — not to mention child rearing — constituted a full-time occupation. Working yet another job for wages outside the home had limited appeal for most married women unless the earnings were essential for family survival. The homemaker's managerial skills, however, enabled the working-class couple to maximize their personal well-being.

The woman's guidance of the household went hand in hand with the increased pride in the home and family and the emotional importance attached to them in working- and middle-class families alike. According to one historian, by 1900 the English song "Home, Sweet Home" had become "almost a second national anthem."[8] Domesticity and family ties were now central to the lives of millions of people of all classes.

Child Rearing

Another striking sign of deepening emotional ties within the family was a growing emphasis on the love and concern that mothers gave their babies. Early emotional bonding and a willingness to make real sacrifices for the welfare of the infant became increasingly important among the comfortable classes by the end of the eighteenth century, though the ordinary mother of modest means adopted new attitudes only as the nineteenth century progressed.

The surge of maternal feeling was shaped by and reflected in a wave of specialized books on child rearing and infant hygiene, such as French family reformer Gustav Droz's phenomenally successful *Papa, Mama, and Baby*, which went through 121 editions between 1866 and 1884. Droz urged fathers to become affectionate toward their children and pitied those "who do not know how to roll around on the carpet, play at being a horse and a great wolf, and undress their baby."[9] Following expert advice, mothers increasingly breast-fed their infants, rather than paying wet nurses to do so. Another sign, from France, of increased parental affection was that fewer illegitimate babies were abandoned as foundlings after about 1850. Moreover, the practice of swaddling — wrapping babies in clothes or blankets so tightly they could not move — fell from favor. Instead, ordinary mothers allowed their babies freedom of movement and delighted in their spontaneity.

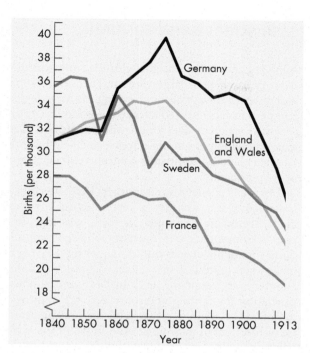

FIGURE 22.2 **The Decline of Birthrates in England and Wales, France, Germany, and Sweden, 1840–1913** Women had fewer babies for a variety of reasons, including the fact that their children were increasingly less likely to die before reaching adulthood. How do these numbers compare with those in Figure 22.1 on page 666? What does that comparison reveal about demographic trends in the nineteenth century?

The loving care lavished on infants was matched by greater concern for older children and adolescents. They, too, were bound in the strong emotional ties of a more intimate and protective family. For one thing, European women began to limit the number of children they bore in order to care adequately for those they had (Figure 22.2). By the end of the nineteenth century, the birthrate was declining across Europe, and it continued to do so until after World War II. The Englishwoman who married in the 1860s, for example, had an average of about six children; her daughter marrying in the 1890s had only four; and her granddaughter marrying in the 1920s had only two or possibly three.

The most important reason for this revolutionary reduction in family size, in which the comfortable and well-educated classes took the lead, was parents' desire to improve their economic and social position and that of their children. Children were no longer an economic asset in the late nineteenth century. By having fewer youngsters, parents could give those they had valuable advantages, from music lessons and summer vacations to long, expensive university educations. Thus the growing use in the late nineteenth century

of a variety of contraceptive methods — the rhythm method, the withdrawal method, and mechanical devices, including after the 1840s condoms and diaphragms made of vulcanized rubber — reflected increased concern for children.

In middle-class households, parents expended considerable effort to ensure that they raised their children according to prevailing family values. Indeed, many parents, especially in the middle classes, probably became too concerned about their children, unwittingly subjecting them to an emotional pressure cooker. Professional family experts, including teachers, doctors, and reformers like Droz, produced a vast popular literature on child rearing that encouraged parents to focus on developing their children's self-control, self-fulfillment, and sense of Christian morality. Family specialists recommended against corporal punishment — still common in worker and peasant households — but even though they typically escaped beatings, the children of the wealthy grew up under constant observation and discipline, a style of parenting designed to teach the self-control necessary for adult success. Parents carefully monitored their children's sexual behavior, and masturbation — according to one expert "the most shameful and terrible of all vices" — was of particular concern.[10]

Attempts to repress the child's sexuality generated unhealthy tension, often made worse by the rigid division of gender roles within the family. At work all day, the father could be a stranger to his offspring; his world of business was far removed from the maternal world of spontaneous affection. Although fathers became more overtly loving during this period, the man of the house often set demanding rules, making his approval conditional on achievement. This kind of distance was especially the case in the wealthiest families, in which domestic servants, nannies, and tutors did much of the work of child rearing. Many wealthy parents saw their children only over dinner, or on special occasions like birthdays or holidays.

The children of the working classes probably had more avenues of escape from such tensions than did those of the middle classes. Unlike their middle-class counterparts, who remained economically dependent on their families until a long education was finished or a proper marriage secured, working-class boys and girls went to work when they reached adolescence. Earning wages on their own, by the time they were sixteen or seventeen they could bargain with their parents for greater independence. If they were unsuccessful in these negotiations, they could and did leave home to live cheaply as paying lodgers in other working-class homes. Not until the twentieth century would middle-class youths be equally free to break away from the family when emotional ties became oppressive.

What were the most important changes in science and culture?

Major changes in intellectual life accompanied the emergence of urban society. Breakthroughs in the sciences, especially chemistry, physics, and electricity, spurred the creation of new products and entire industries. The natural and social sciences were also established as highly respected fields of study. In addition, between about the 1850s and the 1890s European arts and literature underwent a shift from soaring Romanticism to tough-minded Realism, which reflected the joys and burdens of everyday life in the emerging urban society.

The Triumph of Science in Industry

As the pace of scientific advancements quickened and resulted in greater practical benefits, science exercised growing influence on human thought. The intellectual achievements of the Scientific Revolution had resulted in few such benefits, and theoretical knowledge had also played a relatively small role in the Industrial Revolution in England. But breakthroughs in industrial technology in the late 1700s enormously stimulated basic scientific inquiry, as researchers sought to explain how such things as steam engines and blast furnaces actually worked. The result was an explosive growth of fundamental scientific discoveries from the 1830s onward. In contrast to earlier periods, these theoretical discoveries were increasingly transformed into material improvements for the general population.

A perfect example of the translation of better scientific knowledge into practical human benefits was the work of Louis Pasteur and his followers in biology and the medical sciences (see "The Bacterial Revolution"). Another was the development of the branch of physics known as **thermodynamics**. Building on Isaac Newton's laws of mechanics and on studies of steam engines, thermodynamics investigated the relationship between heat and mechanical energy. By midcentury, physicists had applied the results to mechanical engineering, chemical processes, and many other technologies.

The study and application of chemistry and electricity—fields in which science was put in the service of industry—likewise progressed rapidly. Chemists devised ways of measuring the atomic weight of different elements, and in 1869 the Russian chemist Dmitri Mendeleev (mehn-duh-LAY-uhf) (1834–1907) codified the rules of chemistry in the periodic law and the periodic table. Chemistry was subdivided into many specialized branches, including organic chemistry—the study of carbon compounds.

Applying theoretical insights gleaned from this new field, researchers in large German chemical companies discovered ways of transforming the dirty, useless coal tar that accumulated in coke ovens into beautiful, expensive synthetic dyes for the world of fashion. German production of synthetic dyes soared, and by 1900 German chemical companies controlled 90 percent of world production.

Electricity, a scientific curiosity in 1800, was totally transformed by a century of technological advancement. It became a commercial form of energy, first used in communications (the telegraph, which spurred quick international communication with the laying of underwater cables), then in electrochemistry (refining aluminum, for example), and finally in central power generation for lighting, transportation, and industrial motors. (See "Thinking Like a Historian: The Promise of Electricity," page 684.) And by 1890 the internal combustion engine fueled by petroleum was an emerging competitor to steam and electricity alike.

The successful application of scientific research in the fast-growing electrical and organic chemical industries between 1880 and 1913 provided a model for other uses. Systematic "R&D"—research and development—was born in the late nineteenth century. Above all, the burst of industrial creativity and technological innovation, often called the **Second Industrial Revolution**, promoted the strong economic growth in the last third of the nineteenth century that drove the urban reforms and the rising standard of living considered in this chapter.

The triumph of science and technology had three other significant consequences. First, though ordinary citizens continued to lack detailed scientific knowledge, everyday experience and innumerable articles in newspapers and magazines impressed the importance of science on the popular mind. Second, as science became more prominent in popular thinking, the philosophical implications of science formulated in the Enlightenment spread to broad sections of the population. Natural processes appeared to be determined by rigid laws, leaving little room for either divine intervention or human will. Yet scientific and technical advances had also fed the Enlightenment's optimistic faith in human progress, which now appeared endless and automatic to growing numbers of people. Third, the methods of science acquired unrivaled prestige after 1850. For many, the union of practical experiment and abstract theory was the only reliable route to truth and objective reality. The "unscientific" intuitions of the poets and the mystical revelations of the saints seemed hopelessly inferior.

Darwin and Natural Selection

Scientific research also progressed rapidly outside of the world of industry and technology, sometimes putting forth direct challenges to traditional religious beliefs. In geology, for example, Charles Lyell (1797–1875) effectively discredited the long-standing view that the earth's surface had been formed by short-lived cataclysms, such as biblical floods and earthquakes. Instead, according to Lyell's principle of uniformitarianism, the same geological processes that are at work today slowly formed the earth's surface over an immensely long time. Similarly, the evolutionary view of biological development, first proposed by the Greek Anaximander in the sixth century B.C.E., re-emerged in a more modern form in the work of French naturalist Jean-Baptiste Lamarck (1744–1829). Lamarck asserted that all forms of life had arisen through a long process of continuous adjustment to the environment, a dramatic challenge to the belief in divine creation of species.

Lamarck's work was flawed — he believed that the characteristics parents acquired in the course of their lives could be inherited by their children — and was not accepted, but it helped prepare the way for Charles Darwin (1809–1882), the most influential of all nineteenth-century evolutionary thinkers. As the official naturalist on a five-year scientific voyage to Latin America and the South Pacific beginning in 1831, Darwin carefully collected specimens of the different animal species he encountered on the voyage. Back in England, convinced by fossil evidence and by his friend Lyell that the earth and life on it were immensely ancient, Darwin came to doubt the general belief in a special divine creation of each species of animal. Instead, he concluded, all life had gradually evolved from a common ancestral origin in an unending struggle for survival. After long hesitation, Darwin published his research, which immediately attracted wide attention.

Darwin's great originality lay in suggesting precisely how biological evolution might have occurred. His theory of **evolution** is summarized in the title of his work *On the Origin of Species by the Means of Natural Selection* (1859). Decisively influenced by the gloomy assertions of Thomas Malthus (MAL-thuhs) that populations naturally grow faster than their food supplies (see "Industry and Population" in Chapter 20), Darwin argued that chance differences among the individual members of a given species helped some survive while others died. The variations that proved useful in the struggle for survival persisted in individuals through a process of natural selection, and they gradually spread to the entire species through reproduction.

Darwin's controversial theory had a powerful and many-sided influence on European thought and the European middle classes. Because his ideas seemed to suggest that evolution moved along without God's intervention, and that humans were simply one species among many others, some conservatives accused Darwin of anti-Christian beliefs and mocked him for suggesting that humans descended from apes. Others hailed Darwin as the great scientist par excellence, the "Newton of biology," who had revealed once again the powers of objective science.

Some thinkers went a step further and applied Darwin's theory of biological evolution to human affairs. English philosopher Herbert Spencer (1820–1903) saw the human race as driven forward to ever-greater specialization and progress by a brutal economic struggle that determined the "survival of the fittest." The poor were the ill-fated weak; the prosperous were the chosen strong. Spencer's **Social Darwinism** gained adherents among nationalists, who viewed global competition between countries as a grand struggle for survival, as well as among imperialists, who used Social Darwinist ideas to justify the rule of the supposedly more civilized West over its colonial subjects and territories.

The Modern University and the Social Sciences

By the 1880s major universities across Europe had been modernized, enlarged, and professionalized. Education now emphasized controlled research projects in newly established clinics and laboratories; advanced students conducted independent research in seminar settings. An increasingly diversified professoriate established many of the academic departments still found in today's universities, from anthropology to zoology.

Faculty devoted to the newly instituted human or social sciences took their place alongside the hard

---

■ **thermodynamics** A branch of physics built on Newton's laws of mechanics that investigated the relationship between heat and mechanical energy.

■ **Second Industrial Revolution** The burst of technological innovation and science-driven industrialization that promoted strong economic growth in the last third of the nineteenth century.

■ **evolution** Darwin's theory that chance differences among the individual members of a given species that prove useful in the struggle for survival are selected naturally, and they gradually spread to the entire species through reproduction.

■ **Social Darwinism** A body of thought, based on the ideas of Charles Darwin, that applied the theory of biological evolution to human affairs and saw the human race as driven by an unending economic struggle that would determine the "survival of the fittest."

The Promise of Electricity

The commercialization and widespread use of electricity around 1900 made possible a broad spectrum of new technologies in the late nineteenth century, including telephones, telegraphs, and radio; electric lights in public and private space; electric railroads, trams, and subways; electrochemistry and electrometallurgy; power plants, generators, and batteries; and electric motors and machines. How did the arrival of electricity revolutionize the lives of ordinary people?

1 **The Palace of Electricity, 1900 Universal Exhibition, Paris.** The ever-popular world fairs and expositions organized around the turn of the century typically included brightly lit pavilions dedicated to the wonders of electricity. At the top of the Palace of Electricity in Paris, illuminated by electric light, the "Electric Fairy" held up a torch powered by 50,000 volts.

(Archives Charmet/Bridgeman Images)

(© Fine Art Images/AGE Fotostock)

2 **"Luks'—The Least Expensive and Brightest Lighting for All Occasions,"** **ca. 1900.** This Russian poster advertising lighting systems from the Luks' (Deluxe) lighting company in Riga promotes "kerosene and incandescent lights and bulbs" and so marks a transitional period, when lighting companies encouraged consumers to switch from gas to electricity. The poster portrays a princess of light holding an electric bulb that illuminates first the Russian Empire and then the rest of the globe. The small scene at the bottom shows the street lights around the historic Tauride Palace in St. Petersburg and suggests the revolutionary effect of electric light in public spaces.

ANALYZING THE EVIDENCE

1. How did the commercialization of electricity reflect and/or contribute to the late-nineteenth-century faith in progress, rationalism, and reform?
2. What sort of research and development model did it take to electrify Europe? What sort of business model? How were the two connected?
3. Even in 1900, it was hard to predict that electricity would be more popular than gas or coal as a source for energy use at home or in the workplace. In Sources 1, 2, and 3, how do electricity's boosters strive to popularize the residential and commercial use of electricity?

3 **"Electrical Progress in Great Britain During 1909."** A U.S. journal for electricians offered glowing approval of the electrification of Great Britain. Along with the United States, Britain was a world leader in electrification around 1900; other European nations were not far behind.

〜 The most noticeable and at the same time the most hopeful, feature of the year 1909 in the United Kingdom, has been the great progress made in bringing electricity within the compass of the "small man." This movement, which means so much for the future of all electrical industry, has occupied the close attention of a large proportion of the electricity works managers and engineers and of most manufacturing and importing businesses. . . .

[T]he forward movement [of the filament lamp] is now in full swing. The wire lamp is everywhere working wonders in reducing the cost of electric lighting on existing installations and that fact together with the very strong support that is being given by other influences, is making it easier to get electrical applications adopted in many places where it seemed impossible before. . . .

[The London power companies] are now jointly using the daily press in an advertising campaign so conducted as to command the attention of all who read, educating them as to the rightful claims of electricity. One of the companies has opened a model "Electric Home" in its area, fitted throughout with electric lighting, heating, and small power. The house is occupied by a tenant who is under special arrangement to admit the public between certain hours every day, to demonstrate to them the manifold domestic applications of electricity and their convenience and cleanliness. Neither coal nor gas is used for any purpose whatsoever in the house. . . . This popularizing work is still very necessary indeed, for really the public does not know yet much that it ought to know. . . .

[The report then describes a number of technological advances, including newly built electric-generating plants, electric-powered steel mills, and the use of electric motors in a variety of industrial applications.]

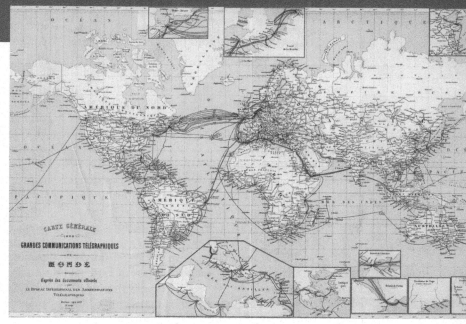

4 **"General Map of Large-Scale World Telegraph Communications, 1901/03."** After some equipment failures, British and U.S. engineers successfully completed the first transatlantic telegraph cable, fired by electric current, in 1858. By 1900 underwater telegraph cables circled the globe. (Bridgeman Images)

5 **Electric trams and lines in Piazza del Duomo, Milan, Italy, ca. 1900.** Electric streetcar and subway systems made quick travel through urban spaces accessible and inexpensive. In Milan, the tracks and streetcars, and the installation of electric streetlights, strike a modern contrast to the Gothic cathedral and Neoclassical triumphal arch that frame the central square.

(DEA PICTURE LIBRARY/AGE Fotostock)

PUTTING IT ALL TOGETHER

Using the sources above, along with what you have learned in class, in Chapter 22, and in the sections on the Industrial Revolution in Chapter 17, write a short essay that describes the various ways electrification changed everyday life and European society. Would you conclude that electricity was a fundamental driving force in the history of Western society? Or were developments in technology generally less important than, say, the results of major wars or the programs of leading politicians?

Source: (3) Albert H. Bridge, "Electrical Progress in Great Britain in 1909," *Electrical Review and Western Electrician*, January 1, 1910, pp. 17–19.

sciences. Using critical methods often borrowed from natural science, social scientists studied massive sets of numerical data that governments had begun to collect on everything from birthrates to crime and from population to prostitution. Like Karl Marx, they were fascinated by the rise of capitalism and modernity; unlike Marx, they preferred to understand rather than revolutionize society.

Sociology, the critical analysis of contemporary or historical social groups, emerged as a leading social science. Perhaps the most prominent and influential late-nineteenth-century sociologist was the German Max Weber (1864–1920). In his most famous book, *The Protestant Ethic and the Spirit of Capitalism* (1890), Weber argued that the rise of capitalism was directly linked to Protestantism in northern Europe. Pointing to the early and successful modernization of countries like the Netherlands and England, he concluded that Protestantism gave religious approval to hard work, saving, and investing—the foundations for capitalist development—because Protestant belief saw worldly success as a sign of God's approval.

This famous argument seriously challenged the basic ideas of Marxism: ideas, for Weber, were just as important as economics or class struggle in the rise of capitalism. Yet like Marx, Weber felt that people were alienated from their own humanity, trapped in what he called the "iron cage" of capitalist relations. Modern industrial society, according to Weber, had turned people into "specialists without spirit, hedonists without heart." An ambitious scholar, Weber wrote extensively on capitalist rationalization, modern bureaucracy, industrialization and agriculture, and the forms of political leadership.

In France, the prolific sociologist Émile Durkheim (1858–1917) earned an international reputation for his wide-ranging work. His study of the psychic and social basis of religion, *The Elementary Forms of Religious Life* (1912), remains a classic of social-scientific thought. In his pioneering work of quantitative sociology, *Suicide* (1897), Durkheim concluded that ever-higher suicide rates were caused by widespread feelings of what he called anomie, or rootlessness. Because modern society had stripped life of all sense of tradition, purpose, and belonging, Durkheim believed, anomie was inescapable; only an entirely new moral order might offer some relief.

Other sociologists contributed to the critique of modern society. The German Ferdinand Tönnies (1855–1936) argued that with industrialization Western civilization had undergone a fundamental transformation from "community" to "society." Rationalized self-interest had replaced traditional values, and selfish individualism had replaced generous

communal support, leading to intensified alienation and a cold bureaucratic age. In *The Crowd* (1895), French sociologist Gustav Le Bon (1841–1931) wrote that alienated individuals were prone to gathering in mass crowds, where they lost control over their emotions and actions. According to the deeply conservative Le Bon, a strong, charismatic leader could easily manipulate the crowd's collective psyche and turn the servile mass into a violent and dangerous revolutionary mob.

The new sociologists cast a bleak light on urban industrial society. While they acknowledged some benefits of rationalization and modernization, they bemoaned the accompanying loss of community and tradition. In some ways, their diagnosis of the modern individual as an isolated atom suffering from anomie and desperately seeking human connection was chillingly prescient: the powerful Communist and Fascist movements that swept through Europe after World War I appeared to generate popular support precisely by offering ordinary people a renewed sense of identity and community.

Realism in Art and Literature

In art and literature, the key themes of **Realism** emerged around 1850 and continued to dominate Western culture until the 1890s. Deeply influenced by the social changes that had accompanied rapid industrialization, Realist artists and writers believed that artistic works should depict ordinary life exactly as it was. They forsook the grand historical subjects favored by academy artists as well as the personal, emotional viewpoint of the Romantics for strict, supposedly factual objectivity. The controversial and shocking Realists observed and recorded the world around them—often to expose the sordid reality of modern life.

Emphatically rejecting the Romantic search for the exotic and the sublime, Realism (or "Naturalism," as it was often called) energetically pursued the typical and the commonplace. Beginning with a dissection of the middle classes, from which most of them sprang, many Realists eventually turned to the lives of working men and women, which had been largely ignored in imaginative literature before this time. Realist works portrayed slums and factories, and exposed unexplored and taboo subjects, including labor strikes, violence, sexuality, and alcoholism. Shocked middle-class critics denounced Realism as ugly sensationalism wrapped in pseudoscientific declarations and crude language—even as the movement attracted middle-class readers who were fascinated by the sensationalist view "from below."

The Realist movement began in France, where Romanticism had never been completely dominant.

■ **Realism** A literary movement that, in contrast to Romanticism, stressed the depiction of life as it actually was.

Artists like Gustave Courbet, Jean-François Millet, and Honoré Daumier painted scenes of laboring workers and peasants in somber colors and simple compositions, exemplified in Courbet's 1849 painting *Burial at Ornans.* Horrified critics rejected this painting because it depicted ordinary people in everyday life and entirely challenged established preferences for heroic compositions.

Literary Realism also began in France, where Honoré de Balzac, Gustave Flaubert, and Émile Zola became internationally famous novelists. Balzac (1799–1850) spent thirty years writing a vastly ambitious panorama of postrevolutionary French life. Known collectively as *The Human Comedy,* this series of nearly one hundred stories, novels, and essays vividly portrays more than two thousand characters from virtually all sectors of French society. Balzac pictured urban society as grasping, amoral, and brutal. In his novel *Father Goriot* (1835), the hero, a poor student from the provinces, eventually surrenders his idealistic integrity to feverish ambition and society's pervasive greed.

Madame Bovary (1857), the masterpiece of Gustave Flaubert (floh-BEHR) (1821–1880), is far narrower in scope than Balzac's work but is still famous for its psychological insight and critique of middle-class values. Unsuccessfully targeted by government censors as an outrage against public morality and religion, Flaubert's novel tells the story of Emma Bovary, a middle-class housewife who fantasizes about a life of romance and luxury. Her attempts to escape through love affairs and extravagant purchases destroy her family and herself. Flaubert portrays the provincial middle class as materialistic and dull, while taking aim at the influence of Romantic novels and theater.

Novelist Émile Zola (1840–1902) was most famous for his seamy, animalistic view of working-class life, expressed in novels such as *Nana* (1880), about the triumphs and tragedy of a high-class prostitute, and *The Earth* (1887), about the brutal life of a family of downtrodden French peasants. But he also wrote gripping, carefully researched stories featuring the stock exchange, the big department store, and the army, as well as urban slums and bloody battles between police and striking coal miners. Like many later Realists, Zola sympathized with socialism, a view evident in his overpowering novel *Germinal* (1885). (See "Viewpoints: Émile Zola and Naturalism/Realism in Western Literature," page 688.)

Realism quickly spread beyond France. In England, Mary Ann Evans (1819–1880), who wrote under the pen name George Eliot, brilliantly achieved a deeply felt, less sensational kind of Realism in her great novel *Middlemarch: A Study of Provincial Life* (1871–1872). The novels of Thomas Hardy (1840–1928), such as *Tess of the D'Urbervilles* (1891) and *The Return of the Native* (1878), depict ordinary men and women

Realism in the Arts   Realist depictions of gritty everyday life challenged the Romantic emphasis on nature and the emotions, as well as the Neoclassical focus on famous men and grand events. French painter Gustave Courbet's twenty-two-foot-long *Burial at Ornans* (1849) is a famous example of Realism in the arts. It portrays a bleak funeral in the artist's hometown. The painting's rejection of heroic subjects or grand themes shocked contemporary critics. When the organizers of a major exhibition in Paris in 1855 refused to show the work, claiming it was too large and too coarse, Courbet, already a leading figure in the Realist movement, withdrew all his paintings from the exhibition and staged a private exhibition that featured his own work. (Universal History Archive/UIG/Shutterstock)

The famous novels written by the great Realist (or Naturalist) author Émile Zola describe the struggles of ordinary people, but he also wrote manifestos that challenged Romanticism and called for a turn to Realism in the arts. The first selection here—from the preface to one of Zola's plays—casts Realism as an historical inevitability that will sweep aside all remnants of the Romantic worldview. Yet Zola's focus on the underside of everyday life angered conservative cultural critics such as the English literary scholar W. S. Lilly, whose scathing critique of Zola and Naturalism is excerpted below.

From Zola's Preface to *Thérèse Raquin*, 1873

[T]he great movement toward truth and experimental science which has since the last century been on the increase in every manifestation of the human intellect . . . was started by the new methods of science; thence, Naturalism revolutionized criticism and history, in submitting man and his works to a system of precise analysis. . . . Then, in turn, art and letters were carried along with the current. . . . [T]he novel, that social and individual study with its extremely loose framework, after growing and growing, took up all the activities of man. . . . These are all undeniable facts. We have come to the birth of the true, that is the great, the only force of the century. Everything advances in a literary epoch. Whoever wishes to retreat or turn to one side, will be lost in the general dust. . . .

There should no longer be any school, no more formulas, no standards of any sort; there is only life itself, an immense field where each may study and create as he likes. . . . Of course, the past is dead. We must look to the future, and the future will have to do with the human problems studied in the frame-work of reality. We must cast aside fables of every sort, and delve into the living drama of the two-fold life of the character and its environment, bereft of every nursery tale, historical trapping, and the usual conventional stupidities. The decayed scaffoldings of the [Romantic] drama of yesterday will fall of their own accord. We must clear the ground.

From W. S. Lilly, "The New Naturalism," 1885

The great aim and object of the New Naturalism, according to M. Zola, is a return to nature. The novelist,

the dramatist, he says, ought to be the photographers of phenomena. Their business is to study the world—to observe, to analyze humanity as they find it. But this is best done in its most vulgar types. The human animal—"la bête humaine," a phrase which our author employs with damnable iteration—is the same in all social varieties and conditions. . . . Everywhere at the bottom there is filth. . . .

[The New Naturalism] is strictly materialistic and frankly professes atheism. . . . Not less decisively does [Zola] cast aside ethical considerations. You have nothing to do with them, he tells his disciples. Sympathy with good or hatred of evil are as much out of place in your work as would be a chemist's anger against nitrogen as inimical to life. . . .

The especial value of the writings of M. Zola and his school seems to me that they are the most popular literary outcome of the doctrine which denies the personality, liberty, and spirituality of man and the objective foundation on which these rest, which empties him of the moral sense, the feeling of the infinite, the aspiration towards the Absolute. . . .

It is beyond question—look at France if you want overwhelming demonstration of it—that the issue of what M. Zola calls the Naturalistic Evolution is the banishing from human life of all that gives it glory and honour.

QUESTIONS FOR ANALYSIS

1. What are the main features of the new literature demanded by Zola?
2. Why does Lilly claim that the New Naturalism destroys the "glory and honor" of human life? How does Lilly's criticism contrast with Zola's assertion that "there is only life itself, an immense field where each may study and create as he likes"?
3. How do the style and subject matter of Realism compare and contrast with those of Romanticism?

Sources: Émile Zola, "Preface to Thérèse Raquin," trans. Barrett H. Clark, in *European Theories of the Drama*, ed. Barrett H. Clark (Cincinnati: Stewart & Kidd, 1918), pp. 400–401; W. S. Lilly, "The New Naturalism," in *Documents of Modern Literary Realism*, ed. George J. Becker (Princeton, N.J.: Princeton University Press, 1963).

frustrated and crushed by social prejudice, sexual puritanism, and bad luck. Russia's Count Leo Tolstoy (1828–1910) combined Realism in description and character development with an atypical moralizing, especially in his later work. In *War and Peace* (1864–1869), a monumental novel set against the background of Napoleon's invasion of Russia in 1812, Tolstoy developed his fatalistic theory of human history, which regards free will as an illusion and the achievements of even the greatest leaders as only the channeling of historical necessity. Yet Tolstoy's central message is one that most of the people discussed in this chapter would have readily accepted: human love, trust, and everyday family ties were life's enduring values.

NOTES

1. S. Marcus, "Reading the Illegible," in *The Victorian City: Images and Realities*, ed. H. J. Dyos and Michael Wolff, vol. 1 (London: Routledge & Kegan Paul, 1973), p. 266.

2. J. McKay, *Tramways and Trolleys: The Rise of Urban Mass Transport in Europe* (Princeton, N.J.: Princeton University Press, 1976), p. 81.

3. Bonnie S. Anderson and Judith P. Zinsser, *A History of Their Own: Women in Europe from Prehistory to the Present*, rev. ed., vol. 2 (New York: Oxford University Press, 2000), p. 195.

4. Quoted in R. P. Neuman, "The Sexual Question and Social Democracy in Imperial Germany," *Journal of Social History* 7 (Winter 1974): 276.

5. Quoted in J. A. Banks, "The Contagion of Numbers," in *The Victorian City: Images and Realities*, ed. H. J. Dyos and Michael Wolff, vol. 1 (London: Routledge & Kegan Paul, 1973), p. 112.

6. Quoted in J. Frykman and O. Löfgren, *Culture Builders: A Historical Anthropology of Middle-Class Life* (New Brunswick, N.J.: Rutgers University Press, 1987), p. 134.

7. See J. de Vries, *The Industrious Revolution: Consumer Behavior and the Household Economy* (Cambridge: Cambridge University Press, 2008), especially pp. 186–237.

8. R. Roberts, *The Classic Slum: Salford Life in the First Quarter of the Century* (Manchester, U.K.: University of Manchester Press, 1971), p. 35.

9. Quoted in T. Zeldin, *France, 1848–1945*, vol. 1 (Oxford: Clarendon Press, 1973), p. 328.

10. Quoted in Frykman and Löfgren, *Culture Builders*, p. 114.

LOOKING BACK　LOOKING AHEAD

When the peoples of northwestern Europe looked out at the economic and social landscape in the early twentieth century, they had good reason to feel that the promise of the Industrial Revolution was being realized. The dark days of urban squalor and brutal working hours had given way after 1850 to a gradual rise in the standard of living for all classes. Scientific discoveries were combined with the applied technology of public health and industrial production to save lives and drive continued economic growth.

Moreover, social and economic advances seemed to be matched by progress in the political sphere. The years following the dramatic failure of the revolutions of 1848 saw the creation of unified nation-states in Italy and Germany, and after 1870, as we shall see in the following chapter, nationalism and the nation-state reigned in Europe. Although the rise of nationalism created tensions among the European countries, these tensions would not explode until 1914 and the outbreak of the First World War. Instead, the most aggressive and destructive aspects of European nationalism found their initial outlet in the final and most powerful surge of Western overseas expansion. Thus Europe, transformed by industrialization and nationalism, rushed after 1875 to seize territory and build new or greatly expanded colonial empires in Asia and Africa.

Make Connections

Think about the larger developments and continuities within and across chapters.

1. What were the most important changes in everyday life from the end of the eighteenth century (Chapter 18) to the end of the nineteenth century? What main causes or agents drove these changes?

2. Did the life of ordinary people improve, stay the same, or even deteriorate over the nineteenth century when compared to the previous century? What role did developments in science, medicine, and urban planning play in this process?

3. How did the emergence of a society divided into working and middle classes affect the workplace, homemaking, and family values and gender roles? Are the values and behaviors associated with the nineteenth-century lower, middle, and upper classes — in all their diversity — still around today? How have they changed?

22 REVIEW & EXPLORE

Identify Key Terms

Identify and explain the significance of each item below.

utilitarianism (p. 664)

"Great Stink" (p. 664)

U.K. Vaccination Acts (p. 664)

germ theory (p. 665)

professionalization (p. 670)

labor aristocracy (p. 672)

sweated industries (p. 673)

companionate marriage (p. 676)

separate spheres (p. 679)

thermodynamics (p. 682)

Second Industrial Revolution (p. 682)

evolution (p. 683)

Social Darwinism (p. 683)

Realism (p. 686)

Review the Main Ideas

Answer the section heading questions from the chapter.

1. What were the main changes in urban life in the nineteenth century? (p. 660)

2. How did class and gender reinforce social difference in the nineteenth century? (p. 668)

3. How did urbanization affect family life and gender roles? (p. 676)

4. What were the most important changes in science and culture? (p. 682)

Suggested Resources

BOOKS

- Barnes, David S. *The Great Stink of Paris and the Nineteenth-Century Struggle Against Filth and Germs.* 2006. An outstanding introduction to sanitary developments and attitudes toward public health.

- Cioc, Mark. *The Rhine: An Eco-Biography, 1815–2000.* 2002. An environmental history focused on the Rhine River, Europe's most important commercial waterway.

- Coontz, Stephanie. *Marriage, a History: From Obedience to Intimacy, or How Love Conquered Marriage.* 2005. A lively investigation of the historical background to current practice.

- Crook, Tom. *Governing Systems: Modernity and the Making of Public Health in England, 1830–1910.* 2016. This account "from below" emphasizes the impact of public health reform on ordinary lives.

- Davidoff, Leonore, and Catherine Hall. *Family Fortunes: Men and Women of the English Middle Class, 1780–1850.* 1991. A groundbreaking classic that places gender at the center of the construction of middle-class values, lifestyles, and livelihoods.

- De Vries, Jan. *The Industrious Revolution: Consumer Behavior and the Household Economy, 1850 to the Present.* 2008. A major interpretative analysis focusing on married couples and their strategies.

- Johnson, Steven. *The Ghost Map: The Story of London's Most Terrifying Epidemic — and How It Changed Science, Cities, and the Modern World.* 2007. This entertaining national bestseller explains the way the reaction to the Broad Street cholera outbreak of 1854 transformed public health and urban planning.

- Kelly, Alfred. *The German Worker: Working-Class Autobiographies from the Age of Industrialization.* 1987. A superb collection of firsthand, primary source accounts of working-class life, with an excellent introduction on German workers in general.

- Lees, Andrew, and Lynn Hollen Lees. *Cities and the Making of Modern Europe, 1750–1914.* 2008. An informative survey of European urbanization from the eighteenth century to World War I.

- Maynes, Mary Jo. *Taking the Hard Road: Life Course in French and German Workers' Biographies in the Era of Industrialization.* 1995. Includes fascinating accounts that provide insight into how workers saw themselves.

- Perrot, Michelle, ed. *A History of Private Life*, vol. 4: *From the Fires of Revolution to the Great War.* 1994. A fascinating multivolume and multiauthor work that puts private life and family at the center of the history of the long nineteenth century.
- Walkowitz, Judith. *Prostitution and Victorian Society: Women, Class, and the State.* 1980. This important work changed the way historians think about sexuality and prostitution in the second half of the nineteenth century.
- Weiner, Jonathan. *The Beak of the Finch: The Story of Evolution in Our Time.* 1994. A prize-winning, highly readable account of Darwin and evolution.

MEDIA

- *Anna Karenina* (Joe Wright, 2012). Based on Leo Tolstoy's famous novel, the film focuses on Anna Karenina's affair with Count Vronsky.
- *Charles Darwin and the Tree of Life* (BBC, 2009). Marking the bicentennial of Darwin's birth, the BBC produced this television documentary about Charles Darwin and his important theory of evolution.
- *Cholera and the Thames.* A captivating website where one can learn about the problem of cholera in London in the nineteenth century. Includes essays, games, educational resources, and a gallery of images related to the topic. **www.choleraandthethames.co.uk**
- *Germinal* (Claude Berri, 1993). Nineteenth-century coal miners in northern France go on strike in response to repression by the authorities in this film based on Émile Zola's classic Realist novel.
- *Haussmann.* An overview of the life of Georges Haussmann and his transformation of Paris from 1858 to 1870. **http://worldimages.sjsu.edu/gallery/paris/architecture/Haussman.html**
- *History of Contraception: Nineteenth Century.* A discussion of contraception, abortion, and other issues surrounding sexuality in the nineteenth century. **www.glowm.com/?p=glowm.cml/section_view&articleid=375#21001**
- *The Literature Network: Realism.* An extended essay about Realism in literature. The site also has biographies and links to works by several Realist authors, including Balzac, Eliot, Flaubert, Hardy, Tolstoy, and Zola. **www.online-literature.com/periods/realism.php**
- *Madame Bovary* (Tim Fywell, 2000). A frustrated middle-class housewife named Emma Bovary has an adulterous love affair in this film adaptation of Gustave Flaubert's novel.

23

The Age of Nationalism

1850–1914

In the years that followed the revolutions of 1848, nationalism—mass identification with the nation-state—emerged as an effective organizing principle capable of channeling the many-sided challenges of the unfinished industrial and political revolutions and the new urban society. Nationalism had been a powerful force since the early nineteenth century, but the goal of creating independent nation-states, inhabited by people sharing a common ethnicity, language, history, and territory, had repeatedly proved elusive, most spectacularly in the revolutions of 1848. By 1914, however, most Europeans lived in nation-states, and nationalism had become an almost universal faith in the Western world.

The governments of the new nation-states took various forms, from conservative authoritarianism to parliamentary monarchy to liberal republicanism. Whatever the political system, nationalism remade territorial boundaries and forged new relations between the nation-state and its citizens. In most cases the nation-state became increasingly responsive to the needs of its people, opening the political franchise and offering citizens at least rudimentary social and economic benefits. Yet the nation-state demanded much from its citizens: rising income taxes, universal military service, and allegiance to the national idea. Nationalism, which before 1848 appealed primarily to liberals seeking political reform or national independence, became an ever more conservative ideology. At its worst, populists and fanatics manipulated and sometimes abused the patriotism of ordinary people to justify exclusionary policies against Jews and other ethnic minorities and to promote expansion in overseas colonies. ▪

CHAPTER PREVIEW

- What were the main features of the authoritarian nation-state built by Napoleon III?

- How were strong nation-states forged in Italy and Germany?

- How did Russian and Ottoman leaders modernize their states and societies?

- How did the relationship between government and the governed change after 1871?

- What were the costs and benefits of nationalism for ordinary people?

- How and why did revolutionary Marxism evolve in the late nineteenth century?

Popular Solidarity in the Age of Nationalism

In this 1878 painting titled *The Departure of the 1866 Conscripts*, men who responded to the national call to arms in an Italian village cheer a speech by a local military official. In the foreground a soldier bids farewell to his family before joining the army in the field. This portrait pays homage to the Italian peasant, willing to fight for his newborn country. This idealized scene depicts the changing relationship between state and citizen as nationalism came to permeate all levels of society. (DeAgostini/DEA/ A. DAGLI ORTI/Getty Images)

What were the main features of the authoritarian nation-state built by Napoleon III?

Early nationalism was generally liberal and idealistic and could be democratic and radical (see Chapter 21). Yet nationalism also flourished in authoritarian states, which imposed social and economic changes from above. Napoleon Bonaparte's France had already combined national feeling with authoritarian rule. Napoleon's nephew, Louis Napoleon (1808–1873), revived and extended this combination.

France's Second Republic

Although Louis Napoleon had played no part in French politics before 1848, he won three times as many votes as the four other presidential candidates combined in the French presidential election of December 1848. Louis Napoleon enjoyed popular support at a time of universal male suffrage for several reasons. First, he bore the famous name of his uncle, whom romantics had transformed into a demigod after 1820. Second, as Karl Marx stressed at the time, middle-class and peasant property owners feared the socialist challenge of urban workers and the chaos of the revolution of 1848, and they wanted a tough ruler to provide stability and protect their property. Third, Louis Napoleon advertised a positive social-economic program for the French people in pamphlets widely circulated before the election.

Above all, Louis Napoleon promoted a vision of national unity and social progress, in which the government stressed the interests of the nation rather than the individual, promised economic and social benefits to all, and appealed to France's past glories. But how, he asked, could these tasks be accomplished when corrupt French politicians mostly supported the interests of wealthy elites? Only a strong, even authoritarian, leader, like the wildly popular first Napoleon, could solve this problem. Louis Napoleon cast himself in this mold. He promised that his rule would be linked to each citizen by direct democracy, his sovereignty uncorrupted by politicians and legislative bodies, his acts approved by mass plebiscites, referendums in which all citizens would cast votes to approve or disapprove of important questions of public policy. To his many enthusiastic supporters, Louis Napoleon was a strong and forward-looking champion of popular interests.

Elected to a four-year term by an overwhelming majority, Louis Napoleon was required by the constitution to share power with the National Assembly, which was overwhelmingly conservative. With some misgivings, he signed bills that increased the role of the Catholic Church in primary and secondary education and deprived many poor men of the right to vote. In return Louis Napoleon hoped that the Assembly would vote for funds to pay his personal debts and change the constitution so he could run for a second term.

But after the Assembly failed to cooperate with that last aim, Louis Napoleon conspired with key army officers to overthrow the government. On December 2, 1851, he illegally dismissed the legislature and seized power in a coup d'état. Acting in tandem with the coup, the national army crushed armed resistance in Paris and widespread insurrection in southern France. Louis Napoleon craftily wrapped himself in the mantle of his famous uncle. Claiming to be above political bickering, he restored universal male suffrage and proclaimed the arrival of the Second French Empire, a proud continuation of the mighty First Empire established by Bonaparte during the Napoleonic Wars. As the first Napoleon had done, Louis Napoleon asked the French people to legalize his actions. They did: 92 percent voted to make him president for ten years. A year later, in a plebiscite, 97 percent voted to approve the Second French Empire and make Louis Napoleon its hereditary emperor.

Napoleon III's Second Empire

Louis Napoleon — now proclaimed Emperor Napoleon III — experienced both success and failure between 1852 and 1870, when he fell from power during the Franco-Prussian War. In the 1850s his policies encouraged economic growth. His government promoted the new investment banks and massive railroad construction that drove the Industrial Revolution on the continent. The French state fostered general economic expansion through an ambitious program of public works, which included rebuilding Paris to improve the urban environment. Business profits soared, rising wages of workers outpaced inflation, and unemployment declined greatly.

Initially, economic progress reduced social and political tensions as Louis Napoleon had hoped. Until the mid-1860s the emperor enjoyed support from France's most dissatisfied group, the urban workers. They appreciated the 1850s reforms, such as the regulation of pawnshops, support for credit unions, and better working-class housing. In the 1860s Louis Napoleon granted workers the right to form unions and the right to strike.

TIMELINE

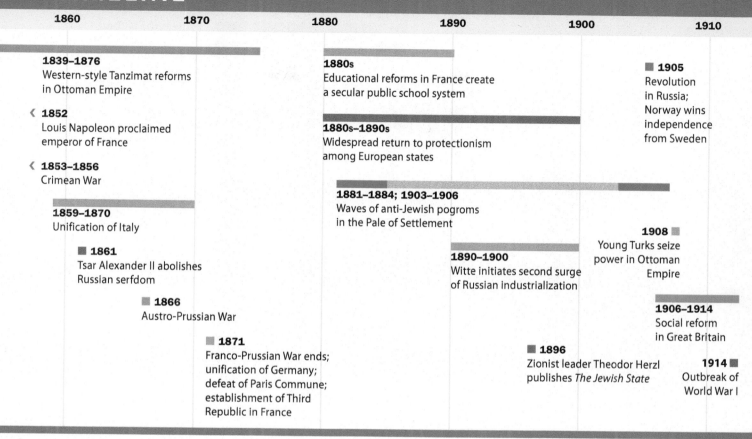

| 1860 | 1870 | 1880 | 1890 | 1900 | 1910 |

1839–1876
Western-style Tanzimat reforms
in Ottoman Empire

1852
Louis Napoleon proclaimed
emperor of France

1853–1856
Crimean War

1859–1870
Unification of Italy

1861
Tsar Alexander II abolishes
Russian serfdom

1866
Austro-Prussian War

1871
Franco-Prussian War ends;
unification of Germany;
defeat of Paris Commune;
establishment of Third
Republic in France

1880s
Educational reforms in France create
a secular public school system

1880s–1890s
Widespread return to protectionism
among European states

1881–1884; 1903–1906
Waves of anti-Jewish pogroms
in the Pale of Settlement

1890–1900
Witte initiates second surge
of Russian industrialization

1896
Zionist leader Theodor Herzl
publishes *The Jewish State*

1905
Revolution
in Russia;
Norway wins
independence
from Sweden

1908
Young Turks seize
power in Ottoman
Empire

1906–1914
Social reform
in Great Britain

1914
Outbreak of
World War I

Although he repeatedly claimed that the Second Empire stood for peace, Louis Napoleon maintained an aggressive foreign policy. He was deeply committed to "the principle of nationalities," which meant redrawing European state borders on the basis of shared national characteristics. He led France to victory in the Crimean War (see "The 'Great Reforms' in Russia" later in this chapter) and then, in 1859, waged war against Austria for the cause of Italian unification (see "The Unification of Italy" ahead in this chapter). During the U.S. Civil War, he meddled unsuccessfully in internal Mexican politics, which drew intense criticism in France.

At first, political power remained in the hands of the emperor. Louis Napoleon alone chose his ministers, who had great freedom of action. Yet in order to win popular support, he retained the legislative Assembly and senate, although with reduced powers. Members were elected by universal male suffrage every six years, and the government took these elections seriously. It tried to entice notable people, even those who had opposed the regime, to stand as candidates to expand the base of support. Government officials and appointed mayors spread the word that

election of mainstream candidates—and defeat of the opposition—would provide tax rebates, roads, and a range of other local benefits.

In elections in 1857 and again in 1863, Louis Napoleon's system produced overwhelming electoral victories for government-backed candidates. In the late 1860s, however, this electoral system gradually disintegrated. With increasing effectiveness, the middle-class liberals who had always wanted a less authoritarian regime denounced his rule. Napoleon was always sensitive to the public mood. Public opinion, he once said, always wins the last victory, and he responded to critics with ever-increasing liberalization. He granted freedom of the press and gave the Assembly greater powers and opposition candidates greater freedom, which they used to good advantage. In 1869 the opposition, consisting of republicans, monarchists, and liberals, polled almost 45 percent of the vote.

The next year, a sick and weary Louis Napoleon again granted France a new constitution, which combined a basic parliamentary regime with a hereditary emperor as chief of state. In a final plebiscite on the eve of the disastrous war with Prussia, 7.3 million Frenchmen approved the new constitution—only

Paris in the Second Empire The flash and glitter of unprecedented prosperity in the Second Empire come alive in this vibrant contemporary painting. Writers and intellectuals chat with elegant women and trade witticisms with financiers and government officials at the Café Tortoni, a favorite rendezvous for fashionable society. Horse-drawn omnibuses with open top decks mingle with cabs and private carriages on the broad new boulevard. (Sepia Times/Universal Images Group/Getty Images)

1.5 million opposed it. Napoleon III's ability to rally voters' support for a strong central state and an emperor rather than a republic and an elected leader showed that popular nationalism was compatible with authoritarian government, even as France moved in an increasingly democratic direction.

How were strong nation-states forged in Italy and Germany?

Napoleon III's authoritarian rule in the 1850s and 1860s provided the old ruling classes of Europe with a new model in politics, in which the expanding middle classes and even portions of the working classes supported a unified, conservative national state that promised economic growth and social benefits. Would this model work elsewhere? This was one of the great political questions in the 1850s and 1860s. In Europe, the national unification of Italy and Germany offered a resounding answer. As in the United States, where a bloody civil war increased the power of the federal government and built the foundations of the modern nation, it often took conflict and violence to inspire popular nationalism and forge a strong central state.

The Unification of Italy

The various kingdoms on the Italian peninsula had never been united. Often a battleground for Europe's Great Powers, Italy was reorganized in 1815 at the Congress of Vienna into a hodgepodge of different states, each with its own government, and the wealthy northern Italian-speaking territories of Lombardy and Venetia were incorporated into the Austrian Empire. Austrian foreign minister Prince Klemens von Metternich captured the essence of the situation when he dismissed the notion of "Italy" as "only a geographical expression" (Map 23.1).

Yet the struggle for a unified Italian nation—the **Risorgimento**—captured the imagination of many Italians. The appeal of Italian nationalism was exemplified in the Young Italy secret society founded by the radical and idealistic patriot Giuseppe Mazzini, who called for a centralized democratic republic based on universal male suffrage. In *Duties Towards Your County* (1858), Mazzini argued that language, historic traditions, and divine purpose defined a national people. He called for the liberation of Italian territories from foreign governments (such as Austria) and unification based on "harmony and brotherhood."

MAP 23.1 The Unification of Italy, 1859–1870 The leadership of Sardinia-Piedmont, nationalist fervor, and Garibaldi's attack on the Kingdom of the Two Sicilies were decisive factors in the unification of Italy.

Catholicism and the papacy offered another potential source of shared belonging and even a potential foundation for an Italian nation-state. Yet after the upheavals of 1848, the reactionary Pope Pius IX (pontificate 1846–1878) opposed unification and most modern trends. In the 1864 *Syllabus of Errors*, Pius IX denounced rationalism, socialism, separation of church and state, and religious liberty. The Catholic Church could not stop unification, but it resisted liberalism and progressive reform for the next two decades.

By the 1850s, many Italian nationalists embraced the promise of a national federation led by Victor Emmanuel II, the autocratic king of Sardinia-Piedmont. They looked to Piedmont for national leadership, much as German liberals looked to Prussia, because Piedmont boasted one of the most industrialized, wealthy, and socially advanced territories on the Italian peninsula. Victor Emmanuel, crowned in 1849, had retained the liberal constitution granted by his father under duress during the revolutions of 1848. This constitution combined a strong monarchy with a fair degree of civil liberties and parliamentary

government, though deputies were elected by a limited franchise based on income. To some of the Italian middle classes, the Kingdom of Sardinia-Piedmont appeared to be a liberal, progressive state ideally suited to drive Austria out of northern Italy and lead the drive to Italian unification. By contrast, Mazzini's brand of democratic republicanism seemed idealistic and too radical.

The struggle for Italian unification under Emmanuel II was supported by Count Camillo Benso di Cavour (ka-VOOR), a brilliant statesman who served as prime minister of Sardinia-Piedmont from 1852 until his death in 1861. A nobleman who had made a substantial fortune in business before entering politics, Cavour had limited and realistic national goals. Until 1859 he sought unity only with the states of northern and perhaps central Italy, which would nonetheless greatly expand the existing kingdom.

In the 1850s Cavour helped turn Sardinia-Piedmont into a liberal constitutional state capable of leading

■ **Risorgimento** The nineteenth-century struggle for Italian independence and unification.

Garibaldi and Victor Emmanuel II: The Right Leg in the Boot at Last   The symbolic 1860 meeting in Naples between the leader of Italy's revolutionary nationalists and the king of Sardinia sealed the unification of northern and southern Italy. In later years Garibaldi became a folk hero, but his vision of Italy united under a revolutionary republican government gave way to the conservative nationalism of Emmanuel II, leaving millions of Italians mired in poverty. The idealized patriotism evident in this painting of Garibaldi and Emmanuel, completed in 1866 (left), testifies to the growing appeal of popular nationalism. On the other hand, the English political cartoon (right) mocks the famous meeting between the two. In the cartoon, a subservient Garibaldi has put down his sword and is fitting the boot of Italy on the king's leg. "If it won't go on, Sire, try a little more powder," he says in the cartoon's original caption (not pictured here), a cutting reference to the gunpowder that the state used to quell popular unrest. (painting: Photo © Raffaello Bencini/Bridgeman Images; cartoon: Sarin Images/Granger)

northern Italy. His program of building highways and railroads, expanding civil liberties, and opposing clerical privilege increased support for his efforts throughout northern Italy. Yet because Sardinia-Piedmont could not drive Austria out of the north without the help of a powerful ally, Cavour established a secret alliance with Napoleon III against Austria in July 1858.

Cavour then goaded Austria into attacking Piedmont in 1859, and Louis Napoleon came to Italy's defense. After defeating the Austrians at the Battles of Magenta and Solferino, however, Napoleon did a sudden about-face. Worried by criticism from French Catholics for supporting the pope's declared enemy, he abandoned Cavour and made a compromise peace with the Austrians in July 1859. The Kingdom of Sardinia-Piedmont received only Lombardy, the area around Milan, from Austria. The rest of Italy remained essentially unchanged.

The skillful maneuvers of Cavour's allies in the moderate nationalist movement nonetheless salvaged plans for Italian unification. While the war against Austria raged in the north, pro-unification nationalists in Tuscany and elsewhere in central Italy led popular revolts that easily toppled their ruling princes.

Encouraged by and appropriating these popular movements, middle-class nationalist leaders in central Italy called for fusion with Sardinia-Piedmont. In early 1860, Cavour regained Napoleon III's support by ceding Savoy and Nice to France. The people of central Italy then voted overwhelmingly to join a greatly enlarged kingdom under Victor Emmanuel. Cavour had achieved his original goal, a united northern Italian state (see Map 23.1).

For superpatriots such as Giuseppe Garibaldi (1807–1882), however, the unification of the north left the job half done. The son of a poor sailor, Garibaldi personified the romantic, revolutionary nationalism and republicanism of Mazzini and 1848. Leading a corps of volunteers against Austria in 1859, Garibaldi emerged in 1860 as an independent force in Italian politics.

Partly to use him and partly to get rid of him, Cavour secretly supported Garibaldi's bold plan to "liberate" the Kingdom of the Two Sicilies. Landing in Sicily in May 1860, Garibaldi's guerrilla band of a thousand Red Shirts inspired the peasantry, who rose in bloody rebellion against their landlords. Outwitting the twenty-thousand-man royal army, the guerrilla leader won battles, gained volunteers, and took

Palermo. Then Garibaldi and his men crossed to the mainland, marched triumphantly toward Naples, and prepared to attack Rome and the pope. The wily Cavour quickly sent Sardinian forces to occupy most of the Papal States (but not Rome) and to intercept Garibaldi.

Cavour realized that an attack on Rome would bring war with France, and he feared Garibaldi's radicalism and popular appeal. He immediately organized a plebiscite in the conquered territories. Despite the urging of some radical supporters, the patriotic Garibaldi did not oppose Cavour, and the people of the south voted to join the kingdom of Sardinia. When Garibaldi and Victor Emmanuel II rode together through Naples to cheering crowds in October 1860, they symbolically sealed the union of north and south, of monarch and nation-state.

Cavour had successfully controlled Garibaldi and turned popular nationalism in a conservative direction. The new kingdom of Italy, which expanded to include Venice in 1866 and Rome in 1870, was a parliamentary monarchy under Victor Emmanuel II. The new nation was hardly democratic or prosperous. Only a half million out of 22 million Italians had the right to vote, and great social inequalities divided the propertied classes and the common people. A deep and growing economic gap separated the progressive, industrializing north from the stagnant, agrarian south. Italy was united on paper, but profound divisions remained.

The Austro-Prussian War

In the aftermath of 1848 the German states were locked in a political stalemate. After Austria and Russia blocked Prussian king Friedrich Wilhelm IV's attempt in 1850 to unify Germany, tension grew between Austria and Prussia as they struggled to dominate the German Confederation (see "Prussia, the German Confederation, and the Frankfurt National Assembly" in Chapter 21).

Economic differences exacerbated this rivalry. Austria had not been included in the German Customs Union, or *Zollverein* (TZOLE-fur-ayne), when it was founded in 1834 to stimulate trade and increase state revenues. By the end of 1853 Austria was the only state in the German Confederation outside the union. As middle-class and business groups profited from participation in the Zollverein, Prussia's leading role within the customs union gave it a valuable advantage in its struggle against Austria.

Prussia had emerged from the upheavals of 1848 with a weak parliament that by 1859 was in the hands of the wealthy middle classes, who favored liberal state policies. Longing for national unification, these representatives wanted to establish that the parliament, not the king, held ultimate political power, including control of the army. At the same time, the national uprising in Italy in 1859 made a profound impression on Prussia's tough-minded Wilhelm I (r. 1861–1888). Convinced that great political change and war — perhaps with Austria, perhaps with France — were quite possible, Wilhelm I and his top military advisers pushed to raise taxes and increase the defense budget in order to double the size of the army. The Prussian parliament rejected the military budget in 1862, and the liberals triumphed completely in new elections, creating a deadlocked constitutional crisis. Wilhelm I then appointed Count Otto von Bismarck as Prussian prime minister and encouraged him to defy the parliament. This was a momentous choice.

Otto von Bismarck (1815–1898) was a master of **Realpolitik**, a German term referring to political practice based on a careful calculation of real-world conditions rather than ethical ideals or ideological assumptions. Bismarck had honed his political skills as a high-ranking diplomat for the Prussian government. Born into the landowning aristocracy and devoted to his sovereign, he had a strong personality and an unbounded desire for power. Yet in his drive to secure power for himself and for Prussia, Bismarck remained extraordinarily flexible and pragmatic. Keeping his options open, he moved with determination and cunning toward his goal.

When he took office as prime minister in 1862, in the midst of the constitutional crisis caused by the deadlock on the military budget, Bismarck made a strong but unfavorable impression. Declaring that Wilhelm's government would rule without parliamentary consent, he lashed out at the liberal opposition: "The great questions of the day will not be decided by speeches and resolutions — that was the blunder of 1848 and 1849 — but by blood and iron."

Denounced by liberals for his view that "might makes right," Bismarck had the Prussian bureaucracy go right on collecting taxes, even though the parliament refused to approve the budget. Bismarck also reorganized the army. And for four years, from 1862 to 1866, voters continued to express their opposition by sending large liberal majorities to the parliament.

Opposition at home spurred Bismarck to search for success abroad. The extremely complicated question of Schleswig-Holstein — two provinces on the disputed border between Denmark and Germany, populated by a large majority of ethnic Germans — provided a welcome opportunity. In 1864 the Danish king tried, as he had in 1848, to bring these two provinces into a more centralized Danish state against the will of the

---

■ **Realpolitik** A German term referring to political practice based on a careful calculation of real-world conditions rather than ethical ideals or ideological assumptions, employed by Bismarck and other nineteenth-century politicians.

MAP 23.2 The Unification of Germany, 1864–1871

This map shows how Prussia expanded and a new German Empire was created through wars with Denmark (1864), Austria (1866), and France (1870–1871).

ANALYZING THE MAP What losses did Austria experience in 1866? What territories did France lose as a result of the Franco-Prussian War?

CONNECTIONS Why would the unification of Germany pose a problem for the traditional balance of power on the European continent?

German Confederation. In response, Prussia enlisted Austria in a short and successful war against Denmark (Map 23.2).

Bismarck, however, was convinced that Prussia had to control completely the northern, predominantly Protestant part of the confederation, which meant expelling Austria from German affairs. After the victory over Denmark, Bismarck's clever Realpolitik maneuvering left Prussia in a position to force Austria out by war. Recognizing that Russia, France, and Italy might come to Austria's defense, Bismarck persuaded them to remain neutral through a skillful blend of territorial promises and reminders of past Prussian support.

The Austro-Prussian War of 1866 that followed lasted only seven weeks. Using railroads to quickly mobilize troops, who were armed with new and more efficient breech-loading rifles, the Prussian army defeated Austria decisively at the Battle of Sadowa (SAH-daw-vah) in Bohemia on July 3. Anticipating Prussia's future needs, Bismarck offered Austria generous peace terms. Austria paid no reparations and lost no territory to Prussia, although Venetia was ceded to Italy. But the existing German Confederation was dissolved, forcing Austria out of German affairs. Prussia conquered and annexed several small states north of the Main River and completely dominated the remaining principalities in the newly formed North German Confederation. The mainly Catholic states of the south remained independent but allied with Prussia. Bismarck's fundamental goal of Prussian expansion was partially realized (see Map 23.2).

Taming the German Parliament

Bismarck had long been convinced that the old order he so ardently defended would have to make peace with the liberal middle class and nationalists. Impressed with Napoleon III's example in France, he realized that nationalists were not necessarily hostile to conservative, authoritarian government. Moreover, the events of 1848 convinced Bismarck that the German middle class could be led to prefer national unity under conservative leadership rather than endure a long, uncertain battle for a truly liberal state. Thus during the Austrian war, he increasingly identified Prussia's fate with what he called the "national development of Germany."

To consolidate Prussian control, Bismarck fashioned a federal constitution for the new North German Confederation. Each state retained its own local government, but the king of Prussia became president of the confederation, and the new imperial chancellor—Bismarck—was responsible only to the president. The federal bureaucracy, under Wilhelm I and Bismarck, controlled the army and foreign affairs. A weak federal legislature, with members of the lower house elected by universal male suffrage, gave some voice to popular opinion. With this radical innovation, Bismarck opened the door to the possibility of going over the head of the middle class directly to the people, as Napoleon III had done in France. Ultimate power, however, still rested with the Prussian king and army.

In Prussia itself, Bismarck held out an olive branch to the parliamentary opposition. Marshalling all his diplomatic skill, he asked the parliament to pass a special indemnity bill to approve, after the fact, all the government's spending between 1862 and 1866. With German unity in sight, most of the liberals cooperated. The constitutional struggle in Prussia ended, and

the German middle class came to accept the monarchical authority that Bismarck represented.

The Franco-Prussian War and German Unification

The final act in the drama of German unification followed quickly. Bismarck calculated that a patriotic war with France would drive the south German states into his arms. He manipulated a minor diplomatic issue—whether a distant relative of Prussia's Wilhelm I might become king of Spain, in defiance of French interests—to goad the leaders of the Second French Empire into a declaration of war on Prussia.

As soon as the war began, Bismarck enlisted the support of the south German states. While other governments maintained their neutrality— Bismarck's generosity to Austria in 1866 paid big dividends—combined German forces under Prussian leadership decisively defeated the main French army at Sedan on September 1, 1870. Napoleon III was captured and humiliated. Three days later, French patriots in Paris proclaimed yet another French republic and vowed to continue fighting. But after five months, in January 1871, a besieged and starving Paris surrendered, and France accepted Bismarck's harsh peace terms.

By this time, the south German states had agreed to join a new German Empire. With Chancellor Bismarck by his side, Wilhelm I was proclaimed emperor of Germany in the Hall of Mirrors in the palace of Versailles (see "Evaluating Visual Evidence: The Proclamation of the German Empire, January 1871," page 702). As in the 1866 constitution, the king of Prussia and his ministers had ultimate power in the new German Empire, and the lower house of the legislature was elected by universal male suffrage.

Bismarck imposed a severe penalty on France: payment of a colossal indemnity of 5 billion francs and loss of the rich eastern province of Alsace and part of Lorraine to Germany. The French viewed these territorial losses as a terrible crime (see Map 23.2). They could never forget and never forgive, and relations between France and Germany were poisoned after 1871.

The Franco-Prussian War, which many Europeans saw as a test of nations in a pitiless Darwinian struggle for existence, released a surge of patriotic feeling in the German Empire. United Germany had become the most powerful state in Europe in less than a decade, and most Germans were enormously proud of Bismarck's genius and the supposedly invincible Prussian army. Semi-authoritarian nationalism and a new conservatism, based on an alliance of the landed nobles and middle classes, had triumphed in Germany.

The Proclamation of the German Empire, January 1871

(Schloss Friedrichsruhe, Germany/Bridgeman Images)

This famous commemorative painting by Anton von Werner testifies to the nationalistic intoxication in Germany after the victory over France at Sedan. Wilhelm I of Prussia stands on a platform surrounded by princes and generals in the famous Hall of Mirrors in the palace of Versailles, while officers from all the units around a besieged Paris cheer and salute him with uplifted swords as emperor of a unified Germany. Bismarck, in white (center), stands between king and army. The painting was commissioned by Wilhelm I as a gift for Bismarck's seventieth birthday in 1885.

EVALUATE THE EVIDENCE

1. How does this painting compare to work by Realist artists such as Gustave Courbet (see Chapter 22)?
2. Von Werner actually attended the ceremony depicted here, but he changed some of the details in his painting. Bismarck, for example, was dressed in a blue (not white) uniform. Why would von Werner make such changes? Is there anything else that seems unrealistic, exaggerated, or staged for effect?
3. What sort of subjective impact would this painting have on a viewer? What message is von Werner trying to impart? How does the decorated frame contribute to that message?

How did Russian and Ottoman leaders modernize their states and societies?

The Russian and Ottoman Empires experienced profound political crises in the mid-nineteenth century. These crises differed from those in Italy and Germany, for both empires were vast multinational states built on long traditions of military conquest and absolutist rule by the dominant Russians and Ottoman Turks. In the early nineteenth century the governing elites in both empires strongly opposed representative government and national independence for ethnic minorities, concentrating on absolutist rule and competition with other Great Powers. For both states, however, relentless power politics led to serious trouble. Their leaders recognized that they had to "modernize" and embrace economic, military, and social-political reforms that might enable their countries to compete effectively with leading European nations such as Great Britain, Germany, and France.

The Crimean War, 1853–1856

The "Great Reforms" in Russia

In the 1850s Russia was a poor agrarian society with a rapidly growing population. Almost 90 percent of the people lived off the land, and industrialization developed slowly. Bound to the lord from birth, the peasant serf had virtually no rights, and by the 1840s serfdom had become a central moral and political issue for the government. Discontent led to hundreds of peasant uprisings in Russia in the first half of the century, and in general the slow pace of modernization encouraged the growth of protest movements, from radical Marxists clamoring for socialist revolution to middle-class intellectuals who sought a liberal constitutional state. Then a humiliating Russian defeat in the Crimean War underscored the need for modernizing reforms.

The **Crimean War** (1853–1856) grew out of general Great Power competition in the Middle East and Russian attempts to grab lands from the declining Ottoman Empire, which shared extensive and disputed borders with Russia. The initial cause was an apparently minor dispute between France and Russia over the protection of Christian shrines in Jerusalem, but the dispute escalated into a full-blown war in which France and Britain joined the Ottomans to halt Russian expansion into the Ottoman Empire's European territories.

Famous for incompetent leadership on all sides, the Crimean War revealed the awesome power of modern weaponry, particularly artillery, in ways that anticipated the U.S. Civil War. Massive naval engagements, doomed cavalry charges, and staggering casualties — Russia alone lost about 450,000 soldiers — captured the imagination of home-front audiences, who followed events in the national press. The Crimean War also brought professional women nurses to the front lines for the first time, exemplified most famously in the British volunteer nurse Florence Nightingale. Her advocacy of simple sanitary precautions, such as washing hands before medical procedures, helped reduce mortality rates among wounded soldiers. By 1856 the French-led alliance had decisively defeated Russia.

The conflict between Russia and the French and British helped break down the European balance of power established after the Napoleonic Wars at the Congress of Vienna. Austria had refused to come to Russia's aid in the war, so Russia turned its back on its former ally. Cooperation among the Great Powers was replaced by competition and hostility. The destruction of the old international system, the isolation of Austria, and tensions between Russia and France smoothed the way to Italian and German unification.

Defeat by superior armies and weaponry furthermore convinced Russia's leaders that they had fallen behind the nations of western Europe. Russia needed railroads, better armaments, and military reform to remain a Great Power. Military disaster thus forced liberal-leaning Tsar Alexander II (r. 1855–1881) and his ministers along the path of rapid social change and modernization.

In a bold move, Alexander II abolished serfdom on privately held estates in 1861 and on state-owned lands in 1866. Russian serfs — about a third of the total population and about one-half of the peasantry — were technically not enslaved, but existing legal codes tied them to the land they lived on, typically the property of noble landowners. For reformers, their condition symbolized Russian backwardness of the sort that led to defeat in Crimea. Under Alexander II's emancipation statutes, some 50 million emancipated peasants received the rights of free citizens, the right to own

■ **Crimean War** A conflict fought between 1853 and 1856 over Russian desires to expand into Ottoman territory; Russia was defeated by France, Britain, and the Ottomans, underscoring the need for reform in the Russian Empire.

Street Scene from a Russian Village This portrayal of everyday life in a rural Russian village at the turn of the century, with dirt streets, idle peasants, and ramshackle wooden homes, seems to underscore Russian backwardness and the need for the modernizing reforms of the late nineteenth century. The photo here is from a card designed for a stereoscope, a device that gained immense popularity in the second half of the nineteenth century. With its dual-image cards viewed through a pair of lenses, the stereoscope gave the viewer the illusion that the scene portrayed came alive in three-dimensional space; companies marketed hundreds of thousands of cards with images of famous landmarks, epic landscapes, exotic foreigners, and natural wonders. Why, in your opinion, would a western European or American be interested in a scene from the Russian hinterland? (Universal History Archive/Getty Images)

property and businesses, and the chance to purchase some of the land they cultivated.

Yet the new freedoms were quite limited. Landlords received government compensation for the serfs they lost, but the newly freed peasants received no support. They had to borrow money, sign mortgages, and pay high prices for lots of relatively unproductive land that were chosen by the landowning class. Many peasants remained in debt for the rest of their lives. The tsar's government furthermore reorganized local government structures to create the *mir*, or village commune, which collected taxes and kept order in the countryside. Most peasant families continued to live on their former lands, now in deep debt, in one-story log cabins with a single living room, a storage room (sometimes shared with animals), and a shallow cellar.

Thus in the end, efforts to modernize life in the countryside through emancipation mostly failed: the reforms went too far for conservatives wishing to preserve the old order, and they did not go far enough for progressives who sought a more radical transformation of Russian society.

Although Alexander II's relatively successful legal reforms unified Russia's antiquated judicial system, established independent courts and jury trials, and gave equal rights to all parties in criminal proceedings, other reforms were halfway measures. In 1864 the government established a new institution of local representative government, the *zemstvo*, to manage local issues and concerns. Members were elected by a three-class system of townspeople, peasant villagers, and noble landowners. Russian liberals hoped that this reform would lead to an elected national parliament, but it did not. The zemstvos remained subordinate to the traditional bureaucracy and the local nobility. Alexander II's government relaxed but did not remove press censorship. It relaxed some anti-Semitic law codes and granted Jews who had graduated from secondary school the right to leave the Pale of Settlement, even as attempts to "Russify" Jewish culture increased.

Russian efforts to promote economic modernization proved more successful. Transportation and industry, both vital to the military, were transformed in two industrial surges. The first came after 1860, when the government subsidized private railway companies. The railroads linked important cities in the western territories of the empire and enabled Russia to export grain and thus earn money to finance further development. The jewel in the crown of the Russian rail system was the 5,700-mile-long Trans-Siberian Railway. Passing through seven time zones from Moscow to Vladivostok, this crucial rail line brought millions of immigrant peasants from western Russia into the lightly populated areas to the east. The grain they grew was moved west along the line, to help feed the growing cities in Russia's heartland (Map 23.3). Industrial suburbs grew up around Moscow and St. Petersburg, and a class of modern factory workers began to take shape. These workers helped spread Marxist thought, and a Russian revolutionary movement began to emerge after 1890.

Strengthened by industrial development, the tsarist state began to seize territories in Russia's borderlands. It took control of territory in far eastern Siberia, on the border with China, and in Central Asia, north of Afghanistan. It also encroached upon the Islamic lands of the Caucasus, along the northeast border of the Ottoman Empire. Russian peasants, offered the chance to escape the small plots of their ancestral homes, used the new rail systems to move to and

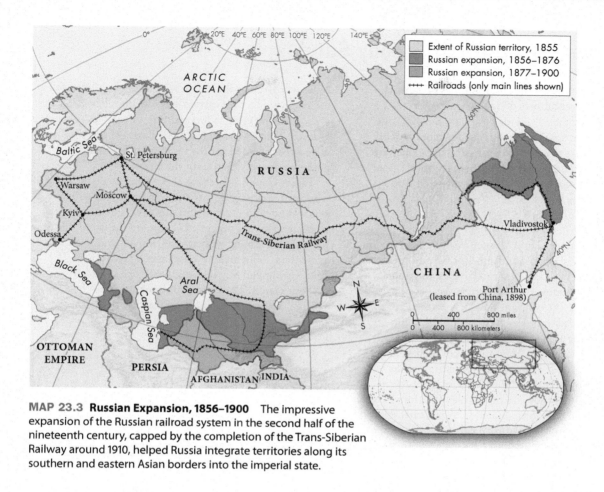

MAP 23.3 Russian Expansion, 1856–1900 The impressive expansion of the Russian railroad system in the second half of the nineteenth century, capped by the completion of the Trans-Siberian Railway around 1910, helped Russia integrate territories along its southern and eastern Asian borders into the imperial state.

settle in the newly colonized areas, at times displacing local residents (see Map 23.3). The rapid expansion of the Russian Empire to the south and east excited ardent Russian nationalists and superpatriots, who became some of the government's most enthusiastic supporters. Alexander II consolidated imperial control by suppressing nationalist movements among Poles, Ukrainians, and Baltic peoples in east-central Europe. By 1900 the Russian Empire commanded a vast and diverse array of peoples and places.

Alexander II's political reforms outraged conservatives but never went far enough for liberals and radicals. In 1881 a member of the "People's Will," a small anarchist group, assassinated the tsar, and the reform era came to an abrupt end. The new tsar, Alexander III (r. 1881–1894), was a determined reactionary. Nevertheless, from 1890 to 1900 economic modernization and industrialization again surged ahead, led by Sergei Witte (suhr-GAY VIH-tuh), finance minister from 1892 to 1903. The tough, competent Witte believed that industrial backwardness threatened Russia's greatness. Under his leadership, the government doubled the network of state-owned railways to thirty-five thousand miles. Witte established high

protective tariffs to support industry, and he put the country on the gold standard to strengthen finances.

Witte's greatest innovation was to use Westerners to catch up with the West. He encouraged foreigners to build factories in Russia, believing that "the inflow of foreign capital is . . . the only way by which our industry will be able to supply our country quickly with abundant and cheap products."[1] His efforts were especially successful in southern Russia. There, in eastern Ukraine, foreign entrepreneurs and engineers built an enormous and up-to-date steel and coal industry. In 1900 peasants still constituted the great majority of the population, but Russia was catching up with the more industrialized West.

The Russian Revolution of 1905

Catching up in part meant further territorial expansion, for this was the age of Western imperialism. By 1903 Russia had established a sphere of influence in Chinese Manchuria and was eyeing northern Korea, which put Russia in conflict with an equally imperialistic Japan. When Tsar Nicholas II (r. 1894–1917), who replaced his father in 1894, ignored their

Eyewitness Account of Bloody Sunday

Newspaper reporters for the London *Times* expressed shock at the rapid outbreak of deadly violence in St. Petersburg on Bloody Sunday (January 22, 1905), one of the events that sparked the Russian Revolution of 1905. The Cossacks referred to in the excerpt below were soldiers recruited from Russia's southern steppes. Father Gapon, also mentioned in the report, was an Orthodox priest who led the march.

Event has succeeded event with such bewildering rapidity that the public is staggered and shocked beyond measure. The first trouble began at 11 o'clock, when the military tried to turn back some thousands of strikers at one of the bridges . . . where the constant flow of workmen pressing forward refused to be denied access to the common rendezvous in the Palace Square. The Cossacks at first used their knouts [whips], then the flat of their sabers, and finally they fired. The strikers in the front ranks fell on their knees and implored the Cossacks to let them pass, protesting that they had no hostile intentions. They refused, however, to be intimidated by blank cartridges, and orders were given to load with ball.

The passions of the mob broke loose like a bursting dam. The people, seeing the dead and dying carried away in all directions, the snow on the streets and pavements soaked with blood, cried aloud for vengeance. Meanwhile the situation at the Palace was becoming momentarily worse. The troops were reported to be unable to control the vast masses which were constantly surging forward. Re-enforcements were sent, and at 2 o'clock here also the order was given to fire. Men, women, and children fell at each volley, and were carried away in ambulances, sledges, and carts. The indignation and fury of every class were aroused. Students, merchants, all classes of the population alike were inflamed. At the moment of writing, firing is going on in every quarter of the city.

Father Gapon, marching at the head of a large body of workmen, carrying a cross and other religious emblems, was wounded in the arm and shoulder. The two forces of workmen are now separated. Those on the other side of the river are arming with swords, knives, and smiths' and carpenters' tools, and are busy erecting barricades. The troops are apparently reckless, firing right and left, with or without reason. The rioters continue to appeal to them, saying, "You are Russians! Why play the part of blood-thirsty butchers?" . . .

A night of terror is in prospect.

EVALUATE THE EVIDENCE

1. Can you begin to reconstruct the events of Bloody Sunday from this report? Who seems to be responsible for the violence?
2. Why would press accounts from London seem more sympathetic to the protesters than to the soldiers, who represent the power of the Russian state?
3. Did popular protest help Russians win civil rights from the tsarist government?

Source: James Harvey Robinson and Charles Beard, eds., *Readings in Modern European History*, vol. 2 (Boston: Ginn and Company, 1909), pp. 373–374.

diplomatic protests, the Japanese launched a surprise attack on Port Arthur, a Russian naval base in northern China, in February 1904. In a series of naval and land campaigns, Japan scored repeated victories, and a humiliated Russia agreed to peace terms negotiated by U.S. president Theodore Roosevelt in September 1905. The victory presaged the rise of Japan as a predominant East Asian power.

In Russia military disaster abroad again brought political upheaval at home. The business and professional classes had long wanted a liberal, representative government. Urban factory workers were organized in a radical and still-illegal labor movement. Peasants had gained little from emancipation and suffered from poverty and lack of land. The empire's minorities and subject nationalities, such as Poles, Ukrainians, and Latvians, continued to call for self-rule. With the Russian army pinned down in Manchuria, these currents of discontent converged in the revolution of 1905.

On a Sunday in January 1905, a massive crowd of workers and their families marched peacefully on the Winter Palace in St. Petersburg to present a petition to Nicholas II. Suddenly troops opened fire, killing and wounding hundreds. The Bloody Sunday massacre produced a wave of general indignation that turned many Russians against the tsar. (See "Evaluating Written Evidence: Eyewitness Account of Bloody Sunday.")

By the summer of 1905 strikes and political rallies, peasant uprisings, revolts among minority nationalities, and mutinies by troops were sweeping the country. The **Russian Revolution of 1905** culminated in October that year in a paralyzing general strike that forced the government to capitulate. The tsar then issued the October Manifesto, which granted full civil rights and promised a popularly elected **Duma** (DO-mah, or parliament) with real legislative power. The manifesto helped split opposition to the tsarist government. Frightened middle-class leaders embraced the liberal reforms and turned their backs on the radical labor movement. Divisions in the revolutionary coalition—similar to those that had emerged in 1848—helped the government repress the popular uprising and contributed to its survival as a constitutional monarchy.

On the eve of the first Duma in May 1906, the government issued the new constitution, the so-called Fundamental Laws, which represented an enormous change and a step toward constitutional monarchy in Russia. Yet the tsar retained great powers: he maintained control of the army and foreign policy. The Duma, elected indirectly by universal male suffrage with a largely appointive upper house, could debate and pass laws, but, as in other representative systems, the tsar had an absolute veto. As in Bismarck's Germany, the tsar appointed his ministers, who did not need to command a majority in the Duma.

The predominantly middle-class liberals, the largest group in the newly elected Duma, saw the Fundamental Laws as a step backward. Cooperation with Nicholas II's ministers soon broke down, and after months of deadlock the tsar dismissed the Duma. Thereupon he and his advisers, including the talented prime minister Pyotr Stolypin, unilaterally rewrote the electoral law to greatly increase the electoral weight of the conservative propertied classes. When new elections were held, the tsar could count on a legislative majority loyal to the monarchy. The government then pushed through important agrarian reforms designed to break down collective village ownership of land and encourage the more enterprising peasants—Stolypin's "wager on the strong and sober," meant to encourage economic growth. The government reformed the education and banking systems, but these acts were accompanied by harsh repression of dissidents and radicals. About three thousand suspected revolutionaries were executed by the state, and the hangman's noose became known as "Stolypin's necktie." In 1914, on the eve of the First World War, Russia was partially modernized, a repressive constitutional monarchy with a peasant-based but industrializing economy and significant pockets of discontent.

Reform and Readjustment in the Ottoman Empire

By the early nineteenth century the economic and political changes reshaping Europe were also at play in the Ottoman Empire, which stretched around the northeastern, eastern, and southern shores of the Mediterranean Sea. The borderlands of this vast empire experienced constant flux and conflict (Map 23.4). Russia had already grabbed Bessarabia during the Napoleonic Wars, thereby taking control of the Danube River's access to the Black Sea. In 1816 the Ottomans were forced to grant Serbia local autonomy. In 1830 the Greeks won independence, and French armies began their long and bloody takeover of Ottoman Algeria. Yet the Ottomans also achieved important victories. Forces under Muhammad Ali, the Ottoman governor in Egypt, restored order in the Islamic holy lands and conquered significant portions of Sudan, south of Egypt.

Muhammad Ali, a ruthless and intelligent soldier-politician, ruled Egypt in the name of the Ottoman sultan from 1805 to 1848. His modernizing reforms of agriculture, industry, and the military helped turn Egypt into the most powerful state in the eastern Mediterranean. In time, his growing strength directly challenged the Ottoman sultan and Istanbul's ruling elite. From 1831 to 1840 Egyptian troops under the leadership of Muhammad Ali's son Ibrahim occupied the Ottoman province of Syria and Palestine and threatened to depose the Ottoman sultan Mahmud II (r. 1808–1839).

This conflict forced the Ottomans to seek European support. Mahmud II's dynasty survived, but only because the European powers, led by Britain, allied with the Ottomans to discipline Muhammad Ali. The European powers preferred a weak and dependent Ottoman Empire to a strong, economically independent state under dynamic leadership.

Faced with growing European military and economic competition, liberal Ottoman statesmen in 1839 launched the **Tanzimat**, or "Reorganization." The radical Tanzimat reforms, borrowed from western European models, were designed to modernize the empire. The high point of reform came when the new liberal-minded sultan, Abdul Mejid (r. 1839–1861), issued the Imperial Rescript of 1856, just after the Ottoman victory in the Crimean War. Articles in the decree called for equality before the law regardless of religious faith, a modernized administration and army, and private ownership of land. As part of the reform policy, and under economic pressure from the European powers that had paid for the empire's war against Russia in Crimea, Ottoman leaders adopted free-trade policies. New commercial laws removed tariffs on

■ **Russian Revolution of 1905** A series of popular revolts and mass strikes that forced the tsarist government to grant moderate liberal reforms, including civil rights and a popularly elected parliament.

■ **Duma** The Russian parliament that opened in 1906, elected indirectly by universal male suffrage but controlled after 1907 by the tsar and the conservative classes.

■ **Tanzimat** A set of reforms designed to remake the Ottoman Empire on a western European model.

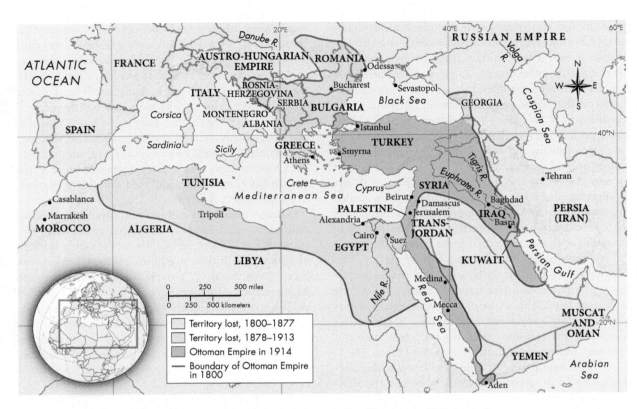

MAP 23.4 Ottoman Contraction, 1800–1914   In the nineteenth and early twentieth centuries, internal national movements and the European powers forced the Ottoman Empire to give up significant territories in North Africa, the Caucasus, and the Balkans. Territorial loss encouraged reform efforts that stabilized the empire but failed to stop its collapse at the end of the First World War.

foreign imports and permitted foreign merchants to operate freely throughout the empire.

This turn to nineteenth-century liberal capitalism had mixed effects. With the growth of Western-style banking and insurance systems, elite Christian and Jewish businessmen prospered. Yet most profits went to foreign investors rather than Ottoman subjects. In addition, the elimination of traditional state-controlled monopolies sharply cut imperial revenues. In 1851 Sultan Mejid was forced to borrow 55 million francs from British and French bankers to cover state deficits. Other loans followed, and intractable indebtedness led to the bankruptcy of the Ottoman state two decades later.

The Tanzimat reforms brought partial recovery but fell short of their goals. The Ottoman initiatives failed to curtail the appetite of Western imperialists, who secured a stranglehold on the imperial economy by issuing loans. The reforms also failed to halt the growth of nationalism among some Christian subjects in the Balkans, which resulted in crises and increased pressure from neighboring Austria and Russia, eager to gain access to the Balkans and the eastern Mediterranean.

Finally, equality before the law for all citizens, regardless of religious affiliation, actually exacerbated religious disputes, which were often encouraged and manipulated by the European powers eager to seize any pretext for intervention. This development embittered relations between religious conservatives and social liberals, a struggle that ultimately distracted the government from its reform mission. Religious conservatives in both the Muslim and Greek Orthodox communities detested the religious reforms, which they viewed as an impious departure from tradition. These conservatives became dependable supporters of Sultan Abdülhamid II (ahb-dool-hah-MEED) (r. 1876–1909), who halted the reform movement and turned away from European liberalism in his long and authoritarian reign.

Abdülhamid II's government failed to halt foreign efforts to fragment and ultimately take control over key Ottoman territories. Defeated in the Russo-Turkish War (1877–1878), the Ottomans ceded districts in the Caucasus to Russia; saw the Balkan territories of Romania, Montenegro, and Serbia declare independence; and granted the establishment of an autonomous Bulgaria, still nominally under the Ottoman sultan's control. By the 1890s the government's failures had encouraged a powerful resurgence of the modernizing impulse under the banner

Abbas Hilmi Pasha Receives the Grand Cross of the French Legion of Honor In 1892, Abbas Hilmi Pasha, the khedive (or viceroy) of the Ottoman Empire in Egypt, received the Grand Cross of the Legion of Honor, France's highest order of merit, from the French consul in Cairo. The award was meant to cement French ties with the Ottomans in Egypt, despite British interests in the region. As this cover of a contemporary French illustrated magazine suggests, Ottoman leaders were well versed in European languages and culture. They mastered the game of power politics, playing one European state against another in attempts to secure the Ottoman Empire's survival. (World History Archive/Alamy)

of the Committee of Union and Progress (CUP), an umbrella organization that united multiethnic reformist groups from across the empire. These fervent patriots, unofficially called the **Young Turks**, seized power in a 1908 coup and forced the sultan to implement new reforms. Although they failed to stop the rising tide of anti-Ottoman nationalism in the Balkans, the Young Turks helped prepare the way for the rise of modern secular Turkey after the defeat and collapse of the Ottoman Empire in World War I.

How did the relationship between government and the governed change after 1871?

The decades after 1870 brought rapid change to European politics. Despite some major differences among countries, European domestic politics had a new common framework, the nation-state. The nation-state made new demands on its citizens but also offered them new benefits, embodied in growing state institutions and bureaucracies.

The Responsive National State

Common themes within the framework of the new nation-state were the emergence of mass politics and growing popular loyalty toward the nation. Traditional elites were forced into new arrangements in order to exercise power, and new, pragmatic politicians took leading roles. The major states of western Europe adopted constitutions of some sort, and the right to vote — for men — was extended in Britain, France, Germany, and elsewhere, at least in elections for the

lower houses of parliament. New political parties representing a broad spectrum of interests and groups, from workers and liberals to Catholics and conservatives, now engaged in hard-fought election campaigns.

Powerful bureaucracies emerged to govern growing populations, manage modern economies, and administer social programs. The responsive national state offered its citizens free education and some welfare and public health benefits, and for good reason many ordinary people felt increasing loyalty to their governments.

Building support for nation-states also had a less positive side. Elite leaders only reluctantly extended the popular vote to male citizens, and they dismissed women's demands for political equality. Young men

■ **Young Turks** Fervent patriots who seized power in a 1908 coup in the Ottoman Empire, forcing the conservative sultan to implement reforms.

were forced to serve in the national military. Although the British maintained an all-volunteer army until the First World War, most continental countries had established conscription systems by the 1870s. They also began to levy income taxes to pay for the expansion of national bureaucracies.

In addition, both conservative and moderate leaders found that workers who voted socialist — whose potential revolutionary power they feared — would rally around the flag in a diplomatic crisis or cheer when colonial interests seized a distant territory. Therefore, governing elites increasingly used antiliberal militarist and imperialist policies to unite national populations and overcome or mask intractable domestic conflicts. The failure to resolve internal conflicts and the tendency to manipulate foreign policy to win popular support inflamed the domestic and international tensions that erupted in the cataclysms of World War I and the Russian Revolution.

The German Empire

The history of Germany after 1871 exemplified many of the political developments associated with the formation of nation-states. Like the United States, the new German Empire adopted a federal system: a union of Prussia and twenty-four smaller states, each with separate legislatures. Much of the business of government was conducted at the state level, but there was a strong national government, dominated by Prussia. Imperial Germany had a chancellor — until 1890, Bismarck — and a popularly elected parliament called the **Reichstag** (RIKES-tahg). Although Bismarck frequently ignored the wishes of the parliamentary majority, he preferred to win the support of the Reichstag to lend legitimacy to his policy goals. This situation gave the political parties opportunities to influence national policy. Until 1878 Bismarck relied mainly on the National Liberals, who supported legislation useful for economic growth and the unification of the country.

Less wisely, the National Liberals backed Bismarck's attack on the Catholic Church, the so-called Kulturkampf (kool-TOOR-kahmpf), or "culture struggle."

Like Bismarck, the middle-class National Liberals were alarmed by Pius IX's declaration of papal infallibility in 1870. That dogma seemed to ask German Catholics to put loyalty to their church, a foreign power, above their loyalty to their newly unified nation. Kulturkampf initiatives aimed to make the Catholic Church subject to government control. However, only in Protestant Prussia did the Kulturkampf have even limited success.

In 1878 Bismarck abandoned his attack on the church and instead courted the Catholic Center Party, whose supporters included many Catholic small farmers in western and southern Germany. By revoking liberal free-trade policies and enacting high tariffs on cheap grain from the United States, Canada, and Russia, he won over both the Center Party and the conservative Protestant Junkers, nobles with large landholdings in East Prussia.

Other governments followed Bismarck's lead, and the 1880s and 1890s saw a widespread return to protectionism in Europe. France, in particular, established high tariffs to protect agriculture and industry. European governments thus offered an effective response to foreign competition in a way that won popular loyalty. But the rise of protectionism exemplified the dangers of self-centered nationalism: new tariffs led to international name-calling and nasty trade wars.

After the failure of the Kulturkampf, Bismarck's government tried to stop the growth of the **German Social Democratic Party (SPD)**, Germany's Marxist, working-class political party that was established in the 1870s. Both conservative elites and middle-class liberals feared the SPD's revolutionary language and allegiance to a Marxist movement that promised to upend established social and economic hierarchies. In 1878 Bismarck pushed the Reichstag to approve the Anti-Socialist Laws, which banned Social Democratic associations, meetings, and publications. The Social Democratic Party was driven underground, but it maintained substantial influence, and Bismarck decided to try another tack.

To win working-class support, Bismarck urged the Reichstag to enact state-supported social welfare measures. Big business and some conservatives accused him of creating "state socialism," but Bismarck carried the day, and his conservative nation-state was among the first to set up extensive social welfare programs. In 1883 the Reichstag enacted the first of several social security laws to help wage earners by providing national sickness insurance. Other laws established accident insurance, old-age pensions, and retirement benefits. Henceforth sick, injured, and retired workers could look forward to some regular benefits from the state. This national social security system, paid for through compulsory contributions by wage earners

■ **Reichstag** The popularly elected lower house of government of the new German Empire after 1871.

■ **German Social Democratic Party (SPD)** A German working-class political party founded in the 1870s, the SPD championed Marxism but in practice turned away from Marxist revolution and worked instead in the German parliament for social benefits and workplace reforms.

■ **Dreyfus affair** A divisive case in which Alfred Dreyfus, a Jewish captain in the French army, was falsely accused and convicted of treason. The Catholic Church sided with the anti-Semites against Dreyfus; after Dreyfus was declared innocent, the French government severed all ties between the state and the church.

and employers as well as grants from the state, was the first of its kind anywhere. The German social security system did not wean workers from voting socialist, but it did give them a small stake in the system and protect them from some of the uncertainties of the competitive industrial economy. This enormously significant development was a product of political competition and conservative efforts to win popular support by defusing the SPD's radical appeal.

Increasingly, the key issue in German domestic politics was socialism and the rapid growth of the SPD. In 1890 the new emperor, the young, idealistic, and unstable Wilhelm II (r. 1888–1918), opposed Bismarck's attempt to renew the Anti-Socialist Laws. Eager to rule in his own right and to earn the support of the workers, Wilhelm II forced Bismarck to resign. Afterward, German foreign policy became far more aggressive — in part to distract the population from ongoing internal conflicts — but the government did legalize socialist political activity and passed new laws to aid workers.

Yet Wilhelm II was no more successful than Bismarck in getting workers to renounce socialism. Social Democrats won more and more seats in the Reichstag, becoming Germany's largest single party in 1912. Though this victory shocked aristocrats and their wealthy, conservative allies, who held exaggerated fears of an impending socialist upheaval, the revolutionary socialists had actually become less radical. In the years before World War I, the SPD broadened its base by adopting a more patriotic tone, allowing for greater military spending and imperialist expansion. German socialists abandoned revolutionary aims to concentrate instead on gradual social and political reform.

Republican France and the Third French Republic

Although Napoleon III's reign reduced some antagonisms between classes, the Franco-Prussian War undid these efforts. In 1871 France seemed hopelessly divided once again. The patriotic republicans who proclaimed the Third Republic in Paris after the military disaster at Sedan refused to admit defeat by the Germans. They defended Paris with great heroism for weeks, until they were starved into submission by German armies in January 1871.

The next national elections sent a large majority of conservatives and monarchists to the National Assembly, and France's new leaders decided they had no choice but to surrender Alsace (al-SAS) and Lorraine to Germany. The traumatized Parisians exploded in patriotic frustration and proclaimed the Paris Commune in March 1871. Its radical leaders wanted to establish a revolutionary government in Paris and rule without interference from the conservative French countryside. Their program included workplace reforms, the separation of church and state, press censorship, and radical feminism. The National Assembly, led by aging politician Adolphe Thiers (TEE-ehr), ordered the French army into Paris and brutally crushed the Commune. Twenty thousand people died in the fighting. As in June 1848, it was Paris against the provinces, French against French.

Out of this tragedy, France slowly formed a new national unity under the banner of the Third Republic, achieving considerable stability before 1914. How do we account for this? Luck played a part. Until 1875 the monarchists in the ostensibly republican National Assembly had a majority but could not agree on who should be king. The compromise Bourbon candidate refused to rule except under the white flag of his absolutist ancestors — a completely unacceptable condition for many supporters of a constitutional monarchy. In the meantime, Thiers's destruction of the Commune and his other firm measures showed the fearful provinces and the middle classes that the Third Republic could be politically moderate and socially conservative. Another stabilizing factor was the skill and determination of moderate republican leaders in the early years. France therefore reluctantly retained republican government, with a presidential system rather than a parliamentary monarchy. As President Thiers cautiously said, this was "the government which divides us least." By 1879 most members of both the upper and lower houses of the National Assembly were republicans, giving the Third Republic firm foundations.

The moderate republicans sought to preserve the Third Republic by winning the allegiance of the next generation. The Assembly legalized trade unions, and France expanded its colonial empire. More important, a series of laws between 1879 and 1886 greatly broadened the state system of public, tax-supported schools and established free compulsory elementary education for both girls and boys. In the past, most elementary and much secondary education had occurred in Catholic schools, which had long been hostile to republicanism and secularism. Now free compulsory elementary education became secular republican education. Throughout the Western world, the expansion of public education was a critical nation-building tool in the late nineteenth century.

Although the educational reforms of the 1880s disturbed French Catholics, many of them rallied to the republic in the 1890s. The limited acceptance of the modern world by the more liberal Pope Leo XIII (pontificate 1878–1903) eased conflicts between church and state. Unfortunately, the **Dreyfus affair** renewed church-state tensions.

In 1894 Alfred Dreyfus, a Jewish captain in the French army, was falsely accused and convicted of treason. His case enlisted the support of prominent republicans and intellectuals, including novelist Émile Zola. In 1898 and 1899 the Dreyfus affair split France apart. On one side was the army, which had manufactured evidence against Dreyfus, joined by anti-Semites, conservative nationalists, and most of the Catholic establishment. On the other side stood liberals and most republicans.

Dreyfus was eventually declared innocent, but the battle revived republican animosity toward the Catholic Church. Between 1901 and 1905 the government severed all ties between the state and the church. It stopped paying priests' and bishops' salaries and placed committees of lay Catholics in control of all churches. Suddenly on their own financially, Catholic schools soon lost a third of their students, greatly increasing the state school system's reach and thus its power of indoctrination. In short, deep religious and political divisions, as well as a growing socialist movement, challenged the apparent stability of the Third Republic.

Great Britain and Ireland

Historians once cast late-nineteenth-century Britain as a shining example of peaceful and successful political evolution, where an effective two-party Parliament skillfully guided the country from classical liberalism to full-fledged democracy with hardly a misstep. This "Whig view" of British history is not so much wrong as it is incomplete. After the right to vote was granted to wealthy middle-class males in 1832, opinion leaders and politicians wrestled with further expansion of the franchise. In 1859 the Whig Party merged with other groups to form the Liberal Party, which advocated social reform and laissez-faire economics and would continue to challenge the opposing Conservative Party into the twentieth century. In the Second Reform Bill of 1867, Benjamin Disraeli and the Conservative Party extended the vote to all middle-class males and the best-paid workers to broaden their base of support beyond the landowning class. After 1867 English political parties and electoral campaigns became more modern, and the "lower orders" appeared to vote as responsibly as their "betters." Hence the Third Reform Bill of 1884, introduced by Liberal prime minister William Gladstone (1809–1898), gave the vote to almost every adult male. The long reign of Queen Victoria (r. 1837–1901), whose role in Britain's evolving constitutional monarchy became increasingly symbolic, offered the British a sense of pride and stability in an era of political change.

While the House of Commons drifted toward democracy, the House of Lords was content to slumber nobly. Between 1901 and 1910, however, the Lords tried to reassert themselves. Acting as supreme court of the land, they ruled against labor unions in two important decisions. And after the Liberal Party came to power in 1906, the Lords vetoed several measures passed by the Commons, including the so-called People's Budget, designed to increase spending on social welfare services. When the king threatened to create enough new peers to pass the bill, the Lords finally capitulated, as they had with the Reform Bill of 1832. Aristocratic conservatism yielded slowly to popular democracy.

Extensive social welfare measures, previously slow to come to Great Britain, were passed in a spectacular rush between 1906 and 1914. During those years the Liberal Party, inspired by the fiery Welshman David Lloyd George (1863–1945), enacted the People's Budget and substantially raised taxes on the rich. This income helped the government pay for national health insurance, unemployment benefits, old-age pensions, and a host of other social measures, although the refusal to grant women the right to vote encouraged a determined and increasingly militant women's suffrage movement.

This record of accomplishment was only part of the story, however. On the eve of World War I, the unanswered question of Ireland brought Great Britain to the brink of civil war. The terrible Irish famine of the 1840s and early 1850s had fueled an Irish revolutionary movement. The Irish Republican Brotherhood, established in 1858 and known as the "Fenians," engaged in violent campaigns against British rule. The British responded with repression and arrests. Seeking a way out, the English slowly granted concessions, such as rights for Irish peasants and abolition of Anglican Church privileges. Gladstone, who twenty years earlier had proclaimed, "My mission is to pacify Ireland," introduced bills to give Ireland self-government, or **home rule**, in 1886 and in 1893, though they failed to pass.

Ireland was on the brink of achieving self-government, but while the Catholic majority in the southern counties wanted home rule, the Protestants of the northern counties of Ulster opposed it. The Ulster Protestants (or Ulsterites) refused to submerge themselves in a majority-Catholic Ireland, just as Irish Catholics had refused to submit to a Protestant Britain.

By December 1913 the Ulsterites had raised one hundred thousand armed volunteers, and much of English public opinion supported their cause. In 1914 the Liberals in the House of Lords introduced a compromise home-rule bill that did not apply to the

■ **home rule** The late-nineteenth-century movement to give Ireland a government independent from Great Britain; it was supported by Irish Catholics and resisted by Irish Protestants.

Irish Home Rule   In December 1867 members of the "Fenians," an underground group dedicated to Irish independence from British rule, detonated a bomb outside Clerkenwell Prison in London. Their attempt to liberate Irish Republican activists failed. Though the bomb blew a hole in the prison walls, damaged nearby buildings, and killed twelve innocent bystanders, no Fenians were freed. The British labeled the event the "Clerkenwell Outrage," and its violence evokes revealing parallels with the radical terrorist attacks of today. (akg-images/Newscom)

northern counties. This bill, which openly betrayed promises made to Irish nationalists, was rejected in the Commons, and in September the original home-rule bill passed but with its implementation delayed. The Irish question had been overtaken by the world war that began in August 1914, and final resolution was suspended for the duration of the hostilities.

Irish developments illustrated once again the power of national feeling and national movements. Moreover, they demonstrated that central governments could not elicit greater loyalty unless they could capture and control that elemental current of national feeling. Though Great Britain had power, prosperity, and parliamentary rule, none of these availed in the face of the conflicting nationalisms created by Irish Catholics and Protestants. Similarly, progressive Sweden was powerless to stop a Norwegian national movement, which culminated in Norway's leaving Sweden and becoming fully independent in 1905.

The Ottoman Empire confronted similar difficulties in the Balkans in the late nineteenth century. It was only a matter of time before the Serbs, Bulgarians, and Romanians would break away.

The Austro-Hungarian Empire

The dilemma of conflicting nationalisms in Ireland or the Ottoman Empire helps one appreciate how desperate the situation in the Austro-Hungarian Empire had become by the early twentieth century. In 1848 Magyar nationalism had driven Hungarian patriots to declare an independent Hungarian republic, which Russian and Austrian armies savagely crushed in the summer of 1849. Throughout the 1850s Hungary was ruled by Austria as a conquered territory, and Emperor Franz Joseph and his bureaucracy tried hard to centralize the state and Germanize the language and culture of the different ethnic groups there.

Then, in the wake of its defeat by Prussia in 1866 and the loss of northern Italy, a weakened Austria agreed to a compromise and in 1867 established the so-called dual monarchy. The Austrian Empire was divided in two, and the Magyars gained virtual independence for Hungary. Henceforth each half of the empire dealt with its own ethnic minorities. The two states, now called the Austro-Hungarian Empire or Austria-Hungary, still shared the same monarch and common ministries for finance, defense, and foreign affairs.

In Austria, ethnic Germans were only one-third of the population, and many Germans saw their traditional dominance threatened by Czechs, Poles, and other Slavs. The language used in local government and elementary education became a particularly emotional issue in the Austrian parliament. From 1900 to 1914 the legislature was so divided that ministries generally could not obtain a majority and ruled instead by decree. Efforts by both conservatives and socialists to defuse national antagonisms by stressing economic issues that cut across ethnic lines were largely unsuccessful.

In Hungary, the Magyar nobility in 1867 restored the constitution of 1848 and used it to dominate both the Magyar peasantry and the minority populations until 1914. Only the wealthiest one-fourth of adult males had the right to vote, making the parliament the creature of the Magyar elite. Laws promoting the Magyar language in schools and government were bitterly resented, especially by Croatians and Romanians. While Magyar extremists campaigned for total separation from Austria, the radical leaders of their subject nationalities dreamed of independence from Hungary. Unlike countries that harnessed nationalism to strengthen the state after 1871, the Austro-Hungarian Empire was progressively weakened by it.

What were the costs and benefits of nationalism for ordinary people?

Although the familiar boundaries of Europe's nation-states were mostly in place by the 1870s, national leaders faced a unique problem: how could they encourage ordinary people to identify with the state? While shared languages and institutions and new national symbols helped build popular support, some people were marginalized, either excluded from political representation or turned into scapegoats.

Making National Citizens

Responding to national unification, an Italian statesman famously remarked, "We have made Italy. Now we must make Italians." His comment captured the dilemma faced by political leaders in the last third of the nineteenth century. As the nation-state extended voting rights and welfare benefits to more and more people, the question of national loyalty became increasingly important. How could the new nation-states win the people's heartfelt allegiance?

The issue was pressing. The recent unification of Italy and Germany, for example, had brought together a patchwork of previously independent states with different customs, loyalties, and in some cases languages. In Italy, only about 2 percent of the population spoke the language that would become official Italian. In Germany, regional and religious differences and strong traditions of local political autonomy undermined collective feeling. In Great Britain, deep class differences still dampened national unity, and across the territories of central and eastern Europe, overlapping ethnic groups with distinct languages and cultures challenged the logic of nation building. Even in France, where national boundaries had been fairly stable for several centuries, only about 50 percent of the people spoke the version of French that would ultimately become the official language of the national state. The 60 percent of the population that still lived in rural areas often felt stronger allegiance to their village or region than to the distant nation headquartered in Paris.

Yet by the 1890s most ordinary people had accepted, if not embraced, the notion of national belonging, for various reasons. For one, centralized institutions imposed across entire territories reached even the lowliest citizen. Universal military conscription, introduced in most of Europe after the Franco-Prussian War (Britain was an exception), yanked peasants off their land and workers out of their factories and exposed young male conscripts to patriotic values. Free compulsory education leveled out language differences and taught children about glorious national traditions. In Italy and Germany, the introduction of a common currency, standard weights and measurements, and a national post office eroded regional differences. Boasting images of grand historical events or prominent leaders, even postage stamps and banknotes could impart a sense of national solidarity.

Improved transportation and communication networks broke down regional differences and reinforced the national idea as well. The extension of railway service into hinterlands and the improvement of local roads shattered rural isolation, boosted the growth of national markets for commercial agriculture, and helped turn "peasants into Frenchmen."[2] Literacy rates and compulsory schooling advanced rapidly in the late nineteenth century, and more and more people read about national history or the latest political events in newspapers, magazines, and books.

Intellectuals, politicians, and ideologues of all stripes eagerly promoted national pride. At Berlin University, prominent history professor Heinrich von Treitschke championed German superiority, especially over archrival Great Britain. Scholars like Treitschke sought to find the deep roots of national identity in ancient folk traditions; in shared language, customs, race, and religion; and in historic attachments to national lands. Such accounts, often based on flimsy historical evidence, were popularized in the classroom and the press. Few nationalist thinkers sympathized with French philosopher Ernest Renan, who suggested that national identity was based more on a people's current desire for a "common life" and an invented, idealized past than on actual, true-to-life historical experiences.

New symbols and rituals brought nationalism into the lives of ordinary people. Each nation had its own unique capital city, flag, military uniform, and national anthem. New symbols, such as Britain's doughty John Bull, France's republican Marianne, America's stern Uncle Sam, and Germany's stolid Michel, supposedly embodied shared national characteristics. All citizens could participate in newly invented national holidays, such as Bastille Day in France, first held in 1880 to commemorate the French Revolution, or Sedan Day in Germany, created to celebrate Germany's victory over France in 1871. Royal weddings, coronations, jubilees, and funerals brought citizens into the streets to celebrate the nation's leaders — British Queen Victoria's 1887 Golden Jubilee set a high standard. Public squares and parks received prominent commemorative statues and monuments, such as the grand memorial to Victor Emmanuel II in central Rome, or the ostentatious Monument to the Battle of Nations built in Leipzig to honor German victory in the Napoleonic Wars. Surrounded by these inescapable elements of everyday nationalism, most ordinary people grew to see themselves as members of their national communities.[3] (See "Thinking Like a Historian: How to Build a Nation," page 716.)

The Feminist Movement

Facing discrimination in education and employment and a lack of legal rights, some women began to demand that the nation-state guarantee the rights of women and the equality of the sexes. Women had much to fight for in the late nineteenth century. The ideal of separate spheres and the rigid gender division of labor meant that middle-class women faced great obstacles when they needed or wanted to move into the man's world of paid employment. Married women were subordinated to their husbands by law and lacked many basic legal rights. In England, a wife had no legal identity and hence no right to own property in her own name. Even the wages she might earn belonged to her husband. In France, the Napoleonic Code enshrined the principle of female subordination and gave the wife few legal rights regarding property, divorce, and custody of the children.

Following women such as Mary Wollstonecraft, middle-class feminists campaigned for equal legal rights for women as well as access to higher education, professional employment, and the vote. They argued that unmarried women and middle-class widows with inadequate incomes simply had to have more opportunities to support themselves. Feminists also argued that paid employment, as opposed to unpaid housework, could relieve the monotony that some women found in their sheltered middle-class existence. Determined organizing and calls for reform helped realize such demands. For example, by 1913 the Federation of German Women's Associations, an umbrella organization for regional feminist groups, had some 470,000 members. Their protests had a direct impact on the revised German Civil Code of 1906, which granted women substantial gains in family law and property rights.

In the late nineteenth century women's organizations scored some significant victories, such as the 1882 law giving English married women full property rights. In the decade before World War I, the British women's **suffrage movement** mounted a militant struggle for the right to vote. Inspired by the slogan "Deeds Not Words," women "suffragettes" marched in public demonstrations, heckled members of Parliament, and slashed paintings in London's National Gallery. Jailed for political activities, they went on highly publicized hunger strikes. Conservatives dismissed "the shrieking sisterhood," and British women received the vote only in 1919.

In most European countries before 1900, women were not admitted as fully registered students at a single university. Switzerland played a pioneering role: women were admitted into some university programs as early as 1867. France and Belgium granted women access to higher education in 1880. In Germany and Austria-Hungary, universities only

---

■ **suffrage movement** A militant movement for women's right to vote led by middle-class British women, which exemplified broader international campaigns for women's political rights around 1900.

How to Build a Nation

Nationalism permeated many aspects of everyday life and became a powerful political ideology in the late nineteenth century. Yet because Europeans were divided by opposing regional and religious loyalties, social and class divisions, and ethnic differences, developing a sense of national belonging among ordinary people posed a problem. How did leaders encourage citizens to embrace national identities?

1 **Ernest Renan, "What Is a Nation?," 1882.** In a famous lecture, French philosopher Ernest Renan argued that national identity depended on an imagined past that had less to do with historical reality than with contemporary aspirations for collective belonging.

A nation is a soul, a spiritual principle. Two things, which in truth are but one, constitute this soul or spiritual principle. One lies in the past, one in the present. One is the possession in common of a rich legacy of memories; the other is present-day consent, the desire to live together, the will to perpetuate the value of the heritage that one has received in an undivided form. . . .

More valuable by far than common customs posts and frontiers conforming to strategic ideas is the fact of sharing, in the past, a glorious heritage and regrets, and of having, in the future, [a shared] programme to put into effect, or the fact of having suffered, enjoyed, and hoped together. These are the kinds of things that can be understood in spite of differences of race and language. I spoke just now of "having suffered together" and, indeed, suffering in common unifies more than joy does. Where national memories are concerned, griefs are of more value than triumphs, for they impose duties, and require a common effort.

A nation is therefore a large-scale solidarity, constituted by the feeling of the sacrifices that one has made in the past and of those that one is prepared to make in the future. It presupposes a past; it is summarized, however, in the present by a tangible fact, namely, consent, the clearly expressed desire to continue a common life. A nation's existence is, if you will pardon the metaphor, a daily plebiscite, just as an individual's existence is a perpetual affirmation of life.

2 **National banknotes and stamps.** Patriotic images turned up in everyday places. An 1881 Italian banknote (below), for example, featured Leonardo da Vinci and King Victor Emmanuel II, while a 1905 Belgian stamp (right) portrayed King Leopold II.

(CSP_Boris15/age-fotostock)

(DeAgostini/DEA/A. DAGLI ORTI/Getty Images)

ANALYZING THE EVIDENCE

1. In Source 1, why does Ernest Renan conclude that "[a] nation's existence is . . . a daily plebiscite"?
2. Consider Sources 2–5. What symbols or ideas are used to promote a sense of national belonging? Why, for example, would an Italian banknote feature an image of the sixteenth-century artist/philosopher Leonardo da Vinci? Why do these sources repeatedly evoke blood, battles, and national leaders?
3. Are nationalists good historians? Do the sources above accurately represent the "true-to-life" historical experiences of specific national peoples?

3 **"The Watch on the Rhine," lyrics 1840, music 1854.** German soldiers sang this triumphal patriotic anthem about the Rhine River, which flows through the borderlands between France and Germany, as they marched to fight in the Franco-Prussian War (1870–1871) and World War I (1914–1918).

A voice resounds like thunder-peal,
'Mid dashing waves and clang of steel:
The Rhine, the Rhine, the German Rhine!
Who guards to-day my stream divine?
    [*Chorus*] Dear Fatherland, no danger thine;
    Firm stand thy sons to watch the Rhine!

They stand, a hundred thousand strong,
Quick to avenge their country's wrong;
With filial love their bosoms swell,
They'll guard the sacred landmark well!
    Chorus

The dead of an heroic race
From heaven look down and meet this gaze;
He swears with dauntless heart, "O Rhine,
Be German as this breast of mine!"
    Chorus

While flows one drop of German blood,
Or sword remains to guard thy flood,
While rifle rests in patriot hand,
No foe shall tread thy sacred strand!
    Chorus

Our oath resounds, the river flows,
In golden light our banner glows;
Our hearts will guard thy stream divine:
The Rhine, the Rhine, the German Rhine!
    Chorus

(adoc-photos/Corbis/Getty Images)

4 **Monument to the Battle of Nations, Leipzig, Germany, 1913.** This colossal monument commemorates the victory of the Prussians and their allies over Napoleon in 1813. A large statue of the archangel Michael underneath an inscription reading "Gott Mit Uns" (God with Us) guards the entrance, while Teutonic knights with drawn swords stand watch around the memorial's crest. The visitors climbing the stairs at the bottom right of the photo give some idea of the monument's size.

5 **The National Monument to King Victor Emmanuel II, Rome, Italy, 1911.** Nicknamed the "wedding cake" by local wits, this memorial/museum features an equestrian statue of the king above a frieze representing the Italian people, and an imposing Roman-style colonnade crowned by two horse-drawn chariots.

(Bailey-Cooper Photography/Alamy)

PUTTING IT ALL TOGETHER

Using the sources above, along with what you have learned about nationalism in class and in Chapters 21 and 23, write a short essay that applies Ernest Renan's ideas about national identity to the spread of nationalism in the late nineteenth century. Can you explain why nationalism might subsume or erode existing regional, religious, or class differences?

Sources: (1) Ernest Renan, "What Is a Nation?" trans. Martin Thom, in *Nation and Narration*, ed. Homi K. Bhabha (New York: Routledge, 2003), pp. 19–20; (3) Eva March Tappan, ed., *The World's Story: A History of the World in Story, Song and Art*, vol. 7, *Germany, the Netherlands, and Switzerland* (Boston: Houghton Mifflin, 1914), pp. 249–250.

First-Wave Feminists in Action   British suffragettes engaged in provocative public acts of civil disobedience in their campaigns for the right to vote, at times resulting in the arrest and imprisonment of women protesters. Once in jail, activists sometimes went on well-publicized hunger strikes. When wardens responded with forced feeding, suffragettes used images of such "torture" in their propaganda campaigns, as this poster published by the National Women's Social and Political Union in 1913 shows. The responsive national state offered benefits to its citizens but only grudgingly extended full political rights to women. (National Institute of Health)

grudgingly began to admit women in the 1890s. Determined pioneers had to fight to break through sexist barriers to advanced education and professional employment.

Women inspired by Marxist socialism blazed an alternative path. Often scorning the reform programs of middle-class feminists, socialist women leaders argued that the liberation of working-class women would come only with the liberation of the entire working class through Marxist revolution. In the meantime, they championed the cause of working women and won some practical improvements,

especially in Germany, where the socialist movement was most effectively organized.

Progress toward women's rights was slow and hard-won, yet the state did respond with more gender-equitable property and family laws, workplace reforms, and civil rights. Women's right to vote, however, was typically only granted in the years after World War I.

Nationalism and Racism

Whereas nationalism in the first two-thirds of the nineteenth century had often promoted liberal reform and peaceful brotherhood, after the 1870s it took on more populist and exclusionary tones. Although nationalism drew on different sources, including a common history or culture, the growing popularity of supposedly scientific understandings of racial difference fueled this animosity. Though we now understand that there is no genetic basis for distinct human races, most people in the late nineteenth century believed that race was a product of heredity or "blood." Many felt pride in their own national racial characteristics — English, German, and others — that were supposedly passed down from generation to generation. Unfortunately, pride in one's own heritage easily led to denigration of someone else's.

Modern attempts to use race to categorize distinct groups of people had their roots in Enlightenment thought (see Chapter 16). Now a new group of intellectuals, including race theorists such as Count Arthur de Gobineau, claimed that their ideas about racial difference were scientific, based on hard biological "facts" about bloodlines and heredity. In *On the Inequality of the Human Races* (1854), Gobineau divided humanity into races based on geographical location. He championed the white "Aryan race" for its supposedly superior qualities. Social Darwinist ideas about the "survival of the fittest" (see "Darwin and Natural Selection" in Chapter 22), when applied to the "contest" between nations and races, further popularized stereotypes about inferior and superior races.

The close links between nationalism and scientific racism helped justify imperial expansion, as we shall see in the next chapter. Nationalist racism also fostered domestic persecution and exclusion, as witnessed in Bismarck's Kulturkampf and the Dreyfus affair. In multiethnic states, minorities were often viewed as outsiders and targets for reform, repression, and relocation. Thus ethnic Russian leaders banned non-Russians from the officer corps and from government administration. They targeted Poles and other minority groups for "Russification," requiring them to learn the Russian language and assimilate into Russian society. Many Germans likewise viewed the ethnic Poles in East Prussia as a national threat that required "Germanization" before they could live alongside the supposedly superior Germans. For many nationalists, driven by ugly currents of race hatred, Jews were the ultimate outsiders and were believed to pose the greatest challenge to national purity.

Jewish Emancipation and Modern Anti-Semitism

Changing political principles and the triumph of the nation-state had revolutionized Jewish life. By the 1870s, Jews across western and central Europe had won emancipation — that is, legal and civic equality with other citizens. In 1871, for example, the constitution of the new German Empire abolished all restrictions on Jewish marriage, choice of occupation, place of residence, and property ownership. Many European Jewish families had improved their economic situation enough to enter the middle classes. They often identified strongly with their respective nation-states and, with good reason, saw themselves as patriotic citizens. Even with these changes, Jews faced discrimination in employment opportunities and social relations.

Vicious anti-Semitism reappeared with force in central and eastern Europe after the stock market crash of 1873. Drawing on long traditions of religious intolerance, segregation into ghettos, and periodic anti-Jewish riots (or pogroms), this anti-Semitism also built on the exclusionary aspects of popular nationalism and the pseudoscience of race. Fanatic anti-Semites whipped up resentment against Jewish achievement and "financial control" and claimed that Jewish "blood" posed a biological threat to Christian peoples. Such ideas were popularized by the repeated publication of the notorious forgery "The Protocols of the Elders of Zion," a fake account of a secret meeting supposedly held at the First Zionist Congress in Basel in 1897, which suggested that Jewish elders planned to dominate the globe. Such anti-Semitic beliefs were particularly popular among conservatives, extreme nationalists, and people who felt threatened by Jewish competition, such as small shopkeepers, officeworkers, and professionals.

Anti-Semites created nationalist political parties that attacked and insulted Jews to win popular support. In one noted example, anti-Semitism combined with a large-scale public works program helped Austrian politician Karl Lueger (LOU-ger) and his Christian Socialist Party win striking electoral victories in

An Anti-Jewish Pogrom in the Pale of Settlement
In April 1903 a violent anti-Semitic riot (or pogrom) broke out in Kishinev, a city in the Pale of Settlement that is the capital of current-day Moldova. In two days of rioting, a mob angered by specious anti-Semitic propaganda murdered at least forty-seven Jews and vandalized and looted hundreds of Jewish homes and businesses. As this cover page from an Italian illustrated magazine suggests, the pogrom focused international media coverage on the violent persecution of Jews in the Russian Empire. (Alfredo Dagli Orti/Shutterstock)

Vienna in the 1890s. Lueger, mayor of Vienna from 1897 to 1910, tried to limit Jewish immigration from the Russian Empire and used fierce anti-Semitic rhetoric to appeal to the worst instincts of the electorate, especially the lower middle class. Future Nazi dictator Adolf Hitler lived in Vienna during this time, and his fervent hatred of Jews drew strength from Lueger's racist rhetoric.

Before 1914 anti-Semitism was most oppressive in eastern Europe, where Jews suffered from rampant poverty. In Europe 4 million of the 7 million Jewish people lived with few legal rights in the western borderlands of the Russian Empire — the Pale

INDIVIDUALS IN SOCIETY

Theodor Herzl

Theodor Herzl in Palestine, 1898. (Imagno/Getty Images)

I n September 1897, only days after his vision had animated the First Zionist Congress in Basel, Switzerland, Theodor Herzl (1860–1904) assessed the results in his diary: "If I were to sum up the Congress in a word — which I shall take care not to publish — it would be this: At Basel I founded the Jewish state. If I said this out loud today I would be greeted by universal laughter. In five years perhaps, and certainly in fifty years, everyone will perceive it."* Herzl's buoyant optimism was prophetic.

Herzl was born in Budapest, Hungary, into an upper-middle-class, German-speaking Jewish family. When he was eighteen, his family moved to Vienna, where he earned a law degree in 1884. Like many well-to-do Viennese Jews, Herzl struggled with his mixed Jewish-German heritage. As a student he embraced German nationalism and joined a German dueling fraternity. But Herzl discovered that full acceptance required an open repudiation of all things Jewish. He resigned.

The popularity of radical anti-Semitism shocked Herzl, as it did many Jewish intellectuals. Moving to Paris in 1891, he worked for Vienna's leading liberal newspaper and studied politics and the history of European anti-Semitism. The Dreyfus affair confirmed his bold conclusions, published in 1896 as *The Jewish State: An Attempt at a Modern Solution to the Jewish Question*. Jewish assimilation had failed, Herzl argued, and attempts to combat European anti-Semitism would never succeed.

Herzl concluded that the Jewish people — like other repressed minorities in Europe — needed their own nation-state in order to flourish. He suggested that this take form in Palestine, a territory in the Ottoman Empire that was the biblical homeland of the Jewish people. He encouraged European Jews to migrate to Palestine; if their numbers increased, they might eventually create an independent nation. Herzl was not deeply religious. Yet he understood the emotional appeal of a Jewish nation, united in the face of Christian persecution, embodied in a Jewish state in the Holy Land with its own national flag.

Many European Jews rejected Zionism. Calls for Jewish separatism, they believed, would bolster accusations that Jews were foreign outsiders in Christian nations and impede Jewish assimilation. Herzl turned for support to youthful idealists and lower-class Jews, who sought civil rights and economic opportunity, but also relief from hostile anti-Semitism. An inspiring man of action, Herzl rallied the delegates at annual Zionist congresses, directed the growth of the

*Theodor Herzl, *The Diaries of Theodor Herzl*, trans. and ed. with an introduction by Marvin Lowenthal (New York: Grosset & Dunlap, 1962), p. 224.

worldwide Zionist organization, and convinced modest numbers of Jews to move to Palestine.

Always ready to promote his Zionist vision before non-Jews and world public opinion, Herzl believed in international diplomacy and political agreements. He eagerly negotiated with European leaders and officials, seeking support in securing territory for the Jewish nation. Herzl proved most successful in Britain. As we will see in Chapter 25, his work paved the way for the 1917 Balfour Declaration, which solemnly pledged British support for a "Jewish homeland" in Palestine.

Herzl died in 1904 so did not witness the foundation of the state of Israel in 1948. Nor could he know that Zionism would become Israel's guiding national philosophy. The results remain controversial. Critics of Zionism claim that Herzl's program drew on the waves of ethnic nationalism and expansionist imperialism that washed through Europe in the late nineteenth century, and they call attention to the role of Zionism in the current Arab-Israeli conflict. Yet Herzl guided the historic steps toward a modern Jewish identity, and it is impossible to imagine the creation of contemporary Israel without him.

QUESTIONS FOR ANALYSIS

1. Why did Herzl believe in the necessity of an independent Jewish state in Palestine, the biblical homeland of the Jewish people? How did his personal experience influence his ideas?
2. Current critics of Zionism argue that Herzl's program was rooted in the late-nineteenth-century European enthusiasm for nationalism and imperialism. Is this a fair critique?

of Settlement (see Chapter 16). In the Pale, officials used anti-Semitism to channel popular discontent away from the government and onto the Jewish minority. Jews were regularly denounced as foreign exploiters who corrupted national traditions, and between 1881 and 1884 a wave of violent pogroms (anti-Jewish riots) commenced in southern Russia. The police and the army stood aside for days while peasants looted and destroyed Jewish property, and official harassment continued in the following decades. Another wave of pogroms broke out in 1903; mass anti-Semitic rioting in Odessa in 1905, which killed at least four hundred Jews, marked the worst event.

The growth of radical anti-Semitism spurred the emergence of **Zionism**, a Jewish political movement whose adherents believed that Christian Europeans would never overcome their anti-Semitic hatred. To escape anti-Semitism, Zionists such as Theodor Herzl advocated the creation of a Jewish state in Palestine — a homeland where European Jews could settle and live free of oppression. (See "Individuals in Society: Theodor Herzl," page 720.) Zionism was particularly popular among Jews living in the Pale. While some embraced the vision of a Zionist settlement in Palestine, many more emigrated to western or central Europe and the United States. About 2.75 million Jews left central and eastern Europe between 1881 and 1914.

How and why did revolutionary Marxism evolve in the late nineteenth century?

Socialist political parties, generally Marxist groups dedicated to international proletarian revolution, grew rapidly in the late nineteenth century. The radical rhetoric of socialist politicians continued to trouble the conservative upper classes. But behind the talk of revolution, Marxism was becoming more mainstream, particularly as the consolidation of labor unions and the turn to Marxist "revisionism" promised real practical improvements for workers.

The Socialist International

The growth of socialist parties after 1871 was phenomenal. In Germany, neither Bismarck's Anti-Socialist Laws nor his extensive social security system checked the growth of the German Social Democratic Party (SPD), which espoused revolutionary Marxism even though it sought reform through legal parliamentary politics. By 1912 the SPD had millions of working-class followers and was the largest party in the Reichstag. Socialist parties grew in other countries as well, though nowhere else with such success. In 1883 Russian exiles in Switzerland founded the Russian Social Democratic Party, and various socialist groups were unified in 1905 in the French Section of the Workers International. Belgium and Austria-Hungary also had strong socialist parties.

Marxist socialist parties strove to join together in an international organization, and in 1864 Marx himself helped found the socialist International Working Men's Association, also known as the First International. In the following years, Marx battled successfully to control the organization and used its annual international meetings to spread his doctrines

of socialist revolution. He endorsed the radical patriotism of the Paris Commune and its terrible struggle against the French state as a giant step toward socialist revolution. Marx's fervent embrace of working-class violence frightened many of his early supporters, especially the more moderate British labor leaders. Internal tensions led to the collapse of the First International in 1876.

Yet even after Marx's death in 1883 international proletarian solidarity remained an important objective for Marxists. In 1889, as the individual parties in different countries grew stronger, socialist leaders came together to form the Second International, which lasted until 1914. Though only a federation of national socialist parties, the Second International had a powerful psychological impact. It had a permanent executive, and every three years delegates from the different parties met to interpret Marxist doctrines and plan coordinated action. May 1 (May Day) — the date in 1886 of a violent labor demonstration in Chicago's Haymarket Square — was declared an annual socialist holiday, a day for strikes, marches, and demonstrations. Prosperous elites and conservative middle-class citizens feared the growing power of socialism and the Second International, but many workers joined the cause.

Labor Unions and the Evolution of Working-Class Radicalism

Was socialism really radical and revolutionary in these years? On the whole, it was not. As socialist parties

■ **Zionism** A movement dedicated to combatting anti-Semitism in Europe by building a Jewish national homeland in Palestine, started by Theodor Herzl.

"Proletarians of All Countries, Unite!"   Quoting the last line in Marx's *Communist Manifesto*, the front page of the 1905 May Day issue of a radical Zurich journal portrays a world harmonious and united under the banner of socialism. Muscular workers from Asia, Australia, Europe, America, and Africa grasp hands under an angel crowned with a halo that reads "freedom"; the angel is also holding a banner proclaiming "equality and brotherhood." May Day — the first of May — was and continues to be an annual celebration of international socialist solidarity. Can you find other meaningful symbols in this proud representation of socialist unity? (bpk Bildagentur/ Dietmar Katz/Art Resource, NY)

Workers were less inclined to follow radical programs for several reasons. As they gained the right to vote and won tangible benefits, they focused more on elections than on revolutions. And workers were not immune to patriotic education and indoctrination during military service. Many responded positively to drum-beating parades and aggressive foreign policy as they loyally voted for socialist parties. Nor were workers by any means a unified group with shared social and political interests — as we saw in Chapter 22.

Perhaps most important of all, workers' standard of living rose gradually but substantially after 1850. The quality of life in urban areas improved dramatically as well. For all these reasons, workers became more moderate: they demanded gains, but they were less likely to take to the barricades in pursuit of them.

The growth of labor unions reinforced the trend toward moderation. In the early stages of industrialization, unions were considered subversive bodies to be hounded and crushed, and they were generally prohibited by law. Determined workers organized and fought back. In Great Britain in 1824 and 1825 unions won the legal right to exist — though generally not the right to strike. Limited primarily to highly skilled workers such as machinists and carpenters, these "new model unions" concentrated on winning better wages and hours through collective bargaining and compromise. This approach helped pave the way to the full acceptance of unions across Europe in the 1870s, and after 1890 unions for unskilled workers developed.

Russia remained an exception to the general trend of working-class moderation. Across the nineteenth century, tsarist autocracy had resisted democratic reform, clamped down on unionization, and granted minimal social benefits. Under the limited constitution granted after the 1905 revolution, most workers still had no right to vote. Radical Russian socialists, including leaders like Vladimir Lenin (see Chapter 25), continued to agitate for violent revolution.

Marxist Revisionism

Germany, the most industrialized and unionized continental country by 1914, offers an instructive case study of the transformation of socialism around 1900. German unions did not receive basic rights until 1869, and until the Anti-Socialist Laws were repealed in 1890, they were frequently harassed by the government. As a result, in 1895 Germany had only about 270,000 union members in a male industrial workforce of nearly 8 million. Then, with almost all legal harassment eliminated,

grew and attracted many members, they looked less and less toward revolution and more and more toward gradual change and steady improvement for the working class. The mainstream of European socialism became militantly moderate. Socialists still liked to alarm mainstream politicians with revolutionary rhetoric. But they increasingly worked within the system, often joining labor unions to win practical workplace reforms.

In 1848 Marx and Engels published *The Communist Manifesto* (see Chapter 21), which predicted that the proletariat or working class would lead a violent revolution to overthrow capitalism. This work, excerpted below, was foundational for the development of the international socialist movement. But by the late nineteenth century criticism of Marx's basic ideas, led by a group of so-called Revisionists, was coming from within the movement itself. German socialist Eduard Bernstein explained why in this excerpt from his book *Evolutionary Socialism*, first published in 1899.

From *The Communist Manifesto*

Owing to the extensive use of machinery and to division of labor, the work of the proletarians has lost all individual character, and consequently, all charm for the workman. He becomes an appendage of the machine. . . .

The lower strata of the middle class—the small tradespeople, shopkeepers, and retired tradesmen generally, the handcraftsmen, and peasants—all these sink gradually into the proletariat. . . .

The modern laborer . . . instead of rising with the progress of industry, sinks deeper and deeper below the conditions of his own class. He becomes a pauper, and pauperism develops more rapidly than population and wealth. And here it becomes evident, that the bourgeoisie is unfit any longer to be the ruling class. . . . It is unfit to rule because it is incompetent to assure an existence to its slave within his slavery, because it cannot help letting him sink into such a state. . . .

The development of Modern Industry, therefore, cuts from under its feet the very foundation on which the bourgeoisie produces and appropriates products. What the bourgeoisie, therefore, produces, above all, is its own grave diggers. Its fall and the victory of the proletariat are equally inevitable. . . .

The Communists . . . openly declare that their ends can be attained only by the forcible overthrow of all existing social conditions. Let the ruling classes tremble at a Communist revolution. The proletarians have nothing to lose but their chains. They have a world to win.

From *Evolutionary Socialism*

I set myself against the notion that we have to expect shortly a collapse of the bourgeois economy, and that social democracy should be induced by the prospect of such an imminent, great, social catastrophe to adapt its tactics to that assumption. . . .

The adherents of this theory of a catastrophe base it especially on the conclusions of the *Communist Manifesto*. This is a mistake in every respect. . . .

Social conditions have not developed to such an acute opposition of things and classes as is depicted in the *Manifesto*. It is not only useless, it is the greatest folly to attempt to conceal this from ourselves. The number of members of the possessing classes is today not smaller but larger. The enormous increase of social wealth is not accompanied by a decreasing number of large capitalists but by an increasing number of capitalists of all degrees. The middle classes change their character but they do not disappear from the social scale. . . .

In all advanced countries we see the privileges of the capitalist bourgeoisie yielding step by step to democratic organizations. . . . [A] social reaction has set in against the exploiting tendencies of capital, a counteraction which, although it still proceeds timidly and feebly, yet does exist, and is always drawing more departments of economic life under its influence. Factory legislation, the democratizing of local government . . . the freeing of trade unions and systems of co-operative trading from legal restrictions, the consideration of standard conditions of labour in the work undertaken by public authorities—all these characterize this phase of the evolution. . . .

No one has questioned the necessity for the working classes to gain the control of government. . . . But the conquest of political power necessitates the possession of political rights; and the most important problem of tactics which German social democracy has at the present time to solve, appears to me to be to devise the best ways for the extension of the political and economic rights of the German working classes.

QUESTIONS FOR ANALYSIS

1. Why does Bernstein label the view advanced in *The Communist Manifesto* a "theory of a catastrophe"? Is this justified?
2. What specific criticisms of Marx does Bernstein offer in support of his argument? Why would Bernstein's approach anger committed Marxist revolutionaries?
3. How do Bernstein's ideas reflect historical changes that had taken place since 1848?

Sources: Marx and Engels, "Manifesto of the Communist Party," in *The Marx-Engels Reader*, 2d ed., ed. Robert C. Tucker (New York: Norton, 1978), pp. 479–480, 483, 501; Eduard Bernstein, *Evolutionary Socialism: A Criticism and Affirmation*, trans. Edith C. Harvey (New York: B. W. Heubsch, 1911), pp. x–xii, xiv, xvi.

union membership skyrocketed, reaching roughly 3 million in 1912.

This great expansion both reflected and influenced the changing character of German unions. Increasingly, union activists focused on bread-and-butter labor issues — wages, hours, working conditions — rather than on fomenting revolution. Genuine collective bargaining, long opposed by socialist intellectuals as a sellout, was officially recognized as desirable by the German Trade Union Congress in 1899. When employers proved unwilling to bargain, strikes forced them to change their minds. In 1913 alone, over ten thousand collective bargaining agreements benefiting 1.25 million workers were signed.

The German trade unions and many of their leaders were in fact, if not in name, thoroughgoing revisionists. **Marxist revisionism** was an effort to update Marx's doctrines to reflect current realities. Thus the socialist Eduard Bernstein (1850–1932) argued in 1899 in his *Evolutionary Socialism* that many of Marx's predictions had been proven false. Socialists, according to thinkers like Bernstein, should reform their doctrines and tactics to meet these changed conditions. They should combine with other progressive forces to win continued steps forward for workers through legislation, unions, and further economic expansion; revolution might happen later, but the movement, not the final goal, was the point. These views were denounced as heresy by hard-core Marxists in the SPD and later by the leaders of the Second International. Yet the revisionist, gradualist approach continued to gain the tacit acceptance of many German socialists, particularly in the trade unions. (See "Viewpoints: Marxist Revisionism," page 723.)

Moderation found followers elsewhere. In France, the famous socialist leader Jean Jaurès (1859–1914) formally repudiated revisionism in order to establish a unified socialist party, but he remained at heart a gradualist and optimistic secular humanist. Questions of revolution or revisionism also divided Russian Marxists on the eve of the Russian Revolution, as we shall see in Chapter 25.

By the early twentieth century socialist parties had clear-cut national characteristics. Russians and socialists in the Austro-Hungarian Empire tended to be the most radical. The German party talked revolution and practiced reformism, greatly influenced by its enormous trade-union movement. The French party talked revolution and tried to practice it, unrestrained by a trade-union movement that was both very weak and very radical. In Britain, the socialist but non-Marxist Labour Party, reflecting the well-established union movement, was formally committed to gradual reform. In Spain and Italy, Marxist socialism was very weak. There anarchism, seeking to smash the state rather than the bourgeoisie, dominated radical thought and action.

In short, socialist policies and doctrines varied from country to country. Although leaders liked to talk about "socialist internationalism," the notion of international unity was more myth than reality. This helps explain why when war came in 1914, almost all socialist parties and most workers supported their national governments and turned away from international solidarity.

NOTES

1. Quoted in J. McKay, *Pioneers for Profit: Foreign Entrepreneurship and Russian Industrialization, 1885–1913* (Chicago: University of Chicago Press, 1970), p. 11.
2. E. Weber, *Peasants into Frenchmen: The Modernization of Rural France, 1870–1914* (Stanford, Calif.: Stanford University Press, 1976).
3. See E. Hobsbawm, "Mass Producing Traditions: Europe, 1870–1914," in *The Invention of Tradition*, ed. E. Hobsbawm and T. Ranger (New York: Cambridge University Press, 1992), pp. 263–307.

LOOKING BACK LOOKING AHEAD

In 1900 the triumph of the national state in Europe seemed almost complete. In the aging Austro-Hungarian, Russian, and Ottoman Empires, ethnic minorities continued to fight for national independence. Class, religion, and ethnicity still divided people across the rest of

---

■ **Marxist revisionism** An effort by moderate socialists to update Marxist doctrines to reflect the realities of the late nineteenth century.

Europe. But in most places, the politically unified nation-state governed with the consent and even the devotion of many citizens. Many men and women embraced patriotism and identified as members of a national group. This newfound sense of national identity could be ugly and exclusionary, but it also eroded traditional social differences.

Responsive and capable of tackling many practical problems, the European nation-state of 1900 was in part the realization of patriotic ideologues and the middle-class liberals active in the unsuccessful revolutions of 1848. Yet whereas early nationalists had envisioned a Europe of free peoples and international peace, the nationalists of 1900 had been nurtured in an atmosphere of competition between European states and the wars of unification in the 1850s and 1860s. This new generation of nationalists reveled in the strength of their unity, and the nation-state became the foundation of a new system of global power.

Thus after 1870, even as the responsive nation-state brought both benefits and burdens to ordinary people, Europe's leading countries extended their imperial control around the globe. In Asia and Africa, Europeans seized territory, fought brutal colonial wars, and built authoritarian empires. Moreover, in Europe itself, the universal faith in nationalism, which usually reduced social tensions within national borders, promoted a bitter competition between states. In this way European nationalism threatened the very progress and unity it had helped to build. In 1914 the power of unified nation-states would turn on itself, unleashing the First World War and doling out self-inflicted wounds of enormous proportions to all of Europe's peoples.

Make Connections

Think about the larger developments and continuities within and across chapters.

1. By 1900 most countries in Europe and North America had established modern nation-states, but the process of nation building varied dramatically. Which countries were most successful in building viable nation-states? What accounts for the variation?

2. The new nation-state made demands on its citizens but also offered them benefits and a new way to think about and experience social community. How would you evaluate the balance? Was the consolidation of the nation-state good for most people?

3. Liberalism, socialism, and nationalism first emerged as coherent ideologies in the decades around 1800 (Chapter 21). How had they changed by 1900?

---

23   REVIEW & EXPLORE

Identify Key Terms

Identify and explain the significance of each item below.

Risorgimento (p. 696)

Realpolitik (p. 699)

Crimean War (p. 703)

Russian Revolution of 1905 (p. 706)

Duma (p. 707)

Tanzimat (p. 707)

Young Turks (p. 709)

Reichstag (p. 710)

German Social Democratic Party (SPD) (p. 710)

Dreyfus affair (p. 711)

home rule (p. 712)

suffrage movement (p. 715)

Zionism (p. 721)

Marxist revisionism (p. 724)

Review the Main Ideas

Answer the section heading questions from the chapter.

1. What were the main features of the authoritarian nation-state built by Napoleon III? (p. 694)

2. How were strong nation-states forged in Italy and Germany? (p. 696)

3. How did Russian and Ottoman leaders modernize their states and societies? (p. 703)

4. How did the relationship between government and the governed change after 1871? (p. 709)

5. What were the costs and benefits of nationalism for ordinary people? (p. 714)

6. How and why did revolutionary Marxism evolve in the late nineteenth century? (p. 721)

Suggested Resources

BOOKS

- Anderson, Benedict. *Imagined Communities: Reflections on the Origin and Spread of Nationalism.* 1991. Famous for its argument about the social construction of nationalism.
- Baer, Mark David. *The Ottomans: Khans, Caesars, and Caliphs.* 2021. A highly readable account of the Ottoman Empire in long-term perspective that emphasizes its place in the history of Europe.
- Calhoun, Craig. *Nationalism.* 1997. A clear and concise overview of recent theories of nationalism and national identity.
- Clyman, Toby W., and Judith Vowles, eds. *Russia Through Women's Eyes: Autobiographies from Tsarist Russia.* 1999. An eye-opening collection detailing women's experiences in Russia.
- Fink, Carole. *Defending the Rights of Others: The Great Powers, the Jews, and International Minority Protection, 1878–1938.* 2004. Skilled consideration of the cruelty and tragedy of ethnic conflict and minority oppression.
- Geary, Dick, ed. *Labour and Socialist Movements in Europe Before 1914.* 1989. An excellent collection that examines labor movements in several different countries.
- Hennock, E. P. *The Origin of the Welfare State in England and Germany, 1850–1914.* 2007. Compares Germany's statist approach with England's response to demands from below.
- Hobsbawm, Eric, and Terrence Ranger, eds. *The Invention of Tradition.* 1992. An influential collection of articles on the invented nature of modern nationalism.
- Merriman, John. *Massacre: The Life and Death of the Paris Commune.* 2014. An engaging narrative account of a key revolutionary moment.

- Mosse, George. *Nationalism and Sexuality: Respectability and Abnormal Sexuality in Modern Europe.* 1985. A pathbreaking and still-relevant work that calls attention to the links between nationalism, racism, and sexuality.

- Riall, Lucy. *Garibaldi: Invention of a Hero.* 2008. A biography of the Italian revolutionary that also examines the ways he became a folk hero after his death.

MEDIA

- *La Commune (Paris 1871)* (Peter Watkins, 2000). A unique dramatic film about the Paris Commune that features hundreds of nonprofessional actors in the roles of the revolutionaries.

- *Discover the Ottomans.* An extensive website on the history of the Ottoman Empire that offers pages on the timeline of the empire, the history of military campaigns, rulers of the empire, and the art and culture of the Ottomans. **www.theottomans.org/english/index.asp**

- *Fall of Eagles* (BBC, 1974). A thirteen-part television drama about the fall from power of the Habsburgs, Romanovs, and Hohenzollerns in the nineteenth century.

- *The Internationale* (Peter Miller, 2000). This documentary tells the story of a song written in 1871 after the suppression of the Paris Commune, and how that song went on to inspire many other groups and movements.

- *The Leopard* (Luchino Visconti, 1963). An epic film about the aristocracy of Sicily struggling in the midst of major social upheaval during Garibaldi's invasion in 1860.

- *Lorraine Beitler Collection of the Dreyfus Affair.* Information about the Dreyfus affair, including essays and examples of sources that are part of the Lorraine Beitler Collection at the University of Pennsylvania. **sceti.library.upenn.edu/dreyfus/**

- *Napoleon.org.* The history of the rule of Napoleon I and Napoleon III through texts, images, and timelines. **https://www.napoleon.org/en/history-of-the-two-empires/**

- *The Wandering Jew* (Otto Kreisler, 1920). An early pro-Zionist film that tells the story of Theodor Herzl's life.

24

The West and the World

1815–1914

While industrialization and nationalism were transforming urban and rural life throughout Europe, western Europeans were reshaping the world. At the peak of its power and pride, the West entered the third and most dynamic phase of the aggressive expansion that had begun with the Crusades and continued with the rise of seaborne colonial empires. Millions of Europeans emigrated abroad, primarily to North and South America but also to Australia, North and South Africa, and Asiatic Russia. An ever-growing stream of people, products, and ideas flowed into and out of Europe in the nineteenth century. Hardly any corner of the globe was left untouched.

The most spectacular manifestations of Western expansion came in the late nineteenth century when the leading European nations established or enlarged their colonial empires. This political annexation of territory in the 1880s—the "New Imperialism"—was the capstone of Europe's underlying economic and technological transformation. Europe's New Imperialism rested on a formidable combination of superior military might and strong authoritarian rule, and it posed a brutal challenge to African and Asian peoples, who met this challenge in different ways. By 1914 Indigenous elites in many lands were leading an anti-imperialist struggle for dignity and independence that would eventually triumph after 1945. ◼

CENTRA

CHAPTER PREVIEW

- **What were the global consequences of European industrialization?**

- **How was massive migration an integral part of Western expansion?**

- **How did the New Imperialism change Western colonialism?**

- **How did non-Westerners respond to Western expansion?**

Entangled Lives on the Imperial Frontier
Colonialism brought together Europeans, Indigenous peoples, and immigrants, as seen in this 1886 painting of the city of Durban in the British colony of South Africa, the site of a minor gold rush. The diversity of peoples in colonial encounters is suggested by the figures in the image, identifiable by the traditional clothes they wear. As Europeans view an exhibit of gold nuggets dug out of local mines, passing by are (from left to right) a Zulu man, a South Asian migrant laborer, a Sikh, and a Muslim. (Prisma/Universal Images Group/Getty Images)

What were the global consequences of European industrialization?

The Industrial Revolution created a tremendously dynamic economic system. In the nineteenth century, that system expanded across the face of the earth. Some of this extension into non-Western areas was peaceful and beneficial, for the new industries produced many goods and techniques that the rest of the world desired. If peaceful methods failed, however, Europeans used their superior military power to force non-Western nations to open their doors to Western economic interests. In general, Europeans fashioned the global economic system so that the largest share of the ever-increasing gains from trade, technology, and migration flowed to the West and its propertied classes.

The Rise of Global Inequality

The Industrial Revolution in Europe marked a momentous turning point. Those regions that industrialized, mainly Europe and North America, increased their wealth and power enormously in comparison to those that did not. A gap between the core industrializing regions and the soon-to-be colonized or semi-colonized regions outside the European–North American core (Africa, Asia, the Middle East, and Latin America) emerged and widened throughout the nineteenth century. Moreover, this pattern of uneven global development became institutionalized, or built into the structure of the world economy. Thus a "lopsided world" evolved, a world with a rich north and a poor south—albeit with regional variations.

In recent years economic historians have charted the long-term evolution of this gap, and Figure 24.1

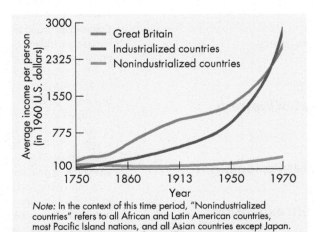

Note: In the context of this time period, "Nonindustrialized countries" refers to all African and Latin American countries, most Pacific Island nations, and all Asian countries except Japan. "Industrialized countries" refers to all European countries, Canada, the United States, and Japan.

FIGURE 24.1 The Growth of Average Income per Person in Industrialized Countries, Nonindustrialized Countries, and Great Britain, 1750–1970   Growth is given in 1960 U.S. dollars and prices.

summarizes the results. Three main points stand out. First, in 1750 the average standard of living was no higher in Europe as a whole than in the rest of the world. Second, it was industrialization that opened the gaps in average wealth and well-being among countries and regions. Third, income per person stagnated in the colonized world before 1913, in striking contrast to the industrializing regions. Only after 1945, in the era of decolonization and political independence, did former colonies make economic progress and begin the process of industrialization. These enormous income disparities brought striking disparities in food and clothing, health and education, and life expectancy and general material well-being.

The World Market

Commerce between nations typically stimulates economic development. In the nineteenth century European development brought an enormous increase in international trade. Great Britain took the lead in cultivating export markets for its booming industrial output, as British manufacturers sought consumers for their growing numbers of mass-produced goods, first in Europe and then around the world.

Take the case of cotton textile markets in Great Britain and India. In 1820 Britain was exporting 50 percent of its production. Europe bought about one-half of these exports, while India bought only 6 percent and had its own well-established textile industry with international markets. After continental European nations and the United States erected tariff barriers on textiles to promote domestic industry, British cotton manufacturers aggressively sought other foreign markets in non-Western areas. By 1850 India was buying 25 percent and Europe only 16 percent of a much larger volume of production. As a British colony, India could not raise tariffs to protect its ancient cotton textile industry, which collapsed, leaving thousands of Indian weavers unemployed.

In addition to its dominance in the export market, Britain was also the world's largest importer of goods and the largest trader of agricultural products, raw materials, and manufactured goods. Under free-trade policies, open access to Britain's market stimulated the development of mines and plantations in many non-Western areas.

Improved transportation systems fostered international trade. Wherever railroads were built, they drastically reduced transportation costs, opened new economic opportunities, and called forth new skills

TIMELINE

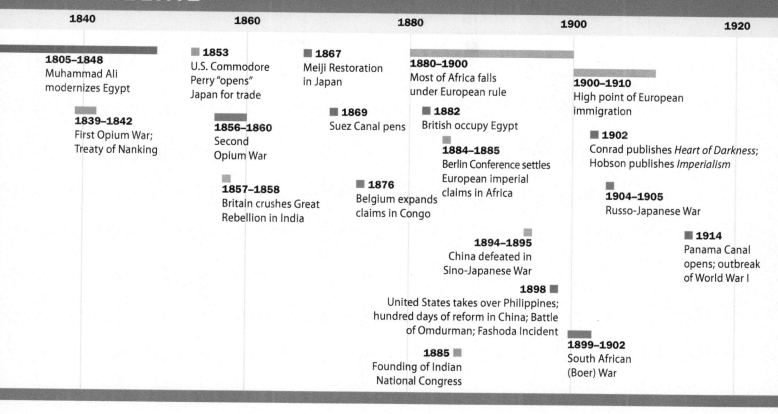

1840   1860   1880   1900   1920

1805–1848
Muhammad Ali modernizes Egypt

1839–1842
First Opium War; Treaty of Nanking

1853
U.S. Commodore Perry "opens" Japan for trade

1856–1860
Second Opium War

1857–1858
Britain crushes Great Rebellion in India

1867
Meiji Restoration in Japan

1869
Suez Canal pens

1876
Belgium expands claims in Congo

1880–1900
Most of Africa falls under European rule

1882
British occupy Egypt

1884–1885
Berlin Conference settles European imperial claims in Africa

1894–1895
China defeated in Sino-Japanese War

1898
United States takes over Philippines; hundred days of reform in China; Battle of Omdurman; Fashoda Incident

1885
Founding of Indian National Congress

1900–1910
High point of European immigration

1902
Conrad publishes *Heart of Darkness*; Hobson publishes *Imperialism*

1904–1905
Russo-Japanese War

1914
Panama Canal opens; outbreak of World War I

1899–1902
South African (Boer) War

and attitudes. European investors funded much of the railroad construction in Latin America, Asia, and Africa, where railroads typically connected seaports with resource-rich inland cities and regions, as opposed to linking and developing cities and regions within a given country. Thus railroads served Western economic interests by facilitating the inflow and sale of Western manufactured goods and the export and development of local raw materials.

The power of steam revolutionized transportation by sea as well as by land. Steam power began to supplant sails in the late 1860s. Passenger and freight rates tumbled as ship design became more efficient and the intercontinental shipment of low-priced raw materials became feasible. The time needed to cross the Atlantic dropped from three weeks in 1870 to about ten days in 1900, and the opening of the Suez and Panama Canals (in 1869 and 1914, respectively) shortened transport time to other areas of the globe considerably. Improved port facilities made loading and unloading cargo less expensive, faster, and more dependable.

The revolution in land and sea transportation encouraged European entrepreneurs to open up and exploit vast new territories in Asia, Africa, and Latin America. The ongoing export of familiar agricultural products supplied by these "primary producers" — spices, tea, sugar, coffee — was now joined by the extraction of new raw materials for

industry, such as jute, rubber, cotton, and coconut oil. The extraction of raw materials for Western manufacturers boosted economic growth in Europe and North America but did little to establish independent industry in the developing world.

New communication systems directed the flow of goods across global networks. Transoceanic telegraph cables, in place by the 1880s, enabled rapid communications among the financial centers of the world. While a British tramp freighter steamed from Calcutta to New York, a broker in London could arrange by telegram for it to carry American cargo to Australia. The same communications network conveyed world commodity prices instantaneously.

As their economies grew, Europeans began to make massive foreign investments beginning in about 1840. By the outbreak of World War I, Europeans had invested more than $40 billion abroad. Great Britain, France, and Germany were the principal investing countries (Map 24.1). The great gap between rich and poor within Europe meant that the wealthy and moderately well-to-do could and did send great sums abroad in search of interest and dividends.

Most of the capital exported did not go to European colonies or protectorates in Asia and Africa. About three-quarters of total European investment went to other European countries, or to settler

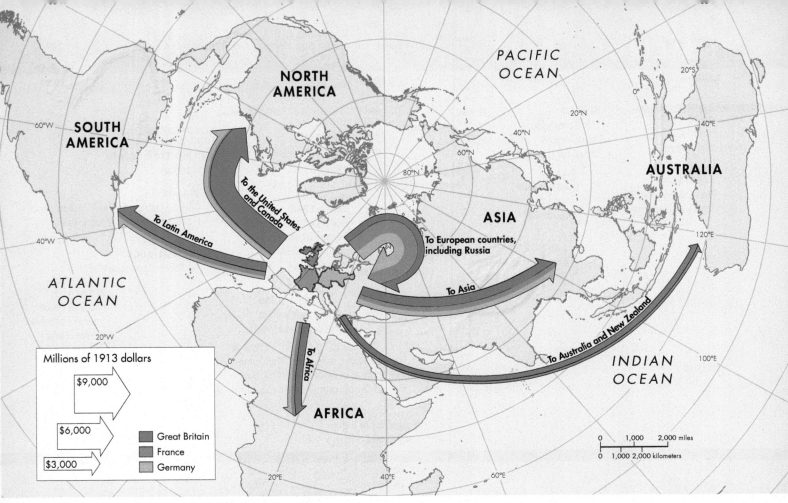

MAP 24.1 European Investment to 1914 Foreign investment grew rapidly after 1850, and Great Britain, France, and Germany were the major investing nations, with Britain in the lead. As this map suggests, most European investment was not directed to the African and Asian areas seized in the New Imperialism after 1880.

colonies—so-called **neo-Europes**, a term coined by historian Alfred Crosby to describe regions where the climate and topography resembled the European homeland, including the United States, Canada, Australia, New Zealand, Latin America, and parts of Siberia. In these relatively developed regions, which had already attracted significant European settler populations, Europe found its most profitable opportunities for investment in the construction of railroads and ports and in resource extraction of cheap food and raw materials.

Much of this investment in European settler colonies was peaceful and mutually beneficial for lenders and borrowers. The extension of Western economic power and the construction of neo-Europes, however, were disastrous for Indigenous peoples. Native Americans and Australian Aborigines especially were decimated by the diseases, liquor, and weapons of an aggressively expanding Western society. In other regions, as we will see, the impact of Western expansion was often immensely destructive of established societies and lifestyles.

Western Pressures on China

Europe's development of robust offshoots in North America, Australia, and Latin America absorbed huge quantities of goods, investments, and migrants. Yet Europe's economic and cultural penetration of old, densely populated civilizations was also significant. Interaction with such civilizations increased the Europeans' trade and profit, and they frequently used force to attain their desires. China provides a striking example of European intrusion into non-Western lands.

For centuries China had sent more goods and inventions to Europe than it had received, and such was still the case in the early nineteenth century. Trade with Europe was carefully regulated by the Chinese imperial government, ruled by the Qing (ching) or Manchu Dynasty in the nineteenth century. Qing officials required all foreign merchants to live in the southern port of Guangzhou (formerly Canton) and to buy and sell only to licensed Chinese merchants. Practices considered harmful to Chinese interests were strictly forbidden.

Commissioner Lin Zexu Overseeing the Destruction of Opium at Guangzhou, 1839   A formidable Chinese bureaucrat known for his competence and high moral standards, Lin Zexu was sent to Guangzhou (Canton) as imperial commissioner in late 1838 to halt the illegal importation of opium by the British. He made a huge impact on the opium trade within a matter of months. As a result, British troops invaded China, and the ultimate British victory in the Opium Wars forced China to grant European merchants one-sided trade agreements. (Pictures From History/CPA Media Pte Ltd/Alamy Stock Photo)

For years the little community of foreign merchants in Guangzhou had to accept this system. By the 1820s, however, the dominant merchants, the British, were flexing their muscles. In the following decades the British used opium — that "destructive and ensnaring vice" denounced by Chinese decrees — to break China's self-imposed isolation. British merchants smuggled opium grown legally in British-occupied India into China, where its use and sale were illegal. Huge profits and growing addiction led to a rapid increase in sales. By 1836 the British merchants in Guangzhou were demanding the creation of an independent British colony in China and "safe and unrestricted liberty" in their Chinese trade. Spurred on by economic motives, they pressured the British government to take decisive action and enlisted the support of British manufacturers with visions of vast Chinese markets to be opened to their goods.

The Qing government tried to stamp out the opium trade. It was ruining the people and stripping the empire of its silver, which went to British merchants to pay for the drug. The government began to vigorously prosecute Chinese drug dealers, and in 1839 it sent special envoy Lin Zexu to Guangzhou to

deal with the crisis. Lin Zexu punished Chinese people who purchased opium and seized the opium supplies of the British merchants, who then withdrew to the barren island of Hong Kong. He sent a famous letter justifying his policy to Queen Victoria in London.

The wealthy, well-connected British merchants appealed to their allies in London for support, and the British government responded with force. London also wanted free, unregulated trade with China and sought to establish diplomatic relations on the European model, complete with ambassadors, embassies, and published treaties. Using troops from India and taking advantage of its control of the seas, Britain occupied several coastal cities and in the first of two **Opium Wars** forced China to give in to British demands. In the Treaty of Nanking in 1842, the

---

■ **neo-Europes** Settler colonies with established populations of Europeans, such as North America, Australia, New Zealand, and Latin America, where Europe found outlets for population growth and its most profitable investment opportunities in the nineteenth century.

■ **Opium Wars** Two mid-nineteenth-century conflicts between China and Great Britain over the British trade in opium, which were designed to "open" China to European free trade. In defeat, China gave European traders and missionaries increased protection and concessions.

imperial government was required to cede the island of Hong Kong to Britain, pay an indemnity of $100 million, and open up four large cities to unlimited foreign trade with low tariffs.

With Britain's new power over Chinese commerce, the opium trade flourished, and Hong Kong developed rapidly as an Anglo-Chinese enclave. But disputes over trade between China and the Western powers continued. Finally, the second Opium War (1856–1860) culminated in the occupation of Beijing by seventeen thousand British and French troops, who burned down the emperor's summer palace. Another round of one-sided treaties gave European merchants and missionaries greater privileges and protection and forced the Chinese to accept trade and investment on unfavorable terms in several more cities. Thus did Europeans use opium addiction and military aggression to blow a hole in the wall of Chinese seclusion and open the country to foreign ideas and uneven foreign trade.

Japan and the United States

China's neighbor Japan had its own highly distinctive civilization and even less use for Westerners. European traders and missionaries first arrived in Japan, an archipelago nation slightly smaller than California, in the sixteenth century. By 1640 Japanese leaders had decided to expel all foreigners and seal off the country from all European influences in order to preserve traditional Japanese culture and society. When U.S. and British whaling ships began to appear off Japanese coasts almost two hundred years later, the policy of exclusion was still in effect. An order of 1825 commanded Japanese officials to "drive away foreign vessels without second thought."[1]

The West, particularly the United States, perceived Japan's unbending isolationism as hostile. It complicated the practical problems of ensuring the safety of shipwrecked American sailors and the provisioning of whaling ships and China traders sailing in the eastern Pacific. It also thwarted American business leaders' hope of trade and profit. Moreover, Americans shared the self-confidence and dynamism of expanding Western society, and they felt destined to play a major role in the Pacific. To Americans it seemed the duty of the United States to force the Japanese to open their ports.

After several unsuccessful American attempts to establish commercial relations with Japan, Commodore Matthew Perry steamed into Edo (now Tokyo) Bay in 1853. Relying on **gunboat diplomacy** by threatening to attack, Perry demanded diplomatic negotiations with the emperor. Some Japanese military leaders urged resistance, but senior officials

realized how defenseless their cities were against naval bombardment. They reluctantly signed a treaty with the United States that opened two ports and permitted trade. Over the next five years, more treaties spelled out the rights and privileges of the Western nations and their merchants in Japan. The country was "opened." What the British had done in China with two wars, the Americans had achieved in Japan with the threat of one.

Western Intervention in Egypt

Egypt's experience illustrates not only the explosive power of the expanding European economy but also its appeal for local elites. Since 1517 Egypt had been under the rule of the Ottoman sultans, and in 1798 French armies under Napoleon Bonaparte invaded and occupied the territory for three years. Into the power vacuum left by the French withdrawal stepped an extraordinary Albanian-born, Turkish-speaking general, Muhammad Ali (1769–1849).

First appointed governor of Egypt in 1805 by the Ottoman sultan, Muhammad Ali set out to build his own state based on European models. He built a large army by drafting illiterate Egyptian peasants, and he hired French and Italian army officers to train these raw recruits and their Turkish officers in modern military methods. He reformed the government bureaucracy, cultivated new lands, and improved communication networks. By the end of his reign in 1848, Muhammad Ali had established a strong and virtually independent Egyptian state, to be ruled by his family on a hereditary basis within the Ottoman Empire (see "Reform and Readjustment in the Ottoman Empire" in Chapter 23).

To pay for his ambitious plans, Muhammad Ali encouraged the development of commercial agriculture. This move had profound implications. Egyptian peasants were poor but largely self-sufficient, growing food for their own consumption on state-owned lands allotted to them by tradition. When high-ranking officials and members of Muhammad Ali's family began carving large private landholdings out of the state domain, they forced peasants to grow cash crops such as cotton and rice geared to European markets. Egyptian landowners "modernized" agriculture, but to the detriment of peasant living standards.

These trends continued under Muhammad Ali's grandson Ismail (ihs-MAH-eel), who in 1863 began his sixteen-year rule as Egypt's khedive (kuh-DEEV), or prince. Educated at France's leading military academy, Ismail was a westernizing autocrat. The large irrigation networks he promoted boosted cotton production and exports to Europe, and with his support a French company completed the Suez Canal in 1869. The Arabic of the Egyptian masses replaced the Turkish spoken by Ottoman rulers as the official

■ **gunboat diplomacy** The use or threat of military force to coerce a government into economic or political agreements.

Building the Suez Canal   Workers dig through a clay bank during construction of the Suez Canal in Egypt. The canal, which took ten years and the labor of some 1.5 million people to build, connects the Mediterranean and Red Seas. Built by the French-owned Suez Canal Company and financed by international investors, the canal opened in 1869 and dramatically reduced shipping time between Europe and Asia. (Otto Herschan/Getty Images)

language. Young Egyptians educated in Europe implemented reforms, and Cairo acquired modern boulevards and Western hotels. As Ismail proudly declared, "My country is no longer in Africa, we now form part of Europe."[2]

Europeans saw opportunities for work and profit in modernizing Egypt. By 1864 more than fifty thousand Europeans lived in the port city of Alexandria, where they worked as army officers, engineers, doctors, government officials, and police officers. Others turned to trade, finance, and shipping.

Ismail's projects were enormously expensive, and by 1876 Egypt owed foreign bondholders a colossal debt that it could not pay. France and Great Britain intervened and forced Ismail to appoint French and British commissioners to oversee Egyptian finances. This decision marked a sharp break with the past.

The Suez Canal, 1869

Mediterranean Sea

•Alexandria

Cairo   Bitter Lakes   Suez Canal   SINAI

EGYPT

Nile R.   Gulf of Suez   OTTOMAN EMPIRE

O T T O M A N   Red Sea

Throughout most of the nineteenth century, Europeans had used military might and political force primarily to make sure that non-Western lands would accept European trade and investment. Now Europeans were going to effectively rule Egypt.

Foreign financial control evoked a violent nationalistic reaction among Egyptian army officers, religious leaders, and young intellectuals. In 1879, under the leadership of Colonel Ahmed Arabi, they formed the Egyptian Nationalist Party. When in 1882 the French and British forced Ismail to abdicate in favor of his ineffectual son, Mohamed Tewfik Pasha (r. 1879–1892), riots broke out in Alexandria. A number of Europeans were killed, and Tewfik (TAW-fik) and his court had to flee to British ships for safety. When the British fleet bombarded Alexandria, more riots swept the country, and Colonel Arabi led a revolt. But a British expeditionary force put down the rebellion and occupied all of Egypt that year.

Although they claimed their occupation was temporary, the British maintained control of Egypt until 1956. Before the First World War (1914–1918), they preserved the façade of Egypt as an autonomous province of the Ottoman Empire; the khedive, however, generally carried out the bidding of the British colonial authorities. British rule did result in tax reforms and somewhat better conditions for peasants, and foreign bondholders received interest on their loans. But Egyptians saw the British as foreign occupiers, and anticolonial resistance grew during and after the First World War.

The British takeover in Egypt provided a new model for European expansion in densely populated lands. Such expansion was based on military force, political domination, and a self-justifying ideology of beneficial reform. This model predominated until at least 1914. In China, Japan, and Egypt, and across the globe, Europe's Industrial Revolution and subsequent expansion contributed to fundamental economic, political, and social changes. Yet in an age of imperialism the profits generated by industrialization were almost entirely one-sided: development benefited Europe but offered much less to China, Egypt, and other European colonies.

How was massive migration an integral part of Western expansion?

A poignant human drama accompanied European expansion: millions of people left their ancestral lands in history's greatest migration. To ordinary Europeans for whom the opening of China and the interest on the Egyptian debt had not the slightest significance, this great movement was the central experience in the saga of Western expansion. It was, in part, because of this **global mass migration** that the West's

impact on the world in the nineteenth century was so powerful and many-sided.

The Pressure of Population

In the early eighteenth century European population growth entered its third and decisive stage, which continued unabated until the early twentieth century. Birthrates declined in the nineteenth century, but so did death rates, mainly because of the revolution in public health that led to rising living standards. During the hundred years before 1900 the population of Europe (including Asiatic Russia) more than doubled, from approximately 188 million to roughly 432 million.

These figures actually understate Europe's population explosion, for between 1815 and 1932 more than 60 million Europeans left the subcontinent. These emigrants went primarily to the rapidly growing neo-Europes—North and South America, Australia, New Zealand, and Siberia. Since the population of Indigenous Africans, Asians, and Americans grew more slowly than that of Europeans, the number of Europeans and people of predominantly European origin jumped from about 24 percent of the world's total in 1800 to about 38 percent on the eve of World War I.

Population growth in Europe drove more and more people to emigrate. As in the eighteenth century, the rapid increase in numbers led to relative overpopulation in area after area. In most countries, emigration increased twenty years after a jump in population as children grew up, saw little available land and few economic opportunities, and departed. This pattern was especially prevalent when rapid population increase predated extensive industrial development, which offered the best long-term hope of creating jobs

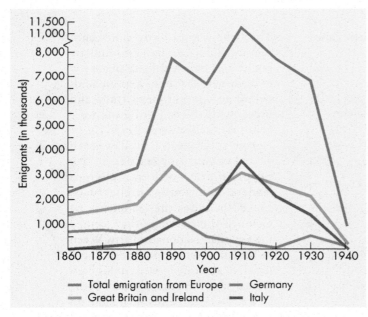

FIGURE 24.2 Emigration from Europe by Decade, 1860–1940
Emigration from Europe followed regional economic trends, as the comparison in this chart suggests. Overall, emigration from Europe grew quickly until the outbreak of World War I in 1914, after which it declined rapidly.

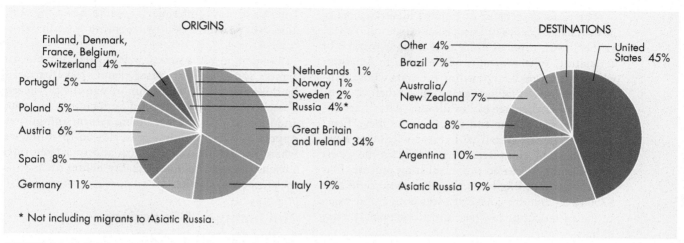

FIGURE 24.3   Origins and Destinations of European Emigrants, 1851–1960   European emigrants came from many countries; almost half of them went to the United States.

and reducing poverty. Thus millions of country folk in industrialized parts of Europe moved to cities in search of work, while those in more slowly industrializing regions moved abroad.

Three facts about this emigration stand out. First, the number of men and women who left Europe increased rapidly at the end of the nineteenth century and leading up to World War I. As Figure 24.2 shows, more than 11 million left in the first decade of the twentieth century, over five times the number departing in the 1850s. Large-scale emigration was a defining characteristic of European society at the turn of the century.

Second, different countries had very different patterns of migration. People left Britain and Ireland in large numbers from the 1840s on. This outflow reflected not only rural poverty but also the movement of skilled industrial technicians and the preferences shown to British migrants in the overseas British Empire. Ultimately, about one-third of all European emigrants between 1840 and 1920 came from the British Isles. German emigration was quite different. It grew irregularly after about 1830, reaching a first peak in the early 1850s and another peak in the early 1880s. Then it declined rapidly, for at that point Germany's rapid industrialization provided adequate jobs at home. This pattern contrasted sharply with that of Italy. More and more Italians left the country right up to 1914, forced out by relatively slow industrial growth and poor living standards in Italian villages. In short, migration patterns mirrored social and economic conditions in the various European countries and provinces.

Third, although the United States did absorb the largest overall number of European emigrants, fewer than half of all these emigrants went to the United States. Asiatic Russia, Canada, Argentina, Brazil,

Australia, and New Zealand also attracted large numbers, as Figure 24.3 shows. Moreover, immigrants accounted for a larger proportion of the total population in Argentina, Brazil, and Canada than in the United States. The common U.S. assumption that European emigration meant immigration to the United States is quite inaccurate.

European Emigration

What kind of people left Europe, and what were their reasons for doing so? The European emigrant was generally an energetic small farmer or skilled artisan trying hard to stay ahead of poverty, not a desperately impoverished landless peasant or urban proletarian. Small peasant landowners and village craftsmen typically left Europe because of the lack of available land and the growing availability of inexpensive factory-made goods, which threatened their traditional livelihoods. Immigrants brought great benefits to the countries that received them, largely because the vast majority were young, unmarried, and ready to work hard to improve their lives in their new homes.

Many Europeans moved but remained within Europe, settling temporarily or permanently in another European country. Jews from central Europe and peasants from Ireland moved to Great Britain; Poles sought work in Germany; Spaniards, Portuguese, and Italians went to France. Many Europeans returned home after some time abroad. One in two immigrants to Argentina and probably one in three to the United States eventually returned to their native lands. Unlike the Irish or Russian Jews, these Europeans might be able to buy land and did not face persecution back at home.

■ **global mass migration** The mass movement of people from Europe in the nineteenth century; one reason that the West's impact on the world was so powerful and many-sided.

The mass movement of Italians illustrates many of the characteristics of European emigration. As late as the 1880s, three of every four Italians worked in agriculture. With the influx of cheap North American wheat, many small landowning peasants whose standard of living was falling began to leave their country. Some called themselves "swallows." After harvesting their own wheat and flax in Italy, they "flew" to Argentina or Brazil to harvest wheat between December and April. Returning to Italy for the spring planting, they repeated this exhausting process. This was a very hard life, but a frugal worker could save $250 to $300 in the course of a season, at a time when an Italian agricultural worker earned less than $1 a day in Italy.

Ties of family and friendship played a crucial role in the emigration process. Many people from a given province or village settled together in rural enclaves or tightly knit urban neighborhoods thousands of miles away. Very often a prominent individual—a businessman, a religious leader, an ambitious family member—would blaze the way, and others would follow, forming a "migration chain."

Emigration was a radical way to gain basic human rights. Some landless young people felt frustrated by the power of the small minority in the privileged classes, which often controlled both church and state and resisted demands for liberal reform and greater opportunity. Emigration rates slowed in countries where the people won political and social reforms, such as the right to vote, equality before the law, or social security benefits.

The Immigrant Experience in the United States

As we have seen, not all European immigrants moved to North America, but about one-half of the 60 million Europeans who left their homelands did come to the United States. Their work and lives had a major impact on Europe and the United States alike.

Migrants Crossing the Atlantic to Reach the United States Between 1800 and 1930, about 30 million Europeans left home to seek better lives in the United States, and today over 40 percent of Americans are descendants of people who went through immigration control on Ellis Island, the country's main immigration station in New York City harbor. Although advertising posters like the one pictured here promised colorful and adventurous passage to South America as well as the United States, the many people who bought tickets in the least expensive "steerage" compartment faced a crowded and uncomfortable journey. Yet poor job prospects at home, political or ethnic persecution, and the lure of the booming U.S. economy led many to take the trip. (poster: National Archives; photo: Granger)

Between 1890 and 1925 over 20 million men, women, and children passed through the Ellis Island Immigration Station in New York City harbor. During these years, southern and eastern Europeans, such as Italians, Poles, and Russian Jews, far outnumbered the northern Europeans who had predominated in the mid-nineteenth-century wave of migration to the United States. Transporting migrants across the North Atlantic was big business. Well-established steamship companies such as Cunard, White Star, and Hamburg-America advertised inexpensive fares and good accommodations. The reality was usually different. For the vast majority who could afford only third-class passage in the steerage compartment, the eight- to fourteen-day journey from Naples, Hamburg, or Liverpool was cramped, cold, and unsanitary.

Once they arrived at Ellis Island, steerage passengers were subjected to a four- to five-hour examination in the Great Hall. Physicians checked their health. Customs officers inspected legal documents. Bureaucrats administered intelligence tests and evaluated the migrants' financial and moral status. The exams worried and sometimes insulted the new arrivals. As one Polish-Jewish immigrant remembered, "They asked us questions. 'How much is two and one? How much is two and two?' But the next young girl, also from our city, went and they asked her, 'How do you wash stairs, from the top or from the bottom?' She says, 'I don't come to America to wash stairs.'"[3]

Migrants with obvious illnesses were required to stay in the island's hospital as long as several weeks to see if they improved. Sick passengers whom officials judged either a threat to public health or a likely drain on public finances were sent home. Suspected anarchists and, later, Bolsheviks were also deported.

By today's standards, it was remarkably easy to move to the United States — only about 2 percent of all migrants were denied entry. After they cleared processing, the new arrivals were ferried to New York City, where they either stayed or departed for other industrialized cities in the Northeast and Midwest. Migrants typically took unskilled jobs for low wages, and by keeping labor costs down they helped fuel the rapid industrialization of late-nineteenth-century America. They also transformed the United States from a land of predominantly British and northern European settlers into a vibrant multiethnic society.

Asian Emigration

Not all emigration was from Europe. Many Chinese, Japanese, Indians, and Filipinos — to name only four key groups — also responded to rural hardship with temporary or permanent emigration. At least 3 million Asians moved abroad before 1920. Most went as indentured laborers to work under difficult conditions on the plantations or in the gold mines

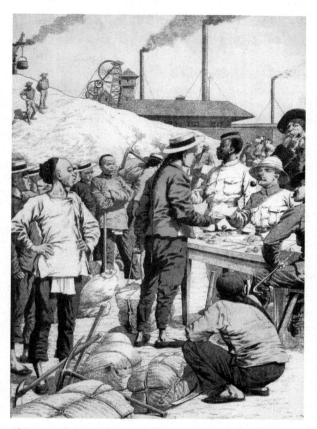

Chinese Laborers in South Africa Western industrialization and imperial expansion contributed to the mass migration of peoples across the globe. In 1904, labor shortages in South Africa, in part a result of the South African (Boer) War, led to the importation of over 60,000 Chinese laborers to work in the local gold mines. This illustration from *Le Petit Journal* (August 1904) shows Chinese workers arriving on the docks near Johannesburg, where they sign work contracts offered by British colonial officials. (Chris Hellier/Corbis/Getty Images)

of Latin America, southern Asia, Africa, California, Hawaii, and Australia. In a new global trend, white estate owners often used Asian immigrants to replace or supplement Black workers after the suppression of the slave trade.

In the 1840s, for example, the Spanish government recruited Chinese laborers to meet the strong demand for field hands in Cuba. Between 1853 and 1873, when such immigration was stopped, more than 130,000 Chinese people had moved to Cuba, where they performed coercive and poorly paid agricultural labor on large plantations. Peruvian plantation and mine owners likewise brought in more than 100,000 workers from China in the nineteenth century, and there were similar movements of Asians elsewhere.

Emigration from Asia would undoubtedly have grown much more if planters and mine owners had been able to hire as many Asian workers as they wished. But the original European settlers, disturbed

Nativism in the United States

In this 1896 Senate speech, the dynamic and well-respected Republican senator Henry Cabot Lodge expressed nativist anxieties about race in the United States and called for strict immigration restrictions. Most Europeans who immigrated to the United States in the late nineteenth century were Roman Catholics from Italy and central Europe, Slavs from Poland and Russia, and Jews from the Russian-controlled Pale of Settlement (in today's Poland, Belarus, and Ukraine). Nativists thought that these "races" were superior to Asians and Africans but far below the Anglo-Saxon Protestants from northern Europe, who constituted the majority of U.S. immigrants before the 1870s.

Restricting Immigration

~ This bill is intended to amend the existing law so as to restrict still further immigration to the United States. Paupers, diseased persons, convicts, and contract laborers are now excluded. By this bill it is proposed to make a new class of excluded immigrants, and to add to those which have just been named the totally ignorant. . . .

[We propose] to exclude all immigrants who could neither read nor write, and this is the plan which was adopted by the committee. . . . In their report the committee have shown by statistics, which have been collected and tabulated with great care, the emigrants who would be affected by this illiteracy test. . . . It is found . . . that the illiteracy test will bear most heavily upon the Italians, Russians, Poles, Hungarians, Greeks, and Asiatics, and very lightly, or not at all, upon English-speaking emigrants, or Germans, Scandinavians, and French. In other words, the races most affected by the illiteracy test are those whose emigration to this country has begun within the last twenty years and swelled rapidly to enormous proportions, races with which the English-speaking people have never hitherto assimilated, and who are most alien to the great body of the people of the United States. . . .

Immigration and the Economy

~ There is no one thing which does so much to bring about a reduction of wages and to injure the American wage earner as the unlimited introduction of cheap foreign labor through unrestricted immigration. . . .

Immigration and Citizenship

~ When we speak of a race, . . . we mean the moral and intellectual characters, which in their association make the soul of a race, and which represent the product of all its past, the inheritance of all its ancestors. . . .

[I]t is on the moral qualities of the English-speaking race that our history, our victories, and all our future rest. There is only one way in which you can lower those qualities or weaken those characteristics, and that is by breeding them out. If a lower race mixes with a higher in sufficient numbers, history teaches us that the lower race will prevail. . . . The lowering of a great race means not only its own decline, but that of civilization. . . .

Mr. President . . . The time has certainly come, if not to stop, at least to check, to sift, and to restrict those immigrants. . . . The gates which admit men to the United States and to citizenship in the great republic should no longer be left unguarded.

EVALUATE THE EVIDENCE

1. How does Lodge's understanding of race drive his enthusiasm for limits on immigration?
2. Why would nativist arguments win popular support in the late nineteenth century? Are such arguments still relevant in Europe and the United States today?

Source: Henry Cabot Lodge, *Speeches and Addresses, 1884–1909* (Boston: Houghton Mifflin, 1909), pp. 245, 247, 249–250, 262, 264–266.

by the presence of Asians who had moved beyond the fields and mines into towns, demanded a halt to Asian immigration. In 1882, the U.S. government enacted the Chinese Exclusion Act, and Australia followed suit in 1901 with the Immigrant Restriction Act—discriminatory laws designed to keep Asians from entering the country.

In fact, the explosion of mass mobility in the late nineteenth century, combined with the growing appeal of nationalism and scientific racism (see "Nationalism and Racism" in Chapter 23), encouraged a variety of attempts to control immigration flows and seal off national borders. Passports and custom posts were created so state governments could monitor travelers across increasingly tight national boundaries. National governments established strict rules for granting citizenship and asylum to foreigners. Such attempts were often inspired by **nativism**, beliefs that led to policies giving preferential treatment to native-born inhabitants above immigrants. Thus French nativists tried to limit the influx of Italian migrant workers, German nativists stopped Poles from crossing eastern borders, and American nativists restricted immigration from southern and eastern Europe and banned it outright from much of Asia. (See "Evaluating Written Evidence: Nativism in the United States.")

A crucial factor in migration patterns before 1914 was, therefore, immigration policies that offered preferred status to "acceptable" racial and ethnic groups in the open lands of possible permanent settlement. This, too, was part of Western dominance in the increasingly lopsided world. Largely successful in monopolizing the best overseas opportunities, Europeans and people of European ancestry reaped the main benefits from the mass migration. By 1913 people in Australia, Canada, and the United States had joined the British in having the highest average incomes in the world, while incomes in Asia and Africa lagged far behind.

How did the New Imperialism change Western colonialism?

The expansion of Western society reached its apex between about 1880 and 1914. In those years, the leading European nations not only continued to send massive streams of migrants, money, and manufactured goods around the world, but also rushed to create or enlarge vast empires. This political empire building, under direct European rule, contrasted sharply with economic intervention in non-Western territories between 1816 and 1880, which had, for example, "opened" China and Japan to international trade on unequal terms but left these countries politically independent. By contrast, the direct political control of the empires of the late nineteenth century recalled the old European colonial empires of the sixteenth to eighteenth centuries. Because this renewed imperial push came after a long pause in European expansionism, contemporaries called it the **New Imperialism**.

Characterized by a frantic rush to plant the flag over as many people and as much territory as possible, the New Imperialism had momentous consequences. By the early twentieth century almost 84 percent of the globe was dominated by European nations, and Britain alone controlled one-quarter of the earth's territory and one-third of its population. Aimed primarily at Africa and Asia, the New Imperialism created tensions among competing European states and led to wars and threats of war with non-European powers.

The European Presence in Africa Before 1880

Prior to 1880, Europeans controlled only about 10 percent of Africa. The slave trade had decimated African populations: by 1850, one historian concluded, Africa's population was about one-half of what it would have been without centuries of forced human trafficking.[4] Yet direct European possession of African lands was still relatively limited.

There were exceptions. The French had begun the conquest of Algeria in 1830, and by 1880 French, Italian, and Spanish colonists had settled among the overwhelming Arab majority there. The Dutch had established small colonies on the southern tip of the continent in the 1650s, and Britain had taken possession of the Dutch settlements in and around Cape Town during the Napoleonic Wars. This takeover had led disgruntled Dutch cattle ranchers and farmers in 1835 to make their Great Trek into the interior, where they fought the Zulu and Xhosa (KO-sah) peoples for land. After 1853 the Boers, or **Afrikaners** (a-frih-KAH-nuhrz), as the descendants of the Dutch in the Cape Colony were beginning to call themselves, proclaimed their independence and defended it against British armies. By 1880 Afrikaner and British settlers, who detested each other and lived in separate areas, had wrested control of much of South Africa from the Zulu, Xhosa, and other African peoples.

In addition to the French in the north and the British and Afrikaners in the south, the Portuguese maintained a loose hold on their old possessions on the coast of West Africa and in Angola and Mozambique. Elsewhere, over the great mass of the continent, Europeans did not rule.

The Berlin Conference and the "Scramble for Africa"

Between 1880 and 1900 the situation changed drastically. In a spectacular manifestation of the New Imperialism, Britain, France, Belgium, Germany, and Italy sought African possessions as if their national livelihoods depended on it (Map 24.2). By 1900 the Europeans had carved up nearly the whole continent and placed it under their rule. Only Ethiopia, which fought off Italian invaders, and Liberia, which had been settled by free and freed people from the United States, remained independent.

In the complex story of the European seizure of Africa, certain events and individuals stand out. Of enormous importance was the British occupation of Egypt in 1882, which established a new model of formal political control. King Leopold II of Belgium (r. 1865–1909), an energetic, strong-willed monarch of a tiny country with a lust for distant territory, also

---

■ **nativism** Policies and beliefs, often influenced by nationalism, scientific racism, and mass migration, that give preferential treatment to established inhabitants over immigrants.

■ **New Imperialism** The late-nineteenth-century drive by European countries to create vast political empires abroad.

■ **Afrikaners** Descendants of the Dutch settlers in the Cape Colony in southern Africa.

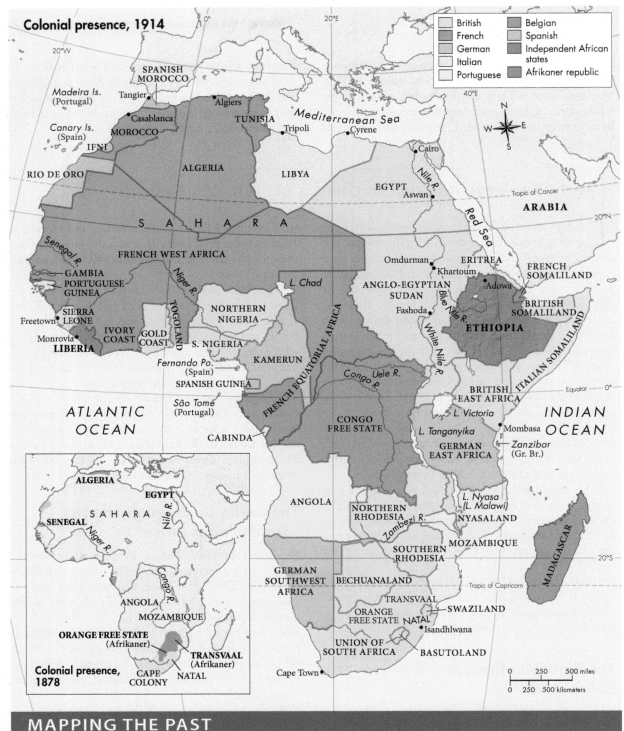

Colonial presence, 1914

Legend:
- British
- French
- German
- Italian
- Portuguese
- Belgian
- Spanish
- Independent African states
- Afrikaner republic

SPANISH MOROCCO
Madeira Is. (Portugal)
Tangier
Casablanca
Algiers
TUNISIA
Canary Is. (Spain)
MOROCCO
IFNI
RIO DE ORO
ALGERIA
LIBYA
Tripoli
Cyrene
Mediterranean Sea
Cairo
Nile R.
EGYPT
Aswan
Tropic of Cancer
ARABIA
20°N
SAHARA
FRENCH WEST AFRICA
Senegal R.
GAMBIA
PORTUGUESE GUINEA
SIERRA LEONE
Freetown
Niger R.
L. Chad
NORTHERN NIGERIA
TOGOLAND
Red Sea
Omdurman
Khartoum
ERITREA
FRENCH SOMALILAND
ANGLO-EGYPTIAN SUDAN
Adowa
Fashoda
Blue Nile R.
BRITISH SOMALILAND
ETHIOPIA
Monrovia
IVORY COAST
GOLD COAST
LIBERIA
S. NIGERIA
KAMERUN
FRENCH EQUATORIAL AFRICA
Congo R.
Uele R.
White Nile R.
ITALIAN SOMALILAND
Fernando Po. (Spain)
SPANISH GUINEA
São Tomé (Portugal)
CABINDA
CONGO FREE STATE
BRITISH EAST AFRICA
L. Victoria
Equator 0°
INDIAN OCEAN
Mombasa
Zanzibar (Gr. Br.)
GERMAN EAST AFRICA
L. Tanganyika
ATLANTIC OCEAN
ANGOLA
NORTHERN RHODESIA
Zambezi R.
L. Nyasa (L. Malawi)
NYASALAND
MOZAMBIQUE
MADAGASCAR
20°S
GERMAN SOUTHWEST AFRICA
BECHUANALAND
SOUTHERN RHODESIA
Tropic of Capricorn
TRANSVAAL
SWAZILAND
ORANGE FREE STATE
NATAL
Isandhlwana
UNION OF SOUTH AFRICA
BASUTOLAND
Cape Town

Inset map: Colonial presence, 1878
ALGERIA
EGYPT
SAHARA
Nile R.
SENEGAL
Niger R.
Congo R.
ANGOLA
MOZAMBIQUE
ORANGE FREE STATE (Afrikaner)
TRANSVAAL (Afrikaner)
CAPE COLONY
NATAL

0   250   500 miles
0   250   500 kilometers

MAPPING THE PAST

MAP 24.2 The Partition of Africa

The European powers carved up Africa after 1880 and built vast political empires. European states also seized territory in Asia in the nineteenth century, although some Asian states and peoples managed to maintain their political independence (see Map 24.3). Compare the patterns of European imperialism in Africa and Asia, using this map and Map 24.3.

ANALYZING THE MAP What European countries were leading imperialist states in both Africa and Asia, and what lands did they hold? What countries in Africa and Asia maintained their independence?

CONNECTIONS The late nineteenth century marked the high point of European imperialism. What conditions made the European rush for land and empire in Africa and Asia so successful?

played a crucial role. As early as 1861, he had laid out his vision of expansion: "The sea bathes our coast, the world lies before us. Steam and electricity have annihilated distance, and all the nonappropriated lands on the surface of the globe can become the field of our operations and of our success."[5]

By 1876 Leopold's expansionism focused on central Africa. He formed a financial syndicate under his personal control to send Henry M. Stanley, a sensation-seeking journalist and part-time explorer, to the Congo basin. Stanley established trading stations, signed unfair treaties with African leaders, and established Belgian control. Leopold's actions alarmed the French, who sent out an expedition under Pierre de Brazza to prevent Belgium from taking the entire region. In 1880 de Brazza signed a treaty with the ruler of the large Teke kingdom that exchanged territory for protection, and he also established a French protectorate on the north bank of the Congo River.

To lay down some basic rules for this new and dangerous global competition for territory in Africa, French statesman Jules Ferry, an ardent republican who also embraced imperialism, and German chancellor Otto von Bismarck arranged for the competing European powers to meet in Berlin in 1884 and 1885. The **Berlin Conference**, attended by over ten Western powers, including the United States, established the principle that European claims to African territory had to rest on "effective occupation" (a strong presence on the ground) to be recognized by other states. The conference basically legitimized British claims in Egypt and southern Africa. With Bismarck's tacit approval, the French could now press southward from Algeria, eastward from their old forts on the Senegal coast, and northward from their protectorate on the Congo River to take control of parts of West and Central Africa.

At the conference, European statesmen agreed to work to stop slavery and the slave trade in Africa and recognized King Leopold's personal rule over a supposedly neutral Congo Free State. In reality, conditions in Leopold's Congo Free State—a territory about the size of the United States east of the Mississippi River—exemplified some of the worst abuses perpetrated against Indigenous peoples by any European imperial power. Belgian colonial administrators sought to enrich themselves by harvesting Congo's ample supplies of elephant ivory and rubber, both in high demand in European markets. Africans in the Congo were coerced by the *Force Publique*, Leopold's private army, to labor in the jungle, where working conditions were little better than slavery. The *Force Publique* punished Congolese who resisted colonial demands or simply failed to meet the quotas for rubber collection by torturing, dismembering, and even murdering them.

As reports and photos of the atrocities — often collected by appalled white Christian missionaries —

Atrocities on a Rubber Plantation in the Belgian Congo   Congolese rubber workers display the severed hands of two of their countrymen murdered by plantation overseers in 1904. The white men are Baptist missionaries, who documented many such atrocities for publication by anti-imperialist critics in Europe. The Congo Free State controlled by the Belgians stands as one of the most violent and brutal examples of European imperialism. (Everett Collection Historical/Alamy Stock Photo)

made their way back to Europe, a public scandal ensued. Widespread outrage and the determined efforts of the anticolonial Congo Reform Association (whose members included Mark Twain and Booker T. Washington) ultimately forced Leopold in 1908 to end his personal rule. The Congo Free State became a formal colony of the Belgian state, and the *Force Publique* was disbanded, but only after 5 to 10 million Africans had lost their lives to Leopold's pursuit of profit and power.

The Berlin Conference coincided with Germany's sudden emergence as an imperial power. Before about 1880, Bismarck had seen little value in establishing overseas colonies. In 1884 and 1885, as nationalist agitation for colonial expansion increased, Bismarck did an abrupt about-face. Germany established protectorates over a number of small African kingdoms in Togo, the Cameroons region, and southwest and east-central Africa. Revolts against exploitative German rule in the colonies of German Southwest Africa (present-day Namibia) and German East Africa (present-day Burundi, Rwanda, and Tanzania) led to German military intervention and full-scale warfare. In German Southwest Africa, German troops massacred some 100,000 Herero and Nama Africans. Some historians view this colonial war as the twentieth-century's first genocide, a dreadful example of racial extermination that would be followed by the mass murder of Armenians and European Jews in the First and Second World Wars, respectively.

> ■ **Berlin Conference** A meeting of European leaders held in 1884 and 1885 in order to lay down some basic rules for imperialist competition in sub-Saharan Africa.

A Map of the British Empire, 1886

(Pictures From History/CPA Media Pte Ltd/Alamy Stock Photo)

This colorful map, by English illustrator Walter Crane, was published by the Imperial Federation League as a large color supplement in a London-based illustrated weekly in 1886. The map exalts the extent of Britain's imperial territories, which are highlighted in red. Small inset boxes list statistics about the geographical area, volume of trade, and population of each colony, and black lines represent the main trade routes to Great Britain, the colonial power. The banners across the top reading "Freedom, Fraternity, Federation" represent the goals of the Federation League, which sought but failed to achieve a federated union among Britain and its colonies.

EVALUATE THE EVIDENCE

1. How does Crane use visual allegories — symbolic fictional figures that represent larger human characteristics or "truths" — to portray Great Britain's commanding role in the world colonial system? What role, for example, do the soldiers play in the overall message of the map?

2. The inset boxes on the map provide basic demographic information about the colonies, including imports from and exports to the United Kingdom. Why did the artist include this information?

3. The critical scholar of maps and cartography Brian Harley once asserted, "As much as guns and warships, maps have been the weapons of imperialism," and he used this map to support his claim. Evaluate the validity of this statement. Based on your analysis, is it fair to call the map a "weapon"?

The British in Africa After 1885

By the time of the Berlin Conference the British Empire was already extensive, and it was poised for dramatic expansion, beginning in its own African colonies at the southern tip of the African continent. (See "Evaluating Visual Evidence: A Map of the British Empire, 1886," page 744.) Led by Cecil Rhodes (1853–1902), prime minister of Britain's Cape Colony, British colonists leapfrogged over the two Afrikaner states—the Orange Free State and the Transvaal (see Map 24.2)—in the early 1890s and established protectorates over Bech-uanaland (bech-WAH-nuh-land; now Botswana) and Rhodesia (now Zimbabwe and Zambia), named in honor of its founder. (See "Individuals in Society: Cecil Rhodes," page 746.)

English-speaking capitalists like Rhodes developed fabulously rich gold and diamond mines in the Transvaal, and this unilateral territorial and economic expansion heightened tensions between the British and the Afrikaners. In 1899 the conflict erupted in the bloody **South African War**, or **Boer War** (1899–1902). After a series of defeats at the hands of the determined Afrikaners, the British shipped some 180,000 troops to southern Africa. During the fighting, both sides enlisted or coerced the support of Black South African soldiers, and the British put Black Africans to work doing forced labor for the war effort. Overwhelming British forces placed the Afrikaners on the defensive, and they responded with an intensive guerrilla war that took two years to put down. The British forces resorted to "scorched earth" policies, burning the crops and villages of Boers and Indigenous Africans alike in Afrikaner regions. Most notoriously, in an attempt to halt the guerrilla campaign, the British forced Afrikaners and Indigenous Africans suspected of supporting them into concentration camps, where tens of thousands of Black African and Boer noncombatants died from disease and malnutrition. News of these tactics provoked liberal outrage at home in Britain.

The war ended with a British victory in 1902. In 1910 the Afrikaner-Boer territories were united with the old Cape Colony and the eastern province of Natal in a new Union of South Africa, established as a largely "self-governing" colony but still under British control. Gradually, however, the defeated Afrikaners used their numerical superiority over the British settlers to take political power. British leaders had lured Black African support with the reward of political rights once the war was over, but the peace treaties never made good on such promises. Instead, the British cooperated with the Boers' efforts to establish white-minority rule.

The British also fought to enlarge their colonies in central Africa, expanding northward from the Cape Colony, westward from Zanzibar, and southward from Egypt. British incursions into Sudan sparked the 1881 Mahdi uprising, in which Sudanese Muslims fought against British control. Eight years of war ensued, which included a Mahdist victory over British forces stationed in the Sudanese city of Khartoum, an outpost on the Nile that protected imperial interests in Egypt.

In 1897 General Sir Herbert Kitchener (who would serve Britain as secretary of state for war during World War I) sent a well-armed force up the Nile River, which built a railroad to supply arms and reinforcements as it went. In 1898 these British troops confronted the poorly armed Mahdist army at the Battle of Omdurman (ahm-duhr-MAHN) (see Map 24.2). Sudanese soldiers charged the British lines time and time again, only to be cut down by the recently invented Maxim machine gun. In the solemn words of one English observer, "It was not a battle but an execution. The bodies were . . . spread evenly over acres and acres." In the end, about 10,000 Sudanese soldiers lay dead, while 28 Britons had been killed and 145 wounded.[6]

Continuing up the Nile after the battle, Kitchener's armies found that a small French force had already occupied the village of Fashoda (fuh-SHOH-duh). Locked in imperial competition with Britain ever since the British occupation of Egypt, France had tried to be first to reach one of Africa's last areas unclaimed by Europeans—the upper reaches of the Nile. The result was a serious diplomatic crisis known as the **Fashoda Incident**, which brought the threat of war between two major European powers. Wracked by the Dreyfus affair (see "Republican France and the Third French Republic" in Chapter 23) and unwilling to fight, France eventually backed down and withdrew its forces, allowing the British to take over.

The British conquest of Sudan exemplifies the general process of empire building in Africa. Like the Mahdist army at Omdurman, or the Herero and Nama in German Southwest Africa, Indigenous peoples who openly resisted European control were defeated by vastly superior military force. But as the Fashoda Incident showed, however much the European powers squabbled for territory around the world, they stopped short of actually fighting one another. Imperial ambitions were not worth a great European war.

Imperialism in Asia

As they raced for territory in Africa, Europeans also exerted political control over much of Asia. Along with the British in India, the Dutch in present-day

---

■ **South African (Boer) War** Conflict in 1899–1902 in which British troops defeated rebellious Afrikaners, ancestors of Dutch colonialists, leading to consolidation of South African territories.

■ **Fashoda Incident** French colonial troops backed down in this 1898 diplomatic crisis caused by British-French competition over African territory in present-day South Sudan, preventing a European Great Power war over imperialist ambitions.

Cecil Rhodes epitomized the dynamism and the ruthlessness of the New Imperialism. He built a corporate monopoly, claimed vast tracts in Africa, and established the famous Rhodes scholarships to educate British (and American) colonial leaders who would love and strengthen the British Empire. But to Africans, he left a bitter legacy.

Rhodes came from a large middle-class family and at seventeen went to southern Africa to seek his fortune. He earned his first riches in the colonial South African diamond industry in the 1870s. Rhodes entered Oxford University, where he studied while returning periodically to Africa. His musings crystallized in a Social Darwinist belief in progress through racial competition and territorial expansion. "I contend," he wrote, "that we [English] are the finest race in the world and the more of the world we inhabit the better it is for the human race."[*]

By 1888 Rhodes's De Beers Consolidated Mines had monopolized southern Africa's diamond production and earned fabulous profits. Rhodes entered the Cape Colony's legislature and became the colony's prime minister from 1890 to 1896. During his tenure he used wealth requirements to prevent Black Africans from voting in elections. He also used government legislation to expropriate African lands and to force Black people to work at white-owned farms and industries.

Rhodes's belief in British expansion never wavered. His main objective was to annex the Afrikaner republics and impose British rule on as much land as possible beyond their northern borders. Working through a state-approved private company financed in part by De Beers, Rhodes's agents forced and cajoled African kings to accept British "protection," and then put down rebellions with machine guns. Britain thus obtained a great swath of empire on the cheap.

But Rhodes, like many imperialists obsessed with power and personal aggrandizement, went too far. He encouraged, and then declined to call back, the 1896 Jameson Raid, a failed British invasion of the Afrikaner Transvaal that was designed to topple the Dutch-speaking republic. Repudiated by top British leaders who had encouraged his plan, Rhodes had to resign as prime minister. In declining health, he continued to agitate against the Afrikaner republics. He died at age forty-nine as the South African War (1899–1902) ended.

In accounting for Rhodes's remarkable but flawed achievements, biographers stress his imposing physical size,

This statue of Cecil Rhodes at the University of Cape Town, South Africa, was removed after mass protests in April 2015. (Roger Sedres/ImageSA/Alamy Stock Photo)

enormous energy, and charismatic personality. He was a confident and powerful orator, and he could persuade and inspire others to follow his lead. According to his most insightful biographer, Rhodes's homosexuality — discreet, partially repressed, but undeniable — was also "a major component of his magnetism and his success."[†] Never comfortable with women, he loved male companionship. He drew together a "band of brothers," both gay and straight, who shared in his pursuit of power.

Rhodes cared nothing for the rights of Black Africans, and he looked forward to an eventual reconciliation of Afrikaners and British in a united white front. He thus helped lay the foundation for the Union of South Africa's brutal policy of racial segregation known as apartheid after 1948. In 2015, students started a "Rhodes Must Go" campaign against institutionalized racism at the University of Cape Town. The initial target of the movement — a 1934 statue of Rhodes on the university campus — was soon taken down. The movement expanded across South Africa and inspired similar protests in the United Kingdom and the United States.

QUESTIONS FOR ANALYSIS

1. In what ways did Rhodes's career epitomize the New Imperialism in Africa?
2. How did Rhodes relate to Afrikaners and to Black Africans? How do you account for the differences and the similarities in his attitudes toward them?

---

[*]Quoted in Robert I. Rotberg, *The Founder: Cecil Rhodes and the Pursuit of Power* (New York: Oxford University Press, 1988), p. 150.

[†]Rotberg, *The Founder*, p. 408.

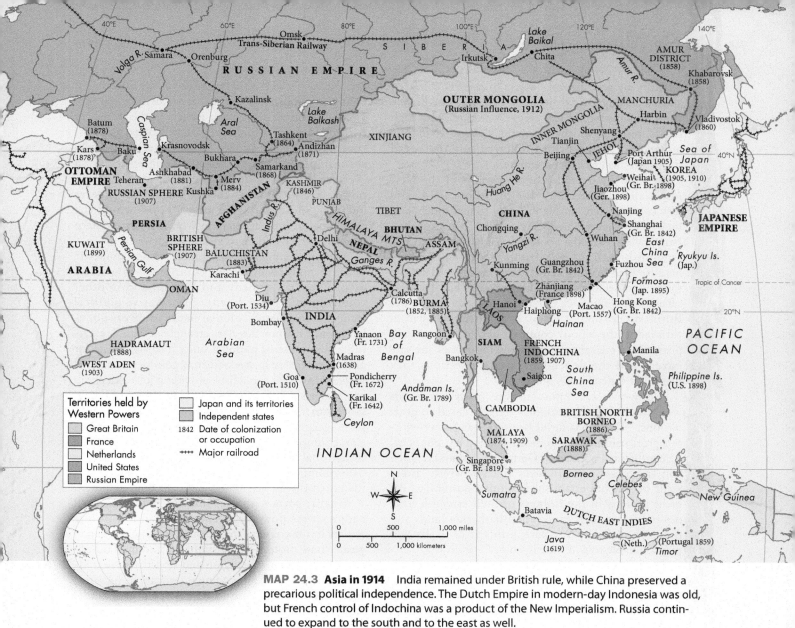

MAP 24.3 Asia in 1914 India remained under British rule, while China preserved a precarious political independence. The Dutch Empire in modern-day Indonesia was old, but French control of Indochina was a product of the New Imperialism. Russia continued to expand to the south and to the east as well.

Indonesia were major players. In 1815 the Dutch ruled little more than the island of Java in the East Indies. Thereafter they gradually brought almost all of the three-thousand-mile Malay Archipelago, including the islands of Indonesia, under their political authority, though—in good imperialist fashion—they had to share some of the spoils with Britain and Germany. In the critical decade of the 1880s, the French under the leadership of Jules Ferry took Indochina (Map 24.3).

Russians also acquired territories in Asia, moving steadily forward on two fronts throughout the nineteenth century. To the south they conquered Muslim areas in the Caucasus and in Central Asia, reaching the border of Afghanistan in 1885. To the east they nibbled on China's outlying provinces, especially in the 1890s.

The United States likewise widened its imperialist sights, taking Puerto Rico and the Philippines from Spain in 1898 through the Spanish-American War.

When it quickly became clear that the United States had no intention of granting the independence it had promised, Philippine patriots rose in revolt and were suppressed only after long, bitter fighting. Some Americans protested the taking of the Philippines, but to no avail. Thus another Western power joined the imperialist ranks in Asia.

Causes of the New Imperialism

Many factors contributed to the late-nineteenth-century rush for empire. First, economic motives enticed European leaders to extend their colonial empires, especially in Great Britain. By the late 1870s France, Germany, and the United States were industrializing rapidly behind rising tariff barriers. Britain was losing its early economic lead and facing increasingly tough competition in foreign markets. In this changing economic climate, the seizure of Asian and African territory by continental powers in the 1880s raised alarms among British leaders. Fearing that France and Germany would seal off their empires with high tariffs, resulting in the permanent loss of economic opportunities, the British followed suit and began their own push to expand empire.

In fact, the overall economic gains of the New Imperialism proved fairly limited before 1914. The new colonies were simply too poor to buy much, and they offered few immediately profitable investments. Nonetheless, even the poorest, most barren desert was jealously prized, and no territory was ever abandoned because each leading country saw colonies as crucial to national security and military power. For instance, safeguarding the Suez Canal played a key role in the British occupation of Egypt, and protecting Egypt in turn led to the bloody conquest of Sudan. Far-flung possessions guaranteed ever-growing navies the safe havens and the dependable coaling stations they needed in time of crisis or war.

Along with economic motives, many Europeans were convinced that colonies were essential to great nations. "There has never been a great power without great colonies," concluded one French publicist. The influential nationalist German historian Heinrich von Treitschke spoke for many when he wrote: "Every virile people has established colonial power. . . . All great nations in the fullness of their strength have desired to set their mark upon barbarian lands and those who fail to participate in this great rivalry will play a pitiable role in time to come."[7]

Treitschke's harsh statement reflects not only the increasing aggressiveness of European nationalism after Bismarck's wars of German unification, but also Social Darwinian theories of brutal competition among races and nations. The strongest nation, in this view, would always conquer the weaker in the grand race for national survival and domination. Thus European nations — in their imagined role as racially distinct representatives of the superior white race — had to seize colonies to show they were strong and powerful. Moreover, because they believed that victory of the fittest in the struggle for survival was nature's inescapable law, Europeans considered the conquest of so-called "inferior" peoples to be just. "The path of progress is strewn with the wreck . . . of inferior races," wrote one professor in 1900. "Yet these dead peoples are, in very truth, the stepping stones on which mankind has risen to the higher intellectual and deeper emotional life of today."[8] Social Darwinism and pseudoscientific racial doctrines fostered imperialist expansion.

So did the Western world's unprecedented technological and military superiority. Three aspects were particularly important. First, the rapidly firing Maxim machine gun, so lethal at Omdurman, was an ultimate weapon in many another unequal battle.

Second, newly discovered quinine proved effective in controlling mosquito-borne malaria, which had previously decimated European settlers in the tropics in Africa and Asia such that they had labeled the west coast of Africa the "white man's grave." Third, the steamship and the international telegraph allowed Western powers to quickly concentrate their firepower in a given area when it was needed. Never before — and never again after 1914 — would the technological gap between the West and non-Western regions of the world be so great.

Attempts to manage social tensions and domestic political conflicts in Europe contributed to overseas expansion. In Germany and Britain, and in other countries to a lesser extent, conservative political leaders manipulated colonial issues to divert popular attention from the class struggle at home, creating a false sense of national unity. Propagandists for empire relentlessly stressed that colonies benefited workers as well as capitalists, providing jobs and cheap raw materials that raised workers' standard of living. Government leaders and their allies in the tabloid press successfully encouraged the masses to savor foreign triumphs and to glory in the supposed increase in national prestige. In short, conservative leaders defined imperialism as a national necessity, which they used to justify the status quo and their hold on power.

Finally, certain special-interest groups in each country were powerful agents of expansion. White settlers in the colonial areas demanded more land and greater state protection. Missionaries and humanitarians wanted to spread religion and stop the slave trade within Africa. Shipping companies wanted lucrative subsidies to protect rapidly growing global trade. Military men and colonial officials foresaw rapid advancement and highly paid positions in growing empires. The actions of such groups pushed the course of empire forward.

A "Civilizing Mission"

Western society did not rest the case for empire solely on naked conquest and a Darwinian racial struggle, or on power politics and the need for naval bases on every ocean. Imperialists developed additional arguments for imperialism to satisfy their consciences and answer their critics. A favorite idea was that Westerners could and should civilize other peoples. According to European imperialists, colonized Africans and Asians would receive the benefits of industrialization and urbanization, Western education, Christianity, advanced medicine, and finally higher standards of living. In time, they might be ready for self-government and Western democracy. Thus the French repeatedly spoke of their imperial endeavors as a sacred "civilizing mission." As one German missionary put it, prayer

Tools for Empire Building   Western technological advances aided Western political ambitions in Africa and Asia. The Maxim machine gun shown at right was highly mobile and could lay down a steady stream of bullets that would decimate charging enemies, as in the slaughter of Mahdist soldiers at the Battle of Omdurman in Sudan. Quinine (left) was also very important to empire building. First taken around 1850 to prevent the contraction of deadly malaria, quinine enabled European soldiers and officials to move safely into the African interior and conquer Indigenous peoples. (quinine: Science Museum London UK/Wellcome Images; gun: PHILIP DE BAY [STAPLETON COLLECTION]/Private Collection/Bridgeman Images)

and hard work under German direction would lead "the work-shy native to work of his own free will" and thus lead him to "an existence fit for human beings."[9] Another argument was that imperial government protected Indigenous people from tribal warfare as well as from cruder forms of exploitation by white settlers and business people. In 1899 Rudyard Kipling (1865– 1936), who wrote numerous stories and poems about life in the "Raj" (the British term for colonial society in the Indian subcontinent) and was perhaps the most influential English writer of the 1890s, summarized such ideas in his poem "The White Man's Burden." (See "Viewpoints: White Man's Burden or Capitalist Exploitation?" on page 750.)

Outside of Europe, many Americans also accepted the ideology of the **white man's burden**. It was an important factor in their decision to rule, rather than liberate, the Philippines after the Spanish-American War. Like their European counterparts, these Americans believed that their civilization had reached unprecedented heights and that they had unique benefits to bestow on peoples they believed were less advanced.

Justifications for Europe's civilizing mission depended on widespread notions of Western superiority. The West, many Europeans believed, was modern, while the non-West was "primitive." The West was white, the non-West "colored"; the West was Christian, the non-West pagan or Islamic—and it was better in Western eyes to be modern, white, and Christian. These stereotypical ideas informed North American and European scholarship, arts, and literature in the

late nineteenth century. The emergence of ethnography and anthropology as academic disciplines in the 1880s was part of the process. Inspired by a new culture of collecting, scholars and adventurers went into the field, where they studied non-Western peoples and traded for, bought, or stole artifacts from them. The results of their work were reported in scientific articles and books, and intriguing objects filled the display cases of new public museums of ethnography and natural history. A slew of novels published around 1900 portrayed romance and high adventure in the colonies. Artists followed suit, and dramatic paintings of Arab warriors, African farms, and the sultan's harem adorned museum walls and wealthy middle-class parlors.

European imperialism also facilitated the spread of Christianity. Catholic and Protestant missionaries— both men and women—believed that their religion was superior to that of colonized peoples, who had their own complex religious beliefs. Christian missionaries competed with Islam and Indigenous religions south of the Sahara, seeking converts and building schools. Many Africans' first real contact with whites was in mission schools. Some peoples, such as the Ibo in Nigeria, became highly Christianized.

Such occasional successes in sub-Saharan Africa contrasted with the general failure of missionary efforts in India, China, and the Islamic world. There

---

■ **white man's burden** The idea that Europeans could and should "civilize" nonwhite people and that imperialism would eventually provide nonwhite people with modern achievements and higher standards of living.

When it was first published in an American illustrated magazine for the middle classes in 1899, Rudyard Kipling's well-known poem was read as encouragement for U.S. occupation of the Philippines in the aftermath of the Spanish-American War. It has since been understood as a forceful if somewhat anxious justification for Western imperialism in general that emphasizes the supposed backwardness of Indigenous peoples and the benefits they might gain under Western rule. Such views drew mockery from anti-imperialist intellectuals and politicians, including the Polish-German Marxist Rosa Luxemburg. In a scathing critique published in 1913, Luxemburg argued that the idealization of imperial domination masked the underlying need for the expansion of Western capitalism and the violent exploitation of colonial subjects.

Rudyard Kipling, "The White Man's Burden"

Take up the White Man's Burden —
   Send forth the best ye breed —
Go, bind your sons to exile
   To serve your captive's need;
To wait, in heavy harness,
   On fluttered folk and wild —
Your new-caught sullen peoples,
   Half devil and half child. . . .

Take up the White Man's burden —
   The savage wars of peace —
Fill full the mouth of Famine,
   And bid the sickness cease;
And when your goal is nearest
   (The end for others sought)
Watch sloth and heathen folly
   Bring all your hope to nought.

Take up the White Man's burden —
   No iron rule of kings,
But toil of serf and sweeper —
   The tale of common things.
The ports ye shall not enter,
   The roads ye shall not tread,
Go, make them with your living
   And mark them with your dead.

Take up the White Man's burden,
   And reap his old reward —
The blame of those ye better
   The hate of those ye guard —
The cry of those ye humor
   (Ah, slowly!) toward the light: —
"Why brought ye us from bondage,
   Our loved Egyptian night?"

Take up the White Man's burden —
   Ye dare not stoop to less —
Nor call too loud on Freedom
   To cloak your weariness.
By all ye will or whisper,
   By all ye leave or do,
The silent sullen peoples
   Shall weigh your God and you.

Take up the White Man's burden!
   Have done with childish days —
The lightly-proffered laurel,
   The easy ungrudged praise:
Comes now, to search your manhood
   Through all the thankless years,
Cold, edged with dear-bought wisdom,
   The judgment of your peers.

Rosa Luxemburg, from *The Accumulation of Capital*

From the very beginning, the forms and laws of capitalist production aim to comprise the entire globe as a store of productive forces. Capital, impelled to appropriate productive forces for purposes of exploitation, ransacks the whole earth, it procures its means of production from all levels of civilization and from all forms of society. . . .

Since capitalist production can develop fully only with complete access to all territories and climes, it can no more confine itself to the natural resources and productive forces of the temperate zone than it can manage with white labor alone. Capital needs other races to exploit territories where the white man cannot work. . . . Since the primitive associations of the natives are the strongest protection for their social organizations and for their material bases of existence, capital must begin by planning for the systematic destruction and annihilation of all the non-capitalist social units which obstruct its development. . . .

Each new colonial expansion is accompanied, as a matter of course, by a relentless battle of capital against the social and economic ties of the natives, who are forcibly robbed of their means of production and labor power. . . . The most important of these productive forces is of course the land, its hidden mineral treasure, and its meadows, woods, and water. . . . Force is the only solution open to capital. The accumulation of capital, seen as a historical process, employs force as a permanent weapon, not only at its genesis, but further down to the present day. . . . Hence permanent occupation of the colonies by the military, native risings, and punitive expeditions are the order of the day for any colonial regime. . . .

Force, fraud, oppression, looting are openly displayed without any attempt at concealment, and it requires an effort to discover within this tangle of political violence and contests of power the stern laws of the economic process.

QUESTIONS FOR ANALYSIS

1. What, exactly, is the "white man's burden"? What, according to Kipling, are the costs and rewards of undertaking the "civilizing mission"?
2. How do Luxemburg's assertions about the development of global capitalism challenge the ideas underlying Kipling's poem? What, according to Luxemburg, drives the imperial project?

Sources: Reprinted in "The White Man's Versus the Brown Man's Burden," *The Literary Digest*, vol. 18, no. 8 (New York: Funk and Wagnalls, 1899), p. 219; Rosa Luxemburg, "Capitalism Depends on the Non-Capitalist World," from *The Accumulation of Capital* in Alice L. Conklin and Ian Christopher Fletcher, *European Imperialism, 1830–1930* (Boston: Houghton Mifflin, 1999), pp. 29–36.

A Missionary School
A schoolboy leads his classmates in a reading lesson in Dar es Salaam in German East Africa (now Tanzania) in 1903; portraits of Emperor Wilhelm II and his wife look down on the classroom, a reminder of imperial control. Europeans argued that they were spreading the benefits of a superior civilization with schools like this one, which is unusually well built and furnished because of its strategic location in the German-controlled territory's capital city. Schoolrooms were typically segregated by sex, and lessons for young men and women adhered to Western notions of gender difference.
(ullstein bild/Granger)

Christians often preached in vain. Yet the number of Christian believers around the world did increase substantially in the nineteenth century, and missionary groups kept trying.

Gender and Empire

Colonization was in many ways a masculine endeavor. Europeans believed that it took male vigor and fortitude to meet the challenges of empire building. Men typically outnumbered women in the colonies by more than two to one—sometimes by much more. Service in colonial outposts offered a cure for the supposed emasculating effects of Western civilization. On the frontier, at least according to stereotypes, European soldiers could defeat Indigenous armies and European farmers could "civilize" supposedly primitive lands. Men could also make professional careers in the colonies as soldiers, administrators, merchants, and scholars.

Though the colonies were mostly managed by men, European women played a central role in the "civilizing mission." Europeans who embraced the "white man's burden" typically believed that the presence of white women in the colonies might help stop European men's tendency to engage in casual and often abusive sexual relationships with Indigenous women, which sometimes led to longer partnerships and occasionally interracial marriage. Proponents of imperial expansion therefore actively encouraged European women to serve in the colonies, and many answered the call. Some women worked as colonial missionaries, teachers, and nurses; others accompanied

their husbands overseas. If they stayed in the colonies long enough to establish a semipermanent household, European women might oversee servants, including men—an apparent violation of the notion of "separate spheres," which still dominated European gender relations (see Chapter 22). Colonial encounters thus established complicated social hierarchies that entangled race, class, and gender. (See "Thinking Like a Historian: Women and Empire," page 752.)

British women played an important part in the imperial enterprise, especially after the opening of the Suez Canal in 1869 made it much easier for civil servants and businessmen to bring their wives and children with them to India. British families tended to live in separate communities, where they occupied large houses with well-shaded porches, handsome lawns, and a multitude of servants. It was the wife's responsibility to manage this complex household. Many officials' wives learned to relish their duties, and they directed their households and servants with the same self-confident authoritarianism that characterized their husbands' political rule.

A small minority of colonial women—feminists, social reformers, and missionaries, both married and single—sought to go further and shoulder what they saw as the "white women's burden."[10] These women tried to improve the lives of Indigenous women in Africa, Asia, and India, promoting education and legislation to move them closer to the better conditions they believed Western women had attained. Reform-minded women led campaigns against polygamy and female genital mutilation. In India they helped outlaw the

Women and Empire

Though men played dominant roles in colonial territories, European women also worked as educators, missionaries, nurses, and housewives. What was life like for European women in the colonies?

1 *The Complete Indian Housekeeper & Cook*, **1898.** This book on household management described the domestic duties of the elite British woman (the "memsahib") in colonial India. It is shot through with notions of racial difference and superiority.

〜 This book, it is hoped, will meet the very generally felt want for a practical guide to young housekeepers in India. A large proportion of English ladies in this country come to it newly married, to begin a new life, and take up new responsibilities under absolutely new conditions. . . .

The first duty of a mistress is, of course, to be able to give intelligible orders to her servants; therefore it is necessary she should learn to speak Hindustani. . . .

The second duty is obviously to insist on her orders being carried out. And here we come to the burning question, "how is this to be done?" . . . The secret lies in making rules, and keeping to them. The Indian servant is a child in everything save age, and should be treated as a child; that is to say, kindly, but with the greatest firmness. . . . [F]irst faults should never go unpunished. By overlooking a first offence, we lose the only opportunity we have of preventing it becoming a habit. . . .

In their own experience the authors have found a system of rewards and punishments perfectly easy of attainment. One of them has for years adopted the plan of engaging her servants at so much a month — the lowest rate at which such service is obtainable — and so much extra as buksheesh [a tip or bribe], conditional on good service. . . . Of course common sense is required to adjust the balance of rewards and punishments, for here again Indian servants are like children, in that they have an acute sense of justice. . . .

We do not wish to advocate an unholy haughtiness; but an Indian household can no more be governed peacefully, without dignity and prestige, than an Indian empire.

2 **Elspeth Huxley, *The Flame Trees of Thika*, 1959.** In her memoir, Elspeth Huxley described her childhood in British Kenya on the eve of the First World War.

〜 Juma [the family's male Kenyan servant] had a patronizing air that [my mother] resented, and she doubted if he was showing enough respect. Those were the days when to lack respect was a more serious crime than to neglect a child, bewitch a man or steal a cow, and was generally punishable by beating. Indeed respect was the only protection available to Europeans who lived singly, or in scattered families, among thousands of Africans accustomed to constant warfare and armed with spears and poisoned arrows, but had themselves no barricades, and went about unarmed. This respect preserved them [the Europeans] like an invisible coat of mail, or a form of magic, and seldom failed; but it had to be very carefully guarded.

3 **Arguments for interracial relationships in Germany's African colonies.** When Germans first claimed African colonies in the mid-1880s, settlers often married or had close relations with African women.

〜

Max Buchner, *colonial bureaucrat*
As for free social intercourse with the daughters of the country [African colonial subjects], it is to be seen as more helpful than harmful to health. The eternal feminine, also under dark skin, is an excellent charm against low spirits, to which one is so vulnerable in the solitude of Africa.

Carl Büttner, *prominent missionary*
Frau Kleinschmidt [the Nama wife of a German missionary] is *highly respected* by whites and natives. . . . [H]er household could be a *model* for all the whites living in Damaraland [central Namibia]. . . . In short, this entire family [with seven children], descended from a mixed marriage, has had an *important* role in the development of this land and one can only wish that there be more like it.

ANALYZING THE EVIDENCE

1. What does the evidence presented in Sources 1–2 and 5–6 reveal about the relationships between European women and colonial subjects? What are the main points of contact and concern?
2. Why was respect viewed by Europeans as a key element in the relationship between colonizers and colonized (Sources 1 and 2)? Why would it be particularly important to women like Elspeth Huxley?
3. In Sources 3 and 4, what are the main arguments for and against "race mixing" in the German colonies? How do they draw on stereotypes about Europeans and Africans?

4 **Arguments against interracial relationships in Germany's African colonies.** After about 1900, colonial authorities tried to halt "race mixing" by condemning and outlawing interracial sexual relations and marriage, and encouraging German women to move to colonial Africa.

~

Paul Rohrbach, *colonial bureaucrat*

[German men are ruined by] keeping a filthy house with the lazy, ignorant, indolent, in a word barbaric and in almost every respect base colored wenches. [German men] for years and years have had no other contact with women besides this intercourse that is down-dragging, demoralizing, and nothing but coarse sensuality.

Editorial, *Hamburg News,* **1912**

The tolerance of mixed marriages would deeply degrade the prestige of the white race in Central Africa and would severely endanger the white women. Mixed marriages would then be permissible for white women as well, with native men. The white woman would thereby lose the only thing that offers her an unconditional protection from attacks in the colonies today, the respect of the colored.

Editorial, *Usambara Post,* **1912**

The European woman alone can solve the problem [of race mixing]. Only she can accomplish something positive, all so-called disciplinary measures belong to the realm of prohibitive and negative decrees, in which no real value resides: nature cannot be driven out with a pitchfork.

(Mansell Collection/The LIFE Picture Collection/Shutterstock)

5 **Photograph of a British tea party in India, 1896.** Class, race, and gender come together in this revealing photograph of an elite group of British colonists enjoying their tea, accompanied by Indian servants. The British "memsahib" at the center of the picture rests her feet on a tiger-skin rug and holds a tiger cub in her lap.

6 **Timetable for the Christian Missionary Society Girl's School, Ibadan, Nigeria, 1908.** Nigerian schoolchildren learned Western domestic tasks at European missionary schools.

5:00 A.M.	Prepare food, fetch water from river for baths, house, and kitchen
6:15–7:00	Quiet time and prayers
7:00	Domestic Work*
8:00	School
12:00 P.M.	Dinner
1:30	School
3:30	Recreation
4:00	Domestic Work*
6:00	Supper
7:15	Home Lessons
8:15	Prayers

Total time devoted to course work (including domestic subjects): 6 hours
Total time devoted to domestic chores: 4 hours, 15 minutes

*Note: "Domestic Work" tasks varied day by day and could include housework, laundry, ironing, preparing food, gardening, and cleaning.

PUTTING IT ALL TOGETHER

European women played a major role in the colonies during the era of New Imperialism. Using the sources above, along with what you have learned in class and in this chapter, write a short essay that describes their experience. How did ideas about race and gender help define the relationship between European colonizers and their colonial subjects?

Sources: (1) F. A. Steel and G. Gardiner, *The Complete Indian Housekeeper & Cook* (London: Heinemann, 1898), pp. 1–4, 9; (2) Quoted in Margaret Strobel, *European Women and the Second British Empire* (Bloomington: Indiana University Press, 1991), p. 23; (3, 4) All quotes from Lora Wildenthal, *German Women for Empire, 1884–1945* (Durham, N.C.: Duke University Press, 2001), pp. 81, 86–87, 103, 120–121; (6) "Timetable" in LaRay Denzer, "Domestic Science Training in Colonial Yorubaland, Nigeria," in *African Encounters with Domesticity,* ed. Karen Tranberg Hansen (New Brunswick, N.J.: Rutgers University Press, 1992), p. 119.

Hindu practice of sati, in which a widow was burned to death on the funeral pyre of her husband. European women enlisted Indigenous women in the cause, who sometimes established their own reform movements for women's rights in the colonies.

European Critics of Imperialism

In Europe, the expansion of empire aroused sharp, even bitter, criticism. A forceful attack was made by radical English economist J. A. Hobson (1858–1940) in *Imperialism* (1902), a work that influenced Lenin and others. Deeply angered by British tactics during the unpopular South African (Boer) War, Hobson contended that the rush to acquire colonies was due to the economic needs of unregulated capitalism, particularly the need of the rich to find outlets for their surplus capital. Yet, Hobson argued, only unscrupulous special-interest groups profited from imperial possessions, at the expense of both European working-class taxpayers and Indigenous peoples. Moreover, the quest for empire diverted popular attention away from domestic reform and the need to reduce the great gap between rich and poor.

Like Hobson, Marxist critics offered a thorough critique of Western imperialism. Rosa Luxemburg, a radical member of the German Social Democratic Party, argued that capitalism needed to expand into noncapitalist Asia and Africa to maintain high profits. The Russian Marxist and future revolutionary leader Vladimir Lenin concluded that imperialism represented the "highest stage" of advanced monopoly capitalism and predicted that its onset signaled the decay and coming collapse of capitalist society. These and

similar arguments were not very persuasive, however. Most people then (and now) were sold on the idea that imperialism was profitable for the homeland and beneficial to the colonized.

Hobson and other critics struck home, however, with their moral condemnation of whites' imperious rule of nonwhites. They rebelled against crude Social Darwinian thought. "O Evolution, what crimes are committed in thy name!" cried one foe. Another sardonically coined a new beatitude: "Blessed are the strong, for they shall prey on the weak."[11] Kipling and his kind were lampooned as racist bullies whose rule rested on brutality, racial contempt, and the Maxim gun. (See "Viewpoints: White Man's Burden or Capitalist Exploitation?" on page 750.) Similarly, in 1902 in the novel *Heart of Darkness*—a demolishing critique of the Belgian exploitation of the Congo—Polish-born novelist Joseph Conrad (1857–1924) castigated the "pure selfishness" of Europeans in supposedly civilizing Africa.

Critics charged Europeans with applying a degrading double standard and failing to live up to their own noble ideals. At home, Europeans had won or were winning representative government, individual liberties, and a certain equality of opportunity. In their empires, Europeans imposed military dictatorships. Colonial administrators forced Africans and Asians to work involuntarily in slavery-like conditions and subjected them to shameless discrimination. Critics insisted that Europeans could only live up to their own traditions if they renounced imperialism and allowed colonized peoples the freedoms Western society had struggled for since the French Revolution.

How did non-Westerners respond to Western expansion?

To Africans and Asians, Western expansion was a profoundly disruptive assault on existing and long-standing ways of life. Non-Western peoples experienced imperialism as an invasion, one made all the more painful by the arrogance and military power of the European intruders. Their responses to conquest ranged broadly from open rebellion to cooperation to appropriation of Western technologies and ideologies.

Impacts and Patterns of Response

Imperial conquest wrought immense changes in colonized lands. In the late nineteenth century, colonial authorities in Africa, India, and East Asia built cities, roads, railroads, and ports to facilitate the exchange of goods: raw materials flowed out, and European manufactured products poured in. Cash economies replaced existing systems of exchange. Indigenous

farmers began to grow cash crops for export, including tobacco, chocolate, and coffee.

New forms of control replaced or overlaid existing political structures. British administrators tended to establish systems of indirect rule, in which Indigenous elites and local troops enforced imperial authority. The French generally favored more direct rule and appointed Frenchmen as colonial governors. Everywhere Indigenous peoples lost political freedom and became subjects of a dictatorial colonial state.

Patterns of response to European invasion ranged from all-out rebellion to various forms of cooperation. African and Asian rulers often tried to drive the unwelcome foreigners away. Violent anticolonial rebellions exploded again and again in China, Japan, and Africa and in the lengthy U.S.–Native American wars. But as the Opium Wars and the Battle of Omdurman showed, the superior military technology of the industrialized

Zulu Workers at De Beers Consolidated Mines Indigenous peoples could eke out livelihoods in colonial enterprises, but the work was often exploitative: coerced, unskilled, unhealthy, and poorly paid. Here a group of Zulu "boys"—so labeled by their British supervisors—haul away rubble at a South African diamond mine in the mid-1880s. In 1888 Cecil Rhodes, working with British financiers, merged this and other regional mining companies into De Beers Consolidated Mines. Today, this global corporation remains the world's largest diamond mining, production, and distribution company. (Ann Ronan Pictures/Print Collector/Getty Images)

West almost always prevailed. The violence of the colonizing process uprooted lives, destroyed cultures, and devastated local economies. Even so, open resistance constantly threatened colonial rule.

Colonized lands were primarily peasant societies, and much of the burden of colonization fell on small farmers who tenaciously fought for some measure of autonomy. When colonists demanded extra taxes or crops, peasants hid the extent of their harvest; when colonists asked for increased labor, peasants dragged their feet. These everyday forms of evasion and resistance stopped short of open defiance, but nonetheless presented a real challenge to Western control.

Other groups and individuals cooperated with colonial administrators. Work for colonial enterprises, especially plantations and mines, could be brutally exploitative, but many farmers, traders, and laborers could earn a living in the new colonial markets. Some colonial subjects served as soldiers in European-led armies. The limited number of Europeans "on the ground" meant that Indigenous elites were needed to staff colonial administrations. Some regional rulers, landowners, and religious leaders earned considerable wealth and preserved much of their elite status by assisting colonial authorities. Such local intermediaries were crucial for the exercise of imperial power.

Some leaders in Africa and Asia—such as Ismail of Egypt—concluded that they would need to copy European achievements if they wished to escape foreign control. These "modernizers" could learn about Western society in missionary schools, and some traveled to Europe to earn university degrees. Western colonizers

thus received considerable support from local elites and an emerging group of Western-educated professional classes and civil servants.

Nevertheless, imperial rule was an imposing edifice built on sand. Support for European rule among subjugated peoples was shallow and weak. Indigenous leaders emerged who demanded human dignity, economic emancipation, and political independence. They ironically found in the Western world ideologies that justified their demands. Liberalism, with its credos of civil liberties and political self-determination, offered a stinging critique of Western domination. After 1917, anti-imperialist revolt would find another European-made weapon in Lenin's version of Marxist socialism.

Above all, anticolonial activists found themselves attracted to nationalism, which asserted that every people had the right to control their own destiny. Indigenous peoples organized nationalist political parties, boycotted European goods, published anticolonial newspapers, and championed non-European cultures and religions. The anti-imperialist search for dignity thus drew strength from resistance and from a complex blend of Western and non-Western sources, as was revealed by imperial expansion in India, Japan, and China.

The British Empire in India

India was the jewel of the British Empire, and no colonial area experienced a more profound British impact. Unlike Japan and China, which maintained a real if precarious independence, and unlike African territories, which Europeans annexed only at the end

The Great Rebellion, 1857–1858

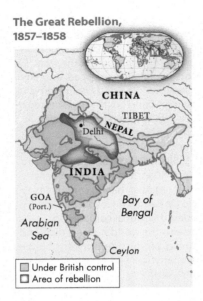

☐ Under British control
☐ Area of rebellion

of the nineteenth century, India was ruled more or less absolutely by Britain for a very long time.

Arriving in India on the heels of the Portuguese in the seventeenth century, the British East India Company had conquered the last independent Indian state by 1848. The last open revolt by the existing ruling groups against British rule was defeated in 1857 and 1858 in the **Great Rebellion** (which the British called a "mutiny"). This insurrection by Muslim and Hindu mercenaries in the British army spread throughout northern and central India before it was finally put down, primarily by Indigenous troops from southern India. Britain then established direct control until Indian independence was gained in 1947.

India was ruled by the British Parliament in London and administered by a tiny, all-white civil service in India. In 1900 this elite consisted of fewer than 3,500 top officials, who controlled a population of 300 million. The white elite, backed by white officers and Indigenous troops, was competent and generally well disposed toward the welfare of the Indian population. Yet it practiced strict job discrimination and social segregation, and most of its members saw the jumble of Indian peoples and castes as racially inferior. Elite colonial administrators and military leaders like Lord Kitchener believed in the "inherent superiority of the European" in India. As Kitchener put it, "however well educated and clever a native may be, and however brave he may prove himself, I believe that no rank we can bestow on him would cause him to be considered an equal of the British officer."[12]

Inspired by the "civilizing mission" and strong feelings of racial superiority, British imperialists worked energetically to westernize Indian society. Realizing that they needed well-educated Indians to serve as skilled subordinates in both the government and the army, the British established a modern system of secondary education, with all instruction in English. Thus some Indians gained excellent opportunities for economic and social advancement. High-caste Hindus, particularly quick to respond, emerged as skillful intermediaries between the British rulers and the Indian people, and soon they formed a new elite profoundly influenced by Western thought and culture.

This new Indian elite joined British officials and businessmen to promote modern economic development, constructing irrigation projects for agriculture, building the world's third-largest railroad network, and forming large tea and jute plantations geared to the world economy. Unfortunately, the lot of the Indian masses improved little because the profits went to Indigenous and British elites. Finally, the British created a unified, powerful state with a well-educated, English-speaking Indian bureaucracy. They placed under the same system of law and administration the different Hindu and Muslim peoples and the vanquished kingdoms of the entire subcontinent. This transformation of India engendered a decisive reaction to European rule: the rise of national resistance among the Indian elite. No matter how anglicized and necessary a member of the Indigenous educated classes became, he or she could never become truly equal in the eyes of the British. The top jobs, the best clubs, the modern hotels, and even certain railroad compartments were off limits to Indians. Racial discrimination meant injured pride and bitter injustice. It flagrantly contradicted the cherished Western concepts of human rights and equality that the Indian elite had learned about in Western schools. Moreover, it was based on dictatorship, no matter how benign.

By 1885, when educated Indians came together to found the predominantly Hindu **Indian National Congress**, demands were increasing for the equality and self-government that Britain had already granted white-settler colonies, such as Canada and Australia. By 1907, emboldened in part by Japan's success (see the next section, "Reforming Japan"), a radical faction in the Indian National Congress called for Indian independence. Although Hindus and Muslims disagreed on what shape the Indian future should take, Indians were finding an answer to the foreign challenge. The experience of discriminatory British rule and exposure to liberal Western ideals, along with the revitalization of the Hindu religion and the determined resistance to colonial abuse, had created a genuine movement for national independence.

Reforming Japan

When Commodore Matthew Perry arrived in Tokyo in 1853 with his crude but effective gunboat diplomacy, Japan was a complex feudal society. At the top stood a figurehead emperor, but real power was in the hands of a hereditary military governor, the shogun. With the help of a warrior nobility known as samurai, the shogun governed a country of hard-working, productive peasants and city dwellers. The intensely proud samurai were deeply angered by the sudden American intrusion and the unequal treaties with Western countries that followed.

The Russo-Japanese War, 1904–1905   This 1904 Japanese print portrays the surprise Japanese naval attack on the Russian fleet at Port Arthur as a glorious victory. Though the opening battle was in fact inconclusive, with few losses on either side, the Japanese won the war. The Japanese victory over a European "Great Power" inspired anticolonial independence movements in East Asia. In Russia, defeat by a supposedly "primitive" Asian nation encouraged reform movements in the Russian Empire and became a factor in the outbreak of the Russian Revolution of 1905 (see Chapter 23). (Universal Images Group/Getty Images)

When foreign diplomats and merchants began to settle in Yokohama, radical samurai reacted with a wave of antiforeign terrorism and antigovernment assassinations that lasted from 1858 to 1863. In response, U.S., British, Dutch, and French warships demolished key forts, further weakening the power and prestige of the shogun's government. Then in 1867 a coalition led by patriotic samurai seized control of the government with hardly any bloodshed and restored the political power of the emperor in the **Meiji Restoration**, a great turning point in Japanese history.

The battle cry of the Meiji (MAY-jee) reformers was "Enrich the state and strengthen the armed forces," and their immediate goal was to meet the foreign threat. In a remarkable about-face, the leaders of Meiji Japan dropped their antiforeign attacks. Convinced that Western civilization was indeed superior in its military and industrial aspects, they initiated a series of measures to reform Japan along modern lines. In the broadest sense, the Meiji leaders tried to harness Western models of industrialization and political reform to protect their country and catch up with Europe. In 1871 the new leaders abolished

the old feudal structure of aristocratic, decentralized government and formed a strong unified state. They created a robust, competitive economy, stimulated by government support, and skillfully adapted Western science and technology, particularly in industry, medicine, and education.

The overriding concern of Japan's political leadership was always to maintain a powerful state and a strong military. The government created a powerful modern navy and completely reorganized the army along European lines, forming a professional officer corps and requiring three years of military service of all males. This army of draftees effectively put down disturbances in the countryside, and in 1877 it crushed a

■ **Great Rebellion** The 1857 and 1858 insurrection by Muslim and Hindu mercenaries in the British army that spread throughout northern and central India before finally being crushed.

■ **Indian National Congress** An Indian nationalist movement, founded in 1885 and dedicated to independence from the British Empire.

■ **Meiji Restoration** The restoration of the Japanese emperor to power in 1867, leading to the subsequent modernization of Japan.

Demonizing the Boxer Uprising   The Sunday supplement to *Le Petit Parisien*, a popular French newspaper, ran a series of gruesome front-page pictures of ferocious Boxers burning buildings, murdering priests, and slaughtering Chinese Christians. In this 1910 illustration, Boxer rebels invade a church in Mukden, Manchuria, and massacre the Christian worshippers. Whipping up European outrage about Chinese atrocities was a prelude to harsh reprisals by the Western powers. (Print Collector/Getty Images)

major rebellion by feudal elements protesting the loss of their privileges.

By 1890, when the new state was firmly established, the wholesale borrowing of the early restoration had given way to a more selective emphasis on foreign elements that were in keeping with Japanese tradition. Following the model of the German Empire, Japan established an authoritarian constitution and rejected democracy. The power of the emperor and his ministers was vast, that of the legislature limited.

Japan also copied Western imperialism. Expansion proved that Japan was strong and cemented the nation together in a great mission. Having "opened" Korea with its own gunboat diplomacy in 1876, Japan

decisively defeated China in the Sino-Japanese War fought over Korean territory in 1894 and 1895 and took Formosa (modern-day Taiwan). In the next years, Japan competed aggressively with European powers for influence and territory in China, particularly in Manchuria, where Japanese and Russian imperialism collided. In 1904 Japan launched the Russo-Japanese War (1904–1905) by attacking Russia without a formal declaration of war. After a series of bloody battles, Japan took over Russia's former protectorate in Port Arthur and emerged with a valuable foothold in China (see Map 24.3). By 1910, with the annexation of Korea, Japan had become a major imperial power.

Japan exemplified the way non-Western countries could combine European-style economic and political reforms with their own long-standing values and traditions in order to meet the many-sided challenge of Western expansion. Moreover, Japan demonstrated that an Asian nation could defeat and humble Russia, a major Western power. Japan's achievement fascinated Chinese and Vietnamese nationalists and provided patriots throughout Asia and Africa with an inspiring example of national recovery and liberation.

Toward Revolution in China

In 1860 the two-hundred-year-old Qing Dynasty in China appeared on the verge of collapse. Efforts to repel foreigners had failed, and rebellion and chaos wracked the country. A series of midcentury popular revolts—including the great Taiping rebellion (1859–1864)—weakened state authority, caused enormous loss of life, and created severe economic dislocation. Attempts to cooperate with the Western imperialist powers hardly stopped incursions on Chinese autonomy. The implementation of domestic "self-strengthening" reforms, in which the Qing adopted some aspects of liberal government and modern technology while maintaining traditional Chinese values, led to a period of stability. But they failed to halt the dynasty's decline.

The parallel movement toward domestic reform and limited cooperation with the West collapsed under the blows of Japanese imperialism. Defeat in the Sino-Japanese War (1894–1895) and the subsequent harsh peace treaty revealed China's helplessness in the face of aggression, triggering a rush by foreign powers for concessions and protectorates.

China's precarious position after the war with Japan led to a renewed drive for fundamental reforms. Like the leaders of the Meiji Restoration, some modernizers saw salvation in Western institutions. In 1898 they convinced the young emperor to launch a desperate hundred days of reform in an attempt to meet the foreign challenge. More radical reformers, such as the revolutionary Sun Yatsen (1866–1925), who came from the peasantry and was educated in Hawaii

■ **Boxer Uprising** A violent revolt from 1899 to 1901 against foreigners and imperialists in China encouraged by the Qing court, which was quelled by large-scale Western intervention.

by Christian missionaries, sought to overthrow the dynasty altogether and establish a republic.

The efforts at radical reform by the young emperor and his allies threatened the Qing establishment and the empress dowager Cixi (see-SHEE), who had dominated the court for a quarter of a century. In a palace coup, she and her supporters imprisoned the emperor, rejected the reform movement, and put reactionary officials in charge. Hope for reform from above was crushed.

Between 1899 and 1901, the **Boxer Uprising** — a violent revolt against foreigners and imperialists encouraged by the Qing court — swept through the country. The patriotic Boxers blamed China's ills on foreigners, charging Christian missionaries with undermining reverence for ancestors and thereby threatening the Chinese family and society as a whole. In northeastern China, the Boxers killed more than two hundred foreign missionaries and several thousand Chinese Christians, prompting threats and demands from Western governments. The empress dowager answered by declaring war on the foreign powers, hoping that the Boxers might help limit European influence and control.

The imperialist response was swift and harsh. After the Boxers besieged the embassy quarter in Beijing, foreign governments — including Japan, Britain, France, Germany, and the United States — organized an international force of twenty thousand soldiers to rescue their diplomats and punish China. These troops defeated the Boxers and occupied and plundered Beijing. In 1901 China was forced to accept a long list of penalties, including a heavy financial indemnity payable over forty years.

The years after this heavy defeat were ever more troubled. Anarchy and foreign influence spread as the power and prestige of the Qing Dynasty declined still further. Antiforeign, antigovernment revolutionary groups agitated and plotted. Finally, in 1912 a spontaneous uprising toppled the Qing Dynasty. After thousands of years of emperors, a loose coalition of revolutionaries proclaimed a Western-style republic and called for an elected parliament. The transformation of China under the impact of expanding Western society entered a new phase, and the end was not in sight.

NOTES

1. Quoted in J. W. Hall, *Japan: From Prehistory to Modern Times* (New York: Delacorte Press, 1970), p. 250.
2. Quoted in Earl of Cromer, *Modern Egypt* (London: Macmillan, 1911), p. 48.
3. Quoted in Brooke Hauser, *The New Kids: Big Dreams and Brave Journeys at a High School for Immigrant Teens* (New York: Free Press, 2011), title page.
4. Howard W. French, *Born in Blackness: Africa, Africans, and the Making of the Modern World, 1471 to the Second World War* (New York: Liveright, 2021), p. 320.
5. Quoted in W. L. Langer, *European Alliances and Alignments, 1871–1890* (New York: Vintage Books, 1931), p. 290.
6. Quoted in J. Ellis, *The Social History of the Machine Gun* (New York: Pantheon Books, 1975), pp. 86, 101. The numbers given for British casualties at the Battle of Omdurman vary; the total casualties quoted here come from an original British army report. See Lieutenant General H. M. L. Rundle, M.G., Chief of Staff, "Herewith Returns of Killed and Wounded of the Expeditionary Force at the Battle of Khartum, on September 2, 1898," Khartum, September 9, 1898, at North East Medals, http://www.britishmedals.us/kevin/other/lgomdurman.html.
7. Quoted in G. H. Nadel and P. Curtis, eds., *Imperialism and Colonialism* (New York: Macmillan, 1964), p. 94.
8. Quoted in W. L. Langer, *The Diplomacy of Imperialism*, 2d ed. (New York: Alfred A. Knopf, 1951), pp. 86, 88.
9. Quoted in S. Conrad, *Globalisation and the Nation in Imperial Germany* (New York: Cambridge University Press, 2010), p. 78.
10. A. Burton, "The White Women's Burden: British Feminists and 'The Indian Women,' 1865–1915," in *Western Women and Imperialism: Complicity and Resistance*, ed. N. Chauduri and M. Strobel (Bloomington: Indiana University Press, 1992), pp. 137–157.
11. Quoted in Langer, *The Diplomacy of Imperialism*, p. 88.
12. Quoted in K. M. Panikkar, *Asia and Western Dominance: A Survey of the Vasco da Gama Epoch of Asian History* (London: George Allen & Unwin, 1959), p. 116.

LOOKING BACK LOOKING AHEAD

In the early twentieth century educated Europeans had good reason to believe that they were living in an age of progress. The largest wave of mass migration in human history had spread Europeans and their ideas around the world, even as it relieved social pressures at home. The ongoing triumphs of industry and science and the steady improvements in the standard of living beginning about 1850 were undeniable, and it was generally assumed that these favorable trends would continue. There had also been progress in the political realm. The bitter class conflicts that culminated in the bloody civil strife of 1848 had given way in most European countries to stable nation-states with elected legislative bodies that responded to real problems and enjoyed popular support. Moreover, there had been no general European war since Napoleon's defeat in 1815. Only the brief, limited wars connected with German and Italian unification at midcentury had broken the peace in the European heartland.

In the global arena, peace was much more elusive. In the name of imperialism, Europeans (and North

Americans) used war and the threat of war to open markets and punish foreign governments around the world. Although criticized by some intellectuals and leftists such as J. A. Hobson, these foreign campaigns resonated with European citizens and stimulated popular nationalism. Like fans in a sports bar, the peoples of Europe followed their colonial teams and cheered them on to victories that were almost certain. Thus imperialism and nationalism reinforced and strengthened each other in Europe, especially after 1875.

This was a dangerous development. Easy imperialist victories over weak states and poorly armed non-Western peoples encouraged excessive pride and led Europeans to underestimate the fragility of their accomplishments as well as the murderous power of their weaponry. Imperialism also made nationalism more aggressive and militaristic. At the same time that European imperialism was dividing the world, the leading European states were also dividing themselves into two opposing military alliances. Thus when the two armed camps stumbled into war in 1914, there would be a superabundance of nationalistic fervor, patriotic sacrifice, and cataclysmic destruction.

Make Connections

Think about the larger developments and continuities within and across chapters.

1. How did the expansion of European empires transform everyday life around the world?

2. Historians often use the term *New Imperialism* to describe the globalization of empire that began in the later nineteenth century. Was the New Imperialism really that different from earlier waves of European expansion (Chapters 14 and 17)?

3. In what ways does the global impact of European imperialism in the late nineteenth century continue to shape world relations and conflicts today?

24 REVIEW & EXPLORE

Identify Key Terms

Identify and explain the significance of each item below.

neo-Europes (p. 732)
Opium Wars (p. 733)
gunboat diplomacy (p. 734)
global mass migration (p. 736)
nativism (p. 740)
New Imperialism (p. 741)
Afrikaners (p. 741)
Berlin Conference (p. 743)

South African (Boer) War (p. 745)
Fashoda Incident (p. 745)
white man's burden (p. 749)
Great Rebellion (p. 756)
Indian National Congress (p. 756)
Meiji Restoration (p. 757)
Boxer Uprising (p. 759)

Review the Main Ideas

Answer the section heading questions from the chapter.

1. What were the global consequences of European industrialization? (p. 730)

2. How was massive migration an integral part of Western expansion? (p. 736)

3. How did the New Imperialism change Western colonialism? (p. 741)

4. How did non-Westerners respond to Western expansion? (p. 754)

Suggested Resources

BOOKS

- Bagchi, Amiya Kumar. *Perilous Passage: Mankind and the Global Ascendancy of Capital.* 2005. A spirited radical critique of the "rise of the West."
- Bayley, C. A. *The Birth of the Modern World, 1780–1914.* 2004. A broad survey that puts European imperialism and nationalism in a global context.
- Brantlinger, Patrick. *Taming Cannibals: Race and the Victorians.* 2019. Explores Victorian-era British literature to uncover the contradictory paradoxes at the heart of the European "civilizing mission."
- Conklin, Alice, Sarah Fishman, and Robert Zaretsky. *France and Its Empire Since 1870.* 2010. An outstanding general survey of French imperialism that brings the story up to the present.
- Conrad, Sebastian. *Globalisation and the Nation in Imperial Germany.* 2010. Places German nationalism and imperialism in the context of the wave of globalization that took place in the late nineteenth century.
- Crews, Robert. *For Prophet and Tsar: Islam and Empire in Russia and Central Asia.* 2006. Considers neglected aspects of Russian imperialism.
- Davis, Mike. *Late Victorian Holocausts: El Niño Famines and the Making of the Third World.* 2002. A passionate condemnation of the links among imperialist policy, environmental catastrophe, and mass starvation in European colonies around 1900.
- Goodlad, Graham. *British Foreign and Imperial Policy, 1865–1919.* 2000. Examines Britain's leading role in European imperialism.
- Hochschild, Adam. *King Leopold's Ghost: A Story of Greed, Terror, and Heroism in Colonial Africa, 1895–1930.* 1997. A chilling account of Belgian imperialism in the Congo.
- Maier, Charles S. *Among Empires: American Ascendancy and Its Predecessors.* 2006. Explores imperial power in history and how well the United States measures up.
- Midgley, Clare, ed. *Gender and Imperialism.* 1998. Examines the complex questions related to European women and imperialism.
- Pomeranz, Kenneth. *The Great Divergence: China, Europe, and the Making of the Modern Economy.* 2001. This influential book explores the rise of European global influence after 1800.

MEDIA

- *Berlin 1885: The Scramble for Africa* (Joël Calmettes, 2010). A re-enactment of and documentary about the Berlin Conference, where European powers divided up the African continent into colonies.
- *Congo: White King, Red Rubber, Black Death* (Peter Bate, 2003). This television documentary covers King Leopold II's horrific exploitation of the Congo.
- *The Four Feathers* (Shekhar Kapur, 2002). In this feature film, a British officer resigns his post just before his regiment goes to the Sudan to fight the "rebels." Seen as a coward because of the resignation, the officer goes undercover to regain his honor.
- *Internet Modern History Sourcebook: Imperialism.* A vast array of primary sources on imperialism across the globe. **https://sourcebooks.fordham.edu/mod/modsbook34.asp**
- *Opium War* (Jin Xie, 1997). An epic historical movie that depicts the dramatic conflicts between the British and Chinese surrounding the opium trade in the nineteenth century.
- *Queen Victoria's Empire* (Paul Bryers, 2001). A PBS four-part series about Queen Victoria and her empire, which included one-fifth of the world's population.
- *Rhodes* (BBC, 1996). An eight-part television drama about the British imperialist Cecil Rhodes, known for his success in the diamond industry and his passionate pursuit of British rule in southern Africa.
- *Slavery and the "Scramble for Africa"* (BBC History). Explores the role abolition played in British interests in the colonization of Africa in the nineteenth century. **www.bbc.co.uk/history/british/abolition/scramble _for_africa_article_01.shtml**

25

War and Revolution

1914–1919

In the summer of 1914 the nations of Europe went willingly to war, confidently expecting a short war leading to a decisive victory after which life would return to normal. Instead, the First World War was long, indecisive, and tremendously destructive. To the shell-shocked generation of survivors, it was known simply as the Great War because of its unprecedented scope and intensity.

From today's perspective, it is clear that the First World War was closely connected to the ideals and developments of the previous century. Industrialization, which promised a rising standard of living, also produced horrendous weapons that killed and maimed millions. Imperialism, which promised to civilize those the Europeans considered savages, led to intractable international conflicts. Nationalism, which promised to bring compatriots together in a harmonious nation-state, encouraged hateful prejudice and chauvinism. The extraordinary violence of world war shook nineteenth-century idealism to its core.

The war would have an enormous impact on European society. The need to provide extensive supplies and countless soldiers created mass suffering, encouraged the rise of the bureaucratic state, and brought women in increasing numbers into the workplace. Millions were killed or wounded at the front, and millions more grieved these losses. Grand states collapsed: the Russian, Austro-Hungarian, and Ottoman Empires passed into history, and the Russian Revolution ushered in a radically new Communist state and society. The trauma of war contributed to the rise of extremist politics that would ultimately lead to another world war. ■

CHAPTER PREVIEW

- **What caused the outbreak of the First World War?**

- **How did the First World War differ from previous wars?**

- **In what ways did the war transform life on the home front?**

- **Why did world war lead to a successful Communist revolution in Russia?**

- **What were the benefits and costs of the postwar peace settlement?**

What caused the outbreak of the First World War?

Historians have long debated why Europeans so readily pursued a war that was long and costly and failed to resolve the problems faced by the combatant nations. There was no single most important cause. Competition over colonies and world markets, a belligerent arms race, and a series of diplomatic crises and blunders sharpened international tensions. On the home front, growing populist nationalism strengthened people's unquestioning belief in "my country right or wrong." Ongoing domestic conflicts encouraged governments to pursue aggressive foreign policies in attempts to bolster national unity. All helped pave the road to war.

Growing International Conflict

The First World War began, in part, because European statesmen failed to resolve the diplomatic problems created by Germany's rise to Great Power status. The Franco-Prussian War and German unification opened a new era in international relations. By the war's end in 1871, France was defeated, and Bismarck had made Prussia-Germany the most powerful nation in Europe (see "The Franco-Prussian War and German Unification" in Chapter 23). After 1871 Bismarck declared that Germany was a "satisfied" power. Within Europe, he stated, Germany had no territorial ambitions and wanted only peace.

But how was peace to be preserved? Bismarck's first concern was to keep France—bitter over its defeat and the loss of Alsace and Lorraine—diplomatically isolated and without allies. His second concern was the threat to peace posed by the enormous multinational empires of Austria-Hungary and Russia, particularly in southeastern Europe, where the waning strength of the Ottoman Empire had created a threatening power vacuum in the disputed border territories of the Balkans.

Bismarck's accomplishments were effective, but only temporary. From 1871 to the late 1880s, he maintained German leadership in international affairs, and he signed a series of defensive alliances with Austria-Hungary and Russia designed to isolate France. Yet in 1890 the new emperor Wilhelm II dismissed Bismarck, in part because he disagreed with the chancellor's friendly policy toward Russia. Wilhelm II was an impulsive and bombastic leader, given to making bold and tactless statements on sensitive international affairs, and under his leadership Bismarck's carefully planned alliance system began to

unravel. Germany refused to renew a nonaggression pact with Russia, the centerpiece of Bismarck's system, in spite of Russian willingness to do so. This fateful move prompted long-isolated republican France to court absolutist Russia, offering loans, arms, and diplomatic support. In early 1894 France and Russia became military allies. As a result, continental Europe was divided into two rival blocs. The **Triple Alliance** of Austria, Germany, and Italy faced an increasingly hostile Dual Alliance of Russia and France, and the German general staff began secret preparations for a war on two fronts (Map 25.1).

As rivalries deepened on the continent, Great Britain's foreign policy became increasingly crucial. After 1891 Britain was the only uncommitted Great Power. Many Germans and some Britons felt that the industrially advanced, ethnically related Germanic and Anglo-Saxon peoples were natural allies. However, the good relations that had prevailed between Prussia and Great Britain since the mid-eighteenth century gave way to a bitter Anglo-German rivalry.

There were several reasons for this ill-fated development. Commercial competition in world markets between Germany and Great Britain increased sharply in the 1890s, as Germany became a global industrial power. Germany's ambitious pursuit of colonies further threatened British interests. Above all, Germany's decision in 1900 to expand its battle fleet challenged Britain's long-standing naval supremacy. In response to German expansion, British leaders prudently sought new alliances. Britain improved its often-strained relations with the United States, concluded an alliance with Japan in 1902, and joined France in the Anglo-French Entente of 1904, which settled all outstanding colonial disputes between the two countries.

Alarmed by Britain's closer ties to France, Germany's leaders decided to test the strength of their alliance. In 1905 Wilhelm II declared that Morocco—where France had colonial interests—was an independent, sovereign state, and demanded that Germany receive the same trading rights as France. In March the German emperor paid a surprise visit to Tangier on the Moroccan coast, toured the city on a white stallion, and declared his support for Moroccan independence. This rather awkward proclamation initiated an international crisis that almost led to war between Germany and France. Then Wilhelm II insisted on an international conference in hopes that his saber rattling would settle the Moroccan question to Germany's benefit. But his crude bullying only brought France and Britain closer together, and Germany left the conference empty-handed.

The result of the First Moroccan Crisis in 1905 was something of a diplomatic revolution. Britain, France,

■ **Triple Alliance** The alliance of Austria, Germany, and Italy. Italy left the alliance when war broke out in 1914.

■ **Triple Entente** The alliance of Great Britain, France, and Russia prior to and during the First World War.

TIMELINE

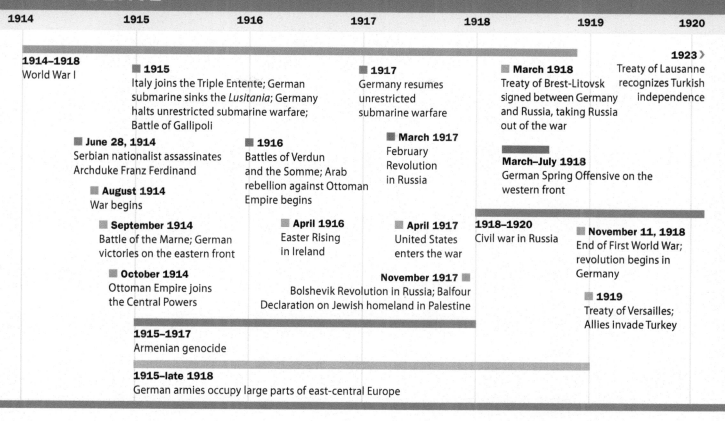

| 1914 | 1915 | 1916 | 1917 | 1918 | 1919 | 1920 |

1914–1918
World War I

1915
Italy joins the Triple Entente; German submarine sinks the *Lusitania*; Germany halts unrestricted submarine warfare; Battle of Gallipoli

June 28, 1914
Serbian nationalist assassinates Archduke Franz Ferdinand

August 1914
War begins

September 1914
Battle of the Marne; German victories on the eastern front

October 1914
Ottoman Empire joins the Central Powers

1916
Battles of Verdun and the Somme; Arab rebellion against Ottoman Empire begins

April 1916
Easter Rising in Ireland

1915–1917
Armenian genocide

1915–late 1918
German armies occupy large parts of east-central Europe

1917
Germany resumes unrestricted submarine warfare

March 1917
February Revolution in Russia

April 1917
United States enters the war

November 1917
Bolshevik Revolution in Russia; Balfour Declaration on Jewish homeland in Palestine

March 1918
Treaty of Brest-Litovsk signed between Germany and Russia, taking Russia out of the war

March–July 1918
German Spring Offensive on the western front

1918–1920
Civil war in Russia

1923 ›
Treaty of Lausanne recognizes Turkish independence

November 11, 1918
End of First World War; revolution begins in Germany

1919
Treaty of Versailles; Allies invade Turkey

Russia, and even the United States began to see Germany as a potential threat. At the same time, German leaders now saw sinister plots to encircle Germany and block its development as a world power. In 1907 Russia, battered by its disastrous war with Japan and the revolution of 1905, agreed to settle its quarrels with Great Britain in Persia (Iran) and Central Asia and signed the Anglo-Russian Agreement. This agreement laid the foundation of the **Triple Entente** (ahn-TAHNT), an alliance among Britain, Russia, and France.

Animosity between the German-led Triple Alliance and the Triple Entente sharpened in 1911, when French troops went into the Moroccan hinterland to put down an anticolonial rebellion and Germany sent a gunboat to a Moroccan port in response. International agreements to resolve this Second Moroccan Crisis allowed France to claim Morocco as a permanent protectorate and gave Germany some territorial concessions in the Congo, but the Triple Entente viewed Germany as a worrisome aggressor.

Germany's decision to expand its navy with a large, enormously expensive fleet of big-gun battleships, known as "dreadnoughts" because of their great size and power, heightened international tensions. German patriots saw a large navy as the legitimate right of a grand world power and as a source of national pride. But British leaders saw the German buildup as a military challenge that forced them to spend the "People's Budget" (see "Great Britain and Ireland" in Chapter 23) on battleships rather than social welfare. In 1909

the London *Daily Mail* hysterically informed its readers that "Germany is deliberately preparing to destroy the British Empire."[1] By then Britain had sided psychologically, if not yet officially, with France and Russia, and the leading nations of Europe were divided into two hostile camps, both ill-prepared to deal with growing international tensions (see Map 25.1).

The Mood of 1914

Diplomatic rivalries and international crises played key roles in the rush to war, but a complete understanding of the war's origins requires an account of the "mood of 1914"—the attitudes and convictions of Europeans around 1914.[2] Widespread militarism and nationalism encouraged leaders and citizens alike to see international relations as an arena for the testing of national power, with war if necessary.

Germany was especially famous for its powerful and aggressive army, but military institutions played a prominent role in affairs of state and in the lives of ordinary people across Europe. In a period marked by diplomatic tensions, politicians relied on generals and military experts to help shape public policy. All the Great Powers built up their armed forces and designed mobilization plans to rush men and weapons to the field of battle. Universal conscription in Germany, France, Italy, Austria-Hungary, and Russia—only Britain still relied on a volunteer army—exposed hundreds of thousands of young men each year to military culture and discipline.

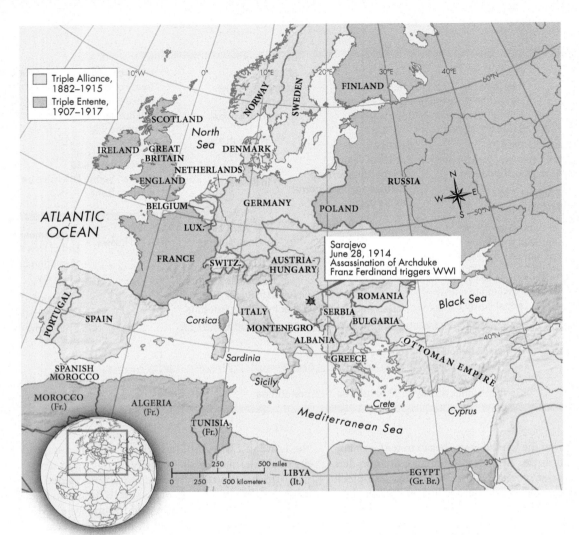

MAP 25.1 European Alliances at the Outbreak of World War I, 1914 At the start of World War I, Europe was divided into two hostile alliances: the Triple Entente of Britain, France, and Russia, and the Triple Alliance of Germany, Austria-Hungary, and Italy. Italy never fought with the Triple Alliance but instead joined the Entente in 1915.

The continent had not experienced a major conflict since the Franco-Prussian War (1870–1871), so Europeans vastly underestimated the destructive potential of modern weapons. Encouraged by the patriotic national press, many believed that war was glorious, manly, and heroic. If they expected another conflict, they thought it would be over quickly. Leading politicians and intellectuals likewise portrayed war as a test of strength that would lead to national unity and renewal. Such ideas permeated European society. As one German volunteer wrote in his diary as he left for the front in 1914, "this war is a challenge for our time and for each individual, a test by fire, that we may ripen into manhood, become men able to cope with the coming stupendous years and events."[3]

Support for military values was closely linked to the growth of popular nationalism, the notion that one's country was superior to all others. Since the 1850s the spread of the idea that members of an ethnic group should live together in a homogeneous, united nation-state had provoked all kinds of international conflicts over borders and citizenship rights. Nationalism drove the spiraling arms race and the struggle over colonies. Broad popular commitment to national interests above all else weakened groups that thought in terms of international communities and consequences. Expressions of antiwar sentiment by socialists, pacifists, and women's groups were seen as a betrayal of country in time of need. Inspired by nationalist beliefs, much of the population was ready for war.

Leading statesmen had practical reasons for promoting militarism and nationalism. Political leaders had long used foreign adventurism and diplomatic posturing to distract the people from domestic

The British Fleet Assembled at Spithead, July 1914   Starting in about 1906, Germany and Great Britain engaged in an all-out arms race focused on naval fleets, which raised international tensions and exemplified the militarism that paved the road to war. Two weeks before the start of the war, King George V reviewed the British fleet and supporting forces assembled at the Portsmouth (Spithead) naval base. Twenty-two miles of warships ranging from dreadnoughts to destroyers passed before the king and his entourage. (Chronicle/Alamy Stock Photo)

conflicts. In Great Britain, leaders faced civil war in Northern Ireland and a vocal and increasingly radical women's movement. In Russia, defeat in the Russo-Japanese War (1904–1905) and the revolution of 1905 had greatly weakened support for the tsarist regime. In Germany, the victory of the Marxist Social Democratic Party in the parliamentary elections of 1912 led government authorities to worry that the country was falling apart. The French likewise faced domestic labor and budget problems.

Determined to hold on to power and frightened by rising popular movements, ruling classes across Europe were willing to gamble on diplomatic brinksmanship and even war to postpone dealing with internal social and political conflicts. Victory promised to preserve the privileged positions of elites and rally the masses behind the national cause. The patriotic nationalism bolstered by the outbreak of war did bring unity in the short run, but the wealthy governing classes underestimated the risk of war to themselves. They had forgotten that great wars and great social revolutions very often go hand in hand.

The July Crisis and the Outbreak of War

On June 28, 1914, Archduke Franz Ferdinand, heir to the Austro-Hungarian throne, was assassinated by a Serbian revolutionary during a state visit to the Bosnian capital of Sarajevo (sar-uh-YAY-voh). After failed attempts to bomb the archduke's motorcade, Gavrilo Princip, a fanatical member of the radical group Young Bosnia, shot the archduke and his wife, Sophie, in their automobile. After his capture, Princip remained defiant: "I am a Yugoslav nationalist, aiming for the unification of all Yugoslavs, and I do not care what form of state, but it must be free from Austria."[4]

Princip's deed, in the crisis-ridden borderlands between the weakened Ottoman and Austro-Hungarian Empires, led Europe into world war. In the early years of the twentieth century, war in the Balkans—"the powder keg of Europe"—seemed inevitable. Between 1900 and 1914 the Western powers had successfully forced the Ottoman rulers to give up their European territories. Serbs, Bulgarians, Albanians, and others now sought to consolidate their independent nation-states in the redrawn map of southeastern Europe, and the threat of wars loomed (Map 25.2).

Independent Serbia was eager to build a state that would include all ethnic Serbs and was thus openly hostile to Austria-Hungary and the Ottoman Empire, since both states included substantial Serbian minorities. To block Serbian expansion, Austria in 1908 annexed the territories of Bosnia and Herzegovina (hehrt-suh-goh-VEE-nuh). The southern part of the Austro-Hungarian Empire now

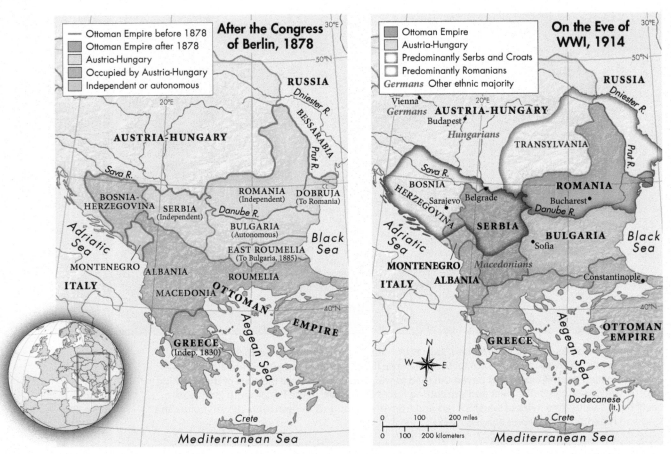

MAP 25.2 The Balkans, 1878–1914   After the Congress of Berlin in 1878, the Ottoman Empire suffered large territorial losses but remained a power in the Balkans. By 1914 Ottoman control had collapsed. New national borders divided long-standing ethnic populations, contributing to the growth of Serbian national aspirations that threatened Austria-Hungary.

included an even larger Serbian population. Serb leaders expressed rage but could do nothing without support from Russia, their traditional ally.

The tensions in the Balkans soon erupted into regional warfare. In the First Balkan War (1912), Serbia joined Greece and Bulgaria to attack the Ottoman Empire and then quarreled with Bulgaria over the spoils of victory. In the Second Balkan War (1913), Bulgaria attacked its former allies. Austria intervened and forced Serbia to give up Albania. After centuries, nationalism had finally destroyed the Ottoman Empire in Europe. Encouraged by their success against the Ottomans, Balkan nationalists increased their demands for freedom from Austria-Hungary. The leaders of that multinational empire viewed such demands as a serious threat.

Within this complex international context, the assassination of Archduke Franz Ferdinand instigated a five-week period of intense diplomatic activity known as the July Crisis. The leaders of Austria-Hungary concluded that Serbia was implicated in the assassination and deserved severe punishment.

On July 23 Austria-Hungary sent the Serbs an unconditional ultimatum that would violate Serbian sovereignty. When Serbia replied moderately but evasively, Austria mobilized its armies and declared war on Serbia on July 28. In this way, multinational Austria-Hungary, desperate to save its empire, deliberately chose war to stem the rising tide of hostile nationalism within its borders.

Commitments made under the existing alliance system helped turn a little war into a world war. Bethmann-Hollweg, the German chancellor, promised Austria-Hungary that Germany would "faithfully stand by" its ally in case of war. This "blank check" of unconditional support encouraged the prowar faction in Vienna to take a hard line against the Serbs, at a time when moderation might still have limited the crisis. At the same time, Serbia's traditional ally Russia — backed by France — encouraged the Serbs to refuse Austrian demands. Such decisions made the outbreak of war almost inevitable.

The complicated diplomatic situation spiraled out of control as military plans and timetables began to dictate policy. Vast Russia required much more time to mobilize its armies than did Germany and Austria-Hungary. And since the complicated mobilization plans of the Russian general staff assumed a two-front war with both Austria and Germany, Russia could not mobilize against one without mobilizing against the other. Therefore, on July 30 Tsar Nicholas II ordered full mobilization, which in effect declared war on both Austria-Hungary and Germany; formal declarations of war among the combatant nations followed over the next few days.

The German general staff had long thought in terms of a two-front war. Their misguided **Schlieffen Plan** called for a quick victory over France after a lightning attack through

The Schlieffen Plan

- ◄ - - Planned German offensive
- ◄— Actual German offensive
- ☐ Neutral nations

GREAT BRITAIN • NETHERLANDS • BELGIUM • Brussels • GERMANY • Rhine R. • LUX. • Reims • Metz • Seine R. • Paris • Marne R. • FRANCE • SWITZ.

0   100   200 mi.
0   100   200 km

neutral Belgium — the quickest way to reach Paris — before turning on Russia. On August 3 German armies invaded Belgium. Great Britain, infuriated by the German violation of Belgian neutrality, declared war on Germany the following day.

The speed of the July Crisis created shock, panic, and excitement. In the final days of July and the first few days of August, massive crowds thronged the streets of Paris, London, St. Petersburg, Berlin, and Vienna, seeking news and shouting prowar slogans. Events proceeded rapidly, and those who opposed the war could do little to prevent its arrival. In a little over a month, a limited Austrian-Serbian conflict had become a European-wide war, and the First World War had begun.

How did the First World War differ from previous wars?

When the Germans invaded Belgium in August 1914, they and many others thought that the war would be short and relatively painless. Many sincerely believed that "the boys will be home by Christmas." They were wrong. On the western front in France and the eastern front in Russia, and on the borders of the Ottoman Empire, the belligerent armies bogged down in a new and extremely costly kind of war, later labeled **total war** by German general Erich Ludendorff. Total war meant new roles for soldiers and civilians alike. At the front, it meant long, deadly battles fought with all the destructive weapons a highly industrialized society could produce. At home, national economies were geared toward the war effort. Governments revoked civil liberties, and many civilians lost lives or livelihoods as occupying armies moved through their towns and cities. The struggle expanded outside Europe, and the Middle East, Africa, East Asia, and the United States were all brought into the maelstrom.

Stalemate and Slaughter on the Western Front

In the face of the German invasion, the Belgian army defended its homeland and fell back in good order to join a rapidly landed British army corps near the Franco-Belgian border. At the same time, Russian armies attacked eastern Germany, forcing

the Germans to transfer much-needed troops to the east. Instead of quickly capturing Paris as per the Schlieffen Plan, by the end of August dead-tired German soldiers were advancing slowly along an enormous front in the scorching summer heat. Afraid that armed Belgian partisans (called *francs-tireurs*) were attacking German troops behind the lines, the German occupiers dealt harshly with local resistance. German soldiers executed civilians suspected of joining the partisans and, in an out-of-control tragedy, burned the medieval core of the Belgian city of Louvain. Entente propaganda made the most of the German "Rape of Belgium" and the atrocities committed by German troops.

On September 6 the French attacked a gap in the German line in the Battle of the Marne. For three days, France threw everything into the attack. At one point, the French government desperately requisitioned all the taxis of Paris to rush reserves to the front. Finally, the Germans fell back. France had been miraculously saved (Map 25.3).

■ **Schlieffen Plan** Failed German plan calling for a lightning attack through neutral Belgium and a quick defeat of France before attacking Russia.

■ **total war** A war in which distinctions between the soldiers on the battlefield and civilians at home are blurred, and where massive government intervention in society and the economy ensures support for the war effort.

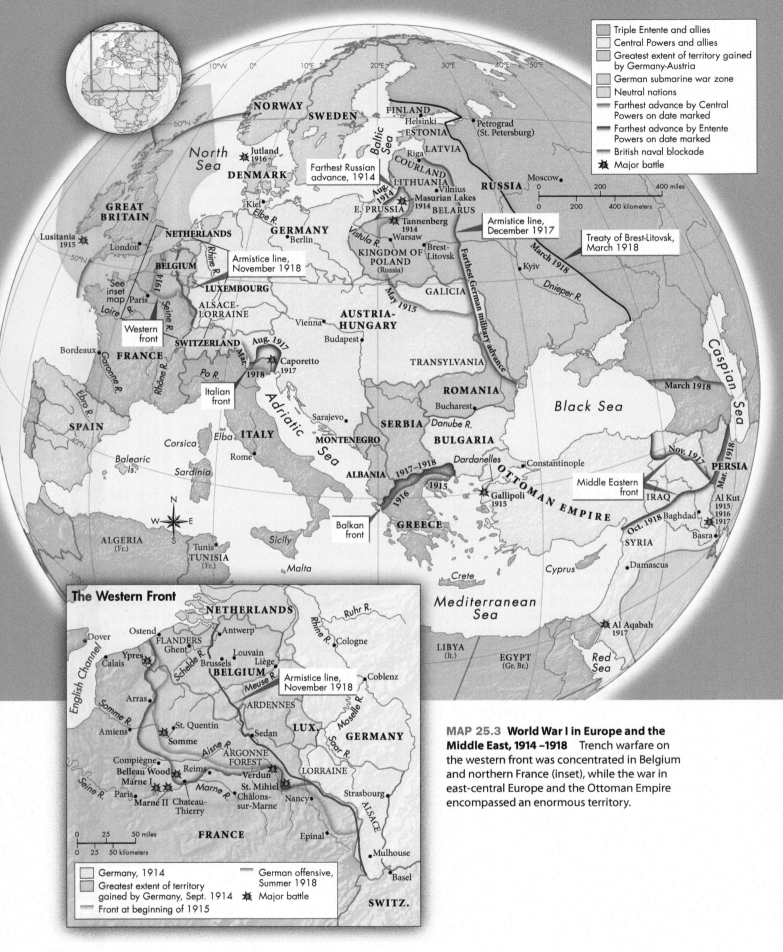

Legend:
- Triple Entente and allies
- Central Powers and allies
- Greatest extent of territory gained by Germany-Austria
- German submarine war zone
- Neutral nations
- Farthest advance by Central Powers on date marked
- Farthest advance by Entente Powers on date marked
- British naval blockade
- Major battle

200   400 miles
0   200   400 kilometers

NORWAY
SWEDEN
FINLAND
Helsinki
Petrograd (St. Petersburg)
ESTONIA
LATVIA
Riga
COURLAND
North Sea
Jutland 1916
DENMARK
Kiel
Elbe R.
LITHUANIA
Vilnius
RUSSIA
Moscow
Farthest Russian advance, 1914
Aug. 1914
Masurian Lakes 1914
E. PRUSSIA
BELARUS
Tannenberg 1914
Armistice line, December 1917
GREAT BRITAIN
Lusitania 1915
London
NETHERLANDS
GERMANY
Berlin
Vistula R.
Warsaw
Brest-Litovsk
March 1918
Treaty of Brest-Litovsk, March 1918
BELGIUM
Rhine R.
Armistice line, November 1918
LUXEMBOURG
KINGDOM OF POLAND (Russia)
Kyiv
Dnieper R.
See inset map
Paris
1914
Seine R.
Loire R.
ALSACE-LORRAINE
Western front
SWITZERLAND
GALICIA
Farthest German military advance
Bordeaux
Garonne R.
FRANCE
Mar. 1918
Aug. 1917
AUSTRIA-HUNGARY
Vienna
Budapest
TRANSYLVANIA
March 1918
Caspian Sea
Caporetto 1917
Po R.
Italian front
Rhône R.
Adriatic Sea
Sarajevo
ROMANIA
Bucharest
Black Sea
SPAIN
Ebro R.
Corsica
Elba
ITALY
Rome
MONTENEGRO
SERBIA
Danube R.
1917–1918
BULGARIA
Constantinople
Nov. 1917
PERSIA
Balearic Is.
Sardinia
ALBANIA
1915
1916
Dardanelles
OTTOMAN EMPIRE
Middle Eastern front
IRAQ
Al Kut 1915 1916 1917
Mar. 1918
Gallipoli 1915
GREECE
Balkan front
Baghdad
Basra
ALGERIA (Fr.)
Tunis
TUNISIA (Fr.)
Sicily
Malta
Crete
Cyprus
Oct. 1918
SYRIA
Damascus
Mediterranean Sea
LIBYA (It.)
EGYPT (Gr. Br.)
Al Aqabah 1917
Red Sea

The Western Front

Germany, 1914
Greatest extent of territory gained by Germany, Sept. 1914
Front at beginning of 1915
German offensive, Summer 1918
Major battle

0   25   50 miles
0   25   50 kilometers

NETHERLANDS
Ruhr R.
Rhine R.
Dover
Ostend
Antwerp
Cologne
FLANDERS
Ghent
Ypres
Calais
Schelde R.
Brussels
Louvain
Liège
BELGIUM
Coblenz
English Channel
Arras
Meuse R.
Armistice line, November 1918
Somme R.
ARDENNES
LUX.
Amiens
St. Quentin
Aisne R.
Sedan
Moselle R.
GERMANY
Somme
Compiègne
ARGONNE FOREST
Saar R.
Belleau Wood
Reims
Verdun
St. Mihiel
Marne I
Marne R.
LORRAINE
Seine R.
Paris
Marne II
Chateau-Thierry
Châlons-sur-Marne
Nancy
Strasbourg
Epinal
ALSACE
FRANCE
Mulhouse
Basel
SWITZ.

MAP 25.3 World War I in Europe and the Middle East, 1914–1918 Trench warfare on the western front was concentrated in Belgium and northern France (inset), while the war in east-central Europe and the Ottoman Empire encompassed an enormous territory.

"Greetings from the front." This British postcard shows a soldier writing to his wife or girlfriend at home. The post was typically the only connection between soldiers and their relatives, and over 28 billion pieces of mail passed between home and front on all sides during the war. Patriotic, mass-produced postcards like the one pictured here often played on the connections between absent loved ones and national duty. (Lordprice Collection/Alamy)

Trench Warfare on the Western Front In this famous photograph apparently taken by an infantryman at the front, three German soldiers in a half-destroyed trench fight off an attack by four Frenchmen during the Battle of Verdun in October 1916. Such candid photographs are quite rare, because conditions on the western front made it extremely dangerous to take pictures in a live combat situation. How does this candid photograph compare to more "official" visions of the war, like those portrayed in the posters in "Evaluating Visual Evidence: Wartime Propaganda Posters," page 776? (Bettmann/Getty Images)

With the armies stalled, both sides began to dig trenches to protect themselves from artillery and machine-gun fire. By November 1914 an unbroken line of four hundred miles of defensive positions extended along the western front, from the Belgian coast through northern France and on to the Swiss frontier. Armies on both sides dug in behind rows of trenches, mines, and barbed wire.

The cost in lives of **trench warfare** was staggering, the gains in territory minuscule. Conditions in the trenches were atrocious. Enlisted men rotated in and out of position, at best spending two weeks at base, two weeks in reserve positions, and two weeks in the trenches. They had little leave time to visit loved ones at home, though they exchanged billions of letters and postcards with friends and family. At the front, mud and vermin, bad food, damp and cold, and wretched living

quarters were the norm. Soldiers spent most of their time repairing rough trenches and dugouts and standing watch for an enemy they rarely saw.

During combat, recently invented weapons, the products of the industrial age, made battle impersonal, traumatic, and deadly. The machine gun, hand grenades, poison gas, flamethrowers, long-range artillery, the airplane, and the tank were all used to murderous effect. Military units were often decimated in poorly planned frontal assaults, and comrades could rarely retrieve the wounded and dead from no-man's land between the lines. Bodies, mangled by high explosives, were ground into the mud and disappeared, or became part of the earthworks themselves. (See "Viewpoints: Poetry in the Trenches," page 772.)

The leading generals of the combatant nations, who had learned military tactics and strategy in the nineteenth century, struggled to understand trench warfare. For four years they mostly repeated the same mistakes, mounting massive offensives designed to achieve decisive breakthroughs. Brutal frontal assaults against highly fortified trenches might overrun the enemy's frontline, but because of the extent of the defensive trench system, attacking soldiers rarely captured any substantial territory. The French and British offensives of 1915 never gained more than three miles of territory. In 1916 the German campaign against

---

■ **trench warfare** A type of fighting used in World War I behind rows of trenches and barbed wire; the cost in lives was staggering and the gains in territory minimal.

VIEWPOINTS

Poetry in the Trenches

The trauma of the First World War generated an outburst of cultural creation, and each nation had its favored group of artists and writers. Among the most famous were Britain's "trench poets," including John McCrae, Wilfred Owen, and many others. McCrae and Owen served in France. McCrae, a medical officer, died of an infection contracted in a field hospital close to the front. Owen was killed in action one week before the end of the war.

John McCrae, "In Flanders Fields," 1915

In Flanders fields the poppies blow
  Between the crosses, row on row
   That mark our place; and in the sky
   The larks, still bravely singing, fly
Scarce heard amid the guns below.

We are the Dead. Short days ago
We lived, felt dawn, saw sunset glow,
  Loved and were loved, and now we lie
     In Flanders fields.

Take up our quarrel with the foe:
To you from failing hands we throw
  The torch; be yours to hold it high.
   If ye break faith with us who die
We shall not sleep, though poppies grow
     In Flanders fields.

Wilfred Owen, "Dulce et Decorum Est," 1917/18

Bent double, like old beggars under sacks,
Knock-kneed, coughing like hags, we cursed through
   sludge,
Till on the haunting flares we turned our backs
And towards our distant rest began to trudge.
Men marched asleep. Many had lost their boots,
But limped on, blood-shod. All went lame; all blind;
Drunk with fatigue; deaf even to the hoots
Of gas-shells dropping softly behind.

Gas! GAS! Quick, boys!—An ecstasy of fumbling
Fitting the clumsy helmets just in time,
But someone still was yelling out and stumbling
And flound'ring like a man in fire or lime.—
Dim through the misty panes and thick green light,
As under a green sea, I saw him drowning.

In all my dreams before my helpless sight
He plunges at me, guttering, choking, drowning.

If in some smothering dreams, you too could pace
Behind the wagon that we flung him in,
And watch the white eyes writhing in his face,
His hanging face, like a devil's sick of sin,
If you could hear, at every jolt, the blood
Come gargling from the froth-corrupted lungs
Obscene as cancer, bitter as the cud
Of vile, incurable sores on innocent tongues,—
My friend, you would not tell with such high zest
To children ardent for some desperate glory,
The old Lie: *Dulce et decorum est
Pro patria mori.**

QUESTIONS FOR ANALYSIS

1. These poems were both written during the war. How do the authors use the traditional language and rhythm of poetry to capture the costs and brutality of modern warfare?
2. What messages do the poems have for the reader at home? If McCrae and Owen happened to meet each other, do you think they would agree about the goals and costs of the war?
3. What do these poems reveal about the effects of World War I on the fine arts and literature?

Sources: John McCrae, *In Flanders Fields and Other Poems* (New York: G. P. Putnam's Sons/Knickerbocker Press, 1919), p. 15; Wilfred Owen, *Poems by Wilfred Owen* (New York: Viking Press, 1921), p. 15.

*This line in Latin is taken from a poem by the Roman poet Horace, written in the first decades of the first century C.E. Translation: "It is sweet and fitting to die for one's country."

Verdun left over 700,000 soldiers killed or wounded and ended with the combatants in their original positions. The results in 1917 were little better. In hard-fought battles on all fronts, millions of young men were wounded or died for no real gain.

The Battle of the Somme, a great British offensive undertaken in the summer of 1916 in northern France, exemplified the horrors of trench warfare. The battle began with a weeklong heavy artillery bombardment on the German lines, intended to cut the barbed

wire fortifications, decimate the enemy trenches, and prevent the Germans from making an effective defense. For seven days and nights, the British artillery fired nonstop on the German lines, delivering about 1.5 million shells. On July 1 the British went "over the top," climbing out of the trenches and moving into no-man's land toward the German lines, dug into a series of ridges about half a mile away.

During the bombardment, the Germans had fled to their dugouts—underground shelters dug deep into the trenches—where they suffered from lack of water, food, and sleep. But they survived. As the British soldiers neared the German lines and the shelling stopped, the Germans emerged from their bunkers, set up their machine guns, and mowed down the approaching troops. Traversing the gently sloping farmland of the Somme River district, the attackers made easy targets. About 20,000 British men were killed and 40,000 more were wounded on just the first day, a crushing loss that shook troop morale and public opinion at home. The battle lasted until November, and in the end the British did push the Germans back—a whole seven miles. Some 420,000 British, 200,000 French, and 600,000 Germans were killed or wounded fighting over an insignificant scrap of land.

The Widening War

On the eastern front, the slaughter did not immediately degenerate into trench warfare, and the fighting was dominated by Germany. Repulsing the initial Russian attacks, the Germans won major victories at the Battles of Tannenberg and the Masurian Lakes in August and September 1914. Russia put real pressure on the relatively weak Austro-Hungarian army, but by 1915 the eastern front had stabilized in Germany's favor. A staggering 2.5 million Russian soldiers had been killed, wounded, or captured. German armies occupied huge swaths of the Russian Empire in central Europe, including ethnic Polish, Belorussian, and Baltic territories (see Map 25.3). Yet Russia continued to fight, marking another wrong assumption of the Schlieffen Plan.

To govern these occupied territories, the Germans installed a vast military bureaucracy, with some 15,000 army administrators and professional specialists. Anti-Slavic prejudice dominated the mind-set of the occupiers, who viewed the local Slavs as ethnic "mongrels." German military administrators used prisoners of war and refugees as forced labor. They stole animals and crops from local farmers to supply the occupying army or send home to Germany. About one-third of the

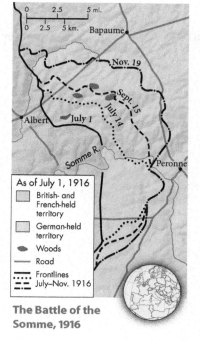

The Battle of the Somme, 1916

The Battle of Gallipoli, 1915

civilian population died or became refugees under this brutal occupation. In the long run, the German state hoped to turn these territories into German possessions, a chilling forerunner of Nazi policies in World War II.[5]

The changing tides of victory and hopes for territorial gains brought neutral countries into the war. Italy, a member of the Triple Alliance since 1882, had declared its neutrality in 1914 on the grounds that its ally Austria had violated the pact by launching a war of aggression. Then in May 1915 Italy switched sides to join the Triple Entente in return for promises of Austrian territory. The war along the Italian-Austrian front was bitter and deadly and cost some 600,000 Italian lives.

In October 1914 the Ottoman Empire joined Austria and Germany, by then known as the Central Powers. The following September Bulgaria followed the Ottoman Empire's lead in order to settle old scores with Serbia. The Balkans, with the exception of Greece, were occupied by the Central Powers. The Austro-Hungarian invasion and occupation of Serbia, aided by the Bulgarians, was particularly vicious.

The entry of the Ottomans carried the war into the Middle East. Heavy fighting between the Ottomans and the Russians in the Caucasus enveloped the Armenians, who lived on both sides of the border and had experienced brutal pogroms in 1894 and 1909. When in 1915 some Armenians welcomed Russian armies as liberators, the Ottoman government ordered a mass deportation of its Armenian citizens from their homeland. In this early example of modern ethnic cleansing, often labeled genocide, about 1 million Armenians died from murder, starvation, and disease. The causes and consequences of these mass deaths continue to elicit heated controversy.

In 1915, at the Battle of Gallipoli, British forces tried and failed to take the Dardanelles and Constantinople from the Ottoman Turks. The invasion force was pinned down on the beaches, and the ten-month-long battle cost the Ottomans 300,000 and the British 265,000 men killed, wounded, or missing.

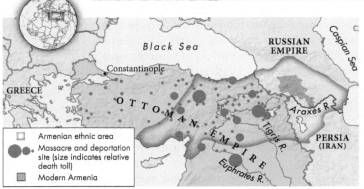

The Armenian Genocide, 1915 –1917

Deportation of Ottoman Armenians   When some Armenians welcomed Russian armies as liberators after years of persecution, the Ottoman government ordered a mass deportation of its Armenian citizens from their homeland in the empire's eastern provinces. This photo shows Armenian refugees forced by Turkish militias to cross the Anatolian hinterland in 1915, under conditions designed to lead to their deaths. About 1 million civilians perished from murder, starvation, and disease during the Armenian genocide, the deliberate and systematic destruction of the Armenian population of the Ottoman Empire during World War I. (Pictures from History/Bridgeman Images)

The British were more successful at inciting the Arabs to revolt against their Ottoman rulers. They opened negotiations with the foremost Arab leader, Hussein ibn-Ali (1856–1931). In the name of the Ottoman sultan, Hussein ruled much of the Ottoman Empire's territory along the Red Sea (in today's Saudi Arabia), an area known as the Hejaz that included Mecca, the holiest city in the Muslim world (see the maps in "Thinking Like a Historian," page 793). In 1915, Hussein managed to win vague British commitments for an independent postwar Arab kingdom. Fulfilling his promise to the British, in 1916 Hussein rebelled against the Turks, proclaiming himself king of the Arabs. He was aided by the British liaison officer T. E. Lawrence, who helped lead Arab soldiers in a guerrilla war against the Turks on the Arabian peninsula.

The British, aided by colonial troops from India, enjoyed similar victories in the Ottoman province of Mesopotamia (today's Iraq). British troops quickly occupied the southern Iraqi city of Basra in 1914, securing access to the region's oil fields. After a series of setbacks at the hands of Ottoman troops, the British captured Baghdad in 1917. In September 1918 British armies and their Arab allies rolled into Syria, a large and diverse Ottoman territory that included the holy lands of Palestine and the present-day countries of Syria, Lebanon, Jordan, and Israel. This offensive culminated in the triumphal entry of Hussein's son Faisal into Damascus. Arab patriots in Syria and Iraq now expected a large, unified Arab nation-state to rise from the dust of the Ottoman collapse—though they would later be disappointed by the Western powers (see "The Peace Settlement in the Middle East" later in this chapter).

The war spread to East Asia and colonial Africa as well. Japan declared war on Germany in 1914, seized Germany's Pacific and East Asian colonies, and used the opportunity to expand its influence in China. In Africa, instead of rebelling as the Germans hoped, colonial subjects of the British and French generally supported the Allied powers and helped British and French armies, staffed primarily by Black African conscripts, take over German colonies.

As the European world war spilled out of European borders, it brought non-European peoples into the conflict. More than a million Africans and Asians served in the various armies of the warring powers; more than double that number served as porters to carry equipment and build defenses. The French, facing a shortage of young men, made especially heavy use of colonial troops from North Africa. Soldiers from India played a key role in Britain's campaigns against the Ottomans, though under the command of British officers. And large numbers of soldiers came from the British Commonwealth, a voluntary association of former British colonies. Canadians, Australians, and New Zealanders fought with the British; those from Australia and New Zealand (the ANZAC Army Corps) fought in the failed Allied assault on Gallipoli.

After three years, the United States was finally drawn into the expanding conflict. American intervention grew out of the war at sea and general sympathy for the Triple Entente. At the beginning of the war, Britain and France established a naval blockade to strangle the Central Powers. No neutral cargo ship was permitted to sail to Germany. In early 1915 Germany retaliated with attacks on the Entente's supply ships with a murderously effective new weapon, the submarine.

In May 1915 a German submarine sank the British passenger liner *Lusitania*, claiming 1,198 lives, including 128 U.S. citizens. President Woodrow Wilson protested vigorously, using the tragedy to incite American public opinion against the Germans. To avoid almost-certain war with the United States, Germany halted its unrestricted submarine campaign for almost two years.

Early in 1917 the German military command — hoping that improved submarines could starve Britain into submission before the United States could come to its rescue — resumed unrestricted submarine warfare. Instead of weakening the British, however, the move tipped the balance against the Central Powers by prompting the United States to declare war on Germany. The first U.S. troops reached France in June 1917.

In what ways did the war transform life on the home front?

The war's impact on civilians was no less massive than it was on the men crouched in the trenches. Total war encouraged the growth of state bureaucracies, transformed the lives of ordinary women and men, and by the end inspired mass antiwar protest movements.

Mobilizing for Total War

In August 1914 many people believed that their nation was right to defend itself from foreign aggression and so greeted the outbreak of hostilities enthusiastically. With the exception of those on the extreme left, even socialists supported the war. Yet by mid-October generals and politicians had begun to realize that they had underestimated the demands of total war. Heavy casualties and the stalemate meant that each combatant country experienced a desperate need for men and weapons. To keep the war machine moving, national leaders aggressively intervened in society and the economy.

By the late nineteenth century the nation-state had already shown an eagerness to manage the welfare of its citizens (see "The Responsive National State" in Chapter 23). Now, confronted by the crisis of total war, the state intruded even further into people's daily lives. New state ministries mobilized soldiers and armaments, established rationing programs, and provided care for war widows and wounded veterans. Propaganda and censorship offices controlled news and information about the war and tried to drum up popular support for the cause. (See "Evaluating Visual Evidence: Wartime Propaganda Posters," page 776.) Government planning boards set mandatory production goals and limits on wages and prices, and thus temporarily abandoned free-market capitalism. Government management of highly productive industrial economies worked: it yielded an effective and immensely destructive war effort on all sides.

Germany went furthest in developing a planned economy to wage total war. As soon as war began, the industrialist Walter Rathenau convinced the government to set up the War Raw Materials Board to ration and distribute various goods. Under Rathenau's direction, every useful material from foreign oil to barnyard manure was inventoried and rationed. Moreover, the board launched successful attempts to produce substitutes, such as synthetic rubber and nitrates, for scarce war supplies. Food was rationed in accordance with physical need. Germany failed to tax the

Wartime Propaganda Posters

(The Stapleton Collection/Bridgeman Images)

(Library of Congress Prints and Photographs Division, Washington, D.C.)

This famous French propaganda poster from 1918 (left) proclaims "They shall not pass!" and expresses the French determination to hold back the German invaders at any cost. The American recruitment poster from 1917 (right) features a provocatively dressed woman and encourages men to "do it" and join the U.S. Navy. In an era before radio or television, such posters, prominently displayed in public places, were a common way for national governments to reach ordinary people with official news and messages.

EVALUATE THE EVIDENCE

1. Summarize the visual imagery presented in each poster. How do the artists present the war?
2. The French poster was published after France had been at war for four years, while the U.S. naval recruitment poster probably came out before American troops were actively engaged overseas. How might the country of origin, the experience of war, and the date of publication have affected the messages conveyed in each poster?
3. Artist Maurice Neumont created the French poster; Howard Chandler Christy did the American poster. Do a quick Internet search for these artists. Does additional information about their lives and work shed light on these two posters?

Women Workers Building a Truck in a London Workshop, 1917 Millions of men on all sides were drafted to fight in the war, creating a serious labor shortage on the home front. When women began to fill jobs formerly reserved for men, they challenged middle-class gender roles. (Hulton Deutsch/Corbis/Getty Images)

war profits of private firms heavily enough, however. This failure contributed to massive deficit financing, inflation, the growth of a black market, and the eventual re-emergence of class conflict.

Following the terrible Battles of Verdun and the Somme in 1916, German military leaders forced the Reichstag to accept the Auxiliary Service Law, which required all males between seventeen and sixty to work only at jobs considered critical to the war effort. Women also worked in war factories, mines, and steel mills, where they labored, like men, at heavy and dangerous jobs. While war production increased, people lived on little more than one thousand calories a day—about half the normal average.

After 1917 Germany's leaders ruled by decree. Generals Paul von Hindenburg and Erich Ludendorff—heroes of the Battle of Tannenberg—drove Chancellor Bethmann-Hollweg from office. With the support of the newly formed ultraconservative Fatherland Party, the generals established a military dictatorship. Hindenburg called for the ultimate mobilization for total war. Germany could win, he said, only "if all the treasures of our soil that agriculture and industry can produce are used exclusively for the conduct of War. . . . All other considerations must come second."[6] Thus in Germany total war led to attempts to establish history's first "totalitarian" society, a model for future National Socialists, or Nazis.

Although only Germany was directly ruled by a military government, leaders in all the belligerent nations took power from parliaments, suspended civil liberties, and ignored democratic procedures. After 1915 the British Ministry of Munitions organized private industry to produce for the war, allocated labor, set wage and price rates, and settled labor disputes. In France, a weakened parliament met without public oversight, and the courts jailed pacifists who dared criticize the state. Once the United States entered the war, new federal agencies such as the War Labor Board and the War Industries Board regulated industry, labor relations, and agricultural production, while the Espionage and Sedition Acts weakened civil liberties. The war may have been deadly for citizen armies, but it was certainly good for the growth of the bureaucratic nation-state.

The Social Impact of Total War

The social changes wrought by total war were no less profound than the economic impact, though again there were important national variations. Conscription

INDIVIDUALS IN SOCIETY

Vera Brittain

Although the Great War upended millions of lives, it struck Europe's young people with the greatest force. Vera Brittain (1893–1970), who was in her twenties during the war years, captured this life-changing experience in her best-selling autobiography, *Testament of Youth* (1933).

Brittain grew up in a wealthy business family in northern England, bristling at small-town conventions and discrimination against women. Very close to her brother Edward, two years her junior, Brittain read voraciously and dreamed of being a successful writer. Finishing boarding school and overcoming her father's objections, she prepared for Oxford's rigorous entry exams and won a scholarship to its women's college. Brittain fell in love with her brother's best friend, Roland Leighton, who was also a brilliant student. All three, along with two other close friends, Victor Richardson and Geoffrey Thurlow, confidently prepared to enter Oxford in late 1914.

When war suddenly loomed in July 1914, Brittain shared with millions of Europeans a surge of patriotic support for her government, a prowar enthusiasm she later downplayed in her published writings. She wrote in her diary that her "great fear" was that England would declare its neutrality and commit the "grossest treachery" toward France.* She supported Leighton's decision to enlist, agreeing with his glamorous view of war as "very ennobling and very beautiful." Later, exchanging anxious letters with Leighton in France in 1915, Brittain began to see the conflict in personal, human terms. She wondered if any victory could be worth her fiancé's life.

Struggling to quell her doubts, Brittain redoubled her commitment to England's cause and volunteered as an army nurse. For the next three years, she served with distinction in military hospitals in London, Malta, and northern France, repeatedly torn between the vision of noble sacrifice and the reality of human tragedy. Having lost sexual inhibitions while caring for mangled male bodies, she longed to consummate her love with Leighton. Awaiting his return on leave on Christmas Day in 1915, she was greeted instead with a telegram: he had been killed two days before.

Vera Brittain was marked forever by her wartime experiences. (Vera Brittain fonds, William Ready Division of Archives and Research Collections, McMaster University Library)

Leighton's death was the first of several devastating blows that eventually overwhelmed Brittain's idealistic patriotism. In 1917 Thurlow and then Richardson died from gruesome wounds. In early 1918, as the last great German offensive covered the floors of her war-zone hospital with maimed and dying German prisoners, the bone-weary Brittain felt a common humanity and saw only more victims. A few weeks later her brother Edward died in action. When the war ended, she was, she said, a "complete automaton," with her "deepest emotions paralyzed if not dead."

Returning to Oxford, Brittain gradually recovered. She formed a deep, restorative friendship with another talented woman writer, Winifred Holtby; published novels and articles; and became a leader in the feminist campaign for women's equality. She also married and had children. But her wartime memories were always with her. Finally, Brittain succeeded in coming to grips with them in *Testament of Youth*. The unflinching narrative spoke to the experiences of an entire generation and became a runaway bestseller. Above all, Brittain captured the contradictory character of the war, in which millions of young people found excitement, courage, and common purpose but succeeded only in destroying their lives with futile sacrifices. Increasingly committed to pacifism, Brittain opposed England's entry into World War II.

QUESTIONS FOR ANALYSIS

1. What were Brittain's initial feelings toward the war? How and why did they change as the conflict continued?
2. Why did Brittain volunteer as a nurse, as many women did? How might wartime nursing have influenced women of her generation?
3. In portraying the contradictory character of World War I for Europe's youth, was Brittain describing the character of all modern warfare?

*Quotations from P. Berry and M. Bostridge, *Vera Brittain: A Life* (London: Virago Press, 2001), pp. 59, 80, 136.

sent millions of men to the front, exposing many to foreign lands for the first time in their lives. The insatiable needs of the military created a tremendous demand for workers, making jobs readily available. This situation—seldom, if ever, seen before 1914, when unemployment and poverty had been facts of urban life—brought momentous changes.

The need for workers meant greater power and prestige for labor unions. Unions cooperated with war governments on workplace rules, wages, and production schedules in return for real participation in important decisions. The entry of labor leaders and unions into policymaking councils paralleled the entry of socialist leaders into war governments. Both reflected a new government openness to the needs of those at the bottom of society.

The role of women changed dramatically. The production of vast amounts of arms and ammunition required huge numbers of laborers, and women moved into skilled industrial jobs long considered men's work. Women became highly visible in public—as munitions workers, bank tellers, and mail carriers, and even as police officers, firefighters, and farm laborers. Women also served as auxiliaries and nurses at the front. (See "Individuals in Society: Vera Brittain," page 778.)

The war expanded the range of women's activities and helped change attitudes about proper gender roles, but the long-term results were mixed. Women gained experience in jobs previously reserved for men, but at war's end millions of demobilized soldiers demanded their jobs back, and governments forced women out of the workplace. Thus women's employment gains were mostly temporary, except in nursing and social work, already considered "women's work."

The dislocations of war loosened sexual morality, and some women defied convention and expressed their new-found freedom by bobbing their hair, shortening their skirts, and smoking in public. Yet supposedly "loose" women were often criticized for betraying their soldier-husbands away at the front. As a result of women's many-sided war effort, the United States, Britain, Germany, Poland, and other countries granted women the right to vote immediately after the war. Yet women's rights movements faded in the 1920s and 1930s, in large part because feminist leaders found it difficult to regain momentum after the wartime crisis.

To some extent, the war promoted greater social equality, blurring class distinctions and lessening the gap between rich and poor. In Great Britain, the bottom third of the population generally lived better than they ever had, for the poorest gained most from the severe shortage of labor. Elsewhere, greater equality was reflected in full employment, distribution of scarce rations according to physical needs, and a sharing of hardships. In general, despite some war

profiteering, European society became more uniform and egalitarian.

Death itself had no respect for traditional social distinctions. It savagely decimated the young aristocratic officers who led the charge, and it fell heavily on the mass of drafted peasants and unskilled workers who followed, leading postwar commentators to speak of a "lost generation." Yet death often spared highly skilled workers and foremen. Their lives were too valuable to squander at the front, for they were needed to train the newly recruited women and older unskilled men laboring in war plants at home.

Growing Political Tensions

During the first two years of war, many soldiers and civilians supported their governments. Patriotic nationalism and belief in a just cause united peoples behind their national leaders. Each government used rigorous censorship and crude propaganda to bolster popular support. German propaganda falsely pictured Black soldiers from France's African empire abusing German women, while the French and British ceaselessly recounted and exaggerated German atrocities in Belgium and elsewhere. Patriotic posters and slogans, slanted news, and biased editorials inflamed national hatreds, helped control public opinion, and encouraged soldiers to keep fighting.

Political and social tensions re-emerged, however, and by the spring of 1916 ordinary people were beginning to crack under the strain of total war. Strikes and protest marches over war-related burdens and shortages flared up on every home front. On May 1, 1916, several thousand demonstrators in Berlin heard the radical socialist leader Karl Liebknecht (1871–1919) attack the costs of the war effort. Liebknecht was arrested and imprisoned, but his daring action electrified Europe's far left. In France, Georges Clemenceau (zhorzh kleh-muhn-SOH) (1841–1929) established a virtual dictatorship, arrested strikers, and jailed without trial journalists and politicians who dared to suggest a compromise peace with Germany.

In April 1916 Irish republican nationalists took advantage of the tense wartime crisis to step up their rebellion against British rule. During the great **Easter Rising**, armed republican militias took over parts of Dublin and proclaimed an independent Irish Republic. After a week of bitter fighting, British troops crushed the rebels and executed their leaders. Though the republicans were defeated, the punitive aftermath fueled anti-British sentiment in Ireland. The Rising set the stage for the success of the nationalist Sinn

■ **Easter Rising** Rebellion of Irish nationalists in April 1916 that was quickly repressed by British troops, but contributed to the Irish independence movement of the 1920s.

Fein Party and a full-scale civil war for Irish independence in the early 1920s.

On all sides, soldiers' morale began to decline. Numerous French units mutinied and refused to fight after the disastrous French offensive of May 1917. Only tough military justice, including death sentences for mutiny leaders, and a tacit agreement with the troops that there would be no more grand offensives, enabled the new general-in-chief, Henri-Philippe Pétain (pay-TAN), to restore order. Facing defeat, wretched conditions at the front, and growing hopelessness, numerous Russian soldiers began to desert, providing fuel for the Russian Revolution of 1917. After the murderous Battle of Caporetto in northern Italy, which lasted from October to November in 1917, the Italian army collapsed in despair. In the massive battles of 1916 and 1917, the British armies had been "bled dry." Only the promised arrival of fresh troops from the United States stiffened the resolve of the Allies.

The strains were worse for the Central Powers. In October 1916 a young socialist assassinated the chief minister of Austria-Hungary. The following month, when the aging emperor Franz Joseph died, a symbol of unity disappeared. In spite of absolute censorship, political dissatisfaction and conflicts among

nationalities grew. Both Czech and Balkan leaders demanded independent states for their peoples. The Austro-Hungarian people and army grew increasingly exhausted.

Germans likewise suffered immensely. The British naval blockade greatly limited food imports, which forced the heavy rationing of everyday goods such as matches, bread, cooking oil, and meat. Some 750,000 German civilians starved to death as a result. A growing minority of moderate socialists in the Reichstag gave voice to popular discontent when they called for a compromise "peace without annexations or reparations."

Such a peace was unthinkable for the Fatherland Party. Yet Germany's rulers faced growing unrest. When the bread ration was further reduced in April 1917, more than 200,000 workers and women struck and demonstrated for a week in Berlin, returning to work only under the threat of prison and military discipline. That same month, radicals left the Social Democratic Party to form the Independent Social Democratic Party; in 1918 they would found the German Communist Party. Thus Germany, like its ally Austria-Hungary (and its enemy France), was beginning to crack in 1917. Yet it was Russia that collapsed first and saved the Central Powers—for a time.

Why did world war lead to a successful Communist revolution in Russia?

Growing out of the crisis of the First World War, the Russian Revolution of 1917 was one of modern history's most momentous events. For some, the revolution was Marx's socialist vision come true; for others, it was the triumph of a despised Communist dictatorship. To all, it presented a radically new prototype of state and society.

The Fall of Imperial Russia

Like their allies and enemies, many Russians had embraced war with patriotic enthusiasm in 1914. At the Winter Palace, throngs of people knelt and sang "God Save the Tsar!" while Tsar Nicholas II (r. 1894–1917) repeated the oath Alexander I had sworn in 1812 during Napoleon's invasion of Russia, vowing never to make peace as long as the enemy stood on Russian soil. Russia's lower house of parliament, the Duma, voted to support the war. Conservatives anticipated expansion in the Balkans, while liberals and most socialists believed that alliance with Britain and France would bring democratic reforms. For a moment, Russia was united.

Enthusiasm for the war soon waned as better-equipped German armies inflicted terrible losses. By 1915 substantial numbers of Russian soldiers were being sent to the front without rifles; they were told to find their arms among the dead. Russia's battered peasant army nonetheless continued to fight, and Russia moved toward full mobilization of the home front. The government set up special committees to coordinate defense, industry, transportation, and agriculture. These efforts improved the military situation, but overall Russia mobilized less effectively than the other combatants.

One problem was weak leadership. Under the constitution resulting from the revolution of 1905 (see "The Russian Revolution of 1905" in Chapter 23), the tsar had retained complete control over the bureaucracy and the army, and he resisted popular involvement in government. Excluded from power, the Duma, the educated middle classes, and the masses became increasingly critical of the tsar's leadership. In September 1915 a group of political parties formed the Progressive bloc, which called for a completely new government responsible to the Duma instead of the tsar. In response, Nicholas temporarily

The Radicalization of the Russian Army   Russian soldiers inspired by the Bolshevik cause carry banners with Marxist slogans calling for revolution and democracy, around July 1917. One reads, "All Power to the Proletariat," a telling response to the provisional government's failure to pull Russia out of the war. Sick of defeat and wretched conditions at the front, the tsar's troops welcomed Lenin's promises of "Peace, Land, and Bread" and were enthusiastic participants in the Russian Revolution. (Hulton Archive/Getty Images)

adjourned the Duma. The tsar then announced that he was traveling to the front to lead and rally Russia's armies, leaving the government in the hands of his wife, the Tsarina Alexandra.

His departure was a fatal turning point. In his absence, Alexandra arbitrarily dismissed loyal political advisers. She turned to her court favorite, the disreputable and unpopular Rasputin, an uneducated Siberian preacher whose influence with the tsarina rested on his purported ability to heal Alexis — the royals' only son and heir to the throne — from his hemophilia. In a desperate attempt to right the situation, three members of the high aristocracy murdered Rasputin in December 1916. The ensuing scandal further undermined support for the tsarist government.

Imperial Russia had entered a terminal crisis that led to the **February Revolution** of 1917. (Though the events happened in March, the name of the revolution conforms to the traditional Julian calendar, used in Russia at the time.) Tens of thousands of soldiers deserted, swelling the number of the disaffected at home. By early 1917 the cities were wracked by food shortages, heating fuel was in short supply, and the economy was breaking down. In March violent street demonstrations broke out in Petrograd (now named

St. Petersburg), spread to the factories, and then engulfed the city. From the front, the tsar ordered the army to repress the protests, but the soldiers joined the revolutionary crowd instead. The Duma declared a provisional government on March 12, 1917. Three days later, Duma members convinced Tsar Nicholas to abdicate for the good of the country.

The Provisional Government

The February Revolution was the result of an unplanned uprising of hungry, angry people in the capital, but it was eagerly accepted throughout the country. The patriotic upper and middle classes embraced the prospect of a more determined war effort, while workers anticipated better wages and more food. After generations of autocracy, the provisional government established equality before the law, granting freedoms of religion, speech, and assembly, as well as the right of unions to organize and strike.

■ **February Revolution** Unplanned uprisings accompanied by violent street demonstrations begun in March 1917 (old calendar February) in Petrograd, Russia, that led to the abdication of the tsar and the establishment of a provisional government.

Yet the provisional government made a crucial mistake: though the people were sick of fighting, the new liberal leaders kept Russia in the war. For the patriotic agrarian socialist Alexander Kerensky, who became prime minister in July, the continuation of war was a national duty. Kerensky refused to confiscate large landholdings and give them to peasants, fearing that such drastic action would complete the disintegration of Russia's peasant army. Human suffering and war-weariness grew, testing the limited strength of the provisional government.

From its first day, the provisional government had to share power with a formidable rival — the **Petrograd Soviet** (or council) of Workers' and Soldiers' Deputies. Modeled on the revolutionary soviets of 1905, the Petrograd Soviet comprised two to three thousand workers, soldiers, and socialist intellectuals. Seeing itself as a true grassroots product of revolutionary democracy, the Soviet acted as a parallel government. It issued its own radical orders, weakening the authority of the provisional government.

The most famous edict of the Petrograd Soviet was Army Order No. 1, which stripped officers of their authority and placed power in the hands of elected committees of common soldiers. Designed to protect the revolution from resistance by the aristocratic officer corps, the order led to a collapse of army discipline.

In July 1917 the provisional government ordered a poorly considered summer offensive against the Germans. The campaign was a miserable failure. Peasant soldiers deserted in droves, returning home to help their families get a share of the land that peasants were seizing in a grassroots agrarian revolt. By the summer of 1917 Russia was descending into anarchy.

Lenin and the Bolshevik Revolution

Vladimir Ilyich Lenin (1870–1924), one of Russia's many revolutionary leaders, rose to power as the provisional government faltered. Born into the middle class, Lenin turned against imperial Russia when his older brother was executed in 1887 for plotting to kill archconservative Tsar Alexander III. As a law student, Lenin eagerly studied Marxist socialism, which began to win converts among radical intellectuals during Russia's industrialization in the 1890s. A pragmatic and flexible thinker, Lenin updated Marx's revolutionary philosophy to address existing conditions in Russia.

Three interrelated concepts were central for Lenin. First, he stressed that only violent revolution could destroy capitalism. He tirelessly denounced all "revisionist" theories of a peaceful evolution to socialism (see "Marxist Revisionism" in Chapter 23) as a betrayal of Marx's message of violent class conflict. Second, Lenin argued that under certain conditions a Communist revolution was possible even in a predominantly agrarian country like Russia. Peasants, who were numerous, poor, and exploited, could take the place of Marx's traditional working class in the coming revolutionary conflict. Third, Lenin believed that the possibility of revolution was determined more by human leadership than by historical laws. He called for a highly disciplined workers' party strictly controlled by a small, dedicated elite of intellectuals and professional revolutionaries that would not stop until revolution brought it to power. Lenin's version of Marxism had a major impact on events in Russia and ultimately changed the way future revolutionaries engaged in radical revolt around the world.

Other Russian Marxists challenged Lenin's ideas. At meetings of the Russian Social Democratic Labor Party in London in 1903, matters came to a head. Lenin demanded a small, elitist party dedicated to Communist revolution, while his more revisionist opponents wanted a democratic, reformist party with mass membership (like the German Social Democratic Party). The Russian Marxists split into two rival factions. Lenin labeled his camp the **Bolsheviks**, or "majority group"; his opponents were Mensheviks, or "minority group." The Bolsheviks had only a tenuous majority of a single vote, but Lenin kept the name for propaganda reasons and they became the revolutionary party he wanted: tough, disciplined, and led from above.

Lenin left Russia in 1907 to escape the tsar's police, and unlike other socialists he refused to support the war in 1914. Observing events from neutral Switzerland, Lenin viewed the war as a product of imperialist rivalries and an opportunity for socialist revolution. After the February Revolution of 1917, the German government provided Lenin with safe passage in a sealed train across Germany and back into Russia. The Germans hoped Lenin would undermine the sagging war effort of the provisional government. They were not disappointed.

Arriving triumphantly at Petrograd's Finland Station on April 3, Lenin attacked at once. He rejected all cooperation with what he called the "bourgeois" provisional government. His slogans were radical in the extreme: "All power to the soviets"; "All land to the peasants"; "Stop the war now." Lenin was a superb tactician. His promises of "Peace, Land, and Bread" spoke to the expectations of suffering soldiers, peasants, and workers and earned the Bolsheviks substantial popular support. The moment for revolution was at hand.

Yet Lenin and the Bolsheviks almost lost the struggle for Russia. A premature attempt to seize power in July

■ **Petrograd Soviet** A huge, fluctuating mass meeting of two to three thousand workers, soldiers, and socialist intellectuals modeled on the revolutionary soviets (or councils) of 1905.

■ **Bolsheviks** Lenin's radical, revolutionary arm of the Russian party of Marxist socialism, which successfully installed a dictatorial socialist regime in Russia.

Lenin Rallies the Masses
Bolshevik leader Vladimir Lenin, known for his fiery speeches, addresses a crowd in Moscow's Red Square. (Sovfoto/Getty Images)

collapsed, and Lenin went into hiding. However, this temporary setback made little difference in the long run. The army's commander in chief, General Lavr Kornilov, led a feeble coup against the provisional Kerensky government in September. In the face of this rightist counter-revolutionary threat, the Bolsheviks re-emerged. Kornilov's forces disintegrated, but Kerensky lost all credit with the army, the only force that might have saved democratic government in Russia.

Trotsky and the Seizure of Power

Throughout the summer, the Bolsheviks greatly increased their popular support. Party membership soared from 50,000 to 240,000, and in October the Bolsheviks gained a fragile majority in the Petrograd Soviet. Now Lenin's supporter Leon Trotsky (1879–1940), a spellbinding revolutionary orator and radical Marxist, brilliantly executed the Bolshevik seizure of power.

Painting a vivid but untruthful picture of German and counter-revolutionary plots, Trotsky convinced the Petrograd Soviet to form a special military-revolutionary committee in October and make him its leader. Thus military power in the capital passed into Bolshevik hands.

On the night of November 6, militants from Trotsky's committee joined with trusted Bolshevik

soldiers to seize government buildings in Petrograd and arrest members of the provisional government. Then they went on to the Congress of Soviets, where a Bolshevik majority — roughly 390 of 650 excited delegates — declared that all power had passed to the soviets and named Lenin head of the new government. John Reed, a sympathetic American journalist, described the enthusiasm that greeted Lenin at the congress:

> Now Lenin, gripping the edge of the reading stand . . . stood there waiting, apparently oblivious to the long-rolling ovation, which lasted several minutes. When it finished, he said simply, "We shall now proceed to construct the Socialist order!" Again that overwhelming human roar.[7]

The Bolsheviks came to power for three key reasons. First, by late 1917 democracy had given way to anarchy: power was there for those who could take it. Second, in Lenin and Trotsky the Bolsheviks had an utterly determined and superior leadership, which both the tsarist and the provisional governments lacked. Third, as Reed's comment suggests, Bolshevik policies appealed to ordinary Russians. Exhausted by war and weary of tsarist autocracy, they were eager for

KEY EVENTS OF THE RUSSIAN REVOLUTION

August 1914	Russia enters World War I
1916–1917	Tsarist government in crisis
March 1917	February Revolution; establishment of provisional government; tsar abdicates
April 1917	Lenin returns from exile
July 1917	Bolshevik attempt to seize power fails
October 1917	Bolsheviks gain a majority in the Petrograd Soviet
November 6–7, 1917	Bolsheviks seize power; Lenin named head of new Communist government
1918–1920	Civil war
March 1918	Treaty of Brest-Litovsk; Trotsky becomes head of the Red Army
1920	Civil war ends; Lenin and Bolshevik-Communists take control of Russia

radical changes. (See "Evaluating Written Evidence: Peace, Land, and Bread for the Russian People," page 785.) The Bolsheviks appealed to the hope for peace, better living conditions, and a more equitable society.

Dictatorship and Civil War

The Bolsheviks' truly monumental accomplishment was not taking power, but keeping it. Over the next four years, they conquered the chaos they had helped create and began to build a Communist society. How was this done?

Lenin made it seem that the Bolsheviks were directing events over which they actually had little control. Since summer, a peasant revolt had swept across Russia, as impoverished peasants had seized for themselves the estates of the landlords and the church. Thus when Lenin mandated land reform, he merely approved what peasants were already doing. Similarly, urban workers had established their own local soviets or committees and demanded direct control of individual factories. This, too, Lenin ratified with a decree in November 1917.

The Bolsheviks proclaimed their regime a "provisional workers' and peasants' government," promising

■ **Treaty of Brest-Litovsk** Peace treaty signed in March 1918 between the Central Powers and Russia that ended Russian participation in World War I and ceded territories containing a third of the Russian Empire's population to the Central Powers.

that a freely elected Constituent Assembly would draw up a new constitution. But free elections in November produced a stunning setback: the Bolsheviks won only 23 percent of the elected delegates. The Socialist Revolutionary Party — the peasants' party — had a clear plurality with about 40 percent of the vote. After the Constituent Assembly met for one day, however, Bolshevik soldiers acting under Lenin's orders disbanded it. By January 1918 Lenin had moved to establish a one-party state.

Lenin acknowledged that Russia had effectively lost the war with Germany and that the only realistic goal was peace at any price. That price was high. Germany demanded that the Soviet government give up all its western territories, areas inhabited primarily by Poles, Ukrainians, Belarusians, and other non-Russians — people who had been conquered by the tsars over three centuries and put into the "prisonhouse of nationalities," as Lenin once called the Russian Empire.

At first, Lenin's fellow Bolsheviks refused to accept such great territorial losses. But when German armies resumed their unopposed march into Russia in February 1918, they accepted the demands. A third of old Russia's population was sliced away by the **Treaty of Brest-Litovsk**, signed with Germany in March 1918. With peace, Lenin escaped the disaster of continued war and could pursue his goal of absolute power for the Bolsheviks — now also called Communists — within Russia.

The peace treaty and the abolition of the Constituent Assembly inspired armed opposition to the Bolshevik regime. People who had supported self-rule in November saw that once again they were getting dictatorship. The officers of the old army organized the so-called White opposition to the Bolsheviks in southern Russia, Ukraine, Siberia, and the area west of Petrograd. The Whites came from many social groups and were united only by their hatred of communism and the Bolsheviks — the Reds.

By the summer of 1918 Russia was in a full-fledged civil war. Eighteen self-proclaimed regional governments — several of which represented minority nationalities — challenged Lenin's government in Moscow. By the end of the year White armies were on the attack. In October 1919 they closed in on central Russia from three sides, and it appeared they might triumph. They did not.

Lenin and the Red Army beat back the counter-revolutionary White armies for several reasons. Most important, the Bolsheviks had quickly developed a better army. Once again, Trotsky's leadership was decisive. At first, the Bolsheviks had preached democracy in the military and had even elected officers in 1917. But beginning in March 1918, Trotsky became war commissar of the newly formed Red Army. He

Peace, Land, and Bread for the Russian People

Lenin wrote this dramatic manifesto in the name of the Congress of Soviets in Petrograd, the day after Trotsky seized power in the city. The Bolsheviks boldly promised the Russian people a number of progressive reforms, including an immediate armistice, land reform, democracy in the army, self-determination for imperial subjects, and ample food for all. They also issued a call to arms. The final paragraphs warn of counter-revolutionary resistance and capture the looming descent into all-out civil war.

~

To Workers, Soldiers, and Peasants!

The . . . All-Russia Congress of Soviets of Workers and Soldiers' Deputies has opened. The vast majority of the Soviets are represented at the Congress. A number of delegates from the Peasants' Soviets are also present. . . . Backed by the will of the vast majority of the workers, soldiers, and peasants, backed by the victorious uprising of the workers and the garrison which has taken place in Petrograd, the Congress takes power into its own hands.

The Provisional Government has been overthrown. The majority of the members of the Provisional Government have already been arrested.

The Soviet government will propose an immediate democratic peace to all the nations and an immediate armistice on all fronts. It will secure the transfer of the land of the landed proprietors, the crown and the monasteries to the peasant committees without compensation; it will protect the rights of the soldiers by introducing complete democracy in the army; it will establish workers' control over production; it will ensure the convocation of the Constituent Assembly at the time appointed; it will see to it that bread is supplied to the cities and prime necessities to the villages; it will guarantee all the nations inhabiting Russia the genuine right to self-determination.

The Congress decrees: all power in the localities shall pass to the Soviets of Workers', Soldiers' and Peasants' Deputies, which must guarantee genuine revolutionary order.

The Congress calls upon the soldiers in the trenches to be vigilant and firm. The Congress of Soviets is convinced that the revolutionary army will be able to defend the revolution against all attacks of imperialism until such time as the new government succeeds in concluding a democratic peace, which it will propose directly to all peoples. The new government will do everything to fully supply the revolutionary army by means of a determined policy of requisitions and taxation of the propertied classes, and also will improve the condition of the soldiers' families.

The Kornilov men — Kerensky, Kaledin and others — are attempting to bring troops against Petrograd. Several detachments, whom Kerensky had moved by deceiving them, have come over to the side of the insurgent people.

Soldiers, actively resist Kerensky the Kornilovite! Be on your guard!

Railwaymen, hold up all troop trains dispatched by Kerensky against Petrograd!

Soldiers, workers in factory and office, the fate of the revolution and the fate of the democratic peace is in your hands!

Long live the revolution!

> November 7, 1917
> The All-Russia Congress of Soviets
> Of Workers' and Soldiers' Deputies
> The Delegates from the Peasants' Soviets

EVALUATE THE EVIDENCE

1. How does Lenin's manifesto embody Bolshevik political goals? Why might it appeal to ordinary Russians in the crisis of war and revolution?
2. What historical conditions made it difficult for the Bolsheviks to fulfill the ambitious promises made at the 1917 congress?

Source: Marxists Internet Archive Library, http://www.marxists.org/archive/lenin/works/1917/oct/25-26/25b.htm.

---

re-established strict discipline and the draft. Soldiers deserting or disobeying an order were summarily shot. Trotsky made effective use of former tsarist army officers, who were actively recruited and given unprecedented powers over their troops. Trotsky's disciplined and effective fighting force repeatedly defeated the Whites in the field.

Ironically, foreign military intervention helped the Bolsheviks. For a variety of reasons, but primarily to stop the spread of communism, the Western Allies (including the United States, Britain, France, and Japan) sent troops to support the White armies. Yet they never sent enough aid to tip the balance, and the Bolsheviks used the specter of foreign intervention to attract former tsarist army officers to their side.

Other conditions favored a Bolshevik victory as well. Strategically, the Reds controlled central Russia and the crucial cities of Moscow and Petrograd. The Whites attacked from the fringes and were hopelessly divided. Moreover, the poorly defined political program of the Whites was a mishmash of conservatism and monarchism, incapable of uniting the Bolsheviks' enemies

"The Deceived Brothers Have Fallen upon Us!" This pro-Bolshevik propaganda poster from the Russian civil war is loaded with symbolism. It draws on the Greek myth of Hercules battling the Hydra to depict the enemies of the revolution as a many-headed snake. Ugly caricatures of Germany, France, Tsar Nicholas, Britain, and the church bleed from the blows of a powerful Russian worker, who embodies the revolutionary working class. At the bottom of the page, a lengthy poem calls on the Russian people to stand together to defeat the "deceived brothers," meaning Russians tricked by the western powers into fighting against the Bolshevik takeover. In the background a booming industrial landscape represents the economic development that will follow Bolshevik victory. (The New York Public Library)

ОБМАНУТЫМЪ БРАТЬЯМЪ

or generating much popular enthusiasm. And while the Bolsheviks promised ethnic minorities in Russian-controlled territories substantial autonomy, the nationalist Whites sought to preserve the tsarist empire.

The Bolsheviks mobilized the home front for the war by establishing a harsh system of centralized controls called **War Communism**. The leadership nationalized banks and industries and outlawed private enterprise. Bolshevik commissars introduced rationing, seized grain from peasants to feed the cities, and maintained strict workplace discipline. Although normal economic activity broke down, these measures maintained labor discipline and kept the Red Army supplied with men and material.

■ **War Communism** The application of centralized state control during the Russian civil war, in which the Bolsheviks seized grain from peasants, introduced rationing, nationalized all banks and industry, and required strict workplace discipline.

Revolutionary terror also contributed to the Communist victory. Lenin and the Bolsheviks set up a fearsome secret police known as the Cheka, dedicated to suppressing counter-revolutionaries. During the civil war, the Cheka imprisoned and executed without trial tens of thousands of supposed "class enemies." Victims included clergymen, aristocrats, the wealthy Russian bourgeoisie, deserters from the Red Army, and political opponents of all kinds. Even Tsar Nicholas, Alexandra, and their children were secretly executed, their bodies disfigured and hidden in a forest to avoid public outrage. The "Red Terror" of 1918 to 1920 helped establish the secret police as a central tool of the emerging Communist government.

By the spring of 1920 the White armies were almost completely defeated, and the Bolsheviks had retaken much of the territory ceded to Germany under the Treaty of Brest-Litovsk. The Red Army reconquered Belarus and Ukraine, both of which had fought for independence in 1918–1920. The Bolsheviks then moved westward into Polish territory, but they were halted on the outskirts of Warsaw in August 1920 by troops under the leadership of the Polish field marshal and chief of state Jozef Pilsudski. This defeat—in a decisive battle for Europe's future—halted Bolshevik attempts to spread communism farther into central Europe. The Russian civil war was over, and the Bolsheviks had won an impressive victory.

What were the benefits and costs of the postwar peace settlement?

Even as civil war raged in Russia and chaos engulfed much of central and eastern Europe, the war in the west came to an end in November 1918. Early in 1919 the victorious Western Allies came together in Paris, where they worked out terms for peace with Germany and created the peacekeeping League of Nations. Expectations were high; optimism was almost unlimited. Nevertheless, the peace settlement of 1919 turned out to be a disappointment for peoples and politicians alike. Rather than lasting peace, the immediate postwar years brought economic crisis and violent political conflict.

The End of the War

In early 1918 the German leadership decided that the time was ripe for a last-ditch, all-out attack on France. The defeat of Russia had released men and materials for the western front. The looming arrival of the first U.S. troops and the growth of dissent at home quickened German leaders' resolve. In the Spring Offensive of 1918, Ludendorff launched an extensive attack on the French lines. German armies came within thirty-five miles of Paris, but the exhausted, overextended forces never broke through. They were stopped in July at the second Battle of the Marne, where 140,000 U.S. soldiers saw action. The late but massive U.S. intervention bolstered the Allied victory.

By September British, French, and U.S. armies were advancing steadily on all fronts. Hindenburg and Ludendorff realized that Germany had lost the war. Not wanting to shoulder the blame, they insisted that moderate politicians should take responsibility for the defeat. On October 4 the German emperor formed a new, more liberal civilian government to sue for peace.

As negotiations over an armistice dragged on, frustrated Germans rose up in revolt. On November 3 sailors in Kiel mutinied, and throughout northern

Germany soldiers and workers established revolutionary councils modeled on the Russian soviets. The same day, Austria-Hungary surrendered to the Allies and began breaking apart. Revolution erupted in Germany, and masses of workers demonstrated for peace in Berlin. With army discipline collapsing, Wilhelm II abdicated and fled to Holland. Socialist leaders in Berlin proclaimed a German republic on November 9 and agreed to tough Allied terms of surrender. The armistice went into effect on November 11, 1918. The war was over.

Revolution in Austria-Hungary and Germany

Military defeat brought turmoil and revolution to Austria-Hungary and Germany, as it had to Russia. Having started the war to preserve an imperial state, the Austro-Hungarian Empire perished in the attempt. The independent states of Austria, Hungary, and Czechoslovakia, and a larger Romania, Italy, and Poland, were carved out of its territories (Map 25.4). For four months in 1919, until conservative nationalists seized power, Hungary became a Marxist republic along Bolshevik lines. The Serbs greatly expanded their territory by gaining control of the western Balkans; the enlarged state, the Kingdom of Serbs, Croats, and Slovenes, would be renamed Yugoslavia in 1929.

In late 1918 Germany experienced a dramatic revolution that resembled the Russian Revolution of March 1917. In both cases, a genuine popular uprising welled up from below, toppled an authoritarian monarchy, and created a liberal provisional republic. In both countries, liberals and moderate socialist politicians struggled with more radical workers' and soldiers' councils (or soviets) for political dominance. In Germany, however, moderates from the Social

Boundaries of German, Russian, and Austro-Hungarian Empires in 1914
New and reconstituted nations
Demilitarized or Allied occupation zone

MAPPING THE PAST

MAP 25.4 Territorial Changes After World War I

World War I brought tremendous changes to eastern Europe. New nations and new boundaries were established, and a dangerous power vacuum was created by the relatively weak states established between Germany and Soviet Russia.

ANALYZING THE MAP What territory did Germany lose, and to whom? Why was Austria referred to as a head without a body in the 1920s? What new independent states were formed from the old Russian and Austrian Empires?

CONNECTIONS How were the principles of national self-determination applied to the redrawing of the map of Europe after the war? Why didn't this theory work in practice? How would you evaluate the relative geopolitical strength of the new nations in central Europe, such as Poland, Czechoslovakia, and the Baltic States?

Democratic Party and their liberal allies held on to power and established the Weimar Republic—a democratic government that would lead Germany for the next fifteen years. Their success was a deep disappointment for Russia's Bolsheviks, who had hoped that a more radical revolution in Germany would spread communism across the European continent.

There were several reasons for the German outcome. The majority of the Marxist politicians in the Social Democratic Party were moderate revisionists, not revolutionaries. They wanted political democracy and civil liberties and favored the gradual elimination of capitalism. They were also German nationalists, appalled by the prospect of civil war and revolutionary terror. The moderate Social Democrats quickly came to terms with the army and big business, which helped prevent total national collapse.

Yet the triumph of the Social Democrats brought violent chaos to Germany in early 1919. The new republic was attacked from both sides of the political spectrum. Radical Communists led by Karl Liebknecht and Rosa Luxemburg tried to seize control of the government in the Spartacist Uprising in Berlin in January 1919. The Social Democrats called in nationalist Free Corps militias, bands of demobilized soldiers who had kept their weapons, to crush the uprising. Liebknecht and Luxemburg were arrested and then brutally murdered by Free Corps soldiers. In Bavaria, a short-lived Bolshevik-style republic was violently overthrown on government orders by the Free Corps. Nationwide strikes by leftist workers and a short-lived, right-wing military takeover—the Kapp Putsch—were repressed by the central government.

By the summer of 1920 the situation in Germany had calmed down, but the new republican government faced deep discontent. Communists and radical socialists blamed the Social Democrats for the murders of Liebknecht and Luxemburg and the repression in Bavaria. Right-wing nationalists, including the new National Socialist German Workers (or Nazi) Party, founded in 1920, despised the government from the start. They spread the myth that the German army had never actually lost the war on the battlefield—instead, the nation had been "stabbed in the back" by socialists and pacifists at home. In Germany, the end of the war brought only a fragile sense of political stability.

The Treaty of Versailles

In January 1919 over seventy delegates from twenty-seven nations met in Paris to hammer out a peace accord. The conference produced several treaties, including the **Treaty of Versailles**, which laid out the terms of the postwar settlement with Germany. The peace negotiations inspired great expectations. A young British diplomat later wrote that the victors

"were journeying to Paris . . . to found a new order in Europe. We were preparing not Peace only, but Eternal Peace."[8]

This idealism was strengthened by U.S. president Wilson's January 1918 peace proposal, the **Fourteen Points**. The plan called for open diplomacy, a reduction in armaments, freedom of commerce and trade, and the establishment of a **League of Nations**, an international body designed to provide a place for peaceful resolution of international problems. Perhaps most important, Wilson demanded that peace be based on the principle of **national self-determination**, meaning that peoples should be able to choose their own national governments through democratic majority-rule elections and live free from outside interference in territories with clearly defined, permanent borders. Despite the general optimism inspired by these ideas, the conference and the treaty itself quickly generated disagreement.

The "Big Three"—the United States, Great Britain, and France—controlled the conference. Germany, Austria-Hungary, and Russia were excluded, though their lands were placed on the negotiating table. Italy took part, but its role was quite limited. Representatives from the Middle East, Africa, and East Asia attended as well, but their concerns were largely ignored.

Almost immediately, the Big Three began to quarrel. Wilson, who was wildly cheered by European crowds as the champion of democratic international cooperation, insisted that the matter of the League of Nations should come first, for he passionately believed that only a permanent international organization could avert future wars. Wilson had his way—the delegates agreed to create the League, though the details would be worked out later and the final structure was too weak to achieve its grand purpose. Prime Ministers Lloyd George of Great Britain and Georges Clemenceau of France were unenthusiastic about the League. They were primarily concerned with punishing Germany.

The question of what to do with Germany in fact dominated discussions among the Big Three.

■ **Treaty of Versailles** The 1919 peace settlement that ended war between Germany and the Allied powers.

■ **Fourteen Points** Wilson's 1918 peace proposal calling for open diplomacy, a reduction in armaments, freedom of commerce and trade, the establishment of the League of Nations, and national self-determination.

■ **League of Nations** A permanent international organization, established during the 1919 Paris Peace Conference, designed to protect member states from aggression and avert future wars.

■ **national self-determination** The notion that peoples should be able to choose their own national governments through democratic majority-rule elections and live free from outside interference in nation-states with clearly defined borders.

Clemenceau wanted Germany to pay for its aggression. The war in the west had been fought largely on French soil, and like most French people, Clemenceau wanted revenge, economic retribution, and lasting security for France. This, he believed, required the creation of a buffer state between France and Germany, the permanent demilitarization of Germany, and vast reparation payments. Lloyd George supported Clemenceau in part, but was less harsh. Wilson despised German militarism but felt that Clemenceau's demands seemed vindictive. Harsh punishment for Germany violated Wilson's sense of Christian morality and the principle of national self-determination. By April the conference was deadlocked. Wilson packed his bags to go home.

In the end, Clemenceau agreed to a compromise. He gave up the French demand for a Rhineland buffer state in return for French military occupation of the region for fifteen years and a formal defensive alliance with the United States and Great Britain. Both Wilson and Lloyd George promised that their countries would come to France's aid in the event of a German attack. The Allies moved quickly to finish the settlement, believing that further adjustments would be possible within the dual framework of a strong Western alliance and the League of Nations.

The various agreements signed at Versailles redrew the map of Europe, and the war's losers paid the price. The new independent nations of Poland, Czechoslovakia, Finland, the Baltic States, and the future Yugoslavia were carved out of the Austro-Hungarian and Russian Empires. The Ottoman Empire was also split apart, or "partitioned," its territories placed under the control of the victors.

The Treaty of Versailles, signed by the Allies and Germany, was key to the settlement. Germany's African and Asian colonies were given to France, Britain, and Japan as League of Nations mandates or administered territories, though Germany's losses within Europe were relatively minor, thanks to Wilson. Alsace-Lorraine was returned to France. Ethnic Polish territories seized by Prussia during the eighteenth-century partition of the Polish-Lithuanian Commonwealth (see "Catherine the Great of Russia" in Chapter 16) were returned to a new independent Polish state. Predominantly German Danzig was also placed within the Polish border but as a self-governing city under League of Nations protection. Germany had to limit its army to 100,000 men, agree to build no military fortifications in the Rhineland, and accept temporary French occupation of that region.

More harshly, in Article 231, the **war guilt clause**, the Allies declared that Germany (with Austria) bore sole responsibility for the war and so had to pay reparations equal to all civilian damages caused by the fighting. This much-criticized clause expressed French and to some extent British demands for revenge. For the Germans,

reparations were a crippling financial burden and a cutting insult to German national pride. Many Germans believed wartime propaganda that had repeatedly claimed that Germany was an innocent victim, forced into war by a circle of aggressive enemies. When presented with these terms, the new German government protested vigorously but to no avail. On June 28, 1919, representatives of the German Social Democrats signed the treaty in Louis XIV's Hall of Mirrors at Versailles, where Bismarck's empire had been joyously proclaimed almost fifty years before (see "The Franco-Prussian War and German Unification" in Chapter 23).

The rapidly concluded Versailles treaties were far from perfect, but within the context of war-shattered Europe they were a beginning. Germany had been punished but not dismembered. A new world organization complemented a traditional defensive alliance of satisfied powers: Britain, France, and the United States. The remaining serious problems, the Allies hoped, could be worked out in the future. Allied leaders had seen speed as essential because they feared that the Bolshevik Revolution might spread. The best answer to Lenin's unending calls for worldwide upheaval, they believed, was peace and tranquility.

Yet the great hopes of early 1919 had turned to ashes by the end of the year. The Western alliance had collapsed, and a grandiose plan for permanent peace had given way to a fragile truce, for several reasons. First, the U.S. Senate and, to a lesser extent, the American people rejected Wilson's handiwork. Republican senators led by Henry Cabot Lodge believed that the treaty gave away Congress's constitutional right to declare war and demanded changes in the articles. In failing health after extensive travel to drum up popular support for the treaty, Wilson rejected all compromise. In doing so, he ensured that the Senate would never ratify the treaty and that the United States would never join the League of Nations. Moreover, the Senate refused to ratify treaties forming a defensive alliance with France and Great Britain. The United States had turned its back on Europe; the new gospel of isolationism represented a tragic renunciation of international responsibility. Using U.S. actions as an excuse, Great Britain too refused to ratify its defensive alliance with France. Bitterly betrayed by its allies, France stood alone.

A second cause for the failure of the peace was that the principle of national self-determination, which had engendered such enthusiasm, was good in theory but flawed in practice. In Europe, the borders of new states such as Poland, Czechoslovakia, and Yugoslavia cut through a jumble of ethnic and religious groups that often despised each other. The new central European nations — relatively small and powerless countries trapped between a resurgent Germany and the Soviet Union — would prove to be economically weak and politically unstable, the source of conflict in the years to come. In the colonies, desires for self-determination were simply ignored, leading to problems particularly in the Middle East.

The Peace Settlement in the Middle East

Although Allied leaders at Versailles focused mainly on European issues, they also imposed a political settlement on what had been the Ottoman Empire. Their decisions, made in Paris and at other international conferences, brought radical and controversial changes to the region. The Allies dismantled or partitioned the Ottoman Empire, Britain and France expanded their influence in the region, Jewish peoples were promised a "national homeland" in British-controlled Palestine, and Arab nationalists felt cheated and betrayed.

The British government had encouraged the wartime Arab revolt against the Ottoman Turks and had even made vague promises of an independent Arab kingdom. But when the fighting stopped, the British and the French chose instead to honor their own secret wartime agreements to divide and rule the Ottoman lands. Most important was the Sykes-Picot Agreement of 1916, named after the British and French diplomats who negotiated the deal.

In the secret accord, Britain and France agreed that the lands of the Ottoman Empire would be administered by the European powers under what they called the **mandate system**. Under the terms of the mandates, granted to individual European powers by the League of Nations, former Ottoman territories (and former German colonies) would be placed under the "tutelage" of European authorities until they could "stand alone." France would receive a mandate to govern modern-day Lebanon and Syria and much of southern Turkey, and Britain would control Palestine, Transjordan, and Iraq. Though the official goal of the mandate system was to eventually grant these regions national independence, it quickly became clear that the Allies hardly intended to do so. Critics labeled the system colonialism under another name, and when Britain and France set about implementing their agreements after the armistice, Arab nationalists reacted with understandable surprise and resentment.

British plans for the former Ottoman lands that would become Palestine (and later Israel) further angered Arab nationalists. The **Balfour Declaration** of November 1917, written by British foreign secretary Arthur Balfour, had announced that Britain favored a "National Home for the Jewish People" in Palestine, but without discriminating against the civil and religious rights of the non-Jewish communities already living in the region. Some members of the British cabinet believed the declaration would appeal to German,

Austrian, and U.S. Jews and thus help the British war effort. Others sincerely supported the Zionist vision of a Jewish homeland (see "Jewish Emancipation and Modern Anti-Semitism" in Chapter 23), which they hoped would also help Britain maintain control of the Suez Canal. Whatever the motives, the declaration enraged the region's Arabs.

In 1914 Jews accounted for about 11 percent of the population in the three Ottoman districts that the British would lump together to form Palestine; the rest of the population was predominantly Arab. Both groups understood that Balfour's "National Home" implied the establishment of some kind of Jewish state that would violate majority rule. Moreover, a state founded on religious and ethnic exclusivity was out of keeping with Islamic and Ottoman tradition, which had historically been more tolerant of religious diversity and minorities than Christian Europe had been.

Though Arab leaders attended the Paris Peace Conference, their efforts to secure autonomy in the Middle East came to nothing. Only the kingdom of Hejaz—today part of Saudi Arabia—was granted independence. In response, Arab nationalists came together in Damascus as the General Syrian Congress in 1919 and unsuccessfully called again for political independence. The congress proclaimed Syria an independent kingdom; a similar congress declared Iraqi independence.

The Western reaction was swift and decisive. A French army stationed in Lebanon attacked Syria, taking Damascus in July 1920. The Arab government fled, and the French took over. Meanwhile, the British bloodily put down an uprising in Iraq and established control there. Brushing aside Arab opposition, the British mandate in Palestine formally incorporated the Balfour Declaration and its commitment to a Jewish national home. Western imperialism, in the form of the mandate system authorized by the League of Nations, appeared to have replaced Ottoman rule in the Middle East. In the following decades, deadly anti-imperial riots and violent conflicts between Arabs and Jews would repeatedly undermine the region's stability. (See "Thinking Like a Historian: The Partition of the Ottoman Empire and the Mandate System," page 792.)

The Allies sought to impose even harsher terms on the defeated Turks than on the "liberated" Arabs. A treaty forced on the Ottoman sultan dismembered

---

■ **war guilt clause** An article in the Treaty of Versailles that declared that Germany (with Austria) was solely responsible for the war and had to pay reparations equal to all civilian damages caused by the fighting.

■ **mandate system** The plan to allow Britain and France to administer former Ottoman territories, put into place after the end of the First World War.

■ **Balfour Declaration** A 1917 British statement that declared British support of a National Home for the Jewish People in Palestine.

The Partition of the Ottoman Empire and the Mandate System

During and after the First World War, representatives of the Entente governments made various agreements to carve up Ottoman territories into spheres of interest and "mandates," managed much like colonies by the European powers. Such agreements were subject to competing claims and criticism, including wartime strategic needs, Zionist desires for an independent state in Palestine, and Arab aspirations for national independence. The outcome satisfied no one. What were the mandate system's strengths and weaknesses?

1 **Resolution of the General Syrian Congress at Damascus, July 2, 1919.** President Woodrow Wilson insisted at Versailles that the right of self-determination should be applied to the conquered Ottoman territories. In the selection below, a group of Arab nationalists from Syria offer their response to the King-Crane Commission, a group of Americans on a fact-finding mission to investigate the partition of the Ottoman Arab territories. The Arabs demand national independence and critique the League of Nations mandate system and the Balfour Declaration.

〜 We the undersigned members of the General Syrian Congress . . . provided with credentials and authorizations by the inhabitants of our various districts, Moslems, Christians, and Jews, have agreed upon the following statement of the desires of the people of the country who have elected us to present them to the American Section of the International Commission. . . .

1. We ask absolutely complete political independence for Syria within these boundaries. [Request includes the present-day states of Syria, Lebanon, Israel, and Jordan; the congress rejected any French rule or interference in the area and requested "complete independence" for present-day Iraq.]

2. We ask that the Government of this Syrian country should be a democratic civil constitutional Monarchy on broad decentralization principles, safeguarding the rights of minorities, and that the King be the Emir Faisal, who carried on a glorious struggle in the cause of our liberation and merited our full confidence and entire reliance.

3. Considering the fact that the Arabs inhabiting the Syrian area are not naturally less gifted than other more advanced races and that they are by no means less developed than the Bulgarians, Serbians, Greeks, and Romanians at the beginning of their independence, we protest against Article 22 of the Covenant

of the League of Nations, placing us among the nations in their middle stage of development which stand in need of a mandatory power. . . .

7. We oppose the pretensions of the Zionists to create a Jewish commonwealth in the southern part of Syria, known as Palestine, and oppose Zionist migration to any part of our country; for we do not acknowledge their title but consider them a grave peril to our people from the national, economical, and political points of view. Our Jewish compatriots shall enjoy our common rights and assume the common responsibilities. . . .

The noble principles enunciated by President Wilson strengthen our confidence that our desires emanating from the depths of our hearts, shall be the decisive factor in determining our future; and that President Wilson and the free American people will be our supporters for the realization of our hopes, thereby proving their sincerity and noble sympathy with the aspiration of the weaker nations in general and our Arab people in particular.

2 **Article 22 of the Covenant of the League of Nations, ratified January 1920.** In one of its first acts, the League of Nations defined the terms of the mandate system, under which the victors in the First World War would govern territories disrupted by the war, primarily former lands of the Ottoman and German Empires.

〜 To those colonies and territories which as a consequence of the late war have ceased to be under the sovereignty of the States which formerly governed them and which are inhabited by peoples not yet able to stand by themselves under the strenuous conditions of the modern world, there should be applied the principle that the well-being and development of such peoples form a sacred trust of civilisation and that securities for the performance of this trust should be embodied

ANALYZING THE EVIDENCE

1. Compare and contrast the maps in Sources 3 and 4. What are the key differences? What historical events account for these differences?
2. In Source 1, why do the representatives at the Syrian Congress appeal to the "noble principles" associated with U.S. president Wilson? How did the mandate system deal with demands for national self-determination?
3. The sources above present contradictions that proved difficult if not impossible for contemporary negotiators to resolve. What were the sticking points? In what ways did the partition of the Ottoman Empire leave unresolved problems for future generations?

3 **Entente proposals for the partition of the Ottoman Empire, 1915–1917.** In secret treaties and agreements negotiated during the war, Britain, France, Russia, and Italy planned to divide up the territories of the Ottoman Empire.

4 **The partition of the Ottoman Empire, 1914–1923.** The division of the Ottoman Arab states between Britain and France and the creation of a separate Palestinian state under British mandate would set the stage for decades of conflict.

in this Covenant. . . . [T]he tutelage of such peoples should be entrusted to advanced nations who by reason of their resources, their experience or their geographical position can best undertake this responsibility, and who are willing to accept it, and that this tutelage should be exercised by them as Mandatories on behalf of the League.

The character of the mandate must differ according to the stage of the development of the people, the geographical situation of the territory, its economic conditions and other similar circumstances. Certain communities formerly belonging to the Turkish Empire have reached a stage of development where their existence as independent nations can be provisionally recognized subject to the rendering of administrative advice and assistance by a Mandatory until such time as they are able to stand alone. The wishes of these communities must be a principal consideration in the selection of the Mandatory.

5 **The British mandate for Palestine, July 24, 1922.** The League of Nations granted Britain the mandate for Palestine, a disputed territory that included significant Christian, Jewish, and Islamic holy lands and sites.

~ Whereas His Britannic Majesty has accepted the Mandate in respect of Palestine and undertaken to exercise it on behalf of the League of Nations in conformity with the following provisions. . . .

Article 1. The Mandatory shall have full powers of legislation and of administration [in Palestine].

Article 2. The Mandatory shall be responsible for placing the country under such political, administrative, and economic conditions as will secure the establishment of the Jewish National Home . . . and the development of self-governing institutions, and also for safeguarding the civil and religious rights of all the inhabitants of Palestine, irrespective of race and religion. . . .

Article 4. An appropriate Jewish Agency shall be recognized as a public body for the purpose of advising and co-operating with the Administration of Palestine in such economic, social and other matters as may affect the establishment of the Jewish National Home and the interests of the Jewish population in Palestine. . . . The Zionist organization . . . shall be recognized as such agency. . . .

Article 6. The Administration of Palestine, while ensuring that the rights and position of other sections of the population are not prejudiced, shall facilitate Jewish immigration under suitable conditions and shall encourage, in co-operation with the Jewish Agency . . . close settlement by Jews on the land.

PUTTING IT ALL TOGETHER

Notions of national self-determination, Western superiority, and strategic diplomacy inspired the European powers who dissolved the Ottoman Empire. Few could predict the intractable conflicts that followed. Using the sources above, along with what you have learned in class and in Chapters 24 and 25, write a short essay that evaluates the motivations of these actors. Was the mandate system a fair way to resolve their conflicting needs and interests?

Sources: (1) "Resolution of the General Syrian Congress at Damascus, 2 July 1919," from the King-Crane Commission Report, in *Foreign Relations of the United States: Paris Peace Conference, 1919*, 12:780–781; (2) The Covenant of the League of Nations, Yale Law School, The Avalon Project: Documents in Law, History and Diplomacy, http://avalon.law.yale.edu/20th_century/leagcov.asp; (5) Charles D. Smith, *Palestine and the Arab-Israeli Conflict: A History with Documents*, 8th ed. (Boston: Bedford/St. Martin's, 2013), pp. 100–102.

The War in the Middle East   An Ottoman camel corps prepares for action in Beersheba, a settlement in the Negev Desert in southern Palestine (now Israel), in 1915. The defeat of the Ottoman Empire in the First World War helped shape the modern Middle East as we know it today. (Library of Congress Prints and Photographs Division, Washington, D.C.)

the Turkish heartland. Great Britain and France occupied parts of modern-day Turkey, and Italy and Greece claimed shares. There was a sizable Greek minority in western Turkey, and Greek nationalists wanted to build a modern Greek empire modeled on long-dead Byzantium. In 1919 Greek armies carried by British ships landed on the Turkish coast at Smyrna (SMUHR-nuh; today's Izmir) and advanced unopposed into the interior, while French troops moved in from the south. Turkey seemed finished.

Yet Turkey survived the postwar invasions. A Turkish National Movement emerged, led by Mustafa Kemal (1881–1938), a prominent general in the successful Turkish defeat of the British at the Battle of Gallipoli. The leaders of the movement overthrew the sultan and refused to acknowledge the Allied dismemberment of their country. Under Kemal's direction, a revived Turkish army gradually mounted a forceful resistance, and despite staggering losses, his troops repulsed the invaders. The Greeks and British sued for peace. In 1923, after long negotiations, the resulting Treaty of Lausanne (loh-ZAN) recognized the territorial integrity of Turkey. The treaty abolished the hated unequal treaties and capitulations that the European powers had imposed in the nineteenth century to give their citizens special privileges in the Ottoman Empire.

The peace accords included an agreement for a shattering example of what we would now call "ethnic cleansing," under which Greek Orthodox Catholics were forced to leave Turkish-majority lands for Greece, while Muslims moved from Greece and former Balkan territories to the Turkish mainland. The result, driven by ideals of national self-determination and long-standing tension between Christians and Muslims in Ottoman territories, was a humanitarian disaster. Greeks constituted about 16 percent of the Turkish population, and now between 1.5 and 2 million people had to pick up and move west. At the same time, 500,000 to 600,000 Muslims moved out of Greece and Bulgaria to the Anatolian peninsula (modern-day Turkey). Very few wanted to leave their homes, and though the authorities set up transit camps, refugees faced harsh conditions, rampant looting, and physical abuse. The population exchange — based primarily on religious identity rather than ethnicity — destroyed a vital, multicultural ethnic patchwork. The agreements at Lausanne became a model for future examples of ethnic cleansing, most notably the exchange of Germans and Slavs in central Europe after the Second World War, as well as the exchange of Hindus and Muslims that followed Indian independence in 1947.

Kemal, a secular nationalist, believed that Turkey should modernize and secularize along Western lines. He established a republic, was elected president, and created a one-party system—partly inspired by the Bolshevik example—to transform his country. The most radical reforms pertained to religion and culture. For centuries, Islamic religious authorities had regulated most of the intellectual, political, and social activities of Ottoman citizens. Profoundly influenced by the example of western Europe, Kemal set out to limit the place of religion and religious leaders in daily affairs. He decreed a controversial separation of church and state, promulgated law codes inspired by European models, and established a secular public school system. Women received rights that they never had before. By the time of his death in 1938, Kemal had implemented much of his revolutionary program and had moved the former Ottoman heartland much

closer to Europe, foretelling later Turkish efforts to join the European Union as a full-fledged member.

The Human Costs of the War

World War I broke empires, inspired revolutions, and changed national borders on a world scale. It also had immense human costs, and men and women in the combatant nations struggled to deal with its legacy in the years that followed. The raw numbers are astonishing: estimates vary, but total deaths on the battlefield numbered about 8 million soldiers. Russia had the highest number of military casualties, followed by Germany. France had the highest proportionate number of losses; about one out of every ten adult males died in the war. The other belligerents paid a high price as well (Figure 25.1). Between 7 and 10 million civilians died because of the war and war-related

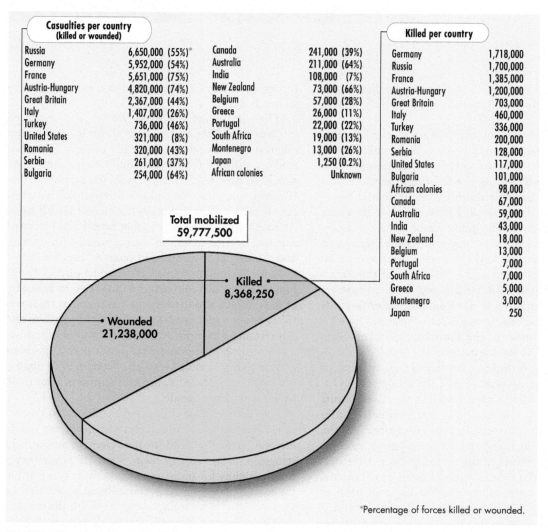

Casualties per country (killed or wounded)				Killed per country	
Russia	6,650,000 (55%)*	Canada	241,000 (39%)	Germany	1,718,000
Germany	5,952,000 (54%)	Australia	211,000 (64%)	Russia	1,700,000
France	5,651,000 (75%)	India	108,000 (7%)	France	1,385,000
Austria-Hungary	4,820,000 (74%)	New Zealand	73,000 (66%)	Austria-Hungary	1,200,000
Great Britain	2,367,000 (44%)	Belgium	57,000 (28%)	Great Britain	703,000
Italy	1,407,000 (26%)	Greece	26,000 (11%)	Italy	460,000
Turkey	736,000 (46%)	Portugal	22,000 (22%)	Turkey	336,000
United States	321,000 (8%)	South Africa	19,000 (13%)	Romania	200,000
Romania	320,000 (43%)	Montenegro	13,000 (26%)	Serbia	128,000
Serbia	261,000 (37%)	Japan	1,250 (0.2%)	United States	117,000
Bulgaria	254,000 (64%)	African colonies	Unknown	Bulgaria	101,000
				African colonies	98,000
				Canada	67,000
				Australia	59,000
				India	43,000
				New Zealand	18,000
				Belgium	13,000
				Portugal	7,000
				South Africa	7,000
				Greece	5,000
				Montenegro	3,000
				Japan	250

Total mobilized
59,777,500

Killed
8,368,250

Wounded
21,238,000

*Percentage of forces killed or wounded.

FIGURE 25.1 Casualties of World War I   The losses of World War I—not including the millions who died in the Russian civil war—were the highest ever for a war in Europe. These numbers are approximate because of problems with record keeping caused by the destructive nature of total war.

The Human Costs of War   The war killed millions of soldiers and left many more permanently disabled, making the sight of men missing limbs or disfigured in other ways a common one in the 1920s. Attempts to heal war wounds brought advances in reconstructive surgery, but the field was still relatively primitive. Some wounded veterans — like this decorated French soldier — wore lifelike masks to hide their facial injuries. (CBW/Alamy Stock Photo)

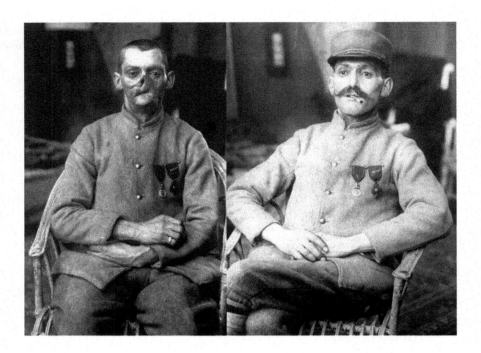

hardships, and another 20 million people died in the worldwide influenza epidemic that followed the war in 1918.

The number of dead, the violence of their deaths, and the nature of trench warfare had made proper burials difficult, if not impossible. When remains were gathered after or during the fighting, the chaos and danger of the battlefield limited accurate identification. Soldiers were typically interred close to where they fell, and by 1918 thousands of ad hoc military cemeteries were scattered across northern France and Flanders. After the war, the bodies were moved to more formal cemeteries, but hundreds of thousands remained unidentified. British and German soldiers ultimately remained in foreign soil, in graveyards managed by national commissions. After some delay, the bodies of most of the French combatants were brought home to local cemeteries.

Millions of ordinary people grieved, turning to family, friends, neighbors, and the church for comfort. Towns and villages across Europe raised public memorials to honor the dead and held ceremonies on important anniversaries: on November 11, the day the war ended, and in Britain on July 1, to commemorate the Battle of the Somme. These were poignant and often tearful moments for participants. For the first time, many nations built a Tomb of the Unknown Soldier as a site for national mourning. Memorials were also built on the main battlefields of the war. All expressed the general need to

recognize the great sorrow and suffering caused by so much death.

The victims of the First World War included millions of widows and orphans and huge numbers of emotionally scarred and disabled veterans. Countless soldiers suffered from what the British called "shell shock" — now termed post-traumatic stress disorder (PTSD). Contemporary physicians and policymakers poorly understood this complex mental health issue. Although some soldiers suffering from PTSD received medical treatment, others were accused of cowardice and shirking and were denied veterans' benefits.

Some 10 million soldiers came home physically disfigured or mutilated. Governments tried to take care of the disabled and the survivor families, but there was rarely enough money to adequately fund pensions and job-training programs. Artificial limbs were expensive, uncomfortable, and awkward, and some employers refused to hire disabled workers. Veterans with disabilities were often forced to beg on the streets, a common sight for the next decade.

The German case is illustrative. Nearly 10 percent of German civilians were direct victims of the war in one way or another, and the new German government struggled to take care of them. Veterans' groups organized to lobby for state support, and fully one-third of the federal budget of the Weimar Republic was tied up in war-related pensions and benefits. With the onset of the Great Depression in 1929, benefits were cut, leaving bitter veterans vulnerable to Nazi propagandists, who paid homage to the sacrifices of the war while calling for the overthrow of the republican government. The human cost of the war thus had another steep price. Across Europe, newly formed radical right-wing parties, including the German Nazis and the Italian Fascists, successfully manipulated popular feelings of loss and resentment to undermine fragile parliamentary governments.

NOTES

1. Quoted in J. Remak, *The Origins of World War I* (New York: Holt, Rinehart & Winston, 1967), p. 84.
2. On the mood of 1914, see J. Joll, *The Origins of the First World War* (New York: Longman, 1992), pp. 199–233.
3. Quoted in G. L. Mosse, *Fallen Soldiers: Reshaping the Memory of the World Wars* (New York: Oxford University Press, 1990), p. 64.
4. Quoted in N. Malcolm, *Bosnia: A Short History* (New York: New York University Press, 1996), p. 153.
5. V. G. Liulevicius, *War Land on the Eastern Front: Culture, National Identity, and German Occupation in World War I* (New York: Cambridge University Press, 2000), pp. 54–89.
6. Quoted in F. P. Chambers, *The War Behind the War, 1914–1918* (London: Faber & Faber, 1939), p. 168.
7. J. Reed, *Ten Days That Shook the World* (New York: International Publishers, 1967), p. 126.
8. Quoted in H. Nicolson, *Peacemaking 1919* (New York: Grosset & Dunlap Universal Library, 1965), pp. 8, 31–32.
9. Quoted in C. Barnett, *The Swordbearers: Supreme Command in the First World War* (New York: Morrow, 1964), p. 40.

LOOKING BACK LOOKING AHEAD

When chief of the German general staff Count Helmuth von Moltke imagined the war of the future in a letter to his wife in 1905, his comments were surprisingly accurate. "It will become a war between peoples which will not be concluded with a single battle," the general wrote, "but which will be a long, weary struggle with a country that will not acknowledge defeat until the whole strength of its people is broken."[9] As von Moltke predicted, World War I broke peoples and nations. The trials of total war brought down the Austro-Hungarian, Ottoman, and Russian Empires, and a Communist dictatorship took over Russia and remained in power until 1991. The brutal violence shocked and horrified observers across the world; ordinary citizens were left to mourn their losses.

Despite high hopes for Wilson's Fourteen Points, the Treaty of Versailles hardly brought lasting peace. The war's disruptions encouraged radical political conflict in the 1920s and 1930s and the rise of fascist and Communist totalitarian regimes across Europe, which led to the even more extreme violence of the Second World War. Indeed, some historians believe that the years from 1914 to 1945 might most accurately be labeled a modern Thirty Years' War, since the problems unleashed in August 1914 were only really resolved in the 1950s. This strong assertion contains a great deal of truth. For all of Europe, World War I was a revolutionary conflict of gigantic proportions with lasting traumatic effects.

Make Connections

Think about the larger developments and continuities within and across chapters.

1. While the war was being fought, peoples on all sides of the fighting often referred to the First World War as "the Great War." Why would they find this label appropriate?

2. How did long-standing political rivalries and tensions among the European powers contribute to the outbreak of the First World War (Chapters 19, 23, and 24)?

3. In what ways are current conflicts in the Middle East related to the peace treaties of the First World War and the partition of the Ottoman Empire?

25　REVIEW & EXPLORE

Identify Key Terms

Identify and explain the significance of each item below.

Triple Alliance (p. 764)
Triple Entente (p. 765)
Schlieffen Plan (p. 769)
total war (p. 769)
trench warfare (p. 771)
Easter Rising (p. 779)
February Revolution (p. 781)
Petrograd Soviet (p. 782)
Bolsheviks (p. 782)

Treaty of Brest-Litovsk (p. 784)
War Communism (p. 786)
Treaty of Versailles (p. 789)
Fourteen Points (p. 789)
League of Nations (p. 789)
national self-determination (p. 789)
war guilt clause (p. 790)
mandate system (p. 791)
Balfour Declaration (p. 791)

Review the Main Ideas

Answer the section heading questions from the chapter.

1. What caused the outbreak of the First World War? (p. 764)

2. How did the First World War differ from previous wars? (p. 769)

3. In what ways did the war transform life on the home front? (p. 775)

4. Why did world war lead to a successful Communist revolution in Russia? (p. 780)

5. What were the benefits and costs of the postwar peace settlement? (p. 787)

Suggested Resources

BOOKS

* Barthas, Louis. *Poilu: The World War I Notebooks of Corporal Louis Barthas, Barrelmaker, 1914–1918.* Trans. Edward M. Strauss. 2014. This French corporal's wartime diary offers a gritty yet humane description of daily life in the trenches.

* Clark, Christopher. *The Sleepwalkers: How Europe Went to War in 1914.* 2013. This narrative-driven, comprehensive view of the political-diplomatic crises that led to the First World War suggests that all of Europe's Great Powers—not just Germany and Austria-Hungary—bore responsibility for the war's outbreak.

* Davis, Belinda J. *Home Fires Burning: Food, Politics, and Everyday Life in Berlin in World War I.* 2000. A moving account of women struggling to feed their families on the home front and their protests against the imperial German state.

* Fitzpatrick, Sheila. *The Russian Revolution, 1917–1932.* 1982. An important interpretation that considers the long-term effects of the revolution.

* Fromkin, David. *A Peace to End All Peace.* 2001. A brilliant reconsideration of the collapse of the Ottoman Empire and its division by the Allies.

* Grayzel, Susan R. *Women and the First World War.* 2002. A thorough overview of women's experience of war across Europe.

* Joll, James. *The Origins of the First World War.* 1992. A thorough review of the causes of the war that brings together military, diplomatic, economic, political, and cultural history.

* Leonhard, Jörn. *Pandora's Box: A History of the First World War.* 2018. A comprehensive account that covers the global history of the war and its aftermath.

* Liulevicius, Vejas Gabriel. *War Land on the Eastern Front: Culture, National Identity, and German Occupation in World War I.* 2000. An important and pathbreaking work on the eastern front.

* Macmillan, Margaret. *Paris, 1919: Six Months That Changed the World.* 2001. A comprehensive, exciting account of all aspects of the peace conference.

* Mosse, George L. *Fallen Soldiers: Reshaping the Memory of the World Wars.* 1990. An innovative yet accessible account of how Europeans remembered the world wars.

* Rogan, Eugene. *The Fall of the Ottomans: The Great War in the Middle East.* 2015. A readable narrative on the key role played by the Ottoman Middle East in the conflict.

* Whalen, Robert Weldon. *Bitter Wounds: German Victims of the Great War.* 1984. An excellent treatment of the human costs of the war in Germany.

MEDIA

* *1914–1918-Online: International Encyclopedia of the First World War.* This open access encyclopedia, with authors from over fifty countries, is an impressive and comprehensive collection of recent scholarly articles on all aspects of the war. **http://www.1914-1918 -online.net/**

* *A Farewell to Arms* (Frank Borzage, 1932). The tragic story of a romance between an American ambulance driver and a Red Cross nurse, set on the Italian front. This feature film is based on a novel by Ernest Hemingway.

* *All Quiet on the Western Front* (Lewis Milestone, 1930). This graphic antiwar film about the frontline experiences and growing disillusionment of a young German volunteer is based on the famous novel of the same name by Erich Maria Remarque, first published in 1928.

* *The Battle of the Somme* (Geoffrey Malins, 1916). One of the very first wartime propaganda films, this famous documentary was originally released in August 1916. Though several scenes are clearly staged, the realistic battle sequences shocked contemporary audiences.

* *Imperial War Museums.* These five famous museums and a research center were founded in 1917 to preserve artifacts and record events from the then-ongoing world war. Its world-class collections include materials from all conflicts involving Great Britain, the British Commonwealth, and former colonies, from the First World War to the present day. **www .iwm.org.uk**

* *J'Accuse* (Abel Gance, 1938). This French remake, based on a film first produced in 1919, tells the story of an angry veteran who travels to the former front-lines and calls forth the ghosts of the war dead to help him prevent a second world war.

* *Paris 1919: Inside the Peace Talks That Changed the World* (BFS Entertainment and Multimedia, 2009). Through historical re-enactments, archival footage, and contemporary photos, this documentary takes viewers "behind the scenes" at the Paris Peace Conference to explore the controversial decisions made in 1919.

* *They Shall Not Grow Old* (Peter Jackson, 2018). A documentary on the British experience in the First World War that makes extensive use of original film, including *The Battle of the Somme*. Colorization and the addition of sound effects and voice acting lend impact to this acclaimed reconstruction.

26

Opportunity and Crisis in the Age of Modernity

1880–1940

When Allied diplomats met in Paris in early 1919 with their optimistic plans for building a lasting peace, many people looked forward to happier times. After the terrible trauma of total war, they hoped that life would return to normal and would make sense in the familiar prewar terms of peace, progress, and prosperity. Yet life would never be the same. World War I and the Russian Revolution had changed too many things. Instead of a return to past certainties, Europeans faced the ambiguities and contradictions of the modern age.

While faith in science and progress remained strong, late-nineteenth-century thinkers had already called attention to the uncertainty and irrationalism that accompanied modern life. By 1900 developments in philosophy and the sciences had substantiated and popularized such ideas. The modernist movement had begun its sweep through literature, music, and the arts, as avant-garde innovators rejected old cultural forms and began to experiment with new ones. Radical innovations in the arts and sciences dominated Western culture in the 1920s and 1930s and remained influential after World War II. An emerging consumer society, and the new media of radio and film, transformed the habits of everyday life and leisure time.

As modern science, art, and culture challenged received wisdom of all kinds, the system of international relations established under the Treaty of Versailles began to unravel. Despite some progress in the mid-1920s, political stability was short-lived, and the Great Depression that began in 1929 shocked the status quo. Democratic liberalism was besieged by the rise of authoritarian and Fascist governments, and another world conflict seemed imminent. ■

CHAPTER PREVIEW

- How did intellectual developments reflect the ambiguities of modernity?

- How did modernism revolutionize Western culture?

- How did consumer society change everyday life?

- What obstacles to lasting peace did European leaders face?

- What were the causes and consequences of the Great Depression?

Street Life in Soviet Moscow
This Moscow square bustles with big city energy. A cigarette vendor hawks her wares in the foreground, passersby and cars crowd the busy streets, and modernist buildings emblazoned with advertising placards frame the background. This 1927 photo of everyday life in the capital of the Soviet Union — a revealing image from the age of modernity — was taken by Alexander Rodchenko, one of the founders of Russian Constructivism, an avant-garde art movement that flourished after the Bolshevik Revolution. In the 1920s, in the hands of Rodchenko and many others, photography came into its own as a form of modern art. (© 2022 Estate of Alexander Rodchenko/UPRAVIS, Moscow/ARS, NY/The Art Institute of Chicago/Art Resource, NY)

How did intellectual developments reflect the ambiguities of modernity?

The decades surrounding the First World War—from the 1880s to the 1930s—brought intense cultural and intellectual experimentation. As people grappled with the costs of the war and the challenges of postwar recovery, philosophers and scientists questioned and even abandoned many of the cherished values and beliefs that had guided Western society since the eighteenth-century Enlightenment and the nineteenth-century triumph of industry and science.

Modern Philosophy

In the 1920s many people still embraced Enlightenment ideals of progress, reason, and scientific rationalism. At the turn of the century supporters of these philosophies had some cause for optimism. Women and workers were gradually gaining support in their struggles for political and social recognition, and the rising standard of living, the taming of the city, and the growth of state-supported social programs suggested that life was indeed improving. The bloodbath of the First World War had shaken faith in progress, but the notion that the rational human mind could discover the laws of society and then wisely act on them remained strong.

Nevertheless, as Western society entered the age of modernity, people faced growing uncertainties and contradictions. They discovered that modernity—generally defined by historians as the highly industrialized, urbanized class society that had arrived in most of Europe and North America by 1900—brought pessimism and crisis as well as opportunity and promise. Modernity, they realized, was in essence "Janus faced." Janus, a Roman god, is typically depicted as a single head with two opposing faces—one happy, one sad. Modernity also had at least two sides, a positive one embodied in the developments associated with science and the spread of reason, and a negative one embodied in persistent irrationalism and pessimism and the violence and destruction of modern war.

Modern philosophy echoed the Janus face of modernity. By the late nineteenth century a small group of serious thinkers had mounted a determined attack on the optimism of Enlightenment rationality. These critics rejected the general faith in progress and the rational human mind. The German philosopher Friedrich Nietzsche (NEE-chuh) (1844–1900) was particularly influential, though not until after his death. Never a systematic philosopher, Nietzsche wrote more as a prophet in a provocative and poetic style. In the first of his *Untimely Meditations* (1873), he argued that ever since classical Athens, the West had overemphasized rationality and stifled the authentic passions and animal instincts that drive human activity and true creativity.

Nietzsche questioned the conventional values of Western society. He believed that reason, progress, and respectability were outworn social and psychological constructs that suffocated self-realization and excellence. Though he was the son of a Lutheran minister, Nietzsche famously rejected religion. In his 1887 book *On the Genealogy of Morals*, he claimed that Christianity embodied a "slave morality" that glorified weakness, envy, and mediocrity. In one of his most famous lines, an apparent madman proclaims that "God is dead," metaphorically murdered by lackadaisical modern Christians who no longer really believed in him. (See "Evaluating Written Evidence: Friedrich Nietzsche Pronounces the Death of God," page 804.)

Nietzsche painted a dark world, perhaps foreshadowing his own loss of sanity in 1889. He

Philosophy with a Hammer   German philosopher Friedrich Nietzsche claimed that his "revaluation of all values" was like writing "philosophy with a hammer." His ideas posed a radical challenge to conventional Western thought and had enormous influence on later thinkers. (akg-images/Newscom)

TIMELINE

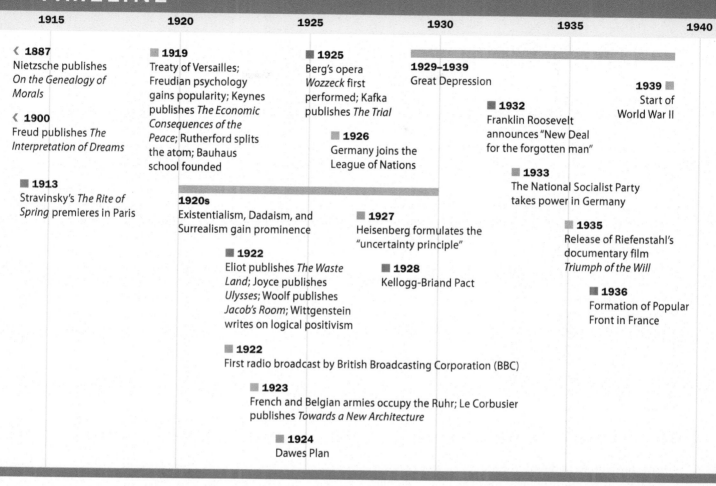

1915   **1920**   **1925**   **1930**   **1935**   **1940**

1887
Nietzsche publishes *On the Genealogy of Morals*

1900
Freud publishes *The Interpretation of Dreams*

1913
Stravinsky's *The Rite of Spring* premieres in Paris

1919
Treaty of Versailles; Freudian psychology gains popularity; Keynes publishes *The Economic Consequences of the Peace*; Rutherford splits the atom; Bauhaus school founded

1920s
Existentialism, Dadaism, and Surrealism gain prominence

1922
Eliot publishes *The Waste Land*; Joyce publishes *Ulysses*; Woolf publishes *Jacob's Room*; Wittgenstein writes on logical positivism

1922
First radio broadcast by British Broadcasting Corporation (BBC)

1923
French and Belgian armies occupy the Ruhr; Le Corbusier publishes *Towards a New Architecture*

1924
Dawes Plan

1925
Berg's opera *Wozzeck* first performed; Kafka publishes *The Trial*

1926
Germany joins the League of Nations

1927
Heisenberg formulates the "uncertainty principle"

1928
Kellogg-Briand Pact

1929–1939
Great Depression

1932
Franklin Roosevelt announces "New Deal for the forgotten man"

1933
The National Socialist Party takes power in Germany

1935
Release of Riefenstahl's documentary film *Triumph of the Will*

1936
Formation of Popular Front in France

1939
Start of World War II

---

warned that Western society was entering a period of nihilism — the grim idea that human life is entirely without meaning, truth, or purpose. Nietzsche asserted that all moral systems were invented lies and that liberalism, democracy, and socialism were corrupt systems designed to promote the weak at the expense of the strong. The West was in decline; false values had triumphed; the death of God left people disoriented and depressed. According to Nietzsche, the only hope for the individual was to accept the meaninglessness of human existence and then make that very meaninglessness a source of self-defined personal integrity and hence liberation. In this way, at least a few superior individuals could free themselves from the humdrum thinking of the masses and become true heroes.

Little read during his active years, Nietzsche's works attracted growing attention in the early twentieth century. Artists and writers experimented with his ideas, which were fundamental to the rise of the philosophy of existentialism in the 1920s. Subsequent generations remade Nietzsche to suit their own needs, and his influence remains enormous to this day.

The growing dissatisfaction with established ideas before 1914 was apparent in other important thinkers as well. In the 1890s French philosophy professor Henri Bergson (1859–1941), for one, argued that immediate experience and intuition were as important as rational and scientific thinking for understanding reality. According to Bergson, a religious experience or mystical poem was often more accessible to human comprehension than a scientific law or a mathematical equation.

The First World War accelerated the revolt against established certainties in philosophy, but that revolt went in two very different directions. In English-speaking countries, the main development was the acceptance of logical positivism in university circles. In the continental countries, the primary development in philosophy was existentialism.

Logical positivism was truly revolutionary. Adherents of this worldview argued that what we know about human life must be based on rational facts and direct observation. They concluded that theology

> ■ **logical positivism** A philosophy that sees meaning in only those beliefs that can be empirically proven and that therefore rejects most of the concerns of traditional philosophy, from the existence of God to the human search for happiness, as meaningless.

Friedrich Nietzsche Pronounces the Death of God

In this selection from philosopher Friedrich Nietzsche's *The Gay Science* (1882), one of the best-known passages in his entire body of work, a "madman" pronounces the death of God and describes the anxiety and despair — and the opportunities — faced by people in a world without faith.

The Madman. Haven't you heard of that madman, who on a bright morning day lit a lantern, ran into the marketplace, and screamed incessantly: "I am looking for God! I am looking for God!" Since there were a lot of people standing around who did not believe in God, he only aroused great laughter. Is he lost? asked one person. Did he lose his way like a child? asked another. Or is he in hiding? Is he frightened of us? Has he gone on a journey? Or emigrated? And so they screamed and laughed. The madman leaped into the crowd and stared straight at them. "Where has God gone?" he cried. "I will tell you! *We have killed him.* You and I! All of us are his murderers! But how did we do this? How did we manage to drink up the sea? Who gave us the sponge to wipe away the entire horizon? What were we doing when we unchained this earth from its sun? Where is it going now? Where are we going? Away from all the suns? Aren't we ceaselessly falling? Backward, sideways, forward, in all directions? Is there an up or a down at all? Aren't we just roaming through an infinite nothing? Don't you feel the breath of this empty space? Hasn't it gotten colder? Isn't night and ever more night falling? Don't we have to light our lanterns in the morning? Do we hear anything yet of the noise of the gravediggers who are burying God? Do we smell anything yet of the rot of God's decomposition? Gods decompose too! God is dead! God will stay dead! And we have killed him! How do we console ourselves, the murderers of all murderers? The holiest and mightiest the world has ever known has bled to death against our knives — who will wipe the blood off? Where is the water to cleanse ourselves? What sort of rituals of atonement, what sort of sacred games, will we have to come up with now? Isn't the greatness of this deed too great for us? Don't we have to become gods ourselves simply to appear worthy of it? There has never been a greater deed, and whoever will be born after us will belong to a history greater than any history up to now!"

EVALUATE THE EVIDENCE

1. Does Nietzsche believe that the "death of God" is a positive experience? In what ways can people come to grips with this "great deed"?
2. How does the nihilism expressed in this passage foreshadow many of the main ideas in the philosophy of existentialism?

and most traditional philosophy were meaningless because even the most cherished ideas about God, eternal truth, and ethics were impossible to prove using logic. This outlook is often associated with the Austrian philosopher Ludwig Wittgenstein (VIHT-guhn-shtine) (1889–1951), who later immigrated to England, where he trained numerous disciples.

In his pugnacious *Tractatus Logico-Philosophicus* (*Essay on Logical Philosophy*), published in 1922, Wittgenstein argued that philosophy is only the logical clarification of thoughts and that therefore it should concentrate on the study of language, which expresses thoughts. In his view, the great philosophical issues of the ages — God, freedom, morality, and so on — were quite literally senseless, a great waste of time, for neither scientific experiments nor mathematical logic could demonstrate their validity. Statements about such matters reflected only the personal preferences of a given individual. As Wittgenstein put it in the famous last sentence of this work, "Of what one cannot speak, of that one must keep silent." Logical positivism, which has remained central in England and the United States to this day, drastically reduced the scope of philosophical inquiry and offered little solace to ordinary people.

On the continent, others looked for answers in **existentialism**. This new philosophy loosely united highly diverse and even contradictory thinkers in a search for usable moral values in a world of anxiety and uncertainty. Modern existentialism had many nineteenth-century forerunners, including Nietzsche, the Danish religious philosopher Søren Kierkegaard (1813–1855), and the Russian novelist Fyodor Dostoyevsky (1821–1881). The philosophy gained recognition in Germany in the 1920s when philosophers Martin Heidegger (1889–1976) and Karl Jaspers (1883–1969) found a sympathetic audience among disillusioned postwar university students.

These writers placed great emphasis on the loneliness and meaninglessness of human existence and the need to come to terms with the fear caused by this situation.

Most existential thinkers in the twentieth century were atheists. Often inspired by Nietzsche, they did not believe that a supreme being had established humanity's fundamental nature and given life its meaning. In the words of French existentialist Jean-Paul Sartre (SAHR-truh) (1905–1980), "existence precedes essence." By that, Sartre meant that there are no God-given, timeless truths outside or independent of individual existence. Only after they are born do people struggle to define their essence, entirely on their own. According to thinkers like Sartre and his lifelong intellectual partner Simone de Beauvoir (1908–1986), existence itself is absurd. Human beings are terribly alone, for there is no God to help them. They are left to confront the inevitable arrival of death and so are hounded by despair. The crisis of the existential thinker epitomized the modern intellectual crisis—the shattering of beliefs in God, reason, and progress.

At the same time, existentialists recognized that human beings must act in the world. Indeed, in the words of Sartre, "man is condemned to be free." Because life is meaningless, existentialists believe that individuals are forced to create their own meaning and define themselves through their actions. Such radical freedom is frightening, and Sartre concluded that most people try to escape it by structuring their lives around conventional social norms. According to Sartre, to escape is to live in "bad faith," to hide from the hard truths of existence. To live authentically, individuals must become "engaged" and choose their own actions in full awareness of their responsibility for their own behavior. Existentialism thus had a powerful ethical component. It placed great stress on individual responsibility and choice, on "being in the world" in the right way.

Existentialism had important precedents in the late nineteenth and early twentieth centuries, but the philosophy really came of age in France during and immediately after World War II. The terrible conditions of that war, discussed in the next chapter, reinforced the existential view of and approach to life. After World War II, French existentialists such as Sartre and Albert Camus (1913–1960) became enormously influential. They offered powerful but unsettling answers to the profound moral issues and the crises of the first half of the twentieth century.

The Revival of Christianity

Although philosophers such as Nietzsche, Wittgenstein, and Sartre believed that religion had little to teach people in the modern age, the decades after the First World War witnessed a tenacious revival of Christian thought. Christianity—and religion in general—had been on the defensive in intellectual circles since the Enlightenment. In the years before 1914 some theologians, especially Protestant ones, had felt the need to interpret Christian doctrine and the Bible so that they did not seem to contradict science, evolution, and common sense. They saw Christ primarily as a great moral teacher and downplayed the mysterious, spiritual aspects of his divinity. Indeed, some modern theologians were embarrassed by the miraculous, unscientific aspects of Christianity and rejected them.

Especially after World War I, a number of thinkers and theologians began to revitalize the fundamental beliefs of Christianity. Sometimes called Christian existentialists because they shared the loneliness and despair of atheistic existentialists, they stressed human beings' sinful nature, their need for faith, and the mystery of God's forgiveness. The revival of Christian belief after World War I was fed by the rediscovery of the work of the nineteenth-century Danish theologian Søren Kierkegaard (KIHR-kuh-gahrd), whose ideas became extremely influential. Kierkegaard believed it was impossible for ordinary people to prove the existence of God, but he rejected the notion that Christianity was an empty practice. In his classic *Sickness unto Death* (1849), Kierkegaard mastered his religious doubts by suggesting that people must take a "leap of faith" and accept the existence of an objectively unknowable but nonetheless awesome and majestic God.

In the 1920s the Swiss Protestant theologian Karl Barth (1886–1968) propounded similar ideas. In brilliant and influential writings, Barth argued that human beings were imperfect, sinful creatures whose intellectual abilities and will are hopelessly flawed. Religious truth is therefore made known to human beings only through God's grace, not through reason. People have to accept God's word and the supernatural revelation of Jesus Christ with awe, trust, and obedience, not reason or logic.

Among Catholics, the leading existential Christian was Gabriel Marcel (1889–1973). Born into a cultivated French family, Marcel found in the Catholic Church an answer to what he called the postwar "broken world." Catholicism and religious belief provided the hope, humanity, honesty, and piety for which he hungered. Marcel denounced anti-Semitism and supported closer ties with non-Catholics.

After 1914 religion became much more meaningful to intellectuals than it had been before the war. Between about 1920 and 1950, poets T. S. Eliot and W. H. Auden, novelists Evelyn Waugh and Aldous Huxley, historian Arnold Toynbee, writer C. S. Lewis, psychoanalyst Karl Stern, and physicist Max Planck all either

■ **existentialism** A philosophy that stresses the meaninglessness of existence and the importance of the individual in searching for moral values in an uncertain world.

converted to a faith or became attracted to religion for the first time. Religion, often of an existential variety, offered one meaningful answer to the horrific costs of the First and Second World Wars and the ambiguities of the age of modernity. In the words of English novelist Graham Greene, a Roman Catholic convert, "One began to believe in heaven because one believed in hell."[1]

The New Physics

Ever since the Scientific Revolution of the seventeenth century, scientific advances and their implications had greatly influenced the beliefs of thinking people. In the late nineteenth century science was one of the main pillars supporting Western society's optimistic and rationalistic worldview. Progressive minds believed that science, unlike religion or philosophical speculation, was based on hard facts and controlled experiments. Unchanging natural laws seemed to determine physical processes and permit useful solutions to more and more problems. All this marked the upside of the modern age, especially for people no longer committed to traditional religious beliefs.

By the 1920s, developments in the science of physics had begun to cast doubt on the unchanging, factual basis of natural law. An important first step came at the end of the nineteenth century with the discovery that atoms were not like hard, permanent little billiard balls. They were actually composed of many far-smaller, fast-moving, unstable particles, such as electrons and protons. Polish-born physicist Marie Curie (1867–1934) and her French husband, Pierre, for example, discovered that radium constantly emits subatomic particles and thus does not have a constant atomic weight. Building on this and other work in radiation, German physicist Max Planck (1858–1947) showed in 1900 that subatomic energy is emitted in uneven little spurts, which Planck called "quanta," and not in a steady stream, as previously believed. Planck's discovery called into question the old sharp distinction between matter and energy: the implication was that matter and energy might be different forms of the same thing. The view of atoms as the stable basic building blocks of nature, with a different kind of unbreakable atom for each of the ninety-two chemical elements, was badly shaken.

In 1905 the German-Jewish genius Albert Einstein (1879–1955) further challenged the mathematical laws at the base of Newtonian physics. Einstein's **theory of special relativity** postulated that time and space are relative to the viewpoint of the observer and that only the speed of light is constant for all frames of reference in the universe. In order to make his revolutionary and paradoxical idea somewhat comprehensible to the nonmathematical layperson, Einstein used analogies involving moving trains: if a woman in the middle of a moving car got up and walked forward to the door, she had gone, relative to the train, a half car length. But

relative to an observer on the embankment, she had gone farther. To Einstein, this simple example showed that time and distance were not natural universals but depended on the position and motion of the observer.

In addition, Einstein's theory stated that matter and energy were interchangeable and that even a particle of matter contains enormous levels of potential energy. These ideas unified an apparently infinite universe with the incredibly small, fast-moving subatomic world. In comparison, the closed framework of the Newtonian physics developed during the Scientific Revolution, exemplified by Newton's supposedly immutable laws of motion and mechanics, was quite limited (see "Newton's Synthesis," Chapter 16).

The 1920s opened the "heroic age of physics," in the apt words of Ernest Rutherford (1871–1937), one of its leading pioneers. Breakthrough followed breakthrough. In 1919 Rutherford showed that the atom could be split. By 1944 seven subatomic particles had been identified, the most important of which was the neutron. Physicists realized that the neutron's capacity to shatter the nucleus of another atom could lead to chain reactions of shattered atoms that would release unbelievable force. This discovery was fundamental to the subsequent development of the nuclear bomb.

Although few nonscientists truly understood the revolution in physics, its implications, as presented in newspapers and science fiction, fascinated millions of men and women in the 1920s and 1930s. As radical as Einstein's ideas was a notion popularized by German physicist Werner Heisenberg (HIGH-zuhn-buhrg) (1901–1976). In 1927 Heisenberg formulated the "uncertainty principle," which postulates that nature itself is ultimately unknowable and unpredictable. He suggested that the universe lacked any absolute objective reality. Everything was "relative," that is, dependent on the observer's frame of reference. Such ideas challenged familiar certainties: instead of Newton's dependable, rational laws, there seemed to be only tendencies and probabilities in an extraordinarily complex and uncertain universe. Like modern philosophy, physics no longer provided comforting truths about natural laws or optimistic answers about humanity's place in an understandable world.

Freudian Psychology

With physics presenting an uncertain universe so unrelated to ordinary human experience, questions regarding the power and potential of the rational human mind assumed special significance. The findings and speculations of Sigmund Freud were particularly influential, yet also deeply provoking. (See "Individuals in Society: Sigmund Freud," page 808.)

Before Freud, poets and mystics had probed the unconscious and irrational aspects of human behavior. But most scientists assumed that the conscious mind

En amerikansk tecknares bekymmer för framtiden.

Då professorn äntligen efter årslånga experiment lyckades sönderdela en atom.

Unlocking the Power of the Atom   Many of the fanciful visions of science fiction came true in the twentieth century, although not exactly as first imagined. This 1927 Swedish reprint of a drawing by American cartoonist Robert Fuller satirizes a pair of professors who have split the atom and unwittingly destroyed their building and neighborhood in the process. In the Second World War, professors indeed harnessed the atom in bombs and decimated faraway cities and foreign civilians. (Chronicle/Alamy Stock Photo)

processed sense experiences in a rational and logical way. Human behavior in turn was the result of rational calculation — of "thinking." Beginning in the late 1880s Freud developed a very different view of the human psyche. Basing his insights on the analysis of dreams and of "hysteria," a sort of nervous breakdown, Freud concluded that human behavior was basically irrational, governed by the unconscious, a mental reservoir that contained vital instinctual drives and powerful memories. Though the unconscious profoundly influenced people's behavior, it was unknowable to the conscious mind, leaving people unaware of the source or meaning of their actions. Freud explained these ideas in his magisterial book *The Interpretation of Dreams*, first published in 1900.

Freud eventually described three structures of the self — the **id,** the **ego,** and the **superego** — that were basically at war with one another. The primitive, irrational id was entirely unconscious. The source of sexual, aggressive, and pleasure-seeking instincts, the id sought immediate fulfillment of all desires and was totally amoral. Keeping the id in check was the superego, the conscience or internalized voice of parental or social control. For Freud, the superego was also irrational. Overly strict and puritanical, it was constantly in

conflict with the pleasure-seeking id. The third component was the ego, the rational self that was mostly conscious and worked to negotiate between the demands of the id and the superego.

For Freud, the healthy individual possessed a strong ego that effectively balanced the id and superego. Neurosis, or mental illness, resulted when the three structures were out of balance. Since the id's instinctual drives were extremely powerful, the danger for individuals and indeed whole societies was that unacknowledged drives might overwhelm the control mechanisms of the ego in a violent, distorted way. Freud's "talking cure" — in which neurotic patients lay back on a couch and shared their innermost thoughts with the psychoanalyst — was an attempt to resolve such unconscious tensions and restore the rational ego to its predominant role.

Freudian psychology and clinical psychiatry had become an international medical movement by 1910, but only after 1919 did they receive more public attention, especially in northern Europe. In the United States, Freud's ideas attained immense popularity after the Second World War. Many opponents and even some enthusiasts interpreted Freud as saying that the first requirement for mental health was an uninhibited sex life; popular understandings of Freud thus reflected and encouraged growing sexual experimentation, particularly among middle-class women. For more serious students, the psychology of Freud and his followers weakened the old easy optimism about the rational and progressive nature of the human mind.

■ **theory of special relativity**   Albert Einstein's theory that time and space are relative to the observer and that only the speed of light remains constant.

■ **id, ego, and superego**   Freudian terms to describe the three parts of the self and the basis of human behavior, which Freud saw as basically irrational.

INDIVIDUALS IN SOCIETY

Sigmund Freud

In the course of his long and brilliant career, Sigmund Freud developed psychological theories and therapeutic techniques that revolutionized contemporary understandings of the human mind. Freud was born in 1856 to a middle-class Jewish merchant family and moved to Vienna when he was four years old. He entered the University of Vienna to study physiology and biology, and earned a medical degree in 1881 with a dissertation titled "The Spinal Cord of Lower Fish Species."

In 1885–1886 Freud studied in Paris at the clinic of the leading French neurologist Jean-Martin Charcot. Charcot's work on hysteria — fainting spells in women — inspired Freud to turn to mental health and psychology. From Charcot, Freud learned to treat patients with hypnosis. In 1886 he married Martha Bernays, the daughter of the chief rabbi in Hamburg. The same year Freud opened a medical practice in Vienna, where he continued to believe that hypnosis could help reveal psychological damage lodged somewhere in the unconscious.

Freud's collaboration with Viennese psychologist Dr. Joseph Breuer marked a breakthrough in the development of psychoanalysis, the label Freud would use to designate his thought and practice. Freud and Breuer worked together to treat "Anna O.," a deeply neurotic patient whose symptoms included radical mood swings, hallucinations, and psychosomatic disorders. Her partial recovery — achieved through the so-called talking cure, in which patients described their experiences and the symptoms began to go away — was described in their coauthored book, *Studies in Hysteria* (1895). The psychologists suggested that the goal of therapy was to decode the logic of the unconscious. No symptom was accidental. To bring relief, the therapist needed to discover and explain the links between repressed experience and the symptom.

Freud worked hard on what he saw as his great mission: to propagate the message of psychoanalysis. He published a series of famous books, including case studies about his patients and detailed explanations of his theories and methods. In 1910 he cofounded the International Psychoanalytic Association, an umbrella group for like-minded colleagues, designed to promote Freudian theories.

The great slaughter of World War I confirmed for Freud the role of aggressive irrationality at the core of the human personality, and after the war Freud began to apply his theories to human society at large. Most famously, in his book *Civilization and Its Discontents* (1930), Freud argued that civilization was possible only when individuals renounced their irrational

Sigmund Freud and his wife, Martha Bernays, about 1890. (Sigmund Freud/ullstein bild/Getty Images)

instincts in order to live peaceably in groups. Such renunciation made communal life possible, but it left basic instincts unfulfilled and so resulted in widespread unhappiness. Freud gloomily concluded that Western civilization was itself inescapably neurotic.

Although Freud was a nonpracticing Jew, he was appalled by the anti-Semitism of the German Nazi Party. When the Nazis took over Austria in 1938, he emigrated to London. Suffering from long-term mouth cancer, the eighty-three-year-old Freud died by physician-assisted suicide in September 1939. Although the science of psychology has in many ways moved on, Freud's ideas about the role of the unconscious in human motivation, as well as his famous "talking cure," have had a lasting impact on the Western intellectual tradition.

QUESTIONS FOR ANALYSIS

1. Using the material in the biography above and in the chapter text, summarize the main features of psychoanalysis. Why was the unconscious so central to Freud's ideas?
2. How do Freud's theories and therapies reflect the "Janus face" of the modern age?

How did modernism revolutionize Western culture?

Like the scientists and intellectuals who were part of an increasingly unsettled modern culture, creative artists rejected old forms and values. **Modernism** in architecture, art, literature, and music meant constant experimentation and a search for new kinds of expression. Many artists produced critical, challenging works that called attention to the irrational aspects of Western society. Their work was strikingly original, and the era of early-twentieth-century modernism is widely viewed as one of the greatest in Western art.

Architecture and Design

Already in the late nineteenth century, architects inspired by modernism had begun to transform the physical framework of urban society. The United States, with its rapid urban growth and lack of rigid building traditions, pioneered the new architecture. In the 1890s the Chicago School of architects, led by Louis H. Sullivan (1856–1924), used inexpensive steel, reinforced concrete, and electric elevators to build skyscrapers and office buildings lacking almost any exterior ornamentation. In the first decade of the twentieth century, Sullivan's student Frank Lloyd Wright (1867–1959) built a series of radically modern houses featuring low lines, open interiors, and mass-produced building materials. European architects were inspired by these and other American examples of modern construction.

Modern architects believed that buildings and living spaces in general should be ordered according to a new principle: **functionalism**. Buildings, like industrial products, should be "functional" — that is, they should serve, as well as possible, the purpose for which they were made. According to the Franco-Swiss architect Le Corbusier (luh cowr-booz-YAY) (1887–1965), one of the great champions of modernism, "a house is a machine for living in."[2] Le Corbusier's polemical work *Towards a New Architecture*, published in 1923, laid out guidelines meant to revolutionize building design. Le Corbusier argued that architects should affirm and adopt the latest scientific technologies. Rejecting fancy ornamentation, they should find beauty in the clean, straight lines of practical construction and efficient machinery. The resulting buildings, fashioned according to what was soon called the "International Style," were typically symmetrical rectangles made of concrete, glass, and steel.

In Europe, architectural leadership centered in German-speaking countries until Hitler took power in 1933. In 1911 twenty-eight-year-old Walter Gropius (1883–1969) broke sharply with the past in his design of the Fagus shoe factory at Alfeld, Germany — a clean, light, elegant building of glass and iron. In 1919 Gropius merged the schools of fine and applied arts at Weimar into a single interdisciplinary school, the **Bauhaus**. The Bauhaus brought together many leading modern architects, designers, and artists.

The impact of the Bauhaus on everyday life, from architecture to interior design, was immense. Working as an effective, inspired team, Bauhaus instructors and students sought to revolutionize product design by unifying art, craft, and technology. They combined the study of fine art, including painting and sculpture, with the study of applied art in the crafts of printing, weaving, and furniture making. Bauhaus adherents argued that everyday objects should reflect the highly rationalized, industrialized, and modern society in which — and for which — they were made. No object was too insignificant to be treated as an object of high design, and the industrial ethos of the Bauhaus was brought to bear on textiles, typography, dishware, and furniture. Such goods were mass-produced and marketed at affordable prices, bringing high-concept design into the lives of ordinary Europeans. Bauhaus architects applied the same principles in designing buildings, from factories to working-class housing projects and private homes.

Another leading modern architect, Ludwig Mies van der Rohe (1886–1969), followed Gropius as director of the Bauhaus in 1930. Like many modernist intellectuals, after 1933 he moved to the United States to escape the repressive Nazi regime. His classic steel-frame and glass-wall Lake Shore Apartments in Chicago, built between 1948 and 1951, epitomized the spread and triumph of the modernist International Style in the great building boom that followed the Second World War.

New Artistic Movements

In the decades surrounding the First World War, the visual arts also entered a phase of radical experimentation. For the previous several centuries, most artists had tried to produce accurate representations of reality. Now a committed avant-garde emerged to challenge that practice. From Impressionism and Expressionism to Dadaism and Surrealism, a sometimes bewildering array of artistic movements followed one after another.

■ **modernism** A label given to the artistic and cultural movements of the late nineteenth and early twentieth centuries, which were typified by radical experimentation that challenged traditional forms of artistic expression.

■ **functionalism** The principle that buildings, like industrial products, should serve as well as possible the purpose for which they were made, without excessive ornamentation.

■ **Bauhaus** A German interdisciplinary school of fine and applied arts that brought together many leading modern architects, designers, and artists.

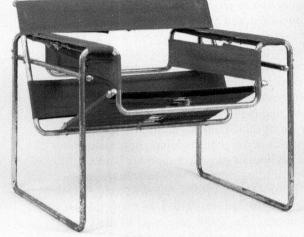

The Bauhaus Movement   European design movements of the early twentieth century such as the Bauhaus, an institute for arts and crafts founded in Germany in 1919, had a lasting impact on everyday lifestyles. Bauhaus adherents believed that form should follow function and that, as director Ludwig Mies van der Rohe put it in a famous aphorism, "less is more." The results, including the Bauhaus School of Design (above) in Dessa, Germany, and this "Wassily" armchair (left) by Marcel Breuer, were streamlined, functional buildings and objects stripped of all ornamentation. They were nonetheless works of beauty, whose design and materials expressed the values of the modern age. (school: CALLUM VELLACOTT/Bridgeman Images; chair: Marcel Breuer/FISCHER FINE ART/Private Collection/Bridgeman Images)

Photography and collage emerged as new experimental fields. Painting and sculpture became increasingly abstract as modern artists turned their backs on figurative representation and began to break down form into its constituent parts: lines, shapes, and colors.

Berlin, Munich, Vienna, Moscow, New York, and especially Paris became famous for their radical art scenes. Commercial art galleries and exhibition halls promoted the new work, and schools and institutions, such as the Bauhaus, emerged to train a generation in modern techniques. Young artists flocked to these cultural centers to participate in the new movements, earn a living making art, and perhaps change the world with their revolutionary ideas.

One of the earliest modernist movements was Impressionism, which blossomed in Paris in the 1870s. French artists such as Claude Monet (1840–1926) and Edgar Degas (1834–1917), and the American Mary Cassatt (1844–1926), who settled in Paris in 1875, tried to portray their sensory "impressions" in their work. Impressionists looked to the world around them for subject matter, turning their backs on traditional

themes such as battles, religious scenes, and wealthy elites. Monet's colorful and atmospheric paintings of farmland haystacks and Degas's many pastel drawings of ballerinas exemplify the way Impressionists moved toward abstraction. Capturing a fleeting moment of color and light, in often blurry and quickly painted images, was far more important than making a heavily detailed, precise rendering of an actual object.

An astonishing array of art movements followed Impressionism. Postimpressionists and Expressionists, such as Vincent van Gogh (1853–1890), built on Impressionist motifs of color and light but added a deep psychological element to their pictures, reflecting the attempt to search within the self and express inner feelings on the canvas.

After 1900 a new generation of artists overturned the art world status quo. In Paris in 1907 painter Pablo Picasso (1881–1973), along with others, established Cubism — a highly analytical approach that concentrated on a complex geometry of zigzagging lines and sharply angled overlapping planes. Cubism exemplified the ongoing trend toward abstract, nonrepresentational art. In 1909 Italian Filippo Tommaso Marinetti (1876–1944) announced the arrival of Futurism, a movement in art and literature determined to glorify modernity

■ **Dadaism** An artistic movement of the 1910s and 1920s that attacked all accepted standards of art and behavior and delighted in outrageous conduct.

and destroy the burdens of the past. According to Marinetti, traditional culture could not adequately deal with the advances of modern technology — automobiles, radios, telephones, phonographs, ocean liners, airplanes, the cinema, the newspaper — and the way these had changed human consciousness. Marinetti embraced the future, championing the speed and confusion of modernity and calling for new art forms that could express the modern condition.

The shock of World War I encouraged further radicalization. In 1916 a group of international artists and intellectuals in exile in Zurich, Switzerland, championed a new movement they called **Dadaism**, which attacked all the familiar standards of art and delighted in outrageous behavior. The war had shown once and for all that life was meaningless, the Dadaists argued, so art should be meaningless as well. Dadaists tried to shock their audiences with what they called "anti-art," works and public performances that were insulting and entirely nonsensical. A well-known example is a reproduction of Leonardo da Vinci's *Mona Lisa* in which the masterpiece is ridiculed with the addition of a hand-drawn mustache and an obscene inscription. After the war, Dadaism became an international movement, spreading to Paris, New York, and particularly Berlin in the early 1920s.

During the mid-1920s some Dadaists turned to Surrealism, a movement deeply influenced by the Freudian idea of the unconscious. Surrealists painted fantastic worlds of wild dreams and uncomfortable symbols, where watches melted and giant metronomes beat time in precisely drawn but impossibly alien landscapes.

Many modern artists sincerely believed that art had a transformative mission. By calling attention to the bankruptcy of mainstream society, they thought art had the power to change the world. The sometimes-nonsensical manifestos written by members of the Dadaist, Futurist, and Surrealist movements were meant to spread their ideas, challenge conventional assumptions, and foment social change.

By the 1920s art and culture had become increasingly politicized. Many avant-garde artists sided with the far left; some became committed Communists. (See "Evaluating Visual Evidence: Georg Grosz, *Eclipse of the Sun*, 1926," page 813.) Such artists and modern art movements in general had a difficult time surviving the political crises of the 1930s. In 1933 the National Socialist (Nazi) Party came to power in Germany; in 1939 they started the Second World War. The Nazis despised the abstract ambiguities of modernism, and hundreds of artists and intellectuals — often Jews and leftists — fled to the United States to escape Nazi repression. After World War II, New York benefited from this transfusion of talent and replaced Paris and Berlin as the world capital of modern art.

Twentieth-Century Literature

In the decades that followed the First World War, Western literature was deeply influenced by the turn toward radical experimentation that swept through the other arts. The great nineteenth-century novelists had typically written as all-knowing narrators, describing realistic characters and their relationships to an understandable, if sometimes harsh, society. Modernist writers developed new techniques to express new realities. In the twentieth century many authors adopted the limited, often confused viewpoint of a single individual. Like Freud, they focused on the complexity and irrationality of the human mind, where feelings, memories, and desires were forever scrambled. French novelist Marcel Proust (PROOST) (1871–1922), in his semi-autobiographical, multivolume *Remembrance*

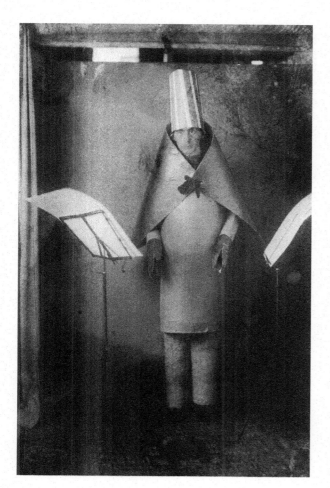

The Shock of the Avant-Garde   German Dadaist Hugo Ball recites his nonsense poem "Karawane" at the notorious Cabaret Voltaire in Zurich, Switzerland, in 1916. Avant-garde artists such as Ball consciously used their work to overturn familiar artistic conventions and challenge the assumptions of the European middle classes. (Apic/Getty Images)

Salvador Dali, *The Persistence of Memory*, 1931 Dali was a leader of the Surrealist art movement, which emerged in the late 1920s. Surrealists were deeply influenced by the theories of Sigmund Freud and used strange and evocative symbols to capture the inner workings of dreams and the unconscious in their work. Melting clocks, swarming ants, and a misshapen human body — all signature features of Dali's art — dominate this 1931 painting. What mysterious significance, if any, lies behind this surreal reordering of everyday reality? (© 2022 Salvador Dalí, Fundació Gala–Salvador Dalí, Artists Rights Society/M. Flynn/Alamy Stock Photo)

of Things Past, published in 1927, recalled bittersweet memories of childhood and youthful love and tried to discover their innermost meaning. To do so, Proust lived like a hermit in a soundproof Paris apartment for ten years, withdrawing from the present to dwell on the past.

Some novelists used the **stream-of-consciousness technique**, relying on internal monologues to explore the human psyche. In *Jacob's Room* (1922), the English author Virginia Woolf (1882–1941) created a novel made up of a series of such monologues in which she tried to capture the inner voice in prose. In this and other stories, Woolf portrayed characters whose ideas and emotions from different periods of their lives bubble up as randomly as from a patient on a psychoanalyst's couch. William Faulkner (1897–1962), one of America's great novelists, used the same technique in *The Sound and the Fury* (1929), with much of its intense drama confusedly seen through the eyes of a man who is mentally disabled.

The most famous and perhaps most experimental stream-of-consciousness novel was *Ulysses* (1922) by Irish novelist James Joyce (1882–1941). Into an account of a single day in the life of an ordinary man, Joyce weaves an extended ironic parallel between the aimless wanderings of his hero through the streets and pubs of Dublin and the adventures of Homer's hero Ulysses on his way home from Troy. *Ulysses* was surely one of the most difficult novels of its generation. Abandoning any sense of a conventional plot, breaking rules of grammar, and blending foreign words, puns, bits of knowledge, and scraps of memory together in bewildering confusion, *Ulysses* is intended to mirror modern life: a gigantic riddle impossible to unravel. Since Joyce included frank descriptions of the main character's sexual thoughts and encounters, the novel was considered obscene in Great Britain and the United States and was banned there until the early 1930s.

As creative writers turned their attention from society to the individual and from realism to psychological relativity, they rejected the idea of progress. Some described "anti-utopias," nightmare visions of things to come, as in the T. S. Eliot poem *The Waste Land* (1922), which depicts a world of growing desolation:

April is the cruelest month, breeding
Lilacs out of the dead land, mixing
Memory and desire, stirring
Dull roots with spring rain.
. . .

What are the roots that clutch, what branches grow
Out of this stony rubbish? Son of man,
You cannot say, or guess, for you know only
A heap of broken images, where the sun beats,
And the dead tree gives no shelter, the cricket no
    relief,
And the dry stone no sound of water.[3]

■ **stream-of-consciousness technique** A literary technique, found in works by Virginia Woolf, James Joyce, and others, that uses interior monologue — a character's thoughts and feelings as they occur — to explore the human psyche.

Georg Grosz, *Eclipse of the Sun*, 1926

Berlin Dadaist artist Georg Grosz served in the German army in the First World War and was discharged after experiencing a nervous breakdown. He supported the postwar revolution and joined the Communist Party in 1921. An apocalyptic visionary, Grosz grappled in his art with the violence and destruction of the war and the corruption and crises of postwar Germany. His *Eclipse of the Sun*, a large, almost 6-by-7-foot painting finished in 1926, reveals his typical concerns with the effects of militarism, political corruption, and capitalist exploitation. The dollar sign on the sun represents the Dawes Plan of 1924, which attempted to resolve German reparations issues by extending American loans to the German government so it could pay its war debt to France, as mandated by the Treaty of Versailles.

EVALUATE THE EVIDENCE

1. What does this painting reveal about the connections between works of art and the crises of postwar German society?
2. The artist Georg Grosz once wrote that his goal was to be "understood by everyone." How does he use relatively accessible symbols to convince viewers that his view of society and politics should be taken seriously?
3. How does the imagery of the painting express the artist's leftist or Communist worldview?

(© 2022 Estate of George Grosz/Licensed by VAGA at Artists Rights Society (ARS), NY/akg-images/Newscom)

Modern Dance   Dancers in Russian composer Igor Stravinsky's avant-garde ballet *The Rite of Spring* perform at the Paris premiere. The dissonant music, wild sets and costumes, and unpredictable dance movements shocked and insulted the audience, which rioted on the opening night in May 1913.
(Charles Gerschel/Lebrecht Music & Arts/Alamy Stock Photo)

With its biblical references, images of a ruined and wasted natural world, and general human incomprehension, Eliot (1888–1965) expressed the crisis of confidence that followed the First World War. The Czech writer Franz Kafka (1883–1924) likewise portrayed an incomprehensible, alienating world. Kafka's novels *The Trial* (1925) and *The Castle* (1926) are stories about helpless people crushed by inexplicably hostile forces, as is his famous novella *The Metamorphosis* (1915), in which the main character turns into a giant insect. The German-Jewish Kafka died young, at forty-one, and was spared the horror of seeing the world of his nightmares materialize in the Nazi state. In these and many other works, authors between the wars used new literary techniques and dark imagery to capture the anxiety of the modern age.

Modern Music

Developments in modern music paralleled those in art and literature. Composers and performers captured the emotional intensity and shock of modernism in radically experimental forms. The ballet *The Rite of Spring* by Russian composer Igor Stravinsky (1882–1971), for example, practically caused a riot when it was first performed in Paris in 1913. The

combination of pulsating rhythms and dissonant sounds from the orchestra pit with earthy representations of lovemaking by the strangely dressed dancers on the stage shocked audiences accustomed to traditional ballet.

After the First World War, when irrationality and violence had seemed to pervade human experience, modernism flourished in opera and ballet. One of the most powerful examples was the opera *Wozzeck*, by Alban Berg (1885–1935), first performed in Berlin in 1925. Blending a half-sung, half-spoken kind of dialogue with harsh, atonal music, *Wozzeck* is a gruesome tale of a soldier driven by inner terrors and vague suspicions of infidelity to murder his mistress.

Some composers turned their backs on long-established musical conventions. Just as abstract painters arranged lines and color but did not draw identifiable objects, so modern composers arranged sounds without creating recognizable harmonies. Led by Viennese composer Arnold Schönberg (SHURN-buhrg) (1874–1951), they abandoned traditional harmony and tonality. The musical notes in a given piece were no longer united and organized by a key; instead they were independent and unrelated. Schönberg's twelve-tone music of the 1920s arranged all twelve notes of the scale in an abstract mathematical pattern, or "tone row." This pattern sounded like no pattern at all to the ordinary listener and could be detected only by a highly trained eye studying the musical score. Accustomed to the harmonies of classical and romantic music, audiences generally resisted atonal music. Only after the Second World War did it begin to win acceptance.

How did consumer society change everyday life?

Fundamental innovations in the basic provision and consumption of goods and services accompanied the radical transformation of artistic and intellectual life. A range of new mass-produced objects, from telephones to vacuum cleaners, and the arrival of cinema and radio, heralded the first steps toward a consumer revolution that would be fully consolidated in the 1950s and 1960s.

Modern Mass Culture

The emerging consumer society of the 1920s is a good example of the way technological developments inform widespread social change. The arrival of a highly industrialized manufacturing system dedicated to mass-producing inexpensive goods, the establishment of efficient transportation systems that could bring these products to national markets, and the rise of professional advertising experts to sell them were all part of a revolution in the way everyday items were made, marketed, and used by ordinary people.

Contemporaries viewed the new mass culture as a distinctly modern aspect of everyday life. It seemed that consumer goods themselves were modernizing society by changing so many ingrained habits. Some people embraced the new ways; others worried that these changes threatened familiar values and precious traditions.

Critics had reason to worry. Mass-produced goods had a profound impact on the lives of ordinary people. Housework and private life were increasingly organized around an array of modern appliances, from electric ovens, washing machines, and refrigerators to telephones and radios. The aggressive marketing of fashionable clothing and personal care products, such as shampoo, perfume, and makeup, encouraged a cult of youthful "sex appeal." Advertisements increasingly linked individual attractiveness to the use of brand-name products. The mass production and marketing of automobiles and the rise of tourist agencies opened roads to increased mobility and travel.

Commercialized mass entertainment likewise prospered and began to dominate the way people spent their leisure time. Movies and radio thrilled millions. Professional sporting events drew throngs of fans. Thriving print media brought readers an astounding variety of newspapers, inexpensive books, and glossy illustrated magazines. Flashy restaurants, theatrical revues, and nightclubs competed for evening customers.

Department stores epitomized the emergence of consumer society. Already well established across Europe and the United States by the 1890s, they had become veritable temples of commerce by the 1920s. The typical store sold an enticing variety of products, including clothing, housewares, food, and spirits. Larger stores included travel bureaus, movie theaters, and refreshment stands. Aggressive advertising campaigns, youthful and attractive salespeople, and easy credit and return policies helped attract customers in droves.

The emergence of modern consumer culture both undermined and reinforced existing social differences. On one hand, consumerism helped democratize Western society. Since anyone with the means could purchase any item, consumer culture helped break down old social barriers based on class, region, and religion. Yet it also reinforced social differences. Manufacturers soon realized they could profit by marketing goods to specific groups. Catholics, for example, could purchase their own popular literature and inexpensive devotional items; young people eagerly bought the latest fashions marketed directly to them. In addition, the expense of many items meant that only the wealthy could purchase them. Automobiles and, in the 1920s, even vacuum cleaners cost so much that ownership became a status symbol.

The changes in women's lives were particularly striking. The new household items transformed how women performed housework. Advice literature of all kinds encouraged housewives to rush out and buy the latest appliances so they could "modernize" the home. Consumer culture brought growing public visibility to women, especially the young. Girls and young women worked behind the counters and shopped in the aisles of department stores, and they went out on the street alone in ways unthinkable in the nineteenth century.

Contemporaries spoke repeatedly about the new **"modern girl,"** an independent young woman who could vote and held a job, spent her salary on the latest fashions, applied makeup and smoked cigarettes, and used her sex appeal to charm any number of modern men. "The woman of yesterday" yearned for marriage and children and "honor[ed] the achievements of the 'good old days,'" wrote one German feminist in 1929.

■ **"modern girl"** The somewhat stereotypical image of the modern and independent working woman popular in the 1920s.

A Typical Café Scene in Berlin, 1924. (bpk, Bildagentur/Bildarchiv Preussischer Kulturbesitz/Art Resource, NY)

A German Perfume Advertisement, ca. 1925. (Lordprice Collection/Alamy Stock Photo)

A young woman enjoys a dessert at the Romanesque Café in Berlin in 1924. The independence of this "modern girl," wearing fashionable clothes with a revealing hemline and without a male escort, transgressed familiar gender roles and shocked and fascinated contemporaries. Images of the modern girl appeared in movies, illustrated magazines, and advertisements, such as this German poster promoting "this winter's perfume."

QUESTIONS FOR ANALYSIS

1. Why would the appearance and behavior of the "modern girl," as reflected in these images, challenge conventional understandings of women's gender roles?
2. Look closely at the images. How would you characterize the relationship between advertising, consumer goods, and individual behavior?
3. Did the emerging consumer society of the 1920s open doors to liberating behavior for women, or did it set new standards that limited women's options?

The "woman of today," she continued, "refuses to be regarded as a physically weak being . . . and seeks to support herself through gainful employment. . . . Her task is to clear the way for equal rights for women in all areas of life."[4]

Despite such enthusiasm, the modern girl was in some ways a stereotype, a product of marketing campaigns dedicated to selling goods. Few young women could afford to live up to this image, even if they did have jobs. Yet the changes in women's roles associated with the First World War and the emergence of consumer society did loosen traditional limits on women's behavior. (See "Viewpoints: The Modern Girl: Image or Reality?")

The emerging consumer culture generated a chorus of complaint from cultural critics of all stripes. On the left, socialist writers worried that its appeal undermined working-class radicalism, because mass culture created passive consumers rather than active, class-conscious revolutionaries. On the right, conservatives complained that money spent on frivolous consumer goods sapped the livelihood of industrious artisans and undermined proud national traditions. Religious leaders protested that modern consumerism encouraged rampant individualism and that greedy materialism was replacing spirituality. Many bemoaned the supposedly loose morals of the modern girl and fretted over the decline of traditional family values.

Despite such criticism — which continued after World War II — consumer society was here to stay. Ordinary people enjoyed the pleasures of mass consumption, and individual identities were tied ever more closely to modern mass-produced goods. Yet the Great Depression of 1929 soon made active participation in the new world of goods elusive. The promise of prosperity would only truly be realized during the economic boom that followed the Second World War.

The Appeal of Cinema

Nowhere was the influence of mass culture more evident than in the rapid growth of commercial entertainment, especially cinema and radio. Both became major industries in the interwar years, and an eager public enthusiastically embraced them, spending their leisure hours watching movies or listening to radio broadcasts. These mass media overshadowed and began to replace the traditional amusements of people in cities, and then in small towns and villages, changing familiar ways of life.

By the late 1870s experiments with "moving pictures" were taking place in Europe and the United States. In 1888 the Frenchman Louis le Prince took out the first patents on an early motion picture camera and projector. By 1910 American directors and business people had set up "movie factories," at first in the New York area and then in Los Angeles. Europeans were quick to follow. By 1914 small production companies had formed in Great Britain, France, Germany, and Italy, among others. World War I quickened the pace. National leaders realized that movies offered distraction to troops and citizens and served as an effective means of spreading propaganda. Audiences lined up to see *The Battle of the Somme*, a British film released in August 1916 that was frankly intended to encourage popular support for the war. (This film, which now seems quite primitive, can be seen on various YouTube pages.)

Cinema became a true mass medium in the 1920s, the golden age of silent film. The United States was a world leader, but European nations also established important national film industries. Germany's Universal Film Company (or UFA) was particularly renowned. In the massive Babelsberg Studios just outside Berlin, talented UFA directors produced classic Expressionist films such as *Nosferatu* (1922), a creepy vampire story, and *Metropolis* (1927), about a future society in the midst of a working-class revolt. Such films made use of cutting-edge production techniques, thrilling audiences with fast and slow motion, montage sequences, unsettling close-ups, and unusual dissolves.

Film making became big business on an international scale. Studios competed to place their movies on foreign screens, and European theater owners were sometimes forced to book whole blocks of American films to get the few pictures they really wanted. In response, European governments set quotas on the number of U.S. films they imported. By 1926 U.S. money was drawing German directors and stars to Hollywood and consolidating America's international domination. These practices put European producers at a disadvantage until "talkies" permitted a revival of national film industries in the 1930s, particularly in France.

Motion pictures would remain the central entertainment of the masses until after the Second World War and the rise of television. People flocked to the gigantic movie palaces built across Europe in the mid-1920s, splendid theaters that could seat thousands. There they viewed the latest features, which were reviewed by critics in newspapers and flashy illustrated magazines. Cinema audiences grew rapidly in the 1930s. In Great Britain in the late 1930s, one in every four adults went to the movies twice a week, and two in five went at least once a week. Audience numbers were similar in other countries.

As these numbers suggest, motion pictures could be powerful tools of indoctrination, especially in countries with dictatorial regimes. In the Soviet Union, Lenin encouraged the development of the movie industry, believing that the new medium was essential to the social and ideological transformation of the country. Beginning in the mid-1920s, a series of epic films, the most famous of which were directed by Sergei Eisenstein (1898–1948), brilliantly dramatized the Communist view of Russian history. In Nazi Germany, the film maker Leni Riefenstahl (REE-fuhn-shtahl) (1902–2003) directed a masterpiece of documentary propaganda, *Triumph of the Will*, based on the 1934 Nazi Party rally at Nuremberg. Riefenstahl combined stunning aerial photography with mass processions of young Nazi fanatics and images of joyful crowds welcoming Adolf Hitler. Her film, released in 1935, was a brilliant yet chilling documentary of the rise of Nazism.

The Arrival of Radio

Like film, radio became a full-blown mass medium in the 1920s. Experimental radio sets were first available in the 1880s; the work of Italian inventor Guglielmo Marconi (1874–1937) around 1900 and the development of the vacuum tube in 1904 made possible primitive transmissions of speech and music. But the first major public broadcasts of news and special events occurred only in the early 1920s, in Great Britain and the United States.

Every major country quickly established national broadcasting networks. In the United States such networks were privately owned and were financed by advertising, but in Europe the typical pattern was direct control by the government. In Great Britain, Parliament set up an independent public corporation, the British Broadcasting Corporation (BBC), supported by licensing fees. Whatever the institutional framework, radio enjoyed a meteoric growth in popularity. By the late 1930s more than three out of every four households in both democratic Great Britain and dictatorial Germany had at least one radio. (See "Thinking Like a Historian: The Radio Age," page 820.)

Like the movies, radio was well suited for political propaganda. Dictators such as Hitler and Italy's Benito Mussolini could reach enormous national audiences with their dramatic speeches. In democratic countries, politicians such as U.S. president Franklin Roosevelt and British prime minister Stanley Baldwin effectively used informal "fireside chats" to bolster their popularity.

What obstacles to lasting peace did European leaders face?

Arts and culture reflected the opportunities and crises of the modern age — and so did politics. The Versailles settlement had established a shaky truce to end World War I, not a solid postwar peace. In the 1920s, leaders faced a gigantic task as they sought to create a stable international order within the general context of social crisis, halting economic growth, and political turmoil.

Germany and the Western Powers

Germany was the key to lasting stability. Yet to Germans of all political parties, the Treaty of Versailles represented a harsh dictated peace, to be revised or repudiated as soon as possible. Germany still had the potential to become the strongest country in Europe, but its future remained uncertain. Moreover, with ominous implications, France and Great Britain did not see eye to eye on Germany.

Immediately after the war, the French struggled to implement the harsh elements in the Treaty of Versailles. Most of the war in the west had been fought on French soil, and the expected costs of reconstruction, as well as of repaying war debts to the United States, were staggering. Thus French politicians believed that massive reparations from Germany were vital for economic recovery. After having compromised with President Wilson only to be betrayed by America's failure to ratify the treaty, many French leaders saw strict implementation of all provisions of the Treaty of Versailles as France's last best hope.

Large reparation payments could hold Germany down indefinitely, ensuring French security.

The British soon felt differently. Before the war Germany had been Great Britain's second-best market in the world; after the war a healthy, prosperous Germany appeared to be essential to the British economy. Many Britons agreed with the analysis of the English economist John Maynard Keynes (1883–1946), who eloquently denounced the Treaty of Versailles in his book *The Economic Consequences of the Peace* (1919). According to Keynes, astronomical reparations and harsh economic measures would impoverish Germany, encourage Bolshevism, and increase economic hardship in all countries. Only a complete revision of the treaty could save Germany — and Europe. Keynes's influential critique engendered much public discussion and helped create sympathy for Germany in the English-speaking world.

In addition, British politicians were suspicious of France's expansive foreign policy and the French army — the largest in Europe, and authorized at Versailles to occupy the German Saarland until 1935. Since 1890 France had looked to Russia as a powerful ally against Germany. But with Russia hostile and Communist, and with Britain and the United States unwilling to make any firm commitments, France turned to the newly formed states of central Europe for diplomatic support. In 1921 France entered a mutual defense pact with Poland and associated itself closely with the so-called Little Entente, an alliance that joined Czechoslovakia, Romania, and Yugoslavia against defeated and bitter Hungary. French concerns with Germany increased when the German government signed the Treaty of Rapollo with Soviet Russia in 1922.

■ **Dawes Plan** War reparations agreement that reduced Germany's yearly payments, made payments dependent on economic growth, and granted large U.S. loans to promote recovery.

The treaty renounced war reparations and established diplomatic relations between the two countries. It also paved the way for secret military cooperation between the two, in violation of the Versailles treaties.

While French and British leaders drifted in different directions, the Allied commission created to determine German reparations completed its work. In April 1921 it announced that Germany had to pay the enormous sum of 132 billion gold marks ($33 billion) in annual installments of 2.5 billion gold marks. Facing possible occupation of more of its territory, the young German republic—generally known as the Weimar Republic—made its first payment in 1921. Then in 1922, wracked by rapid inflation and political assassinations and motivated by hostility and arrogance as well, German leaders announced their inability to pay more. They proposed a moratorium on reparations for three years, with the clear implication that thereafter the payments would be either drastically reduced or eliminated entirely.

The British were willing to accept a moratorium, but the French were not. Led by their tough-minded prime minister, Raymond Poincaré (1860–1934), they decided they had to either call Germany's bluff or see the entire peace settlement dissolve to France's great disadvantage. If the Germans refused to pay reparations, France would use military occupation to paralyze Germany and force it to accept the Treaty of Versailles. So, despite strong British protests, in early January 1923 French and Belgian armies moved out of the Rhineland and began to occupy the Ruhr district, the heartland of industrial Germany, creating the most serious international crisis of the 1920s.

Strengthened by a wave of German patriotism, the German government ordered the people of the Ruhr to stop working, a way to passively resist the French occupation. The coal mines and steel mills of the Ruhr fell silent, leaving 10 percent of Germany's population out of work. The French responded by sealing off the Ruhr and the Rhineland from the rest of Germany, letting in only enough food to prevent starvation. German public opinion was incensed when the French sent over forty thousand colonial troops from North and West Africa to control the territory. German propagandists labeled these troops the "black shame" and claimed that the African soldiers would brutalize civilians and assault German women. These racist attacks, though entirely unfounded, nonetheless intensified tensions between Germany and France.

By the summer of 1923 France and Germany were engaged in a great test of wills. French armies could not collect reparations from striking workers at gunpoint, but the occupation was paralyzing Germany and its economy. To support the workers and their employers, the German government began to print money to pay its bills, causing runaway inflation. Prices soared as German money rapidly lost all value. People went to the store with bags of banknotes; they returned home with handfuls of groceries. Catastrophic inflation cruelly mocked the old middle-class virtues of thrift, caution, and self-reliance as savings were wiped out. Many Germans felt betrayed. They hated and blamed the Western governments, their own government, big business, the Jews, and the Communists for their misfortune. Right-wing nationalists—including Adolf Hitler and the newly established Nazi Party—eagerly capitalized on the widespread discontent.

In August 1923, as the mark lost value and unrest spread throughout Germany, Gustav Stresemann (SHTRAY-zuh-mahn) (1878–1929) assumed leadership of the government. Stresemann tried compromise. He called off passive resistance in the Ruhr and in October agreed in principle to pay reparations, but asked for a re-examination of Germany's ability to pay. Poincaré accepted. His hard line had become unpopular in France, and it was hated in Britain and the United States. In addition, power in both Germany and France was passing to more moderate leaders who realized that continued confrontation was a destructive, no-win situation. Thus, after five long years of hostility and tension, culminating in a kind of undeclared war in the Ruhr in 1923, Germany and France both decided to try compromise. The British, and even the Americans, were willing to help. The first step was to reach an agreement on the reparations question.

French Occupation of the Ruhr, 1923–1925

Hope in Foreign Affairs

In 1924 an international committee of financial experts headed by American banker Charles G. Dawes met to re-examine German reparation payments from a broad perspective. The resulting **Dawes Plan** (1924) was accepted by France, Germany, and Britain. Germany's yearly reparation payments were reduced and linked to the level of German economic output. Germany would also receive large loans from the United States to promote economic recovery. In short, Germany would get private loans from the United States in order to pay reparations to France

The Radio Age

In the late 1920s and 1930s radio became a mass medium that reached millions of people around the world. How did the arrival of radio change the way Europeans and others experienced everyday life?

1 **John Reith, *Broadcast over Britain*, 1924.** In a spirited defense of public radio, published shortly after the BBC's first official broadcast, the corporation's founding director championed the potential of wireless broadcasting.

～ Broadcasting brings relaxation and interest to many homes where such things are at a premium. It does far more; it carries direct information on a hundred subjects to innumerable men and women who will after a short time be in a position to make up their own minds on many matters of vital moment, matters which formerly they had either to receive according to the dictated and partial versions and opinions of others, or to ignore altogether. . . .

As we conceive it, our responsibility is to carry into the greatest possible number of homes everything that is best in every department of human knowledge, endeavour and achievement, and to avoid the things which are, or may be hurtful. It is occasionally indicated to us that we are apparently setting out to give the public what we think they need—and not what they want, but few know what they want, and very few what they need. There is often no difference. . . .

I expect the day will come when, for those who wish it, in the home or office, the news of the world may be received in any quarter of the globe. . . .

Because we broadcast certain items with no permanent value, ethical or educational, it does not follow that we have failed in an ideal to transmit good things, and such as will tend to raise the general ethical or educational standard. There is no harm in trivial things; in themselves they may even be unquestionably beneficial for they may assist the more serious work by providing the measure of salt which seasons. . . .

The whole service which is conducted by wireless broadcasting may be taken as the expression of a new and better relationship between man and man. . . . The genius and the fool, the wealthy and the poor listen simultaneously, and to the same extent, and the satisfaction of the one may be as great as that of the other. . . . There need be no first and third class. . . .

Broadcasting may help to show that mankind is a unity and that the mighty heritage, material, moral, and spiritual, if meant for the good of any, is meant for the good of all, and this is conveyed in its operations.

2 ***The Broadcaster*, ca. 1925.** Radio transformed the way millions of listeners spent their leisure time and organized their households, and fan magazines like *The Broadcaster* helped broaden its appeal. As this cover illustration suggests, excited listeners would often install a radio set in a prominent location in the family living room.

(The Advertising Archives/Bridgeman Images)

ANALYZING THE EVIDENCE

1. What, according to director John Reith in Source 1, are the main goals of the BBC?
2. What do Sources 2–5 reveal about radio's impact on everyday life? Does this evidence help explain the larger impact of modern consumer culture on Western society?
3. How would listening to radio change the experience of a "traditional" Christmas (see Source 3)? Who is the target audience for this holiday broadcast?
4. Consider the figures in Source 5. Do these numbers accurately represent the number of listeners in the radio audience? Can historians use them to estimate the popularity of radio in the 1920s and 1930s?

3 **Christmas Day radio programming in western Germany, 1928.** By the late 1920s the radio audience in the Münster-Cologne-Aachen region could enjoy a full day of Christmas Day programming. (The schedule is lightly edited for clarity.)

Tuesday, 25 December

6:00   **Broadcast of the Christmas Mass from the [Protestant] Mother Church in Unterbarmen.** Community and choir singing, a Christmas sermon, and organ music by J. S. Bach.

9:00   **Ringing Church Bells from St. Gereon's Basilica, Cologne.**

9:05   **Catholic Morning Service.** A sermon on the "Christmas Message," with solo and choir performances of Christmas music.

11:00   **University Professor Dr. J. Verweyen: On the Origins of the Christmas Holiday.**

12:35   **Hanns Brauckmann, Christmas in the Holy Lands.**

2:40   **Pastor Dr. Girkon Soest: Christmas in the Fine Arts.**

3:30   **Children's Hour. "The Christ Child's Way Home."**

4:40   **Broadcast of the Glockenspiel Concert from St. John's Cathedral in Hertogenbosch [Holland].** Church and family Christmas carols.

5:40   **Christmas Songs.** A trio of vocalists sings "Oh Christmas Tree" and other carols.

7:00   **"Holy Night."** A Christmas legend by Ludwig Thoma recited in Upper Bavarian dialect with zither.

8:00   **Christmas Concert.** A variety of classical Christmas music.

Intermission: An Hour for the Betrothed. Wedding music by famous composers. [Note: It was customary for Germans to get engaged on Christmas Eve and Day.]

Until

1:00 A.M.   **Evening Music and Dance Music.** Waltz, foxtrot, slowfox, tango, and one-step ballroom dance music.

(akg-images/Newscom)

4 **Listening to the radio in a Romanian village, ca. 1935.** Radio took some time to penetrate Europe's less wealthy, rural areas. Eventually, however, broadcasting's transformative effects reached the European hinterlands.

5 **Official listening numbers, Germany, 1923–1938.** When Germans bought a radio, they were supposed to register it with state authorities and pay a small fee to support the national broadcasting system. This chart gives the number of radios registered in Germany from 1923 to 1938.

Number of Radios Registered in Germany, 1923–1938

Year	Number	Year	Number
1923	467	1931	3,509,509
1924	1,580	1932	3,981,000
1925	548,749	1933	4,307,722
1926	1,022,299	1934	5,052,607
1927	1,376,564	1935	6,142,921
1928	2,009,842	1936	7,192,000
1929	2,635,567	1937	8,167,975
1930	3,066,682	1938	9,087,454

PUTTING IT ALL TOGETHER

According to BBC director John Reith, radio broadcasts embodied a "new and better relationship between man and man." Radio, for Reith, had the potential to level social differences by bringing the "material, moral, and spiritual" heritage of Western society to broad groups of ordinary people. Using the sources above, along with what you have learned in class and in this chapter, write a short essay explaining whether or not you agree. Did radio fulfill its democratic promise?

Sources: (1) John Reith, *Broadcast over Britain* (London: Hodder and Stoughton, 1924), pp. 19, 34, 212–213, 217–218; (3) "Die Ründfunkwoche," *Die Sendung*, December 21, 1928, p. 12, translated by Joe Perry; (5) Kate Lacey, *Feminine Frequencies: Gender, German Radio, and the Public Sphere, 1923–1945* (Ann Arbor: University of Michigan Press, 1996), p. 247.

Hyperinflation in Germany   Catastrophic inflation shattered the German economy in the early 1920s. Here a woman fires up her stove with paper money because it was more cost-efficient to burn banknotes than use them to purchase coal. In 1923, at the height of the inflation, a U.S. dollar was worth 800 million German marks. (Everett Collection Inc./Alamy Stock Photo)

and Britain, thus enabling those countries to repay the large war debts they owed the United States.

This circular flow of international payments was complicated and risky, but for a while it worked. With continual inflows of American capital, the German republic experienced a shaky economic recovery. Germany paid about $1.3 billion in reparations in 1927 and 1928, enabling France and Britain to repay the United States. In this way the Americans belatedly played a part in the general settlement that, though far from ideal, facilitated precarious economic growth in the mid-1920s.

A political settlement accompanied the economic accords. In 1925 the leaders of Europe signed a number of agreements at Locarno, Switzerland. Germany

and France solemnly pledged to accept their common border, and both Britain and Italy agreed to fight either France or Germany if one invaded the other. Stresemann reluctantly agreed to settle boundary disputes with Poland and Czechoslovakia by peaceful means, although he did not agree on permanent borders to Germany's east. In response, France reaffirmed its pledge of military aid to those countries if Germany attacked them. The refusal to settle Germany's eastern borders angered the Poles, and though the "spirit of Locarno" lent some hope to those seeking international stability, political tensions deepened in central Europe.

Other developments suggested possibilities for international peace. In 1926 Germany joined the League of Nations, and in 1928 fifteen countries signed the Kellogg-Briand Pact, initiated by French prime minister Aristide Briand and U.S. secretary of state Frank B. Kellogg. The signing states agreed to "renounce [war] as an instrument of international policy" and to settle international disputes peacefully. The pact made no provisions for disciplinary action in case war actually broke out and would not prevent the arrival of the Second World War in 1939. In the late 1920s, however, it fostered a cautious optimism and encouraged the hope that the United States would accept its responsibilities as a great world power by contributing to European stability.

Hope in Democratic Government

Domestic politics also offered reason to hope. During the occupation of the Ruhr and the great inflation, republican government in Germany had appeared on the verge of collapse. In 1923 Communists momentarily entered provincial governments, and in November an obscure politician named Adolf Hitler leaped onto a table in a beer hall in Munich and proclaimed a "national socialist revolution." But the young republican government easily crushed Hitler's Beer Hall "Putsch" (a violent attempt to overthrow a government), and he was sentenced to a short term in prison. In the late 1920s liberal democracy seemed to take root in Weimar Germany. Elections were held regularly, and republican democracy appeared to have growing support among a majority of Germans. A new currency was established, and the economy stabilized. The moderate businessmen who tended to dominate the various German coalition governments were convinced that economic prosperity demanded good relations with the Western powers, and they supported parliamentary government at home.

Sharp political divisions remained, however. Throughout the 1920s the Nazi Party attracted support from fanatical anti-Semites, ultranationalists, and disgruntled veterans. Many unrepentant monarchists supported the far right. On the left, members of Germany's recently formed Communist Party were noisy and active. The Communists, directed from Moscow, reserved their greatest hatred and sharpest barbs for their cousins the Social Democrats, whom they accused of betraying the revolution. Though the working class was divided, a majority supported the nonrevolutionary Social Democrats.

The situation in France was similar to that in Germany. Communists and Socialists battled for workers' support. After 1924 the democratically elected government rested mainly in the hands of coalitions of moderates, with business interests well represented. France's great accomplishment was the rapid rebuilding of its war-torn northeastern region. The expense of this undertaking led, however, to a large deficit and substantial inflation. By early 1926 the franc had fallen to 10 percent of its prewar value, causing a severe crisis. Poincaré was recalled to office, while Briand remained minister for foreign affairs. Poincaré slashed spending and raised taxes, restoring confidence in the economy. The franc was stabilized at about one-fifth of its prewar value, and the economy remained fairly stable until 1930.

Britain, too, faced challenges after 1920. The great problem was unemployment. In June 1921 almost 2.2 million people — or 23 percent of the labor force — were out of work, and throughout the 1920s unemployment hovered around 12 percent, leading to a massive general strike in 1926. Yet the state provided unemployment benefits and supplemented the

payments with subsidized housing, medical aid, and increased old-age pensions. These and other measures kept living standards from seriously declining, helped moderate class tensions, and pointed the way toward the welfare state Britain would establish after World War II.

Relative social harmony was accompanied by the rise of the Labour Party, founded in 1900 as a determined champion of greater social equality and the working class. Committed to the kind of moderate revisionist socialism that had emerged before World War I, the Labour Party replaced the Liberal Party as the main opposition to the Conservatives. This shift reflected the decline of old liberal ideals of competitive capitalism, limited government control, and individual responsibility. In 1924 and from 1929 to 1931, the Labour Party under Ramsay MacDonald (1866–1937) governed the country with the support of the smaller Liberal Party. Yet Labour moved toward socialism gradually and democratically, so as not to antagonize the middle classes.

The British Conservatives showed the same compromising spirit on social issues. In 1922, after a bitter guerrilla war, Britain granted southern, Catholic Ireland full autonomy, thereby removing a key source of prewar friction. Despite conflicts such as the 1926 strike by hard-pressed coal miners, which led to an unsuccessful general strike, social unrest in Britain was limited in the 1920s and 1930s. Developments in both international relations and the domestic politics of the leading democracies across western Europe gave some cause for optimism in the late 1920s.

What were the causes and consequences of the Great Depression?

This fragile optimism was short-lived. Beginning in 1929, a massive economic downturn struck the entire world with ever-greater intensity. Recovery was slow and uneven, and contemporaries labeled the economic crisis the **Great Depression**, to emphasize its severity and duration. Only with the Second World War did the depression retreat in much of the world. The prolonged economic collapse shattered the fragile political stability of the mid-1920s and encouraged the rise of extremists on both ends of the political spectrum.

The Economic Crisis

Though economic activity was already declining moderately in many countries by early 1929, the crash of the stock market in the United States in October of that year initiated a worldwide crisis. The U.S.

economy had prospered in the late 1920s, but there were large inequalities in income and a serious imbalance between actual business investment and stock market speculation. Thus net investment — in factories, farms, equipment, and the like — actually fell from $3.5 billion in 1925 to $3.2 billion in 1929. In the same years, as money flooded into stocks, the value of shares traded on the exchanges soared from $27 billion to $87 billion. Such inflated prices should have raised serious concerns about economic solvency, but even experts failed to predict the looming collapse.

This stock market boom — or "bubble" in today's language — was built on borrowed money. Many wealthy investors, speculators, and people of modest means bought stocks by paying only a small

■ **Great Depression** A worldwide economic depression from 1929 through 1939, unique in its severity and duration and with slow and uneven recovery.

fraction of the total purchase price and borrowing the remainder from their stockbrokers. Such buying "on margin" was extremely risky. When prices started falling in 1929, the hard-pressed margin buyers had to either put up more money, which was often impossible, or sell their shares to pay off their brokers. Thousands of people started selling all at once. The result was a financial panic. Countless investors and speculators were wiped out in a matter of days or weeks.

The consequences were swift and severe. Stripped of wealth and confidence, battered investors and their fellow citizens started buying fewer goods. Prices fell, production began to slow down, and unemployment began to rise. Soon the entire U.S. economy was caught in a spiraling decline.

The financial panic triggered an international financial crisis. Throughout the 1920s American bankers and investors had lent large amounts of capital to many countries. Once the panic broke, U.S. bankers began recalling the loans they had made to foreign businesses. Gold reserves began to flow rapidly out of European countries, particularly Germany and Austria, toward the United States. It became very hard for European businesses to borrow money, and panicky Europeans began to withdraw their savings from banks. These banking problems eventually led to the crash of the largest bank in Austria in 1931 and then to general financial chaos. The recall of loans by American bankers also accelerated a collapse in world prices when businesses dumped industrial goods and agricultural commodities in a frantic attempt to get cash to pay their loans.

The financial crisis led to a general crisis of production: between 1929 and 1933 world output of goods fell by an estimated 38 percent. As this happened, each country turned inward and tried to manage the crisis alone. In 1931, for example, Britain went off the gold standard, refusing to convert banknotes into gold, and reduced the value of its money. Britain's goal was to make its goods cheaper and therefore more salable in the world market. But more than twenty other nations, including the United States in 1934, also went off the gold standard, so few countries gained a real advantage from this step—though Britain was an exception. Similarly, country after country followed the example of the United States when in 1930 it raised protective tariffs to their

highest levels ever in an attempt to preserve shrinking national markets for domestic producers. Such actions further limited international trade. Within this context of fragmented and destructive economic nationalism, a recovery did not begin until 1933, and it was a halting one at that.

Although opinions differ, two factors probably best explain the relentless slide to the bottom from 1929 to early 1933. First, the international economy lacked leadership able to maintain stability when the crisis came. Neither Britain nor the United States—the world's economic leaders at the time—successfully stabilized the international economic system in 1929. The American decisions to cut back on international lending and erect high tariffs, as we have seen, had damaging ripple effects.

The second factor was poor national economic policy in almost every country. Governments generally cut their budgets when they should have raised spending and accepted large deficits in order to stimulate their economies. After World War II, this "counter-cyclical policy," advocated by John Maynard Keynes, became a well-established weapon against downturn and depression. But in the 1930s orthodox economists who believed balanced budgets to be the key to economic growth generally regarded Keynes's prescription with horror.

Mass Unemployment

The lack of large-scale government spending contributed to the rise of mass unemployment. As the financial crisis led to production cuts, workers lost their jobs and had little money to buy goods. In Britain, where unemployment had averaged 12 percent in the 1920s, it averaged more than 18 percent between 1930 and 1935. Far worse was the case of Germany, where in 1932 one in every three workers was jobless. In the United States, unemployment had averaged only 5 percent in the 1920s. In 1933 it soared to about 30 percent: almost 13 million people were out of work (Map 26.1).

Mass unemployment intensified existing social problems. Poverty increased dramatically, although in most countries unemployed workers generally received some kind of meager unemployment

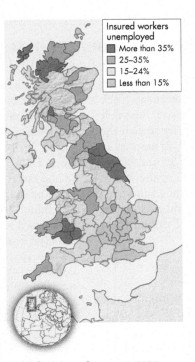

Insured workers unemployed
- More than 35%
- 25–35%
- 15–24%
- Less than 15%

British Unemployment, 1932

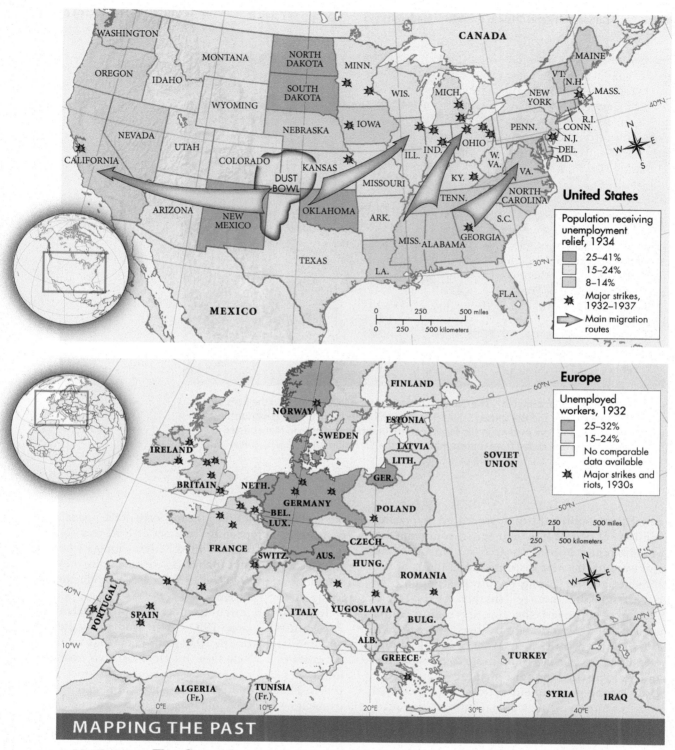

MAPPING THE PAST

MAP 26.1 The Great Depression in the United States and Europe, 1929–1939

These maps show that unemployment was high almost everywhere but that national and regional differences were also substantial.

ANALYZING THE MAP Which European countries had the highest rate of unemployment? How do the numbers of people on unemployment relief in the United States compare to the percentage of unemployed workers in Europe? How do you account for those differences?

CONNECTIONS What tactics of reform and recovery did European nations use to combat the deprivations of the Great Depression? How did events and government policies associated with the Great Depression in the United States contribute to economic problems in Europe?

Unemployment in Manchester   The Great Depression of the 1930s disrupted the lives of millions across Europe and the United States. The frustration and pain of being without work and "on the dole" are evident in the faces of these unemployed men in Manchester, England, receiving free coffee from representatives of the Salvation Army. (Photo by Staff/Mirrorpix/ Getty Images)

benefits or public aid that prevented starvation. Millions of people lost their spirit, condemned to an apparently hopeless search for work. Homes and ways of life were disrupted in millions of personal tragedies. Young people postponed marriages, and birthrates fell sharply. As poverty or the threat of poverty became a grinding reality, cases of suicide and mental illness increased. In 1932 a union official in Manchester, England, called on city officials to do more to provide work and warned that "hungry men are angry men."[5] Only strong government action could deal with mass unemployment, a social powder keg ready to explode.

The New Deal in the United States

The Great Depression and the government response to it marked a major turning point in U.S. history. President Herbert Hoover (U.S. pres. 1929–1933) and his administration initially reacted to the stock market crash and economic decline with dogged optimism

but limited action. When the full force of the financial crisis struck Europe in the summer of 1931 and boomeranged back to the United States, people's worst fears became reality. Banks failed; unemployment soared. Between 1929 and 1932 industrial production fell by about 50 percent.

In these dire circumstances, Franklin Delano Roosevelt (U.S. pres. 1933–1945) won a landslide presidential victory in 1932 with grand but vague promises of a "New Deal for the forgotten man." Roosevelt's goal was to reform capitalism in order to save it. Though Roosevelt rejected socialism and government ownership of industry, he advocated forceful government intervention in the economy and instituted a broad range of government-supported social programs designed to stimulate the economy and provide jobs.

In the United States, innovative federal programs promoted agricultural recovery, a top priority. Almost half of the U.S. population still lived in rural areas, and the depression hit farmers hard. Roosevelt took the United States off the gold standard and devalued the dollar in an effort to rescue farmers. The Agricultural Adjustment Act of 1933 aimed at raising prices — and thus farm income — by limiting

■ **Works Progress Administration (WPA)** An American government agency, designed as a massive public jobs program, established in 1935 as part of Roosevelt's New Deal.

agricultural production. These measures worked for a while, and in 1936 farmers repaid Roosevelt with overwhelming support in his re-election campaign.

The most ambitious attempt to control and plan the economy was the National Recovery Administration (NRA). Intended to reduce competition among industries by setting minimum prices and wages, the NRA broke with the cherished American tradition of free competition. Though participation was voluntary, the NRA aroused conflicts among business people, consumers, and bureaucrats and never worked well. The program was abandoned when declared unconstitutional by the Supreme Court in 1935.

Roosevelt and his advisers then attacked the key problem of mass unemployment. The federal government accepted the responsibility of employing as many people as financially possible. New agencies like the **Works Progress Administration (WPA)**, set up in 1935, were created to undertake a vast range of projects. One-fifth of the entire U.S. labor force worked for the WPA at some point in the 1930s, constructing public buildings, bridges, and highways. The WPA was enormously popular, and the opportunity of taking a government job helped check the threat of social revolution in the United States.

In 1935 the U.S. government also established a national social security system with old-age pensions and unemployment benefits. The National Labor Relations Act of 1935 gave union organizers the green light by guaranteeing rights of collective bargaining. Union membership more than doubled from 4 million in 1935 to 9 million in 1940. In general, between 1935 and 1938 government rulings and social reforms tried to help ordinary people and chipped away at the privileges of the wealthy.

Programs like the WPA were part of the New Deal's fundamental commitment to use the federal government to provide relief welfare for all Americans. This commitment marked a profound shift from the traditional stress on family support and community responsibility. Embraced by a large majority in the 1930s, this shift in attitudes proved to be one of the New Deal's most enduring legacies.

Despite undeniable accomplishments in social reform, the New Deal was only partly successful in responding to the Great Depression. At the height of the recovery in May 1937, 7 million workers were still unemployed—better than the high of about 13 million in 1933 but way beyond the numbers from the 1920s. The economic situation then worsened seriously in the recession of 1937 and 1938, and unemployment had risen to a staggering 10 million when

Oslo Breakfast   Scandinavian Social Democrats championed cooperation and practical welfare measures, playing down strident left-wing rhetoric and theories of class conflict. The "Oslo Breakfast" program portrayed in this pamphlet from the mid-1930s exemplified the Scandinavian approach. It provided every schoolchild in the Norwegian capital with a good breakfast free of charge. (Courtesy, Directorate for Health and Social Affairs, Oslo)

war broke out in Europe in September 1939. The New Deal never pulled the United States out of the depression; it took the government spending associated with the Second World War to do that.

The Scandinavian Response to the Depression

Of all the Western democracies, the Scandinavian countries under Social Democratic leadership responded most successfully to the challenge of the Great Depression. Having grown steadily in the late nineteenth century, the Social Democrats had become the largest political party in Sweden and then in Norway after the First World War. In the 1920s they passed important social reform legislation that benefited both farmers and workers and developed a unique kind of socialism. Flexible and nonrevolutionary, Scandinavian socialism grew out of a strong tradition of cooperative community action. Even before 1900 Scandinavian agricultural cooperatives had shown how individual peasant families could join together for everyone's benefit. Labor leaders and capitalists were also inclined to cooperate with one another.

When the economic crisis struck in 1929, socialist governments in Scandinavia built on this pattern of cooperative social action. Sweden in particular pioneered in the use of large-scale deficits to finance public works and thereby maintain production and employment. In ways that paralleled some aspects of

Roosevelt's New Deal, Scandinavian governments also increased public benefit programs such as old-age pensions, unemployment insurance, subsidized housing, and maternity allowances. All this spending required a large bureaucracy and high taxes, first on the rich and then on practically everyone. Yet both private and cooperative enterprise thrived, as did democracy. Some observers saw Scandinavia's welfare socialism as an appealing middle way between sick capitalism and cruel communism or fascism.

Recovery and Reform in Britain and France

In Britain, MacDonald's Labour government and then, after 1931, the Conservative-dominated coalition government followed orthodox economic theory. The budget was balanced, spending was tightly controlled, and unemployed workers received barely enough welfare to live. Nevertheless, the economy recovered considerably after 1932. By 1937 total production was about 20 percent higher than in 1929. In fact, for Britain the years after 1932 were actually somewhat better than the 1920s had been, the opposite of the situation in the United States and France.

This good but by no means brilliant performance reflected the gradual reorientation of the British economy. After going off the gold standard in 1931 and establishing protective tariffs in 1932, Britain concentrated increasingly on the national, rather than the international, market. The old export industries of the Industrial Revolution, such as textiles and coal, continued to decline, but new industries, such as automobiles and electrical appliances, grew in response to demand at home. Moreover, low interest rates encouraged a housing boom. By the end of the decade, there were highly visible differences between the old, depressed industrial areas of the north and the new, growing areas of the south.

Because France was relatively less industrialized and thus more isolated from the world economy, the Great Depression came to it late. But once the depression hit France, it persisted. Decline was steady until 1935, and a short-lived recovery never brought production or employment back up to predepression levels.

Economic stagnation both reflected and heightened an ongoing political crisis. The French parliament was made up of many political parties that could never cooperate for long. While divisions between the

Socialist and Communist Parties undermined any successful leadership from the left, French Fascist organizations agitated against parliamentary democracy and turned to Mussolini's Italy and Hitler's Germany for inspiration. In 1933 alone, for example, five coalition cabinets formed and fell in rapid succession. In February 1934 a loose coalition of right-wing groups rioted in Paris and threatened to take over the republic. Moderate republicanism was weakened by attacks from both sides.

The February riot encouraged politicians on the left to join forces in defense of a democratic reform program. Frightened by the growing strength of the Fascists at home and abroad, and encouraged by a new line from Moscow that encouraged Socialists and Communists to join together to face the Fascist threat, the French Communist and Socialist Parties formed an alliance — the **Popular Front** — for the national elections of May 1936. Their clear victory reflected the trend toward polarization. The number of Communists in the parliament jumped dramatically from 10 to 72, while the Socialists, led by Léon Blum, became the strongest party in France, with 146 seats. The Radicals — who were actually quite moderate — slipped badly, and the conservatives lost ground to the far right.

In the next few months, Blum's Popular Front government made the first and only real attempt to deal with the social and economic problems of the 1930s in France. Inspired by Roosevelt's New Deal, it encouraged the union movement and launched a far-reaching program of social reform, complete with paid vacations and a forty-hour workweek. Supported by workers and the lower middle class, these measures were quickly sabotaged by rapid inflation and accusations of revolution from Fascists and frightened conservatives. Wealthy people sneaked their money out of the country, labor unrest grew, and France entered a severe financial crisis. Blum was forced to announce a "breathing spell" in social reform.

Political polarization in France was encouraged by the Spanish Civil War (1936–1939), during which authoritarian Fascist rebels overthrew the democratically elected republican government. French Communists demanded that the government support the Spanish republicans, while many French conservatives would gladly have joined Hitler and Mussolini in aiding the Spanish Fascists. Extremism grew, and France itself was within sight of civil war. Blum was forced to resign in June 1937, and the Popular Front quickly collapsed. An anxious and divided France drifted aimlessly once again, preoccupied by Hitler and German rearmament.

■ **Popular Front** A short-lived New Deal–inspired alliance in France, led by Léon Blum, that encouraged the union movement and launched a far-reaching program of social reform.

NOTES

1. G. Greene, *Another Mexico* (New York: Viking Press, 1939), p. 3.
2. C. E. Jeanneret-Gris (Le Corbusier), *Towards a New Architecture* (London: J. Rodker, 1931), p. 15.
3. From *The Waste Land* by T. S. Eliot.
4. E. Herrmann, *This Is the New Woman* (1929), quoted in *The Weimar Republic Sourcebook*, ed. A. Kaes, M. Jay, and E.

Dimendberg (Berkeley: University of California Press, 1994), pp. 206–208.
5. Quoted in S. B. Clough et al., eds., *Economic History of Europe: Twentieth Century* (New York: Harper & Row, 1968), pp. 243–245.
6. S. Freud, *Civilization and Its Discontents* (New York: W. W. Norton, 1961), p. 112.

LOOKING BACK LOOKING AHEAD

The decades before and especially after World War I brought intense intellectual and cultural innovation. The results were both richly productive and sometimes deeply disturbing. From T. S. Eliot's poem *The Waste Land* to Einstein's theory of special relativity to the sleek glass and steel buildings of the Bauhaus, the intellectual products of the time stand among the highest achievements of Western arts and sciences. At the same time, mass culture, embodied in cinema, radio, and an emerging consumer society, transformed everyday life. Yet the modern vision was often bleak and cold. Modern art and consumer society alike challenged traditional values, contributing to feelings of disorientation and pessimism that had begun late in the nineteenth century and were exacerbated by the searing events of the war. The situation was worsened by ongoing political and economic turmoil. The Treaty of Versailles had failed to create a lasting peace or resolve the question of Germany's role in Europe. The Great Depression revealed the fragility of the world economic system and cast millions out of work. In the end, perhaps, the era's intellectual achievements and the overall sense of crisis were closely related.

Sigmund Freud captured the general mood of gloom and foreboding in 1930. "Men have gained control over the forces of nature to such an extent that . . . they would have no difficulty in exterminating one another to the last man," he wrote. "They know this, and hence comes a large part of their current unrest, their unhappiness and their mood of anxiety."[6] Freud's dark words reflected the extraordinary human costs of World War I and the horrific power of modern weaponry. They also expressed his despair over the growing popularity of repressive dictatorial regimes. During the interwar years, many European nations — including Italy, Germany, Spain, Poland, Portugal, Austria, and Hungary — would fall one by one to authoritarian or Fascist dictatorships, succumbing to the temptations of totalitarianism. Liberal democracy was severely weakened and European stability was threatened by the radical programs of Soviet Communists on the left and Fascists on the right. Freud uncannily predicted the great conflict to come.

Make Connections

Think about the larger developments and continuities within and across chapters.

1. How did trends in politics, economics, culture, and the arts and sciences come together to create a general sense of crisis but also opportunity in the 1920s and 1930s?

2. To what extent did the problems of the 1920s and 1930s have roots in the First World War (Chapter 25)?

3. What made modern art and intellectual thought "modern"?

26   REVIEW & EXPLORE

Identify Key Terms

Identify and explain the significance of each item below.

logical positivism (p. 803)

existentialism (p. 804)

theory of special relativity (p. 806)

id, ego, and superego (p. 807)

modernism (p. 809)

functionalism (p. 809)

Bauhaus (p. 809)

Dadaism (p. 811)

stream-of-consciousness technique (p. 812)

"modern girl" (p. 815)

Dawes Plan (p. 819)

Great Depression (p. 823)

Works Progress Administration (WPA) (p. 827)

Popular Front (p. 828)

Review the Main Ideas

Answer the section heading questions from the chapter.

1. How did intellectual developments reflect the ambiguities of modernity? (p. 802)

2. How did modernism revolutionize Western culture? (p. 809)

3. How did consumer society change everyday life? (p. 815)

4. What obstacles to lasting peace did European leaders face? (p. 818)

5. What were the causes and consequences of the Great Depression? (p. 823)

Suggested Resources

BOOKS

- Brown, Frederick. *The Embrace of Unreason: France, 1914–1940.* 2014. A fast-paced account of culture and politics in France during World War I and the interwar period that focuses on avant-garde culture and the emergence of French fascism.

- Burrow, J. W. *The Crisis of Reason: European Thought, 1848–1914.* 2002. A rewarding intellectual history.

- Durozoi, Gerard, and Vincent Bouvet. *Paris Between the Wars, 1919–1939: Art, Life, and Culture.* 2010. A cultural history of the Parisian avant-garde in a defining period and place for Western art.

- Eksteins, Modris. *Rites of Spring: The Great War and the Birth of the Modern Age.* 1989. A penetrating analysis of the links between World War I and modern culture and politics.

- Gay, Peter. *Modernism: The Lure of Heresy.* 2008. An encyclopedic compendium by a renowned cultural

historian that covers modernism in arts and culture from the mid-nineteenth century to the 1960s.

- Jackson, Julian. *The Popular Front in France: Defending Democracy, 1934–38.* 1990. Explores the rise and fall of the political, social, and cultural aspects of the Popular Front.

- Mazower, Mark. *Dark Continent: Europe's Twentieth Century.* 2000. A sophisticated survey that pays close attention to the crises of the interwar era.

- Rothermund, Dietmar. *The Global Impact of the Great Depression, 1929–1939.* 1996. A compact account that examines the causes and consequences of the Great Depression and covers events in the United States, Europe, Asia, and Latin America.

- Slater, Don. *Consumer Culture and Modernity.* 1997. An informative introduction to scholarly interpretations of consumer society.

- Weinbaum, Alys Eve, et al., eds. *The Modern Girl Around the World: Consumption, Modernity, and Globalization*. 2008. A collection of essays on how the "modern girl" of the 1920s and 1930s challenged conventions in major cities across the globe.

- Weitz, Eric D. *Weimar Germany: Promise and Tragedy*. 2007. A thorough exploration of modern art, culture, and politics in Weimar Germany.

MEDIA

- *The Artist* (Michel Hazanavicius, 2011). A romantic comedy film about two actors who must grapple with the end of the silent film era and the emergence of the talkies. Winner of the 2012 Academy Award for Best Picture.

- *Un Chien Andalou* (Luis Buñuel, 1929). Written by Buñuel and his Surrealist collaborator Salvador Dalí, this short silent film is a Surrealist classic that seems to portray the Freudian, dreamlike fantasies of a young man. The sixteen-minute film is available free online at several websites.

- *The Grapes of Wrath* (John Ford, 1940). Set in the United States during the 1930s, this famous film adaptation of John Steinbeck's novel shows the suffering of a family displaced by the Great Depression.

- *Internet Encyclopedia of Philosophy: Friedrich Nietzsche*. Provides a look at the life and theories of Friedrich Nietzsche. **www.iep.utm.edu/nietzsch**

- *Internet Encyclopedia of Philosophy: Sigmund Freud*. Examines the life and theories of Sigmund Freud. **www.iep.utm.edu/freud**

- *Metropolis* (Fritz Lang, 1927). Famous for its early use of special effects, this silent sci-fi classic film from UFA studios in Berlin portrays a working-class revolution in a city of the future.

- *Modernism: Searching for Utopia*. The Victoria and Albert Museum of Art and Design offers an overview of modernist experimentation and links to primary and secondary sources, focused on modernism in material culture, the decorative arts, and architecture. **www.vam.ac.uk/content/articles/m/modernism/**

- *Picasso and Braque Go to the Movies* (Arne Glimcher, 2010). This documentary film depicts the influence of early film making on modern art — especially Cubism.

- *The Rules of the Game* (Jean Renoir, 1939). A favorite of cinema buffs, this dark comedy portrays the banality and corruption of the French aristocracy and subtly anticipates the brutality of the Second World War.

- *Triumph of the Will* (Leni Riefenstahl, 1935). A chilling Nazi propaganda film that covers the 1934 Nuremberg rally and demonstrates the new political possibilities of the mass media.

27

Dictatorships and the Second World War

1919–1945

The intense wave of artistic and cultural innovation in the 1920s and 1930s, which shook the foundations of Western thought, was paralleled by radical developments in the world of politics. Totalitarian regimes took power in the Communist Soviet Union, Fascist Italy, and Nazi Germany, where they practiced a dynamic but ruthless tyranny. On the eve of the Second World War, popularly elected governments in Europe survived only in Great Britain, France, Czechoslovakia, the Low Countries, Scandinavia, and Switzerland.

Totalitarian regimes promised to greatly improve the lives of ordinary citizens by pursuing radical utopian schemes of social engineering. Their attempts to revolutionize state and society went far beyond traditional forms of conservative authoritarianism, and their drive for territorial expansion threatened neighboring nations. The human costs of these policies were appalling. Millions died as Stalin forced communism on the Soviet Union in the 1930s. Attempts to build a "racially pure" New Order in Europe by Hitler's Nazi Germany led to the deaths of tens of millions more in World War II and the Holocaust, a scale of destruction far beyond that of World War I. ■

CHAPTER PREVIEW

- **What were the most important characteristics of Communist and Fascist ideologies?**

- **How did Stalinism transform state and society in the Soviet Union?**

- **What kind of government did Mussolini establish in Italy?**

- **What policies did Nazi Germany pursue, and why did they appeal to ordinary Germans?**

- **What explains the success and then defeat of Germany and Japan during World War II?**

Forced Labor at Auschwitz Concentration Camp
This rough painting by an anonymous inmate of the Auschwitz-Birkenau Nazi concentration camp is preserved on the ceiling of a camp barracks. Guarded by SS officers, prisoners labor on a drainage canal under horrific conditions, while two carry a dead worker off the field. (De Agostini/ Getty Images)

What were the most important characteristics of Communist and Fascist ideologies?

The end of World War I and the postwar treaties brought drastic changes to European politics. Age-old monarchies and empires crumbled, replaced by the nation-state, and professional politicians and bureaucracies replaced kings and royal courts. Political systems across Europe ranged from liberal democracy to conservative authoritarianism. Yet the crises of the interwar years brought something new: radical dictatorships in the Communist Soviet Union and in Fascist Italy and Nazi Germany that sought the total reconstruction of society. (National Socialism in Germany, also called Nazism, was one variant of the larger Fascist movement.) Communist and Fascist political parties were also established in all major European nations, where they challenged democratic rule. The great midcentury conflict between communism and fascism was one of the key reasons for the disaster of World War II, and it had a chilling precursor in the Spanish Civil War.

Conservative Authoritarianism and Radical Totalitarian Dictatorships

Governments based on conservative authoritarianism had deep roots in the early modern era. After the First World War new forms of modern authoritarianism emerged, based on strongman leaders supported by large state bureaucracies, especially in eastern Europe. In Hungary, for example, the nationalist Miklós Horthy took control of the government in 1920. Hungary retained a popularly elected parliament, but Horthy and his conservative administration retained sweeping powers. In Poland, postwar democratic government ended in 1926 when a coup led by statesman and general Józef Piłsudski established the one-party Sanacja (san-NATS-ya) regime. These authoritarian regimes pursued determined right-wing nationalist policies, yet the radical Communist and Fascist dictatorships that took power in the Soviet Union, Italy, and Germany intervened even more aggressively in social life and foreign affairs.

Some scholars use the term **totalitarianism** to describe these radical dictatorships, which made unprecedented "total claims" on the beliefs and behavior of their citizens. The totalitarian model emphasizes the characteristics that Fascist and Communist dictatorships had in common. One-party totalitarian states used violent political repression and intense propaganda to gain complete power. The state aimed to dominate the economic, social, intellectual, and cultural aspects of people's lives.

Most historians agree that totalitarianism drew on the experience of total war in 1914 to 1918 (see

Chapter 25). World War I required state governments to limit individual liberties and intervene in the economy in order to achieve one supreme objective: victory. Totalitarian leaders drew inspiration from this example. They greatly expanded the power of the state in pursuit of social control and showed a callous disregard for human life.

Communist and Fascist dictatorships shared other characteristics. Both rejected parliamentary government and liberal values. Classical liberals (see "Liberalism and the Middle Class" in Chapter 21) sought to limit the power of the state and protect individual rights. Totalitarians believed that individualism undermined national unity, and they rejected democracy in favor of one-party political systems.

A charismatic leader typically dominated the totalitarian state — Joseph Stalin in the Soviet Union, Benito Mussolini in Italy, Adolf Hitler in Germany. All three led political parties of a new kind, dedicated to promoting idealized visions of collective harmony. They used force and terror to intimidate and destroy political opponents and pursued policies of imperial expansion to exploit other lands. They censored the mass media and instituted propaganda campaigns to advance their goals. Finally, and perhaps most important, totalitarian governments engaged in massive projects of state-controlled social engineering dedicated to replacing individualism with a unified "people" capable of exercising the collective will.

Communism and Fascism

Communism and fascism shared a desire to revolutionize state and society. Yet some scholars have argued that the differences between the two systems are more important than the similarities. To understand those differences, it is important to consider the way ideology, or a guiding philosophy, was linked to political radicalism.

Following Marx, Soviet Communists strove to create an international brotherhood of workers. In the Communist utopia ruled by the revolutionary working class, economic exploitation would supposedly disappear and society would be based on fundamental social equality. Under **Stalinism** — the name given to the Communist system in the Soviet Union during Stalin's rule — the state aggressively intervened in all walks of life to pursue this social leveling. Using brute force to destroy the upper and middle classes, the Stalinist state nationalized private property, pushed rapid industrialization, and collectivized agriculture. Attempts to eliminate the upper classes led to the

TIMELINE

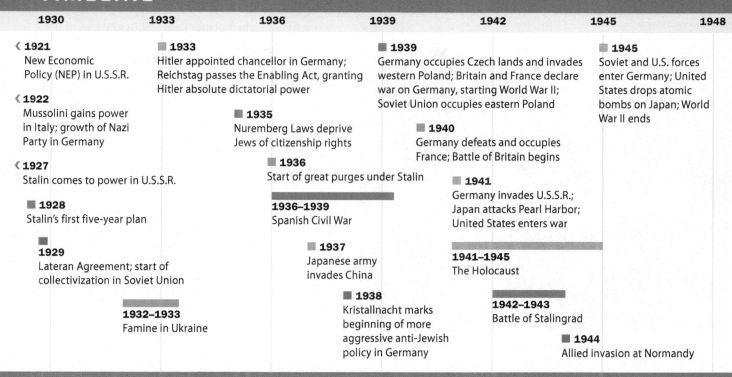

1930   1933   1936   1939   1942   1945   1948

1921
New Economic
Policy (NEP) in U.S.S.R.

1922
Mussolini gains power
in Italy; growth of Nazi
Party in Germany

1927
Stalin comes to power in U.S.S.R.

1928
Stalin's first five-year plan

1929
Lateran Agreement; start of
collectivization in Soviet Union

1932–1933
Famine in Ukraine

1933
Hitler appointed chancellor in Germany;
Reichstag passes the Enabling Act, granting
Hitler absolute dictatorial power

1935
Nuremberg Laws deprive
Jews of citizenship rights

1936
Start of great purges under Stalin

1936–1939
Spanish Civil War

1937
Japanese army
invades China

1938
Kristallnacht marks
beginning of more
aggressive anti-Jewish
policy in Germany

1939
Germany occupies Czech lands and invades
western Poland; Britain and France declare
war on Germany, starting World War II;
Soviet Union occupies eastern Poland

1940
Germany defeats and occupies
France; Battle of Britain begins

1941
Germany invades U.S.S.R.;
Japan attacks Pearl Harbor;
United States enters war

1941–1945
The Holocaust

1942–1943
Battle of Stalingrad

1944
Allied invasion at Normandy

1945
Soviet and U.S. forces
enter Germany; United
States drops atomic
bombs on Japan; World
War II ends

---

killing of millions of innocent people in the Soviet Union.

The Fascist vision of a new society was quite different. Leaders who embraced **fascism**, such as Mussolini and Hitler, claimed that they were striving to build a new community on a national — not an international — level. Extreme nationalists, and often racists, Fascists glorified war and the military. For them, the nation was the highest embodiment of the people, and the powerful leader was the materialization of the people's collective will.

Like Communists, Fascists promised to improve the lives of ordinary workers. Fascist governments intervened in the economy, but unlike Communist regimes they accepted inequalities and did not try to level class differences and nationalize private property. Instead, they championed a vision of national belonging. In the ideal Fascist state, all social strata and classes would join together to build a harmonious national community.

Communists and Fascists differed in another crucial respect: the question of race. Where Communists sought to build a new world around the eradication of class differences, Fascists typically sought to build a new national community grounded in ideas about racial difference. Fascists and particularly National Socialists embraced the doctrine of **eugenics**, a pseudoscience that maintained that the selective breeding of human beings could improve the general characteristics of a national population. Though widely

recognized today as both unscientific and immoral, eugenics enjoyed widespread popularity throughout the Western world in the 1920s and 1930s and was viewed by many as a legitimate reform program. But Fascists, especially the German National Socialists, or Nazis, pushed such ideas to the extreme.

Adopting a radicalized view of eugenics, the Nazis maintained that the German nation had to be "purified" of groups of people deemed "unfit" by the regime. Following state policies intended to support what they called "racial hygiene," Nazi authorities attempted to control, segregate, or eliminate those of "lesser value," including Jews, Slavs, Sinti and Roma (historically called "Gypsies," a term that has pejorative connotations), and other ethnic minorities; homosexual people; and people suffering from chronic

---

■ **totalitarianism** A radical dictatorship that exercises "total claims" over the beliefs and behavior of its citizens by taking control of the economic, social, intellectual, and cultural aspects of society.

■ **Stalinism** The name given to the Communist system in the Soviet Union during the rule of Joseph Stalin.

■ **fascism** The name given to political movements, including German National Socialism, characterized by extreme nationalism, anti-socialism, a charismatic leader, and the glorification of war and the military.

■ **eugenics** A pseudoscientific doctrine saying the selective breeding of human beings can improve the general characteristics of a national population, which helped inspire Nazi ideas about national unity and racial exclusion and ultimately contributed to the Holocaust.

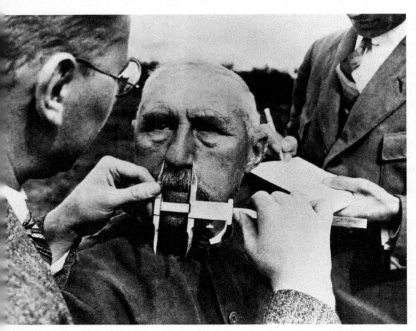

Eugenics in Nazi Germany   Nazi "race scientists" believed they could use the eugenic methods of social engineering to build a powerful Aryan race. In this photograph, published in a popular magazine in 1933, a clinician measures a man's nose. Such pseudoscientific methods were used to determine an individual's supposed "racial value." (Hulton Deutsch/Corbis/Getty Images)

mental or physical disabilities. The Nazis' pursuit of "racial hygiene" ultimately led to the Holocaust, the attempt to purge Germany and Europe of all Jews and other groups deemed undesirable by mass killing during World War II. Though the Soviets readily persecuted specific ethnic groups they believed were disloyal to the Communist state, they justified these attacks using ideologies of class rather than race.

Communists and Fascists were sworn enemies. The result was a clash of ideologies, which was in large part

responsible for the horrific destruction and loss of life in the middle of the twentieth century. The nature of totalitarian dictatorships and the varied reasons ordinary people supported or resisted such regimes thus remain crucial questions for historians, even as they look more closely at the ideological differences between communism and fascism.

The Spanish Civil War

The great clash of ideologies just described drove the **Spanish Civil War** (1936–1939), which began after a right-wing coup attempt failed to unseat a democratically elected government formed by a group of liberal republicans, socialists, and Communists. The right, led by Fascist rebel and general Francisco Franco, opened a full-scale military campaign against the Spanish Republic. Despite heroic bravery on the part of the republic's defenders, the Fascist army took the capital Madrid in 1939 and ended the bloody war that April. Franco established a repressive one-party Fascist state that ruled Spain until his death in 1975.

Germany and Italy sent troops and weapons to help Franco's revolutionary Fascist movement, but republican Spain's only official aid came from the Soviet Union because anticommunist sentiment in Britain, France, and the United States stalled any effort to intervene. Tens of thousands of volunteers from Germany, France, the United States, and Italy went to Spain to fight fascism, but they failed to halt Franco's advance. Tensions on the left between anarchists, socialists, and Soviet Communists undermined the government's war effort. A republican victory might have warned Nazi Germany against starting a war of aggression, but instead the war encouraged Fascists across Europe and served as a prelude to the ideologically inspired conflict to follow.

How did Stalinism transform state and society in the Soviet Union?

Lenin's harshest critics claim that he established the basic outlines of a modern totalitarian dictatorship after the Bolshevik Revolution and during the Russian civil war. If so, Joseph Stalin (1879–1953) certainly finished the job. After he consolidated his power in the mid-1920s, Stalin and his government undertook a radical attempt to transform Soviet society into a Communist state.

From Lenin to Stalin

By spring 1921 Lenin and the Bolsheviks had won the civil war, but they ruled a shattered and devastated

land. Many farms were in ruins, and food supplies were exhausted. In southern Russia, drought combined with the ravages of war to produce the worst famine in generations. Industrial production had broken down completely. In the face of economic disintegration, riots by peasants and workers, and an open rebellion by previously pro-Bolshevik sailors at Kronstadt, Lenin was tough but, as ever, flexible. The new regime repressed the Kronstadt rebels, and in March 1921 replaced War Communism with the **New Economic Policy (NEP)**, which re-established limited economic freedom in an attempt to rebuild agriculture and industry. During the civil war, the Bolsheviks

A Republican Militia in the Spanish Civil War   The enthusiasm of the republican forces of the democratically elected government of Spain could not overcome the rebel Fascist armies of Francisco Franco during the Spanish Civil War (1936–1939). Once in power, Franco ruled over a repressive dictatorial state in Spain until his death in 1975. Women combatants like the *milicianas* pictured here, carrying rifles with their male comrades, made a significant contribution to the republican cause. (Universal History Archive/Getty Images)

had simply seized grain without payment. Now peasant producers were permitted to sell their surpluses in free markets, and private traders and small handicraft manufacturers were allowed to reappear. Heavy industry, railroads, and banks, however, remained wholly nationalized. The NEP was a political and economic success. It quelled discontent in rural areas and brought rapid economic recovery. By 1926 industrial output surpassed and agricultural production almost equaled prewar levels.

In 1924, as the economy recovered and the government partially relaxed its censorship and repression, Lenin died without a chosen successor, creating an intense struggle for power in the inner circles of the Communist Party. The principal contenders were Joseph Stalin and Leon Trotsky. Stalin was a good organizer but a poor speaker and writer, and he had no experience outside of Russia. Trotsky, an inspiring leader who had planned the 1917 Bolshevik takeover and then led the victorious Red Army, appeared to have the advantage in the power struggle. Yet Stalin won because he was more effective at gaining the all-important support of the party. Having risen to general secretary of the party's Central Committee in 1922, he used his office to win friends and allies with jobs and promises.

Stalin also won because he was better able to relate Marxist teaching to Soviet realities in the 1920s. He developed a theory of "socialism in one country,"

which was more appealing to the majority of party members than Trotsky's doctrine of "permanent revolution." Stalin argued that the Russian-dominated Soviet Union had the ability to build socialism on its own. Trotsky maintained that communism in the Soviet Union could only succeed if revolution swept across Europe. To many Russian Communists, this view sold their country short and promised risky conflicts with capitalist countries. Stalin's willingness to revoke NEP reforms furthermore appealed to young party militants, who detested the NEP's reliance on capitalist free markets.

With cunning skill, Stalin achieved supreme power between 1922 and 1927. First he allied with Trotsky's personal enemies to crush his rival, and then he moved against all who might challenge his ascendancy, including former allies. Stalin's final triumph came at the party congress of December 1927, which condemned all "deviation from the general party line" that he had formulated. The dictator and his followers were ready to launch "the revolution from above," radically changing the lives of millions of people.

■ **Spanish Civil War** A war from 1936 to 1939 that led to the overthrow of the left-leaning democratic government of Spain and the establishment of a Fascist state under the general Francisco Franco.

■ **New Economic Policy (NEP)** Lenin's 1921 policy to re-establish limited economic freedom in an attempt to rebuild agriculture and industry in the face of economic disintegration.

MAP 27.1 The Formation of the U.S.S.R. When the Bolsheviks successfully overthrew the tsarist government and won the civil war that followed, they inherited the vast territories of the former Russian Empire. Following policies instituted by Stalin, they established a Union of Soviet Socialist Republics (U.S.S.R.) that gave limited cultural autonomy but no real political independence to the Soviet republics now under Communist control.

Stalin and the Nationalities Question

Stalin's ascendancy had a momentous impact on the policy of the new Soviet state toward non-Russians. The Communists had inherited the vast multiethnic territories of the former Russian Empire. Lenin initially argued that these ethnic groups should have the right to self-determination even if they claimed independence from the Soviet state. In 1922, reflecting such ideas, the Union of Soviet Socialist Republics (or U.S.S.R.) was organized as a federation of four Soviet republics: the Russian Soviet Federative Socialist Republic, Ukraine, Belorussia, and a Transcaucasian republic. The last was later split into Armenia, Azerbaijan, and Georgia, and five Central Asian republics were established in the 1920s and 1930s (Map 27.1).

In contrast to Lenin, Stalin argued for more centralized Russian control of these ethnic regions. This view would dominate state policy until the breakup of the Soviet Union in the early 1990s. The Soviet republics were granted limited cultural independence but no true autonomy. Party leaders allowed the use of non-Russian languages in regional schools and government institutions, but the right to secede was a fiction. Real authority remained in Moscow, in the hands of the Russian Communist Party. The Stalinists thus established a far-flung Communist empire on the imperial holdings of the former tsars.

The Five-Year Plans

The party congress of 1927, which ratified Stalin's consolidation of power, marked the end of the NEP. The following year brought the start of the era of the Communist five-year plans. The first **five-year plan** had staggering economic and social objectives. In just

Ethnic Minorities in the U.S.S.R.
The Soviet Union inherited the vast and diverse territories of the former Russian Empire. This 1921 propaganda poster, titled "Unfurling the Flag of Freedom in Every Land," champions the arrival of Bolshevism in Central Asia. It depicts a Muslim Tartar woman waving a red flag. She has torn off her headscarf and turned her back on members of the older generation, who point imploringly toward a mosque, while two men beckon toward the open door to the Communist future. This idealized testament to peaceful coexistence within the Soviet empire masked the conflicts aroused by Russian domination in the Soviet republics. (Album/British Library/Alamy Stock Photo)

five years, total industrial output was to increase by 250 percent, with heavy industry, the preferred sector, growing even faster. Agricultural production was slated to rise by 150 percent, and one-fifth of the peasants in the Soviet Union were to give up their private plots and join collective farms. The five-year plans, imposed from above, successfully dragged Soviet society into the modern age, but the cost in disrupted livelihoods and ended lives was enormous.

Stalin unleashed this "second revolution" to realize interrelated economic and ideological goals. Soviet leaders were deeply committed to communism, as they understood it. They feared a gradual restoration of capitalism and wished to promote the working classes. The regime was eager to abolish the remnants of the free market, embodied in the NEP's private traders, independent artisans, and property-owning peasants. The planned development of industry and agriculture would theoretically allow the U.S.S.R. to catch up with the West and so overcome traditional Russian "backwardness," and the Soviet Union began to train a new class of Communist engineers and technicians to manage the transition.

The independent peasantry remained a major problem. For centuries the peasants had wanted to own their own land, and finally they had it. Sooner or later, Stalinists reasoned, landowning peasants would embrace conservative capitalism and pose a threat to the regime. At the same time, committed Communists — mainly city dwellers — believed that the feared and despised "class enemy" in the villages could be squeezed to provide the enormous sums needed for all-out industrialization.

To resolve these issues, in 1929 Stalin ordered the **collectivization of agriculture** — the forced consolidation of individual peasant farms into large, state-controlled enterprises that served as agricultural factories. Peasants across the Soviet Union were compelled to move off their small plots onto large state-run farms, where their tools, livestock, and produce would be held in common and central planners could control all work.

The increasingly repressive measures instituted by the state first focused on the **kulaks**, the class of well-off peasants who had benefited the most from the NEP. The kulaks were small in number, but propagandists cast them as the great enemy of progress. Stalin called for their "liquidation" and seizure of their property. Stripped of land and livestock, many starved or were deported to forced-labor camps for "re-education."

Forced collectivization brought disaster. Large numbers of peasants opposed to the change slaughtered their animals and burned their crops rather than turn them over to state commissars. Between 1929 and 1933 the number of horses, cattle, sheep, and goats in the Soviet Union fell by at least half. Nor were the state-controlled collective farms more productive. During the first five-year plan, the output of grain

■ **five-year plan** A plan launched by Stalin in 1928 and termed the "revolution from above," aimed at modernizing the Soviet Union and creating a new Communist society with new attitudes, new loyalties, and a new socialist humanity.

■ **collectivization of agriculture** The forcible consolidation of individual peasant farms into large state-controlled enterprises in the Soviet Union under Stalin.

■ **kulaks** The better-off peasants who were stripped of land and livestock under Stalin and were generally not permitted to join collective farms; many of them starved or were deported to forced-labor camps for "re-education."

Famine and Recovery on a Soviet Collective Farm in Ukraine

Fedor Belov describes daily life on a kolkhoz, or collective farm, in Soviet Ukraine during the famine of the early 1930s. Belov, a former collective farm chairman, fled the Soviet Union for the West, where he published this critical account in 1955.

In these kolkhozes the great bulk of the land was held and worked communally, but each peasant household owned a house of some sort, a small plot of ground and perhaps some livestock. All the members of the kolkhoz were required to work on the kolkhoz a certain number of days each month; the rest of the time they were allowed to work on their own holdings. They derived their income partly from what they grew on their garden strips and partly from their work in the kolkhoz. . . .

By late 1932 more than 80 per cent of the peasant households in the raion [district] had been collectivized. . . . That year the peasants harvested a good crop and had hopes that the calculations would work out to their advantage and would help strengthen them economically. These hopes were in vain. The kolkhoz workers received only 200 grams of flour per labor day for the first half of the year; the remaining grain, including the seed fund, was taken by the government. The peasants were told that industrialization of the country, then in full swing, demanded grain and sacrifices from them.

That autumn the "red broom" [government agents who requisitioned grain] passed over the kolkhozes and the individual plots, sweeping the . . . "surpluses," [and] everything was collected. . . . As a result, famine, which was to become intense by the spring of 1933, already began to be felt in the fall of 1932.

The famine of 1932–1933 was the most terrible and destructive that the Ukrainian people have ever experienced. The peasants ate dogs, horses, rotten potatoes, the bark of trees, grass—anything they could find. Incidents of cannibalism were not uncommon. The people were like wild beasts, ready to devour one another. And no matter what they did, they went on dying, dying, dying. . . .

There was no one to gather the bumper crop of 1933, since the people who remained alive were too weak and exhausted. More than a hundred persons—office and factory workers from Leningrad—were sent to assist on the kolkhoz; two representatives of the Party arrived to help organize the harvesting. . . .

That summer (1933) the entire administration of the kolkhoz—the bookkeeper, the warehouseman, the manager of the flour mill, and even the chairman himself—were put on trial on charges of plundering the kolkhoz property and produce. All the accused were sentenced to terms of seven to ten years, and a new administration was elected. . . .

After 1934 a gradual improvement began in the economic life of the kolkhoz and its members. . . . In general, from the mid-1930s until 1941, the majority of kolkhoz members in the Ukraine lived relatively well.

EVALUATE THE EVIDENCE

1. How did the organization of the collective farm express the basic ideas of Communist ideology?
2. How did party leaders respond to widespread starvation? Did government policy contribute to the intensity of the famine in 1932?

Source: *History of a Soviet Collective Farm* by Fedor Belov, Research Program on the U.S.S.R. (Praeger, 1955), pp. 11–12.

---

barely increased, and collectivized agriculture was unable to make any substantial financial contribution to Soviet industrial development.

Collectivization in the fertile farmlands of Ukraine was particularly rapid and violent. The drive against peasants snowballed into an assault on Ukrainians in general, who had sought independence from Soviet rule after the First World War. Stalin and his associates viewed this resistance as an expression of unacceptable anti-Soviet nationalism. In 1932, as collectivization and deportations continued, party leaders set levels of grain deliveries for the Ukrainian collectives at excessively high levels and refused to relax those quotas or allow food relief when Ukrainian Communist leaders reported staggering rates of mass starvation. A terrible man-made famine in 1932 and 1933—known as the Holodomor in Ukraine—claimed 3 to 3.5 million lives. (See "Evaluating Written Evidence: Famine and Recovery on a Soviet Collective Farm in Ukraine.")

Collectivization was a cruel but substantial victory for Stalinist ideologues. Though millions died, by the end of 1938 government representatives had forced 93 percent of peasant households onto collective farms, neutralizing their political threat. Peasant resistance had nonetheless forced the supposedly all-powerful state to make modest concessions. Peasants secured the right to limit a family's labor on the state-run farms and to cultivate tiny family plots, which provided them with much of their food. In 1938 these family plots produced 22 percent of all

Day Shift at Magnitogorsk Beginning in 1928, Stalin's government issued a series of ambitious five-year plans designed to rapidly industrialize the Soviet Union. The plans focused primarily on boosting heavy industry and included the building of a gigantic steel complex at Magnitogorsk in the Ural Mountains. Here steelworkers review production goals at the Magnitogorsk foundry. (Sovfoto/Getty Images)

Soviet agricultural produce on only 4 percent of all cultivated land.

The rapid industrialization mandated by the five-year plans likewise transformed Soviet society, at great cost. A huge State Planning Commission, the "Gosplan," was created to set production goals and control deliveries of raw and finished materials. This was a complex and difficult task, and production bottlenecks and slowdowns often resulted. In addition, Stalinist planning favored heavy industry over the production of consumer goods, which led to shortages of basic necessities. Despite such problems, Soviet industry produced about four times as much in 1937 as it had in 1928. No other major country had ever achieved such rapid industrial growth.

Steel was the idol of the Stalinist age. The state needed heavy machinery for rapid development, and an industrial labor force was created almost overnight. In the 1930s, millions of peasant immigrants moved into the Soviet Union's rapidly expanding cities. An internal passport system, meant to ensure that individuals could change locations or jobs only with official permission, hardly controlled the ensuing chaos. Peasants became industrial workers in huge steel mills and other new factories, under the direction of a small number of skilled foremen and engineers. This flood of peasant migrants lived in deplorable conditions in hastily built industrial cities such as Magnitogorsk (Magnetic Mountain City), which was built around a massive steel foundry in the Ural Mountains. If they

were lucky, they found shelter in crowded, dormitory-style barracks. Many lived in mud huts, tent cities, or shantytowns, and most had no running water or sewage facilities and only primitive heating or lighting. The authorities slowly worked to provide basic amenities, including better apartments, stores, schools, public baths, and sports facilities.

The new workers often lived in deplorable conditions, yet they also experienced some benefits. This young working class, recruited almost entirely from the rural population, escaped the worst results of collectivization—deportation or death from famine. It included growing numbers of women, who by 1939 made up about 40 percent of the workforce. Uneducated peasants gained new skills and autonomy as they became the backbone of the new working class. As one peasant turned factory electrician explained, "From a common laborer I have turned into a skilled worker. . . . I live in a country where one feels like living and learning."[1] As one historian wrote, the new factories "became a kind of frontier, a gateway between town and country, between the nineteenth and twentieth centuries."[2] The great industrialization drive of 1928 to 1937 was an awe-inspiring achievement, purchased at enormous sacrifice on the part of the Soviet people.

Life and Culture in Soviet Society

Daily life was difficult in Stalin's Soviet Union. As we have seen, millions were moving into the cities, but the government built few new apartments, leading to a serious shortage of adequate housing. There were constant shortages of consumer goods as well. The average standard of living improved little in the years before World War II, and the average nonfarm wage purchased only about half as many goods in 1932 as it had in 1928. After 1932 real wages rose slowly, but by 1937 workers could still buy only about 60 percent of what they had bought in 1928 and less than they could purchase in 1913. Collectivized peasants experienced greater hardships.

Life was by no means hopeless, however. Idealism and ideology had real appeal for many Communists and ordinary people, who saw themselves heroically building the world's first socialist society while capitalism crumbled in a worldwide depression and degenerated into fascism in the West. On a more practical level, Soviet workers received social benefits, such as old-age pensions, free medical services, free education, and day-care centers for children. Unemployment was almost unknown. This optimistic vision of the Soviet future attracted many disillusioned Westerners to communism in the 1920s and 1930s.

Stalinism also opened possibilities for personal advancement. Rapid industrialization required massive numbers of skilled workers, engineers, and plant managers. In the 1930s the Stalinist state broke with the egalitarian policies of the 1920s and offered tremendous incentives to those who could serve its needs. It paid the mass of unskilled workers and collective farmers very low wages but provided high salaries and special privileges to its growing technical and managerial elite. This group joined with the political and artistic elites in a new upper class, whose members grew rich and powerful.

The radical transformation of Soviet society had a profound impact on women's lives. Marxists had traditionally believed that both capitalism and middle-class husbands exploited women, and the Russian Revolution of 1917 immediately proclaimed complete equality for women. In the 1920s divorce and abortion were easily available, and women were urged to work outside the home. After Stalin came to power, he reversed these trends. The government revoked many laws supporting women's emancipation in order to strengthen the traditional family and build up the state's population.

Soviet leaders encouraged women to enter the workforce in unprecedented numbers. The Soviets opened higher education to women, who could now enter the ranks of the better-paid specialists in industry and science. Medicine practically became a woman's profession. By 1950, 75 percent of all doctors in the Soviet Union were female. Alongside such advances, however, Soviet society demanded great sacrifices from women. Wages were so low that it was almost impossible for a family or couple to live on the husband's earnings, so most women had to work outside the home. Peasant women continued to work on farms, and millions of women toiled in factories and in heavy construction, building dams, roads, and steel mills in summer heat and winter frost. Men continued to dominate the very best jobs. Finally, rapid change and economic hardship led to many broken families, creating further physical and emotional strains for women.

In the U.S.S.R. culture was thoroughly politicized. Party activists lectured workers in factories and peasants on collective farms, while newspapers, films, and radio broadcasts endlessly revealed capitalist plots and recounted socialist achievements. Whereas the 1920s had seen considerable modernist experimentation in the arts, in the 1930s intellectuals were ordered by Stalin to become "engineers of human minds." Following the dictates of Socialist Realism, they were instructed to exalt the lives of ordinary workers and glorify communism. Russian history was rewritten so that early tsars such as Ivan the Terrible and Peter the Great became worthy forerunners of the greatest Russian leader of all—Stalin. Writers and artists who could effectively combine genuine creativity and political propaganda became the darlings of the regime.

Stalin seldom appeared in public, but his presence was everywhere—in portraits, statues, books, and quotations from his writings. Although the government persecuted those who practiced religion and turned churches into "museums of atheism," the state had both an earthly religion and a high priest—Marxism-Leninism and Joseph Stalin.

The Purges and the Great Terror of 1937–1938

In the mid-1930s the great offensive to build socialism and a new society culminated in ruthless state terror and a massive purging of the Communist Party. First used by the Bolsheviks in the civil war to maintain their power, terror as state policy was revived in the collectivization drive against the peasants. Top members of the party and government publicly supported Stalin's initiatives, but there was internal dissent. In late 1934 a top Soviet official, Sergei Kirov, was mysteriously killed. Stalin—who probably ordered Kirov's murder—blamed the assassination on "Fascist agents" within the party. He used the incident to launch a reign of terror that purged the Communist Party of supposed traitors and solidified his own control.

Murderous repression picked up steam over the next two years. It culminated in the "Great Terror" of 1937–1938. In those years alone, the security police arrested some 2 million people. About 1.3 million were sent to camps and labor colonies in the Soviet gulag, the system of forced-labor camps already crowded with victims of the collectivization campaign. Almost 700,000 people were murdered by the regime, and at least 1 million more died in the gulag.

The terror opened with a series of spectacular public show trials in which false evidence, often gathered using torture, was used to incriminate top party administrators and Red Army leaders. In August 1936 sixteen "Old Bolsheviks"—prominent leaders who had been in the party since the Russian Revolution—confessed to all manner of contrived plots against Stalin. All were executed. In 1937 the secret police arrested a mass of lesser party officials and newer members, using torture to extract confessions.

In addition to the party faithful, victims of the terror included army officers, union officials, technical experts and factory managers, and intellectuals. They were accused of counter-revolutionary activities such as spying, sabotaging factory production lines, and organizing anti-Soviet uprisings. Communist bureaucrats and mid-level managers were hard hit, yet the majority of the victims were ordinary people who were not party members. They were persecuted primarily because they belonged to the "wrong" social class or were members of an ethnic group supposedly hostile to Soviet power. The terror claimed tens of thousands of Germans, Poles, Latvians, and others who had settled and found work in the Soviet Union and were now labeled "anti-Soviet elements."

The Great Terror remains baffling, for most historians believe that the victims posed no threat and were innocent of their supposed crimes. Some scholars have argued that the terror was a defining characteristic of the totalitarian state, which must always fight real or imaginary enemies. Certainly the highly publicized purges sent a warning: no one was secure; everyone had to serve the party and its leader with redoubled devotion.

The long-standing interpretation that puts most of the blame for the purges on Stalin has been confirmed by recent research in newly opened Soviet archives. Apparently fearful of active resistance, Stalin and his allies used the harshest measures against their political enemies, real or imagined. Moreover, many people in the general population—bombarded with ideology and political slogans—shared such fears. Investigations and trials snowballed into mass hysteria, resulting in a modern witch-hunt that claimed millions of victims. In this view of the 1930s, a deluded Stalin found large numbers of willing collaborators.[3]

The terror seriously weakened the Soviet Union in military, economic, and intellectual terms. But it left Stalin in command of a vast new state apparatus, staffed by the 1.5 million new party members enlisted to replace the victims. Thus more than half of all Communist Party members in 1941 had joined since the purges. Taking the place of those forced out by the regime, they experienced rapid social advance. Often the children of workers, some studied in the new technical schools, and they soon proved capable of managing the government and large-scale production. Despite the human costs, the Great Terror brought practical rewards to a new generation of committed Communists. They would serve Stalin effectively until his death in 1953, and they would govern the Soviet Union until the early 1980s.

What kind of government did Mussolini establish in Italy?

Mussolini's Fascist movement and his seizure of power in 1922 were important steps in the rise of dictatorships in Europe between the two world wars. Mussolini and his supporters were the first to call themselves "Fascists"—revolutionaries determined to create a new totalitarian state based on extreme nationalism and militarism.

The Seizure of Power

In the early twentieth century, Italy was a liberal constitutional monarchy. On the eve of World War I, the parliament granted universal male suffrage, and Italy appeared to be moving toward democracy. But there were serious problems. Much of the population lived in poverty, and many peasants were more attached to their villages and local interests than to the national state. Vast gaps between rich and poor led to the development of a powerful revolutionary socialist movement. Moreover, the papacy, many devout Catholics, conservatives, and landowners remained strongly opposed to liberal institutions, and relations between church and state were often tense.

World War I worsened the situation. To win support for the war effort, the Italian government had promised territorial expansion as well as social and land reform, which it failed to deliver. Instead, the postwar treaties brought only limited territorial gains, and soaring unemployment and inflation after the war created mass hardship. In response, the Italian Socialist Party followed the Bolshevik example, and radical workers and peasants began occupying factories and seizing land in 1920. These actions mobilized the property-owning classes. Thus by 1921 socialists, conservatives, Catholics, and property owners were all opposed — though for different reasons — to the liberal government.

Into these crosscurrents of unrest and fear stepped bullying, blustering Benito Mussolini (1883–1945). Mussolini began his political career before World War I as a Socialist Party leader and radical newspaper editor. In 1914 he had urged that Italy join the Allies, a stand for which he was expelled from the Socialist Party. Returning home after being wounded at the front in 1917, Mussolini began organizing bitter war veterans like himself into a band of Fascists — from the Italian word *fascio* (derived from the Latin *fasces*), a bundle of wooden rods that symbolized national strength in a united Fascist state.

At first Mussolini's program combined nationalist and socialist demands. As such, it competed directly with the well-organized Socialist Party and failed to get off the ground. After Mussolini's violent verbal assaults on rival Socialists won him growing support from conservatives and the middle classes, he shifted gears in 1920 and became a sworn enemy of socialism. Mussolini and his private militia of **Black Shirts** grew increasingly violent. Few people were killed, but Socialist Party newspapers, union halls, and local headquarters were destroyed, and the Black Shirts managed to push Socialists out of city governments in northern Italy.

Fascism soon became a mass movement, one that Mussolini claimed would help the little people against the established interests. In 1922, in the midst of chaos largely created by his Black Shirt militias, Mussolini stepped forward as the savior of order and property. Striking a conservative, anticommunist note in his speeches and gaining the support of army leaders, Mussolini demanded the resignation of the existing government. In October 1922 a group of armed Black Shirts marched on Rome to threaten the king and force him to appoint Mussolini prime minister of Italy. The threat worked. Victor Emmanuel III (r. 1900–1946) — who himself had no love for the liberal regime — asked Mussolini to take over the government and form a new cabinet. Thus, after widespread violence and a threat of armed uprising, Mussolini seized power using the legal framework of the Italian constitution.

The Fascist Regime in Action

Mussolini became prime minister in 1922 and moved cautiously in his first two years in office to take control of the government. At first, he promised a "return

to order" and consolidated his support among Italian elites. Fooled by Mussolini's apparent moderation, the Italian parliament passed an electoral law that gave two-thirds of the representatives in the parliament to the party that won the most votes. This change allowed the Fascist Party and its allies to win an overwhelming majority in April 1924. Shortly thereafter, a group of Fascist extremists kidnapped and murdered the leading Socialist politician Giacomo Matteotti (JAHK-oh-moh mat-tee-OH-tee). Alarmed, a group of prominent parliamentary leaders called for the dissolution of Mussolini's armed squads and a crackdown on political violence.

Mussolini may not have ordered Matteotti's murder, but he took advantage of the resulting crisis. Declaring his desire to "make the nation Fascist," he imposed a series of repressive measures. The government ruled by decree, abolished freedom of the press, and organized fixed elections. Mussolini arrested his political opponents, disbanded all independent labor unions, and put dedicated Fascists in control of Italy's schools. Mussolini trumpeted his goal in a famous slogan: "Everything in the state, nothing outside the

Mussolini and Hitler   In September 1937 Italian dictator Benito Mussolini traveled to Germany to cement the Rome-Berlin Axis alliance. In this picture from an Italian propaganda photo album, Mussolini (left) and Nazi leader Adolf Hitler salute a military parade in front of a Munich memorial to Nazis killed in the Beer Hall Putsch. (Pictorial Press Ltd/Alamy Stock Photo)

■ **Black Shirts** Mussolini's private militia, which destroyed socialist newspapers, union halls, and Socialist Party headquarters, eventually pushing Socialists out of the city governments of northern Italy.

■ **Lateran Agreement** A 1929 agreement that recognized the Vatican as an independent state, with Mussolini agreeing to give the church heavy financial support in return for public support from the pope.

Fascist Youth on Parade   Totalitarian governments in Italy and Nazi Germany established mass youth organizations to instill the values of national unity and train young soldiers for the state. These members of the Balilla, Italy's Fascist youth organization, raise their rifles in salute at a mass rally in 1939. (Hulton Deutsch/Corbis/Getty Images)

state, nothing against the state." By the end of 1926 Italy was a one-party dictatorship under Mussolini's unquestioned leadership.

Mussolini's Fascist Party drew support from broad sectors of the population, in large part because he was willing to compromise with the traditional elites that controlled the army, the economy, and the state. He left big business to regulate itself, and there was no land reform. Mussolini also drew increasing support from the Catholic Church. In the **Lateran Agreement** of 1929, he recognized the Vatican as an independent state, and he agreed to give the church significant financial support in return for the pope's allegiance. Because he was forced to compromise with these conservative elites, Mussolini never established complete totalitarian control.

Italy's Ethiopian Campaign, 1935–1936

SUDAN (Gr. Br.)
ERITREA (It.)
FRENCH SOMALILAND
Addis Ababa
BRITISH SOMALILAND
ETHIOPIA
ITALIAN SOMALILAND
KENYA (Gr. Br.)
INDIAN OCEAN

→ Italian campaigns, 1935–1936

Mussolini's government nonetheless proceeded with attempts to bring fascism to Italy. The state engineered popular consent by staging massive rallies and sporting events, organizing Fascist youth and women's groups, and providing new social benefits. Newspapers, radio, and film promoted a "cult of the Duce" (DU-chay, or leader), portraying Mussolini as a powerful strongman who embodied the best qualities of the Italian people. Like other Fascist regimes, his government was vehemently opposed to liberal feminism and promoted traditional gender roles. Mussolini gained support by manipulating popular pride in the grand history of the ancient Roman Empire—as one propagandist put it, "Fascism, in its entirety, is the resurrection of Roman-ness."[4]

Mussolini matched his aggressive rhetoric with military action: Italian armies invaded the African nation of Ethiopia in October 1935. After surprising setbacks at the hands of the poorly armed Ethiopian army, the Italians won in 1936, and Mussolini could proudly declare that Italy again had its empire. Although it shocked international opinion, the war resulted in close ties between Italy and Nazi Germany. After a visit to Berlin in the fall of 1937, the Italian dictator pledged support for Hitler and promised that Italy and Germany would "march together right to the end."[5]

Deeply influenced by Hitler's example (see the next section), Mussolini's government passed a series of anti-Jewish racial laws in 1938. Though the laws were unpopular, Jews were forced out of public schools and dismissed from professional careers. Nevertheless, extreme anti-Semitic persecution did not occur in Italy until late in World War II, when Italy was under Nazi control. Though Mussolini's repressive tactics were never as ruthless as those in Nazi Germany, his government did much to establish a Fascist state in Italy before the war.

What policies did Nazi Germany pursue, and why did they appeal to ordinary Germans?

German National Socialism (Nazism) shared characteristics with Italian fascism, but Nazism was far more interventionist. Under Hitler, the Nazi dictatorship smashed or took over most independent organizations, established firm control over the German state, and violently persecuted Jews and other non-German peoples. Truly totalitarian in aspiration, Nazi Germany's policies of racial aggression and territorial expansion led to history's most destructive war.

The Roots of National Socialism

National Socialism grew out of many complex developments, of which the most influential were nationalism and racism. These two ideas captured the mind of the young Adolf Hitler (1889–1945), who became the leader of the Nazi Party after World War I. The son of an Austrian customs official, Hitler was a mediocre student who dropped out of school at age fourteen. He moved to Vienna, where he developed an unshakable belief in the crudest distortions of Social Darwinism, the superiority of Germanic races, and the inevitability of racial conflict. He claimed that Jews directed an international conspiracy of finance capitalism and Marxist socialism against the German people.

Hitler was not alone. As we have seen, racist anti-Semitism became wildly popular on the far-right wing of European politics in the decades surrounding the First World War. Such irrational beliefs, rooted in centuries of Christian anti-Semitism, were bolstered by nineteenth-century developments in biology and eugenics. These ideas came to define Hitler's worldview and would play an immense role in the ideology and actions of National Socialism.

Hitler greeted the outbreak of the First World War as a salvation. The struggle and discipline of war gave life meaning, and Hitler served as a dispatch carrier on the western front. Germany's defeat shattered his world. Convinced that Jews and Marxists had "stabbed Germany in the back," he vowed to fight on. In late 1919 he joined a tiny extremist group in Munich called the German Workers' Party. In addition to denouncing Jews, Marxists, and democrats, the party promised a uniquely German National Socialism that would abolish the injustices of capitalism and create a mighty "people's community." By 1921 Hitler had gained control of this small but growing party, renamed the National Socialist German Workers' Party, or Nazis for short. Hitler became a master of political showmanship. His wild, histrionic speeches, filled with demagogic attacks on the Versailles treaty, Jews, war profiteers, and the Weimar Republic, thrilled audiences eager to escape the crises that followed German defeat in World War I.

In late 1923, when the Weimar Republic seemed on the verge of collapse, Hitler organized an armed uprising in Munich—the so-called Beer Hall Putsch. Despite the failure of the poorly planned coup and Hitler's arrest, National Socialism had been born.

Hitler's Road to Power

At his trial, Hitler gained enormous publicity by denouncing the Weimar Republic. He used his brief prison term to dictate his book *Mein Kampf* (My Struggle), where he laid out his basic ideas on "racial purification" and territorial expansion that would define National Socialism. In *Mein Kampf*, Hitler claimed that Germans were a "master race" that needed to defend its "pure blood" from groups he labeled "racial degenerates," including Jews, Slavs, and others. The German race was destined to grow and triumph,

■ **National Socialism** A movement and political party driven by extreme nationalism and racism, led by Adolf Hitler; its adherents ruled Germany from 1933 to 1945 and forced Europe into World War II.

and, according to Hitler, it needed *Lebensraum* (living space). The future dictator outlined a sweeping vision of war and conquest in which the German master race would colonize east and central Europe and ultimately replace the "subhuman" Jews and Slavs living there. Hitler championed the idea of the leader-dictator, or *Führer* (FYOUR-uhr), whose unlimited power would embody the people's will and lead the German nation to victory. These ideas would ultimately propel the world into the Second World War.

In the years of relative prosperity and stability between 1924 and 1929, Hitler built up the Nazi Party. After the failed beer hall revolt, he had concluded that the Nazis had to come to power through electoral competition rather than armed rebellion. To appeal to middle-class voters, Hitler de-emphasized the anticapitalist elements of National Socialism and vowed to fight communism. The Nazis still remained a small splinter group in 1928, when they received only 2.6 percent of the vote in the general elections.

The Great Depression of 1929 brought the ascent of National Socialism. Now Hitler promised German voters economic as well as political salvation. His appeals for "national rebirth" appealed to a broad spectrum of voters, including middle- and lower-class groups — small business owners, officeworkers, artisans, peasants, and skilled workers. Seized by panic as bankruptcies increased, unemployment soared, and the Communists made dramatic election gains, voters deserted conservative and moderate parties for the Nazis. In the election of 1930 the Nazis won 6.5 million votes and 107 seats, and in July 1932 they gained 14.5 million votes — 38 percent of the total. They were now the largest party in the Reichstag, where Nazi deputies pursued the legal strategy of using democracy to destroy democracy.

The breakdown of democratic government helped the Nazis seize power. Chancellor Heinrich Brüning (BROU-nihng) tried to overcome the economic crisis by cutting back government spending and ruthlessly forcing down prices and wages. His conservative economic policies intensified Germany's economic collapse and convinced many voters that the country's republican leaders were incompetent and corrupt, adding to Hitler's appeal.

Division on the left contributed to Nazi success. Even though the two left-wing parties together outnumbered the Nazis in the Reichstag, the Communists refused to cooperate with the Social Democrats. Failing to resolve their differences, the left could not mount an effective opposition to the Nazi takeover.

Finally, Hitler excelled in the dirty backroom politics of the decaying Weimar Republic. In 1932 he gained backing from the conservative politicians in power, who thought they could use the Nazi leader for their own advantage to defuse the political crisis

EVENTS LEADING TO WORLD WAR II	
1919	Treaty of Versailles signed
1922	Mussolini gains power in Italy
1927	Stalin takes control in the Soviet Union
1931	Japan invades Manchuria
January 1933	Hitler appointed chancellor of Germany
October 1933	Germany withdraws from the League of Nations
March 1935	Hitler announces German rearmament
October 1935	Mussolini invades Ethiopia
1936–1939	Civil war in Spain, culminating in establishment of Fascist regime under Franco
March 1936	German armies move unopposed into the Rhineland
October 1936	Rome-Berlin Axis created
1937	Japan invades China
March 1938	Germany annexes Austria
September 1938	Munich Conference: Britain and France agree to German seizure of the Sudetenland from Czechoslovakia
March 1939	Germany occupies Czech territories; appeasement ends in Britain
August 1939	Nazi-Soviet pact signed
September 1, 1939	Germany invades Poland
September 3, 1939	Britain and France declare war on Germany

and clamp down on leftists. They accepted Hitler's demand to be appointed chancellor in a coalition government, believing that they could use and control him. On January 30, 1933, Adolf Hitler, leader of the most popular political party in Germany, was appointed chancellor by President Hindenburg.

State and Society in Nazi Germany

Hitler moved rapidly to establish a dictatorship that would pursue the Nazi program of racial segregation and territorial expansion. First, Hitler and the Nazi Party worked to consolidate their power. To maintain appearances, Hitler called for new elections. In

February 1933, in the midst of an electoral campaign plagued by violence—much of it caused by Nazi thugs—the Reichstag building was partly destroyed by fire. Hitler blamed the Communists and convinced Hindenburg to sign emergency acts that abolished freedom of speech and assembly as well as most personal liberties.

The façade of democratic government was soon torn asunder. When the Nazis won only 44 percent of the vote in the elections, Hitler outlawed the Communist Party and arrested its parliamentary representatives. Then on March 23, 1933, the Nazis pushed through the Reichstag the Enabling Act, which gave Hitler dictatorial power for four years. The Nazis' deceitful stress on legality, coupled with divide-and-conquer techniques, disarmed the opposition until it was too late for effective resistance.

Germany became a one-party Nazi state. The new regime took over the government bureaucracy, installing Nazis in top positions. At the same time, it created a series of overlapping Nazi Party organizations responsible solely to Hitler. The resulting system of dual government was riddled with rivalries, contradictions, and inefficiencies. The poorly organized Nazi state lacked the all-encompassing unity that its propagandists claimed. Yet this fractured system suited Hitler and his purposes. The lack of unity encouraged competition among state administrators, who worked to outdo each other to fulfill Hitler's vaguely expressed goals. The Führer thus played the established bureaucracy against his personal party government and maintained dictatorial control.

Once the Nazis were firmly in command, Hitler and the party turned their attention to constructing a National Socialist society defined by national unity and racial exclusion. First they eliminated political enemies. Communists, Social Democrats, and trade-union leaders were forced out of their jobs or arrested and taken to hastily built concentration camps. The Nazis outlawed strikes and abolished independent labor unions, which were replaced by the Nazi-controlled German Labor Front.

Hitler then purged the Nazi Party itself of its more extremist elements. The Nazi storm troopers (the SA)—the quasi-military band of 3 million toughs in brown shirts who had fought Communists and beaten up Jews before the Nazis took power—now expected top positions in the army. Some SA radicals even talked of a "second revolution" that would create equality among all Germans by sweeping away capitalism. Now that he was in power, however, Hitler was eager to win the support of the traditional military and maintain social order. He decided that the leadership of the SA had to be eliminated. On the night of June 30, 1934, Hitler's elite personal guard—the SS—arrested and executed about one hundred SA

leaders and other political enemies. Afterward, the SS grew rapidly. Under its methodical, ruthless leader Heinrich Himmler (1900–1945), the SS took over the political police and the concentration camp system.

By 1934 the Nazi dictatorship was largely in place. The Nazis instituted a policy called "coordination" that forced existing institutions to conform to National Socialist ideology. Professionals—doctors and lawyers, teachers and engineers—saw their previously independent organizations swallowed up by Nazi associations, and universities, publishers, and writers were quickly brought into line. Democratic, socialist, and Jewish literature was put on ever-growing blacklists. Passionate students and radicalized professors burned forbidden books in public squares. Modern art and architecture—which the Nazis considered "degenerate"—were prohibited. As a result, Germany lost its status as a world leader in science and the arts.

Acting on its vision of so-called "racial hygiene," the party now opened a many-faceted campaign against those they deemed incapable of making positive contributions to the development of the supposedly superior "master race." The results were monstrous, a barbaric violation of the ethical norms most of us take for granted. Thousands of innocent people faced social ostracism and then brutal repression. Jews were always the main targets of the Nazis' eugenicist measures, but Slavs, Sinti and Roma, and Jehovah's Witnesses also faced harsh repression, and the state persecuted and imprisoned homosexual people.

Nazi bureaucrats furthermore invented two categories targeted for "racial hygiene": the "hereditarily ill" and "asocials." The "hereditarily ill" included people with chronic mental or physical disabilities, such as people with schizophrenia, bipolar disorder, epilepsy, and what Nazi physicians called "congenital feeblemindedness." The catchall category of "asocials" included common criminals, alcoholics, prostitutes, the "work shy" (chronically unemployed), beggars, vagrants, and others on the margins of German society. Nazi medical workers forcibly sterilized some 400,000 German citizens, mainly people with disabilities and "asocials," because they wanted to prevent them from having children who might "weaken" the "Aryan race"—the Nazis' name for the so-called master race, which was supposed to have "pure" German blood. This eugenics campaign reached a crescendo in 1939, when the authorities initiated a coldhearted euthanasia program—dubbed "mercy killing" by Nazi physicians and administrators—and systematically murdered about 70,000 Germans with chronic disabilities (see "The Holocaust" later in the chapter) .

From the beginning, German Jews were a special target of Nazi persecution. Ugly propaganda posters;

feature films and documentaries about the so-called Jewish "menace"; signs in shop windows, banks, and parks forbidding Jewish entry; schoolroom lessons; articles in the popular press; feature films; traveling expeditions; and even children's board games — all and more were used to stigmatize German Jews. (See "Thinking Like a Historian: Normalizing Eugenics and 'Racial Hygiene' in Nazi Germany," page 850.)

Such means were backed up with harsh legal oppression. Shortly after they took power, Nazi authorities issued the Professional Civil Service Restoration Act, which banned Jews from working in government jobs; by 1934 many Jewish civil servants, lawyers, doctors, and professors had been summarily dismissed from their jobs. In 1935 the infamous Nuremberg Laws classified as Jewish anyone having three or more Jewish grandparents, outlawed marriage and sexual relations between Jews and those defined as German, and deprived Jews of all rights of citizenship. Conversion to Christianity and abandonment of the Jewish faith made no difference.

In late 1938 the assault on the Jews accelerated. During a well-organized wave of violence known as Kristallnacht (or the Night of Broken Glass pogrom), Nazi gangs smashed windows and looted over 7,000 Jewish-owned shops, destroyed many homes, burned down over 200 synagogues, and killed dozens of Jews. German Jews were then arrested and made to pay for the damage. By 1939 some 300,000 of Germany's 500,000 Jews had emigrated, sacrificing almost all their property to escape persecution. Some Germans privately opposed these outrages, but most went along or looked the other way. Historians still debate the degree to which this lack of opposition expressed popular anti-Semitism. In any case, it revealed widespread acceptance of the Nazi government.

Popular Support for National Socialism

Why did millions of Germans back a brutally repressive, racist regime? A combination of coercion and reward enlisted popular support for the Nazi state. Using the secret police and the growing concentration camp system in a reign of ruthless terror, the regime persecuted its political and "racial enemies." Yet for the large majority of ordinary German citizens who were not Jews, Communists, or members of other targeted groups, Hitler's government brought opportunities. Many Germans benefited from Nazi policies and programs. Even the creation of demonized outsider groups contributed to feelings of national unity and support for the Hitler regime, at least for those who belonged to the socially dominant group.

Hitler promised the masses economic recovery, and he delivered. The Nazi state launched a large public

Mothers in the Fatherland Nazi ideologues promoted strictly defined gender roles for men and women, and the Nazi state implemented a variety of social programs to encourage "racially correct" women to stay home and raise "Aryan" children. This colorful poster portrays the joy of motherhood and calls for donations to the Mother and Child division of the National Socialist People's Welfare office. A woman who had four children was awarded the bronze Cross of Honor for the German Mother (left). The medal came with a letter of appreciation signed by Hitler. (medal: Private Collection/Peter Newark Military Pictures/Bridgeman Images; poster: Joachim Schich/akg-images/Newscom)

Unterstützt das Hilfswerk
Mutter und Kind

works program to pull Germany out of the depression. Work began on public buildings, superhighways, and gigantic sports stadiums, which created jobs and instilled pride in national recovery. By 1938 unemployment had fallen to 2 percent, and there was a shortage of workers. Between 1932 and 1938 the standard of living for the average worker increased moderately. Business profits rose sharply.

The persecution of Jews brought economic benefits to some ordinary Germans as well. As Jews were

Normalizing Eugenics and "Racial Hygiene" in Nazi Germany

The Nazi regime issued a number of laws and regulations that institutionalized racial eugenics, including the Civil Service Restoration Act (1933) and the Nuremberg Laws (1935). Notions of "racial hygiene" also penetrated the very fabric of everyday life in the Third Reich. What means did Nazi supporters use to teach Germans that racial engineering was legitimate and even desirable?

1 **Adolf Hitler, *Mein Kampf* (My Struggle).** The dictator of the Nazi state explained the importance of racial education in his infamous political manifesto, first published in 1925.

~ If, as the first task of the State in the service and for the welfare of its nationality we recognize the preservation, care, and development of the best racial elements, it is natural that this care must not only extend to the birth of every little national and racial comrade, but that it must educate the young sapling to become a valuable link in the chain of future reproduction.

2 **Joseph Goebbels, party rally speech.** Propaganda Minister Goebbels sums up his view of welfare benefits in a 1938 speech, delivered to functionaries working in the Nazi welfare agency.

~ Our starting point is not the individual, and we do not subscribe to the view that one should feed the hungry, give drink to the thirsty, or clothe the naked—those are not our objectives. Our objectives are entirely different. They can be put most crisply in the sentence: we must have a healthy people [*Volk*] in order to prevail in the world.

(akg-images)

3 **An anti-Semitic children's book.** In this scene from a notorious 1936 anti-Semitic children's book, blond-haired schoolchildren laugh and jeer as a Jewish schoolteacher and a group of Jewish students are forcibly ejected from a German grade school. The portrayal of the Jewish teacher and students draws on the most ugly racist stereotypes. Approximately 100,000 copies of the book were printed by a Nazi publisher, and it was used in many German schoolrooms.

ANALYZING THE EVIDENCE

1. In Source 1, why does Hitler emphasize the importance of education for the development of "the best racial elements"?
2. Review Goebbels's statement on the relationship between the individual and the "people" in Source 2. How do his ideas, and those expressed in Sources 5 and 6, challenge the rationale behind Christian charity and/or liberal-democratic ideals of individual human rights?
3. How do Sources 3–6 bring Nazi assumptions about "racial hygiene" to ordinary Germans?
4. The evidence presented here is "top down"—it was created by propagandists who supported the Nazis' racial ideas. Given these limitations, how can historians tackle the question of reception? Can we really know what ordinary people in Germany thought about these sources?

4 **A lesson in racial biology.** In 1935 educator Jakob Graf wrote a series of exercises designed to teach young students to identify what he termed a person's "racial soul" by observing his or her habits and physical characteristics.

How We Can Learn to Recognize a Person's Race

ASSIGNMENTS

1. Summarize the spiritual characteristics of the individual races.
2. Collect from stories, essays, and poems examples of ethnological illustrations. Underline those terms which describe the type and mode of the expression of the soul.
3. What are the expressions, gestures, and movements which allow us to make conclusions as to the attitude of the racial soul?
4. Determine also the physical features which go hand in hand with the specific racial soul characteristics of the individual figures.
5. Try to discover the intrinsic nature of the racial soul through the characters in stories and poetical works in terms of their inner attitude. Apply this mode of observation to persons in your own environment.
6. Collect propaganda posters and caricatures for your race book and arrange them according to a racial scheme. . . .
7. Collect from illustrated magazines, newspapers, etc., pictures of great scholars, statesmen, artists, and others who distinguish themselves by their special accomplishments (for example, in economic life, politics, sport). Determine the preponderant race and admixture, according to physical characteristics. Repeat this exercise with the pictures of great men of all nations and times.

. . .

9. Observe people whose special racial features have drawn your attention, also with respect to their bearing when moving or when speaking. Observe their expressions and gestures.
10. Observe the Jew: In his way of walking, his bearing, gestures, and movements when talking.
11. What strikes you about the way a Jew talks and sings?
12. What are the occupations engaged in by the Jews of your acquaintance?
13. What are the occupations in which Jews are not to be found? Explain this phenomenon on the basis of the character of the Jew's soul.

(bpk, Bildagentur/Art Resource, NY)

5 **Envisioning "racial decline."** Visitors to the 1935 Wonders of Life eugenics exposition in Berlin could view this poster titled "The Qualitative Decline of the Population Due to Weak Reproduction Rates Among the Highly Valued." The poster graphs population rates. It depicts a man labeled "Lowly Valued" who grows to tower over the "Highly Valued" figure. The text claims that "This Is How It Will End" after 120 years if each "Lowly Valued" family continues to have four children while each "Highly Valued" family has only two.

6 **A lesson in mathematics.** A great variety of Nazi propaganda materials — including feature films, traveling exhibits, and these 1936 math exercises — brought home the message that people with physical or mental disabilities were an expensive and ultimately unnecessary burden on German society.

Question 95: The construction of a lunatic asylum costs 6 million RM [Reich Marks]. How many houses at 15,000 RM each could have been built for that amount? . . .

Question 97: To keep a mentally ill person costs approx. 4 RM per day, a cripple 5.50 RM, a criminal 3.5 RM. Many civil servants receive only 4 RM per day, white-collar employees barely 3.5 RM, unskilled workers not even 2 RM per head for their families.

(a) Illustrate these figures with a diagram.

According to conservative estimates there are 300,000 mentally ill, epileptics, etc., in care.

(b) How much do these people cost to keep in total, at a cost of 4 RM per head?
(c) How many marriage loans at 1,000 RM each . . . could be granted from this money?

PUTTING IT ALL TOGETHER

Historians have often argued that victims of Nazi racial policy and the Holocaust — Jews, homosexual people, people with mental or physical disabilities, and others considered "less worthy" — were subjected to processes of dehumanization before they were persecuted or even murdered. Using the sources above, along with what you have learned in class and in this chapter, write a short essay that outlines this process. What ideas about race and eugenics were most widespread in Nazi society, and how were these ideas "normalized" — made acceptable to ordinary people — in Nazi propaganda?

Sources: (1, 2) Michael Burleigh and Wolfgang Wippermann, *The Racial State: Germany 1933–1945* (New York: Cambridge University Press, 1991), pp. 202, 69; (4) George Mosse, ed., *Nazi Culture: A Documentary History* (New York: Schocken Books, 1981), pp. 80–81; (6) Burleigh and Wippermann, *The Racial State*, p. 154.

forced out of their jobs and compelled to sell their homes and businesses, other Germans stepped in to take their place in a process known as "Aryanization." For millions of so-called Aryans, a rising standard of living—at whatever ethical price—was tangible evidence that Nazi promises were more than show and propaganda.

Economic recovery was accompanied by a wave of social and cultural innovation intended to construct what Nazi propagandists called the *Volksgemeinschaft* (FOLKS-ge-MINE-shaft)—a "people's community" for racially pure Germans. The party set up mass organizations to spread Nazi ideology and enlist volunteers for the Nazi cause. Millions of Germans joined the Hitler Youth, the League of German Women, and the German Labor Front. Mass rallies, such as annual May Day celebrations and Nazi Party conventions in Nuremberg, brought together thousands of participants. Glowing reports on such events in the Nazi-controlled press brought the message home to millions more.

As the economy recovered, the government also proudly touted an array of inexpensive and enticing people's products. Items such as the *Volksempfänger* (the "People's Radio") and the Volkswagen (the "People's Car") were intended to link individuals' desire for consumer goods to the collective ideology of the "people's community." The Volkswagen "Beetle" was sold by subscription: Germans eager to purchase their own car could pay a small monthly amount into a state-run account until they had paid the full price. Thousands signed up, but although the Volkswagen was the subject of flashy marketing campaigns, not one single car was ever delivered to a private consumer. Such programs to ramp up the production of consumer goods faltered as the state increasingly focused on rearmament for the approaching war. Even so, they suggested to all that the regime was working hard to improve German living standards. (See "Evaluating Visual Evidence: Nazi Propaganda and Consumer Goods: The 'People's Car,'" page 853.)

Women played a special role in the Nazi state. Promising to "liberate women from women's liberation," Nazi ideologues championed a return to traditional family values. They outlawed abortion, discouraged women from obtaining higher education or holding jobs, and glorified domesticity and motherhood. Women were cast as protectors of the hearth and home and were instructed to raise young boys and girls in accordance with Nazi ideals. In the later 1930s, facing labor shortages, the Nazis had to reluctantly reverse course and encourage women to enter the labor force. Whatever the employment situation,

the millions of women enrolled in Nazi mass organizations, which organized charity drives and other social programs, experienced a sense of freedom and community in these social activities.

Nazi propagandists continually played up the supposed accomplishments of the regime. Economic growth, the vision of the *Volksgemeinschaft*, national pride in recovery, and feelings of belonging created by acts of racial exclusion led many Germans to support the regime. Hitler himself remained popular with broad sections of the population well into the war.

Not all Germans supported Hitler, however, and a number of groups actively resisted him after 1933. They were never unified, which helps explain their lack of success. Furthermore, the regime harshly clamped down on dissidents: tens of thousands of political enemies were imprisoned, and thousands were executed. After Communists and socialists were smashed by the SS system, a second group of opponents arose in the Catholic and Protestant churches. Their efforts, however, were directed primarily at preserving religious life, not at overthrowing Hitler. In 1938 and again during the war, a few high-ranking army officers, who feared the consequences of Hitler's reckless aggression, plotted against him, but their plans were unsuccessful.

Aggression and Appeasement

The Nazification of German society fulfilled only part of the Nazi agenda. While building the "people's community," the regime aggressively pursued territorial expansion for the supposedly superior German race. Although Germany withdrew from the League of Nations in 1933, at first Hitler carefully camouflaged his expansionist goals. Germany was still militarily weak, and the Nazi leader loudly proclaimed his peaceful intentions. Then in March 1935 Hitler declared that Germany would no longer abide by the disarmament clauses of the Treaty of Versailles. He established a military draft and began to build up the German army.

France and Great Britain protested, but any hope of a united front against the Nazis quickly collapsed. Britain adopted a policy of **appeasement**, granting Hitler what he demanded to avoid war. British appeasement, which practically dictated French policy, was largely motivated by the pacifism of a population still horrified by the memory of the First World War. As in Germany, powerful conservatives in Britain underestimated Hitler. They believed that Soviet communism was the real danger and that Hitler could be used to stop it. Such strong anticommunist feelings made an alliance between the Western powers and the Soviet Union against Nazi Germany highly unlikely.

When Hitler suddenly marched his armies into the demilitarized Rhineland in March 1936,

■ **appeasement** The British policy toward Germany prior to World War II that aimed at granting Hitler's territorial demands, including western Czechoslovakia, in order to avoid war.

Nazi Propaganda and Consumer Goods: The "People's Car"

It is easy to forget that the Volkswagens that zip around North America's streets today got their start in Hitler's Germany, introduced as part of a Nazi campaign to provide inexpensive but attractive consumer goods to the *Volk* (people). Marketed to "Aryans," but not to Jews or to other people whom the Nazis considered "racial enemies," the Volkswagen ("People's Car") symbolized a return to German prosperity. As the advertisement shown here suggests, the appeal of material abundance was a central plank in Nazi propaganda. Yet despite Hitler's promise that a "new, happier age" would "make the German people rich," many of the consumer goods promoted by the Nazi state remained out of reach of ordinary Germans.*

EVALUATE THE EVIDENCE

1. What does this image suggest about everyday life in Nazi Germany? What does it reveal about the aspirations of the German people for a good life in the 1930s?
2. Consider why both the government and commercial businesses attached the prefix *Volk*, or "people," to products like the Volkswagen. What larger message did these two groups seek to convey through the use of this prefix?
3. How is this advertising image similar to ads today? What makes it different?

*Peter Fritzsche, *Life and Death in the Third Reich* (Cambridge, Mass.: Harvard University Press, 2008), p. 59.

(Shawshots/Alamy Stock Photo)

brazenly violating the treaties of Versailles and Locarno (Map 27.2), Britain refused to act. France could do little without British support. Emboldened, the Nazis moved ever more aggressively, enlisting powerful allies in international affairs. Italy and Germany established the Rome-Berlin Axis in 1936. Japan, also under the rule of an ultranationalist dictatorship, joined the Axis alliance that same year. As we have seen, Germany and Italy also intervened in the Spanish Civil War (1936–1939).

In late 1937 Hitler moved forward with plans to seize Austria and Czechoslovakia as the first step in his long-contemplated drive for "living space" in the east. By threatening Austria with invasion, Hitler forced the Austrian chancellor to put local Nazis in control of the government in March 1938. The next day, in the Anschluss (annexation), German armies moved in unopposed, and Austria became part of Greater Germany (see Map 27.2).

Simultaneously, Hitler demanded that territories inhabited mostly by ethnic Germans in western Czechoslovakia — the Sudetenland — be ceded to Nazi Germany. Though democratic Czechoslovakia was allied with France and the Soviet Union and prepared to defend itself, appeasement triumphed again. In negotiations British prime minister Neville Chamberlain and the French agreed with Hitler that Germany should immediately take over the

MAP 27.2 The Growth of Nazi Germany, 1933–1939 Until March 1939 Hitler's conquests brought ethnic Germans into the Nazi state; then he turned on the Slavic and Jewish peoples he had always hated. He stripped Czechoslovakia of its independence and then attacked Poland in September 1939.

Sudetenland. Returning to London from the Munich Conference in September 1938, Chamberlain told cheering crowds that he had secured "peace with honor [and] peace for our time." Sold out by the Western powers, Czechoslovakia gave in.

Chamberlain's peace was short-lived. In March 1939 Hitler's armies invaded and occupied the Czech lands of Bohemia and Moravia. The effect on Western public opinion was electrifying. This time, there was no possible ethnic rationale for Nazi aggression, since Hitler was seizing ethnic Czechs and Slovaks—not Germans—as captive peoples. When Hitler next used the question of German minorities in Danzig as a pretext to confront Poland, a suddenly militant Chamberlain declared that Britain and France would fight if Hitler attacked his eastern neighbor. Hitler did not take these warnings seriously.

In August 1939, in an about-face that stunned the world, Nazi Germany and the Soviet Union—determined enemies—signed a nonaggression pact that paved the road to war. Each dictator promised to remain neutral if the other became involved in open hostilities. An attached secret protocol ruthlessly divided Poland, the Baltic nations, Finland, and Romania into German and Soviet spheres of influence. Stalin agreed to the pact because he remained distrustful of Western intentions and because Hitler offered immediate territorial gain.

For Hitler, everything was now set. On September 1, 1939, German armies and warplanes invaded Poland from three sides. Two days later, Britain and France, finally true to their word, declared war on Germany. The Second World War had begun.

What explains the success and then defeat of Germany and Japan during World War II?

Nazi Germany's actions unleashed an apocalyptic cataclysm. German armies quickly conquered much of western and eastern Europe, while the Japanese overran much of Southeast Asia. This reckless aggression brought together a coalition of unlikely but powerful allies determined to halt the Fascist advance: Britain, the United States, and the Soviet Union. After years of slaughter and genocide that decimated much of Europe and East Asia, this "Grand Alliance" decisively defeated the Axis powers.

German Victories in Europe

Using planes, tanks, and trucks in the first example of what German propagandists called blitzkrieg, or "lightning war," Hitler's armies crushed Poland in four weeks. The Soviet Union invaded and occupied the eastern half of Poland, as per the terms of the nonaggression pact. While the French and British armies prepared their defenses in the west, the Soviets undertook a violent campaign of political repression against Polish political and military leaders and intellectuals. In April and May 1940 the Soviets executed some 22,000 Polish army officers in what became known as the Katyn massacre, named after a forest in western Russia where some of the killings took place.

In spring 1940 the Nazi blitzkrieg struck again. After Germany occupied Denmark, Norway, and Holland, motorized columns broke into France through southern Belgium, split the Franco-British forces, and trapped the British army on the French beaches of Dunkirk. In a hard-pressed evacuation, the British withdrew their troops — although equipment could not be saved. Soon after, France was taken by the Nazis. By July 1940 Hitler ruled practically all of continental Europe. Italy was a German ally. Romania, Hungary, and Bulgaria joined the Axis alliance, and the Soviet Union, Spain, Switzerland, and Sweden were neutral powers. Only Yugoslavia and Britain, the latter led by the uncompromising Winston Churchill (1874–1965), remained unconquered.

To prepare for an amphibious invasion of Britain, Germany sought to gain control of the air. In the Battle of Britain, which began in July 1940, up to a thousand German planes a day attacked British airfields and key factories, dueling with British defenders high in the skies. Losses were heavy on both sides. In September 1940 Hitler turned from military objectives to indiscriminate bombing of British cities in an attempt to break British morale. British aircraft factories increased production, and, encouraged by the words of the ever-determined Churchill, the heavily bombed people of London defiantly dug in. (See "Viewpoints: Oratory and Ideology in World War II," page 858.) By October Britain was beating Germany three to one in the air war, and the Battle of Britain was over. Stymied there, the Nazi war machine invaded and occupied Greece and Yugoslavia.

Hitler now allowed his lifetime obsession of creating a vast eastern European empire ruled by Germany to dictate policy. On June 22, 1941, he broke his pact with Stalin and invaded the Soviet Union (Map 27.3). By October German troops had conquered most of Ukraine, surrounded Leningrad, and besieged Moscow. But the Soviets did not collapse, and when a severe winter struck German armies outfitted only in summer uniforms, the invaders retreated. Nevertheless, Hitler and his allies now ruled over a European empire stretching from eastern Europe to the English Channel. Hitler, the Nazi leadership, and the loyal German army were positioned to accelerate the construction of their so-called New Order in Europe.

Churchill Inspects Bomb Damage at Coventry Cathedral   British prime minister Winston Churchill (center), with members of the English Anglican clergy, visits the ruins of Coventry Cathedral, which was destroyed by German bombing in November 1940. Before halting their bombing raids in summer 1941, the Germans inflicted significant damage in the Battle of Britain, the first full-scale military campaign fought entirely by air forces. (Galerie Bilderwelt/Hulton Archive/Getty Images)

Map legend:

- Axis powers and their allies
- Occupied by Germany and its allies
- Allied powers and their allies
- Neutral nations
- — Boundary of Greater Germany
- ✹ Major battle

Siege of Leningrad, Sept. 1941–Jan. 1944

Germans repulsed, Dec. 1941

Moscow Oct. 1941–Jan. 1942

Siege of Stalingrad, Aug. 21, 1942– Jan. 31, 1943

Russian front, spring 1944

Russian front, Nov. 1942

Russian front, Dec. 1941

Battle of Britain, fall 1940

Germany surrenders, May 8, 1945

Siege of Warsaw, Sept. 1939 Ghetto Uprising, Apr.–May 1943 Warsaw Uprising, Aug.–Sept. 1944

Kursk July–Aug. 1943

Dnieper Aug.–Dec. 1943

Invasion of Normandy, June 6, 1944

Battle of the Bulge Dec. 1944

Western front, Feb. 1945

Russian front, Feb. 1945

Axis troops occupy Vichy France, Nov. 10 and 11, 1942

Italian front Feb. 1945

Rome (Liberated June 1944)

Monte Cassino May 1944

Salerno Sept. 1943

Allies invade Sicily and Italy, July–Sept. 1943

Casablanca Nov. 1942

Axis troops evacuated, May 1943

Sicily July 1943

Battle for Crete, May 20–June 1, 1941

El Alamein autumn 1942

Joined Allies, Nov. 1942

Countries and places labeled: NORWAY, SWEDEN, FINLAND, Helsinki, Leningrad, Oslo, Stockholm, ESTONIA, NORTHERN IRELAND, North Sea, DENMARK, Copenhagen, Riga, LATVIA, LITHUANIA, Smolensk, SOVIET UNION, Tula, Volga R., IRELAND, GREAT BRITAIN, NETHERLANDS, London, Berlin, Posen, BELARUS, Warsaw, Vistula R., POLAND, Dunkirk, BELGIUM, Kyiv, Dnieper R., Don R., Stalingrad, Paris, Battle of the Bulge, GERMANY, Kraków, UKRAINE, ATLANTIC OCEAN, FRANCE, Danube R., SLOVAKIA, Vienna, HUNGARY, Budapest, Vichy, SWITZERLAND, VICHY FRANCE, Bologna, Po R., CROATIA, ROMANIA, Bucharest, Danube R., Yalta, PORT., Madrid, Ebro R., ITALY, SERBIA, Black Sea, Lisbon, SPAIN, Corsica, Adriatic Sea, Sofia, BULGARIA, ALBANIA, SPANISH MOROCCO, GIBRALTAR (Gr. Br.), Sardinia, Ankara, TURKEY, MOROCCO (Fr.), ALGERIA (Vichy France), Sicily, GREECE, Athens, SYRIA (Fr. Mandate), IRAQ (Br. Mandate), Cyprus (Gr. Br.), LEBANON (Fr. Mandate), TRANS-JORDAN (Br. Mandate), PALESTINE (Br. Mandate), TUNISIA (Fr.), Malta (Gr. Br.), Crete (Gr.), SAUDI ARABIA, Suez Canal, Nile R., Cairo, LIBYA (It.), EGYPT, Mediterranean Sea

Scale: 0–400 miles / 0–400 kilometers

MAPPING THE PAST

MAP 27.3 World War II in Europe and Africa, 1939–1945

This map shows the extent of Hitler's empire before the Battle of Stalingrad in late 1942 and the subsequent advances of the Allies until Germany surrendered on May 8, 1945. Compare this map with Map 27.2 to trace the rise and fall of the Nazi empire over time.

ANALYZING THE MAP What was the first country conquered by Hitler (see Map 27.2)? Locate Germany's advance and retreat on the Russian front in December 1941, November 1942, spring 1944, and February 1945. How do these points compare to the position of British and U.S. forces on the battlefield at similar points in time?

CONNECTIONS What implications might the battle lines on February 1945 have had for the postwar settlement in Europe?

Europe Under Nazi Occupation

Hitler's **New Order** was based firmly on the guiding principle of National Socialism: racial imperialism. Occupied peoples were treated according to their place in the Nazi racial hierarchy. All were subject to harsh policies dedicated to ethnic cleansing and the expropriation of resources for the Nazi war effort. A flood of plunder reached Germany, helping maintain high living standards and preserving home-front morale well into the war. Nazi victory, furthermore, placed national Jewish populations across Europe under German control, allowing the mass murder of Europe's Jews.

Within the New Order, the "Nordic" peoples — the Dutch, Danes, and Norwegians — received preferential treatment, for the Germans believed they were related to the Aryan master race. In Holland, Denmark, and Norway, the Nazis established puppet governments of various kinds. Though many people hated the conquerors, the Nazis found willing collaborators who ruled in accord with German needs. France was divided into two parts. The German army occupied the north, including Paris. The southeast remained nominally independent. There the aging First World War general Marshal Henri-Philippe Pétain formed a new French government — the Vichy (VIH-shee) regime — that supported Germany, adopted many aspects of National Socialist ideology, and willingly placed French Jews in the hands of the Nazis.

In central-eastern Europe, the war and German rule were far more ruthless and deadly than in the west. From the start, the Nazi leadership had cast the war in the east as one of annihilation. The Nazis now set out to build a vast colonial empire where Jews would be exterminated and Poles, Belorussians, Ukrainians, and Russians would be enslaved and forced to die out. According to the plans, ethnic German peasants would resettle the resulting abandoned lands. In pursuit of such goals, large parts of western Poland were incorporated into Germany. Another part of Poland

Vichy France, 1940

□ Occupied by Germany
■ Annexed by Germany

Nazi Occupation of Poland and East-Central Europe, 1939–1942

— Boundary of Poland, 1938
■ Germany, 1938
■ Annexed by Germany, 1939
□ German civil administration, 1942
■ German military occupation, 1942
— Boundary of Greater Germany, 1942

was placed under the rule of a merciless civilian administration.

With the support of military commanders, Himmler's elite SS corps now implemented a program of destruction and annihilation to create a "mass settlement space" for supposedly racially pure Germans. Nazi occupation forces destroyed cities and factories, stole crops and farm animals, and subjected conquered peoples to forced starvation and mass murder. Nazi occupation in Poland and Belarus destroyed the lives of millions.[6]

Small but determined underground resistance groups fought back against these atrocities. They were hardly unified. Communists and socialists often disagreed with more centrist or nationalist groups on long-term goals and short-term tactics. In Yugoslavia, for example, Communist and royalist military resistance groups attacked the Germans, but also each other. In occupied Soviet territories, organized partisan groups undertook sustained guerrilla war against Nazi forces. Poland, under German occupation longer than any other nation, had the most determined and well-organized resistance. The Nazis had closed all Polish universities and outlawed national newspapers, but the Poles organized secret classes and maintained a thriving underground press. Underground members of the Polish Home Army, led by the government in exile in London, passed intelligence about German operations to the Allies and committed sabotage. The famous French resistance undertook similar actions, as did groups in Italy, Greece, and the Netherlands.

The resistance presented a real challenge to the Nazi New Order, and the German response was swift and deadly. The Nazi army and the SS tortured captured resistance members and executed hostages in reprisal for attacks. Responding to actions undertaken by resistance groups, the German army murdered the male populations of Lidice

■ **New Order** Hitler's program based on racial imperialism, which gave preferential treatment to the "Nordic" peoples; the French, an "inferior" Latin people, occupied a middle position; and Slavs and Jews were treated harshly as "subhumans."

In times of intense warfare, political leaders do their utmost to convince the nation's citizens to fight on to victory. In "Their Finest Hour," British prime minister Winston Churchill called on the people to defend Great Britain from German attack. The speech was given in the House of Commons on June 18, 1940, just after the British defeat at Dunkirk and just at the beginning of the Battle of Britain. Nazi propaganda minister Joseph Goebbels's speech "Storm Break Loose," delivered to a sympathetic crowd at the Berlin Sports Palace on February 18, 1943, followed the critical German defeat at the Battle of Stalingrad.

Winston Churchill, "Their Finest Hour"

⤳ I cannot accept the drawing of any distinctions between Members of the present Government. It was formed at a moment of crisis in order to unite all the Parties and all sections of opinion. It has received the almost unanimous support of both Houses of Parliament. Its Members are going to stand together, and, subject to the authority of the House of Commons, we are going to govern the country and fight the war. . . .

[T]he Battle of France is over. I expect that the Battle of Britain is about to begin. Upon this battle depends the survival of Christian civilization. Upon it depends our own British life, and the long continuity of our institutions and our Empire.

The whole fury and might of the enemy must very soon be turned on us. Hitler knows that he will have to break us in this Island or lose the war. If we can stand up to him, all Europe may be free and the life of the world may move forward into broad, sunlit uplands.

But if we fail, then the whole world, including the United States, including all that we have known and cared for, will sink into the abyss of a new Dark Age made more sinister, and perhaps more protracted, by the lights of perverted science.

Let us therefore brace ourselves to our duties, and so bear ourselves that, if the British Empire and its Commonwealth last for a thousand years, men will still say,

"This was their finest hour."

Joseph Goebbels, "Nation, Rise Up, and Let the Storm Break Loose!"

⤳ The German people, raised, educated and disciplined by National Socialism, can bear the whole truth. It knows the gravity of the situation, and its leadership can therefore demand the necessary hard measures, yes even the hardest measures. . . .

The goal of Bolshevism is Jewish world revolution. They want to bring chaos to the Reich and Europe, using the resulting hopelessness and desperation to establish their international, Bolshevist-concealed capitalist tyranny.

I do not need to say what that would mean for the German people. A Bolshevization of the Reich would mean the liquidation of our entire intelligentsia and leadership, and the descent of our workers into Bolshevist-Jewish slavery. . . . [T]he storm from the East that breaks against our lines daily in increasing strength is nothing other than a repetition of the historical devastation that has so often in the past endangered our part of the world. . . .

This explains, by the way, our consistent Jewish policies. We see Jewry as a direct threat to every nation. . . . Germany . . . has no intention of bowing before this threat, but rather intends to take the most radical measures, if necessary, in good time. . . .

I am firmly convinced that the German people have been deeply moved by the blow of fate at Stalingrad. It has looked into the face of hard and pitiless war. It knows now the awful truth, and is resolved to follow the Führer through thick and thin. . . .

We promise you, we promise the front, we promise the Führer, that we will mold together the homeland into a force on which the Führer and his fighting soldiers can rely on absolutely and blindly. We pledge to do all in our life and work that is necessary for victory. . . .

Now, people rise up and let the storm break loose!

QUESTIONS FOR ANALYSIS

1. Compare and contrast the two speeches. What are the most obvious similarities and differences? What threats and sources of strength do Churchill and Goebbels evoke?

2. How do the assertions made in these two famous speeches reflect the political values of Great Britain and Nazi Germany?

Sources: Winston Churchill, "Their Finest Hour," June 18, 1940; "Goebbels' 1943 Speech on Total War," ed. and trans. Randall Bytwerk, Calvin College Propaganda Archive, http://research.calvin.edu/german-propaganda-archive/goeb36.htm.

MAP 27.4 The Holocaust, 1941–1945   The leaders of Nazi Germany established an extensive network of ghettos and concentration and extermination camps to persecute their political opponents and those people deemed "racially undesirable" by the regime. The death camps, where the Nazi SS systematically murdered millions of European Jews, Soviet prisoners of war, and others, were located primarily in Nazi-occupied territories in eastern Europe, but the conditions in the concentration camps within Germany's borders were almost as brutal.

(Czechoslovakia) and Oradour (France) and leveled the entire towns. Despite such reprisals, Nazi occupiers were never able to eradicate popular resistance to their rule.

The Holocaust

The ultimate abomination of Nazi racism was the condemnation of all European Jews and other peoples to extreme racial persecution and then annihilation in the **Holocaust**, a great spasm of racially inspired mass murder. The Nazis began to use cultural, legal, and economic means to persecute Jews and other "undesirable" groups immediately after taking power in Germany. Between 1938 and 1940 persecution turned deadly in the Nazi euthanasia (mercy killing) campaign, an important step toward genocide.

Just as Germany began the war, some 70,000 people with physical and mental disabilities were forced into special hospitals, barracks, and camps. Deemed by Nazi administrators to be "unworthy lives" who might "pollute" the German race, they were murdered in cold blood. The victims were mostly ethnic Germans, and the euthanasia campaign was stopped in 1940 after church leaders and ordinary families spoke out. The staff involved took what they learned in this program to the extermination camps the Nazis would soon build in the east (Map 27.4).

The German victory over Poland in 1939 brought some 3 million Jews under Nazi control. Jews in

■ **Holocaust** The systematic effort of the Nazi state to exterminate all European Jews and other groups deemed racially inferior during the Second World War.

A "Transport" Arrives at Auschwitz   Upon arrival at Auschwitz in May 1944, Hungarian Jews undergo a "selection" managed by Nazi officers and prisoners in striped uniforms. Camp guards will send the fittest people to the barracks, where they will probably soon die from forced labor under atrocious conditions. The aged, ill, very young, or otherwise infirm will be murdered immediately in the Auschwitz gas chambers. The tower over the main gate to the camp, which today opens onto a vast memorial complex, is visible in the background. (Galerie Bilderwelt/Getty Images)

German-occupied territories were soon forced to move into urban districts termed "ghettos." In walled-off ghettos in cities large and small—two of the most important were in Warsaw and Lodz—hundreds of thousands of Polish Jews lived in crowded and unsanitary conditions, without real work or adequate sustenance. Over 500,000 people died, imprisoned in the ghettos.

The racial violence reached new extremes when Germany invaded the Soviet Union in 1941. Four military death squads known as Special Task Forces (*Einsatzgruppen*) and other military units, assisted by local collaborators, followed the advancing German armies. They moved systematically from town to town, shooting Jews and other target populations. The victims of these mobile killing units were often forced to dig their own graves in local woods or fields before they were shot. In this way the German armed forces murdered some 2 million civilians.

In late 1941 Hitler and the Nazi leadership, in some still-debated combination, ordered the SS to implement the mass murder of all Jews in Europe. What the Nazi leadership called the "final solution of the Jewish question" had begun. The Germans set up

an industrialized killing machine that remains unparalleled, with an extensive network of concentration camps, factory complexes, and railroad transport lines to imprison and murder Jews and other so-called undesirables and to exploit their labor before they died. In the occupied east, the surviving residents of the ghettos were loaded onto trains and taken to camps such as Auschwitz-Birkenau, the best known of the Nazi killing centers, where over 1 million people—the vast majority of them Jews—were murdered in gas chambers. Some few were put to work as expendable laborers. The Jews of Germany and occupied western and central Europe were rounded up, put on trains, and sent to the camps. Even after it was quite clear that Germany would lose the war, the killing continued.

Given the scope and organization of Nazi persecution, there was little opportunity for successful Jewish resistance, yet Jews did evade or challenge the killing machine. Some brave Jews went underground or masqueraded as Christians to escape Nazi persecution; others fled to rural areas and joined bands of anti-Nazi partisans. Jews also organized secret resistance groups in ghettos and concentration camps.

INDIVIDUALS IN SOCIETY
Primo Levi

The vast majority of Jews deported to Auschwitz-Birkenau were murdered soon after arriving, but the Nazis used some prisoners as slave laborers, and a few of them survived. Primo Levi (1919–1987), one of these laborers, lived to become one of the most influential witnesses to the Holocaust.

Like much of Italy's small Jewish community, Levi's family belonged to the urban professional classes. Levi graduated from the University of Turin with highest honors in chemistry in 1941. Growing discrimination against Italian Jews led him to join the antifascist resistance two years later. Captured, he was deported to Auschwitz with 650 Italian Jews in February 1944. Stone-faced SS men picked 96 men, Levi among them, and 29 women from this group to work in labor camps; the rest were gassed upon arrival.

Levi and his fellow prisoners were kicked, punched, stripped, branded with tattoos, crammed into huts, and worked unmercifully. Hoping for some prisoner solidarity, Levi found only a desperate struggle of each against all and enormous status differences among prisoners. Many bewildered newcomers, beaten and demoralized by their bosses — the most privileged prisoners — collapsed and died. Others struggled to secure their own privileges, however small, because food rations and working conditions were so abominable that prisoners who were not bosses usually perished in two to three months.

Sensitive and noncombative, Levi found himself sinking into oblivion. But instead of joining the mass of the "drowned," he became one of the "saved"— a complicated surprise with moral implications that he would ponder all his life. As Levi explained in *Survival in Auschwitz* (1947), the usual road to salvation in the camps was some kind of collaboration with German power. German criminals were released from prison to become brutal camp guards; non-Jewish political prisoners competed for jobs entitling them to better conditions; and, especially troubling for Levi, a few Jews plotted and struggled to become "bosses," who gained not only better rations but also the power of life and death over other Jewish prisoners.

Though not one of these Jewish bosses, Levi believed that he, like almost all survivors, had entered the "gray zone" of moral compromise. "Nobody can know for how long and under what trials his soul can resist before yielding or breaking," Levi wrote. "The harsher the oppression, the more widespread among the oppressed is the willingness, with all its infinite nuances and motivations, to collaborate."* The camps held no saints, he believed: the Nazi system degraded

Primo Levi never stopped thinking, writing, and speaking about the Holocaust. (Gianni Giansanti/Getty Images)

its victims, forcing them to commit sometimes-bestial acts against their fellow prisoners in order to survive.

For Levi, salvation came from his education. Interviewed by a German technocrat for work in the camp's synthetic rubber program, Levi was chosen for this relatively easy labor because he spoke fluent German, including scientific terminology. Work in the warm camp laboratory offered Levi opportunities to pilfer equipment he could then trade to other prisoners for food and necessities. Levi also gained critical support from three prisoners who refused to do wicked and hateful acts. And he counted luck as essential for his survival: in the camp infirmary with scarlet fever in January 1945 as advancing Russian armies prepared to liberate the camp, Levi was not evacuated by the Nazis and shot to death like most Jewish prisoners.

After the war, Levi was haunted by the nightmare that the Holocaust would be ignored or forgotten. Ashamed that so many people whom he considered better than himself had perished, and wanting the world to understand the genocide in all its complexity so that people would never again tolerate such atrocities, he turned to writing about his experiences. Primo Levi, while revealing Nazi guilt, tirelessly grappled with his vision of individual responsibility and moral ambiguity in a hell designed to make the victims collaborate and persecute each other.

QUESTIONS FOR ANALYSIS

1. Describe Levi's experience at Auschwitz. What does he mean by the "gray zone"?
2. Will a vivid historical memory of the Holocaust help prevent future genocide?

*Primo Levi, *The Drowned and the Saved* (New York: Vintage, 1989), pp. 43, 60. See also Levi, *Survival in Auschwitz: The Nazi Assault on Humanity* (London: Collier Books, 1961). These powerful testimonies are highly recommended.

As news of German-perpetrated mass murder reached the Warsaw Ghetto, Jews living there began to organize underground resistance groups. On April 19, 1943, the poorly armed resisters attacked the vastly superior German forces. The resisters surrendered on May 16; afterwards, German troops burned the ghetto to the ground and took the remaining Jewish inhabitants to extermination camps. In Auschwitz itself, in October 1944, a group of Jewish prisoners revolted and burned down one of the camp's crematoriums before being captured and summarily executed.

The murderous attack on European Jews was the ultimate monstrosity of Nazi "racial hygiene" in action. By 1945 the Nazis had killed about 6 million Jews and some 5 million other Europeans, including millions of ethnic Poles and Russian prisoners of war. (See "Individuals in Society: Primo Levi," page 861.) Who exactly was responsible for this terrible crime? Historians continue to debate this critical question. Some lay the guilt on Hitler and the Nazi leadership, arguing that ordinary Germans had little knowledge of the extermination camps or were forced to participate by Nazi terror and totalitarian control. Other scholars conclude that far more Germans knew about and were at best indifferent to the fate of the Jews and other people targeted for extermination. The question remains: what motivated those who actually worked in the killing machine—the "desk murderers" in Berlin who sent trains to the east, the soldiers who shot Jews in the Polish forests, the guards at Auschwitz? Some historians believe that widely shared anti-Semitism led ordinary Germans to become Hitler's "willing executioners." Others argue that heightened peer pressure, the desire to advance in the ranks, and the need to prove their strength under the most brutalizing wartime violence turned average Germans into reluctant killers. The conditioning of racist Nazi propaganda clearly played a role. Whatever the cause, numerous Germans were prepared to follow Nazi ideology and perpetrate ever-greater crimes, from mistreatment to incarceration to mass murder.[7]

Japanese Empire and the War in the Pacific

The racist war of annihilation in Europe was matched by racially motivated warfare in East Asia. In response to political divisions and economic crisis, a Fascist government had taken control of Japan in the 1930s. As in Germany and Italy, the Japanese government was highly nationalistic and militaristic, and it was deeply committed to imperial expansion. According to Japanese race theory, the Asian races were far superior to Western ones. In speeches, schools, and newspapers, ultranationalists eagerly voiced the extreme anti-Western views that had risen in the 1920s and 1930s. They glorified the warrior virtues of honor and sacrifice and proclaimed that Japan would liberate East Asia from Western colonialists.

Japan soon acted on its racial-imperial ambitions. In 1931 Japanese armies invaded and occupied Manchuria, a vast territory in northeastern China. In 1937 Japan brutally invaded the Chinese mainland. Seeking to cement ties with the Fascist regimes of Europe, in 1940 the Japanese entered into a formal alliance with Italy and Germany, and in summer 1941 Japanese armies occupied southern portions of the French colony of Indochina (now Vietnam, Laos, and Cambodia).

The Japanese proudly proclaimed what they called the Greater East Asia Co-Prosperity Sphere. Under the slogan "Asia for Asians," Japanese propagandists maintained that their expansion would free Asians from hated Western imperialists. By promising to create a mutually advantageous union for long-term development, the Japanese tapped currents of nationalist sentiment, and most local populations were glad to see the Westerners go.

But the Co-Prosperity Sphere was a sham. Real power remained in the hands of the Japanese. They exhibited great cruelty toward civilian populations and prisoners of war, subjected China and Korea to full-scale military occupation and dreadful atrocities, and exploited other peoples for Japan's wartime needs, arousing local populations against them. Nonetheless, the ability of the Japanese to defeat the Western colonial powers set a powerful example for national liberation groups in Asia, which would become important in the decolonization movement that followed World War II.

Japanese expansion evoked a sharp response from U.S. president Franklin Roosevelt, and Japan's leaders came to believe that war with the United States was inevitable. After much debate, they decided to launch a surprise attack on the U.S. fleet based at Pearl Harbor in the Hawaiian Islands. On December 7, 1941, the Japanese sank or crippled every U.S. battleship, but by chance all the U.S. aircraft carriers were at sea and escaped unharmed. Pearl Harbor brought the Americans into the war in a spirit of anger and revenge.

As the Americans mobilized for war, Japanese armies overran more European and American colonies in Southeast Asia. By May 1942 Japan controlled a vast empire (Map 27.5) and was threatening Australia. The United States pushed back and engaged the Japanese in a series of hard-fought naval battles. In July 1943 the Americans and their Australian allies opened a successful island-hopping campaign that slowly forced Japan out of its conquered territories. The war in the Pacific was extremely brutal—a "war without mercy," in the words of a leading American scholar—and soldiers on both sides committed atrocities. A product of spiraling violence, mutual hatred, and dehumanizing

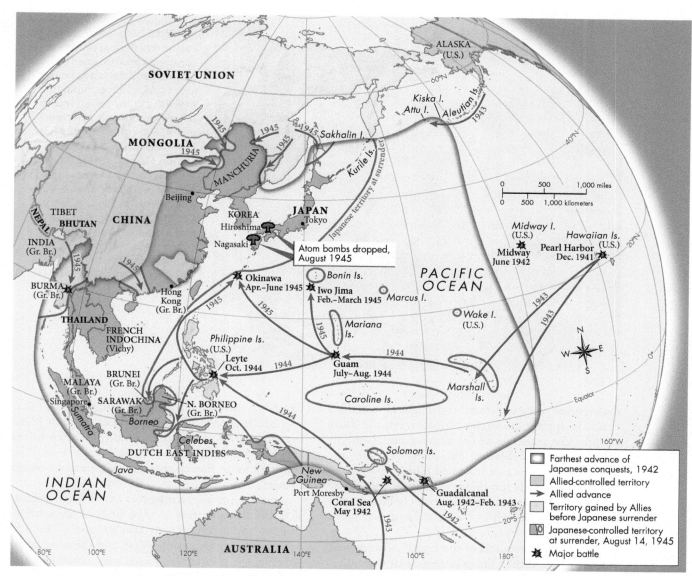

MAP 27.5 World War II in the Pacific In 1942 Japanese forces overran an enormous amount of territory, which the Allies slowly recaptured in a long, bitter struggle. As this map shows, Japan still held a large Asian empire in August 1945, when the unprecedented devastation of atomic warfare suddenly forced it to surrender.

racial stereotypes, the fighting intensified as the United States advanced toward Japan.[8]

The Grand Alliance and the "Hinge of Fate"

While the Nazis and the Japanese built their savage empires, Great Britain, the United States, and the Soviet Union joined together in a military pact Churchill termed the Grand Alliance. This was a matter of circumstance more than choice. It had taken the Japanese surprise attack to bring the isolationist United States into the war. Moreover, the British and Americans were determined opponents of Soviet

communism, and disagreements between the Soviets and the capitalist powers during the course of the war sowed mutual distrust. Stalin repeatedly urged Britain and the United States to open a second front in France to relieve pressure on Soviet forces, but Churchill and Roosevelt refused until the summer of 1944. Despite such tensions, the overriding goal of defeating the Axis powers brought together these reluctant allies.

In one area of agreement, the Grand Alliance concurred on a policy of "Europe first." Only after Hitler was defeated would the Allies mount an all-out attack on Japan, seen as the lesser threat. The Allies also agreed to concentrate on immediate military needs, postponing tough political questions about

The Anders Army at the Battle of Monte Cassino, 1944   Although Poland was the first country to be conquered and occupied by Nazi Germany and the last to be liberated by Allied forces, thousands of Polish soldiers served with the Allies in hard-fought campaigns in the Soviet Union, North Africa, the Middle East, and western Europe. Members of the "Anders Army"—named after commanding general Władysław Anders—played a key role in the Battle of Monte Cassino, a desperate struggle to take a German stronghold in a hilltop medieval monastery in southern Italy in 1944. (GIANCARLO COSTA/Private Collection/Bridgeman Images)

the eventual peace settlement that might have divided them. To further encourage mutual trust, the Allies adopted the principle of the unconditional surrender of Germany and Japan. This policy cemented the Grand Alliance because it denied Hitler any hope of dividing his foes. It also meant that Soviet and Anglo-American armies would almost certainly be forced to invade and occupy all of Germany, and that Japan would fight to the bitter end.

The military resources of the Grand Alliance were awesome. The United States harnessed its vast industrial base to wage global war and in 1943 outproduced not only Germany, Italy, and Japan, but all the rest of the world combined. Great Britain became an impregnable island fortress, a gigantic staging area for a decisive blow to the heart of Germany. After a determined push, the Soviet Union's military strength was so great that it might well have defeated Germany without Western help. Stalin drew heavily on the resolve of the Soviet people, especially those in the central Russian heartland. Broad-based Russian nationalism, as opposed to narrow Communist ideology, became a powerful unifying force in what the Soviet state called the Great Patriotic War of the Fatherland.

The combined might of the Allies forced back the Nazi armies on all fronts (see Map 27.3). At the Second Battle of El Alamein (el al-uh-MAYN) in October–November 1942, British forces decisively defeated combined German and Italian armies and halted the Axis penetration of North Africa. Winston Churchill called the battle the "hinge of fate" that opened the door to Allied victory. Fearful of an Allied invasion across the Mediterranean, German forces occupied Vichy France in November 1942, and the collaborationist French government effectively ceased to exist.

After driving the Axis powers out of North Africa, U.S. and British forces invaded Sicily in the summer of 1943 and mainland Italy that autumn. Mussolini was overthrown by a coup d'état, and the new Italian government publicly accepted unconditional surrender. In response, Nazi armies invaded and seized control of northern and central Italy, and German paratroopers rescued Mussolini in a daring raid and put him at the head of a puppet government. Facing stiff German resistance, the Allies battled their way slowly up the Italian peninsula. The Germans were everywhere on the defensive.

The spring of 1943 brought crucial Allied victories at sea and in the air. In the first years of the war, German submarines had successfully attacked North Atlantic shipping, severely hampering the British war effort. New antisubmarine technologies favored the Allies, and soon massive convoys of hundreds of ships were streaming across the Atlantic, bringing much-needed troops and supplies from the United States to Britain.

The German air force had never really recovered from its defeat in the Battle of Britain. With almost unchallenged air superiority, the United States and Britain now mounted massive bombing raids on German cities to maim industrial production

Soviet Troops After the Battle of Stalingrad   Triumphant Soviet soldiers march through the center of bomb-damaged Stalingrad after the end of the battle on February 2, 1943. In the background stands the destroyed department store that housed the headquarters of German Field Marshal von Paulus before his Sixth Army was surrounded and forced to surrender. Hundreds of thousands of soldiers on both sides lost their lives, and of the approximately 100,000 German prisoners taken by the Red Army, only about 5,000 returned home after the war. (Emmanuel Yevzerikhin/Slava Katamidze Collection/Getty Images)

and break civilian morale. By the war's end, hardly a German city of any size remained untouched, and many — including Dresden, Hamburg, and Cologne — lay in ruins.

Great Britain and the United States had made critical advances, but the worst German defeats came at the hands of the Red Army on the eastern front. Although the Germans had almost captured the major cities of Moscow and Leningrad in early winter 1941, they were forced back by determined Soviet counterattacks. The Germans mounted a second and initially successful invasion of the Soviet Union in the summer of 1942, but the campaign turned into a disaster. The downfall came at the **Battle of Stalingrad**, when in November 1942 the Soviets surrounded and systematically destroyed the entire German Sixth Army of 300,000 men. In January 1943 only 123,000 soldiers were left to surrender. Hitler, who had refused to allow a retreat, suffered a catastrophic defeat. For the first time, German public

opinion turned decisively against the war. In summer 1943 the larger, better-equipped Soviet armies took the offensive and began to push the Germans back along the entire eastern front (see Map 27.3).

Allied Victory

The balance of power was now clearly in Allied hands, yet bitter fighting continued in Europe for almost two years. The German war industry, under the Nazi minister of armaments Albert Speer, put to work millions of prisoners of war and slave laborers from across occupied Europe. Between early 1942 and July 1944, German war production tripled despite heavy Anglo-American bombing.

German resistance against Hitler failed to halt the fighting. An unsuccessful attempt by conservative

■ **Battle of Stalingrad** A Russian victory over Germany in winter 1942–1943 and a major turning point in the war, which led to the ultimate defeat of the Germans in May 1945.

Nuclear Wasteland at Hiroshima   Only a handful of buildings remain standing in the ruins of Hiroshima in September 1945. Fearing the costs of a prolonged ground and naval campaign against the Japanese mainland, the United States dropped atomic bombs on Hiroshima and Nagasaki in August 1945. The bombings ended the war and opened the nuclear age. (AP Photo)

army officers to assassinate Hitler in July 1944 only brought increased repression by the fanatic Nazis who had taken over the government. Closely disciplined by the regime, frightened by the prospect of unconditional surrender, and terrorized by Nazi propaganda that stereotypically portrayed the advancing Russian armies as rapacious Slavic beasts, the Germans fought on.

On June 6, 1944, American and British forces under General Dwight Eisenhower landed on the beaches of Normandy, France, in history's largest naval invasion. In a hundred dramatic days, more than 2 million men and almost half a million vehicles broke through the German lines and pushed inland. Rejecting proposals to strike straight at Berlin in a massive attack, Eisenhower moved forward cautiously on a broad front. Not until March 1945 did American troops cross the Rhine and enter Germany. By spring of 1945 the Allies had finally forced the Germans out of the Italian peninsula. That April, Mussolini was captured in northern

Italy by Communist partisans and executed, along with his mistress and other Fascist leaders.

The Soviets, who had been advancing steadily since July 1943, reached the outskirts of Warsaw by August 1944. Anticipating German defeat, the Polish underground Home Army ordered an uprising, so that the Poles might take the city on their own and establish independence from the Soviets. The Warsaw Uprising was a tragic miscalculation. Citing military pressure, the Red Army refused to enter the city. Stalin and Soviet leaders thus allowed the Germans to destroy the Polish insurgents, a cynical move that paved the way for the establishment of a postwar Communist regime. Only after the decimated Home Army surrendered did the Red Army continue its advance. Warsaw lay in ruins, and between 150,000 and 200,000 Poles—mostly civilians—had lost their lives.

Over the next six months, the Soviets moved southward into Romania, Hungary, Bulgaria, and Yugoslavia. In January 1945 the Red Army crossed Poland into

Germany, and on April 26 it met American forces on the Elbe River. The Allies had overrun Europe and closed their vise on Nazi Germany. As Soviet forces fought their way into Berlin, Hitler died by suicide, and on May 8 the remaining German commanders capitulated.

The war in the Pacific also drew to a close. Despite repeated U.S. victories through the summer of 1945, Japanese troops had continued to fight with enormous courage and determination. American commanders believed the invasion and conquest of Japan itself might cost 1 million U.S. casualties and claim 10 to 20 million Japanese lives. In fact, Japan was almost helpless, its industry and dense, fragile wooden cities largely destroyed by intense American bombing. Yet the Japanese seemed determined to fight on, ready to die for a hopeless cause.

After intense planning, American planes dropped atomic bombs on Hiroshima and Nagasaki in Japan on August 6 and 9, 1945. The number of victims is incalculable, but about 200,000 residents died, and the city centers were destroyed in massive firestorms. The mass bombing of cities and civilians, one of the terrible new practices of World War II, now ended in the final nightmare—unprecedented human destruction in a single blinding flash. On August 14, 1945, the Japanese announced their surrender. The Second World War, which had claimed the lives of more than 60 million soldiers and civilians, was over.

NOTES

1. Quoted in S. Kotkin, *Magnetic Mountain: Stalinism as a Civilization* (Berkeley: University of California Press, 1997), pp. 221–222.
2. Karl Schlögel, *Moscow 1937* (Malden, Mass.: Polity Books, 2012), p. 417.
3. R. Thurston, *Life and Terror in Stalin's Russia, 1934–1941* (New Haven, Conn.: Yale University Press, 1996), esp. pp. 16–106; also M. Malia, *The Soviet Tragedy: A History of Socialism in Russia, 1917–1991* (New York: Free Press, 1995), pp. 227–270.
4. Quoted in C. Duggan, *A Concise History of Italy* (New York: Cambridge University Press, 1994), p. 227.
5. Quoted in Duggan, *A Concise History of Italy*, p. 234.
6. See, for example, the population statistics on the German occupation of Belarus in C. Gerlach, "German Economic Interests, Occupation Policy, and the Murder of the Jews in Belorussia, 1941–43," in *National Socialist Extermination Policies: Contemporary German Perspectives and Controversies*, ed. U. Herbert (New York: Berghan Books, 2000), pp. 210–239. See also M. Allen, *The Business of Genocide: The SS, Slave Labor, and the Concentration Camps* (Chapel Hill: University of North Carolina Press, 2002), pp. 270–285.
7. D. Goldhagen, *Hitler's Willing Executioners: Ordinary Germans and the Holocaust* (New York: Vintage Books, 1997); for an alternate explanation, see C. Browning, *Ordinary Men: Reserve Police Battalion 101 and the Final Solution in Poland* (New York: Harper, 1992).
8. J. Dower, *War Without Mercy: Race and Power in the Pacific War* (New York: Pantheon, 1986).
9. E. Hobsbawm, *The Age of Extremes: A History of the World, 1914–1991* (New York: Vintage, 1996), p. 21.

LOOKING BACK LOOKING AHEAD

The first half of the twentieth century brought almost unimaginable violence and destruction, leading historian Eric Hobsbawm to label the era the "age of catastrophe."[9] Shaken by the rapid cultural change and economic collapse that followed the tragedy of World War I, many Europeans embraced the radical politics of communism and fascism. Some found appeal in visions of a classless society or a racially pure national community, and totalitarian leaders like Stalin and Hitler capitalized on these desires for social order, building dictatorial regimes that demanded total allegiance to an ideological vision. Even as these regimes rewarded supporters and promised ordinary people a new age, they violently repressed their enemies, real and imagined. The vision proved fatal: the great clash of ideologies that emerged in the 1920s and 1930s led to history's most deadly war, killing millions and devastating large swaths of Europe and East Asia.

Only the reluctant Grand Alliance of the liberal United States and Great Britain with the Communist Soviet Union was able to defeat the Axis powers. After 1945 fascism was finished, discredited by total defeat and the postwar revelation of the Holocaust. To make sure, the Allies would occupy the lands of their former enemies. Rebuilding a devastated Europe proved a challenging but in the end manageable task: once recovery took off, the postwar decades brought an economic boom that led to levels of prosperity unimaginable in the interwar years. Maintaining an alliance between the capitalist West and the Communist East was something else. Trust quickly broke down. Europe would be divided into two hostile camps, and Cold War tensions between East and West would dominate European and world politics for the next forty years.

Make Connections

Think about the larger developments and continuities within and across chapters.

1. Historians continue to disagree on whether "totalitarianism" is an appropriate way to describe Communist and Fascist dictatorships in Europe. How would you define this term? Is it a useful label to describe state and society under Stalin, Mussolini, and Hitler? Why is the debate over totalitarianism still important today?

2. Why would ordinary people support dictatorships that trampled on democracy, political freedoms, and civil rights?

3. Summarize the key issues in the origins of World War II and the key turning points in the war itself. Was political ideology the main driving force behind these events, or were other factors at play?

27 REVIEW & EXPLORE

Identify Key Terms

Identify and explain the significance of each item below.

totalitarianism (p. 834)

Stalinism (p. 834)

fascism (p. 835)

eugenics (p. 835)

Spanish Civil War (p. 836)

New Economic Policy (NEP) (p. 836)

five-year plan (p. 838)

collectivization of agriculture (p. 839)

kulaks (p. 839)

Black Shirts (p. 844)

Lateran Agreement (p. 845)

National Socialism (p. 846)

appeasement (p. 852)

New Order (p. 857)

Holocaust (p. 859)

Battle of Stalingrad (p. 865)

Review the Main Ideas

Answer the section heading questions from the chapter.

1. What were the most important characteristics of Communist and Fascist ideologies? (p. 834)

2. How did Stalinism transform state and society in the Soviet Union? (p. 836)

3. What kind of government did Mussolini establish in Italy? (p. 843)

4. What policies did Nazi Germany pursue, and why did they appeal to ordinary Germans? (p. 846)

5. What explains the success and then defeat of Germany and Japan during World War II? (p. 855)

Suggested Resources

BOOKS

◆ Aly, Götz. *Hitler's Beneficiaries: Plunder, Racial War, and the Nazi Welfare State*. 2005. A controversial interpretation of popular support for the Hitler regime, focused on the material benefits of wartime plunder.

◆ Bergen, Doris L. *War and Genocide: A Concise History of the Holocaust*, 3d ed. 2016. A concise and accessible discussion of National Socialism and the murderous Nazi assault on European Jews and other groups.

◆ Bosworth, R. J. B. *Mussolini's Italy: Life Under the Fascist Dictatorship, 1915–1945*. 2007. An outstanding study of Italy under Mussolini.

◆ Browning, Christopher R. *Ordinary Men: Reserve Police Battalion 101 and the Final Solution in Poland*, 2d ed. 2001. A carefully researched, unnerving account of German atrocities in Poland during World War II.

◆ Fitzpatrick, Sheila. *Everyday Stalinism: Ordinary Life in Extraordinary Times: Soviet Russia in the 1930s*. 2000. An excellent study of what it was like to live in Stalin's Soviet Union.

◆ Geyer, Michael, and Sheila Fitzpatrick, eds. *Beyond Totalitarianism: Stalinism and Nazism Compared*. 2009. A collection of essays that compares the two dictatorships and challenges the usefulness of the totalitarian model.

◆ Kaplan, Marion A. *Between Dignity and Despair: Jewish Life in Nazi Germany*. 1998. A deeply moving book about the Jewish response to the Holocaust, with a compelling focus on women's history.

◆ Kotkin, Stephen. *Magnetic Mountain: Stalinism as a Civilization*. 1997. An extraordinary account of Stalinism and forced industrialization in the 1930s.

◆ Merridale, Catherine. *Ivan's War: Life and Death in the Red Army, 1939–1945*. 2007. An in-depth look at the lives of ordinary Soviet soldiers.

◆ Roberts, David D. *The Totalitarian Experiment in Twentieth-Century Europe: Understanding the Poverty of Great Politics*. 2006. Makes a case for the totalitarian model by comparing Stalinism, Nazism, and Italian fascism.

◆ Schlögel, Karl. *Moscow 1937*. 2014. This prize-winning history reconstructs the Soviet terror and offers an extensive and disturbing account of the Stalinist purges in Moscow in 1937.

◆ Snyder, Timothy. *Bloodlands: Europe Between Hitler and Stalin*. 2010. A synthesis that examines the murderous policies and practices of Nazi and Soviet authorities in east-central Europe before and during World War II.

◆ Weinberg, Gerhard L. *World at Arms: A Global History of World War II*, new ed. 2005. A masterful military history of World War II.

MEDIA

◆ *Burnt by the Sun* (Nikita Mikhalkov, 1994). In a subtle, Oscar-winning feature film that ably expresses Russian attempts to come to grips with memories of Stalinism, Commander Sergei Kotov, an "Old Bolshevik," senior Red Army officer, and civil war hero, is unexpectedly trapped in his summer house by the great purges of the late 1930s.

◆ *Come and See* (Elem Klimov, 1985). A harrowing anti-war film, produced in the Soviet Union, that tells the story of a young Belorussian boy who joins the Soviet partisans and witnesses the horror of Nazi reprisals against a harmless peasant village.

◆ *The Conformist* (Bernardo Bertolucci, 1970). This art film explores the Fascist mentality through an investigation of a young man who joins the Fascist secret police and helps assassinate his former professor.

◆ *Eyewitness to History: World War II*. A remarkable collection of firsthand accounts from a variety of people, covering all theaters of the war. **www.eyewitnessto history.com/w2frm.htm**

◆ *A Film Unfinished* (Yael Hersonski, 2010). This documentary takes a critical look at the infamous Nazi propaganda film of the Warsaw Ghetto.

◆ *Gulag: Many Days, Many Lives*. Explores the history of the Soviet gulags through various exhibits, such as "Days and Lives," "Soviet Forced Labor Camps and the Struggle for Freedom," and "Tour a Gulag Camp." **gulaghistory.org**

◆ *History of World War II* (BBC, 2005). With thirty hours of programming, this collection of ten BBC programs offers a wide-ranging analysis of World War II.

◆ *Night and Fog* (Alain Resnais, 1955). A justly famous, existentialism-influenced documentary about the Holocaust by a noted French film director.

◆ *United States Holocaust Memorial Museum*. A vast collection of material on all aspects of the Holocaust and other acts of genocide. **www.ushmm.org**

28

Cold War Conflict and Consensus

1945–1965

The defeat of the Nazis and their allies in 1945 left Europe in ruins. In the immediate postwar years, as people struggled to overcome the effects of rampant death and destruction, the victorious Allies worked to shape an effective peace accord. Disagreements between the Soviet Union and the Western allies emerged during this process and quickly led to an apparently endless Cold War between the two new superpowers: the United States and the Soviet Union. This conflict split much of Europe and then the world into a Soviet-aligned Communist bloc and a U.S.-aligned capitalist bloc and spurred military, economic, and technological competition.

Amid these tensions, battered western European countries fashioned a remarkable recovery, building stable democratic institutions and vibrant economies. In the Soviet Union and the East Bloc—the label applied to central and eastern European countries governed by Soviet-backed Communist regimes—Communist leaders repressed challenges to one-party rule but also offered limited reforms, leading to stability there as well.

The postwar decades brought fundamental change on a global scale, as people living in Europe's colonies won liberation from imperialist rule. Cold War hostilities had an immense impact on this process of decolonization. At the same time, evolving class structures, new migration patterns, and new roles for women and youths remade European society, laying the groundwork for major transformation in the decades to come. ■

CHAPTER PREVIEW

- Why was World War II followed so quickly by the Cold War?

- What were the sources of postwar recovery and stability in western Europe?

- What was the pattern of postwar development in the Soviet bloc?

- How did decolonization proceed in the Cold War era?

- What were the key changes in social relations in postwar Europe?

The Idealization of Work in the East Bloc

This relief sculpture, a revealing example of Socialist Realism from 1952, portrays (from left to right) a mail carrier, a builder, a miner, and a farmer, with their proud wives behind them. It adorns the wall of the central post office in Banská Bystrica, a regional capital in present-day Slovakia (formerly part of Czechoslovakia). Citizens in the Soviet Union and its satellite countries of the East Bloc saw many such works of public art, which idealized the dignity of ordinary workers and the advantages of communism. (© Georgios Makkas/Alamy Stock Photo)

Why was World War II followed so quickly by the Cold War?

In 1945 the Allies faced the momentous challenges of rebuilding a shattered Europe, dealing with Nazi criminals, and creating a lasting peace. Allied cooperation proved elusive, and Great Britain and the United States were soon at loggerheads with the Soviet Union (U.S.S.R.). By 1949 most of Europe was divided into East and West Blocs allied with the U.S.S.R. and the United States, respectively. For the next forty years, the competing superpowers engaged in the **Cold War**, a determined competition for political and military superiority around the world.

The Legacies of the Second World War

In the summer of 1945 Europe lay in ruins. Across the continent, the fighting destroyed cities and landscapes and obliterated buildings, factories, farms, rail tracks, roads, and bridges. Many cities — including Leningrad, Warsaw, Vienna, Budapest, Rotterdam, and Dresden — were completely devastated. Postwar observers compared the piles of rubble to moonscapes. Surviving cities such as Prague and Paris were left relatively unscathed, mostly by chance.

The human costs of the Second World War are almost incalculable (Map 28.1). The death toll in Europe far exceeded the mortality figures for World War I. At least 20 million Soviets, including soldiers and civilians, died in the war. German armies and occupiers murdered between 9 and 11 million noncombatants, including approximately 6 million Jews. One out of every five Poles died in the war, including 3 million of Poland's 3.25 million Jews. German deaths numbered 5 million, 2 million of them civilians. France and Britain both lost fewer soldiers than in World War I, but about 350,000 French civilians were killed in the fighting. Over 400,000 U.S. soldiers died in the European and Pacific campaigns, and other nations across Europe and the globe lost staggering numbers. In total, about 50 million human beings perished in the conflict.

The destruction left tens of millions homeless — 25 million in the U.S.S.R. and 20 million in Germany alone. Some 30 million people lost their homes in the hardest-hit war zones of central and eastern Europe. The end of the war and the start of the peace increased their numbers. Some 13 million ethnic Germans fled west before the advancing Soviet troops or were expelled from eastern Europe under the terms of Allied agreements. Forced laborers from Poland, France, the Balkans, and other nations, brought to Germany by the Nazis, now sought to go home. A woman in Berlin

Displaced Persons in the Ruins of Berlin The end of the war in 1945 stopped the fighting but not the suffering. For the next two years, millions of displaced persons—"small, tired, caravans of people"— wandered across Europe searching for sustenance, lost family members, and a place to call home. (Fred Ramage/Getty Images)

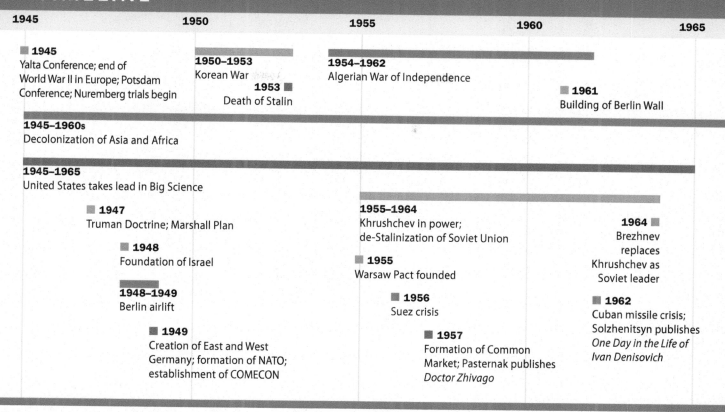

■ **1945**
Yalta Conference; end of World War II in Europe; Potsdam Conference; Nuremberg trials begin

1950–1953
Korean War

1953 ■
Death of Stalin

1954–1962
Algerian War of Independence

■ **1961**
Building of Berlin Wall

1945–1960s
Decolonization of Asia and Africa

1945–1965
United States takes lead in Big Science

■ **1947**
Truman Doctrine; Marshall Plan

■ **1948**
Foundation of Israel

1948–1949
Berlin airlift

■ **1949**
Creation of East and West Germany; formation of NATO; establishment of COMECON

1955–1964
Khrushchev in power; de-Stalinization of Soviet Union

■ **1955**
Warsaw Pact founded

■ **1956**
Suez crisis

■ **1957**
Formation of Common Market; Pasternak publishes *Doctor Zhivago*

1964 ■
Brezhnev replaces Khrushchev as Soviet leader

■ **1962**
Cuban missile crisis; Solzhenitsyn publishes *One Day in the Life of Ivan Denisovich*

---

described the "small, tired caravans of people" passing through the city in spring 1945 pulling "pitiful handcarts piled high with sacks, crates, and trunks." The elderly refugees were particularly wretched, "pale, dilapidated, apathetic. Half-dead sacks of bones."[1]

These **displaced persons** or DPs — their numbers increased by concentration camp survivors and freed prisoners of war, and hundreds of thousands of orphaned children — searched for food and shelter. From 1945 to 1947 the newly established United Nations Relief and Rehabilitation Administration (UNRRA) opened over 760 DP camps and spent $10 billion to house, feed, clothe, and repatriate the refugees.

For DPs, going home was not always the best option. Soviet citizens who had spent time in the West were seen as politically unreliable by political leaders in the U.S.S.R. Many DPs faced prison terms, exile to labor camps in the Siberian gulag, and even execution upon their return to Soviet territories. Jewish DPs faced unique problems. Their families and communities had been destroyed, and persistent anti-Semitism often made them unwelcome in their former homelands. Many stayed in special Jewish DP camps in Germany for years. After the creation of Israel in 1948, over 330,000 European Jews left for the new Jewish nation-state. By 1952 about 100,000 Jews

had also immigrated to the United States. When the last DP camp closed in 1957, the UNRRA had cared for and resettled many millions of refugees, Jews and non-Jews alike.

When the fighting stopped, Germany and Austria had been divided into four occupation zones, each governed by one of the Allies — the United States, the Soviet Union, Great Britain, and France. The Soviets collected substantial reparations from their zone in eastern Germany and from former German allies Hungary and Romania. Occupation administrators seized factories and equipment, even tearing up railroad tracks and sending the rails to the U.S.S.R.

The authorities in each zone tried to punish those guilty of Nazi atrocities. Across Europe, almost 100,000 Germans and Austrians were convicted of war crimes. Many more were investigated or indicted. In Soviet-dominated central and eastern Europe — where the worst crimes had taken place — retribution was particularly intense. There and in other parts of Europe, collaborators, non-Germans who had assisted

---

■ **Cold War** The rivalry between the Soviet Union and the United States that divided much of Europe into a Soviet-aligned Communist bloc and a U.S.-aligned capitalist bloc between 1945 and 1989.

■ **displaced persons** Postwar refugees, including 13 million Germans, former Nazi prisoners and forced laborers, and orphaned children.

MAP 28.1 The Aftermath of World War II in Europe, ca. 1945–1950

By 1945 millions of people displaced by war and territorial changes were on the move. The Soviet Union and Poland took land from Germany, which the Allies partitioned into occupation zones. Those zones subsequently formed the basis of the East and West German states. Austria was detached from Germany and similarly divided, but the Soviets later permitted Austria to reunify as a neutral state.

ANALYZING THE MAP Which groups fled west? Who went east? How would you characterize the general direction of most of these movements?

CONNECTIONS What does the widespread movement of people at the end of the war suggest about the war? What does it suggest about the ensuing political climate?

---

the German occupiers during the war, were also punished. In the days and months immediately after the war, spontaneous acts of retribution brought some collaborators to account. In both France and Italy, unofficial groups seeking revenge summarily executed some 25,000 persons. French women accused of "horizontal collaboration" — having sexual relations with German soldiers during the occupation — were publicly humiliated by angry mobs. Newly established postwar governments also formed official courts to sanction collaborators or send them to prison. A small number received the death sentence.

In Germany and Austria, occupation authorities set up "denazification" procedures meant to identify and punish former Nazi Party members responsible for the worst crimes and eradicate National Socialist ideology from social and political institutions. At the Nuremberg trials (1945–1946), an international military tribunal organized by the four Allied powers tried the highest-ranking Nazi military and civilian leaders who had survived the war, charging them with war crimes and crimes against humanity. After chilling testimony from victims of the regime, which revealed the full systematic horror of Nazi atrocities, twelve were sentenced to death and ten more to lengthy prison terms.

The Nuremberg trials marked the last time the four Allies worked closely together to punish former Nazis. As the Cold War developed and the Soviets and the Western Allies drew increasingly apart, each carried out separate denazification programs in their own zones of occupation. In the Western zones, military courts at first actively prosecuted leading Nazis. But the huge numbers implicated in Nazi crimes, German opposition to the proceedings, and the need for stability in the looming Cold War made thorough denazification impractical. Except for the worst offenders, the Western authorities had quietly shelved denazification by 1948. The process was similar in the Soviet zone. At first, punishment was swift and harsh. About 45,000 former party officials, upper-class industrialists, and large landowners identified as Nazis were sentenced to prison or death. As in the West, however, former Nazis who cooperated with the Soviet authorities could avoid prosecution. Thus many former Nazis found positions in government and industry in both the Soviet and Western zones.

The Peace Settlement and Cold War Origins

In the years immediately after the war, as ordinary people across Europe struggled to recover, the victorious Allies — the U.S.S.R., the United States, and Great Britain — tried to shape a reasonable and lasting peace. Yet the Allies began to quarrel almost as soon as the unifying threat of Nazi Germany disappeared, and the interests of the Communist Soviet Union and the capitalist Britain and United States increasingly diverged. The hostility between the Eastern and Western superpowers was the sad but logical outgrowth of military developments, wartime agreements, and long-standing political and ideological differences that stretched back to the Russian Revolution.

Once the United States entered the war in late 1941, the Americans and the British had made

The Big Three   In 1945 a triumphant Winston Churchill, an ailing Franklin Roosevelt, and a determined Stalin met at Yalta in Soviet Crimea to plan for peace. Cooperation soon gave way to bitter hostility, and the decisions made by these leaders transformed the map of Europe. (Franklin D. Roosevelt Presidential Library and Museum of the National Archives and Records Administration)

military victory their highest priority. They did not try to take advantage of the Soviet Union's precarious position in 1942 because they feared that hard bargaining would encourage Stalin to consider making a separate peace with Hitler. Together, the Allies avoided discussion of postwar aims and the shape of the eventual peace settlement and focused instead on pursuing a policy of German unconditional surrender to solidify the alliance. By late 1943 negotiations about the postwar settlement could no longer be postponed. The conference that the "Big Three" — Stalin, Roosevelt, and Churchill — held in the Iranian capital of Tehran in November 1943 proved crucial for determining the shape of the postwar world.

At Tehran, the Big Three jovially reaffirmed their determination to crush Germany, and this was followed by tense discussions of Poland's postwar borders and a strategy to win the war. Stalin, concerned that the U.S.S.R. was bearing the brunt of the fighting, asked his allies to relieve his armies by opening a second front in German-occupied France. Churchill, fearing the military dangers of a direct attack, argued that U.S. and British forces should follow up their Italian campaign with an indirect attack on Germany through the Balkans, which had the potential to save the region from Soviet control after the war. Roosevelt, however, agreed with Stalin that an American-British assault through France would be better, though the date for the invasion was set later than the Soviet leader desired.

The decision to invade France had momentous implications for the Cold War. While the delay in opening a second front fanned Stalin's distrust of the Allies, the agreement on a British-U.S. invasion of France ensured that the American-British and Soviet armies would come together in defeated Germany along a north-south line and that Soviet troops would play the predominant role in pushing the Germans out of eastern and central Europe. Thus the basic shape of postwar Europe was cast even as the fighting continued.

When the Big Three met again in February 1945 at Yalta, on the Black Sea in southern Russia, advancing Soviet armies had already occupied Poland, Bulgaria, Romania, Hungary, part of Yugoslavia, and much of Czechoslovakia and were within a hundred miles of Berlin. The stalled American-British forces had yet to cross the Rhine into Germany. Moreover, the United States was far from defeating Japan. In short, the U.S.S.R.'s position on the ground was far stronger than that of the United States and Britain, which played to Stalin's advantage.

The Allies agreed at Yalta that each of the four victorious powers would occupy a separate zone of Germany and that the Germans would pay heavy reparations to the Soviet Union. At American insistence, Stalin agreed to declare war on Japan after Germany's defeat. As for Poland, the Big Three agreed that the U.S.S.R. would permanently incorporate the eastern Polish territories its army had occupied in 1939 under the Molotov-Ribbentrop pact and that Poland would be compensated with German lands to the west. They also agreed in an ambiguous compromise that the new governments in Soviet-occupied Europe would be freely elected but "friendly" to the Soviet Union.

The Yalta compromise over elections in these countries broke down almost immediately. Even before the conference, Communist parties were taking control in Bulgaria and Poland. Elsewhere, the Soviets formed coalition governments that included Social Democrats and other leftist parties but reserved key government posts for Moscow-trained Communists. At the Potsdam Conference of July 1945, the differences over elections in Soviet-occupied Europe surged to the fore. Roosevelt had died and had been succeeded by Harry Truman (U.S. pres. 1945–1953), who demanded immediate free elections throughout central and eastern Europe. Stalin refused point-blank. "A freely elected government in any of these East European countries would be anti-Soviet," he admitted simply, "and that we cannot allow."[2]

Here, then, were the keys to the much-debated origins of the Cold War. While fighting Germany, the Allies could maintain an alliance of necessity. As the war drew to a close, long-standing hostility between East and West re-emerged. Mutual distrust, security concerns, and antagonistic desires for economic, political, and territorial control began to destroy the former partnership.

Stalin, who had lived through two enormously destructive German invasions, was determined to establish a buffer zone of sympathetic states around the U.S.S.R. and at the same time expand the reach of communism and the Soviet state. Stalin believed that only Communists could be dependable allies and that free elections would result in independent and possibly hostile governments on his western border. With Soviet armies in central and eastern Europe, there was no way short of war for the United States to control the region's political future, and war was out of the question. The United States, for its part, pushed to maintain democratic capitalism in western Europe. The Americans quickly showed that they, too, were willing to use their vast political, economic, and military power to maintain predominance in their sphere of influence.

West Versus East

The Cold War took shape over the next five years, as both sides hardened their positions. After Japan's surrender in September 1945, Truman cut off aid to the ailing U.S.S.R. In October he declared that the United States would never recognize any government established by force against the will of its people. In March 1946 former British prime minister Churchill ominously informed an American audience that an "iron curtain" had fallen across the continent, dividing Europe into two antagonistic camps (Map 28.2).

The Soviet Union was indeed consolidating its hold on central and eastern Europe. In fact, the Soviets enjoyed some popular support in the region, though this varied from country to country. The Red Army had thrown out the German invaders, and after the abuses of fascism the ideals of Communist equality retained some appeal. Yet the Communist parties in these areas quickly recognized that they lacked enough support to take power in free elections. In Romania, Bulgaria, Poland, and Hungary, Communist politicians, backed by Moscow, repressed their liberal opponents and engineered phony elections that established Communist-led regimes. They purged the last remaining noncommunists from the coalition governments set up after the war and by 1948 had established Soviet-style, one-party Communist dictatorships.

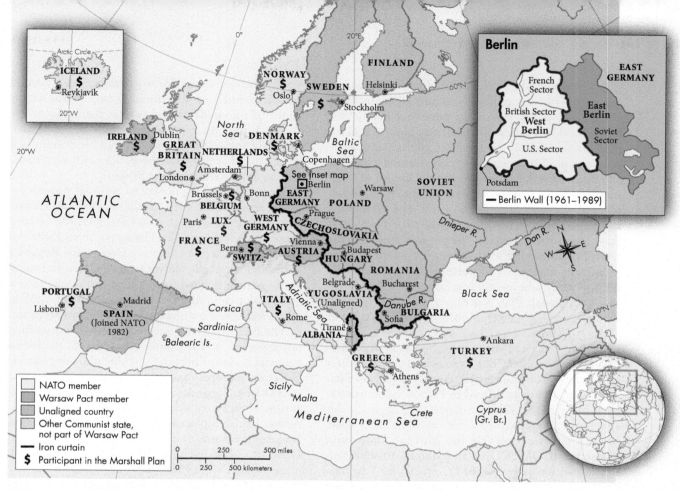

MAP 28.2 Cold War Europe in the 1950s The Cold War divided Europe into two hostile military alliances that formed to the east and west of the "iron curtain," the border between the two blocs.

The pattern was somewhat different in Czechoslovakia, where Communists enjoyed success in open elections and initially formed a coalition government with other parties. When the noncommunist ministers resigned in February 1948, the Communists took over the government and began Stalinizing the country. This seizure of power in Czechoslovakia contributed to Western fears of limitless Communist expansion.

In western Europe, communism also enjoyed some support. In Italy, which boasted the largest Communist Party outside of the Soviet bloc, Communists won 19 percent of the vote in 1946; French Communists earned 28 percent of the vote the same year. These large, well-organized parties criticized the growing role of the United States in western Europe and challenged their own governments with violent rhetoric and large strikes. At the same time, bitter civil wars in Greece and China pitted Communist revolutionaries against authoritarian leaders backed by the United States.

By early 1947 it appeared to many Americans that the U.S.S.R. was determined to export communism by subversion throughout Europe and around the world. The United States responded with the **Truman Doctrine**, aimed at "containing" communism to

areas already under Communist governments. The United States, President Truman promised, would use diplomatic, economic, and even military means to resist the expansion of communism anywhere on the globe. In the first examples of containment policies in action, Truman asked Congress to provide military aid to anticommunist forces in the Greek Civil War (1944–1949) and counter the threat of Soviet expansion in Turkey. With American support, both countries remained in the Western bloc.

The American determination to enforce containment hardened when the Soviets exploded their own atomic bomb in 1949, raising popular fears of a looming nuclear holocaust. At home and abroad, the United States engaged in an anticommunist crusade. Emotional, moralistic denunciations of Stalin and Communist regimes became part of American public life. By the early 1950s the U.S. government was restructuring its military to meet the Soviet threat, pouring money into defense spending and testing nuclear weapons that dwarfed the destructive power of atomic bombs.

■ **Truman Doctrine** America's policy geared to containing communism to those countries already under Soviet control.

Military aid and a defense buildup were only one aspect of Truman's policy of containment. In 1947 western Europe was still on the verge of economic collapse. Food was scarce, inflation was high, and black markets flourished. Recognizing that an economically and politically stable western Europe would be an effective block against the popular appeal of communism, U.S. secretary of state George C. Marshall offered Europe economic aid — the **Marshall Plan** — to help it rebuild. As Marshall wrote in a State Department bulletin, "Its purpose should be the revival of a working economy in the world so as to permit the emergence of political and social conditions in which free institutions can exist."[3]

The Marshall Plan was one of the most successful foreign aid programs in history. When it ended in 1951, the United States had given about $13 billion in aid (equivalent to about $140 billion in 2022 dollars) to fifteen western European nations, and Europe's economy was on the way to recovery. Marshall Plan funding was initially offered to East Bloc countries as well, but fearing Western interference in the Soviet sphere, they rejected the offer. In 1949 the Soviets established the **Council for Mutual Economic Assistance (COMECON)**, an economic organization of Communist states intended to rebuild the East Bloc independently of the West. Thus the generous aid of the Marshall Plan was limited to countries in the Western bloc, which further widened Cold War divisions.

In the late 1940s Berlin, the capital city of Germany, was on the frontline of the Cold War. Like the rest of Germany and Austria, Berlin had been divided into four zones of occupation. In June 1948 the Western allies replaced the currency in the western zones of Germany and Berlin, an early move in plans to establish a separate West German state sympathetic to U.S. interests. The currency reform violated the peace settlement and raised Stalin's fears of the American presence in Europe. In addition, growing ties among Britain, France, Belgium, and the Netherlands convinced Stalin that a Western bloc was forming against the Soviet Union. In response, the Soviet dictator used the one card he had to play — access to Berlin — to force the allies to the bargaining table. Stalin blocked all traffic through the Soviet zone of Germany to Berlin in an attempt to win concessions and perhaps

reunify the city under Soviet control. Acting firmly, the Western allies coordinated around-the-clock flights of hundreds of planes over the Soviet roadblocks, supplying provisions to West Berliners and thwarting Soviet efforts to swallow up the western half of the city. After 324 days, the Berlin airlift succeeded, and the Soviets reopened the roads.

Success in breaking the Berlin blockade had several lasting results. First, it paved the way for the creation of two separate German states in 1949: the Federal Republic of Germany (West Germany), aligned with the United States, and the German Democratic Republic (East Germany), aligned with the U.S.S.R. Germany would remain divided for the next forty-one years, a radical solution to the "German problem" that satisfied people fearful of the nation's possible military resurgence.

The Berlin crisis also seemed to show that containment worked, and thus strengthened U.S. resolve to maintain a strong European and U.S. military presence in western Europe. In 1949 the United States formed **NATO** (the North Atlantic Treaty Organization), an anti-Soviet military alliance of Western governments. As one British diplomat put it, NATO was designed "to keep the Russians out, the Americans in, and the Germans down."[4] With U.S. backing, West Germany joined NATO in 1955 and was allowed to rebuild its military to help defend western Europe against possible Soviet attack. That same year, the Soviets countered by organizing the **Warsaw Pact**, a military alliance among the U.S.S.R. and its Communist satellites. In both political and military terms, most of Europe was divided into two hostile blocs.

The superpower confrontation that emerged from the ruins of World War II took shape in Europe, but it quickly spread around the globe. The Cold War turned hot in East Asia. When Soviet-backed Communist North Korea invaded South Korea in 1950, President Truman swiftly sent U.S. troops. In the end, the Korean War was indecisive: the fragile truce in 1953 left Korea divided between a Communist north and a capitalist south. The war nonetheless showed that though the superpowers might maintain a fragile peace in Europe, they were perfectly willing to engage in open conflict in non-Western territories. By the early 1950s the confrontation between the Soviet Union and its satellite states and the United States and its European allies had become an apparently permanent feature of world affairs. (See "Viewpoints: Cold War Propaganda," page 879.)

Big Science in the Nuclear Age

Cold War hostilities helped foster a nuclear arms race, a space race, and the computer revolution, all made possible by stunning advances in science and technology. During the Second World War, theoretical

---

■ **Marshall Plan** American plan for providing economic aid to western Europe to help it rebuild.

■ **Council for Mutual Economic Assistance (COMECON)** An economic organization of Communist states meant to help rebuild East Bloc countries under Soviet auspices.

■ **NATO** The North Atlantic Treaty Organization, an anti-Soviet military alliance of Western governments.

■ **Warsaw Pact** Soviet-backed military alliance of East Bloc Communist countries in Europe.

VIEWPOINTS

Cold War Propaganda

During the 1950s and 1960s, East and West Bloc propagandists sought to demonize their Cold War opponents, exemplified in these contemporary posters. The first poster (right), from a 1953 West German election campaign, warns that "All Paths of Marxism Lead to Moscow!" and exhorts voters to choose the Christian Democratic Party (CDU) over the left-leaning Social Democrats. The Soviet poster (below) depicts Americans masking their nuclear threat as the dove of peace. The text reads, "Washington 'Dove'—Though cleverly disguised, it does not hide its nasty insides."

West German Election Poster, 1953. (Photo 12/Universal Images Group/ Getty Images)

Soviet Propaganda Poster, ca. 1955. (Peter Newark Military Pictures/Bridgeman Images)

QUESTIONS FOR ANALYSIS

1. Although these are drawings, both posters tell a story. What are those stories?
2. How do the propagandists play on the fears of those who might see their work?
3. Which poster, in your view, is most graphically compelling? Why?

science lost its innocence when it was joined with practical technology (applied science) on a massive scale. Many leading university scientists went to work on top-secret projects to help their governments fight the war. The development by British scientists of radar to detect enemy aircraft was a particularly important outcome of this new kind of sharply focused research. The air war also stimulated the development of rocketry and jet aircraft. The most spectacular and deadly result of directed scientific research during the war was the atomic bomb, which showed the world both the awesome power and the heavy moral responsibilities of modern science.

The impressive results of this directed research inspired a new model for science — Big Science. By combining theoretical work with sophisticated engineering in a large bureaucratic organization, Big Science could tackle extremely difficult problems, from new and improved weapons for the military to better products for consumers. Big Science was extremely expensive, requiring large-scale financing from governments and large corporations.

After the war, scientists continued to contribute to advances in military technologies, and a large portion of postwar research supported the expanding arms race. New weapons such as missiles, nuclear submarines, and spy satellites demanded breakthroughs no less remarkable than those responsible for radar and the first atomic bomb. After 1945 roughly one-quarter of all men and women trained in science and engineering in the West — and perhaps more in the Soviet Union — were employed full-time in the production of weapons to kill other humans. By the 1960s both sides had enough nuclear firepower to destroy each other and the rest of the world many times over.

Sophisticated science, lavish government spending, and military needs came together in the space race of the 1960s. In 1957 the Soviets used long-range rockets developed in their nuclear weapons program to launch Sputnik, the first man-made satellite to orbit the earth. In 1961 they sent the world's first cosmonaut circling the globe. Embarrassed by Soviet triumphs, the United States caught "Sputnik-itis" and made an all-out commitment to catch up with the Soviets. The U.S. National Aeronautics and Space Administration (NASA), founded in 1958, won a symbolic victory by landing a manned spacecraft on the moon in 1969. Five more moon landings followed by the end of 1972.

Advanced nuclear weapons and the space race were made possible by the concurrent revolution in computer technology. The search for better weaponry in World War II boosted the development of sophisticated data-processing machines, including the electronic Colossus computer used by the British to break German military codes. The massive mainframe ENIAC (Electronic Numerical Integrator and Computer), built for the U.S. Army at the University of Pennsylvania, went into operation in 1945. The invention of the transistor in 1947 further advanced computer design. From the mid-1950s on, this small, efficient electronic switching device increasingly replaced bulky vacuum tubes as the key computer components. By the 1960s sophisticated computers were indispensable tools for a variety of military, commercial, and scientific uses, foreshadowing the rise of personal computers in the decades to come.

Big Science had tangible benefits for ordinary people. During the postwar green revolution, directed agricultural research greatly increased the world's food supplies. Farming was industrialized and became more and more productive per acre, resulting in far fewer people being needed to grow food. The application of scientific advances to industrial processes made consumer goods less expensive and more available to larger numbers of people. The transistor, for example, was used in computers but also in portable radios, kitchen appliances, and many other consumer products. In sum, in the nuclear age, Big Science created new sources of material well-being and entertainment as well as destruction.

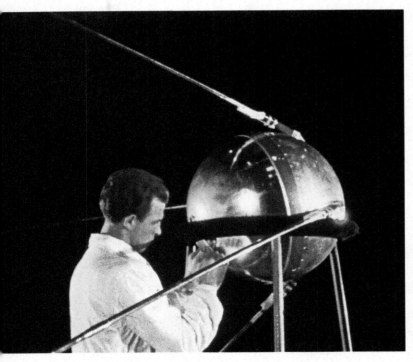

Sputnik and the Space Race   A Soviet technician prepares the Sputnik space satellite for its trial run in October 1957. The successful launch of the Sputnik, which orbited earth for about three months before falling back into the atmosphere and disintegrating, surprised Western observers and overturned the notion that the U.S.S.R. was technologically inferior to the United States. It inspired a full-blown space race that ultimately saw U.S. astronauts land on the moon in 1969. (Sovfoto/Getty Images)

What were the sources of postwar recovery and stability in western Europe?

In the late 1940s the outlook for Europe appeared bleak. Yet the continent recovered, with the nations of western Europe in the lead. In less than a generation, many western European countries constructed democratic political institutions, while a period of unprecedented economic growth and a consumer revolution brought a sense of prosperity to ever-larger numbers of people. Politicians entered collective economic agreements and established the European Economic Community, the first steps toward broader European unity.

The Search for Political and Social Consensus

In the first years after the war, economic conditions in western Europe were terrible. Infrastructure of all kinds barely functioned. Runaway inflation and a thriving black market testified to severe shortages and hardships. In 1948, as Marshall Plan dollars poured in, the battered economies of western Europe began to improve. The outbreak of the Korean War in 1950 further stimulated economic activity, and Europe entered a period of rapid economic progress that lasted into the late 1960s. Never before had the European economy grown so fast. By the late 1950s contemporaries were talking about a widespread **economic miracle** that had brought robust growth to most western European countries.

There were many reasons for this stunning economic performance. American aid got the process off to a fast start. Moreover, economic growth became a basic objective of all western European governments, for leaders and voters alike were determined to avoid a return to the dangerous and demoralizing stagnation of the 1930s.

The postwar governments in western Europe thus embraced new political and economic policies that led to a remarkably lasting social consensus. They turned to liberal democracy and generally adopted Keynesian economics (see "Germany and the Western Powers" in Chapter 26) in successful attempts to stimulate their economies. In addition, whether they leaned to the left or to the right, national leaders typically applied an imaginative mixture of government planning and free-market capitalism to promote economic growth. They nationalized — or established government ownership of — significant sectors of the economy, used economic regulation to encourage growth, and established generous social benefits programs, paid for with high taxes, for all citizens. This consensual

framework for good government lasted until the middle of the 1970s.

In politics, a new team of European leaders emerged to guide the postwar recovery. Across the West, newly formed Christian Democratic parties became important power brokers. Rooted in the Catholic parties of the prewar decades, the **Christian Democrats** offered voters tired of radical politics a center-right vision of reconciliation and recovery. Socialists and Communists, active in the resistance against Hitler, also increased their power and prestige, especially in France and Italy. They, too, provided fresh leadership as they pushed for social change and economic reform.

Across much of continental Europe, the centrist Christian Democrats defeated their left-wing competition. In Italy, the Christian Democrats were the leading party in the first postwar elections in 1946, and in early 1948 they won an absolute majority in the parliament in a landslide victory. In France, the Popular Republican Movement, a Christian Democratic party, took power after General Charles de Gaulle (duh GOHL) resigned from his position as head of the provisional government in January 1946. West Germans, too, elected a Christian Democratic government from 1949 until 1969.

As they provided effective leadership for their respective countries, Christian Democrats drew inspiration from a common Christian and European heritage. They firmly rejected authoritarianism and narrow nationalism and placed their faith in democracy and liberalism. At the same time, the anticommunist rhetoric of these steadfast cold warriors was unrelenting. Rejecting the class-based politics of the left, they championed a return to traditional family values, a vision with great appeal after a war that left many broken families and destitute households; the Christian Democrats often received a majority of women's votes.

Following their U.S. allies, Christian Democrats advocated free-market economics and promised voters prosperity and ample supplies of consumer goods. They established education subsidies, family and housing allowances, public transportation, and public health insurance throughout continental Europe. When necessary, Christian Democratic leaders accepted the need for limited government planning. In France, the government established modernization

---

■ **economic miracle** Term contemporaries used to describe rapid economic growth, often based on the consumer sector, in post–World War II western Europe.

■ **Christian Democrats** Center-right political parties that rose to power in western Europe after the Second World War.

commissions for key industries, and state-controlled banks funneled money into industrial development. In West Germany, the Christian Democrats broke decisively with the straitjacketed Nazi economy and promoted a "social-market economy" based on a combination of free-market liberalism, limited state intervention, and generous social-welfare benefits.

Though Portugal, Spain, and Greece generally supported NATO and the United States in the Cold War, they proved exceptions to the rule of democratic transformation outside the Soviet bloc. In Portugal and Spain, nationalist authoritarian regimes had taken power in the 1930s. Portugal's authoritarian state was overthrown in a left-wing military coup only in 1974, while Spain's dictator Francisco Franco remained in power until his death in 1975. The authoritarian monarchy established in Greece when the civil war ended in 1949, bolstered by military support and kept in power in a series of army coups, was likewise replaced by a democratic government only in 1975.

By contrast, the Scandinavian countries and Great Britain took decisive turns to the left. Norway, Denmark, and especially Sweden earned a global reputation for long-term Social Democratic governance, generous state-sponsored benefit programs, tolerant lifestyles, and independent attitudes toward Cold War conflicts.

Even though wartime austerity and rationing programs were in place until the mid-1950s, Britain offered the most comprehensive state benefit programs outside Scandinavia. The social-democratic Labour Party took power after the war and ambitiously established a "cradle-to-grave" welfare state. Many British industries were nationalized, including banks, iron and steel industries, and utilities and public transportation networks. The government provided free medical services and hospital care, generous retirement pensions, and unemployment benefits, all subsidized by progressive taxation that pegged tax payments to income levels, with the wealthy paying significantly more than those below them. Although the Labour Party suffered defeats throughout much of the 1950s and early 1960s, its Conservative opponents maintained much of the welfare state when they came to power. Across western Europe, economic growth and state-sponsored benefits systems raised living standards higher than ever before.

Toward European Unity

Though there were important regional differences across much of western Europe, politicians and citizens supported policies that brought together limited state planning, strong economic growth, and

democratic government, and this political and social consensus accompanied the first tentative steps on the long road toward a more unified Europe.

A number of new financial arrangements and institutions encouraged slow but steady moves toward European integration, as did cooperation with the United States. To receive Marshall Plan aid, the European states were required by the Americans to work with one another, leading to the creation of the Organization for European Economic Cooperation and the Council of Europe in 1948, both of which promoted commerce and closer ties among European countries.

Idealistic European federalists hoped that the Council of Europe would evolve into a European parliament with sovereign rights over individual states, but this did not happen. Britain, with its still-vast empire and its close relationship with the United States, consistently opposed conceding sovereignty to the council. On the continent, many prominent politicians agreed with the British view.

Frustrated in political consolidation, European federalists turned to economics as a way of working toward genuine unity. Christian Democratic governments in France, West Germany, Italy, Belgium, the Netherlands, and Luxembourg founded the European Coal and Steel Community in 1951 (the British steadfastly refused to join). The founding states quickly attained their immediate economic goal — a single, transnational market for steel and coal without national tariffs or quotas. Close economic ties, advocates hoped, would eventually bind the six member nations so closely together that war among them would become unthinkable.

In 1957, the six countries of the Coal and Steel Community signed the Treaty of Rome, which created the European Economic Community, or **Common Market**. The first goal of the treaty was a gradual reduction of all tariffs among the six in order to create a single market. Other goals included the free movement of capital and labor and common economic policies and institutions. The Common Market encouraged trade among member states, promoted global exports, and helped build shared resources for the modernization of national industries. European integration thus meant not only increased transnational cooperation but also economic growth on the national level.

In the 1960s, hopes for rapid progress toward political as well as economic union were frustrated by a resurgence of nationalism. French president Charles de Gaulle, elected to office in 1958, viewed the United States as the main threat to genuine French (and European) independence. He withdrew all French military forces from what he called an "American-controlled" NATO, developed France's own nuclear weapons, and vetoed the scheduled advent of majority rule within the Common Market. Thus, the 1950s and 1960s established a lasting

■ **Common Market** The European Economic Community, created by six western and central European countries in the West Bloc in 1957 as part of a larger search for European unity.

Traffic Jam in Paris   The consumer revolution of the late 1950s brought a rapid increase in the number of privately owned automobiles across western Europe. Major European cities began to experience one of the more unfortunate but increasingly common aspects of postwar life: the traffic jam. Contemporary advertisements, like this 1952 French ad for the Dyna Panhard Junior 130 Sprint, played up the youthful, sporty aspects of the new auto-mobility. (traffic: akg-images/Paul Almasy/Newscom; advertisement: akg-images/Newscom)

pattern: Europeans would establish ever-closer economic ties, but the Common Market remained a union of independent, sovereign states.

The Consumer Revolution

In the late 1950s western Europe's rapidly expanding economy led to a rising standard of living and remarkable growth in the number and availability of standardized consumer goods. Modern consumer society had precedents in the decades before the Second World War, but the years of the "economic miracle" saw the arrival of a veritable consumer revolution: as the percentage of income spent on necessities such as housing and food declined dramatically, near full employment and high wages meant that more Europeans could buy more things than ever before. Shaken by war and eager to rebuild their homes and families, western Europeans embraced the new products of consumer society. Like North Americans,

they filled their houses and apartments with modern appliances such as washing machines, and they eagerly purchased the latest entertainment devices of the day: radios, record players, and televisions.

The consumer market became an increasingly important engine for general economic growth. For example, the European automobile industry expanded phenomenally after lagging far behind that of the United States since the 1920s. In 1948 there were only 5 million cars in western Europe; by 1965 there were 44 million. No longer reserved for the elites, car ownership became possible for better-paid workers. With the expansion of social security safeguards reducing the need to accumulate savings for hard times and old age, ordinary people were increasingly willing to take on debt, and new banks and credit unions and even retail outlets increasingly offered loans — or "credit" — for consumer purchases on easy terms.

Visions of consumer abundance became a powerful weapon in an era of Cold War competition.

Politicians in both East and West claimed that their respective systems could best provide citizens with ample consumer goods. In the competition over consumption, Western capitalism clearly surpassed Eastern planned economies in the production and distribution of inexpensive products. Western leaders boasted about the abundance of goods on store shelves and promised new forms of social equality in which all citizens would have equal access to consumer items — rather than encouraging equality through state-enforced social leveling, as in the East Bloc. The race to provide ordinary people with higher living standards would be a central aspect of the Cold War, and the Communist East Bloc consistently struggled to catch up to Western standards of prosperity.

What was the pattern of postwar development in the Soviet bloc?

In the counties of the East Bloc, the Soviet Union established firm control over the peoples it had supposedly "liberated" during the Second World War. Although reforms after Stalin's death in 1953 led to economic improvement and limited gains in civil rights, postwar recovery in Communist central and eastern Europe was deeply influenced by developments in the U.S.S.R.

Postwar Life in the East Bloc

The "Great Patriotic War of the Fatherland" had fostered Russian nationalism and a partial relaxation of dictatorial terror. Even before the war ended, however, Stalin was moving the U.S.S.R. back toward rigid dictatorship, disappointing citizens who hoped for greater freedoms and perhaps a turn to democracy. By early 1946 Stalin maintained that another war with the West was inevitable as long as capitalism existed. Working to extend Communist influence across the globe, the Soviets established the Cominform, or Communist Information Bureau, an international organization dedicated to maintaining Russian control over Communist parties abroad, in western Europe and the East Bloc. Stalin's new superpower foe, the United States, served as an excuse for re-establishing a harsh dictatorship in the U.S.S.R. itself. Stalin reasserted the Communist Party's control of the government and his absolute mastery of the party. Rigid ideological indoctrination, attacks on religion, and the absence of civil liberties were soon facts of life for citizens of the Soviet empire. Millions of supposed political enemies were sent to prison, exile, or forced-labor camps.

As discussed earlier, in the satellite states of central and eastern Europe — including East Germany, Poland, Hungary, Czechoslovakia, Romania, Albania, and Bulgaria — national Communist parties remade state and society on the Soviet model. Though there were significant differences in these East Bloc countries, postwar developments followed a similar pattern. Popular Communist leaders who had led the resistance against Germany were ousted and replaced by politicians who supported Stalinist policies. With Soviet backing, national Communist

Nowa Huta, A Model Polish Steel Town   Steel was the idol of the Stalinist era, and model steel factory cities were established across the East Bloc. Nowa Huta (New Foundry), erected in the early 1950s on the outskirts of the Polish city of Kraków, epitomized the model. The monumental Central Square, pictured here, was the center of the planned city. Streets radiated out into blocks of modern apartment buildings that housed the men and women who worked in the massive steel complex in the background. (Sovfoto/Universal Images Group/Shutterstock)

parties absorbed their Social Democratic rivals and established one-party dictatorships subservient to the Communist Party in Moscow. State security services arrested, imprisoned, and sometimes executed dissenters. Show trials of supposedly disloyal Communist Party leaders took place across the East Bloc from the late 1940s into the 1950s, but were particularly prominent in Bulgaria, Czechoslovakia, Hungary, and Romania. The trials testified to the influence of Soviet advisers and the unrestrained power of the domestic secret police in the satellite states, as well as Stalin's urge to establish complete control—and his increasing paranoia.

Yugoslavia was an exception to the general rule of Communist takeover. There Josip Broz Tito (TEE-toh) (1892–1980), a Communist leader active in the anti-Nazi resistance, successfully resisted Soviet domination and established an independent Communist state. Because there was no Russian army in Yugoslavia, the country remained outside of the Soviet bloc and remained a one-party, multiethnic state until it began to break apart in 1991.

Within the East Bloc, the newly installed Communist governments moved quickly to restructure national economies along Soviet lines, introducing five-year plans to cope with the enormous task of economic reconstruction. Most industries and businesses were nationalized. These efforts transformed prewar patterns of everyday life, even as they laid the groundwork for industrial development later in the decade.

In their attempts to revive the economy, Communist planners gave top priority to heavy industry and the military. East Bloc planners neglected consumer goods and housing, because they lacked industrial plants and were generally suspicious of Western-style consumer culture. A glut of consumer goods, they believed, created waste, encouraged rampant individualism, and led to social inequality. Thus, for practical and ideological reasons, the provision of consumer goods lagged in the East Bloc, leading to complaints and widespread disillusionment with the constantly deferred promise of socialist prosperity.

Communist regimes also moved aggressively to collectivize agriculture, as the Soviets had done in the 1930s (see "The Five-Year Plans" in Chapter 27). By the early 1960s independent farmers had virtually disappeared in most of the East Bloc. Poland was the exception: there the government abandoned collectivization and tolerated private agriculture, hoping to maintain stability in the large and potentially rebellious country.

For many people in the East Bloc, everyday life was hard throughout the 1950s. Socialist planned economies often led to production backlogs and persistent shortages of basic consumer goods. Party leaders encouraged workers to perform almost superhuman labor to "build socialism," often for low pay and under poor conditions. In East Germany, popular discontent with this situation led to open revolt in June 1953. A strike by Berlin construction workers protesting poor wages and increased work quotas led to nationwide demonstrations that were put down with Soviet troops and tanks. At least fifty-five protesters were killed and about five thousand were arrested during the uprising. When the revolt ended, the authorities rescinded the increased work quotas, but hardliner Stalinists within the East German government used the conflict to strengthen their position.

Communist censors purged culture and art of independent voices in aggressive campaigns that imposed

Rebellion in East Germany In June 1953 disgruntled construction workers in East Berlin walked off the job to protest low pay and high work quotas, setting off a nationwide rebellion against the Communist regime. The protesters could do little against the Soviet tanks and troops that put down the revolt. (Deutsches Historisches Museum, Berlin, Germany/© DHM/ Bridgeman Images)

"Building the Republic": Socialist Realism in Postwar East Berlin

(Andreas Teich/Agencja Fotograficzna Caro/Alamy Stock Photo)

The 60-foot mural "Building the Republic" (of which this is a detail) was installed by East German painter and graphic artist Max Lingner on the Communist House of Ministries (now united Germany's Federal Finance Ministry) in 1952. A classic example of Socialist Realism, the mural glorifies social harmony, the liberation of women, the joys of youth, and the leading role of the working class in building a socialist republic.

EVALUATE THE EVIDENCE

1. How do the activities of the people pictured in the mural represent the goals of East German communism? How, for example, would you interpret the meaning of the three men at the right of the picture?
2. Based on what you have learned in this chapter, does Lingner's mural accurately represent the everyday life experience of ordinary people in East Germany?

rigid anti-Western ideological conformity. In the 1950s most Communist states required artists and writers to conform to the dictates of **Socialist Realism**, which idealized the working classes, Marxism-Leninism, and the Soviet Union. Party propagandists denounced artists who strayed from the party line and forced many talented writers, composers, and film directors to produce works that conformed to the state's political goals. (See "Evaluating Visual Evidence: 'Building the Republic': Socialist Realism in Postwar East Berlin.") In short, the postwar East Bloc resembled the U.S.S.R. in the 1930s, although police terror was far less intense.

Reform and De-Stalinization

In 1953 the ailing Stalin died, and the dictatorship that he had built began to change. Even as Stalin's

heirs struggled for power, they realized that reforms were necessary because of the widespread hardship created by Stalinist repression. The new leadership curbed the power of the secret police, gradually closed forced-labor camps, and tried to spur economic growth, which had sputtered in the postwar years.

The Soviet leadership was badly split on the question of just how much change could be permitted while still preserving the system. Conservatives wanted to move slowly. Reformers, led by the remarkable Nikita Khrushchev (1894–1971), argued for major innovations. Khrushchev (kroush-CHAWF), who had joined the party as a coal miner in 1918 and risen to a high-level position in Ukraine in the 1930s, became first party secretary in 1953 and consolidated his hold on power by 1955.

To strengthen his position and that of his fellow reformers, Khrushchev launched a surprising attack

De-Stalinization and Khrushchev's "Secret Speech"

In this famous speech, Soviet leader Khrushchev initiated the de-Stalinization movement. Khrushchev delivered the speech, which according to the official transcript was punctuated with surprise, indignation, and "tumultuous applause," at a closed session at the Twentieth Party Congress in February 1956. Khrushchev attacked Stalin's legacy and reputation and criticized his cult of personality, his role in the repressive purges of the 1930s, and his failures of leadership in the Second World War. The speech was later read aloud at party meetings but was never openly published in the U.S.S.R. until 1989.

After Stalin's death, the Central Committee began to implement a policy of explaining concisely and consistently that it is impermissible and foreign to the spirit of Marxism-Leninism to elevate one person, to transform him into a superman possessing supernatural characteristics, akin to those of a god. Such a man supposedly knows everything, sees everything, thinks for everyone, can do anything, is infallible in his behavior.

Such a belief about a man, and specifically about Stalin, was cultivated among us for many years. . . . At present, we are concerned with a question which has immense importance for the Party now and for the future—with how the cult of the person of Stalin . . . became at a certain specific stage the source of a whole series of exceedingly serious and grave perversions of Party principles, of Party democracy, of revolutionary legality. . . .

Stalin originated the concept "enemy of the people." This term automatically made it unnecessary that the ideological errors of a man or men engaged in a controversy be proven. It made possible the use of the cruelest repression, violating all norms of revolutionary legality, against anyone who in any way disagreed with Stalin. . . .

Arbitrary behavior by one person encouraged and permitted arbitrariness in others. Mass arrests and deportations of many thousands of people, execution without trial and without normal investigation created conditions of insecurity, fear and even desperation. . . . The [false] confessions of guilt of many of those arrested and charged with enemy activity were gained with the help of cruel and inhuman tortures. . . . Mass arrests of Party, Soviet, economic and military workers caused tremendous harm to our country and to the cause of socialist advancement. . . .

The power accumulated in the hands of one person, Stalin, led to serious consequences during the Great Patriotic War. When we look at many of our novels, films and historical-scientific studies, the role of Stalin in the Patriotic War appears to be entirely improbable. Stalin had foreseen everything . . . the Soviet Army, supposedly thanks only to Stalin's genius, turned to the offensive and subdued the enemy. . . .

Very grievous consequences, especially with regard to the beginning of the war, followed Stalin's annihilation of many military commanders and political workers during 1937–1941 because of his suspiciousness and through slanderous accusations. . . . [T]he threatening danger which hung over our Fatherland in the initial period of the war was largely due to Stalin's very own faulty methods of directing the nation and the Party. . . . Even after the war began, the nervousness and hysteria which Stalin demonstrated while interfering with actual military operations caused our Army serious damage. . . .

Not Stalin, but the Party as a whole, the Soviet Government, our heroic Army, its talented leaders and brave soldiers, the whole Soviet nation—these are the ones who assured victory in the Great Patriotic War.

EVALUATE THE EVIDENCE

1. What accusations does Khrushchev level at Stalin? What does he leave out? Why would the new Soviet leader make these choices?
2. This speech was read at various low-level party meetings, where it generated support but also shock, disillusionment, and outrage. Why would the arguments Khrushchev advances evoke a range of responses?
3. Why would the speech encourage a thaw in the Soviet Union and open revolt in Poland and Hungary?

Source: "Speech to the 20th Party Congress of the CPSU," Marxists Internet Archive, https://www.marxists.org/archive/khrushchev/1956/02/24.htm.

on Stalin and his crimes at a closed session of the Twentieth Party Congress in 1956. In his famous "secret speech," Khrushchev told Communist delegates startled by his open admission of errors that Stalin had "supported the glorification of his own person with all conceivable methods" to build a propagandistic "cult of personality." The delegates applauded when Khrushchev reported that Stalin had bungled the country's defense in World War II and unjustly imprisoned and tortured thousands of loyal Communists. (See "Evaluating Written Evidence: De-Stalinization and Khrushchev's 'Secret Speech.'")

■ **Socialist Realism** Artistic movement that followed the dictates of Communist ideals, enforced by state control in the Soviet Union and East Bloc countries in the 1950s and 1960s.

The U.S.S.R. now entered a period of genuine liberalization — or **de-Stalinization**, as it was called in the West. Khrushchev's speech was read at Communist Party meetings held throughout the country, and it strengthened the reform movement. The party maintained its monopoly on political power, but Khrushchev enlisted younger, reform-minded members. Calling for a relaxation of tensions with the West, the new leader announced a policy of "peaceful coexistence." In domestic policies, state planners shifted resources from heavy industry and the military toward consumer goods and agriculture, and they relaxed Stalinist workplace controls. Leaders in some other Communist countries adopted similar reforms, and the East Bloc's generally low standard of living began to improve.

Khrushchev was proud of Soviet achievements and liked to boast that East Bloc living standards and access to consumer goods would soon surpass those of the West. Soviet and East Bloc reforms did spark a limited consumer revolution. Consumers' options were more modest than those in the West, but people in Communist countries also purchased automobiles, televisions, and other consumer goods in increasing numbers in the 1960s.

Writers and intellectuals saw de-Stalinization as a chance to push against the constraints of Socialist Realism. Russian author Boris Pasternak (1890–1960), for example, published his classic novel *Doctor Zhivago* in 1957, which appeared in the West but not in the Soviet Union until 1988. *Doctor Zhivago* was both a literary masterpiece and a powerful challenge to communism. It tells the story of a talented poet who rejects the brutality of the Bolshevik Revolution and the Stalinist years. Mainstream Communist critics denounced Pasternak, whose book was circulated in secret — but in an era of liberalization he was neither arrested nor shot. Other talented writers followed Pasternak's lead, and courageous editors let the sparks fly. Aleksandr Solzhenitsyn (sohl-zhuh-NEET-suhn) (1918–2008) created a sensation when his *One Day in the Life of Ivan Denisovich* was published in the U.S.S.R. in 1962. Solzhenitsyn's novel, a damning indictment of the Stalinist past, portrays in grim detail life in a Soviet labor camp — a life to which Solzhenitsyn himself had been unjustly condemned.

Foreign Policy and Domestic Rebellion

Khrushchev also de-Stalinized Soviet foreign policy. "Peaceful coexistence" with capitalism was possible, he argued, and war was not inevitable. As a result, Cold War tensions relaxed considerably between 1955 and 1957. At the same time, Khrushchev began wooing the new nations of Asia and Africa — even those that were not Communist — with promises of support and economic aid.

In the East Bloc states, Communist leaders responded in complex ways to de-Stalinization. In East Germany the regime stubbornly resisted reform, but in Poland and Hungary de-Stalinization stimulated rebelliousness. Poland took the lead in 1956, when extensive popular demonstrations brought a new government to power. The new first secretary of the Polish Communist Party proclaimed that there were "many roads to socialism," and by promising to remain loyal to the Warsaw Pact, Poland managed to win greater autonomy from Soviet control. The new leadership maintained the Communist system even as it tolerated a free peasantry and an independent Catholic Church.

Hungary experienced an ultimately tragic revolution the same year. In October 1956, the people of Budapest installed Imre Nagy (im-rey nadge), a liberal Communist, as the new prime minister. Encouraged by extensive popular protests and joined by other Communist reformers, Nagy proposed to democratize Hungary. Though never renouncing communism, he demanded open, multiparty elections, the relaxation of political repression, and other reforms. Bold moves in Hungary raised widespread hopes that Communist states could undergo substantial but peaceful change, driven from within.

At first, it seemed that the Soviets might negotiate, but the breathing space was short-lived. When Nagy announced that Hungary would leave the Warsaw Pact and asked the United Nations to protect the country's neutrality, the Soviets grew alarmed about the possibility that Hungary's independent course would affect other East Bloc countries. On November 4 Soviet troops moved in on the capital city of Budapest and crushed the revolution. Around 2,700 Hungarians died in the crackdown. Fighting was bitter until the end, for the Hungarians hoped that the United Nations would come to their aid. This did not occur — in part because the Western powers were involved in the Suez crisis (see "Independence and Conflict in the Middle East" ahead) and were, in general, reluctant to directly confront the Soviets in Europe with military force. When a newly installed Communist regime executed Nagy and other protest leaders and sent thousands more to prison, many people in the East Bloc concluded that their best hope was to strive for internal reform without openly challenging Soviet control.

The outcome of the Hungarian uprising weakened support for Soviet-style communism in western Europe — the brutal repression deeply discouraged those who still believed in the possibility of an equitable socialist society, and tens of thousands of Communist Party members in the West resigned in disgust. At the same time, Western politicians recognized that the U.S.S.R. would use military force to defend its control of the East Bloc, and that only open war between East and West had the potential to overturn Communist rule there. This price was too high, and it seemed that Communist domination of the satellite states was there to stay.

The Limits of Reform

By late 1962 Khrushchev's Communist colleagues began to see de-Stalinization as a dangerous threat to the authority of the party, and opposition to Khrushchev's reformist policies gained momentum in party circles. Moreover, Khrushchev's policy toward the West was erratic and ultimately unsuccessful. In 1958, in a failed attempt to staunch the flow of hundreds of thousands of disgruntled East German residents who used the open border between East and West Berlin to move permanently to the West, Khrushchev tightened border controls and ordered the Western allies to evacuate the city within six months. In response, the allies reaffirmed their unity in West Berlin, and Khrushchev backed down. Then, with Khrushchev's support, in 1961 the East German authorities built a wall that surrounded West Berlin, sealing off the city, in clear violation of existing access agreements between the former Allies. The recently elected U.S. president, John F. Kennedy (pres. 1961–1963), insisted publicly that the United States would never abandon Berlin. Privately hoping that the wall would ease hostilities in Berlin and lessen Cold War tensions, Kennedy did little to prevent its construction.

Emboldened by American acceptance of the Berlin Wall and seeing a chance to change the balance of

military power decisively, First Secretary Khrushchev secretly ordered missiles with nuclear warheads installed in Fidel Castro's Communist Cuba in 1962. When U.S. intelligence discovered missile sites under construction, Kennedy ordered a naval blockade of Cuba. After a tense diplomatic crisis, Khrushchev agreed to remove the Soviet missiles in return for American pledges not to disturb Castro's regime. In a secret agreement, Kennedy also promised to remove U.S. nuclear missiles from Turkey.

Khrushchev's influence in the party, already slipping, declined rapidly after the Cuban missile crisis. In 1964 the reformist leader was displaced in a bloodless coup, and he spent the rest of his life under house arrest. Under his successor, Leonid Brezhnev (1906–1982), the U.S.S.R. began a period of limited re-Stalinization and economic stagnation. Almost immediately, Brezhnev (BREHZH-nehf) and his supporters started talking quietly of Stalin's achievements and downplaying his crimes, disappointing people eager for further liberalization. Soviet leaders, determined never again to suffer Khrushchev's humiliation in the face of American nuclear superiority, launched a massive arms buildup in the mid-1960s. Even so, the Soviets cautiously avoided direct confrontation with the United States.

Despite popular protests and changes in leadership, the U.S.S.R. and its satellite countries had achieved some stability by the late 1950s. Communist regimes addressed dissent and uprisings with an effective combination of military force, political repression, and limited reform. East and West traded propaganda threats, but both sides basically accepted the division of Europe into spheres of influence. Violent conflicts now took place in the developing world, where decolonization was opening new paths for Cold War confrontation.

How did decolonization proceed in the Cold War era?

In one of world history's great turning points during the Cold War era, Europe's long-standing overseas expansion was dramatically reversed. The retreat from imperial control—a process Europeans called **decolonization**—remade the world map in ways that were profoundly influenced by Cold War conflicts. In just two decades, over fifty new nations joined the global community (Map 28.3). In some cases, decolonization proceeded relatively smoothly. In others, colonized peoples won independence only after long and violent struggles. Decolonization often involved armed conflict, with atrocities and terrorist attacks on civilian populations, perpetrated by colonizers and colonized peoples alike.

Decolonization and the Global Cold War

The most basic cause of imperial collapse was the rising demand of non-Western peoples for national self-determination, racial equality, and personal dignity. This demand spread from intellectuals to ordinary people in nearly every colonial territory after the

---

■ **de-Stalinization** The liberalization of the post-Stalin Soviet Union led by reformer Nikita Khrushchev.

■ **decolonization** The postwar reversal of Europe's overseas expansion caused by the rising demand of the colonized peoples themselves, the declining power of European nations, and the freedoms promised by U.S. and Soviet ideals.

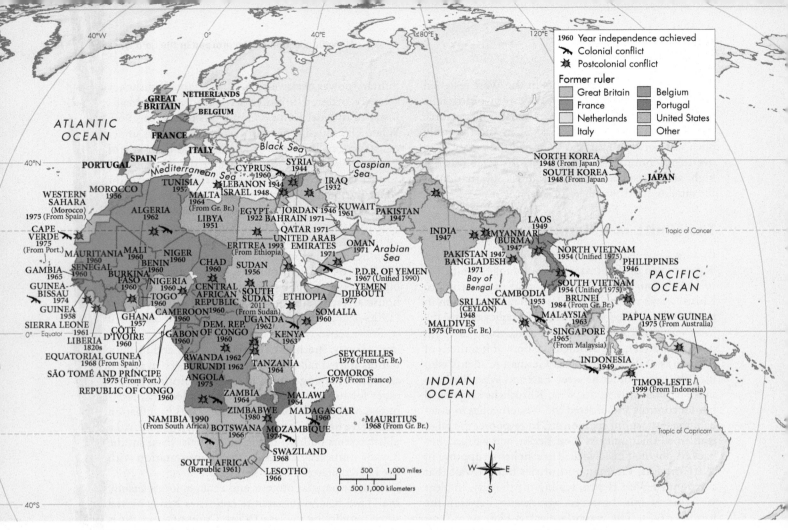

MAP 28.3 Decolonization in Africa and Asia, 1945 to the Present Divided primarily along religious lines into two states, British India won political independence in 1947, serving as an example for other decolonizing nations. Most African territories achieved statehood by the mid-1960s as European empires passed away, unlamented.

First World War. By 1939 the colonial powers were already on the defensive; the Second World War paved the way for the eventual triumph of independence movements.

European empires had been based on an enormous power differential between the rulers and the ruled, a difference that had greatly declined by 1945. Western Europe was economically devastated and militarily weak immediately after the war. Moreover, the Japanese had driven imperial rulers from large parts of East Asia during the war in the Pacific, shattering the myth of European superiority and invincibility. In Southeast Asia, European imperialists confronted strong anticolonial nationalist movements that re-emerged with new enthusiasm after the defeat of the Japanese.

To some degree, the Great Powers regarded their empires very differently after 1945. Empire had rested on self-confidence and self-righteousness; Europeans had believed their superiority to be not only technical and military but also spiritual, racial, and moral.

The horrors of the First and Second World Wars undermined such complacent arrogance and gave opponents of imperialism much greater influence in Europe. Increasing pressure from the United States, which had long presented itself as an enemy of empire despite its own imperialist actions in the Philippines and the Americas, encouraged Europeans to let go. Indeed, Americans were eager to extend their own influence in Europe's former colonies. Economically weakened, and with their political power and moral authority in tatters, the imperial powers preferred to avoid bloody colonial wars and generally turned to rebuilding at home.

Furthermore, the imperial powers faced dedicated anticolonial resistance. Popular politicians, including China's Mao Zedong, India's Mohandas Gandhi, Egypt's Gamal Abdel Nasser, and many others provided determined leadership in the struggle against European imperialism. A new generation of intellectuals, such as Jomo Kenyatta of Kenya and Aimé Césaire and Frantz Fanon, both from Martinique, wrote trenchant critiques of imperial power, often rooted in Marxist ideas. Anticolonial politicians and intellectuals alike helped inspire colonized peoples to resist and overturn imperial rule.

Around the globe, the Cold War had an inescapable impact on decolonization. Liberation from colonial rule had long been a central goal for proponents of Communist world revolution. The Soviets and, after 1949, the Communist Chinese advocated rebellion in the developing world. They promised to help end colonial exploitation and bring freedom and equality in a socialist state and supported Communist independence movements with economic and military aid. The guerrilla insurgent armed with a Soviet-made AK-47 machine gun became the new symbol of Marxist revolution.

Western Europe and particularly the United States offered a competing vision of independence, based on free-market economics and, ostensibly, liberal democracy — though the United States was often willing to support authoritarian regimes that voiced staunch anticommunism. Like the U.S.S.R., the United States extended economic aid and weaponry to decolonizing nations. The Americans promoted cautious moves toward self-determination in the context of containment, attempting to limit the influence of communism in newly liberated states.

After they had won independence, the leaders of the new nations often found themselves trapped between the superpowers, compelled to voice support for one bloc or the other. Many new leaders followed a third way and adopted a policy of **nonalignment**, which emphasized neutrality in the Cold War and the unity of states emerging out of colonial domination.

The Struggle for Power in Asia

The first major fight for independence that followed World War II, between the Netherlands and anticolonial insurgents in Indonesia, in many ways exemplified decolonization in the rest of the Cold War world. The Dutch had been involved in Indonesia since the early seventeenth century (see "The Birth of the Global Economy" in Chapter 14) and had extended their colonial power over the centuries. During World War II, however, the Japanese had overrun the archipelago, encouraging hopes among the locals for independence from Western control. Following the Japanese defeat in 1945, the Dutch returned, hoping to use Indonesia's raw materials, particularly rubber, to support economic recovery at home. But Dutch imperialists faced a determined group of rebels inspired by a powerful combination of nationalism, Marxism, and Islam. Four years of deadly guerrilla war followed, and in 1949 the Netherlands reluctantly accepted Indonesian independence. The new Indonesian

president, Sukarno, became an effective advocate of nonalignment. He had close ties to the Indonesian Communist Party but received foreign aid from the United States as well as the Soviet Union.

A similar combination of communism and anticolonialism inspired the independence movement in parts of French Indochina (now Vietnam, Cambodia, and Laos), though noncommunist nationalists were also involved. France desperately wished to maintain control over these prized colonies and tried its best to re-establish colonial rule after the Japanese occupation collapsed. Despite substantial American aid, the French army fighting in Vietnam was defeated in 1954 by forces under the guerrilla leader Ho Chi Minh (hoh chee min) (1890–1969), who was supported by the U.S.S.R. and China. Vietnam was divided. As in Korea, a shaky truce established a Communist North and a pro-Western South Vietnam, which led to civil war and subsequent intervention by the United States. Cambodia and Laos also gained independence under noncommunist regimes, though Communist rebels remained active in both countries.

India — Britain's oldest, largest, and most lucrative imperial possession — played a key role in the decolonization process. Nationalist opposition to British rule coalesced after the First World War under the leadership of British-educated lawyer Mohandas (sometimes called "Mahatma," or "Great-Souled") Gandhi (1869–1948), one of the twentieth century's most influential figures. In the 1920s and 1930s Gandhi (GAHN-dee) built a mass movement preaching nonviolent "noncooperation" with the British. In 1935 he wrested from the frustrated and unnerved British a new, liberal constitution that was practically a blueprint for independence. The Second World War interrupted progress toward Indian self-rule, but when the Labour Party came to power in Great Britain in 1945, it was ready to relinquish sovereignty. British socialists had long been critics of imperialism, and the heavy cost of governing India had become a large financial burden on the war-wracked country.

The British withdrew peacefully, but conflict between India's Hindu and Muslim populations posed a lasting dilemma for South Asia. As independence neared, the Muslim minority grew increasingly anxious about their status in an India dominated by the Hindu majority. Muslim leaders called for partition — the division of India into separate Hindu and Muslim states — and the British agreed. When independence was made official on August 15, 1947, predominantly Muslim territories on India's eastern and western borders became Pakistan (the eastern section is today's Bangladesh). Seeking relief from

---

■ **nonalignment** Policy of postcolonial governments that emphasized neutrality in the Cold War and the unity of states emerging out of colonial domination.

A Refugee Camp During the Partition of India   A young Muslim man, facing an uncertain future, sits above a refugee camp established on the grounds of a medieval fortress in the northern Indian city of Delhi. In the camp, Muslim refugees wait to cross the border to the newly founded Pakistan. The chaos that accompanied the mass migration of Muslims and Hindus during the partition of India in 1947 cost the lives of up to 1 million migrants and disrupted the livelihoods of millions more. (Margaret Bourke-White/The LIFE Picture Collection/Shutterstock)

the violence that erupted, millions of Muslim and Hindu refugees fled both ways across the new borders, a massive population exchange that left mayhem and death in its wake. In just a few summer weeks, up to 1 million people lost their lives (estimates vary widely). Then in January 1948 a radical Hindu nationalist opposed to partition assassinated Gandhi, and Jawaharlal Nehru became Indian prime minister.

Under the leadership of Nehru, India successfully maintained a policy of nonalignment. India became a liberal, if socialist-friendly, democratic state that dealt with both the United States and the U.S.S.R. As the Cold War heated up in the early 1950s, Pakistan, an Islamic republic, developed close ties with the United States. Pakistan and India both joined the British Commonwealth, a voluntary and cooperative association of former British colonies that already included Canada, Australia, and New Zealand.

Where Indian nationalism drew on Western parliamentary liberalism, Chinese nationalism developed and triumphed in the framework of Marxist-Leninist ideology. After the withdrawal of the occupying Japanese army in 1945, China erupted again in open civil war. The authoritarian Guomindang (National People's Party), led by Jiang Jieshi (traditionally called Chiang Kai-shek; 1887–1975), fought to repress the Chinese Communists, led by Mao Zedong (MA-OW zuh-DOUNG) and supported by a popular grassroots uprising.

During the revolutionary war that ensued, the Soviets gave Mao aid, and the Americans gave Jiang much more. Winning the support of the peasantry by promising to expropriate the holdings of the big landowners, the Communists forced the Guomindang to retreat to the island of Taiwan in 1949. Mao and the Communists united China's 550 million inhabitants in a strong centralized state, and the "Red Chinese" began building a new society that adapted Marxism to Chinese conditions. The new government promoted land reform, extended education and health-care programs to the peasantry, and introduced Soviet-style five-year plans that boosted industrial production. It also brought Stalinist-style repression — mass arrests, forced-labor camps, and ceaseless propaganda campaigns — to the Chinese people.

Independence and Conflict in the Middle East

In some areas of the Middle East, the movement toward political independence went relatively smoothly. The French League of Nations mandates in Syria and Lebanon had collapsed during the Second World War, and Saudi Arabia and Transjordan had already achieved independence. But events in the British mandate of Palestine and in Egypt showed that decolonization in the Middle East could lead to violence and lasting conflict.

As part of the peace accords that followed World War I, the British government had advocated a Jewish homeland alongside the Arab population (see "The Peace Settlement in the Middle East" in Chapter 25). This tenuous compromise unraveled after World

War II. Neither Jews nor Arabs were happy with British rule, and violence and terrorism mounted on both sides. In 1947 the British decided to leave Palestine, and the United Nations voted in a nonbinding resolution to divide the territory into two states—one Arab-Palestinian and one Jewish. The Jews accepted the plan and founded the state of Israel in 1948.

The Palestinians and the surrounding Arab nations viewed Jewish independence as a profound betrayal, enforced by Western colonial interests. Palestinian militias, joined by Arab troops from Egypt, Transjordan, Syria, Lebanon, and Iraq, attacked the Jewish state as soon as it was proclaimed. Over ten months of fighting, the Israeli army pushed back the Arab forces and took control of about 60 percent of the territory the UN had assigned for the Palestinian state. Over 700,000 Palestinians fled or were expelled from their homes, creating an ongoing refugee problem. Holocaust survivors from Europe streamed into Israel, as Theodor Herzl's Zionist dream came true (see "Jewish Emancipation and Modern Anti-Semitism" in Chapter 23). The next sixty years brought five more Arab-Israeli wars (in 1956, 1967, 1973, 1982, and 2006) and innumerable clashes between Israelis and Palestinians.

The 1948 Arab defeat triggered a nationalist revolution in Egypt in 1952, led by the young army officer Gamal Abdel Nasser (1918–1970). The revolutionaries drove out the pro-Western king, and in 1954 Nasser became president of an Egyptian republic. A crafty politician, Nasser advocated nonalignment and expertly played the superpowers against each other, securing loans from the United States and purchasing Soviet arms.

In July 1956 Nasser abruptly nationalized the foreign-owned Suez Canal Company, a major remnant of Western power in the Middle East. Infuriated, the British and the French, along with the Israelis, planned a secret military operation. The Israeli army invaded the Sinai Peninsula bordering the canal, and British and French bombers attacked Egyptian airfields. World opinion was outraged, and the United States feared that such a blatant show of imperialism would encourage the

Israel, 1948

The Suez Crisis, 1956

Arab states to join the Soviet bloc. The Americans joined with the Soviets to force the British, French, and Israelis to back down. Egyptian nationalism triumphed: Nasser got his canal, and Israel left the Sinai. The Suez crisis, a watershed in the history of European imperialism, revealed the Europeans' weakening control over their global empires.

Decolonization in Africa

In less than a decade, most of Africa won independence from European imperialism, a remarkable movement of world historical importance. The new African states were quickly caught up in the struggles between the Cold War superpowers, and decolonization all too often left a lasting legacy of economic decline and political struggle (see Map 28.3).

Starting in 1957, most of Britain's African colonies achieved independence with relatively little bloodshed and then entered a very loose association with Britain as members of the British Commonwealth. Ghana, Nigeria, Tanzania, and other countries gained independence in this way, but there were exceptions. In Kenya, British forces brutally crushed the nationalist Mau Mau rebellion in the early 1950s, but nonetheless recognized Kenyan independence in 1963. In South Africa, the white-dominated government left the Commonwealth in 1961 and declared an independent republic in order to preserve apartheid—an exploitative system of racial segregation enforced by law.

The decolonization of the Belgian Congo was one of the great tragedies of the Cold War. Belgian leaders, profiting from the colony's wealth of natural resources and proud of their small nation's imperial status, maintained a system of apartheid there and dragged their feet in granting independence. These conditions sparked an anticolonial movement that grew increasingly aggressive in the late 1950s under the able leadership of the charismatic Patrice Lumumba. In January 1960 the Belgians gave in and hastily announced that the Congo would be independent six months later, a schedule that was irresponsibly fast. Lumumba was chosen

Egyptian President Nasser Greets a Crowd
The charismatic president was immensely popular with ordinary Egyptians and enjoyed mingling with his supporters. Here, on August 20, 1956, Nasser greets a cheering crowd in Cairo, the Egyptian capital. That July, ignoring French and British protests, Nasser had announced that Egypt would nationalize the all-important Suez Canal, a crucial event in the history of postwar decolonization. (RUE DES ARCHIVES (RDA)/Bridgeman Images)

prime minister in democratic elections, but when the Belgians pulled out on schedule, the new government was unprepared. Chaos broke out when the Congolese army attacked Belgian military officers who remained in the country.

With substantial financial investments in the Congo, the United States and western Europe worried that the new nation might fall into Soviet hands. U.S. leaders cast Lumumba as a Soviet proxy, an oversimplification of his nonalignment policies. American anxiety increased when Lumumba asked the U.S.S.R. for aid and protection. In a troubling example of containment in action, the CIA helped implement a military coup against Lumumba. With U.S. support, Congolese army officers took him prisoner and then executed him by firing squad, under Belgian supervision. The Congolese military then established a U.S.-backed dictatorship under the corrupt general Joseph Mobutu. Mobutu ruled until 1997 and became one of the world's wealthiest men, while the Congo remained one of the poorest, most violent, and most politically torn countries in the world.

French colonies and protectorates in North Africa followed several roads to independence. Like the British, the French offered most of their African territories, including Tunisia, Morocco, and Senegal, the choice of a total break or independence within a kind of French commonwealth. All but one of the new states chose the latter option, largely because they wanted aid from their former colonizer, although two years later they all opted for total independence. The French were eager to maintain close ties, at least on French terms. As in the past, the French and their Common Market partners, who helped foot the bill, saw themselves as continuing their "civilizing mission" in sub-Saharan Africa. More important, they saw in Africa raw materials for their factories, markets for their industrial goods,

outlets for profitable investment, and good temporary jobs for their engineers and teachers.

Things were far more difficult in the French colony of Algeria, a large Islamic state on the Mediterranean Sea where some 1.2 million white European settlers, including some 800,000 French, had taken up permanent residency by the 1950s. Nicknamed pieds-noirs (literally "black feet"), many of these Europeans had raised families in Algeria for three or four generations, and they enforced a two-tiered system of citizenship, dominating politics and the economy. Algerian rebels, inspired by anticolonialism and Algerian nationalism, established the National Liberation Front (FLN) and revolted against French colonialism in the early 1950s. The presence of the pieds-noirs complicated matters. Worried about their position in the colony, the pieds-noirs pressured the French government to help them. In response, France sent some 400,000 troops to crush the FLN and put down the revolt. (See "Thinking Like a Historian: Violence and the Algerian War," page 896.)

The resulting Algerian War—long, bloody, and marred by atrocities committed by both sides—lasted from 1954 to 1962. FLN radicals repeatedly attacked pied-noir civilians, while the French army engaged in systematic torture, mass arrests (often of innocent suspects), and the forced relocation and internment of millions of Muslim civilians suspected of supporting the insurgents.

By 1958 French forces had successfully limited FLN military actions, but their disproportionate use of force encouraged many Algerians to support or join the FLN. News reports about torture and abuse of civilians turned French public opinion against the war, and international outrage further pressured French leaders to end the conflict. Efforts to open peace talks led to a revolt by the Algerian French and threats of a coup d'état by the French army. In 1958 the immensely popular General Charles de Gaulle was reinstated as French president as part of the movement to keep Algeria French. His appointment at first calmed the army, the pieds-noirs, and the French public.

Yet to the dismay of the pieds-noirs and army hardliners, de Gaulle pragmatically moved toward Algerian self-determination. In 1961 furious pieds-noirs and army leaders formed the OAS (Secret Army Organization) and began a terrorist revolt against Muslim Algerians and the French government. In April of that year the OAS mounted an all-out but short-lived putsch, taking over Algiers and threatening the government in Paris. Army units loyal to the French government defeated the rebellion, the leading generals were purged, and negotiations between the French government and FLN leaders continued. In April 1962, after more than a century of exploitative French rule and a decade of brutal anticolonial warfare, Algeria became independent under the FLN. Then in a massive exodus, over 1 million pieds-noirs fled to France and the Americas.

By the mid-1960s most African states had won independence, some through bloody insurrections. There were exceptions: Portugal, for one, waged war against independence movements in Angola and Mozambique into the 1970s. Black people in South Africa still sought liberation from apartheid, and white rulers in Rhodesia continued a bloody civil war against African insurgents until 1979. Even in liberated countries, the colonial legacy had long-term negative effects. African leaders may have expressed support for socialist or democratic principles in order to win aid from the superpowers. In practice, however, corrupt and authoritarian African leaders like Mobutu in the Congo often established lasting authoritarian dictatorships and enriched themselves at the expense of their populations.

Despite decolonization, in the 1960s and 1970s western European countries managed to increase their economic and cultural ties with their former African colonies. Above all, they used the lure of special trading privileges and provided heavy investment in

Decolonization in the Democratic Republic of the Congo   Flushed with victory, the democratically elected Congolese premier Patrice Lumumba waves as he leaves the National Senate on September 8, 1960. Lumumba had just received a 41–2 vote of confidence that confirmed his leadership position. Four months later he was assassinated in a military coup. (Bettmann/Getty Images)

French- and English-language education to bolster the Western presence in the new African states. This situation led a variety of leaders and scholars to charge that western Europe (and the United States) had imposed a system of **neocolonialism** on the former colonies. According to this view, neocolonialism was a system designed to perpetuate Western economic domination and undermine the promise of political independence, thereby extending to Africa (and much of Asia) the kind of economic subordination that the United States had imposed on Latin America in the nineteenth century.

What were the key changes in social relations in postwar Europe?

While Europe staged its astonishing recovery from the Nazi nightmare and colonized peoples won independence, changing class structures, new patterns of global migration, and evolving roles for women and youths had dramatic impacts on everyday life, albeit with different effects in the East Bloc and western Europe.

Changing Class Structures

The combination of rapid economic growth, growing prosperity and mass consumption, and the provision of generous, state-sponsored benefit programs went

a long way toward creating a new society in Europe after the Second World War. Old class barriers relaxed, and class distinctions became fuzzier.

Changes in the structure of the middle class were particularly important. In the nineteenth and early twentieth centuries, the model for the middle class had been the independent, self-employed individual who owned a business or practiced a liberal profession such as law or medicine. Ownership of property—

■ **neocolonialism** A postcolonial system that perpetuates Western economic exploitation in former colonial territories.

Violence and the Algerian War

In the course of the eight-year-long Algerian War, French soldiers and police, FLN insurgents, and OAS militiamen all used ferocious violence to pursue their military-political objectives. Though casualty numbers were small at the start, the Algerian War would ultimately claim the lives of hundreds of thousands of people. What sort of tactics did the combatants use, and how did they justify their actions?

1 **An argument for revolutionary violence.** While thinkers like Frantz Fanon called for anti-imperial violence in historical-psychological terms, radicals like Brazilian guerrilla Carlos Marighella laid out the justification in chilling, practical terms. Similar ideas inspired the FLN.

〜 It is necessary to turn political crisis into armed conflict by performing violent actions that will force those in power to transform the political situation of the country into a military situation. That will alienate the masses, who, from then on, will revolt against the army and the police and blame them for the state of things.

2 **An argument for torture.** French soldiers and police routinely tortured FLN members and other Algerians suspected of supporting the insurgents in order to gain information and intimidate the general population. Colonel Antoine Argoud, a commander of a French paratroop force sent to Algeria, argued for the necessity of torture.

〜 Muslims will not talk . . . as long as we do not inflict acts of violence on them. . . . They will rally [to] our camp only if it [justice] responds to their respect and thirst for authority. . . . From our perspective, torture and capital executions are acts of war. Now, war is an act of violence aimed at compelling the enemy to execute our will, and violence is the means [by which to do it]. . . .

Torture is an act of violence just like the bullet shot from a gun, the [cannon] shell, the flame-thrower, the bomb, napalm, or gas. Where does torture really start, with a blow with the fist, the threat of reprisal, or electricity? Torture is different from other methods in that it is not anonymous. . . . Torture brings the torturer and his victim face to face. The torturer at least has the merit of operating in the open. It is true that with

torture the victim is disarmed, but so are the inhabitants of a city being bombed, aren't they? . . .

It is my choice. I will carry out public executions, I'll shoot those absolutely guilty. Justice will therefore be just. It will conform to the first criterion of Christian justice. I'll expose their corpses to the public . . . not out of some sadist feeling, but to enhance the virtue of exemplary justice. . . .

To the great astonishment of my men, I then decided to bring the corpses [of presumed insurgents killed in an air strike] back to M'sila to expose them to the population. . . . I ordered the driver to unload [the corpses] in M'sila on the main square [where they remained exposed for twenty-four hours]. When we left, the ambiance had completely changed. No more attacks, and the population, initially mute, opened up, and information began to pour out.

3 **The Philippeville massacres, August 20, 1955.** Faced with setbacks, the FLN decided to mount an open attack on the coastal region of Philippeville. A violent group, encouraged by FLN insurgents, massacred 123 European settlers. Enraged by the atrocities — the mob had brutally assaulted elderly men, women, and children — French army units, police, and settler vigilantes retaliated by killing at least 1,273 insurgents and Muslim-Arab residents; the FLN claimed that the actual number was 12,000. A French paratrooper described the scene.

〜 [Catching up with a group of "rebels," mingled with civilians,] we opened fire into the thick of them, at random. Then as we moved on and found more bodies [of French colonial settlers], our company commanders finally gave us the order to shoot down every Arab we met. You should have seen the result. . . . For two hours all we heard was automatic rifles spitting fire into the crowd. Apart from a dozen *fellagha* ["bandit,"

ANALYZING THE EVIDENCE

1. What are the main arguments made for the use of violence and terror in Sources 1 and 2? Are any of these arguments legitimate?
2. Review the firsthand accounts by French soldiers who fought against FLN insurgents (Sources 2 and 3). What is their attitude toward Algerian Muslims?
3. Consider Sources 2–5. Did the use of violence and terror by both French forces and the FLN have consequences that they did not intend?

or FLN insurgent] stragglers, weapons in hand, whom we shot down, there were at least a hundred and fifty *boukaks* [another derogatory term for Muslims]. . . .

At midday, fresh orders: take prisoners. That complicated everything. It was easy when it was merely a matter of killing. . . . At six o'clock next morning all the l.m.g.s [light machine guns] and machine-guns were lined up in front of the crowd of prisoners, who immediately began to yell. But we opened fire; ten minutes later, it was practically over. There were so many of them they had to be buried with bulldozers.

(ullstein bild/akg-images)

4 **A 1956 FLN terror bombing in Algiers.** The violence continued to escalate after the Philippeville massacres, and in 1956 the FLN formally embraced terrorism, expanding its attacks on the colonial state to include European civilians. This FLN bomb attack, intended to strike a French police patrol in a working-class district of Algiers, missed its target and hit customers in a coffeehouse instead. In the background, suspects are under arrest.

(AFP/Getty Images)

5 **Pacification of the Algerian countryside.** Fighting took place in the capital of Algiers and other cities, but the Algerian War was largely fought in the countryside. In attempts to "pacify" the Algerian peasantry, French forces undertook numerous campaigns in rural areas like the one pictured here. Soldiers checked identity cards, searched for weapons, arrested villagers and moved them to internment centers, and at times tortured and summarily executed those they suspected of supporting the FLN.

PUTTING IT ALL TOGETHER

War inevitably involves the use of deadly, unrestrained violence, but historians agree that the Algerian War was particularly brutal. Using the sources above, along with what you have learned in class and in this chapter, write a short essay that explores the use of violence in the process of decolonization. Why was violence so central in the Algerian struggle for independence?

Sources: (1) Alejandro Colás and Richard Saull, eds., *The War on Terrorism and the American "Empire" After the Cold War* (New York: Routledge, 2007), p. 190; (2) Marnia Lazreg, *Torture and the Twilight of Empire: From Algiers to Baghdad* (Princeton, N.J.: Princeton University Press, 2008), pp. 89–92; (3) Alistair Horne, *A Savage War of Peace: Algeria 1954–1962* (New York: Viking, 1978), p. 121.

frequently inherited property—and strong family ties had often been the keys to wealth and standing within the middle class. After 1945 this pattern changed drastically in western Europe. A new breed of managers and experts—so-called white-collar workers—replaced property owners as the leaders of the middle class. The ability to earn an ample income largely replaced inherited property and family connections in determining an individual's social position in the middle and upper-middle classes. At the same time, the middle class grew massively and became harder to define.

There were several reasons for these developments. Rapid industrial and technological expansion and the consolidation of businesses created a powerful demand for technologists and managers in large corporations and government agencies. Moreover, the old propertied middle class lost control of many family-owned businesses. Numerous small businesses (including family farms) could no longer turn a profit, so their former owners regretfully joined the ranks of salaried employees.

Similar processes were at work in the East Bloc, where class leveling was an avowed goal of the authoritarian socialist state. The nationalization of industry, expropriation of property, and aggressive attempts to open employment opportunities to workers and equalize wage structures effectively reduced class differences. Communist Party members typically received better jobs and more pay than nonmembers, but by the 1960s the income differential between the top and bottom strata of East Bloc societies was far smaller than in the West.

In both East and West, managers and civil servants represented the model for a new middle class. Well paid and highly trained, often with professional degrees, these pragmatic experts were primarily concerned with efficiency and practical solutions to concrete problems.

The structure of the lower classes also became more flexible and open. Continuing trends that began in the nineteenth century, large numbers of people left the countryside for the city. The population of one of the most traditional and least mobile groups in European society—farmers—drastically declined. Meanwhile, the number of industrial workers in western Europe began to fall, as new jobs for white-collar and service employees grew rapidly. This change marked a significant transition in the world of labor. The social benefits extended by postwar governments also helped promote greater equality because they raised lower-class living standards and were paid for in part by higher taxes on the wealthy. In general,

European workers were better educated and more specialized than before, and the new workforce bore a greater resemblance to the growing middle class of salaried specialists than to traditional industrial workers.

Patterns of Postwar Migration

The 1850s to the 1930s had been an age of global migration, as countless Europeans moved around the continent and the world seeking economic opportunity or freedom from political or religious persecution (see "European Emigration" in Chapter 24). The 1950s and 1960s witnessed new waves of migration that had a significant impact on European society.

Some postwar migration took place within countries. Declining job prospects in Europe's rural areas encouraged small farmers to seek better prospects in cities. In the poorer countries of Spain, Portugal, and Italy, millions moved to more developed regions of their own countries. The process was similar in the East Bloc, where the forced collectivization of agriculture and state subsidies for heavy industry opened opportunities in urban areas. And before the erection of the Berlin Wall in 1961, some 3.5 million East Germans moved to the Federal Republic of Germany, seeking higher pay and political freedom.

Many other Europeans moved across national borders seeking work. The general pattern was from south to north. Workers from less developed countries like Italy, Spain, and socialist Yugoslavia moved to the industrialized north, particularly to West Germany, which—having lost 5 million people during the war—was in desperate need of able-bodied workers. In the 1950s and 1960s West Germany and other prosperous countries implemented **guest worker programs** designed to recruit much-needed labor for the booming economy. West Germany signed labor agreements with Italy, Greece, Spain, Portugal, Yugoslavia, Turkey, and the North African countries of Tunisia and Morocco. By the early 1970s there were 2.8 million foreign workers in Germany and another 2.3 million in France, where they made up 11 percent of the workforce.

Most guest workers were young, unskilled single men who labored for low wages in entry-level jobs and sent much of their pay to their families at home. (See "Individuals in Society: Armando Rodrigues," page 899.) According to government plans, these guest workers were supposed to return to their home countries after a specified period. Many built new lives, however, and, to the dismay of the authorities and conservative nationalists, chose to live permanently in their adoptive countries.

Europe was also changed by **postcolonial migration**, the movement of people from the former colonies and the developing world into prosperous Europe. In contrast to guest workers, who enlisted in

---

■ **guest worker programs** Government-run programs in western Europe designed to recruit labor for the booming postwar economy.

■ **postcolonial migration** The postwar movement of people from former colonies and the developing world into Europe.

Popping flashbulbs greeted Portuguese worker Armando Rodrigues when he stepped off a train in Cologne in September 1964. Celebrated in the national media as West Germany's 1 millionth guest worker, Rodrigues was met by government and business leaders — including the Christian Democratic minister of labor — who presented him with a motorcycle and a bouquet of carnations.

In most respects, Rodrigues was hardly different from the many foreign workers recruited to work in West Germany and other northern European countries. Most foreign laborers were nobodies, written out of mainstream historical texts and treated as statistics. Yet in his moment of fame, Rodrigues became the face of a troubled labor program that helped turn Germany into a multiethnic society.

By the late 1950s the new Federal Republic desperately needed able-bodied men to fill the low-paying jobs created by rapid economic expansion. The West German government signed labor agreements with several Mediterranean countries to meet this demand. Rodrigues and hundreds of thousands of other young men signed up for the employment program and then submitted to an arduous application process. Rodrigues traveled from his village to the regional Federal Labor Office, where he filled out forms and took written and medical exams. Months later, after he had received an initial one-year contract from a German employer, Rodrigues and twelve hundred other Portuguese and Spanish men boarded a special train reserved for foreign workers and embarked for West Germany.

For labor migrants, life was hard in West Germany. In the first years of the guest worker program, most recruits were men between the ages of twenty and forty who were either single or willing to leave their families at home. They typically filled low-level jobs in construction, mines, and factories, and they lived apart from West Germans in special barracks close to their workplaces, with six to eight workers in a room.

West Germans gave Rodrigues and his fellow migrants a mixed reception. Though they were a welcome source of inexpensive labor, the men who emigrated from what West Germans called "the southern lands" faced discrimination and prejudice. "Order, cleanliness, and punctuality seem like the natural qualities of a respectable person to us," wrote one official in 1966. "In the south, one does not learn or know this, so it is difficult [for a worker from the south] to adjust here."*

According to official plans, the so-called guest workers were supposed to return home after a specified period of

*Quoted in Rita Chin, *The Guest Worker Question in Postwar Germany* (New York: Cambridge University Press, 2007), p. 43.

Armando Rodrigues received a standing ovation and a motorcycle when he got off the train in Cologne in 1964.
(Horst Ossinger/picture-alliance/dpa/AP Photo)

time. Rodrigues, for one, went back to Portugal in the late 1970s. Others did not. Resisting government pressure, millions of temporary "guests" raised families and became permanent West German residents, building substantial ethnic minorities in the Federal Republic. Because of strict naturalization laws, however, they could not become West German citizens.

Despite the hostility they faced, foreign workers established a lasting and powerful presence in West Germany, and they were a significant factor in the country's swift economic recovery. More than fifty years after Rodrigues arrived in Cologne, his motorcycle is on permanent display in the House of History Museum in Bonn. The exhibit is a remarkable testament to one man's history, to the contribution of migrant labor to West German economic growth, and to the ongoing struggle to come to terms with ethnic difference and integration in a democratic Germany.

QUESTIONS FOR ANALYSIS

1. How did Rodrigues's welcome at his 1964 reception differ from the general attitude toward guest workers in West Germany at the time?
2. What were the long-term costs and benefits of West Germany's labor recruitment policies?

formal recruitment programs, postcolonial migrants could often claim citizenship rights from their former colonizers and moved spontaneously. Immigrants from the Caribbean, India, Africa, and Asia went to Britain; people from North Africa, especially Algeria, and from sub-Saharan countries such as Cameroon and the Ivory Coast moved to France; Indonesians migrated to the Netherlands.

These new migration patterns had dramatic results. Immigrant labor helped fuel economic recovery, while growing ethnic diversity changed the face of Europe and enriched the cultural life of the continent. The new residents were not always welcome, however. Adaptation to European lifestyles could be difficult, and immigrants often lived in separate communities where they spoke their own languages. They faced employment and housing discrimination, as well as the harsh anti-immigrant rhetoric and policies of xenophobic politicians. Even prominent European intellectuals worried aloud that Muslim migrants from North Africa and Turkey would never adopt European values and customs. The tensions that surrounded changed migration patterns would pose significant challenges to social integration in the decades to come.

New Roles for Women

The postwar culmination of a one-hundred-year-long trend toward early marriage, early childbearing, and small family size in wealthy urban societies had revolutionary implications for women. Above all, pregnancy and child care occupied a much smaller portion of a woman's life than in earlier times. The postwar baby boom did make for larger families and fairly rapid population growth of 1 to 1.5 percent per year in many European countries, but the long-term decline in birthrates resumed by the 1960s. By the early 1970s about half of Western women were having their last baby by the age of twenty-six or twenty-seven. When the youngest child trooped off to kindergarten, the average mother had more than forty years of life in front of her.

This was a momentous transition. Throughout history male-dominated society insisted on defining most women as mothers or potential mothers, and motherhood was very demanding. In the postwar years, however, motherhood no longer absorbed the energies of a lifetime, and more and more married women looked for new roles in the world of work outside the family.

Three major forces helped women searching for jobs in the changing post–World War II workplace. First, the economic boom created strong demand for labor. Second, the economy continued its gradual shift away from the old male-dominated heavy industries, such as coal, steel, and shipbuilding, and toward the white-collar service industries in which some women already worked, such as government, education, sales, and health care. Third, young women shared fully in the postwar education revolution and so were positioned to take advantage of the growing need for officeworkers and well-trained professionals. Thus more and more married women became full-time and part-time wage earners.

In the East Bloc, Communist leaders opened up numerous jobs to women, who accounted for almost half of all employed persons. Many women made their way into previously male professions, including factory work but also medicine and engineering. In western Europe and North America, the percentage of married women in the workforce rose from a range of roughly 20 to 25 percent in 1950 to anywhere from 30 to 60 percent in the 1970s.

All was not easy for women entering paid employment. Married women workers faced widespread discrimination in pay, advancement, and occupational choice in comparison to men. Moreover, many women could find only part-time work. As the divorce rate rose in the 1960s, part-time work, with its low pay and scanty benefits, meant poverty for many women with children. Finally, married women who held jobs in both the East and West still shouldered most of the child-rearing and housekeeping responsibilities and were left with an exhausting "double burden." Trying to live up to society's seemingly contradictory ideals was one reason that many women accepted part-time employment.

The injustices that women encountered as wage earners contributed greatly to the feminist movement that emerged in the 1960s. Sexism and discrimination in the workplace—and in the home—grew loathsome and evoked the sense of injustice that drives revolutions and reforms.

Youth Culture and the Generation Gap

The bulging cohort of so-called baby boomers born after World War II created a distinctive and very international youth culture that brought remarkable changes to postwar youth roles and lifestyles. That subculture, found across Europe and the United States, was rooted in behaviors, fashions, and musical tastes that set its members off from their elders and fueled anxious comments about a growing "generation gap."

Youth styles in the United States often provided inspiration for movements in Europe. Groups like the British Teddy boys, the West German *Halbstarken* (half-strongs), and the French *blousons noirs* (black jackets) modeled their rebellious clothing and cynical attitudes on the bad-boy characters played by U.S. film stars such as James Dean and Marlon Brando. American jazz and rock 'n' roll spread rapidly in western Europe, aided by the invention of the long-playing record album (or LP) and the 45-rpm "single" in the late 1940s, as well as the growth of the corporate music industry. American musicians such as Elvis Presley, Bill Haley and His Comets,

Postwar Youth Subcultures   By the early 1960s, the postwar baby boom had brought remarkable changes to the lives of teenagers and young adults. New styles and behaviors, often based on American models, embraced youthful rebelliousness and challenged adult conventions. The Rockers pictured here, for example, were British motorcycle enthusiasts who wore leather jackets and traveled in gangs. Their rivals the Mods rode scooters (not motorcycles) and wore trendy suits and "Parka" coats. In places where their territory overlapped, Mods and Rockers sometimes clashed, and English seaside resorts were sites of riots started by fighting between these rival gangs. (Paul Popper/Popperfoto/Getty Images)

and Gene Vincent thrilled European youths and worried parents, teachers, and politicians.

Youths played a key role in the consumer revolution. Marketing experts and manufacturers quickly recognized that the young people they now called "teenagers" had money to spend due to postwar prosperity. An array of advertisements and products consciously targeted the youth market. In France, for example, magazine advertising aimed at adolescents grew by 400 percent between 1959 and 1962. As the baby boomers entered their late teens, they eagerly purchased trendy clothing and the latest pop music hits, as well as record players, transistor radios, magazines, hair products, and makeup, all marketed for the "young generation."

The new youth culture became an inescapable part of Western society. One clear sign of this new presence was the rapid growth in the number of universities and college students. Before the 1960s, in North America and Europe, only a small elite received a university education. In 1950 only 3 to 4 percent of western European youths went on to higher education; numbers in the United States were only slightly higher. Then, as government subsidies made education more affordable to ordinary people, enrollments skyrocketed. By 1960 at least three times more European

students attended some kind of university than they had before World War II, and the number continued to rise sharply until the 1970s.

The rapid expansion of higher education opened new opportunities for the middle and lower classes, but many students felt that they were not getting the kind of education they needed for jobs in the contemporary world. At the same time, some reflective students feared that universities were doing nothing but turning out docile technocrats both to stock and to serve "the establishment." Thus it was no coincidence that students became leaders in a counterculture that attacked the ideals of the affluent society of the postwar world and rocked the West in the late 1960s.

NOTES

1. Anonymous, *A Woman in Berlin: Eight Weeks in the Conquered City: A Diary* (New York: Metropolitan Books, 2005), pp. 239–240.
2. Quoted in N. Graebner, *Cold War Diplomacy, 1945–1960* (Princeton, N.J.: Van Nostrand, 1962), p. 17.
3. From a speech delivered by G. Marshall at Harvard University on June 5, 1947, reprinted in *Department of State Bulletin* (June 15, 1947), pp. 1159–1160.
4. Quoted in T. Judt, *Postwar: A History of Europe Since 1945* (New York: Penguin, 2005), p. 150.

LOOKING BACK LOOKING AHEAD

The unprecedented human and physical destruction of World War II left Europeans shaken, searching in the ruins for new livelihoods and a workable political order. A tension-filled peace settlement left the continent divided into two hostile political-military blocs, and the resulting

Cold War, complete with the threat of atomic annihilation, threatened to explode into open confrontation. Albert Einstein voiced a common anxiety when he said, "I do not know with what weapons World War III will be fought, but World War IV will be fought with sticks and stones."

Despite such fears, Cold War divisions led to relative stability on the European continent. In the West Bloc, economic growth, state provision of social benefits, and the strong NATO alliance engendered social and political consensus. In the East Bloc, a combination of political repression and partial reform likewise limited dissent and potential change. During the height of the Cold War, Europe's former colonies won liberation in a process that was often flawed but that nonetheless resulted in political independence for millions of people. And large-scale transformations, including the rise of Big Science and rapid economic growth, opened new opportunities for women and immigrants and contributed to stability on both sides of the iron curtain.

By the early 1960s Europeans had entered a remarkable age of affluence that almost eliminated real poverty on most of the continent. Superpower confrontations had led not to European war but to peaceful coexistence. The following decades, however, would see substantial challenges to this postwar consensus. Youth revolts and a determined feminist movement, an oil crisis and a deep economic recession, and political dissent and revolution in the East Bloc would shake and remake Western society.

Make Connections

Think about the larger developments and continuities within and across chapters.

1. How did the Cold War shape politics and everyday life in the United States and western Europe, the U.S.S.R. and the East Bloc, and the decolonizing world? Why was its influence so pervasive?

2. How were the postwar social transformations in class structures, patterns of migration, and the lives of women and youths related to the broad political and economic changes that followed World War II? How did they differ on either side of the iron curtain?

3. Compare and contrast the treaties and agreements that ended the First and Second World Wars (Chapter 25). Did the participants who shaped the peace accords face similar problems? Which set of agreements did a better job of resolving outstanding issues, and why?

28 REVIEW & EXPLORE

Identify Key Terms

Identify and explain the significance of each item below.

Cold War (p. 872)	Christian Democrats (p. 881)
displaced persons (p. 873)	Common Market (p. 882)
Truman Doctrine (p. 877)	Socialist Realism (p. 886)
Marshall Plan (p. 878)	de-Stalinization (p. 888)
Council for Mutual Economic Assistance (COMECON) (p. 878)	decolonization (p. 889)
NATO (p. 878)	nonalignment (p. 891)
Warsaw Pact (p. 878)	neocolonialism (p. 895)
economic miracle (p. 881)	guest worker programs (p. 898)
	postcolonial migration (p. 898)

Review the Main Ideas

Answer the section heading questions from the chapter.

1. Why was World War II followed so quickly by the Cold War? (p. 872)

2. What were the sources of postwar recovery and stability in western Europe? (p. 881)

3. What was the pattern of postwar development in the Soviet bloc? (p. 884)

4. How did decolonization proceed in the Cold War era? (p. 889)

5. What were the key changes in social relations in postwar Europe? (p. 895)

Suggested Resources

BOOKS

- Berstein, Serge. *The Republic of de Gaulle, 1958–1969.* 2006. An outstanding work on postwar France.

- Chin, Rita. *The Guest Worker Question in Postwar Germany.* 2007. An engaging interpretation of postwar migration patterns in West Germany.

- de Grazia, Victoria. *Irresistible Empire: America's Advance Through Twentieth-Century Europe.* 2005. A lively, provocative account of the Americanization of Europe from 1900 to the 1950s.

- de Senarclens, Pierre. *From Yalta to the Iron Curtain: The Great Powers and the Origins of the Cold War.* 1995. A valuable work on the Cold War.

- Hitchcock, William I. *The Struggle for Europe: The Turbulent History of a Divided Continent, 1945 to the Present.* 2004. A valuable general study with extensive bibliographies.

- Jähner, Harald. *Aftermath: Life in the Fallout of the Third Reich, 1945–1955.* 2021. Accessible account of West German efforts to rebuild and come to terms with the legacies of Nazism after World War II.

- Jansen, Jan C., and Jürgen Osterhammel. *Decolonization: A Short History.* 2017. A concise account that explores the collapse of European, American, and Japanese colonies and the long-term consequences of decolonization.

- Judt, Tony. *Postwar: A History of Europe Since 1945.* 2006. A masterful reconsideration, especially strong on smaller countries.

- Kertzer, David I., and Marzio Barbagli, eds. *Family Life in the Twentieth Century: The History of the European Family*, vol. 3. 2003. A distinguished collection of essays by experts.

- Lomax, Bill. *Hungary 1956.* 1976. A gripping and still important book on the failed Hungarian revolution that explores the actions of ordinary people as well as prominent leaders.

- Westad, Odd Arne. *The Global Cold War: Third World Interventions and the Making of Our Times.* 2007. An up-to-date study of the Cold War's global impact.

MEDIA

- *The Battle of Algiers* (Gillo Pontecorvo, 1966). A justly famous and fairly accurate feature film about the "Battle of the Casbah" during the Algerian War, shot in black-and-white documentary style.

- *BBC: History: Cold War.* A great resource for overviews on the Korean War, Cuban missile crisis, weapons of the Cold War, and the fall of the Soviet Union. **www.bbc.co.uk/history/worldwars/coldwar/**

- *The Bicycle Thief* (Vittorio De Sica, 1948). This classic example of Italian Neorealist cinema explores the tribulations of ordinary Italian workers dealing with the hardships of the immediate postwar period.

- *The Death of Stalin* (Armando Iannucci, 2017). This dark comedy examines the power struggle of high-level Soviet politicians, including future leader Nikita Khrushchev, as they scheme to take control after Stalin's death in 1953.

- *Dr. Strangelove or: How I Learned to Stop Worrying and Love the Bomb* (Stanley Kubrick, 1964). A feature film by an acclaimed director that satirizes the fear of a nuclear holocaust.

- *North Atlantic Treaty Organization.* NATO's homepage provides information about its origins and the nature of the organization today. **www.nato.int/cps/en/natolive/index.htm**

- *Nuremberg Trials.* Legal resources pertaining to the Nuremberg trials. **www.loc.gov/rr/frd/Military_Law/Nuremberg_trials.html**

- *Sputnik Mania* (David Hoffman, 2007). A documentary looking at the Soviet Union's launch of Sputnik and its worldwide effects.

- *Wilson Center: Cold War International History Project.* This website offers government documents from all sides of the Cold War. The project seeks to integrate materials and perspectives from the former East and West Blocs. **www.wilsoncenter.org/program/cold-war-international-history-project**

29

Challenging the Postwar Order

1960–1991

As Europe entered the 1960s, the political and social systems forged in the postwar era appeared sound. Centrist politicians in western Europe generally agreed that managed economic expansion, abundant jobs, and state-sponsored benefit programs would continue to improve living standards and promote social consensus. In the Soviet Union and the East Bloc, although conditions varied by country, modest economic growth and limited reforms amid continued political repression likewise contributed to a sense of stability. Cold War tensions diminished, and it seemed that a remarkable age of affluence would ease political differences and lead to social harmony.

By the mid-1960s, however, this hard-won sense of stability had begun to disappear as popular protest movements in East and West arose to challenge dominant certainties. In the early 1970s the astonishing postwar economic boom ground to a halt, with serious consequences. In western Europe, a new generation of conservative political leaders advanced transformative policies to deal with economic stagnation and global competition. Political groups across the political spectrum, from feminists and environmentalists to national separatists and right-wing populists, added to the atmosphere of crisis and conflict.

In the East Bloc, leaders vacillated between central economic control and liberalization and left in place tight controls on social and political freedom, leading to widespread frustration. In the 1970s popular dissident movements emerged in Poland and other satellite states, and efforts to reform the Communist system in the Soviet Union from the top down snowballed out of control. In 1989, as revolutions swept away Communist rule throughout the entire Soviet bloc, the Cold War reached a dramatic conclusion. ■

CHAPTER PREVIEW

- Why did the postwar consensus of the 1950s break down?

- What were the consequences of economic stagnation in the 1970s?

- What led to the decline of "developed socialism" in the East Bloc?

- What were the causes and consequences of the 1989 revolutions in the East Bloc?

Life in a Divided Europe
Watchtowers, armed guards, and minefields controlled the Communist eastern side of the Berlin Wall, a familiar symbol of Cold War division in Europe. In the liberal West, to the contrary, ordinary folk turned what was an easily accessible blank space into an ad hoc art gallery — whimsical graffiti art, like the examples pictured here, covered the western side of the wall. (Bernd Kammerer/picture-alliance/dpa/akg-images)

Why did the postwar consensus of the 1950s break down?

In the early 1960s politics and society in prosperous western Europe remained relatively stable. East Bloc governments, bolstered by modest economic growth and state-enforced political conformity, and committed to generous welfare benefits for their citizens, maintained control. As the 1960s progressed, politics in the West shifted noticeably to the left, and amid this more liberalized society, a youthful counterculture emerged to critique the status quo. In the East Bloc, Khrushchev's limited reforms also inspired rebellions. Thus activists around the world rose in protest against the perceived inequalities of both capitalism and communism, leading to dramatic events in 1968, exemplified in Paris and Prague.

Cold War Tensions Thaw

In western Europe, the first two decades of postwar reconstruction had been overseen for the most part by center-right Christian Democrats, who successfully built postwar stability around Cold War politics, free-market economics with limited state intervention, and welfare provisions. Beginning in the mid-1960s, buoyed by the rapidly expanding economy, much of western Europe moved politically to the left. Socialists entered the Italian government in 1963. In Britain, the Labour Party returned to power in 1964, after thirteen years in opposition. In West Germany, the

aging postwar chancellor Konrad Adenauer (1876–1967) retired in 1963, and in 1969 Willy Brandt (1913–1992) became the first Social Democratic West German chancellor; his party would govern Germany until 1982. There were important exceptions to this general trend. Though the tough-minded, independent French president Charles de Gaulle resigned in 1969, the centrist Gaullists remained in power in France until 1981. And in Spain, Portugal, and Greece, authoritarian regimes remained in power until the mid-1970s.

Despite these exceptions, the general leftward drift eased Cold War tensions. Western European leaders took major steps to normalize relations with the East Bloc. Willy Brandt took the lead. In December 1970 he flew to Poland for the signing of a historic treaty of reconciliation. In a dramatic moment, Brandt laid a wreath at the tomb of the Polish unknown soldier and another at the monument commemorating the armed uprising of Warsaw's Jewish ghetto against occupying Nazi armies. Standing before the ghetto memorial, a somber Brandt fell to his knees as if in prayer. "I wanted," Brandt said later, "to ask pardon in the name of our people for a million-fold crime which was committed in the misused name of the Germans."[1]

Brandt's gesture at the Warsaw Ghetto memorial and the treaty with Poland were part of his broader, conciliatory foreign policy termed **Ostpolitik**

A West German Leader Apologizes for the Holocaust In 1970 West German chancellor Willy Brandt knelt before the Jewish Heroes' Monument in Warsaw, Poland, to ask forgiveness for the German mass murder of European Jews and other groups during the Second World War. Brandt's action, captured in photo and film by the onlooking press, symbolized the chancellor's policy of Ostpolitik, the normalization of relations between the East and West Blocs. (bpk, Bildagentur/Hanns Hubmann/Art Resource, NY)

TIMELINE

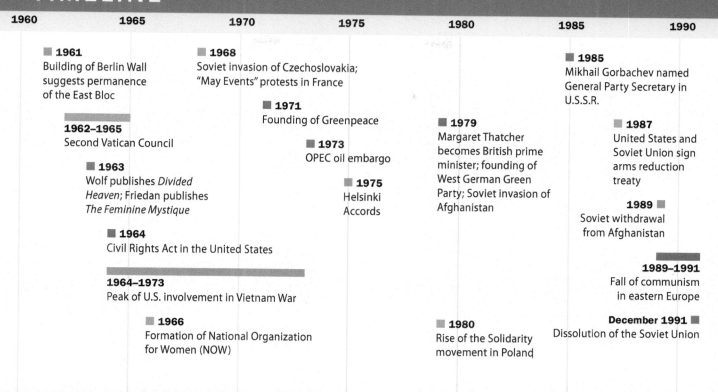

1960 — **1965** — **1970** — **1975** — **1980** — **1985** — **1990**

1961
Building of Berlin Wall suggests permanence of the East Bloc

1962–1965
Second Vatican Council

1963
Wolf publishes *Divided Heaven*; Friedan publishes *The Feminine Mystique*

1964
Civil Rights Act in the United States

1964–1973
Peak of U.S. involvement in Vietnam War

1966
Formation of National Organization for Women (NOW)

1968
Soviet invasion of Czechoslovakia; "May Events" protests in France

1971
Founding of Greenpeace

1973
OPEC oil embargo

1975
Helsinki Accords

1979
Margaret Thatcher becomes British prime minister; founding of West German Green Party; Soviet invasion of Afghanistan

1980
Rise of the Solidarity movement in Poland

1985
Mikhail Gorbachev named General Party Secretary in U.S.S.R.

1987
United States and Soviet Union sign arms reduction treaty

1989
Soviet withdrawal from Afghanistan

1989–1991
Fall of communism in eastern Europe

December 1991
Dissolution of the Soviet Union

(German for "Eastern policy"). Brandt sought a comprehensive peace settlement for central Europe and the two postwar German states. Rejecting West Germany's official hard line toward the East Bloc, the chancellor negotiated new treaties with the Soviet Union and Czechoslovakia, as well as Poland, that formally accepted existing state boundaries — rejected by West Germany's government since 1945 — in return for a mutual renunciation of force or the threat of force. Using the imaginative formula of "two German states within one German nation," he broke decisively with past policy and opened direct relations with East Germany.

Brandt's Ostpolitik was part of a general relaxation of East-West tensions, termed **détente** (day-TAHNT), that began in the early 1970s. Though Cold War hostilities continued in the developing world, diplomatic relations between the United States and the Soviet Union grew less strained. The superpowers agreed to limit the testing and proliferation of nuclear weapons and in 1975 mounted a joint U.S.-U.S.S.R. space mission.

The move toward détente reached a high point in 1975 when the United States, Canada, the Soviet Union, and all European nations (except isolationist Albania and tiny Andorra) met in Helsinki to sign the Final Act of the Conference on Security and Cooperation in Europe. Under what came to be called the Helsinki Accords, the thirty-five participating nations agreed that Europe's existing political frontiers could not be changed by force. They accepted provisions guaranteeing the civil rights and political freedoms of their citizens, which lowered Cold War tensions. Although Communist regimes continued to curtail domestic freedoms and violate human rights guarantees, the accords encouraged East Bloc dissidents, who could now demand that their governments respect international agreements on human rights. (See "Evaluating Written Evidence: Human Rights Under the Helsinki Accords," page 908.)

Newly empowered center-left leaders in western Europe also pushed through reforms at home. Building on the benefit programs established in the 1950s, they increased state spending on public services even further. Center-left politicians did not advocate "socialism" as practiced in the Soviet bloc, where strict economic planning, the nationalization of key economic sectors, and one-party dictatorships ensured state control. To the contrary, they maintained a firm commitment to capitalist free markets and democracy. At the same time, they viewed state-sponsored benefits as a way to ameliorate the inequalities of a competitive market economy. As a result, western European

---

■ **Ostpolitik** German for Chancellor Willy Brandt's new "Eastern policy"; West Germany's attempt in the 1970s to ease diplomatic tensions with East Germany, exemplifying the policies of détente.

■ **détente** The progressive relaxation of Cold War tensions that emerged in the early 1970s.

Human Rights Under the Helsinki Accords

At the conclusion of the two-year-long Conference on Security and Cooperation in Europe (1973–1975), the representatives of thirty-five West and East Bloc states solemnly pledged to "respect each other's sovereign equality" and to "refrain from any intervention, direct or indirect . . . in the internal or external affairs . . . of another participating state." East Bloc leaders, pleased that the West had at last officially accepted the frontiers and territorial integrity of the Communist satellite states established after World War II, agreed to recognize a lengthy list of "civil, political, economic, social, cultural and other rights and freedoms."

~

Principle VII on Human Rights and Freedoms, from the Final Act of the Conference on Security and Cooperation in Europe (August 1, 1975)

VII. Respect for human rights and fundamental freedoms, including the freedom of thought, conscience, religion or belief

The participating States will respect human rights and fundamental freedoms, including the freedom of thought, conscience, religion or belief, for all without distinction as to race, sex, language or religion.

They will promote and encourage the effective exercise of civil, political, economic, social, cultural and other rights and freedoms all of which derive from the inherent dignity of the human person and are essential for his free and full development.

Within this framework the participating States will recognize and respect the freedom of the individual to profess and practice, alone or in community with others, religion or belief acting in accordance with the dictates of his own conscience.

The participating States on whose territory national minorities exist will respect the right of persons belonging to such minorities to equality before the law, will afford them the full opportunity for the actual enjoyment of human rights and fundamental freedoms and will, in this manner, protect their legitimate interests in this sphere.

The participating States recognize the universal significance of human rights and fundamental freedoms, respect for which is an essential factor for the peace, justice and well-being necessary to ensure the development of friendly relations and co-operation among themselves as among all States.

They will constantly respect these rights and freedoms in their mutual relations and will endeavor jointly and separately, including in co-operation with the United Nations, to promote universal and effective respect for them.

They confirm the right of the individual to know and act upon his rights and duties in this field.

In the field of human rights and fundamental freedoms, the participating States will act in conformity with the purposes and principles of the Charter of the United Nations and with the Universal Declaration of Human Rights. They will also fulfill their obligations as set forth in the international declarations and agreements in this field, including *inter alia* the International Covenants on Human Rights, by which they may be bound.

EVALUATE THE EVIDENCE

1. How do the Helsinki Accords express the guiding principles of liberal democracy?
2. Why would Communist representatives publicly agree to recognize a list of rights that clearly challenged many of the repressive aspects of one-party rule in the East Bloc?

Source: "The Final Act of the Conference on Security and Cooperation in Europe, Aug. 1, 1975, 14 I.L.M. 1292 (Helsinki Declaration)," University of Minnesota Civil Rights Library, http://www1.umn.edu/humanrts/osce/basics/finact75.htm.

---

democracies spent more and more state funds on health care, education, old-age insurance, and public housing, all paid for with high taxes.

By the early 1970s state spending on such programs hovered around 40 percent of the gross domestic product in France, West Germany, and Great Britain, and even more in Scandinavia and the Netherlands. Center-right politicians generally supported increased spending on entitlements—as long as the economy prospered. The economic downturn in the mid-1970s, however, undermined support for the welfare state consensus.

The Affluent Society

While politics shifted to the left in the 1960s, western Europeans enjoyed a period of economic growth and high wages, which meant that an expanding middle class could increasingly enjoy the benefits of the consumer revolution that began in the 1950s. This so-called age of affluence had clear limits. The living standards of workers and immigrants did not rise as fast as those of the educated middle classes, and the expanding economy did not always reach underdeveloped regions, such as southern Italy. The 1960s nonetheless brought general prosperity to millions, and the consolidation of a full-blown consumer society had a profound impact on daily life.

Many people now had more money to spend on leisure time and recreational pursuits, which encouraged the growth of the tourist industry. With month-long paid vacations required by law in most western European countries and widespread automobile ownership, travel to beaches and ski resorts came within the reach of the middle class and much of the working class. By the late 1960s package tours with cheap group airfares and bargain hotel accommodations made even distant lands easily accessible.

Consumerism also changed life at home. Household appliances that were still luxuries in the 1950s were now commonplace. Televisions overtook radio as the most popular form of domestic entertainment, while vacuum cleaners, refrigerators, and washing machines transformed women's housework. Studies later showed that these new "laborsaving devices" caused women to spend even more time cleaning and cooking to new exacting standards, but at the time electric appliances were considered indispensable to what contemporaries called a "modern lifestyle." The establishment of U.S.-style self-service supermarkets across western Europe changed the way food was produced, purchased, and prepared and threatened to force independent bakers, butchers, and neighborhood grocers out of business. (See "Evaluating Visual Evidence: The Supermarket Revolution," page 910.)

Intellectuals and cultural critics greeted the age of affluence with a chorus of criticism. Some worried that rampant consumerism created a bland conformity that wiped out regional and national traditions. The great majority of ordinary people, they argued, now ate the same foods, wore the same clothes, and watched the same programs on television, sapping creativity and individualism. Others complained bitterly that these changes threatened to Americanize Europe. Neither group could do much to stop the spread of consumer culture.

Worries about the Americanization of Europe were overstated. European nations preserved distinctive national cultures even during the consumer revolution, but social change nonetheless occurred. The moral authority of religious doctrine lost ground before the growing materialism of consumer society. In predominantly Protestant lands — Great Britain, Scandinavia, and parts of West Germany — church membership and regular attendance both declined significantly. Even in traditionally Catholic countries, such as Italy, Ireland, and France, outward signs of popular belief seemed to falter. At the **Second Vatican Council**, convened from 1962 to 1965, Catholic leaders agreed on a number of reforms meant to democratize and renew the church and broaden its appeal. They called for new openness in Catholic theology

Mini-Skirts and Ruffled Shirts   The 1960s counterculture helped popularize the use of kaleidoscopic fluorescent colors and wild shapes in the fine arts, advertising, and fashion — such as the styles worn by these young men and women in "Swinging London," circa 1966. (Chronicle/Alamy Stock Photo)

and declared that masses would henceforth be held in local languages rather than in Latin, which few could understand. These resolutions, however, did little to halt the slide toward secularization.

Family ties also weakened in the age of affluence. The number of adults living alone reached new highs, men and women married later, the nuclear family became smaller and more mobile, and divorce rates rose rapidly. By the 1970s the baby boom of the postwar decades was over, and population growth leveled out across Europe and even began to decline in prosperous northwestern Europe.

The Counterculture Movement

The dramatic emergence of a youth counterculture accompanied growing economic prosperity. The "sixties generation" angrily criticized the comforts of the affluent society and challenged the social and political status quo.

Simple demographics played an important role in the emergence of the counterculture. Young soldiers returning home after World War II in 1945 eagerly established families, and the next two decades brought a dramatic increase in the number of births per year in Europe and North America. The children born during the postwar baby boom grew up in an era of relative political liberalism and unprecedented material abundance, yet many

■ **Second Vatican Council** A meeting of Catholic leaders convened from 1962 to 1965 that initiated a number of reforms, including the replacement of Latin with local languages in church services, designed to democratize the church and renew its appeal.

The Supermarket Revolution

For centuries most Europeans had bought food from local butchers, bakers, and produce dealers. In tiny neighborhood stores, a specialized shopkeeper greeted regular customers, shared gossip, took an order for items on display behind the counter, wrapped the goods, and calculated the price. Around 1960, the arrival in Europe of U.S.-style supermarkets transformed the shopping experience. As this advertisement for Sainsbury's suggests, consumers now entered a well-lit, much larger store and filled their baskets from open shelves stocked with pre-packaged, pre-priced goods. Frozen meat and canned vegetables meant that once-seasonal items were available year-round, while competing brands introduced many versions of the same product.

EVALUATE THE EVIDENCE

1. Although they never entirely displaced small grocers or dominated the food retail sector as in the United States, by the 1980s supermarkets were a normal part of everyday life across Europe. How did the supermarket as pictured here transform the way Europeans shopped for, ate, and thought about food?
2. How do the benefits of the self-service supermarket touted in the advertisement exemplify the consumer revolution that swept through Europe in the 1950s and 1960s?

(ADVERTISING ARCHIVES/Bridgeman Images)

came to challenge the growing conformity that seemed to be a part of consumer society and the unequal distribution of wealth that arose from market economics.

Counterculture movements in both Europe and the United States drew inspiration from the American civil rights movement. In the late 1950s and early 1960s African Americans effectively challenged institutionalized inequality, using the courts, public demonstrations, sit-ins, and boycotts to throw off a deeply entrenched system of segregation and repression. If dedicated African Americans and their white supporters could successfully reform entrenched power structures, student leaders reasoned, so could they. In 1964 and 1965, at the University of California, Berkeley, students consciously adapted the tactics of the civil rights movement, including demonstrations and sit-ins, to challenge limits on free speech and academic freedom at the university. Soon students across the United States and western Europe, where rigid rules controlled student activities at overcrowded universities, were engaged in active protests. The youth movement had come of age, and it mounted a determined challenge to the Western consensus.

Eager for economic justice and more tolerant societies, student activists in western Europe and the United States embraced new forms of Marxism, creating a multidimensional movement that came to be known as the **New Left**. In general, adherents of the various strands of the New Left believed that Marxism in the Soviet Union had been perverted to serve the needs of a repressive totalitarian state but that Western capitalism, with its cold disregard for social equality, was little better. What was needed was a more humanitarian style of socialism that could avoid the worst excesses of both capitalism and Soviet-style communism. New Left critics further attacked what they saw as the conformity of consumer society.

New Left ideas inspired student intellectuals, but much counterculture activity revolved around a lifestyle rebellion that had broad appeal, a process captured in the popular 1960s slogan "the personal is political." Nowhere was this more obvious than in the so-called sexual revolution. The 1960s brought frank discussion about sexuality, a new willingness to engage in premarital sex, and a growing acceptance of homosexuality. Sexual experimentation was facilitated by the development of the birth control pill, which helped eliminate the risk of unwanted pregnancy for millions of women after it went on the market in most Western countries in the 1960s. Much of the new openness about sex crossed generational lines, but for the young the idea of sexual emancipation was closely linked to radical politics. Sexual openness and "free love," the sixties generation claimed, moved people beyond traditional norms and towards a more humane society.

The revolutionary aspects of the sexual revolution are easily exaggerated. According to a poll of West German college students taken in 1968, for example, the overwhelming majority wished to establish permanent families on traditional middle-class models. Yet the sexual behavior of young people did change in the 1960s and 1970s. More young people engaged in premarital sex, and they did so at an earlier age than ever before. A 1973 study reported that only 4.5 percent of West German youths born in 1945 and 1946 had sexual relations before their seventeenth birthday, but that 32 percent of those born in 1953 and 1954 had done so.[2] Such trends were found in other Western countries and continued in the following decades.

Along with sexual freedom, drug use and rock music encouraged lifestyle rebellion. Taking drugs challenged conventional morals; in the infamous words of the U.S. cult figure Timothy Leary, users could "turn on, tune in, and drop out." The popular music of the 1960s championed alternative lifestyles. Rock bands like the Beatles, the Rolling Stones, and many others sang songs about drugs and casual sex. Counterculture "scenes" developed in cities such as San Francisco, Paris, and West Berlin. Carnaby Street, the center of "swinging London" in the 1960s, was world famous for its clothing boutiques and record stores, underscoring the connections between generational revolt and consumer culture.

The United States and Vietnam

The growth of the counterculture movement was closely linked to the escalation of the Vietnam War. Although many student radicals at the time argued that imperialism was the main cause, U.S. involvement in Vietnam was more clearly a product of the Cold War policy of containment. After Vietnam won independence from France in 1954, president Dwight D. Eisenhower

(U.S. pres. 1953–1961) refused to sign the Geneva Accords that temporarily divided the country into a Communist north and an anticommunist south. When the South Vietnamese government declined to hold free elections that would unify the two zones, Eisenhower provided the south with military aid to combat guerrilla insurgents in South Vietnam who were supported by the Communist north.

John F. Kennedy (U.S. pres. 1961–1963) increased the number of U.S. "military advisers" to 16,000, and in 1964 President Lyndon B. Johnson (U.S. pres. 1963–1969) greatly expanded the U.S. role in the conflict, providing South Vietnam with massive military aid and eventually some 500,000 American troops. Although the United States bombed North Vietnam with ever-greater intensity, it never invaded the north with troops on the ground.

In the end, U.S. intervention backfired. The undeclared war in Vietnam, fought nightly on television, eventually divided the nation. Initial support was strong. The politicians, the media, and the population as a whole saw the war as part of a legitimate defense against the spread of communism. But an antiwar movement that believed that the United States was fighting an immoral and imperialistic war against a small country and a heroic people quickly emerged on college campuses. In October 1965 student protesters joined forces with old-line socialists, New Left intellectuals, and pacifists in antiwar demonstrations in fifty U.S. cities. The protests spread to western Europe. By 1967 a growing number of U.S. and European critics denounced the U.S. presence in Vietnam as a criminal intrusion into another people's civil war.

Criticism reached a crescendo after the Vietcong staged the Tet Offensive in January 1968, the Communists' first comprehensive attack on major South Vietnamese cities. The Vietcong, an army of Communist insurgents and guerrilla fighters located in South Vietnam, suffered heavy losses, but the Tet Offensive signaled that the war was not close to ending, as Washington had claimed. Widespread public disapproval pressured President Johnson to end the war. Within months of Tet, Johnson announced that he would not stand for re-election and called for negotiations with North Vietnam.

Richard M. Nixon (U.S. pres. 1969–1974) sought to gradually disengage from Vietnam once he took office. Nixon intensified the bombing campaign against the north, opened peace talks, and pursued a policy of "Vietnamization" designed to give the South Vietnamese responsibility for the war and reduce the U.S. presence. He suspended the draft and cut U.S. forces in Vietnam from 550,000 to 24,000 in four years. In 1973 Nixon finally reached

■ **New Left** A 1960s counterculture movement that embraced updated forms of Marxism to challenge both Western capitalism and Soviet-style communism.

The "May Events" in Paris, 1968 Rebellious students built this barricade of overturned cars to hinder police action on a major thoroughfare in Paris during the 1968 riots. Graffiti on the wall on the left reads "Up the Revolution." Other slogans sprayed on the city's walls during the revolt and the general strike that followed included "Underneath the Paving Stones, the Beach" and "Be Realistic, Demand the Impossible." (Bettmann/Getty Images)

a peace agreement with North Vietnam that allowed the remaining U.S. forces to complete their withdrawal and gave the United States the right to resume bombing if the accords were broken. Fighting declined markedly in South Vietnam, where the South Vietnamese army appeared to hold its own against the Vietcong.

Although the storm of criticism in the United States slackened with the peace settlement, U.S. disillusionment with the war had far-reaching repercussions. In late 1974, when North Vietnam launched a successful invasion against South Vietnamese armies, the U.S. Congress refused to permit any American military response. In April 1975 the last U.S. troops were evacuated from Saigon, the South Vietnamese capital, and in July 1976 North and South Vietnam were unified under a Communist regime, ending a conflict that had begun with the anticolonial struggle against the French at the end of World War II.

Student Revolts and 1968

While the Vietnam War raged, U.S. escalation engendered worldwide opposition, and the counterculture became increasingly radical. In western European and North American cities, students and sympathetic followers organized massive antiwar demonstrations and then extended their protests support colonial independence movements, demand an end to the nuclear arms race, and call for world peace and liberation from social conventions of all kinds.

Political activism erupted in 1968 in a series of protests and riots that circled the globe. African Americans rioted across the United States after the assassination of civil rights leader Martin Luther King, Jr., and antiwar demonstrators battled police at the Democratic National Convention in Chicago. Young protesters marched for political reform in Mexico City, where

police responded by shooting and killing several hundred. Students in Tokyo rioted against the war and for university reforms. Protesters clashed with police in the West and East Blocs as well. Berlin and London witnessed massive, sometimes violent demonstrations, students in Warsaw protested government censorship, and youths in Prague were in the forefront of the attempt to radically reform communism from within.

One of the most famous and perhaps most far-reaching of these revolts occurred in France in May 1968, when massive student protests coincided with a general strike that brought the French economy to a standstill. The "May Events" began when a group of students dismayed by conservative university policies and inspired by New Left ideals occupied buildings at the University of Paris. Violent clashes with police followed. When police tried to clear the area around the university on the night of May 10, a pitched street battle took place. At the end of the night, 460 arrests had been made by police, 367 people were wounded, and about 200 cars had been burned by protesters.

The May Events might have been a typically short-lived student protest against overcrowded universities, U.S. involvement in Vietnam, and the abuses of capitalism, but the demonstrations triggered a national revolt. By May 18 some 10 million workers were out on strike, and protesters occupied factories across France. For a brief moment, it seemed as if counterculture hopes for a revolution from below would come to pass. The French Fifth Republic was on the verge of collapse, and a shaken President de Gaulle surrounded Paris with troops.

In the end, however, the New Left goals of the radical students contradicted the bread-and-butter demands of the striking workers. When the government promised workplace reforms, including immediate pay raises, the strikers returned to work. President de Gaulle dissolved the French parliament and called for new elections. His conservative party won almost 75 percent of the seats, showing that the majority of the French people supported neither general strikes nor student-led revolutions. The universities shut down for the summer, administrators enacted educational reforms, and the protests had dissipated by the time the fall semester began. The May Events marked the high point of counterculture activism in Europe; in the early 1970s the movement declined.

As the political enthusiasm of the counterculture waned, committed activists disagreed about the best way to continue to fight for social change. Some followed what West German student leader Rudi Dutschke called "the long march through the institutions" and began to work for change from within the system. They ran for office and joined the emerging feminist, antinuclear, and environmental groups that would gain increasing prominence in the following decades.

Others followed a more radical path. Across Europe, but particularly in Italy and West Germany, fringe New Left groups tried to bring radical change by turning to violence and terrorism. Like the American Weather Underground, the Italian Red Brigades and the West German Red Army Faction robbed banks, bombed public buildings, and kidnapped and killed business leaders and conservative politicians. After spasms of violence in the late 1970s — in Italy, for example, the Red Brigades murdered former prime minister Aldo Moro in 1978 — security forces succeeded in incarcerating most of the terrorist leaders, and the movement fizzled out.

Counterculture protests generated a great deal of excitement, helped end the Vietnam War, and trained a generation of activists. In general, however, the protests of the sixties generation resulted in short-term and mostly limited political change. Lifestyle rebellions involving sex, drugs, and rock music certainly expanded the boundaries of acceptable personal behavior, but they hardly overturned the existing system.

The 1960s in the East Bloc

The building of the Berlin Wall in 1961 suggested that communism was there to stay, and NATO's refusal to intervene showed that the United States and western Europe basically accepted this premise. In the West, the wall became a symbol of the repressive nature of communism in the East Bloc, where halting experiments with economic and cultural liberalization brought only limited reform.

East Bloc economies clearly lagged behind those of the West, exposing the weaknesses of central planning. To address these problems, in the 1960s Communist governments implemented cautious forms of decentralization and limited market policies. The results were mixed. East Germany's New Economic System, inaugurated in 1963, brought moderate success, though it was reversed when the government returned to centralization in the late 1960s. Hungary's so-called New Economic Mechanism, which broke up state monopolies, allowed some private retail stores, and encouraged private agriculture, was perhaps most successful. In other East Bloc countries, however, economic growth flagged; in Poland the economy stagnated in the 1960s.

Recognizing that ordinary people in the East Bloc were growing tired of the shortages of basic consumer goods caused by the emphasis on heavy industry, Communist planning commissions began to redirect resources to the consumer sector. Again, the results varied. By 1970, for example, ownership of televisions in the more developed nations of East Germany, Czechoslovakia, and Hungary approached that of the

The East German Trabant
This small East German passenger car, pictured here in a 1980s advertisement, was one of the best-known symbols of everyday life in East Germany. Produced between 1963 and 1990, the cars were notorious for their poor engineering. The growing number of "Trabis" on East German streets nonetheless testified to the increased availability of consumer goods in the East Bloc in the 1960s and 1970s.

(akg-images/Newscom)

affluent nations of western Europe, and other consumer goods were also more available. In the more conservative Albania and Romania, where leaders held fast to Stalinist practices, provision of consumer goods faltered.

In the 1960s Communist regimes cautiously granted cultural freedoms. In the Soviet Union, the cultural thaw allowed dissidents like Aleksandr Solzhenitsyn to publish critical works of fiction, and this relative tolerance spread to other East Bloc countries as well. In East Germany, for example, during the Bitterfeld Movement—named after a conference of writers, officials, and workers held at Bitterfeld, an industrial city south of Berlin—the regime encouraged intellectuals to take a more critical view of life in the East Bloc, as long as they did not directly oppose communism. Christa Wolf's novel *Divided Heaven* (1963), which explores workplace problems in a typical East German factory, exemplified the literature of the Bitterfeld Movement and the larger shift to cultural reform.

Cultural openness only went so far, however. The most outspoken dissidents were harassed and often forced to emigrate to the West; others went underground, creating books, periodicals, newspapers, and pamphlets that were printed secretly and passed hand to hand by dissident readers. This

The Invasion of Czechoslovakia   Armed with Czechoslovakian flags and Molotov cocktails, courageous Czechs in downtown Prague in August 1968 try to stop a Soviet tank and repel the invasion and occupation of their country by the Soviet Union and its Warsaw Pact allies. Realizing that military resistance would be suicidal, the Czechs capitulated to Soviet control. (Libor Hajsky/CTK/AP Photo)

samizdat ("self-published") literature emerged in Russia, Poland, and other countries in the mid-1960s and blossomed in the 1970s. These unofficial networks of communication kept critical thought alive and built contacts among dissidents, creating the foundation for the reform movements of the 1970s and 1980s.

The citizens of East Bloc countries sought political liberty as well, and the limits on reform were sharply revealed in Czechoslovakia during the 1968 "Prague Spring" (named for the country's capital city). In January 1968 reform elements in the Czechoslovak Communist Party gained a majority and voted out the long-time Stalinist leader in favor of Alexander Dubček (1921–1992), whose new government launched dramatic reforms. Educated in Moscow, Dubček (DOOB-chehk) was a dedicated Communist, but he and his allies believed that they could reconcile genuine socialism with personal freedom and political democracy. They called for relaxed state censorship and replaced rigid bureaucratic planning with local decision making by trade unions, workers' councils, and consumers. The reform program—labeled "Socialism with a Human Face"—proved enormously popular.

Remembering that the Hungarian revolution had revealed the difficulty of reforming communism from within, Dubček constantly proclaimed his loyalty to the Soviet Union and the Warsaw Pact. But his reforms nevertheless threatened hard-line Communists, particularly in Poland and East Germany, where leaders knew full well that they lacked popular support. Moreover, Soviet authorities feared that a liberalized Czechoslovakia would eventually be drawn to neutrality or even to NATO. Thus the East Bloc leadership launched a concerted campaign of intimidation against the reformers. Finally, in August 1968, five hundred thousand Soviet and East Bloc troops occupied Czechoslovakia. The Czechoslovaks made no attempt to resist militarily, and the arrested leaders surrendered to Soviet demands. The Czechoslovak experiment in humanizing communism from within came to an end.

Shortly after the invasion of Czechoslovakia, Soviet leader Leonid Brezhnev (1906–1982) announced that the U.S.S.R. would now follow the so-called **Brezhnev Doctrine**, under which the Soviet Union and its allies had the right to intervene militarily in any East Bloc country whenever they thought doing so was necessary to preserve Communist rule and the interests of the U.S.S.R. The 1968 invasion of Czechoslovakia was the crucial event of the Brezhnev era: it demonstrated the determination of the Communist elite to maintain the status quo throughout the Soviet bloc, which would last for another twenty years. At the same time, the Soviet crackdown encouraged dissidents to change their focus from reforming Communist regimes from above to building a grassroots civil society that might bring internal freedoms independent of Communist repression.

What were the consequences of economic stagnation in the 1970s?

The great postwar economic boom came to a close in the early 1970s, opening a long period of economic stagnation, widespread unemployment, and social dislocation. By the end of the 1980s the postwar consensus based on prosperity, modest government regulation, and generous welfare provisions had been deeply shaken. Led by a new generation of conservative politicians, the West restructured its economy and entered the information age.

Economic Crisis and Hardship

Starting in the early 1970s the West entered into a long period of economic decline. One of the early causes of the downturn was the collapse of the international monetary system, which since 1945 had been based on the American dollar, valued in gold at $35 an ounce. In the postwar decades the United States spent billions of dollars on foreign aid and foreign wars, weakening the value of American currency. In 1971 President Nixon attempted to reverse this trend by abruptly stopping the exchange of U.S. currency for gold. The value of the dollar fell sharply, and inflation accelerated worldwide. Countries abandoned fixed rates of currency exchange, and great uncertainty replaced postwar predictability in international trade and finance.

Even more damaging to the global economy was the dramatic increase in the price of energy and a decrease in its availability. The great postwar boom had been fueled in large part by cheap and plentiful oil from the Middle East, and the main energy supplies of the developed world were thus increasingly linked to this turbulent region. In 1967, in the Six-Day War, Israel defeated Egypt, Jordan, and Syria and occupied more of the former territories of Palestine, angering Arab leaders and exacerbating anti-Western feeling in the Arab states. Tension between Arab states and the West was also fueled by economics. Over the years **OPEC**, the Organization of Petroleum Exporting Countries, had watched the price of crude oil decline compared with the rising price of Western manufactured goods. OPEC decided to reverse that trend by presenting a united front against Western oil companies.

The stage was thus already set for a revolution in energy prices when Egypt and Syria launched a surprise attack on Israel in October 1973, setting off the fourth Arab-Israeli war. With the help of U.S. weapons, Israel again achieved a quick victory. In response, the Arab members of OPEC declared an embargo on oil shipments to the United States and other industrialized nations that supported Israel in the war, and

they simultaneously raised oil prices. Within a year, the cost of crude oil quadrupled. Western nations realized that the rapid price increase was economically destructive, but together they did nothing. Thus governments, industry, and individuals dealt piecemeal with the so-called oil shock—a "shock" that turned out to be an earthquake.

Coming on the heels of the upheaval in the international monetary system, the revolution in energy prices plunged the world into its worst economic crisis since the 1930s. Energy-intensive industries that had driven the economy up in the 1950s and 1960s now dragged it down. Unemployment rose, productivity and living standards declined, and inflation soared. Economists coined a new term — **stagflation** — to describe the combination of low growth and high inflation that drove the worldwide recession. By 1976 a modest recovery was in progress, but in 1979 a fundamentalist Islamic revolution overthrew the shah of Iran. When oil production in that country collapsed, the price of crude oil doubled again, and the world economy succumbed to another oil shock. Unemployment and inflation rose dramatically before another uneven recovery began in 1982.

Anxious observers, recalling the disastrous consequences of the Great Depression, worried that the European Common Market would disintegrate in the face of severe economic dislocation and that economic nationalism would halt steps toward European unity. Yet the Common Market continued to attract new members. In 1973 Britain finally joined, as did Denmark and Ireland. After replacing authoritarian regimes with democratic governments in the 1970s, Greece joined in 1981, and Portugal and Spain entered in 1986. The nations of the Common Market cooperated more closely in international undertakings, and the movement toward western European unity stayed alive.

The developing world was hit hard by slow growth, and the global economic downturn widened the gap between rich and poor countries. Governments across South America, sub-Saharan Africa, and South Asia borrowed heavily from the United States and western Europe in attempts to restructure their economies, setting the stage for a serious

---

■ **Brezhnev Doctrine** Doctrine created by Leonid Brezhnev that held that the Soviet Union had the right to intervene in any East Bloc country when necessary to preserve Communist rule.

■ **OPEC** The Organization of Petroleum Exporting Countries.

■ **stagflation** Term coined in the early 1980s to describe the combination of low growth and high inflation that led to a worldwide recession.

international debt crisis. At the same time, the East Asian countries of Japan and then Singapore, South Korea, and Taiwan started exporting high-tech consumer goods to the West. Competition from these East Asian "tiger economies," whose labor costs were comparatively low, shifted manufacturing jobs away from the highly industrialized countries of northern Europe and North America. Even though the world economy slowly began to recover in the 1980s, western Europe could no longer create enough jobs to replace those that were lost.

By the end of the 1970s, the foundations of economic growth in the industrialized West had begun shifting to high-tech information industries, such as computing and biotechnology, and to services, including medicine, banking, and finance. Scholars spoke of the shift as the arrival of "the information age" or **postindustrial society**. Technological advances streamlined the production of many goods, making many industrial jobs superfluous. In western Europe, heavy industry, such as steel, mining, automobile manufacture, and shipbuilding, lost ground. Factory closings led to the emergence of "rust belts"—formerly prosperous industrialized areas that were now ghost lands, with vacant lots, idle machinery, and empty inner cities. The highly industrialized Ruhr district in northwest West Germany and the once-extensive factory regions around Birmingham (Great Britain) and Detroit, Michigan, were classic examples. By 1985 the unemployment rate in western Europe had risen to its highest level since the Great Depression. Nineteen million people were jobless.

The crisis struck countless ordinary people, upending lives and causing real hardship. The punk rock songs of the late 1970s captured the mood of hostility and cynicism among young people. Yet on the whole, the welfare system fashioned in the postwar era prevented mass suffering and degradation. The responsive, socially concerned national state undoubtedly contributed to the preservation of political stability and democracy in the face of economic difficulties that might have brought revolution and dictatorship in earlier times.

■ **postindustrial society** A society that relies on high-tech and service-oriented jobs for economic growth rather than heavy industry and manufacturing jobs.

■ **neoliberalism** Philosophy of 1980s conservatives who argued for privatization of state-run industries and decreased government spending on social services.

■ **privatization** The sale of state-managed industries such as transportation and communication networks to private owners; a key aspect of broader neoliberal economic reforms meant to control government spending, increase private profits, and foster economic growth, which were implemented in western Europe in response to the economic crisis of the 1970s.

With the commitment of governments to supporting social needs, government spending in most European countries continued to rise sharply during the 1970s and early 1980s. In 1982 western European governments spent an average of more than 50 percent of all national income on social programs, as compared to 37 percent fifteen years earlier. Across western Europe, people supported increased government spending, but they resisted higher taxes. This imbalance contributed to the rapid growth of budget deficits, national debts, and inflation. While increased spending was generally popular, a powerful reaction against government's ever-increasing role had set in by the late 1970s that would transform governance in the 1980s.

The New Conservatism

The transition to a postindustrial society was led to a great extent by a new generation of conservative political leaders who believed they could restore economic growth by restructuring the relations between the state and the economy. During the thirty years following World War II, both Social Democrats and the more conservative Christian Democrats had usually agreed that growth and social stability were best achieved through full employment and high wages, some government regulation, and generous social benefit programs. In the late 1970s, however, with a weakened economy and increased global competition, this consensus began to unravel. Whether politics turned to the right, as in Great Britain, the United States, and West Germany, or to the left, as in France and Spain, leaders moved to cut government spending and regulation in attempts to improve economic performance.

The new conservatives of the 1980s followed a philosophy that came to be known as **neoliberalism** because of its roots in the free market, laissez-faire policies favored by eighteenth-century liberal economists such as Adam Smith (see "Adam Smith and Economic Liberalism" in Chapter 17). Neoliberal theorists like U.S. economist Milton Friedman argued that governments should cut support for social services, including housing, education, and health insurance; limit business subsidies; and retreat from regulation of all kinds. (Neoliberalism should be distinguished from modern American liberalism, which generally supports social programs and some state regulation of the economy.) Neoliberals also called for **privatization**—the sale of state-managed industries to private owners. They argued that placing government-owned industries, including transportation and communication networks and heavy industry, in private hands would both reduce government spending and lead to greater workplace efficiency. A central goal was to increase private profits, which neoliberals believed were the real engine of economic growth.

The Social Consequences of Thatcherism
During the National Miners Strike of 1984, reports of open conflict between striking miners and police typified acts of popular protest. Prime Minister Margaret Thatcher broke the strike, weakening the power of Britain's trade unions and easing the turn to free-market economic reforms. Thatcher's neoliberal policies revived economic growth but cut state subsidies for welfare benefits and heavy industries, leading to lower living standards for many working-class Britons and, as this image attests, to popular protest. (Trevor Smith/Alamy Stock Photo)

The effects of neoliberal policies are best illustrated by events in Great Britain. The broad shift toward greater conservatism, coupled with growing voter dissatisfaction with high taxes and runaway state budgets, helped elect Margaret Thatcher (1925–2013) prime minister in 1979. A member of the Conservative Party and a convinced neoliberal, Thatcher was determined to scale back the role of government, and in the 1980s — the "Thatcher years" — she pushed through a series of controversial free-market policies that transformed Britain. Thatcher's government cut spending on health care, education, and public housing; reduced taxes; and privatized or sold off government-run enterprises. In one of her most popular actions, Thatcher encouraged low- and moderate-income renters in state-owned housing projects to buy their apartments at rock-bottom prices. This initiative, part of Thatcher's broader privatization campaign, created a new class of property owners, thereby eroding the electoral base of Britain's socialist Labour Party. (See "Individuals in Society: Margaret Thatcher," page 918.)

Though Thatcher never eliminated all social programs, her policies helped replace the interventionist ethos of the welfare state with a greater reliance on private enterprise and the free market. This transition involved significant human costs. In the first three years of her government, heavy industries such as steel, coal mining, and textiles shut down, and unemployment rates in Britain doubled to over 12 percent. The gap between rich and poor widened, and increasing poverty led to discontent and crime.

Strikes and working-class protests sometimes led to violent riots, and street violence often had racial overtones. Immigrants from former British colonies in

Africa, India, and the Caribbean, dismayed with poor jobs and racial discrimination, clashed repeatedly with police. Thatcher successfully rallied support by leading a British victory over Argentina in the brief Falklands War (1982), but over time her position weakened. By 1990 Thatcher's popularity had fallen to record lows, and she was replaced by Conservative Party leader John Major.

In the United States, two-term president Ronald Reagan (U.S. pres. 1981–1989) followed a similar path, though his success in cutting government was more limited. Reagan's campaign slogan — "government is not the solution to our problem, government is the problem" — summed up a movement in line with Thatcher's ideas, which was labeled the conservative movement in the United States. With widespread popular support and the agreement of most congressional Democrats as well as Republicans, Reagan pushed through major cuts in income taxes in 1981. But Reagan and Congress failed to limit government spending, which increased as a percentage of national income in the course of his presidency. A massive military buildup was partly responsible, but spending on social programs — despite Reagan's pledges to rein it in — also grew rapidly. The harsh recession of the early 1980s required the government to spend more on unemployment and welfare benefits and on medical treatment for the poor. Moreover, Reagan's antiwelfare rhetoric mobilized the liberal opposition and eventually turned many moderates against him. The budget deficit soared, and U.S. government debt tripled in a decade.

West Germany also turned to the right. After more than a decade in power, the Social Democrats foundered, and in 1982 Christian Democrat Helmut

INDIVIDUALS IN SOCIETY

Margaret Thatcher

Margaret Thatcher, the first woman elected to lead a major European state, was known as the "Iron Lady" for her uncompromising conservatism. She attacked socialism, promoted capitalism, and changed the face of modern Britain.

Raised in a lower-middle-class family in a small city in southeastern England, Thatcher entered Oxford in 1943 to study chemistry. She soon discovered a passion for politics and was elected president of student conservatives. Four years after her graduation, she ran for Parliament in 1950 in a solidly Labour district to gain experience. Articulate and attractive, she won the attention of Denis Thatcher, a wealthy businessman who drove her to campaign appearances in his Jaguar. Married a year later, the new Mrs. Thatcher abandoned chemistry, went to law school, gave birth to twins, and became a tax attorney. In 1959 she returned to politics and won a seat in that year's Conservative triumph.

For the next fifteen years Thatcher served in Parliament and held various ministerial posts when the Conservatives governed. In 1974, as the economy soured and the Conservatives lost two close elections, a rebellious Thatcher adroitly ran for the leadership of her party and won. Five years later, as the Labour government faced rampant inflation and crippling strikes, Thatcher promised to reduce union power, lower taxes, and promote free markets. Attracting swing votes from skilled workers, the Conservatives gained a majority, and she became prime minister.

A self-described "conviction politician," Thatcher rejected postwar Keynesian efforts to manage the economy, arguing that governments created inflation by printing too much money. Thus her government reduced the supply of money and credit and refused to retreat when interest rates and unemployment soared. Her popularity plummeted. But Thatcher remained in office, in part through an aggressive foreign policy. In 1982 the generals ruling Argentina suddenly seized the nearby Falkland Islands, home to 1,800 British citizens. A staunch nationalist, Thatcher detached a naval armada that recaptured the islands without a hitch. Britain admired Thatcher's determination and patriotism, and she was re-elected in 1983.

Margaret Thatcher as prime minister.
(Dave Caulkin/AP Photo)

Thatcher's second term was the high point of her influence. Her commitment to privatization transformed British industry. More than fifty state-owned companies, ranging from the state telephone monopoly to the nationalized steel trust, were sold to private investors. Small investors were offered shares at bargain prices to promote "people's capitalism." Thatcher also curbed the power of British labor unions, most spectacularly in 1984, when the once-mighty coal miners rejected more mine closings and doggedly struck for a year; the "Iron Lady" stood firm and beat them. This outcome had a profound psychological impact on the public, who blamed her for growing unemployment. Thatcher was also accused of mishandling a series of protest hunger strikes undertaken by the Irish Republican Army — in 1981 ten IRA members starved themselves to death in British prisons — but she refused to compromise with those she labeled criminals. As a result, the revolt in Northern Ireland entered one of its bloodiest phases.

Despite these problems, an increasingly stubborn and overconfident Thatcher was elected to a third term in 1987. Working with her ideological soul mate, U.S. president Ronald Reagan, she opposed greater political and economic unity within the European Community. This, coupled with rising inflation, stubborn unemployment, and an unpopular effort to assert financial control over city governments, proved her undoing. In 1990, as in 1974, party stalwarts suddenly revolted and elected a new Conservative leader. The transformational changes of the Thatcher years nonetheless endured, consolidated by her Conservative successor, John Major, and largely accepted by the next Labour prime minister, the moderate Tony Blair, who served in office from 1997 to 2007.

QUESTIONS FOR ANALYSIS

1. How did the policies promoted by Thatcher's government embody neoliberal ideas?
2. Would you say that Thatcher was a successful British leader? Why or why not?

Kohl (1930–2017) became the new chancellor. Like Thatcher, Kohl cut taxes and government spending. His policies led to increasing unemployment in heavy industry but also to solid economic growth. By the mid-1980s West Germany was one of the most prosperous countries in the world. In foreign policy, Kohl drew close to President Reagan. The chancellor agreed to deploy U.S. cruise missiles and nuclear-armed Pershing missiles on West German territory, a decision that contributed to renewed superpower tensions. In power for sixteen years, Kohl and the Christian Democrats governed during the opening of the Berlin Wall in 1989, the reunification of East and West Germany in 1990, and the end of the Cold War.

The most striking temporary exception to the general drift to the right in European politics was François Mitterrand (1916–1996) of France. After his election as president in 1981, Mitterrand and his Socialist Party led France on a lurch to the left. This marked a significant change in French politics, which had been dominated by center-right parties for some twenty-five years. Working at first in a coalition that included the French Communist Party, Mitterrand launched a vast program of nationalization and public investment designed to spend the country out of economic stagnation. By 1983 this attempt had clearly failed, and Mitterrand's Socialist government made a dramatic about-face. The Socialists were compelled to reprivatize industries they had just nationalized. They imposed a wide variety of austerity measures and maintained those policies for the rest of the decade.

Despite persistent economic crises and high social costs, by 1990 the developed nations of western Europe and North America were far more productive than they had been in the early 1970s. Western Europe was at the center of the emerging global economy, and its citizens were far richer than those in Soviet bloc countries. Even so, the collapse of the postwar consensus and the remaking of Europe in the transitional decades of the 1970s and 1980s helped generate new forms of protest and dissent across the political spectrum.

Challenges and Victories for Women

The 1970s marked the arrival of a diverse and widespread feminist movement devoted to securing genuine gender equality and promoting the general interests of women. Three basic reasons accounted for this dramatic development. First, ongoing changes in underlying patterns of motherhood and paid work created novel conditions and new demands. Second, a vanguard of feminist intellectuals articulated a

Feminist Protest in Amsterdam, ca. 1970   Members of the Dutch branch of the Women's Liberation Movement burn brassieres in front of a statue of Dutch feminist Wilhelmina Drucker. In the 1970s and 1980s, women's groups across western Europe and North America repeatedly organized public protests for women's rights, including an end to sexism, equal pay, and access to abortion. (Central Press/Getty Images)

powerful critique of gender relations that stimulated many women to rethink their assumptions and challenge the status quo. Third, taking a lesson from the civil rights movement in the United States and protests against the Vietnam War, dissatisfied women recognized that they had to organize if they were to influence politics and win fundamental reforms.

Feminists could draw on a long heritage of protest, stretching back to the French Revolution and the women's movements of the late nineteenth century. They were also inspired by recent writings, such as the foundational book *The Second Sex* (1949) by the French writer and philosopher Simone de Beauvoir (1908–1986). Beauvoir, who worked closely with the existentialist philosopher Jean-Paul Sartre, analyzed the position of women within the framework of existential thought. Drawing on history, philosophy, psychology, biology, and literature, Beauvoir argued that women had almost always been trapped by inflexible and limiting conditions. Only through courageous action and self-assertive creativity could a woman become a completely free person and escape the role of the inferior "other" that men had constructed for her gender.

The Second Sex inspired a generation of women intellectuals, and in the late 1960s and 1970s **second-wave feminism** spread through North America and Europe. The U.S. writer and organizer Betty Friedan's (1921–2006) pathbreaking study *The Feminine Mystique* (1963) pointed the way. Friedan called attention to the stifling aspects of women's domestic life, devoted to the service of husbands and children. Housewives lived in a "gilded cage," she concluded, because they were usually not allowed to hold professional jobs or become mature adults and genuine human beings. In 1966 Friedan helped found the National Organization for Women (NOW) to press for women's rights. NOW flourished, growing from seven hundred members in 1967 to forty thousand in 1974.

Many other women's organizations rose in Europe and North America. The diverse groups drew inspiration from Marx, Freud, or political liberalism, but in general feminists attacked patriarchy (the domination of society by men) and sexism (the inequalities faced by women simply because they were female). Throughout the 1970s publications, conferences, and institutions devoted to women's issues reinforced the emerging international movement. Advocates of women's rights pushed for new statutes governing the workplace: laws against discrimination, acts requiring equal pay for equal work, and measures such as maternal leave and affordable day care designed to help women combine careers and family responsibilities.

The movement also addressed women's rights beyond the workplace, including the right to divorce (in some Catholic countries), legalized abortion, the needs of single mothers, and protection from rape and physical violence. In almost every country, the effort to decriminalize abortion served as a catalyst in mobilizing an effective, self-conscious women's movement—and an opposition to it.

In countries that had long placed women in a subordinate position, the legal changes were little less than revolutionary. In Italy, for example, new laws abolished restrictions on divorce and abortion that had been strengthened by Mussolini and defended energetically by the Catholic Church in the postwar era. Yet while the women's movement of the 1970s won new rights for women, subsequently it became more diffuse, a victim of both its successes and the resurgence of an antifeminist opposition.

The Rise of the Environmental Movement

Like feminism, environmentalism had roots in the 1960s counterculture. Early environmentalists drew inspiration from writers like U.S. biologist Rachel Carson, whose book *Silent Spring*, published in 1962, was quickly translated into twelve European languages. Carson's chilling title referred to a future in which people in developed society would wake up one spring morning and hear no birds singing because they had all been killed by the rampant use of pesticides. The book had a striking impact on the growth of environmental movements in Europe and North America.

By the 1970s the destructive environmental costs of industrial development in western Europe and the East Bloc were everywhere apparent. The mighty Rhine River, which flows from Switzerland, past France, and through Germany and the Netherlands, was an industrial sewer. The forests of southwestern Germany were dying from acid rain, a result of smokestack emissions. The pristine coast of Brittany, in northwest France, was fouled by oil spills from massive tanker ships. Rapid industrialization in the East Bloc, undertaken with little regard for environmental impact, severely polluted waterways, contaminated farmlands and forests, and degraded air quality. Nuclear power plants across Europe were generating toxic waste that would last for centuries; serious accidents at nuclear plants—at Three Mile Island in Pennsylvania (1979) and at Chernobyl in Soviet Ukraine (1986)—revealed nuclear power's potential to create human and environmental disaster. These were just some examples of the environmental threats that inspired a growing environmental movement to challenge government and industry to clean up their acts.

Environmentalists had two main agendas. First, they worked to lessen the ill effects of unbridled industrial development on the natural environment. Second, they argued that local environmental problems often increased human poverty, inequality, and violence around the globe, and they sought ways to ameliorate the impact of environmental decline on human well-being. Environmental groups pursued their goals in various ways. Some used the mass media to reach potential supporters; some worked closely with politicians and public officials to change government policies. Others took a more confrontational stance. (See "Thinking Like a Historian: The New Environmentalism," page 922.)

In North America and western Europe, environmentalists also built new institutions. In 1971 Canadian activists established Greenpeace, a nongovernmental organization dedicated to environmental conservation and protection. Greenpeace quickly

---

■ **second-wave feminism**   Label given to the revitalized feminist movement that emerged in the United States and western Europe in the late 1960s and 1970s.

grew into an international organization, with strong support in Europe and the United States. In West Germany the environmentalist Green Party, founded in 1979, met with astounding success when it elected members to parliament in 1983, the first time in sixty years that a new political party had been seated in Germany. Its success was a model for like-minded activists in Europe and North America, and Green Party members were later elected to parliaments in Belgium, Italy, and Sweden. In the East Bloc, government planners increasingly recognized and tried to ameliorate environmental problems in the 1980s, but official censorship meant that groups like the Greens would not emerge there until after the end of Communist rule.

Separatism and Right-Wing Extremism

The 1970s also saw the rise of determined separatist movements across Europe. In Ireland, Spain, Belgium, and Switzerland — and in Yugoslavia and Czechoslovakia in the East Bloc — regional ethnic groups struggled for special rights, political autonomy, and even national independence. This separatism was most violent in Spain and Northern Ireland, where well-established insurgent groups used terrorist attacks to win government concessions. In the ethnic Basque region of northern Spain, the ETA (short, in the Basque language, for Basque Homeland and Freedom) tried to use bombings and assassinations to force the government to grant independence. After the death in 1975 of Fascist dictator Francisco Franco, who had ruled Spain for almost forty years, a new constitution granted the Basque region special autonomy, but it was not enough. The ETA stepped up its terrorist campaigns, killing over four hundred people in the 1980s.

The Provisional Irish Republican Army (IRA), a paramilitary organization in Northern Ireland, used similar tactics. Though Ireland had won autonomy in 1922, Great Britain retained control of six primarily Protestant counties in the north of the island. In the late 1960s violence re-emerged as the IRA, hoping to unite these counties with Ireland, attacked British security forces, which it saw as an occupying army. On "Bloody Sunday" in January 1972, British soldiers shot and killed thirteen demonstrators who had been protesting anti-Catholic discrimination in the town of

Violence in Northern Ireland   A silent crowd fills the streets of Derry to join the funeral procession of the thirteen young men killed on "Bloody Sunday," when British soldiers shot into a crowd during a peaceful protest against British military activities in Northern Ireland. Although British army representatives claimed the soldiers had fired in response to gun and nail bomb attacks, a 2010 investigation concluded that the demonstrators were unarmed. In a subsequent statement, Prime Minister David Cameron explained that "what happened on Bloody Sunday was both unjustified and unjustifiable" and apologized on behalf of the British government. (PA Images/Getty Images)

Derry, and the violence escalated. For the next thirty years the IRA attacked soldiers and civilians in Northern Ireland and in Britain itself. Over three thousand British soldiers, civilians, and IRA members were killed during the "Time of Troubles" before negotiations between the IRA and the British government opened in the late 1990s; a settlement was finally reached in 1998.

In the 1970s and 1980s mainstream European politicians also faced challenges from newly assertive political forces on the far right, including the National Front in France, the Northern League in Italy, the Austrian Freedom Party, and the National Democratic Party in West Germany. Populist leaders such as Jean-Marie Le Pen, the founder of the French National Front, opposed European integration and called for an embrace of nationalism, often at the expense of the non-European immigrants who were a growing proportion of western Europe's working-class population. New right-wing politicians promoted themselves as the champions of ordinary white workers, complaining that immigrants swelled welfare rolls and stole jobs from native-born Europeans. Though their programs at times veered close to open racism, in the 1980s they began to win seats in national parliaments.

The New Environmentalism

The environmentalism of the late 1960s and 1970s readily drew on earlier nineteenth-century concerns about the effects of an emerging industrial-urban society on human health and the natural landscape. Yet as the negative impact of industrial development became ever more apparent, arguments that stewardship of the environment should be a fundamental concern of humankind grew increasingly angry — and more widespread. How did a new generation of activists respond to the environmental degradation of the late twentieth century?

1 **Rachel Carson, *Silent Spring*, 1962.** Rachel Carson's highly readable polemic specifically targeted the U.S. pesticide industry, though the pathbreaking marine biologist and conservationist made larger claims about the great chains of being that enmeshed humans in their natural environment.

For each of us, as for the robin in Michigan or the salmon in the Miramichi, this is a problem of ecology, of interrelationships, of interdependence. We poison the caddis flies in a stream and the salmon runs dwindle and die. We poison the gnats in a lake and the poison travels from link to link of the food chain and soon the birds of the lake margins become its victims. We spray our elms and the following springs are silent of robin song, not because we sprayed the robins directly but because the poison traveled, step by step, through the now familiar elm leaf–earthworm–robin cycle. These are matters of record, observable, part of the visible world around us. They reflect the web of life — or death — that scientists know as ecology. . . .

We stand now where two roads diverge. But unlike the roads in Robert Frost's familiar poem, they are not equally fair. The road we have long been traveling is deceptively easy, a smooth superhighway on which we progress with great speed, but at its end lies disaster. The other fork of the road — the one less traveled by — offers our last, our only chance to reach a destination that assures the preservation of the earth.

The choice is, after all, ours to make.

2 **Arne Naess, "The Deep Ecology Platform," 1984.** Norwegian philosopher Arne Naess was a founder of the Deep Ecology wilderness movement. His vision of "biospheric egalitarianism" rejected notions that humans stood above or outside of nature and called on activists to take a radical stand in defense of the natural world.

1. The well-being and flourishing of human and nonhuman life on Earth have value in themselves (synonyms: inherent worth, intrinsic value, inherent value). These values are independent of the usefulness of the nonhuman world for human purposes.

2. Richness and diversity of life forms contribute to the realization of these values and are also values in themselves.

3. Humans have no right to reduce this richness and diversity except to satisfy vital needs.

4. Present human interference with the nonhuman world is excessive, and the situation is rapidly worsening.

5. The flourishing of human life and cultures is compatible with a substantial decrease of the human population. The flourishing of nonhuman life requires such a decrease.

6. Policies must therefore be changed. The changes in policies affect basic economic, technological, and ideological structures. The resulting state of affairs will be deeply different from the present.

7. The ideological change is mainly that of appreciating life quality (dwelling in situations of inherent worth) rather than adhering to an increasingly higher standard of living. There will be a profound awareness of the difference between big and great.

8. Those who subscribe to the foregoing points have an obligation directly or indirectly to participate in the attempt to implement the necessary changes.

ANALYZING THE EVIDENCE

1. Compare and contrast the arguments made in Sources 1, 2, and 3. What do they share? What are the most significant differences?
2. In Sources 4 and 5, how do environmental activists use visual presentation and symbolism to assert their political beliefs? In Source 5, how do the more traditionally dressed members of the parliament react to the Green Party members in their midst?
3. Do the arguments in these sources express continuities with the ideas of the 1960s counterculture, or was the environmentalism of the 1970s and 1980s something new?

3 **Rudolf Bahro, "Some Preconditions for Resolving the Ecology Crisis," 1979.** Rudolf Bahro, a founding member of the West German Green Party who compared the earth's environment to the doomed ocean liner *Titanic*, called for radical intervention in the structures of corporate capitalism to prevent the looming disaster.

～ The ecology crisis is insoluble unless we work at the same time at overcoming the confrontation of military blocs. It is insoluble without a resolute policy of détente and disarmament, one that renounces all demands for subverting other countries. . . .

The ecology crisis is insoluble without a world order on the North-South axis. And we must realize that our entire standard of living [in the North] is largely based on the exploitation and suppression of the rest of humanity. . . .

The ecology crisis is insoluble without a decisive breakthrough towards social justice in our own country and without a swift equalization of social differences throughout Western Europe. . . . The ecology crisis is insoluble without progress in human emancipation here and now, even while capitalism still exists. It is insoluble without countless individuals managing to rise above their immediate and compensatory interests. . . .

If all this is brought to a common denominator, the conclusion is as follows: The ecology crisis is insoluble under capitalism. We have to get rid of the capitalist manner of regulating the economy and above all of the capitalist driving mechanism, for a start at least bringing it under control. In other words, there is no solution to the ecology crisis without the combination of all anticapitalist and socialist tendencies for a peaceful democratic revolution against the dominant economic structure.

(Keystone/Getty Images)

4 **"Please Save Me from Lead Pollution," 1978.** A nine-year-old schoolgirl stands in front of the British prime minister's residence to protest the proposed extension of the M25 highway through her local playing fields, warning that children will be hurt by lead poisoning if the project goes through.

(Peter Strack/bpk Bildagentur/Art Resource, NY)

5 **Green Party representatives enter the West German parliament, 1983.** Members of the West German "Greens" won enough votes to send several representatives to the Bundestag (parliament) for the first time in 1983, a significant victory for the environmental movements that emerged in the 1970s.

PUTTING IT ALL TOGETHER

The environmental activists of the 1970s and 1980s were a diverse group with diverse opinions about the ways to address environmental issues. Using the sources above, along with what you have learned in class and in Chapters 28 and 29, write a short essay that explores the impact of environmentalism on political debate in the late twentieth century. How did environmental activists combine ethical, economic, and scientific critiques?

Sources: (1) Rachel Carson, *Silent Spring* (New York: Houghton Mifflin, 2002), pp. 189, 277; (2) Bill Devall and George Sessions, *Deep Ecology* (Salt Lake City, Utah: G. M. Smith, 1985), p. 70; (3) Rudolf Bahro, *Socialism and Survival* (London: Merlin Books, 1982), pp. 41–43.

What led to the decline of "developed socialism" in the East Bloc?

In the postwar decades the Communist states of the East Bloc had achieved a shaky social consensus based on a rising standard of living, an extensive welfare system, and political repression. In the long run, leaders promised, "developed socialism" would prove better than capitalism. But such claims were an attempt to paper over serious tensions in socialist society. When Mikhail Gorbachev burst on the scene in 1985, the new Soviet leader opened an era of reform that was as sweeping as it was unexpected.

State and Society in the East Bloc

By the 1970s many of the professed goals of communism had been achieved. Communist leaders in central and eastern Europe and the Soviet Union adopted the term **developed socialism** (sometimes called "real existing socialism") to describe the accomplishments of their societies. Agriculture had been thoroughly collectivized, and although Poland was an exception, 80 to 90 percent of Soviet and East Bloc farmers worked on huge collective farms. Industry and business had been nationalized, and only a small portion of the economy remained in private hands in most East Bloc countries. The state had also done much to level class differences. Though some people—particularly party members—clearly had greater access to opportunities

and resources, the gap between rich and poor was far smaller than in the West. An extensive system of government-supported social benefits included free medical care, guaranteed employment, inexpensive public transportation, and large subsidies for entertainment, rent, and food.

Everyday life under developed socialism was often an uneasy mixture of outward conformity and private disengagement—or apathy. The Communist Party dominated public life. Party-led mass organizations for youth, women, workers, and sports groups staged huge rallies, colorful festivals, and new holidays that exposed citizens to the values of the socialist state. But while East Bloc citizens might participate in public events, at home, and in private, they often grumbled about and sidestepped the Communist authorities.

East Bloc living standards were well above those in the developing world, but below those in the West. Centralized economic planning continued to result in shortages, and people complained about the poor quality and lack of choice of the most basic goods. Under these conditions, informal networks of family and friends helped people find hard-to-get goods and offered support beyond party organizations. Though the secret police persecuted those who openly challenged the system and generated mountains of files on

Crossing the Border Between East and West Berlin   It was relatively easy for Westerners to get into East Germany to visit friends and relatives, but the Communist state tightly controlled the border. Most East Germans were never allowed to visit the West. In this 1964 photo, a group of West Berliners cross the border to return home after a trip to East Berlin. The glass and steel building in the background—the East German border-crossing station—was nicknamed the "Palace of Tears" by local residents. Here departing West Germans and their East German relatives who could not leave East Germany said many tearful farewells. The limits on travel to the West were one of the most hated aspects of daily life in the East Bloc. (ADN-Bildarchiv/ullstein bild Dtl./Getty Images)

ordinary people, they generally left alone those who demonstrated the required conformity.

Women in particular experienced the contradictions of the socialist system. Official state policy guaranteed equal rights for women and encouraged them to join the workforce in positions formerly reserved for men, and the gender gap between men's and women's pay was less than in the West. Divorce and abortion were free and legal, and an extensive system of state-supported child care eased the work of parenting and freed women to accept employment opportunities. Yet women rarely made it into the upper ranks of business or politics, and despite holding jobs they did most of the housework. In addition, government control of the public sphere meant that the independent groups dedicated to feminist reform that emerged in the West in the 1970s barely emerged in the East Bloc and the Soviet Union. Women could complain to the Communist authorities about unequal or sexist conditions at work or at home, but they could not set up private, nongovernmental organizations to lobby for change.

Though everyday life was fairly comfortable in the East Bloc, a number of deeply rooted structural problems undermined popular support for Soviet-style communism, which contributed to the re-emergence of civic dissent and ultimately to the revolutions of 1989. East Bloc countries — like those in the West — were hard hit by the energy crisis and stagflation of the 1970s. For a time, access to inexpensive oil from the Soviet Union, which had huge resources, helped prop up faltering economies, but this cushion began to fall apart in the 1980s.

For a number of reasons, East Bloc leaders refused to make the economic reforms that might have made developed socialism more effective. First, a move toward Western-style postindustrial society would have required fundamental changes to the Communist system. As in the West, it would have hurt the already weakened living standard of industrial workers. But Communist East Bloc states were publicly committed to supporting the working classes, including coal miners, shipbuilders, and factory and construction workers. To pursue the neoliberal reforms undertaken in the West would have destroyed support for the government among these important constituencies, which was already tenuous at best. In addition, East Bloc regimes refused to cut spending on social benefits because that was, after all, one of the proudest achievements of socialism.

Second, East Bloc economies faltered. High-tech industries failed to take off in Communist Europe, in part because the West maintained embargoes on technology exports. The state continued to provide subsidies to heavy industries such as steel and mining, even though the industrial goods produced in the East Bloc were increasingly uncompetitive in the changing global system. To stave off total collapse, governments borrowed massive amounts of hard currency from Western banks and governments, helping to convince ordinary people that communism was bankrupt and setting up a cycle of indebtedness that helped bring down the entire system in 1989.

Economic decline was hardly the only reason people increasingly questioned one-party Communist rule. The best career and educational opportunities were reserved for party members or handed out as political favors, leaving many talented people underemployed and resentful. Tight controls on travel continually called attention to the burdens of daily life in a repressive society. The one-party state had repeatedly quashed popular reform movements, retreated from economic liberalization, and jailed or exiled dissidents, even those who wished to reform communism from within. Though many East Bloc citizens still found the promise of Marxist egalitarian socialism appealing, they increasingly doubted the legitimacy of Soviet-style communism: the dream of distributing goods "from each according to his means, to each according to his needs" (as Marx had once put it) hardly made up for the deficiencies of developed socialism.

Dissent in Czechoslovakia and Poland

Stagnation in the East Bloc encouraged small numbers of dedicated people to try to change society from below. Developments in Czechoslovakia and Poland were the most striking and significant, and determined protest movements re-emerged in both countries in the mid-1970s. Remembering a history of violent repression and Soviet invasion, dissenters carefully avoided direct challenges to government leaders. Nor did they try to reform the Communist Party from within, as Dubček and his followers had attempted in Prague in 1968. Instead, they worked to build a civil society from below — to create a realm of freedom beyond formal politics, where civil liberties and human rights could be exercised independently of the Communist system.

In Czechoslovakia in 1977 a small group of citizens, including future Czechoslovak president Václav Havel (VAH-slahf HAH-vuhl) (1936–2011), signed a manifesto that came to be known as Charter 77. The group criticized the government for ignoring the human rights provision of the Helsinki Accords and called on Communist leaders to respect civil and political liberties. They also criticized censorship and argued for improved environmental policies. Despite immediate state repression, the group challenged passive

■ **developed socialism** A term used by Communist leaders to describe the socialist accomplishments of their societies, such as nationalized industry, collective agriculture, and extensive social welfare programs.

acceptance of Communist authority and voiced public dissatisfaction with developed socialism.

In Poland, an unruly satellite from the beginning, the Communists had failed to dominate society to the extent seen elsewhere in the East Bloc. Most agricultural land remained in private hands, and the Catholic Church thrived. The Communists also failed to manage the economy effectively. The 1960s brought stagnation, and in 1970 Poland's working class rose again in angry protest. A new Communist leader came to power, and he wagered that massive inflows of Western capital and technology, especially from rich and now-friendly West Germany, could produce a Polish economic miracle. Instead, bureaucratic incompetence and the first oil shock in 1973 sent the economy into a nosedive. Workers, intellectuals, and the church became increasingly restive. Then the real Polish miracle occurred: Cardinal Karol Wojtyła (voy-TIH-wah), archbishop of Kraków, was elected pope in 1978 as John Paul II. In June 1979 he returned to Poland from Rome, preaching love of Christ and country and the "inalienable rights of man." The pope drew enormous crowds and electrified the Polish nation.

In August 1980 strikes broke out across Poland; at the gigantic Lenin Shipyards in Gdansk (formerly known as Danzig) sixteen thousand workers laid down their tools and occupied the plant. As other workers joined "in solidarity," the strikers advanced the ideals of civil society, including the right to form trade unions free from state control, freedom of speech and religion,

the release of political prisoners, and economic liberalization. After the strikers occupied the shipyard for eighteen days, the government gave in and accepted the workers' demands in the Gdansk Agreement. In a state in which the Communist Party claimed to rule on behalf of the proletariat, a working-class revolt had won an unprecedented, even revolutionary, victory.

Led by feisty Lenin Shipyards electrician and devout Catholic Lech Wałęsa (lehk vah-WEHN-suh) (b. 1943), the workers organized a free and democratic trade union called **Solidarity**. As in Czechoslovakia, Solidarity worked cautiously to shape an active civil society from below. Joined by intellectuals and supported by the Catholic Church, it became a national union with a full-time staff of 40,000 and 9.5 million members. Cultural and intellectual freedom blossomed in Poland, and Solidarity enjoyed tremendous public support. But Solidarity's leaders pursued a self-limiting revolution, meant only to defend the concessions won in the Gdansk Agreement. Solidarity practiced moderation, refusing to challenge directly the Communist monopoly on political power. At the same time, the ever-present threat of calling a nationwide strike gave it real leverage in negotiations with the regime.

Solidarity's combination of strength and moderation postponed a showdown, as the Soviet Union played a waiting game of threats and pressure. After a confrontation in March 1981, Wałęsa settled for minor government concessions, and Solidarity dropped plans for a massive general strike. Criticism of Wałęsa's moderate leadership gradually grew, and Solidarity lost its cohesiveness. The worsening economic crisis also encouraged radical actions among disgruntled Solidarity members, and the Polish Communist leadership shrewdly denounced the union for promoting economic decline and provoking a possible Soviet invasion. In December 1981 Wojciech Jaruzelski (VOY-chehk yahr-oo-ZEHL-skee), the general who led Poland's Communist government, suddenly proclaimed martial law and arrested Solidarity's leaders.

Outlawed and driven underground, Solidarity survived in part because of the government's unwillingness (and probably its inability) to impose full-scale terror. Moreover, millions of Poles decided to continue acting as if they were free—the hallmark of civil society—even though they were not. Cultural and intellectual life remained extremely vigorous as the Polish economy continued to deteriorate dramatically. Popular support for outlawed Solidarity remained strong under martial law in the 1980s, preparing the way for the

Lech Wałęsa and Solidarity   An inspiration for fellow workers at the Lenin Shipyards in the dramatic and successful strike against the Communist leaders in August 1980, Wałęsa played a key role in Solidarity before and after it was outlawed. Here he speaks at a protest rally in the port city of Gdansk during the strike. Wałęsa personified the enduring opposition to Communist rule in eastern Europe. (STR/Reuters/Forum/Erazm Ciolek/Newscom)

union's political rebirth toward the end of the decade.

The rise and survival of Solidarity showed that ordinary Poles would stubbornly struggle for greater political and religious liberty, cultural freedom, trade-union rights, patriotic nationalism, and a more humane socialism. Not least in importance, Solidarity's challenge encouraged fresh thinking in the Soviet Union, ever the key to lasting change in the East Bloc.

From Détente Back to Cold War

Soviet and East Bloc leaders faced challenges from abroad as optimistic hopes for détente in international relations faded in the late 1970s. Brezhnev's Soviet Union ignored the human rights provisions of the Helsinki agreement, and East-West political competition remained very much alive outside Europe. Western critics became convinced that the Soviet Union was taking advantage of détente, steadily building up its military might and pushing for political gains and revolutions in Africa, Asia, and Latin America. The Soviet invasion of Afghanistan in December 1979, designed to save an increasingly unpopular Marxist regime, alarmed the West. Some feared that the oil-rich states of the Persian Gulf would be next, and once again they looked to the NATO alliance and military might to thwart Communist expansion.

President Jimmy Carter (U.S. pres. 1977–1981) tried to lead NATO beyond verbal condemnation of the Soviet Union and urged economic sanctions against it, but only Great Britain among the European allies supported the U.S. initiative. The alliance furthermore failed to support the Solidarity movement in Poland. Some observers concluded that NATO had lost the will to act decisively in dealing with the Soviet bloc.

The Atlantic alliance endured, however, and the U.S. military buildup launched by Carter in his last years in office was greatly accelerated by President Reagan, who was swept into office in 1980 by a wave of patriotism and economic discontent. The new American leadership acted as if the military balance had tipped in favor of the Soviet Union, which Reagan anathematized as the "evil empire." Increasing defense spending enormously, the Reagan administration deployed short-range nuclear missiles in western Europe and called for an expensive space-based missile defense system; this "Strategic Defense Initiative" was nicknamed the "Star Wars program" in popular slang. The broad shift toward greater conservatism in

The Soviet War in Afghanistan, 1979–1989

the 1980s gave Reagan invaluable allies in western Europe. Like the U.S. president, Margaret Thatcher was a forceful advocate for a revitalized Atlantic alliance, and under Helmut Kohl West Germany likewise worked with the United States to coordinate military and political policy toward the Soviet bloc.

Gorbachev's Reforms in the Soviet Union

Cold War tensions aside, the Soviet Union's Communist elite seemed safe from any challenge from below in the early 1980s. A firmly entrenched administrative system stretched downward from the central ministries and state committees to provincial cities and from there to factories, neighborhoods, and villages. At each level of this massive state bureaucracy, the overlapping hierarchy of the 17.5-million-member Communist Party maintained tight control. Organized opposition was impossible, and average people left politics to the bosses.

Although the massive state and party bureaucracy safeguarded the elite, it promoted widespread apathy and stagnation. When Brezhnev died in 1982, his successors Konstantin Chernenko (who died himself a year later) and then the long-time chief of the secret police, Yuri Andropov (1914–1984), tried to invigorate the system. Relatively little came of such efforts, but they combined with a sharply worsening economic situation to set the stage for the emergence in 1985 of Mikhail Gorbachev (b. 1931), the most vigorous Soviet leader in a generation.

A lawyer and experienced Communist Party official, Gorbachev believed in communism but realized that the Soviet Union was failing to keep up with the West and was losing its superpower status. Thus he tried to revitalize the Soviet system with fundamental reforms. An idealist who wanted to improve conditions for ordinary citizens, Gorbachev understood that the enormous expense of the Cold War arms race had had a disastrous impact on living conditions in the Soviet Union; improvement at home, he realized, required better relations with the West.

In his first year in office, Gorbachev consolidated his power, attacked corruption and incompetence in the bureaucracy, and tried to reduce alcoholism, which was widespread and lethal in Soviet society. He worked out an ambitious reform program designed to restructure the economy to provide for the real needs

■ **Solidarity** Independent Polish trade union that worked for workers' rights and political reform throughout the 1980s.

The Dissolution of the Soviet Union   General Party Secretary Mikhail Gorbachev (at podium) gives an address to a crowd of delegates at the twenty-eighth and last congress of the Soviet Communist Party in July 1990. Gorbachev took office in 1985 with the goal of reforming communism from within. His plans spiraled out of control. By 1991 the Soviet Union and the East Bloc had disintegrated into independent, non-communist states. (World History Archive/Alamy Stock Photo)

public discourse, the newfound openness, or **glasnost** (GLAS-nohst), of the government and the media marked an astonishing break with the past. Long-banned émigré writers sold millions of copies of their works in new editions, while denunciations of Stalin and his terror became standard fare in plays and movies. In another example of glasnost in action, after several days of hesitation the usually secretive Soviet government issued daily reports on the 1986 nuclear plant accident at Chernobyl, one of the worst environmental disasters in history. Indeed, the initial openness in government pronouncements quickly went much further than Gorbachev intended and led to something approaching free speech, a veritable cultural revolution.

Democratization was another element of reform. Beginning as an attack on corruption in the Communist Party, it led to the expansion of the ballot, with candidates outside the Communist Party for the first time in the Soviet Union since 1917. Gorbachev and the party remained in control, but a minority of critical independents was elected in April 1989 to a revitalized Congress of People's Deputies. Millions of Soviets then watched the new congress for hours on television as Gorbachev and his ministers saw their proposals debated and even rejected. An active civil society was emerging—a new political culture at odds with the Communist Party's monopoly of power and control.

of the Soviet population. To accomplish this economic restructuring, or **perestroika** (pehr-uh-STROY-kuh), Gorbachev and his supporters eased government price controls on some goods, gave more independence to state enterprises, and created profit-seeking private cooperatives to provide personal services. These small-scale reforms initially produced improvements, but shortages grew as the economy stalled at an intermediate point between central planning and free-market mechanisms. By late 1988 widespread consumer dissatisfaction posed a serious threat to Gorbachev's leadership and the entire reform program.

Gorbachev's bold and far-reaching campaign for greater freedom of expression was much more successful. Very popular in a country where censorship, dull uniformity, and outright lies had long characterized

Democratization ignited demands for greater political and cultural autonomy and even national independence among non-Russian minorities living in the fifteen Soviet republics. The Soviet population numbered about 145 million ethnic Russians and 140.6 million non-Russians, including 55 million Muslims in the Central Asian republics and over 44 million Ukrainians. Once Gorbachev opened the doors to greater public expression, tensions flared between central Soviet control and national separatist movements. Independence groups were particularly active in the Baltic Soviet socialist republics of Lithuania, Latvia, and Estonia; in western Ukraine; and in the Transcaucasian republics of Armenia, Azerbaijan, and Georgia.

Finally, Gorbachev brought reforms to the field of foreign affairs. Of enormous importance, the Soviet leader sought to halt the arms race with the United States and convinced President Reagan of his sincerity. In a Washington summit in December 1987, the two leaders agreed to eliminate all land-based

■ **perestroika** Economic restructuring and reform implemented by Soviet leader Mikhail Gorbachev in 1985.

■ **glasnost** Soviet leader Mikhail Gorbachev's popular campaign for openness in government and the media.

A pair of famous speeches marked the beginning of the end of the Cold War: U.S. president Ronald Reagan's address at the Berlin Wall (June 12, 1987) and U.S.S.R. general party secretary Mikhail Gorbachev's address to the United Nations General Assembly (December 7, 1988). In a resounding call for freedom, Reagan demanded that the East Bloc open its borders. Gorbachev shocked his audience when he spoke openly of the need for "the principle of freedom" — a move that encouraged East Bloc nations to seek independence from Soviet control.

Reagan's Speech at the Berlin Wall

Behind me stands a wall that encircles the free sectors of this city, part of a vast system of barriers that divides the entire continent of Europe. From the Baltic South, those barriers cut across Germany in a gash of barbed wire, concrete, dog runs, and guard towers. Farther south, there may be no visible, no obvious wall. But there remain armed guards and checkpoints all the same — still a restriction on the right to travel, still an instrument to impose upon ordinary men and women the will of a totalitarian state. . . .

[I]n the West today, we see a free world that has achieved a level of prosperity and well-being unprecedented in all human history. In the Communist world, we see failure, technological backwardness, declining standards of health, even want of the most basic kind — too little food. . . . After these four decades, then, there stands before the entire world one great and inescapable conclusion: Freedom leads to prosperity. Freedom replaces the ancient hatreds among nations with comity and peace. Freedom is the victor.

And now — now the Soviets themselves may, in a limited way, be coming to understand the importance of freedom. We hear much from Moscow about a new policy of reform and openness. . . . Are these the beginnings of profound changes in the Soviet state? Or are they token gestures intended to raise false hopes in the West, or to strengthen the Soviet system without changing it? . . .

There is one sign the Soviets can make that would be unmistakable, that would advance dramatically the cause of freedom and peace.

General Secretary Gorbachev, if you seek peace, if you seek prosperity for the Soviet Union and Eastern Europe, if you seek liberalization: Come here to this gate.

Mr. Gorbachev, open this gate.

Mr. Gorbachev — Mr. Gorbachev, tear down this wall!

Gorbachev's Address to the UN General Assembly

Today we have entered an era when progress will be based on the interests of all mankind. Consciousness of this requires that world policy, too, should be determined by the priority of the values of all humanity. . . .

Further world progress is now possible only through the search for a consensus of all humanity, in movement toward a new world order. . . . The formula of development "at another's expense" is becoming outdated. In light of present realities, genuine progress by infringing upon the rights and liberties of man and peoples, or at the expense of nature, is impossible. . . .

The compelling necessity of the principle of freedom of choice is also clear to us. The failure to recognize this . . . is fraught with very dire consequences, consequences for world peace. Denying that right to the peoples, no matter what the pretext, no matter what the words are used to conceal it, means infringing upon even the unstable balance that is, [that] has been possible to achieve. . . .

Finally, being on U.S. soil . . . I cannot but turn to the subject of our relations with this great country. . . . Relations between the Soviet Union and the United States of America span 5 1/2 decades. . . . For too long they were built under the banner of confrontation, and sometimes of hostility, either open or concealed. But in the last few years, throughout the world people were able to heave a sigh of relief, thanks to the changes for the better in the substance and atmosphere of the relations between Moscow and Washington.

QUESTIONS FOR ANALYSIS

1. Where do Reagan and Gorbachev draw on familiar Cold War rhetoric? Where do they move beyond it?
2. American historians sometimes argue that Reagan's Berlin Wall speech was a major reason for the ultimate collapse of the Soviet system. How would you evaluate such claims? Were there other, equally important causes?

Sources: "Ronald Reagan, Remarks at the Brandenburg Gate," June 12, 1987, American Rhetoric/Top 100 Speeches, http://www.americanrhetoric.com/speeches/ronaldreaganbrandenburggate.htm; "Gorbachev's Speech to the U.N." December 7, 1988, https://astro.temple.edu/~rimmerma/gorbachev_speech_to_UN.ht.

intermediate-range missiles in Europe, setting the stage for more arms reductions. In February 1989 the U.S.S.R. withdrew its troops from Afghanistan. Gorbachev also repudiated the Brezhnev Doctrine and pledged to respect the political choices of the peoples of East Bloc countries, which encouraged reform movements in Poland, Czechoslovakia, and Hungary. By early 1989 it seemed that if Gorbachev held to his word, the tragic Soviet occupation of eastern Europe might wither away, taking the long Cold War with it once and for all. (See "Viewpoints: 'Mr. Gorbachev, Tear Down This Wall!'")

What were the causes and consequences of the 1989 revolutions in the East Bloc?

In 1989 Gorbachev's plan to reform communism from within snowballed out of control. A series of largely peaceful revolutions swept across eastern Europe, overturning existing Communist regimes (Map 29.1). The peoples of the East Bloc gained political freedom, West Germany absorbed its East German rival, and as Gorbachev's reforms boomeranged, a complicated anti-communist revolution swept through the Soviet Union. The Cold War came to an end, and the United States suddenly stood as the world's only superpower.

MAPPING THE PAST

MAP 29.1 Democratic Movements in Eastern Europe, 1989

Countries that had been satellites in the orbit of the Soviet Union began to set themselves free in 1989.

ANALYZING THE MAP Why did the means by which communism was overthrown in the East Bloc vary from country to country? What accounts for the rapid spread of these democratic movements?

CONNECTIONS How did Gorbachev's reforms in the Soviet Union contribute to the spread of democratic movements in eastern Europe, and how did his actions hasten the end of the Cold War?

The Collapse of Communism in the East Bloc

The collapse of Communist rule in the Soviet satellite states surprised many Western commentators, who had expected Cold War divisions to persist for many years. Yet while the revolutions of 1989 appeared to erupt quite suddenly, long-standing structural weaknesses in the Communist system had prepared the way. East Bloc economies never really recovered from the economic catastrophe of the 1970s. State spending on outdated industries and extensive social benefits led to massive indebtedness to Western banks and undermined economic growth, while limits on personal and political freedoms fueled a growing sense of injustice.

In this general climate of economic stagnation and popular anger, Solidarity and the Polish people led the way to revolution. In 1988 widespread strikes, raging inflation, and the outlawed Solidarity's refusal to cooperate with the military government had brought Poland to the brink of economic collapse. Poland's frustrated Communist leaders offered to negotiate with Solidarity if the outlawed union's leaders could get the strikers back to work and resolve the political crisis. The subsequent agreement in April 1989 legalized Solidarity and declared that a large minority of representatives to the Polish parliament would be chosen by free elections that June. Still guaranteed a parliamentary majority and expecting to win many of the contested seats, the Communists believed that their rule was guaranteed for four years and that Solidarity would keep the workers in line.

Lacking access to the state-run media, Solidarity succeeded nonetheless in mobilizing the country and winning all but one of the contested seats in an overwhelming victory. Moreover, many angry voters crossed off the names of unopposed party candidates, so that the Communist Party failed to win the majority its leaders had anticipated. Solidarity members jubilantly entered the Polish parliament, and a dangerous stalemate quickly developed. But Lech Wałęsa, a gifted politician who always repudiated violence, adroitly obtained a majority by securing the allegiance of two minor procommunist parties that had been part of the coalition government after World War II. In August 1989 Tadeusz Mazowiecki (ta-DAY-ush MAH-zoe-vee-ETS-key) (1927–2013), the editor of one of Solidarity's weekly newspapers, was sworn in as Poland's new noncommunist prime minister.

In its first year and a half, the Solidarity government cautiously introduced revolutionary political changes. It eliminated the hated secret police, the Communist ministers in the government, and finally Communist Party leader Jaruzelski himself, but it did so step-by-step to avoid confrontation with the army or the Soviet Union. In economics, however, the Solidarity

THE COLLAPSE OF COMMUNISM	
1977	Charter 77 reform movement founded in Czechoslovakia
1980	Polish Solidarity movement formed
1981	Solidarity outlawed by Communist leaders
1982	Soviet leader Leonid Brezhnev dies
1985	Mikhail Gorbachev becomes Soviet general party secretary and institutes perestroika and glasnost reforms
1988	Polish workers strike throughout country
1989	
April	Solidarity legalized in Poland
June	Free elections in Poland
August	Noncommunist prime minister takes power in Poland
November	Berlin Wall opened
November–December	Velvet Revolution ends communism in Czechoslovakia
December	Communist dictator of Romania executed
1990	
February	Communist Party defeated in Soviet elections
March	Free elections in Hungary
May	Boris Yeltsin elected leader of Russian Soviet Republic
October	Reunification of Germany
November	Paris Accord: arms reductions across Europe
1991	
August	Communist hardliners kidnap Gorbachev and try to overthrow Soviet government
December	Soviet Union dissolved

government was radical from the beginning. It applied economic shock therapy, an intense dose of neoliberal policy designed to make a clean break with state planning and move quickly to market mechanisms and private property. The government abolished controls on many prices on January 1, 1990, and drastically reformed the monetary system.

Hungary followed Poland. Hungary's moderate Communist Party leader János Kádár (KAH-dahr)

The Opening of the Berlin Wall The sudden and unanticipated opening of the Berlin Wall on November 10, 1989, dramatized the spectacular fall of communism throughout east-central Europe. Here East German border guards look on as a man takes a sledge-hammer to the much-despised barrier. Millions of East German citizens visited West Berlin and the Federal Republic of Germany in the first few days after the surprise relaxation of inter-German travel controls. (Pictorial Press Ltd/Alamy Stock Photo)

had permitted liberalization of the rigid planned economy after the 1956 uprising in exchange for political loyalty and continued Communist control. In May 1988, in an effort to retain power by granting modest political concessions, the party replaced the ill and aging Kádár with a reform-minded Communist. But liberal opposition groups rejected piecemeal progress, and in the summer of 1989 the Hungarian Communist Party agreed to hold free elections the following March. Welcoming Western investment and moving rapidly toward multiparty democracy, Hungary's Communists now enjoyed considerable popular support, and they believed, quite mistakenly, that they could defeat the opposition in the upcoming elections.

In an effort to strengthen their support at home, the Hungarians opened their border to East Germans and tore down the barbed wire curtain separating

Hungary from Austria. Tens of thousands of dissatisfied East German "vacationers" then poured into Hungary, crossed into Austria as refugees, and continued on to immediate resettlement in West Germany.

The flight of East Germans fed the rapid growth of a homegrown, spontaneous protest movement in East Germany. Workers joined intellectuals, environmentalists, and Protestant ministers in huge candlelight demonstrations. While some activists insisted that a democratic but still socialist East Germany was both possible and desirable, numerous East German citizens continued to depart en masse. In a desperate attempt to stabilize the situation, the East German government opened the Berlin Wall in November 1989, allowing free travel across the former border. A new, reformist government took power and scheduled free elections.

In Czechoslovakia, Communist rule began to dissolve peacefully in November to December 1989. This so-called **Velvet Revolution** grew out of popular demonstrations led by students and joined by intellectuals and a dissident playwright-turned-moral-revolutionary named Václav Havel. When the protesters took control of the streets, the Communist government resigned, leading to a power-sharing arrangement termed the "Government of National Understanding." As 1989 ended, the Czechoslovakian assembly elected Havel president.

In Romania, popular revolution turned violent and bloody. There the dictator Nicolae Ceaușescu (chow-SHESS-koo) (1918–1989) had long combined tight party control with stubborn independence from Moscow. Faced with mass protests in December 1989, Ceaușescu ordered his ruthless security forces to quell unrest, sparking an armed uprising. Perhaps 750 people were killed in the fighting; the numbers were often exaggerated. After the dictator and his wife were captured and executed by a military court, Ceaușescu's forces were defeated. A coalition government emerged, although the legacy of Ceaușescu's long and oppressive rule left a troubled country.

German Unification and the End of the Cold War

The dissolution of communism in East Germany that began in 1989 reopened the "German question" and raised the threat of renewed Cold War conflict

■ **Velvet Revolution** The term given to the relatively peaceful overthrow of communism in Czechoslovakia; the label came to signify the collapse of the East Bloc in general in 1989 to 1990.

Revolution in Romania A man holding a Romanian flag with the Communist symbol torn from its center stands on a balcony overlooking the tanks, soldiers, and citizens filling Palace Square in Bucharest, the capital city, during the revolution of 1989. Deadly violence accompanied the overthrow of communism in Romania. Elsewhere the collapse of the East Bloc was relatively peaceful. (Peter Turnley/Corbis/VCG/Getty Images)

over Germany. Taking power in October 1989, East German reform Communists, enthusiastically supported by leading intellectuals and former dissidents, wanted to preserve socialism by making it genuinely democratic and responsive to the needs of the people. They argued for a "third way" that would go beyond the failed Stalinism they had experienced and the ruthless capitalism they saw in the West. These reformers supported closer ties with West Germany but feared unification, hoping to preserve a distinct East German identity with a socialist system.

Over the next year, however, East Germany was absorbed into an enlarged West Germany, much as a faltering company is swallowed by a stronger rival and ceases to exist. Three factors were particularly important in this outcome. First, in the first week after the Berlin Wall was opened, almost 9 million East Germans—roughly half of the total population—poured across the border into West Germany. Almost all returned to their homes in the east, but the exhilaration of crossing a long-closed border aroused long-dormant hopes of unity among ordinary citizens.

Second, West German chancellor Helmut Kohl and his closest advisers skillfully exploited the historic opportunity handed them. Sure of support from the United States, whose leadership he had steadfastly followed, in November 1989 Kohl presented a ten-point plan for step-by-step unification in cooperation with both East Germany and the international community. Kohl then promised the struggling citizens of East

Germany an immediate economic bonanza—a generous though limited exchange of East German marks in savings accounts and pensions into much more valuable West German marks. This offer helped popularize the Alliance for Germany, a well-financed political party established in East Germany with the support of Kohl's West German Christian Democrats. In March 1990 the Alliance won almost 50 percent of the votes in an East German parliamentary election, outdistancing the Party of Democratic Socialism (the renamed East German Communist Party) (16 percent) and the revived Social Democratic Party (22 percent). The Alliance for Germany quickly negotiated an economic and political union on favorable terms with Kohl. The rapid pace of reunification quickly overwhelmed those who argued for the preservation of an independent socialist society in East Germany.

Third, in the summer of 1990 the crucial international aspect of German unification was successfully resolved. Unification would once again make Germany the strongest state in central Europe and would directly affect the security of the Soviet Union. But Gorbachev swallowed hard—Western cartoonists showed Stalin turning over in his grave—and negotiated the best deal he could. In a historic agreement signed by Gorbachev and Kohl in July 1990, Kohl solemnly affirmed Germany's peaceful intentions and pledged never to develop nuclear, biological, or chemical weapons. The Germans sweetened the deal by promising enormous loans to the hard-pressed Soviet Union. In October

1990 East Germany merged into West Germany, forming a single nation under the West German laws and constitution.

The peaceful reunification of Germany accelerated the pace of agreements to liquidate the Cold War. In November 1990 delegates from twenty-two European countries joined those from the United States and the Soviet Union in Paris and agreed to a scaling down of all their armed forces. The delegates also solemnly affirmed that all existing borders in Europe, including those of unified Germany and the emerging Baltic States, were legal and valid. The Paris Accord was for all practical purposes a general peace treaty that ended the forty-five-year-old Cold War.

Peace in Europe encouraged the United States and the Soviet Union to scrap a significant portion of their nuclear weapons. In September 1991 a confident President George H. W. Bush canceled the around-the-clock alert status for American bombers outfitted with atomic bombs, and Gorbachev quickly followed suit with his own forces. For the first time in four decades, Soviet and American nuclear weapons were not standing ready for mutual destruction.

The Disintegration of the Soviet Union

As 1990 began, the tough work of dismantling some forty-five years of Communist rule had begun in all but two East Bloc states — tiny Albania and the vast Soviet Union. The great question now became whether the Soviet Union would follow its former satellites.

In February 1990, as competing Russian politicians noisily presented their programs and nationalists in the non-Russian republics demanded autonomy or independence from the Soviet Union, the Communist Party suffered a stunning defeat in local elections throughout the country. As in East Bloc countries, democrats and anticommunists won clear majorities in the leading cities of the Russian Soviet Republic, by far the largest republic in the Soviet Union. Moreover, in Lithuania, a newly chosen parliament declared the nation's independence from the U.S.S.R.

Gorbachev responded by placing an economic embargo on Lithuania, but after popular protests stopped a Soviet-sponsored coup in January 1991, the

The Reunification of Germany, 1990

— Former boundary between East and West Germany

separatist government remained in place. The result was a tense political standoff that undermined popular support for Gorbachev. Separating himself further from Communist hardliners, Gorbachev asked Soviet citizens to ratify a new constitution that formally abolished the Communist Party's monopoly of political power and expanded the power of the Congress of People's Deputies. While retaining his post as party secretary, Gorbachev then convinced a majority of deputies to elect him president of the Soviet Union.

Despite his victory, Gorbachev's power continued to erode, and his unwillingness to risk a universal suffrage election for the presidency strengthened his archrival, Boris Yeltsin (1931–2007). A radical reform Communist, Yeltsin embraced the democratic movement, and in May 1990 he was elected parliamentary leader of the Russian Soviet Republic. He boldly announced that Russia would put its interests first and declare its independence from the Soviet Union, broadening the base of the anticommunist movement by joining the patriotism of ordinary Russians with the democratic aspirations of big-city intellectuals. Gorbachev tried to save the Soviet Union with a new treaty that would link the member republics in a looser, freely accepted confederation, but six of the fifteen Soviet republics rejected his plan.

Opposed by democrats and nationalists, Gorbachev was also challenged by the Communist old guard. In August 1991 a gang of hardliners interned him and his family while on vacation in Crimea and tried to seize the Soviet government. The attempted coup collapsed in the face of massive popular resistance that rallied around Yeltsin. As a spellbound world watched on television, Yeltsin defiantly denounced the rebels from atop a stalled tank in central Moscow and declared the "rebirth of Russia." The army supported Yeltsin, and Gorbachev was rescued and returned to power as head of the Soviet Union.

The leaders of the coup had wanted to preserve Communist power, state ownership, and the multinational Soviet Union; they succeeded in destroying all three. An anticommunist revolution swept Russia as Yeltsin and his supporters outlawed the Communist Party and confiscated its property. Locked in a personal and political duel with Gorbachev, Yeltsin and his democratic allies declared Russia independent, withdrew from the Soviet Union, and changed the country's name from the Russian Soviet Republic to the Russian Federation. All the other Soviet republics also withdrew. Gorbachev resigned on December 25, 1991, and the next day the Supreme Soviet dissolved itself, marking the end of the Soviet Union. The independent republics of the old Soviet Union then established a loose confederation, the Commonwealth of Independent States, which played only a minor role in the 1990s.

NOTES

1. Quoted in Kessing's Research Report, *Germany and East Europe Since 1945: From the Potsdam Agreement to Chancellor Brandt's "Ostpolitik"* (New York: Charles Scribner's Sons, 1973), pp. 284–285.
2. M. Mitterauer, *The History of Youth* (Oxford: Basil Blackwell, 1992), p. 40.

LOOKING BACK LOOKING AHEAD

The unexpected collapse of Communist Europe capped three decades of turbulent change. In the 1960s the consensus established after the Second World War was challenged by protest movements in the East and West Blocs alike. In the 1970s a global recession had devastating effects across the globe. In the 1980s conservative Western leaders pushed neoliberal plans to revive growth and meet growing global competition. In the East Bloc, structural problems and spontaneous revolt brought down communism, dissolved the Soviet Union, and ended the Cold War.

With the world economy on the road to recovery and new free-market systems in place across the former East Bloc, all of Europe would now have the opportunity to enter the information age. After forty years of Cold War division, the continent regained an underlying unity as faith in democratic government and market economics became the common European creed. In 1991 hopes for peaceful democratic progress were almost universal. According to philosopher Francis Fukuyama, the world had reached "the end of history" — the end

of the Cold War, he argued, would lead to peaceful development based on growing tolerance, free-market economics, and liberal democracy.

The post–Cold War years saw the realization of some of these hopes, but the new era brought its own problems and tragedies. In the former Yugoslavia, ethnic and nationalist tensions flared, leading to a disastrous civil war. The struggle to rebuild the shattered societies of the former East Bloc countries was far more difficult than the people living in them had hoped. Poor economic growth continued to complicate attempts to deal with the wide-open global economy. New conflicts with Islamic nations in the Middle East involved some European nations in war. The European Union expanded, but political disagreements, environmental issues, increased anxiety about non-Western immigrants, and a host of other problems undermined moves toward true European unity. History was far from over — the realities of a post–Cold War world continued to yield difficult challenges as Europe entered the twenty-first century.

Make Connections

Think about the larger developments and continuities within and across chapters.

1. How did the revolts that shook western European countries and the East Bloc develop out of issues left unresolved in the 1950s era of postwar reconstruction (Chapter 28)?

2. Both East and West Blocs faced similar economic problems in the 1970s, yet communism collapsed in the East and capitalism recovered. How do you account for the difference? Were economic problems the main basis for popular opposition to communism?

3. What were some of the basic ideas behind the neoliberal economic policies that emerged in the West in the 1970s and 1980s? Why are they still popular today?

29 REVIEW & EXPLORE

Identify Key Terms

Identify and explain the significance of each item below.

Ostpolitik (p. 906)

détente (p. 907)

Second Vatican Council (p. 909)

New Left (p. 910)

Brezhnev Doctrine (p. 914)

OPEC (p. 915)

stagflation (p. 915)

postindustrial society (p. 916)

neoliberalism (p. 916)

privatization (p. 916)

second-wave feminism (p. 920)

developed socialism (p. 924)

Solidarity (p. 926)

perestroika (p. 928)

glasnost (p. 928)

Velvet Revolution (p. 932)

Review the Main Ideas

Answer the section heading questions from the chapter.

1. Why did the postwar consensus of the 1950s break down? (p. 906)

2. What were the consequences of economic stagnation in the 1970s? (p. 915)

3. What led to the decline of "developed socialism" in the East Bloc? (p. 924)

4. What were the causes and consequences of the 1989 revolutions in the East Bloc? (p. 930)

Suggested Resources

BOOKS

+ Ash, Timothy Garton. *The Magic Lantern: The Revolution of '89 Witnessed in Warsaw, Budapest, Berlin, and Prague.* 1993. An exciting firsthand narrative of the collapse of the East Bloc in 1989 and 1990.

+ Cohen, Stephen F. *Soviet Fates and Lost Alternatives: From Stalinism to the New Cold War.* 2011. An up-to-date book by an acclaimed historian that challenges conventional interpretations of the rise and fall and aftermath of the Soviet Union.

+ Evans, Eric. J. *Thatcher and Thatcherism.* 2018. A critical study of the origins and impact of Thatcherism, inside and outside Great Britain.

+ Gahrton, Per. *Green Parties, Green Future: From Local Groups to the International Stage.* 2015. Explores the history, ideologies, and governmental roles of environmentalist Green parties around the world.

+ Guha, Ramachandra. *Environmentalism: A Global History.* 2000. A powerful and readable overview

of environmentalism that puts Europe in a world context.

+ Kurlansky, Mark. *1968: The Year That Rocked the World.* 2003. Popular history at its best; a gripping account of the 1960s generation and 1968 across the globe.

+ Okey, Robin. *The Demise of Communist East Europe: 1989 in Context.* 2004. A measured overview of the collapse of the East Bloc that avoids accusatory Cold War rhetoric.

+ Pittaway, Mark. *Eastern Europe, 1939–2000.* 2004. A survey of east-central Europe from the start of World War II to the end of communism, with a welcome emphasis on social history.

+ Port, Andrew I. *Conflict and Stability in the German Democratic Republic.* 2007. A penetrating analysis of popular support for communism in this major East Bloc country.

- Reitan, Earl A. *Tory Radicalism: Margaret Thatcher, John Major, and the Transformation of Modern Britain, 1979–1997*. 1997. Clear, concise, and very useful.
- Smith, Bonnie G. *Global Feminisms Since 1945*. 2000. A broad overview of feminism after World War II that puts European and American movements in global context.

- Williams, Kieran. *The Prague Spring and Its Aftermath: Czechoslovak Politics, 1968–1970*. 1997. Explores the events of the Prague Spring and the political changes that followed the revolt.
- Zubok, Vladislav M. *A Failed Empire: The Soviet Union in the Cold War from Stalin to Gorbachev*. 2008. An in-depth account of Soviet leaders and elites during the Cold War.

MEDIA

- *Apocalypse Now* (Francis Ford Coppola, 1979). In this famous film, loosely based on Joseph Conrad's *Heart of Darkness*, a special operations captain undertakes a secret mission into the jungle of Cambodia that reveals the cruelty and absurdity of the war in Vietnam.
- *BBC News Special Report: The Thatcher Years in Statistics*. An interactive website that allows users to compare and contrast various sets of economic and social statistics in Britain during the Thatcher years. **news .bbc.co.uk/2/hi/in_depth/4447082.stm**
- *The Iron Lady* (Phyllida Lloyd, 2011). A film about the life of Great Britain's first female prime minister, Margaret Thatcher (played by Meryl Streep), who is renowned for her neoliberal policies in the 1980s.
- *Making the History of 1989*. Primary sources, scholarly interviews, and case studies on the fall of communism in eastern Europe. **chnm.gmu.edu/1989/**

- *Man of Marble* (Andrzej Wajda, 1977). By a noted Polish director, this film tells the story of the first decade of Communist rule in Poland through the experiences of a young bricklayer and a documentary film maker who seeks to make a film about the bricklayer's life and times.
- *MSU Billings Library Research Guide: Europe in the 1960s*. A library research guide, hosted by Montana State University, that includes a wide variety of links to online primary and secondary sources on all aspects of Europe's experience of the 1960s. **http://libguides .msubillings.edu/c.php?g=242173&p=1610604**
- *My Perestroika* (Robin Hessman, 2010). Documents the story of five individuals who were born in the Soviet Union and came of age during its collapse.

30

Life in an Age of Globalization

1990 to the present

On November 9, 2009, the twentieth anniversary of the opening of the Berlin Wall, jubilant crowds filled the streets around the Brandenburg Gate at the former border between East and West Berlin. World leaders and tens of thousands of onlookers applauded as former Polish president Lech Wałęsa pushed over a line of one thousand eight-foot-tall foam dominos, symbolizing the collapse of communism.

The crowd had reason to celebrate. The revolutions of 1989 had opened a new chapter in European and world history. Capitalism spread across the former East Bloc and Soviet Union (now the Russian Federation and fourteen other republics), along with the potential for political reform. Some of these hopes were realized, but the new era also brought problems and tragedies. The process of remaking formerly Communist societies was more difficult than expected. At the same time, across the West and around the world, globalization, the digital revolution, and the ongoing flow of immigrants into western Europe had impacts both positive and negative.

As Europeans faced serious tensions and complex changes in the twenty-first century, they also came together to form a strong new European Union (EU) that would prove a formidable economic competitor to the United States. Ties between western Europe and the United States began to loosen, but Europe and North America—as well as the rest of the world—confronted common challenges. Finding solutions to problems in the Middle East and addressing the growth of authoritarian populism, environmental degradation, energy needs, and human rights would require not only innovation but also creative cooperation. ■

CHAPTER PREVIEW

- How did life change in Russia and the former East Bloc countries after 1989?

- How did globalization affect European life and society?

- How is growing ethnic diversity changing contemporary Europe?

- What challenges will Europeans face in the coming decades?

Life in a Globalizing World
In a global art project titled *Inside Out*, French photographer JR installed large-scale photographs of ordinary people in public locations around the world. This version, from the floor of the Panthéon in Paris, champions the ethnic diversity and cultural variety of EU and French citizens in the third decade of the twenty-first century. (DENIS/REA/Redux Pictures)

How did life change in Russia and the former East Bloc countries after 1989?

Establishing stable democratic governments in the former East Bloc countries and the fifteen diverse republics of the former Soviet Union was not easy. While Russia initially moved toward economic reform and political openness, by 2010 it had returned to its authoritarian traditions. The transformation of the Communist East Bloc was also difficult. After a period of tense reform, some countries, such as Poland and the Czech Republic, established relatively prosperous democracies and joined NATO and then the European Union. Others lagged behind. In multiethnic Yugoslavia, the collapse of communism and the onset of a disastrous civil war broke the country apart.

Economic Shock Therapy in Russia

Politics and economics were closely intertwined in Russia after the dissolution of the Soviet Union. President Boris Yeltsin (r. 1991–1999), his supporters, and his economic ministers wanted to create conditions that would prevent a return to communism and right the faltering economy. Agreeing with neoliberal Western advisers who argued that a quick turn to free markets would speed economic growth, Russian reformers opted in January 1992 for liberalization at breakneck speed—so-called **shock therapy**, a set of

economic policies adopted by Poland and other former Communist countries.

To implement the plan, the Russians abolished price controls on most consumer goods, with the exception of bread, vodka, oil, and public transportation. The government launched a rapid privatization program, selling formerly state-owned industries and agricultural concerns to private investors. Thousands of factories and mines were turned over to new private companies. In an attempt to share the wealth privatization was expected to generate, each citizen received a voucher worth 10,000 rubles (about $22) to buy stock in these private companies. Ownership of these assets, however, usually remained in the hands of the old bosses—the managers and government officials from the Communist era—undermining the reformers' goal of worker participation.

Instead of reviving production and bringing widespread prosperity, shock therapy brought hardship. Prices immediately soared, increasing by a factor of twenty-six in the course of 1992. Production fell a staggering 20 percent. Nor did the situation stabilize quickly. After 1995 inflation still raged, though at slower rates, and output continued to fall. According to most estimates, Russia produced from one-third to one-half less in 1996 than it had in 1991. The Russian economy crashed again in 1998 in the wake of Asia's financial crisis.

Shock therapy worked poorly for several reasons. Soviet industry had been highly monopolized and strongly tilted toward military goods. Production of many items had been concentrated in one or two gigantic factories or in interconnected combines. With privatization, these powerful state monopolies became powerful private monopolies that cut production and raised prices in order to maximize profits. Moreover, Yeltsin's government handed out enormous subsidies to corporate managers and bureaucrats, ostensibly to reinforce faltering firms and avoid bankruptcies, but also to buy political allegiance. New corporate leaders included criminals who intimidated would-be rivals

Rich and Poor in Postcommunist Russia   A woman sells knitted scarves in front of a department store window in Moscow in September 2005. The collapse of the Soviet Union and the use of shock therapy to reform the Russian economy created new poverty as well as new wealth. (Sovfoto/Universal Images Group/Shutterstock)

TIMELINE

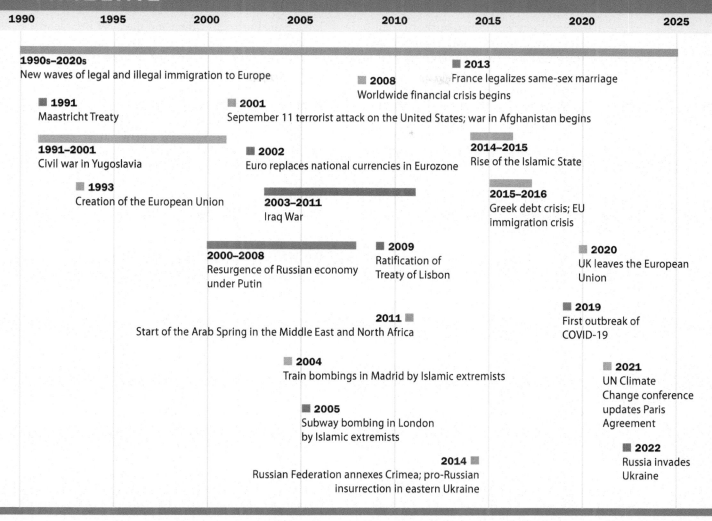

1990   1995   2000   2005   2010   2015   2020   2025

1990s–2020s
New waves of legal and illegal immigration to Europe

2013
France legalizes same-sex marriage

2008
Worldwide financial crisis begins

1991
Maastricht Treaty

2001
September 11 terrorist attack on the United States; war in Afghanistan begins

1991–2001
Civil war in Yugoslavia

2002
Euro replaces national currencies in Eurozone

2014–2015
Rise of the Islamic State

1993
Creation of the European Union

2003–2011
Iraq War

2015–2016
Greek debt crisis; EU immigration crisis

2000–2008
Resurgence of Russian economy under Putin

2009
Ratification of Treaty of Lisbon

2020
UK leaves the European Union

2011
Start of the Arab Spring in the Middle East and North Africa

2019
First outbreak of COVID-19

2004
Train bombings in Madrid by Islamic extremists

2021
UN Climate Change conference updates Paris Agreement

2005
Subway bombing in London by Islamic extremists

2014
Russian Federation annexes Crimea; pro-Russian insurrection in eastern Ukraine

2022
Russia invades Ukraine

---

in attempts to prevent the formation of competing businesses.

Runaway inflation and poorly executed privatization brought a profound social revolution to Russia. The new capitalist elite — the so-called Oligarchs — acquired great wealth and power, while large numbers of people struggled to make ends meet. The Oligarchs, Yeltsin's main supporters, maintained control with corrupt business practices and rampant cronyism.

At the other extreme, the vast majority of people saw their savings become practically worthless. Pensions lost much of their value, living standards drastically declined, and many people sold their personal goods to survive. Under these conditions, effective representative government failed to develop, and many Russians came to equate democracy with the corruption, poverty, and national decline they experienced throughout the 1990s. Yeltsin became increasingly unpopular; only the backing of the Oligarchs kept him in power.

Russian Revival Under Vladimir Putin

This widespread disillusionment set the stage for the rise of Vladimir Putin (POO-tihn) (b. 1952), who was elected president as Yeltsin's chosen successor in 2000 and re-elected in a landslide in March 2004. A colonel in the secret police during the Communist era, Putin maintained relatively liberal economic policies but re-established tight political controls. Critics labeled Putin's system an "imitation democracy," and indeed a façade of democratic institutions masked authoritarian rule.[1] Putin's government stayed in power with rigged elections, a weak parliament, and the intimidation of political opponents. The ongoing distribution of state-owned public assets won the support of the new elite. The Russian president also increased military spending and expanded the secret police.

■ **shock therapy** Economic policies set in place in Russia and some former East Bloc countries after the collapse of communism, through which a quick turn to free markets was meant to speed economic growth.

Putin's government combined authoritarian politics with economic reform. The regime clamped down on the worst excesses of the Oligarchs, lowered corporate and business taxes, and re-established some government control over key industries. Such reforms—aided greatly by high world prices for oil and natural gas, Russia's most important exports—led to a decade of economic expansion, encouraging the growth of a new middle class. In 2008, however, the global financial crisis and a rapid drop in the price of oil caused a downturn, and the Russian stock market collapsed. The government initiated a $200 billion rescue plan, and the economy stabilized and returned to modest growth in 2010.

Throughout his long rule, Putin's government decisively limited political opposition. Though the Russian constitution guaranteed freedom of the press, the government cracked down on the independent media. Using a variety of tactics, officials and progovernment businessmen influenced news reports and intimidated critical journalists. The suspicious murder in 2006 of journalist Anna Politkovskaya, a prominent critic of the government's human rights abuses and its war in Chechnya, and the attempted poisoning and imprisonment of Putin's political rival Alexei Navalny in 2021–2022, were only two of many flagrant attacks on critics of Putin's Russia. Such moves reinforced Western worries that the country was returning to Soviet-style press censorship, but faced with blanket denials there was little the West could do to rein in Russian tactics. (See "Individuals in Society: Alexei Navalny," page 943.)

In foreign relations, Putin led Russia on an ambitious and at times interventionist stance toward the Commonwealth of Independent States, a loose confederation of most of the former Soviet republics. Russia replaced the weak military it had inherited from the U.S.S.R. with an effective force armed with the latest battlefield and cyber-warfare technologies. Further abroad, Putin generally championed assertive anti-Western policies in an attempt to bolster Russia's status as a great Eurasian power and world player. He forcefully opposed the expansion of NATO into the former East Bloc and regularly challenged U.S. and NATO foreign policy goals. In the Syrian civil war that broke out in 2011, for example, Russian backing of Syrian president Bashar al-Assad flew in the face of U.S. attempts to depose him. In a dramatic turn of events, Western security services accused Russia of using social media, fake websites, and stolen e-mails to interfere in the 2016 U.S. presidential elections, as well as Great Britain's 2016 "Brexit" referendum on

leaving the European Union and the 2017 presidential elections in France.

Putin's domestic and foreign policies proved quite popular with a majority of Russians. His housing, education, and health-care reforms significantly improved living standards. Capitalizing on Russian patriotism, Putin repeatedly evoked the glories of Russian history, expressed pride in the accomplishments of the Soviet Union, and downplayed the abuses of the Stalinist system. Putin's carefully crafted manly image and his aggressive international diplomacy soothed the country's injured pride and symbolized its national revival.

Political Instability and Russian Intervention in the Former Soviet Republics

The collapse of the Soviet Union led to the establishment of the Russian Federation and fourteen other newly independent republics, and brought major changes to east-central Europe and south-central Asia (Map 30.1). In some ways, the transformation of this vast and diverse region paralleled the experience of the former East Bloc countries and Russia itself. Though most of the fourteen new republics, which included almost one-half of the former Soviet Union's total population, adopted some sort of market capitalism, political reforms varied broadly. In the Baltic republics, where Gorbachev's perestroika had quickly encouraged powerful separatist movements, reformers established working democratic government. Ukraine, Armenia, Georgia, and Moldova likewise embraced democracy. In Russia, Belarus, Azerbaijan, and the Central Asian republics, systems of "imitation democracy" or outright authoritarian rule took hold. Here former Communist bosses built virtual monarchies, with family members in numerous top positions.

Though Putin encouraged the former Soviet republics to join the Commonwealth of Independent States, a loose confederation dominated by Russia that supposedly represented regional common interests, stability proved elusive. Popular protests and revolts challenged regional politicians and Russian interests alike. In the independent state of Georgia, which won independence when the Soviet Union collapsed in 1991, the so-called Rose Revolution (November 2003) brought a pro-Western, pro-NATO leader to power. In Ukraine, the Orange Revolution (November 2004–January 2005) challenged the results of a national election and expressed popular nationalist desires for more distance from Russia. Similar **Color Revolutions** in Kyrgyzstan and Moldova exemplified the unpredictable path toward democratization in the new republics that bordered the powerful Russian Federation.

■ **Color Revolutions** A series of popular revolts and insurrections that challenged regional politicians and Russian interests in the former Soviet republics during the first decade of the twenty-first century.

Russian politician and dissident Alexei Navalny, cast by *Time* magazine as "the man Putin fears," received a multiyear prison sentence in 2021 on trumped-up charges of corruption and antistate terrorism.* His outspoken criticism of Putin and Russia's authoritarian government brought him worldwide attention and determined attempts by the Russian government to shut him up.

Born in 1976 in a small city southwest of Moscow, Navalny earned a law degree in 1998. In 2000 he married economist Yulia Navalnaya, sometimes labeled the "First Lady" of the Russian democratic opposition because of her prominent role as an activist reformer. In the following decades, Navalny became an increasingly prominent figure in Russian politics. A self-labeled "nationalist democrat," Navalny held positions that were not particularly liberal. He supported cuts in government spending, gun rights, and restrictive immigration policies to prevent Muslims from Central Asia from entering Russia. Putin accused Navalny of right-wing radicalism. Yet Navalny's calls for democracy cemented his reputation as the leading critic of the Putin regime and the ruling United Russia Party, which Navalny nicknamed the "Party of Crooks and Thieves" for its greed and corruption.

In 2011 Navalny founded the Anti-Corruption Foundation (FBK), an activist group dedicated to exposing the self-dealing of Putin's Kremlin cronies. The FBK became famous for its investigations of prominent Russian officials, ranging from members of parliament to Dmitry Medvedev, the Russian prime minister. FBK videos on social media, watched by millions, exposed the wealthy lifestyles of Russian leaders, showing drone footage of their extensive villas and luxury yachts.

In 2013 a criminal court convicted Navalny for embezzling timber, which barred the reformer from running for political office. After the European Court of Human Rights ruled that his trial was unfair, Russia's Supreme Court overturned the conviction. The same year Navalny ran for mayor of Moscow. Putin's chosen candidate won, but Navalny got over 27 percent of the vote, a sign of his growing popularity.

In December 2016 Navalny announced his intention to run for president in the 2018 elections. Russia's election commission barred him from running, and he was arrested again in the summer of 2019. The Russian Ministry of Justice declared the FBK a "foreign agent," and in June 2021 Moscow's City Court forced the group to shut down.

Navalny was no stranger to harsh repression, but it was still a surprise when this famous dissident was the victim of a near-fatal poisoning attempt in August 2020. Navalny recovered in Berlin. He had been poisoned with Novichok, a nerve agent commonly used by the Soviet-era secret police to murder its opponents, which raised suspicions that Putin had ordered the assassination attempt.

Once he recovered in January 2021, Navalny returned to Moscow. He was immediately arrested for violating parole

Alexei Navalny and his wife Yulia (right) join protesters in Moscow at a February 2020 demonstration in memory of murdered Putin critic Boris Nemtsov. (KIRILL KUDRYAVTSEV/AFP/Getty Images)

and sentenced to two and a half years in a labor colony. This move unleashed mass protests across Russia and was condemned by the Western press. Two days later Navalny's supporters released a YouTube video, viewed by millions, that showed drone footage of a lavish palace and other properties purportedly built for Putin on Russia's Black Sea coast; Putin denied any involvement.[†] In prison, Navalny complained of inhumane treatment and went on a three-week-long hunger strike. In February 2022 he was accused of new charges of embezzling campaign donations, and in March he was sentenced to nine additional years in prison.

In prison, Navalny continued to communicate with a group of dissident exiles dedicated to removing Putin from office and bolstering Russian democracy. In 2022, his YouTube channel had 6.25 million subscribers.[‡] While their reach is difficult to evaluate, their struggle exemplifies the ongoing fight for democratic governance in contemporary Russia.

QUESTIONS FOR ANALYSIS

1. Why do you think Navalny returned to Moscow after the assassination attempt?
2. How does Navalny's story exemplify the "imitation democracy" practiced in Putin's Russian Federation?

*Simon Shuster, "The Man Putin Fears: Letter from Alexei Navalny, Russia's Imprisoned Dissident," *Time*, January 19, 2022, https://time.com/6140102/alexei-navalny-russia-profile/.

[†]You can watch this famous video here: https://www.youtube.com/watch?v=ipAnwilMncl.

[‡]Alex Ward, "Alexei Navalny, the Russian Dissident Challenging Putin, Explained," *Vox*, April 23, 2021, https://www.vox.com/22254292/alexei-navalny-prison-hunger-strike-end-russia-protests-vladimir-putin.

MAP 30.1 Russia and the Successor States, 1991–2022 After the failure of an attempt in August 1991 to depose Gorbachev, an anticommunist revolution swept the Soviet Union. The republics that formed the Soviet Union each declared their sovereignty and independence, with Russia, under President Boris Yeltsin, being the largest. Eleven of the fourteen republics then joined with Russia to form a loose confederation called the Commonwealth of Independent States (CIS), but the integrated economy of the Soviet Union dissolved into separate national economies, each with its own goals and policies. Conflict continued to simmer over these goals and policies, as evidenced by the ongoing civil war in Chechnya, the struggle between Russia and Georgia over South Ossetia and Abkhazia, the Russian annexation of Crimea, and the Russian invasion of Ukraine in 2022.

Putin took an aggressive and at times interventionist stance toward anti-Russian revolt in the Commonwealth of Independent States and the Russian borderlands, seeking to rebuild Russian influence in eastern Europe and slow the expansion of NATO. Conflict was intense in the oil-rich Caucasus, where an unstable combination of nationalist separatism and ethnic and religious tensions challenged Russian dominance. Russian troops have repeatedly invaded Chechnya (CHEHCH-nyuh), a tiny Muslim republic with 1 million inhabitants on Russia's southern border that declared its independence in 1991. The cost of the conflict was high. Thousands lost their

lives, and both sides committed serious human rights abuses. Moscow declared an end to military operations in April 2009, and the fighting eventually stopped.

In 2008 Russian troops invaded Georgia to support separatist movements in South Ossetia (oh-SEE-shuh or oh-SET-tia) and Abkhazia (Ahb-KAZ-ee-ah). Both states established breakaway independent republics, recognized only by Russia and a handful of small states.

Revolution broke out again in Ukraine in February 2014. When popular protests brought down the pro-Russian government, Putin sent Russian troops into Crimea, Ukraine's strategically valuable peninsula on the Black Sea where pro-Russian sentiment ran high. The territory, with a major naval base in the city of Sevastopol and a large oil and natural gas company, was incorporated into the Russian Federation. Then, in response to the anti-Russian policies of the new Ukrainian government, in April 2014 a group of armed rebels took over the regional capital Donetsk and other cities in eastern Ukraine and declared the establishment of the separatist, pro-Russian Donetsk and Luhansk "People's Republics" (see Map 30.1). A full-scale military assault by Ukrainian government troops failed to push back or defeat the separatist forces, which were supported by Russian weapons and troops. In response, the United States and the European Union placed economic sanctions on Russia, and a shaky ceasefire was imposed in February 2015.

Tensions flared again when about 150,000 Russian troops invaded Ukraine in February 2022. Putin justified the attack by baselessly proclaiming the need to "denazify" and demilitarize the country. Russian troops made quick territorial gains in the northern, eastern, and southern regions of Ukraine, unleashing the largest refugee crisis since the Second World War: over 11 million Ukrainians were displaced internally and over 4 million left the country to avoid the fighting.

Under President Joe Biden (U.S. pres. 2021–), the United States joined with the EU and other nations to impose harsh sanctions on the Putin regime. Such actions did not stop the war, but they did contribute to the global economic downturn associated with the conflict. Most countries condemned the invasion, although China and India maintained a neutral stance and Iran and Belarus supported Russian goals. NATO members supplied Ukraine with weapons and humanitarian support, but such support was limited by the need to avoid risking a full-scale nuclear war with

Russia. By April 2022 a Ukrainian counteroffensive had forced the Russian army back from the Ukrainian capital Kyiv, and global outrage greeted accounts of atrocities reportedly carried out by Russian forces in Kyiv's suburbs. Yet intense fighting continued in the south and east, especially in Donetsk and Luhansk. The outcome of the conflict remained uncertain, a revealing example of the way Great Power conflicts continued to create instability in the former Soviet republics.

Economic and Political Transformations in the Former East Bloc

Developments in the former East Bloc paralleled those in Russia in numerous ways. The newly independent states replaced Soviet-style planned economies with market-based economic systems and grappled with the geopolitical challenges of the post–Cold War era.

Economic reforms varied from country to country. Encouraged by Western institutions such as the International Monetary Fund and the World Bank, Poland's new leaders were the first in eastern Europe to adopt shock therapy policies. Starting in 1990, the Poles liberalized prices and trade policies, raised taxes, cut state spending to reduce budget deficits, and quickly sold state-owned industries, businesses, and farms to private investors. As they would in Russia a few years later, these radical moves at first brought high inflation and a rapid decline in living standards, which generated public protests and strikes. But because the plan had the West's approval, Poland received Western financial support that eased the pain of transition. In its first five years of reform, Poland created twice as many

Ukrainian Civilians Volunteer to Repel Russian Invasion When Russian troops invaded Ukraine in February 2022, civilians with no military training volunteered to fight back. Here a group of men receive arms at a Ukrainian weapons storage facility on February 25, 2022. (Brendan Hoffman/The New York Times/Redux Pictures)

new businesses as did Russia in a comparable period, despite having only a quarter of Russia's population.

Economic reform and growth varied in the former Communist countries, but most observers agreed that Poland, the Czech Republic, and Hungary were the most successful. Each met the critical challenge of economic reconstruction more successfully than Russia. The reasons for these successes included considerable experience with limited market reforms before 1989, flexibility and lack of dogmatism in government policy, and an enthusiastic embrace of capitalism by a new entrepreneurial class.

In the years that followed 1989, Poland, the Czech Republic, and Hungary also did far better than Russia in creating new civic institutions, legal systems, and independent media outlets that reinforced political moderation and national revival. Lech Wałęsa in Poland and Václav Havel in Czechoslovakia were elected presidents of their countries and proved as remarkable in power as in opposition. After Czechoslovakia's Velvet Revolution in 1989, the Czechoslovak parliament accepted a "velvet divorce" in 1993, when Slovakian nationalists wanted to break off and form their own state, creating the separate Czech and Slovak Republics.

In 1999 Poland, Hungary, and the Czech Republic were accepted into NATO, and in 2004 they and Slovakia gained admission to the European Union; Slovakia joined NATO the same year. Economic growth lagged behind in Romania and Bulgaria but improved after 2000, and both countries joined NATO in 2004 and the EU in 2007.

The social consequences of rebuilding the former East Bloc were similar to those in Russia, though people were generally spared the widespread shortages and misery that characterized Russia in the 1990s. Ordinary citizens and the elderly were once again the big losers, while the young and former Communist Party members were the big winners. Inequalities between richer and poorer regions also increased. Capital cities such as Warsaw, Prague, and Budapest concentrated wealth, power, and opportunity, while provincial centers stagnated and old industrial areas declined. Crime, corruption, and gangsterism increased in both the streets and the executive suites.

Though few former East Bloc residents wanted to return to communism, some expressed longings for the stability of the old system. They missed the guaranteed jobs and generous social benefits provided by the Communist state, and they found the individualism and competitiveness of capitalism cold and difficult. One Russian woman living on a small monthly pension in 2003 summed up the dilemma: "What we want is for our life to be as easy as it was in the Soviet Union, with the guarantee of a good, stable future and low prices — and at the same time this freedom that did not exist before."[2]

The question of whether or how to punish former Communist leaders who had committed political crimes or abused human rights emerged as a pressing issue in the former East Bloc. Germany tried major offenders and opened the records of the East German secret police (the Stasi) to the public, and by 1996 more than a million former residents had asked to see their files.[3] Other countries designed various means to deal with former Communist elites who might have committed crimes, with conservative politicians generally taking a more punitive stand. The search for fair solutions proceeded slowly and with much controversy, a reminder of the troubling legacies of communism and the Cold War.

Civil War in Yugoslavia

Postcommunism turned tragic in Yugoslavia, which under Josip Broz Tito had been a federation of republics under centralized Communist rule. After Tito's death in 1980, power passed increasingly to the sister republics. This process revived regional, religious, and ethnic conflicts that were exacerbated by charges of ethnically inspired massacres during World War II and a dramatic economic decline in the mid-1980s.

The revolutions of 1989 accelerated the breakup of Yugoslavia. Serbian president Slobodan Milošević (1941–2006), a former Communist bureaucrat, wished to strengthen the federation's centralized government under Serbian control. In 1989 Milošević (mee-LOH-sheh-veech) severely limited the right of self-rule in the territory of Kosovo, an autonomous province that was established in the Republic of Serbia after the Second World War. In Kosovo ethnic Albanians constituted the overwhelming majority of residents, but the province included a medieval battleground that nationalists like Milošević claimed was sacred to Serbian identity. Religious differences reinforced ethnic and regional tensions: most Albanians were Muslims, while the vast majority of Serbs were Eastern Orthodox Christians.

In 1990 Milošević called for the unification of all Serbs in a "Greater Serbia," regardless of where they lived in the weakening Yugoslavian federation. This aggressive move strengthened the cause of national separatism, and in June 1991 the relatively wealthy federal republics of Slovenia and Croatia declared their independence. Milošević ordered the Yugoslavian federal army to invade both areas to assert Serbian control. The Serbs were quickly repulsed in Slovenia, but they managed to conquer about 30 percent of Croatia.

In 1992 the civil war spread to Bosnia-Herzegovina, which had also declared its independence. Serbs — about 30 percent of that region's population — refused to live under the more numerous Bosnian Muslims, or

1990 to the present

How did life change in Russia and the former East Bloc countries after 1989?

947

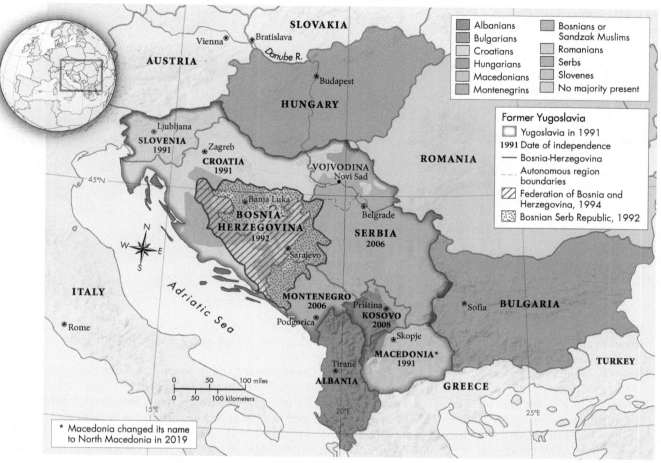

MAP 30.2 The Breakup of Yugoslavia, 1991–2006 Yugoslavia had the most ethnically diverse population in eastern Europe. The Republic of Croatia had substantial Serbian and Muslim minorities, while Bosnia-Herzegovina had large Muslim, Serbian, and Croatian populations, none of which had a majority. In June 1991 Serbia's brutal effort to seize territory and unite all Serbs in a single state brought a tragic civil war.

Bosniaks (Map 30.2). Yugoslavia had once been a tolerant and largely successful multiethnic state with different groups living side by side and often intermarrying. But the new goal of both sides in the Bosnian civil war was **ethnic cleansing**: the attempt to establish ethnically homogeneous territories by intimidation, forced deportation, and killing. The Yugoslavian army and irregular militias in particular attempted to "cleanse" the territory of its non-Serb residents, unleashing ruthless brutality, with murder, rape, destruction, and the herding of refugees into concentration camps. Before the fighting in Bosnia ended, some three hundred thousand people were dead, and millions had been forced to flee their homes.

While appalling scenes of horror not seen in Europe since the Holocaust shocked the world, the Western nations had difficulty formulating an effective, unified response. The turning point came in July 1995 when Bosnian Serbs overran Srebrenica

(sreb-reh-NEET-suh) — a Muslim city previously declared a United Nations safe area. Serb forces killed about eight thousand of the city's Bosniak civilians, primarily men and boys. Public outrage prompted NATO to bomb Bosnian Serb military targets intensively, and the Croatian army drove all the Serbs from Croatia. In November 1995 U.S. president Bill Clinton helped the warring sides hammer out the Dayton Accords, a complicated agreement that gave Bosnian Serbs about 49 percent of Bosnia and gave Bosniaks and the Roman Catholic Bosnian Croats the rest.

The Kosovo Albanians, who hoped to establish self-rule, gained little from the Dayton Accords. Frustrated Kosovar militants formed the Kosovo Liberation Army (KLA) and began to fight for independence. Serbian repression of the Kosovars

■ **ethnic cleansing** The attempt to establish ethnically homogeneous territories by intimidation, forced deportation, and killing.

Srebrenica Refugees More than 2,300 Bosnian Muslims packed into NATO trucks to flee the Serbian encirclement of Srebrenica in the spring of 1995. That July, the Serbian army massacred approximately 8,000 civilians in the city, and outraged public opinion in western Europe and North America finally led to decisive intervention against Serbia. (Michel Euler/ AP Photo)

increased, and in 1998 Serbian forces attacked both KLA guerrillas and unarmed villagers, displacing 250,000 people.

When Milošević refused to withdraw Serbian militias from Kosovo and accept self-government (but not independence) for Kosovo, NATO began bombing Serbia in March 1999. Serbian paramilitary forces responded by driving about 865,000 Albanian Kosovars into exile. NATO redoubled its destructive bombing campaign, which eventually forced Milošević to withdraw and allowed the Kosovars to regain their homeland. A United Nations and NATO peacekeeping force occupied Kosovo, ending ten years of Yugoslavian civil wars. Although U.S.-led NATO intervention finally brought an end to the conflict, the failure to take a stronger stand in the early years led to widespread and unnecessary suffering in the former Yugoslavia.

The war-weary and impoverished Serbs eventually voted the still-defiant Milošević out of office, and in July 2001 a new pro-Western Serbian government turned him over to a war crimes tribunal in the Netherlands to stand trial for crimes against humanity. After blustering his way through the initial stages of his trial, Milošević died in 2006 before the proceedings were complete. In 2008, after eight years of administration by the United Nations and NATO peacekeeping forces, the Republic of Kosovo declared its independence from Serbia. The United States and most states of the European Union recognized the declaration. Serbia and Russia did not, and the long-term status of this troubled emerging state remained uncertain.

How did globalization affect European life and society?

The era of **globalization** that emerged in the last decades of the twentieth century shaped new international economic, cultural, and political networks. Multinational corporations restructured national economies on a global scale, and an array of international governing bodies, such as the European Union, the United Nations, and the World Trade Organization, increasingly set policies that challenged the autonomy of traditional nation-states. At the same time the expansion and ready availability of highly efficient computer and media technologies led to ever-faster exchanges of goods, information, and entertainment around the world.

The Global Economy

Though large business interests had long profited from international trade and investment, multinational corporations grew and flourished in a world economy increasingly organized around free-market neoliberalism, which relaxed barriers to international trade. Multinational corporations built global systems of production and distribution that generated unprecedented wealth and generally escaped the control of regulators and politicians acting on the national level.

Conglomerates such as Siemens and Vivendi exemplified this business model. Siemens, with international headquarters in Berlin and Munich and offices around the globe, is one of the world's largest engineering companies, with vast holdings in energy, construction, health care, financial services, and industrial production. Vivendi, an extensive media and telecommunications company headquartered in Paris, controls an international network of producers and products, including music and film, publishing, television broadcasting, pay-TV, Internet services, and video games.

The development of personal computers and the Internet at the end of the twentieth century, coupled with the deregulation of national and international financial systems, encouraged the growth of international trade. The ability to rapidly exchange information and capital meant that economic activity was no longer centered on national banks or stock exchanges, but rather flowed quickly across international borders. Large cities like London, Moscow, New York, and Hong Kong consolidated their hold on international networks of banking, trade, and financial services. The influence of financial and insurance companies, communications conglomerates, and energy and legal firms headquartered in these global cities extended far beyond the borders of the traditional nation-state.

At the same time, the close connections between national economies also made the entire world increasingly vulnerable to economic panics and downturns. In 1997 a banking crisis in Thailand spread to Indonesia, South Korea, and Japan and then echoed around the world. The resulting slump in oil and gas prices hit Russia especially hard, leading to high inflation, bank failures, and the collapse of the Russian stock market. The crisis then spread to Latin America, plunging most countries there into a severe economic downturn. A decade later in 2008, a global recession triggered by a crisis in the U.S. housing market and financial system created the worst international economic crisis since the Great Depression of the 1930s, followed by yet another worldwide economic slowdown after the outbreak of the COVID-19 pandemic in winter 2020.

The New European Union

Global economic pressures encouraged the expansion and consolidation of the European Common Market, which in 1993 proudly rechristened itself the **European Union (EU)** (Map 30.3). Following the terms of the 1985 Schengen Agreement, the EU added the free movement of capital and services and eventually individuals across national borders to the existing free trade in goods. In addition, member states sought to create a monetary union in which all EU countries would share a single currency. Membership in the monetary union required states to meet strict

financial criteria defined in the 1991 **Maastricht Treaty**, which also set legal standards and anticipated the development of common policies on defense and foreign affairs.

Western European elites and opinion makers generally supported the economic integration embodied in the Maastricht Treaty. They felt that membership requirements, which imposed financial discipline on national governments, would bolster European economies, while the proposed establishment of a single European currency was seen as an irreversible historic step toward basic political unity. This unity would allow Europe as a whole to regain its place in world politics and to deal on equal footing with the United States.

Support for the Maastricht Treaty, however, was hardly universal. Ordinary people, leftist political parties, and right-wing nationalists expressed considerable opposition to the new rules. Many people resented the EU's ever-growing bureaucracy in Brussels, which imposed common standards on everything from cheese production to day care, supposedly undermining national customs and local traditions. Moreover, increased unity meant yielding still more power to distant "Eurocrats" and political insiders, which limited national sovereignty and democratic control.

Above all, many citizens feared that the European Union would operate at their expense. Joining the monetary union required national governments to meet stringent fiscal standards, impose budget cuts, and contribute to the EU operating budget. The resulting reductions in health care and social benefits hit ordinary citizens and did little to reduce high unemployment. When put to the public for a vote, ratification of the Maastricht Treaty was usually very close. In France, for example, the treaty passed with just 50.1 percent of the vote. Even after the treaty was ratified, battles over budgets, benefits, and high unemployment continued throughout the EU in the 1990s.

Then in 2002, brand-new euros finally replaced the national currencies of all Eurozone countries. The establishment of the European monetary union built confidence in member nations and increased their willingness to accept new members. On May 1, 2004, the European Union began admitting its former East Bloc neighbors. This rapid expansion underscored the need to reform the EU's unwieldy governing structure,

---

■ **globalization** A label for the new international economic, cultural, and political connections that emerged in the last decades of the twentieth century.

■ **European Union (EU)** The economic, cultural, and political alliance of twenty-eight European nations.

■ **Maastricht Treaty** The basis for the formation of the European Union, which set financial and cultural standards for potential member states and defined criteria for membership in the monetary union.

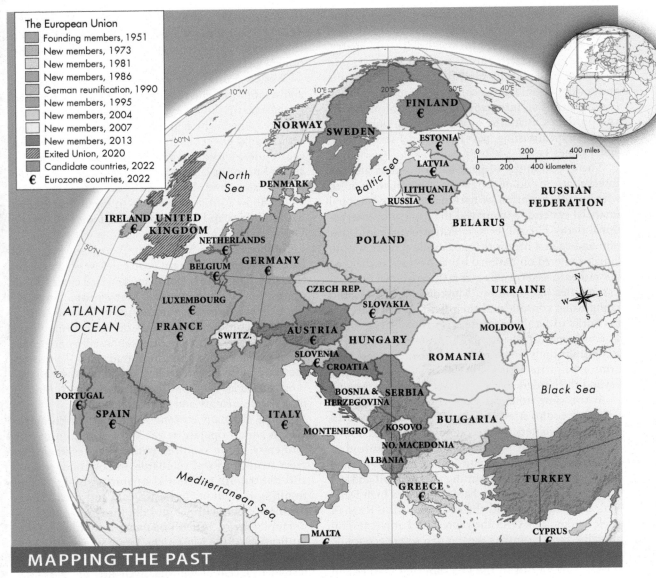

The European Union
- Founding members, 1951
- New members, 1973
- New members, 1981
- New members, 1986
- German reunification, 1990
- New members, 1995
- New members, 2004
- New members, 2007
- New members, 2013
- Exited Union, 2020
- Candidate countries, 2022
- € Eurozone countries, 2022

MAPPING THE PAST

MAP 30.3 The European Union, 2022

No longer divided by ideological competition and the Cold War, much of today's Europe has banded together in a European Union that facilitates the open movement of people, jobs, and currency across national borders.

ANALYZING THE MAP Trace the expansion of membership from its initial founding as the European Economic Union to today. How would you characterize the most recent members? Whose membership is still pending?

CONNECTIONS Which countries are and are not part of the Eurozone, and what does this suggest about how successful the European Union has been in adopting the euro?

and in 2007 the member nations signed the Treaty of Lisbon, which streamlined the EU bureaucracy and reformed its political structure.

When the Treaty of Lisbon went into effect on December 1, 2009, it capped a remarkable fifty-year effort to unify what had been a deeply divided and war-torn continent. By 2019 the EU was home to about 500 million citizens in twenty-eight countries. It included most of the former East Bloc and, with the Baltic nations, three republics of the former Soviet Union. Yet profound questions about the meaning of European unity and identity remained. How would the European Union deal with disruptive membership issues, maintain its democratic ethos in the face of growing right-wing populism, and manage general economic and political crises? We return to these issues later in the chapter.

Supranational Organizations

Beyond the European Union, the trend toward globalization empowered a variety of other supranational organizations that had tremendous reach. National governments still played the leading role in defining and implementing policy, but they increasingly had to take the policies of institutions such as the United Nations and the World Trade Organization into consideration.

The United Nations (UN), established in 1945 after World War II, remains an important player on the world stage. Representatives from all independent countries meet in the UN General Assembly in New York City to try to forge international agreements. UN agencies deal with issues such as world hunger and poverty, and the International Court of Justice in The Hague, Netherlands, hears cases that violate international law. The UN also sends troops in attempts to preserve peace between warring parties—as in Yugoslavia in the 1990s. While the smaller UN Security Council has broad powers, including the ability to impose sanctions to punish uncooperative states and even to endorse military action, its five permanent members—the United States, Russia, France, Great Britain, and China—can each veto resolutions introduced in that body. The predominance of the United States and western European powers on the Security Council has led some critics to accuse the UN of implementing Western neocolonial policies. Others, including U.S. president Donald Trump, have argued that UN policies should never take precedence over national needs, and UN resolutions are at times ignored or downplayed.

Nonprofit international financial institutions have also gained power. Like the United Nations, the World Bank and the International Monetary Fund (IMF) were established in the years following World War II to help rebuild war-torn Europe, and these organizations now provide loans to the developing world. Their funding comes primarily from donations from the United States and western Europe, and they typically extend loans on the condition that recipient countries adopt neoliberal economic reforms, including budget reduction, deregulation, and privatization. In the 1990s the World Bank and the IMF played especially active roles in shaping economic and social policy in the former East Bloc.

The **World Trade Organization (WTO)** is one of the most powerful supranational financial institutions.

It sets trade and tariff agreements for over 150 member countries, thus helping manage a large percentage of the world's import-export policies. Like the IMF and the World Bank, the WTO generally promotes neoliberal policies.

Life in the Age of Social Media

The growing sophistication of rapidly proliferating information technologies has had a profound and rapidly evolving effect on patterns of communications, commerce, politics, and entertainment. As the Internet grew in scope and popularity, more and more people organized their everyday lives around the use of ever-more-powerful high-tech devices.

Leisure-time pursuits were a case in point. Digital media changed popular forms of entertainment and replaced many physical products. The arrival of cable television, followed swiftly by DVDs and then online video streaming, let individuals watch movies or popular television shows on their personal computers or smartphones at any time. Europe's once-powerful public broadcasting systems, such as the BBC, were forced to compete with a variety of private enterprises, including Netflix, a U.S. online video provider that entered the European media market in 2014. Music downloads and streaming audio files replaced compact discs, vinyl records, and cassettes; digital cameras eliminated the need for expensive film; e-book readers and tablets offered a handheld portable library; and smartphone apps provided an endless variety of conveniences and distractions.

Digitalization and the Internet, which began its rapid expansion in the 1980s, transformed familiar forms of communication in a few short decades. Early in the twenty-first century, the evolution of the cell phone into the smartphone, with its multimedia telecommunications features, hastened the change. The growing popularity of communication tools such as e-mail, text messaging, and social media changed the way friends, families, and businesses kept in touch. The launch of the Chinese social media platform TikTok, which allowed users to post short homemade videos, became a sensation among youths across the globe, exemplifying China's controversial push into world markets. The old-fashioned "landline," connected to a stationary telephone, seemed ready to join the vinyl LP and the handwritten letter in the junk bin of history.

Entire industries were dramatically changed by the emergence of the Internet and the giant tech

---

■ **World Trade Organization (WTO)** A powerful supranational financial institution that sets trade and tariff agreements for over 150 member countries and so helps manage a large percentage of the world's import-export policies. Like the IMF and the World Bank, the WTO promotes neoliberal policies around the world.

Life in the Digital Age Attendees at the Mobile World Congress in Barcelona in 2018 react to a virtual reality headset demonstration. The annual conference, which explores the impact of mobile information and artificial intelligence technologies on individuals and businesses, is the world's largest trade fair for wireless industries and a telling example of the way digitalization has transformed everyday life. (Simon Dawson/Bloomberg/Getty Images)

companies Apple, Google, Facebook, Amazon, and Microsoft. With faster speeds and better online security, people increasingly purchased goods from clothes to computers to groceries on the Web. Online file sharing of books and popular music transformed the publishing and music industries, while massive online retailers such as Amazon and eBay, which sell millions of goods across the globe without physical storefronts, undermined local retail outlets.

The rapid growth of the Internet and social media raised complex questions related to politics and personal privacy. (See "Viewpoints: Debating the Impact of Social Media and the Internet," page 953.) Individuals and groups could use social media to organize protest campaigns for social justice. Facebook and Twitter, for example, helped mobilize demonstrators in Egypt during the Arab Spring. Online platforms also provided a ready means for the spread of hate speech and disinformation of all kinds. The Internet thus played a key role in driving political polarization and extremism across the Western world. A number of authoritarian states from North Korea to Iran to Cuba, recognizing the disruptive powers of the Internet, strictly limited online access.

Governments and Web businesses, such as Facebook and Google, regularly used online tracking systems to amass an extraordinary amount of information on individuals, including political and personal activities; this information could be sold for targeted advertising in a system some observers labeled "surveillance capitalism." Hackers also attacked large databases, exposing the private information of millions of people to criminal use. Such abuses of data did not go unchecked. The revelation, for example, that the British consulting firm Cambridge Analytica had acquired the personal data of millions of Facebook users for use in the U.S. 2016 presidential campaign led to a political scandal and calls for tighter regulation of data collection.

In general, online privacy rules developed along with the Internet and were more stringent in Europe than in the United States, as exemplified by the General Data Protection Regulation instituted by the EU in May 2018. According to this broad mandate, tech companies had to clearly describe their information-gathering practices and their use of private data; the new regulations required Internet users to specifically "opt in" before companies could collect their personal data. In the United States, to the contrary, simply clicking on a link generally exposed personal information to website managers. Yet by 2020 the U.S. government followed the EU and attempted to increase regulation of the largest Internet companies. In fall of 2020, for example, the U.S. Justice Department brought an antitrust suit against Google for illegally protecting its market dominance; other antitrust bills followed. Facebook changed its corporate name to Meta in October 2021 and began to place new emphasis on developing virtual products, but such moves hardly stopped regulators from investigating business practices and violations of privacy in the EU and the United States alike.

The vast amount of information circulating on the Internet also led to the exposure of government and business secrets, with mixed results. The classified U.S. National Security Agency information leaked in 2013 by former CIA contractor Edward Snowden embarrassed U.S. diplomats and fueled debates about Internet surveillance, national security, and privacy protection. The materials posted online by the nonprofit organization WikiLeaks, dedicated to the publication of secret information and news leaks, documented numerous examples of government and corporate misconduct. In the U.S. presidential elections of 2016, however, WikiLeaks published e-mails hacked from Hillary Clinton's campaign chairman, leading to accusations of election meddling and ongoing congressional investigations.

The Costs and Consequences of Globalization

Globalization transformed the lives of millions of people, as the technological changes associated with postindustrial society remade workplaces and lifestyles around the world. Widespread adoption of neoliberal

The Internet revolution and the ever-growing popularity of social media brought profound changes and generated intense debates about the potential impacts on people and their relationships. In the selections below, Harvard Law School professor Yochai Benkler emphasizes the creative possibilities supposedly inherent in the emerging digital information networks, a popular stance among early supporters of the Web. Computer scientist and philosopher Jaron Lanier disagrees. By 2010, according to Lanier, the original creativity and room for self-expression associated with the early years of the Internet had been overtaken by crass commercialization, undermining the very meaning of personhood.

Yochai Benkler, from *The Wealth of Networks*, 2006

In the past decade and a half, we have begun to see a radical change in the organization of information production. Enabled by technological change, we are beginning to see a series of economic, social, and cultural adaptations that make possible a radical transformation of how we make the information environment we occupy as autonomous individuals, citizens, and members of cultural and social groups. . . .

These newly emerging practices have seen remarkable success in areas as diverse as software development and investigative reporting, avant-garde video and multiplayer online games. Together, they hint at the emergence of a new information environment, one in which individuals are free to take a more active role than was possible in the industrial information economy of the twentieth century. This new freedom holds great practical promise: as a dimension of individual freedom; as a platform for better democratic participation; as a medium to foster a more critical and self-reflective culture; and, in an increasingly information dependent global economy, as a mechanism to achieve improvements in human development everywhere. . . .

This does not mean that [personal computers and network connections] cannot be used for markets, or that individuals cease to seek market opportunities. It does mean, however, that whenever someone, somewhere, among the billion connected human beings, and ultimately among all those who will be connected, wants to make something that requires human creativity, a computer, and a network connection, he or she can do so—alone, or in cooperation with others. . . . The result is a flourishing nonmarket sector of information, knowledge, and cultural production, based in the networked environment, and applied to anything that the many individuals connected to it can imagine.

Jaron Lanier, from *You Are Not a Gadget*, 2010

Something started to go wrong with the digital revolution around the turn of the twenty-first century. . . . The way the Internet has gone sour . . . is truly perverse. The central faith of the web's early design has been superseded by a different faith in the centrality of imaginary entities epitomized by the idea that the Internet as a whole is coming alive and turning into a superhuman creature. . . . The early waves of web activity were remarkably energetic and had a personal quality. People created personal "homepages," and each of them was different, and often strange. The web had flavor.

Entrepreneurs naturally sought to create products that would inspire demand . . . where there was no lack to be addressed and no need to be filled, other than greed. . . . An endless series of gambits backed by gigantic investments encouraged young people entering the online world for the first time to create standardized presences on sites like Facebook. Commercial interests promoted the widespread adoption of standardized designs like the blog, and these designs encouraged pseudonymity in at least some aspects of their designs, such as the comments, instead of the proud extroversion that characterized the first wave of web culture.

Instead of people being treated as the sources of their own creativity, commercial aggregation and abstraction sites presented anonymized fragments of creativity as products that might have fallen from the sky or been dug up from the ground, obscuring the true sources. . . . The deep meaning of personhood is being reduced by illusions of bits.

QUESTIONS FOR ANALYSIS

1. Compare the arguments presented above. What are the strengths and weaknesses of each? Where are the main sources of disagreement?
2. Drawing on the material above and in this chapter, and in your own experience with the Internet, would you say that Internet technologies lead to more passive or more active social interaction?

Sources: Yochai Benkler, *The Wealth of Networks: How Social Production Transforms Markets and Freedom* (New Haven, Conn.: Yale University Press, 2006), pp. 1–2, 6–7; Jaron Lanier, *You Are Not a Gadget: A Manifesto* (New York: Knopf, 2010), pp. 6, 13–14, 17.

free-trade policies, combined with low labor costs in developing countries — including the former East Bloc, Latin America, and East Asia — made it less expensive to manufacture steel, automotive parts, computer components, and all manner of consumer goods in developing countries and then import them for sale in the West. Many international corporations, seeking to save costs, shifted manufacturing operations — and jobs — from western Europe and the United States to the developing world.

In the 1990s China, with its low wages and rapidly growing industrial infrastructure, emerged as an economic powerhouse that supplied goods across the world as the West's industrial heartlands continued to decline. By the 2010s China had become a global economic superpower and in 2020 replaced the United States as the EU's largest trading partner. Growing bonds between China and other authoritarian states like Russia caused concern in the West, as did China's aggressive foreign policy, particularly in East Asia. For some observers, China's rise and its dismal human rights record posed an economic and military threat to Europe and the United States. Western politicians accused the Chinese government of predatory business practices and the systematic use of cyber hacking to steal intellectual property and mislead public opinion. Anti-China sentiment increased across the West, among ordinary people and leaders alike.

The rise of China as a global industrial leader and the outsourcing of manufacturing jobs from the West

to the East dramatically changed the nature of work in western Europe and North America. In France in 1973, for example, some 40 percent of the employed population worked in industry — in mining, construction, manufacturing, and utilities. About 49 percent worked in services, including retail, hotels and restaurants, transportation, communications, financial and business services, and social and personal services. In 2004 only 24 percent of the French worked in industry, and a whopping 72 percent worked in services. The numbers varied country by country, yet across Europe the general trend was clear: by 2016 only about 15 percent of employed workers were still working in the once-booming manufacturing sector; in the United States, less than 9 percent of workers held such jobs.[4]

The deindustrialization of the West established a multitiered society with winners and losers. At the top was a small, affluent group of experts, executives, and professionals — about one-quarter of the total population — who managed the new global enterprises. In the second, larger tier, the middle class struggled with stagnating incomes and a declining standard of living as once-well-paid industrial workers faced stubborn unemployment and cuts in both welfare and workplace benefits. Many were forced to take low-paying jobs in the retail service sector.

In the bottom tier — in some areas as much as a quarter of the population — a poorly paid underclass performed the unskilled jobs of a postindustrial economy or were chronically unemployed. In western Europe and North America, inclusion in this lowest segment of society was often linked to race, ethnicity, and a lack of educational opportunity. Recently arrived immigrants had trouble finding jobs and often lived in unpleasant, hastily built housing, teetering on the edge of poverty. In London, unemployment rates among youths and particularly young Black men soared above those of their white compatriots. Frustration over these conditions, coupled with anger at a police shooting, boiled over in immigrant neighborhoods across the city in August 2011, when angry youths rioted in the streets, burning buildings and looting stores.

A similar wave of riots broke out in the multiethnic immigrant suburbs of Stockholm, Sweden, in May 2013, spurred by growing economic inequality and discrimination, and in late 2018 protests by so-called Yellow Vests brought street violence to cities across France over economic problems facing the working and middle classes. Police powers generally brought such unrest under control. While parliamentarians recognized that poverty, unemployment, and perceived racism inspired unrest, they struggled to find solutions to problems generated by large-scale economic trends.

Geographic contrasts further revealed the unequal aspects of globalization. Urban redevelopment and

Antiglobalization Activism   French protesters carry the figure of Ronald McDonald through the streets to protest the trial of José Bové, a prominent leader in campaigns against the human and environmental costs associated with globalization. Bové was accused of demolishing a McDonald's franchise in a small town in southern France. With its worldwide fast-food restaurants that pay little attention to local traditions, McDonald's has often been the target of antiglobalization protests. (Witt/Haley/Sipa)

gentrification forced poorer people out of the downtown cores of major Western cities. Regions in the United States and Europe that had successfully shifted to a postindustrial economy, such as Silicon Valley or northern Italy and southern Germany and Austria, enjoyed prosperity. Lagging behind were regions dependent on heavy industry, such as the former East Bloc countries and the factory districts north of London, and historically underdeveloped areas, such as rural sections of southern Italy, Spain, and Greece. In addition, a global north-south divide increasingly separated Europe and North America — both still affluent despite their economic problems — from the industrializing nations of Africa and Latin America. Though India, China, and other East Asian nations experienced solid growth, other industrializing nations struggled to overcome decades of underdevelopment.

How is growing ethnic diversity changing contemporary Europe?

The ethnic makeup of European communities shifted in key ways in the early twenty-first century. Western Europe's remarkable decline in birthrates seemed to predict a shrinking and aging population in the future, yet the peaceful, wealthy European Union attracted rapidly growing numbers of refugees and immigrants from the former Soviet Union and East Bloc, North Africa, and the Middle East. The unexpected arrival of so many newcomers raised perplexing questions about ethnic diversity and the costs and benefits of multiculturalism, exacerbating issues that Europeans had confronted at least since the late nineteenth century.

The Prospect of Population Decline

In 2022 population rates were still growing rapidly in many poor countries but not in the world's industrialized nations. In 2000 families in developed countries had only 1.6 children on average; only in the United States did families have, almost exactly, the 2.1 children necessary to maintain a stable population. In Europe, where birthrates had been falling since the 1950s, national fertility rates ranged from 1.2 to 1.8 children per woman of childbearing age. By 2013 Italy and Ireland, once known for large Catholic families, had each achieved one of Europe's lowest birthrates — a mere 1.3 babies per woman. None of the twenty-eight countries in the EU had birthrates above 2.0; the average fertility rate was about 1.55 children per woman.[5]

If the current baby bust continues, the long-term consequences could be dramatic, though hardly predictable. At the least, Europe's population would decline and age. For example, total German population, barring much greater immigration, would gradually decline from about 83 million in 2019 to about 66 million around 2050.[6] The number of people of working age would fall, and because of longer life spans, nearly a third of the population would be over sixty. Social security taxes paid by the shrinking labor force would need to soar to meet the skyrocketing costs of pensions and health care for seniors — a recipe for generational conflict. As the premier of Bavaria, Germany's biggest state, has warned, the prospect of demographic decline is a "ticking time bomb under our social welfare system and entire economy."[7]

Why, in times of peace, did Europeans fail to reproduce? Studies showed that European women and men in their twenties, thirties, and early forties still wanted two or even three children — like their parents. But unlike their parents, young couples did not achieve their ideal family size. Many families postponed having children in order to finish their education and establish careers. And because balancing a child and a career was more difficult than anticipated, many mothers tended to postpone and eventually forgo having a second child. The better educated and the more economically successful a woman was, the more likely she was to have just one child or no children at all. The uneven, uninspiring European economic conditions since the mid-1970s also played a role. High unemployment fell heavily on young people, especially after the recession of 2008, convincing youths to delay settling down and having children.

By 2013 some population experts concluded that European birthrates had stabilized, though families continued to delay having children. Moreover, the frightening economic implications of dramatic population decline emerged as a major public issue. Some opinion leaders, politicians, and the media started advocating for larger families and proposed policies to provide more support for families with children. Europeans may yet respond with enough vigor to reverse their population decline and avoid societal crisis.

Changing Immigration Flows

As European demographic vitality waned in the 1990s, a new surge of migrants from the former Soviet bloc, Africa, and then the Middle East headed for western Europe. Some migrants entered the

European Union legally, with proper documentation, but undocumented or irregular immigration into the European Union also exploded, as increasing numbers of people were smuggled in despite beefed-up border patrols. Large-scale immigration, both documented and undocumented, emerged as a critical and controversial issue.

The collapse of communism in the East Bloc and civil wars in Yugoslavia drove hundreds of thousands of refugees westward in the 1990s, as did equally brutal conflicts in Somalia. Later, immigration flows shifted to reflect the dislocation that emerged in North Africa and the Middle East in the wake of the U.S.-led invasions of Afghanistan and Iraq, the Arab Spring of 2011, and the war against the Islamic State. Smugglers with a callous disregard for the well-being of their charges demanded thousands of euros to bring undocumented migrants from these troubled regions across the Mediterranean to Greece, Spain, and Italy.

In the summer of 2015, during the height of the Syrian civil war, the migration issue reached crisis proportions. Counting undocumented migrants is always difficult, but estimates suggest that in 2015–2016 more than 2.3 million people, mostly from Syria and Iraq, illegally entered the European Union. Many traveled across Turkey and crossed the Mediterranean Sea to the relatively accessible Greek islands. From there they passed through Serbia into Hungary and then struggled to travel north into more hospitable Austria, Germany, and northern Europe. Others continued to enter the EU from North Africa into Italy or Spain (Map 30.4).

When in 2015 Germany's first woman chancellor, Angela Merkel (r. 2005–2021), responded to the crisis by promising homes for 800,000 migrants and encouraged other EU nations to take a share, tens of thousands of migrants trying to reach Germany choked train and bus stations on the Hungarian-Austrian border. Others languished in quickly established refugee camps built in northern Greece and the Hungarian countryside, and Hungary's anti-immigrant government quickly built a 108-mile razor-wire fence along the border with Serbia to squelch further movement.

The 2015 discovery of seventy-one dead migrants locked in an abandoned truck on an Austrian highway — and the deaths of thousands more who attempted to cross the Mediterranean in rudimentary rubber rafts and leaky boats — underscored the venality of the smugglers and the human costs of uncontrolled immigration. Yet by 2020 the number of annual illegal crossings to Europe had dropped to 114,300, the lowest level in six years and far below the numbers from 2015–2016. In part, the decline reflected the impact of the COVID-19 pandemic, as countries closed borders, placed new restrictions on legal migration, and scaled back programs to care for refugees. Stricter border controls, the growth of popular anti-immigration sentiment across western Europe, and the election of far-right anti-immigrant governments in Hungary and Italy, which moved to close their national borders, contributed to the decline.[8] Nonetheless, European leaders struggled to contain the multiple challenges caused by the largest movement of peoples across Europe since the end of World War II. EU leaders sought to better manage the zone's borders and combat migrant smuggling along irregular routes, while fostering humane pathways to legal migration and asylum.[9]

Why was Europe such an attractive destination for non-European migrants? First, economic opportunity in relatively prosperous western Europe undoubtedly was one attraction. Germans, for example, earned on average three and a half times more than neighboring Poles, who in turn earned much more than people farther east and in North Africa. In 1998 most EU states abolished all border controls; entrance into one country allowed for unimpeded travel almost anywhere

Europe's Refugee Crisis A Kurdish refugee family from northern Iraq seeks shelter in May 2018 in a refugee camp in Thessaloniki, Greece. People in the camp complained about lack of food, water, and a secure place to sleep. At the height of the refugee crisis in the fall and early winter of 2015–2016, about five thousand refugees reached Europe each day. While the number of migrants has declined, the crisis stoked anti-immigrant tensions across Europe and called into question the internal open-border system. (Nicolas Economou/ NurPhoto/Getty Images)

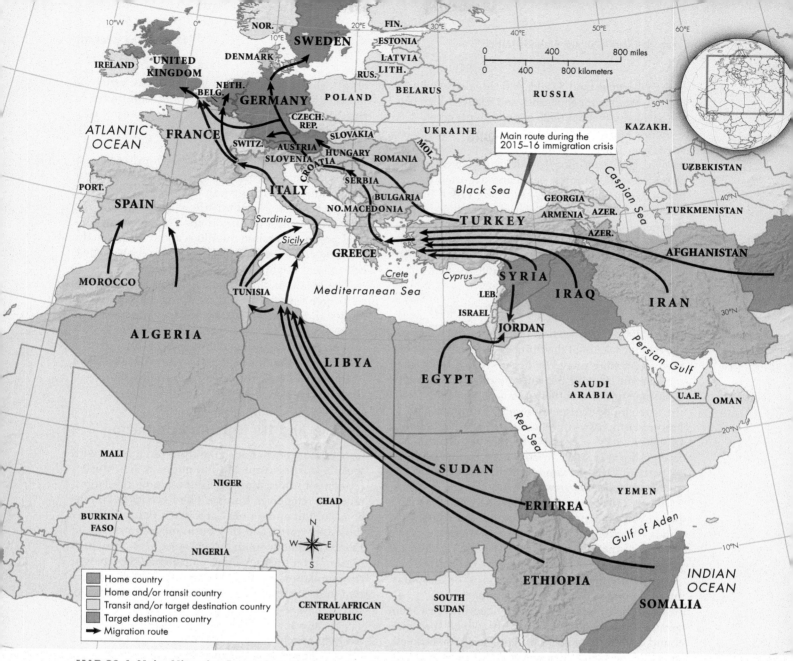

MAP 30.4 Major Migration Routes into Contemporary Europe In the wake of wars and the collapse of the Arab Spring, migration from northern Africa and the Middle East into Europe reached crisis proportions. Aided by smugglers, thousands of migrants traveled two main routes: through Libya and across the Mediterranean Sea into southern Italy, and across Turkey to close-by Greek islands and then north through the Balkans. Wealthy countries with relatively lenient refugee regulations, such as Sweden and Germany, were favorite destinations. Under the Schengen Agreement, the EU's open-border policy made travel through Europe fairly easy. As the number of migrants increased in the fall of 2015 and the spring of 2016, however, European politicians began to close national borders, and many migrants were stranded in hastily built refugee camps.

(though Ireland and the United Kingdom opted out of this agreement). This meant that undocumented migrants could enter across the relatively lax borders of Greece and south-central Europe and then move north across the continent in search of refuge and jobs. And because Europe was simply closer to North Africa and the Middle East than other wealthy countries such as the United States or Japan, it was a more accessible destination for desperate migrants.

Second, EU immigration policy offered migrants the possibility of acquiring asylum status if they could demonstrate that they faced severe persecution based on race, nationality, religion, political belief, or membership in a specific social group in their home countries. Many migrants turned to Europe as they fled civil wars in North Africa and the Middle East, as well as poverty and political repression in other parts of Africa. The rules for attaining asylum status varied by nation, though Germany and Sweden offered relatively liberal policies, housing for applicants, and relatively high benefit payments—about $425 per month per adult.

Across Europe asylum regulations were nonetheless restrictive. Though numerous migrants applied, after an average fifteen-month wait many were rejected, classified as illegal job seekers, and deported to their home countries. The acceptance rate varied broadly across the different countries in the EU, but the total numbers for 2017 offer some insight into the general plight of the refugees. That year EU countries evaluated about 1 million asylum applications and granted about 538,000 people protected residency status.[10]

Toward a Multicultural Continent

By the 2020s immigration had profoundly changed the ethnic makeup of the European continent, though the effects were unevenly distributed. One way to measure the effect of these new immigrants is to consider the rapid rise of their numbers. Since the 1960s the foreign population of western European nations has grown by two to ten times. In the Netherlands in 1960, only 1 percent of the population was foreign-born. In 2017 foreign-born people made up 12 percent. Over the same years the proportion of foreign-born residents grew from 1.2 percent to almost 15 percent in Germany and from 4.7 percent to 12.2 percent in France. In 2017 non-natives constituted about 10 percent of the population, on average, across Europe—though they typically constituted a far smaller share of the former East Bloc nations.[11] These permanently displaced ethnic groups, or diasporas, brought ethnic diversity to the continent.

The new immigrants were divided into two main groups. A small number of highly trained specialists found work in the upper ranks of education, business, and high-tech industries. Engineers from English-speaking India, for example, could land jobs in international computer companies. Most immigrants, however, had little access to high-quality education or language training, which limited their employment opportunities and made integration more difficult. They often lived in separate city districts marked by poor housing and crowded conditions. Districts of London were home to tens of thousands of immigrants from the former colonies, and in Paris North Africans dominated some working-class suburbs.

The **multiculturalism** associated with ethnic diversity inspired a variety of new cultural forms. Recipes and cooks from former colonies in North Africa enlivened French cooking, while the döner kebab—the Turkish version of a gyro sandwich—became Germany's "native" fast food. Indian restaurants proliferated across Britain, and controversy raged when the British foreign minister announced in 2001 that chicken tikka masala—a spicy Indian stew—was Great Britain's new national dish.[12] Multiculturalism also inspired a rich variety of works in literature, film, and the fine arts; from rap to reggae to rai, it had a profound effect on popular music, a medium with a huge audience.

The growth of immigration and ethnic diversity created vital social and cultural interactions and goods but also generated controversy and conflict. In most EU nations, immigrants can become full citizens if they meet certain legal qualifications; adopting the culture of the host country is not a requirement. This legal process has raised questions about who, exactly, could or should be European and about the way these new citizens might change European society.

The idea that cultural and ethnic diversity could be a force for vitality and creativity ran counter to long-standing, deep-seated beliefs about national homogeneity and unity, particularly among political conservatives. Some commentators accused the newcomers of taking jobs and welfare benefits from unemployed native Europeans, especially in times of economic decline.

Europe and Its Muslim Population

General concerns about migration often fused with specific worries about Muslim migrants and Muslim residents born in Europe. Islam is now the largest minority religion in Europe. The EU's 15 to 20 million Muslims outnumber Catholics in Europe's mainly Protestant north, and they outnumber Protestants in Europe's Catholic south. Major cities have substantial Muslim minorities, who make up about 25 percent of the population in Marseilles and Rotterdam, 15 percent in Brussels, and 10 percent in Paris, Copenhagen, and London.[13]

Tensions increased after the September 11, 2001, al-Qaeda attack on New York's World Trade Center, the subsequent war in Iraq, and a string of terrorist attacks in Europe organized by Islamist extremists. In March 2004, radical Moroccan Muslims living in Spain exploded bombs planted on trains bound for Madrid, killing 191 commuters and wounding 1,800 more. A year later, an attack on the London transit system carried out by British citizens of Pakistani descent killed over 50 people. Since then, a number of attacks have kept Islamist terrorism in the public eye—including the murderous January 2015 assault on the staff of the satiric French magazine *Charlie Hebdo*, which had published critical cartoons depicting the Prophet Muhammad, and the even more deadly attacks in Paris in November 2015, when extremists motivated by the ideologies of the Islamic State killed 130 people.

The vast majority of Europe's Muslims support democracy and reject violent extremism, but these spectacular attacks and other assaults by Islamist militants nonetheless sharpened the debate over immigration. Security was not the only issue. Critics across the political

The Changing Face of London's Arsenal Football Club Growing ethnic diversity is transforming many aspects of everyday life in contemporary Europe, including the ethnic makeup of European football (soccer) teams. In 1950 the Arsenal Football Club of northern London was composed entirely of white ethnic Britons (right). In 2018 its diverse roster included players from around the globe (above). (2018 team: David Klein/Cal Sport Media/Newscom; 1950 team: Bob Thomas/Getty Images)

spectrum warned that Europe's rapidly growing Muslim population posed a dire threat to the West's liberal tradition, which embraced freedom of thought, representative government, toleration, separation of church and state, and, more recently, equal rights for women and LGBTQ+ people. Extremists and radical clerics living in Europe, critics proclaimed, rejected these fundamental Western values and preached the supremacy of Islamic laws for Europe's Muslims.

Radical nationalist politicians exploited widespread doubts that immigrant populations from Muslim countries would ever assimilate into Western culture. Time was on the side of Euro-Islam, far-right critics claimed. Europe's Muslim population, estimated at about 26 million in 2016, appeared likely to increase rapidly in the next several decades. Population rates are difficult to predict, but one recent account suggests that in 2050 the share of Muslims in Europe's total population could range from 11 to 14 percent, with the highest percentages in Sweden, Germany, France, and the United Kingdom and much smaller numbers in Spain and east-central Europe.[14]

Liberal pundits and politicians admitted that Islamist extremism could pose problems, but they emphasized the potential benefits of long-term integration of non-Western Muslim residents. They argued that Europe badly needed newcomers to limit the impending population decline, boost social benefit budgets, and provide valuable technical skills. Some asserted that Europe should recognize that Islam has for centuries been a vital part of European life and culture and that mutual respect might help head off the resentment that can drive a tiny minority to separatism and acts of terror.

Liberal commentators also emphasized the role of economics and religious discrimination as the root cause of terrorist activity. Although the first generation of Muslim migrants had found jobs as unskilled workers in Europe's great postwar boom, they and their children had been hard hit after 1973 by the general economic downturn and the decline of manufacturing. Offered only modest welfare benefits and limited access to education or housing, many second- and third-generation Muslim immigrants felt like outcasts in countries where they had lived their entire lives. For liberal observers, economics and discrimination had more influence on immigrants' attitudes about their host communities than did religion and extremist teachings.

■ **multiculturalism** The mixing of ethnic styles in daily life and in cultural works such as film, music, art, and literature.

Terrorist Attacks in Paris, November 2015   At a makeshift memorial made of flowers, candles, and messages left by mourners and passersby, onlookers observe a moment of silence for the victims of the November 13, 2015, terrorist attacks in central Paris. Islamic State jihadists claimed responsibility for the series of coordinated assaults, which killed 130 people and wounded hundreds more at a concert hall (Le Bataclan), restaurants, and the national stadium. (Jacques Demarthon/ Getty Images)

What challenges will Europeans face in the coming decades?

Beyond Russia's interference in former Soviet territories, uncontrolled immigration, and radical Islamic terrorism, European societies faced a number of other interconnected challenges that posed long-term challenges. At the same time, the relative wealth of European societies provoked serious thinking about European identity and Europe's humanitarian mission in the community of nations.

Growing Strains in U.S.-European Relations

In the fifty years after World War II, the United States and western Europe generally maintained close diplomatic relations. Although they were never in total agreement, they usually worked together to promote international consensus, typically under U.S. guidance, as in the NATO alliance. For example, a U.S.-led coalition that included thousands of troops from France and the United Kingdom and smaller contributions from other NATO allies attacked Iraqi forces in Kuwait in the 1990–1991 Persian Gulf War, freeing the small nation from attempted annexation by Iraqi dictator Saddam Hussein. Over time, however, the growing power of the European Union and the new unilateral thrust of Washington's foreign policy created strains in traditional transatlantic relations.

The growing gap between the United States and Europe had several causes. For one, the European Union was now the world's largest trading block, challenging the predominance of the United States. Prosperous European businesses invested heavily in the United States, reversing a decades-long economic relationship in which investment dollars had flowed the other way.

A values gap between the United States and Europe likewise contributed to cooler relations. Ever-more secular Europeans had a hard time understanding the intense religiosity of many Americans; in a 2017 survey, 76 percent of people identifying as Christians in the United States "believe[d] in God with absolute certainty," compared to 23 percent in western Europe.[15] Relatively lax gun control laws and the use of capital punishment in the United States were viewed with dismay in Europe, where most countries had outlawed private handgun ownership and abolished the death penalty. Despite U.S. president Barack Obama's health-care reforms—which evoked controversy among U.S. citizens—the reluctance to establish a single-payer, state-funded program surprised Europeans, who saw their own programs as highly advantageous.

In addition, under Presidents George W. Bush (U.S. pres. 2001–2009), Barack Obama (U.S. pres. 2009–2017), and Donald Trump (U.S. pres. 2017–2021), the United States often ignored international opinion and policy in pursuit of its own interests. This trend had been escalating at least since 1997, when, citing the economic impact, Washington refused to ratify the Kyoto Protocol intended to limit global warming; nearly two hundred countries had already signed off. Nor did the United States join the International Criminal Court, a global tribunal founded in 2002 that prosecutes individuals accused of crimes against humanity, and which nearly 140 states agreed to join. These positions troubled EU leaders, as did unflagging U.S. support for Israel in the ongoing Palestinian-Israeli crisis.

President Trump's policies of "America First" opened further rifts in U.S.-European relations. Trump announced in June 2017 that the United States would withdraw from the Paris Agreement, intended to control climate change, and his willingness to set tariffs on European imports upset familiar patterns of international trade. When criticized, the U.S. president tweeted blistering attacks on European politicians, including German chancellor Angela Merkel and French president Emmanuel Macron (pres. 2017–). Although U.S. president Joe Biden rejoined the Paris Agreement and promised closer ties, European leaders remained uncertain about the long-term reliability of U.S. foreign policy.

Military considerations further undermined the close relationship between the United States and Europe. U.S.-led wars in Afghanistan and Iraq, undertaken in response to the September 11 terrorist attacks against the United States, were a source of strain. On the morning of September 11, 2001, passenger planes hijacked by terrorists destroyed the World Trade Center towers in New York City and crashed into the Pentagon. Perpetrated by the radical Islamist group al-Qaeda, the attacks took the lives of more than three thousand people from many countries and put the personal safety of ordinary citizens at the top of the West's agenda.

Immediately after the September 11 attacks, the peoples and governments of Europe and the world joined Americans in heartfelt solidarity. Over time, however, tensions between Europe and the United States re-emerged and deepened markedly, particularly after President Bush declared a unilateral U.S. **war on terror**—a determined effort to fight terrorism in all its forms around the world. The wars against Afghanistan (2001–2021) and Iraq (2003–2011) exemplified Bush's war on terror. Both brought down dictatorial regimes, but they also fomented anti-Western sentiment in the Muslim world and encouraged regional violence driven by ethnic and religious differences.

Some European leaders, notably in France and Germany, questioned the rationale for and indeed the very effectiveness of a "war" on terror. Military victory, even over rogue states, would hardly end terrorism, since terrorist groups easily moved across national borders. Terrorism, they concluded, was better fought through police and intelligence measures. Europeans certainly shared U.S. worries about stability in the Middle East, and they faced their own problems with Islamist terrorist attacks. But European leaders worried that the tactics

used in the Iraq War, exemplified by Washington's readiness to use its military without international agreements or UN backing, violated international law.

Tensions over military issues revived under President Trump, who repeatedly derided NATO as an obsolete alliance and pressured European members to do more to support NATO budgets. In response, some European politicians argued that the EU should determine its own military and defense policy without U.S. or NATO guidance. President Biden again reversed course, however, and expressed strong support for the NATO alliance. When Russian troops invaded Ukraine in 2022, the United States and its NATO allies in Europe joined together to express support for Ukraine and impose significant economic sanctions on Russia. Transatlantic ties remained firm, although the future of U.S.-European relations was difficult to predict.

Turmoil in the Muslim World

Over the past decades, Western intervention, civil wars, and flagging political and economic stability have shaken much of the Muslim world in North Africa and the Middle East and given rise to radical political Islam. In many ways, these trends drew from a deep history that included the legacies of European colonialism, Cold War power plays, and the ongoing Palestinian-Israeli conflict. Yet more recent events intensified the tumult in North Africa and the Middle East.

As the western European powers loosened their ties to the Middle East after World War II, the United States stepped in. Applying containment policy to limit the spread of communism and eager to preserve steady supplies of oil, the United States supported secular, authoritarian regimes friendly to U.S. interests in Egypt, Saudi Arabia, Iran, and elsewhere. Such regimes were generally unpopular with local residents.

U.S. policies in the Middle East produced "blowback"—unforeseen and unintended consequences. One example was the Iranian revolution of 1979, when Islamist radicals, antagonized by Western intervention, state corruption, and secularization, overthrew the U.S.-supported shah and established an Islamic republic. The successful revolution encouraged militant Islamists elsewhere, as did the example of the mujahideen, the Muslim guerrilla fighters in Afghanistan who successfully fought off the Soviet army from 1979 to 1989. During that conflict, the United States supplied the mujahideen with military aid as part of Cold War containment policies, but this support also generated blowback. Many of the U.S.-armed mujahideen would go on to support the Taliban, a militant Islamist faction that came to rule Afghanistan in 1996. The Taliban established a strict Islamist state based on shari'a, Islamic

---

■ **war on terror** American policy under President George W. Bush to fight global terrorism in all its forms.

religious law. They denied women's right to education, banned Western movies and music, and provided a safe haven for Saudi-born millionaire Osama bin Laden's al-Qaeda terrorist network.

During the 1990s the United States and western Europe became the main targets for Islamist militants angered by Western intervention in the Middle East; al-Qaeda's attack on the World Trade Center was one tragic result. The Bush administration hoped that the invasions of Afghanistan and Iraq would end the terrorist attacks and bring peace and democracy to the Middle East, but both brought chaos instead. The military campaign in Afghanistan quickly defeated the Taliban, and the United States installed a friendly government. But U.S. troops failed to disable al-Qaeda, and Taliban insurgents mounted a determined and lasting guerrilla war. Although U.S. commandos killed Osama bin Laden in Pakistan in May 2011, the apparently unwinnable guerrilla war in Afghanistan became increasingly unpopular in the United States and among NATO allies in Europe. U.S. forces withdrew in August 2021, ending the longest war in U.S. history. The Taliban then immediately returned to power, underscoring the difficulty faced by U.S. attempts to enact lasting change in the Middle East.

With heavy fighting still under way in Afghanistan in late 2001, the Bush administration turned its attention to Saddam Hussein's Iraq, arguing that it was necessary to expand the war on terror to other hostile regimes in the Middle East. U.S. leaders' claims that Hussein was developing weapons of mass destruction turned out to be false. Yet even though they failed to win UN approval, in March 2003 the United States and Britain, with token support from a handful of other European states, invaded Iraq.

The invasion quickly overwhelmed the Iraqi army, and Saddam's dictatorship collapsed in April. Yet America's subsequent efforts to establish a stable pro-American Iraq proved difficult. Poor postwar planning and management by administration officials undermined U.S. attempts at nation building. In addition, Iraq, a creation of Western imperialism after the First World War, was a fragile state with three distinct groups: non-Arab Kurds, Arab Sunni Muslims, and Arab Shi'ite Muslims. Sectarian conflicts among these groups led to a protracted civil war. Although the Obama administration withdrew U.S. forces in 2011, the shaky Iraqi government continued to struggle with ethnic divisions and terrorist violence.

In early 2011 an unexpected chain of events that came to be called the **Arab Spring** further destabilized the

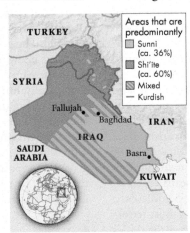

Iraq, ca. 2010

Middle East and North Africa. In a provincial town in Tunisia, Mohamed Bouazizi, a poor fruit vendor, set himself on fire to protest official harassment. His death eighteen days later unleashed a series of spontaneous mass protests that brought violence and regime change; six weeks later, Tunisia's authoritarian president fled the country, opening the way for reform.

Massive popular demonstrations calling for democratic government and social tolerance broke out across the Middle East. In Egypt, demonstrators forced the resignation of President Hosni Mubarak, a U.S.-friendly leader who had ruled for thirty years. An armed uprising in Libya, supported by NATO air strikes, brought down the dictatorial government of Muammar Gaddafi that October. A civil war broke out in Syria in July 2011, when President Bashar al-Assad (elected 2000), with Russian support, hurled his army at the rebels and Western powers disagreed about what to do. Protests arose in other countries in the region as well, evoking a mixed response of repression and piecemeal reform.

As the popular movements inspired by the Arab Spring faltered, the emergence of the **Islamic State** (sometimes called IS or ISIS) brought insurgent violence to new heights. The Islamic State, an extremist Islamist militia dedicated to the establishment of a new caliphate to unify Muslims around the world, grew out of al-Qaeda and the various other insurgent groups fighting in Iraq and the Syrian civil war. By summer 2015 IS soldiers had taken control of substantial parts of central Syria and Iraq. Over 4 million Syrians and Iraqis lost their homes during the fighting, and hundreds of thousands streamed north in attempts to find asylum in Europe.

In the territories under their control, IS militants set up a terroristic government based on an extremist reading of shari'a law. Islamic State terror tactics included the violent persecution of sectarian religious groups; mass executions and beheadings of military, political, or sectarian enemies; and the "cultural cleansing" (destruction and looting) of ancient cultural monuments and shrines that failed to meet its stringent religious ideals. All these actions were documented in widespread Internet propaganda campaigns intended to demonstrate IS power and entice recruits.

By 2019 the U.S. military and its allies had defeated the Islamic State in the field, yet the militant group could still mount isolated terrorist attacks across the globe, and much of the Middle East was still struggling to find peace and stability. The Arab Spring was, for the most part, a dismal failure. The young activists who sought political reforms quickly lost control of the changes they unleashed. Multiple players now vied for power: military leaders and old elites, local chieftains representing ethnic or sectarian interests, and moderate and radical Islamists. In Egypt, the first open elections in decades brought to power representatives of the moderate wing of the Muslim Brotherhood; a year later, military leaders overthrew this elected government. In Libya, Syria, and Yemen, persistent civil wars continued.

Western and especially U.S. policymakers grappled in vain for effective ways to help bring order to the region, even as their own policies contributed to the turmoil. Their efforts were especially freighted because problems in the Muslim world were at the center of many of Europe's problems. These included the immigration emergency of 2015–2016, ongoing Islamist terrorist attacks, and the disastrous human rights crisis faced by millions of Middle East residents.

The Global Recession and the Viability of the European Union

While chaos in the Muslim world caused concern in the West, economic crisis shattered growth and political unity in Europe and North America. In 2008 the United States entered a deep recession, caused by the burst of the housing boom, bank failures, and an overheated financial securities market. The U.S. government spent massive sums to recharge the economy, giving banks, insurance agencies, auto companies, and financial services conglomerates billions of dollars in federal aid. By 2012 the economy had improved and much of the housing market had recovered, though some critics claimed that income inequality was higher than ever.

The 2008 recession swept into other parts of the world and across Europe, where a housing bubble, high national deficits, and a weak bond market made the crisis particularly acute. One of the first countries affected, and one of the hardest hit, was Iceland, where the currency and banking system collapsed outright. Other countries followed—Ireland and Latvia made deep and painful cuts in government spending to balance national budgets. By 2010 Britain was deeply in debt, and Spain, Portugal, and especially Greece were close to bankruptcy.

This sudden "euro crisis" put the very existence of the Eurozone in question. The common currency grouped together countries with vastly divergent economies. Germany and France, the zone's two strongest economies, felt pressure to provide financial support to ensure the stability of far weaker countries, including Greece and Portugal. They did so with strings attached: recipients of EU support were required to reduce deficits through austerity measures. Even so, the transfer of monies within the Eurozone angered the citizens of wealthier countries, who felt they were being asked to subsidize countries in financial difficulties of their own making. Such feelings

were particularly powerful in Germany, encouraging Chancellor Merkel to move cautiously in providing financial stimulus to troubled Eurozone economies.

The difficulty dealing with the stubborn Greek debt crisis prompted debates about the viability of a single currency for nations with vastly different economies as well as widespread speculation that the Eurozone might fall apart. In 2010 and 2012 Greece received substantial bailouts from the IMF, the European Common Bank, and the European Union (the so-called Troika). In return for loans and some debt relief, the Troika required Greece to implement a painful austerity plan—which meant raising taxes, privatizing state-owned businesses, reforming labor markets, and drastically reducing government spending on popular social benefits. Greek unemployment hit a record 25 percent in 2012, and more than half of young adults lacked jobs. Rampant joblessness meant declining tax revenues, and the Greek economy continued to weaken. As the government cut popular social programs, demonstrators took to the streets to protest declining living standards and the lack of work; in Athens, protests large and small were almost a daily occurrence.

The 2015 Greek elections brought the left-wing, populist Syriza Party to power. Syriza promised voters a tough stand against the Troika's fiscal demands and an end to austerity, yet Troika negotiators, led by Germany, maintained an uncompromising line: if Greece failed to meet its debt payments, it would be forced into a "Grexit" (a Greek exit from the Eurozone). Syriza backtracked and accepted further austerity measures in return for yet another bailout loan. Among other conditions, Greek leaders promised to sell off about 50 billion euros' worth of government-owned property, including airports, power plants and energy assets, roads and railroads, and the national post office. (See "Evaluating Written Evidence: The Thessaloniki Programme," page 964.)

Even as the Greek crisis shook European unity, in June 2016 residents of the United Kingdom narrowly voted to leave the EU altogether. The campaign for the referendum on **Brexit** (the informal name for the British exit from the EU) was intense, with populists on the right promising "Leavers" autonomy from the EU's economic and trade ties and freedom from the EU's relatively open immigration policies. The victory of those wanting out showed that many Brits did not

---

■ **Arab Spring** A series of popular revolts in several countries in the Middle East and North Africa that sought an end to authoritarian, often Western-supported regimes.

■ **Islamic State** A radical Islamist militia in control of substantial parts of central Syria and Iraq, where it applies an extremist version of shari'a law.

■ **Brexit** The informal name for Great Britain's exit from the European Union.

The Thessaloniki Programme

Under the leadership of soon-to-be Greek prime minister Alexis Tsipras, in September 2014 the left-wing Syriza Party unanimously adopted the Thessaloniki Programme, which fundamentally challenged demands for neoliberal reform. The reformist manifesto called for a "European Debt Conference" to write down Greece's public debt and end the austerity policies enforced by bailout deals with the EU, and it announced a series of measures to grow the Greek economy. In elections in January 2015, Syriza took power from the center-right government led by Prime Minister Antonis Samaras. Though Tsipras boldly announced that the terms of the Programme were "non-negotiable," in July 2015 his government accepted a new EU bailout and a new round of strict austerity requirements.

~

We demand immediate parliamentary elections and a strong negotiation mandate with the goal to:

Write-off the greater part of public debt's nominal value so that it becomes sustainable in the context of a "European Debt Conference." It happened for Germany in 1953. It can also happen for the South of Europe and Greece.

Include a "growth clause" in the repayment of the remaining part so that it is growth-financed and not budget-financed.

Include a significant grace period ("moratorium") in debt servicing to save funds for growth.

Exclude public investment from the restrictions of the Stability and Growth Pact.

A "European New Deal" of public investment financed by the European Investment Bank.

Quantitative easing by the European Central Bank with direct purchases of sovereign bonds.

Finally, we declare once again that the issue of the Nazi Occupation forced loan from the Bank of Greece is open for us. Our partners know it. It will become the country's official position from our first days in power.

On the basis of this plan, we will fight and secure a socially viable solution to Greece's debt problem so that our country is able to pay off the remaining debt from the creation of new wealth and not from primary surpluses, which deprive society of income.

With that plan, we will lead with security the country to recovery and productive reconstruction by:

Immediately increasing public investment by at least €4 billion.

Gradually reversing all the Memorandum injustices.

Gradually restoring salaries and pensions so as to increase consumption and demand.

Providing small and medium-sized enterprises with incentives for employment, and subsidizing the energy cost of industry in exchange for an employment and environmental clause.

Investing in knowledge, research, and new technology in order to have young scientists, who have been massively emigrating over the last years, back home.

Rebuilding the welfare state, restoring the rule of law and creating a meritocratic state.

We are ready to negotiate and we are working towards building the broadest possible alliances in Europe.

The present Samaras government is once again ready to accept the decisions of the creditors. The only alliance which it cares to build is with the German government.

This is our difference and this is, at the end, the dilemma:

European negotiation by a SYRIZA government, or acceptance of the creditors' terms on Greece by the Samaras government.

EVALUATE THE EVIDENCE

1. How did the Thessaloniki Programme challenge the economic policies promoted by international organizations like the European Union and the International Monetary Fund?
2. Why did Tsipras and the Syriza Party drop these demands? How do you think the Greek public responded to that action?

Source: "Syriza: The Thessaloniki Programme," Syriza, https://www.syriza.gr/article/id/59907/SYRIZA---THE-THESSALONIKI-PROGRAMME.html.

---

want "Eurocrats" in Brussels intruding on national policy. The debates helped elect Prime Minister Boris Johnson in 2019. A Tory (Conservative Party) politician often compared to Donald Trump, Johnson championed the supposed benefits of a rapid break with the EU.

Once implemented on January 1, 2021, Brexit brought major changes. The EU lost its second-largest economy and a major contributor to EU budgets. The U.K. would no longer have to set numerous laws and policies in accordance with EU rules and regulations, including international trade, immigration, and fishing rights. U.K. citizens could no longer freely cross EU borders or take jobs in other EU countries without residency permits. Under the terms of the Brexit deal negotiated between the EU and the U.K., goods could cross the U.K. border without added taxes or tariffs. But new customs requirements meant backups at border crossings and supply-chain delays, and sales of British-made goods plummeted in Europe. In 2022, a lasting solution to the open border between Ireland (part of the EU) and Northern Ireland (part of the U.K.) was still elusive.

The New Populism

One of the most significant aspects of Western politics after the turn of the century was the emergence of new forms of political populism in Europe and the United States. Populism, identified in the United States with President Trump, is typically based on an appeal to the needs and virtues of ordinary people, who stand in determined opposition to a corrupt or exploitative elite and the broad effects of globalization.

In the 2000s powerful populist voices and political parties emerged on both sides of the political spectrum. On the left, the Greek Syriza Party, with its challenge to EU austerity policies, calls for increased public investment, and celebration of the ordinary worker, exemplified leftist populism in Europe. In the United States leftist populism found expression in the Occupy movement, which began in the United States in 2011 and quickly spread to over eighty countries before it fizzled out.

The new populism has had a greater impact on the politics of the far right. In the United States, New York businessman Donald Trump rode a wave of populist sentiment to win the presidency in 2016, surprising pollsters and complacent Democrats alike. Drawing on themes articulated by the Tea Party, which emerged in 2009, Trump's winning platform called for an end to oppressive taxation, strong immigration controls, the relaxation of government regulation of the economy and environment, support for fading rustbelt industries and jobs, and a foreign policy that put "America First."

In Europe, although far-right populist parties, including the French National Front (renamed the National Rally in 2018) and the Austrian Freedom Party, had already enjoyed electoral success in the 1990s, right-wing populism has grown dramatically in recent decades. European populists typically oppose membership in the European Union and the Eurozone. They champion nationalism, demand an end to immigration and tolerant refugee policies, and decry the growth of Islam in Europe. Whatever the cause, the number of Europeans voting for populists on the left and the right swelled from 7 percent in 2000 to over 25 percent in 2018.[16]

In Germany, for example, tens of thousands of people joined the anti-immigrant movement called Pegida (Patriotic Europeans Against the Islamization of the West) or the Alternative for Germany (AfD), a far-right political party that won about 10 percent of the vote in the 2021 federal elections. In Britain, an upstart populist movement including far-right members of the Tory Party successfully campaigned for Brexit. (See "Evaluating Visual Evidence: 'John Bull' Supports Brexit," page 966.) In both Italy and Austria,

government coalitions in 2019 included populist parties. In the United States, the willingness of far-right supporters to challenge the liberal rule of law was revealed on January 6, 2021, when a group of pro-Trump protesters stormed the U.S. Capitol building in an attempt to overturn the results of the presidential election, which Trump lost to Joe Biden.

In the former East Bloc, right-wing populism has been especially strong: in 2018, populist, authoritarian governments ruled Poland and Hungary, where they worked to undermine freedom of the press and judicial independence. Hungary under Prime Minister Viktor Orban exemplified the trend. Openly calling for the construction of an "illiberal democracy," Orban introduced a new constitution that violated EU principles, clamped down on press freedoms, demonized LGBTQ+ people, and overhauled the court system to preserve conservative power. Orban's criticism of immigration and the EU apparently appealed to Hungarian voters, since he easily won a fourth term in April 2022 elections. At the same time, EU leaders struggled to find ways to encourage — or force — Hungary and Poland to adhere to EU conventions with little success, further revealing cracks in the façade of EU unity.

Far-right populist success has been aided by bigotry and widespread misconceptions about immigration and the nature of Muslim faith. Polls show that Europeans routinely overestimate the number of Muslims in Europe. In France, for example, the public believed that 31 percent of the population is Muslim, when the actual number is about 8 percent.[17] Immigration and the supposed "Islamization" of Europe, along with fundamentalist terrorism, have become highly charged political issues, and conservative and far-right pundits and politicians across Europe offer a variety of diagnoses of and solutions to these perceived problems. (See "Thinking Like a Historian: The Conservative Reaction to Immigration and Islamist Terrorism," page 968.)

As the political fringe grows in power, support for traditional centrist parties has shrunk, remaking the political structures that emerged in the post–World War II decade. Center-right parties certainly suffered, but the real losers have been Europe's social democratic parties. In fall 2018, center-left social democrats were included in only six governments in the twenty-eight EU member states. In 2017 the center-left French Socialist Party received just 7.4 percent in national elections, and the Dutch Labour Party won 5.7 percent. That same year Germany's once-mighty Social Democrats received just over 20 percent of the vote in the national elections, only one-half of what they won in 1998.[18] The outcome of these trends remains unclear. Yet the consensus politics shaped around neoliberal socioeconomic policies, state-sponsored benefits, multiculturalism and (relatively) open borders,

"John Bull" Supports Brexit

In a referendum in June 2016, 51.89 percent of residents of the United Kingdom voted to leave the European Union. After various setbacks and negotiations, on January 1, 2021, the plan was carried out. The pro- and anti-Brexit campaigns were bitter and hard fought. In this photo, a pro-Brexit supporter dressed as John Bull, the traditional personification of England and the U.K., calls for an accelerated exit from the EU.

EVALUATE THE EVIDENCE

1. Why would the protester include references to Great Britain in 1940, along with pictures of Winston Churchill (who was prime minister during World War II) at the bottom of his flag?
2. How does the protester use familiar symbols of British pride and power to attract attention and make his case?

(Nick Maslen/Alamy Stock Photo)

and the EU project itself—embraced by center-left and center-right parties alike—no longer had much appeal to voters shaken by sweeping social change, economic stagnation, and mass migration.

The COVID-19 Pandemic

Although other viral pandemics have traversed the globe in the last decades, the outbreak of the COVID-19 pandemic has had particularly damaging effects. The virus causes severe respiratory disease that has often proven deadly, overwhelming hospitals and clinics. Its multiple variants, including Delta and Omicron, are highly contagious.

COVID-19 emerged in Wuhan province in China in 2019, and it then spread quickly around the world. In Europe, northern Italy was hit first, and by March 2020 the virus was basically everywhere. Health departments struggled to find ways to slow its spread, including masking, social distancing, and full-scale shutdowns of public events and gathering spaces. The quick development and release of vaccines helped limit the virus's impact, at least to some extent. At the same time, governments across Europe and North America pumped money into programs designed to address COVID-related unemployment and health needs. Even so, the disruptions caused by the virus led to supply-chain breakdowns and a global economic downturn.

Managing COVID quickly turned political. In general, conservatives favored fewer restrictions while liberals sought more thorough controls. Such differences led to popular protests against government-mandated attempts to manage the pandemic. In Germany, for example, anti-vaxxers, neo-Nazis, and members of the AfD party led demonstrations against government shutdowns in 2020. And in February 2022, Canadian truck drivers used their trucks to barricade the Canadian-U.S. border in an effort to force the government to relax stringent restrictions.

From 2020 until the present, major waves of infection have continued to evade the most determined efforts to control the pandemic. In 2022, after more than 1 million U.S. citizens had died of the disease, many people had accepted that the virus would become endemic, a recurring and severe but manageable illness.

Dependence on Fossil Fuels, Climate Change, and Environmental Degradation

One of the most significant long-term challenges facing Europe and the world in the early twenty-first century was the need for adequate energy resources. Maintaining standards of living in industrialized countries and modernizing the developing world required extremely high levels of energy use, and supplies were heavily dependent on fossil fuels: oil, coal, and natural gas. In 2011 Europe had about 12 percent of the world's population but annually consumed about 34 percent of the world's natural gas production, 22 percent of oil production, and 13 percent of coal output. Scientists warned that such high levels of usage were unsustainable over the long run and predicted that fossil fuel supplies will eventually run out, especially as the countries of the developing world—including giants such as India and China—increased their own rates of consumption.[19]

Struggles to control and profit from these shrinking resources often resulted in tense geopolitical conflicts. The need to preserve access to oil, for example, has led to a transformation in military power in the post–Cold War world. Between 1945 and 1990 the largest areas of military buildup were along the iron curtain in Europe and in East Asia, as U.S. forces formed a bulwark against the spread of communism.

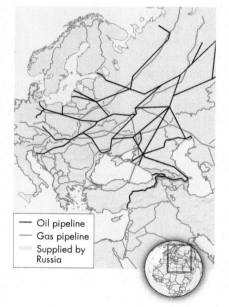

Primary Oil and Gas Pipelines to Europe, ca. 2005

— Oil pipeline
— Gas pipeline
　 Supplied by Russia

Today military power is increasingly concentrated in oil-producing areas such as the Middle East, which holds about 65 percent of the world's oil reserves. One scholar labeled conflicts in the Persian Gulf and Central Asia "resource wars" because they were fought, in large part, to preserve the West's access to the region's energy supplies.[20]

Beyond questions of supply, dependence on fossil fuels has led to serious environmental problems. Burning oil and coal releases massive amounts of carbon dioxide (CO_2) into the atmosphere, the leading cause of **climate change**, or global warming. While the future effects of climate change are difficult to predict, the vast majority of climatologists agree that global warming is proceeding far more quickly than previously predicted and that some climatic disruption is now unavoidable. Rising average temperatures already play havoc with familiar weather patterns, driving wildfires, melting glaciers and polar ice packs, and drying up freshwater resources. Moreover, in the next fifty years rising sea levels may well flood low-lying coastal areas around the world.

Environmental degradation encompasses a number of problems beyond climate change. Overfishing and toxic waste threaten the world's oceans and freshwater lakes, which once seemed to be inexhaustible sources of food and drinking water. The disaster that resulted when an offshore oil rig exploded in the Gulf of Mexico in April 2010, spewing millions of gallons of oil into the gulf waters, underscored the close connections between energy consumption and water pollution. Deforestation, land degradation, soil erosion, and overfertilization; species extinction related to habitat loss; the accumulation of toxins in the air, land, and water; the disposal of poisonous nuclear waste—all will continue to pose serious problems in the twenty-first century.

Since the 1990s the EU has spearheaded efforts to control energy consumption and contain climate change. EU leaders have imposed tight restrictions on CO_2 emissions, and Germany, the Netherlands, and Denmark have become world leaders in harnessing alternative energy sources such as solar and wind power. Despite these and other measures, the overall effort to control energy consumption

---

■ **climate change** Changes in long-standing weather patterns caused primarily by carbon dioxide emissions from the burning of fossil fuels.

The Conservative Reaction to Immigration and Islamist Terrorism

The impact of immigration on European values and society, the connections between immigration and Islamist terrorism, and the best means to stop terrorist attacks are among the most critical and controversial issues in contemporary Europe. In these selections, conservative politicians offer their diagnoses and prescriptions. What are the main problems, according to these leaders? What solutions do they propose?

1 **Immigration and the German welfare state.** Former Social Democratic senator and German central bank board member Thilo Sarrazin's bestselling book *Germany Does Itself In* (2010), a radical critique of the Muslim presence in Germany, generated heated controversy. Sarrazin explained his views in an interview with the newspaper *Kurier*.

KURIER: What does [Germany's national debt crisis] have to do with immigration?

SARRAZIN: At this time in Berlin there is massive influx of Roma and Bulgarian Turks. In 2014 they will all have permanent residence rights and a claim on the German benefits system. It won't work, financing the growing burdens of demographic aging as well as further uncontrolled immigration on the German welfare state by raising taxes on the so-called rich. . . .

2 **Popular opposition to the "islamization" of Europe.** The programs offered by conservative politicians evoked substantial popular support, as seen in demonstrations across Europe, such as this April 2016 anti-immigrant/anti-Islam rally in Warsaw, Poland. The banner in the foreground, surrounded by the Polish national flag and bearing an eagle and the Polish coat of arms, reads, "No to Islam in Poland."

KURIER: And you would very much like to stop it. How?

SARRAZIN: First: change the benefits system — immigrants receive no benefits for at least ten years. Second: change the permanent residency law — only those able and willing to make a long-term, highly skilled contribution to Germany receive residency rights. Third: social and family benefits in Germany should be dependent on adequate knowledge of the language and efforts at integration. Fourth: we must clearly say to the Muslim immigrants who are already here: at some point you become German, even if you obviously continue to cook Turkish food and go to the mosque, and if you don't want to do that, it's best you return home. Opinion polls show that more than 60 percent of Turks in Germany speak no German at all or cannot speak it well, and a third would leave Germany immediately if there were no German welfare benefits.

(Franciszek Mazur/Agencja Gazeta/Reuters/Newscom)

ANALYZING THE EVIDENCE

1. Why and how do the conservative politicians evoke Western values and ideals in their critiques of Islamist extremism?
2. Why would conservative critics of Islamic fundamentalism, as represented in the sources here, be more likely to challenge the immigration policies of the European Union than more left-wing politicians would?
3. Examine the statistics in Source 3. What conclusions can you draw about popular concerns with Islamist extremism in contemporary Europe?

3 **Islamist extremism in Europe: some statistics on popular attitudes.** This Pew Research Center poll taken in the spring of 2015 suggested that popular concerns about Islamist extremism varied significantly across national borders and that gender, age, and ideology were statistically significant factors in such concerns.

Percentage responding they are very concerned about Islamic extremism in their country:

	Total %	By age (percent)			By gender (percent)		By ideology (percent)		
		18–29	30–49	50+	Male	Female	Left	Moderate	Right
Germany	46	22	39	56	42	50	33	48	55
U.K.	52	33	49	64	51	52	37	53	56
Spain	61	47	55	70	54	67	52	65	61
France	67	54	63	74	62	71	52	68	73
Italy	53	49	48	58	46	59	48	61	52
Poland	22	18	18	27	21	23	30	21	22
Russia	23	16	18	32	24	23	—	—	—

4 **The Dutch government turns away from multiculturalism.** The 2010 Dutch elections brought to power a conservative government that announced plans to restrict immigration, ban face-covering garments for Muslim women, and ensure that immigrants "integrate" into Dutch society. The new interior minister, P. H. Donner, mounted a trenchant critique of multiculturalism.

The government distances itself explicitly from the relativism contained in the concept of a multicultural society and envisions a society which may change, also through the influence of immigrants who settle here, but is not interchangeable with any other society. The fundamental elements which determine Dutch society are rooted in its history and constitute reference points which many Dutchmen share and which cannot be discarded.

5 **The British crackdown on Islamic extremism.** In July 2015 British prime minister David Cameron announced that his Conservative Party government would seek new policies to combat Islamist extremism. The key problem, he argued, was a "radical ideology" that was violent and subversive of Western liberal values but also an exciting temptation for youths facing identity crises and failures of integration.

We should expose their extremism for what it is—a belief system that glorifies violence and subjugates its people—not least Muslim people. We should contrast their bigotry, aggression and theocracy with our values. . . . We are all British. We respect democracy and the rule of law. We believe in freedom of speech, freedom of the press, freedom of worship, equal rights regardless of race, sex, sexuality or faith. . . . Whether you are Muslim, Hindu, Jewish, Christian or Sikh . . . we can all feel part of this country—and we must now all come together and stand up for our values with confidence and pride. . . .

We must . . . deglamorize the extremist cause, especially ISIL [the Islamic State]. . . . This isn't a pioneering movement—it is vicious, brutal, and a fundamentally abhorrent existence. And here's my message to any young person here in Britain thinking of going out there. . . . You are cannon fodder for them. . . . If you are a boy, they will brainwash you, strap bombs to your body and blow you up. If you are a girl, they will enslave and abuse you. That is the sick and brutal reality of ISIL. . . .

We need our internet companies to go further in helping us identify potential terrorists online. . . . It's now time for [Internet companies] to protect their users from the scourge of radicalization. . . .

Government has a key role to play in this. It's why we ban hate preachers from our country. . . . We need to put out of action the key extremist influencers who are careful to operate just inside the law, but who clearly detest British society and everything we stand for. . . . So as part of our Extremism Bill, we are going to introduce new narrowly targeted powers to enable us to deal with these facilitators and cult leaders, and stop them peddling their hatred. . . . This is not about clamping down on free speech. It's just about applying our shared values uniformly.

PUTTING IT ALL TOGETHER

Using the sources above, along with what you have learned in class and in Chapters 29 and 30, write a short essay that summarizes the conservative viewpoint on Islamist extremism. Are the conservative critics able to reconcile Western democratic traditions of freedom and tolerance with the perceived need to limit immigration, clamp down on fundamentalism, and prevent terrorist attacks?

Sources: (1) Andreas Schwarz, "Thilo Sarrazin legt nach," *Kurier*, December 5, 2011, http://kurier.at/politik/thilo-sarrazin-legt-nach/731.594, translated by Joe Perry; (3) Spring 2015 Global Attitudes survey, Q23, Pew Research Center, http://www.pewglobal.org/2015/07/16/extremism-concerns-growing-in-west-and-predominantly-muslim-countries/extremism-concerns-08; (4) Quoted in Geert Wilders, *Marked for Death: Islam's War Against the West and Me* (Washington, D.C.: Regnery, 2011), p. 206; (5) David Cameron extremism speech, at Nonestiles School in Birmingham, July 20, 2015.

Global Warming in the Austrian Alps   This photo, taken in August 2016, shows the melting and rock-covered Pasterze glacier in the Austrian Alps in the distant background and a sign in the foreground indicating the location of the glacier in 2015 — the prior year. The Pasterze glacier is shrinking rapidly and has receded in length by at least three kilometers since the nineteenth century. Although glaciers across Europe have been receding since the 1870s, the process began accelerating in the early 1980s, a phenomenon many scientists attribute to global warming. (Sean Gallup/Getty Images)

has been an especially difficult endeavor, underscoring the interconnectedness of the contemporary world. Rapidly industrializing countries such as India and China — the latter surpassed the United States in 2008 as the largest emitter of CO_2 — have had a difficult time balancing environmental concerns and the energy use necessary for economic growth. Because of growing demand for electricity, for example, China currently accounts for about 47 percent of the world's coal consumption, causing hazardous air pollution in Chinese cities and contributing to climate change.[21]

Can international agreements and good intentions make a difference? In December 2015 representatives of almost two hundred nations met at the annual United Nations Climate Change Conference in Paris, France. The resulting Paris Agreement set ambitious goals for the reduction of CO_2 emissions by 2020 and promised to help developing countries manage the effects of climate change. The world's nations met again in Glasgow in November 2021 to set stricter targets for cutting fossil fuel emissions, but the ultimate success of ambitious plans to limit human energy consumption and slow global warming was still uncertain.

Promoting Human Rights

Though regional differences persisted in the twenty-eight EU member states, Europeans entering the twenty-first century enjoyed some of the highest living standards in the world, the sweet fruit of more than fifty years of peace, security, and overall economic growth. Nevertheless, the recent agonies of barbarism and war in the former Yugoslavia, as well as the memories of the horrors of World War II and the Holocaust,

were reminders of the ever-present possibility of collective violence. For some Europeans, the realization that they had so much and so many others had so little kindled a desire to help. European intellectuals and opinion makers began to envision a new historic mission for Europe: the promotion of domestic peace and human rights in lands plagued by instability, violence, and oppression.

European leaders and humanitarians believed that more global agreements and new international institutions were needed to set moral standards and to regulate countries, leaders, armies, corporations, and individuals. In practice, this meant more curbs on the sovereign rights of the world's states, just as the states of the European Union had imposed increasingly strict standards of behavior on themselves to secure the rights and welfare of EU citizens. As one EU official concluded, the European Union has a "historical responsibility" to make morality "a basis of policy" because "human rights are more important than states' rights."[22]

In practical terms, this mission raised questions. Europe's evolving human rights policies would require military intervention to stop civil wars and to prevent tyrannical governments from slaughtering their own people. Thus the EU joined the United States to intervene militarily to stop the killing and protect minority rights in Bosnia, Croatia, and Kosovo. The EU states vigorously supported UN initiatives to verify compliance with anti–germ warfare conventions, outlaw the use of land mines, and establish a new international court to prosecute war criminals.

Europeans also broadened definitions of individual rights. Having abolished the death penalty in the EU, they condemned its continued use in China, the United States, and other countries. At home, Europe

Memorial to the Murdered Jews of Europe in Berlin   Berlin's Memorial to the Murdered Jews of Europe, a somber monument of 2,711 concrete slabs on a vast, uneven plain, stands at the city's center, just footsteps away from the American Embassy and the famous Brandenburg Gate. Opened in 2005, the memorial commemorates the 6 million Jews murdered by the Nazis during the Holocaust of World War II. Its blank walls and forbidding, rolling passageways symbolize the brutality of crimes against humanity that stretch the limits of understanding. (Jens Kalaene/AFP/dpa/Getty Images)

expanded personal rights. The pacesetting Netherlands gave pensions and workers' rights to prostitutes and provided assisted suicide (euthanasia) for the terminally ill. The Dutch recognized same-sex marriage in 2001. By the time France followed suit in 2013, nine western European countries had legalized same-sex marriage and twelve others had recognized alternative forms of civil union. (The U.S. Supreme Court guaranteed the right to same-sex marriage in June 2015.) The countries of the former East Bloc, where people were generally less supportive of LGBTQ+ rights, lagged behind in this regard.

Europeans extended their broad-based concept of human rights to the world's poorer countries, often criticizing globalization and unrestrained neoliberal capitalism. For example, Europe's moderate social democrats joined human rights campaigners in 2001 to secure drastic price cuts from international pharmaceutical corporations selling drugs to combat Africa's AIDS crisis. Advocating greater social equality and state-funded health care, European socialists embraced morality as a basis for the global expansion of human rights.

The record was inconsistent. Critics accused the European Union (and the United States) of selectively promoting human rights in their different responses to the Arab Spring—the West was willing to act in some cases, as in Libya, but dragged its feet in others, as in Egypt and Syria. The conflicted response to the immigration emergency of 2015 underscored the difficulties of shaping unified human rights policies that would satisfy competing political and national interests. Attempts to extend rights to women, Indigenous peoples, and immigrants remained controversial, especially on the far right. Even so, the general trend suggested that most of Europe's leaders and peoples took very seriously the ideals articulated in the 1948 UN Universal Declaration of Human Rights. In an era defined by sharp political conflicts, riven by growing social inequality, and troubled by environmental decline, this commitment to basic human rights offered some hope for meeting ongoing and future challenges.

NOTES

1. P. Anderson, "Managed Democracy," *London Review of Books*, August 27, 2015, pp. 19–27.
2. Quoted in T. Judt, *Postwar: A History of Europe Since 1945* (New York: Penguin, 2005), p. 691.
3. Judt, *Postwar*, pp. 698–699.
4. *Quarterly Labor Force Statistics*, vol. 2004/4 (Paris: OECD Publications, 2004), p. 64; "Which Sector Is the Main Employer in the EU Member States?" *Eurostat: Your Key to European Statistics*, October 24, 2017, https://ec.europa.eu/eurostat/web/products-eurostat-news/-/DDN-20171024-1; Robert E. Scott, "The Manufacturing Footprint and the Importance of U.S. Manufacturing Jobs," *Economic Policy Institute Briefing Paper No. 338*, January 22, 2015, https://www.epi.org/publication/the-manufacturing-footprint-and-the-importance-of-u-s-manufacturing-jobs/.
5. "Fertility Statistics," *Eurostat: Statistics Explained*, accessed August 7, 2015, http://ec.europa.eu/eurostat/statistics-explained/index.php/Fertility_statistics.

Demonstrating for Peace
Holding torches, some 3,500 people form the peace sign in Heroes Square in central Budapest, the capital of Hungary, in 2006. The rally marked the third anniversary of the U.S.-led invasion of Iraq. Millions long for peace, but history and current events suggest that bloody conflicts will continue. Yet Europeans have cause for cautious optimism: despite episodes of intense violence and suffering, since 1945 wars have been localized; cataclysmic catastrophes like World Wars I and II have been averted; and Europe has become a world leader in the push for human rights. (Karoly Arvai/Reuters/Newscom)

6. "Germany: More Babies?" *The Economist*, January 6, 2001, p. 6.

7. Quoted in "Germany: More Babies?" p. 6.

8. *Asylum and Migration in the EU: Facts and Figures* (European Parliament News, 2021), https://www.europarl.europa.eu/news/en/headlines/society/20170629STO78630/asylum-and-migration-in-the-eu-facts-and-figures.

9. European Commission, Report on Migration and Asylum, September 29, 2012, p. 1, https://ec.europa.eu/info/sites/default/files/report-migration-asylum.pdf.

10. "Asylum Statistics," *Eurostat*, April 2018, https://ec.europa.eu/eurostat/statistics-explained/index.php/Asylum_statistics#Final_decisions_taken_in_appeal.

11. Mark Mazower, *Dark Continent: Europe's Twentieth Century* (New York: Vintage, 2000), p. 415; United Nations, *International Migration Report 2017* (New York: UN Department of Economic and Social Affairs, 2017), pp. 28–29.

12. L. Collingham, *Curry: A Tale of Cooks and Conquerors* (London: Oxford University Press, 2006), pp. 2, 9.

13. J. Klausen, *The Islamic Challenge: Politics and Religion in Western Europe* (New York: Oxford University Press, 2006), p. 16; Malise Ruthven, "The Big Muslim Problem!" *New York Review*, December 17, 2009, p. 62.

14. "Europe's Growing Muslim Population," Pew Research Center, November 29, 2017, http://www.pewforum.org/2017/11/29/europes-growing-muslim-population/.

15. Jonathan Evans, "U.S. Adults Are More Religious Than Western Europeans," Pew Research Center, September 5, 2018, http://www.pewresearch.org/fact-tank/2018/09/05/u-s-adults-are-more-religious-than-western-europeans/.

16. Jon Henley, "How Populism Emerged as an Electoral Force in Europe," *theguardian.com*, November 20, 2018, https://www.theguardian.com/world/ng-interactive/2018/nov/20/how-populism-emerged-as-electoral-force-in-europe.

17. "Islam in Europe," *The Economist*, January 7, 2015, http://www.economist.com/blogs/graphicdetail/2015/01/daily-chart-2.

18. Henley, "How Populism Emerged," p. 12.

19. Statistics in *BP Statistical Review of World Energy June 2012*, http://www.bp.com/en_no/norway/media/press-releases-and-news/2012/bp-statistical-review-of-world-energy-2012.html.

20. M. T. Klare, *Resource Wars: The New Landscape of Global Conflict* (New York: Henry Holt, 2001), pp. 25–40.

21. Edward Wong, "Beijing Takes Steps to Fight Pollution as Problem Worsens," *New York Times*, January 31, 2013, p. A4.

22. Quoted in *International Herald Tribune*, June 15, 2001, p. 6.

LOOKING BACK LOOKING AHEAD

The twenty-first century opened with changes and new challenges for the Western world. The collapse of the East Bloc brought more representative government to central and eastern Europe, but left millions struggling to adapt to a different way of life in market economies. Digital technology and information systems that quickened the pace of communications and the global reach of new supranational institutions made the world a smaller place, yet globalization left some struggling to maintain their livelihoods. New contacts between peoples, made possible by increased migration, revitalized European society, but the massive influx of refugees in 2015–2016 raised concerns about cultural tolerance and the EU's open internal borders policy, while the COVID-19 pandemic underscored the sometimes fraught interconnections among the world's peoples and nations.

Despite the success of European democracy and liberalism, and despite the high living standards enjoyed by most Europeans, the challenges won't go away. The search for solutions to environmental degradation and conflicts between ethnic and religious groups, as well as the promotion of human rights across the globe, will clearly occupy European and world leaders for some time to come.

However these issues play out, the study of the past puts the present and the future in perspective. Others before us have witnessed uncertainty and crisis, and the historian's ability to analyze and explain the choices they made helps us understand our current situation and may save us from exaggerated self-pity in the face of our own predicaments. We stand, momentarily, at the head of a long procession of Western and world civilization. Now it is our turn to decide which path the procession takes next.

The study of history, of mighty struggles and fearsome challenges, of shining achievements and tragic failures, gives a sense of the essence of life itself: the process of change over time. Again and again we have seen how peoples and societies evolve, influenced by ideas, human passions, and material conditions. This process of change will continue as the future becomes the present and then the past. Students of history are well prepared to make sense of this unfolding process because they have closely observed it. They understand that change is rooted in existing historical forces, and they have tools to explore the intricate web of activity that propels life forward. Students of history can anticipate the new and unexpected in human development, for they have already seen great breakthroughs and revolutions. They have an understanding of how things really happen.

Make Connections

Think about the larger developments and continuities within and across chapters.

1. Did people's lives really change dramatically during the wave of globalization that emerged in the late twentieth century? How have they stayed the same?

2. The globalization of today's world seems inseparable from advances in digital technology. How are the two connected? Were there other times in the history of Western society during which technological developments drove social, political, or cultural change?

3. How are the challenges that confront Europeans in the twenty-first century rooted in events and trends that came before?

30 REVIEW & EXPLORE

Identify Key Terms

Identify and explain the significance of each item below.

shock therapy (p. 940)

Color Revolutions (p. 942)

ethnic cleansing (p. 947)

globalization (p. 948)

European Union (EU) (p. 949)

Maastricht Treaty (p. 949)

World Trade Organization (WTO) (p. 951)

multiculturalism (p. 958)

war on terror (p. 961)

Arab Spring (p. 962)

Islamic State (p. 962)

Brexit (p. 963)

climate change (p. 967)

Review the Main Ideas

Answer the section heading questions from the chapter.

1. How did life change in Russia and the former East Bloc countries after 1989? (p. 940)

2. How did globalization affect European life and society? (p. 948)

Suggested Resources

BOOKS

- Caldwell, Christopher. *Reflections on the Revolution in Europe: Immigration, Islam, and the West.* 2009. A controversial and thought-provoking book that emphasizes the problems associated with growing numbers of Muslim immigrants in Europe.

- Gillingham, John. *European Integration, 1950–2003: Superstate or New Market Economy?* 2003. A brilliant interpretive history.

- Jordan, Andrew. *Environmental Policy in the European Union: Actors, Institutions and Processes.* 2005. A critical look at the European Union's response to major environmental problems.

- Klausen, Jytte. *The Islamic Challenge: Politics and Religion in Western Europe.* 2006. Reviews the goals of Europe's Islamic leaders and takes a positive view of future Muslim integration in western Europe.

- Laqueur, Walter. *Putinism: Russia and Its Future with the West.* 2015. A critical look at Russia's leader and Russian-U.S. relations after the Cold War, by a renowned historian.

- Noueihed, Lin, and Alex Warren. *The Battle for the Arab Spring: Revolution, Counter-Revolution, and the Making of a New Era.* 2012. Explores the causes and results of the popular revolutions in the Middle East and North Africa.

- Patel, Ian. *We're Here Because You Were There: Immigration and the End of Empire.* 2021. A history of the connections among decolonization, immigration, and social change and prejudice in Britain after 1945.

- Pinder, John, and Simon Usherwood. *The European Union: A Very Short Introduction*, 4th ed. 2018. A readable overview of the history, institutions, and policies of the European Union.

- Ryan, Johnny. *A History of the Internet and the Digital Future.* 2011. An accessible review of the way electronic communications are changing commercial, political, and cultural life.

- Stiglitz, Joseph E. *Making Globalization Work.* 2006. An excellent overview of the successes and failures of globalization, by a distinguished economist.

- Tarrow, Sidney. *The New Transnational Activism.* 2005. A sympathetic account of the transnational activism opposed to corporate globalization.

- Ther, Philip. *Europe Since 1989: A History.* 2016. Focused on the effects of liberalization and privatization in east-central Europe, this book explores social and economic changes after the end of the Cold War.

MEDIA

- *Citizenfour* (Laura Poitras, 2014). A documentary about Edward Snowden and the NSA leaks scandal.

- *The Class* (Laurent Cantet, 2008). In this feature film a teacher attempts to connect with his ethnically diverse students in a working-class neighborhood in Paris.

- *Debtocracy* (Aris Chatzistefanou and Katerina Kitidi, 2011). A documentary that explores the causes of the Greek debt crisis and critiques the government austerity plans intended to resolve it.

- *European Union.* A website sponsored by the European Union that explains "How the EU Works" and gives access to documents pertaining to the EU, among other resources. **europa.eu/**

- *Global Warming: The Signs and the Science* (PBS, 2005). Documents the evidence and effects of global warming; includes interviews with scientists on particular ways people can cope with or change this environmental problem.

- *The History Place: Genocide in the 20th Century: Bosnia-Herzegovina.* An overview of the ethnic cleansing in Bosnia in the 1990s. **www.historyplace.com/worldhistory/genocide/bosnia.htm**

- *Leviathan* (Andrey Zvyagintsev, 2014). This moving film explores the challenges faced by ordinary people in postcommunist Russia.

- *Once Brothers* (ESPN, 2010). A dramatized documentary about Drazen Petrovic and Vlade Divac, friends who played together on the Yugoslavian National Basketball team but ended up on separate sides of the civil war.

- *World Trade Organization.* The homepage of the World Trade Organization, which includes official documents pertaining to the WTO. **www.wto.org/**

ACKNOWLEDGMENTS

CHAPTER 1

Enheduana's "Exaltation of Innana": J. A. Black et al., *Electronic Text Corpus of Sumerian Literature* (http://etcsl.orinst.ox.ac.uk/), Oxford 1998–2006. Reprinted by permission of the University of Oxford Oriental Studies Faculty.

Pyramid text of King Unas: Miriam Lichtheim, *Ancient Egyptian Literature: A Book of Readings. Volume I: The Old and Middle Kingdoms* (Berkeley: University of California Press, 1973), p. 31. Copyright © 1973 by University of California Press. Republished with permission of University of California Press; permission conveyed through Copyright Clearance Center, Inc. All rights reserved.

Hymn to Aton: John A. Wilson, trans., from James B. Pritchard, ed., *Ancient Near Eastern Texts: Relating to the Old Testament,* Third Edition. Copyright © 1969 by Princeton University Press. Republished with permission from Princeton University Press. Permission conveyed through Copyright Clearance Center, Inc.

Excerpt beginning "Hail to Thee, O Nile": From James B. Pritchard (ed.), *Ancient Near Eastern Texts Relating to the Old Testament*, Third Edition with Supplement, p. 171. © 1950, 1955, 1969, renewed 1978 by Princeton University Press. Republished with permission of Princeton University Press. Permission conveyed through Copyright Clearance Center, Inc.

CHAPTER 2

The Egyptian *Book of the Dead:* Miriam Lichtheim, *Ancient Egyptian Literature: A Book of Readings. Volume II: The New Kingdom.* © 2006 by the Regents of the University of California. Published by the University of California Press. Reprinted by permission.

Zoroaster's teachings in the Avesta: M. L. West, *The Hymns of Zoroaster: A New Translation of the Most Ancient Sacred Texts of Iran.* Copyright © 2010 by M. L. West, 2010, I. B. Tauris, used by permission of Bloomsbury Publishing Plc.

The Cyrus cylinder: Cylinder inscription translation by Irving Finkel, curator of Cuneiform Collections at the British Museum, www.britishmuseum .org. Copyright © 2021 The Trustees of the British Museum. Used by permission of The British Museum. All rights reserved.

The Book of Isaiah, Chapter 45: Reproduced from *Tanakh: The Holy Scriptures* by permission of the University of Nebraska Press. Copyright © 1985 by The Jewish Publication Society.

Excerpt beginning "As to Hezekiah, the Jew": From James B. Pritchard (ed.), *Ancient Near Eastern Texts Relating to the Old Testament*, Third Edition with Supplement, p. 288. © 1950, 1955, 1969, renewed 1978 by Princeton University Press. Republished with permission of Princeton University Press. permission conveyed through Copyright Clearance Center, Inc.

CHAPTER 3

Thucydides on the Great Plague at Athens: Excerpt from *The History of the Peloponnesian War*, by Thucydides, translated by Rex Warner, with an introduction and notes by M. I. Finley (Penguin Classics 1954; revised edition 1972). Translation copyright © Rex Warner, 1954. Introduction and Appendices copyright © M. I. Finley, 1972. Reprinted by permission of Penguin Books Limited.

Aeschylus, *Agamemnon:* From *The Oresteian Trilogy: Agamenon, The Choephori, The Eumenides*, by Aeschylus, translated by Philip Vellacott, 1986. Published by Penguin Classics. Reprinted by permission of Penguin Books Limited.

Sophocles, *Antigone:* Elizabeth Wyckoff, *Sophocles I: Antigone in the Complete Greek Tragedies* (Chicago: Phoenix Books, 1954), pp. 173–174, 190, 191. Copyright © 1954 by The University of Chicago Press. Republished with permission of The University of Chicago Press. Permission conveyed through Copyright Clearance Center, Inc. All rights reserved.

Sappho, excerpt beginning "He appears to me, that one, equal to the gods": "Sappho Fragment 31" from *The Ancient Greek Hero in 24 Hours* (Cambridge, Mass.: Harvard University Press, 2013). Translated by Gregory Nagy. Copyright © 2013 by Gregory Nagy. All rights reserved.

CHAPTER 4

Diodorus of Sicily, excerpt beginning "They feed their children": *Diodorus of Sicily: Volume I,* translated by C. H. Oldfather, Loeb Classical Library Volume 279, Cambridge, Mass.: Harvard University Press, first published 1933. Loeb Classical Library® is a registered trademark of the President and Fellows of Harvard College. Used by permission. All rights reserved.

A Hellenistic spell of attraction: Bernadette J. Brooten, *Love Between Women: Early Christian Responses to Female Homoeroticism* (Chicago: University of Chicago Press, 1996), pp. 83–87. Copyright © 1966 by The University of Chicago Press. Republished with permission of The University of Chicago Press; permission conveyed through Copyright Clearance Center, Inc.

Hippocratic writings, *On the Nature of Man:* From *Hippocratic Writings,* edited by G. E. R. Lloyd, translated by J. Chadwick and W. N. Mann, published by Penguin Classics. Translations copyright © 1950, J. Chadwick and W. N. Mann. Reproduced by permission of Penguin Books Limited.

CHAPTER 5

The Turia Inscription: Mary R. Lefkowitz and Maureen B. Fant, eds. *Women's Life in Greece and Rome: A Source Book in Translation*, pp. 135–137. © 1992 Mary R. Lefkowitz and Maureen B. Fant. Reprinted with permission from Bloomsbury Academic, an imprint of Bloomsbury Publishing Plc., and Johns Hopkins University Press.

CHAPTER 6

Pliny the Younger, excerpt beginning "My uncle was stationed at Misenum": *Letters* 6.16, from *Letters of the Younger Pliny,* translation copyright © by Betty Radice 1976. Published by Penguin Classics. Reprinted by permission of Penguin Books Limited.

CHAPTER 7

Gregory of Tours on the veneration of relics: *Gregory of Tours, Glory of the Martyrs,* trans. Raymond Van Dam (Liverpool: Liverpool University, 1988), pp. 22, 107–108. Reproduced with permission of the Liverpool University Press through PLSclear.

CHAPTER 8

Treaty of Tudmir, from 713: Olivia Remie Constable, ed., *Medieval Iberia: Readings from Christian, Muslim, and Jewish Sources*, pp. 30–31, 37–38. Copyright © 2012 Liverpool Press. Reprinted with permission of the Liverpool University Press.

The Death of Beowulf: Maria Dahvana Headley, excerpts from *Beowulf: A New Translation.* Copyright © 2020 by Maria Dahvana Headley. Reprinted by permission Farrar, Straus and Giroux. All Rights Reserved.

Inscriptions from Runestones: English translations from R. I. Paige, *Runes: Reading the Past* (Berkeley: University of California Press, 1987), pp. 46–51. © 1987 The Trustees of the British Museum. With kind permission of the family of R. I. Page. All rights reserved.

CHAPTER 9

Pope Boniface VIII, *Unam Sanctam:* Henry Bettenson, ed., *Documents of the Christian Church.* Copyright © 1963 by Oxford University Press. Reproduced with permission of Oxford University Press through PLSclear.

Ibn al-Athir on the Fall of Antioch: *Arab Historians of the Crusades,* edited and translated by Francesco Gabrieli. Copyright © 1984 by the Regents of the University of California. Published by the University of California Press. Reprinted by Permission.

CHAPTER 10

Poem by Arnaut Daniel: Leonardo Malcovati, from "Sol sui qui sai lo sobrafan qu'em sortz" by Arnaut Daniel, translated. Copyright © by Leonardo Malcovati, from *Prosody in England and Elsewhere: A Comparative Approach.* Reprinted by permission of Gival Press. All rights Reserved.

CHAPTER 11

Henry Knighton, excerpt beginning "Then that most grievous pestilence penetrated": Translated by Mary Martin McLaughlin, "The Impact of the Black Death," from *The Portable Medieval Reader,* edited by James Bruce Ross and Mary Martin McLaughlin. Copyright © 1949 by Viking Penguin, Inc.; copyright renewed © 1976 by James Bruce Ross and Mary Martin McLaughlin. Used by permission of Viking Books, an imprint of Penguin Publishing Group, a division of Penguin Random House LLC. All rights reserved.

Judicial inquiry of a labor organizer in Florence, 1345, and Chronicle of the Ciompi Revolt, 1378: Gene Brucker, ed., *The Society of Renaissance Florence: A Documentary Study* (New York: Harper Torchbooks, 1971), pp. 235, 237–239. Reprinted by permission.

CHAPTER 12

Marin Sanudo on Venice, 1493: David Chambers, Brian S. Pullan, & Jennifer Fletcher, *Venice: A Documentary History, 1450–1630.* Copyright © by The Renaissance Society of America. All rights reserved. Used with permission.

Benedetto Dei on Florence, 1472: Gertrude Randolph Bramlette Richards, *Florentine Merchants in the Age of the Medici: Letters and Documents from the Selfridge Collection of Medici Manuscripts,* edited by Gertrude Randolph Bramlette Richards, Cambridge, Mass.: Harvard University Press, Copyright © 1932 by the President and Fellows of Harvard College. Used by permission. All rights reserved.

Cassandra Fedele, "Oration on Learning," 1487: Cassandra Fedele, *Letters and Orations,* ed. and trans. Diana Robin. Copyright © 2000 by The University of Chicago Press. Republished with permission of The University of Chicago Press. Permission conveyed through Copyright Clearance Center, Inc.

Christine de Pizan, *The Treasure of the City of Ladies,* published by Penguin Classics Translation. Copyright © Sarah Lawson, 1985. Reprinted by permission of Penguin Books Ltd.

CHAPTER 14

Columbus Describes His First Voyage: *The Four Voyages of Christopher Columbus,* edited and translated by J. M. Cohen, published by Penguin Classics. Copyright © J. M. Cohen, 1969. Reprinted by permission of Penguin Books Limited.

The *Florentine Codex:* Miguel Leon-Portilla, excerpt from *The Broken Spears: The Aztec Account of the Conquest of Mexico.* Copyright © 1962, 1990 by Miguel Leon-Portilla. Expanded and Updated Edition © 1992 by Miguel Leon-Portilla. Reprinted by permission of Beacon Press, Boston. All rights reserved.

Aztec Response to the Franciscans' 1524 Explanation of Mission, 1564: "The Lords and Holy Men of Tenochtitlan Reply to the Franciscans Bernardino de Sahagún, Coloquios y doctrina Cristiana," ed. Miguel León-Portilla, in *Colonial Spanish America: A Documentary History,* ed. Kenneth Mills and William B. Taylor, pp. 20–21. Reproduced with permission of Rowman & Littlefield Publishers.

CHAPTER 17

Parlement of Paris, Argument Against the Edict Suppressing the Guilds, March 1776: Keith Michael Baker, ed., *University of Chicago Readings in Western Civilization, Vol. 7: The Old Regime and the French Revolution.* Copyright © 1987 by University of Chicago Press. Republished with permission of The University of Chicago Press. Permission conveyed through Copyright Clearance Center, Inc.

CHAPTER 18

Louis-Sébastien Mercier, *Tableau de Paris,* Chapter 39: How the Day Goes, from *Panorama of Paris: Selections from "Le Tableau de Paris,"* based on the translation by Helen Simpson, edited with a new preface and translations by Jeremy D. Popkin. Republished with permission of The Pennsylvania State University Press. Copyright © 1999 The Pennsylvania State University Press; permission conveyed through Copyright Clearance Center, Inc.

CHAPTER 22

W. S. Lilly, "The New Naturalism": Republished with permission of Princeton University Press from George J. Becker, ed., *Documents of Modern Literary Realism.* Copyright © 1963 by Princeton University Press; permission conveyed through Copyright Clearance Center, Inc.

CHAPTER 23

The Communist Manifesto: Marx and Engels, "Manifesto of the Communist Party," from *The Marx-Engels Reader,* Second Edition by Karl Marx and Friedrich Engels, edited by Robert C. Tucker. Copyright © 1978, 1972 by W. W. Norton & Company. Used by permission of W. W. Norton & Company, Inc.

CHAPTER 26

Friedrich Nietzsche Pronounces the Death of God: *Fritzsche, Nietzsche and the Death of God: Selected Writings.* Long Grove, IL: Waveland Press, Inc. © 2007; reissued 2013. Reprinted by permission of Waveland Press, Inc. All rights reserved.

CHAPTER 27

Joseph Goebbels, "Nation, Rise Up, and Let the Storm Break Loose!": Goebbels' 1943 Speech on Total War, ed. and translated by Randall Bytwerk, Calvin College Propaganda Archive, http://research.calvin.edu/german-propaganda-archive/goeb36.htm. Reprinted by permission of Randall Bytwerk.

CHAPTER 30

The British Crackdown on Islamic Extremism: David Cameron Extremism Speech at Nonestiles School in Birmingham, July 20, 2015. Licensed under the Open Government Licence. https://www.gov.uk/government/speeches/extremism-pm-speech

Afrikaners Descendants of the Dutch settlers in the Cape Colony in southern Africa. (Ch. 24)

al-Andalus The part of the Iberian Peninsula under Muslim control in the eighth century, encompassing most of modern-day Spain. (Ch. 8)

anticlericalism Opposition to the clergy. (Ch. 13)

Antigonid dynasty Dynasty of rulers established by General Antigonus in Macedonia after Alexander's conquests, which ruled until 168 B.C.E. (Ch. 4)

apostolic succession The doctrine that all bishops can trace their spiritual ancestry back to Jesus's apostles. (Ch. 7)

appeasement The British policy toward Germany prior to World War II that aimed at granting Hitler's territorial demands, including western Czechoslovakia, in order to avoid war. (Ch. 27)

aqueducts Canals, channels, and pipes that brought freshwater into cities. (Ch. 6)

Arab Spring A series of popular revolts in several countries in the Middle East and North Africa that sought an end to authoritarian, often Western-supported regimes. (Ch. 30)

Arianism A theological belief that originated when Arius, a priest of Alexandria, denied that Christ was co-eternal with God the Father. (Ch. 7)

Assyrian Empire An empire that originated in northern Mesopotamia and expanded to encompass much of the Near East in the tenth through the seventh centuries B.C.E. (Ch. 2)

Aztec Empire A large and complex Native American civilization in modern Mexico and Central America that possessed advanced mathematical, astronomical, and engineering technology. (Ch. 14)

Babylonian Captivity The period from 1309 to 1376 when the popes resided in Avignon rather than in Rome. The phrase refers to the seventy years when the Hebrews were held captive in Babylon. (Ch. 11)

Balfour Declaration A 1917 British statement that declared British support of a National Home for the Jewish People in Palestine. (Ch. 25)

baroque style A style in art and music lasting from roughly 1600 to 1750 characterized by the use of drama and motion to create heightened emotion, especially prevalent in Catholic countries. (Ch. 15)

barracks emperors The emperors of the middle of the third century, so called because they were military commanders. (Ch. 6)

Battle of Stalingrad A Russian victory over Germany in winter 1942–1943 and a major turning point in the war, which led to the ultimate defeat of the Germans in May 1945. (Ch. 27)

Bauhaus A German interdisciplinary school of fine and applied arts that brought together many leading modern architects, designers, and artists. (Ch. 26)

Berlin Conference A meeting of European leaders held in 1884 and 1885 in order to lay down some basic rules for imperialist competition in sub-Saharan Africa. (Ch. 24)

bishops Christian Church officials with jurisdiction over certain areas and the power to determine the correct interpretation of Christian teachings. (Ch. 6)

Black Death Plague that first struck Europe in 1347 and killed perhaps one-third of the population. (Ch. 11)

Black Shirts Mussolini's private militia, which destroyed socialist newspapers, union halls, and Socialist Party headquarters, eventually pushing Socialists out of the city governments of northern Italy. (Ch. 27)

blood sports Events such as bullbaiting and cockfighting that involved inflicting violence and bloodshed on animals and that were popular with the eighteenth-century European masses. (Ch. 18)

Bolsheviks Lenin's radical, revolutionary arm of the Russian party of Marxist socialism, which successfully installed a dictatorial socialist regime in Russia. (Ch. 25)

bourgeoisie The upper-class minority who owned the means of production and, according to Marx, exploited the working-class proletariat. (Ch. 21)

Boxer Uprising A violent revolt from 1899 to 1901 against foreigners and imperialists in China encouraged by the Qing court, which was quelled by large-scale Western intervention. (Ch. 24)

boyars The highest-ranking members of the Russian nobility. (Chs. 8, 15)

Brexit The informal name for Great Britain's exit from the European Union. (Ch. 30)

Brezhnev Doctrine Doctrine created by Leonid Brezhnev that held that the Soviet Union had the right to intervene in any East Bloc country when necessary to preserve Communist rule. (Ch. 29)

Bronze Age The period in which the production and use of bronze implements became basic to society. (Ch. 1)

caliph The chief Muslim ruler, regarded as a successor to the Prophet Muhammad. (Ch. 8)

cameralism View that monarchy was the best form of government, that all elements of society should serve the monarch, and that, in turn, the state should use its resources and authority to increase the public good. (Ch. 16)

canon law Church law, which had its own courts and procedures. (Ch. 9)

caravel A small, maneuverable, two- or three-masted sailing ship developed by the Portuguese in the fifteenth century that gave them a distinct advantage in exploration and trade. (Ch. 14)

carnival The few days of revelry in Catholic countries that preceded Lent and that included drinking, masquerading, dancing, and rowdy spectacles that upset the established order. (Ch. 18)

Cartesian dualism Descartes's view that all of reality could ultimately be reduced to mind and matter. (Ch. 16)

cathedral The church of a bishop and the administrative headquarters of a diocese. (Ch. 10)

charivari Degrading public rituals used by village communities to police personal behavior and maintain moral standards. (Ch. 18)

chivalry Code of conduct in which fighting to defend the Christian faith and protecting one's countrymen were declared to have a sacred purpose. (Ch. 9)

Christendom The term used by early medieval writers to refer to the realm of Christianity. (Ch. 9)

Christian Democrats Center-right political parties that rose to power in western Europe after the Second World War. (Ch. 28)

Christian humanists Northern humanists who interpreted Italian ideas about and attitudes toward classical antiquity and humanism in terms of their own religious traditions. (Ch. 12)

civilization A large-scale system of human political, economic, and social organizations; civilizations have cities, laws, states, and often writing. (Ch. 1)

civitas The city and surrounding territory that served as a basis of the administrative system in the Frankish kingdoms, based on Roman models. (Ch. 8)

class-consciousness Awareness of belonging to a distinct social and economic class whose interests might conflict with those of other classes. (Ch. 20)

climate change Changes in long-standing weather patterns caused primarily by carbon dioxide emissions from the burning of fossil fuels. (Ch. 30)

Code of Justinian A collection of laws and legal commentary issued by the emperor Justinian that brought together all existing imperial laws into a coherent whole. (Ch. 7)

Cold War The rivalry between the Soviet Union and the United States that divided much of Europe into a Soviet-aligned Communist bloc and a U.S.-aligned capitalist bloc between 1945 and 1989. (Ch. 28)

collectivization of agriculture The forcible consolidation of individual peasant farms into large state-controlled enterprises in the Soviet Union under Stalin. (Ch. 27)

college of cardinals A special group of high clergy with the authority and power to elect the pope and the responsibility to govern the church when the office of the pope is vacant. (Ch. 9)

Color Revolutions A series of popular revolts and insurrections that challenged regional politicians and Russian interests in the former Soviet republics during the first decade of the twenty-first century. (Ch. 30)

Columbian exchange The exchange of diseases, animals, and plants between the Old and the New Worlds, named after Christopher Columbus, who initiated this contact. (Ch. 14)

Combination Acts British laws passed in 1799 that outlawed unions and strikes, favoring capitalist business people over skilled artisans. Bitterly resented and widely disregarded by many craft guilds, the acts were repealed by Parliament in 1824. (Ch. 20)

comitatus A war band of young men in a barbarian tribe who were closely associated with the chief, swore loyalty to him, and fought with him in battle. (Ch. 7)

comites A senior official or royal companion, later called a count, who presided over the civitas. (Ch. 8)

commercial revolution The transformation of the European economy as a result of changes in business procedures and growth in trade. (Ch. 10)

common law A body of English law established by King Henry II's court that in the next two or three centuries became common to the entire country. (Ch. 9)

Common Market The European Economic Community, created by six western and central European countries in the West Bloc in 1957 as part of a larger search for European unity. (Ch. 28)

communes Sworn associations of free men in Italian cities led by merchant guilds. (Ch. 12)

community controls A pattern of cooperation and common action in a traditional village that sought to uphold the economic, social, and moral stability of the closely knit community. (Ch. 18)

companionate marriage Marriage based on romantic love and middle-class family values that became increasingly dominant in the second half of the nineteenth century. (Ch. 22)

conciliarists People who believed that the authority in the Roman Church should rest in a general council composed of clergy, theologians, and laypeople, rather than in the pope alone. (Ch. 11)

confraternities Voluntary lay groups organized by occupation, devotional preference, neighborhood, or charitable activity. (Ch. 11)

Congress of Vienna A meeting of the Quadruple Alliance (Russia, Prussia, Austria, and Great Britain), restoration France, and smaller European states to fashion a general peace settlement that began after the defeat of Napoleon's France in 1814. (Ch. 21)

conquistadors Spanish for "conquerors"; armed Spaniards such as Hernán Cortés and Francisco Pizarro, who sought to conquer people and territories in the New World for the Spanish Crown. (Ch. 14)

constitutionalism A form of government in which power is limited by law and balanced between the authority and power of the government, on the one hand, and the rights and liberties of the subjects or citizens on the other hand; could include constitutional monarchies or republics. (Ch. 15)

consuls Primary executives in the Roman Republic, elected for one-year terms in the Senate, who commanded the army in battle, administered state business, and supervised financial affairs. (Ch. 5)

consumer revolution The wide-ranging growth in consumption and new attitudes toward consumer goods that emerged in the cities of northwestern Europe in the second half of the eighteenth century. (Ch. 18)

Continental System A blockade imposed by Napoleon to halt all trade between continental Europe and Britain, thereby weakening the British economy and military. (Ch. 19)

Copernican hypothesis The idea that the sun, not the earth, is the center of the universe. (Ch. 16)

Corn Laws British laws governing the import and export of grain, which were revised in 1815 to place high tariffs on imported grain, thus benefiting the aristocracy but making food prices high for working people. (Ch. 21)

Cossacks Free groups and outlaw armies originally comprising runaway peasants living on the borders of Russian territory from the fourteenth century onward. By the end of the sixteenth century they had formed an alliance with the Russian state. (Ch. 15)

cottage industry A stage of industrial development in which rural workers used hand tools in their homes to manufacture goods on a large scale for sale in a market. (Ch. 17)

Council for Mutual Economic Assistance (COMECON) An economic organization of Communist states meant to help rebuild East Bloc countries under Soviet auspices. (Ch. 28)

courts Magnificent households and palaces in Italy where signori and other rulers lived, conducted business, and supported the arts. (Ch. 12)

Covenant An agreement that the Hebrews believed to exist between themselves and Yahweh, in which he would consider them his chosen people if they worshipped him as their only god. (Ch. 2)

craft guild A band of producers in a town that regulated most aspects of production of a good in that town. (Ch. 10)

Crimean War A conflict fought between 1853 and 1856 over Russian desires to expand into Ottoman territory; Russia was defeated by France, Britain, and the Ottomans, underscoring the need for reform in the Russian Empire. (Ch. 23)

Crusades Wars sponsored by the papacy for the recovery of Jerusalem and surrounding territories from the Muslims in the late eleventh to the late thirteenth centuries. (Ch. 9)

Crystal Palace The location of the Great Exhibition in 1851 in London; an architectural masterpiece made entirely of glass and iron. (Ch. 20)

cuneiform Sumerian form of writing; the term describes the wedge-shaped marks made by a stylus. (Ch. 1)

Dadaism An artistic movement of the 1910s and 1920s that attacked all accepted standards of art and behavior and delighted in outrageous conduct. (Ch. 26)

Dawes Plan War reparations agreement that reduced Germany's yearly payments, made payments dependent on economic growth, and granted large U.S. loans to promote recovery. (Ch. 26)

debate about women Debate among writers and thinkers in the Renaissance about women's qualities and proper role in society. (Ch. 12)

debt peonage A form of serfdom that allowed a planter or rancher to keep workers in perpetual debt bondage by periodically advancing food, shelter, and a little money. (Ch. 17)

decolonization The postwar reversal of Europe's overseas expansion caused by the rising demand of the colonized peoples themselves, the declining power of European nations, and the freedoms promised by U.S. and Soviet ideals. (Ch. 28)

deism Belief in a distant, noninterventionist deity; common among Enlightenment thinkers. (Ch. 16)

Delian League A military alliance led by Athens whose aims were to protect the Aegean Islands, liberate Ionia from Persian rule, and keep the Persians out of Greece. (Ch. 3)

democracy A type of Greek government in which all citizens administered the workings of government. (Ch. 3)

de-Stalinization The liberalization of the post-Stalin Soviet Union led by reformer Nikita Khrushchev. (Ch. 28)

détente The progressive relaxation of Cold War tensions that emerged in the early 1970s. (Ch. 29)

developed socialism A term used by Communist leaders to describe the socialist accomplishments of their societies, such as nationalized industry, collective agriculture, and extensive social welfare programs. (Ch. 29)

diocese An administrative unit in the later Roman Empire; adopted by the Christian Church as the territory under the authority of a bishop. (Ch. 7)

displaced persons Postwar refugees, including 13 million Germans, former Nazi prisoners and forced laborers, and orphaned children. (Ch. 28)

Domesday Book A manuscript that records the general inquiry about the wealth of his lands ordered by William of Normandy. (Ch. 9)

Dreyfus affair A divisive case in which Alfred Dreyfus, a Jewish captain in the French army, was falsely accused and convicted of treason. The Catholic Church sided with the anti-Semites against Dreyfus; after Dreyfus was declared innocent, the French government severed all ties between the state and the church. (Ch. 23)

Duma The Russian parliament that opened in 1906, elected indirectly by universal male suffrage but controlled after 1907 by the tsar and the conservative classes. (Ch. 23)

Easter Rising Rebellion of Irish nationalists in April 1916 that was quickly repressed by British troops, but contributed to the Irish independence movement of the 1920s. (Ch. 25)

economic liberalism A belief in free trade and competition based on Adam Smith's argument that the invisible hand of free competition would benefit all individuals, rich and poor. (Ch. 17)

economic miracle Term contemporaries used to describe rapid economic growth, often based on the consumer sector, in post–World War II western Europe. (Ch. 28)

Edict of Nantes A document issued by Henry IV of France in 1598, granting liberty of conscience and of public worship to Calvinists, which helped restore peace in France. (Ch. 13)

enclosure The movement to fence in fields in order to farm more effectively, at the expense of poor peasants, who relied on common fields for farming and pasture. (Ch. 17)

encomienda system A system whereby the Spanish Crown granted the conquerors the right to forcibly employ groups of Native Americans in exchange for providing food, shelter, and Christian teaching. (Ch. 14)

English Peasants' Revolt Revolt by English peasants in 1381 in response to changing economic conditions. (Ch. 11)

enlightened absolutism Term coined by historians to describe the rule of eighteenth-century monarchs who, without renouncing their own absolute authority, adopted Enlightenment ideals of rationalism, progress, and tolerance. (Ch. 16)

Enlightenment The influential intellectual and cultural movement of the late seventeenth and eighteenth centuries that introduced a new worldview based on the use of reason, the scientific method, and progress. (Ch. 16)

Epicureanism A system of philosophy based on the teachings of Epicurus, who viewed a life of contentment, free from fear and suffering, as the greatest good. (Ch. 4)

estates The three legal categories, or orders, of France's inhabitants: the clergy, the nobility, and everyone else. (Ch. 19)

Estates General A legislative body in prerevolutionary France made up of representatives of each of the three classes, or estates. It was called into session in 1789 for the first time since 1614. (Ch. 19)

ethnic cleansing The attempt to establish ethnically homogeneous territories by intimidation, forced deportation, and killing. (Ch. 30)

eugenics A pseudoscientific doctrine saying the selective breeding of human beings can improve the general characteristics of a national population, which helped inspire Nazi ideas about national unity and racial exclusion and ultimately contributed to the Holocaust. (Ch. 27)

European Union (EU) An economic, cultural, and political alliance among European nations, characterized by shared currency, free trade, and free movement across borders. (Ch. 30)

evolution Darwin's theory that chance differences among the individual members of a given species that prove useful in the struggle for survival are selected naturally, and they gradually spread to the entire species through reproduction. (Ch. 22)

excommunication A penalty used by the Christian Church that meant being cut off from the sacraments and all Christian worship. (Ch. 9)

existentialism A philosophy that stresses the meaninglessness of existence and the importance of the individual in searching for moral values in an uncertain world. (Ch. 26)

Factory Acts English laws passed from 1802 to 1833 that limited the workday of child laborers and set minimum hygiene and safety requirements. (Ch. 20)

fascism The name given to political movements, including German National Socialism, characterized by extreme nationalism, anti-socialism, a charismatic leader, and the glorification of war and the military. (Ch. 27)

Fashoda Incident French colonial troops backed down in this 1898 diplomatic crisis caused by British-French competition over African territory in present-day South Sudan, preventing a European Great Power war over imperialist ambitions. (Ch. 24)

February Revolution Unplanned uprisings accompanied by violent street demonstrations begun in March 1917 (old calendar February) in Petrograd, Russia, that led to the abdication of the tsar and the establishment of a provisional government. (Ch. 25)

Fertile Crescent An area of mild climate and abundant wild grain where agriculture first developed, in present-day Lebanon, Israel, Jordan, Turkey, and Iraq. (Ch. 1)

feudalism A term devised by later scholars to describe the political system in which a vassal was generally given a piece of land in return for his loyalty. (Ch. 8)

fief A piece of land granted by a feudal lord to a vassal in return for service and loyalty. (Ch. 8)

First Triumvirate The name later given to an informal political alliance among Caesar, Crassus, and Pompey in which they agreed to advance one another's interests. (Ch. 5)

fiscal-military state Centralized bureaucratic states that appeared in Europe in the seventeenth century and that harnessed domestic resources to maintain large armies. (Ch. 15)

Five Pillars of Islam The five practices Muslims must fulfill according to the shari'a, or sacred law, including the profession of faith, prayer, fasting, giving alms to the poor, and pilgrimage to Mecca. (Ch. 8)

five-year plan A plan launched by Stalin in 1928 and termed the "revolution from above," aimed at modernizing the Soviet Union and creating a new Communist society with new attitudes, new loyalties, and a new socialist humanity. (Ch. 27)

flagellants People who believed that the plague was God's punishment for sin and sought to do penance by flagellating (whipping) themselves. (Ch. 11)

Fourteen Points Wilson's 1918 peace proposal calling for open diplomacy, a reduction in armaments, freedom of commerce and trade, the establishment of the League of Nations, and national self-determination. (Ch. 25)

friars Men belonging to certain religious orders who lived not in monasteries but out in the world. (Ch. 9)

Fronde, the A series of violent uprisings during the early reign of Louis XIV triggered by growing royal control and increased taxation. (Ch. 15)

functionalism The principle that buildings, like industrial products, should serve as well as possible the purpose for which they were made, without excessive ornamentation. (Ch. 26)

German Social Democratic Party (SPD) A German working-class political party founded in the 1870s, the SPD championed Marxism but in practice turned away from Marxist revolution and worked instead in the German parliament for social benefits and workplace reforms. (Ch. 23)

germ theory The idea that disease was caused by the spread of living organisms that could be controlled. (Ch. 22)

Girondists A moderate group that fought for control of the French National Convention in 1793. (Ch. 19)

glasnost Soviet leader Mikhail Gorbachev's popular campaign for openness in government and the media. (Ch. 29)

globalization A label for the new international economic, cultural, and political connections that emerged in the last decades of the twentieth century. (Ch. 30)

global mass migration The mass movement of people from Europe in the nineteenth century; one reason that the West's impact on the world was so powerful and many-sided. (Ch. 24)

Gothic An architectural style typified by pointed arches and large stained-glass windows. (Ch. 10)

Gracchi reforms Land reforms proposed by the Gracchi brothers to distribute public land to the poor of the city of Rome. (Ch. 5)

Grand Empire The empire over which Napoleon and his allies ruled, encompassing virtually all of Europe except Great Britain and Russia. (Ch. 19)

Great Depression A worldwide economic depression from 1929 through 1939, unique in its severity and duration and with slow and uneven recovery. (Ch. 26)

Greater Germany A liberal plan for German national unification that included the German-speaking parts of the Austrian Empire, put forth at the National Assembly in 1848 but rejected by Austrian rulers. (Ch. 21)

Great Famine The result of four years of potato crop failure in the late 1840s in Ireland, a country that had grown dependent on potatoes as a dietary staple. (Ch. 21)

Great Fear The fear of noble reprisals against peasant uprisings that seized the French countryside and led to further revolt. (Ch. 19)

Great Rebellion The 1857 and 1858 insurrection by Muslim and Hindu mercenaries in the British army that spread throughout northern and central India before finally being crushed. (Ch. 24)

Great Schism The division, or split, in church leadership from 1378 to 1417 when there were two, then three, popes. (Ch. 11)

"Great Stink" In the summer of 1858 appalling fumes from the polluted River Thames threatened to shut down London, providing a boost to the emerging public health movement. (Ch. 22)

guest worker programs Government-run programs in western Europe designed to recruit labor for the booming postwar economy. (Ch. 28)

guild system The organization of artisanal production into trade-based associations, or guilds, each of which received a monopoly over its trade and the right to train apprentices and hire workers. (Ch. 17)

gunboat diplomacy The use or threat of military force to coerce a government into economic or political agreements. (Ch. 24)

gynaeceum Women's quarters at the back of an Athenian house where the free and enslaved women of the family worked, ate, and slept. (Ch. 3)

Hammurabi's law code A proclamation issued by Babylonian king Hammurabi to establish laws regulating many aspects of life. (Ch. 1)

Hanseatic League A mercantile association of towns begun in northern Europe that allowed for mutual protection and trading rights. (Ch. 10)

Haskalah The Jewish Enlightenment of the second half of the eighteenth century, led by the Prussian philosopher Moses Mendelssohn. (Ch. 16)

Hellenistic A term that literally means "like the Greek," used to describe the period after the death of Alexander the Great, when Greek culture spread. (Ch. 4)

Hellenization The spread of Greek ideas, culture, and traditions to non-Greek groups across a wide area. (Ch. 4)

helots Unfree residents of Sparta forced to work state lands. (Ch. 3)

heresy A religious practice or belief judged unacceptable by church officials. (Ch. 6)

Holocaust The systematic effort of the Nazi state to exterminate all European Jews and other groups deemed racially inferior during the Second World War. (Ch. 27)

Holy Alliance An alliance formed by the conservative rulers of Austria, Prussia, and Russia in September 1815 that became a symbol of the repression of liberal and revolutionary movements all over Europe. (Ch. 21)

Holy Office The official Roman Catholic agency founded in 1542 to combat international doctrinal heresy. (Ch. 13)

Holy Roman Empire The loose confederation of principalities, duchies, cities, bishoprics, and other types of regional governments stretching from Denmark to Rome and from Burgundy to Poland. (Ch. 9)

home rule The late-nineteenth-century movement to give Ireland a government independent from Great Britain; it was supported by Irish Catholics and resisted by Irish Protestants. (Ch. 23)

hoplites Heavily armed citizens who served as infantry troops and fought to defend the polis. (Ch. 3)

Huguenots French Calvinists. (Ch. 13)

humanism A program of study designed by Italians that emphasized the critical study of Latin and Greek literature with the goal of understanding human nature. (Ch. 12)

Hundred Years' War A war between England and France from 1337 to 1453, with political and economic causes and consequences. (Ch. 11)

id, ego, and superego Freudian terms to describe the three parts of the self and the basis of human behavior, which Freud saw as basically irrational. (Ch. 26)

illegitimacy explosion The sharp increase in out-of-wedlock births that occurred in Europe between 1750 and 1850, caused by low wages and the breakdown of community controls. (Ch. 18)

imperator Title originally given to a Roman general after a major victory that came to mean "emperor." (Ch. 6)

Inca Empire The vast and sophisticated Peruvian empire centered at the capital city of Cuzco that was at its peak from 1438 until 1533. (Ch. 14)

Indian National Congress An Indian nationalist movement, founded in 1885 and dedicated to independence from the British Empire. (Ch. 24)

indulgence A document issued by the Catholic Church lessening penance or time in purgatory, widely believed to bring forgiveness of all sins. (Chs. 9, 13)

Industrial Revolution A term first coined in 1799 to describe the burst of major inventions and economic expansion that began in Britain in the late eighteenth century. (Ch. 20)

industrious revolution The shift that occurred as families in northwestern Europe focused on earning wages instead of producing goods for household consumption; this reduced their economic self-sufficiency but increased their ability to purchase consumer goods. (Ch. 17)

infidel A disparaging term used for a person who does not believe in a particular religion. (Ch. 8)

Institutes of the Christian Religion, The Calvin's formulation of Christian doctrine, which became a systematic theology for Protestantism. (Ch. 13)

Iron Age Period beginning about 1100 B.C.E., when iron became the most important material for tools and weapons. (Ch. 2)

iron law of wages Theory proposed by English economist David Ricardo suggesting that the pressure of population growth prevents wages from rising above the subsistence level. (Ch. 20)

Islamic State A radical Islamist militia in control of substantial parts of central Syria and Iraq, where it applies an extremist version of shari'a law. (Ch. 30)

Jacobin Club A political club in revolutionary France whose members were well-educated radical republicans. (Ch. 19)

Jacquerie A massive uprising by French peasants in 1358 protesting heavy taxation. (Ch. 11)

janissary corps The core of the sultan's army, composed of enslaved conscripts from non-Muslim parts of the empire; after 1683 it became a volunteer force. (Ch. 15)

Jansenism A sect of Catholicism originating with Cornelius Jansen that emphasized the heavy weight of original sin and accepted the doctrine of predestination; it was outlawed as heresy by the pope. (Ch. 18)

Jesuits Members of the Society of Jesus, founded by Ignatius Loyola, whose goal was the spread of the Roman Catholic faith. (Ch. 13)

Junkers The nobility of Brandenburg and Prussia, who were reluctant allies of Frederick William in his consolidation of the Prussian state. (Ch. 15)

just price The idea that prices should be fair, protecting both consumers and producers, and that they should be imposed by government decree if necessary. (Ch. 18)

Karlsbad Decrees Issued in 1819, these repressive regulations were designed to uphold Metternich's conservatism, requiring the German states to root out subversive ideas and suppress any liberal organizations. (Ch. 21)

Kievan Rus A confederation of Slavic territories, with its capital at Kyiv, ruled by descendants of the Vikings. (Ch. 8)

kulaks The better-off peasants who were stripped of land and livestock under Stalin and were generally not permitted to join collective farms; many of them starved or were deported to forced-labor camps for "re-education." (Ch. 27)

Kush Kingdom in Nubia that adopted hieroglyphics and pyramids, and later conquered Egypt. (Ch. 2)

labor aristocracy The highly skilled workers, such as factory foremen and construction bosses, who made up about 15 percent of the working classes from about 1850 to 1914. (Ch. 22)

laissez faire A doctrine of economic liberalism that calls for unrestricted private enterprise and no government interference in the economy. (Ch. 21)

Lateran Agreement A 1929 agreement that recognized the Vatican as an independent state, with Mussolini agreeing to give the church heavy financial support in return for public support from the pope. (Ch. 27)

law of inertia A law hypothesized by Galileo that states that motion, not rest, is the natural state of an object, and that an object continues in motion forever unless stopped by some external force. (Ch. 16)

law of universal gravitation Newton's law that all objects are attracted to one another and that the force of attraction is proportional to the objects' quantity of matter and inversely proportional to the square of the distance between them. (Ch. 16)

League of Nations A permanent international organization, established during the 1919 Paris Peace Conference, designed to protect member states from aggression and avert future wars. (Ch. 25)

liberalism The principal ideas of this movement were equality and liberty; liberals demanded representative government and equality before the law as well as individual freedoms such as freedom of the press, freedom of speech, freedom of assembly, freedom of worship, and freedom from arbitrary arrest. (Ch. 21)

Little Ice Age Period of colder and wetter weather that began in the fourteenth century, leading to poor harvests, famine, and other problems. (Ch. 11)

logical positivism A philosophy that sees meaning in only those beliefs that can be empirically proven and that therefore rejects most of the concerns of traditional philosophy, from the existence of God to the human search for happiness, as meaningless. (Ch. 26)

Luddites Group of handicraft workers who attacked factories in northern England in 1811 and later, smashing the new machines that they believed were putting them out of work. (Ch. 20)

Maastricht Treaty The basis for the formation of the European Union, which set financial and cultural standards for potential member states and defined criteria for membership in the monetary union. (Ch. 30)

ma'at The Egyptian belief in a cosmic harmony that embraced truth, justice, and moral integrity; it gave the kings the right and duty to govern. (Ch. 1)

Magna Carta A peace treaty intended to redress the grievances that particular groups had against King John; it was later viewed as the source of English rights and liberty more generally. (Ch. 9)

mandate system The plan to allow Britain and France to administer former Ottoman territories, put into place after the end of the First World War. (Ch. 25)

manorialism A system in which peasant residents of manors, or farming villages, provided work and goods for their lord in exchange for protection. (Ch. 8)

Marshall Plan American plan for providing economic aid to western Europe to help it rebuild. (Ch. 28)

Marxism An influential political program based on the socialist ideas of German radical Karl Marx, which called for a working-class revolution to overthrow capitalist society and establish a Communist state. (Ch. 21)

Marxist revisionism An effort by moderate socialists to update Marxist doctrines to reflect the realities of the late nineteenth century. (Ch. 23)

Meiji Restoration The restoration of the Japanese emperor to power in 1867, leading to the subsequent modernization of Japan. (Ch. 24)

mercantilism A system of economic regulations aimed at increasing the power of the state based on the belief that a nation's international power was based on its wealth, specifically its supply of gold and silver. (Ch. 15)

merchant guild A band of merchants in a town that prohibited nonmembers from trading in that town. (Ch. 10)

Messiah In Jewish belief, an anointed leader who would bring a period of peace and happiness for Jews. (Ch. 6)

Methodists Members of a Protestant revival movement started by John Wesley, so called because they were so methodical in their devotion. (Ch. 18)

millet system A system used by the Ottomans whereby subjects were divided into religious communities, with each millet (nation) enjoying autonomous self-government under its religious leaders. (Ch. 15)

Mines Act of 1842 English law prohibiting underground work for all women and girls as well as for boys under ten. (Ch. 20)

Minoan A wealthy and vibrant culture on Crete from around 1900 B.C.E. to 1450 B.C.E., ruled by a king with a large palace at Knossos. (Ch. 3)

"modern girl" The somewhat stereotypical image of the modern and independent working woman popular in the 1920s. (Ch. 26)

modernism A label given to the artistic and cultural movements of the late nineteenth and early twentieth centuries, which were typified by radical experimentation that challenged traditional forms of artistic expression. (Ch. 26)

monotheism Worship of a single god. (Ch. 2)

Mountain, the Led by Robespierre, the French National Convention's radical faction, which seized legislative power in 1793. (Ch. 19)

multiculturalism The mixing of ethnic styles in daily life and in cultural works such as film, music, art, and literature. (Ch. 30)

Mycenaean A Bronze Age culture that flourished in Greece from about 1650 B.C.E. to 1100 B.C.E., building fortified palaces and cities. (Ch. 3)

mystery religions Belief systems that were characterized by secret doctrines, rituals of initiation, and sometimes the promise of rebirth or an afterlife. (Ch. 3)

Napoleonic Code French civil code promulgated in 1804 that reasserted the 1789 principles of the equality of all male citizens before the law and the absolute security of wealth and private property, as well as restricting rights accorded to women by previous revolutionary laws. (Ch. 19)

National Assembly The first French revolutionary legislature, made up primarily of representatives of the third estate and a few from the nobility and clergy, in session from 1789 to 1791. (Ch. 19)

nationalism The idea that each people had its own genius and specific identity that manifested itself especially in a common language and history, which often led to the desire for an independent political state. (Ch. 21)

national self-determination The notion that peoples should be able to choose their own national governments through democratic majority-rule elections and live free from outside interference in nation-states with clearly defined borders. (Ch. 25)

National Socialism A movement and political party driven by extreme nationalism and racism, led by Adolf Hitler; its adherents ruled Germany from 1933 to 1945 and forced Europe into World War II. (Ch. 27)

nativism Policies and beliefs, often influenced by nationalism, scientific racism, and mass migration, that give preferential treatment to established inhabitants over immigrants. (Ch. 24)

NATO The North Atlantic Treaty Organization, an anti-Soviet military alliance of Western governments. (Ch. 28)

natural law A Stoic concept that a single law that was part of the natural order of life governed all people. (Ch. 4)

natural philosophy An early modern term for the study of the nature of the universe, its purpose, and how it functioned; it encompassed what we would call "science" today. (Ch. 16)

Navigation Acts A series of English laws that controlled the import of goods to Britain and British colonies. (Ch. 17)

neocolonialism A postcolonial system that perpetuates Western economic exploitation in former colonial territories. (Ch. 28)

neo-Europes Settler colonies with established populations of Europeans, such as North America, Australia, New Zealand, and Latin America, where Europe found outlets for population growth and its most profitable investment opportunities in the nineteenth century. (Ch. 24)

neoliberalism Philosophy of 1980s conservatives who argued for privatization of state-run industries and decreased government spending on social services. (Ch. 29)

Neolithic era The period after 9000 B.C.E., when people developed agriculture, domesticated animals, and used tools made of stone and wood. (Ch. 1)

New Christians A term for Jews and Muslims in the Iberian Peninsula who accepted Christianity; in many cases they included Christians whose families had converted centuries earlier. (Ch. 12)

New Economic Policy (NEP) Lenin's 1921 policy to re-establish limited economic freedom in an attempt to rebuild agriculture and industry in the face of economic disintegration. (Ch. 27)

New Imperialism The late-nineteenth-century drive by European countries to create vast political empires abroad. (Ch. 24)

New Left A 1960s counterculture movement that embraced updated forms of Marxism to challenge both Western capitalism and Soviet-style communism. (Ch. 29)

New Order Hitler's based on racial imperialism, which gave preferential treatment to the "Nordic" peoples;

the French, an "inferior" Latin people, occupied a middle position; and Slavs and Jews were treated harshly as "subhumans." (Ch. 27)

Nicene Creed A statement of belief written by a group of Christian church leaders in 325 that declared God the Father and Jesus to be of the same "substance"; other interpretations were declared heresy. (Ch. 7)

nonalignment Policy of postcolonial governments that emphasized neutrality in the Cold War and the unity of states emerging out of colonial domination. (Ch. 28)

oligarchy A type of Greek government in which citizens who owned a certain amount of property ruled. (Ch. 3)

OPEC The Organization of Petroleum Exporting Countries. (Ch. 29)

open-field system System in which the arable land of a manor was divided into two or three fields without hedges or fences to mark individual holdings. (Ch. 10)

Opium Wars Two mid-nineteenth-century conflicts between China and Great Britain over the British trade in opium, which were designed to "open" China to European free trade. In defeat, China gave European traders and missionaries increased protection and concessions. (Ch. 24)

Orthodox Church Eastern Christian Church in the Byzantine Empire. (Ch. 7)

Ostpolitik German for Chancellor Willy Brandt's new "Eastern policy"; West Germany's attempt in the 1970s to ease diplomatic tensions with East Germany, exemplifying the policies of détente. (Ch. 29)

pagan Originally referring to those who lived in the countryside, it came to mean those who practiced religions other than Judaism or Christianity. (Ch. 6)

Paleolithic era The period of human history up to about 9000 B.C.E., when tools were made from stone and bone and people gained their food through foraging. (Ch. 1)

pastoralism An economic system based on herding flocks of goats, sheep, cattle, or other animals beneficial to humans. (Ch. 1)

paterfamilias The oldest dominant male of the Roman family, who held great power over the lives of family members. (Ch. 5)

patriarchy A social system in which men have more power and access to resources than women of the same social level, and in which some men are dominant over other men. (Ch. 1)

patricians The Roman hereditary aristocracy; they held most of the political power in the republic. (Ch. 5)

patronage Financial support of writers and artists by cities, groups, and individuals, often to produce specific works or works in specific styles. (Ch. 12)

patron-client system An informal system of patronage in which free men promised their votes to a more powerful man in exchange for his help in legal or other matters. (Ch. 5)

pax Romana The "Roman peace," a term invented by the historian Edward Gibbon in the eighteenth century to describe the first and second centuries C.E., which he saw as a time of political stability and relative peace. (Ch. 6)

Peace of Utrecht A series of treaties, from 1713 to 1715, that ended the War of the Spanish Succession, ended French

expansion in Europe, and marked the rise of the British Empire. (Ch. 15)

Peace of Westphalia The name of a series of treaties that concluded the Thirty Years' War in 1648 and marked the end of large-scale religious violence in Europe. (Ch. 15)

perestroika Economic restructuring and reform implemented by Soviet leader Mikhail Gorbachev in 1985. (Ch. 29)

Persian Empire A large empire centered in today's Iran that used force and diplomacy to consolidate its power and that allowed cultural diversity. (Ch. 2)

Peterloo Massacre The British army's violent suppression in 1819 of a protest that took place at Saint Peter's Fields in Manchester in reaction to the revision of the Corn Laws. (Ch. 21)

Petrine Doctrine A doctrine stating that the popes (the bishops of Rome) were the successors of Saint Peter and therefore heirs to his highest level of authority as chief of the apostles. (Ch. 7)

Petrograd Soviet A huge, fluctuating mass meeting of two to three thousand workers, soldiers, and socialist intellectuals modeled on the revolutionary soviets (or councils) of 1905. (Ch. 25)

pharaoh The title given to the king of Egypt in the New Kingdom, from a word that meant "great house." (Ch. 1)

philosophes A group of French intellectuals who proclaimed that they were bringing the light of knowledge to their fellow humans in the Age of Enlightenment. (Ch. 16)

Phoenicians Seafaring people from Canaan who traded and founded colonies throughout the Mediterranean and spread the phonetic alphabet. (Ch. 2)

Pietism A Protestant revival movement in early-eighteenth-century Germany and Scandinavia that emphasized a warm and emotional religion, the priesthood of all believers, and the power of Christian rebirth in everyday affairs. (Ch. 18)

Platonic ideals According to Plato, the eternal unchanging ideal forms that are the essence of true reality. (Ch. 3)

plebeians The common people of Rome; they were free but had few of the patricians' advantages. (Ch. 5)

polis Generally translated as "city-state," it was the basic political and institutional unit of Greece in the Hellenic period. (Ch. 3)

politiques Catholic and Protestant moderates who held that only a strong monarchy could save France from total collapse. (Ch. 13)

polytheism The worship of many gods and goddesses. (Ch. 1)

popolo Disenfranchised common people in Italian cities who resented their exclusion from power. (Ch. 12)

Popular Front A short-lived New Deal–inspired alliance in France, led by Léon Blum, that encouraged the union movement and launched a far-reaching program of social reform. (Ch. 26)

postcolonial migration The postwar movement of people from former colonies and the developing world into Europe. (Ch. 28)

postindustrial society A society that relies on high-tech and service-oriented jobs for economic growth rather than heavy industry and manufacturing jobs. (Ch. 29)

Praetorian Guard Imperial bodyguard created by Augustus. (Ch. 6)

predestination The teaching that God has determined the salvation or damnation of individuals based on his will and purpose, not on their merit or works. (Ch. 13)

primogeniture An inheritance system in which the oldest son inherits all land and noble titles. (Ch. 9)

principate Official title of Augustus's form of government, taken from *princeps*, meaning "first citizen." (Ch. 6)

privatization The sale of state-managed industries such as transportation and communication networks to private owners; a key aspect of broader neoliberal economic reforms meant to control government spending, increase private profits, and foster economic growth, which were implemented in western Europe in response to the economic crisis of the 1970s. (Ch. 29)

professionalization The process in which members of skilled trades and occupations established criteria for training and certification and banded together in professional organizations to defend their interests. (Ch. 22)

proletarianization The transformation of large numbers of small peasant farmers into landless rural wage earners. (Ch. 17)

proletariat The industrial working class who, according to Marx, were unfairly exploited by the profit-seeking bourgeoisie. (Ch. 21)

Protectorate The English military dictatorship (1653–1658) established by Oliver Cromwell following the execution of Charles I. (Ch. 15)

Protestant The name originally given to followers of Luther, which came to mean all non-Catholic Western Christian groups. (Ch. 13)

Ptolemaic dynasty Dynasty of rulers established by General Ptolemy in Egypt after Alexander's conquests, which ruled until 30 B.C.E. (Ch. 4)

Ptolemy's *Geography* A second-century-C.E. work that synthesized the classical knowledge of geography and introduced the concepts of longitude and latitude. Reintroduced to Europeans about 1410 by Arab scholars, its ideas allowed cartographers to create more accurate maps. (Ch. 14)

public sphere An idealized intellectual space that emerged in Europe during the Enlightenment, where the public came together to discuss important issues relating to society, economics, and politics. (Ch. 16)

Punic Wars A series of three wars between Rome and Carthage in which Rome emerged the victor. (Ch. 5)

Puritans Members of a sixteenth- and seventeenth-century reform movement within the Church of England that advocated purifying it of Roman Catholic elements such as bishops, elaborate ceremonials, and wedding rings. (Ch. 15)

putting-out system The eighteenth-century system of rural industry in which a merchant loaned raw materials to cottage workers, who processed them and returned the finished products to the merchant. (Ch. 17)

Qur'an The sacred book of Islam. (Ch. 8)

rationalism A secular, critical way of thinking in which nothing was to be accepted on faith and everything was to be submitted to reason. (Ch. 16)

Realism A literary movement that, in contrast to Romanticism, stressed the depiction of life as it actually was. (Ch. 22)

Realpolitik A German term referring to political practice based on a careful calculation of real-world conditions rather than ethical ideals or ideological assumptions, employed by Bismarck and other nineteenth-century politicians. (Ch. 23)

reconquista The Christian term for the conquest of Muslim territories in the Iberian Peninsula by Christian forces. (Ch. 9)

Reform Bill of 1832 A major British political reform that increased the number of male voters by about 50 percent and gave political representation to new industrial areas. (Ch. 21)

regular clergy Men and women who lived in monastic houses and followed sets of rules, first those of Benedict and later those written by other individuals. (Ch. 7)

Reichstag The popularly elected lower house of government of the new German Empire after 1871. (Ch. 23)

Reign of Terror The period from 1793 to 1794 during which Robespierre's Committee of Public Safety tried and executed thousands suspected of treason and a new revolutionary culture was imposed. (Ch. 19)

relics Bones, articles of clothing, or other objects associated with the life of a saint. (Ch. 7)

religious orders Groups of monastic houses following a particular rule. (Ch. 9)

Renaissance A French word meaning "rebirth," used to describe the rebirth of the culture of classical antiquity in Italy during the fourteenth to sixteenth centuries. (Ch. 12)

representative assemblies Deliberative meetings of lords and wealthy urban residents that flourished in many European countries between 1250 and 1450. (Ch. 11)

republicanism (17th century) A form of government in which there is no monarch and power rests in the hands of the people as exercised through elected representatives. (Ch. 15)

republicanism (19th century) An expanded liberal ideology that endorsed universal democratic voting rights, at least for men, and radical equality for all. (Ch. 21)

Risorgimento The nineteenth-century struggle for Italian independence and unification. (Ch. 23)

Rocket The name given to George Stephenson's effective locomotive that was first tested in 1829 on the Liverpool and Manchester Railway at 35 miles per hour. (Ch. 20)

rococo A style of art and architecture in Europe in the eighteenth century, known for its soft pastels, ornamental decoration, asymmetrical patterns, and its thematic focus on pleasure and sensuality. (Ch. 16)

Romanesque An architectural style with rounded arches and small windows. (Ch. 10)

Romanticism An artistic movement at its height from about 1790 to the 1840s that was in part a revolt against classicism and the Enlightenment, characterized by a belief in emotional exuberance, unrestrained imagination, and spontaneity in both art and personal life. (Ch. 21)

Russian Revolution of 1905 A series of popular revolts and mass strikes that forced the tsarist government to grant moderate liberal reforms, including civil rights and a popularly elected parliament. (Ch. 23)

sacraments Certain rituals defined by the church in which God bestows benefits on the believer through grace. (Ch. 7)

salon Regular social gathering held by talented and rich Parisians in their homes, where philosophes and their followers met to discuss literature, science, and philosophy. (Ch. 16)

sans-culottes The laboring poor of Paris, so called because the men wore trousers instead of the knee breeches of the aristocracy and middle class; the word came to refer to the militant radicals of the city. (Ch. 19)

satraps Administrators in the Persian Empire who controlled local government, collected taxes, heard legal cases, and maintained order. (Ch. 2)

Schlieffen Plan Failed German plan calling for a lightning attack through neutral Belgium and a quick defeat of France before attacking Russia. (Ch. 25)

Scholastics University professors in the Middle Ages who developed a method of thinking, reasoning, and writing in which questions were raised and authorities cited on both sides of a question. (Ch. 10)

Second Industrial Revolution The burst of technological innovation and science-driven industrialization that promoted strong economic growth in the last third of the nineteenth century. (Ch. 22)

second revolution From 1792 to 1795, the second phase of the French Revolution, during which the fall of the French monarchy introduced a rapid radicalization of politics. (Ch. 19)

Second Triumvirate A formal agreement in 43 B.C.E. among Octavian, Mark Antony, and Lepidus to defeat Caesar's murderers. (Ch. 5)

Second Vatican Council A meeting of Catholic leaders convened from 1962 to 1965 that initiated a number of reforms, including the replacement of Latin with local languages in church services, designed to democratize the church and renew its appeal. (Ch. 29)

second-wave feminism Label given to the revitalized feminist movement that emerged in the United States and western Europe in the late 1960s and 1970s. (Ch. 29)

secular clergy Priests and bishops who staffed churches where people worshipped and who were not cut off from the world. (Ch. 7)

Seleucid Empire Large empire established in the Near East by General Seleucus after Alexander's conquests, which remained in power until 63 B.C.E. (Ch. 4)

Senate The assembly that was the main institution of power in the Roman Republic, originally composed only of aristocrats. (Ch. 5)

sensationalism The idea that all human ideas and thoughts are produced as a result of sensory impressions. (Ch. 16)

separate spheres A gender division of labor with the wife at home as mother and homemaker and the husband as wage earner. (Chs. 20, 22)

serfs Peasants bound to the land by a relationship with a manorial lord. (Ch. 8)

shock therapy Economic policies set in place in Russia and some former East Bloc countries after the collapse of communism, through which a quick turn to free markets was meant to speed economic growth. (Ch. 30)

signori Government by one-man rule in Italian cities such as Milan; also refers to these rulers. (Ch. 12)

simony The buying and selling of church offices, a policy that was officially prohibited but often practiced. (Ch. 9)

Social Darwinism A body of thought, based on the ideas of Charles Darwin, that applied the theory of biological evolution to human affairs and saw the human race as driven by an unending economic struggle that would determine the "survival of the fittest." (Ch. 22)

socialism A backlash against the emergence of individualism and the fragmentation of industrial society, and a move toward cooperation and a sense of community; the key ideas were economic planning, greater social equality, and state regulation of property. (Ch. 21)

Socialist Realism Artistic movement that followed the dictates of Communist ideals, enforced by state control in the Soviet Union and East Bloc countries in the 1950s and 1960s. (Ch. 28)

Socratic method A method of inquiry used by Socrates based on asking questions, through which participants developed their critical-thinking skills and explored ethical issues. (Ch. 3)

Solidarity Independent Polish trade union that worked for workers' rights and political reform throughout the 1980s. (Ch. 29)

Sophists A group of thinkers in fifth-century-B.C.E. Athens who applied philosophical speculation to politics and language and were accused of deceit. (Ch. 3)

South African (Boer) War Conflict in 1899–1902 in which British troops defeated rebellious Afrikaners, ancestors of Dutch colonialists, leading to consolidation of South African territories. (Ch. 24)

Spanish Armada The fleet sent by Philip II of Spain in 1588 against England as a religious crusade against Protestantism. Weather and the English fleet defeated it. (Ch. 13)

Spanish Civil War A war from 1936 to 1939 that led to the overthrow of the left-leaning democratic government of Spain and the establishment of a Fascist state under the general Francisco Franco. (Ch. 27)

spinning jenny A simple, inexpensive, hand-powered spinning machine created by James Hargreaves in 1765. (Ch. 20)

stadholder The executive officer in each of the United Provinces of the Netherlands, a position often held by the princes of Orange. (Ch. 15)

stagflation Term coined in the early 1980s to describe the combination of low growth and high inflation that led to a worldwide recession. (Ch. 29)

Stalinism The name given to the Communist system in the Soviet Union during the rule of Joseph Stalin. (Ch. 27)

Statute of Kilkenny Law issued in 1366 that discriminated against the Irish, forbidding marriage between the English and the Irish, requiring the use of the English language, and denying the Irish access to ecclesiastical offices. (Ch. 11)

steam engines A breakthrough invention by Thomas Savery in 1698 and Thomas Newcomen in 1705 that burned coal to produce steam, which was then used to operate a pump; the early models were superseded by James Watt's more efficient steam engine, patented in 1769. (Ch. 20)

Stoicism A philosophy, based on the ideas of Zeno, that people could be happy only when living in accordance with nature and accepting whatever happened. (Ch. 4)

stream-of-consciousness technique A literary technique, found in works by Virginia Woolf, James Joyce, and others, that uses interior monologue—a character's thoughts and feelings as they occur—to explore the human psyche. (Ch. 26)

Struggle of the Orders A conflict in which the plebeians sought political representation and safeguards against patrician domination. (Ch. 5)

suffrage movement A militant movement for women's right to vote led by middle-class British women, which exemplified broader international campaigns for women's political rights around 1900. (Ch. 23)

sultan The ruler of the Ottoman Empire; he owned all the agricultural land of the empire and was served by an army and bureaucracy composed of highly trained enslaved people. (Ch. 15)

sumptuary laws Laws that regulated the value and style of clothing and jewelry that various social groups could wear as well as the amount they could spend on celebrations. (Ch. 10)

sweated industries Poorly paid handicraft production, often carried out by married women paid by the piece and working at home. (Ch. 22)

Tanzimat A set of reforms designed to remake the Ottoman Empire on a western European model. (Ch. 23)

tariff protection A government's way of supporting and aiding its own economy by laying high taxes on imported goods from other countries, as when the French responded to cheaper British goods flooding their country by imposing high tariffs on some imported products. (Ch. 20)

Test Act Legislation passed by the English Parliament in 1673 to secure the position of the Anglican Church by stripping Puritans, Catholics, and other dissenters of the right to vote, preach, assemble, hold public office, and teach at or attend the universities. (Ch. 15)

tetrarchy Diocletian's four-part division of the Roman Empire. (Ch. 7)

theory of special relativity Albert Einstein's theory that time and space are relative to the observer and that only the speed of light remains constant. (Ch. 26)

Thermidorian reaction A reaction to the violence of the Reign of Terror in 1794, resulting in the execution of Robespierre and the loosening of economic controls. (Ch. 19)

thermodynamics A branch of physics built on Newton's laws of mechanics that investigated the relationship between heat and mechanical energy. (Ch. 22)

Torah The first five books of the Hebrew Bible, containing the most important legal and ethical Hebrew texts; later became part of the Christian Old Testament. (Ch. 2)

totalitarianism A radical dictatorship that exercises "total claims" over the beliefs and behavior of its citizens by taking control of the economic, social, intellectual, and cultural aspects of society. (Ch. 27)

total war A war in which distinctions between the soldiers on the battlefield and civilians at home are blurred, and where massive government intervention in society and the economy ensures support for the war effort. (Ch. 25)

transatlantic slave trade The forced migration of Africans across the Atlantic for enslaved labor on plantations and in other industries; the trade reached its peak in the eighteenth century and ultimately involved more than 12 million Africans. (Ch. 17)

Treaty of Brest-Litovsk Peace treaty signed in March 1918 between the Central Powers and Russia that ended Russian participation in World War I and ceded territories containing a third of the Russian Empire's population to the Central Powers. (Ch. 25)

Treaty of Paris The treaty that ended the Seven Years' War in Europe and the colonies in 1763 and that ratified British victory on all colonial fronts. (Ch. 17)

Treaty of Tordesillas A 1494 treaty that settled competing claims to newly discovered Atlantic territories by giving Spain everything to the west of an imaginary line drawn down the Atlantic and giving Portugal everything to the east. (Ch. 14)

Treaty of Verdun Treaty signed in 843 by Charlemagne's grandsons dividing the Carolingian Empire into three parts and setting the pattern for political boundaries in Europe still in use today. (Ch. 8)

Treaty of Versailles The 1919 peace settlement that ended war between Germany and the Allied powers. (Ch. 25)

trench warfare A type of fighting used in World War I behind rows of trenches and barbed wire; the cost in lives was staggering and the gains in territory minimal. (Ch. 25)

tribunes Plebeian-elected officials; tribunes brought plebeian grievances to the Senate for resolution and protected plebeians from the arbitrary conduct of patrician magistrates. (Ch. 5)

Triple Alliance The alliance of Austria, Germany, and Italy. Italy left the alliance when war broke out in 1914. (Ch. 25)

Triple Entente The alliance of Great Britain, France, and Russia prior to and during the First World War. (Ch. 25)

troubadours Poets who wrote and sang lyric verses celebrating love, desire, beauty, and gallantry. (Ch. 10)

Truman Doctrine America's policy geared to containing communism to those countries already under Soviet control. (Ch. 28)

tyranny Rule by one man who took over an existing government, generally by using his wealth to gain a political following. (Ch. 3)

U.K. Vaccination Acts Legislation introduced in the United Kingdom during the nineteenth century requiring that all children be vaccinated against smallpox. (Ch. 22)

Union of Utrecht The alliance of seven northern provinces (led by Holland) that declared its independence from Spain and formed the United Provinces of the Netherlands. (Ch. 13)

utilitarianism The idea of Jeremy Bentham that social policies should promote the "greatest good for the greatest number." (Ch. 22)

vassal A warrior who swore loyalty and service to a noble in exchange for land, protection, and support. (Ch. 8)

Velvet Revolution The term given to the relatively peaceful overthrow of communism in Czechoslovakia; the label came to signify the collapse of the East Bloc in general in 1989 to 1990. (Ch. 29)

vernacular literature Writings in the author's local dialect, that is, in the everyday language of the region. (Ch. 10)

viceroyalties The name for the four administrative units of Spanish possessions in the Americas: New Spain, Peru, New Granada, and La Plata. (Ch. 14)

virtù The quality of being able to shape the world according to one's own will. (Ch. 12)

War Communism The application of centralized state control during the Russian civil war, in which the Bolsheviks seized grain from peasants, introduced rationing, nationalized all banks and industry, and required strict workplace discipline. (Ch. 25)

war guilt clause An article in the Treaty of Versailles that declared that Germany (with Austria) was solely responsible for the war and had to pay reparations equal to all civilian damages caused by the fighting. (Ch. 25)

war on terror American policy under President George W. Bush to fight global terrorism in all its forms. (Ch. 30)

Warsaw Pact Soviet-backed military alliance of East Bloc Communist countries in Europe. (Ch. 28)

water frame A spinning machine created by Richard Arkwright that had a capacity of several hundred spindles and used waterpower; it therefore required a larger and more specialized mill—a factory. (Ch. 20)

wergeld Compensatory payment for death or injury set in many barbarian law codes. (Ch. 7)

wet-nursing A widespread and flourishing business in the eighteenth century in which women were paid to breast-feed other women's babies. (Ch. 18)

white man's burden The idea that Europeans could and should "civilize" nonwhite people and that imperialism would eventually provide nonwhite people with modern achievements and higher standards of living. (Ch. 24)

Works Progress Administration (WPA) An American government agency, designed as a massive public jobs program, established in 1935 as part of Roosevelt's New Deal. (Ch. 26)

World Trade Organization (WTO) A powerful supranational financial institution that sets trade and tariff agreements for over 150 member countries and so helps manage a large percentage of the world's import-export policies. Like the IMF and the World Bank, the WTO promotes neoliberal policies around the world. (Ch. 30)

Yahweh The sole god in the Jewish religion. (Ch. 2)

Young Turks Fervent patriots who seized power in a 1908 coup in the Ottoman Empire, forcing the conservative sultan to implement reforms. (Ch. 23)

Zionism A movement dedicated to combatting anti-Semitism in Europe by building a Jewish national homeland in Palestine, started by Theodor Herzl. (Ch. 23)

Zoroastrianism Religion based on the ideas of Zoroaster that stressed devotion to the god Ahuramazda alone and that emphasized the individual's responsibility to choose between good and evil. (Ch. 2)

INDEX

A History of Western Society: A Brief Overview

	Government	Society and Economy
3000 B.C.E.	Emergence of first cities in Mesopotamia, ca. 3800 Unification of Egypt; Archaic Period, ca. 3100–2600 Old Kingdom of Egypt, ca. 2660–2180 Dominance of Akkadian empire in Mesopotamia, ca. 2331–2200 Middle Kingdom in Egypt, ca. 2080–1640	Neolithic peoples rely on settled agriculture, while others pursue nomadic life, ca. 7000–3000 Expansion of Mesopotamian trade and culture into the modern Middle East and Turkey, ca. 2600
2000 B.C.E.	Babylonian empire, ca. 2000–1595 Code of Hammurabi, ca. 1755 Hyksos invade Egypt, ca. 1640–1570 Hittite Empire, ca. 1600–1200 New Kingdom in Egypt, ca. 1570–1075	First wave of Indo-European migrants, by ca. 2000 Extended commerce in Egypt, by ca. 2000 Horses introduced into Asia and North Africa, by ca. 2500
1500 B.C.E.	Third Intermediate Period in Egypt, ca. 1070–712 Unified Hebrew kingdom under Saul, David, and Solomon, ca. 1025–925	Use of iron increases in western Asia, by ca. 1300–1100 Second wave of Indo-European migrants, by ca. 1200 "Dark Age" in Greece, ca. 1100–800
1000 B.C.E.	Hebrew kingdom divided into Israel and Judah, 925 Assyrian Empire, ca. 900–612 Phoenicians found Carthage, 813 Kingdom of Kush conquers and reunifies Egypt, ca. 800–700 Roman monarchy, ca. 753–509 Medes conquers Persia, 710 Babylon wins independence from Assyria, 626 Dracon issues law code at Athens, 621 Solon's reforms at Athens, ca. 594 Cyrus the Great conquers Medes, founds Persian Empire, 550 Persians complete conquest of ancient Near East, 521–464 Reforms of Cleisthenes in Athens, 508	Phoenician seafaring and trading in the Mediterranean, ca. 900–550 First Olympic games, 776 Concentration of landed wealth in Greece, ca. 750–600 Greek overseas expansion, ca. 750–550 Beginning of coinage in western Asia, ca. 640
500 B.C.E.	Persian wars, 499–479 Struggle of the Orders in Rome, ca. 494–287 Growth of the Athenian Empire, 478–431 Peloponnesian War, 431–404 Rome captures Veii, 396 Gauls sack Rome, 387 Roman expansion in Italy, 390–290 Philip II of Macedonia conquers Greece, 338 Conquests of Alexander the Great, 334–324 Punic Wars, 264–146 Reforms of the Gracchi, 133–121	Growth of Hellenistic trade and cities, ca. 330–100 Beginning of Roman silver coinage, 269 Growth of slavery, decline of small farmers in Rome, ca. 250–100 Agrarian reforms of the Gracchi, 133–121

Religion and Philosophy	Science and Technology	Arts and Letters
Growth of anthropomorphic religion in Mesopotamia, ca. 3000–2000 Emergence of Egyptian polytheism and belief in personal immortality, ca. 2660 Spread of Mesopotamian and Egyptian religious ideas as far north as modern Turkey and as far south as central Africa, ca. 2600	Development of wheeled transport in Mesopotamia, by ca. 3000 Use of widespread irrigation in Mesopotamia and Egypt, ca. 3000 Construction of Stonehenge monument in England, ca. 2500 Construction of first pyramid in Egypt, ca. 2600	Cuneiform and hieroglyphic writing, ca. 3200
Emergence of Hebrew monotheism, ca. 1700 Mixture of Hittite and Near Eastern religious beliefs, ca. 1595	Construction of first ziggurats in Mesopotamia, ca. 2100 Widespread use of bronze in ancient Near East, ca. 1900 Babylonian mathematical advances, ca. 1800	*Epic of Gilgamesh*, ca. 1900
Exodus of the Hebrews from Egypt into Palestine, ca. 1300–1200	Hittites introduce iron technology, ca. 1400	Phoenicians develop alphabet, ca. 1400 Naturalistic art in Egypt under Akhenaton, 1367–1350 Egyptian *Book of the Dead*, ca. 1300
Era of the prophets in Israel, ca. 1100–500 Beginning of the Hebrew Bible, ca. 950–800 Intermixture of Etruscan and Roman religious cults, ca. 753–509 Growing popularity of local Greek religious cults, ca. 700 B.C.E.–337 C.E. Introduction of Zoroastrianism, ca. 600 Babylonian Captivity of the Hebrews, 587–538	Babylonian astronomical advances, ca. 750–400 Construction of Parthenon in Athens begins, 447	Homer, traditional author of *Iliad* and *Odyssey*, ca. 800 Hesiod, author of *Theogony* and *Works and Days*, ca. 800 Aeschylus, first significant Athenian tragedian, ca. 525–456
Pre-Socratic philosophers, ca. 500–400 Socrates executed, 399 Plato, student of Socrates, 427–347 Diogenes, leading proponent of cynicism, ca. 412–323 Aristotle, student of Plato, 384–322 Epicurus, founder of Epicurean philosophy, 340–270 Zeno, founder of Stoic philosophy, 335–262 Emergence of Mithraism, ca. 300 Greek cults brought to Rome, ca. 200 Spread of Hellenistic mystery religions, ca. 200–100	Hippocrates, formal founder of medicine, ca. 430 Building of the Via Appia begins, 312 Aristarchos of Samos, advances in astronomy, ca. 310–230 Euclid codifies geometry, ca. 300 Herophilus, discoveries in medicine, ca. 300–250 Archimedes, works on physics and hydrologics, ca. 287–212	Sophocles, tragedian whose plays explore moral and political problems, ca. 496–406 Herodotus, "father of history," ca. 485–425 Euripides, most personal of the Athenian tragedians, ca. 480–406 Thucydides, historian of Peloponnesian War, ca. 460–440 Aristophanes, greatest Athenian comic playwright, ca. 445–386

	Government	Society and Economy
100 B.C.E.	Dictatorship of Sulla, 88–79 B.C.E. Civil war in Rome, 88–31 B.C.E. Dictatorship of Caesar, 45–44 B.C.E. Principate of Augustus, 31 B.C.E.–14 C.E. "Five Good Emperors" of Rome, 96–180 C.E. "Barracks Emperors," civil war, 235–284 C.E.	Reform of the Roman calendar, 46 B.C.E. "Golden age" of Roman prosperity and vast increase in trade, 96–180 C.E. Growth of serfdom in Roman Empire, ca. 200–500 C.E. Economic contraction in Roman Empire, ca. 235–284 C.E.
300 C.E.	Constantine moves capital of Roman Empire to Constantinople, ca. 315 Visigoths defeat Roman army at Adrianople, 378 Bishop Ambrose asserts church's independence from the state, 380 Odoacer deposes last Roman emperor in the West, 476 Clovis issues Salic law of the Franks, ca. 490	Barbarian migrations throughout western and northern Europe, ca. 378–600
500	Law code of Justinian, 529 Spread of Islam across Arabia, the Mediterranean region, Spain, North Africa, and Asia as far as India, ca. 630–733	Gallo-Roman aristocracy intermarries with Germanic chieftains, ca. 500–700 Decline of towns and trade in the West; agrarian economy predominates, ca. 500–1800
700	Charles Martel defeats Muslims at Tours, 732 Pippin III anointed king of the Franks, 754 Charlemagne secures Frankish Crown, r. 768–814	Height of Muslim commercial activity with western Europe, ca. 700–1300
800	Imperial coronation of Charlemagne, Christmas 800 Treaty of Verdun divides Carolingian kingdom, 843 Viking, Magyar, and Muslim invasions, ca. 850–1000 Establishment of Kievan Rus, ca. 900	Invasions and unstable conditions lead to increase of serfdom in western Europe, ca. 800–900 Height of Byzantine commerce and industry, ca. 800–1000
1000	Seljuk Turks conquer Muslim Baghdad, 1055 Norman conquest of England, 1066 Penance of Henry IV at Canossa, 1077	Decline of Byzantine free peasantry, ca. 1025–1100 Growth of towns and trade in the West, ca. 1050–1300 *Domesday Book* in England, 1086
1100	Henry I of England, r. 1100–1135 Louis VI of France, r. 1108–1137 Frederick I of Germany, r. 1152–1190 Henry II of England, r. 1154–1189	Henry I of England establishes the Exchequer, 1130 Beginnings of the Hanseatic League, 1159

Religion and Philosophy	Science and Technology	Arts and Letters
Mithraism spreads to Rome, 27 B.C.E.–270 C.E. Life of Jesus, ca. 3 B.C.E.–29 C.E.	Engineering advances in Rome, ca. 100 B.C.E.–180 C.E.	Flowering of Latin literature: Virgil, 70–19 B.C.E.; Livy, ca. 59 B.C.E.–17 C.E.; Ovid, 43 B.C.E.–17 C.E.
Constantine legalizes Christianity, 312 Theodosius declares Christianity the official state religion, 380 Donatist heretical movement at its height, ca. 400 St. Augustine, *Confessions*, ca. 390; *The City of God*, ca. 425 Clovis adopts Roman Christianity, 496	Construction of Arch of Constantine, ca. 315	St. Jerome publishes Latin *Vulgate*, late 4th c. Byzantines preserve Greco-Roman culture, ca. 400–1000
Rule of St. Benedict, 529 Life of the Prophet Muhammad, ca. 571–632 Pope Gregory the Great publishes *Dialogues, Pastoral Care, Moralia*, 590–604 Monasteries established in Anglo-Saxon England, ca. 600–700 Publication of the Qur'an, 651 Synod of Whitby, 664	Using watermills, Benedictine monks exploit energy of fast-flowing rivers and streams, by 600 Heavy plow and improved harness facilitate use of multiple-ox teams; harrow widely used in northern Europe, by 600 Byzantines successfully use "Greek fire" in naval combat against Arab fleets attacking Constantinople, 673, 717	Boethius, *The Consolation of Philosophy*, ca. 520 Justinian constructs church of Santa Sophia, 532–537
Bede, *Ecclesiastical History of the English Nation*, ca. 700 Missionary work of St. Boniface in Germany, ca. 710–750 Iconoclastic controversy in Byzantine Empire, 726–843 Pippin III donates Papal States to the papacy, 756		Lindisfarne Gospel Book, ca. 700 *Beowulf*, ca. 700 Carolingian Renaissance, ca. 780–850
Foundation of abbey of Cluny, 909 Byzantine conversion of Russia, late 10th c.	Stirrup and nailed horseshoes become widespread in combat, 900–1000 Paper (invented in China, ca. 150) enters Europe through Muslim Spain, ca. 900–1000	Byzantines develop Cyrillic script, late 10th c.
Schism between Roman and Greek Orthodox churches, 1054 Lateran Council restricts election of pope to College of Cardinals, 1059 Pope Gregory VII, 1073–1085 Theologian Peter Abelard, 1079–1142 First Crusade, 1095–1099 Founding of Cistercian order, 1098	Arab conquests bring new irrigation methods, cotton cultivation, and manufacture to Spain, Sicily, southern Italy, by 1000 Avicenna, Arab scientist, d. 1037	Muslim musicians introduce lute, rebec (stringed instruments, ancestors of violin), ca. 1000 Romanesque style in architecture and art, ca. 1000–1200 *Song of Roland*, ca. 1095
Universities begin, ca. 1100–1300 Concordat of Worms ends investiture controversy, 1122 Height of Cistercian monasticism, 1125–1175	Europeans, copying Muslim and Byzantine models, construct castles with rounded towers and crenellated walls, by 1100	Troubadour poetry, especially of Chrétien de Troyes, circulates widely, ca. 1100–1200 *Rubaiyat of Umar Khayyam*, ca. 1120 Dedication of abbey church of Saint-Denis launches Gothic style, 1144

	Government	Society and Economy
1100 (CONT.)	Thomas Becket, archbishop of Canterbury, murdered 1170 Philip Augustus of France, r. 1180–1223	
1200	Spanish victory over Muslims at Las Navas de Tolosa, 1212 Frederick II of Germany and Sicily, r. 1212–1250 Magna Carta, charter of English political and civil liberties, 1215 Louis IX of France, r. 1226–1270 Mongols end Abbasid caliphate, 1258 Edward I of England, r. 1272–1307 Philip IV (the Fair) of France, r. 1285–1314	European revival, growth of towns; agricultural expansion leads to population growth, ca. 1200–1300 Crusaders capture Constantinople (Fourth Crusade) and spur Venetian economy, 1204
1300	Philip IV orders arrest of Pope Boniface at Anagni, 1303 Hundred Years' War between England and France, 1337–1453 Political disorder in Germany, ca. 1350–1450 Merchant oligarchies or despots rule Italian city-states, ca. 1350–1550	Little Ice Age, European economic depression, ca. 1300–1450 Black Death appears ca. 1347; returns intermittently until ca. 1720 Height of the Hanseatic League, 1350–1450 Peasant and working-class revolts: Flanders, 1328; France, 1358; Florence, 1378; England, 1381
1400	Joan of Arc rallies French monarchy, 1429–1431 Medici domination of Florence begins, 1434 Princes in Germany consolidate power, ca. 1450–1500 Ottoman Turks under Mahomet II capture Constantinople, May 1453 Wars of the Roses in England, 1455–1471 Establishment of the Inquisition in Spain, 1478 Ferdinand and Isabella complete reconquista in Spain, 1492 French invasion of Italy, 1494	Population decline, peasants' revolts, high labor costs contribute to decline of serfdom in western Europe, ca. 1400–1650 Flow of enslaved people from the Balkans into eastern Mediterranean, from Africa into Iberia and Italy, ca. 1400–1500 Christopher Columbus reaches the Americas, 1492 Portuguese gain control of East Indian spice trade, 1498–1511
1500	Charles V, Holy Roman emperor, 1519–1556 Habsburg-Valois Wars, 1521–1559 Philip II of Spain, r. 1556–1598 Revolt of the Netherlands, 1566–1598 St. Bartholomew's Day massacre in France, 1572 English defeat of the Spanish Armada, 1588 Henry IV of France issues Edict of Nantes, 1598	Consolidation of serfdom in eastern Europe, ca. 1500–1650 Balboa discovers the Pacific, 1513 Magellan's crew circumnavigates the earth, 1519–1522 Spain and Portugal gain control of regions of Central and South America, ca. 1520–1550 Peasants' Revolt in Germany, 1524–1525 "Time of Troubles" in Russia, 1598–1613

Religion and Philosophy	Science and Technology	Arts and Letters
Aristotle's works translated into Latin, ca. 1140–1260 Third Crusade, 1189–1192 Pope Innocent III, height of the medieval papacy, 1198–1216	Underground pipes with running water and indoor latrines installed in some monasteries, such as Clairvaux and Canterbury Cathedral Priory, by 1100; elsewhere rare until 1800 Windmill invented, ca. 1180	
Founding of the Franciscan order, 1210 Fourth Lateran Council accepts seven sacraments, 1215 Founding of Dominican order, 1216 Thomas Aquinas, height of scholasticism, 1225–1274	*Notebooks* of architect Villard de Honnecourt, a major source for Gothic engineering, ca. 1250 Development of double-entry bookkeeping in Florence and Genoa, ca. 1250–1340 Venetians purchase secrets of glass manufacture from Syria, 1277 Mechanical clock invented, ca. 1290	*Parzifal, Roman de la rose, King Arthur and the Round Table* celebrate virtues of knighthood and chivalry, ca. 1200–1300 Height of Gothic style, ca. 1225–1300
Pope Boniface VIII declares all Christians subject to the pope in *Unam Sanctam*, 1302 Babylonian Captivity of the papacy, 1309–1376 Theologian John Wyclif, ca. 1330–1384 Great Schism in the papacy, 1378–1417	Edward III of England uses cannon in siege of Calais, 1346 Clocks in general use throughout Europe, by 1400	Paintings of Giotto mark emergence of Renaissance movement in the arts, ca. 1305–1337 Dante, *Divine Comedy*, ca. 1310 Petrarch develops ideas of humanism, ca. 1350 Boccaccio, *The Decameron*, ca. 1350 Jan van Eyck, Flemish painter, 1366–1441 Brunelleschi, Florentine architect, 1377–1446 Chaucer, *Canterbury Tales*, ca. 1387–1400
Council of Constance ends the schism in the papacy, 1414–1418 Pragmatic Sanction of Bourges affirms special rights of French Crown over French church, 1438 Expulsion of Jews from Spain, 1492	Water-powered blast furnaces operative in Sweden, Austria, the Rhine Valley, Liège, ca. 1400 Leonardo Fibonacci's *Liber Abaci* popularizes use of Hindu-Arabic numerals, important in rise of Western science, 1402 Paris and largest Italian cities pave streets, making street cleaning possible, ca. 1450 European printing and movable type, ca. 1450	Height of Renaissance movement: Masaccio, 1401–1428; Botticelli, 1444–1510; Leonardo da Vinci, 1452–1519; Albrecht Dürer, 1471–1528; Michelangelo, 1475–1564; Raphael, 1483–1520
Machiavelli, *The Prince*, 1513 More, *Utopia*, 1516 Luther, "Ninety-five Theses," 1517 Henry VIII of England breaks with Rome, 1532–1534 Merici establishes Ursuline order for education of women, 1535 Loyola establishes Society of Jesus, 1540 Calvin establishes theocracy in Geneva, 1541 Council of Trent shapes essential character of Catholicism until the 1960s, 1545–1563 Peace of Augsburg, official recognition of Lutheranism, 1555	Scientific Revolution in western Europe, ca. 1540–1690: Copernicus, *On the Revolutions of the Heavenly Bodies*, 1543; Galileo, 1564–1642; Kepler, 1571–1630; Harvey, 1578–1657	Erasmus, *The Praise of Folly*, 1509 Castiglione, *The Courtier*, 1528 Baroque movement in arts, ca. 1550–1725: Rubens, 1577–1640; Velasquez, 1599–1660 Shakespeare, West's most enduring and influential playwright, 1564–1616 Montaigne, *Essays*, 1598

	Government	Society and Economy
1600	Thirty Years' War begins, 1618 Richelieu dominates French government, 1624–1643 Frederick William, Elector of Brandenburg, r. 1640–1688 English Civil War, 1642–1649 Louis XIV, r. 1643–1715 Peace of Westphalia ends the Thirty Years' War, 1648 The Fronde in France, 1648–1660	Chartering of British East India Company, 1600 English Poor Law, 1601 Chartering of Dutch East India Company, 1602 Height of Dutch commercial activity, ca. 1630–1665
1650	Anglo-Dutch wars, 1652–1674 Protectorate in England, 1653–1658 Leopold I, Habsburg emperor, r. 1658–1705 English monarchy restored, 1660 Ottoman siege of Vienna, 1683 Glorious Revolution in England, 1688–1689 Peter the Great of Russia, r. 1689–1725	Height of mercantilism in Europe, ca. 1650–1750 Agricultural revolution in Europe, ca. 1650–1850 Principle of peasants' hereditary subjugation to their lords affirmed in Prussia, 1653 Colbert's economic reforms in France, ca. 1663–1683 Cossack revolt in Russia, 1670–1671
1700	War of the Spanish Succession, 1701–1713 Peace of Utrecht redraws political boundaries of Europe, 1713 Frederick William I of Prussia, r. 1713–1740 Louis XV of France, r. 1715–1774 Maria Theresa of Austria, r. 1740–1780 Frederick the Great of Prussia, r. 1740–1786	Foundation of St. Petersburg, 1701 Last appearance of bubonic plague in western Europe, ca. 1720 Growth of European population, ca. 1720–1789 Enclosure movement in England, ca. 1730–1830
1750	Seven Years' War, 1756–1763 Catherine the Great of Russia, r. 1762–1796 Partition of Poland, 1772–1795 Louis XVI of France, r. 1774–1792 American Revolution, 1775–1783 French Revolution, 1789–1799 Insurrection of enslaved people in Saint-Domingue, 1791	Growth of illegitimate births in Europe, ca. 1750–1850 Industrial Revolution in western Europe, ca. 1780–1850 Serfdom abolished in France, 1789
1800	Napoleonic era, 1799–1815 Haitian republic declares independence, 1804 Congress of Vienna re-establishes political power after defeat of Napoleon, 1814–1815 Greece wins independence from Ottoman Empire, 1830 French conquest of Algeria, 1830 Revolution in France, 1830 Great Britain: Reform Bill of 1832; Poor Law reform, 1834; Chartists, repeal of Corn Laws, 1838–1848 Revolutions in Europe, 1848	British takeover of India complete, 1805 British slave trade abolished, 1807 German Zollverein founded, 1834 European capitalists begin large-scale foreign investment, 1840s Great Famine in Ireland, 1845–1851 First public health law in Britain, 1848

Religion and Philosophy	Science and Technology	Arts and Letters
Huguenot revolt in France, 1625	Further development of scientific method: Bacon, *The Advancement of Learning*, 1605; Descartes, *Discourse on Method*, 1637	Cervantes, *Don Quixote*, 1605, 1615 Flourishing of French theater: Molière, 1622–1673; Racine, 1639–1699 Golden age of Dutch culture, ca. 1625–1675: Rembrandt van Rijn, 1606–1669; Vermeer, 1632–1675
Social contract theory: Hobbes, *Leviathan*, 1651; Locke, *Second Treatise on Civil Government*, 1690 Patriarch Nikon's reforms split Russian Orthodox Church, 1652 Test Act in England excludes Roman Catholics from public office, 1673 Revocation of Edict of Nantes, 1685 James II tries to restore Catholicism as state religion, 1685–1688	Tull (1674–1741) encourages innovation in English agriculture Newton, *Principia Mathematica*, 1687	Construction of baroque palaces and remodeling of capital cities, central and eastern Europe, ca. 1650–1725 Bach, great late baroque German composer, 1685–1750 Enlightenment begins, ca. 1690: Fontenelle, *Conversations on the Plurality of Worlds*, 1686; Voltaire, French philosopher and writer whose work epitomizes Enlightenment, 1694–1778 Pierre Bayle, *Historical and Critical Dictionary*, 1697
Wesley, founder of Methodism, 1703–1791 Montesquieu, *The Spirit of Laws*, 1748	Newcomen develops steam engine, 1705 Charles Townsend introduces four-year crop rotation, 1730	
Hume, *The Natural History of Religion*, 1755 Rousseau, *The Social Contract* and *Emile*, 1762 Fourier, French utopian socialist, 1772–1837 Papacy dissolves Jesuits, 1773 Smith, *The Wealth of Nations*, 1776 Church reforms of Joseph II in Austria, 1780s Kant, *What Is Enlightenment?*, 1784 Reorganization of church in France, 1790s Wollstonecraft, *A Vindication of the Rights of Woman*, 1792 Malthus, *Essay on the Principle of Population*, 1798	Hargreaves's spinning jenny, ca. 1765 Arkwright's water frame, ca. 1765 Watt's steam engine promotes industrial breakthroughs, 1780s Jenner's smallpox vaccine, 1796	*Encyclopedia*, edited by Diderot and d'Alembert, published 1751–1765 Classical style in music, ca. 1770–1830: Mozart, 1756–1791; Beethoven, 1770–1827 Wordsworth, English Romantic poet, 1770–1850 Romanticism in art and literature, ca. 1790–1850
Napoleon signs Concordat with Pope Pius VII regulating Catholic Church in France, 1801 Spencer, Social Darwinist, 1820–1903 Comte, *System of Positive Philosophy*, 1830–1842 Height of French utopian socialism, 1830s–1840s List, *National System of Political Economy*, 1841 Nietzsche, radical and highly influential German philosopher, 1844–1900 Marx, *Communist Manifesto*, 1848	First railroad, Great Britain, 1825 Faraday studies electromagnetism, 1830–1840s	Staël, *On Germany*, 1810 Balzac, *The Human Comedy*, 1829–1841 Delacroix, *Liberty Leading the People*, 1830 Hugo, *The Hunchback of Notre Dame*, 1831

Government	Society and Economy
1850 Second Empire in France, 1852–1870	Crédit Mobilier founded in France, 1852
Crimean War, 1853–1856	Japan opened to European influence, 1853
Britain crushes Great Rebellion in India, 1857–1858	Russian serfs emancipated, 1861
Unification of Italy, 1859–1870	First Socialist International, 1864–1871
U.S. Civil War, 1861–1865	
Bismarck leads Germany, 1862–1890	
Unification of Germany, 1864–1871	
Britain's Second Reform Bill, 1867	
Third Republic in France, 1870–1940	
1875 Congress of Berlin, 1878	Full property rights for women in Great Britain, 1882
European "scramble for Africa," 1880–1900	Second Industrial Revolution; birthrate steadily declines in Europe, ca. 1880–1913
Britain's Third Reform Bill, 1884	Social welfare legislation, Germany, 1883–1889
Dreyfus affair in France, 1894–1899	Second Socialist International, 1889–1914
Spanish-American War, 1898	Witte directs modernization of Russian economy, 1892–1899
South African War, 1899–1902	
1900 Russo-Japanese War, 1904–1905	Women's suffrage movement, England, ca. 1900–1914
Revolution in Russia, 1905	Social welfare legislation, France, 1904, 1910; Great Britain, 1906–1914
Balkan wars, 1912–1913	Agrarian reforms in Russia, 1907–1912
1914 World War I, 1914–1918	Planned economics in Europe, 1914
Armenian genocide, 1915	Auxiliary Service Law in Germany, 1916
Easter Rebellion, 1916	Bread riots in Russia, March 1917
U.S. declares war on Germany, 1917	
Bolshevik Revolution, 1917–1918	
Treaty of Versailles, World War I peace settlement, 1919	
1920 Mussolini seizes power in Italy, 1922	New Economic Policy in U.S.S.R., 1921
Stalin comes to power in U.S.S.R., 1927	Dawes Plan for reparations and recovery, 1924
Hitler gains power in Germany, 1933	Great Depression, 1929–1939
Rome-Berlin Axis, 1936	Rapid industrialization in U.S.S.R., 1930s
Nazi-Soviet Non-Aggression Pact, 1939	Start of Roosevelt's New Deal in U.S., 1933
World War II, 1939–1945	
1940 United Nations founded, 1945	Holocaust, 1941–1945
Decolonization of Asia and Africa, 1945–1960s	Marshall Plan enacted, 1947
Cold War begins, 1947	European economic progress, ca. 1950–1970
Founding of Israel, 1948	European Coal and Steel Community founded, 1952
Communist government in China, 1949	European Economic Community founded, 1957
Korean War, 1950–1953	
De-Stalinization of Soviet Union under Khrushchev, 1953–1964	

Religion and Philosophy	Science and Technology	Arts and Letters
Decline in church attendance among working classes, ca. 1850–1914 Mill, *On Liberty*, 1859 Pope Pius IX, *Syllabus of Errors*, denounces modern thoughts, 1864 Marx, *Das Capital*, 1867 Doctrine of papal infallibility, 1870	Modernization of Paris, ca. 1850–1870 Great Exhibition in London, 1851 Freud, founder of psychoanalysis, 1856–1939 Darwin, *On the Origin of Species*, 1859 Pasteur develops germ theory of disease, 1860s Suez Canal opened, 1869 Mendeleev develops periodic table, 1869	Realism in art and literature, ca. 1850–1870 Flaubert, *Madame Bovary*, 1857 Tolstoy, *War and Peace*, 1869 Impressionism in art, ca. 1870–1900 Eliot (Mary Ann Evans), *Middlemarch*, 1872
Growth of public education in France, ca. 1880–1900 Growth of mission schools in Africa, 1890–1914	Emergence of modern immunology, ca. 1875–1900 Electrical industry: lighting and streetcars, ca. 1880–1900 Trans-Siberian Railroad, 1890s Marie Curie, discovery of radium, 1898	Zola, *Germinal*, 1885 Kipling, "The White Man's Burden," 1899
Separation of church and state in France, 1901–1905 Hobson, *Imperialism*, 1902 Schweitzer, *Quest of the Historical Jesus*, 1906	Planck develops quantum theory, ca. 1900 First airplane flight, 1903 Einstein develops theory of special relativity, 1905–1910	Modernism in art and literature, ca. 1900–1929 Conrad, *Heart of Darkness*, 1902 Cubism in art, ca. 1905–1930 Proust, *Remembrance of Things Past*, 1913–1927
Keynes, *Economic Consequences of the Peace*, 1919	Submarine warfare introduced, 1915 Ernest Rutherford splits atom, 1919	Spengler, *The Decline of the West*, 1918
Emergence of modern existentialism, 1920s Revival of Christianity, 1920s–1930s Wittgenstein, *Essay on Logical Philosophy*, 1922 Heisenberg's principle of uncertainty, 1927	"Heroic age of physics," 1920s First major public radio broadcasts in Great Britain and U.S., 1920 First talking movies, 1930 Radar system in England, 1939	Gropius, Bauhaus, 1920s Dadaism and surrealism, 1920s Woolf, *Jacob's Room*, 1922 Joyce, *Ulysses*, 1922 Eliot, *The Waste Land*, 1922 Remarque, *All Quiet on the Western Front*, 1929 Picasso, *Guernica*, 1937
De Beauvoir, *The Second Sex*, 1949 Communists fail to break Catholic Church in Poland, 1950s	U.S. drops atomic bombs on Japan, 1945 Big Science in U.S., ca. 1945–1965 Watson and Crick discover structure of DNA molecule, 1953 Russian satellite in orbit, 1957	Cultural purge in Soviet Union, 1946–1952 Van der Rohe, Lake Shore Apartments, 1948–1951 Orwell, *1984*, 1949 Pasternak, *Doctor Zhivago*, 1956 "Beat" movement in U.S., late 1950s

Government	Society and Economy
1960	
Building of Berlin Wall, 1961	Civil rights movement in U.S., 1960s
U.S. involvement in Vietnam War, 1964–1973	Stagflation, 1970s
Student rebellion in France, 1968	Feminist movement, 1970s
Soviet tanks end Prague Spring, 1968	Collapse of postwar monetary system, 1971
Détente between U.S. and U.S.S.R., 1970s	OPEC oil price increases, 1973, 1979
Soviet occupation of Afghanistan, 1979–1989	
1980	
U.S. military buildup, 1980s	Growth of debt in the West, 1980s
Solidarity in Poland, 1980	Economic crisis in Poland, 1988
Unification of Germany, 1989	Maastricht Treaty proposes monetary union, 1990
Revolutions in eastern Germany, 1989–1990	European Community becomes European Union, 1993
Persian Gulf War, 1990–1991	Migration to western Europe increases, 1990s
Dissolution of Soviet Union, 1991	Former Soviet bloc nations adopt capitalist economies, 1990s
Civil war in Yugoslavia, 1991–2001	
Separatist war breaks out in Chechnya, 1991	
2000	
Vladimir Putin elected president of Russian Federation, 2000	Same-sex marriage legalized in the Netherlands, 2001
Terrorist attacks on U.S., Sept. 11, 2001	Euro enters circulation, 2002
War in Afghanistan, 2001–2021	Voters reject new European Union constitution, 2005
Iraq War, 2003–2011	Immigrant riots in France, 2005, 2009
Angela Merkel serves as chancellor of Germany, 2005–2021	Worldwide financial crisis; European debt crisis, 2008–2011
NATO intervenes in Libyan civil war, 2011	Anti-austerity protests across Europe begin, 2010
Al-Qaeda leader Osama bin Laden killed, 2011	Arab Spring uprisings in the Middle East and North Africa, 2011
Ex-NSA contractor Edward Snowden leaks classified U.S. government information, 2013	France legalizes same-sex marriage, 2013
Russia annexes Crimea (southern Ukraine) and supports pro-Russian Ukrainian rebels, 2014	Occupy movement begins in the United States, spreads to Europe, 2011
Growth of Islamic State, 2014–2015	Greek debt crisis, 2015
Terrorist attacks in Paris organized by Islamic State kill 130 people, 2015	Massive influx of refugees from the Middle East undermines European unity, 2015–2016
Terrorist attacks in London, Barcelona, St. Petersburg, and other European cities, organized by Islamic State, kill at least 115 people, 2017	Austria legalizes same-sex marriage, 2019
Donald Trump serves as U.S. president, takes hard line against NATO and European allies, 2017–2021	European Union home to about 500 million citizens, 2019
First outbreak of COVID-19 in Wuhan, China, 2019	
United Kingdom withdraws from European Union, 2020	
Joe Biden takes office as U.S. president, 2021	
Russian Federation invades Ukraine, 2022	

Religion and Philosophy	Science and Technology	Arts and Letters
Second Vatican Council announces sweeping Catholic reforms, 1962–1965 Pope John II, 1978–2005	European Council for Nuclear Research founded, 1960 Space race, 1960s Russian cosmonaut first to orbit globe, 1961 American astronaut first person on moon, 1969	The Beatles, 1960s Solzhenitsyn, *One Day in the Life of Ivan Denisovich*, 1962 Carson, *Silent Spring*, 1962 Friedan, *The Feminine Mystique*, 1963 Servan-Schreiber, *The American Challenge*, 1967
Revival of religion in Soviet Union, 1985– Growth of Islam in Europe, 1990s Fukuyama proclaims "end of history," 1991	Reduced spending on Big Science, 1980s Computer revolution continues, 1980s–1990s U.S. Genome Project begins, 1990 First World Wide Web server and browser, 1991 Pentium processor invented, 1993 First genetically cloned sheep, 1996	Consolidation and popularization of postmodernism in fine arts and literature, 1980s Solzhenitsyn returns to Russia, 1994; dies 2008 Author Salman Rushdie exiled from Iran, 1989 Gehry, Guggenheim Museum, Bilbao, 1997
Number of Europeans who claim to be religious continues to decline, 2000– Sexual abuse scandal challenges Catholic Church across the globe, 2000– UN announces first World Philosophy Day to "honor philosophical reflection" across the globe, 2002 Ramadan, *Western Muslims and the Future of Islam*, 2004 Pontificate of Benedict XVI, 2005–2013 Jorge Mario Bergoglio elected as Pope Francis, 2013 Noted Slovenian philosopher Slavoj Žižek critiques contemporary Western notions of freedom, 2014	Google emerges as popular Internet search engine, 2000s Growing concern about global warming, 2000s First hybrid car, 2003 Facebook founded, 2004 YouTube founded, 2005 iPhone introduced to consumers, 2007 Copenhagen summit on climate change, 2009 Paris summit on climate change sets Paris Agreement to limit CO_2 emissions, 2015 TikTok introduced in Europe and the U.S., 2017 UN Climate Control conference in Katowice, Poland, updates Paris Agreement, 2018 European Union implements General Data Protection Regulation, 2018 Whistleblower testifies before U.S. Congress about misinformation on Facebook, 2021	Middle East conflict leads to looting and destruction of archaeological sites and museums, 2000– Growing importance of artists and art centers outside of Europe: in Latin America, Africa, and Asia, 2000– Digital methods of production and display grow increasingly popular in works of art, 2000– Movies and books exploring clash between immigrants and host cultures popular: *Bend It Like Beckham*, 2002; *The Namesake*, 2003; *White Teeth*, 2003; *The Class*, 2008; *Brooklyn*, 2015 Memorial to the Murdered Jews of Europe opens in Berlin, 2005

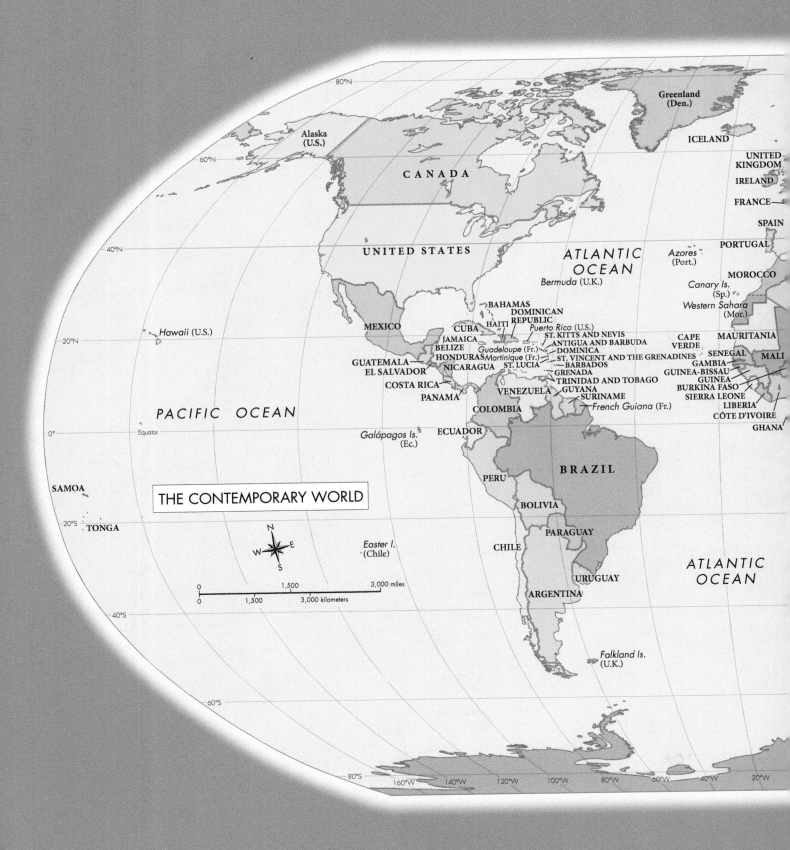

THE CONTEMPORARY WORLD